MW01195749

WEST ACADEMIC PUBLISHING'S
LAW SCHOOL ADVISORY BOARD

JESSE H. CHOPER
Professor of Law and Dean Emeritus
University of California, Berkeley

JOSHUA DRESSLER
Distinguished University Professor Emeritus
Michael E. Moritz College of Law, The Ohio State University

RENÉE McDONALD HUTCHINS
Dean and Joseph L. Rauh, Jr. Chair of Public Interest Law
University of the District of Columbia David A. Clarke School of Law

YALE KAMISAR
Professor of Law Emeritus, University of San Diego
Professor of Law Emeritus, University of Michigan

MARY KAY KANE
Professor of Law, Chancellor and Dean Emeritus
University of California, Hastings College of the Law

LARRY D. KRAMER
President, William and Flora Hewlett Foundation

JONATHAN R. MACEY
Professor of Law, Yale Law School

DEBORAH JONES MERRITT
Distinguished University Professor, John Deaver Drinko/Baker &
Hostetler Chair in Law
Michael E. Moritz College of Law, The Ohio State University

ARTHUR R. MILLER
University Professor, New York University
Formerly Bruce Bromley Professor of Law, Harvard University

GRANT S. NELSON
Professor of Law Emeritus, Pepperdine University
Professor of Law Emeritus, University of California, Los Angeles

A. BENJAMIN SPENCER
Justice Thurgood Marshall Distinguished Professor of Law
University of Virginia School of Law

JAMES J. WHITE
Robert A. Sullivan Professor of Law Emeritus
University of Michigan

BUSINESS ORGANIZATIONS LAW

Fifth Edition

James D. Cox
Brainerd Currie Professor of Law
Duke University

Thomas Lee Hazen
Cary C. Boshamer Distinguished Professor of Law
The University of North Carolina at Chapel Hill

HORNBOOK SERIES®

The publisher is not engaged in rendering legal or other professional advice, and this publication is not a substitute for the advice of an attorney. If you require legal or other expert advice, you should seek the services of a competent attorney or other professional.

Hornbook Series is a trademark registered in the U.S. Patent and Trademark Office.

© 2011 Thomson Reuters
© 2016 LEG, Inc. d/b/a West Academic
© 2020 LEG, Inc. d/b/a West Academic
    444 Cedar Street, Suite 700
    St. Paul, MN 55101
    1-877-888-1330

West, West Academic Publishing, and West Academic are trademarks of West Publishing Corporation, used under license.

Printed in the United States of America

ISBN: 978-1-64242-401-0

Preface

This hornbook is an updated adaptation of *Cox & Hazen on Corporations* (Practitioner's Edition 3d ed. 2010)—a four volume treatise supplemented annually.[1] The first edition of this treatise was selected in 1995 for a national book award by The Association of American Publishers. The first edition and its successors were each built upon the solid foundation laid by the late Henry W. Ballantine in his classic single-volume work, *Ballantine on Corporations*. It has been our aim to examine the law of corporations with care and craftsmanship equal to its predecessor. Though corporate law has undergone a sea change since Ballantine published the last edition of his work, the challenges to the corporate lawyer have not changed over the years. Corporate law is one of the areas most vital to our society, for it regulates the workings of Adam Smith's invisible hand in the allocation of resources among competing uses. Unfortunately, the importance of corporate law is not matched by clarity in its doctrines, principles, and statutes. The field continues to be filled with "trite dogmas, formulas, metaphors, and legal fictions to the fundamental realities and policies of the law."[2]

In this work, we provide a comprehensive analysis of all areas of corporate law and some significant provisions of the federal securities laws. Contrasting judicial and statutory approaches are examined in both a contemporary commercial context and historical evolution of law on each subject examined. We have avoided a state-by-state review on each topic; instead we devote our energies to capturing and critiquing the significance of the differences in approaches. As evident in each of our chapters, we examine the historical fount of doctrines, their contemporary vitality, and qualifications and weaknesses in their impact. This text is not content to recite the empty metaphors and vague incantations that appear with regrettable frequency in the courts' treatment of important issues of corporate law. We emphasize the financial, political, and social considerations that appear to have guided the courts' dispositions in individual cases. Simply stated, we seek to provide a helpful and insightful treatment of the law of corporations.

The text is written and edited to provide an understanding of the law relating to business organizations. Although some leading sources are included, the text is not intended as a research tool. Footnotes from the parent Practitioner's Edition have been edited severely. Readers conducting research and seeking additional citations should consult the four volume *Cox & Hazen on Corporations* (Practitioner's Edition 3d ed. 2010) (with its annual supplements).

Because of the broad impact on the shape of state corporate statutes of the Model Business Corporation Act, close attention is given to the Model Act throughout the text.

---

[1] Although this hornbook contains the same chapters as the multivolume treatise, many of the section numbers and footnotes have been renumbered.

[2] Preface, Henry W. Ballantine, Ballantine on Corporations iii (rev. ed. 1946).

Major non-Model Act jurisdictions, such as California, Delaware, and New York, are also emphasized in our treatment of statutes and doctrine.

James D. Cox
Thomas Lee Hazen

January, 2020

Acknowledgments

We very much appreciate the support and encouragement for this treatise that we have received from our respective deans. A great debt is also due the numerous students who provided invaluable research on this project. Their numbers are far too large to permit each to be singled out here for fear of inadvertent omissions.

A work such as this does not occur without personal sacrifices. We each thank our families for their patience, understanding, and support.

Summary of Contents

Table of Contents

BUSINESS ORGANIZATIONS LAW

Fifth Edition

Chapter 1

FORMS OF BUSINESS ASSOCIATION— DEFINITIONS AND DISTINCTIONS

Table of Sections

§ 1.1   The Corporation

Much of the industrial and commercial development of the nineteenth and twentieth centuries was made possible by the corporate mechanism. By its use investors may combine their capital and participate in the profits of large-or small-scale business enterprises under a centralized management, with their risk limited to the capital contributed and without peril to their other resources and business. The amount of capital needed for modern business could hardly have been assembled and combined in any other way. The corporate device has indeed raised serious questions as to the undue concentration of economic power.

Long ago it was aptly observed that "A corporation is, after all, but an association of individuals under an assumed name and with a distinct legal entity."[1] What, then, is this corporate entity or personality? It should be clearly understood at the outset that it is entirely a matter of convenience to employ the metaphor or figure of speech by which we call a corporation a legal person. A corporation may more realistically be described as a legal unit, a concern separated off with a legal existence, status, or capacity of its own, a legal device or instrument for carrying on some business enterprise, or some social, charitable, religious, or governmental activities.

Other than the corporation, the forms of business association generally available in this country are (1) the partnership, including the joint venture, (2) the limited partnership, (3) the limited liability company, (4) the joint stock company (sometimes referred to as a "joint stock association"), (5) the business trust (which originated with the Massachusetts business trust), and (6) in a few states, the partnership association. These six forms of doing business are distinct from the sole proprietorship in which a single individual owns and operates the business.

§ 1.2 The Concept of Corporate Entity or Personality

A business corporation is a legal device for carrying on a business enterprise for profit, a legal unit with a status or capacity of its own separate from the shareholders or members who own it.

The famous definition of "corporation" given by Chief Justice Marshall emphasizes the notion that the corporation is a legal entity. "A corporation," Marshall said,

> [I]s an artificial being, invisible, intangible, and existing only in contemplation of law. Being the mere creature of law, it possesses only those properties which the charter of its creation confers upon it, either expressly, or as incidental to its very existence. These are such as are supposed best calculated to effect the object for which it was created. Among the most important are immortality, and, if the expression may be allowed, individuality; properties, by which a perpetual succession of many persons are considered as the same, and may act as a single individual. They enable a corporation to manage its own affairs, and to hold property without the perplexing intricacies, the hazardous and endless necessity, of perpetual conveyances for the purpose of transmitting it from hand to hand. It is chiefly for the purpose of clothing bodies of men, in succession, with these qualities and capacities, that corporations were invented, and are in use. By these means, a perpetual succession of individuals are capable of acting for the promotion of the particular object, like one immortal being.[2]

"Business corporation" has sometimes been defined in terms of an *association* of a number of persons in a business enterprise with the object of economic gain. Thus it has been said: "A corporation is, after all, but an association of individuals under an assumed name and with a distinct legal entity."[3] In contrast, an unincorporated association has

---

[1]   *See, e.g.,* Hale v. Henkel, 201 U.S. 43, 76 (1906).

[2]   Trustees of Dartmouth College v. Woodward, 17 U.S. (4 Wheat.) 518, 636 (1819). In the *Dartmouth College* case, *id.* at 667, Justice Story commented: "An aggregate corporation at common law is a collection of individuals united into one collective body, under a special name, and possessing certain immunities, privileges, and capacities in its collective character, which do not belong to the natural persons composing it."

[3]   Hale v. Henkel, 201 U.S. 43, 76 (1906).

no entity status beyond that of its members and ordinarily lacks the legal capacity to sue or be sued in its own name. It should be clearly understood that it is entirely a matter of convenience to employ the metaphor or figure of speech to call the corporation a legal person.

A corporation may be more realistically described as a legal unit, a concern separated off with a legal existence, status, or capacity of its own, a legal device or instrument for carrying on some business enterprise or some social, charitable, religious, or governmental activities. Corporation A is a legal person entirely different from individual shareholder *X*, or, rather, it has a legal capacity that is distinct from *X*'s, even though *X* organized it, manages it, and owns all or practically all of its shares.[4]

Unlike in an individual enterprise or partnership, in a corporation the maximum loss to shareholders or owners due to the business's debts and torts, with rare exceptions, will not exceed the amount that they have invested in the enterprise. If *Y* loans money or otherwise extends credit to A Corporation, he must look to the corporate assets for repayment; ordinarily he cannot recover from the shareholders or levy on their property.[5] The separateness of the corporation is also generally recognized for tax purposes, the corporation usually being considered a taxable entity.

The corporation has also been referred to as "a creature of statute." This reflects the fact that a corporation can only be formed by compliance with requirements set forth in the corporation statute of the state in which the corporation is being organized. Incorporation papers setting forth certain basic information, such as the corporation's name, registered agent, and its capital structure, must be prepared and filed with designated public officials.

§ 1.3   Exceptions to the Separate Legal Personality

The corporate personality is a curious creature, which has led to many confounding questions for the courts. A frequently litigated issue is whether a corporation is a "person" or "citizen" within the purview of various statutory and constitutional provisions. As a general proposition, resolution of such questions depends on the legislative intent and whether subjecting the corporation to the provision at issue would be consistent with both the purpose of the legislation or constitutional provision and the essence of corporate existence. There accordingly can be no formula for determining whether a statute or constitutional provision is directed at only natural persons. Some laws are expressly limited to natural persons.[6] In other instances, corporations are expressly included within the scope of both penal and civil statutes.[7] Difficult problems of construction arise where the inclusion of corporations is not addressed with specificity,

---

[4]   *See* J.B. Heaton, What Injures a Corporation? Toward Better Understanding Corporate Personality, 73 Bus. Law. 1031, 1040–41 (2018):

> The ability to cordon off a set of assets and then build value within that partition is what . . . gives rise to corporate personality. . . . [W]ithout the concept of corporate injury, it would be impossible to (1) protect the going concern value of the corporation; (2) maintain creditor priority; and (3) contract through the corporate form. That is, it would be impossible to maintain the benefits of asset partitioning and locking in capital, the essential aspects of corporate law.

[5]   For a more comprehensive discussion of limited liability and the circumstances in which a court will disregard the separate personality of a corporation and impose liability for the corporation's debts on the shareholder or shareholders, *see* Chapter 7.

[6]   *E.g.*, 11 U.S.C. §§ 1301 et seq. (2006).

[7]   For example, the corporation is included with the definition of "person" in the federal securities acts. 15 U.S.C. § 77b(a)(2) (2006).

as it is not in a large number of statutes. More importantly, the provisions of the Constitution do not include corporations.

§ 1.4   The Corporation and the Constitution

When questions arise concerning the right of corporations to invoke constitutional protections, the Supreme Court resolves the question by examining the nature and purpose of the specific articles, clause, or amendment. Over time, this inquiry has yielded a "corporate personality" for constitutional purposes.[8] Corporations, as artificial persons, are entitled to many, but not all, the protections and guarantees afforded natural persons.

Citizenship. One significant limitation on a corporation's rights under the Constitution is the Supreme Court's historical refusal to grant it citizenship status for the purposes of the privileges and immunities clause of Article IV, section 2, as well as under the Fourteenth Amendment.[9] As a consequence of being denied citizenship status, states may, as a valid exercise of their police powers, regulate foreign corporations conducting business within their borders, provided the regulations do not impermissibly affect commerce.[10]

On the other hand, in a very significant Supreme Court decision, *Citizens United v. Federal Election Commission*,[11] the Court recognized that corporation's enjoy certain freedoms under the First Amendment, one of which is that corporations enjoy the same freedom as individuals to engage in unlimited spending on political issues and campaigns (provided the corporation acts independently of any campaign or candidate) in spending funds to advance its belief.

A corporation is a citizen for the purposes of determining whether the federal court has jurisdiction based on diversity of citizenship under Article III of the Constitution.[12] Specifically, in *Hertz Corp. v. Friend*,[13] the Supreme Court embraced the so-called "nerve center" approach so that a corporation's principal place of business for diversity jurisdiction is where its officers direct, control and coordinate the corporation's activities (which is a location not necessarily where a substantial portion of the corporation's business activities are centered). Whereas a professional corporation is a corporate entity for diversity purposes, so that it is inappropriate to consider its owners' citizenship in determining whether there is diversity of citizenship,[14] the citizenship of an LLC for

---

[8]   *See* John Dewey, The Historic Background of Corporate Legal Personality, 35 Yale L.J. 655, 656 (1926).

[9]   Asbury Hosp. v. Cass County, 326 U.S. 207, 210–12 (1945); Selover, Bates & Co. v. Walsh, 226 U.S. 112, 126 (1912).

[10]   *See, e.g.,* Allenberg Cotton Co. v. Pittman, 419 U.S. 20, 32–34 (1974) (state court does not have jurisdiction over corporation incorporated in another state unless there are sufficient intrastate contacts). *Compare* Eli Lilly & Co. v. Sav-On-Drugs, 366 U.S. 276, 280–81 (1961) (service on foreign corporation upheld where office and 18 employees maintained within state).

[11]   558 U.S. 310 (2010).

[12]   Bank of United States v. Deveaux, 9 U.S. (5 Cranch) 61, 86–88 (1809).

[13]   559 U.S. 77 (2010).

[14]   *See e.g.,* Hoagland ex rel. Midwest Transit, Inc. v. Sandberg, Phoenix & von Gontard, P.C., 385 F.3d 737 (7th Cir. 2004); Schneider ex rel. Estate of Schneider v. Fried, 320 F.3d 396, 60 Fed. R. Evid. Serv. 781, 55 Fed. R. Serv. 3d 245 (3d Cir. 2003); Saxe, Bacon & Bolan, P.C. v. Martindale-Hubbell, Inc., 710 F.2d 87 (2d Cir. 1983)

purposes of diversity jurisdiction is the citizenship of its members.[15] The corporation's citizenship for jurisdictional purposes and its presence for venue purposes is now controlled by statute. Under the federal statute, a corporation's residence is its principal place of business.[16]

Independent of the meaning of "citizenship" is whether suit in a particular federal or state court satisfies the Due Process clause of the Constitution. While venue provisions can be very broad, historically the Due Process clause requires the defendant corporation have "minimum contacts" with the forum.[17] Beginning in 2011, the Supreme Court for general jurisdiction purposes employs an approach in which the focus is having the corporation's "home," which normally means the corporation's place of incorporation or principal place of business, be the determinant whether sufficient contact exists among the forum, the claims and the corporate defendant. The approach has taken form in four Supreme Court decisions:[18]

> The Supreme Court's quartet of decisions in *Goodyear*, *Daimler*, *BNSF*, and *Bristol Myers*, while reaffirming the decision [in *International Shoe*] as "canonical," substantially recast the more flexible *International Shoe* jurisdictional *continuum* into a brighter-line, stricter *dichotomy* that is both reflective of the post-*International Shoe* concepts of "general" versus "specific" jurisdiction and more protective against forum shopping. Under this new dichotomy, for a corporation to be subject to *general* (all-purpose) jurisdiction, the firm must be essentially "at home" in the state, such as being incorporated or having its principal place of business *there*. Otherwise, only *specific* (claim-connected) jurisdiction is constitutionally permissible. Even if the defendant does very substantial, continuous business in a state in which it is not "at home," each plaintiff's claim must "arise out of or relate to" the company's contacts with the state in order to establish personal jurisdiction. The Court also emphasized in the quartet of decisions that general jurisdiction should be the exception to the rule that, ordinarily, jurisdiction should be specific, based on the company's claim-connections to the state.[19]

Person. Various constitutional provisions afford protection to a "person." The Court interprets this language as including artificial persons such as corporations when the provision does not pertain to a "purely personal" guarantee.[20] Thus, a corporation is a person for purposes of the Fourth Amendment's protection against unlawful searches and seizures of its property[21] and the Fifth Amendment's protection against double jeopardy.[22] For example, the Court reasoned that, because a corporation's success

---

[15]   Cosgrove v. Bartolotta, 150 F.3d 729, 731 (7th Cir. 1998). The treatment of LLC's can be traced to the earlier Supreme Court precedents that looked to the owners of unincorporated organizations. *See* Carden v. Arkoma Associates, 494 U.S. 185, 195 (1990).

[16]   28 U.S.C. § 1332(c)(1).

[17]   *See* Int'l Shoe Co. v. Washington, 326 U.S. 310 (1945).

[18]   Goodyear Dunlop Tires Operations, S.A. v. Brown, 564 U.S. 915 (2011); Daimler A.G. v. Bauman, 571 U.S. 117 (2014); BNSF Ry. Co. v. Tyrrell, 137 S.Ct. 1549 (2017); Bristol-Myers Squibb Co. v. Superior Court, 137 S. Ct. 1773 (2017).

[19]   Goodyear Dunlop Tires Operations, S.A. v. Brown, 564 U.S. 915 (2011); Daimler A.G. v. Bauman, 571 U.S. 117 (2014); BNSF Ry. Co. v. Tyrrell, 137 S.Ct. 1549 (2017); Bristol-Myers Squibb Co. v. Superior Court, 137 S. Ct. 1773 (2017).

[20]   *See* United States v. White, 322 U.S. 694, 699 (1944).

[21]   G.M. Leasing Corp. v. United States, 429 U.S. 338, 353 (1977).

[22]   *See, e.g.,* United States v. Martin Linen Supply Co., 430 U.S. 564, 568–71 (1977).

depends heavily on its goodwill, it should be protected by the Fifth Amendment from a second, damaging criminal trial. The corporation is also a person protected by the due process clauses of the Fifth and Fourteenth Amendments,[23] as well as the equal protection clause of the Fourteenth Amendment.[24]

A corporation is not a "person" under the self-incrimination clause of the Fifth Amendment. Because that guaranty is intended to prohibit the use of physical or moral compulsion exerted on the person asserting the privilege, its protection is purely personal in nature and therefore applies only to natural persons.[25]

Corporations, while entitled to many Fourth, Fifth, and Fourteenth Amendment freedoms, do not enjoy the same right of privacy as do individuals.[26] Because a corporation exists solely by the grace of the legislature and "[t]here is a reserved right in the legislature to investigate [a corporation's] contracts and find out whether it has exceeded its powers,"[27] the corporation's books and records carry no personal privacy.[28] This position ensures that under appropriate circumstances, the government can have access to the information needed to regulate corporations. While government agencies have a legitimate right to make inquiries to assure the corporation's behavior is consistent with the law and the public interest, the government must be mindful that the Fourth Amendment does protect the corporation from unreasonable searches and seizures.[29]

The meaning of "person" assumed a central role in *Burwell v. Hobby Lobby Stores, Inc.*[30] where the issue was whether a close corporation was within a "person" within the scope of the Religious Freedom Restoration Act (RFRA) which provides the government "shall not substantially burden a person's exercise of religion" unless such burden that is imposed is the least restrictive means to further a compelling governmental interest.[31] The handful of family members that owned all the shares of Hobby Lobby objected to the requirement of the Affordable Care Act (ACA) that employers must provide medical insurance that would provide coverage to employees for certain types of contraception; the shareholders of Hobby Lobby argued that certain forms of contraception violated their religious beliefs. The Supreme Court held 5–4 that for purposes of the RFRA the Court would disregard the separateness of the entity so that a religious faith could be found among the firm's owners. It remains to be seen whether *Hobby Lobby's* holding will be cabined to the unique facts of that case—a close corporation with all family members of the same belief and the RFRA's connection with the ACA. A possible basis for so limiting *Hobby Lobby* is that the majority opinion emphasized that the Obama Administration, in the case of religious non-profit entities, had itself peered through

---

[23] *See, e.g.,* First Nat'l Bank v. Bellotti, 435 U.S. 765, 780 n.15 (1978).

[24] Bell v. Maryland, 378 U.S. 226, 262 (1964).

[25] *See, e.g.,* United States v. Doe, 465 U.S. 605, 608 (1984) (individual may be entitled to avoid producing document potentially incriminating to him; corporation remains obligated to produce document).

[26] *See, e.g.,* California Bankers Ass'n v. Shultz, 416 U.S. 21, 65–67 (1974); United States v. Morton Salt Co., 338 U.S. 632, 651–52 (1950).

[27] Hale v. Henkel, 201 U.S. 43, 75 (1906).

[28] United States v. White, 322 U.S. 694, 700 (1944).

[29] G.M. Leasing Corp. v. United States, 429 U.S. 338, 353 (1977).

[30] 573 U.S. 682 (2014).

[31] The Religious Freedom Restoration Act of 1993, 42 U.S.C. §§ 2000bb *et. seq.*

entities in reaching accommodations in addressing non-profit entities that had also objected to providing contraceptive coverage.

Liberty. A corporation does not enjoy the full protections of the Fourteenth Amendment's due process guarantees respecting "liberty."[32] The liberties embodied in the Fourteenth Amendment generally are those associated with a natural, not artificial, person. However, in *Grosjean v. American Press Co.,*[33] the Supreme Court held that the Fourteenth Amendment's due process clause accords corporations the protection embodied in the First Amendment.[34] Occasionally the Court recognizes constitutional protections without having to address the corporation's status. For example, in *First National Bank of Boston v. Bellotti,*[35] the Supreme Court avoided the issue as to whether a corporation is entitled to First Amendment protection by rephrasing the issue. It focused on whether the speech involved itself was constitutionally protected. Reasoning "the Constitution often protects interests broader than those of the party seeking their vindication," the Court there concluded that corporate expenditures to support political activity were constitutionally protected.[36]

Legal Process. In *Ross v. Bernhard,*[37] the Court accepted the position that "a corporation's suit to enforce a legal right was an action at common law carrying the right to a jury trial at the time the Seventh Amendment was adopted."[38] Thus the corporation enjoys the right to a jury trial where such right existed at common law. And, relying on the Sixth Amendment, corporations have a constitutional right to effective assistance of counsel.[39] To sue or be sued, however, they must be represented by counsel—that is, a corporation cannot proceed pro se.[40]

§ 1.5　Non-Tax Advantages of Corporations

The principal non-tax advantages customarily given for doing business in the corporate form are: (1) exemption of shareholders from personal liability; (2) continuity of the organization's existence despite changes in its members; (3) centralized management by a board of directors; (4) free transferability of a participant's interest; (5) access of the business to additional capital; (6) the organization's capacity to act as a legal unit in holding property, contracting, and bringing suit; and (7) standardized methods of organization, management, and finance prescribed by corporation statutes for the protection of shareholders and creditors, including a more or less standardized system of shareholder relations, rights, and remedies.

A primary advantage of the corporation is the shareholders' limited liability. Shareholders are immune from personal liability for corporate debts and torts beyond the amount of their agreed investments in the corporation's stock.

---

[32]　Northwestern Nat'l Life Ins. Co. v. Riggs, 203 U.S. 243, 255 (1906).

[33]　Grosjean v. American Press Co., 297 U.S. 233 (1936).

[34]　Grosjean v. American Press Co., 297 U.S. 233, 243–44 (1936).

[35]　First National Bank of Boston v. Bellotti, 435 U.S. 765 (1978).

[36]　First National Bank of Boston v. Bellotti, 435 U.S. 765, 776 (1978). *See also* FEC v. Beaumont, 539 U.S. 146 (2003).

[37]　Ross v. Bernhard, 396 U.S. 531 (1970).

[38]　Ross v. Bernhard, 396 U.S. 531, 533–34 (1970).

[39]　*See, e.g.,* United States v. Rad-O-Lite of Philadelphia, Inc., 612 F.2d 740, 743 (3d Cir. 1979).

[40]　*See, e.g.,* In re Las Colinas Dev. Corp., 585 F.2d 7, 11 (1st Cir. 1978).

Limited liability may be less of a factor in selecting corporate form today than it once was in light of the growing number of alternative business forms which grant limited liability to owners. For example, the limited partnership,[41] the limited liability partnership,[42] and the limited liability company[43] are forms of doing business where the owners can enjoy limited liability. In addition, even in a general partnership, in most states the partners elect to have the business treated as a limited liability partnership to at least some extent.[44] Most states permit a partnership to elect to become a limited liability partnership and thereby eliminate the partners' personal liability for the negligence of the partnership or of the other partners.[45] A growing number of states, and the 1996 version of the Revised Uniform Partnership Act, permit full limited liability of the partners with regard to both tort and contract obligations.

A second important advantage gained by incorporation is continuity of existence. Incorporation creates an entity endowed with the capacity to exist either perpetually or for a fixed period, notwithstanding the death or change of its members. When the membership of a partnership changes—for example, when a partner's interest is transferred or when a partner dies—the partnership is dissolved. Unless appropriate provisions have been made in the partnership agreement for the continuation of the business, the enterprise must be liquidated. In contrast, whenever shareholders transfer their shares, the transferees become shareholders in their place; and when shareholders die, their shares pass like other personal property to successors. Neither the separate existence nor the identity of the corporation as a legal unit is affected by these changes. In the colorful language of Blackstone, a corporation is "a person that never dies: in like manner as the River Thames is still the same river, though the parts which compose it are changing every instant."[46] A further advantage of the entity's continuity is it facilitates the corporation attracting capital. Because the corporate entity is not easy to terminate so that investors cannot easily withdraw their investment, investors need not fear that the entity will be prematurely terminated so that capital is withdrawn before it has had time to achieve the objectives for which the funds were raise. Thus, the continuity of existence is linked to a "lock up of capital."[47]

Because managerial responsibility is lodged with the board of directors and their duly selected officers and agents, the corporation enjoys centralized administration, which, as a practical matter, is of necessity in a large organization. Although the shareholders elect the directors and in theory have ultimate control over actions taken by the corporation, they do not participate as shareholders in the day-to-day management of corporate affairs. Thus, the corporate form facilitates a good amount of efficiency: those with managerial skills and experience are entrusted with the capital of their investors whose skills and experiences may well lie in other areas, thereby allowing

---

[41]   See § 1.9 infra.

[42]   See § 1.7[6] infra.

[43]   See § 1.11 infra.

[44]   See § 1.7 infra.

[45]   E.g., Del. Code Ann. tit. 6, §§ 15–1001 to 15–1105 (2005); N.C. Gen. Stat. Ann. § 59–45(b) (2007). See Prefatory Notes to the 1996 Amendments to the Revised Uniform Partnership Act (1996).

[46]   Blackstone, Commentaries 468 (1783). Unincorporated joint stock companies and business trusts also issue transferable shares and by contract may continue their existence in spite of membership changes.

[47]   Margaret Blair, Locking in Capital: What Corporate Law Achieved for Business Organizers in the Nineteenth Century, 51 U.C.L.A. L. Rev. 387 (2003).

investors to make an optimal use of their energies by devoting themselves to their individual vocations.[48]

In publicly held corporations, free alienation of shares is a distinct advantage of the corporate form of doing business. "A prime requisite for the functioning of the corporation system as a capital-raising device is liquidity for investment. Even with limited liability an investor must still consider the possibility of a change in his own or in corporate circumstances which may affect his investment interest."[49] In a closely held business, however, in which each shareholder often is an active, vital member of the management team and the active participants do not look to outside investors for funds, free transferability of shares may be undesirable.[50]

Great flexibility in financing is available to a corporation. It may issue many different kinds of securities, each with distinct claims and preferences against the corporate income or assets. For instance, a corporation may issue several classes of stock, varieties of bonds, debentures, or notes and hybrid securities having characteristics of both equity securities and debt securities. The great flexibility corporations have in the types of securities they can issue permits corporations to tailor their economic relationships to the demands of particular investors in prevailing market conditions.

Because a corporation is viewed as a legal entity that exists apart from its shareholders, it may sue, be sued, hold property, enter into contracts, and perform most other acts that an individual can perform. Another aspect of the concept of the corporation as a distinct legal person that may prove advantageous is that shareholders, to some extent, can remain anonymous. The corporate name sometimes acts as a mask behind which shareholders can conceal their identities, perhaps even for the purpose of evading their rightful responsibilities. A corporation's list of shareholders is ordinarily a private record, except to the extent that the Securities Exchange Act of 1934[51] and state statutes[52] require disclosure or provide shareholder inspection rights.

At least in large business enterprises, an advantage of corporate organization over some other types of association is the greater standardization of a corporation's organization and operation. Every state statute has detailed provisions on the legal relations of shareholders toward each other and the corporation. Further, an elaborate system of regulation of management and protection of shareholders' and creditors' rights has been established and is constantly under review by the courts.

§ 1.6   Disadvantages of the Corporate Form

The corporate form of doing business has a number of distinct disadvantages. A single owner or small group of owners starting a new business have little appetite for the more formal procedures of operation that accompany incorporation. A disadvantage of the corporate form is the necessity of compliance with various statutory formalities,

---

[48]   Henry Hansmann & Reinier Kraakman, The End of History for Corporate Law, 89 Geo. L. J. 439 (2001).

[49]   Henry G. Manne, Our Two Corporation Systems: Law and Economics, 53 Va. L. Rev. 259, 263–64 (1967). *See also* William L. Cary & Melvin A. Eisenberg, Cases and Materials on Corporations 95 (6th ed. 1988).

[50]   *See generally* 2 F. Hodge O'Neal & Robert Thompson, O'Neal's Close Corporations: Law and Practice, ch. 7 (1991).

[51]   15 U.S.C. §§ 78a to 78*l*–1 (2006).

[52]   Many corporation statutes require production of a list of shareholders at shareholders' meetings. *See, e.g.,* 6 N.Y. Bus. Corp. Law § 607 (McKinney 2003).

which require considerable legal advice and other expert assistance. Examples include the filing of various reports and documents. Further, a corporation experiences greater difficulty in doing business across state lines. A corporation domiciled in one state that does business in other states is invariably required to "qualify" in the other states—that is, obtain authorization from each of the other states to transact business. A partnership can generally operate in another state without the formality of qualification. In some states a corporation is prohibited from engaging in specific kinds of activity—for example, only recently did the accounting profession agree to permit its professionals to incorporate. Generally, corporate income is subject to a double tax burden—first, to the corporation and, second, when distributed as dividends, as personal income to the shareholders. In sum, the sentiment is frequently expressed: "When in doubt don't incorporate."[53]

§ 1.7   Characteristics of the Partnership

[1] Partnership in Context

An unincorporated association, like a firm, is not generally recognized in American law as a *legal* unit or entity having a separate capacity and rights, but, rather, for most purposes it traditionally has been regarded as an aggregation of individuals operating the business as co-owners with individual rights and duties.[54] Thus, for example, a partnership's citizenship for federal diversity jurisdiction is determined by the citizenship of its partners.[55] On some matters, however, such as the continuity of identity of the firm in spite of changes in the personnel or membership, conveyances by and to the firm as if it were a legal unit, and the prior application of the assets of insolvent partnerships to the firm debts in bankruptcy, the Uniform Partnership Act treats the partnership as having, to a certain extent, a separate identity or individuality, as if the partnership were an independent concern or person.[56] The partnership liabilities may be regarded as primarily the liabilities of a separate legal unit. The obligations of a firm are made payable out of its assets in bankruptcy and are given priority over the individual debts that might be owed the partners. Under statutes, partnerships are often treated as if they are an entity for purposes of suing and being sued in the firm name. Aside from the rules governing partners' liabilities, the law of partnership is based on

---

[53]   *See, e.g.,* George C. Seward & W. John Nauss, Basic Corporate Practice 1 (2d ed. 1977):

When in doubt, do not incorporate. Many small corporations are formed unadvisedly. The corporate form of doing business is probably disadvantageous for a small, new venture. The cost of the privilege of limited liability will probably be very high. To determine whether incorporation is advisable, the cost of establishing and maintaining the corporation and the potential tax disadvantages of corporate status should be measured against the advantages of corporate status, principally those of limited liability and relative ease of raising capital. Hence a basic rule: do not incorporate unless the advantages are worth the cost. Time devoted at the outset to determining whether incorporation is advisable will be well spent.

[54]   *See* Donald Weidner, A Perspective to Reconsider Partnership Law, 16 Fla. St. U. L. Rev. 1 (1988).

[55]   Chapman v. Barney, 129 U.S. 677 (1889). *Cf.* Grynberg v. Kinder Morgan Energy Partners, L.P., 805 F.3d 901 (10th Cir. 2015), *cert. denied,* 136 S. Ct. 1714, 194 L. Ed. 2d 825 (2016) (master limited partnerships are partnerships for the purposes of diversity jurisdiction and the citizenship is determined by the citizenship of its partners), relying on Chapman v. Barney, *supra* and subsequent case law.

[56]   *See* In re Groff, 898 F.2d 1475 (10th Cir. 1990) (partnership is entity distinct from partners); Everest Investors 8 v. McNeil Partners, 8 Cal.Rptr.3d 31 (Ct. App. 2003) (" 'California law treats a partnership as a 'hybrid' organization that is viewed as an aggregation of individuals for some purposes, and as an entity for others.' " (Epstein v. Frank, 177 Cal.Rptr. 831 (Ct. App. 1981))).

contract and agency principles.[57] Unlike other forms of doing business, partnership existence is not dependent on filings or other formalities. In contrast, limited liability entities, including the limited liability partnership,[58] require filing or registration in the state of organization.

As discussed more fully later in this section, the 1990s brought major changes in the law relating to partnerships. The Revised Uniform Partnership Act, which has been adopted in whole or in part in a majority of states, has altered many of the traditional partnership concepts. Perhaps most importantly, the Revised Uniform Partnership Act recognizes a partnership as a separate entity rather than an aggregation of its members.[59] Also, as of 1998, 48 states and the District of Columbia permitted partnerships to register as limited liability partnerships and take advantage of at least some limited liability attributes.[60] Most states insulate partners from liability for negligence that they are not involved in, while other states provide a full liability shield for all partnership obligations—both tort and contract—except the partners' own negligence.

[2] Partnership Defined

The Uniform Partnership Act (UPA) and the RUPA similarly define "partnership" as "an association of two or more persons to carry on as co-owners a business for profit."[61] The co-ownership element of this definition entails both profit-sharing and sharing in control. An essential characteristic of the partnership is that it is an association for profit. The Acts provide that in most cases receipt of a share of the profits is prima facie evidence of partnership status.[62] The presumption is rebutted by evidence that the party lacks the power to share in control of the business. That is, profit-sharing alone is not sufficient to establish partnership status.[63] This does not require that such control actually be exercised. Control in this context requires more than discharging ministerial tasks; it requires the power to share in significant managerial tasks.[64] Though a formal written agreement is not necessary for a partnership's existence, more is required than a naked desire to form a partnership, such as an understanding regarding relative responsibilities or the organizational structure of the business. There is authority to the effect that the partnership definition of "carrying on a business" contemplates a continuing or ongoing venture rather than a simple and finite undertaking such as we find in a promissory note, option, or contract.[65]

The existence of a partnership does not depend upon a formal written agreement to that effect. For example, the partnership agreement may be oral.[66] Furthermore, a series

---

[57]   Agency law is discussed § 1.24 *infra. See also* Chapter 8 for discussion of agency in the context of corporate officials.

[58]   *See* § 1.7[6] *infra.*

[59]   RUPA § 204.

[60]   *See* Elizabeth G. Hester, Registered Limited Liability Partnerships, 69 Aspen Law & Business Corporation Guide 1 (No. 6, March 16, 1998).

[61]   Uniform Partnership Act § 6(1) (1969) (hereinafter UPA); Revised Uniform Partnership Act § 101(6) (hereinafter RUPA).

[62]   UPA §§ 6, 7(4) (1969); RUPA §§ 101(6), 202(c)(3).

[63]   *See* Southex Exhibitions, Inc. v. Rhode Island Builders Ass'n, 279 F.3d 94 (1st Cir. 2002).

[64]   Alan R. Bromberg & Larry E. Ribstein, Bromberg & Ribstein on Partnership § 2.14 (2001).

[65]   *See* Kiszely v. Yi, 70 Va. Cir. 364 (2006) (financing arrangement for purchase of house was not a partnership agreement).

[66]   *See* Kansallis Fin. Ltd. v. Fern, 40 F.3d 476, 478–79 (1st Cir. 1994).

of understandings may result in a partnership even in the absence of an agreement. The determination of whether a particular business arrangement is a partnership is a highly factual inquiry and is dependent upon not only the written or oral understandings and agreements between the parties but also upon the conduct of the parties and the surrounding circumstances. Thus, for example, a statement in an agreement that it does not create a partnership, although probative of the party's intent, is not dispositive in determining whether a partnership in fact exists.[67] The determination depends not upon the form of the agreement but rather on the nature of relationship that the parties intended and how the law classifies such a relationship. The failure to duly create a LLC would suggest the fallback description of an arrangement among individuals would be a general partnership, assuming their arrangement meets the definition of a partnership.[68]

When two or more persons share profits in a business venture, there is a presumption that a partnership exists.[69] However, profit-sharing alone will not create a partnership if the profits are shared as joint tenants,[70] under a lease, as a means for repaying a debt,[71] or as part of an employment agreement.[72]

Parties can find themselves in a partnership even if they do not meet the criteria discussed directly above. This can happen for example when a group holds themselves out as a partnership or as an association that possesses partnership attributes. In these cases, if third parties rely on such a holding out, courts may recognize the existence of a partnership by estoppel.[73] Other courts have referred to this as the doctrine of "ostensible partnership."[74]

[3] Fiduciary Nature of Partnership

A partnership is a form of organization suitable only to an association of a few members known to each other, perhaps bound together by ties of friendship, who are able to trust each other. The relationship between partners is a fiduciary one of mutual power and responsibility. It is usually accepted that partners owe each other a fiduciary

---

[67] Apollon v. OCA, Inc., 592 F. Supp. 2d 906 (E.D. La. 2008) ("While the parties to a contract may intend that, between themselves, their relationship is to be governed by the label they affix, that label neither governs the rights of third parties nor affects the legal consequences of the parties' agreement," (citing In re PCH Associates, 804 F.2d 193 (2d Cir. 1986))).

[68] *But cf,* MAS Associates, LLC v. Korotki, 465 Md. 457, 214 A.3d 1076 (Md. Ct. App. 2019) (reversing trial court determination that partnership existed since the parties intent and conduct did not establish a partnership).

[69] *See* RUPA § 202; UPA § 7.

[70] *E.g.,* Bickhardt v. Ratner, 871 F.Supp. 613, 620 (S.D.N.Y. 1994); Johnson v. Wiley, 613 N.E.2d 446 (Ind. App. 1993). *See* RUPA § 202(c)(1); UPA § 7.

[71] *See, e.g.,* Martin v. Peyton, 246 N.Y. 213, 158 N.E. 77 (1927); RUPA § 202(c)(3)(i), (vi).

[72] *See* RUPA § 202(c)(3); UPA § 7. There are other situations where the resumption of partnership does not apply: "A person who receives a share of the profits of a business is presumed to be a partner in the business unless the profits were received in payment: (i) of a debt by installments or otherwise; (ii) for services as an independent contractor or other compensation to an employee; (iii) of rent; (iv) of an annuity or other retirement or health benefit to a beneficiary, representative, or designee of a deceased or retired partner; (v) of interest or other charge on a loan, even if the amount of payment varies with the profits of a business, including a direct or indirect present or future ownership of the collateral, or rights to income, proceeds, or increase in value derived from the collateral; or (vi) for the sale of goodwill of a business or other property by installments or otherwise." RUPA § 202(c)(3).

[73] *See, e.g.,* Gosselin v. Webb, 242 F.3d 412 (1st Cir. 2001).

[74] *See, e.g.,* In re Lona, 393 B.R. 1 (Bankr. N.D. Cal. 2008) (finding no ostensible partnership but an actual partnership).

duty of the "utmost good faith and loyalty."[75] In the classic words of Justice Cardozo, partners:

> owe to one another, while the enterprise continues, the duty of the finest loyalty. Many forms of conduct permissible in a workaday world for those acting at arm's length, are forbidden to those bound by fiduciary ties. A trustee is held to something stricter than the morals of the market place. Not honesty alone, but the punctilio of an honor the most sensitive, is then the standard of behavior.[76]

As further explained in a later New York case,

> it is elemental that a fiduciary owes a duty of undivided and undiluted loyalty to those whose interests the fiduciary is to protect. This is a sensitive and "inflexible" rule of fidelity, barring not only blatant self-dealing, but also requiring avoidance of situations in which a fiduciary's personal interest possibly conflicts with the interest of those owed a fiduciary duty. Included within this rule's broad scope is every situation in which a fiduciary, who is bound to single-mindedly pursue the interests of those to whom a duty of loyalty is owed, deals with a person "in such close relation [to the fiduciary] . . . that possible advantage to such other person might . . . consciously or unconsciously" influence the fiduciary's judgment.[77]

Demanding partnership fiduciary standards have frequently been applied with respect of the duty of majority shareholders to the minority in closely held corporations.[78] A partner's fiduciary duty often involves full candor and disclosure to copartners.[79] As discussed in subsequent sections of this work, when dealing with close corporations and limited liability companies it is appropriate to look to partnership law in evaluating fiduciary duties.

Beginning in the last quarter of the twentieth century, there was a movement in corporate law known as the contractarian movement that challenged fiduciary obligations as a basic tenet of corporate governance.[80] The basis of their argument is that governance and relationships within an organization should be a matter of contract with the freedom of contract that it entails rather than the more limiting norms of fiduciary

---

[75]   *See, e.g.,* South Atl. Ltd. Partnership of Tenn., LP v. Riese, 284 F.3d 518 (4th Cir. 2002).

[76]   Meinhard v. Salmon, 164 N.E. 545, 546 (N.Y. 1928).

[77]   Birnbaum v. Birnbaum, 539 N.E.2d 574, 576 (N.Y. 1989) (citations omitted).

[78]   *E.g.,* Donahue v. Rodd Electrotype Co., 328 N.E.2d 505 (Mass. 1975), *noted in* 61 Cornell L. Rev. 986 (1976); 89 Harv. L. Rev. 423 (1975); Meiselman v. Meiselman, 307 S.E.2d 551 (N.C. 1983).

[79]   *See, e.g.,* Triple Five of Minnesota, Inc. v. Simon, 404 F.3d 1088 (8th Cir. 2005) (failure to disclose material terms of the transaction prevented plaintiff from participating in the sale of ownership in the Mall of America); Meehan v. Shaughnessy, 535 N.E.2d 1255 (Mass. 1989) (secrecy in plotting to leave law firm partnership).

[80]   *E.g.,* Lucien Bebchuk, Contractual Freedom in Corporate Law, 89 Colum. L. Rev. 1395 (1989); Stephen M. Bainbridge, Community and Statism: A Conservative Contractarian Critique of Progressive Corporate Law Scholarship, 82 Cornell L. Rev. 856, 857–58 (1997); Frank Easterbrook & Daniel Fischel Contract and Fiduciary Duty, 36 J. Law & Econ. 425 (1993).

principles.[81] Many commentators have been critical of this movement.[82] The courts have tolerated some contractual restrictions on the partnership fiduciary obligations. Some statutes expressly permit some contractual limitations. For example, the Delaware limited partnership law permits partners to contract out of fiduciary duties up to a point but "the partnership agreement may not eliminate the implied contractual covenant of good faith and fair dealing."[83] Accordingly, a broadly drafted agreement may forgive negligently unfair self-dealing but could not excuse unfair self dealing resulting from gross negligence or bad faith.[84]

The elimination of fiduciary duties among partners would be a wholly undesirable outcome.[85] Thus, you can redefine the duties in the partnership agreement in terms of what partners may do vis-à-vis each other. But even so, they must still acquit those obligations in the utmost good faith and spirit of fairness.[86] Even RUPA, which eliminates the words "fiduciary duty" and takes a relatively restrictive view of partnership duties, retains the basic fiduciary principles recognized by the common law in its express recognition of partners' duties of loyalty[87] and care[88] with regard to partners' conduct vis-à-vis each other and the partnership itself.

The Delaware partnership statute goes even further in permitting the elimination of fiduciary duties. In contrast to the approach to corporations, the Delaware partnership

---

[81]   *See, e.g.,* Wood v. Baum, 953 A.2d 136, 143 n. 23 (Del. 2008), quoting Gale v. Bershad, 1998 WL 118022, at *5 (Del. Ch. 1998) ("[t]o allow a fiduciary duty claim to coexist in parallel with an implied contractual claim, would undermine the primacy of contract law over fiduciary law in matters involving the essentially contractual rights and obligations of [the] shareholders").

[82]   William Bratton, The New Economic Theory of the Firm: Critical Perspectives from History, 41 Stan. L. Rev. 1471 (1989).

[83]   Del. Code Ann. tit. 6, § 17–1101 ("To the extent that, at law or in equity, a partner or other person has duties (including fiduciary duties) to a limited partnership or to another partner or to another person that is a party to or is otherwise bound by a partnership agreement, the partner's or other person's duties may be expanded or restricted or eliminated by provisions in the partnership agreement; provided that the partnership agreement may not eliminate the implied contractual covenant of good faith and fair dealing."). *See generally* Mohsen Manesh, the Default Duty Debate in Delaware, 39 J. Corp. L. 35 (2013).

[84]   Venhill Ltd. Partnership v. Hillman, 2008 WL 2270488 (Del.Ch. 2008).

[85]   Judson A. Crane & Alan R. Bromberg, Law of Partnership 389 (1968).

[86]   *See, e.g.,* RUPA § 404(d) ("A partner shall discharge the duties to the partnership and the other partners under this [Act] or under the partnership agreement and exercise any rights consistently with the obligation of good faith and fair dealing").

[87]   RUPA § 404(b):

A partner's duty of loyalty to the partnership and the other partners is limited to the following:

> (1)   to account to the partnership and hold as trustee for it any property, profit, or benefit derived by the partner in the conduct and winding up of the partnership business or derived from a use by the partner of partnership property, including the appropriation of a partnership opportunity;

> (2)   to refrain from dealing with the partnership in the conduct or winding up of the partnership business as or on behalf of a party having an interest adverse to the partnership; and

> (3)   to refrain from competing with the partnership in the conduct of the partnership business before the dissolution of the partnership.

[88]   RUPA § 404(c):

> A partner's duty of care to the partnership and the other partners in the conduct and winding up of the partnership business is limited to refraining from engaging in grossly negligent or reckless conduct, intentional misconduct, or a knowing violation of law.

RUPA's formulation of the duty of care is an unfortunate watering down of the principles of ordinary care that have traditionally been applicable in partnership operations. Presumably, this gross negligence standard is an attempt to incorporate the business judgment rule as it has evolved in corporate law.

statute permits such contractual provisions without limiting them to duty of care violations.[89] The Delaware statute, however, cautions that "agreement may not eliminate the implied contractual covenant of good faith and fair dealing."[90]

[4] Authority of Partners; Management of Partnership

Authority of partners to act on the partnership's behalf is determined both by agency principles and applicable partnership statutes. Each partner has the apparent authority to contract on behalf of the partnership. In the absence of an agreement providing otherwise, all partners have equal rights in the management and conduct of the business, and persons dealing with a partnership are not affected by private agreements between partners. Thus a partner may bind the partnership on a contract within the apparent scope of the partnership business, even though the partnership agreement expressly denies the contracting partner such authority (unless the person with whom the partner dealt has knowledge of the restriction on the partner's authority). All the partners, even those with a proportionately small interest, are liable jointly and severally for loss or injury caused by the tortious or other wrongful act of any partner or employee of the firm who is acting in the ordinary course of the business.

If a note or contract is made in the partnership's name, it is the obligation of all the partners jointly as individuals and, as sometimes provided by statute or agreement, their liability is joint and several. A partnership's name is not the name of a separate legal unit, although by statute in some jurisdictions partners may sue or be sued under the common name. A judgment obtained against partners may be joint, but attachment or execution may be levied on their separate assets without any duty to resort first to partnership assets. Thus, innocent partners having only a small interest in the business may be "lunged into the unknown depths of unlimited liability"[91] by contracts made by other persons or torts committed by other persons over whom they have no control.

The partnership agreement determines the extent to which partners have a say in the management of the partnership. The statute provides default rules that apply if there is no agreement or if the agreement is silent on the issue. Unless the partnership agreement provides otherwise, partners vote equally on partnership matters regardless of their relative contributions to the partnership.[92] This means that no matter how little a partner contributes in the way of capital, he or she will have significant voting rights unless limited by the partnership agreement. Since this is not ordinarily consistent with the wishes of the larger investors, lawyers must take care to assure that partnership agreements in fact reflect the intent of the partners. The partnership statutes also generally provide that in the absence of an agreement to the contrary, ordinary

---

[89]　Del. Code Ann. tit. 6, § 17–1101(d) (2009):

To the extent that, at law or in equity, a partner or other person has duties (including fiduciary duties) to a limited partnership or to another partner or to another person that is a party to or is otherwise bound by a partnership agreement, the partner's or other person's duties may be expanded or restricted or eliminated by provisions in the partnership agreement; provided that the partnership agreement may not eliminate the implied contractual covenant of good faith and fair dealing.

[90]　Del. Code Ann. tit. 6, § 17–1101(d) (2009).

[91]　Henry W. Ballantine, Corporations 7 (rev. ed. 1946).

[92]　UPA § 18 ("All partners have equal rights in the conduct of the business"); RUPA § 401(f) (same).

governance matters are determined by a majority of the partners.[93] Extraordinary matters, as opposed to those relating to the ordinary business, including amendment of the partnership agreement, require the consent of all partners.[94]

[5] Partners' Liabilities

Under section 17 of the UPA, entering partners are not personally liable on partnership debts contracted before their admission; partnership property, including that in which the newly admitted partner has an interest, can be the source of satisfying such a debt.[95] Section 306(b) of RUPA is to the same effect.[96] Thus, for example, a newly admitted partner was held not liable for construction loan funds drawn upon by a partnership after admitting the new partner when the loan agreement authorizing such advances was entered into before the new partner was admitted.[97] One can better understand this result by envisioning that it is through the partnership entity that individual partners become personally liable on partnership debts. One who is not a partner when the contract giving rise to the obligation was entered into by the partnership is therefore not linked to the agreement giving rise to that contractual claim. It should also be remembered that upon the admittance of a new partner, there is in essence the creation of a new partnership arrangement. Thus it can be said that by shielding the new partner from personal liability on debts that existed prior to his becoming a partner implicitly prefers creditors of the new partnership over the creditors of the old partnership in terms of who should be able to pursue the new partner.[98]

[6] Limited Liability Partnerships

In the 1990s, a revolutionary change occurred in partnership law. As of 1991, all states followed the traditional view that in a general partnership, the partners are joint and severally liable for all of the partnership's tort obligations and had joint liability for contract-based claims. However, by 1997, 48 states had adopted statutes permitting a general partnership to elect to become a limited liability partnership, which at one time in most states meant that the partners are insulated from tort but not contract liability. An increasing number of states, and the most recent version of the Revised Uniform Partnership Act, provide for the same type of limited liability that exists with corporations—the partners are not liable for either the tort or contract obligations of the partnership or of the other partners.[99] An increasing number of states have adopted the full liability shield for limited liability partnerships. Even in states adopting a full liability shield, there may be exceptions. For example, a partner in a limited liability

---

[93]   UPA § 18(h) ("Any difference arising as to ordinary matters connected with the partnership business may be decided by a majority of the partners; but no act in contravention of any agreement between the partners may be done rightfully without the consent of all the partners."); RUPA § 401(j).

[94]   *See* RUPA § 401(j) ("An act outside the ordinary business of a partnership and an amendment to the partnership agreement may be undertaken only with the consent of all of the partners."). *Compare* UPA § 18(h) which is quoted in the preceding footnote.

[95]   UPA § 17 (1969).

[96]   RUPA § 306(b) ("A person admitted as a partner into an existing partnership is not *personally* liable for any partnership obligation incurred before the person's admission as a partner.") (emphasis added).

[97]   Citizens Bank of Mass. v. Parham-Woodman Medical Assoc., 874 F.Supp. 705, 707 (E.D. Va. 1995).

[98]   *Id.*

[99]   RUPA § 306(c).

partnership will remain personally liable for negligent or wrongful conduct, including wrongful supervision.[100]

Limited liability partnership status generally depends upon making a filing in the state of organization and also by appointing a registered agent for service of process.[101] Although the procedures for limited liability registration vary from state to state, most states permit a general partnership to register as a limited liability partnership upon a majority vote of the partners.[102] Limited liability registration, along with the other unincorporated forms of doing business, leaves the general partnership with unlimited liability of its owners as the default form of doing business if no other form is selected.

[7] Dissolution and Dissociation

Partnerships traditionally have had a precarious existence. A partnership is subject to serious risks of dissolution, and to possible liquidation of its assets and termination of its business. Even if a partnership is not a partnership at will but is stated to be for a definite term, any partner may dissolve it at any time in violation of the agreement, subject only to liability for damages for breach of the agreement. A partnership is also dissolved by the death of a partner, by the bankruptcy of a partner, or by a court decree declaring a partner to be insane or guilty of serious misconduct relating to the partnership.[103]

Dissolution (or dissociation) may result a partner's share being terminated and the partner being paid his or her pro rata share of the partnership. In the case of a minority partner, the partner's share may be subject to a minority discount in calculating the value of the minority partner's share.[104]

The Revised Uniform Partnership Act is similar in effect except that these events cause the partner's "dissociation" rather than an automatic dissolution of the partnership.[105] Notwithstanding RUPA's introduction of dissociation as an alternative to dissolution, there are situations in which liquidation will still be required.

A partner's dissociation has several consequences. Dissociation terminates the partner's right to manage or conduct partnership business. Dissociation ends the partner's duty to refrain from competing with the partnership, unless of course the partnership agreement provides otherwise. Dissociation limits the partner's remaining duties of loyalty and care only as to matters or events that occurred before the partner's dissociation.

---

[100] *See, e.g.,* N.Y. Partnership Law § 26 (2009).

[101] Given the growth of non-corporate forms of doing business, many states have recognized the value in adopted standardized provisions for registered agents. In fact, the National Conference on Uniform State Laws adopted a Model Registered Agents Act.

[102] *See* Alan R. Bromberg & Larry E. Ribstein, Bromberg & Ribstein on Limited Liability Partnerships and the Revised Uniform Partnership Act § 2.04(b) (2001); General partnerships that do not seek the limited liability shield do not have to register. *See, e.g.,* Goss v. Bobby D. Assoc., 94 S.W.3d 65 (Tex. Ct. App. 2002).

[103] UPA §§ 31, 32.

[104] Congel v. Malfitano, 31 N.Y.3d 272, 76 N.Y.S.3d 873, 101 N.E.3d 341 (2018) (minority partner's action for wrongful dissolution). When the partnership business was to continue after dissolution, it was appropriate to apply a discount reflecting value of the partnership business's goodwill in determining amount to be paid to minority partner. *Id.*

[105] RUPA §§ 601, 602. *See, e.g.,* McCormick v. Brevig, 96 P.3d 697 (Mont. 2004) (applying the RUPA); Shoemaker v. Shoemaker, 745 N.W.2d 299 (Neb. 2008) (applying the RUPA); Warnick v. Warnick, 76 P.3d 316 (Wyo. 2003) (same).

Dissociation does not of itself discharge the partner for a partnership liability incurred *before* the dissociation. However, the partnership agreement may release a dissociated partner from liability for a partnership obligation to the remaining partners. Release from any liability to partnership creditors requires an agreement with those creditors. A dissociated partner will also be released from liability if a creditor of the partnership, with notice of the dissociation but without the partner's consent, agrees to a material alteration in the nature or time of payment of a partnership obligation.

With respect to obligations incurred by a partner *after* his or her dissociation, a partner remains liable as a partner for transactions the partnership enters into within a specified period following the partner's dissociation if at the time of transacting the other party (1) does not have notice of the partner's dissociation, and (2) reasonably believes that the dissociated partner is still a partner. However, once dissociated, a dissociated partner is not liable for obligations of the partnership's ongoing business merely because the business uses the same the partnership name or uses the dissociated partner's name.

As pointed out above, a dissociated partner has no *actual* authority to act for the partnership; there may be lingering *apparent* authority. Thus, in order to protect innocent third parties for a statutory period following a partner's dissociation, the partnership remains bound for that partner's acts that, before the dissociation, would have bound the partnership under the partner's agency authority. However, the partnership is so bound only if, at the time of the transaction, the other party (1) reasonably believed the dissociated partner was then a partner, and (2) neither had notice of the partner's dissociation nor is deemed to have had knowledge due to filed or recorded limitations on the partner's or dissociated partner's authority.

Although no longer triggered by the events that result in a partner's dissociation, under the Revised Uniform Partnership Act a partnership may still decide to dissolve and wind-up its business. A partner's dissociation is not a condition precedent to dissolution. For example, a RUPA partnership may voluntarily dissolve (as is the case with corporations and other business entities).

Subject to special provisions in the partnership agreement, partners are not at liberty to transfer full partnership. The Uniform Partnership Act and RUPA provide that a partner's assignment of his or her interest in the firm does not of itself dissolve the firm.[106] However, the assignment does not substitute the assignee for the assigning partner as a member of the firm;[107] it merely entitles the assignee to receive the profits to which the assigning partner would otherwise be entitled. Interests of partners are thus not readily transferable.

Usually, disputes among partners can be judicially settled only by a full accounting of all partnership matters. As a general proposition, traditionally and under the Uniform Partnership Act, a partner cannot bring an action against another partner on a particular partnership transaction; the partner must ordinarily resort to a suit for an accounting.[108] The Revised Uniform Partnership Act gives more leeway in suits among

---

[106] UPA § 27(1). The revised Act is similar in providing for transferability of a partner's transferable interest. RUPA § 503(a)(2).

[107] UPA § 18(g). The revised Act is in accord. RUPA § 503(a)(3).

[108] UPA §§ 21, 22.

partners by permitting suits for breach of contract and seeking legal or equitable relief with or without an accounting.[109]

The Revised Uniform Partnership Act provides that "a court may order liquidation upon application of a partner if it is established that it is not otherwise reasonably practicable to carry on the partnership business in conformity with the partnership agreement."[110] The courts have invoked the involuntary dissolution power in appropriate cases.[111]

Many limited partnership statutes provide for involuntary liquidation and winding up, in circumstances that parallel the rule with corporations.[112] For example, under Delaware law in an action by one of the partners, a court "may decree dissolution of a limited partnership whenever it is not reasonably practicable to carry on the business in conformity with the partnership agreement."[113] In this section of the statute, irreconcilable deadlock can provide a basis for dissolution.[114] However, since liquidation is a drastic remedy, it should not be granted lightly.[115] As is the case with limited partnership statutes, limited liability company statutes draw distinctions similar to the partnership statutes between dissociation and dissolution. Also, similar to the partnership statutes, the Delaware act provides that a court may dissolve a limited liability company if it is "not reasonably practicable" to continue the business under the limited liability company agreement.[116]

[8] The Revised Uniform Partnership Act

In August 1992, the National Conference of Commissioners on Uniform State Laws adopted the Revised Uniform Partnership Act (RUPA), which provides both greater stability and certainty in partnership arrangements than occurs under the UPA. RUPA does away with the vestiges of the once widely held view that a partnership is an

---

[109] RUPA § 405(b). *See generally* Pankratz Farms, Inc. v. Pankratz, 95 P.3d 671 (Mont. 2004) (electing an accounting in winding up the partnership).

[110] RUPA § 801(5)(iii).

[111] *See, e.g.,* Navarro v. Perron, 19 Cal.Rptr.3d 198 (Ct. App. 2004) (granting dissolution where elected by plaintiff partner in a case where defendant wrongfully repudiated partnership); Della Ratta v. Dyas, 183 Md.App. 344, 350, 961 A.2d 629, 633 (2008) (holding dissolution appropriate where it was no longer reasonably practicable to carry on the business); Pankratz Farms, Inc. v. Pankratz, 322 Mont. 133, 144–45, 95 P.3d 671, 680–81 (2004) (granting dissolution where animosity affecting the efficient and proper operation of the partnership made it impracticable to continue the partnership in its current form); Horizon/CMS Healthcare Corp. v. Southern Oaks Health Care, Inc., 732 So.2d 1156, 1159–60 (Fla.App. 1999) (upholding dissolution where the partners could no longer work together).

[112] Most corporation statutes provide that in the case of deadlock or oppression, a shareholder can petition a court to dissolve the corporation. *See* § 14.12 *infra*.

[113] Del. Code Ann. tit. 6, § 17–802 (2005) ("On application by or for a member or manager the Court of Chancery may decree dissolution of a limited partnership whenever it is not reasonably practicable to carry on the business in conformity with a limited liability company agreement"). *See, e.g.,* PC Tower Ctr., Inc. v. Tower Ctr. Dev. Assocs. Ltd. P'ship, 1989 WL 63901, at *6 (Del. Ch. 1989) (granting dissolution where the sole purpose of a limited partnership was owning and operating certain real property and that purpose was frustrated because market conditions made finding a tenant "practically impossible").

[114] *See, e.g.,* In re Silver Leaf LLC, 2005 WL 2045641, at * 11 (Del. Ch. 2005) (granting dissolution due to voting deadlock); Haley v. Talcott, 864 A.2d 86, 89 (Del. Ch. 2004) (same).

[115] *See, e.g.,* In re Arrow Investment Advisors, LLC, 2009 WL 1101682 (Del.Ch. 2009) (declining to order dissolution of LLC).

[116] Del. Code Ann. tit. 6, § 18–802 (LexisNexis 2005 & Supp. 2008) ("On application by or for a member or manager the Court of Chancery may decree dissolution of a limited liability company whenever it is not reasonably practicable to carry on the business in conformity with a limited liability company agreement").

aggregate of its members rather than a separate entity.[117] Generally, RUPA continues the UPA approach that the statute's provisions pertaining to the relationship among partners apply only in the absence of a contrary provision in the partnership agreement.[118] Not all of the provisions of RUPA, however, are default rules: There are a few "mandatory" rules that cannot be changed by the partnership agreement. Whereas under the UPA there was much uncertainty over which of its rules are mandatory, RUPA provides certainty in this area by listing those rules that are mandatory.[119]

In broad overview, RUPA introduces five significant changes to the law of partnerships. First, RUPA provides greater stability to partnerships on changes in the partnership membership. Under the UPA, a partner's departure from the partnership "dissolved" the partnership. There is much uncertainty over the meaning of "dissolution" under the UPA, which provides only general guidance as to what dissolution is[120] and what it is not.[121] RUPA clearly delineates the two possible consequences of a partner's departure (referred to as a "dissociation"[122])—either a buyout of the departing partner or a winding up of the partnership. Section 701 of RUPA deals with buy outs of the departing partner and provides default rules for the valuation and payout of that partner's interest. Section 801 of RUPA identifies those instances in which the partnership business must be liquidated and provides default rules for the settlement of partnership accounts.

The second major change introduced by RUPA is a more precise delineation of the nature of the partner's fiduciary obligations. RUPA's version of the duty of loyalty balances the commercial flexibility of allowing partners to pursue their individual self-interest against the need to promote fairness and openness among the partners.[123] RUPA also embraces a standard of gross negligence for partners.[124] A component of the partner's fiduciary obligations *inter se* is the broad information rights of each partner under RUPA that cannot be reduced through the partnership agreement.[125]

The third major change by RUPA concerns the nature and transfer of partnership property, where RUPA unambiguously embraces the entity rather than applying UPA's confusing tenancy-in-partnership approach. Under RUPA, property held in the partnership name is conclusively presumed to be partnership property,[126] and its transfer is pursuant to the individual partners' actual or apparent authority.[127] RUPA's treatment of how the property is held underscores the importance of recording title to

---

[117] RUPA § 201 (declaring the partnership to be an entity distinct from its owners). This is consistent with the growing trend to treat partnerships as entities.

[118] *See generally* Donald J. Weidner & John W. Larson, The Revised Uniform Partnership Act: The Reporters' Overview, 49 Bus. Law. 1 (1993).

[119] *See* RUPA § 103(b).

[120] UPA § 29 ("changes in the relation of the partners").

[121] *See* UPA § 30 ("partnership is not terminated").

[122] RUPA § 601.

[123] *See* RUPA § 404(b). For a critical view of this flexibility, *see* Rutheford B. Campbell, The "New" Fiduciary Standards Under the Revised Uniform Limited Liability Company Act: More Bottom Bumping from NCCUSL, 61 Me. L. Rev. 27 (2009); Rutheford B. Campbell, Bumping Along the Bottom: Abandoned Principles and Failed Fiduciary Standards in Uniform Partnership and LLC Statutes, 96 Ky. L.J. 163 (2007–2008).

[124] *See* RUPA § 404(a).

[125] *See* RUPA §§ 403(b), 103(b)(2).

[126] *See* RUPA § 204(a)(1). Property may also be found to be partnership property if the surrounding circumstances so suggest. *See* RUPA § 204(a)(2).

[127] *See* RUPA §§ 301, 302(a).

property. This allows third parties to rely on the record of title by placing the risk of wrongful transfers on the partnership and thereby protecting the reasonable expectations of third parties.[128]

The fourth significant change found in RUPA is its authorization of the conversion of general partnerships into limited partnerships[129] as well as the merger of partnerships.[130] The conversion and merger provisions not only provide needed certainty for partnership combinations and restructurings but also assure flexibility in the partnership's structure.

The fifth significant change found in RUPA is the recognition of limited liability partnerships.[131] RUPA permits a partnership to elect to register as a limited liability partnership and thereby immunize the partners from liability for the obligations incurred by the partnership and by the other partners. In order to qualify for limited liability, a partnership must register with the state as a limited liability partnership. Most state statutes provide that a registered limited liability partnership ("LLP") will insulate partners from liability for the negligence of their co-partners and employees. Some states impose liability on partners who supervise the negligent partner or employee.[132] A number of other states have adopted a full liability shield that insulates partners from liability, other than their own wrongdoing, for both tort and contract obligations.

§ 1.8   The Joint Venture: A Form of Partnership

Business ventures of limited scope or duration conducted by two or more persons for profit are variously referred to as "joint ventures," "joint adventures," "joint enterprises" and, in some contexts, "syndicates." A "joint venture" has been defined as an association of two or more persons to carry out a *single* business transaction, or a few related transactions, for profit or commercial gain, for which purpose they combine their property, money, efforts, skills, and knowledge.[133] This definition is far from universally accepted, so "joint venture" is "at best a nebulous concept."[134] In broad overview, a joint venture is best distinguished from a partnership in that it has a more limited scope and duration.[135]

Many jurisdictions require the presence of several specific elements to establish a joint venture. The most commonly stated elements of a joint venture are (1) a contract,

---

[128] The partnership can protect itself by filing a statement of authority delineating the partners' actual authority. This destroys the rights of third parties with respect to real property if recorded in the office for recording real property transfers. *See* RUPA § 105(b).

[129] *See* RUPA §§ 902, 903.

[130] *See* RUPA §§ 904, 905.

[131] RUPA §§ 306(c), 1001(b).

[132] *See* Elizabeth G. Hester, Registered Limited Liability Partnerships, 69 Aspen Law & Business Corporation Guide 1 (No. 6, March 16, 1998).

[133] *E.g.,* Trustees of the Graphic Communications International Union Upper Midwest Local 1M Health and Welfare Plan v. Bjorkedal, 516 F.3d 719 (8th Cir. 2008).

[134] *See* In re Groff, 898 F.2d 1475, 1476 (10th Cir. 1990) ("Although its history is not entirely clear, apparently the joint venture concept was developed to extend principles of partnership law to organizations that did not meet the technical requirements of a partnership").

[135] *E.g.,* Sadelmi Joint Venture v. Dalton, 5 F.3d 510, 513 (Fed. Cir. 1993).

(2) a common purpose, (3) a community of interest, (4) an equal right of control, and (5) participation in both profits and losses.[136]

§ 1.9 The Limited Partnership

The limited partnership is a statutorily created method[137] of profit-sharing by passive investors. This form of business organization permits investors to share the profits of a business, with their risk of loss limited to their investment if the investors comply with certain legal formalities. A limited partnership has two classes of partners: (1) one or more general partners, who have complete control, manage the enterprise, and are subject to full liability; and (2) one or more limited partners, who are very similar to firm creditors but are subordinated to creditors if the firm becomes insolvent or is liquidated. The limited partner ordinarily does not take part in the day-to-day control of the business.

The first limited partnership statute in this country was adopted in New York in 1822. The early enactments, however, were filled with pitfalls. A safer and more satisfactory form of limited partnership arrived in 1916 with the Uniform Limited Partnership Act. This statute was enacted by every state.[138] In 1976 the Commissioners on Uniform State Laws approved a Revised Uniform Limited Partnership Act (RULPA) as a recommended replacement. Subsequently, the revised act was adopted in most jurisdictions.[139]

Unlike an ordinary partnership, which can be formed by a mere informal agreement among the participants a limited partnership is formed only by complying with statutory formalities. A verified certificate containing provisions similar to those called for in a corporation's articles of incorporation must be filed with the clerk, recorder, or other designated public official of the county in which the limited partnership's principal place of business is located and sometimes must also be filed in other counties in which it has places of business.[140]

Both the original and revised uniform limited partnership acts limit the liability of persons who attempt to become limited partners. If the statutory requirements for the formation of a limited partnership are *substantially* complied with, or if the persons who attempt to become limited partners in good faith believe themselves to be limited partners, the limited partners enjoy limited liability.[141] Limited partners become subject to liability if they exercise control of the business.[142] As a result of the states having adopted the RULPA, limited partners today have much greater latitude to involve

---

[136] *See* Terra Venture, Inc. v. JDN Real Estate-Overland Park, L.P., 443 F.3d 1240, 1245 (10th Cir. 2006); Sullivan v. Scoular Grain Co., 930 F.2d 798 (10th Cir. 1991) (elements of joint venture are (1) community of interest, (2) joint proprietary interest, (3) right of control, (4) right to share profits, and (5) duty to share losses).

[137] "A limited partnership is strictly a creature of statute, its object being to enable persons not desiring to engage in a particular business, to invest capital in it and to share in the profits which might be expected to result from its use, without becoming liable as general partners for all partnership debts. In other words, it is a form of partnership in which the liability to third persons of one or more of its members is limited to a fixed amount." Hoefer v. Hall, 411 P.2d 230, 232 (N.M. 1965).

[138] 6 U.L.A. 2 (Supp. 1980).

[139] Forty-nine states (all except Louisiana) have adopted some form of the 1976 revised Act. Unif. Ltd. Partnership Act Refs. & Ann., 6A U.L.A. 1 (1995).

[140] Under the Revised Act, filings need be made only in the Office of the Secretary of State.

[141] Uniform Limited Partnership Act § 2(2) (1969) (hereinafter ULPA); RULPA § 201(b) (1976).

[142] ULPA §§ 7, 11 (1969); RULPA §§ 303, 304 (1976 with amendments 1985).

themselves in the partnership without risking their loss of limited liability than they could under the former Uniform Limited Partnership Act.[143]

The 1985 amendments to the Revised Uniform Limited Partnership Act further expanded these safe-harbor activities to include limited partners having the right to approve any matter related to the business of the limited partnership so long as their right to so participate is expressly granted in the limited partnership agreement.[144] Also, the Revised Uniform Limited Partnership Act provides that merely being "an officer, director or shareholder" of a corporate general partner of the limited partnership does not constitute taking part in the control of the partnership.[145]

The Revised Uniform Limited Partnership Act also contains a sweeping provision that restricts the class of persons to whom a limited partner is liable to those persons who transact business with the limited partnership reasonably believing, based on the limited partner's conduct, that the limited partner is a general partner.[146] Under this unconditional "creditor-reliance" standard, the creditor's recovery is justified only when limited partners act like the traditional general partners and have failed to let the creditor know that they were acting solely in their limited partner capacity.[147]

Unlike partners in general partnerships, limited partners are not ordinarily agents of the partnership and thus do not have the authority to bind the partnership simply because of their position as limited partners. A corollary issue is the extent to which limited partners owe fiduciary duties to one another.

As managers of the business, general partners owe fiduciary obligations to the limited partnership.[148] There is authority that permits limiting those fiduciary duties pursuant to contract in the limited partnership agreement.[149] Limited partners who take an active role in the business will incur the same fiduciary duties as general partners.[150] In contrast, where the limited partner is not exercising managerial control, the fiduciary duties to the other partners will be much lower.[151] However, when limited partners exercise their majority control to the detriment of other limited partners, they will be accountable for breach of fiduciary duty[152] in much the same manner as partners in a general partnership and majority shareholders in a closely held corporation.[153]

The uniform acts contain provisions restricting withdrawal of a limited partnership's capital and preserving a kind of trust fund of firm assets for the protection

---

[143] These decisions are highly factual and depend on the type of control asserted by the purported limited partners. *See, e.g.,* Gateway Potato Sales v. G.B. Investment Co., 822 P.2d 490 (Ariz. App. 1991) (denying summary judgment on issue of control by limited partner).

[144] RULPA § 303(b)(6)(ix).

[145] RULPA § 303(b)(1).

[146] *Compare* RULPA (1976), *with* 1985 Amendments to § 303(a).

[147] *See, e.g.,* Shimko v. Guenther, 505 F.3d 987 (9th Cir. 2007).

[148] *See, e.g.,* Jerman v. O'Leary, 701 P.2d 1205 (Ariz. App. 1985).

[149] *See, e.g.,* Werner v. Miller Tech. Mgmt., L.P., 831 A.2d 318 (Del. Ch. 2003).

[150] *See, e.g.,* South Atl. Ltd. Partnership of Tenn., LP v. Riese, 284 F.3d 518 (4th Cir. 2002) (applying North Carolina law).

[151] In re Villa West Associates, 146 F.3d 798 (10th Cir. 1998).

[152] Red River Wings, Inc. v. Hoot, 751 N.W.2d 206, 219, 2008 N.D. 117 (2008) ("limited partners who participate in the business of the partnership or act in concert with the general partner are subject to the fiduciary duties of loyalty and care and the obligations of good faith and fair dealing applicable to partners in a general partnership.").

[153] *See id.*

of firm creditors. These provisions are analogous to the provisions of corporation laws restricting payment of dividends or other distributions to shareholders if the distributions would impair the corporation's capital.

Limited partners' rights to share in profits and to obtain repayment of their capital contributions on distribution of firm assets are subordinated to the claims of firm creditors, but limited partners have priority over general partners in the distribution of profits and capital.[154] Because limited partners are not essential to the firm, their withdrawal does not automatically lead to the firm's dissolution; withdrawal does necessitate amendment of the partnership agreement, however.[155] Absent a contrary provision in the partnership agreement, limited partners may at any time withdraw their capital from the firm, provided they give six months' notice. Limited partners can also assign to another their interests in the firm's capital and profits, but their assignees do not become partners in the firm unless the partnership agreement so provides or the remaining partners consent.

Many limited partnership statutes provide for involuntary dissolution in circumstances that parallel the rules with corporations. For example, under Delaware law in an action by one of the partners, a court "may decree dissolution of a limited partnership whenever it is not reasonably practicable to carry on the business in conformity with the partnership agreement."[156] Additionally, irreconcilable deadlock can provide the basis for dissolution under this section of the statute.[157] However, since dissolution is a drastic remedy, it should not be granted lightly.[158]

The general partner has the same fiduciary duties as would apply in partnerships generally.[159] However, contractual provisions in the partnership agreement may be effective in narrowing those duties. For example, the Delaware limited partnership law permits partners to contract out of fiduciary duties up to a point but "the partnership agreement may not eliminate the implied contractual covenant of good faith and fair dealing."[160] Accordingly, a broadly drafted agreement may forgive negligently unfair self-dealing but not excuse unfair self-dealing resulting from gross negligence or bad faith.[161]

The limited liability company (LLC) has become a more attractive form of business than the partnership or limited partnership; unlike a traditional limited partnership, all of the participants in the LLC, including the general managers, enjoy a complete liability shield. A growing number of states have recognized a new variety of limited partnership

---

[154] ULPA § 23; RULPA § 804. Under the Revised Act, partners to the extent they are also creditors may share equally with the other creditors on dissolution.

[155] ULPA §§ 9(1)(g), 19 to 21; RULPA §§ 202, 301, 402 (1976, amended 1985) (withdrawal procedure applies only to general partners).

[156] Del. Code Ann. tit. 6, § 17–802.

[157] *See, e.g.,* In re Silver Leaf LLC, 2005 WL 2045641, at * 11 (Del. Ch. 2005) (granting dissolution due to voting deadlock); Haley v. Talcott, 864 A.2d 86, 89 (Del. Ch. 2004) (same).

[158] *See, e.g.,* In re Arrow Investment Advisors, LLC, 2009 WL 1101682 (Del.Ch. 2009) (declining to order dissolution of LLC).

[159] *See, e.g.,* Purcell v. Southern Hills Investments, LLC, 847 N.E.2d 991 (Ind. App. 2006) (in assessing LLC fiduciary duties it is appropriate to look to closely held corporation cases: "[i]n line with the district court's opinion in Credentials Plus, we now hold that common law fiduciary duties, similar to the ones imposed on partnerships and closely-held corporations, are applicable to Indiana LLCs"). For discussion of partners' fiduciary duties, *see* § 1.7[3] *supra.*

[160] Del. Code Ann. tit. 6, § 17–1101.

[161] Venhill Ltd. Partnership v. Hillman, 2008 WL 2270488 (Del.Ch. 2008).

known as the limited liability limited partnership.[162] This variation permits partners to become general partners and still stand behind a limited liability shield. In a limited liability limited partnership a limited partner may become a general partner without losing his or her limited liability. This permits limited partners to become general partners and thus have significant say in the day-to-day operations of the partnership business. Further, the limited partner turned general partner would not likely be subject to the securities laws for the same reason that a general partnership interest ordinarily is not a security subject to regulation under federal and state securities laws.[163]

§ 1.10 Tax Considerations in Selecting a Business Form

[1] Tax Considerations in Selecting a Business Form

In broad overview, the partnership is not treated as a tax entity under the federal Internal Revenue Code.[164] The partnership is required to file an information return listing the partners and their share of the partnership income. Each partner's share of the partnership income (whether distributed to the partners or not) is taxed to that partner as personal income. A corporation, in contrast, is usually treated as a taxable unit separate and apart from its shareholders. This commonly results in the same income and same assets being taxed twice, once to the corporation and again to its shareholders. For example, the corporation pays a tax on its income, and dividends received by its shareholders are taxed to the shareholders to the extent they represent distributions from the corporation's earnings and profits. Similarly, the corporation pays state and local property taxes on its assets, and the shareholders often pay property taxes on their shares of stock, which represent, among other things, their interests in the corporation's assets. Therefore, double taxation is a common concern in deciding whether to incorporate a business.

A corporate entity can avoid double taxation by electing to be a Subchapter S corporation. Under the tax laws, an S corporation is similar to a partnership in that the business's income and losses are attributed to its owners (whether distributed or not), and the corporation is not a taxable entity. Only a small business corporation may elect to be an S corporation.[165] A "small business corporation" is a corporation with not more than 75 shareholders; it may issue only a single class of stock, which may be owned only by individuals, estates, and certain trusts; and its shares may not be owned by nonresident aliens or certain ineligible corporations, such as financial institutions.[166] The Subchapter S election must be consented to by all the shareholders and must be made no later than by the fifteenth day of the third month of the taxable year in which the election is to take effect. Absent an election, all corporate entities are taxed as C corporations.[167]

---

[162] *E.g.,* Del. Code Ann. tit. 6, § 17–214 (2005).

[163] For a general discussion of the definition of security, *see* 1 Thomas Lee Hazen, Treatise on the Law of Securities Regulation §§ 1:49 *et seq.* (7th ed. 2016).

[164] An important exception to the partnership not being a taxable entity arises in the case of a publicly traded partnership. I.R.C. § 7704 (2009).

[165] I.R.C. § 1361(a)(1) (2009).

[166] I.R.C. § 1361(b)(1), (2) (2009). Although only one class of stock is permitted, voting rights within that class may be varied.

[167] The terms "C corporation" and "S corporation" appear only in the world of taxation and distinguish corporations that are governed by the special rules sets forth in Subchapter S from the more generally applicable Subchapter C of the Internal Revenue Code.

Substantial change to the tax laws was enacted in late 2017. For example, the basic corporate tax rate was reduced from 35 to 21 percent. Other business forms also reaped benefits. Post 2017, individuals who have taxable income attributed to them as a result of ownership in a partnership, LLC or Subchapter S firm generally can deduct 20 percent of the attributed income (called "qualified business income"). This deduction is not available where the business is that of a profession such as medicine, law or engineering services and phases out totally for income above $315,000. These changes complicate further the decision of entity choice. Corporate dividends are subject to double taxation: the earnings producing the funds from which dividends are paid are taxed at the corporate tax rate (now a maximum of 21 percent) and the dividends upon receipt are taxed at the individual tax rate (a progressive rate with a 37 percent maximum). In contrast, income earned by a partnership, Subchapter S corporation or LLC electing to be taxed as a partnership is "attributed" to its owners according to how they share in profits *regardless* whether the owners receive any distribution. Thus, to the extent that earnings of a corporation are paid to shareholders as dividends those earnings are taxed twice. This of course introduces a negative in the selection of the corporate form (*i.e.*, without a Subchapter S election).

In the end, the tax considerations on the type of business to be formed can, in isolated cases, be quite complex. More generally, however, those forming a small business will be sensitive to non-tax considerations as well, such as shielding its owners from the business's debts. In these situations, the disadvantages of double taxation are ameliorated by the availability of Subchapter S. However, this may come at the irritation of losing some fringe benefits that are available to shareholders of a C corporation.

[2] The Check-the-Box Rules

Formerly, the tax laws imposed severe restrictions on the attributes of entities opting to be taxed other than as a corporation. The IRS, drawing on the guidelines set down by the Supreme Court in *Morrissey v. Commissioner*,[168] identified six factors that were to be considered in deciding whether an association would be taxable as a corporation: (1) associates engaged in a joint venture, (2) the purpose of transacting business and sharing in its gains, (3) continuity of life, (4) centralized management through representatives of its participants, (5) limited liability, and (6) free transferability of interests.[169] An association would not be classified as a corporation unless the association had more corporate characteristics than noncorporate characteristics.[170]

The foregoing six characteristics meant that planners did not have complete freedom in drafting the internal governance and operational rules for noncorporate forms of doing business. All of that changed in 1997 when the IRS replaced the *Morrisey* test with a "check the box" procedure under which an entity may elect to be taxed as a corporation or not.[171] Under the current approach, all that is required at the outset is that a noncorporate form of doing business elect whether or not to be taxed as a corporation. Entities that select noncorporate tax treatment may at a later date elect corporate tax treatment.

---

[168] Morrissey v. Commissioner, 296 U.S. 344 (1935).

[169] *See* Treas. Reg. § 301.7701–2(a) (1988).

[170] Treas. Reg. § 301.7701–2(a)(3) (1988).

[171] Treas. Reg. § 301.7701–3(a) (2008).

§ 1.11 The Limited Liability Company

[1] Nature of Limited Liability Companies

One of the newer forms of business association is the limited liability company (LLC). The Wyoming legislature in 1977 enacted the first statute authorizing the limited liability company.[172] All states now provide for limited liability companies.[173]

The impetus for the state enactments authorizing the creation of LLCs is securing the federal income tax advantages of partnership status while simultaneously preserving the state law benefits of limited liability for the entity's owners. In 1988, in a key ruling, the Internal Revenue Service (IRS) issued Ruling 88–76 classifying a Wyoming LLC as a partnership for federal income tax purposes.[174]

The limited liability company, thus, is a relatively new vehicle by which a business's owners can avoid both double taxation and liability for the business's debts. The "interests" of the members of an LLC are not represented by stock; the members hold interests much like partners in a partnership. LLC members have a right to share in profits as spelled out in the LLC operating agreement. Many statutes provide that if the agreement is silent, members share equally in profits. However, a right to share in profits does not translate into a right to demand a distribution of those profits.

At one time most states required an LLC to have at least two members, although an increasing number of states now permit one member LLCs.[175] The members usually enter into an operating agreement that functions much like a partnership agreement. A primary feature of an LLC is that its members have no liability beyond their initial investment, even if they actively participate in or control the firm's management. Under most LLC statutes, the authority to manage is with the firm's members, but the statutes allow the members to allocate managerial authority so that some members can be assured of being active while others are passive. It is also possible for management to be placed with non-owners. Many states thus authorize both member managed and non-member managed LLCs.[176]

Corporations may divide their operations into various subsidiaries and other affiliated entities. LLCs may accomplish this as well by establishing separate LLC entities. Alternatively, some states, including Delaware, allow the establishment of series LLC that permits the division of the business into divisions with cabined exposure to liability.[177]

---

[172] *See* Wyo. Stat. Ann. §§ 17–15–101 to 17–15–136 (1977). The current version is Wyo. Stat. Ann. §§ 17–15–101 to 17–15–147 (Lexis 2007). *See generally* Hamill, The Origins Behind the Limited Liability Company, 59 Ohio St. L. J. 1459 (1998).

[173] *See, e.g.,* Fla. Stat. Ann. §§ 608.401 to 608.705 (2007); Mich. Comp. Laws Ann. § 450.4101 to 450.5200 (2002); Va. Code Ann. §§ 13.1–1000 to 13.1–1080 (2006).

[174] IRS Ruling 88–76 (1988).

[175] *E.g.,* Del. Code Ann. tit. 6, § 18–101(6) (2005).

[176] *See* § 1.11[4] *infra* for discussion of LLC management.

[177] *See* Del. Code Ann. tit. 6, § 18–215(a) (2009), Tex. Bus. Org. Code § 601.101 (2009). *See also, e.g.,* 35 ILCS § 115/2 (2009) ("A series with limited liability shall be treated as a separate entity to the extent set forth in the articles of organization.").

There is great variety remains among the states in their limited liability company statutes. In addition, as is the case with corporate law, the lack of uniformity does not prevent recognition of entities outside the state of organization.[178]

As a result of the foregoing developments, the limited liability company has become an attractive alternative form for doing business. The LLC is likely to continue as the entity of choice[179] for businesses that formerly would be organized as partnerships.[180] Similarly, the limited liability company may become an attractive alternative to a closely held corporation,[181] especially one that would elect partnership tax treatment under Subchapter S of the Internal Revenue Code.

At one time the federal tax laws were extremely limiting in terms of the restrictions on a limited liability company seeking noncorporate tax treatment. In the late 1990s, the IRS relaxed its restrictions. Some limited liability statutes retain the more restrictive provisions that were necessary under the former IRS rules. Many states have eliminated those restrictions thus making the limited liability company a viable form of unincorporated entity for many more businesses.

Series LLCs

The "series LLC" is a separate legal entity, within which assets, liabilities, operations, earnings and members' rights are allocated via the operating agreement. Delaware was the first state to expressly authorize the Series LLC.[182] A number of other states have followed Delaware in recognizing the series LLC.[183] A core feature of the series LLC is that the operating agreement must set forth the method to account for the assets of each series independent of the LLC itself and in some states there is a requirement that a separate certificate of designation must be filed with the state for each series.[184] The Series LLC is a useful means to accommodate the varying interests of sophisticated investors in capital investments, oil and gas ventures, as well as real estate projects.[185]

Benefit LLCs

As discussed in a subsequent section, many states have enacted statutes to enable benefit corporations which are dedicated to a public benefit purpose.[186] Following this

---

[178] *See, e.g.,* Koh v. Inno-Pacific Holdings, Ltd., 54 P.3d 1270 (Wash. Ct. App. 2002).

[179] *See, e.g.,* J. M. Cunningham, The Limited Liability Company: Entity of Choice for High Tech Start-Ups? 13 Computer Law 11 (1996).

[180] This may not be the case, however, in states that have adopted the broad concept of limited liability for limited liability partnerships under the Revised Uniform Partnership Act. This is known as the "full shield" version of the Revised Uniform Partnership Act, which has been adopted in a number but not a majority of states. *See supra* § 1.7.

[181] *See, e.g.,* Richard A. Booth, The Limited Liability Company and the Search for a Bright Line Between Corporations and Partnerships, 32 Wake Forest Law Review 79 (1997).

[182] Del. Code Ann. tit. 6. § 18–215.

[183] *E.g.,* Code of Alabama Section 10A–5A–11; DC Code Ann. § 29–802.06; 805 ILCS 180/37–40; Iowa Code Ann. § 490A.305; K.S.A. 17–76,143; Mo.Rev.Stat. § 347.186; Montana Ann. Code § 35–8–304 *et seq*; Nev. Rev. Stat. § 86.296; N.D. Cent. Code §§ 10–32–17.5, 10–32–48, 10–32–56.5.a, 10–32–56.7; 18 Okla. St. Ann. §§ 2005(B), 2054.4; Tenn.Code Ann. § 48–249–309; Texas Business Organizations Code §§ 101.601 to 101.621, 21.152(A), (C), (D), 21.153(A), 21.361(A)(2); Utah Revised Limited Liability Company Act § 48–2c–606; Wis. Stat. Ann. § 183.0504.

[184] *See e.g.,* 805 Ill. Comp. Stat. 180/37–40.

[185] *See* Dominick T. Gattuso, Series LLCs, Bus. Law Today 33 (July/Aug. 2008).

[186] Benefit corporations are discussed in § 2.9 *infra*.

model, some states have enacted statutes to enable benefit LLCs where the purpose incudes a public benefit in the LLC's mission.[187]

[2] Fiduciary Duties in Limited Liability Companies

It is appropriate to follow the course of many decisions in looking to partnership and close corporation cases in analyzing the applicable fiduciary duties in the LLC context.[188] Subject to the extent the governing LLC statute authorizes private ordering, the guiding standards for fiduciary obligations are, parallel to their meaning in corporate law's treatment of the duty of care and duty of loyalty. In addition to the freedom the parties have to alter these default rules through the operating agreement, the question then arises whether all participants in an LLC—members and managers, active and inactive, are bound by these duties. Some courts have found the appropriate analogy is not corporate but partnership law, so that at least in a member-managed LLC, partnership fiduciary duties apply.[189] The fiduciary duty of members in a member-managed LLC can also be seen as a parallel to the implied contractual covenant of good faith and fair dealing.[190] This is consistent with the well established concept that managers (whether nor not they are members) of LLCs are subject to fiduciary standards.[191] There is some authority, however, that in a non-member-managed LLC the members do not stand in a fiduciary relation to one another as partners would.[192]

A core fiduciary duty among members, and managers to members is a duty of candor. In a leading case, *VGS, Inc. v. Castiel*,[193] X, a majority owner, was a co-manager with Y and Z. The operating agreement authorized mergers by a majority vote of the managers and also provided that X could remove any manager and appoint a replacement. Y and Z, believing that the company was being mismanaged by X, without advance notice of their plans, approved at a duly convened meeting of the managers to merge the firm with a company controlled by them; the consequence of the merger was that X would thereafter be a minority owner. Vice-Chancellor Steele held that managers owe a duty of loyalty to both the LLC and its members. This duty required Y and Z to give advance notice to X of the merger and its consequential effects on X. New York is among the states to recognize that members have a duty of candor among themselves. Thus, a member who purchases another member's shares without disclosing the firm

---

[187] *See, e.g.*, Mohsen Manesh, Introducing the Totally Unnecessary Benefit LLC, 97 N.C. L. Rev. 603 (2019).

[188] *See, e.g.*, Purcell v. Southern Hills Investments, LLC, 847 N.E.2d 991 (Ind. Ct. App. 2006); McConnell v. Hunt Sports Enterprises, 725 N.E.2d 1193 (Ohio Ct. App. 1999).

[189] *See, e.g.*, Anest v. Audino, 773 N.E.2d 202 (Ill. App. Ct. 2002) (fiduciary duties owed in a member-managed LLC are similar to those owed in partnerships and close corporations).

[190] *See, e.g.*, Fisk Ventures, LLC v. Segal, 2008 WL 1961156 (Del.Ch. 2008).

[191] *See, e.g.*, Bay Center Apartments Owner, LLC v. Emery Bay PKI, LLC, 2009 WL 1124451 (Del. Ch. Ct. 2009) (*Mem. Op.*):

> The Delaware LLC Act gives members of an LLC wide latitude to order their relationships, including the flexibility to limit or eliminate fiduciary duties. But, in the absence of a contrary provision in the LLC agreement, the manager of an LLC owes the traditional fiduciary duties of loyalty and care to the members of the LLC.

[192] *See* Dragt v. Dragt/DeTray, LLC, 161 P.3d 473 (Wash. Ct. App. 2007). *See also* WAKA, LLC v. Humphrey, 73 Va. Cir. 310, 314 (2007) ("The General Assembly's express imposition of fiduciary duties among partners in a partnership, Va. Code Ann. § 50–73.102(A), demonstrates that the General Assembly is conscious of the language needed to impose fiduciary duties if desired. The decision to omit similar duty-imposing language in the LLC Act is clear evidence that the General Assembly intended that LLC members owe no fiduciary duty to other LLC members.").

[193] 2000 WL 1277372 (Del. Ch. 2000).

will be sold to a third party at a very high price breached his fiduciary duty.[194] Another area of concern with fiduciary obligations in LLCs is that of a manager or dominant member taking a business opportunity argued to be within the scope of the LLC's likely interest.[195] However, to date the cases impose such fiduciary obligations only with respects to managers and controlling members and not passive members.[196]

Similar to the result reached in corporate law, a fiduciary duty is not owed to creditors whose rights are contractually based and not founded on equitable principles.[197] In contrast, those who promote the LLC stand in a fiduciary relationship to the LLC as well as its prospective members; so that promoters breach their duty of honesty if they make secret profits in connection with property resold to the LLC.[198]

As discussed in a later section of this work, exculpatory provisions in corporate charters may limit or eliminate liability for duty of care, but not duty of loyalty violations.[199] The Delaware partnership statute, however, cautions that "agreement may not eliminate the implied contractual covenant of good faith and fair dealing."[200] The Delaware statute follows the same approach for limited liability companies.[201]

For example, in *Gatz Props., LLC v. Auriga Capital Corp.*,[202] the operating agreement provided that transactions with members or managers could not be on "terms or conditions which are less favorable to the company than . . . [if entered into at] arms-length." The Delaware Supreme Court affirmed that the provision imposed a fiduciary obligation equivalent to Delaware's "entire fairness" standard that has been developed over the years for corporations. The lower court, in dicta, reasoned that Delaware's LLC Act imposes "default" fiduciary duties on managers and controlling stockholders, unless the operating agreement provides otherwise.[203] In its decision, the Delaware Supreme Court rebuked the lower court for opining on an issue not necessary to resolve the dispute between the parties. Thus, it remains an open question whether there are implicit fiduciary duties within LLCs unless the articles or operating agreement provides otherwise. Nonetheless, in 2012, following *Gatz*, Vice-Chancellor Laster reasoned that, while awaiting definitive resolution of the existence, scope and nature of fiduciary duties of LLC managers and members, lower court precedents provide persuasive reasons to apply fiduciary duties by default.[204]

---

[194] Salm v. Feldstein, 20 A.D. 3d 469, 799 N.Y.S.2d 104 (Sup. Ct. App. Div. 2005).

[195] Grove v. Brown, 2013 WL 4041495 (Del. Ch. Aug. 8, 2013).

[196] *See, e.g.*, Feeley v. NHAOCG, 62 A.3d 649 (Del. Ch. 2012); George Wasserman & Janice Wasserman Goldsten Family v. Kay, 197 Md. App. 586, 14 A.3d 1193 (Md. App. 2011); Strebel v. Wimberly, 371 S.W. 3d 355 (Tex. App. 2012).

[197] *See* Weinstein v. Colborne Foodbotics, LLC, 2013 CO 33, 302 P.3d 263 (Colo. 2013) (dismissing suit by creditors alleging managers who were also sole owners of all the members interest in the LLC breached an alleged fiduciary duty to creditors by approving distributions that rendered LLC insolvent).

[198] Roni LLC v. Arfa, 18 N.Y.3d 846, 939 N.Y.S.2d 746, 963 N.E.2d 123 (2011). Fiduciary duties of promoters generally are discussed in § 5.10 *infra*.

[199] *See, e.g.*, Del. Code Ann. tit. 8, § 102(b)(7) (2009); Model Bus. Corp. Act § 2.02(b)(4).

[200] Del. Code Ann. tit. 6, § 17–1101(d) (2009).

[201] Del. Code Ann. tit. 6, § 18–1101(e) (2009).

[202] 59 A.3d 1206 (Del. 2012).

[203] Auriga Capital corp. v. Gatz Properties, 40 A.3d 839 (Del.Ch. 2012).

[204] Feeley v. NHAOCG LLC, 62 A.3d 649 (Del.Ch. 2012) (allowing claim of gross negligence by a managers to survive a motion to dismiss).

The courts have been unusually receptive to agreements limiting fiduciary duties in LLCs.[205] For example, where the operating agreement provided only that managers owed only the duty of good faith the court interpreted this to require allegations that managers acted in a manner they did not believe was in the best interest of the firm or its unitholders.[206]

[3] Continuity of Existence and Transferability of Limited Liability Interests

Today most, if not all, limited liability company enabling legislation allows for continuity of the LLC existence.[207] Prior to the check-the-box procedure, even more significant in the classification of the LLC for tax purposes was the more common limited liability company statute's provision that the LLC is dissolved "upon the death, retirement, resignation, expulsion, bankruptcy . . ." of a member.[208] Limited liability company statutes with such limitations on the duration of the entity frequently provided that the LLC could continue if all the remaining members consent and such consent is authorized in the articles of incorporation. The "check-the-box" rules mean that continuity of existence will no longer put an LLC's tax status in jeopardy. As a result most LLC statutes today provide for continuity of existence of LLCs in much the same way as corporate statutes operate.

An LLC's existence may be terminated by dissolution. Early statutes did not address a member's right to dissociate from the entity although some follow the partnership analogy. An LLC's member's interest does not necessarily translate into a right to force a dissolution of the limited liability company.[209] However, the LLC operating agreement may provide that withdrawal is a trigger for dissolution of the LLC.[210]

Many limited liability statutes provide for involuntary dissolution in circumstances that parallel the rule with corporations.[211] For example, the Delaware act provides that a court may dissolve a limited liability company if it is "not reasonably practicable" to continue the business under the limited liability company agreement.[212] Irreconcilable deadlock can provide the basis for dissolution under this section of the statute.[213]

---

[205] *See, e.g.,* Gerber v. Enterprise Products Holdings, LLC, 2012 WL 34442 (Del. Ch. 2012); Kelly v. Blum, 2010 WL 629850 (Del. Ch. 2010); Strebel v. Wimberly, 371 S.W. 3d 355 (Tex. App. 2012).

[206] In re Atlas Energy Resources LLC, 2010 Del.Ch. LEXIS 216 (Del. Ch. 2010).

[207] *See, e.g.,* McDonough v. McDonough, 169 N.H. 537, 153 A.3d 187 (2016) (holding that provision of articles of formation setting forth a specific date as the latest date for the LLC to dissolve did not compel dissolution).

[208] Fla. Stat. Ann. § 608.441(c) (2001) (*repealed,* 10/1/99, 1999 Fla. Sess. Law Serv. Ch. 99–315 (C.S.H.B. 1513) (West)).

[209] Lieberman v. Wyoming.com LLC, 11 P.3d 353 (2000) (member had right to withdraw and receive return of his capital contribution but it did not follow that he could force dissolution).

[210] *See* Investcorp, L.P. v. Simpson Investment Co., 983 P.2d 265 (Kan. 1999).

[211] Most corporation statutes provide that in the case of deadlock or oppression, a shareholder can petition a court to dissolve the corporation. *See* § 14.12 *infra.*

[212] Del. Code Ann. tit. 6 § 18–802.

[213] *See, e.g.,* In re Silver Leaf LLC, 2005 WL 2045641, at * 11 (Del. Ch. 2005) (granting dissolution due to voting deadlock).

Transferability of LLC Interests

A member's interest encompasses both economic rights (*e.g.*, flow through of money and tax consequences) and governance rights (participation in the management of the business). The operating agreement can control whether a transfer of a member's interest transfers both types of rights or only the economic interest in the shares.[214] Thus, a creditor to a member who attaches a member's interest through a charging order is only entitled to the economic rights associated with the shares unless the procedures set forth in the operating agreement have been satisfied to extend to the creditor full membership status.[215] Similarly, an heir does not become a member solely by inheritance.[216] Similar to corporate law, the operating agreement can condition transfers on granting other members a right of first refusal. Failure to comply with such restriction can render the transfer invalid.[217]

Many early LLC statutes, provided members could transfer or assign their interests to others, but the transferees did not become members themselves and were not allowed to participate in the firm's management absent the written consent of all the other LLC members.[218] Artful planning and drafting may ameliorate this concern. For example, securing advance consent to transfers, such as obtaining advance consent by the LLC members or articles of incorporation empowering the managers to exercise consent for the owners, will increase free transferability. Prior to the new "check-the-box" tax rules, free transferability of limited liability company interests could have jeopardized the favorable tax status sought by the parties. However, today, limited liability company agreements can readily provide for the free transferability of limited liability company interests without jeopardizing the entity's tax status. Thus, more modern LLC statutes readily permit free transferability.

Notwithstanding the ability to provide for free transferability of LLC interests, the organizers often have business reasons for restricting transferability. As is the case with closely held corporations, LLC members may agree to enforceable restrictions on transfer.[219]

[4] Management of Limited Liability Companies

Centralized management is not an inherent feature of an LLC. LLCs may be organized either as member managed LLC or set up with centralized management as a management managed LLC.[220] Most LLC statutes provide that the firm will be managed by the LLC members unless the articles or operating agreement provide otherwise. An LLC managed by persons who are not members has centralized management. This is

---

[214] *See, e.g.*, Gartner v. Cardio Ventures, 121 A.D.3d 609 (N.Y. App. Div. 2014) (per written consent of majority of the members the transferee was a member); In re Huber, 2013 WL 6184972 (W.D. Wa. Bankr. Nov. 25, 2013) (trustee succeeds to debtor's estate that included 85 percent interest in LLC but could not exercise control rights associated with shares as operating agreement conditioned transfer of membership interest on consent of all owners).

[215] Zokaites v. Pittsburgh Irish Pubs., LLC, 2008 Pa. 281, 962 A.2d 1220 (Pa. Super. Ct. 2008).

[216] Ott v. Monroe, 282 Va. 403, 719 S.E.2d 309 (Va. 2011).

[217] *See, e.g.*, Sherwood Park Bus. Ctr., LLC v. Taggart, 261 Or. App. 609, 323 P.3d 551 (Or. Ct. App. 2014).

[218] *See, e.g.*, Colo. Rev. Stat. § 7–80–702 (2008); Wyo. Stat. Ann. § 17–15–122 (2008).

[219] *See, e.g.*, Eureka VIII LLC v. Niagara Falls Holdings, LLC, 899 A.2d 95 (Del. Ch. 2006) (upholding anti-assignment provision with respect to LLC interest and declaring attempted assignment in violation of the agreement invalid).

[220] *See, e.g.*, Del. Code Ann. tit. 6, § 18–402 (dealing with management of LLCs).

referred to as a non-member managed LLC. Larger, more complex LLCs are likely to be management managed as opposed to member-managed.[221] Smaller LLCs, on the other hand, often prefer the member-managed form so as to operate more as partnerships.[222]

As noted above, many statutes provide that absent an agreement to the contrary, limited liability companies are member managed.[223] Under the default provision, which parallels the law of partnership, in member-managed LLCs, each of the members is an agent of the LLC[224] and has the authority to bind it in the ordinary course of business. As an agency relationship, member managed LLCs result in fiduciary duties of its member-manager agents. These fiduciary duties are subject to reasonable limitation in the LLC operating agreement.[225] More generally, in the absence of a contrary provision in the articles of organization or the operating agreement, a manager's financial interest, whether direct or indirect, in a transaction does not render the manager unavailable to approve that transaction.[226]

In the case of manager-managed LLCs, the managers possess the authority set forth in the operating agreement. This results in agency principles analogous to those in the corporate structure wherein certain titles, such as general manager, will carry with the position certain apparent, implied, and inherent authority. Notwithstanding members' obligations to one another, it has been held that absent a provision in the operating agreement, there is no right to expel an LLC member even for misfeasance in office.[227] The initial focus in resolving whether a member or manager has authority to bind the LLC on a transaction is the operating agreement. As seen, resolving questions of authority begin with whether the LLC is member-managed or manager-managed. A threshold question in a manager-managed LLC is whether the person signing the contract on behalf of the LLC is indeed *a manager*.[228] The authority of managers is guided by standard principles of the law of agency so that managers have the actual authority as set forth expressly in the operating agreement[229] or arises by implication of powers reasonably incident to the manager carrying out the normal business or affairs of the LLC in the usual manner.[230] Managers can bind the LLC pursuant to the doctrine

---

[221] *See, e.g.,* Louis G. Hering, Stanford L. Stevenson, and David A. Harris, Limited Liability Companies: Legal Aspects of Organization, Operation, and Dissolution, § IV (2006).

[222] *See, e.g.,* Larry E. Ribstein and Robert R. Keatinge, Ribstein and Keating on Limited Liability Companies, § 2.3 (1996).

[223] *E.g.,* Del. Code Ann. tit. 6, § 18–402 (2007).

[224] *See, e.g.,* J.M. Equip. & Transp. v. Gemstone, LLC, 1998 WL 573255 (Conn. Super. 1998).

[225] *See, e.g.,* Fisk Ventures, LLC v. Segal, 2008 WL 1961156, at *11 (Del. Ch. 2008) (holding that, under Delaware law, LLC agreements may limit or even eliminate fiduciary duties finding the elimination of fiduciary duties by provision in LLC operating agreement "flatly stating that members have no duties other than those expressly articulated in the Agreement").

[226] Feeley v. NHAOCG LLC, 2012 WL 6840577 (Del. Ch. Oct. 12, 2012) (drawing analogy to the law of corporations where statute expressly provides that vote of interested director can count toward the approval of a transaction in which the director has a financial interest).

[227] Walker v. Resource Dev. Co. Ltd., LLC (DE), 791 A.2d 799 (2000) (plaintiff whose drinking problem interfered with the performance of his duties could not be expelled).

[228] *See, e.g.,* Estate of Collins v. Geist, 143 Idaho 821, 153 P.3d 1167, 1170 (Idaho 2007)(based on oral operating agreement M. Collins was deemed manager based on him initially being the sole member and continuing to act with authority after admitting another as member).

[229] Hibbs v. Berger,430 S.W.2d 296, 304 (E.D. Mo. Ct. App. 2014)(operating agreement provided that managers could enter into contracts and terminate contracts so that either manager could, acting pursuant to the firm's interest, terminate the plaintiff's employment contract).

[230] *See, e.g.,* Protective Life Ins. Co. v. B & K Enterprizes, LLC, 2010 U.S. Dist. LEXIS 31650 (E.D. Wis. Mar. 31, 2010) (authority of manager as set forth in operating agreement to "buy, sell and lease" assets did not include doing so without consideration); Estate of Collins v. Geist, 143 Idaho 821, 153 P.2d 1167, 1173 (Ida.

of apparent authority.[231] Furthermore, any lack of authority by a manager can be cured by ratification of the transaction.[232] When an LLC has member managers, those member managers stand in a fiduciary capacity.[233] If the applicable LLC enabling statute permits, the operating agreement may limit or eliminate some fiduciary duties but not the implied covenant of good faith and fair dealing.[234]

Many LLCs do not avail themselves of the default member-managed LLC arrangement and instead opt for a manager-managed LLC. In a manager-managed LLC, managers act for the LLC in its business and affairs to the extent that the limited liability company agreement vests management power in the managers. Managers can bind the LLC.[235] Managers (and members in member managed LLCs) have the power and authority to delegate rights and powers to manage and control the LLC's business and affairs.[236] The LLC agreement may provide for penalties or other consequences in the event that a manager fails to perform appropriately according to the agreement.[237]

The approach to determining the scope of authority of members in a member-managed LLC is similar to that for manager-managed LLCs. The operating agreement is the initial focal point to determine the scope of authority for an individual member to act.[238] The agency doctrine of apparent authority also is available so that a member manager's act for apparently carrying on the usual way of business of the limited liability company is binding against a third party who is unaware of a limitation of that member's authority.[239] A member's authority to act on behalf of the LLC in a manager-managed

---

2007) (manager has authority to execute deeds to property when business of the LLC is to develop and sell real estate).

[231] Farm & Ranch Services, Ltd. v. LT Farm & Ranch, LLC, 779 F. Supp. 2d 949, 963 (S.D. Iowa 2011) (no apparent authority of one of two managers to sell loan contract where state statute provided that action by managers shall be by majority vote); Zions Gate R.V. Resort, LLC v. Oliphant, 2014 Utah App. 98, 101, 326 P.3d 118,121–22 (Utah Ct. App. 2014) (no apparent authority of single manager to execute 99-year lease where articles of organization required leases to be executed by all managers and state statute provided that articles of organization constitute notice of any limitation of authority); Ly v. Jimmy Carter Commons, LLC, 286 Ga. 831, 832–33, 691 S.E.2d 852, 854 (Ga. 2010)(question of fact whether third party was aware that co-manager's signature was necessary on loan documents).

[232] Farm & Ranch Services, Ltd. v. LT Farm & Ranch, LLC, 779 F. Supp. 2d 949, 964 (S.D. Iowa 2011)(lack of manager's authority ratified by LLC's acceptance of knowing acceptance of benefits of the unauthorized sale); Zions Gate R.V. Resort LLC v. Oliphant, 2014 Utah. App. 98, 103, 326 P.3d 118, 123 (Utah. Ct. App. 2014) (triable issue whether lack of authority to enter into 99-year lease was ratified by managers).

[233] See, e.g., In re Sky Harbor Hotel Properties LLC, 246 Ariz. 531, 443 P.3d 21 (2019) (LLC member owes fiduciary duties if the member has manager authority).

[234] See, e.g., In re Sky Harbor Hotel Properties LLC, 246 Ariz. 531, 443 P.3d 21 (2019) (LLC member owes fiduciary duties if the member has manager authority).

[235] E.g., Del. Code Ann. tit. 6, § 18–402 (2007).

[236] E.g., Del. Code Ann. tit. 6, § 18–407 (2007).

[237] E.g., Del. Code Ann. tit. 6, § 18–405 (2007).

[238] JMM Properties, LLC v. Erie Ins. Co., 548 Fed. Appx. 665 (2d Cir. 2013)(Truman named as managing member in operating agreement and thus had actual authority to submit claim for insurance loss); Pint ex rel. Lehigh One, LLC v. Breckner, 2009 U.S. Dist. WL 4042905 (D. Minn. Nov.19, 2009) (single member in a two-member managed LLC lacked authority mortgage property when operating agreement conditioned action on two-thirds approval of members); Lenticular Europe, LLC v. Van Leeuwen Cunnally, 279 Wis.2d 385, 400, 693 N.W. 2d 302, 308 (Wis. Ct. App. 2005) (because operating agreement did not change the state default rule the vote of the member who is targeted in the suit is disregarded in determining whether the member-managers duly approved suit against the member for his alleged misconduct in office).

[239] See, e.g., JMM Properties, LLC v. Erie Ins. Co., 548 Fed. Appx. 665(2d Cir. 2013); Merrill-Benco Agency, LLC v. HSBC Bank USA, 20 A.D. 3d 605, 799 N.Y.S.2d 590, 592 (App. Div. 3d 2005).

LLC is obviously highly circumscribed.[240] An, even in a member-managed LLC, a managing member who acts outside the scope of authority can thereby incur personal liability to the third party.[241] And, the circumstances including the manner in which the contract is executed can support a finding that a member intended to undertake personal liability to the third person.[242]

Fiduciary obligations among LLC members in member managed LLCs presumably include the duties of care and loyalty.[243] Failure to fully disclose conflicts of interest to fellow LLC members can be a breach of the duty of loyalty.[244] In some jurisdictions, the majority interest holders of an LLC have a fiduciary duty toward the minority.[245]

The voting rights of members of limited liability companies are determined by the LLC operating agreement. However, the statutes contain default provisions. Some states, following the partnership model, provide that in the absence of an agreement to the contrary, LLC members have an equal say in the operation of the business.[246] As of 2000, about half of the states had this per capita default rule.[247] Other states impose the default rule based on proportional ownership.[248] As is the case with other forms of doing business, the statute grants LLC members the right to inspect the LLC's books and records.[249]

Again, following the lead of the corporate statutes, most state LLC statutes provide a procedure for derivative suits.[250] Even without express statutory provisions relating to LLCs, analogy can be drawn to the corporate form in recognizing derivative suits within LLCs.[251] These derivative suits permit members to enforce *inter se* the provisions of the

---

[240] U.S. v. ADT Sec. Serv., Inc., 522 F. Appx. 480, 491–92 (11th Cir. 2013)(member lacks authority to sue government in a manager-managed LLC); Simmons v. Ball, 68 So.3d 831, 835 (Ala. 2011)(non-managing member lacks authority to execute deed in a manager-managed LLC).

[241] Bennett v. A.T. Masterpiece Homes at Broadsprings, LLC, 40 A.3d 145 (Pa. Super. 2012) (personal assurances supported liability on the part of the managing member).

[242] Joseph General Contracting, Inc. v. Couto, 144 Conn. App. 241, 72 A.3d 413 (Conn. Ct. App. 2013)(sole owner and president pressured plaintiff to modify project and thus was personally liable for failure to fulfill the contract as modified); Ubom v. SunTrust Bank, 198 Md. App. 278, 17 A.3d 168 (Md. Ct. App. 2011) (manner in which managing member executed credit agreement supported conclusion parties' intent was that he was personally liable).

[243] *See, e.g.,* Blue Chip Emerald LLC v. Allied Partners, Inc., 299 A.D.2d 278, 750 N.Y.S.2d 291 (2002). Snyder v. Puente, 297 A.D.2d 432, 746 N.Y.S.2d 517 (2002).

[244] *E.g.,* VGS, Inc. v. Castiel, 2000 WL 1277372 (Del. Ch. 2000) (setting aside merger for nondisclosures and breach of duty of loyalty).

[245] *See, e.g.,* Ayres v. AG Processing, Inc., 345 F. Supp. 2d 1200 (D. Kan. 2004); Brazil v. Rickerson, 268 F. Supp. 2d 1091 (W.D. Mo. 2003).

[246] *See* § 1.7[4] *supra.*

[247] *See* Melvin Aron Eisenberg, An Introduction to Agency, Partnerships and LLCs 136 (2000).

[248] *Id.*

[249] *See, e.g.,* Del. Code Ann. tit. 6, § 18–305 (2005).

[250] *E.g.,* Uniform Limited Liability Company Act §§ 1101 to 1104 (1995). *See, e.g.,* Elf Atochem North America, Inc. v. Jaffari, 727 A.2d 286, 293 (Del. 1999) ("The derivative suit is a corporate concept grafted onto the limited liability company form.").

On occasion courts have tolerated deviations from the required derivative suit procedure. *See, e.g.,* Caparos v. Morton, 845 N.E.2d 773 (Ill. App. 2006) (allowing claim filed as direct suit to proceed as derivative suit by limited partners in limited partnership); Bryan D. Scofield, Inc. v. Susan A. Daigle, Ltd., 999 So.2d 311, 315 (La. App. 2008) (finding "a member has a direct right of action against other members individually for a breach of fiduciary duty when such breach is grossly negligent and the damage is to the suing member directly.").

[251] *See, e.g.,* Tzolis v. Wolff, 10 N.Y.3d 100, 884 N.E.2d 1005, 855 N.Y.S.2d 6 (2008) (recognizing LLC derivative suit in the absence of statute).

LLC operating agreement as well as fiduciary duties that may arise from the LLC relation. Some of the statutes authorizing derivative suits with respect to LLCs apply the contemporaneous ownership requirement that is also applicable to corporate derivative suits.[252] Accordingly, in states having such statutes, in order to bring a derivative suit, the LLC member must have been a member both at the time of suit and be a member or an assignee of the limited liability interest at the time the of the alleged wrongdoing.[253] As in the corporate context, a threshold consideration is whether the suit should be prosecuted derivatively because it involves a violation of the LLC's rights or whether it can be a suit by the member individually because the alleged violation directly impacted a member.[254]

[5] Piercing the Limited Liability Veil and Other Entity Issues

Validly formed and properly operated limited liability companies will result in limited liability of the member owners with regard to the obligations of the LLC. Just as courts on appropriate facts have pierced the veil of corporate shareholders' limited liability,[255] a limited liability company that is improperly organized or improperly operated can be similarly attacked.[256] As is the case with corporations to pierce the veil of a limited liability company. It would have to be proved that the LLC was in fact a sham and really the alter ego of the members[257] or that it was a mere instrumentality of the owners.[258]

The veil is subject to piercing when there are representations of personal liability on the part of a member or another LLC for obligations to the third person.[259] Personal liability on the sole member of an LLC can occur when adequate provision was not made for creditors of a former LLC that the member dissolved.[260] Conducting the business of the LLC after its existence has been administratively terminated for failure to pay annual fees can also be a basis for personal liability.[261] In addition to traditional veil

---

[252] *E.g.*, Del. Code Ann. tit. 6, § 18–1003(2); Tex. Bus. Orgs. Code Ann. § 101.459.

[253] *E.g.*, Del. Code Ann. tit. 6, § 18–1003(2); Tex. Bus. Orgs. Code Ann. § 101.459. *See, e.g.*, In re LoneStar Logo & Signs, LLC, 2018 WL 2437601 (Tex. App. Austin 2018) (allowing a former LLC member to bring suit would deprive the current members of their rights, the former member is only a bystander in such a dispute).

[254] *See e.g.*, Bongiorno v. Capone, 330 Conn. 943, 196 A.3d 1212 (Conn. 2018)(direct action permitted where defendant sold 50 percent of ownership in a LLC and then embezzled $17,000 from the firm, reasoning that the defendant thereby failed to provide the plaintiff with full consideration for his membership purchased).

[255] *E.g.*, NetJets Aviation, Inc. v. LHC Communs., LLC, 537 F.3d 168, 176 (2d Cir. 2008) (finding that piercing the corporate veil applies to LLCs in similar instances that apply to corporations *i.e.*, "where there is fraud or where the corporation is in fact a mere instrumentality or alter ego of its owner"). *See also, e.g.*, Calipjo v. Purdy, 439 P.3d 218 (Haw. 2019) (jury question whether sole owner was alter ego of corporation and LLC).

[256] *See, e.g.*, Filo America, Inc. v. Olhoss Trading Co., LLC, 321 F. Supp.2d 1266 (M.D. Ala. 2004) (applying Alabama law, courts may pierce LLC veils on appropriate facts).

[257] Hollowell v. Orleans Regional Hosp. LLC, 217 F.3d 379 (5th Cir. 2000) (alter ego doctrine in case of limited liability company was question of fact).

[258] *See, e.g.*, New Horizons Supply Cooperative v. Haack, 590 N.W.2d 282 (Wis. App. 1999) (failure to establish "mere instrumentality" as basis for piercing veil).

[259] *See, e.g.*, Restaurant of Hattiesburg, LLC v. Hotel & Restaurant Supply, Inc., 84 So. 3d 32 (Miss. Ct. App. 2012) (error to dismiss case where record reflected representations to the plaintiff that entity was part of a larger network of LLCs and one of those entities had made payments on the accounts of that entity).

[260] *See, e.g.*, Mbahaba v. Morgan, 163 N.H. 561, 44 A.3d 472 (2012) (reversing dismissal where defendant could not sufficiently justify what appeared to be an arbitrary decision to dissolve LLC from which plaintiff's claim arose and to transfer its business to a new LLC without having made adequate provision for claims that may exist against the former LLC); Martin v. Freeman, 2012 COA 21, 272 P.3d 1182 (Colo. App. 2012) (same).

[261] AT & T Advertising, L.P. v. Winningham, 2012 OK CIV APP 51, 280 P.3d 360 (Div. 1 2012).

piercing principles, courts have applied reverse-piercing to limited liability companies.[262] Applying reverse veil piercing may be particularly appropriate with respect to LLCs having only one member.[263]

Courts have recognized the LLC as a separate entity distinct from its owners.[264] However, for jurisdictional purposes, courts may look through to the citizenship of the owners. A number of courts have held that for jurisdictional purposes, diversity of citizenship with respect to a limited liability company depends on the citizenship of its members.[265]

[6] Limited Liability Company Interests as Securities

There has been some debate on whether interests in an LLC are securities and thus subject to securities regulation.[266]

When a limited liability company's management agreement or operating agreement is written so as to give the members a significant say in the management of the business, those membership interests will not be securities.[267] In contrast, when a limited liability company structure is based on centralized management with passive investors, the limited liability shares of the passive investors ordinarily will fall within the definition of a security.[268]

[7] Professional Limited Liability Companies

Because the LLC is a relatively new form of doing business, a number of questions remain such as whether law firms and other professionals may use this form of doing business and thereby achieve limited liability. In some states there is express statutory authorization for professional limited liability partnerships (LLPs). It is to be anticipated that the efficacy of professional LLPs (PLLPs) and professional limited liability companies (PLLCs) will be clarified over time. Limited liability statutes are much more diverse than partnership and limited partnership statutes, most of which have uniform acts as models. Thus, there are likely to be more state-by-state variations with LLCs.

---

[262] *See, e.g.,* Sky Cable, LLC v. DIRECTV, Inc., 886 F.3d 375 (4th Cir. 2018) (applying Delaware law). Reverse veil piercing is discussed in § 7.11 *infra.*

[263] Sky Cable, LLC v. DIRECTV, Inc., 886 F.3d 375 (4th Cir. 2018) (applying Delaware law).

[264] Fraser v. Major League Soccer, LLC, 97 F. Supp. 2d 130, 135 (D. Mass. 2000) (since an LLC is a separate entity, it cannot be found to violate anti-trust laws "unless the members are acting not in the interest of the entity, but rather in their own separate self-interest"); In re Bourbeau Custom Homes, Inc., 2017 Vt. 51, 171 A.3d 171 (Vt. 2017)(single member LLC that provides carpentry services to a corporation is not an "individual" for whom the corporation was required to contribute to the state's unemployment insurance fund); Poore v. Fox Hollow Enterprises, 1994 WL 150872 (Del. Super. Ct. 1994) (as a separate entity, an LLC cannot represent itself in court; it must be represented by an attorney).

[265] *See, e.g.,* Harvey v. Grey Wolf Drilling Co., 542 F.3d 1077 (5th Cir. 2008).

[266] *See, e.g.,* Elaine A. Welle, Limited Liability Company Interests as Securities: An Analysis of Federal and State Actions Against Limited Liability Companies Under the Securities Laws, 73 Denv. U.L. Rev. 425 (1996); Park McGinty, The Limited Liability Company: Opportunity for Selective Securities Law Deregulation, 64 U. Cin. L. Rev. 369 (1996).

[267] Robinson v. Glynn, 349 F.3d 166 (4th Cir. 2003); Nelson v. Stahl, 173 F. Supp. 2d 153 (S.D.N.Y. 2001); Endico v. Fonte, 485 F. Supp. 2d 411 (S.D.N.Y. 2007).

[268] *See, e.g.,* SEC v. Shreveport Wireless Cable Television Partnership, 1998 WL 892948, [1998 Transfer Binder] Fed. Sec. L. Rep. (CCH) ¶ 90,322 (D.D.C. 1998) (limited partnership and limited liability company interests would be securities where investors had no control over the enterprise).

§ 1.12 The Limited Liability Company—Operational Issues

States vary widely in their respective treatment of LLC issues. Their most fundamental division arises in their choice between a "flexible statute" and the so-called "bulletproof statute"; the former permits members to enter into any agreements they desire to order their relationship (subject to certain general minimum public policy constraints), whereas the latter severely limits the members' contractual freedom to vary those provisions essential for the business's classification as a partnership for tax purposes. States vary in the default rules they provide on specific matters, such as who manages the firm, the transferability of shares, the life of the LLC, events causing dissolution, and the means by which the members can avoid automatic dissolution.[269]

Though some states require the LLC to have two or more members,[270] other states permit the LLC to have a single member.[271] Most LLC statutes provide that management is vested directly in its members, unless the articles of organization (or, in some states, the operating agreement) specify that such authority will be in a manager or managers.[272] Matters pertaining to the members' powers with respect to the board of directors, such as the power to remove directors and to fill board vacancies, is either provided for by the governing LLC statute[273] or can be specified in the articles of organization.[274] Sometimes the members' authority in such matters is required to be set forth in the operating agreement.[275] Some states, consistent with their general corporate statutes, require the approval of the LLC's members for fundamental changes such as mergers or voluntary dissolution.[276] Many states accord LLCs greater latitude on fundamental changes and allow this power to be vested in the managers by the articles of organization or operating agreement.[277]

LLC statutes typically set forth default provisions governing the LLC's operations and governance. These default provisions may be altered by provisions in the operating agreement. However, care must be taken in drafting the operating agreement to make it clear when the default provisions are to be altered.[278]

---

[269] *See, e.g.,* Meghan Gruebner, Note, Delaware's Answer to Management Deadlock in the Limited Liability Company: Judicial Dissolution, 32 J. Corp. L. 641 (2007).

[270] *See, e.g.,* 805 ILCS § 180/5–1 (West 2004).

[271] *See, e.g.,* Cal. Corp. Code § 17050(b) (2008); Del. Code Ann. tit. 6, § 18–101(6) (2005).

[272] *See, e.g.,* Cal. Corp. Code §§ 17150 & 17151 (2007); Fla. Stat. Ann. § 608.422 (2007); 15 Pa. Cons. Stat. Ann. § 8941 (West 1995 & Supp. 2008).

[273] *See, e.g.,* Cal. Corp. Code § 17152 (2007); N.Y. Ltd. Lib. Co. Law §§ 414 & 416 (McKinney 2007).

[274] *See, e.g.,* Del. Code Ann. tit. 6, § 18–101(10) (2005); Fla. Stat. Ann. § 608.422 (2007); 805 ILCS § 180/15–1 (West 2004).

[275] *See* 15 Pa. Cons. Stat. Ann. § 8941 (West 1995 & Supp. 2002). *Cf.* Bubbles & Bleach, LLC v. Becker, 1997 WL 285938 (N.D. Ill. 1997) (operating agreement determines rights among LLC members but does not bind third parties).

[276] *See, e.g.,* Cal. Corp. Code § 17103 (2007); Del. Code Ann. tit. 6, § 18–209 (2005); 3 Tex. Civ. Stat. Ann. art. 1528n, § 2.23 (Vernon 2003).

[277] *See, e.g.,* 805 ILCS § 180/15–5 (West 2004); N.Y. Ltd. Lib. Co. Law § 402 (McKinney 2007); 15 Pa. Cons. Stat. Ann. § 8957 (West 1995 & Supp. 2008).

[278] *See, e.g.,* Saltzer v. Rolka, 2018 WL 5603050 (Pa. Super. 2018). The Pennsylvania LLC statute's default rule is that an operating agreement requires unanimity to be amended. 15 Pa. C.S.A. § 8942(b).This can be altered in the operating agreement which provided that the operating agreement could be amended at a members' regular or special meeting while a separate provision stated "Except as otherwise provided in this agreement, whenever action is to be taken by vote of the members, it shall be authorized upon the affirmative vote of a majority of the votes cast." The court held that this language was not sufficient to displace the statute's default unanimity provision. *Cf.* In re Nantucket Island Associates Ltd. Partnership Unitholders Litigation,

The operating agreement typically sets forth detailed provisions regarding the management of the LLC. It is important to balance the interest of owners in protecting their economic stake in the company while simultaneously avoiding making all future management decisions to be made by a majority vote. LLC statutes customarily do not restrict the person to whom management is delegated. Managers may operate within a structure similar to the traditional corporation, wherein the managers function much like the board of directors, delegating responsibility over day-to-day operations to officers appointed by the managers. Commonly, the LLC statute's default rule is that each member has the authority to act on behalf of the LLC, unless otherwise provided in the articles of organization or operating agreement.[279]

Because many LLC statutes defer substantially to the operating agreement to define the parties' respective rights and involvement, and some even permit specification of the fiduciary obligations, if any, that will exist among the parties,[280] there is a good deal of uncertainty regarding the nature of legal or equitable protections courts will accord owners and minority holders in LLCs. There is sound reason to believe that the courts, when confronted with a dispute among the owners or with their managers, will draw from the areas of contract, corporate, and partnership law in determining the obligations of managers and majority holders.[281] Though it is expected that the courts would give proper deference to the express terms of the operating agreement, it is also expected that the agreement will not, absent very express language, be interpreted as a license to steal by the managers or majority members.

In some states, the duration of the LLC was limited to a specified term of years,[282] whereas the more permissive statutes permit the LLC to have a perpetual existence.[283] Perpetual existence is now the norm for LLCs in light of the IRS "check the box" rules[284] that replaced the former approach to taxation of unincorporated entities. Though membership generally is freely assignable, whether an assignee of an LLC's member's shares becomes a member customarily depends on unanimous approval of the remaining members; membership status may also be conferred upon assignees by the articles of organization.[285]

The National Conference of Commissioners of Uniform State Laws in 1995 approved the Uniform Limited Liability Company Act (ULLCA).[286] The ULLCA is a flexible act, and among its most distinguishing features is the organizers' authority to choose from

---

810 A.2d 351 (Del. Ch. 2002) (noting that where a limited partnership agreement is drafted by the founding partners, as is often the case, a court is required to resolve ambiguities against the drafting general partner and in favor of the reasonable expectations of the limited partners).

[279] Del. Code Ann. tit. 6, § 18–402 (2005).

[280] *See, e.g.,* Fisk Ventures, LLC v. Segal, 2008 WL 1961156, at *11 (Del. Ch. 2008) (LLC operating agreement may limit or eliminate fiduciary duties).

[281] *E.g.,* Harbison v. Strickland, 900 So.2d 385 (Ala. 2004) (applying contract law to interpret the operating agreement).

[282] *See, e.g.,* Wyo. Stat. Ann. § 17–15–107 (2007) (30 years unless otherwise specified in articles of incorporation).

[283] *See, e.g.,* Del. Code Ann. tit. 6, § 18–801(a)(1) (2005) (default is perpetual existence unless the articles of incorporation provide otherwise).

[284] Treas. Reg. § 301.7701–3(a).

[285] *See, e.g.,* Cal. Corp. Code § 17303 (2007); Del. Code Ann. tit. 6, § 18–704 (2005).

[286] Uniform Limited Liability Company Act (1995), 6A U.L.A. 425 (1995).

four default provisions they wish to apply in satisfying the *Morissey* factors.[287] There appear to be at least two significant impediments to the ULLCA becoming the model around which states craft their own LLC statutes. The first is inertia: Legislatures and the bar are not likely to rush to adopt yet another LLC statute when they are adjusting to their own home-grown LLC statute. Most LLC statutes are of fairly recent origin, and history bears out that corporate statutes tend to be reexamined on a cycle that transcends two or three decades. Thus, many may clearly be of the mind that, "if it ain't broke, don't fix it." The second force retarding the wide adoption of the ULLCA is the increasing flexibility of the Internal Revenue Service in classifying business entities (discussed below). Thus, though there is much to commend the uniformity that would be introduced by wide adoption of the ULLCA, the cry for uniformity, or even a better-drafted statute, may not be sufficient for the states to reconvene their drafting processes.

It remains to be seen what the judiciary's approach will be when confronted with a dispute arising because of lacunae that may arise between the LLC statute and operating agreement. Delaware is the only state that appears to suggest a response, and its fault is that it may unwittingly have suggested two quite different responses. On the one hand, its statute states "[i]t is the policy of this chapter to give the maximum effect to the principle of freedom of contract and to the enforceability of limited liability company agreements."[288] On the other hand, the Delaware statute provides: "In any case not provided for in this chapter, the rules of law and equity, including the law [of] merchant, shall govern."[289] The former provision has been commented on as signaling that courts should seldom restructure arrangements, reasoning that the parties have purposely selected the LLC form; in contrast, the latter provision appears to invite sweeping intervention.[290] It would seem that the two provisions can be seen as being consistent with one another where courts are dealing with cases of filling in gaps that the parties and the LLC statute overlook. In such a case, the court should attribute to the operating agreement, the articles of organization, and the governing statute a result likely to fulfill the parties' expectations. However, restraint is clearly mandated by the first quoted provision where the issue is that a party seeks a result that is antithetical to the form of business they have chosen.

Courts have followed the pattern suggested above. Thus, for example, where a limited liability company's operating agreement clearly permits the members to enter into competition with the LLC, the provision will be enforced notwithstanding a claim that competition breaches the member's duty of loyalty.[291]

§ 1.13 Loan to a Business Proprietor for a Share of the Profits; Sharing of Profits by Lessor or Employee

A creditor may contract to share in the profits of a borrower's business in lieu of receiving interest on the loan. Creditors in such cases will not become partners unless

---

[287] For a nice summary of the ULLCA's approach, *see* James W. Reynolds & Steven G. Frost, ULLCA and Tax Classification, 2 J. Ltd. Liab. Cos. 87 (1995).

[288] Del. Code Ann. tit. 6, § 18–1101 (2005). There is reason for concern that this may result in an undue dilution of fiduciary obligations. *See, e.g.*, Note, Investor Beware: Protection of Minority Stakeholder Interests in Closely Held Limited-Liability Business Organizations: Delaware Law and its Adherents, 40 Washburn L.J. 288 (2001).

[289] Del. Code Ann. tit. 6, § 18–1104 (2005).

[290] Robert B. Thompson, The Taming of Limited Liability Companies, 66 U. Colo. L. Rev. 921, 935 (1995).

[291] McConnell v. Hunt Sports Enterprises, 725 N.E.2d 1193 (Ohio App. 1999).

they participate in the management of the business. Under common law,[292] the Uniform Partnership Act and the Revised Uniform Partnership Act,[293] creditors who share in the profits in lieu of or in addition to interest on a loan do not by that fact alone become subject to unlimited personal liability as partners for debts of the business.[294]

In addition to profit-sharing, co-ownership and joint control are necessary to create a partnership. This means that persons do not become partners unless they have a right to participate in the management of the business. Courts generally hold that a profit-sharing lender's reservation of only a right to information and a right to inspect the firm's books is not sufficient control to make the lender a partner in the enterprise.[295] However, if a lender's veto or other powers are so extensive that they effectively give the lender affirmative control, the lender may be held liable as a general partner.[296] Although an agreement may profess to give the ostensible owner or person in charge absolute control, other provisions in the agreement, even of a negative kind, may give the lender, lessor, or employee effective means for dictating policies and thus result in the lender, lessor, or employee becoming liable as a partner. It is impossible to say just how much control an ostensible lender, lessor, or employee can reserve without becoming a principal or co-owner of the business in the eyes of the law.

§ 1.14   The Joint Stock Company

A variant of the partnership form of doing business is the joint stock company. The core of the joint stock company is its articles of association, essentially a private contract among its members. Through the articles of association the participants approach many of the features common to partnerships as well as the corporate characteristics of free transferability of shares, continuity of existence, and centralized management. The principal disadvantage the joint stock company is the same disadvantage of a common law partnership, namely, even where the joint stock company has been recognized by statute, its members do not enjoy limited liability.[297]

Unincorporated joint stock companies have always been recognized as legal in the United States.[298] Most states enacted statutes that permit suits by or against an officer, trustee, or the company itself.[299] In some states, statutes expressly recognize joint stock companies and give them powers and privileges similar to those of corporations. Joint stock companies organized in these states are sometimes referred to as "statutory joint stock companies."

---

[292] *See* Meehan v. Valentine, 145 U.S. 611 (1892).

[293] UPA § 7(4)(d). RUPA § 202(c)(3).

[294] Alan R. Bromberg & Larry E. Ribstein, Bromberg & Ribstein on Limited Liability Partnerships and the Revised Uniform Partnership Act § 202 (1997).

[295] *E.g.*, Martin v. Peyton, 158 N.E. 77 (N.Y. 1927).

[296] *E.g.*, Minute Maid Corp. v. United Foods, Inc., 291 F.2d 577 (5th Cir.), *cert. denied*, 368 U.S. 928 (1961).

[297] *See, e.g.*, Earlsboro Gas Co. v. Vern H. Brown Drilling Co., 52 P.2d 730 (Okla. 1935); Flint v. Culbertson, 309 S.W.2d 269, 270 (Tex. Civ. App.), *reh'g denied*, 159 Tex. 243, 319 S.W.2d 690 (Tex. 1958).

[298] *See, e.g.*, Mason v. American Express Co., 334 F.2d 392 (2d Cir. 1964) (joint stock company is recognized as separate legal entity for purposes of diversity of citizenship jurisdiction).

[299] *See, e.g.*, Mass. Gen. Laws Ann. ch. 182, § 6 (LexisNexis 2005); Tex. Rev. Civ. Stat. art. 6133 (Vernon 1970 & Supp. 2007).

§ 1.15 The Business Trust (Massachusetts Business Trust)

The business trust, often referred to as the "Massachusetts trust" because of its reputed origin in Massachusetts and its frequent use there, is a business organization created by a deed or declaration of trust under which assets suitable for a business enterprise are transferred to trustees to be managed for the benefit and profit of persons holding transferable certificates evidencing the beneficial interests in the trust estate. The trustees have legal title to the property in trust and act as principals for the certificate holders ("shareholders"). Vesting title to the enterprise's assets in trustees and empowering them to act as representatives of the business create a business organization, if not a legal unit.[300] The business trust, therefore, embodies at least three important characteristics of the corporate form of business: limited liability, centralized management, and transferability of ownership.[301] Moreover, continuity of existence is attained by providing for the remaining trustees or the beneficial owners to appoint new trustees as successors in case of vacancies.

The declaration, or deed of trust, somewhat like a corporation's charter or articles of incorporation, establishes the organization, its business purposes[302], and authorized shares and specifies the powers of the trustees as well as the rights of the certificate holders. The trustees of a business trust perform the same functions as the board of directors of a corporation or joint stock company, although in form they carry on the business in their own names. Trust property is held and conveyed in the names of the trustees, and actions are initiated by and against the trustees. This arrangement gives the enterprise the corporate advantage of centralized management. Incoming shareholders become parties to the trust agreement, or at least claim to be beneficiaries under it. The beneficiaries of the trust are simply passive investors with transferable certificates as shares or units of interest.

One major disadvantage of the business trust is its rather shaky legal status in some jurisdictions. Although a number of state statutes expressly declare that the business trust is a permissible form of association for the conduct of business,[303] and although it would probably be sanctioned by courts in most jurisdictions even in the absence of a statute, the courts in a few states have, in the absence of enabling legislation, treated it like a partnership or joint stock company for purposes of shareholder personal liability.[304]

Recently there has been a resurgence of interest in business trusts because they are particularly well suited for many investor-oriented products such as real estate investment trusts and asset-backed securities. Delaware and Wyoming each have taken

---

[300] *See* In re Vento Dev. Corp., 560 F.2d 2 (1st Cir. 1977); Lafayette Bank & Trust Co. v. Branchini & Sons Constr. Co., 342 A.2d 916 (Conn.Super. 1975).

[301] However, in contrast to a corporation, a business trust's citizenship for the purposes of federal diversity jurisdiction is determined by the citizenship of all of its shareholders. Americold Realty Trust v. Conagra Foods, Inc., 136 S. Ct. 1012 (2016).

[302] A business trust must be created for the proper purpose, namely, for "carrying on some kind of business or commercial activity for profit." In re Kenneth Allen Knight Trust, 303 F.3d 671, 676 (6th Cir. 2002). *See* Richardson v. Commissioner, 509 F.3d 736, 740–41 (6th Cir. 2007) (business trust must have a "valid, non-tax business purpose").

[303] As of 2005, at least 29 states had statutes recognizing the business trust as a form of doing business. *See* Robert H. Sitkoff, Trust as Uncorporation: A Research Agenda, 2005 U. Ill. L. Rev. 31, 35 (2005).

[304] *See, e.g.,* FDIC v. Slinger, 913 F.2d 7 (1st Cir. 1990) (benefits of business trust status is lost where individual is sole trustee and beneficiary).

the lead in enacting modern business trust statutes authorizing unincorporated business trusts.[305] Both statutes accord the trust's organizers unlimited freedom with respect to the powers, selection, and activities of the trustees. However, the fact that this form of doing business is nevertheless a trust limits the ability of the participants to fully contract out of fiduciary norms.[306] More than half the states have adopted business trust statutes.

Exactly what must be done to obtain the corporate advantage of limited liability for shareholders of a business trust? Of paramount importance is that the trustee must be given control and independent powers of management. If they are not so empowered, the "trustees" are in fact mere managing agents, subject to the direction and control of the shareholders (for example, in selecting and fixing the compensation of the enterprise's employees); as such, personal liability will be imposed on the shareholders as partners, principals, or joint venturers.[307] The better view is that indirect control resulting from the mere power to elect trustees at annual meetings, fill vacancies, amend the declaration of trust, or dissolve the trust, as contrasted with direct control over the conduct of the business, should not be regarded as sufficient to make the shareholders liable as partners or joint venturers.[308] In this area, the analogy to the powers limited partners may exercise without jeopardizing their limited liability should be a powerful one.

Even though the declaration of trust gives the trustees full authority to make contracts on behalf of the trust (as it usually does), they become personally liable for trust contracts unless clear stipulations against their liability are included in the contracts. Their own property may be levied against in case of breach.[309] A Massachusetts court explained trustee liability in this way:

> Speaking generally a trust is not a legal personality. With the exception later to be dealt with [a statute], it cannot be sued. It is represented by the trustee. He embodies it. He holds title. He deals with the property in which trust rights exist. Contracts with regard to the rights and property affected by trusts are the contracts of the trustee. He, in person, is liable upon them. He is not acting as representative or agent of another. He is acting for himself, but with fiduciary obligations to others.[310]

Even though in form the business and assets are trust funds owned and operated by the trustees, and even though the trustees contract as principals in the administration of the trust, they do not in fact hold or act for themselves. Instead, they act as representatives and fiduciaries for the shareholders. Technically, trustees are not agents, but their powers and their authority to act are defined in the declaration of trust. They represent the beneficial owners of the business in much the same way as directors of a corporation or joint stock company represent the shareholders. Their acts, within

---

[305] Del. Code Ann. tit. 12, § 3801 (2007); Wyo. Stat. Ann. §§ 17–16–1534, 17–23–101 et seq. (2007).

[306] *See* Tamar Frankel, The Failure of the Delaware Business Trust Act and the New Corporate Law, 23 Cardozo L. Rev. 325 (2001). *See also, e.g.,* Robert H. Sitkoff, Trust as Uncorporation: A Research Agenda, 2005 U. Ill. L. Rev. 31, 35 (2005).

[307] *See* Outlaw v. United States, 494 F.2d 1376 (Ct. Cl.), *cert. denied,* 419 U.S. 844 (1974).

[308] Levy v. Nellis, 284 Ill.App. 228, 235, 1 N.E.2d 251, 254 (1936); In re Winter's Estate, 31 A.2d 769 (N.J. Prerog. Ct. 1943), *aff'd,* 40 A.2d 648 (N.J. Err. App. 1945).

[309] Limouze v. M.M. & P. Maritime Advancement, Training, Educ. & Safety Program, 397 F.Supp. 784, 790 (D. Md. 1975) (law of Maryland and New York).

[310] Larson v. Sylvester, 185 N.E. 44, 45–46 (Mass. 1933).

the scope of their authority, bind the trust property.[311] As a federal court said: "If the contract was properly made by the trustee in the administration of the Trust, he is entitled to indemnity or reimbursement from the trust estate. Thus, where the trust estate is sufficient to discharge the obligation, the trustee's personal liability is ultimately satisfied with funds of the trust."[312]

The beneficial owners of business trust shares have many rights analogous to corporate shareholders. For example, in Delaware there is a statutory right to inspect the trust's books and records that includes the ability to discover the identity the other beneficial owners.[313]

§ 1.16   Public or Government Corporations

A public corporation is a corporation created and controlled by public authority to perform some government or public function as an agency of the government. Public corporations differ from business corporations and nonprofit corporations in a number of ways. A public corporation is not a voluntary association of individuals. Establishing a public corporation, in contrast to a business corporation or nonprofit corporation, does not create contractual relationships between the state and the corporation, the corporation and the individual shareholders, or among the shareholders themselves. The creation and operation of public corporations are now governed by a body of statutory and case law completely separate from the law applicable to business corporations or nonprofit "private" corporations.

A corporation may be public, even though it does not exercise governmental powers, if it is created for some public purpose and is controlled by the government. Examples of this type of corporation include the Tennessee Valley Authority and state universities. Educational institutions, hospitals, and asylums founded by private benefactors for purposes of general or public charity, however, are not considered public corporations, even though the state may contribute to their support through appropriations and donations and may reserve some control over their affairs.[314]

While there is no universally accepted theory or policy governing the creation and regulation of government corporations, a partial explanation for government use of corporations is the ability of a separate corporation to operate with greater autonomy than could an ordinary government bureau or agency. It has been said that a corporation can more efficiently apply the techniques of modern business management.

§ 1.17   Municipal Corporations

"A municipal corporation is a legal institution, formed by charter from sovereign power, erecting a populous community of prescribed area into a body politic and corporate, with corporate name and continuous succession, and for the purpose and with the authority of subordinate self government improvement and local administration of affairs of state."[315] Municipal corporations are thus incorporated cities, towns, and

---

[311]   3 Austin W. Scott, The Law of Trusts §§ 271A.1, 271A.2, 271A.3 (3d ed. 1967).

[312]   Limouze v. M. M. & P. Maritime Advancement, Training, Educ. & Safety Program, 397 F.Supp. 784, 790–91 (D. Md. 1975); Town of Hull v. Tong, 442 N.E.2d 427, 429 (Mass. 1982).

[313]   See Grand Acquisition, LLC v. Passco Indian Springs DST, 145 A.3d 990, 991 (Del. Ch. 2016).

[314]   Trustees of Dartmouth College v. Woodward, 17 U.S. (4 Wheat.) 518 (1819).

[315]   Emmett C. Yokley, Municipal Corporations § 5 (1956 & Cum. Supp. 1987).

villages created to serve the dual role as agents of the state and local governing entities. Their characteristic feature is the power and right to local self-government.

Municipal corporations derive their legitimacy from the state. They are created either by a special enactment of the legislature, through compliance with the state's general municipal corporations law, or by satisfaction of any existing state constitutional or statutory home rule provision.

An integral part of the incorporation process is the municipal charter. It contains the municipal powers and gives the form of governance the entity will have as well as its boundaries, wards, or other subdivisions, and sets forth any classification of powers and duties of its various departments, boards, and officers.[316] Municipalities adopt in their charter one of three forms of government: (1) the mayor-council plan, (2) the commission plan, or (3) the city manager (or council-manager) plan. The mayor-council form of government is further divided into a "weak mayor" or "strong mayor" system. The choice of the form of government is considered a local concern.[317]

Once validly formed, the municipal corporation enjoys the same characteristics as private corporations, such as a continuous existence, capacity to sue, be sued, and contract in its own name. Additionally, by virtue of state constitution or statute, municipal corporations generally have the power to control development within their incorporated area, to raise revenues through taxes, and to participate in state and federal revenue-sharing and grants. Its power to borrow money, however, generally requires voter approval.

§ 1.18 Charitable and Other Nonprofit Corporations

Virtually all states have statutes providing for the formation of charitable, educational, literary, scientific, social, fraternal, religious, recreational, and other non-profit corporations. The nonprofit corporation statutes grew helter-skelter over the years without reference to any statutory model, and at one time they existed in great variety and astonishing combinations.[318]

A number of jurisdictions have adopted the Revised Model Non-Profit Corporation Act (RMNPCA) drafted by the Corporation, Banking and Business Law section of the American Bar Association. The RMNPCA divides nonprofit corporations into three broad categories: public benefit corporations, which include most types of charitable organizations; mutual benefit corporations, which include entities such as trade associations, social clubs, and other organizations that pursue nonprofit activities that are neither charitable nor religious; and religious corporations. In broad overview, the RMNPCA subjects mutual benefit corporations to the most regulation of the three types of nonprofit corporations. The regulation of mutual benefit corporations approximates that of business corporations. Religious corporations enjoy a good deal of autonomy and noninterference under the RMNPCA.

Although most recent legislation dealing with nonprofit corporations has been entirely separate from legislation relating to business corporations, provisions in the

---

[316] Eugene McQuillin, Municipal Corporations § 9.02 (3d ed. 1987).

[317] Osborne M. Reynolds, Jr., Local Government Law § 18 (1982).

[318] Ralph E. Boyer, Nonprofit Corporation Statutes: A Critique and Proposal 1–122 (1957); ABA-ALI Model Non-Profit Corp. Act iv (Rev. 1957). *See also* Howard L. Oleck, Non-Profit Corporations, Associations and Organizations 57–75 (5th ed. 1988).

modern nonprofit corporation acts generally parallel those in the business corporation statutes.[319] Thus, judicial decisions interpreting and applying a nonprofit statute may be helpful in interpreting and applying a business corporation statute, and vice versa.

A corporation does not cease to be classified as "nonprofit" simply because it seeks to make profits from some of its activities. Many nonprofit organizations engage in profit-making activities. For example, a leading law school once owned and reaped profits from a macaroni factory. Similarly, hospitals operate at profit-making rates to subsidize those patients who are unable to pay the full rate. As long as the profits are used to further an organization's educational, charitable, or cultural purposes and are not paid to the members as dividends, the organization is usually classified as "nonprofit," even though its members may reap non-pecuniary or indirect benefits.

§ 1.19 The Corporation Sole

A corporation sole consists of one individual, and his or her successors, who hold a particular office and by virtue of that office assume the legal capacity of a corporation. The fact that all of the shares in a business corporation are held by a single individual does not make the corporation or the owner a corporation sole. According to Blackstone, the "corporation sole" is an English invention developed to assure the right of succession to an office or status, usually religious, without the complications attending transfers of office or property under the feudal system.[320]

§ 1.20 Publicly Held Corporations and Close Corporations

Perhaps the most significant classifications of business corporations are publicly held corporations (sometimes referred to as "public-issue corporations") and close corporations (often referred to as "closely held corporations"). A publicly held corporation is a business corporation, such as IBM or Microsoft, which have numerous shareholders—perhaps hundreds of thousands scattered all over the world—and whose shares (or some classes of shares) are traded on a national securities exchange or at least are traded regularly in the over-the-counter market maintained by securities dealers.[321] The close corporation, on the other hand, is often defined simply as a corporation with relatively few shareholders. Several statutes determine close corporation status by reference to the number of shareholders the corporation has.[322] Another popular definition describes the close corporation as a corporation whose shares are not generally traded in securities markets.[323]

Adopting an economic approach and focusing on one of the most significant characteristics of many corporations with a small number of shareholders, some authorities have defined the close corporation as one in which "management and

---

[319] *See* ABA-ALI, Model Non-Profit Corp. Act vii (rev. ed. 1964).

[320] 1 Blackstone, Commentaries 469–70.

[321] The markets for publicly traded securities are highly regulated. *See* Thomas Lee Hazen, Treatise on the Law of Securities Regulation (7th ed. 2016).

[322] *E.g.*, Del. Code Ann. tit. 8, § 342(a)(1)–(3) (2001) (less than 30 shareholders).

[323] Elvin R. Latty, The Close Corporation and the New North Carolina Business Corporation Act, 34 N.C. L. Rev. 432, 438–39 (1956). In the words of a Massachusetts court, a close corporation is "typified by: (1) a small number of stockholders; (2) no ready market for the corporate stock; and (3) substantial majority stockholder participation in the management, direction and operations of the corporation." Donahue v. Rodd Electrotype Co., 328 N.E.2d 505, 511 (Mass. 1975), noted in 89 Harv. L. Rev. 423 (1975).

ownership are substantially identical."[324] Thus, one leading writer defines the close corporation as "one wherein all the outstanding stock (there being no publicly held securities of any other class) is owned by the persons (or members of their immediate families) who are active in the management and conduct of the business."[325] This definition improperly excludes the large number of corporations in which one or more shareholders supply the lion's share or much of the capital for the enterprise but leave the active management of the business to other shareholders, whose holdings may be relatively small.

Although a close corporation is usually a small enterprise, the amount of its assets, the scope of its operations, the number of persons it employs, or the volume of its sales does not determine whether it is "close." Many close corporations have tremendous assets and worldwide operations. For example, Mars, Inc., producer of candies and other foods, and Hallmark Cards, Inc., a leading manufacturer of greeting cards, are close corporations, and until 1955 the vast Ford Motor Company was also. Most of the incorporated enterprises in this country, perhaps 90 percent or more, are close corporations, but publicly held corporations have far greater economic significance. The great bulk of this nation's productive property is controlled by a few hundred giant, publicly held corporations.

Often the number of shareholders in a close corporation gradually increases: Additional shares are issued to friends or relatives of the founding shareholders; shareholders transfer part of their holdings to their children, or a successful close corporation "goes public" by making a public distribution of its shares. Many corporations, of course, are hybrid or intermediate, having characteristics of both publicly held and close corporations. Thus, in many situations some shares in the corporation are rather widely distributed, but a majority of the voting shares—enough for effective control of the corporation—are retained by a single individual, a single family, or a relatively small number of people.

§ 1.21 One-Person Companies; Family Corporations; Subsidiary Corporations

The "closest" of close corporations is the one-person corporation, in which all stock is owned or controlled by a single shareholder, and the family corporation, in which the stock is owned or controlled by members of a family. Perhaps the corporate device was not originally designed for use by individual entrepreneurs or by family businesses in which substantially all the stock is owned or controlled by the head of the family, but, both in England and in this country, one-person companies and family corporations have received judicial sanction and are now widely prevalent.

A wholly-owned subsidiary corporation is a corporation all the shares of which are held by another company, the "parent company." In other words, it is a one-person corporation. A partly owned subsidiary corporation is a corporation in which the parent company owns a majority of the subsidiary's voting shares, or at least enough shares to give the parent effective control of the subsidiary, but in which some of the subsidiary's shares are owned by other holders.[326] Although a partly owned subsidiary is not referred

---

[324] Carlos L. Israels & Alan H. Hoffman, Corporate Practice 57 (3d ed. 1974).

[325] Chester Rohrlich, Organizing Corporate and Other Business Enterprises § 2A.02 (5th ed. 1975).

[326] *See generally* Elvin R. Latty, Subsidiaries and Affiliated Corporations (1936).

to as a "close corporation," the two types of companies present similar opportunities for the person in control to manipulate the companies' affairs to the prejudice of minority shareholders.[327]

§ 1.22   The Joint Venture Corporation

Individuals engaged in a joint enterprise may incorporate their undertaking, and several corporations may organize a new company to carry out a joint undertaking. When individuals engaged in a joint business or commercial operation decide to conduct their venture in the corporate form, the resulting corporation is sometimes referred to as a "joint venture corporation."[328] The term "joint venture corporation" is ordinarily used, however, to designate a company created by other corporations. Thus, one authority defines "joint venture corporation" as "a corporation whose stock is owned by other corporations and which engages in a business different from that of its parents (even though the difference be only that it sells its products in a foreign territory)."[329] A corporation of this kind is also referred to as a "joint company," a "jointly owned subsidiary," or a "collaborative subsidiary."

§ 1.23   The Professional Corporation and PLLC

Historically, the learned professions were not included in the objects for which corporations could be created. The justification given for this rule was that a professional practice requires personal skills and creates confidential relationships. A corporation, it was reasoned, does not possess the necessary skills and personal qualities.[330]

In recent years, however, a strong movement to permit professionals to incorporate or form limited liability companies has resulted in every state and the District of Columbia enacting legislation authorizing professionals to use the corporate form or, alternatively, to create an association such as an LLC, with corporate characteristics.[331] In most states, in order to avoid conflict with licensing requirements prohibiting the unauthorized practice of a profession,[332] only persons who are qualified members of the particular profession can become shareholders or directors in a professional corporation.[333] Frequently there is a requirement that the expression "professional corporation" or "professional association" or their abbreviations (P.C., P.A.) appear in the corporation's name and on letterheads and other representations to the public.

At one time, the primary purpose of professional corporate legislation was to permit professionals to adopt a business organization that would be treated as a corporation for

---

[327] For discussion of transactions between a parent company and a partly owned subsidiary that may be prejudicial to the subsidiary's minority shareholders, *see, e.g.*, F. Hodge O'Neal & Robert B. Thompson, Oppression of Minority Shareholders § 3.19 (1985).

[328] *See* Adolf A. Berle, Developments in the Pattern of Corporate Joint Enterprise, 14 Bus. Law. 309 (1959).

[329] G. E. Hale, Joint Ventures: Collaborative Subsidiaries and the Antitrust Laws, 42 Va. L. Rev. 927 (1956). Economically, a joint venture corporation "may differ only slightly from contractual cooperation between two operating companies." *Id.*

[330] *See* ALI-ABA Model Business Corp. Act Ann. § 3, Comment at 31 (1966 pocket parts).

[331] Professional corporations are to be treated like any other corporation for diversity of citizenship determinations. *See* Hoagland v. Sandberg Phoenix & Von Gontard, PC, 385 F.3d 737 (7th Cir. 2004).

[332] *See, e.g.*, People v. Painless Parker Dentist, 275 P. 928 (Colo. 1929); State v. Superior Court, 135 P.2d 839 (Wash. 1943).

[333] *See, e.g.*, Schmidt v. Ottawa Med. Ctr., P.C., 155 F. Supp. 2d 919 (N.D. Ill. 2001); Street v. Sugarmen, 202 So.2d 749 (Fla. 1967).

income tax purposes and thus eligible for tax-advantageous profit-sharing, pension, and stock option plans.[334] Most of the unfavorable treatment of partnerships vis-à-vis corporations was eliminated with Congress's enactment of the Tax Equity and Fiscal Responsibility Act of 1982 (TEFRA).[335] Nevertheless, there still remain some isolated areas where the tax laws continue to favor those doing business as a corporation rather than as a partnership.

An increasing motivation for incorporating a professional business is the quest to shield the owners from enterprise liability. The traditional rule that individuals are liable for their own torts applies even in the corporate context. Hence, one's status as a shareholder or employee does not absolve the individual of any liability for one's own malpractice. States, however, vary widely in their treatment of the professional corporation's owners' vicarious liability. Some states provide limited liability to shareholders for both business debts and malpractice claims; others deny limited liability for both types of debts; and some states expose shareholders to limited liability for business debts and recognize limited liability for malpractice claims and vice versa.[336] Absent a definitive statement of the legislature or state courts,[337] professionals may well find they continue to have unlimited liability for their co-owners' torts, even though they do business through a professional corporation.

As discussed in an earlier section,[338] a number of states have enacted statutes recognizing the limited liability company as a form of business. A few states have indicated that this form may be used as an alternative to the professional corporation. Professional limited liability companies (PLLCs) and professional limited liability partnerships (PLLPs) have become common forms of doing business.

§ 1.24　Agency—Core Concepts

Although not a separate business entity, an agency relationship is central to all forms of business association. The rules of agency determine the legal consequences of acts by individuals with respect to the business associations with which those individuals may be associated. As an artificial entity, a corporation[339] or other business entity can act only through its agents.[340] The officers of a corporation in both legal theory and in practice are the agents of the corporation.[341]

Agency principles are referred to throughout this treatise as they apply to the various issues discussed. What follows here is an overview of agency law.

---

[334] *See, e.g.,* United States v. Empey, 406 F.2d 157 (10th Cir. 1969); Street v. Sugarmen, 202 So.2d 749 (Fla. 1967).

[335] *See generally* Michael S. Sirkin & Stuart A. Sirkin, The Effect of the TEFRA Pension Provisions on Closely Held and Professional Business, 7 Rev. Tax. Indiv. 99 (1983).

[336] *See* Karen M. Maycheck, Shareholder Liability in Professional Legal Corporations: A Survey of the States, 47 U. Pitt. L. Rev. 817 (1986).

[337] *See, e.g.,* Henderson v. Hsi Fin. Servs., 471 S.E.2d 885 (Ga. 1996) ("We overrule that strict liability rule today because the legislature has provided that shareholders of professional corporations are not personally liable for corporate debts except by personal conduct.").

[338] *See* § 1.11 *infra.*

[339] *See* Chapter 8 *infra.*

[340] *See, e.g.,* In re Merrill Lynch Trust Co. FSB., 235 S.W.3d 185 (Tex. 2007) (noting that since a corporation can only act through human agents, an arbitration agreement generally includes disputes about their agents' actions).

[341] *See, e.g.,* Wasatch Oil & Gas, LLC v. Reott, 163 P.3d 713 (Utah Ct. App. 2007).

Fiduciary Nature of Agency Relationship

To begin with, agency is a *fiduciary* relationship[342] which permits one person (the agent) to act on behalf of another (the principal).[343] The existence of an agency relationship depends upon the consent of the principal (actual, apparent, or implied) to allow the agent to act on the principal's behalf, as well as the agent's consent to the relationship.[344]

When Does an Agency Relationship Exist?

An agency relationship is based on the mutual consent of the principal and the agent.[345] The existence of the relationship can be based on an express agreement or an inference of such an agreement based on the surrounding facts.[346] Control of the agent by the principle is a key element of an agency relationship. The existence of the relationship need not be known to third parties, although the principal's actions and words vis-à-vis third parties can by itself create apparent authority. It is well established in the law that an agency relationship cannot be recognized without an existing principal.[347] The principal must have a valid existence in order for an agency relationship to exist.[348]

How an Agent Binds the Principal

Within the context of an agency relationship, there are a number of ways in which the principal may be held accountable for the words, acts, or deeds of the agent. The five legal theories for binding a principal are as follows: (1) actual authority,[349] (2) apparent authority,[350] (3) respondeat superior,[351] (4) estoppel,[352] and (5) ratification.[353]

---

[342] For a good discussion of the fiduciary nature of the relationship, *see* Austin W. Scott, The Fiduciary Principle, 37 Cal. L. Rev. 539, 543–54 (1949).

[343] "Agency is the fiduciary relationship that arises when one person ('a principal') manifests assent to another person ('an agent') that the agent shall act on the principal's behalf and subject to the principal's control, and the agent manifests assent or otherwise consents so to act." Restatement (Third) of Agency § 1.01 (2006). *Cf., e.g.,* A. Gay Jenson Farms Co. v. Cargill, Inc., 309 N.W.2d 285 (Minn. 1981) (finding a loan to in fact be an agency relationship).

[344] Restatement (Third) of Agency § 1.01 (2006).

[345] *See* Restatement Agency (third) § 1.01 ("Agency is the fiduciary relationship that arises when one person (a 'principal') manifests assent to another person (an 'agent') that the agent shall act on the principal's behalf and subject to the principal's control, and the agent manifests assent or otherwise consents so to act").

[346] *See, e.g.,* Nichols v. Arthur Murray, Inc., 248 Cal.App.2d 610, 56 Cal.Rptr. 728 (1967) (finding agency relationship). A. Gay Jenson Farms Co. v. Cargill, Inc., 309 N.W.2d 285 (Minn. 1981) (commercial loan with significant control over the borrower rendered the borrower an agent of the creditor).

[347] *See, e.g.,* Warren Abner Seavey, Agency § 34 (1964).

[348] *See, e.g.,* P.I.M.L., Inc. v. Fashion Links, LLC, 428 F. Supp. 2d 961, 970 (D. Minn. 2006) ("Instances where several persons associate to promote a business prior to incorporation, and enter into contracts with third parties for the benefit of that business, can trigger promoter liability. Promoter liability exists when a person enters into a contract for a non-existent corporation.").

[349] Restatement (Third) of Agency § 3.01 (2006).

[350] Restatement (Third) of Agency § 2.03 (2006).

[351] Restatement (Third) of Agency § 2.04 (2006).

[352] Restatement (Third) of Agency § 8B (2006).

[353] Restatement (Third) of Agency § 4.01 (2006).

Authority

Actual authority refers to any express agreement between the principal and agent as well as any agreement that may be implied from the surrounding circumstances.[354] As defined by the Restatement of Agency, an agent acts with actual authority when "the agent reasonably believes, in accordance with the principal's manifestations to the agent, that the principal wishes the agent so to act."[355] Express authority is found in written or spoken words. Implied actual authority can be found on the basis of circumstantial evidence.[356]

Apparent authority results from manifestations, not from the principal to the agent but from the principal to the third party, that the agent has authority to perform the act in question.[357] An agent cannot create his or her own apparent authority. There must at least be a manifestation of acquiescence or agreement from the principal. The principal can thus create apparent authority in an agent by allowing an agent to conduct business in a particular way and thereby create the impression that actual authority in fact exists.[358]

The difference between actual authority (express or implied) and apparent authority can be seen from the following triangle.

Manifestations routed down the side of the triangle from *P* to *A* result in "authority." The agent is told by these manifestations what the principal consents to the agent doing on the principal's behalf. Often the manifestations from the principal to the agent do not spell out in so many words the acts that the agent is authorized to perform; the agent may not be given "express authority" to do a particular act, such as to employ ten workers to install specified machinery in a particular plant. The authority to do that act may have to be inferred or implied from either the title or position the principal has given to the agent or the nature and scope of the task the principal has assigned to the agent. The authority is then referred to as "implied authority." If the agent reasonably believes from the principal's manifestations, interpreted in the setting in which they were made, that the principal wants the agent to perform an act on the principal's behalf, the agent is authorized to perform that act and has the same power to affect the principal's legal

---

[354] *See, e.g.,* Trustees of UIU Health & Welfare Fund v. New York Flame Proofing Co., 828 F.2d 79, 83–84 (2d Cir. 1987) (discussing actual authority stemming from membership in multi-employer bargaining group), In re Northwest Airlines Corp., 383 B.R. 283, 295 (Bankr. S.D.N.Y. 2008) ("a party dealing with an agent cannot proceed in reliance on actual authority if it becomes aware of restrictions on that agent's authority").

[355] Restatement (Third) of Agency § 2.01 (2006).

[356] *E.g.,* Lind v. Schenley Industries, Inc., 278 F.2d 79, 85 (3d Cir. 1960).

[357] Restatement (Third) Agency § 2.03 (2006).

[358] *See, e.g.,* Essco Geometric v. Harvard Industries, 46 F.3d 718 (8th Cir. 1995) (Missouri law).

relations by performing the act as an agent who has been given express authority to perform it.

On the other hand, "apparent authority"—sometimes labeled "ostensible authority"—results from manifestations such as those routed down the side of the triangle from *P* to *T*. By these manifestations the principal is telling another party what authority the agent has to act on behalf of the principal. These manifestations create an appearance of authority, which may or may not accurately reflect the authority actually given. Nevertheless, the agent with apparent authority has the power to bind the principal to the third party. A manifestation that creates apparent authority in an agent can be either a direct communication to a third party or a communication to the public in general, such as by advertisement.[359]

Apparent authority ordinarily cannot be created by the agent's own words or actions, such as by falsely representing to a third party that the agent is authorized.[360]

A principal's acquiescence in an agent's performance of unauthorized acts may create authority in the agent insofar as the agent thereafter reasonably believes that the principal consents to performance of similar acts in the future. The principal's acquiescence may also create apparent authority in the agent, because a third party, aware of the agent's performance of the acts, may reasonably believe from the principal's manifestations (apparent acquiescence) that the agent is authorized to perform such acts on the principal's behalf.[361] Furthermore, acquiescence by the principal may be held to constitute ratification of an unauthorized act. In this area the concept of apparent authority and the doctrine of estoppel tend to intertwine.[362]

Respondeat Superior

Respondeat superior is a concept used by the Restatement of Agency and the courts to impose liability on employers for torts committed by employees.[363]

Estoppel

An agent's authority can also be established using general principles of estoppel.[364]

Ratification

Finally, when an act is without authorization, after the fact approval by the principal can operate as a ratification of the previously unauthorized act.[365] Related to the ratification is the concept of affirmance, whereby a principal's acquiescence with

---

[359] The principal's communications to a third party may or may not specify in so many words the act or acts that the agent is authorized to perform. Where the principal does not specify but the third party reasonably infers from the principal's words or actions that the agent has authority to perform an act, it is proper to refer to the agent's "inferred apparent authority" or "implied apparent authority" to perform that act, although those terms are seldom used by the courts.

[360] Restatement (Third) of Agency § 6.11 (1) (2006).

[361] *See* Foote & Davies, Inc. v. Arnold Craven, Inc., 324 S.E.2d 889 (N.C.App. 1985).

[362] Restatement (Third) of Agency §§ 4.01, 4.03 to 4.08 (2006).

[363] Restatement (Third) of Agency § 2.04 (2006).

[364] *E.g.*, In re Nigeria Charter Flights Contract Litig., 520 F. Supp. 2d 447, 465 (E.D.N.Y. 2007).

[365] Restatement (Third) of Agency § 4.01 (2006). *See also, e.g.,* DKS Ventures, LLC v. Kalch, 2011 WL 4829724 (E.D. Wash. 2011) ("Although a corporation may not technically ratify a contract made on its behalf prior to its incorporation, since it could not at that time have authorized such action on its behalf, it may, after it comes into existence, adopt such contract by its corporate action, which adoption may be express or implied, and thereby become liable for its performance."), quoting Smith v. Ford Motor Co., 289 N.C. 71, 80, 221 S.E.2d 282, 288, 79 A.L.R.3d 651 (1976).

knowledge of an agent's unauthorized act can operate as a ratification.[366] Ratification operates within the corporation and allows an after-the-fact approval of a previously unauthorized act by a corporate official.

The burden of establishing an agent's authority falls on the party trying to charge the principal with liability for the agent's acts. In proving an agency relationship, courts look beyond written and spoken words and will consider all relevant surrounding circumstances to determine both the existence and extent of an agency relationship.[367]

As noted above, agency is a fiduciary relationship, and the agent is subject to certain ensuing obligations.[368] For example, unless there is a contrary agreement between the principal and agent, the agent is under a duty to act *solely* for the benefit of the principal.[369] This is often referred to as the duty of loyalty.[370] A corollary to this is that unless it is otherwise agreed, an agent may not deal with the principal as an adverse party.[371] In other words, absent full disclosure by the agent and the consent of the principal, the agent cannot sit on both sides of the bargaining table to any transaction.[372] A variation of the agent's duty of loyalty is the rule that unless otherwise agreed, an agent who makes a profit while working for a principal is under a duty to give any profit made by the agent to the principal.[373]

---

[366] Chemical Bank v. Affiliated FM Ins. Co., 169 F.3d 121, 128 (2d Cir. 1999) (affirmance may be inferred from failure to timely repudiate actions of unauthorized agent).

[367] State v. Hoshijo, 76 P.3d 550, 563–564 (Hawai'i 2003); Mill Street Church of Christ v. Hogan, 785 S.W.2d 263, 267–68 (Ky. App. 1990), relying on Wedding v. Duncan, 220 S.W.2d 564 (Ky. 1949); Monohan v. Grayson County Supply Co., 54 S.W.2d 311 (Ky. 1932).

[368] *See, e.g.,* Zurich Capital Mkts., Inc. v. Coglianese, 332 F. Supp. 2d 1087, 1120 (N.D. Ill. 2004); Lagen v. Balcor Co., 210 Ill.Dec. 773, 653 N.E.2d 968, 975 (App. 1995) ("A fiduciary duty is the duty of an agent to treat his principal with the utmost candor, rectitude, care, loyalty, and good faith—in fact to treat the principal as well as the agent would treat himself.").

[369] Restatement (Third) of Agency § 8.01 (2006).

[370] *See* Chapter 10 for discussion of the duty of loyalty in the corporate context.

[371] Restatement (Third) of Agency § 8.03 (2006). *See* Television Events & Mktg. v. AMCON Distrib. Co., 526 F. Supp. 2d 1118, 1126–1134 (D. Hawai'i 2007).

[372] *See* Restatement (Third) of Agency § 8.06 (2006) (agent acting as adverse party with principal's consent).

[373] Restatement (Third) of Agency § 8.02 (2006).

Chapter 2

THE EVOLUTION OF CORPORATIONS IN ENGLAND AND AMERICA

Table of Sections

---

§ 2.1   Early American Corporations

State legislatures have plenary powers to create corporations. From the post-Revolutionary War period and into the early nineteenth century, American corporations were created by the enactment of special legislative acts[1]—that is, by acts creating a particular corporation, as distinguished from a general law allowing any persons to organize themselves into and be a corporation by complying with prescribed conditions. To incorporate by special act, a private bill had to be introduced in the state legislature, be considered by the legislative committees, pass both houses, and be signed by the governor. Special acts also were used to grant additional privileges to existing corporations or to make changes in their charters.

Corporations were uncommon prior to the 1800s, and those that existed were specifically chartered by the state to operate banks, insurance companies, and companies to build and operate canals, bridges, and roads.[2] The dominant feature of businesses incorporated in the eighteenth century was their public character.[3] With the charter came the privilege of monopoly status as well as the power to assess members in the locality for any deficiencies or capital requirements. However, as the concept of private property became more and more a part of American society and jurisprudence, the corporation and its members were viewed less and less as simply instruments of the state. For example, the Supreme Court held the Constitution's contract clause prevented the legislature from altering established property rights embodied in the relationship

---

[1]   E. Merrick Dodd, Jr., The First Half Century of Statutory Regulation of Business Corporations in Massachusetts, in Harvard Legal Essays 65–131 (1934).

[2]   Lawrence M. Friedman, A History of American Law 129–130 (3d ed. 2005).

[3]   Of special note is that the greater number of incorporations were of churches, cities, boroughs, and charities. Lawrence M. Friedman, A History of American Law 129–130 (3d ed. 2005).

between the corporation and its members.[4] Further evidence of the decline of the public nature of the corporation was the evolution of the law to the view that members could not be assessed without their assent, and courts began to assume that the corporation's members enjoyed limited liability unless they agreed otherwise.[5] Finally, America's embrace of markets and competition was reflected in the courts' construction of the young country's corporate law by the first half of the nineteenth century. For example, the courts began to hold that the grant of a charter did not carry with it monopoly status.[6] Barely a half a century earlier, a major motivating force for incorporation was the monopoly status it conferred for the activity being incorporated.

With the increasing pressures of industrialization, legislatures found themselves deluged with requests for legislation bestowing corporate status. The early reliance on special legislative acts to confer corporate status on individual entities proved not only inefficient but also was rife with the opportunity for favoritism and corruption.[7] Ultimately, states adopted constitutional provisions declaring that, with specified exceptions, the legislature should not pass any special act creating a corporation. These constitutional provisions permitted corporations to be formed only by compliance with general incorporation laws.[8] General incorporation legislation has now developed to the extent that almost any legitimate enterprise can be conducted in corporate form upon compliance with simple statutory formalities. In states that do not have a constitutional prohibition, however, corporations can still be created by special act.

§ 2.2   Evolution of American General Incorporation Laws

The first American general incorporation act—that is, an act allowing anyone to incorporate by compliance with the terms of the statute, apparently was a statute passed in 1811 in the State of New York. In that year, the New York legislature, seeking to encourage the manufacture of various commodities, enacted a law making incorporation available to organizers of concerns that manufactured specified kinds of products.[9] Corporate existence, however, was limited to 20 years, and the capital of such an enterprise could not exceed $100,000.[10]

Soon after New York's pioneer enactment, other states passed acts authorizing the incorporation of manufacturing companies. The more modern general corporation acts were expansive. Having grown out of the old manufacturing company acts, they covered almost every kind of lawful business. The trend toward use of general acts permitting incorporation by signing and filing articles of incorporation began immediately after 1835.[11] With the arrival of general incorporation laws, in contrast to incorporation by special act, businessmen could with certainty and efficiency gain the benefits of corporate status for their businesses.

---

[4]   Trustees of Dartmouth College v. Woodward, 17 U.S. (4 Wheat.) 518 (1819).

[5]   E. Merrick Dodd, Jr., American Business Corporations Until 1860 75–93 (1954).

[6]   Morton J. Horwitz, The Transformation of American Law 114–139 (1977).

[7]   *Id.*

[8]   *See* William L. Cary, Federalism and Corporate Law: Reflections Upon Delaware, 83 Yale L.J. 663, 663–664 (1974).

[9]   1811 N.Y. Laws ch. 67, "Act Relative to Incorporations for Manufacturing Purposes."

[10]   E. Merrick Dodd, Jr., American Business Association Law a Hundred Years Ago and Today, in 3 Law: A Century of Progress, 1835–1935, 254, 271, 289 (1937).

[11]   *Id.*

In 1888, the New Jersey legislature authorized corporations organized under the law of that state to purchase and hold shares of stock in other corporations,[12] thus making possible the creation of holding companies with numerous subsidiaries. Delaware and many other states soon followed New Jersey's lead and authorized corporations to hold stock in other corporations. Growth of holding companies and parent-subsidiary relationships among companies resulted in small groups of persons holding large concentrations of economic power.

In 1896, New Jersey enacted what may be regarded as the first permissive modern incorporation act—that is, a statute that conferred broad powers on corporations, empowered promoters of corporations to set up almost any kind of corporate structure they desired, granted broad powers to corporate directors and managers, and provided great protection against liability for corporate directors and managers. Soon, New Jersey was referred to as "the Mother of Trusts."

In 1913, however, reform-minded then-governor Woodrow Wilson caused New Jersey to amend its more permissive provisions. Delaware, which had borrowed most of its corporation law from New Jersey, seized the opportunity to assume leadership in providing and keeping up-to-date a body of permissive corporate laws. At various times, several states—Maine, West Virginia, and later Nevada—have attempted to "out-Delaware Delaware" in an effort to attract incorporation business and, more specifically, tax revenues and fees. These imitators, however, have had little success in displacing Delaware's preeminence in the race for the rechartering business. Still other states have liberalized their statutes to encourage their local businesses to "stay at home" by incorporating locally rather than organizing in Delaware, New Jersey, or some other permissive jurisdiction.

It can thus be said that, by the end of the nineteenth century, the states had loosened the bonds that once hobbled the corporation's formation and operation. Populist concerns over the concentration of economic powers in large corporations, frequently networked through interlocking ownership or boards of directors, translated into an unending legislative agenda designed to channel or thwart the economic power of corporations.

It is safe to say that the liberalization trend that began toward the end of the nineteenth century continued throughout the twentieth century so that today all states have broadly permissive enabling corporation statutes with very little evidence in any state statute of regulatory or paternalistic provisions. While in some instances the changes were prompted by competition for incorporation fees and the accompanying tax revenues, a more compelling explanation of the trend is the increasing belief among legislators and local drafting groups that corporations are not monolithic in their needs or operations; one set of rules is not appropriate for all corporate entities. Legislatures, especially since the 1960s, have consistently embraced the philosophy of allowing corporations, within the broad framework of local law, to tailor their governance structure to accommodate their own special needs and relationships.

---

[12]   1888 N.J. Laws ch. 269, § 1, repealed by 1896 N.J. Laws ch. 190, § 10 (*reprinted in* 1 Gen. Stat. of N.J., 1709–1893, at 983).

§ 2.3   Modern Corporation Acts

The first general corporation chartering laws were cumbersome and unartfully drafted. They were overly restrictive in that they imposed burdensome conditions precedent to incorporation and unreasonable limitations on the scope of the corporate franchise. This unfortunate state of affairs led to efforts by legislative drafting committees and committees of concerned business lawyers to formulate clear and precise legislation.

The Model Act first appeared in completed form in 1950.[13] The Model Act continued the liberalizing trend that originated in New Jersey and Delaware and for a long time has been universally viewed as " 'enabling,' 'permissive,' and 'liberal' as distinguished from 'regulatory' and 'paternalistic.' "[14] From time to time, other states have competed for the lead in this type of liberalization (which at times has been referred to as "the race to the bottom" although others view it as a "race to the top").[15] The Delaware legislature, however, continues to be the leader in originating permissive corporate legislation.[16] Delaware's continued popularity among public corporations is documented by the fact that nearly 90 percent of public corporations that change their corporate domicile choose to reincorporate in Delaware.[17] The Model Act was intended not to become a uniform corporation law but rather to serve as a drafting guide for the states. Eventually the Model Act became the pattern for large parts of the corporation statutes in most states (notable exceptions being California, Delaware, and New York). The Committee on Corporate Laws revises the Model Act from time to time, and typically a number of states amend their corporation statutes to adopt the latest revisions.

The first complete revision of the Model Act appears in the Revised Model Business Corporation Act (1984). The Revised Model Act incorporates many simplifying and innovative provisions that the states had experimented with over the years. In addition, the Revised Model Act has through subsequent revisions continued the liberalizing trend that started in Delaware. Slightly more than sixty percent of the states have adopted the Model Act as a basic template.[18] However, in those states that have adopted the Model Act, there are many state by state variations. In 2016, the Model Act underwent substantial editing so as to "harmonize" its terminology with other model acts such as the Uniform Limited Liability Company Act and the Revised Uniform Limited Partnership Act. Several states have already amended their corporate statutes to reflect changes introduced by the 2016 Model Act.

---

[13]   1 Model Business Corp. Act Ann. §§ 1, 2 (2d ed. 1971 & Supp. 1973, 1977).

[14]   Harry G. Henn, Handbook of the Law of Corporations and Other Business Enterprises, 22 n.40 (2d ed. 1970).

[15]   William L. Cary, Federalism and Corporate Law: Reflections Upon Delaware, 83 Yale L.J. 663 (1974).

[16]   *See generally* Ernest L. Folk, The Delaware General Corporation Law, a Commentary and Analysis (1972).

[17]   *See* Note, Is Delaware Still a Haven for Incorporation?, 20 Del. J. Corp. L. 965, 999–1002 (1995); Roberta Romano, Law as a Product: Some Pieces of the Incorporation Puzzle, 1 J.L. Econ. & Org. 225, 244 (1985).

[18]   Thirty states have adopted all or a substantial part of the Model Business Corporation Act including Alabama, Arizona, Arkansas, Connecticut, Florida, Georgia, Hawaii, Idaho, Indiana, Iowa, Kentucky, Maine, Massachusetts, Mississippi, Montana, Nebraska, New Hampshire, North Carolina, Oregon, Rhode Island, South Carolina, South Dakota, Tennessee, Utah, Vermont, Virginia, Washington, West Virginia, Wisconsin, and Wyoming. Alaska, the District of Columbia, and New Mexico have adopted certain provisions. Model Business Corp. Act Ann., at ix (4d ed. & 2008 Supp.).

Most states, in addition to a general business corporation act, have more specialized general chartering acts governing the formation and regulation of corporations in special fields of business such as banking, building and loan associations, insurance, railroads, and public utilities.[19] Similarly, virtually all states now have a separate act for professional corporations.

Modern business corporation statutes are primarily "enabling" acts, which make it easy for businessmen to organize and operate an enterprise, large or small, with the advantages of the corporate mechanism.[20] These enabling acts provide the legal framework and financial structure of the corporate devices by which most modern business is transacted and in which managers' energies and investors' capital can be combined effectively.

Corporation laws deal with such matters as the following: the content of the articles of incorporation; the rights of shareholders; the powers and liabilities of directors; rules governing shareholders' meetings and directors' meetings; restrictions on corporate finance, such as limitations on the withdrawal of funds by way of dividends and share purchases; the keeping and inspection of corporate records; and authorization of organic changes, such as charter amendments, sale of all corporate assets, merger, and consolidation, and dissolution and winding up. Some of these provisions seek to prevent management and majority shareholders from abusing their power to the detriment of minority shareholders and corporate creditors.

North Dakota amended its corporate statute in an attempt to make its chartering provisions the most shareholder-friendly corporate law. The North Dakota provisions include:

- a prohibition on staggered boards of directors—all directors are elected to one-year terms;

- generally, there is no plurality voting—directors must be elected by a majority of the "yes" votes cast;

- shareholders are entitled to a "say on pay";

- 5 percent shareholders who have held their stock for two years have an absolute right to proxy access;

- the board may not be chaired by an executive officer;

- shareholders must be reimbursed proxy expenses for certain successful proposals;

- supermajority provisions are prohibited;

- 10 percent of the shareholders may call a special meeting at any time;

- 5 percent of the shareholders may propose to amend the corporate articles;

- shareholders generally must approve the issuance of shares representing 20 percent or more of the voting power; and

---

[19] *See* Alfred F. Conard, Corporations in Perspective §§ 5, 6 (1976).

[20] E. Merrick Dodd, Jr., Statutory Developments in Business Corporation Law, 1886–1936, 50 Harv. L. Rev. 27, 43, 58 (1937).

- board-adopted "poison pill" takeover defenses are of limited duration, and the shareholders may prohibit the adoption of a poison pill.

§ 2.4 The Race to the Bottom or the Race to the Top?

Modern corporation acts became "enabling," "permissive," and "liberal" as a result of state legislative decisions to eliminate or reduce restrictions that earlier incorporation acts had imposed on corporations. Charters granted by the state legislatures and early general incorporation statutes limited the size of corporations, the scope of their business activities, the amount of capital they could assemble by issuing shares, and the size of the indebtedness they could incur by borrowing.

The early restrictions on corporate activities grew out of a suspicion and fear of the corporate mechanism, an attitude manifested in the reported debates of state constitutional conventions before the year 1890.[21] Legislators remembered the unpleasant experiences with large British corporations—the trading companies that colonized and tried to govern the colonies. The American colonies had fought for their independence, in part to free themselves from the control of these large British companies.[22] In an eloquent dissenting opinion in *Louis K. Liggett Company v. Lee*,[23] Justice Brandeis recounted the evolution of state corporation laws and discussed the many restrictions imposed on corporations. In part, Justice Brandeis stated:

> There was a sense of some insidious menace inherent in large aggregations of capital, particularly when held by corporations. So, at first, the corporate privilege was granted sparingly.... The later enactment of general incorporation laws does not signify that the apprehension of corporate domination had been overcome.... The general laws, which long embodied severe restrictions upon size and upon the scope of corporate activity, were, in part, an expression of the desire for equality of opportunity.

> Limitation upon the amount of the authorized capital of business corporations was long universal. The maximum limit frequently varied with the kinds of business to be carried on....

> Limitations upon the scope of a business corporation's powers and activity were also long universal. At first, corporations could be formed under the general laws only for a limited number of purposes—usually those which required a relatively large fixed capital, like transportation, banking, and insurance, and mechanical, mining, and manufacturing enterprises. Permission to incorporate for "any lawful purpose" was not common until 1875; and until that time the duration of corporate franchises was generally limited to a period of 20, 30, 40, or 50 years. All, or a majority, of the incorporators or directors, or both, were required to be residents of the incorporating state. The powers which the corporation might exercise in carrying out its purposes were sparingly conferred and strictly construed. Severe limitations were imposed on the amount of indebtedness, bonded or otherwise. The power to hold stock in other

---

[21] *See, e.g.,* Del Monte Light & Power Co. v. Jordan, 238 P. 710, 713 (Cal. 1925).

[22] Gerard Carl Henderson, The Position of Foreign Corporations in American Constitutional Law 19 (1918).

[23] Louis K. Liggett Company v. Lee, 288 U.S. 517 (1933).

corporations was not conferred or implied. The holding company was impossible.[24]

In his *Liggett* dissent, Justice Brandeis assailed as highly undesirable the loosening of the restrictions formerly imposed on corporations in this country.

Brandeis's concerns continue to be the subject of debate today over the desirability of our federal system, which allocates control of corporate laws to individual states—or fiefdoms, depending on one's point of view. In a classic work, Professor Cary warned that interstate competition for corporate chartering would lead, as predicted by Gresham's Law, to "bad" corporate law driving out "good" corporation laws.[25] On the other hand, others argue that competition among the states can be seen as necessary to foster an environment for incubating new procedures and mechanisms of corporate governance. Also, diversity of laws among the states allows shareholders and managers to choose the set of rules best suited for their own peculiar position.[26]

Obviously there is a great gulf between these two positions. Those favoring the Cary view believe that ever more permissive corporate laws decrease shareholder wealth by favoring managers over owners. In contrast, those favoring the status quo counsel that permissive statutes actually increase the value of the firm and that Professor Cary and others have overlooked how the markets for capital, the firm's products, and managers constrain any proclivities managers may have to benefit themselves at the expense of shareholders.[27]

There appear to be several weaknesses with the argument that markets have a disciplining effect on managers and state legislatures. First, in order for there to be a realistic threat of a hostile takeover, the corporate laws chosen by managers must produce a substantial decline in the value of the firm. With takeover premiums averaging out at a level of more than 50 percent, the decision—for example, to reincorporate in Delaware—must cause roughly one-third of the firm's value to be lost before there is a realistic threat to the current management's control. Such a decline is not conceivable.

Second, markets are not likely to associate a reincorporation decision necessarily with a value-decreasing motivation. The key to understanding this observation is that reincorporation decisions require the approval of the firm's stockholders, a group not presumed to act against its own interest. We might therefore ask, why would shareholders approve reincorporation in a state whose laws are generally viewed as "lax" or "permissive"? To answer this question we can view a broadly enabling corporate statute like the rain that can fall on the good and the bad alike. The state's corporate laws may facilitate value-increasing mergers and reduce the cost of convening stockholder's meetings while at the same time insulating managerial self-dealing and ineptitude.

---

[24] Louis K. Liggett Co. v. Lee, 288 U.S. 517, 549–557 (1933) (Brandeis, J., dissenting) (footnotes omitted).

[25] *See* William L. Cary, Federalism and Corporate Law: Reflections Upon Delaware, 83 Yale L.J. 663, 663–664 (1974). He recommended federally imposed minimum standards for state corporate codes.

[26] Daniel R. Fischel, The "Race to the Bottom" Revisited: Reflections on Recent Developments in Delaware's Corporation Law, 76 Nw. U. L. Rev. 913, 921–923 (1982).

[27] *See, e.g.*, Ralph K. Winter, Jr., State Law, Shareholder Protection, and the Theory of the Corporation, 6 J. Legal. Stud. 251 (1977).

A third qualification on the ability of markets to deter overly permissive corporate statutes is that not all firms are vulnerable to market influences. A monopolistic or oligopolistic market structure, perhaps facilitated in some respect by patents and franchises, insulates the firm's managers from competition. Also, the cost of capital is not a concern to managers, who can rely on retention of earnings or nurtured banking relationships for expansion needs. Moreover, state anti-takeover laws and self-help defenses such as poison pills further shield managers from the disciplining influence of a hostile takeover. And a management that has taken care of itself at the stockholders' expense may well not have any concern for the market for managers, but rather only for a retirement spa.

Managers who have initiated reincorporation, most frequently in Delaware, have usually not acted as tramps, pirates, or privateers, preying on their shareholders or customers or other citizens. Their overall objective usually is to reduce the cost, formality, and uncertainty of doing business. Such motivation is a commendable quest for achieving reasonable business arrangements to advance the interests of the stockholders.[28]

With the increasing adoption of the Model Business Corporation Act, whose provisions are nearly as permissive as those of Delaware, there is every reason to expect some decline in the incidence of reincorporations. There will, however, continue to be substantial considerations that will tug public corporations to Delaware.[29]

Professor Romano identifies three factors that explain why Delaware is the situs for over one half of all reincorporations.[30] First, because Delaware depends more than any other state on corporate franchise tax revenues, it is more committed than any other state to remaining an attractive incorporation site. "It cannot afford to lose firms to other states by failing to keep its code up-to-date."[31] Second, Delaware's constitution mandates a two-thirds vote of both state legislative houses to change its corporation statute.[32] This provision makes radical reform in its provisions unlikely. At the same time, the state's dependence on franchise revenues assures that the legislature will be responsive to innovations that threaten the state's fiscal health. Finally, Delaware has a corporate legal infrastructure that cannot be easily replicated. Not only does it provide its own specialized Chancery Court staffed with individuals from the corporate bar and a Supreme Court with similar expertise, but its statutes are surrounded by a wealth of legal precedent that assures its corporate law is the most comprehensive body in the land, a consideration that reduces the cost of advising clients. In sum, businesses that quest certainty of result, as well as a sympathetic and experienced ear to the problems of running a public corporation, are assured of finding it in Delaware.

The concentration of most businesses into a relatively few huge incorporated units is not due primarily to lax corporation laws or even to a corporation's privilege to hold shares in other corporations. Whether bigness in business should be curtailed or

---

[28] Edward G. Jennings, Federal Incorporation or Licensing of Interstate Corporate Business, 23 Minn. L. Rev. 710, 712 (1939).

[29] For a suggestion that this will not be the case, see John H. Matheson, Philip S. Garon & Michael Stanchfield, Challenging Delaware's Desirability as a Haven for Incorporation, 32 Wm. Mitchell L. Rev. 769 (2006) (concluding that the MBCA is more flexible and provides greater certainty than the Delaware statute).

[30] Roberta Romano, The State Competition Debate in Corporate Law, 8 Cardozo L. Rev. 709, 721–722 (1987).

[31] Id.

[32] Del. Const. art. IX, § 1.

regulated, and how such controls should be accomplished, are unsettled questions of economic policy, not of corporation law. Various economics issues—for example, whether and the extent to which production, competition, monopoly, labor conditions, profits, and the concentration of wealth should be controlled by government—call for patient, thorough study. This task of regulating corporate bigness and curtailing supposed corporate "evils" should not be confused with the task of establishing modern corporation laws to facilitate incorporation and to define and enforce the rights and duties of shareholders, directors, and officers.[33]

Much of what regulates corporations is not state law, but rather federal law and, in the case of public companies, listing requirements on their home stock exchange. Therefore, the force that likely drives the content of Delaware law is not so much competition from other states, but the preemptive threat of federal incursion.[34] Thus Delaware and other state legislatures proceed with a healthy regard that on big issues, the federal government has either acted or considered acting.[35] Nonetheless, the federal government faces its own constraints; as capital markets become more and more international, each country's securities laws are shaped by the intense pressure regulators face to preserve the relative competitiveness of their markets and home countries.[36]

§ 2.5   Separation of Corporate Ownership from Control

In their classic book on the modern corporation, Adolf Berle and Gardiner Means pointed out that the American corporation is no longer merely a private business tool or device; instead, it has evolved into a dominant institution affecting economic, political, and social conditions in modern society.[37] A large amount of the wealth of individuals has shifted from ownership of actual physical property to ownership of shares of stock representing a set of rights and expectations in an enterprise.

Berle's and Means' view that dispersion of ownership is an inherent characteristic of the public corporation has been seriously questioned by Professor Mark Roe. Professor Roe argues that the present dispersed ownership is the result of a series of political decisions motivated principally out of fear of avoiding the concentration of economic power.[38] Among the most significant regulatory developments that foster dispersed ownership are the various directives that limit, either directly or indirectly, the percentage of stock certain financial institutions can own in a single corporation. His

---

[33] *See* Thomas L. Hazen, Corporate Chartering and the Securities Markets: Shareholder Suffrage, Corporate Responsibility and Managerial Accountability, 1978 Wis. L. Rev. 391.

[34] *See* Mark J. Roe, Delaware's Competition, 117 Harv. L. Rev. 588 (2003).

[35] Mark J. Roe, Delaware and Washington as Corporate Lawmakers, 34 Del. J. Corp. L. 1 (2009). Those who champion state over federal regulation emphasize the greater flexibility of case law doctrine over rigid one-size-fits-all federal rules. *See* Griffith and Steele, On Corporate Law Federalism: Threatening the Thaumatrope, 61 Bus. Law. 1 (2005).

[36] Chris Brummer, Corporate Law Preemption in an Age of Global Capital Markets, 81 S. Cal. L. Rev. 1067 (2008). For a discussion of how the potential for federal incursion affects the actors in Delaware, *see* Mark J. Roe, Delaware Politics, 118 Harv. L. Rev. 2491 (2005).

[37] Adolf A. Berle & Gardiner C. Means, The Modern Corporation and Private Property, at 44–46, 66–69, 121–125, 250, 352–357 (1932). A recent development in some states has been the emergence of a new variety of corporate entity known as the benefit corporation. *See, e.g.,* Cal. Corp. Code § 14610 (2012); N.Y. Bus. Corp. Law § 1706(b) (2012). Benefit corporations are discussed in § 2.9 *infra.*

[38] Mark J. Roe, Strong Managers, Weak Owners: The Political Roots of American Corporate Finance (1994). For a critical review of this book, *see* Stephen M. Bainbridge, The Politics of Corporate Governance, 18 Harv. J.L. & Pub. Poly. 671 (1995).

point is that absent such politically motivated directives, ownership may not have fragmented as it has and the problems of the separation of ownership from management would not be what it has become.

Agency problems flowing from the separation of owners and managers is not necessarily limited to public corporations. Start-up companies also pose these problems (as well as agency costs across investors) such that venture capitalists resort to a variety of contractual provisions and other strategies to minimize agency costs.[39]

The separation of ownership from control gives rise to various conflicts of interest between passive owners and active managers. In the abstract, managers are no different from other individuals when facing an economic choice; so as to maximize their own utility, they can be expected to act like other individuals in exercising discretionary decisions. Utility maximization is an especially interesting problem in the public corporation, where management and ownership are separated. The managers' quest to maximize their utility does not naturally lead to decisions that also maximize the value of the firm.

In a classic article,[40] Ronald Coase developed a powerful model of the firm that explains why firms exist and why they decide to expand. Coase argued that a firm will undertake an activity for itself whenever it is cheaper to do so than to acquire that good or service in the market. A distinct cost of the market is imperfect information about the quality and overall utility of the good or service that others will provide. Further concerns are whether the sellers of goods will be able to produce the desired quantity and make the goods available at competitive prices. Because it is expensive to gather information on these various points and because there may be no economies in relying on the production efforts of others, the firm's managers will decide to provide the good or service itself. The firm thus grows because of its decision to integrate the new activity into the firm's existing operation.

In contrast to Coase's model, Berle and Means take the position that the separation of ownership from management has allowed less economically desirable reasons to distort management's expansion decisions, such as the quest for bigness, as though size itself were a virtue.

The neoclassical economists (sometimes more generally referred to as "the Chicago School") have prodigiously mined the problems posed by separation of ownership from control. Any examination of the issues flowing from the separation of ownership and management should begin by considering the work of Professors Jensen and Meckling,[41] who theorize that managers have strong market-based incentives to contract with shareholders to reduce the managers' misbehavior. In this context the misbehavior need not rise to the level of constituting practices that are fraudulent or even in breach of the manager's fiduciary duties. They can, however, include a range of relatively benign conduct, such as longer lunch hours and directing the corporation's munificence to the manager's alma mater.

---

[39] Robert P. Bartlett, III, Venture Capital, Agency Costs, and the False Dichotomy of the Corporation, 54 UCLA. L. Rev. 37 (2006).

[40] Ronald H. Coase, The Nature of the Firm, 4 Economica (n.s.) 386 (1937).

[41] Michael C. Jensen & William H. Meckling, Theory of the Firm: Managerial Behavior, Agency Costs and Ownership Structure, 3 J. Fin. Econ. 305 (1976).

The cornerstone of the Jensen and Meckling analysis is that the value of the firm's shares will reflect the investors' perceptions of the amount of the firm's earnings that managers will deflect to themselves or will otherwise act adverse to the firm. Simply stated, conduct that is adverse to the stockholders' interests will depress the market value of the firm. A decline in the value of the firm's shares impacts the managers to the extent their compensation is based on changes in the firm's value, the managers' ownership of shares in the company, or whether the decline poses a serious threat of a hostile takeover. Managers therefore have an incentive to dampen the investors' perceptions of the likelihood of managerial misbehavior. But how can the managers mollify the investors' concerns over the dark side of the managers' drive to maximize their own utility? To answer this question one must consider the relative knowledge of the owners and their managers.

Information asymmetries accompany managerial misconduct; that is, managers know the frequency and magnitude of the harm they cause by their misconduct, whereas the outside investors do not. Absent other factors, *ex ante* investors will discount all securities by the average misbehavior committed by all firms' managers, because they otherwise are unable to distinguish *ex ante* among the respective proclivities of a particular firm's managers to misbehave.[42] In general, it would be of little use for managers to proclaim they left their self-interest at the office door, since saints and sinners alike are equally capable of proclaiming their virtue. How then can the firm's managers whose misbehavior is less than the norm effectively convey its message to investors? And why would they wish to do so? What follows is a summary of the neoclassical economists' models within which each of these questions is answered.

A key point in the neoclassical economic view of the firm is that managers must have an incentive compensation arrangement that substantially ties their fortunes to that of the owners. Such an arrangement accomplishes two objectives. First, the typical stock option plan or bonuses based on firm profitability *bonds* the manager to serve the stockholders' interest. Obviously, the strength of the bond is directly proportional to the extent the managers' total compensation packages depend on the changes in the firm's value or profitability. Second, linking the managers' incentives to those of the firm's owners *signals* to the investors the depth of the firm's managers' resolve to maximize the value of the firm.[43] Signaling addresses the information asymmetry problem, so that investors will not discount the firm's securities by the average risk expected for the industry. Consistent with agency theorists' view of the firm is the increasing popularity among public corporations of encouraging or requiring their outside directors to acquire a substantial equity investment in the corporation.[44]

A further step to reduce such discounting is the use of *monitoring* devices designed to police management. Conventional examples of monitoring include that of outside boards of directors and independent accountants. However, monitoring is efficient only

---

[42]   The leading authority for this view is George A. Akerlof, The Market for "Lemons": Qualitative Uncertainty and the Market Mechanism, 84 Q.J. Econ. 488 (1970).

[43]   Stephen Ross, Disclosure Regulation in Financial Markets: Implications of Modern Finance Theory and Signaling Theory Issues in Financial Regulation 177 (Franklin R. Edwards ed. 1979); A. Michael Spence, Market Signaling 88–95 (1974).

[44]   *See* Report of the National Association of Corporate Directors Blue Ribbon Commission on Director Compensation 12 (1995) (recommending that boards of directors establish substantial target stock ownership levels for directors and that director fees be paid in stock or cash. The report also takes the position that benefits such as pension and health care plans for outside directors are likely to make directors less independent because they thereby become more akin to employees in their quest for longevity).

to the extent its marginal benefits exceed its marginal cost. Because monitoring can be expected to pose diminishing marginal benefits, it generally prevents only the more extreme managerial departures.

The costs of bonding, signaling, and monitoring, as well as the amount of misbehavior that continues in the face of these steps to deter managerial indiscretions, are collectively referred to as *agency costs.* In view of these mechanisms for reducing agency costs, the neoclassical economists who view the corporation as a "nexus of contracts" reason that what binds the firm together as an entity is not the fiction of its separate existence but the numerous contractual intersections among owners, managers, creditors, and workers through which they define their respective roles, risks, and rights. Under this view, the corporation is reduced to the means for efficient contracting among the owners, managers, creditors, and laborers. Corporate statutes are viewed by these economists as off-the-rack contractual provisions the parties would have embodied in their contract if contracting could occur costlessly. And judges in resolving disputes should similarly confine their analysis.

Thus the contribution of the neoclassical economists on the separation of ownership from management is more than the vocabulary they use to describe common corporate activities. The neoclassical view has a distinctly prescriptive content that increasingly is finding its way into American corporate jurisprudence. According to Professors Klein and Coffee:

> The neoclassical position is that market forces have minimized the firm's agency costs, and further legal interventions are thus unnecessary and wasteful. In other words, the parties to the corporation are seen as having voluntarily installed those monitoring devices that are cost-efficient (i.e., that will prevent greater losses than they, themselves, cost). Legally mandated reforms ... [are unhelpful because they will] result in inefficient expenditures.[45]

Not surprising, there is abundant criticism of this view of the firm. Certainly, it is correct that firms organize their internal governance and structure to achieve efficient operations, which includes effective monitoring of the performance of all operating units.[46] Even if one accepts the economists' nexus-of-contracts interpretation of the firm, it must be done with a healthy respect for the indeterminacy to its prescription that intramural disputes be resolved by divining the presumed intentions of the parties when the corporation or their relationship was formed.[47]

In the end, the neoclassical view of the corporation is vulnerable to the charges that it is both an empty metaphor and tautological:[48] The neoclassical view allows no room for a higher principle or purpose to resolve corporate law questions; disputes are instead

---

[45] William A. Klein & John C. Coffee, Jr., Business Organization and Finance: Legal and Economic Principles 174 (8th ed. 2002).

[46] *See generally* Oliver E. Williamson, The Modern Corporation: Origins, Evolution, Attributes, 19 J. Econ. Lit. 1537 (1981). In Coase's seminal investigation of the firm, he rationalized the firm as existing when it was the more efficient mechanism for directing production than through exchange transactions in the market. Ronald H. Coase, The Nature of the Firm, 4 Economica (n.s.) 386 (1937).

[47] On this point, consider the disagreement between two leading figures of the neoclassical view, Judges Easterbrook and Posner, in Jordan v. Duff & Phelps, Inc., 815 F.2d 429 (7th Cir. 1987), *cert. denied,* 485 U.S. 901 (1988).

[48] William W. Bratton, Jr., The "Nexus of Contracts" Corporation: A Critical Appraisal, 74 Cornell L. Rev. 407, 410 (1989).

resolved according to the presumed intentions of the contracting parties. Thus law is not an engine for societal change and improvement. The neoclassical view has struck many commentators as antithetical even to the basic premises of corporate law.[49]

The nexus-of-contracts interpretation of the firm provides a free-market approach to the problems posed by the separation of ownership from control. In the meantime, the conflicts of interest inherent in the separation of ownership and control continue to create new concerns, such as the broad public alarm about excessive executive compensation and the competitiveness of American industry. Coupled with these concerns are complaints from public interest and consumer groups about the socially undesirable and scandalous conduct that they attribute to corporations. In combination, they continue to spawn a lively debate and action to improve corporate governance mechanisms.

§ 2.6   Reform Efforts, the American Law Institute's Corporate Governance Project, and a Brief Introduction to the Sarbanes-Oxley Act of 2002

Undeniably, there is broad-based dissatisfaction with traditional corporate governance procedures. Many of the recommendations have questioned the "race to the bottom" in corporate legal principles, discussed earlier in this chapter, and recommend either the federal chartering of corporations or that the content of state laws be improved through the imposition of federal minimum standards. Others have invoked a structural approach of healing the corporation from within itself. Among the approaches suggested by this group are mandating that corporate boards have a critical mass of "outside" directors, that outside directors be armed with a professional staff to assist them in discharging their responsibilities, that the boardroom become more diversified, with membership including representatives from labor, consumer, or creditor groups, or that there be significant representation of institutional holders on the board of directors. Of these many suggestions, the one that has the greatest currency is expanding the role of outside directors on the boards of publicly traded corporations. Indeed, the most significant corporate development in the last quarter century has been the rapid evolution from the inside to the outside board. The change in the composition of the American boardroom was stimulated by the popular perception within management that outside directors have much to contribute to the vision and strength of the organization. Further impetus for the managers' acceptance of outside directors is the courts' increasing dependence on outside directors as evidence of the propriety of corporate conduct. One of the most recent and most notable corporate law reform projects, the American Law Institute's Corporate Governance Project, reflects the evolution and thinking of the prominent role that outside directors can and should play in the governance of the American corporation.

The American Law Institute (ALI), after more than a decade of study and fractious debate, adopted in 1992 a voluminous set of principles, recommendations, and commentary entitled the Principles of Corporate Governance: Analysis and Recommendations. A core feature of the project is its heavy reliance on outside directors.

---

[49] Robert C. Clark, Agency Costs versus Fiduciary Duties, in Principals and Agents: The Structure of Business (John W. Pratt & Richard J. Zeckhauser eds. 1985).

Principles of Corporate Governance is different from earlier ALI projects. It is not merely a restatement of prevailing corporate principles that have developed over time. Many of the ALI's positions have scant support in the states, and in some areas the ALI embraces positions that are a matter of popular practice within corporations but are not legally compelled. It thus has been seen as a reform-minded document, driven by academic theory rather than commercial practicality, and it has been attacked without quarter by the representatives of the managerial class. As a result of the firestorm of protest that met its early version in 1980, the document underwent important changes that muffled its more innovative contributions. Nevertheless, the document continues to offer authoritative guidance of where the law may go on many important corporate law questions.

In broad overview, Principles of Corporate Governance has detailed provisions on the functions, powers, and rights of directors as well as recommendations that for certain-sized corporations, outsiders should compose a majority of the board of directors and that the corporations should also have audit, nominating, and executive compensation committees. The project has sought to bring clarity through rigor to the jurisprudence that surrounds director decision-making. The project therefore has chapters devoted to the duty of care and, more generally, to the business judgment rule, the treatment of conflicts of interest, and the role of directors in hostile attempts to acquire their firm. Finally, there is extensive treatment to all aspects of derivative suit litigation, including the manner for initiating the suit, the corporation's participation in the suit, settlement, damages, and indemnification.

In general, Principles of Corporate Governance carefully distinguishes among what it sets forth as an analysis of the present law, what it asserts the law should be, and what it recommends as good corporate practice though not the law. While its provisions are not likely to be adopted in toto by any state, and it was not drafted with this objective in mind, it surely can be expected to have a distinct impact on the direction of corporate law and good corporate practice. For these reasons, its provisions are examined at appropriate locations throughout this book.

The Sarbanes-Oxley Act of 2002[50] ("SOX") reformed corporate governance in response to corporate scandals. SOX affects the conduct of corporations, accountants, attorneys, officers, and directors. It places an emphasis on internal controls, increased public company disclosure requirements, and director independence. CEOs and CFOs must certify that they reviewed their company's financial reports and that the reports are materially accurate and that they comply with sections 13(a) or 15(d) of the Securities Exchange Act of 1934. Signing the reports potentially makes CEOs and CFOs liable in a claim for securities fraud in connection with the sale of a security because there is an inference of scienter if the signers had reason to know of any material misstatements or omissions in the reports. In addition, section 301 of the Act mandates that independent directors comprise the audit committee. SOX also expands the role of the audit committee, making it a corporate "watchdog."

---

[50] 15 U.S.C. §§ 7211 to 7266 (West Supp. 2009).

§ 2.7   Foreign Corporations

The law of the state of incorporation governs the internal affairs of the corporation.[51] Nevertheless, other states in which the corporation does business may regulate a corporation incorporated in another state as a foreign corporation. There are numerous policy reasons a state may wish to regulate a foreign corporation's intrastate activities. Their authority to do so was recognized early in the nineteenth century,[52] and regulatory steps for a foreign corporation to qualify to do business within a state is today fairly standardized. States may exclude a foreign corporation from carrying on intrastate activities when a foreign corporation has not fulfilled the state's qualification requirements for foreign corporations.[53] Nevertheless, the regulation of foreign corporations is not without limits, especially given the strong commitment to the free movement of goods and services that is embodied in the commerce clause of the Constitution. States thus have the power to forbid foreign corporations from conducting business within the state so long as the business does not constitute interstate commerce and the state otherwise conforms with the due process and equal protection clauses of the Constitution.[54]

A foreign corporation seeking to engage in intrastate activities in a state must obtain a certificate of authority by filing certain information with the state.[55] This requirement applies only to foreign corporations that are "doing business" within the state. About the only matters in the application process that approach substantive requirements are the common requirement that the foreign corporation's name be "distinguishable" from that of other corporations doing business within the state[56] and that the foreign corporation designate a registered agent to receive service of process.[57] Once the certificate is obtained, the foreign corporation enjoys the right to do business within the state.[58]

Most states following the Model Business Corporation Act's approach sanction the failure to comply with the requirements for foreign corporations doing business in the state.[59] To wit, the delinquent corporation is barred from maintaining suit in any court within the state until it has obtained a certificate of authority.[60] These provisions are sometimes referred to as "door closing" statutes.

---

[51]   *See* Willis L.M. Reese & Edward M. Kaufman, The Law Governing Corporate Affairs: Choice of Law and the Impact of Full Faith and Credit, 58 Colum. L. Rev. 1118 (1958).

[52]   *See* Bank of Augusta v. Earle, 38 U.S. 519 (1839). More recently, the Supreme Court reminds states that equal protection and due process require even-handed treatment of foreign corporations. *See* WHYY, Inc. v. Borough of Glassboro, 393 U.S. 117 (1968) (regarding validity of ad valorem taxes).

[53]   Wheeling Steel Corp. v. Glander, 337 U.S. 562 (1949).

[54]   *See* American Motorists Ins. Co. v. Starnes, 425 U.S. 637 (1976).

[55]   All states follow the basic pattern set out in the Model Business Corporation Act. *See* Model Bus. Corp. Act Ann. § 15.02 (2016). *See, e.g.,* Bonnier Corp. v. Jersey Cape Yacht Sales, Inc., 416 N.J. Super. 436, 5 A.3d 799 (App. Div. 2010) (magazine publisher who sent sales representatives into state, but had no office there, is not engaged in intrastate commerce, even if contracts were consummated in the state).

[56]   Model Bus. Corp. Act §§ 4.01 & 15.03 (2016).

[57]   Model Bus. Corp. Act § 15.03(d) (2016). Procedures are set forth as well for changing the designation. *See id.* § 5.02 (2016).

[58]   Model Bus. Corp. Act § 15.02(a) (2016).

[59]   Model Bus. Corp. Act § 15.02(b) (2016) ("A foreign corporation doing business in this state may not maintain a proceeding in any court of this state until it is registered to do business in this state").

[60]   *See, e.g.,* Del. Code Ann. tit. 8, §§ 378, 383 (2001).

Under the approach taken by door closing statutes, the failure to obtain a certificate of authority does not impair the validity of contracts made within the state. The clear intent of this sanction is to encourage the delinquent corporation to bring itself into compliance, rather than to impose a more harsh sanction.

§ 2.8   Choice-of-Law Rule: The Internal Affairs Doctrine

There is a virtually universal rule that the state of incorporation law governs corporate activities. Accordingly, when a corporation reincorporates into another state, it is making a choice of law decision to change the applicable law.[61]

Internal affairs covers all governance and fiduciary issues that arise within the corporation, including relations among stockholders, the rights of stockholders, the duties and obligations of the officers and directors, election and appointment of directors, issuance of shares, meetings, inspection rights, acquisition procedures, dividend regulation, and dissolution. With very limited exceptions discussed below, internal affairs are governed by the law of the state of incorporation. This is customarily referred to as the internal affairs doctrine and is a mainstay of corporate law. Therefore, in a leading case, the Delaware Supreme Court, when called upon to decide whether the Delaware subsidiary of a Panamanian corporation could vote the shares it held in the parent, held that per the internal affairs doctrine, the issue should be resolved according to Panamanian, not Delaware, law.[62] Consequently, the subsidiary was allowed to vote the shares in its parent. Had the court instead opted for Delaware law, the subsidiary would have been barred from voting the shares. Hence, the act of incorporation also involves selecting the body of law that will apply to the corporation's internal affairs. The rigidity of this approach stands in sharp contrast to the revolution in conflicts of law that occurred during the second half of the twentieth century where, under the interest-analysis approach, open-ended standards and flexible methodologies were preferred over rigid territorially bound principles.

In the United States, the internal affairs doctrine has created a dominant body of corporate law principles—the Delaware corporate law. Over forty percent of the corporations listed on the New York Stock Exchange are incorporated in Delaware. Delaware's supremacy is easily understood. Indeed, it enjoys an unerodable advantage over other states.[63] First, it has the largest body of precedent interpreting its provisions. To the extent business-people like certainty, Delaware provides it. Though its present code bears the date of its enactment in 1967, it carried forward significant portions of the earlier law so that pre-1967 decisions continue to illuminate the Delaware statute. Second, Delaware's corporate law cannot be easily amended because the state constitution conditions any change in the corporate law upon a two-thirds vote of the legislature. This stability of the legal landscape provides further certainty. Third, Delaware populates its judiciary with those experienced in the trenches of practicing corporate law. Though they have not themselves been captains of industry, members of

---

[61]   For example, where a Virginia corporation reincorporated in Delaware as a first step in a merger, subsequent steps in the transaction were governed by Delaware Law. Fisher v. Tails, Inc., 289 Va. 69, 767 S.E.2d 710 (2015). A shareholder of the Virginia corporation sought the appraisal remedy under Virginia law. However, the Virginia Supreme Court dismissed the claim under Virginia law since "[o]nce a corporation's state of incorporation is transferred to Delaware, it is subject to Delaware corporate law." Fisher v. Tails, Inc., 289 Va. 69, 75, 767 S.E.2d 710 (2015).

[62]   *See* McDermott, Inc. v. Lewis, 531 A.2d 206 (Del. 1987).

[63]   *See generally* Douglas Branson, Indeterminacy: The Final Ingredient in an Interest Group Analysis of a Corporate Law, 43 Vand. L. Rev. 85 (1990).

the Supreme Court and the Court of Chancery have counseled many who were. Fourth, Delaware's Court of Chancery is not only experienced in handling numerous corporate matters, but its procedures facilitate the litigants' securing a hearing and resolution in the most time-bounded disputes, especially issues that arise in the context of takeovers. And finally, though perhaps not uniformly the most permissive and broadly enabling of all corporate statutes, any differences from the statutes of states are at the margins. Overall, Delaware's success in attracting corporate charters is most understandable, and its success is fed by the vitality of the internal affairs doctrine. Thus, in *VantagePoint Venture Partners 1996 v. Examen, Inc.,*[64] the Delaware Supreme Court held that a preferred stockholder of a Delaware corporation could not invoke its right to a class vote in an acquisition under section 2115, reasoning that the internal affairs doctrine is constitutionally protected.

There are some notable departures from the internal affairs doctrine. New York applies a limited set of its corporate provisions to foreign corporations that have two-thirds of their shares, voting shares, or taxable income in New York.[65] A more sweeping application of local laws to "pseudo-foreign" corporations occurs in California, where corporations with half their taxable income or property and half their shareholders within California are subject to a lengthy list of provisions of the California Corporations Code.[66] Neither the New York nor the California provisions apply to companies listed on a national securities exchange, and the California provisions also exempt certain over-the-counter listed securities.[67] Not surprisingly, a California court has upheld the constitutionality of the state's pseudo-foreign corporation provision,[68] whereas the Delaware courts have enshrined the internal affairs doctrine in the Constitution.[69]

§ 2.9   Benefit Corporations

As discussed later in this hornbook, for profit corporations may elect to consider social responsibility even while sacrificing profit maximization.[70] For profit corporations desiring to be socially responsible can describe that mission as part of its corporate purpose.[71] As an outgrowth of the corporate social responsibility movement, proposals emerged to recognize a new type of corporate entity whose mission was statutorily mandated to include a public benefit in its mission. A number of states, including California, Delaware, and New York have enacted benefit corporation statutes.[72] In 2019, the American Bar Association proposed a new chapter 17 for the Model Business Corporation Act that would address benefit corporations.[73]

---

[64] 871 A.2d 1108 (Del. 2005).

[65] N.Y. Bus. Corp. Law §§ 1317 to 1319 (McKinney 2003 & West Supp. 2009).

[66] *See* Cal. Corp. Code § 2115 (West 1990 & West Supp. 2009).

[67] Cal. Corp. Code § 2115(e) (West 1990 & West Supp. 2009); N.Y. Bus. Corp. Law § 1320 (McKinney 2003 & West Supp. 2009).

[68] Wilson v. Louisiana-Pacific Resources, Inc., 187 Cal.Rptr. 852 (Ct. App. 1983).

[69] Vantagepoint Venture Partners 1996 v. Examen, Inc., 871 A.2d 1108 (Del. 2005); Draper v. Paul N. Gardner Defined Plan Trust, 625 A.2d 859 (Del. 1993).

[70] *See* §§ 4.4, 4.5 *infra.*

[71] *See* §§ 3.6, 4.1–4.2 *infra. See also* Burwell v. Hobby Lobby Stores, Inc., 573 U.S. 682 (2014) (allowing closely held corporation to opt out of medical coverage for abortions based on religious purpose).

[72] Cal. Corp. Code § 14610 (2012); Del. Code Ann. tit. 8, § 362(a) (2013); N.Y. Bus. Corp. Law § 1706(b) (2012).

[73] *See* Corporate Laws Committee, ABA Business Law Section, Proposed Changes to the Model Business Corporation Act—New Chapter 17 on Benefit Corporations, 74 Bus. Law. 820 (2019).

A benefit corporation, also known as a "B Corporation," is a business corporation that has "a purpose of creating general public benefit."[74] B corporation statutes typically define "general public benefit" as "[a] material positive impact on society and the environment, taken as a whole, assessed against a third-party standard, from the business and operations of a benefit corporation."[75] Other distinctive characteristics of a benefit corporation include the directors' requirements to consider the interests of non-shareholder constituencies and to provide an annual benefit report.[76]

In addition to a mandated corporate purpose of creating a general public benefit, benefit corporations have the option to choose one or more "specific public benefit" purposes.[77] A "specific public benefit" is defined to include:

> (1) providing low-income or underserved individuals or communities with beneficial products or services; (2) promoting economic opportunity for individuals or communities beyond the creation of jobs in the normal course of business; (3) preserving the environment; (4) improving human health; (5) promoting the arts, sciences or advancement of knowledge; (6) increasing the flow of capital to entities with a public benefit purpose; and (7) conferring any other particular benefit on society or the environment.[78]

A B Corporation's election to select one or more specific public benefit purposes "does not limit the obligation of a benefit corporation [to create a general public benefit]."[79] Furthermore, the benefit corporation statutes "all declare that the general or specific public benefits . . . 'are in the best interests of the corporation.' "[80]

In most cases, electing benefit corporation status after the entity has been formed requires a two-thirds vote of shareholders.[81] Some states have differing voting thresholds. For example, the New York statute requires an affirmative vote of three-

---

[74] Model Benefit Corp. Legislation §§ 102(a), 201(a) (2012); Cal. Corp. Code § 14601(a) (West, Westlaw through ch. 14 of 2012 Reg. Sess.) (effective Jan. 1, 2012); Haw. Rev. Stat. § 420D–2 (Westlaw through 2011); Md. Code Ann., Corps. & Ass'ns § 5–6C–01(c) (Westlaw through 2011); N.J. Stat. Ann. § 14A:18–1 (West, Westlaw through 2011); N.Y. Bus. Corp. Law § 1702 (McKinney, Westlaw through L. 2012, ch. 1–28) (effective Feb. 10, 2012); Vt. Stat. Ann. tit. 11A, § 21.03(a)(1) (West, Westlaw through 2011); Va. Code Ann. § 13.1–782 (West, Westlaw through 2011).

[75] Model Benefit Corp. Legislation § 102(a); Cal. Corp. Code § 14601(c); Haw. Rev. Stat. § 420D–2; Md. Code Ann., Corps. & Ass'ns § 5–6C–01(c); N.J. Stat. Ann. § 14A:18–1; N.Y. Bus. Corp. Law § 1702(b); Vt. Stat. Ann. tit. 11A, § 21.03(a)(4); Va. Code Ann. § 13.1–782.

[76] William H. Clark, Jr. and Elizabeth K. Babson, How Benefit Corporations are Redefining the Purpose of Business Corporations, 38 Wm. Mitchell L. Rev. 817, 818–19 (2012). See also, e.g., Emily Winston, Benefit Corporations and the Separation of Benefit and Control, 39 Cardozo L. Rev. 1783, 1787 (2018); Miriam F. Weismann, The Missing Metrics of Sustainability: Just How Beneficial Are Benefit Corporations?, 42 Del. J. Corp. L. 1, 13 (2017).

[77] Model Benefit Corp. Legislation § 201(b); Cal. Corp. Code § 14610(b); Haw. Rev. Stat. § 420D–5(b); Md. Code Ann., Corps. & Ass'ns § 5–6C–06(b); N.J. Stat. Ann. § 14A:18–5(b); N.Y. Bus. Corp. Law § 1706(b); Vt. Stat. Ann. tit. 11A, § 21.08(b); Va. Code Ann. § 13.1–787(A).

[78] Model Benefit Corp. Legislation § 102(a); Cal. Corp. Code § 14601(e); Haw. Rev. Stat. § 420D–5(b); Md. Code Ann., Corps. & Ass'ns § 5–6C–01(d); N.J. Stat. Ann. § 14A:18–1; N.Y. Bus. Corp. Law § 1702(e).

[79] Model Benefit Corp. Legislation § 201(b) (2012); Cal. Corp. Code § 14610(b) (West, Westlaw through ch. 14 of 2012 Reg. Sess.) (effective Jan. 1, 2012); Haw. Rev. Stat. § 420D–5(b) (Westlaw through 2011); Md. Code Ann., Corps. & Ass'ns § 5–6C–06(b)(2) (Westlaw through 2011); N.J. Stat. Ann. § 14A:18–5(b) (West, Westlaw through 2011); N.Y. Bus. Corp. Law § 1706(b) (McKinney, Westlaw through L.2012, ch. 1–28) (effective Feb. 10, 2012); Vt. Stat. Ann. tit. 11A, § 21.08(b) (West, Westlaw through 2011).

[80] Dana Brakman Reiser, Benefit Corporations—A Sustainable Form of Organization?, 46 Wake Forest L. Rev. 591, 598 (2011).

[81] William H. Clark, Jr. and Larry Vranka, The Need and Rationale for the Benefit Corporation 15 (Jan. 26, 2012).

quarters of each class of outstanding shares[82] and Virginia demands approval from all shareholders that are entitled to vote.[83] Once a corporation becomes a benefit corporation, the articles of incorporation must report the company's status as a benefit corporation[84] and include any specific public benefit purpose that the corporation chooses.[85] Additionally, benefit corporations remain subject to the portions of the corporation code that are not explicitly mentioned in the benefit corporation legislation.[86]

A benefit corporation can terminate its status by amending the articles to delete the portions identifying the corporation as a benefit corporation and any specific public benefit purposes listed.[87] Termination of benefit corporation status generally requires a two-thirds vote of the outstanding shares of the corporation.[88]

Reasoning Behind Benefit Corporation Statutes

The benefit corporation form of doing business has been said to exist primarily "to break the persistent belief that directors should primarily focus on shareholder wealth maximization in their governance of corporations."[89] Because directors are obligated to consider interests other than shareholders, the model benefit corporation legislation explicitly states that this obligation "is at the heart of what it means to be a benefit corporation."[90]

First created in 1983, constituency statutes are a type of statute that explicitly permits directors of a corporation to consider interests other than the interests of the shareholders.[91] Constituency statutes were primarily created as a mechanism for corporations to defend against a hostile takeover;[92] however, constituency statutes and

---

[82] N.Y. Bus. Corp. Law §§ 1702(d), 1704.

[83] Va. Code Ann. § 13.1–785.

[84] Model Benefit Corp. Legislation § 103 (2012); Cal. Corp. Code § 14610(b) (West, Westlaw through ch. 14 of 2012 Reg. Sess.) (effective Jan. 1, 2012); Haw. Rev. Stat. § 420D–3(a) (Westlaw through 2011); Md. Code Ann., Corps. & Ass'ns § 5–6C–03(a) (Westlaw through 2011); N.J. Stat. Ann. § 14A:18–3(a) (West, Westlaw through 2011); N.Y. Bus. Corp. Law §§ 1703, 1704 (McKinney, Westlaw through L. 2012, ch. 1–28) (effective Feb. 10, 2012); Vt. Stat. Ann. tit. 11A, § 21.03(a)(1) (West, Westlaw through 2011); Va. Code Ann. § 13.1–784 (West, Westlaw through 2011).

[85] Model Benefit Corp. Legislation § 201; Cal. Corp. Code § 14610(b); Haw. Rev. Stat. § 420D–5(b); Md. Code Ann., Corps. & Ass'ns § 5–6C–06(b); N.J. Stat. Ann. § 14A:18–5(b); N.Y. Bus. Corp. Law § 1706(b); Vt. Stat. Ann. tit. 11A, § 21.08(b); Va. Code Ann. § 13.1–787(A).

[86] William H. Clark, Jr. and Larry Vranka, The Need and Rationale for the Benefit Corporation 15 (Jan. 26, 2012) ("The enacting state's benefit corporation statutes are placed within existing state corporation codes so that the enacting state's existing corporation code applies to benefit corporations in every respect except those explicit provisions unique in the benefit corporation form.").

[87] Model Benefit Corp. Legislation § 105; Cal. Corp. Code § 14604; Haw. Rev. Stat. § 420D–4; Md. Code Ann., Corps. & Ass'ns § 5–6C–04; N.J. Stat. Ann. § 14A:18–4; N.Y. Bus. Corp. Law § 1705; Vt. Stat. Ann. tit. 11A, § 21.07; Va. Code Ann. § 13.1–786.

[88] Model Benefit Corp. Legislation § 102; Cal. Corp. Code § 14601; Haw. Rev. Stat. § 420D–2; N.J. Stat. Ann. § 14A:18–1; Va. Code Ann. § 13.1–707; *Cf.* Vt. Stat. Ann. tit. 11A, § 21.07 (requiring the higher of "the vote required by the articles of incorporation" or "two-thirds of the votes entitled to be cast by the outstanding shares of the corporation"). *But cf.* N.Y. Bus. Corp. Law § 1702.

[89] Haskell Murray, Benefit Corporations: New Paradigm, The Conglomerate (May 7, 2012) http://www.theconglomerate.org/2012/05/benefit-corporations-new-paradigm.html.

[90] Model Benefit Corp. Legislation § 301 cmt. (2012).

[91] Steven Munch, Improving the Benefit Corporation: How Traditional Governance Mechanisms can Enhance the Innovative New Business Form, 7 NW J. L. & Soc. Pol'y 170, 180–82 (2012); William H. Clark, Jr. and Elizabeth K. Babson, How Benefit Corporations are Redefining the Purpose of Business Corporations, 38 Wm. Mitchell L. Rev. 817, 828–29 (2012). Other constituency statutes are discussed in § 4.10 *infra*.

[92] William H. Clark, Jr. and Elizabeth K. Babson, How Benefit Corporations are Redefining the Purpose of Business Corporations, 38 Wm. Mitchell L. Rev. 817, 829 (2012).

benefit corporation statutes both modify the fiduciary duties of directors suggesting that the new benefit corporation statutes may be superfluous.[93] Nevertheless, many states that have constituency statutes have either enacted or proposed benefit corporation legislation.[94] In most states where enacted, constituency statutes permit, but do not require, directors of a corporation to consider interests of non-shareholder constituencies.[95] Furthermore, the benefit corporation's requirement to create a general public benefit and any specific public benefit chosen is not considered in the constituency statutes.[96]

Critics still argue the benefit corporation is unnecessary since companies can accomplish the same result as the benefit corporation statutes by adding specific purposes or goals in their articles of incorporation or bylaws.[97] Despite these assertions, the benefit corporation statutes offer additional certainty about the non-shareholder interests included within the fiduciary duty of directors and provide the mechanisms available to shareholders to enforce those considerations.[98]

Director Duties[99]

Section 301 of the model benefit corporation legislation rejects the directors' duty to "maximize the financial value of a corporation" by requiring the interests of non-shareholder constituencies to be considered.[100] However, section 301(d) provides that "[a] director does not have a duty to a person that is a beneficiary of the general public benefit purpose or a specific public benefit purpose. . . ."[101] Even though directors do not have a duty to non-shareholder constituents, section 305(b) "permits a benefit corporation to provide in its articles that an identified category of persons may bring a benefit enforcement proceeding."[102] A "benefit enforcement proceeding" is a claim or action against a benefit corporation for "(1) failure of a benefit corporation to pursue or create

---

[93] Christopher Lacovara, Strange Creatures: A Hybrid Approach to Fiduciary Duty in Benefit Corporations, 2011 Colum. Bus. L. Rev. 815, 834–40 (2011).

[94] Christopher Lacovara, Strange Creatures: A Hybrid Approach to Fiduciary Duty in Benefit Corporations, 2011 Colum. Bus. L. Rev. 815, 834–40 (2011). ("Many of the states that have enacted or are considering B-corp legislations already have a constituency statute—further evidence that B-corp legislation is intended to have a more concrete impact on directors' duties.").

[95] Steven Munch, Improving the Benefit Corporation: How Traditional Governance Mechanisms can Enhance the Innovative New Business Form, 7 NW J. L. & Soc. Pol'y 170, 181 (2012).

[96] Christopher Lacovara, Strange Creatures: A Hybrid Approach to Fiduciary Duty in Benefit Corporations, 2011 Colum. Bus. L. Rev. 815, 840 (2011).

[97] Angus Loten, With New Law, Profits Take a Back Seat, Wall St. J. (Jan. 19, 2012), http://online.wsj.com/article/SB10001424052970203735304577168591470161630.html; Stephanie Strom, A Quest for Hybrid Companies that Profit, but can Tap Charity, N.Y. Times (Oct. 12, 2011), http://www.nytimes.com/2011/10/13/business/a-quest-for-hybrid-companies-part-money-maker-part-nonprofit.html?pagewanted=all. *See also* Haskell Murray, Benefit Corporations: New Paradigm, The Conglomerate (May 7, 2012) http://www.the conglomerate.org/2012/05/benefit-corporations-new-paradigm.html ("In some states, with more flexible notions as to the beneficiaries of director fiduciary duties, the corporate form might also be an appropriate vehicle for social entrepreneurs.").

[98] William H. Clark, Jr. and Larry Vranka, The Need and Rationale for the Benefit Corporation 6 (Jan. 26, 2012).

[99] Directors' and officers' duties are discussed in Chapters 10 and 11 *infra*.

[100] Model Benefit Corp. Legislation § 301 cmt (2012).

[101] Model Benefit Corp. Legislation § 301(d). *See* Cal. Corp. Code § 14623 (West, Westlaw through ch. 14 of 2012 Reg. Sess.) (effective Jan. 1, 2012); Haw. Rev. Stat. § 420D–10 (Westlaw through 2011); N.J. Stat. Ann. § 14A:18–10 (West, Westlaw through 2011); N.Y. Bus. Corp. Law § 1707(c) (McKinney, Westlaw through L. 2012, ch. 1–28) (effective Feb. 10, 2012); Vt. Stat. Ann. tit. 11A, § 21.10 (West, Westlaw through 2011); Va. Code Ann. § 13.1–790 (West, Westlaw through 2011).

[102] Model Benefit Corp. Legislation § 301 cmt.

general public benefit or a specific public benefit purpose set forth in its articles; or (2) violation of any obligation, duty or standard of conduct. . . ."[103] Except for Maryland, all the benefit corporation statutes provide this special right of action.[104]

Benefit corporations deviate from the standard for-profit corporation in the respect that benefit corporations are "legally obligated to promote the public interest."[105] In performing their duties, the board of directors is required to consider the effect that an action or inaction may have on the following:

> (i) the shareholders of the benefit corporation; (ii) the employees and work force of the benefit corporation, its subsidiaries and its suppliers; (iii) the interests of customers as beneficiaries of the general public benefit or specific public benefit purposes of the benefit corporation; (iv) community and societal factors, including those of each community in which offices or facilities of the benefit corporation, its subsidiaries or its suppliers are located; (v) the local and global environment; (vi) the short-term and long-term interests of the benefit corporation, including benefits that may accrue to the benefit corporation from its long-term plans and the possibility that these interests may be best served by the continued independence of the benefit corporation; and (vii) the ability of the benefit corporation to accomplish its general public benefit purpose and any specific public benefit purpose.[106]

The directors are not required to give the interests of a particular person or group priority over other interests unless the articles clearly state the intention "to give priority to certain interests related to its accomplishment of its general public benefit purpose or of a specific public benefit purpose. . . ."[107]

Annual Benefit Report

While the shareholders of a standard corporation can assess performance by analyzing the financial statements, the benefit corporation's performance in achieving a general and specific public benefit "will not be readily apparent from those financial statements."[108] Consequently, benefit corporations are required to prepare an annual benefit report which is meant to provide an evaluation of the corporation's success in creating a general and specific public benefit.[109]

---

[103] Model Benefit Corp. Legislation § 102. *See* Cal. Corp. Code § 14601(b); N.J. Stat. Ann. § 14A:18–1; Vt. Stat. Ann. tit. 11A, § 21.13(c); Va. Code Ann. § 13.1–782.

[104] Dana Brakman Reiser, Benefit Corporations—A Sustainable Form of Organization?, 46 Wake Forest L. Rev. 591, 605 (2011).

[105] Briana Cummings, Benefit Corporations: How to Enforce a Mandate to Promote the Public Interest, 112 Colum. L. Rev. 578, 580 (2012).

[106] Model Benefit Corp. Legislation § 301(a)(1) (2012); N.Y. Bus. Corp. Law § 1707(a) (McKinney, Westlaw through L.2012, ch. 1–28) (effective Feb. 10, 2012); Va. Code Ann. § 13.1–788(A). *See also* Md. Code Ann., Corps. & Ass'ns § 5–6C–07 (Westlaw through 2011) (omitting the sixth and seventh interests required to be considered under the model benefit corporation legislation); N.J. Stat. Ann. § 14A:18–6 (requiring the same interests to be considered under the model benefit corporation legislation except for the seventh item); Vt. Stat. Ann. tit. 11A, § 21.09(a) (obligating interests substantially identical to those in the New Jersey statute). *But see* Haw. Rev. Stat. § 420D–6 (Westlaw through 2011) (requiring only the consideration of shareholders and accomplishment of general and specific public benefits).

[107] Model Benefit Corp. Legislation § 301(a)(3); Cal. Corp. Code § 14620(d); N.J. Stat. Ann. § 14A:18–6(c); N.Y. Bus. Corp. Law § 1707(a)(3); Vt. Stat. Ann. tit. 11A, § 21.09(a)(3); Va. Code Ann. § 13.1–787(A)(3).

[108] Model Benefit Corp. Legislation § 102(a) cmt.

[109] *Id.*

Among other things required to be included in the annual benefit report, the benefit corporation must provide a narrative description of the ways the benefit corporation pursued general public benefit and specific public benefits included in its articles.[110] The benefit corporation must include a description of any hindrances encountered in pursuing general and specific public benefits as well as a statement describing "[t]he process and rationale for selecting ... the third-party standard used to prepare the benefit report."[111] Furthermore, the annual benefit report also provides "[a]n assessment of the overall social and environmental performance of the benefit corporation [which is judged] against a third-party standard."[112] A "third-party standard" is "[a] recognized standard for defining, reporting and assessing corporate social and environmental performance."[113] The Maryland, New Jersey, New York, Vermont, and Virginia statutes only require that the "third-party standard" be independent and transparent.[114] Hawaii, California, and the model benefit corporation legislation demands that the standard be "comprehensive," "independent," "credible," and "transparent."[115] A "comprehensive" standard "assesses the effect of the business and its operations upon the interests listed in section 301(a)(1)(ii), (iii), (iv), and (v)" stated above.[116] A third-party standard is also "credible" if the standard is created by someone who "has access to necessary expertise to assess overall corporate social and environmental performance" and "uses a balanced multistakeholder approach, including a public comment period of at least 30 days to develop the standard."[117]

At the very least, independence is established if the third-party standard "[i]s developed by a person or entity that is independent of the corporation."[118] Maryland does not define "independence" but the statutes enacted afterwards provide more guidance.[119] A standard-setter is independent of the benefit corporation if there are "no material relationships with a benefit corporation or a subsidiary of the benefit corporation."[120]

---

[110] Model Benefit Corp. Legislation § 401(a)(1); Cal. Corp. Code § 14630; Haw. Rev. Stat. § 420D–11; Md. Code Ann., Corps. & Ass'ns § 5–6C–08; N.J. Stat. Ann. § 14A:18–11; N.Y. Bus. Corp. Law § 1708; Vt. Stat. Ann. tit. 11A, § 21.14; Va. Code Ann. § 13.1–788.

[111] Model Benefit Corp. Legislation § 401(a)(1) (2012). *See* Cal. Corp. Code § 14630 (West, Westlaw through ch. 14 of 2012 Reg. Sess.) (effective Jan. 1, 2012); Haw. Rev. Stat. § 420D–11 (Westlaw through 2011); Md. Code Ann., Corps. & Ass'ns § 5–6C–08 (Westlaw through 2011); N.J. Stat. Ann. § 14A:18–11 (West, Westlaw through 2011); N.Y. Bus. Corp. Law § 1708 (McKinney, Westlaw through L.2012, ch. 1–28) (effective Feb. 10, 2012); Vt. Stat. Ann. tit. 11A, § 21.14 (West, Westlaw through 2011); Va. Code Ann. § 13.1–791 (West, Westlaw through 2011).

[112] Model Benefit Corp. Legislation § 401(a)(2). *See* Cal. Corp. Code § 14630; Haw. Rev. Stat. § 420D–11; Md. Code Ann., Corps. & Ass'ns § 5–6C–08; N.J. Stat. Ann. § 14A:18–11; N.Y. Bus. Corp. Law § 1708; Vt. Stat. Ann. tit. 11A, § 21.14; Va. Code Ann. § 13.1–791.

[113] Model Benefit Corp. Legislation § 102(a).

[114] Md. Code Ann., Corps. & Ass'ns § 5–6C–01(e); N.J. Stat. Ann. § 14A:18–1; N.Y. Bus. Corp. Law § 1702(g); Vt. Stat. Ann. tit. 11A, § 21.03(a)(8); Va. Code Ann. § 13.1–782.

[115] Model Benefit Corp. Legislation § 102(a); Cal. Corp. Code § 14601(g); Haw. Rev. Stat. §§ 420D–2, 420D–12.

[116] Model Benefit Corp. Legislation § 102(a) (2012); Cal. Corp. Code § 14601(g) (West, Westlaw through ch. 14 of 2012 Reg. Sess.) (effective Jan. 1, 2012); Haw. Rev. Stat. § 420D–12 (Westlaw through 2011).

[117] Model Benefit Corp. Legislation § 102(a).

[118] Md. Code Ann., Corps. & Ass'ns § 5–6C–01(e)(1) (Westlaw through 2011).

[119] Dana Brakman Reiser, Benefit Corporations—A Sustainable Form of Organization?, 46 Wake Forest L. Rev. 591, 601 (2011).

[120] Va. Code Ann. § 13.1–782 (West, Westlaw through 2011). *See* Cal. Corp. Code § 14601(g)(2); Haw. Rev. Stat. § 420D–2 (Westlaw through 2011); N.J. Stat. Ann. § 14A:18–1 (West, Westlaw through 2011); N.Y. Bus. Corp. Law § 1702(c) (McKinney, Westlaw through L.2012, ch. 1–28) (effective Feb. 10, 2012); Vt. Stat. Ann. tit. 11A, § 21.03(a)(5) (West, Westlaw through 2011).

Material relationships include current and recent employees, "an immediate family member of . . . an executive officer,"[121] and "direct or indirect ownership or management of five percent or more of the benefit corporation's equity."[122]

In order to be transparent, each benefit corporation statute requires that "[s]tandard-setters [ ] publicize 'the factors considered when measuring the performance of a business, the relative weightings of those factors, [ ] the identity of the persons who developed and control changes to the standard, and the process by which those changes were made.' "[123] For example, B Lab, the primary third-party evaluator for benefit corporations, assesses potential benefit corporations based on "corporate accountability, employee policy, products' benefit to consumers, the company's relationship with its community, and its impact on the environment."[124] In addition to conducting an initial evaluation, B Lab audits twenty percent of the companies it certifies every two years.[125]

Purported Advantages of the Benefit Corporation Form

As compared to the general corporate laws, the hybrid organizational form created by the benefit corporation statute offers three potential benefits: "articulating and enforcing a dual mission, expanding funding streams, [and] branding their enterprises. . . ."[126] The benefit corporation form will not provide the greater sustainability social entrepreneurs seek to establish until those three potential benefits are realized.[127]

Articulating and Enforcing a Dual Mission

An increasing number of companies are seeking to create a positive impact on society and/or the environment while maintaining their interest in making profits.[128] However, companies with a "double bottom line"—a desire to achieve financial and social results—or a "triple bottom line"—a desire to achieve financial, social and environmental results—may have better success preserving their dual mission while raising capital.[129] While some believe that the benefit corporation structure provides a "high level of transparency and accountability" to the public,[130] others think the structure may create a lack of accountability because shareholders have limited recourse to challenge a bad

---

[121] Cal. Corp. Code § 14601(g)(2); Haw. Rev. Stat. § 420D–2; N.J. Stat. Ann. § 14A:18–1; N.Y. Bus. Corp. Law § 1702(c); Vt. Stat. Ann. tit. 11A, § 21.03(a)(5); Va. Code Ann. § 13.1–782.

[122] Dana Brakman Reiser, Benefit Corporations—A Sustainable Form of Organization?, 46 Wake Forest L. Rev. 591, 601 (2011).

[123] *Id.*

[124] *Id. at* 602.

[125] *Id.*

[126] *Id.* at 592.

[127] *Id.* at 624.

[128] Stephanie Strom, A Quest for Hybrid Companies that Profit, but Can Tap Charity, N.Y. Times (Oct. 12, 2011), http://www.nytimes.com/2011/10/13/business/a-quest-for-hybrid-companies-part-money-maker-part-nonprofit.html?pagewanted=all. *See* Dana Brakman Reiser, Benefit Corporations—A Sustainable Form of Organization?, 46 Wake Forest L. Rev. 591, 591 (2011) ("Founders of social enterprises believe profits and social good can be produced in tandem and wish to form organizations that will pursue these dual missions.").

[129] Briana Cummings, Benefit Corporations: How to Enforce a Mandate to Promote the Public Interest, 112 Colum. L. Rev. 578, 589 (2012) ("[A] major problem facing hybrid corporations is finding a way to prevent neglect of the social bottom line if the company assumes new leadership (the 'legacy problem'), if controlling shares are acquired by someone who wants to prioritize profit-making, or in response to market pressures.").

[130] Kyle Westaway, New Legal Structures for "Social Entrepreneurs," Wall St. J. (Dec. 12, 2011), http://online.wsj.com/article/SB10001424052970203413304577088604063391944.html.

decision of the benefit corporation's management.[131] Undoubtedly, a high level of transparency and accountability are needed to prevent directorial abuse of non-shareholder interests for personal benefit and to prevent "greenwashing"[132]—"the phenomenon of businesses seeking the cachet of being more environmentally and socially responsible than they actually are."[133] The disclosure requirements of the annual benefit report are meant to protect against "greenwashing" and other abuses "by giving consumers and the general public a means of judging whether a business is living up to its claimed status as a benefit corporation."[134]

Potential Expanded Funding Streams

The benefit corporation form may provide additional access to funding but the additional duties imposed may limit a business corporation's ability to seek profit.[135] On one hand, some observers believe that benefit corporations are capable of successfully seeking funding from "conventional capital markets as well as philanthropy."[136] Benefit corporations may be more successful than other types of social enterprises, because benefit corporation statutes provide more "consistent, clear and flexible statements of purpose and more robust accountability and transparency mechanisms for those purposes."[137]

On the other hand, benefit corporations may have particular difficulty raising capital while maintaining a dual mission.[138] Benefit corporations seeking to raise capital may be able to preserve their dual mission by if they are able to "attract and retain owners equally committed to that dual mission."[139] Even though it is not required,[140]

---

[131] Angus Loten, With New Law, Profits Take a Back Seat, Wall St. J. (Jan. 19, 2012), http://online.wsj.com/article/SB10001424052970203735304577168591470161630.html.

[132] Briana Cummings, Benefit Corporations: How to Enforce a Mandate to Promote the Public Interest, 112 Colum. L. Rev. 578, 588–89 (2012).

[133] Model Benefit Corp. Legislation § 102(a) cmt. (2012).

[134] Model Benefit Corp. Legislation § 102(a) cmt.; William H. Clark, Jr. and Elizabeth K. Babson, How Benefit Corporations are Redefining the Purpose of Business Corporations, 38 Wm. Mitchell L. Rev. 817, 846 (2012).

[135] Steven Munch, Improving the Benefit Corporation: How Traditional Governance Mechanisms can Enhance the Innovative New Business Form, 7 NW J. L. & Soc. Pol'y 170, 188 (2012) ("By imposing additional social duties and potential liabilities, the form arguably limits a business' pursuit of profit.").

[136] Stephanie Strom, A Quest for Hybrid Companies that Profit, but Can Tap Charity, N.Y. Times (Oct. 12, 2011), http://www.nytimes.com/2011/10/13/business/a-quest-for-hybrid-companies-part-money-maker-part-nonprofit.html?pagewanted=all.

[137] William H. Clark, Jr. and Larry Vranka, The Need and Rationale for the Benefit Corporation 28 (Jan. 26, 2012).

[138] Dana Brakman Reiser, Benefit Corporations—A Sustainable Form of Organization?, 46 Wake Forest L. Rev. 591, 607–10 (2011). *See* Briana Cummings, Benefit Corporations: How to Enforce a Mandate to Promote the Public Interest, 112 Colum. L. Rev. 578, 588 (2012) ("Double bottom line corporations struggle to raise capital because they do not fit the settled categories and expectation of existing sources of capital."). *See also* Thomas Kelley, Law and Choice of Entity on The Social Enterprise Frontier, 84 Tul. L. Rev. 337, 352 (2009) ("In a recent study of the emerging fourth sector, social entrepreneurs reported that their most pressing challenge was gaining access to investment capital.").

[139] Dana Brakman Reiser, Benefit Corporations—A Sustainable Form of Organization?, 46 Wake Forest L. Rev. 591, 609 (2011).

[140] Model Benefit Corp. Legislation § 301(a)(3) (2012); Cal. Corp. Code § 14620(d) (West, Westlaw through ch. 14 of 2012 Reg. Sess.) (effective Jan. 1, 2012); N.J. Stat. Ann. § 14A:18–6(c) (West, Westlaw through 2011); N.Y. Bus. Corp. Law § 1707(a)(3) (McKinney, Westlaw through L.2012, ch. 1–28) (effective Feb. 10, 2012); Vt. Stat. Ann. tit. 11A, § 21.09(a)(3) (West, Westlaw through 2011); Va. Code Ann. § 13.1–788(A)(3) (West, Westlaw through 2011).

benefit corporations may be able to protect their dual mission while seeking funding by stating in the articles of incorporation when a particular interest has priority.[141]

Branding

One of the major suggested advantages of being designated a benefit corporation is an improved brand. Effective branding of the benefit corporation status will increase the image and reputation of certified companies by creating "a coherent and marketable image of what it means to be a social enterprise organization."[142] An effective brand may also help benefit corporations attract capital by distinguishing them from other companies holding themselves out as dedicated to social responsibility.[143] However, it has been observed that the benefit corporation status will not operate as an effective brand until it is reliable as "a credible proxy for truly dual mission entities."[144]

---

[141] Dana Brakman Reiser, Benefit Corporations—A Sustainable Form of Organization?, 46 Wake Forest L. Rev. 591, 610 (2011) ("This does not necessarily mean that either profit maximization or social good production must be prioritized every time the two come into conflict. In order to ease the tension inherent in a dual mission organization, some structure is needed for balancing these goals.").

[142] Thomas Kelley, Law and Choice of Entity on Social Enterprise Frontier, 84 Tul. L. Rev. 337, 361 (2009) (quoting Thomas J. Billitteri, Mixing Mission and Business: Does Social Enterprise Need a New Legal Approach? 9 (2007), http://www.nonprofitresearch.org/usr_doc/New_Legal_Forms_Report_FINAL.pdf).

[143] William H. Clark, Jr. and Larry Vranka, The Need and Rationale for the Benefit Corporation 4 (Jan. 26, 2012).

[144] Dana Brakman Reiser, Benefit Corporations—A Sustainable Form of Organization?, 46 Wake Forest L. Rev. 591, 622–23 (2011) ("[B]rands are weak unless and until they become familiar to their target audience."). *See* Thomas Kelley, Law and Choice of Entity on Social Enterprise Frontier, 84 Tul. L. Rev. 337, 352, 361–62 (2009).

Chapter 3

THE INCORPORATION PROCESS

Table of Sections

§ 3.1   Selection of the Corporate Form

After considering the relevant business and financial exigencies of a formative business, the attorney must weigh the relative advantages and disadvantages of the corporate form and then must give careful thought to the choice of a suitable business form. If the enterprise is to be publicly held, the corporate form is practically foreordained. A real choice exists, however, in a closely held enterprise, and the decision to be made is an important one. This section discusses in broad outline the preliminary considerations involved in determining whether a particular closely held business can be conducted most effectively as a corporation or in some other business form. These comments, it is believed, are sufficient to put the lawyer on notice regarding areas in which a more detailed exploration may be desirable.

Giving advice on how to choose a business form for a closely held enterprise is extremely difficult. Much of the difficulty arises from the limitless variations in the characteristics of businesses and the circumstances of the business participants, and from the probability of constant change in those variables. Thus an organizational form may be adapted to a particular business today, but be unsuited to it tomorrow. These changing needs are not a problem because the entity can transform itself into the type of entity best suited for its contemporary needs.

A limited partnership is frequently unsuitable because participants in a closely held enterprise usually want to participate in the management of the business, and limited partners, to retain their limited liability, must refrain from taking part in the control of the business.[1] Furthermore, a limited partnership must have at least one general partner who (except in the case of a limited liability limited partnership) is subject to

---

[1]   Uniform Limited Partnership Act § 7 (1916); Revised Uniform Limited Partnership Act, § 303 (2001).

unlimited liability, and in many businesses no one is willing to become a general partner and assume the risk of liability.[2]

The business trust is not generally a viable alternative to the corporation or partnership, primarily because, in addition to their shaky legal status in some states, business trusts are unfamiliar to most lawyers and entrepreneurs. The joint stock company has the characteristics of a corporation, with the important exception that it does not provide limited liability for the owners. Since a corporation with limited liability can be quickly and easily organized under modern statutes to conduct almost any lawful business, the joint stock company is seldom used.

Beginning in the last quarter of the twentieth century, new forms of business entities developed that have dramatically changed the choice of entity decision. The Wyoming legislature in 1977 enacted the first statute authorizing the limited liability company.[3] The limited liability company form of doing business in essence allows the participants to establish what formerly would have been a general partnership with the unlimited liability of its partners but with a full liability shield. All states now provide for limited liability companies. During the last five years of the twentieth century, another new form of business became recognized. Most states now permit a general partnership to operate under a full liability shield by electing to be organized as a limited liability partnership.[4]

The limited liability company and limited liability partnership are likely to be the entities of choice for many start-up businesses. This is so because the owners will have the protection of limited liability but will not be subject to the burdens of formalities that are necessary to establish and maintain the corporate form.

§ 3.2 Selecting the State of Incorporation

In selecting the state of incorporation, the attorney makes a decision not only as to the relevant statutory law but also as to the case law that will govern all corporate questions, including the duties of the corporation's officers and directors and the rights of its stockholders. As such, it may be advisable to shop for the jurisdiction that will best suit the organizers' needs. On the other hand, the decision of where to incorporate "should be approached with a strong predisposition to incorporate in the state where the corporation's principal business activity will be located."[5] This local preference is due to several economic considerations. First, incorporating in a state where it would otherwise not have a sufficient presence to subject the corporation to the state's taxing authority visits upon the corporation an unnecessary tax burden. Moreover, businesses not locally domiciled have to qualify to do business in each state where they operate.[6] Under such qualification provisions, the "foreign" corporation will be subject to filing requirements, fees, *and taxes*. The corporation also subjects itself to a state's taxing power by incorporating under that state's laws, even though the corporation does not otherwise "do business" in the incorporating state. Thus, needless multiple taxes are incurred when

---

[2]   This disadvantage, however, is often minimized by making a corporation the general partner, a practice which in itself raises serious questions. *See* Larson v. Commissioner, 66 T.C. 159 (1976).

[3]   *See* Wyo. Stat. Ann. §§ 17–15–101 to 17–15–136 (1977).

[4]   *See* Alan R. Bromberg & Larry E. Ribstein, Bromberg & Ribstein on Limited Liability Partnerships and the Revised Uniform Partnership Act § 1.02(a), (b) (2001).

[5]   Chester Rohrlich, Organizing Corporate and Other Business Enterprises at 4.01 (5th ed. 1990).

[6]   *E.g.*, Del. Code Ann. tit. 8, § 371 (2001 & Supp. 2008); Model Business Corp. Act Chapter 15 (2016).

a corporation is formed in a state that otherwise lacks a sufficient taxing nexus with the corporation. It follows that foreign incorporation fees and expenses may be wasted if one has to pay substantially the same fees for the privilege of qualifying and conducting business as a foreign corporation in the home state where the business is conducted. A second consideration is whether the corporation's counsel, although otherwise knowledgeable in corporate law, can be expected to provide legal advice as efficiently on the sister state's corporate law.

In contrast to the localized business, when faced with a larger business that is likely to cross state lines, forum-shopping becomes a necessary part of the lawyer's role. As noted earlier, some state statutes take a permissive approach, while others adopt "a more 'regulatory' or 'paternalistic' attitude."[7] While Delaware has generally been regarded as a permissive haven,[8] the overall trend in other states has also been toward more and more permissive statutes. The piecemeal revisions to the Model Business Corporation Act have similarly been permissive. As state corporate statutes have become more permissive, likely under the influence of changes occurring with the Model Act, state courts have increasingly deferred to Delaware jurisprudence in corporate law.[9]

In selecting the most appropriate corporation domicile, there are several factors to be considered. Although the circumstances of a particular situation will frequently narrow the scope of the inquiry, there are a number of general considerations.

(1) Does the proposed state of incorporation permit the type of business proposed in corporate form?

(2) Does the proposed domicile place restrictions on the residence of incorporators and/or shareholders?

(3) Does the proposed domicile have special rules concerning directors and management norms in general?

(4) What are the rights and liabilities of shareholders?

(5) Do the state's statutes permit the desired capital structure?

(6) Does the proposed domicile have an applicable close corporation statute?

(7) What are the applicable organizational and annual fees and taxes?

Even after the initial incorporation in one state, a corporation may change the state of incorporation and applicable governing law. This reincorporation in another state is often referred to as the process of domestication. When a corporation reincorporates and domesticates in another state, the law of the new state of incorporation governs.[10] Accordingly, after a domestication to Delaware, Delaware law governs the appraisal remedy with respect to subsequent transactions.[11]

---

[7] Alexander H. Frey, Jesse H. Choper, Noyes E. Leech & C. Robert Morris, Jr., Cases and Materials on Corporations 89 (3d ed. 1989). One indication that the choice of domicile is usually a binary one is a study of where firms undertaking an IPO choose to incorporate. Robert Daines, Choices of IPO Firms, 77 N.Y.U. Law Rev. 1559 (2002)(IPO firms tend overwhelmingly either Delaware or their home state).

[8] *See* William L. Cary, Federalism and Corporate Law: Reflections Upon Delaware, 83 Yale L.J. 663 (1974).

[9] *See* Jens Dammann, Deference to Delaware Corporate Law Precedents and Shareholder Wealth: An Empirical Analysis, June 2018 Working Paper, available at, https://ssrn.com/abstract=3384446.

[10] *See* Fisher v. Tails, Inc., 289 Va. 69, 767 S.E.2d 710 (2015).

[11] *See* Fisher v. Tails, Inc., 289 Va. 69, 767 S.E.2d 710 (2015).

§ 3.3 The Usual Steps in the Formation and Organization of a Corporation

Incorporation procedure varies somewhat from state to state, but most states follow a general pattern of requirements for formation. Failure to comply with the necessary formalities can result in a failure to obtain corporate status, but more frequently such failure poses no serious problems.[12] In any event, the lawyer should be thoroughly familiar with the requirements of the state of incorporation as well as the foreign qualification provisions of all states where business activity is contemplated.

The successive steps usually required or advisable for the incorporation and organization of a business corporation under modern corporation statutes are enumerated below:

(1) Taking preliminary options and making promotion and financing arrangements by the organizers or promoters with the aid of competent legal advice;

(2) Soliciting pre-incorporation subscriptions if desired. In many cases this activity will be subject to meeting the requirements of the securities act laws in each state in which shares will be offered for sale as well as the requirements of the Federal Securities Act of 1933;

(3) Reserving the desired corporate name by application to the secretary of state or other designated state office;

(4) Selecting a registered office and registered agent;

(5) Drafting the articles (certificate) of incorporation;

(6) Executing and acknowledging the execution of the articles of incorporation by the incorporators;

(7) Filing the articles of incorporation with the secretary of state along with any required county filings;

(8) Paying the filing or organization fees to the secretary of state and any required franchise tax;

(9) Holding the first organization meeting of the incorporators or of the subscribers for shares to elect directors if the first directors are not named in the articles;

(10) Convening the first meeting of the directors (generally called an "organization meeting") to complete the corporation's organization by electing officers, adopting bylaws, issuing shares, and taking subscriptions, accepting pre-incorporation subscriptions and contracts, adopting the form of stock certificate, establishing a principal office, fixing the place for regular meetings of the directors, authorizing a depository for corporate funds as well as identifying who has authority to execute checks against the company's account, adopting contracts made by the promoters on behalf of the proposed corporation, authorizing the application for a

---

[12] *See* Chapter 6.

permit under state blue sky laws to take subscriptions and issue shares, and appointing a resident agent for the service of process;

(11) Obtaining from the secretary of state or other official any permit needed for taking subscriptions and issuing shares as well as all steps to assure compliance with the Federal Securities Act of 1933;

(12) Preparing of minutes of the directors' meeting and opening of corporate books and records;

(13) Paying the minimum paid-in capital, if required, and performing other conditions precedent to engaging in business operations;

(14) Issuing shares;

(15) Qualifying to do business in any state where the corporate business will be conducted.

Some states require a dual filing—one with the secretary of state and another in the office of the county clerk where the corporation has its principal office. In those states, filing copies of the incorporation papers in the offices of the county clerk or recorder is not a condition precedent to corporate existence.

The secretary of state's acceptance or rejection of articles for filing does not create a presumption of the document's validity or invalidity. Generally, the secretary of state should reject the document if it contains illegal or improper provisions. If doubt exists as to the legality of the articles, the secretary of state may submit them to the state's attorney general and his or her staff.[13] Most states allow a direct appeal of the secretary of state's refusal. Under the older view, still found in a few states, review of the secretary of state's refusal occurs through a writ of mandamus.[14]

§ 3.4   Drafting the Articles of Incorporation

The drafting of the incorporation paper, charter, articles of incorporation, certificate of incorporation, or simply "the articles," as the instrument may be called, is usually the first essential step in the incorporation process (in rare cases the parties may first desire to set forth their understandings in a pre-incorporation agreement). The attorney should carefully review the applicable corporation act, the needs of the business, and the wishes of the organizers; and special emphasis should be given to their plans for controlling, capitalizing, and financing the particular enterprises. For example, it is necessary to examine the statutory requirements for the contents of the articles of incorporation, such as the number, residence, and age of the incorporators (that is, those who are to execute the articles); whether the corporation's initial directors must be set forth in the articles of incorporation; the number of shares that must be subscribed for; and the amount of capital that must be paid in, if any, before commencement of business. Care should also be given to whether, under state statute, the corporation's name as set forth in the articles of incorporation must include an indication that the business is a separate entity,

---

[13] *See, e.g.,* De La Trinidad v. Capitol Indem. Corp., 759 N.W.2d 586, 592 (Wis. 2009) (although secretary of state received a contrary opinion from the state's attorney general regarding the legality of the corporation as a non-profit, the business was in fact a legal non-profit corporation since the secretary of state accepted and filed the articles of incorporation).

[14] *See* Lloyd v. Ramsay, 183 N.W. 333 (Iowa 1921).

for example by including "Corporation," "Incorporated," or a suitable abbreviation of corporateness.[15]

The articles of incorporation should set forth all the provisions required by the corporation act, expressing them as nearly as possible in the order and in the exact language found in the statute. The governing corporate statute ordinarily is quite clear in stating what information must be set forth in the articles. Over the years, states have required less and less to be stated in the articles of incorporation so that in most states today the bare minimum contents of the articles can generally be set forth on a single sheet of paper with room to spare. Even though the particular requirements vary from state to state, the typical act usually calls for the following:

(1) The corporate name.

(2) The purposes, objects, or general nature of the business authorized.[16]

(3) Information relevant to the service of process on the corporation, such as identifying a registered agent and perhaps the corporation's principal office.

(4) Identification of incorporators and/or initial directors.

(5) The types and amount of stock the corporation is authorized to issue.

(6) The proper execution of the articles of incorporation by the incorporators.

The articles of incorporation frequently include optional provisions that regulate the business of the corporation, the powers of the directors, and the rights of shareholders. All such provisions are valid as long as they are not inconsistent with the mandates of the statute or the constitution of the state of incorporation.

§ 3.5 Selection and Protection of a Corporate Name

Choosing a corporate name requires great care. It is advisable to inquire of the names available by contacting the secretary of state or other officer with whom the articles of incorporation must be filed.[17] Most states have procedures that not only allow the availability of names to be learned prior to incorporation but also permit an available name to be reserved for a stated period of time, generally 60 to 90 days, after the payment of a nominal fee.[18] The name must contain words or an abbreviation indicating that the business is an entity.[19]

---

[15] Del. Code Ann. tit. 8, § 102(a)(1) (2001 & Supp. 2008); Model Bus. Corp. Act § 4.01 (2016). The name must also not be misleading as to the nature of the business. Model Bus. Corp. Act § 4.01(a)(2) (2016).

[16] Under the Model Act which is followed in many states, it is no longer necessary to have a purpose clause in the articles of incorporation since it is provided that "Every corporation incorporated under this Act has the purpose of engaging in any lawful business unless a more limited purpose is set forth in the articles of incorporation." Model Bus. Corp. Act § 3.01(a) (2016).

[17] Model Bus. Corp. Act § 4.02 (2016).

[18] *See, e.g.,* N.Y. Bus. Corp. Law § 303(c) (McKinney 2003).

[19] Del. Code Ann. tit. 8, § 102(a)(1) (2001 & Supp. 2008) (the corporate name "shall contain 1 of the words 'association,' 'company,' 'corporation,' 'club,' 'foundation,' 'fund,' 'incorporated,' 'institute,' 'society,' 'union,' 'syndicate,' or 'limited' (or abbreviations thereof, with or without punctuation), or words (or abbreviations thereof, with or without punctuation) of like import of foreign countries or jurisdictions (provided they are written in roman characters or letters)"); Model Bus. Corp. Act § 4.01(a)(1) (the corporation's name "must contain the word 'corporation' 'incorporated,' 'company,' or 'limited,' or the abbreviation 'corp.,' 'inc.,' 'co.,' or 'ltd.,' or other words or abbreviations of like import in another language").

The question of availability of a proposed corporate name is usually determined in the first instance by personnel in the secretary of state's office or other executive department. Under many statutes, the secretary of state must pass on the question of the similarity of a proposed name to those already in use. Under the influence of earlier versions of the Model Business Corporation Act, nearly a majority of the states require that a name not be "the same or deceptively similar." What is deceptively similar is frequently problematic. Because of this concern and the belief that the real concern of the secretary of state's office was limited to avoiding confusing two or more organizations in the *secretary's* records, the Model Business Corporation Act requires only that the "name must be distinguishable upon the records of the secretary of state."[20]

The bare fact that articles of incorporation have been accepted and filed by the secretary of state is not an adjudication of the right to the name and does not confer an exclusive right to the name chosen as against previous rights of other corporations or partnerships. There is a vast body of law under the general heading of unfair competition, which, among other things, protects the use of a trademark or trade name.[21]

There is a requirement in most, if not all, states that the name set forth in the articles of incorporation must contain such words as "Company," "Corporation," "Incorporated," "Inc." or "Limited" to indicate its corporate status.[22] Furthermore, there frequently are limitations on filing articles of incorporation setting forth a name including the words "Bank," "Trust," or "Trustee" or related words indicating that the corporation is a bank or trust company, without the certificate of approval of the proper official.[23]

The registered corporate name does not limit the corporation's use of other trade names. Unless there is some express provision to the contrary in a statute, a corporation may assume a name, just as a natural person may, for the purpose of entering into a contract or executing or receiving a conveyance.

§ 3.6   Statement of Purposes and Powers in the Articles

Under the older statutes it was required that a corporation should be formed for some definite enterprise or line of business; a few states even required specification of a single purpose. This requirement reflects the concession theory of the corporation's existence as well as a carry over of the pre-nineteenth century practice of jealously granting charters. When the states require an explicit statement of the corporation's purpose, the drafters usually respond with a lengthy multipurpose clause that assures that the corporation may engage in any lawful activity. Such drafting frequently also assures that the document is unreadable. With the death of the concession theory and an ever-increasing quest for flexibility and economy of words, many states in the 1960s authorized the articles to simply state that the corporation's purpose was "to engage in any lawful business" without any further elaboration. The most resolute response to prolix powers and purposes clauses is found in California, where all sets of filed articles

---

[20]   Model Bus. Corp. Act § 4.01(d).

[21]   In addition to federal trademark and trade name protection under the Trademark Act of 1946, which is also referred to as the Lanham Act (15 U.S.C. §§ 1051 et seq. (2006)), there is a large body of relevant case law. *See* J. Thomas McCarthy, McCarthy on Trademarks and Unfair Competition (4th ed. 2002).

[22]   *See* Del. Code Ann. tit. 8, § 102(a) (2001 & Supp. 2008); Model Bus. Corp. Act § 4.01 (2016).

[23]   Del. Code Ann. tit. 8, § 102(a) (2001 & Supp. 2008). *But cf.* Snell v. Engineered Systems & Designs, Inc., 669 A.2d 13 (Del. 1995) (statute prohibiting use of "engineered," by other than licensed engineer, did not impose per se ban).

are deemed to include an "all purposes" clause, and any other statements are permitted *only* to *limit* the corporation's powers or purposes.[24] A similar approach is taken by the current version of the Model Act.[25]

Generally, there is no need to limit the purposes to the business actually contemplated, and an "all purposes" clause assures flexibility, certainty, and efficiency. However, the occasion can well arise when a narrow purpose clause is a means for fulfilling the desires of the organizers as well as placing a check on management's ability to change the nature of the business.

The statement of the purposes has, as its principal function, the affirmative authorization of the management to enter into those contracts and business transactions that may be considered as incidental to the attainment of the purposes. It also imposes implied limitations on their authority by excluding lines of activity that are not so covered.[26] It does not, however, serve as evidence that the corporation actually engaged in that type of business.[27] The effect of broad purposes or objects is thus to confer wide discretionary authority on the directors and management as to the kinds of business operations in which they may engage. Dealings that are entirely irrelevant to the purposes are unauthorized. Such dealings are referred to as "*ultra vires.*" Statutes do not require repeating in the articles of incorporation the powers that may be enumerated or embodied in the incorporating statute, such as the power to sue, acquire and convey property, make contracts, borrow money, execute bonds and mortgages, sell the entire assets, adopt bylaws, dissolve, merge or consolidate, or amend the articles. Many practitioners, however, for the sake of certainty continue to state in the articles of incorporation many statutory, implied, and incidental powers that might just as well have been left unstated.

§ 3.7   Registered Agent and Principal Place of Business

Nearly every state requires the corporation to select and retain a registered agent to serve process within the state. A registered agent may be an individual or a corporation; in either case the agent must be a resident of the incorporating state. Most states require the articles of incorporation to identify the name and address of the initial registered agent. Thereafter, new agents are added or substituted through a routine filing with the secretary of state.[28] New York's approach is representative of a handful of states that do not require a registered agent; New York designates the secretary of state as the corporation's agent to receive process.[29]

At one time, courts held that incorporation within a state was a sufficient contact to empower the corporate domicile courts to have broad jurisdiction for suits against the corporation.[30] Recent U.S. Supreme Court cases have taken a more restrictive approach

---

[24]   Cal. Corp. Code § 206 (West 1990).

[25]   Model Bus. Corp. Act §§ 2.02(b)(2)(i) and 3.01(a) (2016).

[26]   For an extreme use of this principle, *see* Cross v. Midtown Club, Inc., 365 A.2d 1227 (Conn. Super. Ct. 1976), where the court construed the purpose of operating a luncheon club as not giving the directors the power to exclude women.

[27]   WBM, LLC v. Wildwoods Holding Corp., 270 Va. 156, 613 S.E.2d 402 (2005).

[28]   *See, e.g.,* Cal. Corp. Code § 1502 (West Supp. 2009).

[29]   The articles of a New York corporation must designate the secretary of state as an agent to receive service of process on the corporation. N.Y. Bus. Corp. Law § 402(a) (McKinney 2003).

[30]   *See* Sternberg v. O'Neil, 550 A.2d 1105, Fed. Sec. L. Rep. (CCH) P 94346 (Del. 1988).

to what makes a corporation amenable to a state's jurisdiction.[31] This development has influenced Delaware to hold that a company is not subject to state jurisdiction for product liability claims solely because it is incorporated in Delaware.[32] The approach is different with respect to an individual officer of a Delaware incorporated entity being amendable to service of process in Delaware. Even after the U.S. Supreme Court's decisions in tort and contract matters requiring contacts with the state beyond incorporation, the Delaware Supreme court held that all officers of Delaware corporations' consent to service of process for suits in Delaware and such consent is not limited to corporate law issues.[33]

§ 3.8   Incorporators and Initial Directors

A timing problem arises in the legal mechanics of appointing or electing the first board of directors and adopting bylaws so that the corporation can conduct its business.[34] The link between the inchoate corporation and the completed organization is often the incorporator. Defined functionally, "incorporators" are those who sign the articles of incorporation. They may or may not be subscribers for shares. Most statutes require only a single incorporator.[35] A number of states require that an incorporator be a natural person of at least 18 years of age.[36]

The incorporator's authority under most state statutes transcends executing the articles of incorporation and includes electing the initial directors if they are not identified in the articles of incorporation and any other steps to "complete the organization."[37] Because most states do not require the articles to set forth the names of the initial directors, the question frequently arises as to when it is desirable to do so.

If the identities of the members of the first board are known, there are some economies to setting forth their names in the articles of incorporation so as to avoid the empty ritual of the incorporator or incorporators designating the initial directors. But, if the initial directors are not identified in the articles of incorporation, until the directors are elected, the incorporators have the power to complete the organization, which includes steps to obtain subscriptions to stock, to fix the issue price of shares, and to adopt bylaws. Because incorporators are frequently only clerks or "dummies" pressed into service to duly execute the articles rather than persons with any economic tie to the firm, one must fully consider in each new incorporation the role the incorporators should play in the entity's formation.

Any meeting of the incorporators or directors must be preceded by notice.[38] Generally three to five days is required under the statutes. However, notice can be waived by all the incorporators or directors either attending the meeting or executing a written waiver of notice. Further flexibility appears in provisions that permit action

---

[31] *See* Daimler AG v. Bauman, 571 U.S. 117 (2014); Goodyear Dunlop Tires Operations, S.A. v. Brown, 564 U.S. 915 (2011).

[32] Genuine Parts Company v. Cepec, 137 A.3d 123 (Del. 2016).

[33] Hazout v. Tsang Mun Ting, 134 A.3d 274 (Del. 2016). *But see,* Chiappinelli, The Myth of Director Consent: After *Shaffer,* Beyond *Nicastro,* 37 Del. J. Corp. L. 784 (2013).

[34] *See* Model Bus. Corp. Act § 2.05 (2016).

[35] *E.g.,* N.Y. Bus. Corp. Law § 401 (McKinney 2003).

[36] Colo. Rev. Stat. § 7–102–101 (2008); D.C. Code § 29–101.46 (2001); N.Y. Bus. Corp. Law § 401 (2003); N.D. Cent. Code § 10–19.1–09 (2005); Utah Code Ann. § 16–10a–201 (2005).

[37] *See, e.g.,* N.Y. Bus. Corp. Law § 404(a) (McKinney 2003); Model Bus. Corp. Act § 2.05(a)(2) (2016).

[38] *See, e.g.,* Ray Townsend Farms, Inc. v. Smith, 207 S.W.3d 557, 565 (Ark. Ct. App. 2005).

without a meeting of the incorporators or directors if each incorporator or director, as the case may be, signs a written consent to the action taken.[39]

An incorporators' meeting is usually a cut-and-dried affair. The minutes are prepared in advance by the promoters or their attorney and are adopted at the meeting. If required by statute, the incorporators take just enough stock to qualify, generally with the understanding that they are not bound to pay but will later assign their subscriptions to others, who will be bound to pay for the shares. Such meetings seem a useless and empty form.

§ 3.9   Optional Provisions in the Articles

Under the corporation acts of most states, wide latitude is given to the organizers to include in the articles certain optional provisions and to make certain special variations on the ordinary rules prescribed by statute. Much of what appears in today's broadly enabling corporate statutes are rules for the internal governance that apply in the event the corporation does not specify otherwise. Thus, most of the provisions of the Uniform Partnership Act fill in gaps in a partnership agreement, and corporate statutes increasingly set forth procedural rules that apply unless the articles of incorporation or bylaws provide otherwise. Care must be taken by the attorney to identify not only which state statutory provisions can be varied by an act of the corporation, but also whether the deviation from the statute must appear in a provision in the articles of incorporation or can appear in either the articles or the bylaws. That is, in some instances the statutes expressly permit variations only in the articles of incorporation. In other instances, the variation may appear in either the articles of incorporation or the bylaws.

The articles of incorporation are not merely a private contract between the incorporators or organizers as to their own individual enterprise. They are much more, *viz.*, the constitution of a continuing statutory business association that consists of a shifting group of associates who are expected to invest their money in the enterprise or take by transfer the places of those who have invested. Future shareholders have no voice in drafting the articles of incorporation that limit and define their rights. Most investors become stockholders without reading the articles of incorporation to ascertain provisions that may deprive shareholders of their customary rights and protections. Special and unusual charter clauses may thus prove traps for unwary investors and give opportunity for abuse and oppression by the management. Grossly unfair or unreasonable provisions will doubtlessly be judicially condemned. There are some limits on the oppressive "contracts" that may have been imposed on a corporation during its infancy by management, who thereby sought to reduce statutory and common law rights and safeguards of future shareholders against fraud.

Under most corporate statutes, most rules as to corporate organization, meetings, and management can be varied by the articles and in many instances by the bylaws.[40] For example, express permission may be granted to regulate various matters such as voting rights, the quorum of shareholders' and directors' meetings, and the authority to fix the price or consideration at which shares without par value may be issued.

---

[39] *See, e.g.*, Del. Code Ann. tit. 8, § 108(c) (2001).

[40] Thus, corporations ordinarily must have a board of directors, Model Bus. Corp. Act § 8.01(a) (2016), but requirements regarding its quorum and voting is guided by default rules. *See e.g.*, Model. Bus. Corp. Act § 8.24 (2016).

§ 3.10   The Corporate Charter as a Contract

The term "charter" is frequently used in this country in various senses different from its meaning of royal or executive grant in English law. Sometimes "charter" refers to the articles of incorporation, the organic instrument that sets out the corporate structure under the requirements of a general incorporation act. The term is more often used in a broader sense as indicating the entire corporate constitution, including the articles of incorporation document and the relevant laws under which the corporation is created. Sometimes the term "charter" is used in the sense of "franchise," or right granted by law to exist as a corporation.[41]

The charter may be regarded as a formal contract made by the organizers with the state under authorization of statute for the benefit of those who shall become shareholders or members. The future parties to the contract are the corporation and the persons who become, from time to time, shareholders or members of the corporation. The incorporators, as such, drop out of the picture as soon as their formal organization functions are performed. The essence of the contract is the corporation's articles of incorporation and the laws of the state of incorporation. The relationships and their corresponding duties and rights that flow through these documents underscore the view, discussed earlier, that the corporation is a "nexus of contracts." The charter is also sometimes said to be a contract among the shareholders. Organizers and promoters may contract to form a corporation, but it is not perceived how the shareholders have any contract *inter se*. Their contract rights are worked out and established through the medium of the corporate entity; those rights include the right to have the business activities confined to the scope of the authorized purposes or the right to vote but, at least conceptually, not as between majority and minority.

§ 3.11   Corporate Bylaws—the New Battleground

The bylaws establish rules for the internal governance of the corporation. Bylaws deal with such matters as how the corporation's internal affairs are to be conducted by its officers, directors, and stockholders. Bylaws also commonly deal with the date of the annual shareholders' meeting, the calling and conducting of shareholders' and directors' meetings, formalities as to proxies and voting, qualifications of directors, executive and other committees of the directors, corporate officers (their duties and spheres of authority), formalities and restrictions as to transfers of shares of stock, execution of papers, reports, and audits, and other internal matters. In order to be valid, the bylaw must be consistent with the charter and applicable corporate statute.[42]

Adoption of corporate bylaws is commonly regarded as one of the steps in the organization of the corporation. In broad overview, bylaws must be reasonable, should not conflict with the law of the state of incorporation, and must not limit unduly the rights of shareholders contrary to the policy of the law. Bylaws are subordinate both to the statutes and the charter. Bylaws that conflict with statutes, the articles of incorporation, or public policy are void. Bylaws must be reasonable and must operate equally on all persons of the same class.

---

[41]   Helvering v. Northwest Steel Rolling Mills, Inc., 311 U.S. 46, 50–51 (1940).

[42]   *See, e.g.*, Gorman v. Salamone, 2015 WL 4719681 (Del. Ch. 2015) (the power to remove officers lies inherently with the directors and that power of officer removal cannot be given to the shareholders even with a duly adopted bylaw to that effect).

The courts exercise a regulating power against provisions deemed contrary to policy. For instance, a bylaws provision that attempts unduly to limit the right of transfer of shares or inspection of the books by shareholders or that requires unanimous voting may be viewed as beyond limits permitted by statute or public policy.[43] In the case of closely held corporations, courts strive to effectuate the intent of the parties and thus may uphold such bylaws as *inter se* contracts between the shareholders.[44] Validation of such restrictions is a reflection of a fundamental change in the way judges and lawyers think about corporations. A board's interpretation of a bylaw is not necessarily conclusive.[45]

The power to approve, amend, or repeal bylaws is primarily vested in the shareholders but may be concurrently delegated to the directors either by statute[46] or charter. The power is sometimes conferred by statute on the incorporators as to the original bylaws. The attorney advising the board of directors that seeks to adopt, amend, or repeal a bylaw provision should carefully consider whether the board can do so without stockholder approval. States vary widely in their approaches to this question. Most states allow board action with respect to the bylaws unless the articles of incorporation provide otherwise.[47]

Frequently, state statutes identify certain areas that can be dealt with by the bylaw provision only if that provision has been approved by the stockholders. The most common areas for such treatment are provisions dealing with the size or composition of the board of directors.[48] Also, in many states a bylaw adopted by the shareholders can be amended or repealed only by the shareholders.[49]

Bylaws may be waived or amended informally. Thus, in a leading case, *Dixie Glass Company v. Pollak,*[50] all the company's owners, directors, and officers at a joint meeting approved awarding the plaintiff a five-year employment contract, even though the bylaws strictly limited all employment contracts to one-year terms. The court held their action was an implied waiver or amendment of the bylaw.

Statutes commonly specify many matters that may be regulated in the bylaws and sometimes give an option to include provisions on certain matters in either the bylaws or the articles of incorporation. Certain matters, such as preferences of different classes of shares, can as a rule be provided for only in the charter, not in the bylaws.[51]

A majority of the states have provisions patterned on the Model Business Corporation Act authorizing the corporation to adopt "emergency bylaws," when, due to a "catastrophic event" a quorum of the directors cannot be readily assembled to act.[52]

---

[43]   *E.g.,* Sensabaugh v. Polson Plywood Co., 342 P.2d 1064 (Mont. 1959); E. K. Buck Retail Stores v. Harkert, 62 N.W.2d 288 (Neb. 1954); Clark v. Dodge, 199 N.E. 641 (N.Y. 1936) (agreement by shareholders and directors in close corporation to vote for certain people as officers was permissible despite statutory policy to the contrary).

[44]   *See* F. Hodge O'Neal, Molding the Corporate Form to Particularize Business Situations: Optional Charter Clauses, 10 Vand. L. Rev. 1, 2021 (1956).

[45]   Matanuska Elec. Ass'n, Inc. v. Waterman, 87 P.3d 820 (Alaska 2004).

[46]   Del. Code Ann. tit. 8, § 109 (2001 & Supp. 2008); N.Y. Bus. Corp. Law § 601(a) (McKinney 2003).

[47]   *See, e.g.,* Model Bus. Corp. Act § 10.20(a) (2016).

[48]   *See, e.g.,* N.Y. Bus. Corp. Law § 702(b) (increasing/decreasing board's size) and § 704 (McKinney 2003) (classifying board).

[49]   *See, e.g.,* 805 ILCS § 5/2.25 (West 2004).

[50]   Dixie Glass Co. v. Pollak, 341 S.W.2d 530 (Tex. Civ. App. 1960), *aff'd,* 347 S.W.2d 596 (Tex. 1961).

[51]   *See, e.g.,* Judah v. Delaware Trust Co., 378 A.2d 624 (Del. Supr. Ct. 1977).

[52]   Model Bus. Corp. Act § 2.07.

The corporation's authority extends only to the period of the emergency and includes only the power to adopt bylaws that address legal requirements that otherwise would prevent convening a meeting under the firm's customary procedures. Thus, during an emergency, the corporation may enact bylaw provisions that relax its quorum requirements or that infuse the board of directors with new members.[53]

A major focus for activist shareholders has been proposals for bylaw amendments that, if adopted by the shareholders, would introduce various changes such as mandating that directors to be elected must receive at least a majority of the votes cast (*i.e.*, reversing the statutory default rule that winning directors are those who receive a bare plurality of the votes), calling for the termination of the firm's outstanding poison pill, providing means for shareholders to nominate directors, and authorizing reimbursement of proxy expenses incurred by non-management nominated directors. Resort to bylaws to introduce such governance changes to the corporation confronts a conflict that exists in all corporate statutes. On the one hand, bylaws can be adopted, amended and repealed by a vote of the stockholders without the approval of the board of directors. (In contrast, any change in the corporation's articles of incorporation must be *initiated* by the board of directors.) On the other hand, a keystone provision of each corporate statute broadly provides that the "affairs of the corporation are managed by or under the direction of the board of directors." Hence, most such governance proposals implicate the conflict between the prerogatives of the shareholders with respect to bylaws and the prerogatives of the board of directors over the affairs of the corporation.[54] A significant decision in this area is *CA, Inc. v. AFSCME Employees Pension Plan*,[55] holding a bylaw proposal calling for reimbursement of an insurgent's proxy campaign expenses was not an unlawful infringement on the broad authority of the board of directors with respect to the corporation's affairs; the court reasoned the bylaw did not infringe on the board's prerogatives since it addressed matters related to the *process* for the shareholders to exercise their franchise and, therefore, did not implicate the conduct of the corporation's business. However, the bylaw proposal was nonetheless invalid because the court reasoned it could have required reimbursement in violation of the directors' fiduciary obligations. The proposal likely would have been valid had it included a "fiduciary out" clause so that reimbursement would be excused if doing so would have violated the directors' fiduciary obligation. Since the decision, Delaware has amended its statute to authorize bylaws providing for both the nomination of directors and the reimbursement of insurgent's proxy contest expenses.[56]

In a highly significant decision, the Delaware Chancery Court held in *Boilermakers Local 154 Ret. Fd. v. Chevron*[57] that the board could, without the concurrence of the shareholders, adopt bylaw provisions that permitted the corporation to choose the forum in which a shareholder-initiated suit would be maintained. Subsequently, in *ATP Tour,*

---

[53]   *See* George D. Gibson, Corporate Management During Nuclear Attack, 17 Bus. Law. 249 (1962).

[54]   *See* Lawrence A. Hamermesh, Corporate Democracy and Stockholder-Adopted Bylaws: Taking Back the Street?, 73 Tulane L. Rev. 409 (1998). *See also*, Brett H. McDonnell, Shareholder Bylaws, Shareholder Nominations, and Poison Pills, 3 Berk. Bus. L. J. 205 (2005).

[55]   953 A.2d 227 (Del. 2008). For a similarly reasoned decision involving the termination of the firm's poison pill and calling for any future pill to be approved by the stockholders, *see* International Brotherhood of Teamsters General Fund v. Fleming Companies, 975 P. 2d 907 (Okla. 1999).

[56]   Del. Code Ann. tit. 8, § 112 (2009).

[57]   73 A.3d 934 (Del.Ch. 2013). *See generally* Joseph A. Grundfest, The History And Evolution Of Intra-Corporate Forum Selection Clauses: An Empirical Analysis, 37 Del. J. Corp. L. 333 (2012) (tracing development and pattern of early forum selection bylaws).

Inc. v. Deutscher Tennis Bund,[58] the Delaware Supreme Court, relying on the reasoning in *Boilermakers*, upheld a board adopted bylaw that abandoned the long-maintained American Rule (whereby litigants bear their own litigation costs) to instead assign the suit's defendant's expenses (which in a derivative suit would include the corporation's costs) to the plaintiff except if the suit proved successful. *Boilermakers* and *ATP Tour, Inc.* each reasoned from the perspective that the shareholders' relationship with the corporation, and in turn their relationship to the board of directors, are contractual so that much of the shareholders' rights can be understood to flow from certain organic documents, and most significantly and pervasively from the company's bylaws. For example, with Delaware corporations the board enjoys the power to amend the bylaws only if granted that authority in the articles of incorporation.[59] With that grant of authority to the board being present in both *Boilermakers* and *ATP Tour, Inc.*, it was a short step for each court to conclude that the board's action was pursuant to the contract shareholders had with their corporation and that the power of the board to amend the bylaws carried with it the power to amend the shareholders' rights.[60] Repeatedly the analysis used by each court referenced the contractual relationship the shareholders had through the articles of incorporation and the bylaws with their corporation;[61] hence, the courts believed that contractual relationship was subject to modification through the mechanism provided by the web of the articles of incorporation's authorization for the board to amend the bylaws. With the courts' focus on the contractual basis for their

---

[58]   91 A.3d 554 (Del. 2014).

[59]   Del. Gen. Corp. Law § 109(a). *See also* N.Y. Bus. Corp. Act § 601(a) (charter or bylaws can authorize board to adopt, amend or repeal bylaws). In contrast, most states follow the pattern of the Model Business Corporation Act and grant both the board of directors and the shareholders co-extensive authority to adopt and amend the bylaws, subject to the articles of incorporation restricting the board's authority. MBCA § 10.20(b)(1). *See also,* Cal. Corp. Code § 211 (shareholders and board empowered to adopt, amend and repeal bylaws).

[60]   For an incisive analysis of why consent cannot be found by the shareholders' grant of authority to the board to amend the bylaws, *see* Deborah A. DeMott, Forum-Selection Bylaws Refracted Through an Agency Lens, 57 Ariz. L. Rev. 269 (2015) (a provision in the articles of incorporation authorizing the board to amend the bylaws is too attenuated to constitute consent in part because "nothing in the DGCL or any other Delaware statute explicitly alerts investors to the downstream prospect that limitations may subsequently be imposed" on the shareholders by the board of directors).

[61]   Delaware's invocation of contract principles is illustrated by the following:

   [T]he board itself may act unilaterally to adopt bylaws . . . Such a change by the board is not extra-contractual simply because the board acts unilaterally; rather it is the kind of change that the overarching statutory and *contractual* regime the stockholders buy into explicitly allows the board to make on its own. In other words, the . . . stockholders have assented to a contractual framework established by the DGCL and the certificate of incorporation [authorizing the board to adopt bylaws] that explicitly recognizes that stockholders will be bound by bylaws adopted unilaterally by their board." (emphasis added). Boilermakers Local 154 Ret. Fd. v. Chevron, 73 A.3d 934, 956 (Del.Ch. 2013).

   Because corporate bylaws are "contracts among the corporation's shareholders," a fee shifting provision in a . . . validly enacted bylaw would . . . not be prohibited under Delaware common law." ATP Tour, Inc. v. Deutscher Tennis Bund, 91 A.3d 554, 558 (Del. 2014) (quoting Airgas, Inc. v. Air Products and Chemicals, Inc., 8 A.3d 1182, 1188 (Del. 2010), "[c]orporate charters and bylaws are contracts among a corporation's shareholders; therefore, our rules of contract interpretation apply.").

Boilermakers also relies on the same broad, undeveloped, state in *Airgas, Inc* as well as a much earlier and less convincing decision, Lawson v. Household Finance Corp., 152 A. 723, 728 (Del. Ch. 1930), upholding the imposition of a right-of-first-refusal transfer restriction set forth in the bylaws where the corporate statute expressly authorized bylaws to restrict shares and the shareholder acquired the shares with full notice of such restriction. Thus, the substantive authority for the bylaw restricting transfer was expressly provided by state statute so that neither *Lawson's* facts nor its reasoning lend themselves to other than a substantive interpretation of a state statute.

reasoning, the opinions avoided the more ticklish question of whether there are areas of the corporate statute that are beyond the power of the board of directors, acting unilaterally, to change. The corporation-as-contract theory supports other board-adopted bylaw initiatives such as requiring shareholder suits to be subject to binding arbitration.[62]

The preoccupation with the contractual focus demonstrated in *Boilermakers* and *ATP Tour, Inc.* can be attributed to the impact of the contractarian orientation widely espoused among corporate commentators.[63] This perspective is commonly captured in the metaphor that the corporation is but a 'nexus of contracts'. The vision builds on Coase's perspective on why firms exist (the view holds that labor, suppliers, customers, investors, and managers arrange their activities to their optimal benefit), scholars embraced private ordering as the desired norm within corporate law. In a world of private ordering, the state corporate statute is understood to have the limited role of providing default rules in those instances where the parties have not otherwise specified how their affairs or activities are to occur. Corporate participants may well not so specify where contracting around the default rule would be more costly than the perceived ex ante burdens of the default rule. In any case, the default rule is tailored toward what the legislature believes most, but not all, people would have agreed to if contracting were efficient.[64] Within the nexus of contracts metaphor, forum selection, fee shifting, and even mandated arbitration are just some areas, among many others, that parties can best provide through their negotiations and agreement. Broadly stated, to nexus of contracts adherents, corporate law as provided by the state is merely facilitative of private bargaining; and under this view, corporate law is not public, but private law. In such a realm, the only issue in doubt is what constitutes consent among the affected parties;[65] after all, it is bargaining leading to consent that Coase and contract theory so heavily depend upon as the basis for the efficiency that lies at its end. Even here, the champions of the nexus of contracts approach salve any unease about there being meaningful consent by their obeisance to the efficient pricing of outcomes being reflected

---

[62] On the topic of arbitration bylaws, *see* Claudia H. Allen, Bylaws Mandating Arbitration of Stockholder Disputes, 39 Del. J. Corp. L. 751 (2015).

[63] While the corporation-as-contract banner was carried by many, Frank Easterbrook and Daniel Fischel as well as the celebrated article by Professors Jensen and Meckling provided the intellectual foundation on which others built their multiple contributions. *See* Frank Easterbrook & Daniel Fischel, Voting in Corporate Law, 26 J. L. & Econ. 395 (1983); Frank Easterbrook & Daniel Fischel, Close Corporations and Agency Costs, 38 Stan. L. Rev. 271 (1986); Frank Easterbrook & Daniel Fischel, Corporate Control Transactions, 91 Yale L. J. 698 (1983); and Michael C. Jensen & Wm. H. Meckling, Theory of the Firm: Managerial Behavior, Agency Costs and Ownership Structure, 3 J. Fin. Econ. 305 (1976). The perspective embodied in the metaphor is now well-entrenched. *See, e.g.,* Jonathan R. Macey, Corporate Governance: Promises Made, Promises Broken 22 (2008) ("It has long been recognized . . . that the corporation . . . should be viewed as a 'nexus of contracts' or set of implicit and explicit contracts."). For an insightful analysis of the nuance that separates the early scholars whose collective work propelled the contractarian view behind the nexus of contracts metaphor, *see* William Bratton, Nexus of Contracts Corporation: A Critical Appraisal, 74 Cornell L. Rev. 407 (1989).

[64] Lucian A. Bebchuk, Limiting Contractual Freedom in Corporate Law: The Desirable Constraints on Charter Amendments, 102 Harv. L. Rev. 1820, 1847 (1989) observes that departure from the statutory norm is most likely with respect to rules addressing problems whose 'resolution varies significantly from company to company and when the desirable solution depends on particular features of each company that are better known to the parties than to public officials'.

[65] *See, e.g.,* Deborah A. DeMott, Forum Selection Bylaws Refracted Through the Agency Lens, 57 Ariz. L. Rev. 269 (2015) (authority in charter or statute by which board of directors can be authorized to amend the bylaws is too attenuated for shareholders to envision that such authority would be exercised by the board to limit shareholder rights); Lawrence A. Hamermesh, Consent in Corporate Law, 70 Bus. Law. 161 (2014–15) (arguing that consent is also a necessary component of governance).

in the price of a firm's securities. Thus, owners and others, for example creditors, who believe the 'bargain' may be tilted against them, can overcome any anticipated disadvantage by discounting charges based on the expected costs of any resulting unfairness or harmful contractual provision. Thus, any advantage gained by one party in bargaining can be expected to give rise to counterparty discounting, *e.g.*, paying less for the shares or charging more for the money, goods, or services exchanged. There are multiple bases for disagreeing with the nexus of contracts view of the corporation.[66]

Sciabacucchi v. Salzberg illustrates one limit on "private ordering" through the bylaws. The case held that an arbitration bylaw can only address matters internal to the corporation and hence could not apply to investor suits under the securities laws.[67] The bylaw adopted by the board reached a wide range of litigation by shareholders, including suits under the federal securities laws which provide for suits in courts. The effect of the opinion is to limit bylaw provisions to matters rooted in the internal affairs and operations of the corporation.

In 2015, the Delaware legislature addressed some of the concerns arising from private ordering. Solomon-like, the Delaware legislature split the baby by amending the Delaware General Corporation Law to authorize forum-selection bylaws and to prohibit charter or bylaw provisions that would shift to the plaintiff defense costs incurred in connection with shareholder suits that were not successfully concluded.[68] In so acting, the legislature gave managers something they wanted, a way to deal with the scourge of multi-forum litigation[69] while pacifying the local bar that feared lucrative shareholder suits would disappear because of the chilling effect of a loser pay rule for shareholder suits. Delaware's action by no means settles the question of the authority for the board of directors to act unilaterally in adopting a forum selection bylaw. And, since private ordering in the shadow of shareholder suits is not isolated to Delaware corporations,[70] the peace that the plaintiff's bar has now reached via the Delaware legislature may only shift their once Delaware-focused angst to other states. Moreover, the Delaware legislation is narrowly focused; it remains to be seen whether board-adopted bylaws can condition shareholder suits on a range of other actions that impede shareholder suits, such as standing criteria that mandates size and length of the suit's plaintiff's share holdings or even mandating arbitration of such claims. A California court has upheld a forum selection bylaw.[71]

The scope of the forum selection bylaw before the court in *Boilermakers* was broad. The attorneys representing Chevron and FedEx, the defendant corporations whose

---

[66] *See, e.g.*, James D. Cox, Corporate Law and The Limits of Private Ordering, 93 Wash. U. L. Rev. 257 (2016); Melvin A. Eisenberg, The Structure of Corporation Law, 89 Colum. L. Rev. 1461 (1989); Jeffrey N. Gordon, The Mandatory Structure of Corporate Law, 89 Colum. L. Rev. 1549 (1989).

[67] 2018 WL 6719718 (Del.Ch. Dec. 19, 2018).

[68] Delaware SB 75, 148th Gen'l Assembly, amending Del. G. Corp. L. §§ 102 & 109 (prohibiting fee shifting provisions in articles of incorporation or bylaws, respectively) and adding Del. G. Corp. L. § 155 (authorizing forum selection bylaws) was signed by Governor Jack Markell June 24, 2015.

[69] Thus, during 1999–2000, only 12% of deals had litigation and most of the deal litigation related to Delaware firms was in Delaware. C.N.V. Krishnan et al., *Shareholder Litigation in Mergers and Acquisitions*, 18 J. Corp. Fin. 1248, 1249–1250 (2012). Deal-focused litigation has since increased. *See, e.g.*, Cornerstone Research, Shareholder Litigation Involving Mergers and Acquisitions (March 2013) (finding shareholder suits accompanying 90 percent of merger and acquisition transactions in excess of $100 million).

[70] For a rich account of a challenge in Maryland to a board requiring, among other items, that shareholder disputes be handled through arbitration, *see* Ann Lipton, Manufactured Consent: The Problem of Arbitration Clauses in Corporate Charters and Bylaws, 104 Georgetown L. J. 583 (2016).

[71] Drullias v. 1st Century Bancshares, Inc., 30 Cal. App.5th 696 (6th Dist. 2018).

forum selection clauses were before the court, stated the clauses were designed to cover four areas of shareholder-based litigation: derivative suits, fiduciary duty suits, suits involving provisions of the Delaware General Corporation Law and the internal affairs of the corporation. The plaintiff shareholder argued that the freedom to select a venue other than Delaware could not be limited by the unilateral action of the board of directors. This argument had been successful earlier in *Galaviz v. Berg*,[72] which reasoned that the rights of shareholders to initiate suit enjoy the status of contract rights, so that their amendment or revocation can occur only by bilateral action.[73] *Boilermakers* deftly neuters this argument by accepting that many shareholders' rights are contractually based; from this premise the court concluded that the right to initiate suit could be modified at any time by unilateral action by the board of directors. Chancellor Strine reasoned that such modification was authorized in the shareholders' contract with the corporation because that contract includes the general corporate statute and the articles of incorporation, which in combination conferred on the board the power to amend the bylaws. If the nexus of contracts is the appropriate lens through which to assess relationships in the corporation, then the Chancellor has the better argument.

Consent, however, may be argued to arrive through the back door. *Boilermakers* and *ATP Tour, Inc.* stand for the broad proposition that boards can act unilaterally to amend the bylaws so as to alter the basic rights of shareholders. Such unilateral action may be argued to entail implicit consent, not by the ongoing reserved powers of the board to amend the bylaws, but rather through the failure of the shareholders to reverse the board's action, by repealing the bylaw earlier adopted by the board. Finding consent, or more likely acquiescence, by the lack of repeal or modification, not only overlooks the burdens such action places on shareholders to act collectively, but overlooks that for many public companies shareholder amendments to the bylaws require a greater than majority vote.[74] Furthermore, supervoting shares and multi-classes of shares further weaken the voice of the residual claimants when such distinctions accord a group disproportionate voting rights. Thus, silence on the part of the shareholders may not always be equated to their consent.

Board adopted bylaws that infringe on the shareholders' franchise are vulnerable in the courts. *Blasius Industries, Inc. v. Atlas Corp.*[75] bears significantly on the disconnection between the nexus of contract paradigm and the corporation and shines a light on a core feature of corporate law—the division of authority between the board and the shareholders. Upon learning that a substantial blockholder was soliciting shareholders for their consent that would expand the board from 7 to 15 and thereupon appoint 8 nominees to Atlas's board who would support a proposed restructuring of Atlas, the Atlas board moved swiftly to thwart a potential shift in control. The Atlas board filled two of the board seats so that Blasius Industries could not quickly wrest

---

[72]   763 F. Supp.2d 1170 (N.D. Cal. 2011). *But see* Roberts v. TriQuint Semiconductor, Inc., 358 Or. 413, 364 P.3d 328 (2015) (reversing trial court's relying on Galaviz v. Berg, *supra*, refusing to enforce Delaware forum selection bylaw).

[73]   763 F. Supp. 2d at 1174–75.

[74]   One study found that 39.1 percent of Russell 3000 firms mandate a supermajority vote for shareholder initiated bylaw changes Young, Beth. 2009. The Limits of Private Ordering: Restrictions on Shareholders' Ability to Initiate Governance Change and Distortions of the Shareholder Voting Process, Council of Institutional Investors, Working Paper.

[75]   564 A.2d 651 (Del. Ch. 1988).

control of Atlas.[76] Chancellor Allen, even though holding that the Atlas board acted in good faith in defending control,[77] nonetheless held the board's actions were beyond the protection of the business judgment rule. He reached this conclusion by observing that the board's actions were not solely steps taken to manage the company but instead they were acts that impacted the relationship between principal and agent "with respect to a matter of internal corporate governance."[78] To so act, he believed the board needed to make a stronger case than merely that it acted in good faith when its decision thwarts the shareholders' franchise; he therefore required the board to establish a compelling justification for interdicting the shareholder franchise to elect or nominate directors. Significantly, the justification advanced by the board is not a purpose narrowly focused on whether the *corporate interest* is advanced by management's unilateral interdiction; the compelling justification that is required must be anchored by how, under the circumstances, the board's action furthers the shareholders' franchise. Allen reasoned:

> A board's decision to act to prevent the shareholders from creating a majority of new board positions and filling them does not involve the exercise of *the corporation's power* over its property, or with respect to *its* rights or obligations; rather, it involves allocation, between shareholders as a class and the board, of effective power with respect to governance of the corporation.... Action designed principally to interfere with the effectiveness of a vote inevitably involves a conflict between the board and a shareholder majority. Judicial review of such action involves a determination of the legal and equitable obligations of an agent towards his principal. This is not, in my opinion, a question that a court may leave to the agent finally to decide so long as he does so honestly and competently; that is, it may not be left to the agent's business judgment.[79]

To be noted as well, *Blasius*' protection of shareholder franchise arises, even though the board is acting in a way that is the exercise of corporate powers; a corporate purpose existed in *Blasius*—to continue the on-going business plan—but a legitimate corporate purpose was not by itself sufficient to justify the board's actions that had the correlative effect of impacting the franchise of shareholders. This observation flows from Chancellor Allen holding the board acted consistent with its obligations for defending the corporation from a threatened change in the board's on-going business policy.

Blasius adheres to the wise advice that "agents whose interests may materially diverge from the interests of their principals should not have the power to unilaterally determine or materially vary the rules that govern those divergencies of interests."[80]

---

[76] Because the Atlas Board was classified, with directors serving staggered three-year terms, the consequence of filling two seats was that it would require two annual meetings for Blasius to have any chance to wrest a majority of the board seats.

[77] *Id.* at 658.

[78] *Id.* at 658–659.

[79] *Id.* at 659–660.

[80] Lucian A. Bebchuk, The Myth of the Shareholder Franchise, 93 Va. L. Rev. 675, 709–710 (2007)("[I]t is necessary to constrain board adopted bylaws that opt out of the provided default arrangement to make it more difficult to replace incumbent directors."). Professor Bebchuk suggests a change in such a default rule be conditioned on the bylaw being approved by the shareholders. He offers as support that the Delaware legislature has set the model for this approach by permitting the bylaws adopted after shares have been issued to classify the board only if the bylaw has been approved by the shareholders. *See* Del. Gen. Corp. Law § 141(d). A higher level of approval is also required to provide directors immunity to damages where such a shield must appear in the articles of incorporation, Del. Gen. Corp. Law § 102(b)(7), so that if adopted after shares have been issued requires amendment with the approval of the stockholders.

That is, in the principal-agent realm, the relationship, and the methods for selecting and controlling the agent, are defined by the principal and not the agent. To this end, and as *Blasius* illustrates, managerial actions that impact the owners' ability to pursue the limited powers owners have to discipline managers—sell, suffrage or sue—are not just of a different order of magnitude; they are within an entirely different sphere of corporate law, that of governance. Because they are not within the board's managerial sphere, they should be judged by a very different standard than applies to questions of management's stewardship of the firm's business. This conclusion, as well as *Blasius'* holding, flow naturally from the fact that corporate statutes, while broadly enabling of the board of directors, restrict the board's powers to matters of the corporation and to the limited areas of the shareholders franchise; under today's statutes, the board, and hence its appointees' authority, with respect to the firm's operations is clearly set forth in the command that "all *corporate* powers shall be exercised by or under the authority of, and the business and affairs of *the corporation* managed by or under the direction of" the board of directors.[81] Simply stated, a general grant of authority to the board of directors to adopt, amend and repeal bylaws is a weak basis to conclude such authority extends to altering rights or protections shareholders customarily enjoy.

Because corporate statutes impose no limit on the content of bylaws except that a bylaw not conflict with the corporate statute or the company's charter, the content of bylaws is open ended.[82] Therefore, bylaws typically and appropriately address a wide-range of matters from internal operations, *e.g.*, description of authority of officers, functioning of the board, *e.g.*, notice and quorum for meetings, and shareholder-related matters such as notice and procedures for meetings. The board unquestionably has authority to act in these areas, but its authority is not the same across all areas. It should be noticed that a natural consequence of courts proceeding on the basis that the shareholders' relationship is contractual and therefore amendable to unilateral change, the courts foreclose themselves from mediating the conflicting interests and allied rights that distinguish owners from managers. Therefore, the nexus of contracts notion that the board has wide-ranging authority to alter the shareholder relation to the board therefore is not only at odds with *Blasius* but ignores the distinctions corporate law makes with respect to institutional prerogatives of the board and those of the shareholders, and more fundamentally, why they are not mirror images of one another. Each has spheres of authority and related spheres of protection from the other's encroachment.[83]

There is an even stronger and broader message behind *Blasius*: there needs to be recognized among corporate law certain mandatory prophylactic rules whose existence and enforcement is understood as necessary to prevent opportunistic insider behavior And, this bundle of rules is beyond private ordering except pursuant to the most scrupulous attention to consent being granted. As in *Blasius*, escape from such rules' protections or requirements must be jealously protected, perhaps by the "compelling

---

[81]   MBCA § 801(b) (emphasis added). *See also* Del. Gen. Corp. Law § 141(a) ("The business and affairs *of every corporation* . . . shall be managed by or under the direction of a board of directors") (emphasis added).

[82]   *See, e.g.* Del. Gen. Corp. Law § 109(b) ("The bylaws may contain any provision, not inconsistent with law or with the certificate of incorporation, relating to the business of the corporation, the conduct of its affairs, and its rights or powers or the rights or powers of its stockholders, directors, officers or employees."). *See also* N.Y. Bus. Corp. Law § 601(b)(same); MBCA § 2.06(b) (same).

[83]   Just as *Blasius* protected the shareholder franchise, Delaware recently acted to protect the board's rights from the shareholders. *See* Gorman v. Salamone, 2015 Del. Ch. LEXIS 202 (Del. Ch., July 31, 2015) (invalidating shareholder adopted bylaw that empowered shareholders to remove company officers).

justification" standard invoked by Chancellor Allen.[84] Minimally, there should be a strong presumption that the rules establish a sacred space for shareholders that can rarely be entered by the board.

---

[84] Unfortunately, the Delaware courts have cabined *Blasius* to the shareholders' right to vote. Moreover, the Delaware Supreme Court has weakened the opinion by laments about its demanding standard. *See* Williams v. Geier, 671 A.2d 1368, 1376 (Del. 1996) ("*Blasius*' burdens of demonstrating 'compelling justification" is quite onerous and . . . therefore [should be] applied rarely"). The Delaware courts appear oblivious to considering whether it is especially appropriate to demand that the board explain conduct thwarting shareholder action when, as in *Blasius*, the circumstances supported the conclusion the board could have sought the approval for its actions from the shareholders.

Chapter 4

THE SCOPE OF THE AUTHORIZED BUSINESS AND DUTIES TO OTHER CONSTITUENCIES

Table of Sections

§ 4.1   Purposes, Powers and Profits

At common law, a corporation had the powers enumerated in its purpose clause as well as the implied powers necessary to the accomplishment of its purpose. If a corporation engaged in conduct not authorized by its express or implied powers, the conduct was deemed *ultra vires* and void.[1] With the decline in the concession theory of corporations and the universal recognition of the serious inequities that accompanied sanctioning *ultra vires* acts, courts over time interpreted corporate powers broadly. Legislatures also addressed these concerns by authorizing a corporation's articles to broadly enable the corporation to engage in "any lawful purpose" and by limiting the relief and sanctions available for *ultra vires* acts.

Corporate purposes and corporate powers, although often confused, are fundamentally different. A purpose clause properly refers to a statement describing the business the corporation is to conduct. The stated purpose or object of a corporation, for instance, may be "to manufacture textiles" or "to conduct a retail shoe business and to buy, sell, and deal in all kinds of shoes." The term "corporate powers," on the other hand, refers to methods the corporation may use to achieve its purpose. The retail shoe company, for instance, must have the power to contract and the power to borrow money.

Even though many corporate statutes still require that a "purpose clause" (or, as it is sometimes called, "specific object clause") be included in a corporation's charter, modern corporate statutes introduce a good deal of economy here by permitting the articles of incorporation simply to authorize the corporation to engage "in any lawful

---

[1]   *See* Kent Greenfield, Ultra Vires! A Stakeholder Analysis of Corporate Illegalilty (with Notes on How Corporate Law Could Reinforce International Law Norms), 87 Va. L. Rev. 1279, 1302–1313 (2001) (providing a thoughtful review of the history of the ultra vires doctrine).

purpose."[2] And states following the Revised Model Business Corporation Act do not even require a statement of the corporation's purpose or object.[3]

A statement in a corporation's charter of its objects or purposes or powers has the practical effect of defining the scope of the authorized corporate enterprise or undertaking. Second, the statement both confers and limits the officers' and directors' authority by impliedly excluding activities that are not in furtherance of the stated purposes.

Quite apart from the formal presentation, if any, in the articles of incorporation of the corporation's purpose is whether the social and legal question whether profits alone must be pursued. The classic decision in *Dodge v. Ford Motor Company* held that "A business corporation is organized and carried on primarily for the profit of the stockholders."[4] This statement is frequently referred to as the "shareholder primacy" rule. The court ordered Ford Motor Company to make a substantial distribution of cash to its shareholders after Henry Ford had caused the company to cease its typical large special dividend. Ford had terminated the dividend so as to expand production facilities and thereby employ more workers; at the trial he had lamented that profits at the company were too high and characterized the profits as "awful profits." More recently, *eBay Domestic Holdings, Inc. v. Newmark*,[5] held that a majority of the board of directors of craigslist, a for-profit corporation, could not justify certain steps that would entrench themselves on the ground that those making up a majority of the board needed to stay in control so they could preserve the craigslist practice of providing free of charge classified advertisements when such advertisements represented the bulk of its on-line service activity. Earlier the Delaware Supreme court held that the board of directors can consider the interests of other constituencies, such as creditors, when acting, provided there "are rationally related benefits accruing to the stockholders."[6]

But does it mean the directors are to act to maximize profits? Can they consider the qualitative way in which the firm pursues profits? Can it donate corporate cash and other assets for charitable purposes? The economist, Milton Friedman asserted that a corporation's social responsibility is to increase profits.[7] While this may certainly be the default rule, it is clear that a corporation may at least through its charter include the pursuit of certain social objectives. But notwithstanding such an extraordinary charter provision there is judicial support that the board can be guided by the dual purposes of pursuing profits and acting in a socially responsible fashion. For example, the Supreme Court, in *Burwell v. Hobby Lobby Stores, Inc.*[8] held that a close corporation could invoke religious freedom to opt out of health insurance that federal law mandated must provide coverage for abortion-inducing drugs that the corporation's owners stated violated their faith. In reaching this conclusion the court stated:

---

[2]   *See, e.g.,* Michael A. Schaeftler, The Purpose Clause in the Certificate of Incorporation: A Clause in Search of a Purpose, 58 St. John's L. Rev. 476, 482–484 (1984).

[3]   Model Bus. Corp. Act Annot. § 3.01 at 3–6 (3d ed. 1994).

[4]   204 Mich. 459, 170 N.W. 668 (Mich. 1919).

[5]   16 A.3d 1 (Del. Ch. 2010).

[6]   Revlon, Inc. v. MacAndrews & Forbes Holdings, Inc., 506 A.2d 173, 176 (Del. 1986).

[7]   Milton Friedman, The Social Responsibility of Business is to Increase Profits, The New York Times Magazine, Sept. 13, 1970.

[8]   573 U.S. 682 (2014).

While it is certainly true that a central objective of for profit corporations is to make money, modern corporate law does not require for-profit corporations to pursue profit at the expense of everything else, and many do not do so. For-profit corporations, with ownership approval, support a wide variety of charitable causes, and it is not at all uncommon for such corporations to further humanitarian and other altruistic objectives. Many examples come readily to mind. So long as its owners agree, a for-profit corporation may take costly pollution-control and energy conservation measures that go beyond what the law requires. A for-profit corporation that operates facilities in other countries may exceed the requirements of local law regarding working conditions and benefits. If for-profit corporations may pursue such worthy objectives, there is no apparent reason why they may not further religious objectives as well.

Hobby Lobby arose in a close corporation with ownership held by a small number of individuals who were all members of the same family. The close corporation raises interesting questions with respect to pursuing profits, if we equate profits to benefits its owners' derive. For example, Professor Elhauge observes that in the non-public corporation the pursuit of profit maximization harms shareholder welfare when the value of incremental profits is less than the utility owners would derive from avoiding moral and social sanctions and in the public corporation where shareholders are removed from such opprobrium managers are not and should enjoy some discretion to balance their pursuit of profits within their moral framework.[9] Thus, owners of a family grocery may be as pleased by charging less so that the needy can eat than if they charged higher market rates and lived in the Hamptons.

As discussed in Chapter 2, a growing number of states have enacted benefit corporation acts which pursue both public benefit and profits. But, as noted in *Hobby Lobby*, this dual-functioning can also be accomplished through a skillfully drafted purpose clause of the corporation organized under the traditional for-profit corporation statute.

§ 4.2   Sources of Corporate Powers

Because the corporation is a creation of state statutes, it is reasonable to inquire as to the source and extent of its powers. Corporations have express and implied powers. The *express powers* are enumerated in the corporation laws of the state of incorporation as well as in the articles of incorporation. At one time it was standard practice to include in the articles of incorporation an extensive list of general powers the corporation was to possess. Even today, attorneys as a matter of habit, but rarely of necessity, sometimes include in the articles of incorporation a lengthy set of "powers" the corporation will have to carry out its purpose or objectives. These powers may include the power to mortgage the corporation's property, guarantee the debt of another, enter into partnerships, and purchase another corporation's stock. Again, this practice derives from an earlier day, in which corporate status was a privilege jealously guarded by the state and the courts so that the inherent powers of corporations were narrowly authorized and recognized.

---

[9]   Einer Elhauge, Sacrificing Corporate Profits in the Public Interest, 80 N.Y.U. L. Rev. 733 (2005).

Today, it is rarely necessary to elaborate the corporation's incidental powers because most modern statutes expressly grant such powers.[10]

The doctrine of implied powers is a general rule that corporate management, in the absence of express restrictions, has discretionary authority to enter into contracts and transactions reasonably incidental to its business purposes. For example, a lumber company with the power to invest in securities cannot operate primarily as an investment trust, but it can invest its excess cash in marketable securities.[11] Courts are usually liberal, however, in finding that corporate acts are within the corporation's incidental or implied powers.

Transactions that are outside the express or implied powers of the corporation are commonly known as "*ultra vires* acts," beyond the powers of the corporation. A more realistic view characterizes such activities as being beyond the actual authority of the directors and other representatives of the corporation under the charter contract. The legal effect of a transaction outside the scope of the actual authority of the management is treated later in this chapter.

§ 4.3   Implied Power—Charitable Contributions and Assistance to Employees

Corporations are regularly solicited to contribute to various charitable enterprises in the communities in which they do business. To refuse such requests entirely would probably excite criticism and injure the goodwill and business of the corporation. Nevertheless, the business of a corporation is primarily to earn a profit for its shareholders. The directors' discretion does not in general extend without limits to humanitarian purposes or to purely philanthropic donations at the expense of the shareholders.[12] A pure gift of funds or property by a corporation not created for charitable purposes is generally unauthorized and in violation of the rights of its shareholders unless authorized by statute.[13] Over the years, however, the courts have become increasingly liberal and have exercised considerable ingenuity in finding a sufficient corporate benefit to sustain contributions for charitable, humanitarian, and educational purposes, though the benefit might be indirect, long-term, or highly conjectural.[14] Today, this power is made explicit in corporate statutes.[15] Corporations routinely make sizable charitable contributions.[16] In 2000, for example, the median for corporate charitable contributions was one percent of the company's pretax income.[17] It

---

[10]   Model Bus. Corp. Act § 3.02 (2016). The Model Act as revised sets out a list of general powers (*id.*) and a list of emergency powers (*id.* § 3.03) (2016). The Model Act also provides "[t]he articles of incorporation need not set forth any of the corporate powers enumerated in this Act." Model Bus. Corp. Act § 2.02(c) (2016).

[11]   Edward Hines W. Pine Co. v. First Nat'l Bank, 61 F.2d 503, 511 (7th Cir. 1932).

[12]   Dodge v. Ford Motor Co., 170 N.W. 668 (Mich. 1919).

[13]   Rogers v. Hill, 289 U.S. 582, 591–592 (1933).

[14]   *See generally* Louis O. Kelso, Corporate Benevolence or Welfare Redistribution?, 15 Bus. Law. 259 (1960).

[15]   Model Bus. Corp. Act § 3.02(m) (2016) ("to make donations for the public welfare or for charitable, scientific, or educational purposes").

[16]   *See, e.g.,* R. Franklin Balotti & James J. Hanks, Jr., Giving at the Office: A Reappraisal of Charitable Contributions by Corporations, 54 Bus. Law. 965 (1999).

[17]   Amy Kao, Corporate Contributions in 2000, The Conference Board (2001).

is estimated that in 2008 corporations gave a total of $14.5 billion to charitable causes, totaling approximately five percent of all charitable donations.[18]

The most eloquent and elucidating opinion on corporate charitable contributions is in *A. P. Smith Manufacturing Company v. Barlow.*[19] At issue was the propriety of a $1500 gift to the trustees of Princeton University. The plaintiff shareholder challenged the gift as a waste of corporate assets since it resulted in no direct economic benefit to the corporation. The court first traced the history of corporations, concluding that the corporate entity has always had a role to play as a responsible societal member.[20] The court validated the gift not only as a donation to society but also as in furtherance of the free enterprise system on which the corporation's success was dependent.[21]

The *Barlow* case is especially significant because it upheld the gift as a matter of common law. The holding has won legislative confirmation as evidence by the Model Business Corporation Act's express recognition of the corporate power "[t]o make donations for the public welfare or for charitable, scientific or educational purpose."[22] Even under such express statutory authority, however, charitable gifts are subject to challenge if clearly unconnected to the corporation's present or prospective welfare.[23]

The Delaware counterpart[24] of the Model Business Corporation Act's provision was scrutinized in *Theodora Holding Corporation v. Henderson,*[25] wherein a shareholder challenged a corporate charitable contribution in excess of $525,000. The Delaware Court of Chancery upheld the validity of the contribution, relying on both the state corporation statute and the parameters of permissible charitable deductions as established by the federal tax code.[26] In a more recent decision, the Delaware Supreme Court reaffirmed its view that reasonable charitable gifts are proper and that the tax code provides the guide of reasonableness.[27] These guidelines in turn support giving corporate directors great leeway in making charitable contributions.

The Delaware Supreme Court, in *Kelly v. Bell,*[28] reaffirmed the corporation's social responsibility, as the court upheld the corporation's voluntary payments to the county following the repeal of county taxation. The corporation agreed to continue making property tax payments to the county if legislation were passed exempting from taxation all acquisitions of machinery after a specified date. The corporation believed that opposition to the legislation stemmed largely from concerns about the county losing much needed revenues and that its commitment to continue making tax payments would make passage of the exempting legislation more likely. Legislation was enacted that exempted *all* property taxes on machinery, and the corporation continued to make the payments to the county in the amount of its former tax assessments. The court

---

[18]   Giving USA Found., U.S. Charitable Giving Estimated to be $307.65 Billion in 2008, at 3 (2009).

[19]   A. P. Smith Manufacturing Company v. Barlow, 98 A.2d 581 (N.J. 1953), *appeal dismissed,* 346 U.S. 861 (1953).

[20]   A. P. Smith Mfg. Co. v. Barlow, 98 A.2d 581, 583–588 (N.J. 1953).

[21]   A. P. Smith Mfg. Co. v. Barlow, 98 A.2d 581, 590 (N.J. 1953).

[22]   Model Bus. Corp. Act § 3.02(m) (2016).

[23]   *See* 6A William M. Fletcher, Cyclopedia of the Law of Private Corporations § 2939 (2008).

[24]   Del. Code Ann. tit. 8, § 122(9) (2009).

[25]   Theodora Holding Corporation v. Henderson, 257 A.2d 398 (Del. Ch. 1969).

[26]   I.R.C. § 170(b)(2) (2002); I.R.C. § 545(b)(2) (2002).

[27]   Kahn v. Sullivan, 594 A.2d 48, 61 (Del. 1991).

[28]   Kelly v. Bell, 266 A.2d 878 (Del.Supr. 1970).

characterized the tax payments as corporate donations. Significantly, the court did not confine its inquiry to the *ultra vires* doctrine but examined the question within the more flexible standards of the business judgment rule. The court upheld the payments because the board of directors had reasonably arrived at a business rationale for continuing to make the payments for a purpose that advanced the corporation's interest.

The court's approach in *Kelly* appears the most sensible and workable approach to questions of *ultra vires* acts because it focuses inquiry on what should be the ultimate question—whether the board of directors acted reasonably in what they believed advanced the corporation's interest.[29]

The general judicial and legislative acceptance of corporate benevolence contrasts sharply with the refusal of the Alabama Supreme Court in *Adams v. Smith*[30] to uphold gifts to the widows of former corporate officers: the court designated the disbursements as an invalid waste of corporate assets. The defendant corporation attempted to support the validity of the payments, notwithstanding the absence of their authorization in either the corporate charter or bylaws, on the ground that they were in furtherance of a valid business purpose,[31] presumably to enable the corporation to continue to attract good executives by demonstrating a concern for the welfare of dependents of executives. The court did not dispute the defendant's argument that such payments would have been valid had they been made under proper procedure but concluded that the absence of an express contract was fatal to the defense.[32]

Today, both by law and by public sentiment, a greatly enlarged social duty and responsibility of businesses exists for the comfort, health, and well-being of their employees. It is not always sufficient merely to pay the actual wage agreed upon.[33] However, if a bonus or other compensation of directors and executives is so large as to have no relation to the value of the services for which it is given, it may be treated as in reality a gift, which even the majority shareholders have no power to make.[34] An important consideration in all cases is whether the compensation arrangement has been approved by outside directors or by the stockholders.

Even though corporate philanthropy is generally praised for its civic mindedness, concerns abound whether the objects and amounts of charitable giving by the corporation reflect the interests of the stockholders or are guided by the narrower personal interests of the firm's CEO. A mechanism to address this concern are bylaws requiring improved disclosure of the object and amounts of the corporation's philanthropy.[35]

§ 4.4   Modern Statutory Treatment of *Ultra Vires* Acts

The ultra vires doctrine is not dead, but its availability today is severely limited. Modern corporation acts severely restrict the relief or sanctions that once accompanied

---

[29]   *Accord, e.g.,* Kahn v. Sullivan, 594 A.2d 48, 58 (Del. 1991).

[30]   Adams v. Smith, 153 So.2d 221 (Ala. 1963).

[31]   Adams v. Smith, *supra,* 153 So.2d at 223–224.

[32]   Adams v. Smith, *supra,* 153 So.2d at 223–224.

[33]   Solimine v. Hollander, 16 A.2d 203, 245–247 (N.J. Ch. 1940).

[34]   Rogers v. Hill, 289 U.S. 582, 591 (1933); Adams v. Smith, 153 So.2d 221 (Ala. 1963); Moore v. Keystone Macaroni Mfg. Co., 87 A.2d 295 (Pa. 1952).

[35]   *See,* Martha Minow, Corporate Charity: An Oxymoron?, 54 Bus. Law. 997 (1999); Gilllmor & Bremer, Disclosure of Corporate Charitable Contributions as a Matter of Shareholder Accountability, 54 Bus Law. 1007 (1999).

ultra vires acts. By doing so, the statutes reject the view that a corporation lacks the *capacity* to act beyond its purposes or powers, and promote stability and certainty in transactions with corporations. In broad overview, the statutes narrowly authorize the relief, if any, available to (1) the corporation, (2) the corporation's stockholders, and (3) the state for *ultra vires* acts. Because most states have either adopted the Model Business Corporation Act's treatment of *ultra vires* transactions or their statutes closely parallel the Model Act's provisions in this area, it is useful to examine closely the Model Act's approach to *ultra vires* acts.

First, the Model Act-type provisions prevent either the corporation or the other party to an *ultra vires* transaction from raising the defense of *ultra vires,* even though the contract is completely executory on both sides—that is, neither party can avoid the contract solely because it is *ultra vires.*[36] This changes the common law, which allowed either party to set up the *ultra vires* defense in a suit on a completely executory contract.

Second, the Model Act-type provisions authorize suit for damages by or on behalf of the corporation against the corporate executive responsible for the *ultra vires* act.[37] In such a suit, defendants can be expected to shield the decision by arguing their actions are within the business judgment rule.

Third, in response to a shareholder suit, "the court may enjoin or set aside the act, if equitable and if all affected persons are parties to the proceeding, and may award damages for loss . . . by the corporation or another party because of enjoining the unauthorized act."[38] Only rarely, however, have such suits met with success. One noteworthy case is *Blue Cross and Blue Shield of Alabama v. Protective Life Insurance Company,*[39] involving a corporation organized for the purpose of providing health care service plans to subscribers. The corporation intended to acquire a subsidiary to provide life insurance. The court reasoned that the acquisition of a subsidiary to provide life insurance was neither necessary nor incidental to the accomplishment of the corporation's stated purpose. The acquisition was therefore *ultra vires,* and the court enjoined the corporation from acquiring the life insurance company. Shareholders who have themselves participated in *ultra vires* acts cannot attack.[40]

The waning effect of the *ultra vires* doctrine can be attributed to the expanding development of fiduciary duties in the corporation. That is, there likely is a causal connection between the impact of the *ultra vires* doctrine when historians observe there was a concomitant rise and expansion of fiduciary duty law.[41] Thus, the issues embraced within the *ultra vires* doctrine now are raised in complaints that the board of directors or officers have acted in violation of their duty of care or duty of loyalty in a transaction that harmed the corporation.

As a means of softening the effects of any injunctive relief, the Model Business Corporation Act provides that in such an action the court may allow the corporation or

---

[36] Cal. Corp. Code § 208 (2009); Conn. Gen. Stat. Ann. § 33–649 (2008); Del. Code Ann. tit. 8, § 124 (2009).

[37] *See* Cal. Corp. Code § 208 (2009); 805 ILCS § 5/3.15 (2009); N.Y. Bus. Corp. Law § 203 (2009).

[38] Model Bus. Corp. Act § 3.04(c) (2016).

[39] Blue Cross and Blue Shield of Alabama v. Protective Life Insurance Company, 527 So.2d 125 (Ala. Civ. App. 1987).

[40] *See* Goodman v. Ladd Estate Co., 427 P.2d 102 (Or. 1967).

[41] *See* Kent Greenfield, Ultra Vires! A Stakeholder Analysis of Corporate Illegality (with Notes on How Corporate Law Could Reinforce International Law Norms), 87 Va. L. Rev. 1279, 1306 (2001).

the other party to the contract compensation for the loss or damage sustained by its action.[42] This provision's major thrust is to compensate the parties for any loss suffered as a consequence of the court enjoining the *ultra vires* activity and as such does not seem to have been well thought through. From whom would the corporation recover damages it suffered from the court's action in enjoining performance of a contract? Recovery from the shareholder bringing the proceedings would discourage such suits and does not appear to be contemplated by the statute, and the case will be rare indeed in which the corporation could justly recover from the other party the losses the corporation suffers from a court's injunction in shareholder-instituted litigation of this kind. Furthermore, awarding damages to the other party appears to disserve both the corporation and the third party. To award damages to the third party, the court must believe the corporation is better off without the *ultra vires* contract even after considering the damages it must pay to the third party. This would appear to be such a rare case that it hardly needs to be contemplated in the statute.

Finally, the Model Business Corporation Act authorizes the state to invoke the corporation's *ultra vires* acts as a grounds for its dissolution.[43]

§ 4.5   Other Constituencies Statutes

More than one half of the states have enacted statutes that allow, and in a few cases even require,[44] the board of directors to take into account the interests of persons or groups other than its stockholders—that is, to consider the interest of other constituencies—when making decisions, especially when the decision relates to a potential change in control. In broad overview, "other-constituencies" statutes authorize the directors to consider the effect of their actions on nonshareholder groups such as employees, creditors, bondholders, suppliers, and communities. Some go further and provide that the directors' judgments may be guided by state or national economic considerations as well as broader societal interests. The overall focus of such provisions is to alter the traditional orientation that corporate decisions are to be adjudged by their impact on stockholder wealth as contrasted with some greater good, such as happier workers and a more vibrant community. The traditional formulation of the directors' fiduciary obligations was summarized nicely by the Delaware Supreme Court as requiring that before directors may take into account other constituencies in arriving at their decision there must "be some rationally related benefit accruing to the stockholders."[45] It was put more strongly by the Michigan Supreme Court in its review of Henry Ford's decision to forgo special dividends so as to reduce the price of automobiles for the public benefit:

> [I]t is not within the lawful powers of the board of directors to shape and conduct the affairs of a corporation for the merely incidental benefit of shareholders and for the primary purpose of benefiting others, and no one will contend that, if the avowed purpose of the defendant directors was to sacrifice the interests of shareholders, it would not be the duty of the courts to interfere.[46]

---

[42] Model Bus. Corp. Act § 3.04(c) (2016); Del. Code Ann. tit. 8, § 124 (2009).

[43] Model Bus. Corp. Act § 3.04(a)(3) (2016).

[44] *See* Conn. Gen. Stat. Ann. § 33–756(d) (West 2009).

[45] Revlon, Inc. v. MacAndrews & Forbes Holdings, Inc., 506 A.2d 173, 176 (Del. 1986).

[46] Dodge v. Ford Motor Co., 170 N.W. 668, 684 (Mich. 1919).

More recently, the Delaware Supreme Court stated rather crisply that "[a] board may have regard for various constituencies in discharging its responsibilities, provided there are rationally related benefits accruing to the stockholders."[47] These observations are in stark contrast to other constituencies' statutes' authorization for the board of directors to consider a wider range of interests that may be impacted by the board's decision. For example, Indiana commands that no one corporate constituency shall be a "dominant or controlling factor" in the board of directors' decisions,[48] and Iowa allows other constituencies' interests to guide the decision where they outweigh the financial interests of the corporation or its shareholders when the board is considering an acquisition proposal.[49]

By comparison, consider the breadth of Pennsylvania's statute, which states "directors . . . shall not be required, in considering the best interests of the corporation or the effects of any action, to regard any corporate interest or the interests of any group affected by such action as a dominant or controlling interest or factor."[50] Soon after the statute was enacted, the federal district court held "[i]t was proper for the company to consider the effects the . . . tender offer would have, if successful, on the Company's employees, customers and community."[51] The propriety of the directors' consideration of interests other than the stockholders is nearly unbridled in Pennsylvania because the legislature provided a nearly conclusive presumption of validity for the directors' decision.[52]

The impetus for the states' sudden interest in other-constituencies statutes was the hostile takeovers in the 1980s that frequently led to plant closures, layoffs, and declines in the value of the target corporation's outstanding bonds due to the acquisition being financed by issuing debentures to be paid from the target corporation's future earnings. In essence, other-constituencies statutes are just one of several novel forms of takeover defenses that were developed in the heat of the takeovers that have come to symbolize the "take and break" days of the 1980s. In this context, the state directive or invitation for directors to look beyond the bottom line loses some of its social responsibility zing, especially under most state statutes, where consideration of other constituencies is couched in precatory language.

Minimally, these statutes are vulnerable to the criticism that it removes the bright beacon of wealth maximization as the standard for management's stewardship and replaces it with multiple and sometimes competing standards, thus allowing the directors to choose the constituency by whose interests the directors' action is to be determined.[53] Thus, in the takeover context, the stockholders are benefited by a high takeover premium and disserved if that premium is reduced because the bidder wishes to retain the target company's workforce rather than close inefficient plants.[54] To be

---

[47]   Revlon, Inc. v. MacAndrews & Forbes Holdings, Inc., 506 A.2d 173, 182 (Del.Supr. 1986).

[48]   Ind. Code Ann. § 23–1–35–1(f) (West 2009).

[49]   Iowa Code Ann. § 491.101B (West 2009).

[50]   15 Pa. Cons. Stat. Ann. § 1715(b) (West 2009).

[51]   Baron v. Strawbridge & Clothier, 646 F.Supp. 690, 697 (E.D. Pa. 1986).

[52]   See 15 Pa. Cons. Stat. Ann. § 1715(d) (2009).

[53]   See A.B.A. Committee on Corporate Laws, Other Constituencies Statutes: Potential for Confusion, 45 Bus. Law 2253, 2268–2270 (1990).

[54]   In this regard, consider § 6.02 of the A.L.I. Principles of Corporate Governance: Analysis and Recommendations (1994), which allows nonshareholder interests to be taken into consideration when there is a hostile bid, provided the shareholder interest is not "significantly" disfavored.

sure, these are tragic choices, but ones that are judged by the more objective (and some would say neutral) standard of wealth maximization.

Other-constituencies statutes invite not simply a kinder, gentler standard, but the unbridled discretion of management to choose when to favor stockholders and when to favor workers or bondholders. One can surely expect that workers will not be favored when the issue is abolishing inefficient work rules but protecting those work rules may well be championed by managers facing a hostile bidder who intends to make reductions not only in the factory workforce but in the target management as well.

Others believe that the courts can fine-tune the other constituencies statutes, with the effect that the statutes require directors' judgments that are Pareto optimal in that no proscribed constituency is worse off and many are better off because of the board of directors' action.[55] This brings to mind the Achilles' heel of other constituencies statutes, which is their inherent indeterminacy because they commit complete discretion to the board of directors without any reliable method to adjudge the appropriateness of its exercise.[56] Thus a committee of the American Bar Association concludes:

> [Constituency statutes may be interpreted] to impose new powers and duties on directors.... [T]hey may radically alter some of the basic premises upon which corporation law has been constructed in this country without sufficient attention having been given to all the economic, social, and legal ramifications of such a change in the law.[57]

Many states now provide an alternative corporate form for so-called benefit corporations that have a social benefit as part of their mission.[58]

§ 4.6   The American Law Institute and Corporate Objectives

Commentators have expressed a good deal of dissatisfaction with the objective of the American corporation.[59] Such commentary provided fuel for the American Law Institute's corporate governance project, particularly section 2.01,[60] which provides:

---

[55]   *See* Morey W. McDaniel, Stockholders and Stakeholders, 21 Stetson L. Rev. 121 (1991).

[56]   For this reason, some commentators have urged that the directors should have the burden of explanation. For example, Professor Mitchell argues that the board of directors should have the burden of explaining why the corporate interest was served whenever a constituency complains it was harmed by the board's action. *See* Lawrence E. Mitchell, A Theoretical and Practical Framework for Enforcing Corporate Constituency Statutes, 70 Tex. L. Rev. 579, 635–636 (1992).

[57]   A.B.A. Committee on Corporate Laws, Other Constituencies Statutes: Potential for Confusion, 45 Bus. Law. 2253, 2270–2271 (1990). *But see* Charles Hansen, Other Constituency Statutes: A Search for Perspective, 46 Bus. Law. 1355 (1991) (other constituency statutes are unlikely to have any significant impact on the law of corporate governance).

[58]   *See, e.g.,* Cal. Corp. Code § 14610 (2012); Del. Code Ann. tit. 8, § 362(a) (2013); N.Y. Bus. Corp. Law § 1706(b) (2012). Benefit corporations are discussed in § 2.9 *supra*.

[59]   *See, e.g.,* David L. Engel, An Approach to Corporate Social Responsibility, 32 Stan. L. Rev. 1 (1979); Edwin M. Epstein, Societal, Managerial, and Legal Perspectives on Corporate Social Responsibility Product and Process, 30 Hastings L.J. 1287 (1979); Alfred F. Conard, Response: The Meaning of Corporate Social Responsibility, Variations on a Theme of Edwin M. Epstein, 30 Hastings L.J. 1321 (1979); Friedman, The Social Responsibility of Business Is to Increase Its Profits, N.Y. Times Magazine, Sept. 13, 1978, at 32.

[60]   ALI 1 Principles of Corporate Governance: Analysis and Recommendations (1994 & Supp. 1998). The ALI's corporate governance project commenced in the late 1970s and culminated in the organization's approval in 1992 of a set of principles forming seven chapters. Though much of the project is consistent with the ALI's efforts in other areas to offer in "restatements of the law" descriptions of prevailing and better trends in the case law and statutes, there are many areas of the corporate governance project that prescribe reform for prevailing practices. Hence, the ALI's work on this project is not called a restatement but a set of "principles." Much of what is in *Principles of Corporate Governance* is not aimed at legislative drafting committees but is

The Objective and Conduct of the Corporation

(a) Subject to the provisions of Subsection (b) and 6.02 (Action of Directors That Has the Foreseeable Effect of Blocking Unsolicited Tender Offers), a corporation [§ 1.12] should have as its objective the conduct of business activities with a view to enhancing corporate profit and shareholder gain.

(b) Even if corporate profit and shareholder gain are not thereby enhanced, the corporation, in the conduct of its business:

(1) Is obliged, to the same extent as a natural person, to act within the boundaries set by law;

(2) May take into account ethical considerations that are reasonably regarded as appropriate to the responsible conduct of business; and

(3) May devote a reasonable amount of resources to public welfare, humanitarian, educational, and philanthropic purposes.

Section 2.01 is the type of provision that is intended to provide guidance to corporations, their executives, and the courts on permissible objectives of corporate activities. Central to the proscribed objective is the view that the corporation is an economic institution for which the economic objectives embodied in subsection 2.01(a) apply. Nevertheless, subsection (b) also underscores that in today's world corporations are also viewed as social institutions, so that in some instances (*i.e.*, those proscribed in section 2.01(b)(1)) the corporation's economic objective *must* be constrained by certain social imperatives, and in other situations (*i.e.*, those set forth in section 2.01(b)(2) and (3)) its managers *may* qualify its economic objectives by social considerations.

The debate that surrounds section 2.01 focuses on the necessity of adding subsection (b) to the overall economic objectives that are embodied in subsection (a). The critiques of subsection (b) argue that staying within the bounds of the law as well as the appropriateness of corporate activity being undertaken for ethical or social good could easily be handled by continuing the common law approach of examining the activity to determine whether it is reasonably related to the corporation's economic objective. The common law approach does this through the business judgment rule, which accords a high presumption of propriety to board decisions, so that decisions guided by ethical or social considerations are examined for their plausible relationship to the corporation's economic objectives. As seen earlier in this chapter, this approach is reflected in numerous cases where an activity has been challenged as *ultra vires*. It appears that section 2.01 makes two significant modifications in the common law in this regard.

First, section 2.01 mandates that the corporation must abide by the law, as must a natural person. Under the common law's strict obeisance to the economic objective of the corporation, corporations may disobey the law and remain true to their objectives if the benefits of disobeying the law exceed the cost of compliance and/or apprehension. Section 2.01 rejects such cost-benefit determinations; the ALI commentary permits disobeyance

---

intended as suggestions for courts in deciding issues related to director, officer, or controlling shareholder fiduciary duties. Thus, *Principles of Corporate Governance* does not have a focus similar to that of the Revised Model Business Corporation Act because the latter is devoted exclusively to guidance in drafting state corporate statutes.

One of the challenges met by the American Law Institute was to express a view of the role of the corporation as a functioning member of society. In this regard, consider Symposium, Corporate Malaise—Stakeholders Statutes: Cause or Cure?, 21 Stetson L. Rev. 1 (1991).

only out of necessity or desuetude.[61] A second modification to the common law arises with those actions covered by section 2.01(b)(2) and (3)—deviations from the profit objective supported by ethical or societal considerations. In place of the economic considerations for judging the propriety of such departures, the ALI substitutes a broad standard of "reasonableness," in which the propriety of a corporation's actions motivated by ethical or societal considerations is tested by such varying considerations as the custom among corporations and the relative nexus between the resources the corporation has committed to the activity and the corporation's business.[62]

Section 2.01 purports to operate solely as a constraint on the corporation, with the likely sanction for a violation being injunctive relief. However, lurking in its shadows is the possibility that responsible directors or officers can be held accountable if their conduct falls outside the protection of the business judgment rule. It would appear, therefore, that directors and officers are well advised to proceed cautiously if their actions fall into one of the narrow sets of circumstances that are driven by ethical or societal concerns but cannot independently be premised on serving the corporation's long-term economic objectives.

---

[61] ALI 1 Principles of Corporate Governance: Analysis and Recommendations § 2.01, commentary g (1994 & Supp. 1998).

[62] ALI 1 Principles of Corporate Governance: Analysis and Recommendations § 2.01, commentary i (1994 & Supp. 1998).

Chapter 5

THE PROMOTION OF THE CORPORATION

Table of Sections

§ 5.1   Functions of Promoters

Promoters discover business opportunities, prepare plans to take advantage of them, and push those plans to completion. They perform an essential economic function in assembling and coordinating the necessary plan, materials, and personnel for new business enterprises. Although there are many professional promoters, people whose life's work is the conception and organization of business enterprises, most business enterprises are conceived and organized by amateur promoters, people who play the role of promoter only once or twice in a lifetime, usually in connection with a business with which they expect to be permanently identified.

The typical promoter performs many varied services in launching an enterprise, often enlisting the aid of experts, lawyers, bankers, solicitors, and other persons. The various activities of the promoter may be classified as follows: (1) the discovery and investigation of a promising business opportunity; (2) the formulation of business and financial plans; (3) the assembling of the enterprise by negotiating and obtaining some control over the subject matter by options or contracts made on behalf of the proposed corporation or on the promoter's credit; (4) the making of arrangements for financing the enterprise and issuing securities; and (5) the arranging of the promoter's own compensation.

The mere fact that a person becomes an incorporator and signs the articles of incorporation of a proposed corporation does not make that person a promoter.[1] Furthermore, lawyers, bankers, accountants, and others who work with promoters in a

---

1   *E.g.*, Wheeler & Motter Mercantile Co. v. Lamerton, 8 F.2d 957 (8th Cir. 1925); Benton v. Minneapolis Tailoring & Mfg. Co., 76 N.W. 265 (Minn. 1898).

professional capacity to bring a business into existence usually are not considered promoters. However, incorporators, attorneys, and others become promoters, and thus subject to promoters' obligations and responsibilities, if they take an active part in launching a new enterprise and if their participation is with a view to sharing in promotion profits.[2]

A promoter often is in a position to sell the enterprise to prospective investors, and thus may seek a speculative profit in securities of the new company. Promoters may further attempt to take advantage of their position and seek unreasonable, undisclosed, and excessive compensation. These "secret profits" are often available to promoters because they are usually in complete control of the enterprise in its early stages. Accordingly, courts have ruled that a promoter owes fiduciary duties to the company and cannot profit unduly at its expense.

§ 5.2   Pre-Incorporation Contracts: Questions Raised

Under modern statutes, formal incorporation is relatively quick, simple, and inexpensive, but promoters may still find it desirable, and in some instances essential, to make arrangements before incorporation of the business to insure that the corporation will have needed property, funds, patent rights, licenses, services, or key employees. Thus, before a corporation is formed, its promoters may enter into contracts to obtain or "tie down" the needed assets and personnel.[3]

Frequently these contracts are made in the name of the corporation being formed but not yet in existence. Usually the other contracting party is aware that the corporation has not yet come into being but understands that the promoter is contracting on its behalf and for its benefit. In most instances, no problems develop out of promoters' contracts. The corporation is formed; it is adequately financed, at least for the "short run"; those controlling the corporation after its formation do not question that the contract binds the corporation; both the corporation and the other party to the contract perform their respective obligations under the contract; and no need arises for the other party to the contract to try to subject the promoters to liability.

§ 5.3   Liability of the Corporation on Pre-Incorporation Contracts

It is well established in the law that an agency relationship cannot be recognized without an existing principal.[4] Accordingly, promoters of a corporation are not considered its agents and, apart from statute,[5] they are not recognized as having the power to bind a proposed but not yet formed corporation to contracts made on its behalf.

---

[2]   *See* Oklahoma-Texas Trust v. SEC, 100 F.2d 888 (10th Cir. 1939) (any person "who takes an active part in inducing the formation" of a company, whether or not he later becomes a shareholder, quoting Ex-Mission Land & Water Co. v. Flash, 32 P. 600, 604 (Cal. 1893)).

[3]   *See, e.g.,* Stanley J. How & Assoc. v. Boss, 222 F.Supp. 936 (S.D. Iowa 1963) (contract with architectural firm to perform services for proposed corporation).

[4]   Warren Abner Seavey, Agency § 34 (1964).

[5]   No American jurisdiction has a statute dealing with promoters' contracts. Michigan and Kansas formerly had statutory sections on that subject, but both statutes have now been repealed. For a proposed statute, *see* Robert A. Kessler, Promoters' Contracts: A Statutory Solution, 15 Rutgers L. Rev. 566 (1961). *See also* Model Bus. Corp. Act § 2.04 (1984).

Furthermore, the incorporation of a company will not in itself render that corporation liable on contracts its promoters made on its behalf before incorporation.[6]

§ 5.4   Theories of Corporate Liability on Promoters' Contracts

American courts have professed difficulty in finding a rational explanation of how a corporation can make itself a party to its promoters' pre-incorporation contracts. A corporation may assume the burdens of a contract by agreement with a promoter on sufficient consideration. But such an assumption of the promoter's obligations under the contract does not give the corporation a right to sue on the contract, a right that it could acquire only by assignment from the promoter or as a third-party beneficiary of the contract.

Five theories have been advanced as to how the liability of the corporation on the promoters' contracts can arise: (1) ratification; (2) adoption; (3) acceptance of a continuing offer; (4) formation of a new contract; and (5) novation.[7]

Adoption. Adoption is a corporation's assent to a contract that was made in contemplation of the corporation's assuming it after organization. In other words, adoption occurs when a corporation takes the contract rights and obligations of the promoter and makes them its own.

Ratification. Ratification is the corporation's acceptance of an act purportedly made on its behalf by an agent. Strictly speaking, a purported principal must have been in existence at the time of a contract in order to have the capacity to ratify it; therefore ratification is only properly applicable to post-incorporation contracts.

Adoption and Ratification Compared. Courts, however, often use the term "ratification" loosely to refer to a corporation's acceptance or adoption of a promoter's contract. Adoption and ratification may be shown by any words or acts of responsible corporate officers showing assent or approval, such as by their knowingly accepting benefits of the contract or proceeding to perform obligations imposed on it.

Some courts have drawn a distinction between the effect of ratification and adoption; a ratified contract relates back to the date the promoter made it,[8] whereas an adopted contract becomes binding on the corporation on the date of adoption.[9] However, nothing seems to prevent a corporation from adopting a promoter's contract as of the date it was originally made if the corporation expressly or impliedly agrees to do so.

Acceptance of a Continuing Offer. On what theory does a person who is not a party to a contract become a party by adoption? One theory is that the original promoter's contract is in the nature of a continuing proposal, which the corporation may accept when it comes into existence.[10]

---

[6]   *See, e.g.,* In re Vortex Fishing Systems, Inc., 277 F.3d 1057, 1070 (9th Cir. 2002) (applying Montana law).

[7]   *See* Annot., 41 A.L.R.2d 477 (1955).

[8]   *See* Rees v. Mosaic Technologies, Inc., 742 F.2d 765 (3d Cir. 1984); Stanton v. N.Y. & E. Ry., 22 A. 300 (Conn. 1890).

[9]   McArthur v. Times Printing Co., 51 N.W. 216 (Minn. 1892).

[10]   Kirkup v. Anaconda Amusement Co., 197 P. 1005 (Mont. 1921): "The adoption of such a contract is on the theory that the contract made by the promoters is a continuing offer . . . and that it may be accepted and adopted by the corporation after it is created." *Id.* at 1008.

Formation of a New Contract. Another theory is that a corporation's adoption of a promoter's contract is nothing more than the making of a new contract for new consideration.[11]

Novation. Still another theory is that whenever the parties to a promoter's contract anticipate that the corporation when formed will accept the contract and take over its performance, the contract is to be viewed as contemplating a novation, by which the corporation, when it assents after organization, is substituted for the promoter.[12] Courts in the past have shown some readiness to take this novation view of a promoter's contract,[13] but more recent decisions have relied on an adoption/ratification theory and have been reluctant to find that such a contract contemplated a novation.[14] Finally, some courts hold corporations liable on promoter's contracts under the principle that one who adopts the benefits of an act that another volunteers to perform in the first person's behalf is bound to take the burdens along with the benefits.[15]

§ 5.5   Adoption and Ratification Theories

In England, courts have held that a promoter's contract made on behalf of a corporation before incorporation binds only the promoters, and that the corporation cannot ratify the contract in order to become a party after incorporation. The courts in almost all the American states have repudiated the English doctrine, holding that promoters' contracts made on behalf of a corporation to be formed may be adopted by the corporation when organized, and that the corporation then becomes liable on each contract itself, and not merely for the benefits received.[16]

A corporation's adoption of a contract made by its promoters need not be by formal vote of the shareholders or directors; adoption may be inferred from any conduct on the part of the corporation's shareholders or officers that shows an intention for the corporation to adopt and be bound by the contract.[17] Formal shareholder or director action is required only if it would be necessary for a similar original contract.[18] Thus, if the board of directors or officers of a corporation have the authority to bind it by contract and they accept a contract made on the corporation's behalf by its promoters before incorporation, such recognition amounts to an adoption of the contract, whether the acceptance is expressed orally or in writing or is inferred from conduct.[19]

---

[11]   Kridelbaugh v. Aldrehn Theatres Co., 191 N.W. 803 (Iowa 1923); McArthur v. Times Printing Co., 51 N.W. 216 (Minn. 1892).

[12]   Elements of novation are listed in Haggar v. Olfert, 387 N.W.2d 45, 50 (S.D. 1986); B & H Apartments Partnership v. Tharp, 466 N.W.2d 694, 696 (Iowa Ct. App. 1990).

[13]   2 Samuel Williston, Contracts § 306 (3d ed. Jaeger 1959). *See* Stanley J. How & Assoc. v. Boss, 222 F.Supp. 936 (S.D. Iowa 1963).

[14]   Hog Heaven Corp. v. Midland Farm Mgmt. Co., 380 N.W.2d 756, 759 (Iowa Ct. App. 1985). *See also* Moody v. Bogue, 310 N.W.2d 655 (Iowa Ct. App. 1981); Jacobson v. Stern, 605 P.2d 198 (Nev. 1980) (courts using strict standards because finding of novation cuts off promoter's liability); Vodopich v. Collier County Dev., Inc., 319 So.2d 43 (Fla. Ct. App. 1975).

[15]   In re Vortex Fishing Systems, Inc., 277 F.3d 1057, 1070 (9th Cir. 2002) (applying Montana law).

[16]   In re Vortex Fishing Systems, Inc., 277 F.3d 1057, 1070 (9th Cir. 2002).

[17]   Lupo v. Share of North Carolina, Inc., 199 N.C. App. 318, 682 S.E.2d 247 (2009)(adoption of a pre-incorporation contract may occur by implication such as accepting the contract's benefits with knowledge of the pre-incorporation agreement).

[18]   In re Super Trading Co., 22 F.2d 480 (2d Cir. 1927).

[19]   Stone v. First Wyo. Bank, 625 F.2d 332 (10th Cir. 1980).

Strictly speaking, ratification[20] cannot apply to preincorporation transactions, since the principal is not in existence at the time of the act or contract; however, facts that might otherwise establish a ratification may establish that the corporation adopted the preincorporation contract.[21]

Standing alone, the corporation's receipt of benefits flowing from a contract is not sufficient to bind the corporation on the contract. However, most American authorities hold the corporation liable in quantum meruit for the fair value of the benefits it actually receives.[22] For a corporation to be liable in contract, its representatives must have knowledge of the contract at the time they permit the corporation to receive the benefits, or, at a minimum, they must have notice that calls for reasonable inquiry.[23]

As a general rule, the secret knowledge of a mere promoter is not imputed to the corporation.[24] Even where promoters become directors and shareholders of the corporation upon its organization, their knowledge is not imputed to it if they have personal interests antagonistic to the corporation and the circumstances are such that they cannot be expected to reveal their knowledge to other directors and corporate officials. However, where promoters become controlling directors and shareholders, it is reasonable to impute their knowledge to the corporation.

Adoption of a preincorporation contract does not relieve the promoter of personal liability unless there has been a novation of the contract.[25]

§ 5.6   The Corporation's Right to Enforce Contracts

Most American courts hold that, if a corporation expressly or impliedly adopts a pre-incorporation contract made for its benefit by its promoters, it makes itself a party to the contract and may sue on it.[26] Some have argued that a corporation cannot claim the benefit of or enforce a promoter's contract made in its name or for its benefit unless it has adopted the contract as its own.[27] The better view is that by bringing an action on the contract, the corporation adopts or ratifies it.[28]

It has been suggested that the corporation might also be allowed to sue as a third-party beneficiary of the promoter's contract. A third-party beneficiary need not be in

---

[20]   See the discussion of ratification in § 1.24 *supra*.

[21]   *See, e.g.*, DKS Ventures, LLC v. Kalch, 2011 WL 4829724 (E.D. Wash. 2011) ("Although a corporation may not technically ratify a contract made on its behalf prior to its incorporation, since it could not at that time have authorized such action on its behalf, it may, after it comes into existence, adopt such contract by its corporate action, which adoption may be express or implied, and thereby become liable for its performance."), quoting Smith v. Ford Motor Co., 289 N.C. 71, 80, 221 S.E.2d 282, 288, 79 A.L.R.3d 651 (1976).

[22]   *See, e.g.*, T.G. Slater & Son v. Donald P. & Patricia A. Brennan LLC, 385 F.3d 836, 843 (4th Cir. 2004).

[23]   Lorillard Tobacco Co. v. American Legacy Found., 903 A.2d 728 (Del.Supr. 2006) (corporation is liable on pre-incorporation agreement that it implicitly adopts by accepting contract's benefits with knowledge of its terms).

[24]   Solomon v. Cedar Acres East, Inc., 317 A.2d 283 (Pa. 1974).

[25]   Quest Engineering Solutions, Inc. v. Wilbur, 79 Mass. App. Ct. 1124, 948 N.E.2d 917 (2011), review denied, 460 Mass. 1110, 951 N.E.2d 351 (2011).

[26]   Boatright v. Steinite Radio Corp., 46 F.2d 385, 388 (10th Cir. 1931); Speedway Realty Co. v. Grasshoff Realty Corp., 216 N.E.2d 845 (Ind. 1966).

[27]   Macy Corp. v. Ramey, 144 N.E.2d 698 (Ohio Com.Pl. 1957) (promoter withdrawing from agreement before ratification by corporation).

[28]   K & J Clayton Holding Corp. v. Keuffel & Esser Co., 272 A.2d 565 (N.J.Super.1971) (one way for corporation to adopt promoters' contract is to institute suit thereon); Restatement (Second) of Agency § 97 (1958).

existence at the time the contract is made.[29] However, a flaw in the third-party beneficiary theory is that the purpose of a promoter's contract is to create mutual obligations after the corporation's formation, with the corporation and the other party becoming bound, rather than merely conferring a naked benefit or right on the corporation. The consideration is usually executory. The better view is that the corporation cannot claim the benefits of the contract without assuming the burden of performance.[30]

§ 5.7   Liability of Promoters on Pre-Incorporation Contracts

In the absence of an express or implied agreement to the contrary, promoters are generally personally liable on their pre-incorporation contracts even though the contracts are made on behalf of the corporation to be formed. As the Supreme Court of Washington has stated, as a general rule "where a corporation is contemplated but has not yet been organized at the time when a promoter makes a contract for the benefit of the contemplated corporation, the promoter is personally liable on it, even though the contract will also benefit the future corporation."[31] However, cases dealing with a promoter's personal liability on contracts made for the benefit of a proposed corporation present a wide array of factual situations and a number of so-called general rules. The better view is that a promoter's personal liability should depend on the intention of the parties and the form in which the arrangement is cast.[32]

Among the forms a pre-incorporation contractual arrangement might reasonably take are the following:[33]

(1)   Promoters may obtain options or offers from third parties for the projected corporation, which it may accept or reject after incorporation. If the promoters enter into an arrangement that expressly excludes their own liability, some courts will view such an arrangement as constituting merely a revocable offer to the projected corporation by the third party or parties.[34] In such a case, a contract does not arise until the corporation comes into existence and accepts the offer.[35]

(2)   Instead of purporting to act on behalf of the corporation, promoters may make a contract in their own names without any provision for it to bind the corporation. Promoters who do this take their chances that the corporation will later assume the contract and indemnify the promoters or otherwise hold them harmless from personal liability.[36]

(3)   Promoters may purport to make a contract with the other party in the proposed company's name—that is, on behalf of the proposed company as if

---

[29]   Kentucky Tobacco Prods. Co. v. Lucas, 5 F.2d 723, 727 (W.D. Ky. 1925).

[30]   *See generally* 2 Samuel Williston, Contracts § 306 (3d ed. Jaeger 1959). In other words, in the face of silence, most promoters' contracts are properly read as implying that corporate adoption of the contract is a condition of performance.

[31]   BRJM, LLC v. Output Systems, Inc., 100 Conn. App. 143, 917 A.2d 605 (Conn. 2007).

[32]   *See* H. F. Philipsborn & Co. v. Suson, 322 N.E.2d 45 (Ill. 1974) (whether liability will be imposed depends on intent of parties).

[33]   *See* Restatement (Second) of Agency § 326, Comment b (1958).

[34]   R.A.C. Realty Co. v. W.O.U.F. Atlanta Realty Corp., 52 S.E.2d 617 (Ga. 1949).

[35]   Manfred W. Ehrich & Lucille C. Bunzl, Promoters' Contracts, 38 Yale L.J. 1011, 1019 (1929). *See also* Restatement (Second) Contracts § 23 (1973).

[36]   *See* O'Rorke v. Geary, 56 A. 541 (Pa. 1903).

they were agents. Under such an arrangement the third party may immediately give or commence performance or may defer performance until the corporation comes into existence and can receive it.[37]

(4) Promoters may make a contract that binds them at the time of contracting, with the stipulation or understanding that if a company is formed it will take their places, and the promoters will be relieved of liability. In other words, the parties may intend an immediate contract between the promoters and the other party but contemplate a novation pursuant to which the corporation will be substituted for the promoters when the corporation is organized and adopts the contract.[38]

(5) Promoters may make a contract that presently binds the promoters, with the stipulation or understanding that if a company is formed and adopts, the promoters thereafter are only secondarily liable as sureties for the performance of the corporation, and will be responsible only if the company becomes judgment-proof or is otherwise unable to fulfill its contractual obligations.[39]

(6) Instead of taking an offer for the corporation to be formed as in (1), which offer a third party can revoke before formation of the corporation and its acceptance, promoters may pay or promise an agreed consideration to the third party for an option in favor of the corporation or one that can be transferred to it. The agreed consideration could be the promoters' promise to use their best efforts to secure the corporation's formation and its adoption of the contract. This arrangement fixes the limits of the promoters' responsibility.[40]

(7) Promoters may make a separate or subsidiary contract under which the third party agrees to contract with the corporation following its formation on specified terms or to hold an offer open which it may accept when organized. The consideration given by the promoters might be, for example, an undertaking to form a corporation and cause it to assent to the main contract or to use their best efforts to organize a corporation and cause it to assent to the contract.

Whenever a promoter entering into a contract on behalf of a projected corporation causes the other contracting party to think the corporation is already in existence and that the promoter is its agent and contracting for it, the promoter may be held liable (1) on the contract, (2) for deceit, (3) for breach of implied warranty of authority from a principal, or (4) for breach of implied warranty of the existence of a principal.[41]

When a promoter makes a contract in the name of a nonexistent corporation, a court may find that either: (1) the parties intended for the promoter to be a party to the contract; (2) the promoter was only to be a party until the corporation is organized and accepts the contract; or (3) the promoter was simply soliciting an offer that the

---

[37]   Columbia Metal Culvert Co. v. Kaiser Indus. Corp., 526 F.2d 724 (3d Cir. 1975).

[38]   *See* Quest Engineering Solutions, Inc. v. Wilbur, 79 Mass. App. 1124, 948 N.E.2d 917 (2011); RKO-Stanley Warner Theatres, Inc. v. Graziano, 355 A.2d 830 (Pa. 1976) (promoter not released from liability on incorporation; intent of parties was to hold promoter personally liable until corporation was formed and had ratified agreement).

[39]   *Cf.* In re Robbins Int'l, Inc., 275 B.R. 456, 468–469 (S.D.N.Y. 2002) (discussing promoter liability and suretyship liability with respect to corporation that was found not liable under either principle).

[40]   William L. Cary, Cases and Materials on Corporations 89 n.2 (4th ed. unabr. 1969).

[41]   *See* Annot., 41 A.L.R.2d 477 (1958); 3 Am. Jur. 2d 654–662, Agency §§ 293 to 300 (1986).

corporation, after formation, could accept or reject.[42] When contracts are ambiguous as to whether the parties intend the promoter to be bound, some jurisdictions allow the use of parol evidence to show the personal liability of the promoter was intended or that the third party was to look only to the corporation.[43] Although most decisions passing on whether a promoter is liable on an ambiguous contract have on one theory or another imposed personal liability on the promoter, a number of the more recent decisions show a greater readiness to interpret nonspecific contracts in a way that shields the promoter from liability, thus reaching a result perhaps more in accord with the intention of the parties.[44]

Absent clear intent on the part of the promoter to be liable on a *post*-incorporation contract, the third party is deemed to have relied on the existing corporation, not on the individual promoter, to pay any claim for services or other performance.[45]

§ 5.8   Promoters' Liability After Corporation Adopts

When promoters bind themselves personally by a contract on behalf of a proposed corporation, the mere fact of corporate adoption or assumption of the contract does not alone relieve them from liability.[46] Many courts have held that even though the corporation becomes liable, the promoters also remain liable; the third party has the double security of the corporation and the promoters, unless that party consents to a novation or substitution of the corporation for the promoters.[47] Under a well-settled principle of contract law, without the consent of the other contracting party, one party to a contract cannot relieve herself of her obligations by substituting another person in her place.[48] This double security is a windfall for the other contracting party because had the corporation been in existence at the time of contracting, the other party normally would not have also contracted for the promoter's liability.

The typical promoters' contract might fairly be interpreted as contemplating a novation, and often the other contracting party may be held to have consented in advance to substitute the corporation in the place of the promoters. If all the parties agree at the time a corporation adopts a promoters' contract that the corporation alone will thereafter be liable and that the promoters will be released, there is an express novation. There is in this case sufficient consideration to support the release of the promoters, and no action will lie against the promoters on the contract. Such a novation may also be implied from the conduct of the parties.

---

[42]   *See* White & Bollard, Inc. v. Goodenow, 361 P.2d 571, 573–574 (Wash. 1961).

[43]   Decker v. Juzwik, 121 N.W.2d 652, 657–658 (Iowa 1963).

[44]   *See, e.g.*, In re Robbins Int'l, Inc., 275 B.R. 456, 468 (S.D.N.Y. 2002); Quaker Hill, Inc. v. Parr, 364 P.2d 1056 (Colo. 1961).

[45]   Television Events & Mktg. v. AMCON Distrib. Co., 484 F. Supp. 2d 1124, 1138 (D. Hawai'i 2006).

[46]   Quest Engineering Solutions, Inc. v. Wilbur, 79 Mass. App. Ct. 1124, 948 N.E.2d 917 (2011), review denied, 460 Mass. 1110, 951 N.E.2d 351 (2011).

[47]   Stanley J. How & Assoc. v. Boss, 222 F.Supp. 936 (S.D. Iowa 1963) (after corporation was formed, it sent two checks to plaintiff in partial payment).

[48]   In re Blaszak, 397 F.3d 386, 392 (6th Cir. 2005) (citing Illinois Controls, Inc. v. Langham, 639 N.E.2d 771 (1994)).

§ 5.9   Statutes Relating to Pre-Incorporation Contracts

No American jurisdiction has a statute specifically dealing with promoters' contracts as such.[49] The 1969 version of the Model Business Corporation Act provided that all persons who presume to act as a corporation without authority to do so shall be jointly and severally liable for all debts and liabilities incurred or arising as a result thereof.[50] A number of states have statutes of this kind.[51] The 2016 version of the Model Business Corporation Act provides: "All persons purporting to act as or on behalf of a corporation, knowing there was no incorporation under this Act, are jointly and severally liable for all liabilities created while so acting."[52] As will be seen in the next chapter, the effect of these statutes on liability under promoters' contracts is unclear.[53] The statutes were designed primarily to eliminate the concept of de facto incorporation.[54] The statute's language clearly imposes personal liability on those who contract for a corporation when it was not then in existence.[55] The language of the 1984 Model Business Corporation Act dealing with preincorporation activity generally seems broad enough to cover promoters' contracts, but even under that act a third party dealing with a promoter may be estopped from asserting that the promoter is personally liable.[56]

§ 5.10   Promoters' Fiduciary Obligations

Promoters have such far-reaching control over the enterprise during its formative stages, and even after incorporation, that the law imposes on them fiduciary obligations toward the company and those who contribute its capital. Their fiduciary obligations begin prior to the formation of the entity, whether it be a partnership, LLC or corporation, and require them to act in good faith and with the utmost fairness in their promotional activities and dealings.[57] The promoters' fiduciary duties antedate the corporation's formation, arising when the promoters form a clear intention to promote the corporation.[58] In broad overview, the fiduciary duty requires the promoters to act with the utmost good faith in all dealings with the corporation and its shareholders.[59] The fiduciary relationship extends to the promoted corporation, its stockholders, and

---

[49]   A number of foreign jurisdictions have legislation designed to avoid the strict English rule that a corporation cannot ratify or adopt a pre-incorporation contract.

[50]   Former Model Bus. Corp. Act § 146 (1969).

[51]   *See, e.g.,* Del. Code Ann. tit. 8, § 329 (2001).

[52]   Model Bus. Corp. Act § 2.04 (2016).

[53]   The cases have been in conflict. *See, e.g.,* Timberline Equip. Co. v. Davenport, 514 P.2d 1109 (Or. 1973), where the court found the language of § 146 ambiguous as to who would qualify as a "person who assume[s] to act as a corporation." The court concluded that anyone having an investment in the organization who actively participates in policy and operational decisions of the organization (not necessarily just those who participate in decisions or acts connected with the obligation on which suit is brought) could be held liable.

[54]   *See* Pharmaceutical Sales & Consulting Corp. v. J.W.S. Delavau Co., 59 F.Supp.2d 408, 414 (D.N.J. 1999); Quaker Hill v. Parr, 364 P.2d 1056 (Colo. 1961); Robertson v. Levy, 197 A.2d 443 (D.C. 1964).

[55]   DBA/Delaware Sys. Corp. v. Greenfield, 636 A.2d 1318 (R.I. 1994).

[56]   While no special provision is made in Model Bus. Corp. Act § 2.04, the section does not foreclose the possibility that persons who urge promoters to execute contracts in the corporate name knowing that no steps to incorporate have been taken may be estopped to impose personal liability on the promoters. *See* Official Comments, Model Bus. Corp. Act § 2.04.

[57]   Roni LLC v. Arfa, 18 N.Y.3d 846, 939 N.Y.S.2d 746, 963 N.E.2d 123 (2011) (promoters of LLCs owe fiduciary duties in the formation process).

[58]   Wisconsin Ave. Assoc. v. 2720 Wis. Ave. Co-op. Ass'n, 441 A.2d 956, 963 (D.C. 1982).

[59]   *See, e.g.,* In re Access Cardiosystems, Inc., 340 B.R. 127, 147–148 (Bankr. D. Mass. 2006). Whaler Motor Inn., Inc. v. Parsons, 363 N.E.2d 493 (Mass. 1977).

fellow promoters.[60] Promoters cannot retain inequitable profits from manipulation of corporate purchases and share issues while the enterprise is under their control or influence.

Although the problem of promoter misconduct is now handled chiefly through state and federal securities regulations,[61] the common law still plays a role in appropriate situations. The common law fiduciary relation is still relevant in resolving disputes where overreaching is alleged that cannot be linked directly to deceit practiced on investors. In this context, the common law not only resolves whether a breach has occurred but also guides what remedies should be allowed to the corporation and to individual investors.

Unifying themes across cases invoking the promoters' fiduciary obligations are the mandating of candor and proscribing the promoters' taking unfair advantage of the promoted corporation or its stockholders. Not only do these two themes complement one another, but also the duty of candor in most cases defines what constitutes an undue advantage. Courts that find promoters have breached their fiduciary obligations invariably base their holdings on the promoters' failure to disclose fully all the material facts to either an independent board of directors or to the corporation's outside stockholders,[62] or even to their fellow promoters.[63] This reflects the general prohibition against promoters reaping a secret profit by virtue of their relationship to the corporation. With the approval of an independent body of directors or stockholders and after full disclosure of all material facts to the transaction, the promoters have discharged their fiduciary obligations. When all material facts have not been disclosed, the promoters bear a substantial burden of proving the transaction's entire fairness and the adequacy of the consideration supporting the transaction.[64] Most cases never reach this stage, however, because the promoters have already failed to disclose the wide disparity in value between what they transferred to the corporation and what they received.[65]

The second component of the promoter's fiduciary duty—that no unfair advantage be taken of the corporation or its stockholders—operates in that narrow band of cases where the promoter is the sole stockholder at the time of the transaction. In cases where either an independent board of directors or outside stockholders exist, the responsibility of the promoter is effectively fulfilled by requiring full disclosure of all the facts. Where such independent decision-makers do not exist, courts focus on the relative fairness of the transaction; accordingly any gross disparity in the exchange between the sole promoter and the corporation is treated by the courts as the promoter having taken unfair advantage of his or her position.

---

[60] Public Inv., Ltd. v. Bandeirante Corp., 740 F.2d 1222 (D.C. Cir. 1984); Topanga Corp. v. Gentile, 58 Cal.Rptr. 713 (App. 1967) (duty of full disclosure among co-promoters); Smith v. Bitter, 319 N.W.2d 196 (Iowa 1982); Lustgarten v. Jones, 371 N.W.2d 668 (Neb. 1985).

[61] *See, e.g.,* Miller v. San Sebastian Gold Mines, Inc., 540 F.2d 807 (5th Cir. 1976).

[62] *See, e.g.,* Public Inv. Ltd. v. Bandeirante Corp., 740 F.2d 1222 (D.C. Cir. 1984); In re Access Cardiosystems, Inc., 340 B.R. 127, 150 (Bankr. D. Mass. 2006).

[63] Topanga Corp. v. Gentile, 58 Cal.Rptr. 713 (App. 1967).

[64] *See* Public Inv. Ltd. v. Bandeirante Corp., 740 F.2d 1222 (D.C. Cir. 1984).

[65] Golden v. Oahe Enterprises, Inc., 295 N.W.2d 160 (S.D. 1980).

§ 5.11   Fraudulent Devices Used by Promoters

The principal devices promoters have used to obtain compensation and speculative profits are:

(1) Selling property, greatly overvalued, to the corporation in return for a large part of the corporation's securities.[66] "The most typical promotion situation is presented when a promoter has acquired property at a nominal price which he turns over to a corporation in exchange for a large block of stock which is resold to the public on the basis of the valuation [of the property] made by the promoter-controlled corporation."[67]

(2) Receiving a substantial block of the promoted corporation's shares for no consideration.[68]

(3) Selling to the corporation, at an amount in excess of its cost to the promoter, an option or contract that the promoter holds on certain property, or intercepting part of the purchase price, which the promoter pretends to pay to the owner on behalf of the corporation.

(4) Forming a management corporation, which the promoter controls, and causing the new corporation to make a contract with it that provides management fees and other profitable returns.[69]

(5) Causing the corporation to issue the corporation's securities to the promoter, or to a corporation the promoter controls.[70]

(6) Taking excessive underwriting fees and commissions on the sale of securities.[71]

(7) Misappropriating assets needed to launch the company's operations.[72]

By using these and similar types of abusive promotion schemes promoters are able to divert money to themselves at the expense of the outside investors.

§ 5.12   The Defense of Full Disclosure

A profit is not secret or unlawful and cannot be successfully challenged if all the parties having an interest in the corporation, including existing and incoming shareholders, actually know of the profit and assent to it. Accordingly, the promoters' successful defense generally depends on (1) full disclosure of all material facts to an independent board of directors, who approve it[73] or (2) full disclosure of all material facts to all existing shareholders and subscribers for shares, and they assent to it.[74]

---

[66] *See, e.g.,* San Juan Uranium Corp. v. Wolfe, 241 F.2d 121 (10th Cir. 1957); Topanga Corp. v. Gentile, 58 Cal.Rptr. 713 (Ct. App. 1967).

[67] Brunson MacChesney, The Securities Act and the Promoter, 25 Cal. L. Rev. 66, 71–79 (1936).

[68] *See* Froehlich v. Matz, 417 N.E.2d 183 (Ill. App. 1981).

[69] *See* Yacker v. Weiner, 263 A.2d 188 (N.J. Super. Ch. 1970).

[70] *See, e.g.,* Bowers v. Rio Grande Inv. Co., 431 P.2d 478 (Colo. 1967) (enforcing an option agreement).

[71] *See, e.g.,* Bovay v. H. M. Byllesby & Co., 38 A.2d 808, 811–814 (Del. 1944).

[72] *See, e.g.,* Post v. United States, 407 F.2d 319 (D.C. Cir. 1968).

[73] *See* Frick v. Howard, 126 N.W.2d 619 (Wis. 1964). An independent board of directors in this context means representatives who are not under the promoter's control or influence.

[74] Tilden v. Barber, 268 F. 587 (D.N.J. 1920); Swafford v. Berry, 382 P.2d 999 (Colo. 1963).

Disclosure to the shareholders is of little value unless disclosure is fully made to every shareholder.[75] Promoters who rely on the defense of impartial stockholder approval must be prepared to meet the line of authorities holding that absence of fraud requires the consent of *all* the shareholders. Therefore, disclosure to existing shareholders at a meeting, with ratification or approval by a majority, should not be considered sufficient to bind dissenting shareholders if the transaction was fraudulent.[76] It has also been declared that "ratification by stockholders cannot render fair what is unfair to general creditors, for they, too, constitute a part of that community of interest in the corporation which the law seeks to protect."[77] Such a demanding standard requires more than promoters profiting through a resale to the corporation. Fraud does not arise solely because the promoters are profiting; it arises when the price of resale to the corporation is above the property's fair market value.

In the classic case of *Old Dominion Copper Mining & Smelting Company v. Lewisohn*,[78] the U.S. Supreme Court, in an opinion by Justice Holmes, refused to permit recovery by the corporation even where the fraud required bringing in new shareholders, provided full disclosure was made to all the shareholders at the time of the transaction. It was explained that the "plaintiff cannot recover without departing from the fundamental conception . . . that a corporation remains unaffected in its identity by changes in its membership."[79] Although this view is a minority one, some state courts have followed it.[80] Justice Holmes reasoned that, as the only existing shareholders, the promoter and associates were the corporation and had assented to their own profit with full knowledge of the scheme at the time of the transaction. Therefore, no wrong was done at that time to anyone, and the rights of the corporation as such were not increased when innocent subscribers subsequently were induced to invest in the corporation. According to this doctrine, the wrong, if any, is the misrepresentation to later investors who acquired their shares without knowledge that the corporation's assets had been overvalued by its promoters.

Justice Holmes's opinion in *Lewisohn* is a highly formalistic view of the corporation as well as the nature of fiduciary obligations. This formalism is captured in his conclusion that the sole duty of the promoter is to the few corrupt insiders who for the moment constitute the company. To be sure, *Lewisohn* reduces fiduciary obligations to a consensual basis. This approach is not inappropriate when a truly independent board of directors or body of stockholders exists who can consider the transaction's merits from the perspective of the corporation's and stockholders' interests served thereby. In such a setting, the invisible hand of self-interest serves the worthy purpose of moving resources to their efficient use—that is, mandating consent after full disclosure of all material facts is a natural complement to market forces in a capitalistic economy. However, where all those within the corporation stand on the same side of the transaction, as they did in *Lewisohn*, they cannot purport to express the interests of future owners as to the worthiness of the property that the promoters seek to transfer to the corporation.

---

[75]   Hughes v. Cadena De Cobre Mining Co., 108 P. 231 (Ariz.Terr. 1910) (a single uninformed shareholder was sufficient to deny a finding of corporate assent).

[76]   *See* Note, 53 Harv. L. Rev. 1368 (1940).

[77]   United Hotels Co. v. Mealey, 147 F.2d 816, 818 (2d Cir. 1945).

[78]   Old Dominion Copper Mining & Smelting Company v. Lewisohn, 210 U.S. 206 (1908).

[79]   210 U.S. at 216.

[80]   *See, e.g.,* Hughes v. Cadena De Cobre Mining Co., 108 P. 231 (Ariz.Terr. 1910); Lilylands Canal & Reservoir Co. v. Wood, 136 P. 1026 (Colo. 1913).

Moreover, by definition, the gains the promoters seek from transferring the property to the corporation owned exclusively by the promoters cannot be realized until interests in the corporation are later sold to outsiders. Until those investors appear, the promoters have reaped no secret profit because the transfer is only to themselves. So viewed, on the facts of *Lewisohn*, it is far more logical to recognize the promoters' fiduciary obligation extended until truly independent parties had consented after full disclosure of all material facts. By so holding, courts provide a meaningful prophylaxis for the protection of those who later invest in the corporation.

The leading authority in opposition to the view Justice Holmes advanced is the Massachusetts decision of *Old Dominion Copper Mining & Smelting Company v. Bigelow*,[81] which arose from the same transaction as *Lewisohn*. By reason of their nondisclosure to incoming subscribers, the promoters were able to exact from the plaintiff corporation a secret profit of 50,000 shares of the corporation's stock. Contrary to the United States Supreme Court's ruling, the Massachusetts court held that the promoter was liable to the corporation as well as to the defrauded subscribers individually, where fraud on future subscribers was contemplated as an essential part of the scheme of promotion. Promoters cannot as shareholders or directors absolve themselves in their capacity as promoters from future liability to the corporation for reaping secret profits from dilution of its shares. In *Bigelow*, the corporate assent was invalid because it had no representatives who were able to act independently. The theory of the Massachusetts case was that the fiduciary relationship of a promoter continues until the corporation is completely established. The obligation of faithfulness is coextensive with the plan for completing the capitalization of the corporation. Following the lead of *Bigelow*, a majority of courts[82] have recognized in such cases a right of action in the corporation for the benefit of all participants.

---

[81] Old Dominion Copper Mining & Smelting Company v. Bigelow, 89 N.E. 193 (Mass. 1909), *aff'd*, 225 U.S. 111 (1912).

[82] *See, e.g.*, San Juan Uranium Corp. v. Wolfe, 241 F.2d 121 (10th Cir. 1957); Topanga Corp. v. Gentile, 58 Cal.Rptr. 713 (Ct. App. 1967).

Chapter 6

DEFECTIVE FORMATION OF CORPORATIONS AND REVIVAL OF EXISTENCE

Table of Sections

§ 6.1 Problems Arising from Defects in Formation

Although the process of organizing a corporation under today's corporation statutes is a simple one, failure to comply carefully with the statutory formalities for incorporation can result in loss of corporate status with the concomitant personal liability of the associates. Corporations cannot be created like partnerships and joint stock companies solely by mutual agreement of the associates. To reap all the advantages, privileges, and incidents of corporateness depends on substantial compliance with conditions set in a general corporation act.

There are various degrees of noncompliance with the statutory formalities, some of which are of more and others of less importance in affecting corporate status. The defect, shortcoming, or irregularity complained of may or may not be accidental, may or may not affect the merits of a case being litigated, and may or may not have harmed the person who seeks to raise questions of defective incorporation. In determining the consequences attaching to defective organization, courts typically speak in terms of "de jure corporation," "de facto corporation," and "corporation by estoppel."[1]

Consider the following possibilities: (1) The associates in a business enterprise may brazenly pretend to be incorporated without attempting to take some or any of the required statutory steps or may assume acting as a corporation with knowledge that the steps taken are incomplete. (2) The associates may execute articles of incorporation but, by some inadvertent mischance, may fail to get them filed in any public office.[2] (3) The associates may file the articles of incorporation with a state official, who may reject them.[3] (4) In one of the few states that still require the articles to be filed in two different government offices, they may file the articles in only one of the two prescribed offices. (5)

---

[1] *See* §§ 6.2, 6.3, 6.15.

[2] *See, e.g.,* Cranson v. International Bus. Machines Corp., 200 A.2d 33 (Md. 1964) (defendant shown articles of incorporation, which corporation's attorney failed to file).

[3] *See, e.g.,* Cantor v. Sunshine Greenery, Inc., 398 A.2d 571 (1979).

The articles as filed may not be in proper form, may omit required provisions, or may be incorrectly executed or acknowledged by the incorporators. (6) The associates may fail to pay in the minimum required capital in a state in which that is still prescribed as a condition precedent to doing business. (7) The associates may fail to hold an organizational meeting of incorporators, shareholders, or directors, or fail to adopt bylaws or to elect directors and officers.[4] (8) The statute under which the associates attempt to incorporate may be unconstitutional or may not authorize formation of corporations to do the kinds of business the corporation is being organized to conduct. (9) The associates may purport to continue to do business as a corporation after its prescribed term of existence has expired, after revocation of its charter, or after it has been dissolved.[5]

If business associates purport to conduct their enterprise as a corporation but have not complied with statutory requirements for the organization of a corporation, or if the organization is otherwise defective in one or more of the respects just enumerated, will their association be treated as a corporation? Or perhaps the more accurate question is, which of the normal corporate attributes and incidents will the association be recognized as having, under what circumstances, and for what purposes?

Among the diverse problems arising from defects in organization, the following are perhaps the most important:

(1) May the association sue as a corporation to enforce a contract if the other party to the contract challenges its capacity to sue or to contract?

(2) May the association's creditors and other persons dealing with it sue it as a corporation? And may the association deny its existence as a corporation to defeat litigation brought against it?

(3) May the purported corporation receive or make conveyances of property?

(4) May the incorporators, subscribers, shareholders, directors, or officers in a seriously defective corporation be held to unlimited personal liability as partners or otherwise? For a debt claim against the business? For a tort committed by an employee of the enterprise? In answering these questions, whether the particular persons charged with liability had knowledge of the defects or actively participated in doing or authorizing the transaction giving rise to the liability may be important considerations.[6]

(5) May the association, although defectively formed, enforce pre-incorporation subscriptions?

(6) May the association exercise the right of eminent domain?

(7) May the purported corporation be dissolved for defective incorporation in an action by the shareholders? In a quo warranto proceeding brought by

---

[4]   *See* Beck v. Stimmel, 177 N.E. 920 (Ohio Ct. App. 1931).

[5]   *See* Adam v. Mt. Pleasant Bank & Trust Co., 355 N.W.2d 868 (Iowa 1984).

[6]   *See, e.g.,* Edward Shoes, Inc. v. Orenstein, 333 F.Supp. 39, 42 (N.D. Ind. 1971) (shareholders purporting to be doing business as corporation under Indiana law will be held personally liable to creditors only if they acted fraudulently or in bad faith).

the attorney general to oust it from the exercise of corporate power and the usurpation of a corporate franchise?

(8)   May a corporation doing business in a state other than its state of incorporation without qualifying to do business in that state nevertheless obtain de facto status in that state?

The answers given in the mass of judicial decisions that have dealt with these questions present a discouraging and baffling maze. To generalize the results of the decisions is indeed a difficult task. Satisfactory formulae or mechanical rules simply do not exist. Perhaps the most important question is under what circumstances the associates, active or passive, with or without knowledge of the defects, will be held personally liable for the debts of the supposed corporation.[7]

§ 6.2   Corporation De Jure

A de jure corporation is recognized as having a corporate existence for all purposes, even as against a direct attack by the state of incorporation. No one, not even the state, can successfully challenge its existence as a corporation. To prove that it is a de jure corporation, it must show not only a valid law under which it might be created, and an attempt to organize under that law, but also compliance with all the mandatory requirements of the law that are conditions precedent to corporate existence.[8]

§ 6.3   The De Facto Doctrine

In the absence of substantial compliance with incorporation requirements, a court may nevertheless treat a defectively organized corporation as a "de facto corporation" and recognize it as having continuity of life, limited liability, and the other corporate attributes. Courts have also recognized that the de facto corporation doctrine can apply to an LLC.[9] Except in a direct action by the state and perhaps in a few other minor instances, a de facto corporation is treated as though it were de jure. The state in quo warranto proceedings can terminate its life, but no one else can successfully challenge its existence.[10]

Under the de facto doctrine as usually stated, a de facto corporation results if the following essentials are met:

(1)   A valid statute under which the corporation could have been formed (or, according to some, an apparently valid statute).

(2)   A good faith attempt to comply with the requirements of the statute.

(3)   A "colorable compliance" with the statutory requirements—that is, a sufficient compliance to give an appearance of validity to the incorporation.

---

[7]   *See* E. Merrick, Dodd, Jr., Partnership Liability of Stockholders in Defective Corporations, 40 Harv. L. Rev. 521 (1927).

[8]   *See, e.g.,* People v. Larsen, 106 N.E. 947 (Ill. 1914); Attorney General, *ex rel.* Joseph L. Miner v. Belle Isle Ice Co., 26 N.W. 311 (Mich. 1886).

[9]   Duray Development, LLC v. Perrin, 288 Mich. App. 143, 792 N.W.2d 749 (2010), appeal denied, 488 Mich. 994, 791 N.W.2d 438 (2010); Global BTG, LLC v. National Air Cargo, Inc., 2011 WL 2672337 (C.D. Cal. 2011).

[10]   *See, e.g.,* Thies v. Weible, 254 N.W. 420, 423 (Neb. 1934).

(4) A use of corporate powers—that is, the transaction of business by the organization as if it were a corporation. This element seems to be of only minor importance. Occasionally, in stating the essentials of the doctrine, a court has omitted the requirement of colorable compliance with the statute, but it is not clear whether this omission is deliberate or inadvertent.[11] On the other hand, courts have sometimes added a fifth requirement—namely:

(5) Good faith in claiming to be a corporation and in doing business as a corporation. Initial good faith may not be sufficient. Later discovery of defects by the associates may thereafter preclude application of the de facto doctrine to their organization.

As discussed in a later section, there is some authority supporting the abolition of the de facto doctrine in states adopting the Model Business Corporation Act; but not all courts agree.

§ 6.4 Basis of the De Facto Doctrine

The incorporation statutes of various states set forth certain conditions precedent to corporate existence. It may well be asked: Why do courts recognize an organization as being a corporation de facto when it has failed to comply with the legislative conditions precedent?

The recognition of de facto existence promotes the security of business transactions and tends to eliminate quibbling over irregularities. Persons dealing with a corporation will rarely be prejudiced if the company is recognized as a corporation in spite of minor omissions or defects in its formation. A wrongdoer should not be allowed to quibble over incorporation defects to escape liability to the corporation. Similarly, a creditor of a supposed company usually should not be allowed to assert the individual liability of innocent, passive investors on the basis of flaws in the formal steps of incorporation when to do so would be contrary to the investors' expectations and the bargained-for agreement. This would simply give the creditor a windfall.

§ 6.5 Corporation by Estoppel

Persons may presume to do business as a corporation without having gone far enough in their incorporation attempt to acquire a de facto standing. Nevertheless, under some circumstances and for some purposes, courts sometimes hold either the purported corporation or persons contracting with it estopped to deny its corporate

---

[11] *See, e.g.,* Municipal Bond & Mortgage Corp. v. Bishop's Harbor Drainage Dist., 182 So. 794 (Fla. 1938); Cranson v. International Bus. Mach. Corp., 200 A.2d 33 (Md. 1964); Paper Prods. Co. v. Doggrell, 261 S.W.2d 127 (Tenn. 1953).

status. The corporation then is often referred to as a "corporation by estoppel."[12] Courts have also recognized that the estoppel approach applies to a LLC.[13]

The use of the term "estoppel" in this type of case may be misleading.[14] When a court says that the other parties to a contract are "estoppel," this may mean nothing more than that it or they are precluded for some reason from denying the corporate capacity. The word "estoppel" does not reveal the reason for the conclusion, as the elements of a true estoppel are lacking in many of the decisions in which the term is used. It might be preferable in some of these decisions to say that the person contracting or dealing with the defective organization is considered to have "admitted" its corporate existence, rather than as being estopped to deny it.

The application of the so-called estoppel doctrine does not mean that the irregular corporation has acquired a corporate status generally and for all purposes. Rather, on the appropriate facts, corporation by estoppel may be used to bar collateral attacks on corporateness in a particular setting even though the de facto doctrine has been abrogated by statute in the state or is inappropriate given the factual setting.[15] The doctrine is limited in its application to the consequences of a particular transaction done in the corporate name by associates assuming to be a corporation. Estoppel requires a reasonable consideration of the equities of each case and whether the defects or irregularities should be open to inquiry in that particular situation. Just as in the de facto corporation doctrine, procedural convenience, the avoidance of inquiry into irrelevant formalities, and fairness to all parties may favor treating a defective association purporting to be a corporation as though it has certain corporate incidents.

In one situation, all the elements of a true estoppel exist. Associates who hold out their association as a corporate body, and thereby induce persons to deal with it as such, are properly said to be estopped from denying their representation where to do so would prejudice those persons.[16] Thus it has long been established that a person contracting with an association that pretends to be a corporation may sue the associates as a corporation, and the principle of estoppel will prevent the associates from setting up as a defense the falsity of their own representation of corporateness.[17] The representation of corporateness can be to the general public, rather than to a specific party, and still

---

[12]   *See* Zoning Comm'n v. Lescynski, 453 A.2d 1144 (Conn. 1982); Harry Rich Corp. v. Feinberg, 518 So.2d 377 (Fla. Dist. Ct. App. 1987). *Cf.* Sullivan v. Buckhorn Ranch P'ship, 119 P.3d 192 (Okla. 2005) (estoppel to deny corporate existence may not be invoked unless corporation had at least de facto existence). Corporation by estoppel was raised when a lease was entered into after the foreign corporation had failed to register to do business in the state so that its capacity to contract had been terminated. Brown v. M Street Five, LLC, 56 A.3d 765 (D.C. 2012). The court refused to permit the defense, as the corporation's manager was aware its capacity had been terminated, so that to hold otherwise would undercut the purpose of the statute of denying such status to corporation's failure to keep their registration current. *Id.*

[13]   Duray Development, LLC v. Perrin, 288 Mich. App. 143, 792 N.W.2d 749 (2010), appeal denied, 488 Mich. 994, 791 N.W.2d 438 (2010); Global BTG, LLC v. National Air Cargo, Inc., 2011 WL 2672337 (C.D. Cal. 2011).

[14]   As one court explained:

This term [corporation by estoppel] was a complete misnomer. There was no corporation, the acts of the association having failed even to colorably fulfill the statutory requirements; there was no estoppel in the pure sense of the word because generally there was no holding out followed by reliance on the part of the other party. Robertson v. Levy, 197 A.2d 443, 445 (D.C. 1964).

[15]   Rubenstein v. Mayor, 41 A.D.3d 826, 839 N.Y.S.2d 170 (2d Dept. 2007).

[16]   *See* United States v. Harrison, 653 F.2d 359 (8th Cir. 1981) (trustees estopped to deny corporate existence to prevent disclosure to IRS of business records pertaining to family trust where separate tax returns had been filed on behalf of trust entity).

[17]   Empire Mfg. Co. v. Stuart, 9 N.W. 527 (Mich. 1881).

give rise to estoppel.[18] Also, an associate who transacts business in the corporate name is estopped to deny the validity of the corporation for the purpose of holding other associates personally liable on contracts entered into between them in carrying on the firm's business.[19]

In a different type of case—where a defective corporation brings suit against the other party to a contract to enforce the contract—courts often say that the party who has contracted with the supposed corporation is estopped from denying its existence. For example, in the leading case, *Cranson v. International Business Machines Corporation*,[20] a contract creditor was estopped to deny the corporation's existence solely by having carried on all dealings with the defectively formed corporation in that corporation's name. The certificate of incorporation had not been filed with the secretary of state until after the plaintiff had delivered several office machines on account to the business. The business's president and substantial shareholder was unaware of the attorney's oversight in making the tardy filing. In contrast, *Don Swann Sales Corporation v. Echols*,[21] on facts identical to those in *Cranson*, the court, although recognizing that the legislature had intended to preserve the corporation by the estoppel doctrine, refused to recognize the doctrine's application to protect an *individual* purporting to act for a nonexistent corporation. The court relied on a state statute imposing liability on anyone who acts on behalf of a corporation before the secretary of state has issued a certificate of incorporation.

§ 6.6   Liability of Participants: Active Versus Passive Participation

Should persons having dealt with a defectively organized corporation on a corporate basis be allowed to assert full individual liability against the associates in the business? Numerous decisions hold that associates who deliberately engage in business under the name and pretense of a corporation should be held individually liable if they have not achieved at least a de facto corporate status.[22] The fact that by their pretense they lead outsiders to contract with them as a corporation is said to be no ground of estoppel in their favor. The associates are the principals and co-owners of a business that is carried on by their authorization and for their benefit.

Under this view, if the attempt to comply with the incorporation law does not go far enough to create a corporation de facto, associates who actively participate in the business are held to full liability on contracts authorized or ratified by them, either as partners or as principals.[23] There is said to be no estoppel of one who deals with business

---

[18]   United States v. Theodore, 347 F.Supp. 1070 (D. S.C. 1972) (claim company records were personal records so privilege against self-incrimination applied denied because business had represented itself to public as corporation).

[19]   Kingsley v. English, 278 N.W. 154 (Minn. 1938); Dargan v. Graves, 168 S.E.2d 306 (S.C. 1969).

[20]   Cranson v. International Business Machines Corporation, 200 A.2d 33 (Md. 1964). Cranson has been followed in a number of cases. *See, e.g.,* Turner v. Turner, 809 A.2d 18, 63 (Md. App. 2002).

[21]   Don Swann Sales Corporation v. Echols, 287 S.E.2d 577 (Ga. Ct. App. 1981). *But see* Gardner v. Marcum, 665 S.E.2d 336 (Ga. Ct. App. 2008) (third party who deals with business as corporation cannot deny its corporate existence and hold principal individually liable).

[22]   *See, e.g.,* Puro Filter Corp. v. Trembley, 41 N.Y.S.2d 472 (App. Div. 1943); Conway v. Samet, 300 N.Y.S.2d 243 (Sup. Ct. 1969).

[23]   *See, e.g.,* Harrill v. Davis, 168 F. 187 (8th Cir. 1909); Clinton Inv. Co. v. Watkins, 536 N.Y.S.2d 270 (App. Div. 1989); Minich v. Gem State Dev., Inc., 591 P.2d 1078 (Idaho 1979); *cf.* Chatman v. Day, 455 N.E.2d 672 (Ohio Ct. App. 1982). *See* E. Merrick, Dodd, Jr., Partnership Liability of Stockholders in Defective

associates masquerading under a name that fails to represent a corporation de facto, because the elements of estoppel, viz., action induced by misrepresentation of the party against whom the estoppel is asserted, do not exist.[24]

§ 6.7   Statutes Pertaining to Defective Corporations

By simplifying the mechanics of incorporation, modern corporation statutes have reduced the number of defective incorporations and thereby the amount of litigation. Furthermore, most modern corporation acts contain provisions designed to clear up some of the problems of defective organization. Such provisions either dictate the moment in the incorporation process that a corporation comes into existence by providing that the filing of the articles of incorporation or the issuance of a certificate of incorporation by the secretary of state is either presumptive evidence or "conclusive evidence" or "conclusive proof" that all conditions precedent to incorporation have been met, or they specify the consequences of particular defects in the organization process, as well as forbidding collateral attack on incorporation in certain types of cases. The effect of some of these provisions on traditional doctrines such as de facto incorporation and corporation by estoppel is far from clear.

In many jurisdictions, the corporation statute states that a corporation comes into existence either when its articles of incorporation are filed or when the secretary of state issues a certificate of incorporation,[25] and in addition provides that either acceptance and filing of articles of incorporation by the secretary of state or the secretary's issuance of a certificate of incorporation shall be "conclusive evidence," except against the state, that all conditions precedent to incorporation have been performed.

Statutes containing "conclusive evidence" or "conclusive proof" language seemingly do away with the necessity of litigating some of the questions that might arise under the de facto doctrine, such as what effect defects in the incorporation papers or their execution have and what amounts to sufficient use of corporate powers. In a "conclusive evidence" or "conclusive proof" jurisdiction, de facto questions can arise only if the articles are not filed or the certificate is not issued, or if a corporation of some other state is involved. On the other hand, in states with statutes providing that a certified copy of the articles is only "prima facie evidence" or "evidence" of corporate existence, presumably only the burden of proof or the amount of proof is changed, and the traditional questions as to colorable compliance, use of the franchise, and the need of dealings on a corporate basis may still be raised.

In addition to adopting the Model Act provision on when corporate existence commences, some states have enacted a provision from the 1950 and 1969 versions of the Model Act, which stated: "All persons who assume to act as a corporation without authority so to do shall be jointly and severally liable for all debts and liabilities incurred or arising as a result thereof." The District of Columbia Court of Appeals held that the impact of this provision and the corporate commencement section, taken together, is "to

---

Corporations, 40 Harv. L. Rev. 521, 558–560 (1927); Edward H. Warren, Corporate Advantages Without Incorporation, 814–825 (1929).

[24]   One of the strongest cases on this point is Harrill v. Davis, 168 F. 187 (8th Cir. 1909), holding that four associates, who had actively engaged in the lumber business under a corporate name before filing the articles of incorporation in any public office and who never issued any shares of stock, could not escape individual liability.

[25]   *See* § 6.2.

eliminate the concepts of estoppel and de facto corporateness."[26] The court reasoned that one purpose of modern corporation statutes is to eliminate problems and confusion inherent in the de jure, de facto, and estoppel concepts. It concluded that under the District of Columbia equivalent of the Model Act there is no corporation de jure, de facto, or by estoppel before a certificate of incorporation is issued[27] and, further, that individuals assuming to act as a corporation before a certificate of incorporation has been issued will be held jointly and severally liable.[28]

In the Maryland case of *Cranson v. International Business Machines,*[29] because of an attorney's oversight the articles of incorporation had not been filed. A creditor of the company sought to hold its president personally liable on the ground that failure to file the articles precluded corporate existence. Although the court did not find it necessary to decide whether the failure to file absolutely ruled out a de facto corporation, the court held that the plaintiff was "estopped" from denying the corporation's existence. At the time of this decision, Maryland had a statutory section similar to the Model Act provision on when corporate existence commences.[30] The approach of the Maryland court seems highly preferable to the mechanistic, nothing-or-all (nothing before certificate issues; unassailable de jure corporation afterward) rule adopted in the District of Columbia.[31]

Statutes in a number of states forbid collateral attack on incorporation. The Delaware statute, for example, provides that "no corporation of this State and no person sued by any such corporation shall be permitted to assert the want of legal organization as a defense to any claim."[32] A provision of this kind seems to be merely declaratory of the common law and does not supersede the usual rules as to de facto corporations and corporations by estoppel.[33]

Correction of Corporate Defects Generally

In 2015, Delaware adopted novel provisions to its corporate law regarding ratification of corporate defects.[34] The statute is not limited to defective incorporation or failure to complete the formalities necessary for valid corporate existence, Section 204 of the Delaware General Corporations Code allows retroactive correction of corporate acts that were not validly approved or that contradicted the corporation's certificate of incorporation.[35] The correction of defects can thus be accomplished after the fact by the board of directors. Curing corporate defects under section 204 is retroactive. Thus, subsequent corporate actions that may have been defective as a result of the initial defective acts similarly are cured. Section 205 of the Delaware Code[36] supplements section 204, self-correction of defects, by allowing an application to the Delaware Court

---

[26]   Robertson v. Levy, 197 A.2d 443, 447 (D.C. 1964).

[27]   197 A.2d at 446.

[28]   197 A.2d at 447.

[29]   Cranson v. International Business Machines, 200 A.2d 33 (Md. 1964).

[30]   Md. Code Ann., Corp. & Ass'ns § 2–102(b) (2009), formerly Md. Code Ann. art. 23, § 131(b) (1966).

[31]   *See, e.g.,* Dargan v. Graves, 168 S.E.2d 306 (S.C. 1969) (recognizing estoppel).

[32]   Del. Code Ann. tit. 8, §§ 329(a) (2009), 7104(a) (2008).

[33]   Davis v. Stevens, 104 F. 235, 238 (D.S.D. 1900). In fact, the Delaware statute itself states that. Del. Code Ann. tit. 8, § 329(b) (2009).

[34]   Del. Code Ann. tit. 8, §§ 204, 205.

[35]   Del. Code Ann. tit. 8, § 204.

[36]   Del. Code Ann. tit. 8, § 205. *See* In re Numoda Corporation Shareholders Litigation, 2015 WL 402265 (Del. Ch. 2015), judgment entered, 2015 WL 1056143 (Del. Ch. 2015) and judgment aff'd, 128 A.3d 991 (Del. 2015) (validating corporation's contested capital structure).

of Chancery rather than internal approval under section 204. The statutory correction process supplements rather than preempts common law ratification. There is authority that section 205 cannot be used to invalidate prior corporate acts[37] nor to validate future acts.[38]

---

[37] In re Genelux Corporation, 126 A.3d 644 (Del. Ch. 2015), appeal dismissed, 2016 WL 3381420 (Del. 2016), subsequent determination, 2016 WL 3866609 (Del. 2016) and vacated in part on other grounds, 2016 WL 3866609 (Del. 2016).

[38] In re Baxter International Inc., C.A. No. 11609-CB, http://www.law360.com/articles/747097/new-del-rule-not-for-oking-future-actions-judge-says (Del. Ch. Jan. 15, 2016) (transcript).

Chapter 7

THE SEPARATE CORPORATE ENTITY: PRIVILEGE AND ITS LIMITATIONS

Table of Sections

§ 7.1 The Corporate Entity

Recognition of a corporate personality generally is considered to be the most distinct attribute of the corporation.[1] To speak of a corporation as "a legal person" is a convenient figure of speech used to describe the corporation as a legal unit, a separate concern with a capacity, like a person's, to hold property and make contracts, to sue and be sued, and to continue to exist notwithstanding changes of its shareholders or members.

If *A, B,* and *C* are incorporated into the A, B & C Co., the entity in its corporate capacity is the holder of the rights and liabilities arising from the transactions of the company. The property or rights acquired, or the liabilities incurred on behalf of the corporation, are treated as the property rights and liabilities of the corporate legal person distinct from those of the shareholders who comprise it.[2] A contract entered into by the shareholders of a corporation is not the contract of the corporation unless adopted by authority of its directors. Thus, if a sole shareholder borrows money on a personal note secured by shares of stock for the company's use and benefit even though the money is used to pay off corporate bills, the corporation is not liable on the note when credit was extended to the sole shareholder.[3] A corporation and its shareholders are not liable on each other's contracts. Shareholders' immunity from corporate obligations is one of the most important incidents and advantages of the separate legal entity and serves a useful

---

[1]   *See* Anderson v. Abbott, 321 U.S. 349, 361 (1944); *supra* § 1.2.

[2]   In Donnell v. Herring-Hall-Marvin Safe Co., 208 U.S. 267, 273 (1908), Justice Holmes observed: "A leading purpose of [corporation] statutes and of those who act under them is to interpose a non-conductor, through which, in matters of contract, it is impossible to see the men behind."

[3]   *E.g.,* In re John Koke Co., 38 F.2d 232 (9th Cir. 1930), *cert. denied,* 282 U.S. 840 (1930).

purpose in business life. Under some circumstances, however, sufficient equity may be shown to disregard the distinct legal personality and thereby pierce the corporate veil.

§ 7.2   Limited Liability Reconsidered

No principle is more engrained in corporate law than that shareholders enjoy limited liability. Indeed, limited shareholder liability is not simply a principle of corporate law, but a cornerstone of capitalism. Because of limited liability, a good deal of the enterprise's risks are shifted from owners to third parties. It is the tort or contractual claimant, not the corporation's shareholders, that bears the loss whenever the corporation's resources are insufficient to satisfy the claim. As seen before, limited liability became well established in this country by the middle of the nineteenth century.

A rich debate has recently ensued among economists and legal commentators (although not by any means divided along those lines) as to the desirability of a limited liability rule.[4] Among the advantages cited in support for limited liability is that it stimulates investment by placing a known cap on the loss any investors can expect to incur. Limited liability therefore encourages risk-taking activity by both managers and investors: managers may more easily raise the funds from investors whose risk in any one venture is limited by the amount invested and whose overall risk is lowered through diversification.

Limited liability also promotes efficiency because it facilitates even greater divisions of labor than would otherwise exist.[5] Investors may commit to others the more specialized tasks of managing a particular business so that investors may pursue full-time the vocation for which they are better suited; thus, limited liability not only spawns the large public corporations that are characterized by the division of ownership and management, but also nurtures the creation of a large managerial class. Additionally, it is argued that to abandon limited liability would increase the agency costs, because shareholders would seek even greater bonding and monitoring activities to assure that their managers' goals with respect to risk exposure are congruent with those of the owners.

It has also been argued that abandonment to limited liability will discourage investment in large corporations by large, wealthy investors.[6] Certainly one must recognize that as the corporation increases in size the potential of the claims it may produce grows exponentially and that in a world without limited liability the likely target for any unsatisfied claim would be the financial institutions that typically hold the largest ownership blocks in public corporations. In this regard, it can be seen that one effect of limited liability is that it nurtures diversification—that is, portfolio investment strategies. If there were unlimited liability, one large claim by the unsatisfied creditors of a company held in an investor's portfolio could well wipe out the investor. This fear could cause investors to reasonably determine that investing in fewer rather than more companies, basically a nondiversification strategy, is wise because to

---

[4]   *See, e.g.,* Kenneth Arrow, Essays on the Theory of Risk Bearing 139–143 (1971); Richard Posner, Economic Analysis of Law § 14.3 (7th ed. 2007); Stephen M. Bainbridge, Abolishing Veil Piercing, 26 Iowa J. Corp. L. 479 (2001).

[5]   Frank Easterbrook & Daniel Fischel, Limited Liability and the Corporation, 52 U. Chi. L. Rev. 89, 93–94 (1985).

[6]   *See* Henry Manne, Our Two Corporation Systems: Law and Economics, 53 Va. L. Rev. 259, 262 (1967).

hold more stocks actually increases the risk of personal liability.[7] The virtue of limited liability is also its vice; limited liability encourages corporations to engage in riskier or more damaging endeavors because owners are allowed to externalize the enterprise's costs (that is, they shift to third parties the costs created by the enterprise beyond its net worth and insurance).

Tort claimants are particularly vulnerable in the damaging wake created by limited liability because they generally lack victims' insurance or other means to spread the risk externalized on to them. Some have further argued that limited liability erodes both the deterrent and compensatory objectives of tort law.[8] More sophisticated claimants, such as bondholders and large creditors, however, may contract around limited liability rules to reduce their risk and may also have a greater capacity to spread their risk, such as through diversification of their lending or the rate of interest charged for loans. The concerns for the impact that a limited liability rule has on spreading risk provides an interesting juxtaposition with how responsibility for torts is addressed in other contexts. Much of our approach to who should be responsible for torts is based on judgments regarding who can more efficiently bear the cost of the activity. A similar inquiry in a context where the corporation is the tortfeasor may well reveal that the shareholders are the most efficient risk bearers, especially if liability is shared on a strict pro rata basis among stockholders.[9]

The above would suggest that the most appealing cases for disregarding the corporation's separate entity and imposing liability on the shareholders would be cases involving tort claimants. As is seen below, this is not the case. Professor Robert Thompson conducted an extensive empirical study of 1600 corporate piercing-the-veil cases.[10] Among his study findings are the following:[11]

---

[7]   See David W. Leebron, Limited Liability, Tort Victims, and Creditors, 91 Colum. L. Rev. 1565, 1597 (1991).

[8]   See Christopher Stone, The Place of Enterprise Liability in the Control of Corporate Conduct, 90 Yale L.J. 1 (1980). Dean Clark has suggested several methods of introducing greater fairness into a liability system. See Robert C. Clark, Duties of the Corporate Debtor to Its Creditors, 90 Harv. L. Rev. 505, 540–553 (1977).

[9]   See David W. Leebron, Limited Liability, Tort Victims, and Creditors, 91 Colum. L. Rev. 1565, 1595 (1991).

[10]   Robert Thompson, Piercing the Corporate Veil: An Empirical Study, 76 Cornell L. Rev. 1036 (1991). For a more recent empirical analysis see Christina L. Boyd & David A. Hoffman, Disputing Limited Liability, 104 Nw. U. L. Rev. (forthcoming 2016).

[11]   Robert Thompson, Piercing the Corporate Veil: An Empirical Study, 76 Cornell L. Rev. 1036, 1058 (1991). Professor Thompson has examined his sample further. See Robert B. Thompson, The Limits of Liability in the New Limited Liability Entities, 32 Wake Forest L. Rev. 1 (1997) (piercing has occurred only within corporate groups or in close corporations with fewer than ten shareholders; most successful piercing cases involve active manager-shareholders or corporate groups in which the parent corporation named managers of the subsidiary). In the latest extension of his sample to 3,800 cases, Professor Thomson concludes courts are less likely to pierce corporate veils in cases involving tort as compared with contract liability. Robert B. Thompson, Piercing the Veil Within Corporate Groups: Corporate Shareholders as Mere Investors, 13 Conn. J. Int'l Law 379 (1999).

Context	Total Cases	Piercing Cases	Cases Not Piercing	% Piercing
Contract	779	327	452	41.98
Tort	226	70	156	30.97
Criminal	15	10	5	66.67
Statute	552	224	328	40.58

Others have also empirically studied veil-piercing in decisions. One study found that courts pierce twice as often to hold individuals liable as they do to hold entities (where a parent-subsidiary relationship exists), that veil piercing arguments are more successful in contract cases than tort cases (whereas, with regression analysis, the type of claim—tort vs. contract—does not bear a statistical relationship to explain *why* the veil was pierced in the context of other factors before a court), that appellate courts are far more likely to pierce the veil than trial courts in cases in which the dominant stockholder is an individual (but no difference was observed in the parent-subsidiary context), and that over time there does not appear to be any statistically significant change in the percentage of cases in which the veil piercing argument succeeds.[12] Another study concluded that (voluntary creditor is 17 percent more likely to succeed in veil piercing claim than involuntary, *e.g.*, tort, claimant and the overall success rate in piercing the veil is inversely related to the number of employees of the entity to be pierced). All studies conclude that doctrine in this area is not clear so that results are difficult to predict, but overall success rates are such that veil piercing remains a most attractive option for those seeking payment of their claims.[13]

The differences in the above contexts in which the issue of piercing the corporate veil arises underscores several important considerations in this area. First, the interest to be served is not the same in each context, so that one should expect to find a greater willingness in some areas to pierce than in others. For example, statutory applications fulfill the legislative policy of regulating all aspects of an economic unit rather than a division that has been discretely carved out of that unit by the entire unit's owners. Second, the consequences of piercing the veil are not the same in all contexts. For example, many of the statutory applications of the doctrine do not involve visiting upon the pierced corporation's owners substantial damages; courts in this context can be expected to be less sympathetic to the defendant than in a case where the consequence of piercing the veil is to cause the corporation's owners to dig deep into their pockets. A third consideration is that the contractual context is far more likely to present the type of facts that make a more appealing case for piercing the veil than does a case involving an unsatisfied tort claimant. What is so surprising is that the above widely varying results have occurred under a doctrine whose content the courts purport to apply evenly in all veil-piercing contexts.

The expanding obligations of bank holding companies is one area of regulation that can be rationalized along the lines of those who argue that the abandonment of limited

---

[12] *See*, John H. Matheson, Why Courts Pierce: An Empirical Study of Piercing the Corporate Veil, 7 Berkeley Bus. L. J. 1 (2010). *But see* Peter B. Oh, Veil Piercing, 89 Tex. L. Rev. 81 (2010) (finding higher percentage of success in tort than contract claims, but documenting that success in either category rises with allegations of fraudulent misrepresentations were committed against the claimant, or that assets were siphoned away by the dominant stockholder, or that the firm was undercapitalized).

[13] Christina L. Boyd & David A. Hoffman, Disputing Limited Liability, 104 Nw. U. L. Rev. 853 (2010).

liability will lead to greater efficiency by forcing corporations to internalize their full costs. During the last part of the twentieth century, the regulatory burdens and accompanying sanctions of bank holding companies expanded as a means to address irresponsible risk taking in their subsidiary banks. This regulatory approach can be seen as a discrete intrusion on the doctrine of limited liability that is justified as a means to address the better access to information that the holding company has than would government regulators and as a means of reducing the moral hazard problem that otherwise accompanies limited liability.[14]

Finally, the existence of an entity, whether it be a corporation or LLC, does not excuse the actor, whether he be a shareholder, director or officer, for his personal misconduct or contractual obligations. Individuals remain responsible for their tortious conduct as well as contracts that are personally entered into with others, despite simultaneously acting in a representative capacity for the corporation or LLC. Thus, a member-manager of an LLC who commits a tort is personally liable to the person harmed, even though acting within the scope of the LLC's business.[15]

§ 7.3   Approaches Used to Disregard the Corporate Entity

In general, a corporation may exist and act as an entity or legal unit separate and apart from its shareholders. In many cases, however, the courts place limitations on this privilege. These limitations usually are expressed in terms of "disregarding the corporate fiction," "piercing the corporate veil," or "looking at the substance of the business operation rather than at its form."[16]

The disregard of the corporate entity occurs in a variety of settings, the most common being to impose personal liability on the corporation's stockholders. If the corporation is insolvent, its unsatisfied creditors, including any tort claimants, can be expected to pursue all reasonable avenues to reach the personal assets of its shareholders by arguing that the corporation is not truly a separate entity. Sometimes it is important to determine whether the real party in interest is the corporation or an individual. For example, state usury laws frequently apply if the borrower is an individual but not if the borrower is a corporation. Cases have therefore posed the question whether the corporate entity should be disregarded for the purpose of applying the state usury law. Another illustration where holding a statute had been violated turned on whether to disregard the separate identity of a corporation arose in *Sundaco, Inc. v. State*,[17] where, to circumvent a state law mandating that businesses close on alternate weekends, a subsidiary corporation was formed to operate the business on the weekends that the business was not being operated by its parent.

If the separate corporate capacity is used dishonestly, such as to evade obligations or statutory restrictions, the courts will intervene to prevent the abuse.[18] The figurative terminology and formulae invoked by the judges to disregard legal fictions often obscure

---

[14]   *See* Howell Jackson, The Expanding Obligations of Financial Holding Companies, 107 Harv. L. Rev. 507, 565–566, 570–571 (1994).

[15]   *See, e.g.*, Mbahaba v. Morgan, 44 A.3d 472 (N.H. 2012).

[16]   *See, e.g.*, Wachovia Securities, LLC v. Banco Panamericano, Inc., 674 F.3d 743 (7th Cir. 2012). Minton v. Cayaney, 364 P.2d 473 (Cal. 1961).

[17]   Sundaco, Inc. v. State, 463 S.W.2d 528 (Tex. Civ. App. 1970).

[18]   *See, e.g.*, Toshiba Am. Med. Sys., Inc. v. Mobile Med. Sys., Inc., 730 A.2d 1219, 1223 (Conn. App. Ct. 1999) (defendant held personally liable after conveying funds from one corporation to another so as to avoid payment on contracts made by first corporation).

the real issues presented.[19] Concepts such as "alter ego" and "instrumentality" do not provide general formulae applicable in all cases; each set of circumstances must be considered by the court on its merits.[20] The facts presented must demonstrate some misuse of the corporate privilege or establish a need to limit it in order to do justice.[21] Disregard of the separate corporate entity privilege for one purpose does not mean necessarily that it will be disregarded for other purposes.[22] The absence of clear-cut rules and the reliance on the equities of each fact situation make it difficult to generalize as to the factors that will lead a court to find individual shareholder liability. Thus, drawing the line between a proper use of corporate form in order to avoid personal liability and an abuse of corporate form to defraud a corporation's creditor is sometimes quite difficult.[23]

There are three primary variants within the "piercing the corporate veil" jurisprudence—(1) the "instrumentality" doctrine, (2) the "alter ego" doctrine, and (3) the "identity" doctrine.[24] The instrumentality doctrine's overall approach focuses on the presence of three factors, as reflected in the frequently cited language of its leading case, *Lowendahl v. Baltimore & Ohio Railroad:*[25]

(1) Control, not merely majority or complete stock control, but complete domination, not only of finances, but of policy and business practices in respect to the transaction attacked so that the corporate entity had at the time no separate mind, will, or existence of its own; and

(2) Such control must have been used by the defendant to commit fraud or wrong, to perpetuate the violation of a statutory or other positive legal duty, or a dishonest and unjust act in contravention of the plaintiff's legal rights; and

(3) The aforesaid control and breach of duty must proximately cause the injury or unjust loss complained of.[26]

The "alter ego" doctrine is stated with a far greater economy of words but with much less precision than the statement of instrumentality doctrine. The alter ego doctrine holds that it is appropriate to pierce the veil when (1) a unity of ownership and interests exists between the corporation and its controlling stockholder such that the corporation has ceased to exist as a separate entity and the corporation has been relegated to the status of the controlling stockholder's alter ego and (2) to recognize the corporation and

---

[19] *See* Robert W. Hamilton, The Corporate Entity, 49 Tex. L. Rev. 979, 983 (1971).

[20] *E.g.,* DeWitt Truck Brokers, Inc. v. W. Ray Flemming Fruit Co., 540 F.2d 681 (4th Cir. 1976) (South Carolina law).

[21] Pepper v. Litton, 308 U.S. 295, 310 (1939).

[22] Cooperman v. Unemployment Ins. Appeals Bd., 122 Cal.Rptr. 127, 132 (Ct. App. 1975).

[23] *Compare* Yacker v. Weiner, 263 A.2d 188 (N.J. Super. Ct. Ch. 1970) (corporate entity disregarded when used as subterfuge) *with* Bartle v. Home Owners Co-op., Inc., 127 N.E.2d 832 (N.Y. 1955) (law permits use of corporate entity to limit liability).

[24] Phillip I. Blumberg, The Law of Corporate Groups: Tort, Contract, and Other Common Law Problems in the Substantive Law of Parent and Subsidiary Corporation 111 (1987).

[25] Lowendahl v. Baltimore & Ohio Railroad, 287 N.Y.S. 62 (App. Div.), *aff'd,* 6 N.E.2d 56 (N.Y. 1936).

[26] *Id. See, e.g.,* Breen v. Judge, 124 Conn. App. 147, 4 A.3d 326 (2010) (listing factors indicative of domination).

its controlling stockholder as separate entities would be sanctioning fraud or would lead to an inequitable result.[27]

The leading case for the "identity" doctrine is *Zaist v. Olson*,[28] where the court states:

> If plaintiff can show that there was such a unity of interest and ownership that the independence of the corporations had in effect ceased or had never begun, an adherence to the fiction of separate identity would serve only to defeat justice and equity by permitting the economic entity to escape liability arising out of an operation of one corporation for the benefit of the whole enterprise.[29]

Although stock ownership is a significant factor under the "identity" approach, a court may impose personal liability on a controlling person even if he or she is not a shareholder.[30]

On close scrutiny, none of the three above variants of "piercing the veil" offers precision or a characteristic that distinguishes it from the other two variants. In practice, they are virtually indistinguishable from one another, and the outcome of the cases does not appear to depend on which standard is applied.[31] As commentators have frequently noted, the results in cases appear guided not so much by the doctrine invoked[32] as by the "mist of metaphors."[33] The imprecision is highlighted by veil piercing courts rarely considering as a threshold matter what is the appropriate choice of law rule to apply in determining whether to disregard the corporate entity. The choice of law issue is relevant because, for example, creditors wishing to establish the controlling stockholder is the corporation's alter ego may not be domiciled in the forum state and the corporation may be also be incorporated elsewhere. Just what law should apply in such a matter? Courts rarely discuss the applicable choice of law rule, even in disputes involving truly foreign corporations.[34]

§ 7.4 Lack of Formality and Confusion of Affairs as Bases for Piercing the Corporate Veil

When the dominant shareholders treat the corporate business and property as their own and the affairs of the corporation and the shareholders are confused or intermingled, the separate corporate entity no longer can be respected. If the shareholders themselves

---

[27] *See*, Southern Cal. Fed. Sav. & Loan Assoc. v. United States, 422 F.3d 1319 (Fed. Cir. 2005) (applying California law) (court may disregard corporate entity to prevent grave injustice, including injustice to shareholders).

[28] Zaist v. Olson, 227 A.2d 552 (1967).

[29] Zaist v. Olson, 227 A.2d 552, 558 (1967).

[30] McCormick v. City of Dillingham, 16 P.3d 735, 744 (Alaska 2001); LFC Marketing Group, Inc. v. Loomis, 8 P.3d 841, 847 (Nev. 2000).

[31] Phillip I. Blumberg, The Law of Corporate Groups: Tort, Contract, and Other Common Law Problems in the Substantive Law of Parent and Subsidiary Corporation 120 (1987).

[32] *See, e.g.*, Elvin R. Latty, Subsidiaries and Affiliated Corporations 157–158 (1936); Robert W. Hamilton, The Corporate Entity, 49 Tex. L. Rev. 979 (1971).

[33] Berkey v. Third Ave. Ry., 155 N.E. 58, 61 (1926) (J. Cardozo).

[34] *See, e.g.*, King Fung Tsang, Applicable Law in Piercing the Corporate Veil in the United States: A Choice With No Choice, 10 J. Private Int'l Law 227 (2014)(73 percent of 2012 veil piercing cases involving diverse residency among the parties including the corporation courts did not conduct a choice of law inquiry).

disregard the separateness of the corporation, the courts also will disregard it so far as necessary to protect individual and corporate creditors.[35]

When the same facts arise in the parent-subsidiary context, courts frequently characterize the parent's control as that of treating the subsidiary as though it is merely a department of the parent company.[36] Similarly, a court may disregard separate entities when related corporations under common control fail to observe the formal barriers between them.[37]

A frequent factor supporting a finding of confusion is the failure to comply with corporate formalities in the conduct of the corporation's business.[38] Lapses in corporate formalities that are emphasized in veil-piercing cases are: failing to hold stockholders' or directors' meetings;[39] directing receipts to the controlling stockholder's bank account and using a single endorsement stamp for all affiliated companies;[40] the parent company's board of directors establishing salaries, appointing auditors, and declaring dividends of its subsidiary;[41] and the parent company's providing interest-free loans to its subsidiary without documenting those loans with promissory notes.[42]

Disregard of corporate formalities, however, does not appear sufficient by itself to pierce the corporate veil.[43] Some have even sought to restrict this factor further by requiring a causal relationship between the failure to observe corporate formalities and the fraud or inequitable result that would follow if the veil were not pierced.[44] The mere fact that the business's affairs have been carried out with strict obeisance to corporate formalities, however, does not immunize the corporation from having its separate entity disregarded if other factors justify piercing the corporate veil.[45] The want of corporate formalities is but one consideration, and courts customarily require some suggestion of fraud, illegality, or unfairness that will result if the veil is not disregarded.[46] A disregard of form standing by itself, thus, will not be enough to pierce the corporate veil.[47]

A related consideration is whether there has been mingling of business or assets of the controlling stockholder and the corporation or among affiliated corporations. *Kramer v. Keys,*[48] for example, found sufficient justification to pierce the corporate veil where the controlling stockholder had included his personal assets among those that were

---

[35]   Gardemal v. Westin Hotel Co., 186 F.3d 588, 593 (5th Cir. 1999) (citing Castleberry v. Branscum, 721 S.W.2d 270, 272 (Tex. 1986)).

[36]   Consolidated Rock Prods. Co. v. Du Bois, 312 U.S. 510 (1941).

[37]   *See* NLRB v. G & T Terminal Packaging Co., 246 F.3d 103, 118–119 (2d Cir. 2001).

[38]   *See, e.g.,* Walter E. Heller & Co. v. Video Innovations, Inc., 730 F.2d 50, 53 (2d Cir. 1984).

[39]   *See, e.g.,* Atelier Constantin Popescu, LLC v. JC Corp., 134 Conn. App. 731, 49 A.3d 1003 (2012); Fiumetto v. Garrett Enters., 749 N.E.2d 992, 1006 (Ill. App. Ct. 2001).

[40]   *See* Brown v. Benton Creosoting Co., 147 So.2d 89, 93 (La. Ct. App. 1962).

[41]   *See, e.g.,* Gentry v. Credit Plan Corp., 528 S.W.2d 571 (Tex. 1975).

[42]   *See* Doe v. Unocal Corp., 248 F.3d 915, 927 (9th Cir. 2001).

[43]   Soloman v. Western Hills Dev. Co., 312 N.W.2d 428, 434 (Mich. Ct. App. 1981).

[44]   *See* Transamerica Cash Reserve, Inc. v. Dixie Power & Water, 789 P.2d 24 (Utah 1990).

[45]   *See, e.g.,* Bridas S.A.P.I.C. v. Government of Turkm., 447 F.3d 411, 419–420 (5th Cir. 2006).

[46]   *See, e.g.,* Pepsi-Cola Metro. Bottling Co. v. Checkers, Inc., 754 F.2d 10 (1st Cir. 1985).

[47]   *See, e.g.,* Rogerson Hiller Corp. v. Port of Port Angeles, 982 P.2d 131, 134 (Wash. App. 1999) ("Corporate disregard requires proof of two elements: 'first, the corporate form must be intentionally used to violate or evade a duty; second, disregard must be "necessary and required to prevent unjustified loss to the injured party" ' "), quoting from and relying on Meisel v. M & N Modern Hydraulic Press Co., 645 P.2d 689 (Wash. 1982).

[48]   Kramer v. Keys, 643 F.2d 382, 385–386 n.4 (5th Cir. 1981).

depreciated on the corporation's tax return, had executed the company leases and had filed other company reports in his own name, and had endorsed company checks by signing his own name. Cases that have pierced the veil because of mingling of assets and affairs customarily involve facts suggesting there has been such control exercised over the corporation's assets by its dominant stockholder that the stockholder has essentially ignored the corporation as a distinct entity.[49]

There are several rationales that can be suggested as to why mingling or a lack of obeisance to corporate formalities should lead to the corporation's separate entity being disregarded. One theory is that logic compels treating the dominated corporation and its controlling stockholder as inseparable because the dominant stockholder has chosen to ignore the corporation as a distinct entity. This reasoning does not itself answer why such draconian results should follow from the fact that the dominant shareholder has caused the corporation to conduct its business informally. One would expect some greater purpose should underlie the imposition of personal liability on the dominant stockholder than the rather hollow purpose of assuring the corporation's separate personality is preserved through a respect for formal operations.

Veil piercing for lack of corporate formalities and the mingling of affairs and assets are most appropriate where the facts are sufficiently strong to create a serious doubt whether creditors have been prejudiced by the transfer of corporate assets without sufficient consideration. This is most easily established in cases where there has been mingling of affairs or assets. A breach of corporate formalities should also be sufficient where the breach is so pervasive as to raise grave concerns that it is not possible to determine whether the corporate assets had ever been transferred to its stockholders without fair consideration or the lack of formalities may have caused a sufficient misimpression of personal rather than corporate responsibility for the debts contracted.

§ 7.5 Dominating the Corporation's Affairs as the Basis for Piercing the Corporate Veil

A frequent consideration in veil-piercing cases is whether the controlling stockholder has so dominated the affairs of the corporation that the corporation has no existence of its own. Usually there is the additional requirement that fraud, illegality, or gross unfairness will result if the corporate existence is not disregarded.[50] Many, if not most, veil-piercing claims pursue a shareholder who has abused the corporate form.[51] Veil-piercing is not, however, limited to controlling shareholders. It can also be applied to others who dominate the corporation even if they are not shareholders, officers or directors.[52] Thus, for example, on appropriate facts a court may disregard the limited

---

[49] *See, e.g.,* NLRB v. Bolivar-Tees, Inc., 551 F.3d 722, 729 (8th Cir. 2008).

[50] *See, e.g.,* Bridas S.A.P.I.C. v. Government of Turkm., 447 F.3d 411, 417 (5th Cir. 2006).

[51] *See, e.g.,* Buckley v. Abuzir, 8 N.E.3d 1166 (Ill. Ct. App. 1st Dist. 2014) (discussing the many jurisdictions with law to the same effect).

[52] Calipjo v. Purdy, 439 P.3d 218 (Haw. 2019) (jury question whether sole owner was alter ego of corporation and LLC); Buckley v. Abuzir, 8 N.E.3d 1166 (Ill. Ct. App. 1st Dist. 2014) (defendant dominated the corporation which was used as a "dummy" and had no directors or officers). *See also, e.g.,* Freeman v. Complex Computing Co., 119 F.3d 1044 (2d Cir.1997) (defendant was not a shareholder, officer, director, or employee of the corporation).

liability shield with respect to the moving force beyond a corporation that never issued shares.[53]

Domination can be the basis of piercing to an individual shareholder[54] as well as to a parent corporation. Domination is far more frequently a consideration in the parent-subsidiary context than in cases in which the veil is being pierced to reach an individual stockholder.[55] The lesser role of domination in veil-piercing cases involving individual-close corporations is a sensible recognition that it defies even metaphysics to expect such a corporate entity to have a mind or soul distinct from its controlling stockholder. In contrast, even though it is equally unrealistic to expect a subsidiary to act independently of its parent corporation's strategies and wishes, both parent and subsidiary corporations can be expected to at least formalistically separate their decision-making so as to avoid creating the false impression that the subsidiary is but a branch or division of the parent corporation. Such an impression assumes significance because it misrepresents the status of the subsidiary to third parties, and also suggests a mingling of assets and affairs of the two entities such that there may be fraud on creditors lurking in the background. There also may be facts supporting the conclusion that the subsidiary has no independent profit objective such that creditors are presented with a corporate debtor that has only down-side risks.[56]

Professor Blumberg identifies four factors that are frequently emphasized in parent-subsidiary veil-piercing cases finding undue domination of the subsidiary's affairs:

(1)   the parent's participation in day-to-day operations;

(2)   the parent's determination of important policy decisions;

(3)   the parent's determination of the subsidiary's business decisions, bypassing the subsidiary's directors and officers;

(4)   the parent's issuance of instructions to the subsidiary's personnel or use of its own personnel in the conduct of the subsidiary's affairs.[57]

§ 7.6   Inadequate Capitalization as a Factor for Piercing the Veil

Inadequate capitalization is frequently a factor considered by courts in veil-piercing cases.[58] This consideration most frequently appears in tort cases involving close

---

[53]   *See, e.g.,* Minton v. Cavaney, 56 Cal.2d 576 (1961) (defendant was attorney who set up corporation that never issued shares); Buckley v. Abuzir, 8 N.E.3d 1166 (Ill. Ct. App. 1st Dist. 2014) (non-shareholder set up dummy corporation and could be subject to a claim based on piercing the corporate veil).

[54]   *See, e.g.,* Carter Jones Lumber Co. v. LTV Steel Co., 237 F.3d 745 (6th Cir. 2001).

[55]   *See, e.g.,* William J. Rands, Domination of a Subsidiary by a Parent, 32 Ind. L. Rev. 421 (1999).

[56]   *See* Clinical Components, Inc. v. Leffler Indus., Inc., 1997 WL 28246, at *6 (Ohio Ct. App. 1997) (creditors efforts to pierce corporate veil withstood summary judgment where alleged that wholly owned subsidiary paid significant fees for consulting services to parent when subsidiary's substantial debts remained outstanding).

[57]   Phillip I. Blumberg, The Law of Corporate Groups: Problems of Parent and Subsidiary Corporations Under Statutory Law of General Application 188 (1989).

[58]   *See, e.g.,* HOK Sport, Inc. v. FC Des Moines, L.C., 495 F.3d 927, 936 (8th Cir. 2007).

corporations and in the parent-subsidiary context.[59] *Minton v. Cavney*[60] is the leading case for a seemingly aggressive use of inadequate capitalization as a grounds to pierce the corporate veil. Plaintiff had secured a $10,000 tort judgment against the corporation for the death of her daughter, who had drowned in the corporation's swimming pool. The corporation operated a public swimming pool in a facility it leased and had received no consideration for its stock. Justice Roger Traynor reasoned that there had been "no attempt to provide adequate capitalization," reasoning the corporation's "capital was 'trifling compared with the business to be done and the risks of loss.' "[61] The court therefore upheld the complaint against a shareholder with a one-third interest who was also an officer and director of the corporation.

Minton stands alone as a case that pierced the veil solely for inadequate capitalization. Subsequent cases have relegated inadequate capitalization to one of many factors courts can consider to determine whether to disregard the corporate entity.[62] Even in *Automotriz Del Golfo De California v. Resnick,*[63] the case heavily relied on by *Minton*, there were factors in addition to the court's finding that $5,000 capital was inadequate for a business whose monthly gross receipts were $100,000–$150,000. *Minton* can therefore be seen as a case where it was not simply a matter of capital inadequacy but where there was no attempt to provide any capitalization. This view brings it closer to the cases that have pierced the veil when the facts suggest the corporation is a sham.[64]

In a leading case, the New York Court of Appeals in *Walkovszky v. Carlton*[65] refused to apply the "thin capitalization" theory of piercing the corporate veil. The individual defendant was the sole shareholder of ten corporations, each of which owned two taxicabs and carried only the minimum amount of automobile insurance allowed by the law. The plaintiff was injured due to the negligence of one of defendant's drivers. The court, despite a vigorous dissent, deferred to the legislature in holding that by maintaining the statutory minimum insurance the corporation was not too thinly capitalized. The only basis for piercing the corporate veil would be on a showing that there was such an intermingling of assets as to constitute an abuse of the corporate privilege.[66] Thus, capital inadequacy alone is not generally enough for the entity to be disregarded.

On close inspection, the role of inadequate capitalization is best left as a surrogate for the promoter's possible bad faith as that factor may relate on the overall equities of

---

[59] *See* Phillip I. Blumberg, The Law of Corporate Groups: Problems of Parent and Subsidiary Corporations Under Statutory Law of General Application 202 (1989).

[60] Minton v. Cavaney, 364 P.2d 473 (Cal. 1961).

[61] 364 P.2d at 475, quoting Automotriz Del Golfo De Cal. v. Resnick, 306 P.2d 1, 4 (Cal. 1957).

[62] *See, e.g.,* Hambleton Bros. Lumber Co. v. Balkin Enters., 397 F.3d 1217, 1229 (9th Cir. 2005) ("The mere fact that the two entrepreneurs began their corporation with a small amount of capital is, without more, insufficient to justify the 'extraordinary remedy' of piercing the veil.").

[63] Automotriz Del Golfo De California v. Resnick, 306 P.2d 1 (1957).

[64] *See, e.g.,* Wesco Mfg. v. Tropical Attractions of Palm Beach, Inc., 833 F.2d 1484 (11th Cir. 1987); Hart v. Steel Products, Inc., 666 N.E.2d 1270 (Ind. Ct. App. 1996) (undercapitalization and fraud justified piercing the veil).

[65] Walkovszky v. Carlton, 223 N.E.2d 6 (N.Y. 1966).

[66] The plaintiff subsequently amended her complaint to comport with this alter-ego rationale, and the cause of action was sustained. Walkovszky v. Carlton, 287 N.Y.S.2d 546 (App. Div.), *aff'd*, 244 N.E.2d 55 (N.Y. 1968). *See, e.g.,* Wachovia Securities, LLC v. Banco Panamericano, Inc., 674 F.3d 743 (7th Cir. 2012)(veil pierced upon evidence of both inadequate capitalization and that the defendants abused the corporate form by engaging in various transactions that constituted a financial shell game).

disregarding the corporate entity.[67] Consider in this regard that the inadequacy of the firm's capital is to be measured at the time of the corporation's inception.[68] Capital must then have been sufficient to meet the prospective risks of the business in which the corporation is to engage.[69]

Testing capital adequacy at the corporation's inception and evaluating its amount strictly in terms of the magnitude of future business risks introduce a good deal of ambiguity and unreasonableness into the equation. Are the risks to be perceived only those that are normal for a business, or do they include a highly unusual tort claim that greatly exceeds the firm's liability insurance?[70] Does the test demand that the total amount the shareholders invest must literally equal the present value of all future liabilities of the firm or does it entail some lesser amount that is simply necessary to launch the firm such that its future cash flows will meet its normal operating expenses? The former is clearly an unreasonable demand because no company can be expected to endow its future operating expenses and liabilities as a precondition to opening its doors. As for gauging capital adequacy in terms of massing assets sufficient to generate a positive cash flow, it must be borne in mind that the mere fact a business fails in terms that it produced a negative, rather than a positive, cash flow is customarily explained by a good many factors other than the relative amount invested in the firm. And to require an investment that assures a positive cash flow surely will have a chilling effect on entrepreneurial activity because a central risk of any business venture is that it will not, because of competition and other market forces, be able to generate a cash flow sufficient to support itself. It would therefore appear that inadequate capitalization has correctly assumed a limited role in veil-piercing cases, that of being a surrogate for the probable bad faith of the firm's promoters.

§ 7.7 Definitions: "Parent Company," "Holding Company," "Subsidiary," and "Affiliate"

Subsidiary and affiliated corporations have become important instruments of large-scale business. The same shareholder or group of shareholders may form or acquire various affiliated corporations for use as related branches of an enterprise under the unified management of common directors and officers. Much the same result is accomplished by subincorporation, when a parent or holding company reincorporates itself and splits its personality into several branches of the business.

A corporation with the power to elect a majority of the directors of another corporation and thus exercise working control is a parent company with reference to the corporation so controlled.[71] The parent company may have this power directly by virtue of its controlling equity interest or indirectly through another corporation or series of

---

[67] *See, e.g.,* Haynes v. Edgerson, 240 S.W.3d 189, 197 (Mo. Ct. App. 2007) ("Such undercapitalization is circumstantial evidence of an improper or reckless disregard for the rights of others.").

[68] *See, e.g.,* Trustees of the Nat'l Elevator Indus. Pension, Health Benefit & Educ. Funds v. Lutyk, 332 F.3d 188, 196 (3d Cir. 2003).

[69] *See* Pfohl Bros. Landfill Site Steering Comm. v. Allied Waste Sys., 255 F. Supp. 2d 134, 181 (W.D.N.Y. 2003) (when piercing the corporate veil in a CERCLA action "the inadequate capitalization factor pertains only to capitalization 'in light of the purposes for which the corporation was organized.' ").

[70] On the question whether liability insurance can serve as a substitute for capital, *see* Walkovszky v. Carlton, 223 N.E.2d 6 (N.Y. 1966).

[71] A "parent corporation" is one that has working control through stock ownership of its subsidiary corporations. Culcal Stylco, Inc. v. Vornado, Inc., 103 Cal.Rptr. 419, 421 (Ct. App. 1972).

corporations. The term "holding company"[72] is used most frequently to refer to a corporation created specifically to acquire and hold shares in other corporations for investment purposes, with or without actual control. However, the term sometimes is used interchangeably with "parent company" when the corporation has sufficient equity interest in, or power of control over, another corporation to elect its directors and influence its management.[73]

A corporation subject to control by a parent or holding company is a "subsidiary"[74] of the controlling company, even when it may in turn be the parent or holding company of a third corporation. Corporations related to each other by common control of voting stock and operated as parts of a system or enterprise are "affiliates."[75]

§ 7.8 Disregarding the Separate Entity in the Parent-Subsidiary Context

Problems regarding the corporate entity frequently arise within the context of parent and subsidiary or between affiliated corporations. The same principles apply here as to individual shareholders and their corporations. There is no general formula that furnishes an objective test to determine shareholder liability for the torts or contracts of controlled corporations. Courts exercise their discretion to prevent abuses and regulate the privilege of separate corporate capacities, and in doing so they weigh various factors in deciding the question.[76] At the same time courts will not ordinarily disregard the separation of corporate entities in the absence of a showing that injustice or unfairness would otherwise result.[77]

---

[72] *See, e.g.,* 12 U.S.C. § 1841(a)(1) (2001) (" 'bank holding company' means any company which has control over any bank").

[73] *E.g.,* Kelley, Glover & Vale, Inc. v. Heitman, 44 N.E.2d 981 (Ind. 1942), *cert. denied,* 319 U.S. 762 (1943).

[74] When a parent owns all of the shares of another company, this is sometimes referred to as a wholly-owned subsidiary. *See* Danziger v. Luse, 815 N.E.2d 658, 669 (Ohio 2004). For a somewhat curious definition, *see* 15 U.S.C. § 80a–2(a)(43) (2009) (" '[w]holly-owned subsidiary' of a person means a company 95 per centum or more of the outstanding voting securities of which are owned by such person, or by a company which, within the meaning of this paragraph, is a wholly-owned subsidiary"). *Cf., e.g.,* the definition of "fully-owned subsidiary" in 17 C.F.R. § 270.17a–3(b) (2008) as a subsidiary *all* of whose securities are owned by the parent corporation or other fully-owned subsidiaries.

[75] A typical definition of affiliate is found in the federal securities laws:

An *affiliate* of, or person affiliated with, a specified person shall mean a person that directly, or indirectly through one or more intermediaries, controls or is controlled by, or is under common control with, the person specified.

SEC Rule 501(b), 17 C.F.R. § 230.501(b) (2008). *Accord, e.g.,* 17 C.F.R. § 230.405 (2008). *See also, e.g.,* the definition of control in SEC Rule 405:

The term *control* (including the terms *controlling, controlled by* and *under common control with*) means the possession, direct or indirect, of the power to direct or cause the direction of the management and policies of a person, whether through the ownership of voting securities, by contract, or otherwise.

Id.

The Delaware Supreme Court defines an "affiliate" as a corporation that is related to another corporation by shareholdings or other means of control. Delaware Ins. Guar. Ass'n v. Christiana Care Health Servs., Inc., 892 A.2d 1073 (Del.Supr. 2006). *See also* League of Women Voters of Fla. v. Browning, 575 F. Supp. 2d 1298, 1317 (S.D. Fla. 2008) ("An affiliate is a person who, or entity which owns or exercises control over or is controlled by, directly or indirectly, another person or entity.").

[76] *See* Corrigan v. United States Steel Corp., 478 F.3d 718, 724 (6th Cir. 2007).

[77] *E.g.,* Corrigan v. United States Steel Corp., 478 F.3d 718, 724–725 (6th Cir. 2007) (noting courts should focus on "whether the relationship is so dominating that respecting it would be unjust").

The issue of dominance of one entity over another is not limited to the corporate arena; veil piercing considerations arise in areas of partnership law. *In re USA Cafes LP Litig.*[78] ushered in a novel development by holding that the directors of a corporation that served as the general partner of a limited partnership owed fiduciary duties to the limited partners. The court reasoned that such a duty was owed to the limited partners because "one who controls property of another may not, without implied or express agreement, intentionally use that property in a way that benefits the holder of the control to the detriment of the property or its beneficial owner."[79] This holding has been criticized on the ground that the holding was not based on facts common in veil piercing, *e.g.*, comingling, but was based on the quest to create an individual duty within an organization structure designed to avoid such responsibility.[80] At the same time such veil piercing is the product of equity so that formalism is not a guiding principle. In these cases the courts appear to disregard the organization's fictional existence to allow the true contestants to litigate the claims. Thus we see that the approach taken in *USA Cafes, L.P.* has been applied to reach the managing member of an LLC that was the general partner of a limited partnership,[81] to reach the general partners of the firm that served as the general partner of the limited partnership,[82] and to reach the sole member of an LLC that was the manager of another LLC.[83]

§ 7.9   The Corporation's Separate Entity Under State and Federal Statutes

A significant number of cases regarding the piercing of the corporate veil are those arising in disputes involving the application of a state or federal statute. The greater frequency of veil-piercing in statutory contexts rather than in the contract claim contexts is due to the different objectives served in the statutory contexts—invariably the objective and policy of state and federal statutes invite a more liberal application of veil-piercing considerations.[84] Furthermore, federal courts are more likely to pierce the veil in order to effectuate federal policy and thereby prevent state corporate laws from being used to frustrate the federal objectives.[85]

Courts do not purport to invoke different standards for piercing the veil in the context of interpreting state or federal statutes than they use in cases involving creditors who seek payment. However, they invoke the creditor-based veil piercing considerations with an eye focused on whether the statutory purpose would be better served by piercing the veil. For example, in *Brotherhood of Locomotive Engineers v. Springfield Terminal*

---

[78]   In re USACafes, L.P. Litigation, 600 A.2d 43, Fed. Sec. L. Rep. (CCH) P 96056 (Del. Ch. 1991).

[79]   In re USACafes, L.P. Litigation, 600 A.2d 43, 47–48, Fed. Sec. L. Rep. (CCH) P 96056 (Del. Ch. 1991).

[80]   Mohsen Manesh, The Case Against Fiduciary Veil Piercing, 72 Bus. Law. 61(2017). *See also*, Leo J. Strine, Jr. & J. Travis Laster, The Siren Song of Unlimited Contractual Freedom, in Research Handbook on Partnerships, LLCs and Alternative Forms of Business Organizations, 11 (Rob't W. Hillman & Mark J. Lowenstein, eds. 2015).

[81]   Paige Capital Mngt., LLC v. Lerner Master Fund, LLC, 22 A.3d 710 (Del. Ch. 2011).

[82]   Bigelow/Diversified Secondary P'ship Fund 1990 v. Damson/Birtcher Partners, 2001 WL 1641239 (Del. Ch. Dec. 4, 2001).

[83]   Bay Ctr. Apartments Owner, LLC v. Emery Bay PKI, LLC, 2009 WL 1124451 (Del. Ch. Apr. 20, 2009).

[84]   An exhaustive study of this subject appears in Phillip I. Blumberg, The Law of Corporate Groups: Problems of Parent and Subsidiary Corporations Under Statutory Law of General Application (1989).

[85]   Illinois Bell Tel. Co. v. Global NAPS Illinois, Inc., 551 F.3d 587, 598 (7th Cir. 2008).

Ry. Co.[86], the First Circuit concluded that evidence of overlapping boards and ownership between two companies basis for treating as single entity so as to maintain the policy surrounding Railway Labor Act. The greater willingness to pierce the veil in the statutory context reflects in part that the financial consequences may not be as severe as in veil-piercing cases where the object is to impose liability on the dominant stockholder for all the insolvent corporation's debts. More important yet is the statutory context that may justify expanding responsibility beyond a single corporate actor so as to include perhaps its sister corporations, its parent corporation, or even an individual controlling stockholder. Such expansion can occur by either piercing the corporate veil or by holding that the act's language reaches controlling stockholders or controlled companies regardless of whether the facts support piercing the veil.

In broad overview, the question that drives veil-piercing in the statutory context is whether the statutory purpose would be furthered or frustrated if the individual controlling stockholder or parent corporation is not swept within the scope of the statute. This question can sometimes be answered in a straightforward fashion by relying on statutory intent; in other instances, however, courts invoke the equitable principles embodied in the traditional standards of the "piercing the corporate veil" doctrine.

§ 7.10 Subordination of Controlling Stockholders' Loans and Guaranties

Shareholders make loans to their corporation for a number of legitimate reasons. Because a corporation is treated as an entity distinct from its stockholders, the stockholder-lender enjoys a priority equal to that of outside creditors. Even claims of a sole shareholder, whether an individual or a corporation, can compete with outside creditors for bona fide advances. In contrast, partners' loans in liquidation are paid only after all outside creditors have been satisfied.

The courts, however, scrutinize a controlling stockholder's claim to determine whether the "advance" should be treated as a loan or as a capital investment and also to judge whether it would be inequitable to accord that claim a priority equal to that enjoyed by outside creditors.[87] There are, therefore, two distinct questions: Are the advances to be treated as loans; and, assuming the advances are bona fide loans, do equitable considerations compel that the controlling stockholder's loans be subordinated to other claimants in the bankruptcy or receivership proceedings?

Whether an advance is viewed as a bona fide loan generally depends on whether it bears the indicia common to loans. In deciding whether advances are loans or capital, substance very much governs over form.[88] In broad overview, the litmus is whether from the totality of the circumstances the advances were made when no other disinterested lender would have extended credit. Courts thus examine the relative riskiness of the enterprise as well as whether the lending stockholder has acted as a third-party lender by demanding the protection and terms a third party would have sought under the circumstances. Advances have been treated as capital where the stockholder has agreed to subordinate its loans to the much smaller loans made by banks,[89] where the firm's

---

[86] 210 F.3d 18 (1st Cir. 2000).

[87] *See, e.g.,* In re Multiponics, Inc., 436 F.Supp. 1065 (E.D. La. 1977); Tanzi v. Fiberglass Swimming Pools, Inc., 414 A.2d 484 (R.I. 1980).

[88] This approach was first enunciated in Pepper v. Litton, 308 U.S. 295 (1939).

[89] Diasonics, Inc. v. Ingalls, 121 B.R. 626 (Bankr. N.D. Fla. 1990).

initial capital is inadequate,[90] when the debt appears to be held proportionally among the stockholders,[91] where investors have shifted a portion of their capital investment to loans in the face of bankruptcy,[92] and where the debt-to-equity ratio was believed too high.[93] One has legitimate cause for concern whether such considerations are too crude to separate reliably legitimate lending practices from investments of capital.

Even though debt is bona fide, it may nonetheless be subordinated to the demands for payment by other claimants.[94] Equitable subordination of stockholder's debt is frequently referred to as the "Deep Rock" doctrine, the reference being to the subsidiary in *Taylor v. Standard Gas & Electric Company*,[95] the leading case on the subject.

The doctrine of equitable subordination is distinct from the analysis followed in veil-piercing cases. In veil-piercing cases, there is an overall concern as to whether the controlling stockholder has respected the corporation as a distinct entity. In cases involving equitable subordination, the focus is whether the controlling stockholder has behaved unfairly to the detriment of the corporation's creditors or even other stockholders. In *Taylor*, the parent company's unfair behavior was failing to adequately capitalize the subsidiary, which operated on the precipice of bankruptcy, extracting above-market rates of interest on intercompany loans, and causing the subsidiary to pay dividends when it was short of cash. Section 510(c) of the Bankruptcy Code codifies the previous law by providing that the bankruptcy court "may . . . under principles of equitable subordination, subordinate . . . all or part of an allowed claim to all or part of another allowed claim."[96]

Courts express in various ways the grounds for subordinating the stockholder's loans. A most widely cited version is that set forth in *In re Mobile Steel Company*:[97]

(1) The claimant must have engaged in some type of inequitable conduct.

(2) The misconduct must have resulted in injury to the creditors of the bankrupt or conferred an unfair advantage on the claimant.

(3) Equitable subordination of the claim must not be inconsistent with the provisions of the Bankruptcy Act.[98]

---

[90] *See, e.g.*, In re Multiponics, Inc., 622 F.2d 709 (5th Cir. 1980).

[91] L & M Realty Corp. v. Leo, 249 F.2d 668 (4th Cir. 1957).

[92] In Costello v. Fazio, 256 F.2d 903 (9th Cir. 1958), on incorporation of a failing partnership, three partners each received $2,000 in the corporation's stock, and the balance of partnership equity by other two partners was represented by notes-payable if the corporation was profitable. The court held that the capital was clearly inadequate, but could also have considered the debt was not truly debt.

[93] The higher the ratio, the easier the case. Thus a ratio of 80:1 permits classification as capital without additional showing. *See* In re Fett Roofing & Sheet Metal Co., 438 F.Supp. 726 (E.D. Va. 1977), but a ratio in the low teens requires other factors to support reclassification. *See* In re Autostyle Plastics, Inc., 269 F.3d 726, 751–752 (6th Cir. 2001); In re Mobile Steel Co., 563 F.2d 692 (5th Cir. 1977).

[94] In the typical bankruptcy or receivership setting where such disputes arise, there is no difference in result between subordinating the debt and recharacterizing it as capital: In either case, the controlling stockholder is paid nothing for the claim because the debtor corporation's estate was insufficient to satisfy all its creditors.

[95] Taylor v. Standard Gas & Electric Company, 306 U.S. 307 (1939).

[96] 11 U.S.C. § 510(c) (2004).

[97] In re Mobile Steel Company, 563 F.2d 692, 699–700 (5th Cir. 1977).

[98] In re Mobile Steel Company, 563 F.2d 692, 700 (5th Cir. 1977) (citations omitted).

While inadequate capitalization is frequently a factor raised in deciding to subordinate the controlling stockholder's loans,[99] it is by no means clear whether capital inadequacy alone is sufficient cause for subordination.[100] Other factors that lead to subordination include control of the subsidiary's dividend policy to bleed and innervate the corporation,[101] imposition on controlled corporation of excessive management or consulting fees,[102] intertwining of the parent's and subsidiary's affairs,[103] and intercompany transactions on terms unfavorable to the subsidiary.[104]

The full flavor of the possible bases for finding unfair behavior in connection with the dominating stockholder's loan to the corporation is reflected in *Gannett Company v. Larry*,[105] where a large newspaper publishing corporation purchased a solvent newspaper and then converted the subsidiary into a supplier of newsprint because the parent believed there would soon be a shortage of newsprint. The feared newsprint shortage never developed; in fact, there was an abundant supply of newsprint. The subsidiary entered bankruptcy. Among the claims before the bankruptcy court were the loans the parent had made to convert the subsidiary's operations. The Second Circuit subordinated the parent's loans, reasoning they were tainted by the parent having controlled the subsidiary for its own interests to the detriment of its creditors. One would expect a different holding if the parent had not itself been a publisher but rather a conglomerate that legitimately believed greater returns would lie in meeting the expected demand for newsprint. Under these facts, the parent's motives, while self-serving in the sense they sought to maximize its return, are of the type the law should nurture; the expected benefits of directing its subsidiary into fields believed to be more profitable than its current lines of business also redound to the benefit of its creditors. Whereas in *Gannett Company* the expected benefits were to be reaped by Gannett and the other publishing companies it controlled by avoiding higher prices and shortages for newsprint; there was no expectation that its subsidiary would have greater profits as a result of the conversion.

§ 7.11   Reverse-Piercing of the Corporate Veil

Inside Reverse Piercing

In what has been referred to as "inside reverse piercing" of the veil,[106] the controlling stockholder urges the court to disregard the corporate entity that otherwise separates the stockholder from the corporation.[107] To illustrate why this may be to the

---

[99] *See* In re Fabricators, Inc., 926 F.2d 1458 (5th Cir. 1991).

[100] *See, e.g.,* In re Autostyle Plastics, Inc., 269 F.3d 726, 747 (6th Cir. 2001) ("Undercapitalization alone is insufficient to justify the subordination of insider claims, however.").

[101] In re Tri-State Bldg. Materials Co., 279 F.Supp. 1020 (D.S.D. 1968).

[102] In re Americana Apparel, Inc., 55 B.R. 160 (Bankr. E.D. Pa. 1985).

[103] Henry v. Dolley, 99 F.2d 94 (10th Cir. 1938).

[104] Bankers Life & Cas. Co. v. Kirtley, 338 F.2d 1006 (8th Cir. 1964) (parent purchased subsidiary's stock).

[105] Gannett Company v. Larry, 221 F.2d 269 (2d Cir. 1955).

[106] *See* Postal Instant Press, Inc. v. Kaswa Corp., 77 Cal.Rptr.3d 96, 101 (Cal. Ct. App. 2008): "The typical 'reverse pierce' case involves a corporate insider, or someone claiming through such individual, attempting to pierce the corporate veil from within so that the corporate entity and the individual will be considered one and the same." (quoting 1 William Fletcher, Cyclopedia of the Law of Corporations (Sept.2007) § 41.70.)

[107] *See, e.g.,* C.F. Trust Inc. v. First Flight Limited Partnership, 306 F.3d 126 (4th Cir.2002) (Virginia court apply same factors to reverse veil piercing as to veil piercing generally); Goya Foods, Inc. v. Unanue, 233 F.3d 38, 43 (1st Cir. 2000) (" 'reverse piercing' (which makes the corporation liable for the debts of its owner or

stockholder's advantage, consider *Cargill, Inc. v. Hedge*,[108] where a husband and wife transferred the family farm to a corporation owned solely by the wife. Later a creditor obtained a judgment against the husband and corporation and successfully bid on the property at the execution sale. The wife sought to protect their dwelling by claiming a homestead exemption, which under state law was available only to individuals, not to corporations. The Minnesota Supreme Court recognized the exemption by allowing the wife to reverse-pierce the corporate veil.

Reverse piercing has been applied in parent-subsidiary relationships.[109] Reverse piercing has been recognized as a possibility with limited liability companies as well.[110]

Not surprisingly, many courts fiercely refuse to allow the veil to be pierced for the benefit of those who have created the corporation.[111] This view reflects the strict view that piercing the veil is an equitable consideration and thus subject to equitable defenses. It would appear that a more flexible approach is appropriate. The overall focus should not be a blanket bar of the corporation's stockholders raising their own deficiencies as a basis to disregard the entity they have created but instead inquiring whether a fairer resolution of the dispute before the court is achieved if the corporation's shareholders are permitted to pierce the veil.[112] In jurisdictions where reverse-piercing is recognized, the factors giving rise to the corporate entity being disregarded are those that apply in traditional veil-piercing cases.[113]

Outside Reverse Piercing

Reverse-piercing may be urged by a creditor rather than a shareholder, especially when a majority shareholder uses the controlled corporation to conceal assets or to avoid his or her preexisting liabilities.[114] In that situation, a creditor may reach the assets of a corporation to satisfy the shareholder's personal obligation by showing that the corporate entity is in reality the alter ego of the individual.[115] However, in doing so, the

---

parent) is allowed under New York law where the assets at issue are held by the target corporation and the liability is that of the individual who dominates the corporation and is using it to perpetrate a fraud or wrong.").

[108] Cargill, Inc. v. Hedge, 375 N.W.2d 477 (Minn. 1985).

[109] *See, e.g.*, Searcy v. Knight (In re Am. Int'l Refinery), 402 B.R. 728, 744 (Bankr. W.D. La. 2008); Leonard v. Coolidge (In re Nat'l Audit Def. Network), 367 B.R. 207, 230 (Bankr. D. Nev. 2007).

[110] *See, e.g.*, Sky Cable, LLC v. DIRECTV, Inc., 886 F.3d 375 (4th Cir. 2019) (affirming outside reversing piercing of LLC under Delaware law); C.F. Trust, Inc. v. First Flight Limited Partnership, 338 F.3d 316 (4th Cir. 2003), *aff'g* 140 F. Supp. 2d 628 (E.D. Va. 2001) (reverse veil piercing can be applied to corporations and limited partnerships under Virginia law); In re Schwab, 378 B.R. 854 (Bankr. D. Minn. 2007) (reverse piercing in the LLC context); Litchfield Asset Mgmt. Corp. v. Howell, 799 A.2d 298 (Conn. App. Ct. 2002). *Accord*, C.F. Trust, Inc. v. First Flight L.P., 580 S.E.2d 806 (Va. 2003) (answer to question certified by federal court).

[111] *See, e.g.*, Reboy v. Cozzi Iron & Metal, Inc., 9 F.3d 1303, 1308 (7th Cir. 1993); Carey v. National Oil Corp., 592 F.2d 673 (2d Cir. 1979); T.V.A. v. Exxon Nuclear Co., 753 F.2d 493 (6th Cir. 1985); Uniboard Aktiebolag v. Acer Am. Corp., 118 F. Supp. 2d 19, 25 (D.D.C. 2000) ("[T]he law generally does not allow the option of 'reverse piercing' the corporate veil when it suits the corporation's owner"); In re Flanagan, 373 B.R. 216, 224 (Bankr. D. Conn. 2007); Acree v. McMahan, 276 Ga. 880, 585 S.E.2d 873 (Ga. 2003) (Georgia law does not permit reverse veil piercing); Trossman v. Philipsborn, 869 N.E.2d 1147, 1174 (Ill. App. Ct. 2007) (Illinois does not allow reverse veil piercing); Sims v. Western Waste Industries, 918 S.W.2d 682, 686 (Tex. App. 1996).

[112] *See* In re Oil Spill by Amoco Cadiz, 699 F.2d 909 (7th Cir.)(1983) (U.S. parent corporation of foreign subsidiary allowed to sue foreign shipbuilder in federal court where evidence was that subsidiary a mere shell).

[113] *See, e.g.*, Chao v. OSHRC, 401 F.3d 355, 364 (5th Cir. 2005); Zahra Spiritual Trust v. United States, 910 F.2d 240 (5th Cir. 1990) (remanding reverse-piercing decision for finding whether taxpayers held ownership interest in corporation whose assets were subject to tax lien).

[114] LFC Marketing Group, Inc. v. Loomis, 8 P.3d 841, 846–847 (Nev. 2000).

[115] LFC Marketing Group, Inc. v. Loomis, 8 P.3d 841, 846–847 (Nev. 2000). *See also* Litchfield Asset Mgmt. Corp. v. Howell, 799 A.2d 298, 312 (Conn. App. Ct. 2002) ("[W]hen the elements of the identity or

courts must consider whether the rights of innocent shareholders or other creditors may be harmed by reverse veil-piercing.[116] A number of courts have allowed reverse piercing in actions by creditors of a shareholder.[117] However, in large part because of the potential harm to innocent shareholders, some state reject reverse piercing in actions brought by creditors.[118] Even states that recognize outside reverse piercing will consider a showing of undue prejudice to innocent investors.[119]

Reverse piercing has not been limited to the corporate form. For example, courts have applied reverse-piercing principles to limited liability companies.[120]

---

instrumentality rule have been established, a reverse pierce is a viable remedy that a court may employ when necessary to achieve an equitable result and when unfair prejudice will not result.").

[116] McKay v. Longman, 2019 WL 3242577 (Conn. 2019); LFC Marketing Group, Inc. v. Loomis, 8 P.3d 841, 846–847 (Nev. 2000).

[117] *See, e.g.*, In re Phillips, 139 P.3d 639, 645 (Colo. 2006) (Colorado permits outside reverse piercing "[d]ue to the similarities and parallel goals achieved in outside reverse piercing and traditional piercing."); Litchfield Asset Management Corp. v. Howell, 70 Conn.App. 133, 149–151, 799 A.2d 298 (Conn. App. 2002) ("We discern from these cases a growing recognition of the doctrine of reverse piercing of the corporate veil"); Sweeney, Cohn, Stahl & Vaccaro v. Kane, 6 A.D.3d 72, 76, 773 N.Y.S.2d 420 (N.Y. App. Div. 2004) (Florida law recognizes reverse piercing in the outsider context).

[118] *See*, Floyd v. I.R.S., 151 F.3d 1295 (10th Cir.1998) (rejecting reverse piercing by a third party under Kansas law); Cascade Energy and Metals Corp. v. Banks, 896 F.2d 1557, 1576–1577 (10th Cir.1990) (rejecting reverse piercing in an action by a third party); Acree v. McMahan, 585 S.E.2d 873 (Ga. 2003) (rejecting reverse piercing in an action by a third party); Lollis v. Turner, 654 S.E.2d 229, 232 (Ga. Ct. App. 2007); Lemus v. Horizon Express, Inc., 196 P.3d 1232 (Kan. Ct. App. 2008).

An earlier decision in California rejected outside reverse piercing. Postal Instant Press, Inc. v. Kaswa Corp., 77 Cal.Rptr.3d 96, 98 (Cal. Ct. App. 2008):

> The reasoning of the cases adopting outside reverse piercing of the corporate veil is flawed, and we join other courts declining to accept it. [O]utside reverse piercing is not a logical extension of the standard alter ego doctrine but instead addresses significantly different concerns. Outside reverse piercing can harm innocent shareholders and corporate creditors, and allow judgment creditors to bypass normal judgment collection procedures. Legal theories (such as agency or respondeat superior) and legal remedies (such as claims for conversion or fraudulent conveyance) adequately protect judgment creditors without the need to distort theories of corporate liability.

A more recent holding distinguished *Postal* on the ground the creditor held 99 percent of the LLC's ownership and expressed a willingness to consider reverse piercing. *See* Curci Inv., LLC v. Baldwin, 14 Cal.App.5th 214, 221 Cal. Rptr. 3d 847 (2017).

[119] McKay v. Longman, 2019 WL 3242577 (Conn. 2019) (recognizing reverse piercing but refusing to apply it on the facts due to prejudice to nonculpable investors that would result from reverse piercing).

[120] *See, e.g.*, Sky Cable, LLC v. DIRECTV, Inc., 886 F.3d 375 (4th Cir. 2018); McKay v. Longman, 332 Conn. 394, 2019 WL 3242577 (Conn. 2019).

Chapter 8

POWERS OF OFFICERS AND AGENTS; TORT AND CRIMINAL LIABILITY OF CORPORATIONS

Table of Sections

§ 8.1   Introduction and a Summary of Rules Regarding the Agent's Authority

As an artificial entity, a corporation can act only through its agents.[1] Officers and other employees act as the corporation's agents. As explained in subsequent sections of this book, the more important corporate officers are usually selected by the board of directors, and the actions of all corporate officers and agents are subject to the supervision and control of the board of directors. The discussion that follows summarizes general agency law.

§ 8.2   Corporate Officers and Their Sources of Power

The chief executive officer, president, vice president, treasurer, and secretary are the traditional officers of the corporation, and these are the officers that were most often

---

[1]   *See, e.g.,* In re Merrill Lynch Trust Co. FSB., 235 S.W.3d 185 (Tex. 2007). (Noting that since a corporation can only act through human agents, an arbitration agreement generally includes disputes about their agents' actions).

mentioned in the corporation statutes.[2] The modern trend is not to be wed to specific statutory nomenclature.[3]

Although most officer functions have remained relatively constant over time, the roles, duties, and titles in corporate management are constantly changing. Many corporations, especially the large publicly held corporations, now have other executives and agents who are denominated "officers." For example, the title of "chief executive officer" ("CEO") was rarely used 50 years ago, and the title of "resident" was reserved for the head corporate officer. Today, presidents are frequently subordinate to the CEO. Many of the older cases use "resident" to describe today's CEO but what is said in those cases for the president applies with equal force to the CEO position. However, it must be borne in mind that when both positions exist within a single corporation, the CEO's power is superior and broader than that of the president. The president in such a situation is likely to be more of a chief operating officer ("COO"). In many respects, the COO resembles the position of general manager[4] that may exist in small business or within corporate divisions.

A large corporation may have a number of vice presidents, assistant vice presidents, assistant secretaries, assistant treasurers, and so on. A number of modern corporation statutes provide flexibility by permitting officer titles and duties to be stated in the bylaws or determined by the board of directors.[5] As the number of vice presidents in corporations has proliferated, super vice presidencies under such titles as "executive vice president" or "senior vice president" have been created in an effort to retain distinctive titles. Most large corporations have a "chairman of the board," and in fact in a considerable number of companies that is the title given the chief executive officer. In some companies, however, where there is a desire to provide a system of checks and balances, different individuals hold the offices of CEO and chairman of the board.

An officer's authority to act is most often derived from the corporation's bylaws, a resolution of the board of directors, or a job description of that particular officer's or agent's duties approved by the board or some superior corporate agent. Much of a large corporation's work is conducted by agents selected and given authority by other corporate agents, who may be a number of levels removed from the corporation's board of directors. An agent so selected often has power to affect the legal relations of the corporation but usually does not have the power to act for or to bind the appointing agent.[6]

§ 8.3   Selection of Officers

The board of directors usually selects a corporation's principal officers. Applicable statutes, however, vary considerably. In some states the corporation statute expressly designates the board of directors as the body to elect or appoint officers. In other states, the statutes are more flexible because they provide that the officers will be selected in

---

[2]   *E.g.,* former Model Bus. Corp. Act § 50 (1969). *Cf.* Model Bus. Corp. Act § 8.40(a) (2016) ("the offices described in its bylaws or appointed by the board of directors in accordance with the bylaws").

[3]   *E.g.,* Model Bus. Corp. Act § 8.40(a).

[4]   *See* § 8.11.

[5]   *See, e.g.,* 805 ILCS § 5/8.50 (Smith-Hurd 1993); Model Bus. Corp. Act §§ 8.40, 8.41.

[6]   *See* Detlev F. Vagts, Basic Corporation Law: Materials-Cases-Text 323 (2d ed. 1979).

the manner provided in the bylaws,[7] or that the officers shall be elected by the board unless the bylaws provide otherwise.

Corporation statutes commonly state that the same person may hold more than one corporate office. The 1969 Model Business Corporation Act, for instance, provided that "any two or more offices may be held by the same person, except the offices of president and secretary."[8] A few state statutes provide that the offices of president and vice president may not be held by the same person.[9] The rationale underlying the foregoing limitations is that under certain circumstances the presence of two separate individuals is designed to establish a system of checks and balances. The modern trend, however, is to be more permissive and to permit corporations to fashion their own rules. Thus, for example, the California and Delaware statutes state that any two offices may be held by the same person unless otherwise provided in the corporation's charter or bylaws.[10] The current version of the Model Act is similar.[11]

§ 8.4   Removal or Resignation of Officers or Agents

The power to remove officers lies inherently with the directors and that power of officer removal cannot be given to the shareholders even with a duly adopted bylaw to that effect.[12] The board of directors can remove an officer, with or without cause, even though the corporation has entered into an employment contract and the term has not expired.[13]

Notwithstanding the power to remove an officer without cause, the corporation may be liable to the officer for damages for breach of an employment contract if the officer is removed without cause before his contract term expires.[14] In many states the corporation statute provides that the board's power of removal does not destroy any rights the removed officer may have under an employment contract, shareholders agreement, or other contract.[15] In general, courts have not challenged the removal of officers by boards of directors unless the directors have clearly abused their discretion as to what is in the corporation's best interest.[16]

§ 8.5   The Chief Executive Officer's and President's Authority

For most of the history of American corporations, the corporation's chief executive officer was its president who simply carried the title of president. Over time corporations, especially publicly held corporations, changed the titles of their officers. The chief executive officer ("CEO") became the official title. Many CEOs have both titles of

---

[7]   *E.g.*, Del. Code Ann. tit. 8, § 142 (2001). *See also* Model Bus. Corp. Act § 8.40(b) (1984) ("[t]he board of directors may elect individuals to fill one or more offices of the corporation").

[8]   Former Model Bus. Corp. Act § 50 (1969).

[9]   Md. Code Ann., Corps. & Ass'ns § 2–415(a) (1999).

[10]   Cal. Corp. Code § 312 (West 1990); Del. Code Ann. tit. 8, § 142(a) (2001).

[11]   Model Bus. Corp. Act § 8.40(d)(2016) ("The same individual may simultaneously hold more than one office in a corporation").

[12]   Gorman v. Salamone, 2015 WL 4719681 (Del. Ch. 2015).

[13]   United Prod. & Consumers Co-op. v. Held, 225 F.2d 615 (9th Cir. 1955) (bylaw stated officers hold office at pleasure of board).

[14]   In re Paramount Publix Corp., 90 F.2d 441 (2d Cir. 1937); Pioneer Specialties, Inc. v. Nelson, 339 S.W.2d 199 (Tex. 1960).

[15]   Statutes frequently clearly state that election or appointment of an officer does not itself create contract rights. Model Bus. Corp. Act § 8.44(b) (1984).

[16]   Franklin v. Texas Int'l Petroleum Corp., 324 F.Supp. 808 (W.D. La. 1971).

president and chief executive officer. Other companies have reserved the title of president for the general manager or chief operating officer ("COO"). Smaller corporations are more likely to retain the traditional nomenclature of president.

Under the traditional governance norms a corporation's CEO or president may be given the authority by the corporation's charter, bylaws,[17] resolutions of the directors, or the board's acquiescence to make particular contracts, including the power to hire employees,[18] to borrow money, or to execute conveyances and mortgages and do other acts.[19] The CEO or president may be expressly given general authority to supervise and manage the business of the corporation, or a particular part of it. In such a case the president's authority extends impliedly to any contract or other act that is incident to the ordinary business of the corporation, or to that part with which he or she is entrusted; thus there is no need for special authority for the particular acts within the ordinary business of the corporation or that part of its operations to be expressly granted. Furthermore, in the absence of express authority a corporation may be estopped to deny the authority of its president where it has created apparent authority in the president to make contracts or do other acts, as when a corporation allows its managing officers generally or habitually to make contracts or perform acts of that type.[20] The president's implied, apparent, or inherent authority is limited to carrying on the corporation's ordinary business and does not extend to extraordinary transactions. In any particular case, the scope of the CEO's authority necessarily boils down to a question of fact.

The decisions of the courts are in conflict regarding a corporate president's power, in the absence of any express or implied conferring of authority, to act on behalf of the corporation.[21] The president of a corporation, as its executive head, is often expressly or impliedly given supervision and control of its business. In view of this general practice, some courts have adopted a doctrine of "inherent authority"—namely, that the president of a business corporation, solely by virtue of the office, may bind the corporation by contract and by other acts in the usual course of its business.[22] Other courts recognize a "presumptive authority," taking the position that contracts entered into or acts performed by the president of a corporation in the ordinary course of the corporation's business are presumed to be within his or her authority until the contrary is proven.[23] The presumption is limited, however, to acts in the ordinary course of business and does not extend to all matters that can be authorized by the board of directors.[24]

---

[17] *See* Squaw Mtn. Cattle Co. v. Bowen, 804 P.2d 1292, 1295 (Wyo. 1991).

[18] Diston v. EnviroPak Medical Products, 893 P.2d 1071 (Utah App. 1995) (president had apparent authority to hire employees); Lee v. Jenkins Bros., 268 F.2d 357, 365 (2d Cir.), *cert. denied*, 361 U.S. 913 (1959) (apparent authority of corporate president was question of fact).

[19] Hellman v. Hellman, 19 Misc.3d 695, 860 N.Y.S.2d 817 (Sup. Ct. 2008), *aff'd as modified*, 60 A.D.3d 1468, 876 N.Y.S.2d 298 (4th Dep't 2009) (president has authority to sign lease under grant of authority to manage the business).

[20] Schmidt v. Farm Credit Servs., Inc., 977 F.2d 511 (10th Cir. 1992). Lettiori v. American Sav. Bank, 437 A.2d 822 (Conn. 1980).

[21] Note, Inherent Power as a Basis of a Corporate Officer's Authority to Contract, 57 Colum. L. Rev. 868 (1957).

[22] In re Lee Ready Mix & Supply Co., 437 F.2d 497 (6th Cir. 1971); DuSesoi v. United Refining Co., 540 F.Supp. 1260 (1982).

[23] Adams v. Barron G. Collier, Inc., 73 F.2d 975 (8th Cir. 1934); (president has prima facie the power "to do any act which the directors could authorize or ratify").

[24] Southwest Forest Indus. v. Sharfstein, 482 F.2d 915 (7th Cir. 1972).

According to a third group of courts,[25] the president's power to act for the corporation is limited to authority conferred by the corporation's charter or bylaws or by action of its board of directors. Nevertheless, even where the strict rule prevails, the president or other officer may of course be given authority to represent the corporation and to contract for it (1) by the corporation's articles or bylaws; (2) by a resolution of the board of directors; or (3) by acquiescence of the directors or shareholders in the known exercise or assumption of power.[26]

§ 8.6   Authority of the Chairman of the Board

Many corporations have an office titled "chairman of the board." The functions of the chairman of the board vary widely from company to company. In some companies the chairman of the board has no other duty than presiding at meetings of the board, a responsibility that of course is not executive in nature.[27] In other companies the chairman of the board provides advise and counsel to the president or the board of directors.[28] In all other companies the chairman is the chief executive officer or general manager, with vast responsibility and power. Whenever a company's chief executive officer is titled "chairman of the board," the title of "resident" is often conferred on the company's chief executive officer. The same person may be both chairman of the board and president. Such appointments create the apparent authority to bind the corporation on transactions within the ordinary course of its business.[29] The same authority applies to one appointed as a managing director.[30]

The title of chairman of the board and chief executive officer, when held by a single person, identifies the center of actual power within the organization. Recently there has been much discussion whether the governance of the public corporation would be improved by separating the two positions and assigning to an outside director the role of chairmanship of the board of directors so as to provide something of a counterweight to the inertial flow of power to the chief executive officer.

Most corporation statutes do not define the responsibilities and powers of the chairman of the board, and the judicial decisions on that subject are few in number and are not very helpful. As many people dealing with a corporation are likely to consider a person with the title of "chairman of the board" to be a principal corporate officer, with authority to enter into important transactions, the courts should hold that a board chairman, even in the absence of an additional title such as "resident" or "general manager," has by virtue of the position and title very broad power (whether classified as implied, inherent, or apparent authority) to act for the corporation.[31] The courts nevertheless are hesitant to accord autonomous power to the chairman of the board. Therefore, even though a corporation's bylaws provide that the president is to exercise

---

[25]   *See, e.g.,* Buxton v. Diversified Resources Corp., 634 F.2d 1313 (10th Cir. 1980); *cert. denied,* 454 U.S. 821 (1981).

[26]   *See* Juergens v. Venture Capital Corp., 295 N.E.2d 398 (Mass. App. Ct. 1973) (finding a combination of apparent authority and ratification).

[27]   Lin, CEOs and Presidents, 47 U.C. Davis L. Rev. 1351 (2014).

[28]   *See* Whitley v. Whitley Constr. Co., 175 S.E.2d 128 (Ga.App. 1970).

[29]   *See, e.g.,* American Express Co. v. Lopez, 340 N.Y.S.2d 82, 84 (Civ. Ct. 1973). FDIC v. Texas Bank of Garland, 783 S.W.2d 604 (Tex.App. 1989).

[30]   *See* Covington Hous. Dev. v. City of Covington, 381 F.Supp. 427 (E.D. Ky. 1974).

[31]   *See* City Nat'l Bank v. Basic Food Indus., 520 F.2d 336 (5th Cir. 1975); American Express Co. v. Lopez, 340 N.Y.S.2d 82 (Civ. Ct. 1973).

general management responsibilities "subject to the direction of the chairman and the board," a court has held that the chairman lacked the authority to strip the president of his authority.[32] Such a result is consistent with the well-established principle that only as a deliberative body, not as individuals, does the board have corporate power.[33]

§ 8.7   The Vice President's Authority

A corporation's vice president is generally held to have no authority merely by virtue of the office to dispose of the corporation's property or to bind the corporation by notes or other contracts.[34] A vice president, however, is sometimes entrusted with management of the business or a particular part of it, and in such a case he or she may bind the corporation by a contract within the scope of express or apparent authority.[35] Even the more liberal courts, however, have held that a vice president does not have power to act on behalf of the corporation in highly important and unusual transactions in the absence of specific authorization in the bylaws or a resolution of the board of directors.[36]

§ 8.8   The Secretary's Authority

The principal duties of a corporation's secretary are to make and keep the corporate records and to properly record votes, resolutions, and proceedings of the shareholders and directors as well as other matters that should be entered on corporate records.[37] The secretary's certification of a corporate resolution or the content of a corporate record is conclusive in favor of a person reasonably relying thereon.[38]

The secretary traditionally has been thought of as "merely a ministerial officer who keeps the books and minutes of the stockholders' and directors' meetings and has charge of the seal of the company."[39] Accordingly, the secretary has no authority merely by virtue of the office to make contracts on behalf of the corporation or to bind it by other acts.[40]

In a modern corporation, however, the secretary is generally more than a functionary with purely ministerial duties. The secretary is often a lawyer by profession and, not uncommonly, is also a director.

---

[32]   *See* Delaney v. Georgia-Pacific Corp., 564 P.2d 277, 288 (Or. 1977).

[33]   *See* Star Corp. v. General Screw Prod. Co., 501 S.W.2d 374, 380 (Tex. Civ. App. 1973).

[34]   Clements v. Coppin, 61 F.2d 552, 557 (9th Cir. 1932).

[35]   Townsend v. Daniel, Mann, Johnson & Mendenhall, 196 F.3d 1140 (10th Cir. 1999) (discussion concerning the apparent authority of a corporate vice president).

[36]   Colish v. Brandywine Raceway Ass'n, 119 A.2d 887 (Del.Supr. 1955) (no implied authority to consummate such extraordinary transaction as employing architect to design new plant); Jennings v. Pittsburgh Mercantile Co., 202 A.2d 51 (Pa. 1964) (officer, who was both vice president and treasurer-comptroller, did not have apparent authority to accept offer of sale-and-leaseback of all corporation's real estate).

[37]   *See* Field v. Oberwortmann, 148 N.E.2d 600 (Ill. App. Ct. 1958), *cert. denied,* 358 U.S. 833 (1958) (discussing secretary's obligations in keeping minutes); Del. Code Ann. tit. 8, § 142(a) (2001) (one officer shall record proceedings of shareholders' and directors' meetings in books kept for that purpose).

[38]   *See, e.g.,* McMan Oil & Gas Co. v. Hurley, 24 F.2d 776 (5th Cir. 1928).

[39]   *See* Meyer v. Glenmoor Homes, Inc., 54 Cal.Rptr. 786, 801 (Ct. App. 1966), *reh'g denied,* 55 Cal.Rptr. 502 (Ct. App. 1966).

[40]   Emmerglick v. Philip Wolf, Inc., 138 F.2d 661 (2d Cir. 1943) (secretary "is merely a ministerial officer" and therefore execution of affidavit by corporation's secretary cannot be deemed execution by corporation).

§ 8.9   The Treasurer's Authority; the Comptroller's Duties

The treasurer of a corporation is the proper officer to receive and keep the moneys of the corporation, and to disburse them as he or she may be authorized.[41] As is the case with the corporate secretary, the treasurer is frequently referred to as a "ministerial" position.[42] As a general rule, a corporation's treasurer has no implied authority, merely by virtue of the office, to bind the corporation by contracts or other acts made or done in its name, or to dispose of its assets except as authorized by the directors or other managing officers.[43]

Just like any other corporate officer, the treasurer may be entrusted with the general management of the corporation's business or a particular part of it; in such a case he or she has the same authority, in the absence of restrictions, as any other manager.[44] Even if the treasurer is not given broad general management powers, the directors or corporate executive officers, by acquiescence in the treasurer's actions or by otherwise leading other persons reasonably to believe that he or she has authority to act for the corporation in particular kinds of transactions, may create an apparent authority to enter into such transactions on the corporation's behalf.[45]

The comptroller or, as this officer is sometimes called, the "controller," is the chief accounting officer.[46] The comptroller's duties are to keep, or cause to be kept, all the corporation's books of accounts and accounting records and to prepare, or have prepared, appropriate financial statements for submission to the board of directors, the board's executive committee, appropriate corporate officers, and the shareholders.[47]

§ 8.10   Ratification of Unauthorized Contracts or Transactions

A corporation can ratify a contract or other act of a corporate officer or agent that was unauthorized if the act is legal and the corporation has the legal capacity to perform it.[48] In general, whoever could have originally authorized a transaction on behalf of a corporation can ratify it. Thus, an unauthorized act of a corporate officer or agent can be ratified for the corporation by its board of directors, its shareholders, or one or more of its officers, depending on which of these has the power to authorize the kind of act in question.[49]

Ratification need not be by formal vote or even by parol assent; as in the case of ratification by a natural person, it may be implied from the acts of the shareholders or officers having authority to ratify, in accepting the benefits with knowledge of the facts or otherwise treating or recognizing the contract or act as binding. Under some

---

[41]   Clark v. Minge, 65 So. 832 (Ala. 1914).

[42]   *E.g.,* Ideal Foods, Inc. v. Action Leasing Corp., 413 So.2d 416 (Fla. Dist. Ct. App. 1982).

[43]   Ideal Foods, Inc. v. Action Leasing Corp., 413 So.2d 416 (Fla. App. 1982) (no authority to bind corporation to third party unless expressly or impliedly authorized).

[44]   Vaught v. Charleston Nat'l Bank, 62 F.2d 817 (10th Cir. 1933).

[45]   Jaraczewski v. Krueger International, Inc., 277 Wis. 2d 873, 690 N.W.2d 884 (Ct. App. 2004).

[46]   This is the general understanding even though the corporation statutes do not mention the comptroller. *See, e.g.,* Model Bus. Corp. Act § 8.40; former Model Bus. Corp. Act § 50 (1969).

[47]   *See* Jennings v. Ruidoso Racing Ass'n, 441 P.2d 42 (N.M. 1968).

[48]   E. Edelmann & Co. v. Amos, 277 F.Supp. 105 (N.D. Ga. 1967), *aff'd per curiam,* Transonic Corp. v. E. Edelmann & Co., 386 F.2d 996 (5th Cir. 1967) (express ratification of all officers' acts for previous year).

[49]   Lewis v. Dansker, 357 F.Supp. 636, 644 (S.D.N.Y. 1973) (shareholders may only ratify corporate agent's unauthorized actions if shareholders could have originally authorized such acts).

circumstances ratification may be implied from a mere failure to repudiate or disaffirm.[50] Where the board of directors has the power to ratify, some courts say that knowledgeable acquiescence by the entire board is necessary to constitute ratification, while other courts say knowledgeable acquiescence by a majority of the directors is sufficient.[51]

The party alleging ratification has the burden of proving it.[52] When ratification is established, it relates back to the time the unauthorized act occurred and is legally equivalent to original authority.[53]

In 2015 Delaware adopted novel provisions to its corporate law regarding ratification of corporate defects.[54] Section 204 of the Delaware General Corporations Code allows retroactive correction of corporate acts that were not validly approved or that contradicted the corporation's certificate of incorporation.[55] The correction of defects can thus be accomplished after the fact by the board of directors. Curing corporate defects under section 204 is retroactive. Thus, subsequent corporate actions that may have been defective as a result of the initial defective acts similarly are cured. Section 205 of the Delaware Code[56] supplements section 204, self-correction of defects, by allowing an application to the Delaware Court of Chancery rather than internal approval under section 204. The statutory correction process supplements rather than preempts common law ratification. Section 204's ratification by the board cure cannot be used to mask a breach of duty or other deliberate wrongdoing. Thus, ratification by the board will not allow a company to "invoke ratification to validate a deliberately unauthorized corporate act."[57]

§ 8.11 Constructive Knowledge of the Corporation

"A corporation cannot see or know anything except by the eyes or intelligence of its officers."[58] It is well settled that if an officer or agent of a corporation acquires or possesses knowledge in the course of her employment as to matters that are within the scope of her authority, this knowledge is imputed to the corporation.[59] As one court has put it, "[t]he knowledge possessed by a corporation about a particular thing is the sum total of all the knowledge which its officers and agents, who are authorized and charged with the doing of the particular thing acquired, while acting under and within the scope of their authority."[60] Conversely, knowledge acquired by a corporate officer or agent in

---

[50] *See, e.g.,* 3 A's Towing Co. v. P & A Well Serv., Inc., 642 F.2d 756 (5th Cir. 1981).

[51] *Compare, e.g.,* Hurley v. Ornsteen, 42 N.E.2d 273 (Mass. 1942) (except in rare circumstances, knowledge and acquiescence by all the directors is necessary) *with* Mickshaw v. Coca Cola Bottling Co., 70 A.2d 467 (Pa. Super. Ct. 1950) (majority of directors was sufficient).

[52] Home Tel. Co. v. Darley, 355 F.Supp. 992, 1000–1001 (N.D. Miss. 1973), *aff'd*, 489 F.2d 1403 (5th Cir. 1974).

[53] 3 A's Towing Co. v. P & A Well Serv., Inc., 642 F.2d 756 (5th Cir. 1981).

[54] Del. Code Ann. tit. 8, §§ 204, 205.

[55] Del. Code Ann. tit. 8, § 204.

[56] Del. Code Ann. tit. 8, § 205. *See* In re Numoda Corporation Shareholders Litigation, 2015 WL 402265 (Del. Ch. 2015), judgment entered, 2015 WL1056143 (Del. Ch. 2015) and judgment aff'd, 128 A.3d 991 (Del. 2015) (validating corporation's contested capital structure).

[57] *See, e.g.,* Nguyen v. View, Inc., 2017 WL 2439074 (Del. Ch. 2017) (ratification by the board could not cure transaction made without adequate disclosure to a shareholder who would have lost control under the transaction which involved preferred stock financing).

[58] Factors' & Traders' Ins. Co. v. Marine Dry-Dock & Shipyard Co., 31 La. Ann. 149, 151 (1879). *Accord,* Schoenbaum v. Firstbrook, 405 F.2d 200, 211 (2d Cir. 1968).

[59] Volkswagen of Am., Inc. v. Robertson, 713 F.2d 1151, 1163 (5th Cir. 1983).

[60] Copeman Labs. Co. v. General Motors Corp., 36 F.Supp. 755, 762 (E.D. Mich. 1941).

relation to a matter that is not within the scope of her authority is usually not imputed to the corporation.[61] If duties do not require transmittal of knowledge to other corporate representatives acting in transactions in which the agent is not involved, the corporation's rights and liabilities arising out of those transactions are not affected by the agent's knowledge.

Courts generally base the doctrine that a principal is chargeable with knowledge of facts known to an agent on the agent's duty to communicate his knowledge to the principal and the presumption that this duty has been performed;[62] the presumption is usually treated as conclusive. According to many courts, such a presumption does not arise if the agent is acting out of self-interest or his interest is adverse to that of the principal. Therefore, whenever a director or officer has an interest adverse to the corporation, his knowledge relevant to the transaction is generally not imputed to the corporation.[63]

§ 8.12   Formal Evidence of an Officer's Authority

In highly important matters, such as the execution of conveyances, mortgages, and long-term contracts, a person dealing with a corporation should insist on evidence of the agent's authority in the form of a certified copy under the corporate seal of a resolution of the board of directors. A certified copy of a duly adopted bylaw is also satisfactory evidence of authority.

In the absence of a contrary charter or bylaw provision, the secretary is the custodian of the corporate seal,[64] and the proper person to affix the seal to an instrument is the secretary or assistant secretary.[65] The affixing of the corporate seal to an instrument is generally held to be prima facie evidence of the corporation's approval of the transaction and of the authority of the officer or officers who signed the instrument. The burden of showing lack of authority is then on the party attacking the instrument.[66]

§ 8.13   Criminal Liability of Corporations

The extent of corporate criminal liability has been in dispute since early days. It was formerly doubted whether a corporation could be prosecuted for any crime. The early cases declared that a corporation could not commit a crime for want of the requisite mens rea or intent,[67] today, it is generally accepted that a corporation may be criminally liable for actions or omissions of its agents in its behalf.[68] While a corporation cannot be imprisoned, it may be fined, and the fine may be enforced against its property, its charter

---

[61]   England v. American Southern Ins. Co., 380 F.2d 137, 140 (4th Cir. 1967) (notice to agent not ascribable to principal unless " 'in regard to matter coming within the sphere of the agent's duty' ").

[62]   *E.g.,* In re Parmalat Securities Litigation, 659 F. Supp.2d 504, 519–521 (S.D.N.Y. 2009).

[63]   American Nat'l Bank v. Miller, 229 U.S. 517 (1913); First Nat'l Bank v. Transamerica Ins. Co., 514 F.2d 981, 986 (8th Cir. 1975).

[64]   Stovell v. Alert Gold Mining Co., 87 P. 1071 (Colo. 1906).

[65]   Meyer v. Glenmoor Homes, Inc., 54 Cal.Rptr. 786 (Ct. App. 1966), *reh'g. denied,* 55 Cal.Rptr. 502 (Ct. App. 1966).

[66]   Meyer v. Glenmoor Homes, Inc., 54 Cal.Rptr. 786, 792–793 (Ct. App. 1966), *reh'g denied,* 55 Cal.Rptr. 502 (Ct. App. 1966).

[67]   1 W. Blackstone, Commentaries 476. *See* Anonymous, 88 Eng. Rep. 1518 (K.B. 1701).

[68]   *See, e.g.,* Gilbert Geis & Joseph F. C. DiMento, Empirical Evidence and the Legal Doctrine of Corporate Criminal Liability, 29 Am. J. Crim. L. 341, 343 (2002).

may be forfeited because of its misuse or abuse, or other sanctions may be imposed as a condition of probation.[69]

Over a century ago, the criticism emerged that that punishments levied on the corporate entity are in reality inflicted on the shareholders for the acts of others out of corporate assets by the prosecution and fining of the corporation.[70] These criticisms reemerged in the twenty-first century.[71] For example, criminal accountability of a large corporation can result in significant losses by innocent employees and retirees as was the case with the demise of Arthur Andersen in the wake of the Enron scandal.[72]

A large number of regulatory statutes—both federal and state—now expressly subject corporations to criminal liability for offenses defined in the statutes,[73] and corporations have often been convicted of violating this kind of regulatory legislation. Instances include violation of a statute punishing usury,[74] violation of statute punishing contractors for exacting from laborers more than a stated maximum number of hours per day,[75] violation of a law regulating child labor,[76] violation of a labor-management relations act,[77] peddling by an agent without a license,[78] violation of the weights and measures law by giving short weight on a sale of ice,[79] violating a price regulation,[80] violation of the antitrust laws,[81] violation of federal campaign contribution statutes,[82] as well as violation of the securities laws.[83] There is a lively debate whether such regulatory matters are appropriate for, and effectively addressed within, the criminal arena rather than the procedurally more flexible civil prosecution.[84]

In some of the legislatively defined offenses the employer is subjected to criminal sanctions for acts of employees without regard to any fault or culpability on his part, even though he may have given his employees instructions to comply with the law.[85] By definition, mens rea on the part of the corporation or its agents is not an element of the

---

[69] *See* Coffee, "No Soul to Damn, No Body to Kick": An Unscandalized Inquiry into the Problem of Corporate Punishment, 79 Mich. L. Rev. 386 (1981).

[70] Lee, Corporate Criminal Liability, 28 Colum. L. Rev. L. 4 (1928).

[71] Hamdani and Klement, Corporate Crime and Deterrence, 61 Stan. L. Rev. 271 (2008); Richard A. Bierschbach & Alex Stein, Overenforcement, 93 Geo. L.J. 1743, 1771–1772 (2005).

[72] *See, e.g.,* Wilson Meeks, Corporate and White-Collar Crime Enforcement: Should Regulation and Rehabilitation Spell an End to Corporate Criminal Liability?, 40 Colum. J.L. & Soc. Probs. 77, 84 (2006).

[73] *See, e.g.,* Federal Food, Drug and Cosmetic Act, 52 Stat. 1040, 21 U.S.C. § 321(e) (1970); N.Y. Evntl. Conserv. Law § 3302(24) (Supp. 1976 to 77).

[74] State v. Security Bank, 2 S.D. 538, 51 N.W. 337 (1892).

[75] United States v. John Kelso Co., 86 F. 304 (N.D. Cal. 1898).

[76] People v. Sheffield Farms-Slawson-Decker Co., 225 N.Y. 25, 121 N.E. 474 (1918).

[77] Korholz v. United States, 269 F.2d 897 (10th Cir. 1959), *cert. denied,* 361 U.S. 929 (1960) (the corporation, its president, and a union official were all convicted).

[78] New Jersey Good Humor, Inc. v. Board of Comm'rs, 123 N.J.L. 21, 7 A.2d 824 (1939).

[79] State v. People's Ice Co., 124 Minn. 307, 144 N.W. 962 (1914).

[80] United States v. Armour & Co., 168 F.2d 342 (3d Cir. 1948).

[81] United States v. General Motors Corp., 121 F.2d 376, 411 (7th Cir.), *cert. denied,* 314 U.S. 618 (1941).

[82] 2 U.S.C. § 441b (1982).

[83] *See* Matthews, Criminal Prosecutions Under The Federal Securities Laws and Related Statutes: The Nature and Development of SEC Criminal Cases, 39 Geo. Wash. L. Rev. 901 (1971).

[84] *See* V.S. Khanna, Corporate Criminal Liability: What Purpose Does It Serve?, 109 Harv. L. Rev. 1477 (1996).

[85] *E.g.,* State v. Zeta Chi Fraternity, 696 A.2d 530, 535 (N.H. 1997) (corporation held responsible even though it had expressly instructed agents not to engage in the prohibited acts).

offense proscribed by a strict liability statute.[86] The criminal penalties often form an integral part of regulatory practice and may be based on pragmatic experience indicating their usefulness. In many cases, however, criminal penalties seem to have been added to legislation hastily and without adequate consideration of their necessity or usefulness.

§ 8.14 Criminal Liability of Officers and Directors

Corporate officers and directors are individually liable for the crimes they commit as well as the crimes the corporation commits in which it has participated and meets the requisite mens rea for the offense.[87] The individual does not have a defense that she committed the crime to further the corporation's interests.[88] Conscious avoidance can be the equivalent to the officer acting with knowledge.[89] Because mens rea has been a staple of English common law,[90] officers and directors in most instances are not vicariously responsible under the criminal law for the violations of their subordinates, unless the officer or director had knowledge of the subordinate's criminal act.[91] However, conscious avoidance can be the equivalent to the officer acting with knowledge.[92] Individuals may invoke impossibility to prevent the criminal act as a defense, although it has not yet been widely adopted.[93] If the business is unlawful, an entity's executive may be held vicariously liable for a subordinate's criminal acts regardless of whether the executive was present or had knowledge of the act.[94] If a statute expressly includes a knowledge requirement, the jury instruction must give effect to that requirement.[95]

However, with the enactment of strict liability criminal provisions in public welfare and regulatory statutes, the traditional bases for criminalizing conduct shifted from punishment of misbehavior to protection of the public from harm. This shift in emphasis has given rise to the "responsible corporate officer" doctrine whereby a corporate official can be criminally responsible without proof of his knowledge of a violation.[96] The doctrine, however, is limited to violation of certain "public welfare" or "regulatory" statutes encompassing a strict liability standard.[97] Expansion of the responsible corporate officer doctrine to areas where it has not already been adopted is guided by

---

[86] For the view that corporate mens rea is not socially useful in proscribing misbehavior, but mens rea can play a useful role in determining the sanction to be imposed upon the corporation, see V.S. Khanna, Is the Notion of Corporate Fault a Faulty Notion? The Case of Corporate Mens Rea, 79 B.U.L. Rev. 355 (1999). A succinct review of the law and economic commentators on this subject appears in Jennifer Arlen. Corporate Crime and Its Control, in New Palgrave Dictionary of Economics and the Law 492 (Peter Newman ed. 1998).

[87] See, e.g., United States v. Sherpix, Inc., 512 F.2d 1361 (D.C. Cir. 1975).

[88] See, e.g., Pugh v. State, 536 So.2d 99 (Ala. Crim. App. 1986).

[89] See, e.g., United States v. Gold, 743 F.2d 800 (11th Cir. 1984).

[90] For an elegant and thorough review of the history of mens rea, see United States v. Cordoba-Hincapie, 825 F.Supp. 485, 489–96 (E.D.N.Y. 1993) (J. Weinstein).

[91] See generally C.J.S. Corporations § 649 (2011).

[92] See, e.g., United States v. Gold, 743 F.2d 800 (11th Cir. 1984); United States v. MacDonald & Watson Waste Oil Co., 933 F.2d 35, 55 (1st Cir. 1991); United States v. Hopkins, 55 F.3d 533, 542 (1995). See generally Ira P. Robbins, The Ostrich Instruction: Deliberate Ignorance as a Criminal Mens Rea, 81 J. Crim. L. & Criminology 191 (1990).

[93] See Amiad Kushner, Applying the Responsible Corporate Officer Doctrine Outside the Public Welfare Context, 93 J. Crim.L. & Criminology 681, 700 (2003); see also, United States v. Park, 421 U.S. 658, 673 (1975).

[94] 18B Am. Jur. 2d Corporations § 16.20.

[95] United States v. MacDonald & Watson Waste Oil Co., 933 F.2d 35, 51–52 (1st Cir. 1991).

[96] See generally Ronald M. Broudy, Note, RCRA and the Responsible Corporate Officer Doctrine: Getting Tough on Corporate Offenders by Sidestepping the Mens Rea Requirement, 80 Ky. L.J. 1055 (1991/92).

[97] United States v. MacDonald & Watson Waste Oil. Co., 933 F.2d 35, 51–52 (1st Cir. 1991).

Meyer v. Holley,[98] where the Supreme Court held that expansion of such vicarious liability is to be guided by whether holding an officer vicariously liable would be supported by legislative intent.

The responsible corporate officer doctrine traces its genesis to two Supreme Court decisions, the most significant being *United States v. Park*.[99] Park was president and CEO of a national food chain whose warehouse was found to have evidence of rodents. He was prosecuted under the Food, Drug and Cosmetic Act's provision that imposed strict liability for adulterated products. The Supreme Court affirmed a jury instruction that he violated the act if the jury found he "had a responsible relation" to the violation.[100] Under the doctrine, the president was liable without the need to establish is action or inaction was with mens rea and arises generally in connection with public health and safety statutes.[101]

The most important limitation on the scope of the responsible corporate officer doctrine is found in *Parks'* facts. A predicate to the Court's holding was its emphasis that the violation was of a "public welfare" statute. Moreover, the offense was a misdemeanor punishable by a very small fine.[102] These factors should have a significant influence in restricting application of the doctrine beyond the food, health, and safety area.[103] The doctrine has been invoked in tax matters,[104] and has been followed in many state court decisions.[105]

Some commentators question whether culpability (blameworthiness) is nonetheless an additional consideration in the responsible corporate officer doctrine.[106] Consider that the responsible corporate officer doctrine is at odds with the approach customarily taken that officers are not under the doctrine of respondeat superior vicariously liable for the acts of subordinates. The majority view is that the Supreme Court has not intended to impose unrestrained vicarious liability on senior officers.[107] Indeed, *Park* supports this restrained view with its observation that the officer to be deemed responsible must have some level of colorable blameworthiness.[108] This is most easily met if the officer had

---

[98]   537 U.S. 280 (2003).

[99]   United States v. Park, 421 U.S. 658 (1975). The other, United States v. Dotterweich, 320 U.S. 277 (1943), is less important because its actual holding was limited to whether individuals were included within the statutory proscription of "persons." Its contribution to the subject is that in reaching its conclusion that they are, the court held that defendants include those who had a "responsible share in the furtherance of the activity." *Id.* at 284. *See* Craig S. Lerner, The Trial of Joseph Dotterweich: The Origins of the "Responsible Corporate Officer" Doctrine, 11 Crim L. & Phil. 493 (2017).

[100]   421 U.S. at 666 n.9.

[101]   *See* United States v. White, 766 F. Supp. 873, 895 (E.D. Wash. 1991).

[102]   The fine for each violation (there were five in *Parks*) was $50. 421 U.S. at 666.

[103]   *See, e.g.,* United States v. MacDonald & Watson Waste Oil Co., 933 F.2d 35 (1st Cir. 1991) (responsible officer doctrine does not apply to felony prosecution involving specific intent). The environmental area is an area of intense efforts to apply the doctrine, with only limited success. *See* Cynthia H. Finn, Comment, The Responsible Corporate Officer, Criminal Liability, and Mens Rea: Limitations on the RCO Doctrine, 46 Am. U. L. Rev. 543, 562–569 (1996).

[104]   *See* Purcell v. United States, 1 F.3d 932, 936 (9th Cir. 1993).

[105]   *See, e.g.,* State v. Kailua Auto Wreckers, 615 P.2d 730 (Hawai'i 1980) (spouse who was figurehead president deemed a responsible party for environmental violations).

[106]   Amiad Kushner, Applying the Responsible Corporate Officer Doctrine Outside the Public Welfare Context, 93 J. Crim. L. & Criminology 681, 700 (2003).

[107]   Amiad Kushner, Applying the Responsible Corporate Officer Doctrine Outside the Public Welfare Context, 93 J. Crim. L. & Criminology 681, 696 (2003).

[108]   Amiad Kushner, Applying the Responsible Corporate Officer Doctrine Outside the Public Welfare Context, 93 J. Crim. L. & Criminology 681, 700 (2003).

notice of the criminal conduct. A different view is that the responsible corporate officer doctrine's fundamental purpose is to impose criminal liability for officer's failure to prevent violations of applicable statutes. This view invokes a public welfare perspective for the scope of criminal responsibility.[109]

---

[109] Todd S. Aagaard, A Fresh Look at the Responsible Relation Doctrine, 96 J. Crim. L. & Criminology 1245, 1263 (2006); Susan F. Mandiberg, Moral Issues in Environmental Crime, 7 Fordham Envtl. L. J. 881, 898 (1996). *See also*, United States v. Ming Hong, 242 F.3d 528, 531 (4th Cir. 2001).

Chapter 9

FUNCTIONS AND POWERS OF DIRECTORS

Table of Sections

§ 9.1   The Traditional Pattern of Corporate Governance

The traditional corporate pattern is triangular, with the shareholders at the base. The shareholders, who are generally viewed as the ultimate or residual owners of the business, select the personnel at the next level—namely, the board of directors.[1] According to accepted wisdom, the board of directors appoints the chief executive officer and other corporate officers, determines corporate policies, oversees the officers' work, and in general manages the corporation or supervises the management of its affairs. The directors' control of a corporation is limited by statutory requirements that shareholder approval be obtained for fundamental corporate acts such as charter amendments, consolidations, mergers, voluntary dissolution, and sale or lease of all or substantially all corporate assets.

The principal corporate officers, or executives, are at the top of the corporate triangle. These officers execute policies that supposedly have been fixed by the board of

---

[1]   This may be by a straight majority vote or under a system of cumulative voting for directors. *See* § 13.16, 13.17, *infra*.

directors. The corporation's executives and operating management are said to derive their authority and legitimacy from the board.[2]

Directors are elected by shareholders. Election of directors traditionally has been by a plurality vote. However, in recent years, an increasing number of corporations require a majority of affirmative votes to elect a director.[3] In 2006, Delaware amended it corporate law to allow a shareholder adopted bylaw (not subject to repeal or amendment by the board) to proscribe the method of director selection.[4] Other states also permit majority election requirements. Directors customarily serve annual terms, though modern statutes permit staggered three-year terms. Although voted into office by the shareholders, the director is not a mere agent of the shareholders. As discussed later in this chapter, the process for a director's removal from office is formal. Directors therefore serve until their terms expire or until duly removed. Thus, a shareholder vote reducing the size of the board of directors does not impact the tenure of a current direction.[5] Similarly, advancing the annual meeting date by many months did not shorten the terms of directors as "annual" was interpreted by the Delaware Supreme Court to mean a date "approximately" one year after the last annual meeting date.[6]

In legal theory, the directors are supreme during their term of office. As will be examined later in this chapter, many modern statutes empower shareholders to remove directors at any time with or without cause[7] and, even in the absence of such a statute, removal power may be conferred on the shareholders by the corporation's charter or bylaws. The power of the removal is not the only mechanism for assuring accountability to the company's owners. Other forces at play here are the demands of product markets, reputational considerations, and changes in control either through a tender offer or proxy solicitation.

Majority rule is the traditional governing principle, and the holders of a majority of the voting shares certainly have the ultimate power to control the corporation.[8] The holders of a majority of the voting shares elect the directors, or most of them.[9] And as can be expected, the board of directors usually acts by majority vote of directors present and voting.

§ 9.2   Continuing Efforts to Strengthen the Monitoring Role of the Board of Directors

The Evolution from Super Management Body to Independent Monitor. How and why corporate governance has evolved for the public corporation in the United

---

[2]   The powers of officers and agents are discussed in Chapter 8.

[3]   Cal. Corp. Code § 708.5 (permitting public companies to adopt a bylaw provision requiring majority election of directors); 8 Del. C. § 216 (same).

[4]   8 Del. C. § 216.

[5]   Crown EMAK Partners, LLC v. Kurz, 992 A.2d 377 (Del. 2010).

[6]   Airgas, Inc. v. Air Products and Chemicals, Inc., 8 A.3d 1182 (Del. 2010).

[7]   *See, e.g.,* Model Bus. Corp. Act § 8.08 (2016) (hereinafter MBCA). *Accord,* Model Bus. Corp. Act § 39 (1969) (hereinafter former MBCA).

[8]   In many publicly held corporations, however, shares are so widely distributed, perhaps with no person holding or controlling over a fraction of 1 percent of shares outstanding, that the shareholders cannot organize into effective political or decision-making units. The consequence is that real control is severed from ownership, and the chief executive officer or a group of the corporation's principal executives actually control the corporation. *See infra* §§ 9.4 to 9.5.

[9]   *See* MBCA §§ 7.21, 8.03 (1984).

States is best illustrated by the contrasting approaches in two leading decisions in Delaware. In a 1963 decision, the Delaware Supreme Court in *Graham v. Allis-Chalmers Manufacturing Co.*,[10] dismissed a derivative action against the directors of a large publicly held corporation that sought to recover from the directors losses the corporation suffered as a consequence of illegal price fixing by subordinates in one of the numerous divisions within the highly decentralized management structure of the large public corporation. The plaintiff argued the directors were remiss in not installing surveillance and compliance programs that would have prevented the antitrust violation. The Court dismissed the action, reasoning:

> [T]he question of whether a corporate director has become liable for losses to the corporation through neglect is determined by the circumstances. If he has recklessly reposed confidence in an obviously untrustworthy employee, has refused or neglected cavalierly to perform his duty as a director, or has ignored either willfully or through inattention obvious danger signs of employee wrongdoing, the law will cast the burden of liability upon him. This is not the case at bar. . . .

> [A]bsent cause for suspicion there is no duty upon the directors to install and operate a corporate system of espionage to ferret out wrongdoing which they have no reason to suspect exists.[11]

Thirty-three years later, the highly respected Chancellor of the Delaware Court of Chancery opined:

> [I]t would, in my opinion, be a mistake to conclude that our Supreme Court's statement in *Graham* concerning "espionage" means that corporate boards may satisfy their obligation to be reasonably informed concerning the corporation, without assuring themselves that information and reporting systems exist in the organization that are reasonably designed to provide senior management and the board itself timely, accurate information sufficient to allow management and the board, each within its scope, to reach informed judgments concerning both the corporation's compliance with law and its business performance. . . .

> Thus, I am of the view that a director's obligation includes a duty to attempt in good faith to assure that a corporate information and reporting system, which the board concludes is adequate, exists, and that failure to do so under some circumstances may, in theory at least, render a director liable for losses caused by non-compliance with applicable legal standards.[12]

Ten years later, in *Stone v. Ritter*,[13] the Delaware Supreme Court expressly approved the standard articulated by the Court of Chancery. Under Delaware law,

---

[10]   Graham v. Allis-Chalmers Manufacturing Co., 188 A.2d 125 (Del. 1963).

[11]   Graham v. Allis-Chalmers Manufacturing Co., 188 A.2d 125, 130 (Del. 1963).

[12]   In re Caremark International, Inc. Derivative Litig., 698 A.2d 959 (Del. Ch. 1996). The case involved a derivative suit seeking damages for the directors' failure to prevent subordinates from engaging in illegal referral payments to physicians. Before trial, the case was settled and Chancellor William T. Allen's opinion was in connection with his approval of the settlement.

[13]   Stone v. Ritter, 911 A.2d 362 (Del. 2006). In that derivative action, the court found that the directors were not personally liability for the failure of bank employees to file suspicious activity reports. The court observed that it is very difficult to establish director liability premised on employee failures in the absence of "red flags."

directors incur personal liability for failing to discharge their oversight responsibilities if they utterly failed to implement any reporting information system or controls or if they implemented a system but consciously failed to monitor or oversee its operations.

The contrasting approaches illustrate the movement from the view that the board of directors is a "super management" body that reviews and approves corporate strategies to today's widely held view that the board's essential function is to monitor the officer's stewardship. That movement did not occur without intense debate. It is a debate that continues to inform the expectations, and hence, demands placed upon the modern board of directors. The move toward outside directors whose role is to monitor management's stewardship has been greatly facilitated by the rise of financial institutions—public and private pension funds, mutual funds, insurance companies endowments, and foundations—who today collectively own more than one-half the shares of all publicly traded firms. Moreover, investors of all types have become increasingly focused on share value as the primary corporate objective.[14] With this focus, and believing directors that are better aligned with shareholder interest, there has been a substantial push in recent years for shareholders to have a means by which to nominate directors to stand for election. This challenges the pervasive practice of boards, with the heavy hand of managers, nominating those who stand for election and elections where rarely investors have any choice other than to vote for those nominated by the essentially self-perpetuating board. In addition to permissive amendments to the Delaware statute that empower shareholder bylaws authorizing their nomination of directors (as well as reimbursement of any expenses in seeking office),[15] the SEC amended its shareholder proposal rule to allow shareholders to include on the company's proxy statement a proposed bylaw setting forth procedures for shareholders to nominate directors.[16]

The heyday for calls for reform was the 1970s. Studies of the composition of boards and how directors discharged their tasks documented serious weaknesses in the operation of the board. Studies revealed that in most public corporations the executive officers carried out most of the functions that were commonly thought to be initiated by the board. Officers set the corporation's goals, develop plans for their achievement, allocate the company's resources, and make important policy decisions, including the selection of their successors and nominees to the board.[17]

Soon the debate shifted from evidence of weaknesses in corporate governance to its cure. Former Supreme Court Justice Arthur J. Goldberg popularized a role for a body of "overseers" composed entirely of outside directors who, with the assistance of a staff of experts (auditors, lawyers, financiers, and scientific experts), would evaluate management performance and yield reports to the stockholders.[18] A prominent

---

[14] Jeffrey Gordon, The Rise of Independent Directors in the United States, 1950–2005: Of Shareholder Value and Stock Market Prices, 59 Stan. L. Rev. 1465 (2007).

[15] As of 2009, the Delaware statute expressly permits bylaws giving shareholders access and also bylaws to provide for reimbursement of expenses incurred by shareholders when soliciting proxies to in an election of directors). Del. Code Ann. tit. 8, §§ 112, 113.

[16] Securities Exchange Act Rule 14a–8(i)(8), 17 C.F.R. § 240.14a–8(i)(8).

[17] See, e.g., Myles L. Mace, Directors: Myth and Reality 51–66 (1971); Myles L. Mace, The President and the Board of Directors, 50 Harv. Bus. Rev. 37, 41–44 (Mar.–Apr. 1972); Melvin A. Eisenberg, the Structure of the Corporation: A Legal Analysis 141–148 (1976).

[18] Arthur J. Goldberg, Debate on Outside Directors, N.Y. Times, Oct. 29, 1972, § 3, at 1, col. 3. ("The board is relegated to an advisory and independent monitoring function that is substantially different from the role of policy maker and guardian of shareholder and public interest contemplated by the law of corporations.").

California lawyer, reflecting Justice Goldberg's view for an increased role for non-management directors, also called for "the increased focus on due diligence requirements for individual directors."[19] Professor Christopher Stone, using insights from organization behavior literature, suggested a number of structural changes within the corporate hierarchy, such as officers who would have responsibility and authority with respect to environmental and product safety.[20] Dean Bayless Manning called for improving the flow of information to the board and the stockholders so that management's performance and leadership could be objectively evaluated.[21] And, consumer gadfly Ralph Nader and others reasoned that large public corporations have too significant an impact upon the nation for their governance practices to be a matter solely of state law; they accordingly called for the federal chartering of the larger and more powerful corporations.[22] Even the SEC entered the debate with its own proposals for improving corporate governance.[23]

The most enduring criticism of the hundreds of commentators is that of Professor William Cary, who called for federally imposed "minimum standards" for conduct by public corporations.[24] Though the object of his criticism is the law and courts of Delaware, the fount of that criticism is the internal affairs doctrine, the most significant of all legal principles. The internal affairs doctrine is essentially a choice of law rule; it holds that questions regarding the relations among shareholders, directors, and officers are governed by the law of the state of incorporation.[25] The emphasis here on the state reflects not only the federal system of government in the United States, but also the inertial forces of history whereby matters of corporate law have been a matter of state, not federal, law. And, unlike the continental "law of the seat" approach,[26] there is no requirement in the United States that incorporation be in a state where the company has its principal place of business or, for that matter, any business. Not only the state of incorporation is a matter of choice; to the extent that material differences exist in corporate governance procedures, there is also freedom to choose the level of rigor of applicable corporate governance rules.[27] And, it should be noted that the choice is one

---

[19] *See* Marshall L. Small, The Evolving Role of the Director in Corporate Governance, 30 Hastings L. J. 1353, 1355–1362 (1979). *See also* Thomas L. Hazen, Corporate Chartering and the Securities Markets: Shareholder Suffrage, Corporate Responsibility and Managerial Accountability, 1978 Wis. L. Rev. 391.

[20] *See* Christopher D. Stone, Where the Law Ends: The Social Control of Corporation Behavior (1975).

[21] Bayless Manning, Thinking Straight About Corporate Law Reform, 41 Law & Contemp. Prob. 3, 27–28 (Summer 1977).

[22] Ralph Nader, Mark Green & Joel Seligman, Taming the Giant Corporation (1976). *See also* Donald E. Schwartz, A Case for Federal Chartering of Corporations, 31 Bus. Law. 1125 (1976).

[23] *See* SEC Rule Proposals Concerning Shareholder Democracy and Corporate Governance, SEC Securities Exchange Act Rel. No. 34–14970 (July 18, 1978) in [1978 Transfer Binder] Fed. Sec. L. Rep. (CCH) ¶ 81,645.

[24] William L. Cary, Federalism and Corporate Law: Reflections Upon Delaware, 83 Yale L.J., 663 (1974).

[25] The internal affairs doctrine is not, however, without qualification. By statute, certain provisions of the corporate law of California and New York apply to certain corporations with a substantial presence in the host state, even though incorporated in another state. *See* Norwood P. Beveridge, Jr., The Internal Affairs Doctrine: The Proper Law of a Corporation, 44 Bus. Law. 693 (1989) (discussing few instances in which host states have applied their law rather than the state of incorporation).

[26] *See* Sorensen, Karsten Engsig, "Prospect for European Company Law After the Judgment of the European Court of Justice in *Centros Ltd.*," in Dashwood, Alan and Ward, Agegla (eds.). The Cambridge Yearbook of European Legal Studies 203 (1999).

[27] For a market-oriented argument in favor of such choice, *see, e.g.*, Roberto Romano, The State Competition Debate in Corporate Law, 8 Cardozo L. Rev. 709 (1987); Ralph Winter, State Law, Shareholder Protection and the Theory of the Corporation, 6 J. Legal Stud. 251 (1977).

made by management.[28] Cary's article introduced into the debate on corporate governance the question whether the result of such choice was a "race to laxity," in which all states were competing for corporate charters by sacrificing protection of stockholders by amending their statutes to provide ever increasing levels of discretion to managers.

In the race for corporate charters, Delaware remains supreme. Over forty percent of the corporations listed on the New York Stock Exchange are incorporated in Delaware. Delaware's supremacy is easily understood. Indeed, it enjoys an unerodable advantage over other states. First, it has the largest body of precedent interpreting a corporate statute. To the extent business people like certainty, Delaware provides it. Though its present code bears the date of its enactment in 1967, it carried forward significant portions of the earlier law so that pre-1967 decisions continue to illuminate the Delaware statute. Second, Delaware's corporate law cannot be easily amended because the state constitution conditions any change in the corporate law upon a two-thirds vote of the legislature.[29] This stability of the legal landscape provides further certainty. Third, Delaware populates its judiciary with those experienced in the trenches of practicing corporate law. Though they have not themselves been captains of industry, members of the Supreme Court and the Court of Chancery have counseled many who were. Fourth, Delaware's Court of Chancery is not only experienced in handling numerous corporate matters, but its procedures facilitate the litigants' securing a hearing and resolution in the most time bounded disputes, especially issues that arise in the context of takeovers. And finally, though perhaps not uniformly the most permissive and broadly enabling of all corporate statutes, any differences from the statutes of states are at the margins.[30] Overall, Delaware's success in attracting corporate charters is most understandable.

Throughout all the commentary in the 1970s there was the theme that the board of directors needed to be more independent of management. The crispest insights into this call were provided by Professor Mel Eisenberg and were ultimately memorialized into an influential book.[31] He wisely advised that the issue was not just that of independence, although independence is a necessary condition. The issue ultimately was melding the outside director to a task that she or he is capable of discharging. Even when outside directors constitute a majority of the board of directors, they face important constraints on time, information, and staff to permit them to perform as super policymakers or managers. Professor Eisenberg suggests that the appropriate aspiration for outside directors be changed to that of evaluating management's stewardship, removing poorly performing managers, and developing and enacting succession plans.[32]

Corporate Governance Reform. As the above quote from *Caremark* indicates, the rest is history. Between the 1960s to the mid 1980s a tremendous change in the composition of the American boardroom occurred. Where in 1960 approximately 63 percent of the corporations could report that a majority of their directors were outsiders,

---

[28]   To be sure, when an existing corporation reincorporates in another state the procedure customarily involves a merger of the existing company with one formed under the new domicile's laws; this transaction requires a vote of the stockholders. However, there is no evidence of successful resistance to management's recommendation that the company reincorporate.

[29]   Del. Const. art. IX, § 1.

[30]   *See* William J. Carney, The Production of Corporate Law, 71 So. Cal. L. Rev. 715 (1998).

[31]   *See* Melvin A. Eisenberg, the Structure of the Corporation: A Legal Analysis (1976).

[32]   Melvin A. Eisenberg, the Structure of the Corporation: A Legal Analysis 159–168 (1976).

by 1989 the percentage had climbed to 86 percent.[33] More generally, the trend that began three decades ago has resulted in (1) boards of directors of publicly held corporations having a higher percentage of independent outside directors; (2) independent outside directors now serve on key committees and on some committees, for example audit and compensation committees, are a majority; (3) director fees have generally increased over time; (4) outside directors are devoting more time to corporate affairs; (5) there is evidence that outside directors are developing greater expertise in the work of the committees on which they serve; and (6) independent outside directors are more engaged in determining policy and monitoring the performance of executives. Corporate law provides a powerful inducement for boards to be not just independent but *very* independent as with greater board independence management decisions are subject to substantially less scrutiny when challenged.[34] Nonetheless, there is on-going criticism of the prevalent practice of public company boards being made up of outside directors as it is believed this results in there being few directors with a deep knowledge and experience with the company; public boards today frequently have the CEO as the only insider with the remaining directors being independent so that they excluding no senior managers, none of its investment bankers, and not its outside lawyer: 'the generations-long "good governance" focus on director independence has marginalized company-specific and industry knowledge and discouraged the retention of directors with financial and emotional ties to the companies they serve.'[35]

Through most of the 1980s, the major forum, and even focal point, of debate on corporate governance was not the epic tales that were to be told in the heyday of takeover contests, but rather the American Law Institute's Corporate Governance Project. Historically, the ALI produced thoughtful restatements of the law whose black letter law and supporting commentary nurtured efforts for greater uniformity among the states, frequently recognizing that the better approaches were not those followed by a minority of the states. The project's reporters, led by Professor Mel Eisenberg, professed (1) to restate the law where judicial authority was deemed satisfactory under modern standards and (2) proffer recommendations where no judicial authority existed or where judicial decisions were unsatisfactory by modern standards.[36] This said, the project's critics believed there was too much reform, certainly in the early drafts of the Corporate Governance Project, so that throughout the project was never seen as the more traditional restatement of the law. This caused it to become the most controversial of all ALI projects and, equally visible, to drop any reference to "restatement" from its title. But the primary theme that public corporations are to have independent directors who are to adhere to an active, monitoring model survived the more than decade long assaults on the project. The membership of the American Law Institute approved the final draft in May 1992.

---

[33] *See* Jeremy Bacon, Membership and Organization of Corporate Boards, tbl. 6 at 8 (N.Y. Conf. Bd. 1990).

[34] *See e.g.,* William T. Allen, Jack B. Jacobs & Leo E. Strine, Function over Form: A Reassessment of Standards of Review in Delaware Corporation Law, 26 Del. J. Corp. L. 859, 874–75 (2001)(decisions involving conflicts of interest are subject to review for entire fairness—procedure and price—as the directors' personal interest are viewed as being potentially adverse to the shareholders so that the directors cannot be presumed to be motivated to achieve the highest transaction price acceptable in the market).

[35] *See e.g.,* Theodore N. Mervis & William Savitt, The Dangers of Independent Directors, 40 Del. J. Corp. L. 481, 487 (2016).

[36] *See* James S. Mofsky & Robert D. Rubin, Introduction: A Symposium on the ALI Corporate Governance Project, 37 U. Miami L. Rev. 169, 170 (1983).

The overarching principle of the ALI is its recognition of the board of directors as a corporate organ that can and should perform a monitoring function, and among other things, to address potential overreaching by management, to replace management if it is not meeting established corporate goals, and to prevent the commission of illegal acts.[37] Significantly, the ALI Project, in addition to calling for an independent audit committee, recommends that large public corporations also have nominating and compensation committees. The project also strengthens the role that independent directors are to play in policing conflicts of interest, usurpation of corporate opportunities, and the conduct of derivative suits.

Among the most recent trends among American boardrooms is the movement toward encouraging, and in some instances requiring, the outside director to have a substantial equity position in the corporation on whose board the director serves. The call is to reduce the customary perquisites enjoyed by the outside director, and particularly providing health and retirement benefits and providing for the director to devote some of his director's fees to the purchase of shares in the company. The obvious objective is to more closely align the outside director with the firm's owners.[38] Another trend has been reexamining certain matters bearing directly on the commitment of outside directors to monitor management as well as internal procedures that nurture a viable monitoring role. In 1996 a Blue Ribbon Commission suggested a number of practices for public corporations that would enhance the effectiveness of their outside directors.[39] Among the Commission's recommendations were the call that directors not serve on more than six boards, that there be procedures for independent review of the CEO's and directors' effectiveness, that there be created a board governance committee, an outside director be designated to chair the board, and that there be periodic executive sessions for outside directors.

---

[37] A.L.I. Corporate Governance Project, § 3.02 dictates the following:

(a) The board of directors of a publicly held corporation [§ 1.31] should perform the following functions:

(1) Select, regularly evaluate, fix the compensation of, and, where appropriate, replace the principal senior executives [§ 1.30];

(2) Oversee the conduct of the corporation's business to evaluate whether the business is being properly managed;

(3) Review and, where appropriate, approve the corporation's financial objectives and major corporate plans and actions;

(4) Review and, where appropriate, approve major changes in, and determinations of other major questions of choice respecting, the appropriate auditing and accounting principles and practices to be used in the preparation of the corporation's financial statements;

(5) Perform such other functions as are prescribed by law, or assigned to the board under a standard of the corporation [§ 1.36].

An earlier draft specifically listed monitoring to deter illegal conduct, stating that the directors should "monitor the conduct of the corporation's business to determine whether the corporation's resources are being managed in a manner that is efficient and consistent with the principles of" Section 2.01 of the Project, which among other features commands that the corporation "is obliged, to the same extent as a natural person, to act within the boundaries set by law."

Comparable specifications for the board of directors are embraced in ABA Committee on Corporate Laws, Corporate Director's Guidebook 3–5 (3d ed. 2001), reprinted in, 56 Bus. Law. 1571, 1578–80 (2001).

[38] See Report of the National Association of Corporate Directors Blue Ribbon Commission on Director Compensation 12 (1995).

[39] See Report of the NACD Blue Ribbon Commission on Director Professionalism (1996).

There is a good deal of intuitive appeal to firming up the bonds between the outside directors and the shareholders. Pursuing strategies to this end is likely to be the area of great attention in the next few years. Several considerations point toward this being a politically viable option. As we are well aware, approximately one-half of all equity investments are held by financial institutions, the most significant group being public and private pension plans.[40] With such institutionalization of ownership, the refrain of Berle and Means[41] that the seriousness of the problem posed by the separation of ownership from management is exacerbated by owners being both numerous and that their holdings are relatively small is only partially true. And, more is involved than simply the institutionalization of share holdings. Because a significant percentage of such institutional holdings are indexed, their holders effectively cannot exit from under-performing or overreaching managers by disposing their shares. Thus, in theory, a significant portion of publicly traded shares are held by investors who not only are sophisticated (or are advised by those that are), but also, by reason of the absolute size of their holdings and the absence in many instances of the possibility of exit, have financial incentives that are best served by their portfolio companies' managers performing well.[42] So viewed, there will likely be on-going discussions of mechanisms that can be used to assure representation of some institutional holders on the board of public companies.[43] One ingenious, but effective suggestion is to restore the prominent role that cumulative voting once had with the American *public* corporation. In a careful study of the cumulative voting, Professor Jeff Gordon finds that the number of states mandating cumulative voting peaked in 1956, but fell into disuse because of the fear that it encouraged proxy contests and would facilitate hostile takeovers.[44] He envisions restoring cumulative voting to the public corporation as a means for institutional holders to secure a voice on the board.

Prior to 1992, the SEC's regulations for proxies stilled the voice of financial institutions.[45] By broadly defining proxies to include any communication that would encourage or discourage a holder in how to vote, and subjecting each such solicitation to nontrivial regulation, institutions faced excessive coordination costs with respect to not only pursuing common objectives, but also simply learning whether they indeed had common objectives or concerns with respect to their portfolio companies. Important steps were taken in 1992 by the SEC to facilitate the institutions in exercising their collective voice within the boardroom.[46] The SEC amended its rules with the overall effect of reducing the restrictions on stockholder communication among themselves. For example, new Rule 14a–2(b)(1) exempts from the filing and format requirements communications by a person who is not seeking proxies and does not have certain

---

[40] *See* NYSE Fact Book for the Year 2000, 61 (50.8% of equity shares are held by financial institutions at the end of the third quarter of 2000).

[41] The reference is to the classic work, Adolf A. Berle & Gardiner C. Means, The Modern Corporation and Private Property (1933).

[42] *See generally* Albert Hirshman, Exit, Voice, and Loyalty (1970) (when exit costs are significant, a rational actor will seek to address the cause for exit by involving himself more in the organization's decision making).

[43] For a proposal in this regard, *see* Ronald J. Gilson & Reinier Kraakman, Reinventing the Outside Director: An Agenda for Institutional Investors, 43 Stan. L. Rev. 863 (1991).

[44] *See* Jeffrey N. Gordon, Institutions as Relational Investors: A New Look at Cumulative Voting, 94 Colum. L. Rev. 124 (1994).

[45] *See* Bernard Black, Shareholder Passivity Reexamined, 89 Mich. L. Rev. 520 (1990).

[46] *See* Securities Exchange Act Release No. 34–31326 (Oct. 16, 1992).

specified types of "substantial interest" in the subject matter.[47] Further, new Rule 14a–1(l)(2)(iv) permits holders to announce how they will vote on any matter. Under these rules, holders, and particularly financial institutions, can more easily coordinate their actions to maximize their influence at stockholders meetings because they no longer face costly and burdensome prefiling and format requirements.[48] In recent years, there has been a new push for shareholder access to the director nomination process.[49] In addition to permissive amendments to the Delaware statute, the SEC adopted rules permitting shareholder access to management's proxy statement for director nominations but those rules have been put on hold pending litigation challenging the SEC's rulemaking.[50]

In the wake of growing concern about the prevalence of "earnings management," restatements of reported income, and massive accounting frauds by public companies, then Chairman of the SEC, Arthur Levitt, in 1998 called for "nothing less than a fundamental cultural change on the part of corporate management as well as the whole financial community."[51] Front and center in this reform initiative were changes that the SEC, with the aid of a Blue Ribbon Committee, brought about for audit committees of corporations listed on the NYSE, AMEX, and Nasdaq. Informing the thrust of the changes for the audit committee was a 1999 study of companies charged by the SEC with financial fraud from 1987 to 1997, which found, among other factors, that 25 percent of the surveyed companies did not have an audit committee, that of those that did have audit committees nearly one-third of the committee members' independence was compromised by close relationship with, or actual participation in, the firm's management, and that 65 percent of the committee members lacked accounting or financial expertise.[52] Though some of the recommendations of the Blue Ribbon Committee[53] were ultimately modified, most of its proposals were embraced by the financial community and are now part of the listing requirements of the NYSE, AMEX, and Nasdaq.[54]

---

[47]   This provision is not available, for example, to officers, directors, director nominees, or a person who has in its Williams Act filing disclosed an intent to control the issuer. A holder of more than $5 million of the company's shares must nevertheless file the communication with the SEC within three days of its circulation.

[48]   However, their communication remains a "proxy solicitation" that is subject to Rule 14a–9's prohibition against material omissions or misstatements in a proxy solicitation.

[49]   *See, e.g.,* CA, Inc. v. AFSCME Employees Pension Plan, 953 A.2d 227 (Del. 2008) (a shareholder proposal relating to procedures regarding director elections was a proper matter for shareholder consideration but not mandating reimbursement of proxy expenses was not proper). As of 2009, the Delaware statute expressly permits bylaws giving shareholders access and also bylaws to provide for reimbursement of expenses incurred by shareholders (when soliciting proxies to in an election of directors). Del. Code Ann. tit. 8, §§ 112, 113.

[50]   *See* Facilitating Shareholder Director Nominations, Sec. Act Rel. No. 33–9136, Sec. Exch. Act Rel. No. 34–62764, Inv. Co. Act Rel. No. IC–29384, 2010 WL 3343532 (SEC Aug. 25, 2010)., Sec. Act Rel. No. 33–9149, Sec. Exch. Act Rel. No. 34–63031, Inv. Co. Act Rel. No. IC–29456 (SEC Oct. 4, 2010) (order granting stay).

[51]   Arthur Levitt, Chairman, SEC, Address to the NYU Center for Law and Business (Sept. 28, 1998), quoted in Edward Brodsky, New Rules for Audit Committees and Quarterly Statements, 223 NYLJ 3 (April 12, 2000).

[52]   *See* Mark S. Beasley *et al.,* Fraudulent Financial Reporting 1987–97, An Analysis of U.S. Companies (COSO 1999).

[53]   *See* Report and Recommendations of the Blue Ribbon Committee on Improving the Effectiveness of Corporate Audit Committees, reprinted in 54 Bus. Law. 1067 (1999).

[54]   The SEC's actions occurred on two fronts. First, it approved amendments to the listing requirements adopted by the NYSE, AMEX and Nasdaq to embrace the reforms for audit committees. *See* SEC Release No. 34–42231 (Dec. 1, 1999). Second, it amended its own disclosure requirements for Regulation S–K. *See* SEC Release No. 34–422266 (Dec. 14, 1999). Both developments are reviewed in Joseph I. Goldstein and Jeffrey F.

The core considerations of each organization's listing requirements pertaining to audit committees are substantially identical: listed firms are to have an audit committee of three "independent" directors (in exceptional circumstances, one member may be non-independent); independence requires, among other features, that the member have not been an employee within three years or received (excluding board fees) compensation greater than $60,000 (the NYSE expresses this more generally in terms of a relationship that will impede independence); each member must be financially literate; one member must have financial sophistication, such as employment experience in finance or accounting; and the committee must have a written charter.[55]

The SEC's disclosure requirements reinforced the listing requirements for audit committees. The audit committee must disclose whether it has recommended to the board that the audited financial statements be included in the company's annual report on Form 10-K.[56] Moreover, the audit committee must acknowledge whether it has had discussions with management and the independent accountants, and whether those discussions were the basis for its recommendations regarding the inclusion of the financial reports.[57] The significance of this is it draws the audit committee members closer to the information contained in any included financial report, thus making it easier to establish they are primary participants with respect to any misrepresentation that may be committed in the financial statements. This may not be that significant a development since all directors must sign the Form 10-Q that is filed with the SEC and at least one circuit has held this is sufficient to make each director a primary participant in any resulting suit under the antifraud provision.[58] A further disclosure requirement is that each proxy statement must disclose whether the company has an audit committee, and once every three years the proxy statement must disclose the responsibilities and duties of the audit committee as embodied in its charter.[59]

The Enron-Era and Sarbanes-Oxley Reforms. A significant boost for better governance for public companies occurred in the aftermath of the collapse in the fall of 2001 of Enron Corporation, a company that was the sixth largest American corporation and which had been ranked the most innovative for five straight years by Fortune 500 executives. Within a few weeks its stock plummeted from a trading in the high $40's to being nearly worthless when it filed for bankruptcy in early November 2001. Enron's final achievement was its becoming the largest bankruptcy every filed; an honor it held only briefly, being dwarfed by the bankruptcy of WorldCom in 2002, another failure that was linked to serious financial fraud by senior executives.[60] Enron, WorldCom, and no fewer than a dozen other large public companies shocked the public conscience, not because they failed, but because of the revelations of extensive reporting frauds,

---

Robertson, Modifications to Audit Committee Requirements May Increase Director Liability, 32 BNA Sec. Reg. L. Rep. 1104 (August 14, 2000).

[55] The charter must, among other matters, specify the scope of the committee's responsibilities, the outside auditor's responsibilities to the board and the audit committee, and the audit committee's responsibility in the selection and oversight of the auditor.

[56] *See* Item 306(a)(4) of Regulation S–K, 17 C.F.R. § 228.306(a)(4) (2009).

[57] 17 C.F.R. § 228.306(a)(4) (2009). This acknowledgment and recommendation are to include the printed names of each member of the audit committee.

[58] *See* Howard v. Everex Sys., Inc., 228 F.3d 1057 (9th Cir. 2000).

[59] *See* Regulation Rule 14a–101(e)(ii) & (iii), 17 C.F.R. § 240.14a–101(e)(ii) & (iii) (2002).

[60] For discussions of Enron and the causes of its collapse, *see, e.g.,* William Bratton, Enron and the Dark Side of Shareholder Value, 76 Tulane L. Rev. 1275 (2002); John C. Coffee, Jr., Understanding Enron: "It's About Gatekeepers, Stupid," 57 Bus. Law. 1403 (2002).

overreaching, and wasteful misbehavior by their most senior executives. Certainly there were multiple failures in the role of each company's outside directors, their certified public accountants, and others. The collapse of Enron et al. came when investors were witnessing a meltdown in market capitalization on Wall Street of approximately 4 trillion dollars. The national mood was not to turn a blind eye to the problems of the American corporation.

The first wave of regulatory responses came from the New York Stock Exchange and Nasdaq, both of which strengthened their corporate governance requirements for listed companies by mandating at least a majority of the board be independent (this requirement does not apply to so-called controlled companies where there is a definite controlling stockholder). Not surprisingly, a central focus of their efforts was the audit committee. Both bodies require listed companies to have a majority of their board of directors to meet the new tightened standard for independence and that the audit committee must be comprised solely of independent directors. The nominating and compensation committees of NYSE listed companies must also be comprised only of independent directors. Nasdaq instead permits nominating committees to have one non-independent member (if disclosed) or nominations can instead be approved by a majority of the independent directors. The NYSE's new requirements provide that the board is to determine whether a director has a "material relationship" that would prevent a director from being independent; the NYSE does not further define specifically what such a relationship would be but asks that the board consider "all relevant facts and circumstances."[61] In 2008 the NYSE further amended its rules to allow for a director to qualify as independent so long as the director has not received compensation, excluding director fees, in excess of $120,000 during any twelve month period within the previous three years. These new independence rules also look to immediate family members of directors, who may not be involved with the company's auditing procedures or likewise have received compensation in excess of $120,000 during any twelve month period within the previous three years. Nasdaq also specifies that a director would not be independent if he or she, or a family member, received payments in excess of $120,000. Both the NYSE and Nasdaq further require that all non-management directors meet regularly in executive sessions. And, subject to certain limitations, shareholders must be allowed to vote on all equity-based compensation plans. Finally, the NYSE mandates that companies adopt corporate governance guidelines, and both the NYSE and Nasdaq require codes of conduct with prompt publication of any waiver of their requirements for senior executive officers. The NYSE requires the CEO to annually certify to the Exchange that the company complies with the governance provisions for listing. Nasdaq enters the field of conflict of interest transactions by requiring the audit committee to approve all related party transactions.

Congress too entered the fray, passing in July 2002 the far-reaching Sarbanes-Oxley Act that, among other features, amended the Securities Act of 1933 and the Securities Exchange Act of 1934. In response to the common practice of auditors to provide substantial non-audit services to their audit clients, section 10A of the Exchange Act was amended to bar auditors from providing certain non-audit services.[62] The amendments also seek to centralize the company-auditor relationship with the audit committee by

---

61   The NYSE does provide for a five-year cooling off period and Nasdaq has a three-year period in the case of former employees before they can be deemed independent.

62   15 U.S.C. § 78j–1(g) (2009).

requiring that all services provided by the auditor be approved by the audit committee, subject to a 5 percent de minimus exemption.[63] And, the auditor is required to make timely reports to the audit committee of all critical accounting policies, alternative treatments that have been discussed, and other material communications with management.[64] Issuers must disclose whether its audit committee has a "financial expert," thus putting pressure on companies to assure that at least one member of the audit committee meets this indirect requirement. Finally, audit partners are to rotate every five years,[65] thereby hopefully avoiding too cozy a relationship from forming between the issuer and the engagement partner. Sarbanes—or the committee to be comprised totally of independent directors (meaning at least one can receive fees other that director fees from the corporation or otherwise be deemed an "affiliate") and the audit committee must establish a process for addressing complaints or reports of accounting irregularities.[66]

Perhaps the most radical step for Sarbanes-Oxley was its entering into an area that heretofore was exclusively the domain of the states. The Act amends section 13 of the Securities Exchange Act to bar reporting companies from making personal loans to directors or officers.[67] The initial issues posed by this bar is what impact it would have on a wide range of standard practices such as advancing relocation expenses, litigation expenses per state indemnification statutes, and stock option plans that envision cashless exercise by their holder.

The Act duplicated efforts already under way at the SEC by mandating the chief executive officer and the chief financial officer to certify that the periodic reports filed with the SEC (1) have been reviewed, (2) to the certifying officer's knowledge the report "does not contain any untrue statement of material fact," and (3) to the certifying officer's knowledge "the report fairly presents in all material respects the financial condition and results of operations of the issuer."[68] The sobering experience of periodically having to so attest may well introduce a bit of conservatism into the dynamics between senior management and the outside auditor that heretofore has been missing.

§ 9.3 Changes in the Statutory Description of Functions of the Board of Directors

Representative of early statutory expressions of the board's power are the early versions of the Model Business Corporation Act that provided simply that "the business and affairs of a corporation shall be *managed* by a board of directors."[69] As discussed in the preceding section, boards as a practical matter do not manage the company's affairs; this is a task commended to its officers, even within the closely held corporation. To reflect this reality, in 1974 the Model Act's language was amended to provide that corporate power was exercised "by or under the authority" of the board and that the corporation's affairs would be managed "under the direction" of the board.[70] This is the

---

[63]   15 U.S.C. § 78j–1(i) (2009).

[64]   15 U.S.C. § 78j–1(k) (2009).

[65]   15 U.S.C. § 78j–1(j) (2009).

[66]   15 U.S.C. § 78j–1(m) (2009).

[67]   15 U.S.C. § 78m(k) (2009).

[68]   15 U.S.C. §§ 78n & 78(d) (2009).

[69]   *See* former Model Business Corporation Act § 33 (1950) & (1960) (emphasis added).

[70]   *See* Model Business Corporation Act Ann. § 8.01 (3d ed. 1994).

pattern of most modern statutes. Hopefully, among the effects of the modern expression of the board's role is to dissuade courts from otherwise harboring the view that the board of directors is to involve itself in the day-to-day management of the corporation or imposing liability for failure to exercise close supervision over the firm's executives.

Another change in the expression of the board's power is the invitation for corporation's to deviate from the statutory norm of a centralized management. This invitation appears in conjunction with language that provides that corporate powers and management occur pursuant to the authority or direction of the board, "except as otherwise provided in the articles of incorporation."[71] The statute's broad invitation recognizes the validity of transferring to the shareholders (and likely a third party, such as a creditor) powers or authority customarily exercised by the board of directors. Because the exact scope of such a transfer has not been litigated, it remains to be seen whether a court might nonetheless impose important limits on the ability of the shareholders to transfer fundamental board powers to themselves. One potential area of conflict arises from the consistent practice of corporate statutes to require board approval as a condition to the stockholders considering certain transactions, such as the amendment of the articles, a merger, or a sale of substantially all the firm's assets.[72] Because the clear reading of the statute calls for board approval, not the approval of someone who has the authority to act for the board, there is a reasonable basis to doubt that a special provision in the articles of incorporation can change this part of the normative structure of the corporation.[73]

§ 9.4   Authority and Powers of the Directors

A corporation's board of directors is legally the supreme authority in matters of the corporation's regular business management. Most corporate statutes provide that the corporate business is managed by or under the direction of the board of directors.[74] The basic management function of directors, as traditionally defined, can be summarized as including: (1) setting the course of the enterprise by determining the company's general objectives, goals, and philosophies; (2) selecting the chief executive and senior officers and seeing that able young executives are developed; (3) determining executive compensation, pension, and retirement policies; (4) delegating to the chief executive and subordinate executives authority for administrative action; (5) providing advice, counsel, and assistance to corporate officers, (6) fixing policies relating to such matters as pricing, labor relations, expansion, and new products; (7) determining the dividend payments, financing, and capital changes; (8) monitoring the company's progress, exercising vigilance for its welfare, and taking appropriate action in light of its progress; (9) submitting for shareholder action proposals requiring their approval; and (10) creating adequate machinery for conducting the board's business.[75]

---

[71]   *See, e.g.*, Mich. Comp. Laws Ann. § 450.1501 (West 1990); Del. Code Ann. tit. 8, § 141(a) (2001) ("except as may be otherwise provide in this chapter or in its certificate of incorporation").

[72]   *See, e.g.*, Del. Code Ann. tit. 8, § 271 (2001); MBCA § 12.02 (2016).

[73]   In Jackson v. Turnbull, 1994 WL 693503, *aff'd*, 653 A.2d 306, the court held the board of directors violated section 251(b) of the Delaware General Corporation Law by delegating to a third party the responsibility for determining the price at which a merger was to occur.

[74]   Many states have varied this formula by permitting restrictions on board authority in the articles or elsewhere. *E.g.*, former MBCA § 35 (1969, as amended). *Accord*, MBCA § 8.01(b) (2016).

[75]   Express authorization for the board of directors to take designated action of various kinds can be found in scattered sections of the Model Business Corporation Act and other corporation statutes.

The board of directors has the power to select corporate officers and to determine their compensation.[76] Perhaps the single most important board function is choosing the company's chief executive officer. The board has authority to direct the use of the corporation's property in the operation of its business.[77] It can sell or otherwise dispose of corporate assets,[78] including real estate,[79] in the normal course of business.[80] The board has the power and responsibility to determine whether the financial condition of the company is such as to warrant the declaration and payment of dividends.[81] It can create and control a corporate pension plan;[82] apply the funds of the corporation to the payment of its debts and agree with creditors on an extension of debts;[83] authorize an assignment of all the corporation's property for the benefit of its creditors or the filing of a voluntary petition in bankruptcy;[84] determine whether the corporation will sue to rectify corporate injuries;[85] and waive the corporation's rights to attorney's fees.[86]

The board of directors, not the shareholders, has the original and supreme authority to make corporate contracts. Thus the board can borrow money needed for corporate business, execute or authorize the execution of negotiable notes or bonds to secure borrowing, pledge or mortgage real or personal corporate property, secure debts lawfully contracted, enter a guaranty contract, enter leases, and execute compromise agreements.

The directors' authority generally is restricted to the management of the corporation's business affairs. Without shareholder approval, they cannot effect fundamental changes in the corporation's charter or organization or dissolve the corporation, since such actions do not relate to ordinary business.

There is one area—the making and amending of bylaws—where the board's power as directors, vis-à-vis the power of the shareholders, has increased in recent years. The power to make bylaws was traditionally with the shareholders as an incident of their ownership of the business.[87] On the other hand, virtually all current statutes grant the directors the power to adopt, amend, and repeal bylaws or provide a method by which they can be given such power, such as by appropriate provision in the articles of incorporation.[88] In fact, originally the Model Business Corporation Act[89] empowered the directors or the incorporators to adopt the initial bylaws and further stated that only the directors shall possess the power to amend or repeal the bylaws, except to the extent

---

[76]   MBCA §§ 8.40, 8.44 (1984).

[77]   Continental Sec. Co. v. Belmont, 99 N.E. 138 (N.Y. 1912).

[78]   Hayes v. Johnson, 299 So.2d 566 (La. Ct. App. 1974) (articles of incorporation granted power to board).

[79]   Jeppi v. Brockman Holding Co., 206 P.2d 847 (Cal. 1949).

[80]   Most jurisdictions have statutes requiring shareholder approval for a sale or other disposition of all or substantially all of a corporation's assets other than in the regular course of business. *E.g.*, N.Y. Bus. Corp. Law § 909 (McKinney 1986); MBCA § 12.01 (1984).

[81]   Liebman v. Auto Strop Co., 150 N.E. 505 (N.Y. 1926).

[82]   Delany v. St. Louis Union Trust Co., 518 S.W.2d 704, 708 (Mo. Ct. App. 1974).

[83]   Puma v. Marriott, 283 A.2d 693 (Del. Ch. 1971).

[84]   Royal Indem. Co. v. American Bond & Mortg. Co., 289 U.S. 165 (1933).

[85]   Burks v. Lasker, 441 U.S. 471 (1979).

[86]   Tasby v. Estes, 416 F.Supp. 644 (N.D. Tex. 1976).

[87]   Rogers v. Hill, 289 U.S. 582, 588–589 (1933); North Milwaukee Town-Site Co., No. 2 v. Bishop, 79 N.W. 785 (Wis. 1899).

[88]   *See, e.g.*, former MBCA § 25 (2001). *But see* MBCA §§ 2.06, 10.20(b) (2016) (shareholder may freely amend bylaws even if adopted by board).

[89]   Former MBCA § 27 (1969); MBCA §§ 2.06, 10.20(b) (2016).

that such power is reserved exclusively to the shareholders by the articles of incorporation.

Directors, as a practical matter, often have almost exclusive control over the corporation's issuance of additional stock. Shareholder approval is required to amend the corporation's charter to increase the kind or amount of stock authorized to be issued. Modern statutes do not require that all authorized stock be issued at once, and the widespread practice is to authorize in the original charter or by charter amendments large amounts of stock in excess of that expected to be issued in the near future.[90]

§ 9.5   Necessity for Board Action in a Lawfully Convened Meeting

The authority to manage the affairs of the corporation is vested in the directors not individually but as a board.[91] The traditional rule, as usually stated, is that directors cannot act individually to bind the corporation but must act as a board at a legally convened meeting. Directors who act collectively at an informal meeting are not considered to have acted at a duly convened meeting. As such, the action is not valid and must await a formal meeting of the board.[92] As will be seen, statutes frequently authorize important exceptions to this rule, and courts have upheld informal director approval where it is equitable to bend the requirements that the board act as a deliberative body.

Many cases have held that if directors act or give their consent separately or if they act at anything other than a legal meeting, their action is not that of the corporation, even though all may consent, and, in the absence of statute, ratification, or estoppel, the corporation is not bound.[93] These holdings proceed on the theory that the directors must meet and counsel with each other, and that any determination affecting the corporation shall only be arrived at after a consultation at a meeting of the board on notice to all and attended by at least a quorum of its members.[94] The shareholders are entitled to the directors' combined wisdom, knowledge, and business foresight, which give efficiency and safety to corporate management.

Modern technology has modified the concept of a board meeting. A number of corporation statutes now specifically provide that meetings of directors can be validly held by conference telephone or similar communications methods.[95] Even in the absence of statutory authorization, a meeting of this kind should be held to be a valid formal meeting, as the directors have full opportunity to consult and counsel with each other.

Courts in many instances have upheld the directors' approval, even though the directors' approval was not the product of a meeting convened in accordance with the

---

[90] The authorization and issuance of shares are discussed in Chapter 16.

[91] *See, e.g.,* American Bank & Trust Co. v. Freeman, 560 S.W.2d 444 (Tex. Civ. App. 1977) (individual director without authorization from the board cannot bind corporation on a promise to secure plaintiff's election to the board). However, liability for misfeasance falls on the directors individually and not on the board as a separate entity. *See, e.g.,* Flarey v. Youngstown Osteopathic Hosp., 783 N.E.2d 582 (Ohio Ct. App. 2002) (holding that the board of directors is not a separate entity capable of suing or being sued and "members of the board are liable in their individual, but not their collective, capacity").

[92] *See* Fogel v. United States Energy Systems, 2008 WL 151857 (Del. Ch. 2008) ("When a corporate action is void, it is invalid *ab initio* and cannot be ratified later").

[93] *See, e.g.,* Hotaling v. Hotaling, 224 P. 455 (Cal. 1924).

[94] In re Rye Psychiatric Hosp. Ctr. v. Schoenholtz, 476 N.Y.S.2d 339 (App. Div. 1984).

[95] *See, e.g.,* Cal. Corp. Code § 307(a), (b) (West Supp. 2001); MBCA § 8.20(b) (2016).

statutes or bylaws.[96] Considerable judicial support exists for the proposition that even in the absence of a statute, the separate consent of all the directors is sufficient to bind the corporation without a formal meeting as a board,[97] and some support exists for the proposition that consent of a majority of the board, although acting separately, will suffice.[98]

If the directors own all of a corporation's shares, a conveyance, mortgage, or contract authorized by them, although not assembled at a meeting, is valid.[99] Courts have repeatedly departed from the traditional rule in order to sustain action taken by owner-directors in family and close corporations.[100]

Waiver by Shareholders. The shareholders may waive the necessity of a board meeting and thereby authorize acts to be done by agents of the corporation or ratify acts already done and thus bind the corporation. Where, by acquiescence, the shareholders vest the executive officers with the powers of the directors as the usual method of doing business and the board is inactive, the acts of such officers, although not authorized by a vote of either shareholders or directors, generally will bind the corporation.[101]

Estoppel. A corporation may be estopped, as against an innocent third person, to deny the validity of a mortgage or other act done or authorized by the directors separately, or otherwise than at a legal meeting, by long acquiescence or voluntary receipt or retention of benefits with either actual or presumed knowledge.[102]

Ratification. Ratification by vote or acquiescence of the shareholders, on full disclosure of the circumstances, is generally held effective to validate irregular or voidable acts of the directors;[103] but not as to action that is void *ab initio*.[104] A few cases hold that the shareholders cannot ratify any irregular or invalid act of the board that they, as shareholders, could not authorize.[105] But even when an effective ratification does not take place, the corporation may be "estopped" by the receipt or retention of benefits to deny its liability.[106]

Single Shareholder Corporations. Many cases hold that where a single shareholder owns substantially all the shares of stock, she may bind the corporation by her acts without a resolution of the board of directors.[107] This is usually based on the ground of disregarding the separate corporate entity but may better be explained as a liberalized agency doctrine and a dispensing with the formalities of usual corporate procedure where they can serve no useful purpose.

---

[96]   *See generally* Matthew N. Perlstein, Note, Corporations: When Informal Action by Corporate Directors Will Be Permitted to Bind the Corporation, 53 B.U. L. Rev. 101 (1973).

[97]   National State Bank v. Sandford Fork & Tool Co., 60 N.E. 699 (Ind. 1901).

[98]   Forrest City Box Co. v. Barney, 14 F.2d 590 (8th Cir. 1926); Holy Cross Gold Mining & Milling Co. v. Goodwin, 223 P. 58 (Colo. 1924).

[99]   Jordan v. Collins, 18 So. 137 (Ala. 1895).

[100]   *See, e.g.,* Haff v. Long Island Fuel Corp., 251 N.Y.S. 67, 71 (App. Div. 1931).

[101]   Galbraith v. First Nat'l Bank, 221 F. 386 (8th Cir. 1915); Cunningham v. German Ins. Bank, 101 F. 977 (6th Cir. 1900); Lahnston v. Second Chance Ranch Co., 968 P.2d 32 (Wyo. 1998).

[102]   Wood Estate Co. v. Chanslor, 286 P. 1001 (Cal. 1930).

[103]   Morisette v. Howard, 63 P. 756 (Kan. 1901); Myhre v. Myhre, 554 P.2d 276, 282 (Mont. 1976).

[104]   *See* Fogel v. United States Energy Systems, 2008 WL 151857 (Del. Ch. 2008).

[105]   Curtin v. Salmon River Hydraulic Gold-Mining & Ditch Co., 62 P. 552, 555 (Cal. 1900).

[106]   New Blue Point Mining Co. v. Weissbein, 244 P. 325 (Cal. 1926).

[107]   Wenban Estate, Inc. v. Hewlett, 227 P. 723 (Cal. 1924), noted in 13 Cal. L. Rev. 235 (1925).

§ 9.6   Statutes Authorizing Informal Board Action

In many states the corporation statutes now depart from the traditional requirement of formal board meetings and permit directors to act informally and without a meeting by signing a written consent.[108]

Under these statutes, *all* the directors must sign for the written consent to be effective. To some extent, the unanimity requirement "precludes the stifling of opposing argument"[109] in that a single director can force a meeting at which she will have an opportunity to reason with her colleagues. The written consent is effective when the last director executes her consent, unless a different date is specified.[110]

§ 9.7   The Notice Requirement for Board Meetings

Subject to the exceptions noted in the preceding sections, directors must act as a board at a legal meeting, regular or special, at which a quorum is present. As a general proposition, all directors must be properly notified of board meetings.[111]

A distinction is made between regular and special meetings. Unless otherwise provided by statute, the charter, or bylaws, if the time and place of regular meetings of the board of directors are fixed in the corporation's charter or bylaws, by resolution of the board or by usage, such meetings may be held without additional notice.[112] It is common practice, however, to send a courtesy notice or reminder to the directors. The great weight of authority is that every director must be given notice of a special meeting of the board.[113] A special meeting held without due notice to all directors is illegal and, though a quorum may be present, action taken at such a meeting is invalid.[114]

Most current statutes provide that the bylaws may prescribe what shall constitute notice of a meeting of the board of directors.[115] Some jurisdictions specify what notice must be given in the absence of a bylaw provision. The bylaws customarily specify how many days in advance of a meeting notice must be given. In the absence of a bylaw authorizing other means of giving notice,[116] the notice of a directors' meeting must be a personal notice,[117] unless, by custom, notice by mail or otherwise is authorized[118] or unless some of the directors are absent and notice cannot be given to them except by mail or telegram.[119] The notice must be given a reasonable length of time before the hour

---

[108]   *See, e.g.*, Del. Code Ann. tit. 8, § 141(f) (2001).

[109]   1 former MBCA Ann. § 44, Comment ¶ 2 (2d ed. 1971).

[110]   Herskowitz v. Pilot House Motor Inns, Inc., 806 S.W.2d 531 (Tenn. Ct. App. 1990).

[111]   *See* Rare Earth, Inc. v. Hoorelbeke, 401 F.Supp. 26 (S.D.N.Y. 1975).

[112]   White v. Penelas Mining Co., 105 F.2d 726 (9th Cir. 1939). Many statutes expressly authorize regular meetings of the board to be held without notice if the bylaws or the board of directors fix the time and place of such meetings. *See, e.g.*, Cal. Corp. Code § 307(a)(2) (West Supp. 2001).

[113]   Rare Earth, Inc. v. Hoorelbeke, 401 F.Supp. 26, 32 (S.D.N.Y. 1975) (Michigan law); Schroder v. Scotten, Dillon Co., 299 A.2d 431 (Del. Ch. 1972); MBCA § 8.22 (2016).

[114]   *See* Whitman v. Fuqua, 549 F.Supp. 315 (W.D. Pa. 1982) (meeting called without notice and purpose given was without authority in law and any action taken was invalid or *ultra vires*).

[115]   *E.g.*, N.Y. Bus. Corp. Law § 711(b) (McKinney 1986); MBCA § 8.22 (1984).

[116]   *See, e.g.*, Johnson v. Busby, 278 F.Supp. 235 (N.D. Ga. 1967) (by telephone).

[117]   Harding v. Vandewater, 40 Cal. 77 (1870).

[118]   Stockton Combined Harvester & Agric. Works v. Houser, 41 P. 809 (Cal. 1895).

[119]   Chase v. Tuttle, 12 A. 874 (Conn. 1888).

or day fixed for the meeting.[120] Bylaws may also call for specificity regarding the nature of the business to be conducted.

In the absence of a contrary provision in the charter or bylaws, general notice of the time and place of a directors' meeting, even though it does not specify the business to be transacted, is sufficient, at least to authorize the transaction of the corporation's ordinary business affairs.[121] Many corporation statutes broadly state that neither the business to be transacted at a meeting of the board, whether regular or special, nor the purpose of the meeting need be specified in the notice unless required by the bylaws, thus apparently eliminating any necessity of reference even to extraordinary business to be transacted at a meeting.[122] In the absence of such broad statutory permission, it is doubtful that extraordinary business may be transacted if not specified in the notice.[123]

If a director has notice of a meeting and fails to attend, he waives his rights.[124] A director has constructive notice when he purposely refuses to accept a registered letter giving notice of the meeting.[125] Similarly, a director may waive notice by signing a written waiver of notice before the meeting. A waiver of notice by an absent director subsequent to a meeting has been held invalid by some courts[126] and valid by others.[127]

What result if a director's attendance at the meeting was obtained by deception regarding the meeting's purpose? In *Klaassen v. Allegro Dev. Corp.*[128] the CEO, Klaassen, was induced to make sure that he obtained the attendance of the firm's general counsel at the upcoming regularly scheduled board meeting. Klaassen was told the counsel's attendance was needed for questions that may arise in redeeming some outstanding shares; in fact, the directors intended to fire Klaassen and wanted counsel present in case there were legal questions related to terminating Klaassen. Klaassen challenged his firing on the ground the meeting was convened on deceptive notice of its purpose was unsuccessful. The Delaware Supreme Court reasoned that since the meeting was a regularly scheduled meeting no advance notice of its subject matter was necessary. Moreover, equitable challenges based on the deception were not successful because such deception rendered the board's actions "voidable," not void, so that Klaassen's cooperation in facilitating a smooth transition in the months following his firing established the equitable defense of acquiescence. However, in an earlier decision, the Delaware Court of Chancery held deception that secured a director's attendance at a *special* meeting established equitable grounds for voiding the action taken (firing the CEO) at that meeting.[129]

---

[120] Hayes v. Canada, Atlantic & Plant S.S. Co., 181 F. 289 (1st Cir. 1910).

[121] In re Argus Co., 34 N.E. 388 (N.Y. 1893).

[122] *E.g.*, N.Y. Bus. Corp. Law § 711(b) (McKinney 1986); 2 MBCA Ann. § 8.22 (3d ed. 1994).

[123] *See* Mercantile Library Hall Co. v. Pittsburgh Library Ass'n, 33 A. 744 (Pa. 1896). Especially where a notice states that the meeting is called for a particular purpose or for ordinary business, extraordinary business outside of such purpose cannot be transacted unless all the directors are present. Fay v. Charles Michel & Sons, 147 N.Y.L.J. 15 (Sup. Ct. 1962).

[124] Potter v. Patee, 493 S.W.2d 58, 64 (Mo. Ct. App. 1973); Avien, Inc. v. Weiss, 269 N.Y.S.2d 836 (Sup. Ct. 1966). *See* Holcombe v. Trenton White City Co., 82 A. 618, 624 (N.J. Ch. 1912), *aff'd mem.*, 91 A. 1069 (N.J. 1913).

[125] Schroder v. Scotten, Dillon Co., 299 A.2d 431 (Del. Ch. 1972).

[126] United States v. Interstate R.R., 14 F.2d 328 (W.D. Va. 1926).

[127] Stafford Springs St. Ry. v. Middle River Mfg. Co., 66 A. 775 (Conn. 1907).

[128] Klaassen v. Allegro Development Corp., 106 A.3d 1035 (Del. 2014).

[129] Fogel v. U.S. Energy Systems, Inc., 2007 WL 4438978 (Del. Ch. 2007) (but inconsistent with result reached in regular meeting in Klaassen v. Allegro Development Corp., 106 A.3d 1035 (Del. 2014)).

§ 9.8   Directors' Meetings: Place, Call, Quorum, Votes, Disqualification by Interest

The time and place of board meetings is usually fixed by the bylaws or by procedures set up therein; however, if no provision on these matters is included in the bylaws, the board of directors may determine the time and place.[130] Most current corporation statutes provide that directors may hold both regular and special board meetings outside the state of incorporation.[131]

A majority of the entire board of directors constitutes a quorum[132] for the purpose of transacting business unless a greater or lesser number is required by statute, the corporation's charter, or its bylaws.[133] The quorum remains the same even though vacancies occur on the board.[134]

Unless authorized by statute, charter, or bylaw, less than a majority of the full number of directors cannot meet and bind the corporation by any act or resolution.[135] All they can do is adjourn.[136] Action at a meeting of directors that was invalid because of the absence of a quorum may be subsequently ratified at a legal directors' meeting or by the shareholders, at least if they could have authorized the action in the first instance.[137]

The attending directors must be personally present and act for themselves. Votes at a directors' meeting cannot be by proxy unless that privilege is conferred by charter or bylaw provision.[138] Although the rule is not settled in most jurisdictions, a meeting at which a quorum is initially present should be able to continue to transact business, notwithstanding the withdrawal of directors, at least if any action taken is approved by a majority of the required quorum for the meeting.

Modern corporation statutes typically provide that a majority of the number of directors fixed in the bylaws or otherwise will constitute a quorum and that the act of a majority of the directors present at a meeting at which a quorum is present shall be the act of the board. Nevertheless, the statutes permit charter provisions requiring a higher quorum or a greater vote or, more liberally, permit such provisions in either charter or bylaws[139] or, even more liberally, in the charter, bylaws, or a shareholder's agreement.[140] Some statutes permit the quorum to be fixed by charter or bylaw provision at *less* than a majority of the entire board but not less than one-third.[141]

---

[130] Bylaws typically specify that regular board meetings be held on a specified day each month.

[131] *See, e.g.*, MBCA § 8.20 (1984).

[132] The term "quorum" refers to the number of members of a body that, when properly assembled, is legally competent to transact business. *See* Model Bus. Corp. Act § 8.24.

[133] In re Webster Loose Leaf Filing Co., 240 F. 779, 784 (D.N.J. 1916).

[134] Currie v. Matson, 33 F.Supp. 454, 456–457 (W.D. La. 1940).

[135] In re Rye Psychiatric Hosp. Ctr. v. Schoenholtz, 476 N.Y.S.2d 339 (App. Div.), *appeal dismissed*, 480 N.Y.S.2d 206, 469 N.E.2d 527 (Ct. App. 1984).

[136] A meeting without notice or a quorum is invalid. Rare Earth, Inc. v. Hoorelbeke, 401 F.Supp. 26, 31–32 (S.D.N.Y. 1975).

[137] Michelson v. Duncan, 407 A.2d 211, 219 (Del. 1979).

[138] Perry v. Tuscaloosa Cotton-Seed Oil-Mill Co., 9 So. 217, 219 (Ala. 1891).

[139] *E.g.*, MBCA § 8.24 (2016).

[140] *See* 1 O'Neal & Thompson, O'Neal's Close Corporations Law and Practice § 1.14.

[141] *E.g.*, Del. Code Ann. tit. 8, § 141(b) (2001).

§ 9.9   The Virtual Board: Melding Electronic Media to the Conduct of Board Meetings

As seen earlier, all states permit a director to participate telephonically in a meeting of the board; this permission is generally conditioned upon prior consent on the part of the corporation, such as authorization in its bylaws, and, furthermore, that each director present, physically or telephonically, be able to hear and speak with each of the other participating directors. As breathtaking as this development was many years ago, it now appears primitive compared with the steps a majority of the states have recently taken to incorporate new communication technologies into their corporate governance procedures. Not surprisingly, the trend to expressly embrace new electronic media began with California's 1995 amendment of its Corporations Code to permit notice of board meetings to be given via "electronic mail or other electronic means"[142] and further provided that members of the board could participate in meetings through "electronic video screen communication, or other communications equipment" so long as each member is able to communicate with all others "concurrently." Without such technical reference, the more general, traditional statutory authorization for remote participation so long as each participating director can "hear each other during the meeting"[143] certainly reaches all imaginable media that transmits the directors' voices. The California-like statute broadens the range of permissible communications to written, not voice, transmissions, provided the technology used meets the requirement that they occur concurrently. Nevertheless, a minority of statutes authorize director participation via "a conference telephone or *similar* communications equipment."[144] These jurisdictions risk an unduly narrow and rigid construction of state statutes that incorporate the language when the medium used is not telephone based, such as a Web cast. It was this concern that prompted Delaware in 2000 to amend its statute to substitute "other" for "similar" when referencing the range of "communications equipment" that could be used.[145]

Most state statutes authorize notice of directors' meetings to be imparted through a broad range of media, including mail, telephone, facsimile, or "other form of wire or wireless communication."[146] A few states broadly defer to the company's bylaws to set forth the manner of giving notice for directors' meetings.[147] Only a handful of states continue to rely upon a paper-based system for notice of directors' meetings by requiring notice to take some tangible form.[148] A common scheme among liberal-notice states is to provide a wider range of media for imparting any required notice to directors than is authorized for any notice required to be directed to the stockholders.

Overall, the Internet and the chip have not changed the fundamental postulates for the board. State statutes that embrace newly developed technologies continue to view the board as a deliberative body. Even the most forward-looking statutes continue the

---

[142] Cal. Corp. Code § 307(a)(2) (West Supp. 2001). California further amended the statute in 2004, replacing the 1995 language and permitting notice "by electronic transmission by the corporation." Cal. Corp. Code § 307(a)(2) (West Supp. 2009).

[143] *See, e.g.,* Colo. Rev. Stat. § 7–108–201(2) (2000).

[144] *See, e.g.,* Alaska Stat. § 10.06.475 (Michie 2009).

[145] *See* Del. Code Ann. tit. 8, § 141(i) (2001).

[146] *See, e.g.,* Ala. Code § 10–2B–1.41(b) (Michie 1999).

[147] *See, e.g.,* 805 ILCS § 5/8.25 (West 2009).

[148] *See, e.g.,* Kan. Stat. Ann. § 17–6008(b) (2009); Ohio Rev. Code Ann. § 1701.61(C) (West 2009).

requirement that each participating director be able simultaneously, or certainly without undue delay, to engage his or her fellow director on the topic before the board. Similarly, modern notice provisions appear to reflect the good sense that the Internet is likely to be both more reliable, and certainly quicker, than the mails.

§ 9.10   Governance and Authority Within the LLC

Determining the governance and management within an LLC is a matter of choice which is exercised in the shadow of the default rule set forth in the governing statute. By far the most common approach among the states is that the LLC is member managed, unless otherwise provided in the articles of organization[149] (a few states permit this designation in the operating agreement).[150] Only a few state's default rule embraces manager-operated firms, unless provided otherwise.[151] Some states expressly recognize that even if the members opt generally for centralized management, that their operating agreement, or even the articles of organization, can provide that as to certain matters, or even broad categories of issues, members not managers have the authority to act.[152] Because the choice of governance is essentially elected, it is logical to assume that even without express statutory recognition that the operating agreement or articles of organization may validly divide authority between the members and managers so that the election need not totally favor manager-or member-management. Such a division, however, may not under certain circumstances be enforceable against third parties who contract with, for example, managers in the reasonable belief that they enjoy the authority to act when in fact the operating agreement provides otherwise.

When the LLC is manager-managed, a decision of the managers may, depending on the statute, require more than a majority of the managers present at a meeting. Some states expressly provide that, in the absence of a contrary provision in the articles of organization, when the company is manager-managed any decision by the managers affecting its business affairs must be by a majority of the managers (not simply a majority of the quorum).[153] Indeed, because LLC statutes typically do not set forth, as do corporate statutes, notice, quorum or even voting requirements that are to apply to manager-operated firms, the operating agreement should address each of these. That is, it is rare among LLC statutes to find default rules regarding the procedures that are to apply for action by managers in manager-operated firms.[154]

Another subject that should be addressed in the operating agreement is the members' power to remove a manager before her term has expired. A few states expressly provide for the managers to be removed by the members.[155] Even in the absence of express statutory recognition, removal by the members should be valid. Certainly the analogy to the inherent rights of stockholders to remove a director for cause is a compelling one. But the broad embrace in most LLC statutes of free and open

---

[149] *See, e.g.,* Larry E. Ribstein & Robt. R. Keatinge, 1 Ribstein and Keatinge on Limited Liability Companies App. 8–1 et seq. (1997).

[150] *See, e.g.,* N.J. Stat. Ann. § 42:2B–27 (West Supp. 2002).

[151] *See* Minn. Stat. Ann. § 322B.606 (West 2009) (managed by a board of governors, unless otherwise set forth in the operating agreement or member control agreement).

[152] For such express statutory recognition, *see* Minn. Stat. Ann. §§ 322B.37 & 322B.60 (West Supp. 2002).

[153] *See* Conn. Gen. Stat. Ann. § 34–142 (West 1997).

[154] For an exception, *see* Tex. Rev. Civ. Stat. Ann. tit. 32, art. 1528n § 2.23 (Vernon 1997).

[155] *See, e.g.,* Cal. Corp. Code § 17152(b) (West Supp. 2002).

contracting, in which members have broad authority to opt for a form of governance structure they prefer, argues strongly for the position that members enjoy inherent rights to remove their managers that are broader than those recognized at common law for shareholders.

LLC statutes customarily list types of transactions that require the approval of the members, even when a firm is manager-managed.[156] Thus, the LLC statutes carry forward the philosophy of corporate statutes that certain transactions are so fundamental, or related to the individual member's investment, that it should not occur without providing each member with an opportunity to vote on the transaction. Care must be taken in drafting the articles of organization and operating agreement because many statutes provide that absent a contrary provision in the articles of organization (and sometimes the operating agreement) such fundamental changes require the consent of all the members, not merely a majority in interest. A further consideration here is when drafting to authorize less than unanimous approval by the members is whether a call for "majority approval" is meant to mean a majority of the members or a majority by interest among the members.

A final wrinkle in the manager-managed LLC is the agency authority of individual managers when there are two or more managers. When the LLC is manager-managed, governing LLC statutes often provide that only managers have the authority to bind the firm. Most states recognize the authority of any manager to bind the firm,[157] even when there are multiple managers.[158] Such authority appears poorly conceived when the operating agreement, or even the articles of organization, clearly express the intent that the multiple managers are to function much like the board of directors, namely as a collective body. In such a case, managers should have no greater authority than does the individual director.

When the LLC is member-managed, the operating agreement should give due attention to governance procedures, such as notice and quorum for member meetings as well as the vote that is required. The default rule of many states is that members vote per capita, rather than by interest.[159] Most LLC statutes permit voting power to be allocated among the members, or even classes of members, as the articles of organization or organization agreement may provide. The members can also provide in the articles of organization or operating agreement for super-majority vote; and, in any case, the careful lawyer needs to be aware that many statutes require unanimous approval of the members unless a lower vote is set forth in the articles of organization or operating agreement.

When the LLC is member-managed, the typical default rule follows the partnership analogy to the effect that each member has the inherent authority to bind the company on any matter within the ordinary scope of its business.[160] When a member acts outside the scope of her actual authority with respect to a transaction within the usual course of

---

[156] *See, e.g.*, Ariz. Rev. Stat. Ann. § 29–681 (West 1998).

[157] *See, e.g.*, Colo. Rev. Stat. Ann. § 7–80–405 (West 2009); *but see* Del. Code Ann. tit. 6, § 8–402 (2009) (both members and managers may bind the LLC unless stated otherwise).

[158] *See, e.g.*, Del. Code Ann. tit. 6, § 18–402 (1999) ("each member or manager has the authority to bind the ... company"); 805 ILCS § 180/13–5(b)(1) (West Supp. 2002) ("Each manager is an agent of the company").

[159] *See, e.g.*, Ariz. Rev. Stat. Ann. § 29–681(D)(1) (1998).

[160] *See, e.g.*, Cal. Corp. Code § 17157(a) (West 1990); Del. Code Ann. tit. 6, § 18–402 (1999); Md. Code Ann. § 4A–401 (1990); N.Y. Ltd. Lib. Co. Law § 412(a) (McKinney Pamp. 2002); and Wis. Stat. Ann. § 183.0301(1)(a) (West Supp. 2001) (no member is an agent of any other members of the LLC).

the LLC's affairs, and the third person is not aware of the limitation on the member's authority, traditional agency principles arise to bind the company on the transaction with the third person.

§ 9.11   The Power of Shareholders to Control the Acts of Directors

Directors are not the servants of a majority of the shareholders. One of the basic advantages of the corporate form of doing business, found also in unincorporated joint stock companies and business trusts, is that the collective interests of the owners (shareholders) are represented by the centralized management of a board of directors. The directors control and supervise the conduct of the business. Individual shareholders generally have little direct voice in determining the corporation's business policies.[161] For example, the power to appoint and remove officers lies exclusively with the board of directors and even a validly adopted bylaw cannot give that power to the shareholders.[162]

Each shareholder has a right to have the corporation's affairs managed by its board of directors. This right is derived from the statute under which the corporation is organized and from the corporation's charter and bylaws. Statutory, charter, and bylaw provisions for management by the directors are viewed as part of a control among the shareholders. Consequently, a majority of the shareholders cannot deprive the minority of their right to the directors' judgment and discretion.

The shareholders' participation in a corporate decision is usually "in the form of an assent, request, or recommendation."[163] Traditionally, they have only limited powers of initiative. Even fundamental corporate action that requires a favorable shareholder vote, such as a charter amendment, merger, consolidation, voluntary dissolution, or sale of substantially all corporate assets other than in the usual course of business is, in practice, usually initiated by the directors, and, in any case, reaches the stockholders

---

[161] There are several possible justifications for centralization of management. First, it eliminates the need for hundreds, even thousands, of stockholders to incur non trivial costs to inform themselves about the company's affairs and, if this were the case, there would be a good deal of free riding on the part of some shareholders on the decisions of those few whose financial stake in the firm was great enough to justify their incurring the expense to inform themselves. *See* Robert Charles Clark, Corporate Law 94 (1986). Equally significant is that centralized management allows for owners to have the time and energy to pursue what they do best. Thus, rather than the shareholder expending effort to "get up to speed" on a matter outside her skill package, she can instead be a dentist, an architect, or a retiree. Thus, separating ownership from management is consistent with putting all resources to their highest use. Furthermore, it is easier to rationalize owners bearing no personal liability when they are not deeply involved in decision making than when they are the actors responsible for the company's affairs.

For a review of the various attempts to rationalize what matters should be conditioned upon stockholder approval and what corporate activities the board of directors itself can approve, *see* Lynne L. Dallas, The Control and Conflict of Interest Voting Systems, 71 N.C. L. Rev. 1 (1992). On this point, Eisenberg suggests one litmus test is whether the heuristics involved are akin to those involved in making an investment, such as the decision to approve a merger. *See* Melvin A. Eisenberg. The Structure of the Corporation 14–16 (1976). On the other hand, Professor Gilson believes the test is whether the transaction involves severing the stockholder from the corporation, which explains the ease with which acquirers can structure transactions to avoid a vote of their stockholders, but such avoidance is difficult in the case of a vote by the company to be acquired. *See* Ronald J. Gilson, The Law and Finance of Acquisitions 578–79 (1986). Those who have a market orientation not surprisingly believe the issue turns on the transaction's relative magnitude. *See* Frank H. Easterbrook and Daniel R. Fischel, Voting in Corporate Law, 26 J. L. & Econ. 395, 416 (1983).

[162] *See, e.g.,* Gorman v. Salamone, 2015 WL 4719681 (Del. Ch. 2015) (the power to remove officers lies inherently with the directors and that power of officer removal cannot be given to the shareholders even with a duly adopted bylaw to that effect).

[163] Continental Sec. Co. v. Belmont, 99 N.E. 138, 141 (N.Y. 1912).

only after approval by the board of directors. Indeed, most statutes expressly require board approval of such action before submission to the shareholders.[164] The shareholders may act as a ratifying or approving body and thereby validate an unauthorized act or voidable corporate contract.[165]

It would be wrong to conclude that shareholders have no capacity to act affirmatively to change corporate policies or practices. A good illustration of effective shareholder initiative is provided by the leading New York case of *Auer v. Dressel*.[166] The corporation's charter provided for eleven directors; the class A shareholders elected nine, and the common shareholders elected two. The directors removed and replaced the corporation's president. A majority of the class A shareholders were displeased with that action and duly invoked a bylaw that imposed a duty on the president to call a meeting when requested in writing by holders of a majority of shares entitled to vote. Among the objectives for the meeting were: (1) to adopt a resolution endorsing the administration of the old president and demanding that he be reinstated; (2) to consider a proposal to amend the charter and bylaws to provide that vacancies in the board of directors caused by shareholder removal of a director or by resignation of a director against whom charges had been proffered, could be filled with the unexpired term only by the shareholders of the class represented by the director; and (3) to hear charges proffered against four of the directors, vote on their removal, and select successors if needed. The court held that all of the reasons advanced were proper purposes for holding a shareholder meeting. Although the shareholders, by endorsing the administration of the old president, would not be able directly to effect a change in officers, they were entitled to express themselves and thus alert the directors who would stand for election at the next annual meeting.[167]

Though the primacy of the board of directors is well recognized, there continues to be uncertainty regarding the ability of the stockholders to tailor governance procedures for the corporation to enhance their voice or participation, or even to qualify the otherwise unconditional authority of the board. The source of this uncertainty is the uneasy fit of two standard provisions of corporate statutes. First is the broad grant of authority to the board of directors to manage or direct the corporation's affairs, except as may be otherwise provided in the statute or the articles of incorporation.[168] Second, statutes authorize bylaws not inconsistent with law or the articles of incorporation, and empower the stockholders to adopt, amend and repeal the bylaws.[169]

> At some point the broad shareholder power to adopt or amend corporate bylaws must yield to the board's plenary authority to manage the business and affairs of the corporation. . . . The difficulty of pinpointing where a proposal falls on

---

[164] *See, e.g.*, MBCA § 10.03 (1984).

[165] *See, e.g.*, Goldboss v. Reimann, 55 F.Supp. 811, 819 (S.D.N.Y. 1943), *aff'd mem.*, 143 F.2d 594 (2d Cir. 1944).

[166] Auer v. Dressel, 118 N.E.2d 590 (N.Y. 1954).

[167] *Id.* The court stated further that shareholders who have the power to elect directors have the inherent power to remove them for cause and that the shareholders can amend corporate bylaws to provide that they will elect successors of such directors as shall be removed or such directors as shall resign pending hearing.

[168] *See, e.g.*, Del. Code Ann. tit. 8, § 141(a) (2009); N.Y. Bus. Corp. Law § 701 (McKinney 2009); MBCA § 8.02(b) (1984).

[169] *See, e.g.*, Del. Code Ann. tit. 8, § 109(a), (b) (2009); N.Y. Bus. Corp. Law § 601 (McKinney 1986); MBCA § 10.20 (1984).

this spectrum of sometimes overlapping authority is exacerbated by the absence of state-law precedent demarcating this boundary.[170]

Just how much restraint can a shareholder-adopted bylaw impose on the broad command that the affairs of the corporation are to be managed by or under the direction of the board of directors? Should the qualification on the board's authority found in the statutory reference to "except as otherwise provided in this statute" incorporate limitations that can be imposed by the bylaws? Professor Lawrence Hamermesh argues that the exception refers only to statutory provisions that deal specifically with the allocation of power between stockholders and the board of directors, such as provisions requiring stockholder approval of mergers or the authority of court appointed trustees or custodians; more generally, he advises the corporate statute must be interpreted in light of the contemporary view of the strong board with limited involvement by the stockholders in the conduct of company affairs.[171] On the other hand, Professor John Coffee argues that stockholders can through their amendment of the bylaws introduce significant, albeit reasonable, departures from the traditional model of the board primacy:

> [T]he bylaws are the appropriate location for constraints that limit the exercise of corporate power, including by the directors. The key distinction then seems to be between affirmative instructions to take specific actions (which generally seem impermissible) and negative constraints that affect the allocation of power between the board and the shareholders (which generally seem permissible).[172]

Not surprisingly, this issue has surfaced in the context of management's steps to prevent a takeover, a subject in which managers frequently are not of the same mind as the company's stockholders. In *International Brotherhood of Teamsters General Fund v. Fleming Companies*,[173] the shareholders proposed a bylaw which would restrict the board of directors from implementing a rights plan (poison pill) that would impede a hostile takeover of the firm. The Oklahoma Supreme Court upheld the shareholders' power to propose the restriction on the directors, reasoning that a rights plan is similar to stock option plans whose approval or content are appropriate for shareholder action. If the court's analogy to the stockholders' power with respect to stock options is not central to its decision, then *Fleming*'s holding is even more profound. *Sans* the analogy to options, there would appear to be few limits upon the stockholders' power to adopt bylaws that either limit the discretionary authority of the board of directors or, as was part of the proposed bylaw in *Fleming*, mandate that the board pursue a specific course of action (in *Fleming*, to redeem the outstanding rights).

---

[170] Randall S. Thomas & Catherine T. Dixon, Aranow & Einhorn on Proxy Contests for Corporate Control § 160.5 (3d ed. 1998).

[171] Lawrence A. Hamermesh, Corporate Democracy and Stockholder-Adopted By-Laws: Taking Back the Street?, 73 Tulane L. Rev. 409, 431 & 452 (1998).

[172] John C. Coffee, Jr., The Bylaw Battlefield: Can Institutions Change the Outcome of Corporate Control Contests?, 51 U. Miami L. Rev. 605, 608 (1997). Professor Coffee believes bright-line tests for legitimacy could be based on consideration whether the bylaw involved ordinary versus fundamental issues, constituted affirmative or negative instructions to the board, deals with procedural or substantive matters, and can be seen as related to corporate governance or business decisions. *Id.* at 613–14. For a reply to these categories, *see* Lawrence A. Hamermesh, Corporate Democracy and Stockholder-Adopted By-Laws: Taking Back the Street?, 73 Tulane L. Rev. 409, 433–442 (1998).

[173] International Brotherhood of Teamsters General Fund v. Fleming Companies, 975 P.2d 907 (Okla. 1999).

The statutory provisions that served as the backdrop for the contest in *Fleming* are consistent with those found in most states. Nevertheless, as reflected in the differing views of Professors Hamermesh and Coffee, discussed above, the area depends heavily upon one's overall approach to governance issues so that a court favoring a strong board can easily and quite reasonably reach a result different from that arrived at in *Fleming*, as was the case in a more recent Delaware case of *CA, Inc. v. AFSCME Employees Pension Plan*.[174]

In *CA, Inc.*, the Delaware Supreme Court addressed the distinction between shareholder proposed bylaws that mandate specific board action and those that are process oriented. CA, Inc. shareholders proposed a bylaw that would require the board to reimburse shareholder expenses associated with director nominations, a decision that was previously entirely within the board's discretion. While the bylaw mandated reimbursement, the Court read it in the larger context of regulating the processes by which board members are elected. Nevertheless, the Court struck down the bylaw because, as drafted, it would cause the board to violate its fiduciary duties under Delaware law.[175]

Effective as of August 2009, the Delaware codified the court's holding in *CA, Inc.* allowing shareholder bylaws for reimbursement for proxy expenses in connection with electing directors.[176] However, to avoid the problems of the shareholders' in *CA, Inc.*, the statute lists appropriate situations where reimbursement may be required, though the list is not inclusive.

A further question is whether the stockholders can provide that the bylaw they have adopted cannot be amended or repealed by the board. This is directly answered in the Model Act which allows the adopting shareholder to place a bylaw beyond the reach of the board of directors.[177] The cases suggest that such a limitation would not be valid when a provision of the articles of incorporation confers broad authority on the board with respect to the bylaws.[178]

An equally uncharted area in which stockholders may presume to act arises when the articles of incorporation expressly authorize action by the stockholders in areas that historically were the exclusive domain of the board of directors. Most corporate statutes provide that "subject to any provision in the articles of incorporation" to the contrary, corporate powers are to be exercised exclusively by or under the authority of the board of directors.[179] It would appear that such statutes expressly authorize the corporate charter to carve out areas in which the board's powers would be shared or assumed by the stockholders. Certainly, on the reasoning that a corporation is a nexus of contractual relationships, such an extraordinary provision in the corporation's charter should be enforced in a manner consistent with the intentions of its drafters; doubly so if the provision is being enforced against conspiring third parties.

---

[174] CA, Inc. v. AFSCME Employees Pension Plan, 953 A.2d 227 (Del. 2008).

[175] *Id.*

[176] Del. Code Ann. tit. 8, § 113 (2009).

[177] *See* MBCA § 10.20(b) (2016).

[178] *See, e.g.*, Centaur Partners, IV v. National Intergroup, Inc., 582 A.2d 923, 929 (Del. 1990).

[179] *See, e.g.*, Del. Code Ann. tit. 8, § 141(a) (2009).

§ 9.12 Board Vacancies

A vacancy on the board can arise through the resignation,[180] resignation, death, or removal of a director. Newly authorized directorships not yet filled are customarily considered creating a "vacancy" on the board. A few corporate statutes specify what constitutes a vacancy, and all states have provisions dealing with how any vacancy is to be filled.[181]

In broad overview, all states variously authorize either the shareholders or the board to fill vacancies on the board.[182] Obviously, once either of these bodies has acted to fill a vacancy the vacancy no longer exists and, hence, there no longer is authority for the other body to appoint someone to fill the formerly vacant seat. When a vacancy arises there can be a question regarding what constitutes a quorum for the board. The first step in addressing this question is the language of the quorum requirement; if it does not set a specific number for a quorum, does it specify a certain percentage of the "authorized" or the number "in office"? The Utah court provided an expedient answer to the quorum issue in resolving the validity of board action taken by a vote of three to one after the articles had been amended expanding the board from four to seven, but before the three new directorships had been filled. The quorum requirement was a majority of the directors. The court held that the unfilled directorships were not to be counted in determining a quorum.[183] This question is directly dealt with in the great majority of the state statutes because they expressly authorize the majority of the directors to fill a vacancy, even though they are less than a quorum.[184] Those states following the Model Business Corporation Act restrict the board's authority to act by a vote of a majority of its remaining members to instances in which "the directors remaining in office constitute fewer than a quorum."[185] The Model Act's provision is consistent with the holding in *Tomlinson v. Loew's Inc.*,[186] arising from a proxy contest for control of MGM. One provision of the company's bylaws provided that the board could act only through a majority vote at a meeting with a quorum present; another bylaw provision provided directors in office could fill a vacancy "although less than a quorum." The court held the latter provision applied only when it was not possible to convene a quorum; it accordingly held that the new directors appointed at a meeting without a quorum were not validly selected since it was under the circumstances possible to convene a quorum.[187] Thus, two of three remaining directors acted properly to fill a vacancy on the five-person board pursuant to a bylaw provision authoring "directors in office" to appoint a "successor or

---

[180] A director's resignation need not be in writing and an oral resignation will be sufficient if in compliance with the bylaws. Biolase, Inc. v. Oracle Partners, L.P., 2014 WL 2619404 (Del. 2014).

[181] *See, e.g.,* In Grossman v. Liberty Leasing Co., 295 A.2d 749 (Del. Ch. 1972) (relying in part on the legislature having eliminated any statutory distinctions among types of vacancies, the court upheld the power of the board to fill a seat that had not, in response to a recommendation by the board of directors, been filled for two years by the shareholders).

[182] *See, e.g.,* Conn. Bus. Corp. Act § 33–744 (West 1997); Idaho Code § 30–1–810 (1999); Or. Rev. Stat. § 60–331 (2001); & Va. Code Ann. § 13.1–682 (2009).

[183] *See* Rocket Mining Corp. v. Gill, 483 P.2d 897 (Utah 1971).

[184] *See, e.g.,* Del. Code Ann. tit. 8, § 223 (2009).

[185] *See* MBCA § 8.10(a)(3) (1984).

[186] Tomlinson v. Loew's, Inc., 134 A.2d 518 (1957).

[187] But, when a statute expressly authorizes a majority of the remaining directors to fill a vacancy, then action to fill vacancies by two of three remaining directors of a board of five under statutes such as the Model Act provisions that expressly provide for a vacancy to be filled by a majority of the directors even though less than a quorum. *See* Avien, Inc. v. Weiss, 269 N.Y.S.2d 836 (Sup. Ct. 1966).

successors," even though the articles of incorporation and bylaws had a general provision requiring seventy-five percent of the directors to be present for a quorum.[188]

§ 9.13   Removal of Directors by Shareholders

Shareholders have the inherent power to remove a director for cause, even in the absence of a statute or a clause in the corporation's charter or bylaws providing for such a removal.[189] Even though a shareholders' agreement provides that a particular director shall be maintained in office, the shareholders usually may remove the director for cause, because the agreement is subject to an implied condition that the director faithfully perform the duties of the office.[190] The inherent right of the shareholders to remove a director for cause, however, can only be exercised by shareholders controlling a majority of the votes or, if the corporation's charter requires a higher vote for shareholder action, such number greater than a majority as is provided in the charter.[191]

A proceeding to remove a director for cause need not be conducted with the same formality as a judicial proceeding, but the accused director must be served with the specific charges, be given adequate notice, and be afforded full opportunity to meet the accusations.[192] In a publicly held corporation, where only a fraction of the shareholders attend meetings in person, an accused director must be afforded an opportunity to communicate with the shareholders. In a leading Delaware case,[193] the chancellor provided a fair hearing by requiring that the accused directors be given an opportunity, at the corporation's expense, to present their defense to the shareholders in the form of a statement that would "accompany or precede the initial solicitation of the proxies seeking authority to vote for the removal of such director for cause."

Whether cause exists for the removal of a director or directors is subject to judicial review.[194] As a general proposition, a director must be guilty of some abuse of trust or malfeasance or nonfeasance in office to justify dismissal. Thus a director's disagreement with shareholders on corporate policy or a mistake by a director is not grounds for dismissal.[195] A desire to take over control of the corporation or failure to cooperate with the president has been held insufficient cause for director removal.[196] On the other hand, improper withdrawal of funds and payment of salaries, commissions, and management fees have been held to constitute an abuse of trust and thus cause for dismissal.[197] Other improprieties that have been held to constitute sufficient cause include a director's

---

[188] *See* Jacobson v. Moskowitz, 261 N.E.2d 613 (N.Y. 1970).

[189] Pardue v. Citizens Bank & Trust Co., 247 So.2d 368 (Ala. 1971).

[190] *See* Springut v. Don & Bob Restaurants of Am., Inc., 394 N.Y.S.2d 971 (App. Div. 1977). The question of whether a corporation's shareholders can by appropriate charter or bylaw provision deprive themselves of their inherent power to remove directors for cause was left open in Campbell v. Loew's, Inc., 134 A.2d 852, 858 (Del. Ch. 1957).

[191] *See* Springut v. Don & Bob Restaurants of Am., Inc., 394 N.Y.S.2d 971 (App. Div. 1977).

[192] Schirmer v. Bear, 672 N.E.2d 1171 (Ill. 1996).

[193] Campbell v. Loew's, Inc., 134 A.2d 852, 861–862 (Del. Ch. 1957), noted in 71 Harv. L. Rev. 1154 (1958).

[194] *See, e.g.,* Grace v. Grace Inst., 226 N.E.2d 531 (N.Y. 1967) (court reluctant to interfere with judgment for or against removal of those running charitable corporation when evidence exists to support each judgment).

[195] *See* Abreu v. Unica Ind. Sales, Inc., 586 N.E.2d 661 (Ill. App. Ct. 1991) (dealing with cause for removal by a court).

[196] Campbell v. Loew's, Inc., 134 A.2d 852, 860–861 (Del. Ch. 1957).

[197] People v. Singer, 85 N.Y.S.2d 727 (Sup. Ct. 1949) (action by attorney general).

allowing the payment of rebates contrary to the board's orders[198] and a director organizing a competing company or accepting employment with a competing company.[199]

In the absence of a controlling statute or valid charter or bylaw provision, courts have generally held that the shareholders do not have the power to remove a director without cause; consequently, a director who is serving the corporation faithfully is privileged to continue in office until the end of the term despite the opposition of a majority of the shareholders.[200] In some states, until recently, the corporation's statute's silence had left this common law rule unchanged.[201] In most states, clear statutory or judicial support exists for the use of a charter or bylaw provision for removal without cause, and such provisions are common.

A large number of corporation statutes now specifically grant power to a majority of the shareholders to remove directors without cause or specifically authorize charter or bylaw provisions granting such power.[202] The Model Business Corporation Act, for example, states in part:

> The shareholders may remove one or more directors with or without cause unless the articles of incorporation provide that directors may be removed only for cause.[203]

Under a statute of this kind, "the right of removal hinges not upon the propriety of a director's conduct but upon the bare question of whether the shareholders desire to retain him as a representative on the board for whatever reason."[204]

In a corporation with a number of classes of shares, with each class electing a specified number of directors, the issue may arise as to whether directors elected by a particular class of stock can be removed by a vote of the shareholders generally or only by a vote of holders of the class of shares that elected the directors. The better view is that shareholders of a specific class should have exclusive power to remove the directors whom they elect,[205] although the case law bearing on this point is sparse.[206] Many corporation statutes now specifically protect directors elected by a particular class of shares under a system of class voting against removal by the votes of holders of other classes of shares.[207]

---

[198] Koppitz-Melchers, Inc. v. Koppitz, 24 N.W.2d 220 (Mich. 1946).

[199] Eckhaus v. Ma, 635 F.Supp. 873 (S.D.N.Y. 1986).

[200] *E.g.,* Toledo Traction, Light & Power Co. v. Smith, 205 F. 643 (N.D. Ohio 1913).

[201] An earlier Illinois corporation statute, for example, did not contain a provision for removing directors without cause. *But see* 805 ILCS § 5/8.35 (1993).

[202] *See, e.g.,* Del. Code Ann. tit. 8, § 141(k) (2009) (permitting removal with or without cause unless provided otherwise in the articles of incorporation).

[203] MBCA § 8.08(a) (1984). *Accord* former MBCA § 39 (1969).

[204] Former MBCA Ann. § 39, Comment ¶ 2 (2d ed. 1971).

[205] *See* Ernest E. Folk, The Delaware General Corporation Law § 141, p. 59 (1972).

[206] *See* Murray v. Conseco, Inc., 795 N.E.2d 454 (Ind. 2003) (a director elected by a specific "voting group" may only removed by that group).

[207] Cal. Corp. Code § 303(a)(2) (West 1990) (removal without cause); Del. Code Ann. tit. 8, § 141(k) (2009) (removal without cause); Mont. Code Ann. § 35–1–424(2) (1993); N.Y. Bus. Corp. Law § 706(c)(2) (McKinney 1986) (removal with or without cause); N.D. Cent. Code § 10–19.1–41(3) (2009) (with or without cause); Ohio Rev. Code Ann. § 1701.58 (West 2009); former MBCA § 39 (1969) (query whether statute covers removal with cause); MBCA § 8.08 (1984) (with or without cause).

The Delaware statute, which seemingly shields directors only against removal without cause, leaves directors elected by a particular class vulnerable to being charged with misconduct and tried by a different and perhaps less friendly forum than the shareholders who elected them. *See* Del. Code Ann. tit. 8, § 141(k) (2009).

Cumulative voting rights also need protection against shareholder removal of directors elected by minority shareholders. To permit majority shareholders to remove, without cause, the directors elected by minority shareholders under cumulative voting would obviously be unfair to the minority. Most modern statutes empowering shareholders to remove directors contain a clause designed to protect cumulative voting rights.[208] A surprising decision held that the articles of incorporation and bylaws could not provide a greater vote to remove a director than the two-thirds vote set forth in the state statute.[209]

A novel question is whether removal without cause is inconsistent with a provision of the articles of incorporation that calls for directors to serve staggered three-year terms.[210] The Delaware Chancery Court held that a bylaw provision providing for removal without cause was invalid in the face of the articles mandating staggered director terms, reasoning that otherwise the bylaws would frustrate the purpose sought by having the directors serve three-year terms.[211] The decision quite likely would have gone the other way if the authority to remove the directors without cause had been included in the articles of incorporation rather than in the bylaws.

Because the process for removing a director exists, indirect methods of removing a director are likely to be unsuccessful when challenged in court. Thus reducing the board size does not shorten the term of directors serving staggered terms[212] and advancing the annual meeting date by many months did not shorten the terms of directors serving staggered three-year terms, so that with respect to measuring the meaning of annual for directors means a date "approximately" one year after the last annual meeting).[213]

§ 9.14   Removal of Directors by Action of the Board of Directors

In the absence of authorization by statute or charter or bylaw, the directors do not have the power to remove one of their members even for cause.[214] Charter and bylaw provisions empowering a board of directors to remove a director for cause probably are valid in most states under statutes broadly authorizing optional charter and special

---

[208] *See, e.g.,* Cal. Corp. Code § 303(a)(1) (West 1990); Del. Code Ann. tit. 8, § 141(k)(2) (2009); N.Y. Bus. Corp. Law § 706(c)(1) (McKinney 1986).

[209] *See* Georgia-Pacific Corp. v. Great Northern Nekoosa Corp., 731 F.Supp. 38 (D.Me. 1990) (citing commentary to Maine statute that "if shareholders have acquired sufficient votes to command a two-thirds majority, they should be able to put in their own board of directors, as a matter of right."). The decision may well be understood as guided by its circumstances, a battle for control, and the court wishing to preserve as best it could a level playing field among the combatants. In Smith v. Orange & Rockland Utilities, Inc., 617 N.Y.S.2d 278 (Sup. Ct. 1994), the court, though critical of the bylaws' imposition of an eighty-percent vote requirement to remove a director, nevertheless permitted the polls to remain open (even after closing the voting on two other agenda items) until the next meeting of the stockholders so that additional votes could be obtain to remove the director.

[210] For a defense of the benefits of a classified board, greater director independence improved long-term planning and increased stability, *see* Richard H. Koppes, Lyle G. Ganske & Charles T. Haag, Corporate Governance Out of Focus: The Debate Over Classified Boards, 54 Bus. Law. 1023 (1999). *But see* Rivka Weill, Declassifying the Classified, 31 Del. J. Corp. L. 891 (2006) (arguing that limiting shareholders' ability to remove board members with staggered terms only for cause unless otherwise provided in the articles achieves stability at the expense of the shareholders' interests in replacing an existing board).

[211] Essential Enter. Corp. v. Automatic Steel Prods., Inc., 159 A.2d 288 (Del. Ch. 1960).

[212] EMAK Partners LLC v. Kurz, 992 A.2d 377 (Del. 2010).

[213] Airgas, Inc. v. Air Prods. And Chems., Inc., 8 A.3d 1182 (Del. 2010).

[214] Dillon v. Berg, 326 F.Supp. 1214, 1225 (D. Del.), *aff'd per curiam on other grounds,* 453 F.2d 876 (3d Cir. 1971).

bylaw provisions. A few statutes specify that a charter or bylaw provision adopted by the shareholders may empower the board of directors to remove a director for cause.[215]

§ 9.15   Judicial Removal of Directors

Modern court decisions are fairly consistent in holding that, absent statutory authorization, there is no judicial power to remove legally elected directors, even on a showing of directors' dishonesty or inability to perform their duties.[216] These holdings are in stark contrast to the result reached during the early formative period of corporate law, when courts were willing to invoke their well-established equity powers to remove trustees for substantial cause, such as misappropriation, long continued absence, and antagonism of interest.[217]

The language of section 8.09 of the Model Act illustrates the high threshold for misbehavior required for a director's removal by the court:

(a) The [name of the court] . . . may remove a director . . . if the court finds that (1) the director engaged in fraudulent or dishonest conduct, or gross abuse of authority or discretion, with respect to the corporation and (2) removal is in the best interest of the corporation.

In 2009, Delaware amended its corporate laws to permit judicial removal of directors, but the process is even more restrictive than the approach proffered in the Model Act.[218] If a director is convicted of a felony or is shown to have breached the duty of loyalty, either the corporation or the shareholders via a derivative suit may apply to the Chancery Court for removal. Upon review, the court may only order removal "if the Court determines that the director or directors did not act in good faith in performing the acts resulting in the prior conviction or judgment and judicial removal is necessary to avoid irreparable harm to the corporation."[219]

The showing required in either circumstance is set high in recognition of the primacy of stockholder suffrage rights that elected the director to office. The exercise of stockholders' voting power should not easily be undone by a court.[220] At the same time access to a court is an important safety valve in those instances in which traditional internal governance procedures cannot reasonably are expected to protect the corporation or its stockholders from the on-going misbehavior by a director.

§ 9.16   Committees of the Board of Directors

Boards of directors of publicly held corporations have long used committees to structure their control and supervision of corporate operations. The committee system

---

[215] Murray v. Conseco, Inc., 795 N.E.2d 454 (Ind. 2003)(director validly removed by board where state statute clearly empowers board to remove director unless articles provide otherwise).*See, e.g.,* N.J. Stat. Ann. § 14A:6–6(3) (Supp. 2000); N.Y. Bus. Corp. Law § 706(a) (McKinney 1986) (except when there is cumulative voting).

[216] *See, e.g.,* Ross Sys. Corp. v. Ross, No. Civ. A. 10378, 1993 WL 49778 (Del. Ch. 1993); Harkey v. Mobley, 552 S.W.2d 79 (Mo. Ct. App. 1977); Danziger v. Allen, 2019 WL 4566961 (Ohio App. 2019).

[217] *See* George G. Bogert, The Law of Trusts and Trustees § 527 (2d rev. ed. 1978); Restatement (Second) of Trusts § 107 (1959).

[218] Del. Code Ann. tit. 8, § 225(c) (2009).

[219] Del. Code Ann. tit. 8, § 225(c) (2009).

[220] *See, e.g.,* Tarin v. Pellonari, 625 N.E.2d 739 (Ill. App. Ct. 1993) (among the statutory conditions is proof of "fraudulent conduct" which requires more than proof of self dealing and must be established by clear and convincing evidence).

permits a board to operate more effectively and expeditiously. Committees can study assigned problems in much greater depth than is possible for the full board;[221] they can develop and utilize specialized knowledge and experience; and they can provide a sharper and more intensive focus on particular business issues and activities.[222] Indeed, the boards of the large, publicly held corporations could not function effectively without committees.

Committees also permit governance of the firm to be improved by parceling out responsibilities among directors in ways that more closely address concerns for good corporate practices.[223] The ALI's Principles of Corporate Governance strongest recommendation in this area is that state statutes should include a provision requiring that "large publicly held corporations"[224] should have an audit committee of at least three disinterested members.[225] All the other ALI provisions concerned with the board's structure and its committees are mild suggestions directed exclusively to corporations and their counselors, not to courts and legislatures. The recommendations in this regard are not normative, so non-compliance is not the basis of liability. For example, the ALI recommends that a majority of the board of directors of large publicly held corporations not have a significant financial relationship to the company's senior executives,[226] and other publicly held corporations should have at least three disinterested directors.[227] An audit committee[228] and a nominating committee[229] are each recommended for all public corporations, and a compensation committee is recommended for large publicly held corporations.[230]

Executive Committee. Historically, the "executive committee"[231] has been the most important and the most widely prevalent committee. The bylaws of most publicly held corporations provide for an executive committee and define its powers, usually in broad and general terms. The bylaws or board resolution setting up an executive committee typically vests the committee with "the powers of the board" or "the full powers of the board." The Model Business Corporation Act limits the authority executive

---

[221] *See, e.g.,* Gaillard v. Natomas Co., 256 Cal.Rptr. 702 (Cal. Ct. App. 1989) (use of committees is intended to enhance level of scrutiny).

[222] *See* The Role and Composition of the Board of Directors of the Large Publicly Owned Corporation: Statement of the Business Roundtable, reprinted in 33 Bus. Law. 2083, 2109 (1978).

[223] The Securities and Exchange Commission, the national stock exchanges, and various persons and organizations concerned with improving corporate governance have tried to enhance the ability and inclination of corporate boards to monitor management performance. One recommendation that has gained wide support is that boards of publicly held corporations appoint a committee composed entirely or largely of independent outside directors to deal with issues in which disinterested oversight is especially important.

[224] The ALI defines this term to mean a corporation having 2000 shareholders and $100 million in assets. ALI, Principles of Corporate Governance Analysis and Recommendations 1.24 (1992).

[225] ALI, Principles of Corporate Governance Analysis and Recommendations. § 3.05. A director is disinterested if the director has not been employed by the company during the preceding two years and has no significant relationship with the company's senior executives.

Both the New York Stock Exchange and Nasdaq require listed corporations have audit committees composed of independent directors. Law. of Corp. Offs. & Dirs.: Rts., Duties & Liabs. § 8:6 (2009). *See generally* Fletcher, Cyclopedia, § 550.

[226] ALI, Principles of Corporate Governance Analysis and Recommendations § 3A.01(a).

[227] ALI, Principles of Corporate Governance Analysis and Recommendations § 3A.01(b).

[228] ALI, Principles of Corporate Governance Analysis and Recommendations § 3A.02.

[229] ALI, Principles of Corporate Governance Analysis and Recommendations § 3A.04.

[230] ALI, Principles of Corporate Governance Analysis and Recommendations § 3A.05.

[231] *See generally* Nancy F. Halliday, Note, Corporation Executive Committees, 16 Clev.-Mar. L. Rev. 167 (1967).

committees can exercise, for example, executive committees cannot fill vacancies in the board and cannot amend either the articles of incorporation or bylaws.[232]

Executive committees once were expected to act only between meetings of the board. The present practice in many corporations is for the executive committee not only to act between meetings of the full board but also to review, before presentation to the full board, virtually all matters going before the board for action, including major policy decisions and long-range planning.

Almost invariably, executive committees are controlled by a small number of key "inside" (management) directors. A typical executive committee, for example, might be composed of the chief executive officer, one or two inside directors, and an outside director.[233] There is little doubt that the use of an executive committee composed entirely or largely of management directors raises a serious question regarding the role of the full board of directors. However, a broadly empowered executive committee composed of entirely inside directors is not necessarily inconsistent with the outside directors serving an aggressive monitoring role of management's stewardship. In such a context, one needs to bear in mind that there is a difference between management and monitoring, and in the public corporation it is the latter role that is commended to outside directors. That role does not require that outside directors be involved in the formulation and execution of corporate decisions. One must, however, be concerned that an executive committee not be the tool to exclude directors representing minority interests from real participation in board decisions.[234]

Executive committees have often been aggressive in exercising powers allegedly granted them. Occasionally, they have even tried to usurp the powers of the full board. Courts have usually condemned such attempts to seize complete control of a corporation and exclude the other directors from their management powers.[235]

Audit Committee. The role of the audit committee has long been an evolving one. There has long been considerable divergence of opinion on what the duties and objectives of such a committee are or should be; these differences continue today.[236] It has been

---

[232] Model Bus. Corp. Act § 8.25(d)(2016).

[233] *See* Avery S. Cohen, The Outside Director—Selection, Responsibilities, and Contributions to the Public Corporation, 34 Wash. & Lee L. Rev. 837, 854 (1997) (recommending that "executive committees draw a majority of their membership from among the outside directors, to serve the same function, in essence, as is served by those directors on the board as a whole.").

[234] This is achieved by reaching decisions at the committee level and then formally convening the full board to summarily approve the committee's recommendations.

[235] *E.g.,* Robinson v. Benbow, 298 F. 561, 570 (4th Cir. 1924).

[236] Functions often performed by an audit committee include:

(1) employing the company's independent auditors or making recommendations to the full board on such employment;

(2) reviewing the engagement of the independent auditors, including the scope and timing of the audit and the auditors fee;

(3) consulting with the company's independent auditors on the plan of audit;

(4) reviewing with the independent auditors the results of the audit;

(5) inquiring into the corporation's financial practices and the adequacy of internal controls; and

(6) consulting with the independent auditors, out of the presence of the management, on the adequacy of internal controls and, if need be, consulting with internal auditors.

Sound advice appears in the calls for the audit committee to be more proactive with respect to the firm's financial reporting. For example, the leading authority on the liability of accountants, envisions an important protective function by the audit committee that includes (1) establishing the right kind of financial reporting environment, (2) assuring that the financial reporting system is physically capable of delivering accurate observed that "[t]he primary purpose and function of the Audit Committee, as originally conceived and, in most cases, as currently intended, is limited to providing an opportunity for direct communication with the Board of Directors by the corporation's independent auditors, thereby tending to strengthen their independence and objectivity."[237]

Compensation Committee. The compensation committee is becoming increasingly common. It approves or recommends to the full board compensation arrangements for the company's senior management and any compensation plans in which the directors or officers are eligible to participate.[238] The compensation committee should be composed exclusively of non-management directors to assure an impartial and independent judgment on the fairness of management compensation.[239] In 1992, the SEC amended the reporting requirements for public corporations so that today a graphic representation of the senior executives' total compensation must be matched against data tracking the company's overall financial performance. The obvious impact of the disclosure rules is to heighten the directors' sense of obligation when establishing executive compensation. An unintended consequence of the new disclosure is to introduce to executive compensation a phenomenon previously enjoyed only in Lake Wobegon, a mythical community where everyone is above average. An observed consequence of the 1992 disclosures is more rapid ratcheting upwards of the executive's compensation, lest they be below the median for their industry.[240] Nevertheless in the years that followed, the SEC has continued to focus on increased and more detailed disclosure concerning executive compensation.[241] The Dodd-Frank Wall Street Reform Act of 2010 addressed shareholders' say on pay by including a requirement that management solicit proxies for non-binding shareholder vote on a resolution seeking shareholder approval of Named Executive Officer (NEO) compensation.[242] This "say-on-pay" shareholder votes must take place on a regular basis—every one, two or three years as determined by a shareholder vote.[243]

---

reports on a timely basis, and (3) assure a system of information flows so that the committee is abreast of financial developments within the firm. *See* Michael R. Young, What Is An Audit Committee To Do, 222 N.Y.L.J. 1 (Dec. 16, 1999). *See generally* Accounting Irregularities and Financial Fraud (M.R. Young ed. 1999).

[237] The Overview Committee of the Board of Directors: A Report by the Committee on Corporate Laws, 34 Bus. Law. 1837, 1861 (1979).

[238] "Its chief function is to monitor compensation arrangements with a view to insuring that the corporation is attracting and retaining highly qualified management through competitive salary and benefit programs and by encouraging extraordinary effort through incentive rewards." The Overview Committee of the Board of Directors, A Report by the Committee on Corporate Laws, 34 Bus. Law. 1837, 1848 (1979). *See, e.g.,* In re Walt Disney Co. Deriv. Litig., 906 A.2d 27 (Del. 2006) (rejecting shareholders' claim that committee breached fiduciary duty of care in approving compensation and severance package for corporate president without informing themselves of full magnitude of potential payout).

[239] One court has held that it is inappropriate to grant the committee members' motion for summary judgment to a challenge to golden parachutes approved by the committee's independent members. Gaillard v. Natomas Co., 256 Cal.Rptr. 702 (Cal. Ct. App. 1989) (the possibility of facts removing the committee's decision from the business judgment rule's protection was present because the golden parachutes were initiated and approved after management had approved the merger).

[240] *See* Randall S. Thomas & Kenneth J. Martin, The Effect of Shareholder Proposals on Executive Compensation, 67 Cinn. L. Rev. 1021 (1999).

[241] *See, e.g.,* Regulation S–K Item 402, 17 C.F.R. § 229.402 (2009).

[242] Dodd-Frank Wall Street Reform and Consumer Protection Act § 951, Pub. Law 111–203, H.R. 4173 (111th Cong. 2d sess. 2010), adding 1934 Act § 14A(a), 15 U.S.C. § 78n–1(a).

[243] *Id.* At least every six years, the company's annual proxy statement must include a separate shareholder resolution to determine how frequently the "say-on-pay" votes will occur. In addition if a company solicits a shareholder vote or consent on a business combination, the company must disclose (i) any agreements or understandings that the soliciting person has with any NEO of the issuer concerning any compensation that is based on or otherwise relates to the transaction being voted on and (ii) the aggregate total of all compensation

Nominating Committee. The nominating committee or, more rarely, the "committee on succession," has greater potential for improving corporate governance. This committee selects, or recommends to the full board, candidates for election to the board. The committee's responsibility should include passing on the performance of incumbent directors and determining whether they should be retained. In some corporations, the nominating committee recommends to the full board the membership of board committees and, even more importantly, the choice of successor to top management posts. The nominating committee might also develop and submit to the full board for approval the criteria for board membership. While a minority view holds that a corporation's chief executive officer should be a member of the nominating committee, the better view, and the one gaining increasing acceptance, is that the committee should be composed exclusively of independent, non-management directors. The benefits of assuring the nominating committee's independence from its CEO has strong empirical support.

§ 9.17   Limitations on Delegation of Board Powers to Committees

Under both common law and statutes, as well as under charter or bylaw provisions, questions arise as to the extent to which the board of directors can delegate its powers to a committee. Does the power to delegate extend to delegation of acts requiring the exercise of judgment and discretion? Is this power limited to delegating authority to act in ordinary business transactions? Or does it extend to important decisions, such as approving a merger and recommending it to the shareholders, adopting a pension or profit-sharing plan, declaring dividends, selecting the company's principal executive officers, fixing the officers' compensation, removing officers, and amending the bylaws?[244]

Some of the earlier cases held that the board could delegate "ministerial" duties to a committee but could not grant authority to a committee to determine matters involving high judgment or discretion or to inaugurate reversals of or departures from fundamental corporate policies.[245] Most modern statutes first state that a committee of the board "shall have and may exercise all the authority of the board" to the extent provided in a resolution of the board or in the corporation's charter or bylaws, but then carve out exceptions by specifying extraordinary acts that cannot be delegated.[246] Many statutes do not permit delegation to a committee of the power to act on fundamental corporate changes, such as approving a charter amendment, adopting a plan of merger or consolidation, recommending to the shareholders the sale, lease, or other disposition of all or substantially all of the corporation's assets, or recommending a voluntary dissolution. Other nondelegable duties in a substantial number of states include filling vacancies on the board or board committees, electing or removing officers, altering

---

that may be paid or payable to that officer and the conditions under which it may be paid or payable, and (2) a separate nonbinding shareholder vote to approve any such agreements, understandings and compensation, unless the agreements or understandings were subject to an earlier nonbinding say-on-pay vote.

[244] *See*, In re Walt Disney Co. Deriv. Litig., 906 A.2d 27 (Del. 2006) (committee may set executive compensation, since nothing in Delaware law mandates that entire board must make compensation decisions).

[245] *E.g.*, Fensterer v. Pressure Lighting Co., 149 N.Y.S. 49, 53 (City Ct. 1914).

[246] *E.g.*, MBCA § 8.25(d) (2016); Del. Code Ann. tit. 8, § 141(c) (2009); N.Y. Bus. Corp. Law § 712(a) (McKinney 2009).

are ones best commended to the business judgment of the board. In contrast, contracts delegating substantially all management powers to outsiders for indefinite or extended periods of time are usually held invalid. Thus a contract between two insurance companies that gave one the "underwriting and executive management" of the other for a period of 20 years was struck down.[261] From the terms of the agreement and the length of time it was to remain in effect, the court concluded that "not only managerial powers were delegated, but the entire policy" of one company was to be fixed and determined by the other.[262] Similarly, an agreement by a corporation giving the purchaser of some of its five-year convertible bonds the power to designate a comptroller for the corporation and providing that the comptroller would have complete charge of all finances of the company and that no expenditures should be made or authorized without his prior approval was declared against public policy and unenforceable.[263] On the other hand, corporations have been permitted to delegate to outsiders at least for a limited period some of the functions usually performed by its directors and officers. For instance, an agreement employing an executive for a period of five years and giving him the position of editor and manager of a large daily newspaper, with power to determine editorial policy, has been held to be permissible.[264] A management contract will be upheld where authorized by a separate provision of the state's general corporation law.[265]

There has developed in recent years a variety of arrangements whereby the debtor corporation grants a creditor an effective veto over certain corporate actions. These are collectively referred to as "poison puts" taking this name from the power the put provides the creditor whereby if the creditor with the put does not consent to the proposed action the maturity date of the underlying debt obligation is accelerated.[266] If the amount of the debt is substantial, the prospect of the creditor company addressing the repayment gives rise to substantial coercion on the board. A poison put can be an effective antitakeover provision; for example, the board of directors in securing a loan can agree to include a provision whereby the maturity of the debt is accelerated if there is a change of control of the board of directors not consented to by the board of directors and the creditor. Even though the poison put effectively restricts the freedom of the board of directors, courts thus far have upheld the arrangements as reasonable commercial lending arrangements.[267] To be sure, the coercion flowing from the creditor's right to put its debt to the corporation no doubt impacts the decision reached by the board of directors. And that decision can well be an important one. Nonetheless, absent some clear evidence of bad faith or self dealing surrounding the put's creation, it is difficult to understand why this is not swept up in the presumptions associated with the business judgment rule. In

---

[261] Sherman & Ellis, Inc. v. Indiana Mut. Cas. Co., 41 F.2d 588 (7th Cir.), *cert. denied,* 282 U.S. 893 (1930).

[262] Sherman & Ellis, Inc. v. Indiana Mut. Cas. Co., 41 F.2d 588, 591 (7th Cir.), *cert. denied,* 282 U.S. 893 (1930).

[263] Marvin v. Solventol Chem. Prods., Inc., 298 N.W. 782 (Mich. 1941).

[264] Jones v. Williams, 39 S.W. 486, 40 S.W. 353 (Mo. 1897).

[265] *See, e.g.,* Cal. Corp. Code § 300(a) (West 1990) ("The board may delegate the management of day-to-day operations of the business of the corporation to a management company. . . .").

[266] *See generally* Sean J. Griffith & Natalie Reisel, Dead Hand Proxy Puts and Shareholder Value, 84 Chi. L. Rev. 1027 (2017); Note, The Spirit of *Blasius: Sandridge* As Antidote To The Poison Put, 115 Colum. L. Rev. 375 (2015).

[267] *See,* Kallick v. San Diego Energy, Inc., 68 A.3d 242 (Del. Ch. 2013)(not a breach of directors' fiduciary duty not to approve the slate of directors proposed by an dissident shareholder); San Antonio Fire & Police Pen. Fd. v. Amylin Pharms., Inc., 983 A.2d 304 (Del. Ch.), aff'd, 981 A.2d 1173 (Del 2009)(same).

one case an attempt to impose a fiduciary obligation on the creditor holding the put was unsuccessful.[268]

§ 9.20   Long-Term Employment Contracts

Corporations often contract with an executive or other key employees,[269] promising employment for life, "permanent employment," for an unusually long term, such as 25 years, or assuring employment as long as the employee holds stock in the corporation. Under a view that must be viewed as dated, and hence, badly out of step with today's business climate, such long-term contracts were of doubtful validity.[270] The rationale behind these early decisions was that (1) the corporation statutes give the board power to manage corporate affairs and one board cannot properly take away from future boards part of that statutorily granted power by "freezing in" the company's agents and employees; and (2) the statutes, by providing for the periodic election of directors by the shareholders, contemplate that the shareholder can elect new directors and through the new directors effectuate a complete change of corporate management, a power that would be frustrated if corporate officers and other key personnel could not be removed from their positions.[271] Today, a successful assault upon the validity of a long-term employment contract is made upon contract, not corporate principles. That is, a considerable number of modern decisions sustain long-term, and even lifetime, employment contracts without mentioning their impinging upon the authority of a future board of directors.[272]

There is no apparent reason for a corporate employer to have less power than an individual to enter into long-term contracts. If the corporation is not permitted to enter into long-term contracts, the directors may not be able to enter into contracts that, in their sound judgment, are in the corporation's best interest, including employment contracts designed to obtain needed key personnel.

The commercial justifications for long-term employment arrangements can easily be understood. Moreover, any blanket prohibition of long-term employment contracts would merely bring about a result similar to that which occurs when you squeeze a balloon. The restraint in one area merely causes the expansion of the compressed air's force to another area of the balloon. There are numerous alternatives available to the firm to attract key employees: a grant of stock options, a promise of substantial compensation upon severance, early vesting retirement benefits, etc. So viewed, the natural question is why should the law single out one approach for attack on principles of governance and defer to the board's business judgment with respect to all other

---

[268] *See,* Franchise Servs. of N. A. v. United States, 891 F.3d 198, 208–09 (5th Cir. 2018)(holding that under Delaware law it believed no fiduciary duty attached to a shareholder unless that shareholder had "actual control" of corporate conduct which requires evidence of effective domination and control). The case involved a "golden share" provision in which as part of a financing plan a minority shareholder who also was an unsecured creditor was granted a right through the debtor company's articles of incorporation to block any filing of a bankruptcy petition by the debtor company. The Fifth Circuit held no fiduciary duty surrounded the golden share as the holder of the right did not enjoy sufficient control.

[269] Executive compensation is discussed *infra* §§ 11.1 to 11.5.

[270] *See generally* Annot., 135 A.L.R. 646 (1941), 35 A.L.R. 1432 (1925).

[271] Beers v. New York Life Ins. Co., 20 N.Y.S. 788, 792–793 (Sup. Ct. 1892).

[272] At least one jurisdiction has a statute that expressly authorizes corporations to enter into long-term employment contracts. Tex. Bus. Corp. Act Ann. § 2.02A(12) (2009).

approaches.[273] This reasoning appears to explain why the lens through which long-term contracts are examined is that of contract and not corporate law.

The first consideration for the validity of a long-term employment contract is whether it satisfies the applicable statute of frauds.[274] Many states also require that the employee's promise should be supported by consideration independent of her promise to competently perform the work called for in the contract.[275] This requirement appears inconsistent with a fundamental tenet of contract law, namely that a binding contract requires not *adequate* consideration, but consideration. A far wiser approach is not to require that the employee provide independent consideration in exchange for the promise of long-term employment.[276] Instead, we should treat the presence or absence of such consideration as evidence bearing upon the existence of an express or implied promise of such employment. That is, the expressions "for life," "for as long as the employee chooses" and "permanent" may be used in a casual sense and may even be understood by the parties to have been effusive puffery, so that the agreement in fact called for employment for an indefinite term so that it was terminable by the will of either party. So viewed, the presumption of being an at will employment contract can be overcome by proof the parties expressly or impliedly agreed that the employee could only be terminated for cause or the contract was supported by consideration independent of the services to be performed.[277]

The further issue is the authority of the officer to enter into the long-term arrangement. Such a contract is rightfully seen as typically beyond the inherent authority of the chief executive officer. Thus, in *Boothby v. Texon, Inc.,*[278] the employee was successful in establishing the validity of a promise of "permanent employment" by the company's president by proving that the president acted with the implied authority of the board of directors. This was established by evidence that the board was informed by the president that "job security" was the issue that most concerned the employee and at a meeting of the board its chair instructed the president to do whatever was necessary to get the employee to join the corporation. A final consideration is that the employment contract should be tied to some test of competency.[279]

---

[273] For a case where the business judgment rule protected the board awarding millions of dollars in severance benefits if the executive should leave because he believed the board was interfering with his management, *see* Grimes v. Donald, 673 A.2d 1207 (Del. 1996) *overruled in part by* Brehm v. Eisner, 746 A.2d 244 (De. 2000).

[274] *See, e.g.,* Merlo v. United Way of America, 43 F.3d 96 (4th Cir. 1994) (employment contract extending beyond one year required by Florida law to be in writing).

[275] *See, e.g.,* Deus v. Allstate Ins. Co., 15 F.3d 506 (5th Cir. 1994) (independent consideration includes employee winding up an existing business, transferring a secret formula, or settling a personal claim in exchange for the promise of lifetime employment).

[276] For a case rejecting the necessity of independent consideration, *see* McInerney v. Charter Golf, Inc., 680 N.E.2d 1347 (Ill. 1997) (recognizing bargained for consideration was that employer gave up right to terminate at will in exchange for employee passing up a lucrative job offer from a third person).

[277] *See* Cunico v. Bowie, 133 F.3d 926 (9th Cir. 1997); S & W Agency, Inc. v. Foremost Ins. Co., 51 F.Supp.2d 959 (N.D. Iowa 1998) (lifetime employment is extraordinary arrangement requiring strong proof of parties' intent).

[278] Boothby v. Texon, Inc., 608 N.E.2d 1028 (Mass. 1993).

[279] *See, e.g.,* McInerney v. Charter Golf, Inc., 680 N.E.2d 1347 (Ill. 1997) (may be discharged for dishonesty or disability).

Chapter 10

DIRECTORS' AND OFFICERS' DUTIES OF CARE AND LOYALTY

Table of Sections

PART A. DILIGENCE, SKILL, AND CARE; LIABILITY FOR NEGLIGENCE IN MANAGEMENT

§ 10.1 Liability for Imprudence and Honest Errors of Judgment: The "Business Judgment Rule"

What is the liability of directors for incompetence? Although directors are commonly said to be responsible both for reasonable care and for prudence, the formula is continually repeated that directors are not liable for losses due to imprudence or honest errors of judgment.[1] This formula is frequently referred to as the "business judgment

---

[1]   In re Reading Co., 711 F.2d 509 (3d Cir. 1983); Lewis v. Curtis, 671 F.2d 779 (3d Cir. 1982).

rule."[2] Taken in its most cynical light, the business judgment rule means that management's position is vindicated.[3]

> Courts do not measure, weigh, or quantify directors' judgments. We do not even decide if they are reasonable in this context. Due care in the decision-making context is *process* due care only. Irrationality is the outer limit of the business judgment rule. Irrationality may be the functional equivalent of the waste test or it may tend to show that the decision is not made in good faith, which is a key ingredient of the business judgment rule.[4]

The above description of the business judgment rule is best understood by distinguishing between the duty of care and the business judgment rule. The former can be seen as embracing a standard for officer and director conduct, whereas the latter embodies a standard of judicial review.[5] The twin features of the business judgment rule's application to a decision of the directors is that the directors will not be liable for any losses proximately caused by that decision and the court will not substitute its judgment or that of the plaintiff for the decision made by the directors. We can therefore understand judicial incantations regarding the care obligations of directors and officers as aspirational, even normative. However, whether the officer's or director's departure from an understood norm results in liability (or the court substituting its judgment for that of the corporate decision maker) depends on how her conduct is assessed under the review standard embraced in the business judgment rule.[6]

In general, courts will not undertake to review the expediency of contracts or other business transactions authorized by the directors. Directors have a large degree of discretion. Questions of value and policy have been said to be part of the directors' business judgment, although their errors may be so gross as to show their unfitness to manage corporate affairs.[7] According to the better view, the business judgment rule presupposes that reasonable diligence and care have been exercised.[8] But are there not, in addition, some limits on the immunity for losses due to honest errors resulting from a director's lack of intelligence, foresight, and business sense? Hasty action by an ill-informed board will not be insulated by the business judgment rule.[9] However, directors and officers do not operate in a world that permits them to have all the information they

---

[2]   *E.g.,* Burks v. Lasker, 441 U.S. 471 (1979); Abbey v. Control Data Corp., 603 F.2d 724 (8th Cir. 1979), *cert. denied,* 444 U.S. 1017 (1980); Auerbach v. Bennett, 393 N.E.2d 994 (N.Y. 1979). *See generally* Myron T. Steele, Judicial Scrutiny Of Fiduciary Duties In Delaware Limited Partnerships And Limited Liability Companies, 32 Del. J. Corp. L. 1 (2007).

[3]   As one commentator has put it, when the court finds no breach of a duty of care "[t]he court in effect [is] applying the business judgment rule." *See* Harry G. Henn, Corporations: Cases and Materials 587 (1974).

[4]   Brehm v. Eisner, 746 A.2d 244, 264 (Del. 2000) (emphasis original).

[5]   *See* Melvin Aron Eisenberg, The Divergence of Standards of Conduct and Standards of Review in Corporate Law, 62 Fordham L. Rev. 437 (1993). Thus, section 8.30(b) of the Model Business Corporation Act sets forth a standard of care for directors, but a breach of that standard assumes legal significance only if the director's decision is not protected pursuant to the review standards set forth in section 8.31. *See* Model Business Corporation Act § 8.31 Official Comment (2008). For an example of a court distinguishing between the business judgment "rule" and the business judgment "doctrine," with the effect that the former was viewed to shield the directors from liability for their decisions and the latter protects the transaction from further scrutiny, *see* Gries Sports Enterprises, Inc. v. Cleveland Browns Football Co., 496 N.E.2d 959, 964 (Ohio 1986).

[6]   *See generally* Joy v. North, 692 F.2d 880, 885 (2d Cir. 1982) (in contrast to actors in common tort cases, corporate officers or directors are rarely responsible for their mistakes in judgment).

[7]   Everett v. Phillips, 43 N.E.2d 18, 20 (N.Y. 1942).

[8]   FDIC v. Stahl, 89 F.3d 1510 (11th Cir. 1996) (business judgment rule assumes that the directors have been diligent and careful; plaintiffs need not establish gross negligence, ordinary negligence is sufficient).

[9]   Smith v. Van Gorkom, 488 A.2d 858 (Del. 1985).

would prefer to have before they act. "The need to make judgments with only imperfect information available, and other elements of risk taking, are often inherent in business decisionmaking."[10] When the board has not acted in breach of a fiduciary duty, its members will be entitled to the protection of the business judgment rule.[11]

The evolution in publicly held corporations of a class of directors who are compensated well and devote substantial time to the affairs of each corporation on whose board they serve, coupled with heavy investor reliance on director competence and diligence, arguably justifies imposing professional-like standards of competence on directors.

Nevertheless, the courts and the legislatures (or, perhaps more accurately, the leaders of the corporate bar who draft statutory standards for directors)[12] apparently are not yet ready to recognize the professional status of directors in publicly held corporations and impose truly professional standards of competence on them.

Courts developed the business judgment rule long before statements on directors' duties were included in the corporation statutes. Even though corporation statutes in most states now contain an express statement defining directors' duties and omit any reference to a business judgment rule, courts continue to apply the rule.[13]

§ 10.2 Standard of Care and Diligence

There has been some difference in the language used by the legislatures and the courts to designate the standard of care and diligence required of the directors of a corporation in the management or supervision of its affairs. It is difficult, however, to tell whether the differing standards, which have been referred to as "semantic,"[14] make much difference in practical application. The particular statute's precise formulation of the director's duty of care does not assume great importance in the court's judgment whether the director has breached her duty.[15]

In New York an early theoretical standard was declared to be the care and diligence that an ordinarily prudent man would exercise in the management of his own affairs.[16] The fairer and more satisfactory rule is that degree of care and diligence that an ordinarily prudent director can reasonably be expected to exercise in a like position under similar circumstances.[17] This standard was adopted by the Model Act, and a great number of states have followed suit.[18]

---

[10] A.L.I., 1 Principles of Corporate Governance: Analysis and Recommendations § 4.01(c), Comment f at 182.

[11] *See, e.g.,* Williams v. Geier, 671 A.2d 1368 (Del. 1996) (business judgment rule applied to independent majority's recommendation of articles amendment relating to voting rights).

[12] *See* Report of Committee on Corporate Laws: Changes in the Model Business Corporation Act, 30 Bus. Law. 501, 505 (1975) (hereinafter Report of Committee on Corporate Laws). *See also* Corporate Director's Guidebook (5th ed. 2007), prepared by the Committee on Corporate Laws, Section of Corporation, Banking and Business Law, American Bar Association (hereinafter Corporate Director's Guidebook).

[13] *See, e.g.,* Smith v. Brown-Borhek Co., 200 A.2d 398, 398–402 (Pa. 1964).

[14] Richard W. Jennings & Richard M. Buxbaum, Corporations; Cases and Materials 178 (5th ed. 1979).

[15] *See* Edward Brodsky & M. Patricia Adamski, The Law of Corporate Officers and Directors: Rights, Duties and Liabilities § 2.04 (1984).

[16] Hun v. Cary, 82 N.Y. 65 (1880).

[17] Briggs v. Spaulding, 141 U.S. 132 (1891); DePinto v. Provident Sec. Life Ins. Co., 374 F.2d 37, 43–44 (9th Cir. 1967), *cert. denied,* 389 U.S. 822 (1967).

[18] MBCA § 8.30 (2016) provides in relevant part:

Directors are to use such care and diligence and give such time and attention as ordinarily careful and prudent persons can reasonably be expected to exercise on behalf of such a corporation under similar circumstances.[19] What is a failure to exercise reasonable care and diligence is always to be determined with reference to the circumstances of the particular corporation and, to some extent, of the particular director. Whether the breach of that duty gives rise to liability depends upon both a more extreme departure from the objective standard so that the business judgment rule does not apply, and a finding that losses were proximately caused because of the breach.

The duty of care can be divided into three distinct segments. First, there is the obligation of directors and officers to be attentive to the corporation's affairs. Second, the duty of care also requires that the directors reasonably inform themselves on all matters coming before the board and that their decision be duly deliberated. Finally, the duty of care has a substantive component—namely, that directors and officers have a rational basis for their decisions. These components are discussed in the next three sections.

§ 10.3   The Directors' Obligation to Be Attentive

The Slumbering Director. A directorship, although conferring prestige and power, comes with the heavy demand that the director regularly attend board meetings and otherwise be attentive to the corporation's affairs.[20] The precise commands of these obligations are gleaned from the few cases that have considered the fate of directors held to have shirked their responsibility. The obligation to attend meetings on a regular basis is breached by the director who is habitually absent.[21] Moreover, there is not one standard for a nonresident director who is retired and another for active resident directors.[22] But the duty of attentiveness commands more than regular attendance at meetings. In the early case of *Barnes v. Andrews,*[23] the court held that Andrews, an outside director whose tenure was less than nine months, breached his duty to inform himself adequately about the newly created company's operations. Even though the firm had raised a substantial amount of capital through a public offering, possessed a well-equipped and staffed factory, and produced enough parts for starter motors, the firm was experiencing dramatic delays in assembling starter motors. The company ultimately failed. The court held Andrews breached his duty by failing to inform himself adequately about the firm's performance and position.[24]

(a) Each member of the board of directors, when discharging the duties of a director, shall act: (i) in good faith, and (ii) in a manner the director reasonably believes to be in the best interests of the corporation.

(b) The members of the board of directors or a board committee, when becoming informed in connection with their decision-making function or devoting attention to their oversight function, shall discharge their duties with the care that a person in a like position would reasonably believe appropriate under similar circumstances.

[19]   In re Illinois Valley Acceptance Corp. v. Martin, 531 F.Supp. 737 (C.D. Ill. 1982).

[20]   For rejection of the notion that the directors' oversight should extend to the personal affairs of its controlling stockholder, *see* Beam v. Stewart, 833 A.2d 961, 971–972 (Del. Ch. 2003).

[21]   *See, e.g.,* Hoye v. Meek, 795 F.2d 893, 896 (10th Cir. 1986).

[22]   Bowerman v. Hamner, 250 U.S. 504, 513 (1919).

[23]   Barnes v. Andrews, 298 F. 614 (S.D. N.Y. 1924).

[24]   *Barnes*'s holding is in sharp contrast with Briggs v. Spaulding, 141 U.S. 132 (1891), where the bank's board of directors allowed its president nearly absolute control without any close supervision. In a few months the bank was wrecked because of loans to the president and his relatives on worthless collateral, and no directors' meetings were held during a nearly six-month period. In a five-to-four decision, the Court excused

Barnes's holding is all the more striking because of an absence of any facts or circumstances known to Andrews that would have imparted reasonable notice to him that the firm was experiencing problems. Since *Barnes* was decided, a good deal of change has occurred in the boardroom of America's public corporations.

There is a collective view in business, government, and academia that we must discard the predominance of the inside board of directors and replace them with substantial monitoring obligations for outside directors.[25] This view is reflected in the reasoning of cases such as *Francis v. United Jersey Bank,*[26] where a director who was unfamiliar with the rudiments of the corporation's business, never read annual reports, and visited the corporation's offices only once during her five-year tenure on the board (during most of which she was in poor physical health), was held liable for the embezzlements committed by her two sons, who were the corporation's officers and remaining directors. *Francis* expresses the prevailing view regarding the director's duty of attentiveness:

> Directors are under a continuing obligation to keep informed about the activities of the corporation. . . . [D]irectors may not shut their eyes to corporate misconduct and then claim that because they did not see the misconduct, they did not have a duty to look. The sentinel asleep at his post contributes nothing to the enterprise he is charged to protect.

> Directorial management does not require a detailed inspection of day-to-day activities, but rather a general monitoring of corporate affairs and policies.[27]

Francis also reflects the prevailing view that directors are not excused because of intellectual or physical incapacity from their obligation to inform themselves on a regular basis on the financial and operational status of the business.[28] But does the obligation to be attentive command more than regular attendance of meetings? Neither *Barnes* nor *Francis* emphasizes the number of meetings missed, but instead focuses on the necessity for the director to stay abreast of the corporation's financial position, progress, and performance.[29] For example, in *Barnes* Judge Learned Hand describes how Andrews, even though a regular commuter into Manhattan each day with the company's president, failed to learn of the company's production problems. And in *Francis* the court stressed that any review of the company's financial statements would have readily revealed the officer's embezzlements.

There indeed are a good many cases imposing the responsibility on directors to investigate and check the possible wrongdoing of co-directors, officers, and subordinates.[30] Where suspicions are aroused, or should be aroused, it is the director's

---

the directors from liability on such questionable grounds as newness to office, ill health, and old age. *Briggs's* bases for excusing the directors' failure to supervise are very much out of step with contemporary decisions.

[25] *See* James D. Cox & Nis Jul Clausen, The Monitoring Duties of Directors Under the EC Directives: A View from the United States Experience, 2 Duke J. Comp. & Int'l L. 29, 31–44 (1992).

[26] Francis v. United Jersey Bank, 432 A.2d 814 (N.J. 1981).

[27] Francis v. United Jersey Bank, 432 A.2d 814, 822 (N.J. 1981). *See also* Hoye v. Meek, 795 F.2d 893, 895 (10th Cir. 1986) (liability imposed on chairman whose attendance at board meetings was irregular).

[28] *Contra,* Berman v. Le Beau Inter-Am., Inc., 509 F.Supp. 156, 161 (S.D.N.Y.), *aff'd mem.,* 679 F.2d 872 (2d Cir. 1981) (director who was "virtual figurehead" not liable).

[29] *See also* Brane v. Roth, 590 N.E.2d 587 (Ind. Ct. App. 1992) (directors of cooperative breached duty by retaining inexperienced manager and failing to reasonably supervise manager to assure adequate hedging against possible declines in price of grain).

[30] *See, e.g.,* Michelsen v. Penney, 135 F.2d 409, 419 (2d Cir. 1943).

duty to make the necessary inquiries; ignorance is no basis for escaping liability.[31] And the director's obligation does not end with a reasonable investigation but carries forward the duty to act reasonably in light of the information gained thereby.[32] However, absent such reasonable suspicion, the director or officer acts reasonably in relying upon others, whether they be officers, employees or outside consultants.[33]

The Rise of Compliance Systems and Caremark. A somewhat different question is whether directors are under an obligation to install systems designed to discourage and detect the fraudulent, illegal, or criminal activities of subordinates. An early decision on the obligation of directors to monitor the activities of subordinates for the purpose of discouraging or detecting illegal activities is *Graham v. Allis-Chalmers Manufacturing Company.*[34] In *Allis-Chalmers* a derivative suit was brought against the company's directors to recover damages the company suffered because its employees engaged in massive bid-rigging with competitors, a flagrant violation of the antitrust laws. One theory of the plaintiff's action was that the directors had acted unreasonably in failing to establish a system to detect and prevent the bid-rigging. The Delaware Supreme Court dismissed the suit, reasoning that within a large multinational firm such as Allis-Chalmers, with over 30,000 employees, it is unreasonable to require the directors to undertake an active investigation of each division of the firm absent their being on adequate notice of any wrongdoing.[35] The court held the directors acted reasonably in relying on the reports and summaries of operations, which they had no reason to believe were untrustworthy.[36] More important, the court held the Allis-Chalmers directors had no responsibility to establish and maintain a system of surveillance unless there was suspicion of wrongdoing.[37]

One finds a good deal of dissonance between the *Allis-Chalmers* holding and the reasoning quoted above from *Francis v. United Jersey Bank.* The difference may likely be explained by their placement in time. *Francis* is far more consistent with the perceived role of today's outside directors as monitors. Moreover, since *Allis-Chalmers* was decided, there is a solid perception that it is good corporate practice for public corporations to design and implement legal compliance systems such as those argued for in *Allis-Chalmers.*[38] In the widely celebrated decision *In re Caremark International, Inc. Derivative Litigation,*[39] involving approval of a settlement of a derivative suit alleging

---

[31]   Hoye v. Meek, 795 F.2d 893, 896 (10th Cir. 1986).

[32]   In re Tri-Star Pictures, Inc., Litig., 1995 WL 106520 (Del. Ch. 1995) (interested directors did not breach their fiduciary obligations by recusing themselves while other directors considered the transaction); Berkman v. Rust Craft Greeting Cards, Inc., 454 F.Supp. 787 (S.D.N.Y. 1978) (failure to warn fellow directors that investment banker had a material financial interest in the transaction on which opinion was being expressed constituted material fact regarding non-disclosing directors' fitness to serve as a director and should have been disclosed in the proxy statement seeking the directors' election).

[33]   *See, e.g.,* Dellastatious v. Williams, 242 F.3d 191 (4th Cir. 2001).

[34]   Graham v. Allis-Chalmers Manufacturing Co., 188 A.2d 125 (Del. 1963).

[35]   The court rejected the plaintiff's argument that antitrust consent decrees 19 years earlier imparted such notice, reasoning in part that the current board of directors were not aware of those decrees. 188 A.2d at 129–130.

[36]   Graham v. Allis-Chalmers Manufacturing Company, 188 A.2d 125, 130 (Del. 1963).

[37]   Graham v. Allis-Chalmers Manufacturing Company, 188 A.2d 125, 130 (Del. 1963). *Cf.* the internal controls reporting obligation of public companies under federal law. *See* 15 U.S.C. § 78m(b)(2) (1988).

[38]   *See* Corporate Director's Guidebook, *supra* § 10.1 note 12, at 27–36; A.B.A., Section on Corporation, Banking and Business Law, The Role and Composition of the Board of Directors of the Large Publicly Owned Corporation, 33 Bus. Law. 2083, 2101 (1978).

[39]   In re Caremark International, Inc. Derivative Litigation, 698 A.2d 959 (Del. Ch. 1996).

directors failed to properly oversee employees who engaged in felonious payments for patient referrals, Chancellor Allen opined that:

> [I]t would be . . . mistake to conclude that . . . corporate boards may satisfy their obligation to be reasonably informed concerning the corporation, without assuring themselves that information and reporting systems exist in the organization that are reasonably designed to provide to senior management and to the board itself timely, accurate information sufficient to allow management and the board, each within its scope, to reach informed judgments, concerning both the corporation's compliance with law and its business performance. . . .

> Thus, I am of the view that a director's obligation includes a duty to attempt in good faith to assure that a corporate information and reporting system, which the board concludes is adequate, exists, and that failure to do so under some circumstances may, in theory at least, render a director liable for losses caused by non-compliance with applicable legal standards.[40]

Though dicta in the matter—the approval of a settlement of a derivative suit—Chancellor Allen appears to accurately reflect the likely result that should be reached today with the monitoring role of the board of directors so widely entrenched in corporate governance practices. If seen as a component of the duty of care, the case would be stronger that the oversight called for by *Caremark* is an objective one, so that the practices prevalent within an industry and across types of corporations would be normative in assessing whether a board of directors has acted properly under the circumstances. We could then more easily marry perceived and practiced good corporate governance to the demands of good faith. The prevalence of compliance programs across all types of companies and industries make the absence of such a program in a particular company appear to be a dangerous departure from custom. Accordingly, there is ample reason to doubt the continuing force of *Allis-Chalmers*'s sweeping rejection of the responsibility of directors to install a compliance system.[41]

Even though the directors may be held to have breached their duty of care by failing to install a certain type of compliance system, their breach does not necessarily mean they are liable for any losses associated with the subordinate's violations. It is a well established principle of corporate law that the plaintiff has the burden of proving not only the breach but also what damages were proximately caused thereby. Even a reasonably designed and superintended compliance program will not detect or deter all misbehavior. Some violators will invariably slide through the screening process, so that the directors' technical breach in failing to install a compliance system may ultimately bear no causal relationship with the harm caused by the subordinates' wrongdoing. In a similar manner, even though Andrews in *Barnes v. Andrews* breached his duty of care by failing to inform himself about the company's operations, the court ultimately held he was not liable because there was no evidence that, had he inquired, he could have prevented the company's failure.[42] In contrast, *Francis* could more easily conclude

---

[40]   In re Caremark International, Inc. Derivative Litigation, 698 A.2d 959, 970 (Del. Ch. 1996).

[41]   Two leading Delaware practitioners (one to become Chief Justice of the Delaware Superior Court) conclude that *Allis-Chalmers* would likely be decided differently today because of the changed perception of the role of outside directors. E. Norman Veasey & William E. Manning, Codified Standard—Safe Harbor or Uncharted Reef? An Analysis of the Model Act Standard of Care with Delaware Law, 35 Bus. Law. 919 (1980).

[42]   Barnes v. Andrews, 298 F. 614, 620 (S. D. N.Y. 1924).

causation was established because the conduct there could have easily been stopped by condemning it as illegal.[43] The major causation question arising in law compliance program disputes is not the illegality of the underlying conduct but whether, in instances of misbehavior not as blatant as that in *Francis,* the violation would be detected at all.

Caremark is qualified by *Stone v. Ritter*[44] where the Delaware Supreme Court rejects the view held by some that *Caremark*'s invocation of the director's duty of good faith introduced a distinct, third, fiduciary duty. *Stone v. Ritter* holds there are only two fiduciary duties: the duty of loyalty and the duty of care, so that good faith is subsumed within the director's duty of loyalty. Earlier the Delaware Chancery Court identified three (nonexclusive) illustrations of conduct not in "good faith:"

> A failure to act in good faith may be shown, for instance, where the fiduciary intentionally acts for the purpose other than that of advancing the best interests of the corporation, where the fiduciary acts with the intent to violate applicable positive law, or where the fiduciary intentionally fails to act in the face of a known duty to act, demonstrating a conscious disregard for his duties. . . .[45]

Thus, good faith entails a consciousness of wrongdoing on the part of the actor; it is this feature that distinguishes the absence of good faith from an extreme departure from the objective standard of care, such as the multiple missteps that occurred on the part of the TransUnion directors in *Smith v. Van Gorkom,* discussed in the next section.

In re Abbott Laboratories Derivative Shareholders Litigation,[46] although addressing the question whether a demand upon the board was excused because the allegations created a reasonable doubt the actions of the board of directors were protected by the business judgment rule, illustrates not only the obligation of the board of directors to reasonably pursue facts that put them on notice of conduct that if not addressed would lead to substantial corporate losses, but also illustrates the consciousness element for a good faith violation. During a six-year period, Abbott Laboratories received formal notices of deviations from FDA requirements with respect to several of its medical diagnostic products as well as four formal certified Warning Letters from the FDA's district director. Ultimately the on-going failure to comply with FDA requirements led to a $100 million fine and the destruction of inventory that caused Abbott to take a $168 million charge against its earnings. The plaintiff alleged that a majority of the board, including the board chairman, was aware of the Warning Letters, and demonstrated gross negligence by ignoring over the six-year period the problems the FDA had repeatedly brought to their attention. The Seventh Circuit excused the demand, reasoning that the plaintiff had successful pleaded director conduct that was beyond the protection of the business judgment rule.

> Given the extensive paper trail in *Abbott* concerning the violations and the inferred awareness of the problems, the facts support a reasonable assumption that there was a "sustained and systematic failure of the board to exercise oversight," in this case intentional in that the directors knew of the violations

---

[43] Francis v. United Jersey Bank, 432 A.2d 814, 829 (N.J. 1981).

[44] Stone v. Ritter, 911 A.2d 362 (Del. 2006).

[45] In re Walt Disney Co. Deriv. Litig., 906 A.2d 27, 67 (Del. 2006). Stone v. Ritter, 911 A.2d 362 (Del.2006), elaborates on the oversight liability.

[46] In re Abbott Laboratories Derivative Shareholders Litigation, 325 F.3d 795 (7th Cir. 2003).

of law, took no steps in an effort to prevent or remedy the situation, and that failure to take any action for such an inordinate amount of time resulted in substantial corporate losses, establishing a lack of good faith.[47]

While the FDA warnings brought the risks within the consciousness of the Abbott Laboratories directors, there is some basis to believe that the nature of the underlying managerial misconduct may, at least in the context of excusing a derivative suit demand on the full board, bear on the scope of the directors' *Caremark* responsibilities. *American Int'l Group, Inc. Consolidated Derivative Litig.*[48] excused a demand in claim that the directors failed to exercise reasonable oversight to prevent allegedly pervasive *fraudulent* and *criminal* conduct. This distinction was emphasized in *In re Citigroup Shareholder Derivative Litig., (AIG)*[49] the first detailed analysis of director responsibility with respect to risk management. The case arose out of the significant losses suffered on subprime mortgages and other investments by Citigroup which pushed the firm to the edge of bankruptcy that was prevented only by a massive injection of federal funds. The Chancery Court's reasoning appears to treat the directors' obligation to monitor business risks differently than criminality. For example, the court distinguished *AIG* as involving failure to monitor for fraudulent and criminal conduct and concluded the oversight duties under Delaware law do not extend to imposing personal liability for the failure to properly evaluate business risk.[50] *City of Birmingham Ret. & Relief Sys. v. Good*, addresses the question whether a board's serial involvement with on-going environmental problems that ultimately caused substantial losses to the corporation supported a claim the directors consciously disregarded their oversight responsibilities.[51] The majority opinion reasoned that the complaint sought to conflate a "bad outcome" with "bad faith;" the court held the facts did not support the charge the directors on-going efforts to inform themselves regarding problems posed by the utility's coal ash ponds was a "conscious disregard" of oversight rather than perhaps *too* deliberate an oversight.[52] The dissent, however, believed sufficient facts were plead to supporting excusing a demand on the board as the facts reflected non-exculpated breaches of the directors fiduciary duty by pursuing business strategy premised in part on flouting environmental laws.[53]

A dramatic instance of *Caremark's* application is *In re Massey Energy Company Derivative and Class Action Litigation*[54] where the complaint withstood defendants' motions to dismiss by alleging facts reflecting that the board repeatedly ignored reports and sanctions of mine safety violations in the years preceding the explosion in its Upper

---

[47]   325 F.3d at 807.

[48]   In re American Int'l Group, Inc. Consolidated Derivative Litig., 965 A.2d 763 (Del. Ch. 2009).

[49]   In re Citigroup Shareholder Derivative Litig., 964 A.2d 106 (Del. Ch. 2009).

[50]   For the view that the highly malleable "good faith" standard provides rhetorical openings for the court to delve from time-to-time into director decision making in response to crisis and scandals, *See* Sean J. Griffith, Good Faith Business Judgment: A Theory Of Rhetoric In Corporate Law Jurisprudence, 55 Duke L. J. 1 (2005).

[51]   City of Birmingham Ret. & Relief Sys. v. Good, 177 A.3d 47 (Del. 2017). The issue before the court was whether the suit should be dismissed for failure of the derivative suit plaintiff to make a demand on the board of directors. This required particularized allegations that a majority of the directors were at substantial risk of liability. Because the directors enjoyed the immunity shield exculpating them for care-based violations the issue of the deliberateness of their breach was central to whether a demand on the board was required.

[52]   *Id.*

[53]   *Id.*

[54]   2011 Del. Ch. LEXIS 83.

Big Branch mine that killed 29 miners—the deadliest mine accident in 40 years. But compliance cases only occasionally meet with such success as there is frequently insufficient evidence that the board has engaged in more than negligent oversight, which is insufficient to overcome the ubiquitous immunity shield discussed above.

Indeed, the Delaware judiciary may even conclude that ignoring red flags is not director negligence. To illustrate, consider *In re Citigroup Inc. Shareholder Derivative Litigation*,[55] holding that the business judgment rule insulated the directors against charges they failed to take precautions to avoid the ensuing financial losses arising from Citigroup's large exposure to the subprime lending markets. The suit alleged various red flags such as an economist's forecast that a speculative bubble was nearing its end, a leading subprime lender closing its 229 offices, another lender filing bankruptcy, analysts downgrading subprime mortgages, and a warning of increasing subprime delinquencies by another lender. The court reasoned:

> . . . [The "red flags"] amount to little more than portions of public documents that reflected the worsening conditions in the subprime mortgage market and in the economy generally. . . . Even while admitting that Citigroup had a risk monitoring system in place, plaintiffs seem to conclude that, because the director defendants were charged with monitoring Citigroup's risk, then they must be found liable because Citigroup experienced losses as a result of exposure to the subprime mortgage market. The only factual support plaintiffs provide for this conclusion are "red flags" that actually amount to nothing more than signs of continuing deterioration in the subprime mortgage market. These types of conclusory allegations are exactly the kinds of allegation that do not state a claim for relief under *Caremark*.[56]

The above reasoning appears consistent with observation made in a widely noted Delaware Supreme Court decision that conduct that offends good corporate governance practices nonetheless is not inherently negligent conduct.[57]

Burden of Proof Considerations. A novel approach to allocating the burden of proof was taken in *Cede & Co. v. Technicolor, Inc.*,[58] where the Delaware Supreme Court held that once the presumptions of the business judgment rule are removed because of the absence of good faith or care on the part of the directors, the directors have the burden of proving the transaction's "entire fairness." Failing this burden, the directors are subject to a full panoply of remedies.[59] *Cede & Co.* does not accord the directors the protection of a presumption of propriety on the part of directors. Nor are they provided the protection of the plaintiff having the burden of proving what damages were proximately caused by the directors' breach of their duty of care.[60] Delaware thus treats causation similarly in cases of directors who breach their duty of loyalty and those who breach their duty of care. It remains to be seen whether Delaware's approach in *Cede & Co.* will be followed in other jurisdictions or will remain, as it was when the case was

---

[55] 964 A.2d 106 (Del. Ch. 2009).

[56] *Id.* at 128–130.

[57] In re the Walt Disney Co. Derivative Litig., 906 A.2d 27 (Del. 2006).

[58] Cede & Co. v. Technicolor, Inc., 634 A.2d 345 (Del. 1993).

[59] Cede & Co. v. Technicolor, Inc., 634 A.2d 345, 371 (1993).

[60] However, not every breach of duty will result in actionable damages. Thus, for example, breaches of disclosure duties that did not result in harm could not support damage recovery. Loudon v. Archer-Daniels-Midland Co., 700 A.2d 135 (Del. 1997).

decided, a unique approach. Even in Delaware, it is uncertain just what range of factors the breaching-directors can invoke to meet the "entire fairness" defense. In *Cede & Co.*, the court reviewed a variety of factors in concluding that the board had met the entire fairness test. Among the factors it considered were many that bore directly upon whether the board had acted negligently, so that its inquiry appears to be more focused on the defendant's rebutting the substantive charge they acted with gross negligence and less on an inquiry to whether their actions caused financial harm to the corporation or its stockholders.[61] Upon the directors' breach of the duty of care being established, *Cede & Co.* clearly invites a review of the substantive merits of the decision for which the directors acted negligently.[62] Consequently, though procedural due care may be lacking, even bumblers can make good decisions. Under the formulation in *Barnes*, once a breach of care is established the inquiry was just what harm flowed proximately from the breach.

§ 10.4 Directors' Actions Should Be the Product of Reasonable Investigation and Consideration

Lessons from **Smith v. Van Gorkom.** Lawyers are well acquainted with the connection between reasonable processes and the quality of decision-making. Not only does procedural due process enhance the validity of a decision but the discipline yields a better decision. These benefits are the object of the courts' preoccupation with whether directors' decision are the product of a reasonable investigation and consideration of facts and issues surrounding any matter before the board.[63] A director is reasonably informed if the director considers the *material* facts that are *reasonably available;* there is no need to pursue immaterial facts or information that could not be acquired reasonably under the circumstances.[64]

Any doubt about the force of this judicial preoccupation is removed by the Delaware Supreme Court's landmark decision in *Smith v. Van Gorkom*,[65] where the court held the directors breached their duty of care in approving the sale of Trans Union Corporation. The sale was approved by the board of directors at a meeting that lasted only two hours. The presentation was completely oral, no written drafts of the acquisition agreement were circulated, and Van Gorkom (Trans Union's president) did not disclose that the sales price was proposed not by the buyer but rather by Van Gorkom. The board was not told that the selling price of $55 per share reflected the price Trans Union's own cash flow would justify if the purchase were a management buyout. Thus, the selling price did not indicate in any way the significant synergies of any profitable firm acquiring Trans Union.[66] Furthermore, there was no evidence in the record of the directors

---

[61]   *See* Lyman Johnson, Rethinking Judicial Review of Director Care, 24 Del. J. Corp. L. 787, 818 (1999) (the analysis of the factors considered in *Cede & Co.* "could and should have been done as part of the threshold duty of care analysis").

[62]   For a highly critical review of *Cede & Co.* for departing from precedent by inviting the court to undertake a review of the substantive merits of the directors' decision so that, because of the substantive quality of the decision, the directors are not accountable for their carelessly rendered decision, *see* Lyman Johnson, The Modest Business Judgment Rule, 55 Bus. Law. 625 (2000).

[63]   *See generally* Corporate Director's Guidebook, *supra* § 10.1 note 12.

[64]   Brehm v. Eisner, 746 A.2d 244, 259 (Del. 2000).

[65]   Smith v. Van Gorkom, 488 A.2d 858 (Del. 1985).

[66]   The major source of any synergies was the large amount of unused investment tax credits that Trans Union had accumulated as a major purchaser of rail cars. The case facts clearly reflect that Trans Union had for many years been unable to realize any benefits from the ever-increasing amount of investment tax credits because its taxes were substantially reduced by the accelerated depreciation charges taken on its assets.

questioning Van Gorkom on the sale. Indeed, the case reflects the board's uncritical acceptance of the senior management's recommendation. Several facts were in evidence that supported the directors' quick approval of the sale. For example, the selling price represented nearly a 50 percent premium over the prevailing market price for Trans Union stock; furthermore, the buyer's offer was open for only 48 hours. These factors appear to explain why the directors so quickly approved the sale and in doing so they did not consult any outside financial consultants regarding the sale. Despite these factors that appeared to call for the board to act quickly, the Delaware Supreme Court held that the directors failed to inform themselves adequately and therefore acted with "gross negligence" in approving Trans Union's sale.[67] The court chastised the directors for failing to inquire how the sales price was determined and for failing to inform themselves of the intrinsic value of the firm.[68] *Smith v. Van Gorkom* does not hold that the directors approved the sale of their firm at too low a price; its holding is that the corporation was deprived of a reasonable determination of the sales price by its directors. The case was therefore remanded for determination of whether any damages in fact befell the stockholders because of the faulty deliberations by the board of directors.[69]

Smith v. Van Gorkom illustrates the *process* component of the duty of care, as contrasted with the substantive component that is discussed later in connection with the rational basis requirement of the duty of care. To meet the duty of care's concern for process, whenever practicable, it is good corporate practice to circulate in advance of the board meeting an agenda of such information as is useful to the board to understand the items to be discussed at the upcoming meeting. Such advance circulation, however, is not a prerequisite for the directors to be deemed to have acted reasonably. Director decisions are within the protection of the business judgment rule, even when made at meetings convened without an agenda or when material has not been circulated earlier, provided the facts otherwise reflect that the board was informed and adequately deliberated the matter.[70]

Just what is required for the board to act reasonably to inform itself varies with the facts. Some decisions and some circumstances may call for less information, and less consideration, than others.

In addition to sparking a good deal of commentary[71] and adding to the demand for consultants such as investment bankers, *Smith v. Van Gorkom* reinforces the importance of the board's counselor to assure that the directors act in as deliberate and thorough manner as is possible under the circumstances. Courts repeatedly accord greater weight to the actions of directors who are informed by outside experts and consultants.[72] Similarly, a board's delegation to or reliance upon a committee of directors

---

[67]   488 A.2d at 874.

[68]   488 A.2d at 874.

[69]   The case was settled for $23.5 million, with $10 million coming from the corporation's directors' and officers' liability policy and most of the remainder from the buyer. Bayless Manning, Reflections and Practical Tips on Life in the Boardroom After Van Gorkom, 41 Bus. Law. 1 (1985).

[70]   Unocal Corp. v. Mesa Petroleum Co., 493 A.2d 946 (Del. 1985) (consultations over 11 hours with legal and financial advisors).

[71]   *See, e.g.,* Daniel R. Fischel, The Business Judgment Rule and the Trans Union Case, 40 Bus. Law. 1437 (1984).

[72]   *See, e.g.,* Pirelli Armstrong Tire Corp. Retiree Med. Benefits Trust v. Raines, 534 F.3d 779, 790 (D.C. Cir. 2008) (reliance on accountant to explain $200 million discrepancy "turned this allegedly red flag into a green flag").

charged with responsibility to handle a matter is a reasonable practice.[73] The consultants need not be from outside the organization; reliance on officers and employees within the organization is appropriate, provided the directors are not on notice of any facts suggesting such reliance is unjustified.[74] Many corporate statutes expressly provide that directors in discharging their duties may rely on information, opinions, and reports of consultants, experts, subordinates, and committees.[75]

The ability of directors to rely on information, opinions, and reports prepared by others is not an open invitation to shirk their responsibilities. Minimally, their duty to act in good faith requires the directors to have read the report or attended the meeting at which the information or opinion was orally presented, or to have otherwise taken reasonable steps to familiarize themselves with its contents.[76] There is also the qualification that the directors have some reason to believe the matter is within the competence or expertise of the consultant, subordinate, or committee on whom they are relying.[77] Thus the directors are not entitled to rely on an attorney's advice that pertains mainly to factual questions for which the attorney is no better equipped to opine than the directors.[78] On the other hand, directors act reasonably in relying on their attorney's advice on either purely legal, as well as a matter that involves a mixture of law and facts, unless the advice is patently incorrect.[79] There is always the substantial qualification that a director may not rely on a consultant's, subordinate's, or committee's report if a director is on notice that such reliance is not warranted.[80] Directors breach their duty of care if they fail to question facts or opinions expressed in a report where the circumstances call for further elucidation or challenge.[81]

Reliance upon Others. Directors' knowledge of the facts raising their suspicions can occur as a result of information gained through their non-director status.[82] Thus, the Second Circuit held in *Hanson Trust PLC v. ML SCM Acquisition, Inc.*[83] that the directors breached their duty of care by uncritically accepting their investment banker's opinion respecting the fair value of a product line without probing how such value was determined; had they made such an inquiry the board would have learned that the advisor had failed to calculate a range of values in determining the fairness of the price.[84]

---

[73] Pogostin v. Rice, 480 A.2d 619 (Del. 1984).

[74] It is on this point that the circumstances that separate the inside from the outside director are significant. For example, in the leading case, Bates v. Dresser, 251 U.S. 524 (1920), Justice Holmes held that a teller's flashy lifestyle should have prompted the bank's president to inquire whether shrinkages in the bank's deposits were the result of the teller's embezzlements. *Id.* at 530. The bank's outside directors, however, not being similarly on notice, were entitled to rely on the reassurances of the president and the government examiner that nothing was amiss. *Id.* at 529.

[75] *See, e.g.,* Cal. Corp. Code § 309(b) (West 1990); Del. Code Ann. tit. 8, § 141(c) (2001); N.Y. Bus. Corp. Law § 717 (McKinney 1986); MBCA § 8.30(b) (2008).

[76] MBCA § 8.30(b), Official Comment (2016).

[77] *See, e.g.,* MBCA § 8.30(b) (2016).

[78] Douglas W. Hawes & Thomas J. Sherrard, Reliance on Advice of Counsel as a Defense in Corporate and Securities Cases, 62 Va. L. Rev. 1, 148 (1976).

[79] Douglas W. Hawes & Thomas J. Sherrard, Reliance on Advice of Counsel as a Defense in Corporate and Securities Cases, 62 Va. L. Rev. 1, 43–47 (1976).

[80] Gould v. American Hawaiian S.S. Co., 351 F.Supp. 853, 865 (D. Del. 1972), *rev'd and remanded on other grounds,* 535 F.2d 761 (3d Cir. 1976).

[81] Spirt v. Bechtel, 232 F.2d 241 (2d Cir. 1956).

[82] *See* Rowen v. Le Mars Mut. Ins. Co., 282 N.W.2d 639, 655 (Iowa 1979).

[83] Hanson Trust PLC v. ML SCM Acquisition, Inc., 781 F.2d 264 (2d Cir. 1986).

[84] Hanson Trust PLC v. ML SCM Acquisition, Inc., 781 F.2d 264, 275 (2d Cir. 1986).

Also, reliance is not reasonable when the expert's advice is clearly inconsistent with all other facts before the directors.[85] Directors do not act reasonably in informing themselves as to a transaction's benefits by relying solely on the representations of a person known to have a financial interest in the transaction.[86]

An important qualification on the directors' ability to rely with impunity on the reports of others appears in a critical passage of *Smith v. Van Gorkom:*

> Under 8 Del. C. 141(e), directors are fully protected in relying in good faith on reports made by officers. . . . However, there is no evidence that any "report" . . . was presented to the Board. . . . Van Gorkom's oral presentation of his understanding of the terms of the proposed Merger Agreement, which he had not seen, and Roman's brief oral statement of his preliminary study regarding the feasibility of a leveraged buy-out of Trans Union do not qualify as 141(e) "reports" for these reasons: The former lacked substance because Van Gorkom was basically uninformed as to the essential provisions of the very document about which he was talking. Roman's statement was irrelevant to the issues before the Board since it did not purport to be a valuation study.[87]

Smith therefore adds to the qualification that the directors not be aware of cause for believing reliance on an officer is unjustified. What *Smith* thus provides is the further requirement that the subordinate's presentation pertain to the very issue before the board (Roman's fairness opinion did not), and the officer must herself be adequately informed regarding the matter addressed. Certainly the latter is far more troubling, because if *Smith* is taken literally, it would deny the protections of the business judgment rule to directors who were otherwise unaware that the officer was not adequately informed on the topic. This clearly is a major departure from established principles[88] and appears inconsistent with provisions that permit directors to rely unless they are on notice of circumstances that make such reliance unjustified. It would appear a far better approach in *Smith* if the court had instead denied the directors' the ability to raise as a defense for failing to be adequately informed that they had relied upon Van Gorkom's and Roman's presentation by the court holding instead that his report did not deal with the substantive fairness of the price. Viewed in this way, it could fairly be said that the board had received no information on which to base its decision.[89]

§ 10.5 Directors' Decisions Should Embody a Rational Basis for Action

The duty of care has both procedural and substantive requirements. The requirements that the directors be attentive and reasonably informed are procedural in nature; the substantive requirement is that their decision have a "rational basis" or, as it is sometimes expressed, be "reasonable."[90] At first glance this requirement would appear to invite a good deal of second-guessing and intrusion by the courts and

---

[85] Harris v. Pearsall, 190 N.Y.S. 61 (Sup. Ct. 1921).

[86] *See* Fitzpatrick v. FDIC, 765 F.2d 569, 577 (6th Cir. 1985).

[87] Smith v. Van Gorkom, 488 A.2d 858, 874–875 (Del. 1985).

[88] *See* Fitzpatrick v. FDIC, 765 F.2d 569, 577 (6th Cir. 1985) (duty to inquire into reasonableness of subordinate's investigation does not arise until directors are already on inquiry notice).

[89] Panter v. Marshall Field & Co., 486 F.Supp. 1168, 1180, 1194 (N.D. Ill. 1980), *aff'd,* 646 F.2d 271 (7th Cir.), *cert. denied,* 454 U.S. 1092 (1981).

[90] Meyers v. Moody, 693 F.2d 1196, 1211 (5th Cir. 1982).

disappointed stockholders. But public policy considerations, discussed earlier, have caused the courts not to apply these standards rigorously but instead to afford directors and officers great latitude in their actions and decision-making.[91] In its most rigorous form, the duty of care requires only that managers have a reasonable basis for their decisions, despite the availability of more compelling alternative choices available to them. One court has held for the standard to be violated, the directors' decision must be "so unwise or unreasonable as to fall outside the permissible bounds of the directors' sound discretion."[92]

To illustrate the wide latitude accorded directors under the rational basis standard, consider the leading case of *Kamin v. American Express Company*.[93] A derivative suit was brought against the directors of American Express Company questioning their decision to distribute as a dividend in kind nearly 2 million shares of Donaldson, Lufken, and Jenrette (DL & J) stock that American Express had acquired for investment at a cost of $29.9 million. The directors decided to distribute the shares as a dividend rather than to realize a $25 million loss by selling the DL & J shares in the market. The derivative suit plaintiff asserted this was a waste of the nearly $8 million American Express would have realized in tax savings had the shares been sold and the loss reported on its tax return. By distributing the DL & J shares to its stockholders, American Express avoided recognizing the loss on either its tax return or income statement.[94] The board of directors rationalized its decision as an attempt to avoid depressing American Express' stock price by reporting a $25 million loss on its income statement, which would have been required if the shares had been sold. As it was, the loss on the DL & J shares was merely reported as a deduction to stockholders' equity on the company's balance sheet. Certainly those who believe capital markets are efficient have good cause to question whether astute investors would overlook the true economic significance of the board's decision. Indeed, a compelling case can be made that the *wiser* course was that advocated in the derivative suit, especially since American Express did not deny that its financial statements would have to give some prominence to removing the DL & J shares from among its assets. Nevertheless, the court held that the directors acted reasonably under the circumstances and dismissed the case.

Kamin clearly underscores that the "rational basis" or "reasonableness" standard does not require directors to reach the best or even optimal result. It is sufficient that the decision have the appearance of being a reasoned response to a situation. Thus, entering into a multi-million dollar settlement with a terminated executive is not waste where alternative was to incur uncertainty whether the executive could be fired and paid less.[95] To be sure, the result is a standard unlikely to command much respect in business schools and executive education programs, where the emphasis is on the optimal or even

---

[91]   *See, e.g.*, Hills Stores Co. v. Bozic, 769 A.2d 88 (Del. Ch. 2000) (directors' decision to reject bid for control upheld, even though as a consequence it triggered contractual rights of officers for substantial severance award).

[92]   Cramer v. General Tel. & Elecs. Corp., 582 F.2d 259, 275 (3d Cir. 1978), *cert. denied*, 439 U.S. 1129 (1979).

[93]   Kamin v. American Express Company, 383 N.Y.S.2d 807 (Sup. Ct.), *aff'd*, 387 N.Y.S.2d 993 (App. Div. 1976).

[94]   Moreover, the American Express stockholders would not be able to recognize the loss because their basis in the shares they received was the fair market value of the shares on the date the DL & J were distributed. Thus the real gainer in the transaction was the U.S. government.

[95]   *See* Brehm v. Eisner, 746 A.2d 244, 266 (Del. 2000).

right response. On the other hand, a more demanding standard would most clearly result in less risk-taking by directors.

Freedman v. Adams[96] further illustrates the weak demands that the rational basis component of the duty of care makes on boards of directors. A derivative suit was initiated to recover more than $130 million in bonuses approved by the board of XTO Energy without the compensation plan including provisions to link the bonuses to performance. The plan lacked performance-based standards then demanded by Internal Revenue Code section 162(m) for compensation in excess of $1 million to deductible business expense on XTO Energy's tax return.[97] After the plaintiff initiated a derivative suit, the board prospectively modified the plan and the plaintiff dropped her derivative suit. In responding to the derivative suit plaintiff's request for fees incident the claim, XTO Energy's argued that the board was fully aware of section 162(m), but made a conscious decision not to avail itself of section 162(m) because it believed its approach to compensation decision should not "be constrained by such a plan." The court denied any award of fees to the plaintiff because a claim had not been stated; the court reasoned, "[e]ven if the decision were a poor one" as alleged by the plaintiff, "it was not unconscionable or irrational." A further message of *Freedman* is that "best practices" are not synonymous with legally culpable conduct.[98]

§ 10.6 Knowing Violations of a Criminal Statute

As has been seen, the commentators have offered many suggested approaches to conform the corporation's behavior to desirable social goals. The cry that corporations must act in a socially responsible manner is in fact an invitation to corporations to act beyond the commands of the law. That is, the call to act in a socially responsible manner seeks more than staying within the bounds of the law by, for example, assuring that their effluents into the air and rivers not violate state or local directives. Corporations are socially responsible when their internal goal is to surpass the minimum standard of acceptable behavior embodied in state and federal directives. A socially responsible corporation thus is one that avoids walking close to the line.

But what corporate-law-based punishment awaits the corporation directors or officers who cross the line by knowingly engaging in a criminal act? For example, what is the liability of directors who knowingly flaunt pollution requirements by failing to install the expensive scrubbers in their plant's chimneys that are mandated by federal law if the corporation is ultimately fined $75,000? Assume, however, that the delay in complying with the law allows the corporation to operate more efficiently, so that over the course of its noncompliance the violation yielded a net savings of $1 million—does corporate law provide its own disciplining force to discourage such conduct, or does crime pay?

Two early decisions appear to remove the protections of the business judgment rule entirely on proof of a knowing violation of a criminal statute. In *Roth v. Robertson*[99] the manager of an amusement park paid hush money to individuals who threatened to

---

[96]   Freedman v. Adams, 58 A.3d 414 (Del. 2013).

[97]   Section 162(m) is discussed in § 11:6 and was repealed in 2017. Nonetheless *Freeman* is highly instructive on the deference accorded decisions by an independent body of directors.

[98]   *See also* In re Walt Disney Derivative Litigation, 906 A.2d 27 (Del. 2006) (failure to adhere to best practices does not translate to breach of duty of care or to act in good faith).

[99]   Roth v. Robertson, 118 N.Y.S. 351 (Sup. Ct. 1909).

prevent the park from operating in violation of the state's Sunday closing laws. Even though the corporation received a large percentage of its total revenues from Sunday operations, the court upheld a jury award of $800, the amount of the hush money payments. The court partially based its holding on the payments being a violation of the state's criminal statutes. Another early leading case is *Abrams v. Allen*,[100] where the criminal violation was the corporation's board of directors' approval of the dismantling of plants for the purpose of intimidating union organizing efforts. One of four possible theories of recovery embraced by the court was the illegality of the board's actions.

The contemporary view of the impact a knowing violation of a criminal statute has on the availability of the business judgment rule is reflected in *Miller v. American Telephone & Telegraph Company*,[101] a derivative suit seeking to recover a $1.5 million phone bill of the Democratic National Committee, which the AT & T directors forgave. The plaintiff attacked the directors' decision as an unlawful political contribution. Reasoning that "directors must be restrained from engaging in activities which are against public policy,"[102] the *Miller* court, relying on *Roth* and *Abrams*, concludes that the business judgment rule's presumption of propriety does not extend to directors who knowingly violate a criminal statute.[103] However, finding a knowing violation did not record an automatic award for the derivative suit plaintiff. *Miller*, a diversity action, was bound by New York law, which since *Roth* and *Abrams* has evolved to require the plaintiff to prove not only that the directors have knowingly violated a criminal statute but also that the corporation has suffered a *net loss* through the acts challenged.[104] Thus, if the overall gains of the violation exceed the losses directly associated with the violation, such as fines and attorneys' fees, there is no liability on the part of the responsible directors or officers. Stated more bluntly, purely from the perspective of corporate law, crime may well pay. As one of the authors has written:

> This limitation prevents the derivative suit from serving as a vehicle for redressing social harms committed by the corporation's managers. However offensive the conclusion that within the derivative suit context "crime pays," the net loss requirement may signal no more than the fact the derivative suit is otherwise a poor medium for enforcing societal directives not devoted exclusively to the corporation's efficient performance. The state's concern for pure air and water, safe consumer products, and fair employment practices implicates protections for a more diverse group than the class of shareholders with standing to maintain a derivative suit. When the deterrence question is instead focused upon a threatened harm to the shareholders themselves, there is a stronger basis to permit some recovery out of prophylactic considerations to remind the directors and officers that their ultimate responsibilities are to the shareholders.[105]

The American Law Institute's Principles of Corporate Governance is resolute in dealing with directors and officers who knowingly participate in illegal conduct. Their

---

[100] Abrams v. Allen, 74 N.E.2d 305 (N.Y. 1947).

[101] Miller v. American Telephone & Telegraph Company, 507 F.2d 759, 762–763 (3d Cir. 1974).

[102] Miller v. American Telephone & Telegraph Company, 507 F.2d 759, 763 (3d Cir. 1974).

[103] Miller v. American Telephone & Telegraph Company, 507 F.2d 759, 762 (3d Cir. 1974).

[104] *See, e.g.,* Smiles v. Elfred, 149 N.Y.L.J., Feb. 20, 1963, at 14, col. 6 (N.Y. Sup. Ct. 1963); Borden v. Cohen, 231 N.Y.S.2d 902 (Sup. Ct. 1962); Clayton v. Farish, 73 N.Y.S.2d 727 (Sup. Ct. 1947).

[105] James D. Cox, Compensation, Deterrence, and the Market as Boundaries for Derivative Suit Procedures, 52 Geo. Wash. L. Rev. 745, 765 (1984).

violations are outside the protections of the business judgment rule[106] and are not within the permissible bounds of a charter provision that otherwise can immunize directors from liability for damages.[107] And when the conduct is the subject of a derivative suit, the recommendation of the board or committee that the suit be dismissed is subject to a higher level of review by the court than are care violations and most categories of overreaching behavior.[108] More generally, the ALI incorporates into its broad duty of care the obligation that directors and officers act within the bounds of the law.[109]

The great hurdle in any suit not premised on the directors' knowing violation of a criminal statute but rather on their negligence in failing to detect the violations of subordinates is the problem of causation. No law compliance program is foolproof, and many violations by subordinates are likely to go undetected even under the most aggressive compliance systems. This poses a serious problem to the plaintiff who seeks to impose liability on the directors on the theory that the directors' failure to install *any* compliance program is a breach of the directors' duty of care. Because the plaintiff has the burden of proving not only that the directors breached their duty of care but also that their breach proximately harmed the corporation, the plaintiff generally will have great difficulty establishing a causal relationship between the absence of a compliance system and the injury to the corporation flowing from the violation.[110] The court may well conclude that the directors' failure to install any law compliance system constitutes only a technical breach, much as Andrew's failure to inform himself was so held in *Barnes v. Andrews,* discussed earlier. Thus the causation requirement lifts some of the pressure of personal liability from the directors' shoulders to aggressively pursue law compliance systems. Because the ALI does not have its own provision on causality, its various provisions dealing with directors' obligations to assure compliance with the law are accordingly weakened.

§ 10.7 Statutory Developments Limiting Directors' Liability for Duty-of-Care Violations

In 1986, the Delaware legislature amended its general corporation law to allow the charters of Delaware corporations to include provisions that limit the liability of directors for damages arising from breaches of their duty of care.[111] Following Delaware's lead, numerous states enacted similar statutory provisions.[112] The standard format of such exoneration statutes is that they authorize the articles of incorporation to include a provision eliminating or limiting the liability of a director, except for certain types of breaches. For example, section 102(b)(7) of the Delaware general corporation statute provides:

> A provision eliminating or limiting the personal liability of a director to the corporation or its stockholders for monetary damages for breach of fiduciary duty as a director . . . [except] (i) for any breach of the director's duty of loyalty

---

[106] ALI Principles of Corporate Governance: Analysis and Recommendations § 4.01 (1994).

[107] ALI Principles of Corporate Governance: Analysis and Recommendations § 7.19(1) (1994).

[108] ALI Principles of Corporate Governance: Analysis and Recommendations § 7.10(a)(2) (1994).

[109] ALI Principles of Corporate Governance: Analysis and Recommendations §§ 2.01(b)(1) and 4.01(a) (1994) and commentary at pp. 195–197.

[110] *See* § 10.4.

[111] *See* Del. Code Ann. tit. 8, § 102(b)(7) (2001).

[112] *See generally* Deborah A. DeMott, Limiting Directors' Liability, 66 Wash. U. L.Q. 295, 297–310 (1988).

to the corporation or its stockholders; (ii) for acts or omissions not in good faith or which involve intentional misconduct or knowing violation of law; (iii) . . . [for unlawful distributions]; (iv) for any transaction from which the director derived an improper personal benefit.

The above excepted categories are typical of those found in other state statutes.[113] Three important facets of the exoneration statutes narrow their impact. First, its protection is limited only to breaches committed as a director. Thus, if a person serves as both a director and an officer and breaches duties in both capacities,[114] he would not be protected by such a provision for any violations of care committed as an officer.[115] Second, the provision's protections are limited to actions for damages. Equitable actions, such as for injunctive relief or rescission, are unaffected by the charter limitation on damages. Finally, the directors remain responsible for damages they cause to third parties; the charter provision protects the directors only from liability to the corporation or its shareholders. The typical exoneration statute is in the nature of an affirmative defense so that the burden is upon the person seeking the protection of the exculpatory provision to demonstrate the conduct fell within that provision.[116]

In one case the Delaware Supreme Court clarified the application of Delaware's immunity shield when damages are sought in connection with a transaction with an interested party for which the "entire fairness" standard is applied.[117] With respect to a *non*-interested director of a corporation having an exculpatory provision in its charter, the suit must be dismissed if the plaintiff is unable to plead non-exculpated conduct on the part of such director. It is not, therefore, sufficient for the plaintiff to allege the directors acted in a grossly negligent manner in approving a self-dealing transaction. The Delaware Supreme Court has held that a plaintiff seeking only monetary damages must plead non-exculpated claims against a director who has invoked the defense of an exculpatory charter provision.[118] Thus, where a suit challenges a self-dealing transaction involving a firm's controlling stockholder so that the entire fairness review standard applies, an independent director who approved that transaction is not presumed to be other than independent so that the suit must be dismissed against her unless the complaint alleges non-exculpated acts that director committed.

Other states have taken a different approach by stating affirmatively the types of actions for which directors can be held personally liable.[119] Thus Florida provides that directors are personally liable only for certain violations of criminal statutes, receiving

---

[113] Notable differences include California's statute, whose section affects actions "brought by or in the right of the corporation," so that they are not applicable to actions brought directly by shareholders. *See* Cal. Corp. Code § 204(a)(10) (West 1990).

[114] *See* Smith v. Van Gorkom, 488 A.2d 858 (Del. 1985) (misconduct by Van Gorkom, who was both director and CEO).

[115] Section 102(b)(7) shields the directors from damages whether they arrive in law or equity for rescission.

[116] *See* Emerald Partners v. Berlin, 726 A.2d 1215, 1224 (Del. 1999) (*dicta* because complaint only alleged a violation of the duty of care).

[117] In re Cornerstone Therapeutics Inc, Stockholder Litigation, 115 A.3d 1173 (Del. 2015).

[118] In re Cornerstone Therapeutics Inc, Stockholder Litigation, 115 A.3d 1173 (Del. 2015); Malpiede v. Townson, 780 A.2d 1075 (Del. 2001).

[119] *See, e.g.,* Ohio Rev. Code Ann. § 1701.59(D) (West Supp. 2001); Wis. Stat. Ann. § 180.0828 (West 2002).

an improper personal benefit, unlawful distributions, consciously disregarding the corporation's interest, and willful misconduct.[120]

There is an interesting interplay between the exoneration statute and the court's review of a transaction alleged to pose a conflict of interest. In *Emerald Partners v. Berlin*,[121] the Delaware Chancery court dismissed the plaintiff's suit against the three directors based upon allegations that a merger of the corporation with thirteen companies owned by the controlling stockholder was unfair to the minority stockholders. The Chancery Court justified the dismissal upon its belief the defendant directors had established their defense under the company's exoneration provision by showing they had received no benefit from the transaction not enjoyed by other stockholders and had acted independently of the controlling stockholder. The Delaware Supreme Court reversed the dismissal, holding that the lower court had proceeded improperly by considering the exoneration provision before first determining whether the merger met the "entire fairness" standard.[122] Thus, *Emerald Partners* requires that in cases where the complaint properly pleads a conflict-of-interest transaction, breach of duty of loyalty, or otherwise a failure to act in good faith that the court must first determine whether the transaction meets the entire fairness standard. If it does not, the court then is to assess the role the directors played in this failure and more particularly whether their lapse was a result of conduct exonerated by the charter provision. The Delaware Supreme Court, in a decision subsequent to *Emerald Partners,* similarly held that a plaintiff seeking only monetary damages must plead non-exculpated claims against a director who has invoked the defense of an exculpatory charter provision.[123] Thus, where a suit challenges a self-dealing transaction involving a firm's controlling stockholder so that the entire fairness review standard applies, an independent director who approved that transaction is not presumed to be other than independent so that the suit must be dismissed against her, unless the complaint alleges non-exculpated acts that director committed.

The ultimate effect of immunity shields is likely to lead not only to closer scrutiny of the transaction but also to the individual director's engagement with the challenged transaction. Under the Delaware entire fairness standard the court evaluates not just the price but the manner in which the transaction was considered. This would appear to result in closer attention to the director's involvement at each stage of the approval process than if the review focused only upon the grounds set forth in the state exoneration statute that removed its protection for the director.

Another variation on statutory responses to director liability is that embraced in Virginia, which in 1987 amended its general corporation law to impose a specific cap on damages that are recoverable from officers and directors in any action brought by or on behalf of the corporation. The specific cap is the *lesser* of (1) the monetary amount stated, if any, in the corporation's articles or bylaws (which must have been adopted by the stockholders) or (2) the greater of $100,000 or the cash compensation received by the

---

[120]   Fla. Stat. Ann. § 607.0831(1) (West 2001). The last offense gives rise to liability only if the action is by the corporation or shareholder. A fifth category of director personal liability arises for reckless or wanton misconduct, omissions committed in bad faith, or wanton and willful disregard of human rights, safety, or property when the action is brought by a plaintiff other than the corporation or its stockholders.

[121]   Emerald Partners v. Berlin, 787 A.2d 85 (Del. 2001).

[122]   Emerald Partners v. Berlin, 787 A.2d 85, 97 (Del. 2001).

[123]   Leal v. Meeks, 115 A.3d 1173 (Del. 2015); *see also,* Malpiede v. Townson, 780 A.2d 1075 (Del. 2001).

officer or director in the 12 months preceding the action or omission charged.[124] A similar cap is suggested by the American Law Institute, except the American Law Institute's approach allows the corporation to opt into the cap, whereas the Virginia statute mandates the cap for all corporations and permits the charter or bylaw merely to prescribe a *lower* cap than would otherwise apply.

Nevada provides the penultimate variation of immunity shield; since 2001 officers and directors of Nevada corporations are not subject to liability for breaches of either their duty of care or loyalty (not involving "intentional misconduct, fraud or knowing violation of law").[125] The statute appears to be the cause for Nevada's rise as a popular incorporation venue; at the same time the social benefits of such a broad immunity shield are not clear. For example, one study found companies migrating to Nevada after the 2001 change experienced an increase in accounting restatements.[126] Another investigator finds value to owners by selecting Nevada's permissive regulatory approach is likely limited to small firms with low institutional ownership and high insider ownership.[127]

The overall effect of such charter provisions is to focus attention on the transaction itself through a prayer for injunctive relief, rather than focusing on the personal liability of the directors. While appearing to be a major retreat from directors' responsibilities, the irony of charter provisions such as Delaware's is that they may actually stimulate an increase in the amount of litigation that questions director judgment. When the object of a suit is damages for the losses related to the directors' breaching their duty of care, there is the ever-present disquiet that the sanction for the breach is disproportionate to the directors' fault. The draconian nature of the suit therefore has caused the courts to insulate the directors through heightened procedural and substantive rules.[128] A charter provision shielding directors from liability for breaches of care may well encourage the courts to scrutinize directors' decisions more closely without fear that substituting the court's judgment for that of the directors will also visit a draconian remedy on the individual director. The object of such a suit is an injunction or rescission.

Moreover, the elimination of a damage recovery does not reduce the incentive for care-based suits, because plaintiffs' attorneys' fees still are awarded on proof that the directors breached their duty of care so that equitable relief is appropriate.[129] Thus the overall impact of the very popular exoneration provisions may well be that of encouraging plaintiffs to sue earlier and more frequently for protective equitable relief as well as lessening modestly the historical reluctance of courts to closely scrutinize director decisions.

---

[124]   Va. Code Ann. § 13.1–692.1 (LexisNexis 2006).

[125]   *See* Nev. Rev. Stat. § 78.138(7). The statute does authorize the provision to be overridden, but this is conditioned on the approval of the firm's management.

[126]   *See* Michal Barzuza, Market Segmentation: The Rise of Nevada as a Liability-Free Jurisdiction, 98 Va. L. Rev. 935, 988–992 (2012).

[127]   Ofer Eldar, Can Lax Corporate Law Increase Shareholder Value?, 61 J. L. & Econ. 555 (2019).

[128]   *See* Kenneth Scott, Corporation Law and the American Law Institute Corporate Governance Project, 35 Stan. L. Rev. 927 (1983); John C. Coffee, Jr. & Donald Schwartz, The Survival of the Derivative Suit: An Evaluation and a Proposal for Legislative Reform, 81 Colum. L. Rev. 261 (1981).

[129]   Tandycrafts, Inc. v. Initio Partners, 562 A.2d 1162, 1164 (Del. 1989).

§ 10.8   Executive Officers; Supervision of Subordinates

The president, cashier, or general manager may come under even greater responsibility for the fraud or neglect of subordinates than do directors.[130] Thus, where it is the duty of the president of a corporation to supervise its affairs and to take and keep bonds from subordinate officers, and the president negligently fails to take the required bond from an officer who is entrusted with funds and becomes a defaulter, it is the president who is liable to the corporation for the loss.[131]

In a leading Supreme Court case[132] a bookkeeper of a small national bank on a salary of $12 per week defrauded the bank during a series of years of over $300,000, aggregating more than the bank's capital and more than the normal average of its deposits. This was accomplished in a novel and ingenious way by falsifying the deposit ledger and making false charges against deposits, thereby diminishing the apparent liability to depositors. The fraud could have been discovered by the cashier had he examined checks as they came from the clearinghouse, or had he compared the deposit ledger with the depositors' pass books. But he negligently placed too much trust in the bookkeeper. The directors, serving gratuitously, were held not to be negligent in accepting the cashier's statements of liabilities and were not bound to inspect the depositors' ledger or call in the pass books and compare them with it. The president, who had received certain warnings that the bookkeeper was living fast and dealing in stocks, was held to have been negligent in failing to make an examination, especially as he was in control of the bank's affairs, with immediate access to the depositors' ledger.[133] Of note is that the Supreme Court upheld the criminal conviction of the president of a 36,000-employee concern with 870 retail outlets where the president's failure to supervise resulted in one of the company's 12 warehouses being in violation of federal sanitary standards.[134]

PART B.   DEALINGS BETWEEN DIRECTORS AND THEIR CORPORATIONS—CONFLICTS OF INTEREST

§ 10.9   The Scope of the Officers' and Directors' Duty of Loyalty

Mapping the scope of the directors' or officers' fiduciary obligations is not easy. The nature of the challenge is concisely stated in the now classic observation by Supreme Court Justice Felix Frankfurter in *Securities and Exchange Commission v. Chenery Corp.*: "[T]o say that a man is a fiduciary only begins the analysis; it gives direction to further inquiry. To whom is he a fiduciary? What obligations does he owe as a fiduciary? In what respect has he failed to discharge these obligations?"[135] In the early formative years of corporate law, it was assumed that the rules governing directors and officers should conform to the strict rules governing trustees and agents. Hence, courts frequently referred to directors as both trustees and agents with the effect of holding directors to the same strict rules of disqualification to contract with their principal the

---

[130] *Cf.* United States v. Park, 421 U.S. 658 (1975) (upholding conviction of president where unsanitary conditions existed at one of twelve warehouses; corporation had 36,000 employees and 874 retail outlets).

[131] Pontchartrain R.R. v. Paulding, 11 La. 41 (1837).

[132] Bates v. Dresser, 251 U.S. 524 (1920).

[133] *Cf.* Bates v. Seeds, 272 N.W. 515 (Iowa 1937).

[134] United States v. Park, 421 U.S. 658 (1975).

[135] SEC v. Chenery Corp., 318 U.S. 80, 85–86 (1943).

corporation.[136] However, the functions performed, and hence the obligations implicit to fulfill the fiduciary's undertakings, are not the same for trustees, guardians, executors, administrators, agents, partners, promoters, directors and officers.[137] The differences in the expressed tasks, and the undertakings implicit for their accomplishment, necessarily weaken the analogy between, on the one hand, trustees and, on the other hand, corporate directors or officers.[138] Nevertheless, an aspect of the relationship of directors and officers to the corporation is a fiduciary relationship, and the corporation's owners are the beneficiaries of the duties owed by the officers and directors.[139] The rhetoric of the director or officers as a trustee, therefore, continues to appear in today's decisions, although the guidance that courts invoke to determine the content of the officer's or director's fiduciary obligation is gleaned not by reference to the law of trusts but to the extensive body of corporate fiduciary case law.[140]

The preceding sections of this chapter have closely examined the many facets of the duty of care. Directors and officers must also comply with their duty of loyalty[141] if they are to enjoy the protective benefits of the business judgment rule. The divide between the duty of care and loyalty is not a sharp one, and the courts frequently blur the distinction between these twin obligations.[142] As seen in the preceding material of this chapter, there are many dimensions to the duty of care. In broad overview, the duty of care is about process by which officers and directors are to reach decisions and, more generally, fulfill their monitoring obligations. Hence the material earlier in this chapter focused upon the obligations to be attentive, make reasonable inquiry and have a rational basis for decision making. In contrast, loyalty is not about the decision making process or, for that matter, monitoring. The duty of loyalty is about the director's or officer's motives, purposes, and the goals that are necessary if his action is to enjoy the protective benefits of the business judgment rule.

The duty of loyalty most certainly includes officer or director self-dealing contracts and transactions which more generally are referred to as conflict-of-interest transactions. But an officer or director can be disloyal to her corporation in many more ways than merely transacting business with the corporation. Material elsewhere in this book reviews many instances in which special doctrines have evolved in situations that raise concern for the director's or officer's loyalty. A prime example of such a situation is the directors' defense of control where the courts uniformly remove the actions of the

---

[136] *See, e.g.,* North Confidence Mining & Dev. Co. v. Fitch, 208 P. 328 (Cal. Ct. App. 1922).

[137] *See* Austin Wakeman Scott, The Trustee's Duty of Loyalty, 49 Harv. L. Rev. 521 (1936). *But see,* Bovay v. H. M. Byllesby & Co., 38 A.2d 808 (Del. 1944).

[138] For early recognition of the problems of extrapolating from the law of trusts obligations for directors and officers, *see* York v. Guaranty Trust Co., 143 F.2d 503, 514 (2d Cir. 1944), *rev'd on other grounds,* 326 U.S. 99 (1945).

[139] Thus, when the shareholder's relationship with the company ends, so does the fiduciary obligation attendant to that relationship.

[140] On the general topic of determining the roots for corporate fiduciary obligations, *see, e.g.,* Deborah A. DeMott, Breach Of Fiduciary Duty: On Justifiable Expectations Of Loyalty And Their Consequences, 48 Ariz. L. Rev. 925 (2006) (duty arises from shareholders' justifiable expectations of loyal conduct); Lyman P.Q. Johnson & David Millon, Recalling Why Corporate Officers Are Fiduciaries, 46 Wm. & Mary L. Rev. 1597 (2005).

[141] The duty of loyalty is equated to the "good faith" requirement that appears in statutes and in court opinions dealing with the obligations of directors and officers. *See, e.g.,* In re Gaylord Container Corp. Shareholders Litigation, 753 A.2d 462, 475–76 n.41 (Del. Ch. 2000).

[142] *See* Mills Acquisition Co. v. Macmillan, Inc., 559 A.2d 1261, 1284 n.32 (Del. 1989) (disinterested directors who abandon their oversight responsibilities in context of takeover breach their duties of care and loyalty).

board of directors from the protective presumption of the business judgment rule for fear that the directors may be acting to protect their personal self-interest and not serving the interests of the corporation or its stockholders. An even more blatant form of loyalty breach arises when the officer or director has usurped a corporate opportunity. The duty of loyalty places directors under a duty of confidentiality. Breaches of the duty of confidentiality can, for example, form the basis of insider trading liability. There also have been highly celebrated instances of board members inappropriately leaking information to the press.[143] Interestingly, in special instances, loyalty violations can even arise when the directors or officers are acting in their good faith belief they are advancing the corporation's interest.[144] Thus, most certainly the duty of loyalty includes more than either self-dealing or usurping corporate opportunities.

An important question regarding the scope of the duty of loyalty is whether it requires more than the absence of self-interest, personal gain, and the like on the part of a director or officer. Or, does the duty of loyalty move beyond such minimalist considerations to require the fiduciary to act positively to advance the corporation's interests? That is, does the duty of loyalty have both negative and positive descriptions for how officers and directors are to behave?[145] For example, the American Law Institute's Corporate Governance Project sweeps the duty of loyalty into its obligation for "fair dealing," which prescribes a course of behavior when an officer, director, or controlling stockholder is financially interested in a matter.[146] Pronouncements of the Delaware Supreme Court can be seen as embodying a more expansive view of the duty of loyalty. For example, in a leading case on the disclosure obligations of officers and directors, the court analogized the duty to a "compass" that is to serve as constant guide for the fiduciary when acting for the corporation.[147] And, in a leading corporate opportunity case, *Guth v. Loft, Inc.,*[148] the court observed that the directors have a duty "affirmatively to protect the interests of the corporation committed to his charge."[149] To so view the duty of loyalty places the obligations of directors and officers on a footing equal to that of contemporary standards for fiduciaries generally where the obligation is not simply to subordinate self-interested behavior, but also to "act exclusively for the benefit of the other party."[150] So viewed, the duty of loyalty is not merely regulatory, but has a strong moral element.

Those who prefer to view the corporation as a web of contract have little regard for the duty of loyalty being morally based. Instead, adherents of such a contractual view of the corporation argue that the source of officer and director obligations is what the

---

[143] Most notable was the scandal involving Hewlett-Packard Corporation. *See, e.g.,* Simon A. Rodell, Note: Plumbing In The Boardroom: Plugging Boardroom Leaks Through A Good Faith Duty Of Confidentiality. 59 Fla. L. Rev. 631 (2007).

[144] *See* Blasius Industries, Inc. v. Atlas Corp., 564 A.2d 651, 663 (Del. Ch. 1988) (even though acting in the good faith belief they are serving the corporation's interest, management must demonstrate a compelling justification for action taken for purpose of thwarting the on-going efforts of a stockholder to exercise its rights of corporate suffrage).

[145] *See* Lyman Johnson, Enron: Loyalty Discourse in Corporate Law, 28 Del. J. Corp. Law 27 (2003).

[146] *See generally* Melvin A. Eisenberg, Corporate Law and Social Norms, 99 Colum. L. Rev. 1253, 1265 & 1273 (1999). Cantor v. Perelman, 414 F.3d 430 (3d Cir. 2005), is instructive.

[147] *See* Malone v. Brincat, 722 A.2d 5, 10 (Del. 1998).

[148] Guth v. Loft, Inc., 5 A.2d 503 (Del. 1939).

[149] Guth v. Loft, Inc., 5 A.2d 503, 510 (Del. 1939).

[150] *See* Gregory S. Alexander, A Cognitive Theory of Fiduciary Relationships, 85 Cornell L. Rev. 767, 776 (2000).

parties would have agreed to ex ante.[151] Even with such a simplified view of the corporate enterprise, it is not clear that owners and their officers and directors would not have embodied in their contract a broad duty of loyalty. Indeed, the information asymmetries that abound when passive owners commit funds to the stewardship of others should minimally give rise to a strong presumption that the stewards were to always act exclusively to benefit the firm and its owners. The difference in the result is that the meaning of the duty of loyalty pursuant to the contractual view is driven exclusively by self-interest of the economic actors, whereas for non-contractarians the content is moral in nature having its roots in the social values of our culture.[152] What may be at risk in making a choice between these two views is that a view anchored so firmly in the methodology of economics, as is the case with the contractual view, may well blind or divert the inquiry from a richer perspective that gives regard to a wider range of social inputs.

An example of a breach of the director's duty of loyalty arises when the director, even though financially disinterested, knowingly fails to warn his fellow directors of material facts relevant to a transaction before the board.[153]

In *Gantler v. Stephens*,[154] the Delaware Supreme Court for the first time held what had long been assumed: officers owe fiduciary duties that mirror the fiduciary obligations of directors. Each must act with good faith which is broadly defined to require that when acting to do so to serve the corporation's interests and not the narrower personal interests of the officer or director. Obviously there is nothing wrong with serving both parties' interests; the breach arises when the officer or director advances his own interests at the expense of the corporation.[155] The breaching conduct in *Gantler* was the directors and officers purposely sabotaged the company's efforts to sell itself to several suitors and then caused the firm to undertaking a less valuable reorganization that benefitted the officers and directors. The facts also showed that outside directors acted to preserve their on-going commercial relationships with the firm.

Among the obligations within the director's duty of loyalty can be to bring information to the attention of the board or officers that will have significant consequences to the company.[156] Somewhat related is that information obtained through

---

[151] *See, e.g.,* Frank H. Easterbrook & Daniel R. Fischel, Contract and Fiduciary Duty, 36 J. L. & Econ. 425 (1993).

[152] Consider here the insight of former Chancellor William Allen: "[C]orporation law exists, not as an isolated body of rules and principles, but rather in a historical setting and as part of a larger body of law premised upon shared values." City Capital Associates Limited Partnership v. Interco, Inc., 551 A.2d 787, 800 (Del. Ch. 1988).

[153] *See, e.g.,* Berkman v. Rust Craft Greeting Cards, Inc., 454 F.Supp. 787 (S.D.N.Y. 1978) (some of the directors failed to disclose to their fellow directors their knowledge that the investment banker whose fairness opinion the board would rely upon had a material financial interest in the outcome of the transaction).

[154] 965 A.2d 695 (Del. 2009).

[155] *See, e.g.,* J.A. Morrissey, Inc. v. Smejkal, 6 A.3d 701 (Vt. 2010)(vice president and director orchestrated a lease of property he owned at higher fit-up costs and billed the company for costs unrelated to its tenancy).

[156] *See* Optimis Corp. v. Waite, 2015 WL 5147038 (Del. Ch., Aug. 26, 2015). Finding a breach of fiduciary duty (but not consequential damages) when directors failed to disclose their knowledge that a non-licensed person was a shareholder in a corporation providing physical therapy services; state law limits share ownership in such professional care companies to licensed physical therapists. The evidence supported finding that they did not disclose this information intentionally and for the directors' personal interest. For a close review of the applicable case law, concluding the content of this obligation is unsettled, *see* Jennifer O'Hare, Private Ordering and Improving Information Flow to the Board of Directors: The Duty to Inform Bylaw, 52 U. Rich. L. Rev. 101 (2018).

serving as a director or officer should not be used for personal advancement at the expense of the corporation.[157]

§ 10.10   Interested Officer and Director Transactions: Defined and Historical Treatment

A few early American decisions adopted the inflexible English rule of disqualification whereby directors were forbidden to enter into contracts in which they have a personal interest that conflicts with their fiduciary duty of loyalty to the corporation. Under this view, unless there had been shareholder ratification, any contract with a director is voidable at the election of the corporation, regardless of whether it is fair and honest.[158] The theory of disqualification was that the corporation is entitled to the advice of each of its directors, and that directors may not abdicate their duty to the corporation and bargain with it in their own interest as a stranger, even if the corporation is represented by an independent majority of its directors.[159] It is argued that there cannot be real bargaining where the same person is acting on both sides of the transaction.[160]

Today, all American jurisdictions have found it impractical to disqualify directors or officers from contracting with their corporation. The earlier fear that a corporate fiduciary's dealings with the corporation was rife with the possibility of dishonesty or unfairness has given way to the belief that there are commercial advantages to such transactions and that regulation, rather than strict prohibition, is the approach with the greatest social welfare. In most jurisdictions, interested directors may be counted toward the quorum necessary for the board to take action on the transaction in which the directors have an interest.[161] An in broad overview, the approach in all states is that a corporation's contract with its director or officer is not voidable if approved by a disinterested body of directors or stockholders, or if the contracting director or officer successfully bears the burden of showing the fairness of the transaction.[162] As discussed below, this rule is now declared by most corporation statutes.[163]

§ 10.11   Burden of Proof of Fairness in Fiduciary Contracts

It has long been the prevailing rule that directors or officers seeking the benefits of a contract or transaction with their corporation have the burden of showing that the transaction meets the requirements of state conflict-of-interest provision. This is the case whether the suit is by the corporation to rescind or by the director or officer to enforce

---

[157] *See* Shocking Technologies, Inc. v. Kosowsky, 2012 WL 4482838 (Del. Ch. 2012) (director breached duty by sharing information regarding company's financial distress to potential investors so as to enhance his stature within the company if that investor demanded improved terms or did not invest with the consequence of raising the stature of the defendant who was opposed to the majority's refinancing strategies), *vacated on other grounds*, Shocking Technologies, Inc. v. Kosowsky, 2015 WL 3465825 (Del. Ch. 2015).

[158] Morgan v. King, 63 P. 416 (Colo. 1900); Pearson v. Concord R. Corp., 62 N.H. 537 (1883).

[159] Rothenberg v. Franklin Washington Trust Co., 13 A.2d 667, 672 (N.J. Ch. 1940).

[160] *See generally* Snead v. United States Trucking Corp., 380 So.2d 1075 (Fla. Dist. Ct. App. 1980) (deal not at arm's length when officer-director-stockholder of one corporation contracted with second corporation of which he was salaried employee).

[161] *See, e.g.,* Karris v. Water Tower Trust & Sav. Bank, 389 N.E.2d 1359 (Ill. App. Ct. 1979).

[162] Pepper v. Litton, 308 U.S. 295 (1939); Norlin Corp. v. Rooney, Pace, Inc., 744 F.2d 255 (2d Cir. 1984).

[163] *See* former MBCA § 41 (1969); *accord,* MBCA § 8.31 (2008).

the contract.[164] However, proof that the transaction was approved by disinterested directors after full disclosure shifts the burden back to the complaining stockholder.[165] Similarly, approval of the transaction by the shareholders[166] or an independent committee will shift the burden back to the person challenging the transaction.[167] However, when the committee lacks independence, the defendants retain the burden of proving the transaction's fairness.[168]

As discussed elsewhere in this treatise,[169] corporate fiduciaries' conflict of interest obligations apply to controlling shareholders of close corporations. The fiduciary's burden of proving fairness in conflict of interest transactions thus applies to the duties of controlling shareholders in closely held corporations.[170]

---

[164] *See, e.g.,* Pepper v. Litton, 308 U.S. 295, 306 (1939); Pappas v. Moss, 393 F.2d 865 (3d Cir. 1968); In re Wheelabrator Technologies Shareholder Litigation, 663 A.2d 1194 (Del. Ch. 1995).

[165] Weiss v. Kay Jewelry Stores, 470 F.2d 1259 (D.C. Cir. 1972).

[166] Solomon v. Armstrong, 747 A.2d 1098, 1117 (Del. Ch. 1999), *aff'd,* 746 A.2d 277 (Del. 2000).

[167] Singh v. Attenborough, 137 A.3d 151 (Del. 2016) (memorandum opinion) (dismissing claims that investment bankers aided and abetted fiduciary duty breaches in connection with sale of company where shareholders had been fully informed); City of Miami General Employees v. Comstock, 2016 WL 4464156 (Del. Ch. 2016) (applying Corwin v. KKR Financial Holdings LLC, 125 A.3d 304 (Del. 2015) and *Singh supra* to apply business judgment rule dismiss derivative suit challenging merger); Larkin v. Shah, 2016 WL 4485447 (Del. Ch. 2016) (applying *Singh* and finding fully informed uncoerced shareholder vote results in the application business judgment rule moving the burden of fairness away from the defendant); In re Volcano Corporation Stockholder Litigation, 2016 WL 3626521 (Del. Ch. 2016) (applying *Singh* and holding the same rule applies to transactions "approved" by fully informed, uncoerced stockholders tendering a majority of shares in a two-step merger pursuant to Del. Code Ann. tit. 8, § 251(h)). *But cf.* Appel v. Berkman, 180 A.3d 1055 (Del. 2018) (disclosures were not as full as they might have been and rendered the vote subject to challenge under Corwin v. KKR Financial Holdings LLC, 125 A.3d 304 (Del. 2015)); In re Straight Path Communications Inc. Consolidated Stockholder Litigation, 2018 WL 3120804 (Del. Ch. 2018) (sufficient allegations that transaction was unfair under entire fairness test); Sciabacucchi v. Liberty Broadband Corporation, 2017 WL 2352152 (Del. Ch. 2017) (the requirements of *Corwin* were not satisfied because the stockholder vote on the transaction at issue was "structurally coercive."); In re Massey Energy Company Derivative and Class Action Litigation, 160 A.3d 484 (Del. Ch. 2017) (the *Corwin* defense was inapplicable to fiduciary claims for pre-merger conduct that was not specifically ratified by a stockholder vote in connection with a merger); Dieckman v. Regency GP LP, 155 A.3d 358 (Del. 2017) (sufficient allegations that general partner misled shareholders in their vote approving the challenged transaction); In re Solera Holdings, Inc. Stockholder Litigation, 2017 WL 57839 (Del. Ch. 2017) (the shareholder challenging the transaction has the burden of proving that the disclosure to shareholders was inadequate); In re Saba Software, Inc. Stockholder Litigation, 2017 WL 1201108 (Del. Ch. 2017), as revised, (Apr. 11, 2017) (shareholder vote without full disclosure rendered transaction subject to challenge); RBC Capital Markets, LLC v. Jervis, 129 A.3d 816 (Del. 2015) (affirming finding that financial advisor aided and abetted directors' breach of fiduciary duty in connection with a sale of control transaction).

Notwithstanding the foregoing cases, a fully informed vote does not preclude a shareholder's request for inspection of corporate books relating to the transaction in question. Lavin v. West Corporation, 2017 WL 6728702 (Del. Ch. 2017), judgment entered, 2018 WL 565492 (Del. Ch. 2018).

[168] Kahn v. Tremont Corp., 694 A.2d 422 (Del. 1997) (lower court erred in shifting the burden of proof to plaintiffs challenging corporation's stock purchase from a related company).

[169] Controlling shareholder fiduciary duties in closely held corporations are discussed in § 14.15 *infra.*

[170] *See, e.g.,* Edelman v. JELBS, 2015-Ohio-5542, 57 N.E.3d 246 (Ohio Ct. App. 10th Dist. Franklin County 2015), appeal not allowed, 145 Ohio St. 3d 1471, 2016-Ohio-3028, 49 N.E.3d 1313 (2016) (in upholding a claim of excessive compensation to the majority, the court noted "when a minority shareholder of a close corporation brings suit against a controlling shareholder for breach of his or her fiduciary duties, a presumption arises that the fiduciary, by virtue of his or her superior position, bears the burden of proof with respect to the fairness of his or her actions. Consistent with this presumption, the fiduciary must demonstrate that his or her actions were fair, reasonable, and based on a full disclosure of relevant information.") (citation omitted), relying on Yackel v. Kay, 95 Ohio App. 3d 472, 642 N.E.2d 1107 (8th Dist. Cuyahoga County 1994) ("there exists a presumption that the one owing a fiduciary duty by virtue of superior position must go forward with the burden of proof on the fairness of business transactions. The fiduciary must demonstrate that the one to whom the fiduciary duty was owed had full knowledge of and approved the transactions.").

§ 10.12 Statutory Treatment of Transactions with Interested Officers and Directors

A provision of the California general corporation law,[171] adopted in 1931, changed the former rule as to the disqualification of directors or officers to represent their corporation. Under that statute, if financially interested directors have to be counted to make up a quorum or majority to authorize a transaction, such transactions would no longer be voidable at the option of the corporation solely because of such director's participation, provided one of three alternative safeguards or conditions is met: (1) ratification by an independent majority of directors, (2) approval or ratification by the shareholders, or (3) a showing that the contract is just and reasonable as to the corporation. The statute thus set forth procedures for contracts between a corporation and its officers or directors, as well as between corporations that have some overlap of directors or officers.

Following the lead of the California statute, each version of the Model Business Corporation Act has embraced the same three alternative safe harbors as were adopted in the path-breaking California provision.[172] For example, under section 8.31 of the 1984 Model Act, an interested director may be counted in the quorum, and a particular contract or transaction is not void or voidable "because of such relationship or interest." The statute does not provide per se validation of all contracts where the statutory procedure has been followed and thus does not preclude further scrutiny.[173] The Model Act deals only with director conflict-of-interest transactions. Conflict-of-interest transactions involving non-director officers or employees are dealt with under the general principles of fiduciary obligations and the law of agency. All states have conflict-of-interest statutes that mirror the approach first taken in California; most of the states have patterned their statutes after the pre-1988 versions of the Model Act.[174] The currency Section 8.31 provides somewhat detailed descriptions of what constitutes an "indirect" conflict-of-interest as well as the voting requirements for *impartial* director or shareholder approval; this section, like earlier vintages of the Model Act, is general, even sometimes vague, in its requirements and scope. Because generality and vagueness necessarily robs transactions of predictability, since 1988 the Model Business Corporations Act substitutes new sections 8:60 to 8:62. The overall philosophy of the 1988 amendments is to adopt a bright-line test and to make the provisions' proscription exclusive (circumstances falling outside the statutory definition of conflicting interests cannot be challenged on the basis of the transaction involves a conflict of interest, although challenges on other grounds are not foreclosed). The most distinguishing characteristics of the 1988 amendments are the level of detail with which they define "conflicting interests"[175] and specify when judicial intervention is appropriate.

---

[171] *See* Henry W. Ballantine & Graham L. Sterling, California Corporation Laws 98–102 (1938). For a more recent version of the California statute, *see* Cal. Corp. Code § 310 (West 1990).

[172] Former MBCA § 41 (1969); *accord*, MBCA § 8.31 (2008).

[173] *See* Remillard Brick Co. v. Remillard-Dandini Co., 241 P.2d 66, 72 (Cal. Ct. App. 1952), where the court held that notwithstanding compliance with statutory formalities, the contract if "unfair and unreasonable to the corporation may be avoided."

[174] Model Bus. Corp. Act Ann. § 8.61 at 8.43 (3d ed. 1994).

[175] Douglas M. Branson, Assault on Another Citadel: Attempts to Curtail the Fiduciary Standard of Loyalty Applicable to Corporate Directors, 57 Fordham L. Rev. 375 (1988).

Scope of Conflict-of-Interest Statutes. In broad overview, conflict-of-interest statutes pose three distinct questions to the practitioner. The first is whether a given transaction falls within the statute's coverage.[176] For example, is a subsidiary's declaration of a dividend in response to the influence of its parent a conflict-of-interest transaction? One may consider that declaring a dividend entails creating a "contract or transaction" between the subsidiary and its parent, on whose board many of the subsidiary's directors are also directors, especially since the declaration of a dividend establishes a distinct contractual relationship between the corporation and the stockholders entitled to the dividend. The Delaware Supreme Court, however, has held that, because a dividend is proportional to all the company's stockholders, it is not a conflict-of-interest transaction.[177] The 1988 amendments to the Model Business Corporation Act strive to provide greater specificity to the questions of what is a conflict of interest transactions, the means for its approval, and the consequences of the transaction being approved as set forth by the statute.[178]

However, even the Model Business Corporation Act does not deal with the more problematic inquiry as to the meaning of a "contract or transaction."[179] Thus, a finder's fee that an officer can earn upon a sale of the company to a third party was held within a conflict-of-interest transaction.[180] The question whether a given contract or transaction falls within a state's conflict-of-interest statute is not purely an academic question. As will be seen below, two distinct philosophies can be attributed to the purpose of conflict-of-interest statutes, one being that compliance with the statute immunizes the transaction from attack on any grounds. Under this view, the conflict-of-interest statute has a broad regulatory purpose. So viewed, one seeking to assure no successful attack can be brought against the transaction on grounds that it is unfair or unreasonable can approach the conflict-of-interest statute's alternative validating mechanisms as desirable and useful safe harbors to shield the transaction from further challenge or scrutiny. On the other hand, a second view of conflict-of-interest statutes is that they serve only as a procedural mechanism to overcoming the automatic voidability that existed at common law. Under this approach, satisfaction of one of the conflict-of-interest provisions merely removes any adverse inference that otherwise would be drawn from the director's interest in the transaction. This narrower construction of the statute's scope means the transaction may still be examined under the broader and less predictable standards of the director's or officer's fiduciary obligations; this approach is thus less attractive to the lawyer who wishes certainty and predictability when planning a transaction.

---

[176] When all the directors, being served as defendants in a suit, voted to advance themselves funds to cover their litigation expenses as authorized by the indemnification provisions of the corporate statute, the courts are split whether the board's action is to be assesses solely by the requirements of the indemnification statute or must also satisfy the fairness requirements of the conflict-of-interest provision.

[177] Sinclair Oil Corp. v. Levien, 280 A.2d 717 (Del. 1971).

[178] MBCA §§ 8.60 to 8.63 (2016).

[179] The Model Act "conflicting interest transaction" reaches "transactions" which the commentary describes as "negotiations or a consensual bilateral arrangement between the corporation and another party or parties that concern their respective and differing economic rights or interests—not simply a unilateral action by the corporation, but rather a 'deal.'" MBCA § 8.60 Comment 1C (2016).

[180] *See,* Ryan v. Tad's Enterprises, Inc., 709 A.2d 682 (Del. Ch. 1996) (consulting agreement secured by dominant stockholders in their sale of restaurant business was linked to their purchase of the two remaining divisions).

Methods of Satisfying the Statute. The second practical question posed by state conflict-of-interest statutes is how to comply with the statute's requirements. The typical conflict-of-interest statute sets forth three *alternative* mechanisms for validating a conflict-of-interest transaction: impartial director approval, impartial shareholder approval, or proof of the transaction's fairness. From the view of counseling a client, the least attractive of the three options is relying on proof of the transaction's fairness or reasonableness to the corporation. Courts uniformly place the burden of establishing fairness on the interested director or officer.[181] Fairness typically requires that the transaction reflect terms one would expect in an arm's length transaction, which means generally that a self-dealing fiduciary must treat his corporation's interest as his own.[182] The fiduciary should neither take any advantage from his position on both sides of the transaction nor act in conflict with the corporation's interest to even the slightest extent.[183] Moreover, fairness is more encompassing than the adequacy of consideration; it includes the entirety of the transaction.[184] An important factor in any such fairness inquiry is the actual consideration paid compared with an independent appraisal of the property's fair market value.[185] Thus, the fairness of a lease transaction was considered in light of evidence of the market price of similar leases, the corporation's need for the property, the absence of any evidence that a better deal was possible with a noninterested party, the possibility that the interested party was diverting gain to himself, and whether full disclosure to the disinterested directors and shareholders was made.[186] The provision of the same benefits to non interested parties is also relevant in concluding the transaction is fair.[187]

As between the two other validating mechanisms—impartial approval by the shareholders and impartial approval by the directors—the latter is certainly the more efficient. One needs to take care when seeking ratification of a completed conflict-of-interest transaction as to whether the applicable statute permits the disinterested directors to *ratify* a consummated conflict-of-interest transaction or merely to *approve* a

---

[181] *See, e.g.,* Cascades West Assocs. Ltd. P'ship v. PRC, Inc., 36 Va. Cir. 324 (1995) (because directors are akin to trustees, they must meet burden of proof pursuant to the clear and convincing evidence standard).

[182] Noe v. Roussel, 310 So.2d 806 (La. 1975); Harris Trust & Sav. Bank v. Joanna-Western Mills Co., 368 N.E.2d 629 (Ill. App. Ct. 1977) (transaction should be one that commended itself to a wholly independent board).

[183] In re Brokers, Inc., 363 B.R. 458, 473 (Bankr.M.D.N.C. 2007).

[184] Johnson v. Witkowski, 573 N.E.2d 513, 521 (Mass. App. Ct. 1991).

Kim v. Grover C. Coors Trust, 179 P.3d 86, 92 (Colo. Ct. App. 2007), lists the following factors in determining whether a self-dealing transaction is fair:

(1) the transaction was accompanied by a full and fair disclosure of the material facts to the shareholders;

(2) the transaction as attended by fraud;

(3) there was adequate consideration for the transaction;

(4) the transaction benefited the corporation; and

(5) directors siphoned corporate benefits.

[185] Straight v. Goss, 678 S.E.2d 443, 453 (S.C. Ct. App. 2009).

[186] *See, e.g.,* Pittsburgh Terminal Corp. v. Baltimore & Ohio R.R. Co., 875 F.2d 549 (6th Cir. 1989) (dominant consideration is fairness of the price and that there is no further requirement of "fair dealing" as occurs under the Delaware jurisprudence); Oberly v. Kirby, 592 A.2d 445 (Del. 1991) (fairness satisfied by evidence of lengthy bargaining, value approached midpoint of both sides, and absence of viable alternatives).

[187] Nalty v. D.H. Holmes Co., Ltd., 882 So.2d 1, 10 (La. Ct. App. 2004).

yet to be consummated conflict-of-interest transaction.[188] It is generally recognized and so expressed in most conflict-of-interest statutes that the shareholders have the inherent power to both approve and ratify conflict-of-interest transactions. Central to the power of the disinterested directors or stockholders to approve or ratify a conflict-of-interest transaction is that their approval be impartial, in good faith, and follow full disclosure of the material facts as to the director's or officer's interest as well as to the transaction itself. Each of these requirements is examined in the following paragraphs.

Many state statutes adhere to the 1984 Model Business Corporation Act's scheme of providing detailed rules for ascertaining whether the approving or ratifying body, whether stockholders or directors, is impartial—that is, disinterested. For example, the Model Business Corporation Act requires that approval be by a majority of the voting shares not owned or under the control of the interested party. In states whose statutes do not so limit the shares that can approve or ratify a conflict-of-interest transaction, the result similar to that achieved in the Model Business Corporation Act can be achieved by a reasonable construction of the "good faith" approval requirement so that good faith minimally requires impartiality on the part of the decisionmaker.[189]

Special care must be taken with respect to the type of vote required to satisfy a state's conflict-of-interest statute via impartial director approval. Different patterns exist among the states. Delaware, for example, requires that the approval be "by a majority of the disinterested directors."[190] On the other hand, some states merely condition approval being by votes normally sufficient after disregarding the votes of the interested directors.[191] Thus, consider the vote necessary at a meeting attended by a corporation's seven authorized directors and approval is sought for a transaction in which four of the directors are interested. The Delaware conflict-of-interest provision would be satisfied if at least two of the disinterested directors vote favorably.[192] But, in a state that merely disregards the votes, but not the physical presence of the interested directors, the transaction would not be approved. A common mechanism for overcoming any problems in securing a proper vote at the board of directors is for the board to exercise its powers under the charter or bylaws to create a committee of disinterested directors and to assign to that committee the responsibility to approve or ratify the conflict-of-interest transaction.[193] A further point is that statutes customarily permit the interested director to count toward a quorum; this feature reflects the somewhat narrow feature of conflict of interest statutes, namely to address self dealing by officers and directors. Hence, if a all a boards directors who vote in approval of a transaction are interested this does not prevent there being board approval of that transaction such that

---

[188] Richard M. Buxbaum, Conflict-of-Interest Statutes and the Need for a Demand on Directors in Derivative Actions, 68 Cal. L. Rev. 1122 (1980) (distinction being that directors are less likely to feel freedom to fully consider and reject a transaction that is consummated than one that remains executory).

[189] Even upon approval of a majority of the disinterested shares, the transaction can still be reviewed under a waste standard meaning "an exchange to which no reasonable person not acting under compulsion and in good faith could agree" that the transaction is fair. See Lewis v. Vogelstein, 699 A.2d 327 (Del. Ch. 1997).

[190] Del. Code Ann. tit. 8, § 144 (2001).

[191] See Weiss Med. Complex v. Kim, 408 N.E.2d 959 (Ill. App. Ct. 1980) (quorum not present when four of seven directors had a personal interest in a matter).

[192] See Rapoport v. Schneider, 278 N.E.2d 642 (N.Y. 1972) (5-to-1 vote deemed approval of transaction when three of yes votes were interested).

[193] But the committee must act in good faith which requires minimally its independence from the interested party.

the transaction is vulnerable to attack for never being authorized.[194] The transaction should be viewed as being approved; nonetheless, there are separate questions whether it is voidable or otherwise protected by the business judgment rule because of the lack of disinterested director approval.

Whether authorization or ratification is by the board of directors or by the stockholders, it is subject to the statute's requirement that the decisionmaker have acted in "good faith." As seen earlier in this chapter, good faith implicates the motives or intentions of the approving or ratifying body. As is true in any area of the law that turns on a person's intentions or motives, good faith is established circumstantially. In this regard, impartiality in terms of the voting directors or shareholders not having a financial interest served by the contract or transaction (except to the extent it is beneficial to the corporation itself) is the best measure of whether their approval or ratification is in good faith. Minimally, therefore, good faith requires impartiality. Thus a shareholder who controlled 99 percent of the corporation's stock and was himself an interested party in the transaction was held not to have acted in good faith in approving that transaction.[195] Lack of good faith was established by the self-interested dominating director convening a special board meeting without notice to ratify the conflict-of-interest transaction.[196] Substantial prior business relations with the interested party or apathy, such as rarely attending meetings at which the transaction was discussed, are each inconsistent with the good faith requirement.[197] Evidence of an ulterior motive hostile to the corporation's best interest also established a lack of good faith.[198] Furthermore, neither the directors nor the stockholders can by a majority vote ratify a fraudulent or wasteful transaction.[199] When the approving body is the board of directors, the inquiry into whether they did so in "good faith" focuses on challenges to their independence.[200]

Disclosure can well be viewed as the sine qua non of conflict-of-interest statutes. Not only have courts equated the absence of disclosure with inherent unfairness,[201] but also the efficacy of impartial director or shareholder approval is necessarily dependent on the reviewing body's knowledge of all material facts.[202] It is that body's independent and thoughtful approval after deliberating on all the facts that is intended by the conflict-of-interest statute to protect the corporation from the director's or officer's conflict of interest. Disclosure requires that the interested director or officer bring to the approving or ratifying body of directors or shareholders all facts material bearing on the transaction, not merely disclosing that the transaction involves self-dealing by the director or officer. Nonetheless, the 1989 Amendments to the Model Business

---

[194] *See, e.g.,* Nalty v. D.H. Holmes Co., Ltd., 882 So.2d 1, 8–9 (La. Ct. App. 2004).

[195] Rivercity v. American Can Co., 600 F.Supp. 908, 921 (E.D. La. 1984).

[196] Groves v. Rosemound Improvement Ass'n, 490 So.2d 348, 350–351 (La. Ct. App. 1986).

[197] *See* Kahn v. Tremont Corp., 694 A.2d 422 (Del. 1997).

[198] *See* Nord v. Eastside Ass'n, 664 P.2d 4, 6 (Wash. Ct. App. 1983).

[199] *See, e.g.,* Wolf v. Frank, 477 F.2d 467 (5th Cir. 1973) (all disinterested directors cannot ratify fraud on part of other directors); Lewis v. Vogelstein, 699 A.2d 327 (Del. Ch. 1997) (wasteful options granted directors cannot be ratified by mere majority vote of stockholders).

[200] *See* Benihana of Tokyo, Inc. v. Benihana, Inc., 891 A.2d 150, 175–177 (Del. Ch. 2005), *aff'd,* 906 A.2d 114 (Del. 2006) (finding the following did not render approving directors not independent: director's interest in retaining office and accompanying directors' fees or having a close friendship to the interested party).

[201] *See, e.g.,* Kim v. Grover C. Coors Trust, 179 P.3d 86, 93–94 (Colo. Ct. App. 2007) (in assessing the transaction's overall fairness, it is relevant that the interested directors made full disclosure but irrelevant to the fairness inquiry that the independent directors did not review all the material information so disclosed).

[202] *See, e.g.,* In re Brokers, 363 B.R. 458 (Bankr.M.D.N.C. 2007).

Corporation Act provide an exception to the conflicted director making full disclosure. Under the Model Act, the full disclosure by the conflicted director that is normally required is excused when the director reasonably believes she has an extrinsic duty of confidentiality that justifies no disclosure.[203] The Official Comment states this provision "will apply to the frequently recurring situation where transacting corporations have common directors (or where a director of one party is an officer of the other)."[204] In this instance, the director must still inform the approving body of directors that there exists on her part a conflict of interest, disclose all information bearing on the transactions that the director can disclose without violating the independent duty of confidentiality, and finally must disclose the nature of the director's confidential duty.[205] This exception, however, applies only when there is an indirect conflict of interest transaction: a transaction between the corporation and an entity in which the director is a director, member, trustee or the like as well as a transaction with an entity that is controlled by the director's employer.[206]

The central consideration for effective approval by the stockholders is the fullness of disclosure of the director's or officer's interest as well as the material facts of the transaction and the independence of the approval. Impartial approval is absent if a majority of the votes favoring the transaction are held or controlled by the interested director or officer.[207] It is possible that the stockholder approval can occur informally, by open acquiescence or accepting the benefits of the transaction, provided there is strong evidence that the holders of a majority of the shares were aware of the material facts bearing on the transaction.[208]

Effect of Compliance with Statute. The final question posed by conflict-of-interest statutes is the effect of complying with one of its alternative validation provisions. The preamble to most conflict-of-interest statutes provides that the contract or transaction will not be voidable solely because of the director's or officer's interest if one of the three validating alternatives is satisfied.[209] Some courts interpret this language literally so that the effect of, for example, good faith independent stockholder approval is that such approval shields the transaction from being rescinded *solely* because it involves a conflict of interest.[210] Thus, under this approach, the effect of a transaction having satisfied one of the conflict-of-interest statute's three authorizing provisions is that such satisfaction removes any adverse inference that otherwise would be drawn because of the director's interest. As a correlative proposition, satisfaction of the statute's authorizing provisions shifts the burden of proof back to the objecting

---

[203] MBCA § 8.62(b) (2016).

[204] MBCA § 8.62(b) Comment 2 (2016).

[205] MBCA § 8.62(b) (2016). *See, e.g.,* Fisher v. State Mutual Ins. Co., 290 F.3d 1256 (11th Cir. 2002) (duty of confidentiality supporting use of procedure in Georgia's version of this section found where defendant was a member of each company's board, even though one of the company allegedly was a shell company).

[206] MBCA §§ 8.62(b) & 8.60(v) & (vi) (2016).

[207] *See, e.g.,* Pappas v. Moss, 393 F.2d 865 (3d Cir. 1968) (burden not shifted by shareholder approval when interested party held a majority of the shares).

[208] *See* Robert A. Wachsler, Inc. v. Florafax Int'l, Inc., 778 F.2d 547 (10th Cir. 1985).

[209] Being phrased in terms of a transaction being possibly "void" or "voidable," the statute lends itself naturally to both offensive and defensive applications. Hicks v. Midwest Transit, Inc., 500 F.3d 647 (7th Cir. 2007).

[210] *See, e.g.,* Fliegler v. Lawrence, 361 A.2d 218 (Del. 1976).

stockholder.[211] The result of such an interpretation is to allow the transaction to be questioned as beyond the protection of the business judgment rule because it was wasteful or not in the corporation's best interests. In such a suit, the plaintiff would bear the burden of proof.[212] Thus, under this view of compliance with the conflict-of-interest statute, the impact of the statute is primarily returning the burden of proof to the one challenging the transaction. If there had not been impartial director or stockholder approval, the burden of proving fairness to the corporation would have been on the director or officer with the conflict of interest.[213]

A different and more sweeping view of satisfying any of the conflict-of-interest statute's validating mechanisms is that it removes the transaction from any further scrutiny. That is, the requirements within the validating mechanisms of the statute that are relied on become the exclusive focus of any judicial attack. Thus, once the court is satisfied that the shareholders have independently and in good faith approved a self-dealing transaction after full disclosure of all material facts, the inquiry is closed.[214] Under this view, proof of the transaction's overall unfairness is pushed aside by deference to the will of the independent approving body acting in good faith. Such a perspective appears to comport with a sound view of the role of the reviewing court. A court should avoid second-guessing the diligent and fair deliberations of the independent stockholders or directors. However, there is ample authority to the contrary. Courts have been much influenced in this area by a leading conflict-of-interest case, *Remillard Brick Co. v. Remillard-Dandini Company*,[215] which held that bare technical compliance with the validating provisions of the California conflict-of-interest statute did not remove the transaction from having to be inherently fair to the corporation. *Remillard Brick Co.* has been consistently relied on as standing for the proposition that good faith impartial approval after full disclosure does not obviate the need for the transaction to also be fair to the corporation. While this view is consistent with the *language* used by *Remillard Brick Co.*, the facts of the case are considerably narrower: the defendants held proxies for most of the voting shares of the company and voted those shares in approval of an arrangement that would allow the defendants to divert much of the company's sales to themselves. The court could easily have found that the approval expressed by the defendants was not granted in "good faith," as expressly required by the statute. Instead, the court assumed the statute was complied with, albeit technically, and proceeded to add its own veneer by requiring that the transaction be fair. Ever since *Remillard Brick Co.*, there has been a good deal of confusion as to the substantive effects of satisfying a conflict-of-interest statute's provisions pertaining to impartial director or shareholder approval. If the statute is not satisfied, there will be an action for rescission or damages. Whether approving non-interested directors would be liable will largely depend on whether they can invoke the protections of an immunity shield.[216]

---

[211] *See, e.g.*, Palumbo v. Deposit Bank, 758 F.2d 113 (3d Cir. 1985); Cohen v. Ayers, 596 F.2d 733 (7th Cir. 1979); Rosenfield v. Metals Selling Corp., 643 A.2d 1253 (Conn. 1994).

[212] *See, e.g.*, Melrose v. Capitol City Motor Lodge, Inc., 705 N.E.2d 985 (Ind. 1998).

[213] *See, e.g.*, Pittsburgh Terminal Corp. v. Baltimore & Ohio R.R. Co., 875 F.2d 549 (6th Cir. 1989); Byelick v. Vivadelli, 79 F. Supp. 2d 610 (E.D. Va. 1999).

[214] *See* Camden v. Kaufman, 613 N.W.2d 335 (Mich. Ct. App. 2000).

[215] Remillard Brick Co. v. Remillard-Dandini Company, 241 P.2d 66 (Cal. Ct. App. 1952).

[216] *See, e.g.*, In re Primedia, Inc. Shareholders Litig., 67 A.3d 455 (Del. Ch. 2013) (liability would arise if the approval arose to breach of duty of loyalty of type beyond immunity shield but not for lesser misconduct of gross negligence).

Loans to Officers and Directors: Sarbanes-Oxley Act of 2002. In 2002, Congress made a historic and significant entry into the historically exclusive state domain of corporate law by enacting section 402 of the Sarbanes-Oxley Act. This provision proscribes the extension of credit "in the form of personal loans" by reporting companies making loans to their executive officers or directors.[217] Generally, personal loans do not reach advances made to further the company's business. And overall "personal loans" can be understood to be a narrower class of transactions than the extension of credit so that many items that are advancements are likely not reached, such as travel advances for reimbursable expenses since such expenses were incurred in furtherance of the firm's business. We might also see that advances of litigation costs are not prohibited since they reflect costs incurred in connection with company service.[218]

§ 10.13   The Power of the Shareholders to Ratify

A fundamental principle of corporate law is that waste, gifts, fraud, and ultra vires acts cannot be approved by a mere majority vote; unanimity is the only means to ratify waste.[219] The presence of waste thus is a major qualification of the fundamental principle of majority rule within the corporation. The analogy to constitutional law is apt in such a case. Just as the Bill of Rights protects the minority from the tyranny or misdirection of the mob, so it is that a requirement of unanimity protects the minority from opportunism or improvidence sought by the majority.[220] It is just such thinking that qualifies the operation of conflict-of-interest statutes, discussed in the preceding section, where the statute's bare language would appear to authorize informed stockholder ratification as a means for validating a self-dealing transactions. As seen there, the effect of such approval is merely to restore the presumption of the business judgment rule so that the transaction can still be subject for challenge on the grounds of waste. Placing the burden on the minority in such a case overcomes concern for the tyranny of the minority.[221]

A heuristic the courts sometimes use in determining what conduct may not be ratified by the majority is whether the complaint implicates the directors' or officers' duty of care or does it raise the specter of a duty of loyalty violation. The approval of an informed majority extinguishes the shareholder's duty of care claim.[222] This result would appear best understood if limited to questions of the process the directors or officers pursued in their consideration and approval of the transaction. Majority approval should not, however, prevent the plaintiff from the option of his bearing the substantial burden

---

[217] 15 U.S.C. §§ 7291 et seq., amending Securities Exchange Act, section 13(k), 15 U.S.C. § 78m(k) (operative language focuses on "to extend or maintain credit, to arrange for the extension of credit, or to renew an extension of credit, in the form of a personal loan to or for any director or executive officer . . ." subject to certain enumerated exceptions for banking institutions as part of their normal business).

[218] *See* Sarbanes-Oxley § 402—Interpretation Issued by 25 Law Firms (Oct. 15, 2002) *available at* http://content.lawyerlinks.com/sec/directors_officers/pdfs/soxact_402_25_firm_mailing.pdf.

[219] *See* Michelson v. Duncan, 407 A.2d 211, 219 (Del. 1979).

[220] *See* Melvin A. Eisenberg, The Structure of the Corporation: A Legal Analysis 392–5 (1976).

[221] For the contrary view, namely, that informed majority ratification should remove the transaction from any further scrutiny, *see* Mary A. Jacobson, Interested Director Transactions and the (Equivocal) Effects of Shareholder Ratification, 21 Del. J. Corp. L. 981, 1021 (1996).

[222] *See, e.g.,* In re Wheelabrator Technologies, Inc. Shareholder Litigation, 663 A.2d 1194 (Del. Ch. 1995) (plaintiff can continue to pursue duty of loyalty claim).

of proof that the transaction is so one-sided as to constitute waste.[223] That is, following shareholder approval with full disclosure, even though there arises a presumption of the business judgment, it can be rebutted by proof that the transaction is so far from the norm as to be unconscionable, fraudulent or waste.[224] When the wasteful transaction is approved by all the stockholders and accompanied by full disclosure, any claim the corporation may have had for the misconduct is released.[225]

To be valid, ratification must be after full disclosure of all material facts.[226] If shares owned or controlled by the interested party are needed to satisfy the majority approval, the better view is that the transaction should be proven to be fair to the corporation.[227] However, absent a fraud on creditors the sole stockholder's approval of her one-sided self-dealing transactions prevented the company's bankruptcy trustee from later seeking to recover for the damages the corporation suffered on the earlier transactions.[228] A purported ratification should not take the form of a blanket or whitewash resolution of approval of everything done by the directors for the past year or more, given by proxies solicited by the management of the corporation for the occasion. The Delaware Supreme Court in *Gantler v. Stephens*[229] held that ratification does not occur by a vote to approve a transaction for which shareholder approval is required by the corporate statute; thus, when the transaction, for example a merger with another company, requires shareholder approval, that approval cannot double as ratification of misconduct by the company's officers in connection with the merger. To be effective ratification, there must be a separate vote approving the conduct of the officer after full disclosure of all relevant facts.

An important distinction exists between the power of a majority of the shareholders to ratify a transaction between the corporation and its director and their power to ratify breaches of the directors' duty of loyalty. Approval by a majority of the shareholders after full disclosure of all the facts of the transaction should not also be viewed as their ratification of any misconduct that occurred in connection with that transaction unless the resolution and accompanying disclosures clearly call for the shareholders to ratify any director's misconduct.[230] When shareholder approval is so expressly sought, and there has been full disclosure of the self-dealing and the surrounding facts, the

---

[223] The one instance where stockholder ratification should itself immunize the challenged conduct is in the instance of a claim the directors lacked authority to take action that was later ratified. *See* Gantler v. Stephens, 965 A.2d 695, 713 n. 54 (Del. 2009).

[224] Seidman v. Clifton Sav. Bank, S.L.A., 205 N.J. 150, 14 A.3d 36 (N.J. 2011).

[225] In re Mi-Lor Corp., 348 F.3d 294 (1st Cir. 2003).

[226] Robert A. Wachsler, Inc. v. Florafax Int'l, Inc., 778 F.2d 547 (10th Cir. 1985) (Delaware conflict-of-interest statute requires vote or acquiescence by majority shareholders after full disclosure); Gantler v. Stephens, 965 A.2d 695, 712 (Del. 2009) (failure to disclose material facts robs vote of essential predicate to apply doctrine of ratification).

[227] *See* Stevens ex rel. Park View Corp. v. Richardson, 755 P.2d 389, 395 (Alaska 1988); Fliegler v. Lawrence, 361 A.2d 218 (Del. 1976).

[228] *See* Dannen v. Scafidi, 393 N.E.2d 1246 (Ill. Ct. App. 1979).

[229] 965 A.2d 695 (Del. 2009).

[230] *See* Gantler v. Stephens, 965 A.2d 695, 713 (Del. 2009) (holding that the doctrine of shareholder ratification "must be limited to its 'classic' form; that is, to circumstances where a fully informed shareholder vote approves director action that does *not* legally require shareholder approval in order to become effective. Moreover, the only director action or conduct that can be ratified is that which the shareholders are specifically asked to approve.") (emphasis original).

ratification of the majority can easily be seen as their determination that the corporate interest is not advanced by pursuing an action against the officers or directors.[231]

§ 10.14 Actions Against Directors and Officers for Mismanagement: Corporate, Individual, and Creditor Grounds to Complain

When directors or officers are guilty of mismanagement or negligence in conducting corporate affairs, the right of action is primarily in the corporation or, in the case of insolvency, in the corporation's receiver or trustee in bankruptcy.[232] It is generally held that the corporation or its receiver may sue the delinquent officers to avoid multiplicity of suits against several officers and to do complete justice in one proceeding.[233] Creditors cannot sue individually for any loss suffered as a consequence of a director's or officer's breach of a duty to the corporation.[234] Individual shareholders cannot sue in their own right for impairment of the value of their shares by mismanagement of directors, but under certain conditions they may sue in a derivative or shareholders' suit for the benefit of the corporation, making the corporation and the guilty officers parties-defendants.[235]

To permit shareholders to sue separately for impairment of the value of their shares by wrongs done to the corporation would ordinarily result in confusion and wasteful multiplicity of actions and, further, would not protect the prior rights of creditors to corporate assets. Directors are liable to those who are injured by the directors' own tortious conduct regardless of whether the corporation is also liable.[236]

It is broadly recognized that the directors of a financially healthy corporation owe their fiduciary obligations to the corporation and its shareholders;[237] creditors' rights are accordingly limited to the fair construction of a creditor's contract with the corporation.

The suggestion has been made that directors do owe a fiduciary duty to creditors when the corporation is insolvent or is approaching insolvency.[238] In 1991, this suggestion was given greater attention by Chancellor Allen in *Credit Lyonnais Bank Nederland, N.V. v. Pathe Communications Corporation*,[239] involving a question of whether the board of directors of a corporation in financial distress acted properly in rejecting pressure from its controlling shareholder to engage in certain asset sales. In upholding the directors' actions, the Chancellor reasoned:

---

[231] *See* Berkwitz v. Humphrey, 163 F.Supp. 78 (N.D. Ohio 1958).

[232] *See, e.g.,* Ross v. Bernhard, 396 U.S. 531, 534–535 (1970); Speer v. Dighton Grain, Inc., 624 P.2d 952 (Kan. 1981) (creditors of insolvent corporation may not sue directors and officers for mismanagement of corporate affairs; right reserved for corporation itself).

[233] Meyers v. Moody, 693 F.2d 1196 (5th Cir. 1982); Baker v. Allen, 197 N.E. 521, 524 (Mass. 1935).

[234] Speer v. Dighton Grain, Inc., 624 P.2d 952 (Kan. 1981).

[235] Shareholder litigation is discussed in Chapter 15. For the distinction between direct or class and derivative suits.

[236] *See* Frances T. v. Village Green Owners Ass'n, 229 Cal.Rptr. 456, 723 P.2d 573 (1986) (directors of nonprofit corporation who have met minimum standard of care owed to corporation are not protected by business judgment rule from liability to third parties if directors have engaged in tortious conduct).

[237] *See, e.g.,* Simons v. Cogan, 549 A.2d 300 (Del. 1988).

[238] *See, e.g.,* Rapids Constr. Co. v. Malone, 139 F.3d 892 (4th Cir. 1998) (shareholders of financially shaky corporation breached fiduciary duty to creditors when they caused corporation to engage in stock repurchase; applying Virginia law).

[239] Credit Lyonnais Bank Nederland, N.V. v. Pathe Communications Corporation, 1991 WL 277613 (Del. Ch. 1991).

At least where a corporation is operating in the vicinity of insolvency, a board of directors is not merely the agent of the residual risk bearers, but owes its duty to the corporate enterprise. . . . [T]he board . . . had an obligation to the community of interest that sustained the corporation, to exercise judgment in an informed, good faith effort to maximize the corporation's long-term wealth creating capacity.[240]

In *Credit Lyonnais* the Chancellor could have easily premised his decision on a finding that an elaborate corporate governance contract entered into between the controlling shareholder and the corporation's major lender would have been violated had the board of directors acceded to the wishes of its controlling stockholder. Subsequently, however, the Delaware Supreme Court in *North American Catholic Educational Programming Fdn., Inc. v. Gheewalla,*[241] held that creditors do not have a *direct* action based on a claim of fiduciary obligation when the company is in the "zone of insolvency" or, for that matter, insolvent. The court reasoned that creditors did not need additional protection; creditors customarily enjoy an array of protections of their claims such as covenants, fraudulent conveyance law, doctrines of good faith and fair dealing, bankruptcy law, commercial law and multiple other creditors' rights. This is not to suggest that creditors cannot recover against the directors. *Quadrant Structured Products Co., Ltd. v. Vertin*[242] provided the following summary of the state of Delaware law on the rights of creditors against directors:

i)   Directors owe a fiduciary duty to creditors only once a corporation is actually insolvent;

ii)   Creditors may only bring a derivative claims to enforce the directors' fiduciary duties;

iii)   Directors do not owe any particular duties to creditors as their duty runs to the corporation for the benefit of all of its residual claimants that include the creditors of the insolvent firm;

iv)   Directors acting within their business judgment, can "favor certain non-insider creditors over others of similar priority;"

v)   Directors' ownership of stock alone does not give rise to a conflict of interest; and

vi)   The theory of deepening insolvency (where directors are alleged to breach their fiduciary duty by continuing to operate the firm with the consequence of increasing the losses to creditors) is rejected.

Quandrant Structured Products ultimately held that creditors do not lose standing to bring the suit if their suit is initiated when the firm is insolvent but subsequently becomes solvent. Moreover, the court rejected the directors' argument that the creditors must establish that not only that the firm was insolvent but "irretrievable insolvent" meaning the corporation has no reasonable prospect of returning to solvency. The court held the creditors have standing to sue upon proving the traditional "balance sheet" test

---

[240] Credit Lyonnais Bank Nederland, N.V. v. Pathe Communications Corporation, 1991 WL 277613 at 226 (Del. Ch. 1991). For well-reasoned arguments in support of the Chancellor's view that directors of a bankrupt or near-bankrupt company owe creditors a fiduciary obligation, *see* Steven L. Schwartz, Rethinking a Corporation's Obligations to Creditors, 17 Cardozo L. Rev. 647 (1996).

[241] North American Catholic Educational Programming Fdn., Inc. v. Gheewalla, 930 A.2d 92 (Del. 2007).

[242] 115 A.3d 535 (Del.Ch. 2015).

of insolvency. In dicta, the Vice Chancellor suggested some flexibility with the balance sheet test, suggesting use of reasonable market values as contrasted with historical cost.

The cases in which creditors have successfully invoked fiduciary obligations owed to them arise in closely held corporations where the directors or those in control of the corporation have been engaged in self-dealing.[243] More specifically, the cases are a variety of fraud on creditors that arises in distinct types of transactions:

> [T]he courts seem to have adopted the narrow version of directors' obligations. All of the decisions in which the courts have allowed creditors to recover for breach of fiduciary duty have involved directors of an insolvent corporation diverting corporate assets for the benefit of insiders or preferred creditors. These cases fall into five general categories: (1) withdrawing assets from the insolvent corporation as alleged payment of claims that the directors had against the corporation, such as loans to the company or unpaid commissions; (2) using corporate funds to pay off the company's loans that the directors had personally guaranteed; (3) engaging in transactions, usually without fair consideration to the company, for the benefit of its parent corporation or related entities; (4) pocketing the proceeds of a sale of all corporate assets to a third party or otherwise transferring property to a related entity, leaving the former corporation insolvent; and (5) other forms of self-dealing in which the directors use assets of the insolvent firm for their own benefit, such as pledging stock owned by the corporation as collateral to finance the directors' personal stock purchases.[244]

The major advantage to creditors of pursuing the directors on the theory that they have breached a fiduciary obligation owed to creditors is that the creditors can potentially recover a greater amount than can be recovered under the more traditional fraudulent-conveyance or preferential-transfer claim, where only the amount of the transfer can be recovered.

§ 10.15 Disclosure Obligations Based upon Fiduciary Principles

A rapidly developing area of fiduciary responsibility is the disclosure duty owed shareholders by directors, officers, and controlling shareholders.[245] Though there has long been a developed body of state law pertaining to directors' and officers' disclosure obligations when trading in their company's shares on the basis of material non-public confidential corporate information, only recently has there been the recognition of broader disclosure obligations for company fiduciaries. In the seminal case, *Lynch v. Vickers Energy Corp.*,[246] the Delaware Supreme Court held that directors owe shareholders a duty of "complete candor," so that the objective was "completeness and not adequacy."[247] From this broad language, Delaware courts have imposed a duty of full

---

[243] Rapids Constr. Co. v. Malone, 139 F.3d 892 (4th Cir. 1998) (repurchase of shares breached fiduciary duty to creditors; applying Virginia law).

[244] Laura Lin, Shift of Fiduciary Duty Upon Corporate Insolvency: Proper Scope of Directors' Duty to Creditors, 46 Vand. L. Rev. 1485, 1513–1518 (1993).

[245] *See generally* Jill Z. Barclift, Senior Corporate Officers and the Duty of Candor: Do the CEO and CFO Have a Duty to Inform, 41 Val. U. L. Rev. 269 (2006); Lawrence A. Hamermesh, Calling Off the *Lynch* Mob: The Corporate Director's Fiduciary Disclosure Duty, 49 Vand. L. Rev. 1087 (1996).

[246] Lynch v. Vickers Energy Corp., 383 A.2d 278 (Del. 1977).

[247] Lynch v. Vickers Energy Corp., 383 A.2d 278, 281 (Del. 1977).

disclosure on directors[248] and controlling shareholders.[249] Courts outside of Delaware also impose a duty of candor in a variety of settings.[250]

Materiality of any alleged misrepresentation is judged by the same standards as apply under the federal securities laws.[251] Materiality is sometimes confused with duty in these cases. There are many items that the reasonable stockholder would consider important; but whether such an item must be disclosed turns on the context. Thus, the relative certainty of a third-party bid to acquire a firm can justify imposing a disclosure obligation to stockholders considering a buyback offer.[252] The duty is most readily applied when shareholder approval has been sought through proxy materials that omit or misstate material facts.[253] The duty to disclose applies to information within the fiduciary's control or possession; it does not require, even in transactions requiring stockholder approval, to disclose either information that does not exist or which could have been created.[254]

Directors who breach the duty are liable for damages that the shareholders suffer as a consequence of their breach, even though they did not benefit personally because of their omission or misstatement.[255] However, a breach of a disclosure duty does not automatically result in damages or for that matter even nominal damages; according to the Delaware Supreme Court damages to be recovered must be "logically and reasonably related to the harm or injury for which compensation is being awarded."[256] Because so often material disclosure violations pose irreparable harm to the shareholders, the much preferred remedy is remediation through an appropriate equitable remedy such as a preliminary injunction.[257] By far the most significant expansion of *Lynch* was made in *Malone v. Brincat*,[258] which held that directors and officers breached their duty of candor by knowingly releasing false financial information regarding the company's performance and financial position. The significance of *Malone* is that the court expressly held that *Lynch*'s duty of candor applied even when shareholders were not being asked to vote or otherwise approve a matter.

A further expansion of the disclosure obligations under state law occurred in *Rossdeutscher v. Viacom, Inc.*[259] The plaintiffs successfully pled a breach of the Viacom directors' disclosure obligations by charging they had released false financial data for

---

[248] *See, e.g.*, Arnold v. Society for Savings Bancorp, Inc., 650 A.2d 1270 (Del. 1994).

[249] *See, e.g.*, Weinberger v. UOP, Inc., 457 A.2d 701, 711–12 (Del. 1983).

[250] *See, e.g.*, Kennedy v. VenRock Associates, 348 F.3d 584 (7th Cir. 2003) (applying Maryland law to conclude reincorporation for which there was full disclosure of material differences in laws of Maryland and new domicile, Delaware).

[251] *See, e.g.*, Zirn v. VLI Corp., 621 A.2d 773, 779 (Del. 1993).

[252] *Compare* Bershad v. Curtiss-Wright Corp., 535 A.2d 840 (Del. 1987) (no disclosure breach where firm not for sale and no third-party offer was ever made); *with* Alessi v. Beracha, 849 A.2d 939 (Del. Ch. 2004) (duty breached where firm for sale and discussions with third party were on-going when shareholders accepted offer of their company to repurchase their shares).

[253] Lacos Land Co. v. Arden Group, Inc., 517 A.2d 271 (Del. Ch. 1986).

[254] In re JCC Holding Co., Inc. Shareholder Litig., 843 A.2d 713 (Del. Ch. 2003) (rejecting argument that directors should have performed a discounted cash flow analysis and made that information available when seeking stockholder approval for a merger).

[255] Zirn v. VLI Corp., 621 A.2d 773 (Del. 1993), *aff'd*, 681 A.2d 1050 (Del. 1996).

[256] In re J.P. Morgan Chase & Co. Shareholder Litig., 906 A.2d 766, 773 (Del. 2006).

[257] *See, e.g.*, In re Transkaryotic Therapies, Inc., 954 A.2d 346, 362 (Del. Ch. 2008).

[258] Malone v. Brincat, 722 A.2d 5 (Del. 1998).

[259] Rossdeutscher v. Viacom, Inc., 768 A.2d 8 (Del. 2001).

the purpose of inflating Viacom's price to the disadvantage of its merger partner, Paramount. Of significance in *Rossdeutscher* was that the plaintiffs were not stockholders in Viacom, but of the merger partner, so that disclosure violation could not be based upon a pre-existing fiduciary relationship. Instead, the duty the court imposed upon the Viacom directors was premised on an implied contract of good faith and fair dealing.

Lynch and its progeny are not without limits. Since the duty of candor is a component of the officers', directors', and dominant stockholders' fiduciary obligation its scope is limited to those to whom there is a fiduciary relationship.[260] Another possible restriction may arise where the unlawful conduct is a matter that historically was regulated by federal securities laws, and not state fiduciary law. Thus, complaints alleging manipulation of securities prices via short selling were dismissed on the ground that market manipulation is beyond the purview of state fiduciary law.[261] The Delaware Chancery Court narrowly construed *Malone* to apply only to shareholders whose injury was not accompanied by a purchase or sale. Thus, the court dismissed an action where the class members exchanged their old shares for new shares in a transaction allegedly tainted by fraudulent representations.[262]

---

[260] Alexandra Global Master Fund, Ltd. v. Ikon Office Solutions, Inc., 2007 WL 2077153 (S.D.N.Y. 2007) (no duty owed to holder of convertible notes to disclose secret intent to redeem the notes shortly after their issuance).

[261] *See* RGC International Investors, LDC v. Greka Energy Corp., 2001 WL 984689 (Del. Ch. 2001).

[262] *See* Derdiger v. Tallman, 773 A.2d 1005 (Del. Ch. 2000) (the case also involved an on-going class action in the federal courts by another set of plaintiffs).

Chapter 11

FIDUCIARY DUTIES FOR EXECUTIVE COMPENSATION, CORPORATE OPPORTUNITIES, AND CONTROLLING STOCKHOLDERS

Table of Sections

PART A.   EXECUTIVE COMPENSATION

§ 11.1   Contracts for Compensation of Directors and Officers

No matter is more delicate or important in a corporation, whether it be closely held or publicly held, than the compensation arrangement between the corporation and its executives. A well-designed and thoughtful compensation arrangement provides incentives for managers to reduce the agency costs that are inherent in a public corporation, and in a close corporation it serves as a significant component of how the stockholders will divide the company's cash flows among themselves. Just as there are perplexing planning problems concerning how best to provide rewards and incentives to managers,[1] there are equally challenging jurisprudential questions of the proper role of the courts when asked to judge the propriety of a particular compensation arrangement.[2]

Courts traditionally have been reluctant to imply contracts for director compensation. It has long been a presumption at common law that directors serve without pay. They cannot recover on an implied contract for the reasonable value of their services because both custom and their fiduciary relationship repel any implication that official services are to be paid for.[3] This presumption also applies to executive officers such as president, vice president, secretary, and treasurer, who are not entitled to recover compensation for performing the ordinary duties of their office as directors in the absence of an express agreement.[4] Similarly, no claim will lie in an action for quantum meruit.[5]

In the absence of a statute[6] or a delegation of authority, the fees for compensation of the directors for their ordinary duties must be fixed by the shareholders or by a provision in the bylaws.[7] However, the clear statutory trend is to authorize the board of directors to set the compensation for directors.[8] Even where no statutory authority exists, the charter or the shareholders frequently authorize directors to fix their own fees or salaries[9] and, as such, the presumptions of the business judgment rule apply to even sizable awards to the directors.[10] Substantial fees are frequently provided for attendance at directors' meetings or at meetings of committees of the board of large corporations.

Typically, the compensation of officers is established yearly by a resolution of the board of directors, although it is not uncommon for executive compensation to be set forth in the bylaws[11] or approved by the stockholders. When a person is selected to be an officer or employee under circumstances indicating an expectation of payment but without any express contract, the law will imply a promise on the part of the corporation

---

[1]   See Subcommittee on Executive Compensation of the ABA Section on Corporation, Banking and Business Law, Executive Compensation: A 1987 Road Map for the Corporate Advisor, 43 Bus. Law. 185 (1987). See also Report of the National Association of Corporate Directors Blue Ribbon Commission on Director Compensation 12 (1995) (recommending that the board establish a substantial target of stock ownership for directors and that director fees be paid in stock or cash; also, the report expresses the view that benefits such as pension and health plans are likely to make directors less independent because they are more like employees who seek longevity).

[2]   See Detlev F. Vagts, Challenges to Executive Compensation: For the Markets or the Courts?, 8 J. Corp. L. 231 (1983).

[3]   Corinne Mill, Canal & Stock Co. v. Toponce, 152 U.S. 405 (1894); Vernars v. Young, 539 F.2d 966 (3d Cir. 1976).

[4]   Savage v. Lorraine Corp., 217 F.2d 378 (9th Cir. 1954) (director-president).

[5]   Air Traffic & Serv. Corp. v. Fay, 196 F.2d 40 (D.C. Cir. 1952).

[6]   See McDonald v. Sealift Terminals, Inc., 505 So.2d 675 (Fla. Ct. App. 1987).

[7]   "It is almost universally held that directors acting as such at their meetings, have no power to vote themselves salaries or compensation for their services, either before or after such services have been rendered." Palmer v. Scheftel, 170 N.Y.S. 588, 590 (N.Y. App. Div. 1918).

[8]   Former Model Bus. Corp. Act § 4(k) (1969) (officers and agents); id. § 35 ("The board of directors shall have the authority to fix the compensation of directors unless otherwise provided in the articles of incorporation."). Accord, Model Bus. Corp. Act §§ 3.02(11), 8.11 (2008) (hereinafter MBCA).

[9]   National Oil Co. v. Reeves, 310 S.W.2d 242 (Ark. 1958); Godley v. Crandall & Godley Co., 105 N.E. 818 (N.Y. 1914).

[10]   See, e.g., In re 3Com Corp. Shareholders Litigation, 1999 WL 1009210 (Del. Ch. 1999) (no waste plead for stockholder approved plan whereby each director received options valued at $650,000 pursuant to stockholder approved plan).

[11]   In Schraft v. Leis, 686 P.2d 865 (Kan. 1984), bylaws required officers' salaries to be approved by the board of directors but court held that agreement between sole owners of company as to salary constituted implied ratification of establishing salaries in manner not authorized in bylaws.

to pay a reasonable compensation.[12] It has long been recognized that officers involved in the active management of the company are entitled to reasonable compensation for services as managers even if no compensation had been previously fixed, because such onerous managerial services could not be expected to be performed for nothing.[13]

By the great weight of authority, the presumption against an implied contract of compensation for the directors and officers of a corporation does not apply to unusual or extraordinary services—that is, services that are not properly incidental to their office and are rendered outside of their regular duties. If directors or other officers perform such services at the request of the board of directors with the understanding that they are to be paid for, the law will, in the absence of any special agreement, imply a promise to pay what they are reasonably worth.[14] Thus the president of a company who acted as the general contractor for the construction of an office building was not entitled to be compensated additionally for the services he rendered as the general contractor where the costs of constructing the building exceeded the funds available and he took on the additional responsibilities to cut costs. Furthermore, the president had not been asked by the stockholders to assume the role of general contractor.[15]

It is well engrained in the law of agency that an agent may be required to forfeit compensation received when the agent in the performance of his duties has breached his fiduciary obligations.[16] Significantly, section 304 of the Sarbanes-Oxley Act provides that if a SEC reporting company makes an earnings restatement as a result of earlier "misconduct" in connection with financial reporting, the company's CEO and CFO must disgorge to the issuer any bonus or other incentive compensation received from the issuer during the 12-month period following the first public release of the financial reports that were later restated. There is no private cause of action under section 304; the SEC enjoys sole right to pursue recoveries under the provision.[17] Courts have consistently held that recoveries under section 304 do not require the SEC to establish that the CEO or CFO was responsible or otherwise implicated in the misconduct that ultimately gave rise to the restatement.[18]

§ 11.2 Methods of Paying Executive Compensation

Traditionally, there have been three basic ways of compensating the corporate executive: (1) salary, (2) bonuses, and (3) a pension or other deferred compensation. As a result of increased sophistication in planning, the variations of the three basic forms of compensation defy exhaustive categorization.[19] The growing use of compensation "packages" arises out of a desire to attract and hold top-flight personnel, provide them with incentives for greater effort and dedication, and fully utilize tax advantages offered

---

[12]   Rocky Mtn. Powder Co. v. Hamlin, 310 P.2d 404 (Nev. 1957) (sales manager not a director or officer).

[13]   Bellehurst Syndicate v. Commissioner, 83 F.2d 801, 803 (9th Cir. 1936).

[14]   Neidert v. Neidert, 637 S.W.2d 296 (Mo. Ct. App. 1982); Rocky Mtn. Powder Co. v. Hamlin, 310 P.2d 404 (Nev. 1957).

[15]   Roach v. Bynum, 403 So.2d 187 (Ala. 1981).

[16]   *See* ALI Restatement (Third) of Agency § 8.01 comment d(2). *See generally* Manning Gilbert Warren III, Equitable Clawback: An Essay On Restoration Of Executive Compensation, 12 U. Penn. J. Bus. L. 1135 (2010)(reviewing recent cases applying the doctrine).

[17]   *See, e.g.,* In re Digimarc Corp. Derivative Litigation, 594 F.3d 1223 (9th Cir. 2008).

[18]   *See, e.g.,* SEC v. Jenkins, 718 F. Supp.2d 1070 (D. Ariz. 2010).

[19]   *See* Lucian A. Bebchuk & Robert J. Jackson, Jr., Executive Pensions, 30 J. Corp. L. 823 (2005) (closely examining various pension practices with a view that pensions add to the performance insensitivity of total executive compensation).

by some forms of compensation. Tailoring the most advantageous compensation plan requires careful consideration of the securities law, tax consequences,[20] and the Federal Employment Retirement Income Security Act (ERISA).[21] There is a widespread use in publicly held corporations, and in the large close corporations for that matter, of various kinds of contingent or deferred compensation[22]—cash bonuses, stock bonuses, stock options, stock purchase plans, profit-sharing plans, pension programs, allowances to surviving spouses and dependents, medical and dental payment plans, and other kinds of employee benefits.[23]

Stock options are a highly popular form of executive compensation in the United States.[24] The granting of stock options does not require a present expenditure of corporate funds, which may be badly needed for business operations or for expansion. Executives find stock options attractive because of their speculative appeal in offering a chance for really large financial gain. Further, under some circumstances, stock options carry substantial tax advantages for executives.[25] When the options are exercised, the proportionate interests of existing shareholders in the company will be diluted, but presumably by that time the employees exercising the options will have proved their worth and have benefitted the shareholders by contributing to an increase in the value of the corporation's shares.

A deferred compensation unit plan ("phantom stock" plan) is sometimes used as an alternative to or in addition to traditional pension arrangements for executive employees. Under a phantom stock plan, the company, instead of requiring the employee to buy stock or giving the employee stock in the company, pays the employee additional annual compensation or gives credit toward retirement benefits equal to dividends paid on a share of the company's stock multiplied by the number of units the employee holds in the plan, and on retirement the employee gets deferred compensation based on the increase, if any, in the market value of the company's stock during the time the employee has held units in the plan.

Restricted stock plans have become more common in recent years. Under this arrangement, stock or units are actually issued to the employee, but subject to conditions related to vesting, transferability and even forfeiture conditions. Lifting of the conditions

---

[20] *See, e.g.,* Susan J. Stabile, Is There a Role of Tax Law in Policing Executive Compensation?, 72 St. John's L. Rev. 81 (1998).

[21] Pub. L. No. 93–406, 88 Stat. 829 (1974).

[22] For the view that compensation based on longer-term performance yields positive benefits to the corporation, *see* John F. Boschen & Kimberly J. Smith, You Can Pay Me Now and You Can Pay Me Later: The Dynamic Response of Executive Compensation to Firm Performance, 68 J. Bus. L. 577 (1995).

[23] *See generally* Thomas J. St. Ville, Stock Options And Other Equity-Based Compensation Arrangements, BNA Corporate Practice Series No. 75; Steve Balsam, An Introduction to Executive Compensation (2002) (practitioner's guide with rich use of examples); Bruce R. Ellig, The Complete Guide to Executive Compensation (2001) (reviews key developments for past two decades as well as current issues for design of plans). *See also* Nitzan Shilon, Replacing Executive Equity Compensation: The Case for Cash for Long-Term Performance, 43 Del. J. Corp. L. 1 (2018)(reasoning that cash awards linked to clearly defined performance benchmarks is both more efficient and effective).

[24] The average CEO stock option grant increased 700 percent between 1980 and 1994 (rising from $155,000 to $1.2 million). *See* Brian J. Hall, A better way to pay CEOs?, in Executive Compensation and Shareholder Value Theory and Evidence 35 (J. Carpenter & D. Yermack eds. 1999).

[25] Dixon v. Pro Image, Inc., 987 P.2d 48, 57 (Utah 1999) (when stock option provision does not indicate whether parties contemplated registered or unregistered stock, court should not presume that parties contracted for unregistered stock; rather, extrinsic evidence is necessary to ascertain parties' intentions).

Stock options are considered in connection with restrictions on a corporation's issuance of its shares.

are service based but frequently are dependent on certain performance requirements. The shares may even be subject to repurchase requirements at a predetermined price. Restricted stock confer ownership immediately to their holders, such as dividends and voting rights, and the corporation's tax deduction equals the value of the shares when the restrictions lapse. Hence, if the stock appreciates in value between the grant date and the date the restriction lapses, the corporation is able to deduct the value of the shares as of the latter date, not the grant date as is the case with qualified stock options whereas the accounting charge to earnings is based on the value of the granted shares less any payment by the recipient. Hence, subsequent price increases do not penalize the company's reported net income by increasing the compensation costs related to the earlier grant.

§ 11.3   Compensation for Past Services

A decision by the directors to pay a bonus or to increase the compensation of an officer or employee for past services (*i.e.*, for services already rendered) was formerly invalid. Such a payment was regarded as a gift and thus a misapplication of corporate funds.[26] The rule against compensation for past services does not apply, however, where the services were rendered with a formal or informal understanding that the fixed salary was only a minimum compensation and that additional allowances or compensation, although indefinite, would be paid.[27] The compensation in such a case can be seen as not in fact being for past services and the courts accordingly permit the directors to pay additional compensation in the exercise of reasonable discretion after the services have been performed or the contract for fixed compensation has been entered into.[28]

In recent years, with respect to payments based on past services, there has been a significant retreat from formalistic attitudes and movement toward a rule of reasonableness.[29] In some states statutes expressly grant authority to provide bonuses and retroactive pension plans.[30]

§ 11.4   Judicial Review of Fairness of Executive Compensation: Self-Dealing and Good Faith

Most states have enacted conflict-of-interest statutes[31] that are sufficiently broad to include board-of-director action establishing the compensation of one of its members. Close judicial scrutiny customarily occurs when those receiving the compensation are

---

[26]   *See, e.g.*, Hurt v. Cotton States Fertilizer Co., 159 F.2d 52 (5th Cir.), *cert. denied*, 331 U.S. 828 (1947).

[27]   *See, e.g.*, Blish v. Thompson Automatic Arms Corp., 64 A.2d 581, 606–607 (Del. 1948) (exception to retroactive compensation arises when the payment is pursuant to an earlier implied contract or the amount is not unreasonable in view of the services rendered).

[28]   *See, e.g.*, Estate of Bogley v. United States, 514 F.2d 1027 (Ct. Cl. 1975).

[29]   *See* Wolf v. Fried, 373 A.2d 734, 736 (Pa. 1977) (board's judgment that manager was "unique and knowledgeable" and worthy of additional compensation is evidence there was adequate consideration supporting additional pay).

[30]   Wis. Stat. Ann. § 180.0302(12) (West 2002); Va. Code Ann. § 13.1–627(11) (LexisNexis 2006 Replacement). *Cf.* MBCA § 3.02(*l*) (2016) (a corporation has power to "pay pensions and establish pension plans, pension trusts, . . . share bonus plans . . . for any or all of its current or former directors, officers, employees, and agents").

[31]   *See, e.g.*, Giannotti v. Hamway, 387 S.E.2d 725, 731 (Va. 1990) (in absence of showing of fraud or bad faith, presumption of propriety applies).

In some states, shareholder approval is required by statute for specified kinds of compensation such as employee stock option or stock purchase plans. *See* former MBCA § 20 (1969); MBCA § 6.24 (2008).

the same individuals approving the compensation.[32] Conflict-of-interest statutes set forth steps that, if satisfied, invoke the protection of the business judgment rule for executive compensation. In broad overview, the steps require good faith impartial approval by the directors or shareholders after full disclosure of all material facts. Where such a statute does not exist, the courts similarly consider the circumstances of the directors' or stockholders' approval of the interested director's executive compensation.[33] Directors' voting on their own compensation is not protected by the business judgment rule because of the inherent conflict of interest. Thus, for example, even where the directors' exercise of discretion in awarding stock options that are within parameters established by the shareholders, the business judgment rule does not apply.[34]

Sometimes an attempt is made to give the illusion of a disinterested quorum and majority by having the directors vote on compensation for each office separately, with each director abstaining from voting on her own compensation but voting on the compensation of her co-directors. It has generally been held that where the directors have the common object of procuring a salary or a salary increase for each of them as officers, the device of passing a separate resolution for each instead of one joint resolution for all will not be effective to validate the salary increases. The mutual back-scratching or reciprocal voting voids the action as to each.[35] Nonetheless, impartial approval pursuant to procedures that produce evidence the compensation decision is consistent with the corporate interest creates a formidable barrier to upsetting the compensation.[36]

Many companies provide "golden parachutes" for their most senior executives. The large payment in the event of a change in control that the arrangement provides is designed to assure greater neutrality on the part of managers when assessing the merits of an offer from the firm's suitor and to secure their services through the uncertainty created by the bid for control. Because the objective of the golden parachute is upon the officers' conduct before the change in control occurs, it is understandable that the courts have not conditioned the validity of a golden parachute upon any requirement that the manager exercise reasonable efforts to find comparable compensated employment.[37] A further concern for golden parachutes is whether they will be seen as violating the "all holders" and "best price" rules that apply to tender offer involving a company registered

---

[32] *See, e.g.,* Freedman v. Redstone, 753 F.3d 416 (3d Cir. 2014) (board's decision as to executive compensation is entitled to great deference and claims of lack of independence between a director and recipient of compensation is fact-specific but cannot be resolved on general allegations); Morrissey v. Curran, 650 F.2d 1267 (2d Cir. 1981); Espinoza v. Zuckerberg, 124 A.3d 47 (Del. Ch. 2015) (holding business judgment rule not invoked where controlling stockholder executed written consent approving of the compensation that directors' had awarded themselves); Calma on Behalf of Citrix Systems, Inc. v. Templeton, 114 A.3d 563 (Del. Ch. 2015) (entire fairness review standard applied for director's self-awarded compensation when compensation package that was approved by shareholders failed to set forth the compensation that would be received by non-employee directors).

[33] *See, e.g.,* Moran v. Edson, 493 F.2d 400 (3d Cir. 1974).

[34] In re Investors Bancorp, Inc. Stockholder Litigation, 177 A.3d 1208 (Del. 2017). This decision clarified decades of Delaware lower court cases.

[35] Angelus Sec. Corp. v. Ball, 67 P.2d 152 (Cal. Ct. App. 1937).

[36] *Donnawell v. Hamburger,* 803 F.3d 912 (7th Cir. 2015), illustrates the deference courts accord director decisions in setting executive compensation. In 2005 the company adopted a key employee incentive plan that permitted option awards not to exceed 150,000 shares per employee. When the board determined that too many options had been granted the CEO, the board reduced the awards made under the 2005 plan, but increased the overall awards to the CEO by drawing on authority to grant options in a 2003 plan. Judge Posner's opinion upheld the grant as a fair exercise of the authority the board had under both plans.

[37] *See* Royal Crown Companies, Inc. v. McMahon, 359 S.E.2d 379 (Ga. App. 1987); Koenings v. Joseph Schlitz Brewing Co., 377 N.W.2d 593 (Wis. 1985) (viewing payment as a type of liquidated damage).

with the SEC. In essence, courts have reasoned that payments to officers in the context of a takeover may be deemed additional consideration paid for shares that should have also been offered to all the company's stockholders.[38] The cases follow the reasoning of *Epstein v. MCA, Inc.*,[39] that at $21 million payment to an executive to secure his support of a takeover offer *might* be considered as being made during the tender offer, even if agreed to before the tender offer commenced and paid after its conclusion.

No compensation case has attracted as much attention in recent years as has the Disney litigation. The case initially arose from the Disney board's approval of an executive compensation contract with Michael Ovitz and its implied approval of a no-fault termination of Ovitz resulting in his receipt of a sum in excess of $140 million after barely one year of employment. The Chancery Court held, based on facts set forth in the complaint that could not be more egregious, that the plaintiff's complaint withstood the defendant's motion to dismiss.[40] Among the facts alleged were that Ovitz was hired pursuant to pressure from Disney's CEO, Michael Eisner; that Eisner and Ovitz had been close friends for 25 years; that Ovitz had never been an executive for a publicly owned entertainment company; that internal documents had warned that Ovitz was unqualified; that a member of the compensation committee received a $250,000 fee to secure Ovitz's employment with Disney; that neither the compensation committee nor the board had received, or had an opportunity to review, either the draft or final employment contract with Ovitz; that the compensation committee and the board had devoted hardly any time at their meetings to reviewing and approving the employment of Ovitz; that the compensation committee and the board had delegated the details of the transaction to Eisner; that the board did not condition it becoming effective upon their final review or approval; that the final version of the employment contract varied significantly from the drafts earlier summarized for the compensation committee; that from the outset of his employment Ovitz performed poorly; that no experts were consulted at any time in either the employment or termination of Ovitz; that the terms for Orvitz's departure were entered into without express committee or board approval; and, finally, that the severance agreement entered into by Eisner, acting for Disney, awarded Ovitz $140 million for being fired, and did so far more quickly than if he had worked through the entire term of his contract for Disney.

The Delaware Supreme Court's initial engagement with the Ovitz compensation dispute occurred in *Brehm v. Eisner*,[41] affirming a prior dismissal by the Chancery Court for failure to state a claim. In so doing, the Supreme Court provided a roadmap by which the plaintiff could, notwithstanding the board's apparent disinterestedness and reliance on outside experts and subcommittees (both facially permitted under DGCL 141(e)), could successfully allege that the board nonetheless breached its duties approving the original contract and the non-fault termination:

> To survive a Rule 23.1 motion to dismiss in a due care case where an expert has advised the board in its decisionmaking process, the complaint must allege particularized facts (not conclusions) that, if proved, would show, for example, that: (a) the directors did not in fact rely on the expert; (b) their reliance was not in good faith; (c) they did not reasonably believe that the expert's advice

---

[38] *See* Millionerrors Inv. Club v. General Elec. Co., 2000 WL 1288333 (W.D. Pa. 2000).

[39] Epstein v. MCA, Inc., 50 F.3d 644 (9th Cir. 1995).

[40] In re Walt Disney Co. Derivative Litig., 825 A.2d 275 (Del. Ch. 2003).

[41] Brehm v. Eisner, 746 A.2d 244 (Del. 2000).

was within the expert's professional competence; (d) the expert was not selected with reasonable care by or on behalf of the corporation, and the faulty selection process was attributable to the directors; (e) the subject matter (in this case the cost calculation) that was material and reasonably available was so obvious that the board's failure to consider it was grossly negligent regardless of the expert's advice or lack of advice; or (f) that the decision of the Board was so unconscionable as to constitute waste or fraud.

The plaintiffs re-pled their complaint, closely tracking the recipe provided three years before in *Brehm*. The defendants moved to dismiss the complaint, this time arguing that the complaint dealt solely with duty of care issues, and that Disney had an "immunity shield" in its charter, authorized under section 102(b)(7) of the Delaware Code, allowing it to shield directors from all monetary liability associated with a breached duty of care.

Chancellor Chandler, however, refused to grant the motion, noting that by its text, section 102(b)(7) provisions do not "eliminate or limit the liability of a director: (i) [f]or any breach of the director's duty of loyalty to the corporation or its stockholders; (ii) for acts or omissions not in good faith or which involve intentional misconduct or a knowing violation of the law . . . or (iv) for any transaction from which the director derived an improper personal benefit."[42]

Focusing on the second exclusion above, Chandler ruled that since the plaintiff had alleged that the Disney board acted without taking into account the welfare of the company, they were essentially making a pleading that fell within one of the exceptions to § 102(b)(7). In denying Disney's demurer and excusing demand, the Chancellor observed:

> These facts, if true, do more than portray directors who, in a negligent or grossly negligent manner. Instead, the facts . . . suggest that the defendant directors consciously and intentionally disregarded their responsibilities, adopting a "we don't care about the risks" attitude concerning a material corporate decision. Knowing or deliberate indifference by a director to his or her duty to act faithfully and with appropriate care is conduct, in my opinion, that may not have been taken honestly and in good faith to advance the best interests of the company.[43]

After a protracted trial, Chancellor Chandler released his opinion in the late summer of 2005, essentially reaffirming his earlier views of the facts.

> Upon long and careful consideration, I am of the opinion that the concept of intentional dereliction of duty, a conscious disregard for one's responsibilities, is an appropriate (although not the only) standard for determining whether fiduciaries have acted in good faith. Deliberate indifference and inaction in the face of a duty to act is, in my mind, conduct that is clearly disloyal to the corporation. It is the epitome of faithless conduct.[44]

In applying this standard, Chancellor Chandler did something that many observers had found surprising (at least in light of his prior holdings in the case): he held that the

---

[42] In re Walt Disney Co. Derivative Litig., 825 A.2d 275 (Del.Ch. 2003).

[43] In re Walt Disney Co. Derivative Litig., 825 A.2d 275, 289 (Del. Ch. 2003).

[44] In re Walt Disney Co. Derivative Litig., 907 A.2d 693 (Del.Ch. 2005).

Disney defendants would still receive protection from the Business Judgment Rule-that is, they would enjoy a strong presumption that they acted with appropriate care and good faith when acting for the corporation. In applying this standard, Chandler found that while Disney's senior executives, board and compensation committee had failed to set themselves up as exemplar paragons of corporate governance best practices, the plaintiffs had not overcome the business judgment rule and demonstrated a dereliction of duties meeting the "deliberate indifference and inaction" standard. In fact, in at least some specific aspects of the case (such as the allegation involving the board's decision to grant Ovitz a non-fault termination), Chandler held that any alternative decision by the board was legally unsupportable and would have been subject to a legitimate legal claim by Ovitz for damages.

A unanimous Supreme Court of Delaware affirmed.[45] In addressing the issue of good faith, the Court found (as did Chandler) that such a doctrine was independently actionable and distinct from the duty of care. Specifically approving the lower court's formulation of bad faith as stemming from "intentional indifference and inaction" in the face of a duty to act, the Supreme Court added a visual metaphor to animate its conception of bad faith. One involves deliberate and subjective motivation to do harm to the corporation and its shareholders.

On the other end of the spectrum, the Court explored grossly negligent conduct, which historically would have triggered duty of care liability. Although Chandler had not definitively answered whether such conduct would also trigger good faith liability, the Supreme Court answered this with an unambiguous "no." In order to violate one's duty to act in good faith, the majority held, one had to do more than breach a duty of care. Justice Jacobs approved of Chandler's "deliberate indifference and inaction" metric for bad faith, but in so doing concluded that such a formulation was possibly too restrictive:

> [W]e uphold the Court of Chancery's definition as a legally appropriate, although not the exclusive, definition of fiduciary bad faith. We need go no further. To engage in an effort to craft (in the Court's words) "a definitive and categorical definition of the universe of acts that would constitute bad faith" would be unwise and is unnecessary to dispose of the issues presented on this appeal.[46]

Significantly, the Court also upheld Chandler's utilization of the business judgment rule presumption when scrutinizing defendants' alleged bad faith.

The *Disney* opinion and its immediate progeny have placed the debate around executive compensation, as well as the emerging doctrine of good faith, in an especially murky territory. Although it now seems possible to challenge executive pay decisions on the grounds that they were made in bad faith, the task of doing so is complicated in at least three ways. First, defendants retain the protection of the business judgment rule, which effectively precludes all but the strongest cases from going forward. Second, because of the business judgment rule's focus on process, it is likely that corporate defendants may feel invited to erect additional procedural measures to insulate them from future liability claims. And finally, at least recent interpretations of Disney have

---

45   In re Walt Disney Co. Derivative Litig., 906 A.2d 27 (2006).
46   In re Walt Disney Co. Derivative Litig., 906 A.2d 27, 67 (2006).

characterized the good faith doctrine, somewhat curiously, as a flavor of the duty of loyalty.

Executives sometimes negotiate and receive side-payments in connection with the sale of the firm.[47] Because the payment is transaction specific in the sense that it arises by agreement with the acquirer, and does not occur automatically upon a change of control as is the case with golden parachutes, such an arrangement is distinguishable from golden parachutes. A chief concern for such side-payments is whether the recipient fiduciary has deflected to herself some of the premium that otherwise would have been paid to the seller's shareholders. Such a payment obviously raises concerns of self-interested behavior, for which the likely bulwark would be disinterested approval by the board of directors.[48]

§ 11.5 Judicial Review of Executive Compensation: Equitable Limits

Directors have wide business discretion in fixing executive compensation.[49] However, in appropriate cases at the suit of a shareholder attacking executive compensation as excessive, courts will review the fairness and reasonableness of compensation of executives and shareholder-employees.[50] A majority shareholder cannot give away the corporate funds in the guise of compensation as against the interest of a dissenting minority or in fraud of creditors.[51] Similarly, even if there are no injured shareholders or creditors, exorbitant compensation withdrawals by corporate officers may be classified in part as dividends and as an attempt to evade taxes. However, judicial reversal of executive compensation decisions in public corporations is rare.[52] However, the Delaware Court of Chancery recently held that entire fairness scrutiny applies to compensation to interested parties in the context of a controlled corporation.[53] Thus, the court allowed a suit to proceed claiming that Elon Musk's compensation package from Tesla was excessive and could not survive entire fairness scrutiny.[54]

A striking factor among the reported decisions holding that a particular executive compensation arrangement is wasteful or excessive is that they almost universally

---

[47] Calma on Behalf of Citrix Systems, Inc. v. Templeton, 114 A.3d 563 (Del. Ch. 2015); Seinfeld v. Slager, 2012 WL 2501105 (Del. Ch. 2012) (same).

[48] *See* In re El Paso Corp. Shareholder Litigation, 41 A.3d 432 (Del. Ch. 2012) (while acknowledging such payment cast the taint of disloyalty on the merger, the court rejected the request to preliminarily enjoin the merger reasoning that with disclosure of the side payment the shareholders had the option of self-help of voting against the merger). The decision did not, however, address a suit against the recipient based on his self-interested conduct.

[49] *See, e.g.,* Cramer v. General Tel. & Elecs. Corp., 582 F.2d 259 (3d Cir. 1978), *cert. denied,* 439 U.S. 1129 (1979); Klaus v. Hi-Shear Corp., 528 F.2d 225 (9th Cir. 1975).

[50] Galler v. Galler, 316 N.E.2d 114 (Ill. App. Ct. 1974).

[51] *See, e.g.,* Rogers v. Hill, 289 U.S. 582 (1933); Delta Star, Inc. v. Patton, 76 F. Supp. 3d 617 (W.D. Pa. 1999) (president and chairman set salaries, including for himself, without consulting the board of directors); Michelson v. Duncan, 407 A.2d 211 (Del. 1979).

[52] *See generally* Randall S. Thomas & Kenneth J. Martin, Litigating Challenges to Executive Pay: An Exercise in Futility, 79 Wash. U.L.Q. 569 (2001) (reporting findings that plaintiffs do win more often than is commonly understood, and especially with respect to challenges of compensation paid in a close corporation).

[53] Tornetta v. Musk, 2019 WL 4566943 (Del. Ch. 2019).

[54] Tornetta v. Musk, 2019 WL 4566943 (Del. Ch. 2019).

involve close corporations.[55] There are several reasons why public corporations are not represented among the decisions upsetting executive compensation arrangements. The first explanation is procedural. As will be seen later in Chapter 15, a precondition to any successful derivative suit is convincing the court that the plaintiff need not make a demand on the board of directors. It is far more likely that there will be outside directors in the public corporation and that their presence will erect an unsurpassable barrier in the plaintiff's quest to challenge executive compensation. Thus, in a leading derivative suit case,[56] the plaintiff challenged the decision to award its aged controlling stockholder a salary of $100,000 per year regardless of whether he performed any service to the corporation. The derivative suit was dismissed because the plaintiff failed to persuade the court that the company's outside directors lacked sufficient independence to respond impartially to the plaintiff's demand. Thus, in a widely watched matter, the Delaware Supreme Court affirmed the dismissal of a derivative suit challenging a severance package valued at approximately $140 million, which not surprisingly the court viewed as "exceedingly lucrative" compensation.[57] The court strongly embraced the view that the size and structure of executive compensation are inherently matters of the directors' judgment, unless they act "irrationally."[58] Thus, the demand requirement for maintaining a derivative suit poses a significant obstacle to challenge compensation in the public corporation.[59]

A second consideration that reduces the viability of a challenge to executive compensation in public corporations is also related to the presence of outside directors. A major concern is whether the arrangement is protected by the business judgment rule. Courts are loath to substitute their judgment for that of the directors in such matters, particularly if the decision carries the imprimatur of a critical mass of independent directors. To this end, compensation decisions are routinely submitted to the outside directors for their separate approval, and compensation plans involving stock options and special bonus arrangements are more frequently approved by the stockholders. Such independent approvals dampen the derivative suit attorney's interest in trying to convince the court that it should substitute its judgment for that of the outside directors, or perhaps that of the stockholders. As a result, the modern cases setting aside executive compensation arrangements arise in the close corporation setting, where such impartial approval is absent.

The courts have had great difficulty in formulating definitive standards to determine the propriety of the amount of compensation paid corporate executives. Indeed, this is an area where the role of the business judgment rule as essentially a rule of abstention and not a legal standard for determining the appropriate level of form of compensation.[60] One court or another has said that controlling shareholders may not take advantage of their control to vote themselves excessive salaries or to cause excessive

---

[55] *See* Mark J. Lowenstein, Reflections on Executive Compensation and a Modest Proposal for (Further) Reform, 50 SMU L. Rev. 201 (1996) (almost no appellate court decisions reducing executive compensation for public companies).

[56] Aronson v. Lewis, 473 A.2d 805 (Del. 1984).

[57] Brehm v. Eisner, 746 A.2d 244, 265 (Del. 2000).

[58] Brehm v. Eisner, 746 A.2d 244, 263 (Del. 2000).

[59] For a decision dismissing the derivative suit challenging executive compensation for failure to make a demand upon the *stockholders, see* Saigh v. Busch, 396 S.W.2d 9 (Mo. Ct. App. 1965).

[60] *See* D. A. Jeremy Telman, The Business Judgment Rule, Disclosure, and Executive Compensation, 81 Tulane L. Rev. 829, 863–65 (2007) (reasoning that one function of a business judgment being a rule of abstention is that is enables cases to be resolved (dismissed) before confidential information is disclosed).

salaries to be voted to them by directors they control;[61] that directors must act honestly and reasonably in fixing executive compensation;[62] that directors may not "waste" the corporation's assets by granting excessive compensation;[63] that compensation must bear a reasonable relation to the value of the services rendered[64] and to the ability of the corporation to pay;[65] and that courts of equity will review the fairness and reasonableness of compensation.[66]

Whether executive compensation is excessive is a fact question.[67] Courts proffer a variety of tests for judging whether the challenged compensation arrangement should be struck down, using such expressions as "fraud," "bad faith," "oppression," "excessive and unreasonable," or "a waste of corporate assets."[68] Such labels at best communicate a sense that when viewed in its totality the compensation arrangement departs substantially from what one can view as normative. A wide range of factors[69] are weighed by courts reviewing executive compensation: the executive's qualifications,[70] the nature, extent, and scope of the executive's work, the size and complexities of the business, economic conditions of the company, industry, and country, comparison of salaries to those of similarly situated executives[71] as well as to the company's dividends, past compensation of the executive,[72] the time devoted to the job, the success of the company, if any, during the executive's tenure,[73] and whether the Internal Revenue Service has disallowed the salary.

Particularly important in weighing these factors is whether the executive compensation has received the impartial approval of the directors or the stockholders. In an attack on allegedly exorbitant compensation, the scope of review depends on whether the recipient officers or directors have participated in fixing the compensation. Where the person compensated does not fix the compensation and the amount is set by directors without any adverse interest or influence that would prevent the exercise of a

---

[61] *See* Segall v. Shore, 236 S.E.2d 316 (S.C. 1977).

[62] *See also* Barrett v. Smith, 242 N.W. 392, 394 (Minn. 1932) (salaries of corporate officers may be so high as to evidence fraud and oppression of minority).

[63] Brehm v. Eisner, 746 A.2d 244, 263–264 (Del. 2000) (although executive compensation is inherently matter of board's business judgment, directors may not irrationally squander or give away corporate assets).

[64] Security-First Nat'l Bank v. Lutz, 322 F.2d 348, 354 (9th Cir. 1963) (executives entitled to receive as salary for services to corporation what those services reasonably worth).

[65] Glenmore Distilleries Co. v. Seideman, 267 F.Supp. 915 (E.D.N.Y. 1967) (judgment creditor of corporation recovered from shareholder-officers as fraudulent conveyances the amounts of excessive salary payments; court considered corporation's ability to pay as well as value of officer's services); Baker v. Cohn, 42 N.Y.S.2d 159 (Sup. Ct. 1942), *modified*, 40 N.Y.S.2d 623 (App. Div. 1943), *aff'd*, 54 N.E.2d 689 (N.Y. 1944).

[66] Valeant Pharmaceuticals Int'l v. Jerney, 921 A.2d 732 (Del. Ch. 2007) (applying entire fairness standard to require return of a $3 million bonus).

[67] Pacific Grains, Inc. v. Commissioner, 399 F.2d 603 (9th Cir. 1968).

[68] *E.g.*, McQuillen v. National Cash Register Co., 112 F.2d 877, 883 (4th Cir.), *cert. denied*, 311 U.S. 695 (1940).

[69] *See, e.g.*, Wilderman v. Wilderman, 315 A.2d 610 (Del. Ch. 1974).

[70] *See, e.g.*, Neidert v. Neidert, 637 S.W.2d 296 (Mo. Ct. App. 1982).

[71] *See* Murphy v. Washington Am. League Base Ball Club, Inc., 324 F.2d 394 (D.C. Cir. 1963) (salaries found in line with what other baseball companies were paying).

[72] *See* Fendelman v. Fenco Handbag Mfg. Co., 482 S.W.2d 461 (Mo. 1972) (that director-officer received less in first years with company than for previous similar work at another company important in determining that salary not excessive).

[73] Hurt v. Cotton States Fertilizer Co., 159 F.2d 52 (5th Cir.), *cert. denied*, 331 U.S. 828 (1947); Wilderman v. Wilderman, 315 A.2d 610 (Del. Ch. 1974) (listing eight factors including IRS determination of permissible salary deduction).

fair judgment, judicial review is very limited.[74] It is considered outside the proper judicial function to go into the business question of the fairness or reasonableness of the compensation as determined by the board of directors. In contrast, if there is self-dealing because the directors stand to gain from their actions, the business judgment rule is not available, and the burden shifts to those receiving the compensation to show good faith and overall fairness to the corporation.[75]

A major portion of an executive compensation package frequently takes the form of a bonus or profit-sharing arrangement, and today more typically pursuant to stock options. Bonus and profit-sharing arrangements are of various types, such as an individual cash or stock bonus based on a percentage of the company's annual earnings, an employees' stock purchase plan, or an interest in a bonus or management fund in which a number of important executives may share. To afford the managers of large companies as well as other key employees some share of the profits is generally considered a good business policy.[76] Certainly by linking the employee's pay, or at least an important component of it, to future increases in the value of the firm, addresses directly the separation of ownership from management problem. However, equity-based compensation while portending significant rewards to the manager also carries with it great costs to the firm.[77] In some smaller companies, however, an undue share of the income is sometimes paid to the principal owners by way of compensation, and little or nothing is paid in dividends. Even in publicly held companies a substantial percentage of the earnings is frequently paid to the executive group. A fundamental issue is raised as to the real relationship between management and the shareholders of publicly held corporations. Should directors be regarded as fiduciaries, representatives of the owners, or managers of the enterprise for the sole benefit of the shareholders? Or should they be viewed as managing partners, conducting the business partly for themselves as well as for the benefit of the passive and silent partners, the shareholders, who contribute the

---

[74] *See, e.g.*, Freedman v. Redstone, 753 F.3d 416 (3d Cir. 2014) (board's decision as to executive compensation is entitled to great deference and claims of strong friendship between a director and recipient of compensation is fact-specific but cannot be resolved on general allegations of long-term relationship); Cohen v. Ayers, 596 F.2d 733 (7th Cir. 1979).

[75] Seinfeld v. Slager, 2012 WL 2501105 (Del. Ch. 2012)(board awarded each member options with value of $1 million for two years of service).

[76] The rationale behind the managing officers' claim to a share of the profits was well stated in a famous New York case, Gallin v. National City Bank, 273 N.Y.S. 87, 113, 114 (N.Y. Sup. Ct. 1934):

We have long since passed the stage in which stockholders, who merely invest capital and leave it wholly to management to make it fruitful, can make absolutely exclusive claim to all profits against those whose labor, skill, ability, judgment, and effort have made profits available. The reward, however, must have reasonable relation to the value of the services for which it is given and must not be, in whole or in part, a misuse or waste of corporate funds, or a gift to a favored few, or a scheme to distribute profits under a mere *guise* of compensation, but in fact having no relation to services rendered. Rogers v. Hill, 289 U.S. 582, 590 (1933); Godley v. Crandall & Godley Co., 105 N.E. 818 (N.Y. 1914). To come within the rule of reason the compensation must be in proportion to the executive's ability, services and time devoted to the company, difficulties involved, responsibilities assumed, success achieved, amounts under jurisdiction, corporation earnings, profits and prosperity, increase in volume or quality of business or both, and in all other relevant facts and circumstances; nor should it be unfair to stockholders in unduly diminishing dividends properly payable.

[77] *See* Calvin H. Johnson, Stock Compensation: The Most Expensive Way to Pay Future Cash, 52 SMU L. Rev. 423 (1999) (demonstrating that deferred compensation is better for the employee and less expensive to the corporation, when an appropriate discount rate and tax effects are considered, than grant of stock options).

capital for an uncertain return, a contingent share of the profits, when and as fixed by management?[78]

The most famous compensation litigation came before the United States Supreme Court in *Rogers v. Hill*.[79] The case challenged the emoluments of the American Tobacco Company's president and executives, who received large fixed salaries and in addition participated in company profits through a huge annual bonus and certain profitable stock subscription plans.[80] The annual bonus, which was calculated as 10 percent of any increase in earnings over the company's earnings of 1910, was to be paid to the president and five vice presidents annually. The market price for stock allotted to the directors voting for the stock allotment plan of 1919 (the president not voting) was nearly $2,000,000 greater than the allotment price; the plan was never submitted to the stockholders for their approval.[81] In June 1930, the directors of the company proposed another and further stock subscription plan for officers and employees that was embodied in a bylaw submitted to and approved by the requisite vote of the shareholders as required by the New Jersey statute. Under this plan the directors in 1931 authorized the sale of some 56,000 shares of stock at the par value of $25 per share, which had a current market price of $112. "Of this number, 32,370, more than half, were allotted to the directors, of which 13,440 were allotted to the president. The remaining 24,342 shares were allotted in relatively small amounts to 525 employees."[82] On the day of the allotment, the market price, $112 per share, was more than four times the subscription price. The value of the rights granted to Mr. Hill, the president, in 1919 was estimated at $705,000, and his 1931 grant at $1,169,000; this was in addition to his other compensation of over $1,000,000. Rogers, a minority shareholder, instituted six suits against the company, its directors, and officers, two of which ultimately came before the United States Supreme Court. One suit attacked the bonus payments, the other, the stock subscription privilege. The bonus case was lost before the Second Circuit Court, with Judge Swan dissenting. The Supreme Court, however, reversed:

> Much weight is to be given to the action of the stockholders, and the by-law is supported by the presumption of regularity and continuity. But the rule prescribed by it cannot, against the protest of a shareholder, be used to justify payments of sums as salaries so large as in substance and effect to amount to spoliation or waste of corporate property. The dissenting opinion of Judge Swan indicates the applicable rule, "If a bonus payment has no relation to the value of services for which it is given, it is in reality a gift in part, and the majority stockholders have no power to give away corporate property against the protest of the minority." 60 F.2d 109, 113. The facts alleged by plaintiff are sufficient to require the District Court, upon a consideration of all the relevant facts brought forward by the parties, to determine whether and to what extent payments to the individual defendants under the by-laws constitute misuse and waste of the money of the corporation.[83]

---

[78] *See* Ferdinand Pecora, Wall Street Under Oath, 113–120, 143–146, particularly at 119 (1939); George Thomas Washington & Henry V. Rothschild, Compensating the Corporate Executive ch. 19 (3d ed. 1962).

[79] Rogers v. Hill, 289 U.S. 582 (1933). *See also* its companion case, Rogers v. Guaranty Trust Co., 288 U.S. 123 (1933).

[80] Rogers v. Hill, 289 U.S. 582, 590 (1933); Rogers v. Guaranty Trust Co., 288 U.S. 123 (1933).

[81] Penn v. Robertson, 115 F.2d 167, 170 (4th Cir. 1940).

[82] Rogers v. Guaranty Trust Co., 288 U.S. 123, 134 (1933) (Stone, J., dissenting).

[83] Rogers v. Hill, 289 U.S. 582, 591–592 (1933).

Rogers v. Hill represents one of the few successful challenges to executive compensation arrangements within a publicly held corporation based exclusively on its excessiveness. The case provides, however, little guidance as to how excessiveness is to be determined. Cases involving public corporations decided after *Rogers v. Hill,* as discussed below, emphasize the process by which the bonus or profit-sharing arrangement was approved over the more indefinite question of whether the amounts actually awarded are excessive.

Over the years the Delaware Supreme Court has been an important influence on the standards to be used in assessing bonus and profit-sharing arrangements. In the leading case concerning stock options, *Beard v. Elster,*[84] the court summarized the tests to be employed as follows:

> All stock option plans must be tested against the requirements that they contain conditions, or that surrounding circumstances are such, that the corporation may reasonably expect to receive the contemplated benefit from the grant of the options. Furthermore, there must be a reasonable relationship between the value of the benefits passing to the corporation and the value of the options granted.[85]

Applying the above, *Beard* upheld lucrative stock options granted to officers and supervisory personnel emphasizing that the option plan had been approved by the disinterested directors, that the terms of the plan required that the optionee must be an employee when the option is exercised, and that most of the beneficiaries of the option plan had remained in the company's employ after the plan had been adopted.

On closer analysis, the above tests provide very little specificity. This observation is best understood by considering the weak distinctions *Beard* offered to set its decision apart from two earlier cases, *Kerbs v. California Eastern Airways*[86] and *Gottlieb v. Heyden Chemical Corporation,*[87] where the court refused to protect stock option plans. *Beard* distinguished its earlier reversal of a stock option plan in *Kerbs* because Kerbs's plan allowed employees to exercise their options anytime within six months *of having worked* for the company. This is not itself a satisfactory distinction between the two plans' terms. The stock option plan's terms in *Beard* did not themselves assure that an employee would remain with the company after being granted the right to exercise her options. That plan required only that the officer be in the company's employ when the option was exercised. It was entirely possible under the terms of the plan for the employee to exercise the options, resign, and begin work with a competitor.[88]

The second *Beard* test—namely, that there be a reasonable relationship between the gains the employee reaps on the exercise of the option and the value the corporation receives from that employee's continued service—is at best problematic. The gain to the employee is the difference between the exercise price and the stock's value on the date of exercise. This amount can be quite significant and can be attributed to a good many

---

    84   Beard v. Elster, 160 A.2d 731 (Del. 1960).

    85   Beard v. Elster, 160 A.2d 731, 737 (Del. 1960).

    86   Kerbs v. California Eastern Airways, 90 A.2d 652 (Del. 1952).

    87   Gottlieb v. Heyden Chemical Corporation, 90 A.2d 660 (Del. 1952).

    88   A liberal, *ex post-view* of this inquiry was taken in Newberger v. Rifkind, 104 Cal.Rptr. 663, 665 (Cal. 1972), where the court reasoned that consideration is given for an option by the employee's continuous service to the company.

exogenous events unrelated to that employee's worth.[89] The *Beard* court reasoned that its earlier holding against the stock option plan in *Gottlieb* was justified because there had not been in that case any "independent appraisal of the value of the services to be retained by means of the options and the value of the options granted."[90] The *Beard* court thus deferred not to its determination of reasonableness but to that of the independent directors.

Beard reveals that the truly significant test for stock options and profitsharing arrangements, and executive compensation generally, is not the content that the courts give to the tests or standards they articulate; the dominant consideration is the *process* by which the corporate decision-maker arrives at the executive compensation package that is awarded. The most important consideration, indeed the sole consideration in the public corporation, is good faith impartial approval by the directors and/or the stockholders.[91] As *Beard* itself illustrates, even a plan that potentially fails solely by its terms to assure the officer's continued service, because the officer could exercise the option and then resign from the company, is saved because the approving directors were not themselves the beneficiaries of the stock option plan and otherwise acted in good faith and with reasonable care. However, the awards approved by the board of directors or compensation committee must be consistent with the constraints embodied in the plan.[92] Nevertheless, in *In re Investors Bancorp, Inc. Stockholder Litigation*, the Delaware Supreme Court held that even though the directors' exercise of discretion in awarding stock options was within parameters established by the shareholders, the business judgment rule does not apply to a claim that the directors' acted inequitably and unfairly.[93]

Good faith ratification by the stockholders after full disclosure also invokes the same presumptions, even if the approving directors lack authority to approve or modify a stock option plan.[94] When a plan receives the impartial approval of the directors or stockholders, the burden of proof is on the challenging party to prove the stock option or profit-sharing plan constitutes waste.[95] Not since *Rogers v. Hill* has there been a reported case involving a public corporation where executive compensation in a public corporation was struck down solely on the basis of being excessive.[96] However, in *Lewis v. Vogelstein*,[97] the derivative suit challenged the directors awarding themselves with

---

[89]   *See* Berkwitz v. Humphrey, 163 F.Supp. 78 (N.D. Ohio 1958) (no reasonable relationship between market gains and officer's contribution); *contra*, Lieberman v. Becker, 155 A.2d 596 (Del. 1959); Orlinsky v. Patraka, 971 So.2d 796 (Fla. Ct. App. 2007).

[90]   90 A.2d at 737.

[91]   It is therefore significant whether executive compensation is dominated by the influence of the CEO or whether other forces are at work to explain increases in executive compensation. *Compare* Lucian Arye Bebchuk, Jesse M. Fried & David I. Walker, Managerial Power and Rent Extraction in the Design of Executive Compensation, 69 U. Chi. L. Rev. 751 (2002) (managerial power plays a key role in the design of executive compensation) *with* Bengt Holmstrom, *Pay Without Performance* And The Managerial Power Hypothesis: A Comment, 30 J. Corp. L. 703 (2005) (rise of shareholder influence, not managerial power, linking compensation to changes in firm value is better explanation of rising executive compensation).

[92]   *See* Sanders v. Wang, 1999 WL 1044880 (Del. Ch. 1999) (awards by the board may not exceed number of shares authorized for the plan).

[93]   In re Investors Bancorp, Inc. Stockholder Litigation, 177 A.3d 1208 (Del. 2017), as revised, (Dec. 19, 2017). This decision clarified decades of Delaware lower court cases.

[94]   *See* Michelson v. Duncan, 407 A.2d 211 (Del. 1979).

[95]   Michelson v. Duncan, 407 A.2d 211 (Del. 1979).

[96]   *See generally* Douglas C. Michael, The Corporate Officer's Independent Duty as a Tonic for the Anemic Law of Executive Compensation, 17 J. Corp. L. 785 (1992).

[97]   Lewis v. Vogelstein, 699 A.2d 327 (Del. Ch. 1997).

highly valuable options that could be exercised immediately. Even though the option plan had been ratified by disinterested, informed stockholders, the court rejected the defendants' motion to dismiss, and set the matter for trial. Defining waste as arising when the "exchange of corporate assets for consideration so disproportionately small as to lie beyond the range at which any reasonable person might be willing to trade,"[98] the court believed it could not rule as a matter of law that facts that could be introduced at the trial may not persuade the reasonable person that under the circumstances the options constituted waste.[99]

§ 11.6 Executive Compensation and the Internal Revenue Code

Because a corporation can deduct salary payments, whereas dividends are paid out of after-tax dollars,[100] there is a powerful tax incentive to pay as much as possible in salary. This is an especially critical factor when dealing with closely held enterprises because of the close identity of ownership and management. Accordingly, there are a good many cases in which the Internal Revenue Service challenges compensation as a disguised dividend.[101] In such cases, excessive compensation, if found, results in the excess payment being treated as a dividend so that the corporation is denied a deduction for that disallowed amount. The traditional approach to determining under the IRC whether compensation is excessive is the multi-factor test. Under this approach, the court weighs a number of considerations, with no single factor being dispositive. Factors include (1) the employee's role, position and qualifications in the corporation, (2) duties of, and hours devoted to company, by the employee, (3) comparison of challenged compensation with that of similar companies, (4) character and financial condition of the company including return on investment and changes in market value of firm, (5) dividend record of the company, and (6) the consistency with which the compensation has been paid.[102] An emerging approach is the so-called "independent investor test," whereby a salary is presumptively reasonable when it is paid by a company whose owners are enjoying a desirable rate of return.[103] Applying this test, a court upheld compensation of $1.3 million in the face of expert evidence that investors would expect a 13% return on their investment and were in fact enjoying a 50 percent return.[104]

An important limitation on senior executive compensation was the addition in 1993 of section 162(m) of the Internal Revenue Code, which denies a federal income tax deduction for all taxable years commencing after January 1, 1994, to publicly held corporations for compensation in excess of $1 million per year to any of the corporation's top five officers.[105] An important exemption to this provision applies to "performance-based compensation" arrangements.[106] This exemption applies when compensation is

---

[98]   Lewis v. Vogelstein, 699 A.2d 327, 336 (Del. Ch. 1997).

[99]   Lewis v. Vogelstein, 699 A.2d 327, 339 (Del. Ch. 1997). *See also, e.g.,* In re Inv'rs Bancorp, Inc. Stockholder Litig., 177 A.3d 1208, 1222–23 (Del. 2017).

[100]   *See* I.R.C. § 162(a)(1) (2000); Treas. Reg. § 1.162–7(a) (2009).

[101]   For an illustrative case on the taxation issue *see* Rapco, Inc. v. Commissioner, 85 F.3d 950, 955 (2d Cir. 1996) (salary of $900,000 to 95 percent owner disallowed where it was not supported by expert testimony, ignored the bylaw's bonus compensation scheme, and was set by its recipient).

[102]   *See, e.g.,* Eberl's Claim Service, Inc. v. Commissioner, 249 F.3d 994 (10th Cir. 2001).

[103]   *See, e.g.,* Exacto Spring Corp. v. Commissioner, 196 F.3d 833 (7th Cir. 1999).

[104]   Exacto Spring Corp. v. Commissioner, 196 F.3d 833 (7th Cir. 1999).

[105]   I.R.C. § 162(m) (2000)(repealed in 2017).

[106]   *See generally* Joseph Antenucci & Peter Woodlock, Types of Compensation Qualified As "Performance Based" Under Code section 162(m), 76 Taxes 27 (Sept. 1998).

awarded pursuant to a predetermined compensation arrangement that contains objective performance goals established by a committee of outside directors and approved by the shareholders after full disclosure of the arrangement's material terms. Also beyond the scope of section 162(m) is deferred compensation that is paid to a person who is no longer one of the five top officers of the corporation. In applying this provision to stock options and other contingent compensation arrangements, the tax consequences are determined on the date of exercise, not on the date the option is granted. There is no evidence that section 162(m) has retarded the rate of increase in executive compensation.[107]

Freedman v. Adams[108] may well illustrate the possible irrelevance of section 162(m) in controlling the forces that feed the ever-increasing levels of executive compensation. A derivative suit was initiated to recover more than $130 million in bonuses approved by the board of XTO Energy without the compensation plan including provisions to link the bonuses to performance. Because the plan lacked performance-based standards, the compensation was not a deductible business expense on XTO Energy's tax return. After the plaintiff initiated a derivative suit, the board prospectively modified the plan and the plaintiff dropped her derivative suit. In responding to the derivative suit plaintiff's request for fees incident to the claim, XTO Energy's argued that the board was fully aware of section 162(m), but made a conscious decision not to avail itself of section 162(m) because it believed its approach to a compensation decision should not "be constrained by such a plan." The court held the plaintiff had not stated a claim, reasoning, "[e]ven if the decision were a poor one" as alleged by the plaintiff, "it was not unconscionable or irrational." *Freedman* is another illustration that failure to follow "best practices" is not synonymous with legally culpable misbehavior.[109]

A further attempt to restrict excessive awards appears in sections 280G and 4999 of the Internal Revenue Code.[110] These provisions, respectively, disallow the tax deduction for a company's "excess parachute payments" and impose a 20 percent excise tax on the recipient. Non-public companies are exempt from the provisions provided the payments approved by holders of 75 percent of the stock (but only after disclosure of the *actual* event that will trigger the parachute). The provision defines excessive compensation as being three times the executive's annual compensation. If the provision applies, not only is the corporation denied a deduction, but the recipient incurs a 20 percent excise tax. The clear intent of section 280G is to reach "excessive" golden parachute arrangements; however, a strategy that is sometimes followed is merely to "gross up" the recipient's award to cover the anticipated tax effects and to forego the deduction.

---

[107] *See* Susan J. Stabile, Is There a Role for Tax Law in Policing Executive Compensation, 72 St. John's L. Rev. 91,89 (1998) (reporting that executive pay grew 29 percent faster in the year after the enactment of section 162(m) than was the rate of growth in the previous 14 years).

[108] Freedman v. Adams, 58 A.3d 414 (Del. 2013).

[109] *See also* In re Walt Disney Co. Derivative Litigation, 906 A.2d 27, 37 Employee Benefits Cas. (BNA) 2756 (Del. 2006) (failure to adhere to best practices does not translate to breach of duty of care or duty to act in good faith).

[110] I.R.C. §§ 280G & 4999.

§ 11.7 Regulating Executive Compensation Through Improved Governance and Disclosure

In recent years, the amount of compensation garnered by executives of publicly held corporations has become a public issue eliciting cries within the Congress demanding either capping of executive compensation or subjecting the compensation to severe tax consequences.[111] Two important corporate responses to this national malaise is the increasing use of compensation committees and enhanced mandatory disclosure rules for public corporations.

Concerns for rising executive compensation fit easily into the "managerial power" thesis which argues executives embrace many initiatives to entrench their positions and thereby preserve the rewards associated with their office. Thus classified boards, poison pills and plurality voting are seen as entrenching managers and making non-performance-based compensation possible.[112] An opposing explanation is rising compensation reflects the natural result of pricing a scarce commodity, talented management. Much like baseball, there are only so many individuals who can hit a 90 miles per hour curveball. The theory of paying for talent is supported by studies finding no strong correlation between, for example, classified boards or poison pills and levels of executive compensation.[113]

Compensation Committees

Nearly all sizable public corporations today have compensation committees.[114] The composition, powers, and practices of compensation committees vary widely across corporations, although increasingly compensation committees are composed exclusively of outside directors and are given the authority to establish compensation policies and particular packages for senior executives. The provisions of the American Law Institute embody a prevalent sphere of authority for the compensation committee:

. . .

(b) The compensation committee should:

(1) Review and recommend to the board, or determine, the annual salary, bonus, stock options, and other benefits, direct and indirect, of the senior executives.

(2) Review new executive compensation programs; review on a periodic basis the operation of the corporation's executive compensation programs to determine whether they are properly coordinated; establish and periodically review policies for the administration of executive compensation programs; and

---

[111] The leading work arguing that compensation is both excessive and due to an imbalance between owners and managers is Lucian Bebchuk & Jesse Fried, Pay Without Performance: The Unfulfilled Promise of Executive Compensation (2004). The popular non-legal work subject is Graef S. Crystal, In Search of Excess (1991).

[112] *See generally* Lucian Bebchuk & Jesse Fried, Pay Without Performance: The Unfilled Promise of Executive Compensation (2004).

[113] K.J. Martijn Cremers, Saura Masconale & Simone M. Sepe, CEO Redux, 96 Tex. L. Rev. 205 (2017)(adoption of defensive measures such as a pill or classified board is not associated changes in executive pay but higher pay is associated with higher firm value).

[114] *See, e.g.*, Heidrick & Struggles, The Changing Board Table 11, 13 (93 percent of surveyed corporations in 1989 had compensation committees). Even as early as 1981 some 72 percent of the proxies surveyed by the SEC revealed the presence of a compensation committee. SEC Staff Report, Corporate Accountability 612–614 (1981).

take steps to modify any executive compensation programs that yield payments and benefits that are not reasonably related to executive performance.[115]

The great virtue of a compensation committee is the independence of judgment its members can bring to compensation questions. This approach, of course, demands that its membership be composed of outside directors and that the committee has broad authority to establish, review, and modify the compensation of senior executives. Nevertheless, there is a distinct disquiet that executive compensation could have soared to such prominence in the national consciousness during a time when most public corporations have had compensation committees. Until studies are made of the actual operation of compensation committees, there will continue to be some doubt as to whether they are an effective fulcrum for balancing the interests of the stockholders against the managers' quest for ever-increasing compensation.

Disclosure

Over the years, the SEC has confronted the issue of executive compensation by adopting successively expanded disclosure requirements for the express purpose of providing a clearer presentation of senior executive compensation.[116] There is also the important collateral and moderating influence that arises with any revealing disclosure requirements such as are now required by the SEC. In this respect, recall Brandeis's wise observation: "Sunlight is said to be the best of disinfectants; electric light the most efficient policeman."[117] Among the executive compensation disclosures required is that the board of directors or compensation committee discuss the relationship of corporate performance to executive compensation with respect to the compensation awarded for the last fiscal year.[118] Even more detailed discussion is required with respect to the relationship of the chief executive officer's compensation to the company's financial performance.[119] The SEC requires a line-graph plotting for five years of the relationship of executive compensation to overall corporate performance as embodied in a measure of cumulative total shareholder return, which itself is contrasted with an acceptable stock index. Matters that may compromise the directors' independence must also be disclosed.[120] The disclosures are required to identify the directors or committee members who had responsibility for making the disclosures mandated by the executive compensation disclosure rules.[121] While disclosure has multiple virtues, there is scant evidence that disclosure retards compensation levels for executives.[122]

---

[115] ALI Principles of Corporate Governance: Restatement and Recommendations § 3A.05(b) (1992).

[116] *See* Executive Compensation Disclosure, Securities Act Release No. 6962 [1992 Transfer Binder] Fed. Sec. L. Rep. (CCH) ¶ 85,056 (Oct. 16, 1992).

[117] Louis D. Brandeis, Other People's Money 92 (Stokes 1932). *See also,* Jeffrey N. Gordon, Executive Compensation: If There's A Problem, What's the Remedy? The Case for "Compensation Discussion and Analysis," 30 J. Corp. L. 675 (2005) (favoring expanded disclosure, similar to the compensation disclosure and analysis adopted by the SEC, discussed later in this section, as well as conditioning compensation on shareholder approval).

[118] Item 402(k)(1) of Regulation S–K, 17 C.F.R. § 229.402(k)(1) (2009).

[119] *See, e.g.,* Item 402(a)(4) and Item 402(k)(2) of Regulation S–K, 17 C.F.R. § 229.402(a)(4) & (k)(2) (2009).

[120] *See* Item 402(j)(3) of Regulation S–K, 17 C.F.R. § 228.402(j)(3) (2009).

[121] Item 402(k)(3), Regulation S–K § 228.402(k)(3) (2009).

[122] *See* Brian R. Cheffins & Randall S. Thomas, The Globalization (Americanization?) of Executive Pay, 1 Berk. Bus. L. J. 233, 262–273 (2004) (comparative study of regulatory strategies to address "excessive" executive compensation and finding that introducing greater disclosure of executive compensation is customarily accompanied by a subsequent spiral in compensation levels).

In 2006, the SEC amended Item 402 of Regulation S–K[123] to significantly expand the disclosure requirements for executive compensation. In broad overview, the 2006 additional disclosure requirements focus on five primary areas:

1. Addition of a "Compensation Discussion and Analysis" ("CD & A") section to SEC filings and a new Compensation Committee Report.

2. Detailed disclosure of compensation for "named executive officers" ("NEOs") for the last fiscal year and the two preceding fiscal years.

3. Extensive disclosure of grants, holdings, and realization of equity-related interests (e.g., stock options, stock appreciation rights) to NEOs.

4. Retirement plans, deferred compensation, and other post-employment payments and benefits for NEOs.

5. Director compensation.

CD&A is a central component of the new disclosure requirements. The rules for this new part of SEC filings is principles based, meaning Item 402 broadly calls for registrants to set forth in a comprehensive way the material factors underlying the company's executive compensation policies and practices (instead of setting forth narrow categories of information that is to be provided). Areas of policy to be addressed include what are the objectives of the company's compensation program, what is sought to be rewarded by the compensation, the elements of the executive's compensation, how did the company determine the amount for each such element, and how does each element fit with the company's overall compensation objectives. The CD&A is also part of the CEO's and CFO's certification requirements.

The Compensation Committee Report must address two items: first, whether the committee has reviewed and discussed the CD&A; and, second, based on any review and discussion, the committee has recommended to the board that the CD&A be included in the company's SEC Filing.

NEOs are the firm's principal executive officer (*e.g.*, CEO) and principal financial officer (*e.g.*, CFO) plus the other three most highly compensated officers (provided the person's compensation exceeds $100,000).

Say on Pay

In July, 2010 Congress enacted the Dodd-Frank Wall Street Reform and Consumer Protection Act which adds section 14A to the Securities Exchange Act to require at least once every three years a non-binding shareholder vote on executive compensation in public companies. The "say on pay,"[124] provision is modeled after one that became mandatory in the United Kingdom in 2002.[125] Studies of U.K. say-on-pay practices have found they tend to improve the link between compensation and performance.[126] Studies of "say on pay" votes for the first two proxy seasons of the provision's required use reflects that say on pay votes fail (the provision receives less than a majority approval) in a very

---

[123] 17 C.F.R. § 229.402 (2009).

[124] H.R. 1257, 110th Cong. (2007) (sponsored by Rep. Barney Frank (D.Mass.)) and modeled.

[125] *See generally* L.C.B. Gower & Paul L. Davies, The Principles of Modern Company Law §§ 14–16 to 14–17, 14–22 to 14–23 (8th ed. 2008).

[126] *See, e.g.,* Fabrizio Ferri & David Maber, Say on Pay Votes and CEO Compensation: Evidence from the U.K. (March 2009) (CEO compensation significantly more sensitive to performance post the introduction of say-on-pay requirement and sensitivity increased as vote in opposition to pay increased).

small percentage of the instances, that proxy advisory firms have a statistically significant impact on the outcome, and that failed or close say on pay votes are correlated with stronger negative votes for directors in those firms who serve on the compensation committee.[127]

Golden Leashes

A relatively recent phenomenon has been payments to directors from third parties who generally are large shareholders.[128] The apparent purpose of such third party payments is to create a loyalty to the third party and his or her interests. This type of third party payment is often referred to as a golden leash and raises concerns about possibly compromising a director's duty of loyalty to his or her corporation. In 2016, the SEC approved amendments to the Nasdaq listing standards to require disclosure of third party compensation to directors and board nominees.[129]

PART B.   CORPORATE OPPORTUNITIES

§ 11.8   Misappropriation of Corporate Opportunities: Disloyal Diversion of Business

Directors and officers as insiders cannot utilize their strategic position for their own preferment or use their powers and opportunities for their own advantage to the exclusion or detriment of the interests they are to represent. Thus directors and officers as corporate insiders cannot utilize their strategic position or their powers and opportunities for their personal advantage to the detriment of other corporate constituencies.[130] They cannot sell their votes or their influence in the management of the corporation. A few cases have employed the corporate opportunity doctrine-type analysis to shareholders.[131] There appears little reason why the test should be limited to fiduciaries who are directors or officers; the policy considerations underlying proscribing some opportunities as belonging to the firm are applicable to all who have a fiduciary relationship to the firm.[132] A fiduciary cannot profit personally from information and knowledge that they have acquired in confidence in their corporate capacity, even though

---

[127] *See,* Randall S. Thomas, Alan R. Palmiter and James F. Cotter, Dodd-Frank's Say on Pay: Will It Lead To A Greater Role For Shareholders In Corporate Governance, 97 Cornell L. Rev. 1213 (2012); James F. Cotter, Alan R. Palmiter & Randall S. Thomas, The First Year of Say-on-Pay Under Dodd-Frank: An Empirical Analysis and Look Forward, 81 Geo. Wash. L. Rev. 967, 998–999 (2013).

[128] *See, e.g.,* Cain, Fisch, Griffith, Solomon, How Corporate Governance is Made: The Case of the Golden Leash. 164 U. Pa. L. Rev. 649 (2016).

[129] Self-Regulatory Organizations; The Nasdaq Stock Market LLC; Notice of Filing of Amendment No. 2 and Order Granting Accelerated Approval of a Proposed Rule Change, as Modified by Amendment No. 2, to Require Listed Companies to Publicly Disclose Compensation or Other Payments by Third Parties to Board of Director's Members or Nominees, Release No. 34-78223; File No. SR-NASDAQ-2016-013 (July 1, 2016).

[130] *See, e.g.,* Pepper v. Litton, 308 U.S. 295 (1939); Gulledge v. Frosty Land Foods Int'l, 414 So.2d 60 (Ala. 1982).

[131] *See, e.g.,* Thorpe by Castleman v. CERBCO, Inc., 676 A.2d 436 (Del. 1996); Lyon v. Campbell, 707 A.2d 850, 864 (Md. App. 1998); A. Teixeira & Co., Inc. v. Teixeira, 699 A.2d 1383 (R.I. 1997) (members of close corporation are analogous to partners in a partnership and hence, as fiduciaries, owe duty not to usurp opportunities).

[132] *See* United Teachers Assoc. Ins. Co. v. MacKeen & Bailey, Inc., 99 F.3d 645 (5th Cir. 1996) (actuary retained by the firm deemed a fiduciary who usurped opportunity to acquire another firm).

the corporation suffers no injury.[133] For similar reasons, partners may be held accountable for taking of partnership opportunities.[134]

Of special concern, and the focus of this section, is that directors and officers not acquire for themselves property or business opportunities that are an opportunity or advantage that belongs to the corporation. In broad overview, corporations have a prior claim vis-à-vis their directors, officers, and agents to opportunities for business and profit that may be regarded as sufficiently incident or connected to the corporation's business, or the director's and officer's acquisition of the opportunity is otherwise accomplished through disloyalty and unfairness to the corporation. What opportunities are so related to the corporation's business, or the behavior that is disloyal or unfair to the corporation, is answered only in the context of the circumstances of the particular case and sometimes depends on the particular test followed by the jurisdiction. In making this determination, the facts and circumstances when the fiduciary acquired the opportunity are considered and not those that exist thereafter. Thus, in a leading Delaware case, a director did not usurp a corporate opportunity by acquiring a cellular phone license when CIS, on whose board he sat, was in financial difficulties and disposing of some of its licenses, even though PriCellular, Inc. had an option to acquire the same license and had commenced a tender offer to acquire CIS.[135]

There are several widely differing tests applied by the courts. While the discussion that follows examines each of the prevalent tests, a word of caution is in order. Courts rarely articulate a specific test[136] and apply it strictly. Instead, courts examine a number of factors common to two or more of the tests described below. And, even when purporting to apply a specific test, the factors of each test are so general that the outcome is more sensitive to the egregiousness of the director's or officer's behavior than to the particular test the court applies. Overall, this area of the law is very fact-specific, and a good deal of uncertainty exists as to what constitutes a usurpation of a corporate opportunity (sometimes also referred to as the taking of a corporate advantage). The articles of incorporation can define the scope of permissible activities by a fiduciary without usurping a corporate opportunity.[137]

Interest or Expectancy Approach. A few cases impose the "interest or expectancy" test first announced in *Lagarde v. Anniston Lime & Stone Company*,[138] where the company had unsuccessfully negotiated with *M* for the purchase of an outstanding one-third interest in a stone quarry in which it already had a one-third interest and a lease on the remaining one-third from *C*. The quarry was located near other lands that the company was operating. The two defendants, directors and officers,

---

[133] *E.g.*, Weigel v. Shapiro, 608 F.2d 268 (7th Cir. 1979).

[134] Triple Five of Minnesota, Inc. v. Simon, 280 F. Supp.2d 895 (D. Minn. 2003) (partner usurped partnership opportunity).

[135] *See* Broz v. Cellular Information Systems, Inc., 673 A.2d 148 (Del. 1996) (the option held by PriCellular provided it would not bar the sale of the license to another who offered at least $500,000 more than the option price for the license).

[136] *See, e.g.*, Rapistan Corp. v. Michaels, 511 N.W.2d 918 (Mich. Ct. App. 1994) (wrongful usurpation of corporate opportunity arises when (1) the opportunity is essential to the corporation, (2) the corporation has an interest or expectancy, or (3) fiduciary has used corporate assets to acquire or develop).

[137] Model Bus. Corp. Act § 2.02(b)(6) (2016). *Cf,* Mulloy v. Mulloy, 2019 WL 5078924 (Tenn. Ct. App. 2019) (an across-the-board elimination of fiduciary duties in an LLC will not preclude a claim based on usurpation of a business opportunity but specifying the activities that an individual may pursue can define the scope of permissible activities).

[138] Lagarde v. Anniston Lime & Stone Company, 28 So. 199 (Ala. 1899).

were held not liable for acquiring *M*'s interest for themselves on information gained by their official position, but they were held liable for breach of duty as to the purchase of *C*'s interest, which had already been under contract and lease to the company such that the company then had an "interest or expectancy" in the property. The court said: "Good faith to the corporation does not require of its officers that they steer from their own to the corporation's benefit enterprises or investments which, though capable of profit to the corporation, have in no way become subjects of their trust or duty."[139]

The court's treatment of the purchase from *M* is questionable because this interest was important to the corporation, and if the company had not abandoned its efforts to acquire this interest, the court clearly should have reached a different result.[140] In any case, *Lagarde* established the "interest or expectancy" test, whereby an officer or director is deemed to usurp a corporate opportunity only where the corporation has an existing interest in the property or an expectancy growing out of an existing right. For example, a corporation was deemed to have an interest or expectancy in a contract with a customer with whom it had an ongoing relationship such that when its former officer contracted with that customer to provide the same services, it was deemed a usurpation of the corporation's opportunity.[141] And, the corporation had an interest in land adjacent to the corporation's existing property, which the stockholders had frequently discussed acquiring at their meetings.[142]

A consideration frequently invoked in connection with the "interest or expectancy" inquiry is whether the opportunity is "essential" to the corporation's operation or existence.[143]

Line of Business. In contrast to the narrowness of the "interest or expectancy" test is the "line of business" test, which treats as belonging to the corporation an opportunity that is related to or is in the company's line of activities and is an activity that the company could reasonably be expected to enter.[144] In the leading line-of-business case, *Guth v. Loft, Inc.*,[145] Guth was the president of Loft, Inc., which was engaged in the manufacture and sale of beverages and candy. Guth bought the Pepsi-Cola secret formula and trademark from a bankrupt corporation and, with *M*, organized a new corporation with the aid of money from Loft. Guth used Loft's capital, plant facilities, materials, credit, and employees to perfect the mixture, and the product was sold to Loft for distribution at cost plus 10 percent. The Delaware court held that Guth had appropriated a business opportunity that belonged in equity to Loft, Inc., and had made profits to which Loft was entitled.[146] The opportunity was so closely associated with the

---

[139] 28 So. at 201.

[140] Warner Fuller, Restrictions Imposed by the Directorship Status on the Personal Business Activities of Directors, 26 Wash. U. L.Q. 189, 205 (1941); Note, 54 Harv. L. Rev. 1191, 1195 (1941).

[141] Southeast Consultants, Inc. v. McCrary Engg. Corp., 273 S.E.2d 112 (Ga. 1980).

[142] Farber v. Servan Land Co., 662 F.2d 371 (5th Cir. 1981).

[143] *See, e.g.,* Design Strategies, Inc. v. Davis, 384 F.Supp.2d 649, 672 (S.D.N.Y. 2005) (stating the test is "whether the consequences of deprivation are so severe as to threaten the viability of the enterprise") (quoting, Alexander & Alexander of New York, Inc. v. Fritzen, 542 N.Y.S.2d 530, 534–35 (Sup.Ct. App. Div. 1989)).

[144] *See, e.g.,* Levy v. Markal Sales Corp., 643 N.E.2d 1206 (Ill. App. Ct. 1994) (also evidence that opportunity first offered in expectation it would be of interest to employer and there was use of company resources in developing opportunity).

[145] Guth v. Loft, Inc., 5 A.2d 503 (Del. 1939).

[146] Guth v. Loft, Inc., 5 A.2d 503, 510 (Del. 1939):

The rule, inveterate and uncompromising in its rigidity, does not rest upon the narrow ground of injury or damage to the corporation resulting from a betrayal of confidence, but upon a broader existing business activities of Loft and so important to those activities as to bring it within the scope of Guth's fiduciary duty, even if Guth had not used Loft's facilities and resources to engage in a competing business.[147]

What is within a corporation's line of business is not always easy to identify *ex ante*. Though the test is broader than the interest or expectancy test, courts can still have a very narrow view of what is within a firm's line of business.[148] Furthermore, fine factual distinctions abound even under the broader line of business test. Thus an opportunity to earn a large profit quickly by purchasing a parcel of land should be considered within the line of business of a company that generally develops land but rarely itself speculates in land.[149] The question would be much closer, however, if the company only developed land and never speculated in land. Of course, the corporation may have in its articles, bylaws, or a resolution of its board of directors a provision that unequivocally identifies the types of business or activity in which the company does not have an interest and that are fair game for its directors or even officers.[150] Such an approach is expressly authorized by the American Law Institute's Corporate Governance Project,[151] which otherwise applies a line-of-business approach to opportunities acquired by senior executive officers.[152] There is another route built on the view that the corporation is but a web of contracts. This school has provided the impetus for statutes authorizing provisions to be included in the corporation's articles of incorporation that prescribe what will not be deemed corporate opportunities.[153]

Multiple Factors. A majority of the cases determine whether the director or officer has usurped a corporate opportunity by weighing a range of factors. Even Delaware, which purports to apply a combined line of business and interest or expectancy test, acknowledges that *Guth* enunciates factors that need to be taken into account by the reviewing court in balancing the equities of the individual case.[154] Among the factors or circumstances having significance in distinguishing between corporate opportunities that impose a "mandate" or duty to act for the corporation and those opportunities that are open to appropriation by corporate officers are: (1) Is the opportunity to acquire real estate, patents, etc., of special and unique value, or needed for the corporate business

---

foundation of a wise public policy that, for the purpose of removing all temptation, extinguishes all possibility of profit flowing from a breach of the confidence imposed by the fiduciary relation. Given the relation between the parties, a certain result follows; and a constructive trust is the remedial device through which precedence of self is compelled to give way to the stern demands of loyalty.

[147] 5 A.2d at 514:

Where a corporation is engaged in a certain business, and an opportunity is presented to it embracing an activity as to which it has fundamental knowledge, practical experience and ability to pursue, which, logically and naturally, is adaptable to its business having regard for its financial position, and is one that is consonant with its reasonable needs and aspirations for expansion, it may properly be said that the opportunity is in the line of the corporation's business.

[148] *See, e.g.,* Autocount, Inc. v. Automated Prescription Sys., Inc., 651 So.2d 308 (La. Ct. App. 1995) (developing a modified version of a device that company was negotiating to acquire not within the same line of business).

[149] *See* Imperial Group (Texas), Inc. v. Scholnick, 709 S.W.2d 358 (Tex. Ct. App. 1986).

[150] *See* American Inv. Co. v. Lichtenstein, 134 F.Supp. 857 (E.D. Mo. 1955).

[151] For an insightful analysis of the efficiency of such ex ante waivers by the corporation, *see* Richard A. Epstein, Contract and Trust in Corporate Law: The Case of Corporate Opportunity, 21 Del. J. Corp. L. 5 (1996).

[152] *See* text accompanying note 157 *infra.*

[153] *See, e.g.,* Del. Code Ann. tit. 8, § 12(17) (2001); ALI, 1 Principles of Corporate Governance: Analysis and Recommendations § 5.09 (1992).

[154] Broz v. Cellular Information Systems, Inc., 673 A.2d 148, 155 (Del. 1996).

and its expansion?[155] (2) Did the discovery or information come to the officer by reason of his official position?[156] (3) Was the company in the market, negotiating for, or seeking such opportunity or advantage, and, if so, has it abandoned its efforts in this regard?[157] (4) Was the officer especially charged with the duty of acquiring such opportunities for his enterprise?[158] (5) Did the officer use corporate funds or facilities in acquiring or developing it?[159] (6) Does taking the opportunity place the director in an adverse and hostile position to his corporation?[160] (7) Did the officer intend to resell the opportunity to the corporation?[161] (8) Was the corporation in a favorable position to take advantage of the opportunity, or was it financially or otherwise unable to do so?[162] Such factors are among those that must be weighed and balanced, but it is not possible for the most part to lay down any hard and fast rules as to their effect in imposing a mandate, and variable results have been reached. The multifactor approach is the least rigorous of the tests and therefore provides the least certainty to the director or officer considering *ex ante* whether she can acquire a business opportunity or whether it must first be offered to the corporation.[163]

The American Law Institute Approach. The American Law Institute's Corporate Governance Project may have a considerable impact on future judicial decisions on corporate opportunity. The Supreme Courts of Maine, Massachusetts, and Oregon have already adopted the definition of "corporate opportunity" as it appeared in a tentative draft of the Governance Project, even though that definition was subject to being revised by the American Law Institute.[164] The American Law Institute defines "corporate opportunity" as follows:

(1)   Any opportunity to engage in a business activity of which a director or senior executive becomes aware, either

(A)   in connection with the performance of functions as a director or senior executive, or under circumstances that should reasonably lead the director or senior executive to believe that the person offering the opportunity expects it to be offered to the corporation;[165] or

---

[155] *See, e.g.,* Central Ry. Signal Co. v. Longden, 194 F.2d 310 (7th Cir. 1952).

[156] *See, e.g.,* Broz v. Cellular Information Systems, Inc., 673 A.2d 148, 155 (Del. 1996) (not dispositive that fiduciary learned of opportunity in individual capacity).

[157] *See, e.g.,* Burg v. Horn, 380 F.2d 897 (2d Cir. 1967).

[158] *See, e.g.,* Burg v. Horn, 380 F.2d 897 (2d Cir. 1967).

[159] *See, e.g.,* Central Ry. Signal Co. v. Longden, 194 F.2d 310 (7th Cir. 1952).

[160] *See, e.g.,* American Fed. Group, Ltd. v. Rothenberg, 136 F.3d 897 (2d Cir. 1998).

[161] *See, e.g.,* Burg v. Horn, 380 F.2d 897 (2d Cir. 1967); Southeast Consultants, Inc. v. McCrary Eng'g Corp., 273 S.E.2d 112 (Ga. 1980).

[162] *See, e.g.,* A. C. Petters v. St. Cloud Enter., 222 N.W.2d 83 (Minn. 1974); Ellzey v. Fyr-Pruf, Inc., 376 So.2d 1328 (Miss. 1979).

[163] In Miller v. Miller, 222 N.W.2d 71 (Minn. 1974), the Minnesota Supreme Court attempted to introduce some rigor to the equitable-factors test by combining it with the line-of-business test in a two-step approach. The first question is whether the business opportunity is a corporate opportunity—that is, whether it is of sufficient importance and is so closely related to the existing or prospective activity of the corporation as to warrant judicial sanctions against its personal acquisition.

[164] *See* Northeast Harbor Golf Club, Inc. v. Harris, 661 A.2d 1146 (Me. 1995).

[165] This is the crucial factor in Northeast Harbor Golf Club, Inc. v. Harris, 661 A.2d 1146 (Me. 1995), where the court appears to emphasize more the intent of the broker offering the opportunity than the reasonable belief of the purchasing company official.

(B) through the use of corporate information or property, if the resulting opportunity is one that the director or senior executive should reasonably be expected to believe would be of interest to the corporation; or

(2) Any opportunity to engage in a business activity of which a senior executive becomes aware and knows is closely related to a business in which the corporation is engaged or expects to engage.[166]

The American Law Institute provides a much broader proscription of business opportunities for senior executive officers than for outside directors, essentially applying a line-of-business test to opportunities before the senior executive officer. The American Law Institute also casts aside the multifactor approach, opting for the more certain inquiries of the circumstances surrounding the fiduciary learning of the opportunity or its acquisition as well as, in the case of senior executive officers, its relationship to a present or contemplated business of the corporation. Although there is not much precedent to support its position, the American Law Institute separately proscribes the fiduciary obligation of controlling stockholders.[167] Finally, the American Law Institute eliminates the possible defenses of incapacity or inability, financial or otherwise, of the corporation to embrace the opportunity.[168] If the activity falls within the ALI's proscription of a corporate opportunity, the sole defense is that the board or stockholders have rejected the opportunity. The truly significant contribution of the Corporate Governance Project's section 5.05 is that it causes the director or senior executive officer to *first* obtain disinterested approval of the board of directors. More significantly, the directors are allowed to approve the director's or senior executive officer's acquisition of the business opportunity only in advance of its acquisition; their approval after the acquisition is given no operative effect under the provision.[169] Absent such approval, the only option is the more cumbersome and expensive process of obtaining shareholder approval or the less predictable burden of proving no unfairness to the corporation.[170]

The Close Corporation Setting. In the close corporation context, there is growing support for greater flexibility in resolving whether a director or officer has usurped a corporate opportunity:

A more flexible approach, however, is dictated when dealing with a small corporation which is generally contractual in nature. . . . [T]he small number

---

[166] Thus, in adopting the ALI approach, the case was remanded to determine how a golf club's president learned of the opportunity to acquire land adjacent to the course. *See* Northeast Harbor Golf Club, Inc. v. Harris, 661 A.2d 1146 (Me. 1995).

[167] ALI, Principles of Corporate Governance: Analysis and Recommendations § 512 (1992). As to controlling stockholders, "corporate opportunity" is defined in terms of the property having been "developed or received by the corporation," or having come to the controlling stockholder because of his relationship to the company, or is of the type that was held out to the stockholder as being an activity within the scope of the company's business. *Id.* § 5.12(b)(1)(2). The absence of case law on whether controlling shareholders can usurp a corporate opportunity may be partly a semantic distinction. *See* Thorpe by Castleman v. CERBCO, Inc., 676 A.2d 436 (Del. 1996) (controlling shareholders not liable for having usurped a corporate opportunity by diverting an offer to buy the corporation so that they instead sold their majority interest in the corporation; however, they would be liable for any damages caused by their breach of duty of loyalty).

[168] *See* Klinicki v. Lundgren, 695 P.2d 906 (Or. 1985).

[169] ALI, Principles of Corporate Governance: Analysis and Recommendations § 5.05(a)(1) (1992). Subsection (e) does allow approval after the fact by the directors where the director or senior executive officer failed to get earlier approval because of a good faith belief the business activity was not a corporate opportunity.

[170] ALI, Principles of Corporate Governance: Analysis and Recommendations §§ 5.05(a)(3)(C), 5.05(c) (1992). Courts also place the burden of proving no usurpation of a corporate opportunity on the officer or director. *See* Independent Distributors, Inc. v. Katz, 637 A.2d 886 (Md. App. Ct. 1994).

of players in a private venture result in better communication between the members. Additionally, agreements are entered into which are tailored to particular situations and objectives.[171]

Factors in a close corporation setting that shape the conclusion that no corporate opportunity was usurped are the co-owners' awareness when the corporation was formed that their defendant-fiduciary actively engaged in similar outside activities[172] and whether the opportunity appeared within the parties' reasonable expectation.[173] Absent strong evidence of prejudice to creditors, there is little reason to hold that the sole shareholder can usurp a corporate opportunity.[174]

The Inability or Incapacity Defense. Directors and officers commonly defend their acquisition of a business opportunity on the grounds that, because of financial distress, or legal restrictions, or otherwise, the corporation was unable itself to acquire the opportunity.[175] In a leading case,[176] the United States Court of Appeals, Second Circuit, invalidated the directors' formation of a syndicate to purchase controlling interests in certain radio patents that the corporation had an option to purchase. The defense was that the corporation was financially unable to take advantage of the opportunity, but it was not clearly shown that greater efforts on their part would not have enabled the corporation to obtain the necessary funds. Judge Swan, in his opinion, said:

> While these facts raise some question whether [the corporation] actually lacked the funds or credit necessary for carrying out its contract, we do not feel justified in reversing the District Court's finding that it did. Nevertheless, they tend to show the wisdom of a rigid rule forbidding directors of a solvent corporation contract on the plea of the corporation's financial inability to perform. If the directors are uncertain whether the corporation can make the outlays, they need not embark it upon the venture; and if they do, they may not substitute themselves for the corporation any place along the line and divert possible benefits into their pockets.[177]

Not all courts would feel impelled to adopt such a rule of "uncompromising rigidity" as to inability.[178] In a later Delaware case,[179] for example, the court rejected a rigid rule but held that the burden of proving financial inability rested with the defendant officers and directors. The approach taken by the Massachusetts Supreme Court appears to be most appropriate:

> [T]o ensure fairness . . . , opportunities must be presented to the corporation without regard to possible impediments, and material facts must be fully

---

[171] Leavitt v. Leisure Sports, Inc., 734 P.2d 1221, 1225 (Nev. 1987).

[172] *See* Noble v. Lubrin, 60 P.3d 1224, 1226 (Wash. Ct. App. 2003).

[173] Graham v. Mimms, 444 N.E.2d 549 (Ill. App. Ct. 1982). In their thoughtful article, Professors Brudney and Chirelstein suggest that the appropriate basis for defining corporate opportunities in close corporations is to consider the reasonable expectations of the parties.

[174] *See* In re Safety Int'l, Inc., 775 F.2d 660 (5th Cir. 1985) (invoking a theory of ratification).

[175] *See, e.g.,* Lange v. Lange, 520 N.W.2d 113 (Iowa 1994).

[176] Irving Trust Co. v. Deutsch, 73 F.2d 121 (2d Cir. 1934), *cert. denied,* 294 U.S. 708 (1935).

[177] Irving Trust Co. v. Deutsch, 73 F.2d 121, 124 (2d Cir. 1934), *cert. denied,* 294 U.S. 708 (1935).

[178] Jenkins v. Jenkins, 64 P.3d 953, 957 (Id. 2003) (listing factors to be considered for the defense).

[179] *See* Noble v. Lubrin, 60 P.3d 1224, 1229 (Wash. Ct. App. 2003).

disclosed, so that the corporation may consider whether and how to address these obstacles.[180]

The above quote supports the view that the better choice is to place the burden of proving financial inability or legal incapacity and the like on the defendant. Recall that the fiduciary has had the chance to present the opportunity to his corporation before taking it for himself. Had this occurred, it would certainly have put the corporation to the test of whether it had a desire to acquire the opportunity as well as the financial and legal capacity to acquire it. Having not taken that course because the fiduciary believed it would have been a useless exercise, it is only appropriate that the fiduciary should later have the burden of proving such futility.

Courts are divided whether a third party's purported refusal to contract or deal with the corporation relieves the director or officer of presenting the opportunity to the corporation.[181] Unless the third party's refusal has at least first been disclosed to the corporation, there is no adequate means to test the assertion the corporation could not have acquired the opportunity had its directors or stockholders desired to take the plunge.[182] Similarly unsuccessful is the bald assertion that the corporation would not have acquired the opportunity if it had been given the chance. As one court reasoned, "if an opportunity is within the scope of a corporation's business, then the only acceptable method of determining whether a corporation would take advantage of the opportunity is by complete disclosure of the opportunity to it. To permit an after-the-fact determination as to whether [plaintiff] would have purchased the [opportunity] under the facts before us would abrogate the full disclosure rule."[183]

Other Considerations. The overall thrust of proscribing the fiduciary's usurpation of a corporate opportunity is to avoid self-seeking behavior to prevail over the fiduciary's loyalty to the corporation.[184] Some business opportunities, however, may be regarded as coming to the officer in his individual capacity or under circumstances free from any prior corporate claim. If the opportunity genuinely came to the director or officer in her individual, nonfiduciary capacity she will not be under a duty to act or contract as a representative of the corporation. This is an important consideration in defending against the charge that her acquisition of the opportunity was a breach of fiduciary duty. Indeed, this is one of two grounds under the ALI approach for proscribing corporate opportunities by non-senior management personnel.[185] For this defense to be successful there should not be countervailing considerations, such as the wrongful use of the corporation's assets or personnel to acquire or nurture the opportunity or that the business opportunity was necessary to the corporation.[186] It should not be a defense that

---

[180] Demoulas v. Demoulas Super Markets, Inc., 677 N.E.2d 159, 181 (Mass. 1997) (the defense to creating separate retail company without the plaintiff's participation was that state law limited the number of licenses for beer and wine that could be held by a single entity).

[181] *Compare* Production Finishing Corp. v. Shields, 405 N.W.2d 171 (Mich. Ct. App. 1987) (not a consideration); Owen v. Hamilton, 843 N.Y.S.2d 298, 301 (Sup.Ct. App. Div. 2007) *with* Moser v. Devine Real Estate, Inc., 839 N.Y.S.2d 843, 848 (Sup.Ct. App. Div. 2007) (is a consideration).

[182] Energy Resources Corp. v. Porter, 438 N.E.2d 391 (Mass. App. Ct. 1982).

[183] Imperial Group (Texas), Inc. v. Scholnick, 709 S.W.2d 358, 363 (Tex. Ct. App. 1986).

[184] *See* Science Accessories v. Summagraphics, 425 A.2d 957 (Del. 1980); Demoulas v. Demoulas Super Markets, Inc., 677 N.E.2d 159, 180 (Mass. 1997) (citing to this treatise).

[185] *See, e.g.,* Northeast Harbor Golf Club, Inc. v. Harris, 661 A.2d 1146 (Me. 1995).

[186] Red Top Cab Co. v. Hanchett, 48 F.2d 236 (N.D. Cal. 1931); Broz v. Cellular Info. Systems, Inc., 673 A.2d 148 (Del. 1996) (the interest is that of the corporation on whose board the outside director served and not that of its prospective acquiror).

the director or officer was not such when the opportunity was acquired if he learned of the opportunity while an officer or director. Resigning from the position does not rid a person of a fiduciary obligation to turn over opportunities discovered while a director or officer.[187]

The ultimate defense is that the board of directors or stockholders have rejected the business opportunity or otherwise have approved or ratified the director's or officer's acquisition of the opportunity.[188] Mere hesitation in response to the third party's terms does not alone amount to a rejection such that the fiduciary may then acquire the opportunity.[189] The approval or ratification need not be formal; it can occur informally by the disinterested directors or stockholders acquiescing in the director's or officer's acquisition of the opportunity.[190] However, the defense of rejection, approval, or ratification is conditioned on *full disclosure* of all material facts to the rejecting, approving, or ratifying body.[191] Disclosure to a lower-level employee does not satisfy the fiduciary's obligation to disclose relevant information to the corporation.[192] Absent such disclosure, the fiduciary has the burden of proving that acquiring the opportunity has not harmed the corporation.[193]

Where there has been a usurpation of a corporate opportunity, the corporation may elect to claim the benefits of the transaction.[194] The property the officer or director has acquired in violation of his fiduciary duty is held in constructive trust for the corporation.[195] Even if the defendant lost money on the usurped opportunity, the corporation is entitled to recover damages from the defendant for the profits it would have made.[196]

Private Ordering. Certainly in close corporations and LLCs there is much to commend private ordering among the firm's owners and managers to clarify the freedom to individually pursue business opportunities. The parties should consider when forming the business to what extent business opportunities that are with the firm's line of business or that could be within its line of business can nonetheless be acquired by an owner or manager. State statutes increasingly authorize such private ordering with respect to delineating the extent to which parties can so pursue business opportunities that might otherwise be deemed to belong to the entity.[197]

---

[187] Comedy Cottage, Inc. v. Berk, 495 N.E.2d 1006 (Ill. App. Ct. 1986).

[188] Massachusetts states this most forcefully. *See* Demoulas v. Demoulas Super Markets, Inc., 677 N.E.2d 159, 183 (Mass. 1997) ("the nondisclosure of a corporate opportunity is, *in itself*, unfair to a corporation and a breach of fiduciary duty") (emphasis added).

[189] CST, Inc. v. Mark, 520 A.2d 469 (Pa. Super. Ct. 1987).

[190] Jundt v. Jurassic Resources Dev., 656 N.W.2d 15, 24 (N.D. 2003).

[191] *See, e.g.,* Ostrowski v. Avery, 703 A.2d 117 (Conn. 1997); Yiannatsis v. Stephanis, 653 A.2d 275 (Del. 1995); Demoulas v. Demoulas Super Markets, Inc., 677 N.E.2d 159, 181 (Mass. 1997).

[192] Production Finishing Corp. v. Shields, 405 N.W.2d 171 (Mich. Ct. App. 1987).

[193] *See, e.g.,* Ostrowski v. Avery, 703 A.2d 117 (Conn. 1997).

[194] *See, e.g.,* Science Accessories Corp. v. Summagraphics Corp., 425 A.2d 957 (Del. 1980).

[195] *See* Restatement of Restitution §§ 194, 195 (1937).

[196] *See* CST, Inc. v. Mark, 520 A.2d 469 (Pa. Super. Ct. 1987).

[197] *See, e.g.,* Del. Code Ann. tit. 8, § 122(17); MBCA § 2.02(b)(6) (2016). *See* Rauterberg & Talley, Contracting Out of the Fiduciary Duty of Loyalty Waivers: An Empirical Analysis of Corporate Opportunity Waivers, 117 Colum. L. Rev. 1075 (2017) (finding opportunity waivers to directors are frequent among public companies and drawing some preliminary conclusions of variables associated with waivers).

§ 11.9 Forbidden Profits: Gains by Abuse of Official Position

Directors and officers are fiduciary representatives and as such are not allowed to obtain or retain a commission, bonus, gift, or personal profit or advantage "on the side" for their official action, as in connection with a purchase, sale, lease, loan, or contract by the corporation.[198] Accordingly, they may not keep such rewards without the knowledge and consent of the corporation.[199] A director or officer who has used corporate property or her position to profit personally cannot avoid disgorgement of the ill-gotten gains by invoking that she acted in good faith.[200] Similarly, the officers and directors may not permit any secret profit to be obtained by others.[201]

The rule against insider secret profits by directors and officers is similar to that which applies to agents generally. If an agent receives anything for his acts as such without the knowledge and consent of his principal, he is subject to liability to deliver it or its value or proceeds to the principal.[202] In a famous federal case,[203] *T*, in order to obtain funds with which to bid at a government sale of steel, offered *D*, president and a director of the *A* bank, a one-half interest in the venture. *D* caused the bank to make large loans to the *Y* corporation which had been organized by *T* to finance the steel transaction. The loans were approved by the bank's loan committee on *D*'s recommendation. They were good loans and were repaid promptly. *D* received from the steel venture $75,000 in salary, $73,000 in dividends, and $200,000 on the sale of his shares. After the bank directors refused to sue, the plaintiff shareholder sued on behalf of the bank to recover the profits received by *D*. The court held that *D* was liable to the bank for the profits so received because of his official relation to the bank. It was immaterial that the bank suffered no actual loss. Compensation paid by third persons to a corporate officer for a loan made by the corporation is properly regarded as part of the consideration for the loan or as a commission given for the officer's supposed influence in obtaining the loan.

A director of a corporation cannot remain silent when she knows that a fraud is being attempted against her corporation (and ultimately against its shareholders). It is her duty to acquaint the other officers of the corporation with the facts and to use every effort to prevent the consummation of the fraud. If by passive acquiescence he permits any part of the assets of the corporation to be fraudulently diverted or secret profits to

---

[198] Delano v. Kitch, 542 F.2d 550 (10th Cir. 1976) (bare disclosure of commission received by director on sale of stock is not sufficient under Kansas law).

[199] D'Addario v. Geller, 129 Fed. Appx. 1, 2 (4th Cir. 2005) (allegation that officers and directors received kickbacks from third person's receipt of valuable shares in exchange for worthless treasure maps sets forth breach of fiduciary duty claim).

[200] *See, e.g.,* Wilshire Oil Co. of Texas v. Riffe, 381 F.2d 646, 651 (10th Cir. 1967).

[201] *See generally* Berkman v. Rust Craft Greeting Cards, Inc., 454 F.Supp. 787 (S.D.N.Y. 1978) (failure of some directors to disclose to other board members that investment banker held an interest in firm's acquisition partner).

[202] Restatement (Third) Agency § 8.02 (2006) provides:

An Agent has a duty not to acquire a material benefit from a third party in connection with transactions conducted or other actions taken on behalf of the principal or otherwise through the agent's use of the agent's position.

[203] Blum v. Fleishhacker, 21 F.Supp. 527 (N.D. Cal. 1937), *aff'd in part, rev'd in part,* 109 F.Supp. 543 (9th Cir. 1940), *cert. denied,* 311 U.S. 665 (1940).

be obtained, she is guilty of neglect of duty to the corporation, for which she is liable in damages notwithstanding the fact that she did not herself profit financially thereby.[204]

Section 504 of the American Law Institute comprehensively addresses the use of corporation property and information by directors and senior executives.[205] In broad overview, the ALI proscribes the use of corporate position, property, or information without proof of harm to the corporation, except when non-proprietary information is used (for other than a transaction in securities) in which case proof of harm to the corporation is required.[206] Under the ALI's formulation, the officer or director can defend the charges by proving authorization or ratification by disinterested directors or shareholders after full disclosure.[207]

§ 11.10   The Duty of Employees Not to Compete

Employees (including officers) are precluded from actively competing with their employer during the course of their employment, even though they are not subject to a covenant not to compete.[208] The application of this universal principle occurs within the conflicting tugs of two important commercial considerations. On the one hand, our society prizes entrepreneurial activity and generally nurtures free and vigorous competition. It is with this spirit that fiduciaries are allowed to make important preparations to compete while still in their company's employ and also are allowed within broad limits to leave with skills and knowledge acquired from the company.[209] On the other hand, there is the strong view that it is unfair for the employing company to compete with the very individuals in whom it then places trust and responsibility for serving its best interests.

To what extent may an employee prepare to compete with his employer? Within the broad principles discussed below, the answer to this question is heavily dependent on the facts of the individual case.[210] Most courts recognize the right of an employee while still an employee to incorporate a rival corporation and procure land, buildings, and equipment for its future operation.[211] Obviously, there is a concern that the employee not usurp any opportunity belonging to the employer company when acquiring assets for the employee's own business.[212] Indeed, many cases that appear to raise questions of an employee competing with her employer are instead examined through the usurpation of corporate opportunity window examined in the preceding section.[213] The employee is not allowed to venture beyond the formation and outfitting while an employee; once the employee terminates his relationship with the employer, however, he may actively

---

[204] Reid v. Robinson, 220 P. 676, 681 (Cal. Ct. App. 1923).

[205] 1 ALI, Principles of Corporate Governance: Analysis and Recommendations § 5.04 (1992).

[206] 1 ALI, Principles of Corporate Governance: Analysis and Recommendations § 5.04(a)(3) (1992).

[207] 1 ALI, Principles of Corporate Governance: Analysis and Recommendations § 5.04(a)(4) (1992).

[208] *See, e.g.*, Maryland Metals, Inc. v. Metzner, 382 A.2d 564, 568 (Md. 1978); Anderson v. Bellino, 658 N.W.2d 645 (Neb. 2003).

[209] This principle has long been recognized. *See* Nichol v. Martyn, 2 Esp. 732, 734 (N.P. 1799).

[210] *See* Bancroft-Whitney Co. v. Glen, 411 P.2d 921, 935 (Cal. 1966).

[211] *See* FoodComm Intern. v. Barry, 328 F.3d 300, 303 (7th Cir. 2003) (under most circumstances an employee can incorporate a rival company and procure assets for future operation).

[212] *See* Chelsea Indus. v. Gaffney, 449 N.E.2d 320 (Mass. 1983); Scanwell Freight Express STL, Inc. v. Chan, 162 S.W.3d 477, 480–81 (Mo. 2005).

[213] *See, e.g.*, American Fed. Group, Ltd. v. Rothenberg, 136 F.3d 897 (2d Cir. 1998) (solicited customers of firm); Patmon v. Hobbs, 280 S.W.3d 589, 596 (Ky. Ct. App. 2009).

compete.[214] Setting up any prospective business involves recruiting employees, and there has been a good deal of litigation whether a departing officer has breached his fiduciary duty by recruiting his employer's employees to work for him in the business to be established. Absent evidence of an intent to cripple the current employer by raiding its key employees, some jurisdictions permit informing fellow workers of an intent to start a competing firm and even permit mild forms of solicitation of co-workers.[215] There are, however, more restrictive jurisdictions that proscribe an employee soliciting co-workers to join him in a competing enterprise before he has severed his own employment relationship with the employer.[216]

Even though employees cannot solicit their employer's customers as long as they are employees, they can advise the customers of their intent to leave and start a competing business.[217] Regardless of whether customers are permanent or continuous or that their business can be obtained only by competitive bidding, solicitation is still a violation of the employee's fiduciary obligation.[218] The corporation has a right to be free from interference with its customers from those employed by the corporation.[219] The line between solicitation and advising is not always a bright one. The question turns upon just how specific the communication is so that the more general the communication the more it appears to be mere preparation to leave and not to compete as such. Merely informing customers of an intent to leave and of a desire for their business in the future does not constitute solicitation.[220] However, pressing the customer for business[221] and *a fortiorari* filling customer orders while still an employee[222] are impermissible solicitations. In *C-E-I-R, Inc. v. Computer Dynamics Corporation*,[223] the court observed that the statement that the "defendants hoped that when they got organized and got in business they'd have an opportunity to compete for the [customer's] business" taken alone was not solicitation, but when repeated and combined with other factors in the case the defendants engaged in solicitation.

Normally, once the employee leaves the corporation, she can solicit its customers.[224] However, if the customer list is confidential or amounts to a trade secret, the former employee cannot use the information to approach customers.[225] As will be seen later, customer lists may become a trade secret when they are unusually sensitive, are not generally known in the trade, or were built after great effort and expense by the plaintiff.

---

[214]   Vernon Library Supplies, Inc. v. Ard, 550 S.E.2d 108 (Ga. Ct. App. 2001).

[215]   The easiest case for finding no breach is when co-workers approach the defendant to inquire if they can also join the new venture. *See* The McCallister Co. v. Lynn Kastella, 825 P.2d 980 (Ariz. Ct. App. 1992).

[216]   *See* Foodcomm Intern. v. Barry, 328 F.3d 300, 303 (7th Cir. 2003).

[217]   The McCallister Co. v. Lynn Kastella, 825 P.2d 980 (Ariz. Ct. App. 1992).

[218]   C-E-I-R, Inc. v. Computer Dynamics Corp., 183 A.2d 374, 379 (Md. 1962).

[219]   *See* ABC Trans Nat'l Transp., Inc. v. Aeronautics Forwarders, Inc., 379 N.E.2d 1228, 1239 (Ill. App. Ct. 1978).

[220]   Ellis & Marshall Assocs. v. Marshall, 306 N.E.2d 712, 714 (Ill. App. Ct. 1973).

[221]   Foodcomm. Intern. v. Barry, 328 F.3d 300, 303 (7th Cir. 2003); Hanson Staple Co., Inc. v. Eckelberry, 677 S.E.2d 321, 324 (Ga. Ct. App. 2009) (informing customers of unhappiness and intent to seek new employment not a breach); Hartung v. Architects Hartung/Odle/Burke, Inc., 301 N.E.2d 240, 245 (Ind. Ct. App. 1973).

[222]   Cross Wood Prods., Inc. v. Suter, 422 N.E.2d 953 (Ill. App. Ct. 1981).

[223]   C-E-I-R, Inc. v. Computer Dynamics Corporation, 183 A.2d 374, 377 (Md. 1962).

[224]   *See* J Bar H, Inc. v. Joanna Johnson, 822 P.2d 849, 861 (Wyo. 1991) (former fifty-percent owner who was squeezed out of the business can commence a competing business).

[225]   Raines v. Toney, 313 S.W.2d 802, 809 (Ark. 1958). Criminal sanctions are now available under the Economic Espionage Act of 1996, 18 U.S.C. §§ 1831 et seq. (1994), for the misappropriation of trade secrets.

For example, when the defendant who was a former employee of the plaintiff's home cleaning business used the list of plaintiff's customers to secure clients for his business, the court held that the list could not be used because the plaintiff had developed it after great effort and expense.[226] After all, it was not common knowledge which houses out of all those in the city would desire a cleaning service. On the other hand, if the names can be ascertained from a phone book or industry listing, there generally is no protection afforded to the list. Thus, when a plaintiff dairy sought to enjoin a former employee from soliciting the dairy's customers, the court reasoned that it was a small town and everyone drank milk. The court refused to issue the injunction.[227] The Ninth Circuit provides a very clear expression of a rule of thumb for whether information is a trade secret: "the most important consideration [in determining whether something is a trade secret]is whether the information is readily accessible to a reasonably diligent competitor or salesman."[228]

Even if the customer list is not a trade secret, the list may still be a protected property right of the defendant's former employer. For example, if the employee copied, physically removed, or intently studied the list, the employee's subsequent use of the list will be enjoined on the theory the list had been converted.[229] But if only "casual memory" is involved, no breach exists if the customers are solicited soon after the employee resigns.[230] As a rule of thumb, the smaller the list, the lower the percentage solicited, or the more widely known are the customers all make less likely the finding of a breach.

The fiduciary may not use the corporation's facilities to compete or prepare to compete,[231] and it is a breach to use corporate trips to evaluate prospective sites for a competing factory or to learn how to design and build a factory similar to the current employer's factory.[232]

Courts deciding whether a director, officer, or employee has unfairly competed frequently do so on the basis of the fiduciary having misappropriated his employer's trade secret. A trade secret is "a plan or process, tool, mechanism or compound known to its owner and those of his employees to whom it is necessary to confide it. In order for the business information to be a trade secret, it must have value to the business; it must take a form different from ordinarily acquired general information."[233] Some factors used to determine if something is a trade secret are: (1) the extent to which the information is known outside the business; (2) the extent to which it is known by employees and others involved in the business; (3) the extent of measures taken by the owner to guard the secrecy of the information; (4) the value of the information to the owner and to its competitor; (5) the amount of effort or money expended in developing the information; and (6) the ease or difficulty with which the information can be properly acquired or

---

[226] Town & Country House & Home Serv. v. Newberry, 147 N.E.2d 724 (N.Y. 1958).

[227] Ameristar Jet Charter, Inc. v. Cobbs, 184 S.W.3d 369, 374–75 (Tex. App. 2006) (finding no breach when ex-employee discovers information independently via extensive exploration of public information on the Internet).

[228] Hollingsworth Solderless Terminal v. Turley, 622 F.2d 1324, 1332 (9th Cir. 1980).

[229] See Leo Silfen, Inc. v. Cream, 278 N.E.2d 636 (N.Y. 1972) (no violation because only 47 of 1100 customers were solicited).

[230] Leo Silfen, Inc. v. Cream, 278 N.E.2d 636, 641 (N.Y. 1972).

[231] Foodcomm Intern. v. Barry, 328 F.3d 300, 303 (7th Cir. 2003).

[232] Chelsea Indus. v. Gaffney, 449 N.E.2d 320, 323 (Mass. 1983).

[233] Bimba Mfg. Co. v. Starz Cylinder Co., 256 N.E.2d 357, 363 (Ill. App. Ct. 1969).

duplicated by others.[234] Public disclosure of the information destroys its confidentiality and hence the information's protection in equity.[235]

When misconduct is found, courts have applied a variety of sanctions and remedies. The employee may be enjoined[236] and a constructive trust imposed on the competing business and profits therefrom.[237] Courts also invoke their equitable powers to substitute the former employer as a party to a contract that the employee wrongfully caused the former employer to lose.[238] The employee can also be required to return any compensation he received from the employer during the period of his breach.[239] In addition, any consequential damages suffered by the employer can be recovered from the employee.[240]

PART C.   CONTROLLING STOCKHOLDER'S FIDUCIARY OBLIGATIONS

§ 11.11   Fiduciary Duties of Controlling Shareholders

Courts and legal scholars have given much attention to the scope of the controlling stockholder's[241] fiduciary duty to the corporation and its minority shareholders.[242] Although there is an emerging debate whether activist, albeit non-controlling, shareholders should be subject to some minimal duties when seeking to influence the corporation or their fellow stockholders,[243] courts have constrained the scope of shareholder fiduciary obligations to those who enjoy a position of control *within* the company.[244]

Control is variously defined. It is certainly present when a person owns a majority of the voting shares. The fiduciary duty of a controlling shareholder is not limited to

---

234   *See* Restatement of Torts § 757, Comment (1939).

235   Bacon v. Volvo Service Center, Inc., 597 S.E.2d 440, 443–44 (Ga. Ct. App. 2004).

236   C-E-I-R, Inc. v. Computer Dynamics Corp., 183 A.2d 374 (Md. 1962); Lawter Int'l, Inc. v. Carroll, 451 N.E.2d 1338, 1347 (Ill. App. Ct. 1983).

237   *See* Genesis Technical and Fin. v. Cast Navigation, 905 N.E.2d 569, 576–77 (Mass. App.Ct. 2009).

238   Sialkot Importing Corp. v. Berlin, 68 N.E.2d 501 (N.Y. 1946).

239   Phansalkar v. Andersen Weinroth & Co., L.P., 344 F.3d 184, 205 (2d Cir. 2003).

240   Phansalkar v. Andersen Weinroth & Co., L.P., 344 F.3d 184, 205 (2d Cir. 2003).

241   In corporate law, "controlling interest" refers to dominant ownership of a corporation's stock. Dixon v. Pro Image, Inc., 987 P.2d 48, 54 (Utah 1999). For a stimulating dissection of the taxonomy of macro impacts of control, *see* Ronald J. Gilson, Controlling Shareholders and Corporate Governance: Complicating the Comparative Taxonomy, 119 Harv. L. Rev. 1642 (2006).

242   *See* Thomas L. Hazen, Transfers of Corporate Control and Duties of Controlling Shareholders— Common Law, Tender Offers, Investment Companies—and a Proposal for Reform, 125 U. Pa. L. Rev. 1023, 1027 (1977).

243   *See, e.g.*, Dammann, The Controlling Shareholders' General Duty of Care: A Dogma That Should Be Abandoned, 2015 Ill. L. Rev. 479 (2015); Kahan and Rock, When the Government Is the Controlling Shareholder, 89 Tex. L. Rev. 1293 (2011) (exploring what systems are available to impose accountability on the government when it assumes control of a company as occurred in some instances in the financial crisis in 2008); Iman Anabtawi & Lynn Stout, Fiduciary Duties For Activist Shareholders, 60 Stan. L. Rev. 1255 (2008) (duties traditionally applied to controlling stockholders should be extended to activist stockholders).

244   An illustration of this focus is *Franchise Servs. of N. A. v. United States*, 891 F.3d 198, 208–09 (5th Cir. 2018), holding that under Delaware law it believed no fiduciary duty attached to a shareholder unless that shareholder had "actual control" of corporate conduct which requires evidence of effective domination and control. The case involved a "golden share" provision in which as part of a financing plan a minority shareholder who also was an unsecured creditor was granted a right through the debtor company's articles of incorporation to block any filing of a bankruptcy petition by the debtor company. The Fifth Circuit held no fiduciary duty surrounded the golden share as the holder of the right did not enjoy sufficient control.

those who own a numerical majority of the shares. When a minority shareholder has sufficient power to exert de facto control, Delaware recognizes the fiduciary duty of such a controlling.[245] The duty customarily is found in instances where less than a majority voting shares are owned but the individual has a demonstrated record of exercising influence or securing the nomination of a majority of the directors. The test of control in Delaware is variously expressed. For example, control is determined by whether the defendant had power such that the directors "could not freely exercise their judgment." *In re KKR Financial Holdings LLC Shareholder Litig.*,[246] KKR, owner of only 1 percent of KFN, was not in control even though KFN's officers were employees of KKR, everyday management of KFN was dependent on KKR affiliate per a contract that had substantial termination fee, and KFN's primary assets were debt securities that arose in connection with KKR transactions. Court believed KKR did not exhibit any "coercive power" over KFN's board. Whereas *In re Morton's Restaurant Group, Inc. Shareholders Litigation*[247] reasoned that when defendant owns less than majority of the voting shares the plaintiff must allege that as a practical matter the defendant is no differently situated than if he were a majority holder.

Typically, the duty is breached because of the effects of a corporate activity instituted in response to the controlling stockholder's influence.[248] Unlike the directors' and officers' fiduciary obligations, where the breach can be found for nonfeasance as well as misfeasance, cases finding breaches by controlling stockholders involve affirmative action that can be traced to the controlling stockholder. Thus, it can be said that the controlling stockholder's fiduciary duty does not require that the controlling stockholder act as a guardian charged with the duty to act affirmatively by encouraging or driving the corporation to take action that will increase the value of the shares.[249] Although this fiduciary duty ordinarily arises in the case of majority shareholders, it can apply to any shareholder who has control over corporate actions even if not majority owners.[250]

The basis for the controlling stockholder's fiduciary obligation is the sound policy that, just as directors are bound by certain fiduciary obligations, one who has the potential to control the board's actions should be subject to an obligation as rigorous as

---

[245] *See, e.g.,* Kahn v. Lynch Commc'n Systems, Inc., 638 A.2d 1110, 1115 (Del. 1994) (minority shareholder with 45% of the shares exercised sufficient control to warrant imposition of a fiduciary duty); Citron v. Fairchild Camera and Instrument Corp., 569 A.2d 53, 70 (Del. 1989); Tornetta v. Musk, 2019 WL 4566943 (Del. Ch. 2019) (Elon Musk with 22% share ownership was considered to have de facto control and thus entire fairness scrutiny applied to his compensation package); Smith v. Atlantic Properties, Inc., 422 NE.2d 798, 802 (Mass. Ct. App. 1981) (minority shareholder with de facto control due to high vote requirement owed fiduciary duty); Zimmerman v. Bogoff, 402 Mass. 650, 524 N.E.2d 849 (1988) (minority shareholder's elf-interested acts breached fiduciary duty); Ehrenhaus v. Baker, 216 N.C.App. 59, 88, 717 S.E.2d 9, 28 (2011) (finding "the Delaware courts' articulation of the non-disclosure principle persuasive[,]").

[246] 101 A.3d 980 (Del. Ch. 2014).

[247] 74 A.3d 656 (Del. Ch. 2013), *See also* In re Crimson Exploration, Inc. Stockholder Litig., 2014 Del. Ch. LEXIS 213 (Del. Ch. Oct. 24,2014) (providing a detailed analysis of Delaware cases on the subject of what constitutes control and concludes that a 33.7 percent owner not control person absent specific allegations of domination).

[248] *See, e.g.,* Crowley v. Communications for Hosps., Inc., 573 N.E.2d 996 (Mass. App. Ct.), *review denied,* 577 N.E.2d 309 (Mass. 1991).

[249] *See, e.g.,* Jones v. H. F. Ahmanson & Co., 460 P.2d 464 (Cal. 1969) (controlling stockholder under no duty to have caused company to split company's shares so all shares were more marketable, but when did act to increase marketability had a duty to assure equal treatment for all shareholders).

[250] *See, e.g.,* Corwin v. KKR Financial Holdings LLC, 125 A.3d 304 (Del. 2015); Calesa Associates, L.P. v. American Capital, Ltd., 2016 WL 770251 (Del. Ch. 2016). *See also* Appel v. Berkman, 180 A.3d 1055 (Del. 2018) (disclosures were not as full as they might have been and rendered the vote subject to challenge under Corwin v. KKR Financial Holdings LLC, 125 A.3d 304 (Del. 2015)).

those applied to the directors. Quite separate is the belief that control in a corporation, whether publicly or closely held, carries with it the potential that the controlling stockholder may choose to exercise control to reap disproportionate benefits at the expense of the corporation or noncontrolling shareholders such that protection of their interests is desirable. That protection arises by imposing the fiduciary standards on the controlling stockholder exercising the controlling influence. The overall objective of the controlling stockholder's fiduciary obligation is not to bar the controlling stockholder from acting in his own self-interest but to assure that when so acting the interests of the corporation are also served.[251]

In the public corporation, the threshold question is invariably whether the challenged activity or transaction is to be judged by the business judgment rule or the "inherent fairness" test. This is essentially a question of whether the activity or transaction is to be viewed somewhat neutrally so that it carries a presumption of propriety, or whether the court will approach the activity or transaction skeptically by placing the burden of proving its overall fairness on the controlling stockholder. The leading case emphasizing this dichotomy is *Sinclair Oil Corporation v. Levien*,[252] where, under the influence of its parent, the subsidiary corporation over a seven-year period had paid $38 million more in dividends than it had earned. The plaintiff argued that the subsidiary's dividend policy was guided exclusively by the parent's need for cash and resulted in the subsidiary company's oil exploration activities contracting at a time that the parent company's exploration activities were dramatically expanding. The Delaware Supreme Court held the Chancellor erred in placing on the parent the burden of proving the dividend policy's intrinsic fairness. The Supreme Court held that the burden of proving intrinsic fairness is imposed only when there is self-dealing: "Self-dealing occurs when the parent, by virtue of its domination of the subsidiary causes the subsidiary to act in such a way that the parent receives something from the subsidiary to the exclusion of, *and* detriment to, the minority stockholders of the subsidiary."[253] The plaintiff has the burden of proving self-dealing.[254]

Sinclair Oil held that because all stockholders shared proportionately in the dividend declarations there was no self-dealing, and hence the dividend policy carried the presumptions of the business judgment rule. Only if the plaintiff could have borne the difficult burden of establishing that the dividends were the product of an improper motive or waste would the parent have been required to prove the subsidiary's dividend policy was intrinsically fair.[255] The plaintiff in *Sinclair Oil* also questioned the parent causing the subsidiary to modify to the parent's advantage contracts that obligated the parent to purchase specified quantities of oil at established prices. Because the parent's contracting with the subsidiary fit within the above definition of self-dealing, the court

---

[251] *See, e.g.*, Chiles v. Robertson, 767 P.2d 903, 912 (Or. Ct. App. 1989) ("The fiduciary best fulfills its duties if it approaches them with the attitude of seeking the beneficiary's interests rather than the personal interests of the fiduciary. . . .").

[252] Sinclair Oil Corp. v. Levien, 280 A.2d 717 (Del. 1971).

[253] 280 A.2d at 720 (emphasis added).

[254] Gabelli & Co. Profit Sharing Plan v. Liggett Group, Inc., 444 A.2d 261 (Del. Ch. 1982). *See also* In re Primedia, Inc. Derivative Litig., 910 A.2d 248 (Del. Ch. 2006) (dominance and self dealing sufficiently pled where parent caused subsidiary to redeem preferred at redemption price before contractually obligated to do so).

[255] The court suggests such would have been established if plaintiff could prove that business opportunity embraced by the parent would otherwise have gone to the subsidiary.

held the parent had the burden of proving the contracts' modification was intrinsically fair.

Sinclair Oil's standard of self-dealing purports to be a test of who should bear the burden of proof in actions challenging transactions undertaken in response to the controlling stockholder's influence. On close inspection one may reasonably question whether the Delaware Supreme Court's standard of self-dealing involves more than deciding who bears the burden of proof. It would appear an extremely rare case where the controlling stockholder will be able to establish the transaction's intrinsic fairness after the court has concluded that the same transaction had allowed the controlling stockholder to receive a benefit "to the exclusion of, and detriment to, the minority stockholders."[256] It may therefore be more appropriate to view *Sinclair Oil*'s test of self-dealing as a test of who prevails in the suit.

Erosion of *Sinclair Oil* at the expense of minority holders occurs in *Thorpe by Castleman v. CERBCO, Inc.*,[257] where the controlling stockholder responded to a third person's offer to acquire the assets of a controlled subsidiary by selling its control in the holding company. The court held that, even though there was a breach of the controlling stockholder's fiduciary obligation by his usurping the opportunity to sell the subsidiary, the damages from the breach were *not* the amount of the purchaser price that would have been allocated to the minority. The court reasoned that since the controlling stockholder could block any sale, damages must be restricted to expenses the controlled company incurred to facilitate the transfer of control to the third party as well as the earnest money the controlling stockholder received.[258] Thus, the defendant's control over the enterprise could be used defensively to reduce the minority's recovery for losses they suffered as a result of the abuse of control.

Should the minority be able to raise the unique circumstances of controlling stockholder as a basis to support a claim the controlling stockholder was pursuing a unique gain, even though the controlling stockholder and the minority holders receive the same amount and type of consideration? *New Jersey Carpenters Pension Fund v. InfoGroup, Inc.*,[259] held that, even though all stockholders received the same type and amount of consideration per share, the controlling stockholder's significant need for cash was itself a unique benefit derived by approving the firm's sale that it triggered an entire fairness review. In contrast, no such conflict was found in *Sythes, Inc. v. Shareholder Litig.*,[260] where the controlling stockholder favored Johnson & Johnson's cash and stock offer over the bid of a private equity firm that required the controlling stockholder to take a substantial position in the private equity buyer. While recognizing that in certain limited instances where "disparate benefits" may be alleged to be garnered by the controlling stockholder notwithstanding the same price and type of consideration being received by all stockholders, there was no evidence that the controlling stockholder was so desperate for cash that the controlled firm's sale exclusively benefitted the controlling stockholder by solving a liquidity crisis. Moreover, the court emphasized the process of negotiating with various suitors not only indicated there was no rush to sale. And, as a result of the board's negotiations, Johnson & Johnson did materially improve its offer.

---

[256]   280 A.2d at 720.

[257]   Thorpe by Castleman v. CERBCO, Inc., 676 A.2d 436 (Del. 1996).

[258]   Thorpe by Castleman v. CERBCO, Inc., 676 A.2d 436, 444 (Del. 1996).

[259]   New Jersey Carpenters Pension Fund v. InfoGroup, Inc., 2011 WL 4825888 (Del. Ch. 2011).

[260]   50 A.3d 1022 (Del. Ch. 2012).

Outside of Delaware, courts adhere to the dichotomy between a presumption of propriety (that is, the business judgment rule) and imposing the burden of proving fairness (that is, the intrinsic fairness standard) but do not have the same rigorous and narrow test for their application as embodied in *Sinclair Oil*. Evidence of disproportionate gains to the controlling stockholder is prima facie evidence of a breach.[261] For example, the California Supreme Court set forth the controlling stockholder's obligation when exercising influence over the corporation's affairs, requiring that they exercise their power to benefit the shareholders proportionately and in a manner that is not in conflict with the proper conduct of the corporation's business.[262] Many jurisdictions therefore choose not to follow *Sinclair Oil*'s requirement that the controlling stockholder's influence must produce both an exclusive benefit to itself as well as a corresponding detriment to the corporation or its noncontrolling stockholders.

In broad overview, transactions shown to produce disproportionate gains to the controlling stockholders are typically judged by a standard of fairness, and the burden of proof is on the controlling stockholder. Thus, the burden of establishing the fairness of the transaction is placed upon the controlling stockholder when it is transacting business with the corporation and when the plaintiff has made a threshold showing that the transaction disproportionately benefits the controlling stockholder.[263] "Fairness" is articulated in many different ways, such as bearing the qualities one would expect in "arms-length bargaining,"[264] or having terms within the "expectations" of the stockholders,[265] or bearing indicia of "objective fairness." As is apparent, none of these standards portends exactness, so the results in individual cases are difficult to predict *ex ante*, and the cases frequently appear in conflict.

The greatest variance across jurisdictions appears in disputes on matters that are inherent and peculiar to parent-subsidiary corporations.[266] The environment of parent-subsidiary corporations is rife with instances where for tax or other regulatory purposes the activities of the parent and subsidiary may be combined. When their joint treatment yields a common benefit, the question frequently arises how that benefit is to be allocated. For example, in *Case v. New York Central Railroad*,[267] the parent filed a consolidated return with its 80 percent owned subsidiary whereby the parent's losses offset the subsidiary's gains, producing a net tax savings to the subsidiary of $3,825,717.43. Pursuant to a preexisting agreement between the two corporations, 97 percent of the tax savings was paid by the subsidiary to the parent. The court found no advantage was gained by the parent corporation at the expense of subsidiary. The court emphasized that the division of the tax savings was pursuant to the preexisting

---

[261] *See, e.g.*, Chiles v. Robertson, 767 P.2d 903 (Or. Ct. App. 1989) (relying upon Sections 5.04 and 5.11 of the ALI Principles of Corporate Governance: Analysis and Recommendations (1992), holds the duty is owed to "use their power to control the corporation in a way that would benefit all shareholders proportionately").

[262] *See* Jones v. H. F. Ahmanson & Co., 460 P.2d 464 (Cal. 1969).

[263] *See* Locati v. Johnson, 980 P.2d 173 (Or. Ct. App. 1999).

[264] *See* Odyssey Partners, Ltd. Partnership v. Fleming Companies, 735 A.2d 386 (Del. Ch. 1999) (need not bid a "fair" price at foreclosure sale at which other possible bidders were present, even though foreclosure proceeding initiated by the controlling stockholder).

[265] Case v. New York Cent. R.R., 204 N.E.2d 643 (N.Y. 1965).

[266] *See* Chanoch Schreiber & Aaron Yoran, Allocating the Tax Savings Derived from Filing Consolidated Corporate Tax Returns, 29 Baylor L. Rev. 243 (1977).

[267] Case v. New York Central Railroad, 204 N.E.2d 643 (N.Y. 1965).

agreement,[268] that the arrangement did produce a benefit of reducing the subsidiary's taxes that it would not have enjoyed but for the agreement, and that the parent's losses were a valuable factor in producing the tax savings. In sum, the arrangement was upheld because the subsidiary was no worse off than it would have been had there been no consolidation.[269]

There is no easy reference point to decide what would be a fair sharing in benefits that can occur only in control relationships.[270] Certainly it is too abstract to judge such transactions by what would occur in arm's-length dealings, because the filing of consolidated tax returns by definition does not involve arm's-length transactions.[271] Moreover, reference to what allocations occur in other parent-subsidiary relationships will only invoke a standard that itself is likely to embody dominance and control. California appears to provide the most certainty by holding that fairness requires the benefit be shared proportionately.[272] There is a good deal of appeal to the view that if the controlling stockholder garners more than its proportionate share, it should at least have the burden of proving circumstances justifying why the allocation was fair to the controlled company.

Much like what occurs when directors contract with their corporation, contracts between the corporation and its controlling stockholder invoke critical review. Absent disinterested approval or ratification, the controlling stockholder has the burden of proving the transaction's overall fairness to the corporation.[273] It is well recognized that disinterested minority shareholder approval of a transaction between the controlling stockholder and the corporation places the burden on the challenging party to prove the transaction's unfairness.[274] There is authority that the same presumption of propriety can attach if the independent body of directors approves the transaction.[275]

The American Law Institute's Corporate Governance Project deals specifically with transactions between the corporation and its controlling stockholder,[276] the controlling

---

[268] *See also* In re Reading Co., 711 F.2d 509 (3d Cir. 1983).

[269] In a more demanding jurisdiction, more is required than not being worse off because of the agreement. In Alliegro v. Pan Am. Bank, 136 So.2d 656 (Fla. Dist. Ct. App. 1962), the allocation arrangement whereby the tax savings were allocated to the loss company was held an improper arrangement unless ratified by the stockholders.

[270] An interesting approach was taken in Chiles v. Robertson, 767 P.2d 903 (Or. Ct. App. 1989), where the issue was the lessee-controlling stockholder extracting from the lessor corporation (which was controlled by the same controlling stockholder but also had as its minority stockholder some individuals who were also minority holders in the lessee corporation) consent for the lessee to assign the lease to a subsidiary owned by the controlling stockholders and the lessee's managers. Upon approval of the assignment, the lessee would begin paying higher rents ("upcharges"). The court held that in determining the fairness the issue was not whether the lessee could ultimately prevail under the law that it could withhold its consent, but whether an independent lessee would have been reasonably demanding in seeking to use the possibility of withholding its consent as a bargaining chip to extract payment for consenting to the assignment. *Id.* 918 & 920.

[271] Meyerson v. El Paso Natural Gas Co., 246 A.2d 789, 794 (Del. Ch. 1967) (allocation of entire tax savings to the parent upheld where court found nature of the issues so problematic that the wisest policy is to commit the allocation to the business judgment rule unless the plaintiff established "gross and palpable overreaching").

[272] Smith v. Tele-Communication, Inc., 184 Cal.Rptr. 571 (Cal. Ct. App. 1982).

[273] Efron v. Kalmanovitz, 38 Cal.Rptr. 148 (Ct. App. 1964).

[274] *See, e.g.,* Rosenblatt v. Getty Oil Co., 493 A.2d 929 (Del. 1985).

[275] *See, e.g.,* Odyssey Partners v. Fleming Companies, 735 A.2d 386 (Del. Ch. 1999) (noting director fees of $24,000 per year not so great as to compromise independence and a director who formerly was employee of, and who had a consulting arrangement with, controlling stockholder deemed independent where his membership on board was requested by directors who were clearly independent).

[276] ALI Principles of Corporate Governance: Analysis and Recommendations § 5.10 (1992).

stockholder's use of corporate assets, information, and influence,[277] and the controlling stockholder's usurpation of a corporate opportunity.[278] In broad overview, the scheme of the American Law Institute places the burden of proving fairness on the controlling stockholder with respect to any challenge to a transaction between the corporation and its controlling stockholder and allegations that the controlling stockholder has usurped a corporate opportunity[279] unless the particular transaction has received disinterested director approval, shareholder approval, or ratification. When the controlling stockholder uses corporate assets or information or otherwise exercises influence over the corporation with the effect of securing an economic benefit, the American Law Institute demands either that value be given to the corporation or that any benefit the controlling shareholder secures is proportionally available to other shareholders similarly situated.[280] In sum, the American Law Institute follows a course that is more protective of stockholder rights on these questions than does Delaware but is well within the approach that appears to apply in most jurisdictions.

In the close corporation setting, the breach can be established on more personal basis, such as by proving that the controlling stockholder had an abrasive or intimidating manner toward the minority stockholders[281] or that the controlling stockholder foreclosed the minority from the opportunity to participate in meetings or receive information about corporate transactions.[282] In the closely held corporation the controlling stockholder's fiduciary obligation is increasingly viewed as being akin to the obligation that partners owe to one another.[283] The close corporation's controlling stockholder owes a duty of "utmost good faith and fairness" to the controlled corporation and its stockholders.[284] To be sure, such a standard is inherently devoid of specifics but nevertheless embodies a tone that carries with it the view that challenges transactions between the controlling stockholder and the corporation, or merely the exercise of influence over corporate activities; each will be subjected to close review for overall fairness and proper motivation.[285]

§ 11.12   Unequal Treatment Among Different Classes of Securities or Holders of the Same Class of Security[286]

Disputes regarding the controlling stockholder's obligations sometimes occur in the context of the conflicting rights between different classes of stock where the focus of the

---

[277] ALI Principles of Corporate Governance: Analysis and Recommendations § 5.11 (1992).

[278] ALI Principles of Corporate Governance: Analysis and Recommendations § 5.12 (1992).

[279] With respect to a controlling stockholder, "corporate opportunity" is defined in terms of whether it was developed or received by the corporation, came to the controlling stockholder *primarily* because of the stockholder's relationship to the corporation, or is business activity the controlling stockholder has represented to the shareholders as being of the type that will be within the corporation's scope of business. *Id.* § 5.12(b). *See* Thorpe by Castleman v. CERBCO, Inc., 676 A.2d 436 (Del. 1996) (controlling stockholders were entitled to obtain a control premium for their shares and in that sense compete with their corporation, but only after disclosing to the corporation that they had received a bid to purchase the corporation).

[280] ALI Principles of Corporate Governance: Analysis and Recommendations § 5.11(a)(1) & (2) (1992).

[281] *See, e.g.,* Evans v. Blesi, 345 N.W.2d 775 (Minn. Ct. App. 1984).

[282] *See, e.g.,* Duncan v. Lichtenberger, 671 S.W.2d 948 (Tex. Ct. App. 1984).

[283] Estate of Schroer v. Stamco Supply, Inc., 482 N.E.2d 975 (Ohio Ct. App. 1984).

[284] Crowley v. Communications for Hosps., Inc., 573 N.E.2d 996 (Mass. App. Ct.), *review denied,* 577 N.E.2d 309 (Mass. 1991).

[285] *E.g.,* Knaebel v. Heiner, 663 P.2d 551 (Alaska 1983).

[286] Material in this section has been adapted from James D. Cox, Equal Treatment For Shareholders: An Essay, 19 Cardozo L. Rev. 615 (1997).

dispute is the power of one class (that is, that held by the controlling stockholder) over the rights of another class of stock (that is, the class held by the minority shareholders) and also among holders of the same class of security where disparate treatment among holders arises as a result of actions by those in control of company. In this context, courts frequently support fiduciary obligations by officers, directors, and controlling stockholders to all classes of stockholders, preferred as well as common.[287] The leading decision involving duties of the controlling shareholder qua shareholder is the Third Circuit's decision in *Zahn v. Transamerica Corporation*.[288] The essence of the complaint was that Transamerica, as the controlling shareholder of the Axton-Fisher Tobacco Company, breached its fiduciary duty to minority shareholders in executing its plan to liquidate Axton-Fisher.[289] The controversy pitted Transamerica, who owned virtually all the Class B common shares, against the holders of the Class A common shares. The Class A common shares were convertible into Class B shares, could be redeemed at $60 (plus any dividends in arrears), by the board after notice, and on liquidation was entitled to receive twice as much as the Class B common shares. Transamerica owned virtually all the Class B common shares and through their greater voting power elected Axton-Fisher's board of directors. Transamerica, with full knowledge of the increased value of Axton-Fisher's inventory of tobacco, proceeded toward a two-step liquidation that took advantage of the Class A shareholders' ignorance of the increased asset value. Transamerica caused the Axton-Fisher board to redeem its Class A shares at a price much lower than their liquidation value and then proceeded to liquidate Axton-Fisher.[290] The notice to the Class A common shareholders of its intent to redeem their shares at $60 per share (plus an additional $20.80 in accrued dividends) did not disclose the board's intention to liquidate Axton-Fisher or the liquidation value of Axton-Fisher.

The Third Circuit held that there was an "unmistakable fiduciary duty of those in control of the corporation."[291] However, the opinion speaks rather vaguely as to why Transamerica breached its fiduciary duty to the holders of the Class A common shares. The opinion strongly suggests that Transamerica breached its duty by causing Axton-Fisher's board of directors to redeem the Class A common shares on the eve of the company's liquidation. If this were in fact the court's holding, it would conflict with the contractual right of Axton-Fisher to redeem the Class A common shares at a set price.

The objective of any redemption provision is to allow those in control of the corporation—*i.e.*, Transamerica—to eliminate an expensive financial appendage—*i.e.*, the Class A common shares—when it is in the best interests of the residual owners of the firm—*i.e.*, the Class B common shares—Transamerica. A far wiser approach in such a case is not to condemn the exercise of one class's contractual rights over another class

---

[287] *See, e.g.*, Eisenberg v. Chicago Milwaukee Corp., 537 A.2d 1051, 1062 (Del. Ch. 1987).

[288] Zahn v. Transamerica Corporation, 162 F.2d 36 (3d Cir. 1947). *See also, e.g.*, Mansfield Hardwood Lumber Co. v. Johnson, 268 F.2d 317 (5th Cir. 1959), *cert. denied*, 361 U.S. 885 (1959); Judah v. Delaware Trust Co., 378 A.2d 624 (Del. 1977).

[289] Transamerica owned virtually all of the Axton-Fisher Class B common stock that had full voting rights. The plaintiffs' Class A shares, in addition to having cumulative dividend and conditional voting rights, were callable at $60 per share plus accrued dividends and were convertible into Class B shares on a one-for-one basis. The Class A shares also contained a liquidation preference and were entitled to receive twice as much as Class B out of the common fund. 162 F.2d at 38–39.

[290] For an analysis of the extent of the plaintiffs' injury and the proper measure of damages, *see* Speed v. Transamerica Corp., 135 F.Supp. 176, 186–194 (D. Del. 1955), *modified on other grounds*, 235 F.2d 369 (3d Cir. 1956).

[291] 162 F.2d at 42.

but to examine the totality of their contractual arrangement to discern whether the exercise is consistent with the relationship they have woven through their relative rights, preferences, and privileges. The resolution of the controlling stockholder's fiduciary obligation to another class of shareholders by reference to their relative rights in the corporation's articles of incorporation is but an application of the more general approach of allowing stockholders the freedom to contract among themselves as to the standards they believe appropriate for their relationship. In both close and public corporations the controlling stockholder does not breach his fiduciary obligation to the other stockholders by engaging in conduct that, though harmful to the noncontrolling stockholder, is nevertheless consistent with the terms of the parties' agreement.[292]

Thus in *In re Reading*[293] the Third Circuit upheld the controlling stockholder being able to acquire services from the corporation at below market rate pursuant to an agreement among all the stockholders, even though the complaining minority stockholder's business had changed such that it could no longer make use of the corporation's services. The court held that as long as the discount was authorized by the stockholders' agreement, the controlling stockholder was not required to recognize the change in circumstances for the minority stockholder.[294] Similarly, the Third Circuit in *Zahn* could easily have concluded that Transamerica's breach was not its causing Axton-Fisher's board to redeem the Class A common shares or liquidating Axton-Fisher; rather, the breach was failing to disclose the liquidation value of Axton-Fisher. Armed with such information, and facing a pending redemption of their shares, the holders of Class A common shares would exercise their right to convert into the Class B common shares, where they would reap more than the $80.80, to be received solely through the redemption of their Class A common shares. That is, the very purpose behind the Class A common shares having a right to convert into Class B common shares, as well as a waiting period between the board's announced intention to redeem the Class A common shares and the actual redemption can easily be seen as having the intent of facilitating the conversion of the Class A common shares into the Class B common shares.[295]

Accordingly, in subsequent proceedings the Third Circuit held that the call of the Class A common shares was valid even though it was driven by the desire to benefit one class of shares over another such that the proper measure of damages was what the Class A stockholders would have received had they converted their shares into Class B common shares.[296] Courts frequently find in such contractual settings an implied condition that the board of directors will give adequate notice to the minority holders so they can exercise their right to convert.[297] Claims of unfair treatment can also arise among shareholders of the same class of security or between different classes of securities where there is no dominant stockholder. What is "fair" is always an intriguing question. In the corporate context, fairness is not a point, but a spectrum of values. Inquiries in this context therefore seek to determine whether the transaction falls within that spectrum. When the question is the rights among stockholders, particularly those

---

[292] *See, e.g.,* Evangelista v. Holland, 537 N.E.2d 589 (Mass. App. Ct. 1989).

[293] In re Reading, 711 F.2d 509 (3d Cir. 1983).

[294] In re Reading, 711 F.2d 509, 520 (3d Cir. 1983).

[295] One may question what then is the purpose behind allowing the Class A common shares to receive twice as much on liquidation as the Class B common shares? This provision assumes significance where the liquidation is involuntary—*e.g.,* bankruptcy, and not at the request of the controlling stockholder.

[296] Speed v. Transamerica Corp., 235 F.2d 369 (3d Cir. 1956).

[297] *See, e.g.,* Van Gemert v. Boeing Co., 520 F.2d 1373 (2d Cir. 1975).

of the same class, there is some authority that there are spectrums within spectrums. For example, in *Nixon v. Blackwell*,[298] the Delaware Supreme Court reversed the Chancery Court's holding that the non-employee holders of Class B stock were entitled to liquidity equal to that which the employee holders of Class B stock enjoyed. More than half of the Class B shares were held by an employee stock ownership plan ("ESOP"). Employees being terminated and those retiring were granted the option to receive their interest in the ESOP in Class B shares or cash; senior officers and directors owned Class A shares and, by agreement, could exchange those shares for Class B shares upon the officer's or director's retirement or death.[299] To facilitate repurchase of Class B shares held by former officers or directors, the corporation purchased "key man" insurance to fund purchases that were triggered by the holder's death.[300] Because a comparable repurchase option was not extended to non-employee Class B stockholders, they sued, alleging they were improperly excluded from the company's share repurchase program.

The *Nixon* case involved self-dealing because directors, as prospective holders of Class B shares, unlike the plaintiffs, enjoyed their shares being redeemed by the corporation with funds provided by insurance policies purchased by the corporation. Nevertheless, Chief Justice Veasey rejected the plaintiff's call for equal treatment, reasoning that "[t]o hold that fairness necessarily requires precise equality is to beg the question."[301] "[S]tockholders," he explained, "need not always be treated equally for all purposes."[302] Nixon answered the question of fair treatment for the non-employee Class B holders by identifying a corporate benefit with the corporation's repurchase of retiring employees' shares—to prevent the shares from passing into the hands of members of the founder's family or descendants of employees.[303] The court believed the arrangement was consistent with the intent underlying the original creation of the Class B stock; the Class B shares were to be held by passive investors with no active voice in the corporation.[304]

One can easily get lost in a vast semantical battle under *Nixon's* approach to fairness, where qualities unrelated to the share terms are considered in evaluating how value is to be distributed among the owners. For example, no one disputes the fact that parties receiving the same, *i.e.*, equal, amount for their shares have each been treated fairly. If one looks beyond a person's status as a shareholder, however, to some other endowment she carries to the transaction, such as longevity, loyalty, or some element of sacrifice for the corporate good, one may argue that the failure to compensate such shareholder for those intangible qualities results in that person's unfair treatment. In this case, equal payment for all shares is unfair because it fails to respect the additional value some holders add to their shares.

Correlatively, if the person who brings additional endowments to the corporation receives a higher price than those who do not, those receiving the lesser amount are not being treated unfairly. Under this type of analysis, the semantical question turns on the context in which "fairness" is being assessed. Should it be evaluated only with respect to the rights of a share, or should it include the characteristics of the shareholder herself?

---

[298] Nixon v. Blackwell, 626 A.2d 1366 (Del. 1993).

[299] Nixon v. Blackwell, 626 A.2d 1366, 1371 (Del. 1993).

[300] Nixon v. Blackwell, 626 A.2d 1366, 1372 (Del. 1993).

[301] Nixon v. Blackwell, 626 A.2d 1366, 1377 (Del. 1993).

[302] Nixon v. Blackwell, 626 A.2d 1366, 1376 (Del. 1993).

[303] 626 A.2d at 1377, 1379.

[304] Nixon v. Blackwell, 626 A.2d 1366, 1379 (Del. 1993).

If the latter theory prevails, the fairness approach advocated by *Nixon* appears to be correct.

Fiduciary duties in the corporate context exist to fill gaps where the parties have not otherwise set forth their rights and relationships. Fiduciary duties are therefore similar to corporate statutes in that they provide convenient off-the-rack rules to simplify the process of contracting, and permit deviations from corporate provisions when the interests of third parties (most notably, creditors) will not be harmed. Though there is much concern and uncertainty regarding the duty owed minority stockholders, the burdens of the directors' and controlling stockholders' fiduciary duties are not great. The commands of corporate fiduciary duties provide a fairly low threshold for what constitutes appropriate behavior in the corporation. Indeed, the most notable feature of corporate fiduciary duty law is the lack of rigor found in its prescriptions.

Far more important than the broad standards by which the courts purport to judge defendants' behavior is whether the court will deprive the challenged transaction of the deferential presumptions dictated by the business judgment rule.[305] The all-important burden of persuasion follows from whether the defendants' conduct falls within the business judgment rule. So viewed, the single most important issue in considering the content of fiduciary duty obligations among stockholders is the threshold consideration whether the challenged transaction enjoys the presumption of propriety.[306] In this context, the question of the content of the fiduciary duty among stockholders is answered by inquiring into what assumptions we should make regarding the rights, privileges, and preferences among stockholders who have not otherwise chosen to deviate from the recognized norm. Armed with this standard, courts can then take the next step of determining what showing is necessary to consider whether the parties before it have chosen to depart from that norm. This is precisely the course followed by Justice Traynor in *Jones v. H.F. Ahmanson & Co.*[307]

In *Jones,* the defendants transferred their Association common stock (which represented eighty-five percent of all outstanding shares) to United Financial, a holding company they had created. For each share exchanged, they received 250 United shares and $927.50 cash. The minority were not provided an opportunity to participate in the exchange. They prevailed in their suit charging that their exclusion was wrongful and effectively destroyed the marketability of their shares. Justice Traynor, reasoning that "whenever control is material" there is a comprehensive rule of good faith and inherent fairness to the minority.[308] After several such incantations of the majority's fiduciary obligations to act in good faith toward the minority, *Jones* applies the standard of equal treatment for the minority, unless the majority invokes a *compelling justification* for deviating from the norm.[309] That is, the most important point for the court was that the minority shareholders were excluded and that there was a consequential disproportionate gain on the part of the majority holders.

---

[305] *See* Cede & Co. v. Technicolor, Inc., 634 A.2d 345 (Del. 1993).

[306] *See* Levien v. Sinclair Oil Corp., 261 A.2d 911 (Del. Ch. 1969), *rev'd,* Sinclair Oil Corp. v. Levien, 280 A.2d 717 (Del. 1971).

[307] Jones v. H.F. Ahmanson & Co., 460 P.2d 464 (Cal. 1969).

[308] Jones v. H.F. Ahmanson & Co., 460 P.2d 464, 474 (Cal. 1969).

[309] Jones v. H.F. Ahmanson & Co., 460 P.2d 464, 476 (Cal. 1969).

Chapter 12

OBLIGATIONS ARISING OUT OF TRANSACTIONS IN SHARES

Table of Sections

PART A. STATE LAW

PART A.   STATE LAW

§ 12.1 The Sale of Corporate Control

A purchaser of a controlling interest in a corporation often pays a premium above the prevailing market price for the stock.[1] Legal scholars, the judiciary, and even Congress have examined the extent to which these premiums are unfair to the remaining shareholders and to the corporation. Over many years, significant scholarly energy has been devoted to the sale of corporate control and the appropriate treatment of the resulting premium, with a view toward providing unifying principles to aid courts in their analysis of control transfers.

In 1932, Professor Berle developed the "corporate asset" theory of control.[2] The essence of this theory is that the premium above the per share market price realized by

---

[1]   How many shares constitute a "controlling" interest must often be determined by a factual inquiry in the particular case. *See, e.g.,* Kings County Dev. Co. v. Buell, 709 F.2d 1516 (9th Cir. 1983) (court held that sale of 14 percent of corporation's outstanding stock to purchaser who already owned 20 percent was not a sale of control).

[2]   *See* Adolf A. Berle, "Control" in Corporate Law, 58 Colum. L. Rev. 1212 (1958); Adolf A. Berle, The Price of Power: Sale of Corporate Control, 50 Cornell LQ 579 (1964).

the seller in return for a controlling block of stock is a corporate asset because it "arises out of the ability which the holder has to dominate property which in equity belongs to others."[3] It follows that the entire premium "if it goes anywhere, must go into the corporate treasury."[4] A major objection to Professor Berle's approach is that the price paid for a controlling block will necessarily be higher than the previous prevailing per share price because the control purchaser creates an increased demand that, combined with a constant supply, results in an upward pressure on the price. Another reason suggested for rejecting a per se prohibition on control premiums is that the ability to exercise control as a vehicle for making the enterprise more valuable is a cognizable property right attaching to a controlling interest rather than a corporate asset.

Another school of thought counsels that the obligation of the controlling stockholder is to assure an equal sharing of the premium among the noncontrol shares as well as the control shares.[5] Under this approach, all stockholders must have an equal opportunity to sell the same portion of shares as the controlling stockholder. Thus, if the existing control stockholder owns 51 percent of the shares and the purchaser wishes to acquire 51 percent, the existing control stockholder may sell only 51 percent of her shares, and the noncontrol stockholders must also have the opportunity to each sell 51 percent of their shares at the same price as that offered to the existing control stockholder. This theory has a parallel in a fundamental principle of corporate law that all shares of the same class are to be treated equally.[6] For example, any discrimination in a merger in the amount paid for shares is unlawful such that the higher amount must be paid to all holders.[7]

Within the equal sharing approach are powerful incentives for the existing control stockholder to closely examine the worthiness of the purchaser of control whenever the new purchaser wishes to acquire less than all the outstanding shares. This vigilance arises under the equal opportunity approach because when the new purchaser acquires less than all the outstanding shares, the former controlling stockholder becomes a minority stockholder such that her holdings are at risk should the new purchaser of control prove to be harmful to the corporation or the minority stockholders. A negative aspect of the equal opportunity approach is that its adoption tends to reduce the frequency of transfers of control because the existing control stockholders do not wish to become minority stockholders but instead prefer the purchase of all their shares.

Under the equal opportunity approach, however, the purchase of all the existing control person's shares can occur only when the purchaser of control is willing to acquire all the company's voting stock. This necessarily raises the cost of the acquisition. A natural economic corollary is that the equal opportunity approach will result in fewer transfers of control. It is wise to view transfers of control, especially at a premium, as desirable because on average the company's resources will be put to a greater use; the very sources of the premium are the financial or operating synergies the purchaser of

---

[3]   Adolf A. Berle & Gardiner C. Means, The Modern Corporation and Private Property 216 (rev. ed. 1968).

[4]   Adolf A. Berle & Gardiner C. Means, The Modern Corporation and Private Property 216–217 (rev. ed. 1968).

[5]   The leading commentator for this view is William Andrews. See William Andrews, The Stockholder's Right to Equal Opportunity in the Sales of Shares, 78 Harv. L. Rev. 505 (1965).

[6]   See, e.g., In re Sea-Land Corp., 642 A.2d 792, 800 n.10 (Del. Ch. 1993) ("all shares of the same type, series, or class are, by definition, equal").

[7]   See Beaumont v. American Can Co., 538 N.Y.S.2d 136, 137 (N.Y. Sup. Ct. 1988).

control contemplates from the acquisition. There is strong empirical support for the view that the value of the noncontrolling stockholders' shares increases following a transfer of control.[8]

While the sale of control provokes a good deal of academic debate, the courts have not embraced any of the above schools of thought and have taken a more ad hoc approach to the facts of a particular case.

Courts generally hold that any premium paid to acquire controlling stock is merely a reflection of the greater value of that stock due to its control potential, and as such it is a natural consequence of stock ownership and cannot be considered a corporate asset.[9] More generally, every stockholder, including the controlling stockholder, is at liberty to dispose of her shares at any price as long as there is no cause to believe or suspect the sale will proximately harm the corporation or its stockholders, or will necessarily interfere or mislead the other stockholders in exercising their same right to sell.[10]

Notwithstanding the courts' rejection of a *per se* equal opportunity rule for control premiums, as pointed out in the next section, fiduciary duties may give rise to an obligation to share a control premium under certain situations. Additionally, contractual agreements or provisions in the corporate charter can give rise to an equal opportunity requirement.[11]

§ 12.2   Fiduciary Duties of Sellers of Corporate Control

Numerous courts have held that a seller of control may become liable in certain circumstances for the harm to the corporation caused by the purchaser. Clearly, however, the liability is far from absolute.[12] In the leading case, *Insuranshares Corporation v. Northern Fiscal Corporation*,[13] after the transfer of a controlling interest, the purchasers proceeded to loot the corporation. The district court held the control sellers liable and reasoned that, at a minimum, the transferor of a controlling block of shares owes a duty to the corporation to protect it when "the circumstances surrounding the proposed transfer are such as to awaken suspicion and put a *prudent* man on his guard—unless a *reasonably adequate* investigation discloses such facts as would convince a *reasonable person* that no fraud is intended or likely to result."[14] When the circumstances do awaken suspicion in the reasonably prudent person, the seller of control has a duty to make such inquiry as a reasonably prudent person would make.[15]

[8]   *See* Clifford G. Holderness & Dennis P. Sheehan, The Role of Majority Shareholders in Publicly Held Corporations, 20 J. Fin. Econ. 317 (1988) (minority shares of 31 studied firms increased 7.3 percent and 12.8 percent in one day and twenty days, respectively, following transfer of controlling block of stock); Michael Bradley, Interfirm Tender Offers and the Market for Corporate Control, 53 J. Bus. 345 (1980) (listed share prices remained significantly above pre-control transfer levels 80 days following sale of control). The gains expected from the transfer of control no doubt support the premium paid to acquire control.

[9]   Martin v. Marlin, 529 So.2d 1174, 1176 (Fla. Dist. Ct. App. 1988).

[10]   *See* Doleman v. Meiji Mut. Life Ins. Co., 727 F.2d 1480 (9th Cir. 1984).

[11]   *See, e.g.*, In re Delphi Financial Group Shareholder Litigation, 2012 WL 729232 (Del. Ch. 2012) (charter provision that two classes of stock would receive the same consideration in any merger could trigger an obligation to share the control premium).

[12]   Clagett v. Hutchison, 583 F.2d 1259 (4th Cir. 1978).

[13]   Insuranshares Corporation v. Northern Fiscal Corporation, 35 F.Supp. 22 (E.D. Pa. 1940).

[14]   35 F.Supp. at 25 (emphasis supplied).

[15]   Harman v. Willbern, 374 F.Supp. 1149 (D. Kan. 1974), *aff'd*, 520 F.2d 1333 (10th Cir. 1975).

Liability does not attach, however, merely for the exercise of poor business judgment.[16] A minority view requires proof that the controlling stockholder had actual knowledge, not inquiry notice.[17] The weakness of requiring actual knowledge is that the standard encourages the seller to place his head in the sand when negotiating with his buyer.[18] On the other hand, the minority shareholders owe no fiduciary obligation to their fellow minority holders.[19]

The circumstances awakening suspicion in *Insuranshares Corporation* were as follows: (1) the sellers' probable knowledge that the purchase would be financed by a pledge of the corporation's assets; (2) the corporation president's clear disposition to allow a sale to be financed by pledging those assets; (3) the sellers' awareness of the purchasers' plan to have a large part of the corporation's assets converted into cash prior to the sale; (4) the inflated price or premium paid for control, especially given the nature of the business, which was an investment trust with no physical assets but only the ready equivalent of cash in the form of marketable securities; (5) warnings from the sellers' attorneys as to their potential liabilities for dealing with little-known purchasers; and (6) the fact that the corporation had been looted five years before by a different group, who had gained control by using the same method of financing.[20]

Insuranshares illustrates the highly factual nature of a court's determination in sale of control litigation. This orientation is embraced by the American Law Institute, whose provision makes the controlling stockholders' fiduciary obligation depend in part on the transfer not occurring when "it is apparent from the circumstances that the purchaser is likely" to violate the purchaser's fiduciary obligations so as to acquire a substantial financial benefit for himself.[21]

Looting and mismanagement by the purchaser of control are classic types of misbehavior that form the backdrop for inquiring whether the seller's suspicions were sufficiently piqued for there to have been a breach in disposing of control. Many cases do not involve looting or mismanagement by the new controlling stockholder but rather the diversion of a potential premium from the noncontrolling stockholders by the former controlling stockholder. This occurs when the purchaser offers to acquire at a substantial premium an asset of the company[22] or all the shares of the company[23] and the controlling stockholder diverts most or all of the premium to himself by converting the offer for the asset or all the shares to a transaction in which the controlling stockholder sells only his shares to the third party at a substantial premium. In these situations, the courts embrace the idea that the fiduciary obligation of controlling stockholders is not to divert or appropriate for themselves an offer or opportunity that a third-party purchaser is

---

[16]   Harman v. Willbern, 374 F.Supp. 1149, 1161–1163 (D. Kan. 1974), *aff'd,* 520 F.2d 1333 (10th Cir. 1975).

[17]   The leading case for this view is *Levy v. American Beverage Corp.,* 38 N.Y.S.2d 517, 526 (App. Div. 1942).

[18]   *See* Swinney v. Keebler Co., 329 F.Supp. 216 (D.S.C. 1971), *aff'd,* 480 F.2d 573, 577 (4th Cir. 1973).

[19]   *See, e.g.,* Priddy v. Edelman, 883 F.2d 438 (6th Cir. 1989).

[20]   480 F.2d at 577. *See also* DeBaun v. First W. Bank & Trust Co., 120 Cal.Rptr. 354 (Ct. App. 1975).

[21]   ALI, Principles of Corporate Governance: Analysis and Recommendations § 5.16(b) (1994) (hereinafter ALI, Principles of Corporate Governance).

[22]   *See, e.g.,* Dunnett v. Arn, 71 F.2d 912 (10th Cir. 1934) (officers who owned controlling block of stock sold their shares at price not available to noncontrol shares after earlier refusing to sell company assets to purchaser of shares).

[23]   Brown v. Halbert, 76 Cal.Rptr. 781 (Ct. App. 1969); Thorpe by Castleman v. CERBCO, Inc., 676 A.2d 436 (Del. 1996).

prepared to extend that would benefit all the stockholders proportionally. The language of the American Law Institute's provisions is broad enough to proscribe the controlling stockholder's appropriation of the corporation's opportunity to sell its asset at a premium,[24] but these provisions appear to proscribe the conversion of an offer for all the stockholders' shares only if the controlling stockholder secretly acquires shares from the noncontrolling shareholders as part of his disposition of a control block to a third party.[25]

No case has held, however, that the controlling stockholder breaches its duty by failing actively to initiate transactions that are likely to yield a premium for the noncontrolling stockholders' shares.[26] The controlling stockholder's fiduciary duty with respect to dispositions of control is breached by commission, not omission. One of the most unusual factual settings where this was demonstrated was in *Jones v. H. F. Ahmanson & Company*,[27] where Chief Justice Roger Traynor invoked an equal-opportunity approach, discussed earlier. The case is unique because the opportunity diverted in *Jones* was created by the controlling stockholder rather than by a third party. In *Jones* the individual defendants together held 85 percent of the stock in the United Savings and Loan Association (Association), a closely held corporation whose stock was rarely marketed beyond the original shareholders. Wanting to take advantage of a bullish market for savings and loan stock, the defendants decided to undertake a public offering. The individual defendants formed United Financial as a holding company for their shares in the savings and loan association, and then caused United Financial to make a public offering of its shares. The minority shareholders, who were not allowed to place their stock in the holding company and participate in the offering, filed suit, claiming that the formation of the holding company and the subsequent public offering constituted a breach of the majority's fiduciary duty to the minority shareholders, as the minority shareholders were denied their share of the benefits resulting from the creation of a public market. Chief Justice Traynor, writing for the court, used broad language in upholding the plaintiffs' complaint: "[T]he comprehensive rule of good faith and inherent fairness to the minority in any transaction where control of the corporation is material properly governs controlling shareholders in this state."[28] The court accordingly held that the minority shareholders of the savings and loan association were entitled to damages on the basis of what they would have received had they been invited to participate on an equal basis in the formation of the holding company and the subsequent public offering.[29]

Two interesting and distinctive facts in *Jones* were the absence of any finding that the minority stockholders were worse off after United Financial was created by the

---

[24] ALI, Principles of Corporate Governance: Analysis and Recommendations § 5.12(b)(1) (1994) (hereinafter ALI, Principles of Corporate Governance).

[25] ALI, Principles of Corporate Governance: Analysis and Recommendations § 5.16(a) (1992):

[T]he controlling stockholder does not satisfy the duty of fair dealing . . . if (a) the controlling stockholder does not make disclosure concerning the transaction . . . to other shareholders with whom the controlling shareholder deals in connection with the transaction.

[26] There is no duty to obtain a premium for the minority's shares, even if the controlling stockholder successfully negotiates for a few of the minority to dispose of their shares at the same premium that the controlling stockholder receives. *See* Shoaf v. Warlick, 298 S.C. 415, 419, 380 S.E.2d 865 (1989) (citing Martin v. Marlin, 529 So.2d 1174, 1179 (Fla. Dist. Ct. App. 1988)).

[27] Jones v. H. F. Ahmanson & Co., 460 P.2d 464 (Cal. 1969).

[28] 460 P.2d at 474 (emphasis supplied; footnote omitted).

[29] The *Ahmanson* decision was heralded as breaking new ground in even its most narrow reading by "chang[ing] the generally accepted theory of stockholders' fiduciary responsibility." 83 Harv. L. Rev. 1904, 1906 (1970).

defendants and that *Jones* is not a true sale-of-control case because the defendants continued to control Association through their control of United Financial. *Jones* is a rare example of a court awarding damages without finding the noncontrolling stockholders or the corporation were worse off after the transaction. The decision appears to be guided by the court's belief that any disproportionate gain the controlling stockholder garners through its controlling position should be proscribed.

When there has been a breach of duty in the transfer of control, the more frequently invoked remedy is to require the vendor of control to disgorge the control premium.[30] The best illustration of this is the classic decision of *Perlman v. Feldmann*,[31] where a controlling block of stock to Newport, a producer of steel, had been sold at a premium to Wilport, a consortium of steel users. The court viewed the premium as a bonus for transfer of the ability to control Newport's steel allocation—an especially valuable asset during the war-time shortage.[32] The court therefore ordered that the control premium be disgorged.[33]

The holding is especially interesting in the absence of any finding that Newport had been harmed by Wilport; there was no evidence that Wilport caused Newport to sell its production to Wilport at less than market prices or that Newport's long-term interests were sacrificed to serve the short-term needs of Wilport. For these reasons *Perlman* remains a provocative decision. It should be observed that compelling the *Perlman* defendants to disgorge their premium could best be justified on prophylactic considerations: the court reasoned that the defendants had committed at least a technical breach of their fiduciary duties by transferring control to a buyer, about whom there was genuine suspicion that the buyer may well not have been committed to nurturing and protecting the long-term interests of Newport. It is hard to believe, for example, that the court would have required the premium to be disgorged if the defendants had sold control to General Foods or to another buyer who was not an end user of steel. But having sold their shares to an end user of the company's product during a time in which that product was in very short supply and not having inquired as to the future treatment of Newport or its noncontrolling stockholders, there is every reason to find the selling defendants had committed a technical breach of their fiduciary obligations.

It is also possible to recover for any assets or profits lost because of the misbehavior of the new controlling stockholder.[34] The purchaser of control is liable for his vendor's breach on a theory of civil conspiracy.[35]

---

[30]   *See, e.g.*, Perlman v. Feldmann, 219 F.2d 173 (2d Cir.), *cert. denied*, 349 U.S. 952 (1955), where it was necessary to also determine the fair value of the shares without their "appurtenant control" over the company's production and marketing. *See* Perlman v. Feldmann, 154 F.Supp. 436 (D. Conn. 1957).

[31]   Perlman v. Feldmann, 219 F.2d 173 (2d Cir.), *cert. denied*, 349 U.S. 952 (1955).

[32]   219 F.2d at 178.

[33]   On remand, the district court found the enterprise value of the corporation, based on its book value and earnings potential, to be $14.67 per share. This amount was then subtracted from the $20 received by Feldman and his fellow sellers, giving rise to a total premium of $2,126,280. The complaining stockholders, who held 63 percent of the stock, were granted a judgment of $1,339,769, their proportionate amount of the control premium Perlman v. Feldmann, 154 F.Supp. 436 (D. Conn. 1957). This amount was paid directly to the noncontrolling stockholders to assure that Wilport was not benefited, but the defendants were allowed to retain their pro rata share of the premium. *Id.* at 446–447.

[34]   *See* DeBaun v. First W. Bank & Trust Co., 120 Cal.Rptr. 354, 362 (Ct. App. 1975).

[35]   Doleman v. Meiji Mut. Life Ins. Co., 727 F.2d 1480 (9th Cir. 1984) (no duty owned directly by purchaser of control for misconduct in transfer of control).

§ 12.3 Resignation of Directors in Connection with the Sale of Control

In general, a director or other officer, even though elected for a fixed term, may resign at any time with definite notice.[36] Unless a future date or acceptance by the corporation is specified, resignation takes effect at once, and no acceptance is necessary.[37] There are occasions, however, when directors and officers are not free to quit with impunity. It continues to be true today that directors cannot accept payment in any form or guise for their resignations and delivery of control or for the substitution of others in their place, and they are accountable for any monies so received.[38]

If directors agree to sell their shares, resign from their offices, procure other shareholders to sell their shares, and hand over control to irresponsible persons, they may be liable under various theories. For example, the directors may be liable to fellow shareholders for the profit or excess price that they received over other shareholders whom they persuaded to sell their shares, or to the corporation for secret profits that were obtained by their official acts and for damages caused by the wrongful acts of their transferees and successors.

§ 12.4 The Sale of a Corporate Office

The vendor of a block of shares may lawfully arrange for sitting directors to resign seriatim and for the nominees of her purchaser to be appointed to the board vacancies created by the resignations, provided the block so transferred represents working control. To be sure, it is always possible for one who purchases control between the annual election of directors to simply wait until the next annual meeting or to seek a special meeting at which the new controlling stockholder's nominees can be elected. This rarely occurs because the new holder of control wishes her influence to be felt immediately. There are sound policy reasons supporting this desire:

> The easy and immediate transfer of corporate control to new interests is ordinarily beneficial to the economy and it seems inevitable that such transactions would be discouraged if the purchaser of a majority stock interest were required to wait some period before his purchase of control could become effective. Conversely, it would greatly hamper the efforts of any existing majority group to dispose of its interests if it could not assure the purchaser of immediate control over corporation operations. I can see no reason why a purchaser of majority control should not ordinarily be permitted to make this control effective from the moment of the transfer of stock.[39]

The above quoted justification is equally sound for a block that represents working control even though it represents less than a majority of the shares.[40] Just such a situation was presented in *Essex Universal Corporation v. Yates*,[41] where the defendant contracted to sell at a premium to the plaintiff more than 28.3 percent of the outstanding shares of Republic Theaters. One clause in the sale agreement provided that the

---

[36] *See* Model Bus. Corp. Act § 8.07(a) (2016) (resignation of directors).

[37] Du Bois v. Century Cement Prods. Co., 183 A. 188 (N.J. 1936).

[38] Mitchell v. Dilbeck, 74 P.2d 233 (Cal. 1937).

[39] Essex Universal Corp. v. Yates, 305 F.2d 572, 578–579 (2d Cir. 1962).

[40] *See, e.g.,* In re Caplan, 246 N.Y.S.2d 913, 915 (N.Y. App. Div.), *aff'd,* 198 N.E.2d 908 (N.Y. 1964).

[41] Essex Universal Corporation v. Yates, 305 F.2d 572 (2d Cir. 1962).

defendant, who was also president and chairman of Republic's board, would resign his offices. The defendant raised the invalidity of the resignation clause and the premium as a defense to the plaintiff's action for breach of the contract. Relying largely on an early New York case, writing separately,[42] Judges Lumbard and Friendly in *Essex Universal Corporation* agreed that directors' agreements to resign were not invalid if they accompanied the transfer of a block that had effective working control, meaning the power to see that a majority of directors were the nominees of the holder of that block of shares.[43]

Delaware, when considering whether an individual is deemed to be such a control person, applies a similar approach. The test in Delaware is whether the defendant had power such that the directors "could not freely exercise their judgment."[44]

Thus a provision calling for directors to resign seriatim, with their replacements being the nominees of the purchasing party, is easily upheld when the block of shares transferred constitutes a majority of the voting shares. However, control frequently is exercised by a minority block of shares, especially in public corporations, so that there is not always numerical certainty whether the transferred block will indeed represent voting control in the hands of its purchaser.[45] Courts have had little problem holding that the premium paid for shares representing only 3 percent[46] or 4 percent[47] was in payment for the directors' resignations and not for working control. When, however, the new nominees were reelected at the first stockholders' meeting following their appointment, the court held there was no wrongful sale of a corporate office, even though the block of shares transferred represented only 10 percent of the voting power.[48]

§ 12.5 Statutory Provisions Affecting Control Transactions

Several states have provisions that empower a stockholder to petition for an election of the directors whenever a majority of the sitting directors have been appointed rather than elected by the stockholders.[49] Such provisions can provide a mechanism for testing whether seriatim resignations and appointments in fact are coupled with a block of shares that represents working control.[50] The true significance of such provisions is that they provide the means for stockholders to reestablish their bond to the board. As a practical matter, such provisions are likely to be invoked only when there is no clear

---

[42]   Barnes v. Brown, 80 N.Y. 527 (1880).

[43]   Judge Lumbard in *Essex Universal* added the additional requirement that this power be established on the assumption that management was neutral in the solicitation of the stockholders' votes.

[44]   In re KKR Financial Holdings LLC Shareholder Litig., 101 A.3d 980 (Del. Ch. 2014). KKR, owner of only 1 percent of KFN, held not in control even though KFN's officers were employees of KKR, everyday management of KFN was dependent on KKR affiliate per a contract that had substantial termination fee, and KFN's primary assets were debt securities that arose in connection with KKR transactions. The court believed KKR did not exhibit any "coercive power" over KFN's board. *See also* In re Crimson Exploration, Inc. Stockholder Litig., 2014 Del. Ch. LEXIS 213 (Del. Ch. Oct. 24, 2014) (providing a detailed analysis of Delaware cases on the subject of what constitutes control and concludes that a 33.7 percent owner not control person absent specific allegations of domination).

[45]   In *Insuranshares Corp. v. Northern Fiscal Corp.*, 35 F.Supp. 22 (E.D. Pa. 1940), the court held 27 percent ownership, when coupled with board membership and incumbency as an officer, represented working control.

[46]   In re Caplan, 246 N.Y.S.2d 913 (App. Div.), *aff'd*, 198 N.E.2d 908 (N.Y. 1964).

[47]   Brecher v. Gregg, 392 N.Y.S.2d 776 (Sup. Ct. 1975).

[48]   Carter v. Muscat, 251 N.Y.S.2d 378 (App. Div. 1964).

[49]   Cal. Corp. Code § 305(c) (West 1990); Del. Code Ann. tit. 8, § 223 (2001).

[50]   *See* Carter v. Muscat, 251 N.Y.S.2d 378 (App. Div. 1964).

group that represents working control, so that the election can be seen as reestablishing the board as the stockholders' representatives.

Section 14(f) of the Securities Exchange Act of 1934 requires extensive disclosures of the new directors' backgrounds whenever a majority of the board of directors is appointed as a consequence of an arrangement with a person required to make the filings required by the Williams Act amendments to the Securities Exchange Act by virtue of its purchases of, or tender offer for, a corporation's shares.[51] The information must be circulated to all voting stockholders not less than ten days before the directors are to take office.

§ 12.6 Other Share Transfers That Trigger Fiduciary Obligations—Greenmail and Equal Opportunity Concerns

"Greenmail" has been defined as the purchase at a premium price of a takeover bidder's or dissident's stock that is not available to other stockholders.[52] Several studies have found that the payment of greenmail causes a net decline in the value of the corporation, a decline that can be attributed to the above-market price paid for the shares as well as providing the unmistakable message that the board of directors does not welcome bids for control of the firm.[53] A traditional analysis examines the board's payment of greenmail for evidence the directors have acted unreasonably or in bad faith and places a slightly higher burden on those directors with a direct financial interest served by the preservation of the status quo.[54] The fact that a board's decision to pay greenmail is made in haste and with little evidence that there has been a genuine threat posed by the dissident shareholder provide powerful circumstantial evidence that the true motive of the directors in paying greenmail is to preserve their control.[55] On the other hand, evidence that the dissidents pose a threat to the corporation or its stockholders overcomes any suggestion that the greenmail payment was prompted solely by managerial self-interest.[56] A few states have enacted anti-greenmail provisions that, for example, condition repurchase of shares above a certain percentage upon stockholder approval.[57] Since 1987, greenmail payments have become much less attractive because section 5881 of the Internal Revenue Code of 1986 imposes a 50 percent excise tax of the gain on the shares' resale to the corporation. For the purpose of this provision, "greenmail" is defined as (1) the payment of any consideration by a corporation to acquire its shares from a stockholder when the shares have been held for less than two years; (2) within two years of their purchase the stockholder or those associated with the stockholder made or threatened to make a tender offer for the company's shares; and (3)

---

[51]   The Williams Act is triggered when market purchases or a tender offer will bring one's ownership of a class of a reporting company's equity securities above 5 percent.

[52]   Unocal Corp. v. Mesa Petroleum Co., 493 A.2d 946 (Del. 1985).

[53]   *See generally* Marcia Walter, *Aiding and Abetting the Breach of Fiduciary Duty: Will the Greenmailer Be Held Liable?*, 39 CASE W. RES. 1271, 1278–1290 (1989) for a discussion of the harms and benefits to shareholders as a result of the payment of greenmail.

[54]   *See, e.g.*, Polk v. Good, 507 A.2d 531 (Del. 1986).

[55]   *See* Heckmann v. Ahmanson, 214 Cal.Rptr. 177 (Ct. App. 1985).

[56]   *See* Polk v. Texaco, Inc., 507 A.2d 531 (Del. 1986).

[57]   *See, e.g.*, Minn. Stat. Ann. § 302A.553(3) (West Supp. 2002); Ariz. Rev. Stat. Ann. § 10–2704 (West 1996).

the buyback offer is not made to all the stockholders. A few states have prohibited greenmail payments unless approved by the stockholders.[58]

Hostile takeovers are a phenomenon only of publicly traded corporations; greenmail does not arise in closely held corporations. When a close corporation purchases shares at a premium, the corporation has a very different and unique concern: whether all the stockholders should have an opportunity to sell their shares to the corporation at the same price.[59] In a leading case, *Donahue v. Rodd Electrotype Company*,[60] a close corporation purchased shares from one of the controlling stockholders without offering to purchase the minority's holdings at the same price. The court analogized the relationship among owners of a close corporation to the relationship among participants in a partnership. The court thus applied the strict partnership standard, which requires "utmost good faith and loyalty" rather than the "less stringent standard of fiduciary duty" for public corporations.[61] It may be possible to extrapolate from *Donahue* the view that control premiums are a *per se* breach in close corporations. However, the facts of the case are much narrower than its rhetoric. In *Donahue* there was no stated business reason for the corporation's purchase of its controlling stockholder's shares or the board's decision not to extend the offer to the noncontrolling stockholders. The case was simply about a grab for company assets by the company's dominant stockholder and those he had elected to the board. Moreover, because a characteristic of close corporations is the relative illiquidity of its owners' shares, there is every reason to require special justification for excluding noncontrol shares from a deep and rich market for the company's shares when that market is the corporation itself. *Donahue*, however, continues to be relied on for the broad proposition that the minority must be given an equal opportunity to dispose of their shares in the same manner as the controlling stockholder when the close corporation is the purchaser.

As discussed in Chapter 10, transactions between a director and the corporation will be subject to a fairness scrutiny. Transactions in shares between a controlling shareholder and the corporation will be subject to a similar intrinsic fairness requirement.[62]

§ 12.7 Common Law Fiduciary Duty of Directors and Officers When Trading in Their Corporation's Shares

State courts are in conflict as to how far and when directors and officers come under a fiduciary duty to disclose inside information to individual shareholders before purchasing their shares. There is a growing tendency to hold officials responsible for taking unfair advantage of the ignorance of selling shareholders by failing to disclose to them non-public corporate information affecting the value of the shares.[63] Nonetheless,

---

[58] *See, e.g.*, Minn. Stat. Ann. § 302A.553(3) (West Supp. 2002); Ariz. Rev. Stat. Ann. § 10–2704 (West 1996).

[59] A full discussion of equal treatment and fairness appears *supra* § 11.13.

[60] Donahue v. Rodd Electrotype Co., 328 N.E.2d 505 (Mass. 1975), noted in 61 Cornell L. Rev. 986; 89 Harv. L. Rev. 423 (1975).

[61] 328 N.E.2d at 521.

[62] Kahn v. Tremont Corp., 694 A.2d 422 (Del. 1997) (existence of special negotiating committee did not relieve the burden of proving intrinsic fairness where one of the committee members had commercial ties to the controlling shareholder).

[63] Though the violation is premised on the defendant's position, such as being an officer or director, with the company, the violation itself is not an act committed in the defendant's capacity as, for example, an officer or director, but in her individual capacity. As such the conduct is properly seen as being outside the

the common law has had some difficulty, however, in consistently imposing liability on unscrupulous directors and officers dealing in a faceless market behind the screen of a stock exchange.

What Is Insider Trading? The insider trading problem can be pointed up by the following example. *D,* a director and president of the *C* Oil Company, knows by virtue of his official position that the corporation, after long efforts, has discovered oil on its land, increasing the value of its assets and its shares many-fold. This discovery is carefully concealed by the management so that the directors themselves can acquire adjoining lands and they and other insiders can buy up as many shares of the company's stock as possible. The shares are listed on a local stock exchange. *D* locates *P,* who is not an insider, and buys certain shares from her privately at the market price, which *D* knows is much less than their actual value. *P* asks no questions, and *D* volunteers no hint of any unusual development. *D* also purchases additional shares from *P* through brokers on the stock exchange before any report of the discovery has been made to the shareholders. Soon the news of the discovery becomes public, and the shares at once quadruple in value. *P,* who would not have sold if she had been informed of the discovery, seeks to have the sales that she made to *D* rescinded or to hold *D* accountable for the profits that *D* gained by his nondisclosure.[64]

Corporate officers and directors, when trading in their corporation's shares, must refrain from any designed or active misrepresentation by word or act. Pursuant to a view that was once the weight of authority, directors and officers are deemed not to stand in a fiduciary relationship to their opposite traders when trading in their corporation's shares, because individual dealing in shares is not corporate business.[65] Formally, the director's or officer's fiduciary relationship is, under this view, seen as being with the corporation and not its shareholders and certainly not with someone who will not become a shareholder until the challenged transaction is completed. Absent a fiduciary duty to the insider's opposite trader there is no basis upon which to premise a duty to disclose material non-public information known to the insider. On the other hand, a director who acts for the *corporation purchasing its own stock* does have a fiduciary relationship to the selling shareholder.[66]

Early Laissez-Faire Approach. Under the not-a-fiduciary view, corporate insiders are free to trade at arm's length, provided they do not commit a deliberate active fraud for the purpose of procuring the sellers' stock.[67] The not-a-fiduciary cases thus hold that officers and directors need not disclose to selling shareholders important corporate information that they possess—at least not in the absence of inquiry.[68] As any action by sellers had to be grounded on common law fraud, it was not only active

---

standard coverage of the liability policy for "acts performed in the capacity of an officer or director." *See, e.g.,* Cincinnati Ins. Co. v. Irwin Co., 2000 WL 1867297 (Ohio Ct. App. 2000).

[64] An analogous situation arose in the SEC v. Texas Gulf Sulphur Co., 401 F.2d 833 (2d Cir. 1968), *cert. denied,* 394 U.S. 976 (1969), where the defendant insiders had advance knowledge of ore discoveries.

[65] *See* Goode v. Powers, 397 P.2d 56 (Ariz. 1964) (director has same right as other shareholders to sell stock as long as director acts in good faith and sale does not injure corporation); Tryon v. Smith, 229 P.2d 251, 254 (Ore. 1951) (same).

[66] Fleetwood Corp. v. Mirich, 404 N.E.2d 38 (Ind. Ct. App. 1980).

[67] Sometimes, however, when officers or directors fail to disclose information that is significant to the transaction, there is a distinct likelihood their omission will be treated as a *tacit* misrepresentation of the facts. *See* Jim Short Ford Sales, Inc. v. Washington, 384 So.2d 83, 86–87 (Ala. 1980).

[68] *See, e.g.,* Hardy v. South Bend Sash & Door Co., 603 N.E.2d 895 (Ind. Ct. App. 1992).

misrepresentation that was required, but also proof of reliance upon the misrepresentation by the selling shareholders thereon in parting with their shares.[69]

The not-a-fiduciary rule unjustly favors unscrupulous and scheming officers and directors who are seeking to take advantage of their positions and official knowledge and are dishonestly concealing favorable information in order to deprive shareholders of the benefit of their holdings. It is a rule of unconscionable laxity that has been condemned by most text writers and commentators as well as by an increasingly large number of the courts. More frequently courts hold that a corporate officer or director is subject to a fiduciary duty to disclose to a shareholder from whom he is purchasing stock any corporate information that materially affects the value of the shares and puts the shareholder at an unfair disadvantage.[70] As will be discussed more fully below, this "modern rule" has continued to gain increasing acceptance and, at least in a qualified form, is generally followed today.[71]

"Special Facts" Doctrine. Not all courts have found it necessary to choose between the rule that officers and directors are always subject to a strict fiduciary duty to the shareholders to volunteer all information and the view that they are always free to trade in their corporation's shares without revealing non-public information. The tendency has been to break down the harsh not-a-fiduciary rule by recognizing exceptions to it in "special facts" or "special circumstances" that give rise to a duty to make disclosure. Circumstances or developments that have been held to constitute "special circumstances" include knowledge by officers or directors of important transactions, such as prospective mergers, probable sales of the entire assets or business, agreements by third parties to buy large blocks of stock at a high price, and impending declarations of unusual dividends.[72] Under such circumstances, it clearly is reasonable to require officials to refrain from taking advantage of the ignorance of the shareholders whom they are supposed to represent and protect. The New York courts, once leaders in maintaining the older position, after first giving cautious recognition of the possibility of imposing an affirmative fiduciary duty of disclosure if the special circumstances are sufficiently strong,[73] now counts among their jurisprudence a far-reaching decision recognizing a strict fiduciary duty.[74]

The "special circumstances" or "special facts" doctrine was applied by the U.S. Supreme Court in a pre-*Erie* decision in the leading case of *Strong v. Repide*.[75] The defendant in that case was the general manager, one of the five directors, and the owner of three-fourths of the shares of a land corporation in the Philippine Islands. He was also the chief negotiator for the sale of the company's lands to the U.S. government and knew of the probable sale of the land at a price that would greatly enhance the value of the shares. Concealing his identity, the defendant obtained the plaintiff's shares through a

---

[69]   Du Pont v. Du Pont, 242 F. 98, 136 (D. Del.), *cert. denied*, 250 U.S. 642 (1919).

[70]   *See* Oliver v. Oliver, 45 S.E. 232 (Ga. 1903).

[71]   *E.g.*, Fisher v. Pennsylvania Life Co., 138 Cal.Rptr. 181 (Ct. App. 1977); Brophy v. Cities Serv. Co., 70 A.2d 5 (Del. Ch. 1949); Blakesley v. Johnson, 608 P.2d 908 (Kan. 1980).

[72]   *See, e.g.*, Jernberg v. Mann, 358 F.3d 131 (1st Cir. 2004) (applying Massachusetts law) (director or officer who approaches stockholder for purpose of buying shares has duty to disclose material facts within his or her peculiar knowledge).

[73]   Fischer v. Guaranty Trust Co., 18 N.Y.S.2d 328, 333, 334 (App. Div. 1940). *See* Lesnik v. Public Indus. Corp., 144 F.2d 968, 977 (2d Cir. 1944); Goodwin v. Agassiz, 186 N.E. 659 (Mass. 1933).

[74]   Diamond v. Oreamuno, 248 N.E.2d 910 (N.Y. 1969).

[75]   Strong v. Repide, 213 U.S. 419 (1909).

broker for about one-tenth of what the shares were worth. The Court granted rescission of the sale, holding that the defendant had a duty to disclose to the plaintiff the special facts and circumstances affecting the value of the shares. The defendant's dishonest concealment of his identity as the purchaser was also an element showing bad faith.

Under the "special facts" doctrine, uncertainties exist as to what developments are sufficiently important to call for disclosure of information if the selling shareholder makes no inquiry about developments that affect the value of the shares. Some courts say that an officer or director need not volunteer information as to the prospects of the company or the probability of dividends, but that the official must give truthful answers to such questions as the shareholder asks. For example, a company officer who stated he was not aware of "any bluebirds of happiness" on the corporate horizon breached a duty to update that statement when he learned the company would sell its patents for an amount that increased cash by 22 percent, even though his secret knowledge that the patents would be sold was not deemed so significant as to trigger a disclosure duty under the special facts doctrine.[76] At common law, if the official undertakes to inform the selling shareholder, he must speak fully and truthfully and is liable for misleading the seller even by expressions of his opinion.[77] It would seem, however, that the official should also be obliged to speak fully if he seeks out the shareholder and is active in inducing the sale or if he knows of overtures to purchase the corporate property or shares or any other matter that ought in all fairness to be disclosed.[78] Under SEC Rule 10b–5[79] and the federal securities acts' antifraud provisions generally, the test of materiality for both misstatements and omissions is whether the reasonable investor would have considered the fact important if the defendant had disclosed the information to him.[80]

In a leading Kansas case for more demanding disclosure by corporate insiders, *Hotchkiss v. Fisher*,[81] the plaintiff wished to sell her shares if no dividend could reasonably be expected in the near future. She sought the advice of *D*, the corporation's president and a director. He declined to express an opinion on whether dividends would be declared at the upcoming meeting of the directors but furnished the plaintiff with copies of the corporation's last financial statements. *D* purchased the plaintiff's shares for $1.25 per share. A week or so later the directors declared a dividend of $1.00 a share. The shareholder sued for damages. The court imposed a strict fiduciary rule, holding it was not sufficient to protect the officer based on the fact that he had truthfully answered the questions the plaintiff had asked. *D* was obligated to point out the significance of the data on the financial statements and volunteer any information that he had bearing on the likelihood of a dividend declaration, such as large earning capacity, large surplus, and liquid assets. The American Law Institutes adopts the approach taken by *Hotchkiss*.[82]

---

[76] In re Wayport, Inc., Litig., 76 A.3d 296 (Del.Ch. 2013).

[77] Ragsdale v. Kennedy, 209 S.E.2d 494 (N.C. 1974); Poole v. Camden, 92 S.E. 454 (W. Va. 1916); Schroeder v. Carroll, 212 N.W. 299 (Wis. 1927).

[78] *See* Hayes v. Kelley, 112 F.2d 897, 901 (9th Cir. 1940).

[79] 17 C.F.R. § 240.10b–5, discussed *infra*.

[80] *See* TSC Indus. v. Northway, Inc., 426 U.S. 438, 449 (1976) (decided under federal proxy rules).

[81] Hotchkiss v. Fisher, 16 P.2d 531 (Kan. 1932), noted in 46 Harv. L. Rev. 847 (1933), s.c., 31 P.2d 37 (Kan. 1934). *Hotchkiss* has been said to reflect a "strict accountability" rule. Amen v. Black, 234 F.2d 12 (10th Cir. 1956). *See also* Blakesley v. Johnson, 608 P.2d 908 (Kan. 1980).

[82] *See* 2 A.L.I., Principles of Corporate Governance: Analysis and Recommendations § 5.04(a) (1992).

There is a problem as to purchases of listed shares by directors and officers through the medium of a stock exchange, as is pointed out in the leading Massachusetts decision of *Goodwin v. Agassiz*.[83] Purchases and sales of shares of stock through brokers on a stock exchange are commonly impersonal affairs. Because the buyer and seller are anonymous, it is not practicable for an officer or director to make a personal disclosure to the buyer or for the buyer to request such a disclosure. *Goodwin* therefore held that given the impersonal nature of the trade between the plaintiff and the defendant, insiders owe no fiduciary duty to disclose their private knowledge of material information about the company. The formalism of the *Goodwin* court's reasoning leaves much to be desired. Any disclosure complications should not confer complete immunity on an officer or director who purchases his company's shares through a stock exchange. If the officer or director is one of the corporate officials implicated in a dishonest or willful failure to report to the shareholders information they need for their guidance, particularly if the nondisclosure is for the very purpose of buying shares for or taking other advantage of outside shareholders or the corporation, he may well be held accountable to the selling shareholders. Dishonest officers or directors should not find absolution from retributive justice by concealing their identity from their victims under the mask of the stock exchange.[84]

Corporate Recovery of Ill-Gotten Gains. The preceding discussion has focused on the duty of candor that officers and directors owe to their sellers or buyers when trading on non-public information. A very distinct duty question is whether the fiduciary breaches his duty *to his corporate employer* when he trades on material non-public information acquired by virtue of his relationship to the corporation. This question was addressed in an early Delaware decision[85] involving a "confidential secretary" who had advance knowledge of a corporation's plans to purchase its own stock on the open market. Armed with this knowledge, the secretary purchased stock on his own account, which he resold at a profit when the information became public. The court allowed the corporation to recover the secretary's profit and explicitly stated that no loss or damage to the corporation by the secretary's trading needed to be alleged.[86] The court reasoned that the fiduciary duty the secretary owed the corporation and the agency doctrine that a principal is entitled to recover from an agent the profits ("fruits") arising out of the agency. The *sine qua non* of a fiduciary's breach in all cases is that the fiduciary traded on the basis[87] of material non-public information[88] that was acquired through a relationship of trust and confidence with the corporation.[89] The fiduciary obligation so recognized is broad enough to include trading in another corporation's shares as long as the information used in so trading was acquired through the defendant's relationship to

---

[83]   Goodwin v. Agassiz, 186 N.E. 659 (Mass. 1933).

[84]   *See* Adolf A. Berle, Studies in Corporation Finance, ch. 9, at 177, 184–185 (1928).

[85]   Brophy v. Cities Serv. Co., 70 A.2d 5 (Del. Ch. 1949). *See generally* Douglas M. Branson, Choosing the Appropriate Default Rule—Insider Trading Under State Law, 45 Ala. L. Rev. 753 (1994).

[86]   In so ruling, the court relied on Restatement of Restitution § 200 comment a (1937) and Austin Wakeman Scott, The Law of Trusts § 505.1 (1939).

[87]   *See* Polin v. Conductron Corp., 552 F.2d 797 (8th Cir. 1977) (sold not because of content of information but because needed cash for new business).

[88]   *See, e.g.,* Thomas v. Roblin Indus., 520 F.2d 1393 (3d Cir. 1975) (information of company's problems publicly available).

[89]   25 *See* Walton v. Morgan Stanley & Co., 623 F.2d 796 (2d Cir. 1980).

the plaintiff corporation.[90] The key to understanding the corporation's recovery of its fiduciary's insider trading profits is that the fiduciary has acted in a manner inconsistent with the trust placed in him by the corporation that the information be used for corporate and not private purposes. Or, stated somewhat differently, disgorgement to the corporation is a necessary disincentive to the fiduciary not to compromise the relationship of trust by extracting non-consented-to benefits from the relationship. Note that the source of the fiduciary obligation is not just the defendant's position in the company, but the access that position provides him to confidential corporate information. Once the defendant has achieved access to such information he should be bound not to compromise either its confidentiality or the trust placed in him by trading on the basis of that information.

In a leading case, *Diamond v. Oreamuno*,[91] the New York Court of Appeals held that the corporation may recover the insider trading profits of two senior officers who traded on material non-public information they acquired through their corporate positions. The court held the corporation could recover the ill-gotten gains of its fiduciaries without proof the corporation had been harmed by the insider trading (although the court did acknowledge the likelihood of a reputational injury is likely to be suffered by any corporation whose high-ranking officers abuse their positions by trading on inside information).[92] In contrast, there is no breach of duty, however, when the board of directors has authorized a selective disclosure of material non-public information for the purpose of encouraging a third party to purchase the company's securities.[93] In 2011, the Delaware Supreme Court, in *Kahn v. Kohlberg, Kravis and Roberts*, used similar reasoning in upholding the corporate cause of to recover.[94]

Not all courts, however, interpret the corporation's rights to recover its fiduciary's insider trading profits. For example, the Florida Supreme Court held in *Schein v. Chasen*[95] that the corporation may recover its directors' and officers' profits made through trading on inside information obtained through their corporate positions only if the corporation is able to prove it was harmed because of its fiduciary's trading. The result in *Schein* thus rejects the position taken in cases such as *Diamond* that disgorgement is needed as a necessary prophylaxis to deter breaches that *could possibly* harm the corporation. A very different approach was taken by the federal court in *Freeman v. Decio*,[96] which held that under the law of the state of the corporation's formation, Indiana, the corporation may recover the insider trading profits of its fiduciaries only when the fiduciary's trading can be seen as being in competition with the corporation's power secretly to use that information to its own advantage. Under this

---

[90] *See, e.g.,* Cambridge Fund v. Abella, 501 F.Supp. 598 (S.D.N.Y. 1980); Gottlieb v. McKee, 107 A.2d 240 (Del.Ch. 1954).

[91] Diamond v. Oreamuno, 248 N.E.2d 910 (N.Y. 1969).

[92] *See* Restatement (Third) of Agency § 8.02 cmt. b (2006) (noting that although it is not necessary to show harm to the principal since the benefit realized by the agent can be more easily calculated, if there *is* harm the principal may also recover compensatory damages from the agent); Restatement (Second) of Agency § 388 cmt. c (1958) (expanding the liability to selling confidential information to a third party even if the principal is not harmed). The Third Restatement took a more general approach to liability than the Second Restatement in order "to make it explicit that a principal's remedies are not limited to recovery of profit from the agent." Restatement (Third) of Agency § 8.02 Reporter's Notes a (2006).

[93] *See* Frigitemp Corp. v. Financial Dynamics Fund, Inc., 524 F.2d 275 (2d Cir. 1975).

[94] 23 A.3d 831, 837–40 (Del. 2010).

[95] Schein v. Chasen, 313 So.2d 739 (Fla. 1975).

[96] Freeman v. Decio, 584 F.2d 186 (7th Cir. 1978).

approach, executives who, similar to the facts of *Diamond*, sell their shares on their secret knowledge that the corporation's income had declined substantially would likely not be liable to the corporation for their profits (*i.e.*, the difference between the price at which the shares were sold and the lower shares' price following disclosure of the decline in the corporation's income) since it is difficult to envision how the corporation could have used such information to its advantage. Moreover, the Second Circuit opined that New Jersey likely would not recognize a corporate recover of its insider's profits absent injury to the corporation.[97] The Delaware courts continue to recognize a derivative corporate claim based on breach of fiduciary duty.[98]

As a practical matter, the state insider trading law is today largely eclipsed by the extensive development of insider trading regulation that has occurred under the federal securities laws. The same can be said of state Blue Sky laws' application to insider trading.[99] Commentators have noted, for example, that state common law has been "overshadowed if not superseded" by section 10(b) of the Securities Exchange Act of 1934.[100]

PART B.   FEDERAL LAW

§ 12.8   Short-Swing Profits Under Section 16 of the Securities Exchange Act

Directors and officers of publicly traded companies are not ordinarily held accountable to the corporation for profits made in the purchase and sale of its shares unless they have taken unfair advantage of information that equitably belonged to the corporation.[101] To prevent the unfair use of inside information for the purpose of speculation, Congress has provided in section 16 of the Securities Exchange Act of 1934 (as amended),[102] that every person who is a director, officer, or beneficial owner of more than 10 percent of any class of "equity security" that is registered pursuant to section 12 of that Act[103] must file a statement and report the changes of ownership that have occurred during that month as to such securities.[104] Any profit[105] realized from any

---

[97]   *See* Frankel v. Slotkin, 984 F.2d 1328, 1337 (2d Cir. 1993).

[98]   *See, e.g.,* Pfeiffer v. Toll, 989 A.2d 683 (Del. Ch. 2010).

[99]   *See, e.g.,* Cal. Corp. Code §§ 25402, 25502, 25502.5 (West 2001).

[100]   William L. Cary & Melvin A. Eisenberg, Corporations Cases & Materials 714 (5th unab. ed. 1980).

[101]   *E.g.,* Weigel v. Shapiro, 608 F.2d 268 (7th Cir. 1979); Bisbee v. Midland Linseed Prods. Co., 19 F.2d 24 (8th Cir.), *cert. denied*, 275 U.S. 564 (1927). *See* § 12.7.

[102]   15 U.S.C. §§ 78p(a), 78p(b) (2015).

[103]   By Virtue of section 12 of the Act, registration is required for a company with any security traded on a national securities exchange or that has net total assets exceeding $10 million and a class of equity securities with 2,000 shareholders of record but retains the former 500 record holder threshold with respect to investors who are not accredited investors. Sections 12(a), (g)(1)(A), 15 U.S.C. § 78l(a), (g)(1)(A) as amended by the Jumpstart Our Business Startups Act (JOBS Act), H.R. 3606, 112 Cong. 2d sess. § 501 (2012). The record holder calculation excludes shareholders who receive shares as part of an employee compensation plan that is exempt from 1933 Act registration. Section 12(g) was also amended to exclude from the shareholder calculation holders of shares issued pursuant to an exempt crowdfunding offering.

[104]   These filings have to be made on the second business day following the transaction in shares. 15 U.S.C. § 78p(a) (2015). Prior to amendments in 2002, the section 16(a) reports had to be filed in the month following the trades in question.

[105]   Courts generally take a broad view of defining "profit" under section 16(b). Which can capture a "profit" even in situations where an out-of-pocket loss for all transactions entered into during the six-month period may exist when there have been a series of transactions within a six-month period. The apparent majority view is to match the lowest purchase price against the highest sales price within that period. Gratz

"purchase and sale" or "sale and purchases" of any such equity security within a period of less than six months is recoverable by the issuer without the need of proving unfair use of official information.[106] Section 16(b) is intended to be a prophylaxis for such trading. The remedy provided in section 16(b) in no way restricts the sanction or recovery that can be obtained pursuant to state law or other provisions of the federal securities law.

Under the early cases, the federal courts consistently interpreted 16(b) to require an objective and mechanical application. The statute continues to be read literally, without a pragmatic eye toward its purpose, except when the transaction is other than a standard securities transaction. When the transaction is of an extraordinary nature in the sense that it does not, for example, fall literally within the common definition of "sale" or "purchase," the courts apply a subjective, pragmatic test pursuant to which they inquire whether the circumstances were such that the defendant might have had access to inside information when she traded.[107] The courts have thus employed a more subjective analysis in such non-cash non-garden variety transactions as mergers, share exchanges, and exercises of stock options. Similarly, a case-by-case analysis has also been used when trying to determine whether someone who is denominated an officer in fact should be given officer status within the context of section 16(b)'s prophylactic provisions. In such cases, before applying 16(b) liability, the courts have looked to the potential for speculative abuse. Section 16(b) was aimed at a particular type of abuse—namely, those instances in which an insider could make a sure-thing short-swing profit by entering into transactions in anticipation of price changes that would lead to a profit at the second stage of the short-swing transaction. In other words, the section was aimed at discouraging insiders from speculating in their own company's stock especially when such speculation is based on special knowledge of facts soon to be made public. Notwithstanding the section's apparent objectivity and supposed ease of application, a number of section 16(b) issues have resulted in protracted litigation. Thus the statute falls far short of providing a predictable rule of thumb.

Stocks with different rights, privileges and preferences, even though each is an equity security, are not paired to give rise to short-swing profits.[108] Section 16(b) provides the so-called "debt exception," providing that "a security . . . acquired in good faith in connection with a debt previously contracted" is outside the provision.[109]

---

v. Claughton, 187 F.2d 46 (2d Cir.1951); Smolowe v. Delendo Corp., 136 F.2d 231 (2d Cir. 1943), *cert. denied*, 320 U.S. 751 (1943). Dreiling v. Jain, 281 F.Supp.2d 1234, 1238–1239 (W.D. Wash. 2003).

In calculating the value of the share for the purpose of determining profit, the courts have looked to the actual price paid or received rather than some other value alleged due to discounts and the like. *See* Olagues v. Icahn, 866 F.3d 70 (2d Cir. 2017). The court noted that it is not improper to structure transactions to purposely avoid section 16(b) liability. *Id.* (profit from options should be based on the actual option premium received rather than also look to alleged improper discounts that were allegedly given to hide the section 16(b) profit; also, these discounts could be the result of the difference between publicly traded options and those private ones in the case at hand).

[106]   15 U.S.C. § 78p(b).

[107]   *See* 2 Louis Loss & Joel Seligman, Securities Regulation 1040 to 1045 (3d ed. 1989); Thomas L. Hazen, The New Pragmatism Under Section 16(b) of the Securities Exchange Act, 54 N.C. L. Rev. 1 (1975); Lewis D. Lowenfels, Section 16(b): A New Trend in Regulating Insider Trading, 54 Cornell L. Rev. 45 (1968).

[108]   Gibbons v. Malone, 703 F.3d 595 (2d Cir. 2013).

[109]   *See, e.g.*, Analytical Surveys, Inc. v. Tonga Partners LP, 684 F.3d 36 (2d Cir. 2012).

One of the more perplexing 16(b) issues has revolved around the statutory definitions of "purchase" and "sale." For example, an early case[110] held that the exercise of conversion rights constituted a 16(b) purchase. Two courts of appeal subsequently took the contrary position and held 16(b) inapplicable.[111] The question of the status of conversions remained in doubt[112] until the adoption of SEC Rule 16b–9, which provides that generally a conversion constitutes neither a sale nor a purchase.[113]

In *Kern County Land Company v. Occidental Petroleum Corporation*,[114] the Court eschewed such an objective approach and opted for a pragmatic analysis.[115] In *Kern County*, the management of the target company opposed a takeover by Occidental Petroleum and reacted with a defensive merger with Tenneco Corporation. As a result of the merger, Occidental was to receive Tenneco preferred stock. Occidental, not wanting to own an interest in one of its competitors, issued to Tenneco an option to repurchase the Tenneco preferred. More than six months after both the purchase by Occidental of the Old Kern stock and Occidental's acquisition via the exchange of the Tenneco stock, Tenneco exercised the option.

Kern County asserted that 16(b) required Occidental to disgorge its short-swing profits. The court thus had to decide (1) whether Occidental's disposition of the Kern stock in exchange for the Tenneco preferred was a sale and (2) whether the subsequent option arrangement resulted in a sale within six months of the purchase. The district court held that Occidental's acquisition of Tenneco stock pursuant to the Old Kern-Tenneco merger was a section 16(b) "sale" within six months of its purchase pursuant to the original tender offer and, further, that the subsequent option agreement was a second "sale" also within the reach of section 16(b).[116] On appeal, the Second Circuit reversed, reasoning that the exchange pursuant to the merger could not properly be classified as a 16(b) "sale" because there had been no potential for speculative abuse, and the court also found that the option did not violate section 16(b).[117] The Supreme Court followed the court of appeals and took a pragmatic approach:

---

[110] Park & Tilford, Inc. v. Schulte, 160 F.2d 984 (2d Cir.), *cert. denied*, 332 U.S. 761 (1947).

[111] Petteys v. Butler, 367 F.2d 528 (8th Cir. 1966), *cert. denied*, 385 U.S. 1006 (1967); Feraiolo v. Newman, 259 F.2d 342 (6th Cir. 1958), *cert. denied*, 359 U.S. 927 (1959). Potter Stewart's opinion in the *Feraiolo* case has been identified as the first of the so-called pragmatic decisions.

[112] *See* Blau v. Lamb, 363 F.2d 507 (2d Cir.), *cert. denied*, 385 U.S. 1002 (1967) (conversion not a sale); Heli-Coil Corp. v. Webster, 352 F.2d 156 (3d Cir. 1965) (conversion is sale of convertible security and purchase of underlying security); Blau v. Max Factor & Co., 342 F.2d 304 (9th Cir.), *cert. denied*, 382 U.S. 892 (1965) (conversion not a purchase).

[113] 17 C.F.R. § 240.16b–9 (2015).

[114] Kern County Land Company v. Occidental Petroleum Corporation, 411 U.S. 582 (1973).

[115] *See generally* Thomas L. Hazen, The New Pragmatism Under Section 16(b) of the Securities Exchange Act, 54 N.C.L. Rev. 1 (1975).

[116] Abrams v. Occidental Petroleum Corp., 323 F.Supp. 570, 579–580 (S.D.N.Y. 1970).

[117] It also rejected the alternative of classifying the option agreement as a "sale" because Occidental's obligation to dispose of the shares had not been fixed until Tenneco exercised the option more than six months later:

It is urged that Occidental possessed the "inside information" that Old Kern might well respond [to its takeover attempt] by arranging a "defensive merger" and that, if the terms were sufficiently favorable, Occidental would not try to top them. But, in contrast to [Newmark v. RKO General, Inc., 425 F.2d 348 (2d Cir.), *cert. denied*, 400 U.S. 854 (1970)] where the buyer knew of the imminent announcement of a merger that would enhance the price of the shares and could largely control its course, Occidental had no knowledge what Old Kern would do, and certainly did not know that Old Kern would be able to arrange an exchange offer exceeding Occidental's bid by $20 per share, with the added benefit of freedom from capital gains tax. We fail to see the possibility of speculative abuse in a situation where such an offeror simply declines to make a still higher offer

In deciding whether borderline [unorthodox] transactions are within the reach of the statute, the courts have come to inquire whether the transaction may serve as a vehicle for the evil which Congress sought to prevent—the realization of short-swing profits based upon access to inside information—thereby endeavoring to implement congressional objectives without extending the reach of the statute beyond its intended limits.[118]

The sale or purchase occurs when the seller's or purchaser's obligations become fixed, which is customarily when the price and number of shares are determined.[119]

Following the Supreme Court's lead, the trend toward pragmatism has continued to flourish in defining "purchase" and "sale" in unorthodox transactions. One court has gone so far as to apply 16(b) to certain statutory insiders but not to others in the same transaction.[120] Thus, for example, in the context of a negotiated merger, a director of one of the constituent companies who was actively involved in the merger negotiations was held to have been subject to section 16(b)'s disgorgement provisions, while an outside director was not.[121] The court reasoned that the outside director, who did not participate in the merger negotiations, did not have access to the type of information that could be the basis of the type of "sure thing" speculation that section 16(b) was designed to prevent.

Another significant 16(b) issue is the question of who is a statutory insider. For example, where a corporation appoints or deputizes one of its officers or directors to sit on another corporation's board, that individual's insider status may be attributed to the deputizing body.[122] Deputization *was* found to be present in *Feder v. Martin Marietta Corp.*[123] Bunker, the president of Martin Marietta (Enterprise A), had become a director of Sperry (Enterprise B), in which Martin Marietta held substantial stock. Bunker was ultimately responsible for the total operation of Martin Marietta, and personally approved all of the firm's financial investments—in particular, its purchase of the Sperry stock. Bunker's control over Martin Marietta, coupled with his membership on Sperry's Board, placed him in a position in which he could acquire inside information concerning Sperry and could utilize such information for Martin. Further, Bunker admitted discussing Sperry's affairs with two officials at Martin Marietta and participating in sessions when Martin Marietta's investment in Sperry was reviewed, and Bunker's ultimate letter of resignation to Martin Marietta's president stated that "When I became a member of the [Sperry] board . . . it appeared to your associates that the Martin Marietta ownership of a substantial number of shares of Sperry Rand should have representation on your Board." On these facts, the Second Circuit concluded that "The control possessed by Bunker, his letter of resignation, the approval by the Martin Board of Bunker's directorship with Sperry and the functional similarity between Bunker's acts as a Sperry director and the acts of Martin's representatives on other boards . . . are all

---

or to attempt a block transaction which it regards as advantageous to all the stockholders including itself.

Abrams v. Occidental Petroleum Corp., 450 F.2d 157, 163 (2d Cir. 1971) (footnotes omitted).

[118] 411 U.S. at 594–595 (footnote omitted).

[119] Magma Power Co. v. Dow Chemical Co., 136 F.3d 316 (2d Cir. 1998) (shares purchased when option acquired that set forth price and amount of shares and not later when option exercised).

[120] Gold v. Sloan, 486 F.2d 340 (4th Cir. 1973), noted in 42 Fordham L. Rev. 852 (1974).

[121] Gold v. Sloan, 486 F.2d 340 (4th Cir. 1973).

[122] Feder v. Martin Marietta Corp., 406 F.2d 260 (2d Cir. 1969).

[123] 406 F.2d 260 (2d Cir.1969), cert. denied 396 U.S. 1036 (1970).

definite and concrete indicatives that Bunker, in fact, was a Martin deputy." Martin Marietta was therefore held liable, as a director, for its short-swing profits in Sperry stock.

A very different result was reached in *Roth v. Perseus LLC*,[124] because the defendant, who had purchased the traded shares from the issuer, Beacon, was able to invoke the exemption provided in Rule 16b–3. Perseus LLC had made a substantial investment in Beacon and as part of the transaction was accorded two nominees to Beacon's board. Within six months, Perseus sold some of the Beacon shares. Rule 16b–3 exempts a transaction between the issuer and its officer or director from section 16(b) if, among other conditions, the transaction is approved by the issuer's board of directors. The Second Circuit held this provision extends to directors by deputization even if that person is also the holder of more than 10 percent of the issuer's equity.

Further interpretive questions arise with respect to trading by a family member of a officer, director or beneficial owner of 10 percent. Notwithstanding the maintenance of separate brokerage accounts and different investment advisers, a spouse's sale may be matched with an insider's purchase to find a 16(b) profit.[125] Similarly, questions arise about what constitutes a "class" of securities for the purpose of calculating whether the defendant is an owner of more than 10 percent of a class.[126]

The SEC has invoked its rule-making power to clarify the meaning of "beneficial ownership." The rules are directed at those persons who can exercise sufficient control over the company's management to justify presuming access to inside information. The tests of beneficial ownership the SEC uses for determining reporting obligations are different from those it uses to decide whether purchases and sales should be matched for the purpose of requiring the disgorgement of short-swing profits. Once 10 percent beneficial holder status is determined, section 16's reporting and short-swing profit provisions apply only to securities in which the insider has a direct or indirect pecuniary interest.[127]

Rule 16a–2(a)(2)[128] begins by setting forth the basic rule that for reporting purposes beneficial ownership hinges on the direct or indirect pecuniary interest in the shares, and that interest may be the result of "any contract, arrangement, understanding, relationship, or otherwise." This includes the opportunity to participate, directly or indirectly, in any profit attributable to transactions in the shares in question. The rule then goes on to list examples of "indirect pecuniary interest" that trigger section 16. Securities held by immediate family members sharing the same household are included. A general partner's proportional interest in securities held by a general or limited partnership is similarly included. In contrast, a shareholder does not have a pecuniary interest in the portfolio securities held by a corporation, limited partnership, or similar entity, as long as he is not a controlling shareholder of the entity and neither has nor shares investment control over the entity's portfolio securities.

---

[124]   522 F.3d 242 (2d Cir. 2008).

[125]   Whiting v. Dow Chem. Co., 523 F.2d 680 (2d Cir. 1975).

[126]   *See, e.g.*, Morales v. Freund, 163 F.3d 763 (2d Cir. 1999) (class A preferred shares were separate class where their vote would have been sufficient to block company's reorganization).

[127]   SEC Release No. 34–28869, Ownership Reports and Trading By Officers, Directors, and Principal Security Holders, Fed. Sec. L. Rep. (CCH) No. 1434 (Feb. 13, 1991).

[128]   17 C.F.R. § 240.16a–2(a)(2) (2015).

Because of the breadth of the beneficial ownership rules, section 16 problems arise when X joins with Y and Z to sell their Alpha shares for Beta shares pursuant to a lock up agreement imposed by Beta whereby for a period of two years they were barred from disposing of the shares. Though X's interest in the Beta shares was less than 2.5 percent, the combined Beta holdings of the three constituted 18 percent of Beta's outstanding shares. While the shares were subject to the agreement, X individually engaged in a number of trades in Beta shares. The Second Circuit,[129] rejecting the view that beneficial ownership by a group required proof of an intent to acquire control, remanded the case for further findings whether X, Y, and Z had combined for the common objective of "acquiring" or "holding" shares as provided by the beneficial ownership rule that is applicable to groups.[130] If so, section 16(b) liability would arise from X's trades.

The question of who is an "officer" or "director" may also lead to a fact inquiry insofar as those terms include persons performing similar functions. An analysis of the relevant cases reveals that when an employee, although denominated an officer, does not possess the type of executive power or decision-making authority likely to give him or her access to inside information, section 16(b) will not be held applicable.[131] This pragmatic analysis is supported by SEC rule-making that provides that section 16 applies to executive officers[132]—that is, those who are clothed with policymaking authority. The focus thus is not on a person's title but whether in discharging his or her duties the individual is likely to obtain information that would be helpful in avoiding the risks ordinarily associated with shortswing speculation.[133]

In *Foremost-McKesson, Inc. v. Provident Securities Company*,[134] the Supreme Court held that a 10 percent beneficial owner was not subject to the Act until after that status was achieved; thus the threshold purchase was not covered by 16(b). This test is met, however, when the holder of a security convertible into more than ten percent of the outstanding common shares converts into the common and disposes of some of the common shares so acquired within six months of the conversion.[135] In contrast to the treatment of owners of more than ten percent, the difference in statutory language for officers and directors led the Second Circuit to apply a stricter rule, holding that officers and directors fall within section 16(b) if they have that status at the time of either purchase or sale.[136] As part of its massive rule-making initiatives in 1992, the SEC has clarified its position on this issue. Transactions by officers and directors prior to taking office do not have section 16 implications.[137] Transactions occurring within the six

---

[129] *See* Morales v. Quintel Entertainment, Inc., 249 F.3d 115 (2d Cir. 2001).

[130] Rule 13d–5, 17 C.F.R. § 240.13d–5 (2015). *See generally* General Aircraft Corp. v. Lampert, 556 F.2d 90 (1st Cir. 1977) (finding a group for section 13d–3 purposes).

[131] Merrill Lynch, Pierce, Fenner & Smith, Inc. v. Livingston, 566 F.2d 1119, 1122 (9th Cir. 1978).

[132] Rule 16a–1(f) includes in the definition of "executive officer" the president, any vice president in charge of a principal unit or division, and the principal financial and accounting officers, as well as any other officer who performs a policymaking function. 17 C.F.R. § 240.16a–1(f) (2015).

[133] Sec. Exch. Act Rel. No. 34–28869 [1990–1991 Transfer Binder] Fed. Sec. L. Rep. (CCH) ¶ 84,709 (Feb. 8, 1991), relying on Colby v. Klune, 178 F.2d 872, 873 (2d Cir. 1949).

[134] Foremost-McKesson, Inc. v. Provident Securities Company, 423 U.S. 232 (1976).

[135] *See* Medtox Scientific, Inc. v. Morgan Capital LLC, 258 F.3d 763 (8th Cir. 2001).

[136] Adler v. Klawans, 267 F.2d 840 (2d Cir. 1959).

[137] 17 C.F.R. § 240.16a–2(a) (2015).

months after leaving office may be matched against purchases or sales occurring while the officer or director was still in office.[138]

Today, trades covered by section 16 must be disclosed within two days, all reports filed pursuant to section 16(a) of the Exchange Act be filed electronically, and issuers must post their reports on the issuer's website not later than the day the report is filed with the SEC.[139]

Section 16(b) authorizes only private suits to recover short-swing profits and provides that "no such suit shall be brought more than two years after the date such profit was realized." Construing this limitation, the Supreme Court in *Credit Suisse Securities LLC v. Simmonds*,[140] held that the two-year period is not automatically tolled for the period in which the insider failed to disclose the trading by not filing the Form 4 as mandated by section 16(a). The SEC can, however, initiate enforcement actions for failure or tardy filing of disclosures mandated by section 16(a). The private suit is a hybrid cause of action that lies somewhere between a derivative suit and a direct action. There is exclusive federal jurisdiction over such suits. The plaintiff shareholder must demand that the corporation sue, and the corporation can bring suit. However, if the corporation fails to respond within 60 days, the shareholder can initiate the suit with any recovery going to the corporation. Unlike the standard derivative suit, a good faith determination by the board of directors that the suit should not be prosecuted cannot bar the shareholder from maintaining the suit to recover short-swing profits. Moreover, the section does not contain a requirement that the plaintiff have been a shareholder at the time of the trading transactions in question.[141] Since the suit can be either at equity or in law, the plaintiff has a choice of whether or not to have a jury trial.[142]

§ 12.9 Section 10(b) and Rule 10b–5 of the Securities Exchange Act of 1934

The 1929 stock market crash, and the fraudulent stock promotions that played a contributing role, provided the impetus for federal regulation. The Securities Act of 1933[143] and the Securities Exchange Act of 1934[144] were enacted to regulate the initial distribution of securities—day-to-day securities trading activities and the securities markets in general. While state general corporation laws are concerned with corporate chartering and the protection of the shareholders' proprietary interest, the federal and state securities laws are geared to investor protection.[145] At the time 1933 and 1934 federal statutes were enacted, state "blue sky" securities statutes combined a general

---

[138] 17 C.F.R. § 240.16a–2(b) (2015).

[139] *See* Mandated Electronic Filing and Website Posting for Forms 3, 4, and 5, Securities Act Rel. No. 33–8230 (May 7, 2003) (filings made before 10 p.m. are deemed made on that date, even though normal closing for EDGAR filings is earlier in the day).

[140] Credit Suisse Securities LLC v. Simmonds, 566 U.S. 221 (2012). However, The Court was equally divided whether the doctrine of equitable tolling applies so that the two-year period would not begin to run until the trading could have been discovered.

[141] In contrast, such a contemporaneous ownership rule generally applies to shareholder derivative suits—*e.g.*, Fed. R. Civ. P. 23.1. *See* Chapter 15.

[142] Arbetman v. Playford & Alaska Airlines, Inc., 83 F.Supp. 335 (S.D.N.Y. 1949); Dottenheim v. Emerson Elec. Mfg. Co., 7 F.R.D. 343 (E.D.N.Y. 1947).

[143] Act of May 27, 1933, ch. 38, tit. 1, 48 Stat. 881 (1933) (current version at 15 U.S.C. §§ 77a to 77bbbb).

[144] Act of June 6, 1934, ch. 404, 48 Stat. 881 (1933) (current version at 15 U.S.C. §§ 77a to 78bb–1).

[145] Although some states had enacted securities acts as far back as 1911, these laws proved ineffective against much of the pervasive securities frauds.

antifraud approach with a merit evaluation or licensing system; Congress considered but rejected a merit approach. Instead, the federal legislation is based on full disclosure and market regulation.[146] The Securities Act of 1933 or "Truth in Securities" Act requires registration and full disclosure for all nonexempt securities distributions.[147] In contrast, the Securities Exchange Act of 1934 is directed at a range of securities market abuses as well as seeking full and fair disclosure in connection with trading in securities. Overall, the 1934 Act seeks to maintain the integrity of the securities markets by regulating exchanges[148] and broker-dealers.

The Exchange Act contains several provisions that are of importance to a corporate attorney who does not specialize in securities law. For example, as has been discussed in the preceding section, the Act provides that insider short-swing profits "shall inure to and be recoverable by the issuer."[149] The Act also regulates practices with respect to the solicitation of proxies.[150] Section 10(b) of the Act[151] contains a general antifraud provision that renders unlawful manipulative and deceptive acts and practices in connection with the sale or purchase of a security. This section specifically empowers the SEC to promulgate rules in order to define the prohibited conduct. Rule 10b–5,[152] which was drawn under this authority, constitutes a catch-all antifraud provision. In addition to prohibiting fraudulent acts and practices in connection with the purchase of a security, this rule expressly renders it unlawful "to make any untrue statement of material fact or to omit to state a material fact" in connection with the purchase or sale of a security.[153] The rule's breadth is great, as it applies to *any* security, regardless of whether the security is subject to the Act's registration and reporting requirements.[154] Further, the rule applies to any transaction utilizing an instrumentality of interstate commerce, including the mails and even intrastate telephone conversations.[155]

By the terms of the statute, violations of Rule 10b–5 subject an offender to civil enforcement proceedings brought by the SEC as well as to criminal prosecution by the Justice Department. Nevertheless, the primary significance of the rule has been its availability for a private right of action by an injured purchaser or seller of a security.[156] Beginning with a 1946 federal district court decision,[157] the implied private right of action for violation of Rule 10b–5 grew from a "legislative acorn" into a "judicial oak."[158] The rule's reach grew rapidly, until the Supreme Court turned to its pruning shears in reshaping the remedy.[159]

---

[146] *See generally* Homer Virgil Cherrington, The Investor and the Securities Act (1942).

[147] *Cf.* Milton H. Cohen, Truth in Securities Revisited, 79 Harv. L. Rev. 1340 (1966).

[148] 15 U.S.C. §§ 78f, 78k (2015).

[149] 15 U.S.C. § 78p(b) (2015), discussed *supra* § 12.8.

[150] 15 U.S.C. § 78n(a) (2015) and Reg. 14A promulgated thereunder.

[151] 15 U.S.C. § 78j(b) (2015).

[152] 17 C.F.R. § 240.10b–5 (2015).

[153] 17 C.F.R. § 240.10b–5 (2015).

[154] *Compare, e.g.,* 15 U.S.C. § 78p(a) (proxy regulation); *id.* § 78m(d) (tender offer regulation), *with id.* § 78p(b) (insider short-swing profits).

[155] *E.g.,* Dupuy v. Dupuy, 511 F.2d 641 (5th Cir. 1975).

[156] *See, e.g.,* 8 Louis Loss & Joel Seligman, Securities Regulation 3680–3726 (1991).

[157] Kardon v. National Gypsum Co., 69 F.Supp. 512 (E.D. Pa. 1946).

[158] Blue Chip Stamps Co. v. Manor Drug Stores, 421 U.S. 723, 737 (1975).

[159] Santa Fe Indus. v. Green, 430 U.S. 462 (1977) (deception requirement); Ernst & Ernst v. Hochfelder, 425 U.S. 185 (1976) (defendant must have acted with scienter); Blue Chip Stamps Co. v. Manor Drug Stores, 421 U.S. 723 (1975) (plaintiff must be a purchaser or seller of the security).

Rule 10b–5's broad language has been applied in a wide variety of fact contexts. Picking up where section 16(b) leaves off, Rule 10b–5 has an impact on trading in securities based on inside information.[160] The rule can be used to regulate the flow of information to the investing public and in many instances to compel corporate disclosure of material facts. The rule has also proved to be a weapon against certain types of corporate mismanagement. This versatility is due to the breadth of the statute's and rule's language.[161] In addition to material misstatements or omissions reasonably calculated to affect an investor's decision in ordinary sales or purchases of securities,[162] Rule 10b–5 applies to a corporation's issuance of stock or bonds,[163] mergers and other organic changes,[164] a corporation's purchase or sale of its own or another company's securities,[165] and the sale of a controlling interest in a corporation.

Because the cause of action is implied, there was not, until 2002, any expressly provided statute of limitations, although at one time courts used the analogous limitations period in the state or securities law.[166] In 2002, the Congress enacted a statute of limitations period requiring private suits be filed within discovery and not later than five years of the commission of the violation.[167]

Federal jurisdiction over suits based on Rule 10b–5 is exclusive.[168] When, as is frequently the case, a particular set of facts gives rise to both a 10b–5 claim and a cause of action under state law, the aggrieved buyer or seller of securities is generally able to combine both in federal court under the doctrine of pendent jurisdiction.[169] As discussed later, in most securities class action state securities fraud claims are preempted.

[1] Materiality

In order for a misstatement or omission to be actionable under Rule 10b–5, it must be a material one. The Supreme Court has defined "materiality" in terms of the type of information that a reasonable investor would consider significant in making an investment decision.[170] Materiality is highly contextual and bright-line tests are not appropriate in determining materiality.[171] Instead courts must look at the misstatements and omissions in light of the total mix of available information. The test of materiality is an objective one and not one that turns upon the unique information

---

[160] *See supra* § 12.8. This fills a significant void in the law of many states. *See supra* § 12.7.

[161] 17 C.F.R. § 230.10b–5 (2015).

[162] Zweig v. Hearst Corp., 594 F.2d 1261 (9th Cir. 1979) (sustaining complaint against financial columnist for alleged material misinformation).

[163] Lanza v. Drexel & Co., 479 F.2d 1277 (2d Cir. 1973).

[164] *E.g.*, Goldberg v. Meridor, 567 F.2d 209 (2d Cir. 1977), *cert. denied*, 434 U.S. 1069 (1978).

[165] Superintendent of Ins. v. Bankers Life & Cas. Co., 404 U.S. 6 (1971) (sale of other issuers' securities).

[166] Stull v. Bayard, 561 F.2d 429, 431 (2d Cir. 1977), *cert. denied*, 434 U.S. 1035 (1978).

[167] *See* § 804 of the Sarbanes-Oxley Act of 2002, Pub. L. No. 107–204 (July 20, 2002), amending 28 U.S.C. § 1658.

[168] 15 U.S.C. § 78aa.

[169] *See* Lewis D. Lowenfels, Pendent Jurisdiction and the Federal Securities Acts, 67 Colum. L. Rev. 474 (1967); Note, The Evolution and Scope of the Doctrine of Pendent Jurisdiction in the Federal Courts, 62 Colum. L. Rev. 1018 (1962).

[170] The standard for materiality is the same for the antifraud provision as it is for other provisions of the securities laws, such as the proxy solicitations. Thus, the leading case for materiality is TSC Indus. v. Northway, Inc., 426 U.S. 438, 449 (1976) (decided under the proxy rules).

[171] Matrixx Initiatives, Inc. v. Siracusano, 563 U.S. 27 (2011) (refusing to require that pharmaceutical study that was omitted was statically significant); Basic, Inc. v. Levinson, 485 U.S. 224 (1988) (rejecting bright-line test to determine materiality of preliminary merger negotiations).

needs of the particular investor. When the misstated or omitted fact is contingent or speculative, such as a prediction, a forecast, or even an appraisal of the value of an asset, the standard definition of materiality must account not solely for the probability that the forecasted event or item will in fact occur. In such a case, the Supreme Court holds that there is to be a balancing of the probability of the event's occurrence and its expected magnitude to make the materiality determination.[172] In such an instance, even though an event might be accorded a low probability of occurrence, a very substantial magnitude should it occur can result in the item being deemed material.[173] Even though an opinion is not a "fact" as such, misrepresenting one's opinion, such as stating that "loan reserves are adequate," can violate Rule 10b–5 if the speaker is aware there is objective evidence that contradicts her opinion.[174] The Supreme Court holds that opinion statements can be materially misleading only when they are "objectively" false, *i.e.*, when the plaintiff can establish by objective evidence that the opinion statement was false.[175] Hence, directors who opine that $40 is a "high" price commit fraud if they have before them evidence that the fair price is $60. However, no violation occurs if the directors have been advised that $40 is the fair price, but the directors' personal belief is that the shares' intrinsic value is higher.

Omnicare, Inc. v. Laborers District Council Construction Industry Pension Fund[176] substantially clarifies, if not qualifies, *Virginia Bankshares, Inc. v. Sandberg*,[177] the Supreme Court's earlier, opaque approach for treatment of the materiality of opinion statements. In *Virginia Bankshares*, the Supreme Court, after quickly concluding shareholders would attach significance to the board of directors' statement that the cash-out merger price was "fair" and "high" so that the statement met the materiality standard, nevertheless emphasized there was another, more perplexing, issue: whether such an opinion statement was a statement of *fact*. On this question, *Virginia Bankshares'* formulation is hopelessly ambiguous except for the rather clear implication arising out of the record before the Court that opinion statements are statements of facts when there is before the defendant objective evidence in direct conflict with the professed opinion. Absent conflicting objective evidence, the opinion statement is not a "fact" but a non-actionable misrepresentation of the defendant's belief or motive.

The facts of *Omnicare* are fairly straight forward. In a registration statement for its public offering, Omnicare stated it "believed" its various contracts were "in compliance with applicable federal and state laws" and "legally and economically valid arrangements." Subsequent to the public offering, several federal government enforcement suits were initiated against Omnicare, alleging that various aspects of its contractual relationships and arrangements violated multiple provisions of federal health care laws. The plaintiff pension funds that purchased shares in the registered offering sued under section 11 of the Securities Act, alleging that the opinion statements were materially misleading. Because securities issuers that commit a material

---

[172] *See* Basic, Inc. v. Levinson, 485 U.S. 224 (1988) (decided under Rule 10b–5 involving the denial of merger negotiations).

[173] *See, e.g.,* Kronfeld v. Trans World Airlines, Inc., 832 F.2d 726 (2d Cir. 1987).

[174] *See, e.g.,* Shapiro v. U.J.B. Financial Corp., 964 F.2d 272 (3d Cir. 1992).

[175] *See* Virginia Bankshares, Inc. v. Sandberg, 501 U.S. 1083 (1991).

[176] 575 U.S. 175 (2015). *See* James D. Cox, "We're Cool" Statements after *Omnicare*: Securities Fraud Suits for Failures to Comply with the Law, 68 S.M.U. L. Rev. 715 (2015) (reviewing the implications of *Omnicare* with a focus on puffery and forward looking statements).

[177] 501 U.S. 1083, 1091–99 (1991).

misrepresentation in their registration statement have absolute liability under section 11 of the Securities Act, the complaint did not allege awareness on the part of Omnicare of facts inconsistent with the professed opinion of compliance with the law. The complaint's failure to allege such awareness clashed with the formulation in *Virginia Bankshares*. The allegations in *Omnicare* therefore posed two distinct questions: who has the burden of establishing the existence of objective facts contrary to the stated opinion of compliance with the law[178] and whether this showing must be accompanied by evidence of knowledge of such conflicting evidence by Omnicare officials.[179] Because section 11 imposes strict liability on a security's issuer, *Virginia Bankshares'* orthodoxy of placing both these burdens on the plaintiff meshes poorly with the absolute liability regime housed in section 11.

A key step in Justice Kagan's majority opinion in *Omnicare* is the opinion was premised on section 11 which similar to other disclosure provisions proscribes both what is misstated as well as what is omitted from what is stated. Thus, she observes that "a reasonable investor may, depending on the circumstances, understand an opinion statement to convey facts about how the speaker has formed the opinion. . . . [I]f the real facts are otherwise, but not provided, the opinion statement will mislead its audience." *Omnicare Inc.* therefore emphasized whether facts related to the opinion needed to be disclosed to prevent the opinion statement from being misleading.

> [A]n investor cannot state a claim by alleging only that an opinion was wrong; the complaint must as well call into question the issuer's basis for offering the opinion. . . . [A] cause of action [exists] only when an issuer's failure to include a material fact has rendered a published statement misleading. . . . The investor must identify particular (and material) facts going to the basis for the issuer's opinion—facts about the inquiry the issuer did or did not conduct or the knowledge it did or did not have—whose omission makes the opinion statement at issue misleading to a reasonable person reading the statement fairly and in context.[180]

Because Omnicare's opinion statements focused on its purported compliance with the law, the opinion applied the above formulation to such statements:

> Consider an unadorned statement of opinion about legal compliance; "We believe our conduct is lawful." If the issuer makes that statement without having consulted a lawyer, it could be misleadingly incomplete . . . [A]n investor, although recognizing that legal opinions can prove wrong in the end, still likely expects such an assertion to rest on some meaningful legal inquiry . . . Similarly, if the issuer made the statement in the face of its lawyers' contrary advice, or with knowledge that the Federal Government was taking the opposite view, the investor again has cause to complain: He expects not just

---

[178] The Sixth Circuit held that though the plaintiffs did not have to establish that Omnicare officials knew their belief was false, the funds were required to allege that the professed beliefs were "objectively false." Ind. State Dist. Council v. Omnicare, Inc, 719 F.3d 498, 506–07 (6th Cir. 2013), *affirmed in part and reversed in part*, 575 U.S. 175, 135 S.Ct. 1318, 191 L.Ed.2d 253 (2015).

[179] *See* Ind. State Dist. Council of Laborers & HOD Carriers Pension & Welfare Fund v. Omnicare, Inc., 2012 U.S. Dist. LEXIS 17526 (E.D. Ky. Feb. 13, 2012) (granting dismissal of case because the complaint failed to allege "the company's officers knew they were violating the law").

[180] 575 U.S. at 194, 135 S.Ct. at 1328–29, 1332.

that the issuer believes the opinion . . . but that it fairly aligns with the information in the issuer's possession at the time.[181]

Thus we can see that the formulation for opinion statements is the orthodox half-truth doctrine where, even under the strict liability standard of section 11, the burden is upon plaintiff to establish under the totality of the circumstances that omitted facts were necessary to disclose in order to render the opinion statement not materially misleading. In the absolute liability context, such as *Omnicare.,* the preceding formulation, while requiring the plaintiff to allege what facts were not disclosed that were needed to render what was said not misleading, the plaintiff is not required to further establish that the issuer was aware of those facts in order to establish that a material misrepresentation had occurred.

An intriguing point opened by *Omnicare's* approach is whether it weakens the doctrinaire bulwark that lower courts have developed that generalized statements of optimism, commonly referred to as puffery, are not material. For example, consider J.P. Morgan's touting that the company's "risk management processes . . . are highly disciplined," a claim it made on the cusp of the recent financial crisis that nearly terminated the firm because of excessive exposure to risk. Before *Omnicare,* courts had ample precedent to support dismissal of the suit on the grounds the claim was non-actionable puffery.[182] After *Omnicare,* the outcome of such a suit is surrounded by a good deal of uncertainty because J.P. Morgan's statement is not distinguishable from Omnicare Inc.'s statement, "[w]e believe our contract arrangements . . . are in compliance with applicable federal and state laws." Each are generalized statements of opinion, and each point toward a body of facts and principles upon which investors can be expected to believe management premised its opinion. Moreover, each appears potentially actionable under *Omnicare's* formulation of considering how the statement is likely understood by the reasonable investor so that the plaintiff can challenge the statement as a half-truth based on facts before the speaker that were materially inconsistent with the professed optimistic statement. In the end, puffery is but an optimistic opinion that the investor can expect the speaker has some factual basis. Absent that factual basis, the opinion is actionable. Similarly raised by *Omnicare* is whether it will impact how cautionary language that accompanies a forward looking statement is to be assessed in determining whether the "bespeaks caution" doctrine protects a misleading forward looking statement because it was accompanied by cautionary language. This issue arises in instances when the actors are aware the forecast is misleadingly optimistic but claim there was cautionary language that rendered that misstatement immaterial.

The materiality of a particular item is determined within the "total mix" of information that is publicly available. Through the total mix lens a statement is assessed in light of the other information available to investors. As seen below, this invites defenses such as "truth on the market" and "bespeaks caution." As materiality questions are highly fact-specific, summary judgment is rarely appropriate. Because of the breadth of the definition of materiality there are many categories of information that can, under the right set of circumstances, be deemed materiality. Broad categories of information

---

[181]   575 U.S. at 188–89, 135 S.Ct. at 1328–29, 1332.

[182]   ECA & Local 134 IBEW Joint Pension Trust of Chi. v. J.P. Morgan Chase Co., 553 F.3d 187, 195 (2d Cir. 2009).

courts have held material include past business failures of the promoters,[183] on-going criminal investigation of the firm's president,[184] and directors' concealment of a bribery and kickback scheme.[185]

Whether a fact is material is a joint question of law and fact and in theory is poorly suited for resolution on the pleadings. However, the courts with some regularity dismiss actions after concluding the alleged omission or misstatement was not material. Aside from their willingness to weigh the likely importance to the objectively qualified investor of an omitted or misstated item, there are several other heuristics that have developed that empower the court to determine the plaintiff has failed to allege a material misrepresentation. The first is the doctrine of "puffing." A puffing statement is a generalized statement of optimism that, in the court's eye, is not material to the investor because the investor would never attribute any importance to statements as "the business is proceeding well."[186] As Judge Richard Posner observed about statements that the quest for a buyer for the firm was going well (when in fact it was going badly): "*Everyone* knows that someone trying to sell something is going to look and talk on the bright side. You don't sell a product by bad mouthing it."[187]

A second tool for addressing whether a statement is materially misleading is the so-called "truth-on-the-market" defense. This defense arises when the court is persuaded that, even though the defendant's representations in isolation were materially misleading, they could not have misled investors in an efficient market because truthful information was publicly available. For example, a company, when touting the contribution its new product lines would make did not commit a material omission by failing to disclose that its established product lines were approaching obsolescence and, hence, would yield smaller and smaller profits; the court noted that the omitted information was set forth in numerous analysts' reports.[188]

The third tool is the "Bespeaks Caution" doctrine that applies only to forward looking statements, such as a forecast or prediction. Pursuant to this doctrine an erroneous forward looking statement is not materially misleading if accompanied by "meaningful cautionary language."[189] In the leading case, *Kaufman v. Trump's Castle Funding*,[190] the prospectus for a bond offering to finance a casino-hotel in Atlantic City stated the firm "believes that funds generated from the operation of the Taj Mahal will be sufficient to cover all of its debt service (interest and principal). . . ." The firm went bankrupt before even the first payment was due. The court found that the forward looking statement was not misleading because the prospectus contained extensive description of a range of uncertainties the firm must overcome to remain solvent.[191] Not

---

[183] *See, e.g.*, SEC v. Carriba Air, Inc., 681 F.2d 1318 (11th Cir. 1981).

[184] *See, e.g.*, SEC v. Electronics Warehouse, Inc., 689 F.Supp. 53 (D. Conn. 1988), *aff'd*, 891 F.2d 457 (2d Cir. 1989).

[185] *See, e.g.*, Weisberg v. Coastal States Gas Corp., 609 F.2d 650 (2d Cir. 1979). But absent evidence of self-dealing behavior, a leading case holds social character of directors' decisions are not material. *See* Gaines v. Haughton, 645 F.2d 761, 778 (9th Cir. 1981).

[186] *See, e.g.*, Makor Issues & Rights, Ltd. v. Tellabs, Inc., 437 F.3d 588 (7th Cir. 2006) (statement that amounts to vague aspiration or unspecific puffery is not material).

[187] Eisenstadt v. Centel Corp., 113 F.3d 738, 745 (7th Cir. 1997).

[188] *See* In re Convergent Technologies Sec. Lit., 948 F.2d 507, 513 (9th Cir. 1991).

[189] In re Stone & Webster, Inc., 414 F.3d 187 (1st Cir. 2005).

[190] Kaufman v. Trump's Castle Funding, 7 F.3d 357 (3d Cir. 1993).

[191] 7 F.3d at 362.

only is the Bespeaks Caution doctrine well established among the various federal circuits,[192] the doctrine is also now part of the statutory safe harbor for forward looking statements. The statutory safe harbor was added to the Securities Act[193] and Securities Exchange Act[194] in 1995 by the Private Securities Litigation Reform Act. These provisions each provide essentially two distinct safe harbors for forward looking statements (in addition, they each provide their own definition for what constitutes a forward looking statement). The first safe harbor essentially codifies the Bespeaks Caution doctrine since it provides a forward looking statement is not actionable if accompanied by meaningful cautionary language. The Conference Committee Report accompanying this provision clarifies that there can be meaningful cautionary language even though the cautionary statements do not include the particular factor that ultimately causes the forward looking statement not to come true.[195] Second, the Conference Report emphasizes that the cautionary statements "must convey substantive information about factors that realistically could cause results to differ materially from those projected," mere boilerplate is insufficient.[196] Neither the Bespeaks Caution doctrine nor the statutory safe harbor protect misrepresentations of historical fact—each applies only to protect forward looking statements.

The second safe harbor arises if the plaintiff fails to prove that the forward looking statement was made with knowledge of its falsity. Juxtaposing this second safe harbor with the first reveals that the first safe harbor applies even if management knows the forward looking statement is false, provided they have surrounded the knowingly false forecast with meaningful cautionary language. Under the Bespeaks Caution doctrine courts, when it is clear the forecast was knowingly false, have either found that the cautionary language was deficient or that the defendants had committed material misrepresentations of fact, *i.e.*, non-forward looking statements.[197] The statutory safe harbor does not apply to forward looking statements made in certain types of transactions, such as initial public offerings or tender offers, although the Bespeaks Caution doctrine would apply in those contexts.

[2] Scienter and Its Pleading

The Supreme Court has definitively held that the enabling language of section 10(b) that authorizes the SEC to proscribe through rule making "deceptive or manipulative devices or contrivances" forecloses § 10(b) and, hence, Rule 10b–5 from reaching conduct that involves no greater fault than mere negligence.[198] Though the Supreme Court has yet to speak on the subject, reckless disregard of the truthfulness, as well as knowledge of the falsity, of the representation are widely recognized by the lower courts as permissible standards for fault, *i.e.*, scienter, in both private and SEC actions under Rule 10b–5. Scienter under the "knowledge" formula does not require, as does the common

---

[192] *See, e.g.,* Romani v. Shearson Lehman Hutton, 929 F.2d 875 (1st Cir. 1991); I. Meyer Pincus & Assoc. v. Oppenheimer & Co., 936 F.2d 759 (2d Cir. 1991); Sinay v. Lamson & Sessions Co., 948 F.2d 1037 (6th Cir. 1991); In re Convergent Technologies Sec. Lit., 948 F.2d 507 (9th Cir. 1991).

[193] *See* § 27A, 15 U.S.C. § 77z–2 (2015).

[194] *See* § 21E, 15 U.S.C. § 78uu–1 (2015).

[195] H.R. Conf. Rep. No. 369, 104th Cong., 2d Sess. 11 (1995).

[196] H.R. Conf. Rep. No. 369, 104th Cong., 2d Sess. 11 (1995).

[197] *See, e.g.,* Franklin High Yield v. County of Martin Minnesota, 152 F.3d 736 (8th Cir. 1998).

[198] This holding was first reached in *Ernst & Ernst v. Hochfelder*, 425 U.S. 185 (1976) for private actions and was soon applied to SEC enforcement actions in Aaron v. Securities and Exchange Commission, 446 U.S. 680 (1980).

law action of deceit, that the defendant have intended that the misrepresentation induced the plaintiff to trade. It is enough that the defendant was aware of the untruth and its likelihood of influencing investor behavior.[199] The area of the greatest uncertainty regarding possible future Supreme Court action is whether representations and statements made with reckless disregard of their truthfulness are actionable under Rule 10b–5. Presently all the circuits recognize recklessness? As a permissible standard of fault. There are various formulations of what constitutes recklessness under Rule 10b–5. Recklessness falls obviously somewhere between intent and negligence. One court has explained its location as "a lesser form of intent [rather] than a merely greater degree of ordinary negligence."[200] Though a somewhat weaker version of recklessness is a standard of "carelessness approaching indifference" to the truth of the representation,[201] courts more frequently impose a somewhat higher hurdle of what could be called "severe recklessness". However recklessness is defined, and even in a case not involving an allegation of recklessness, the true hurdle facing the plaintiff is that heightened pleading requirements that now apply to securities fraud actions.

The passage of the Private Securities Litigation Reform Act of 1995 (PSLRA) (amending the Securities Act and the Securities and Exchange Act) ended the liberal notice pleading requirements for securities litigation. To discourage what Congress believed was frequent baseless securities fraud litigation,[202] the PSLRA requires that the private plaintiff's complaint not only continue in its other portions to meet the specificity requirements of Federal Rule of Civil Procedure 9(b), but also that the complaint "state with particularity facts giving rise to a *strong inference* that the defendant acted with the requisite state of mind."[203] Adding to the plaintiff's difficulties is that the PSLRA bars any discovery until the resolution of any pending motion to dismiss. Consequently, the plaintiff cannot use discovery, as she once could, to obtain the necessary information to amend her earlier complaint so as to meet the particularity requirements that would be in issue following the defendant's motion to dismiss. Not surprisingly, there is a wide variance among the circuits, and one can even find variances among the district court judges within a single circuit, on just what facts or circumstances give rise to a "strong inference." Indeed, following the PSLRA, the question of pleading scienter is the single most litigated issue in a Rule 10b–5 case. Many courts believe that the template for what constitutes a "strong inference" was the pre-PSLRA Second Circuit decision in *In re Time Warner Securities Litigation*[204] where a majority of the panel held that scienter was plead with particularity by facts supporting a "motive or opportunity" to commit fraud on the part of the company's officers. In *Time Warner* such facts were found in the managers' likely desire to prop up the price of the company's shares to facilitate a public offering of the securities. The Conference Report

---

[199] *See, e.g.,* AUSA Life Insurance Co. v. Ernst & Young, 206 F.3d 202 (2d Cir. 2000); SEC v. Falstaff Brewing Co., 629 F.2d 62, 76 (D.C. Cir. 1980).

[200] Sanders v. John Nuveen & Co., 554 F.2d 790, 793 (7th Cir. 1977).

[201] *See* Hoffman v. Estabrook & Co., 587 F.2d 509, 516 (1st Cir. 1978).

[202] There are numerous studies on the impact of the PSLRA. One study focusing on the pleading requirements found that the Ninth Circuit's decision substantially tightening the pleading requirements was greeted favorably by investors, suggesting that investor sentiment believed lax standards that permitted more suits were harmful. *See* Johnson, Nelson & Pritchard, In re *Silicon Graphics, Inc.*: Shareholder Wealth Effects Resulting from the Interpretation of the Private Securities Litigation Reform Act's Pleading Standard, 73 So. Cal. L. Rev. 773 (2000). *See also* Elam v. Neidorff, 544 F.3d 921 (8th Cir. 2008) (PSLRA's heightened pleading requirement was intended to eliminate abusive securities litigation and prevent pleading fraud by hindsight).

[203] 15 U.S.C. § 78u–4(b)(2) (emphasis added).

[204] In re Time Warner Securities Litigation, 9 F.3d 259 (2d Cir. 1993).

accompanying the PSLRA expressly states it did not intend to codify the Second Circuit's case law, although the new standard was there stated to have been based in part on the Second Circuit's standard.[205] Other courts, following what can be seen as an intermediate approach, though finding that motive and opportunity relevant, considered the facts of the particular case.

The Supreme Court elaborated on the requirements for pleading scienter in *Tellabs, Inc. v. Makor Issues & Rights Ltd.*,[206] which although rejecting a stricter standard urged by the defendants, required that the court take into consideration other plausible inferences negating any alleged inferences of scienter.[207] The strong inference of scienter must be more than a plausible one, it must be "cogent."[208] This means that the inference of scienter must be more than merely reasonable and must be persuasive in light of the particular facts of the case.[209] The inference of scienter must be at least as likely as other reasonable inferences that could be drawn from the facts as pleaded. The Court's analysis is far from a bright-line test but appears to strike a balance in requiring more than speculative or reasonable inferences but at the same time not imposing a requirement of firmly requiring unequivocal allegations of a "smoking gun."[210]

[3] Standing—the Purchaser or Seller Requirement

The SEC's standing to sue under the antifraud provision is never in serious doubt since under section 21(d)(1)[211] the agency is authorized to initiate an enforcement action in the federal district court and can proceed internally pursuant to its cease and desist powers under section 21C of the Exchange Act.[212] Private investors seeking a monetary recovery must, however, be either a purchaser or seller of a security in connection with the fraud alleged to have been committed by the defendant. Once known as the *Birnbaum* doctrine,[213] a reference to the leading case first enshrining it within the Rule 10b–5 jurisprudence, it was not until three decades after *Birnbaum* was decided that the Supreme Court in *Blue Chip Stamps v. Manor Drug Stores*[214] affirmed the practice that had been uniformly followed in the circuits. *Blue Chip Stamps* above all other cases denotes the change in attitude toward private securities suits from the earlier more liberal approaches of the Warren Court. It was not just that *Blue Chip Stamps* opted for a technical standing requirement that signaled a new balance within what was then the Burger Court, but it was the Court's reasons for opting for the technical rule. The Court was not guided by what it thought were logical inferences to be drawn from legislative history. Rather the basis for its mandating a purchaser-seller requirement was its belief

---

[205] S. 1260, H.R. Conf. Rep. No. 105–803, 104th Cong., 1st Sess. at 41. For an excellent review of the legislative history on this topic, *see* Joseph A. Grundfest & A.C. Pritchard, Statutes with Multiple Personality Disorders: The Value of Ambiguity in Statutory Design and Interpretation, 54 Stan. L. Rev. 627, 650–665 (2002).

[206] Tellabs, Inc. v. Makor Issues & Rights Ltd., 551 U.S. 308 (2007).

[207] *Id.*

[208] *Id.*

[209] *Id.*

[210] *Id.*

[211] 15 U.S.C. § 78u(d)(1) (2015).

[212] 15 U.S.C. § 78u–3 (2015).

[213] *See* Birnbaum v. Newport Steel Corp., 193 F.2d 461 (2d Cir.), *cert. denied,* 343 U.S. 956 (1952).

[214] Blue Chip Stamps v. Manor Drug Stores, 421 U.S. 723 (1975).

of the need for a rule that would insulate companies and their officers from what the court described as "vexatious litigation."[215]

The purchaser-seller requirement is by far the most rigid fixture of Rule 10b–5 litigation. This requires an executed purchase or sale, not merely a speculative opportunity to trade. Even where the defendant's successful intent to prevent the plaintiff from selling by purposefully misrepresenting material facts is beyond peradventure, suit to recover for the losses suffered is barred, even if the sale occurs later after the true facts are known.[216] The sale that is in connection with the fraud does not have to arise by volition so long as the losses are causally related to the sale. Thus, when control of a company was acquired by fraud practiced upon all its shareholders and thereafter the remaining stockholders are cashed out in a squeeze-out merger, the so-called forced seller doctrine applies to confer standing.[217] Somewhat related to the forced seller is the "aborted purchaser-seller." This arises when the defendant's fraud aborts a formal plan involving the sale or exchange of shares.[218] Following the lead of a leading pre-*Blue Chip Stamps* case,[219] most courts that have been called upon to decide the matter have held that the plaintiff seeking injunctive relief need not be a purchaser or seller of shares.[220] There seems to be little cause to deny standing for prospective injunctive relief to a plaintiff who has neither purchased nor sold if the plaintiff sustains the burden of proving that, if equitable relief is not awarded, the defendant's violation likely will cause the plaintiff to suffer a loss through the purchase or sale of a security.

[4] "In Connection with"

Not only must there be a purchase or sale of a security, but Rule 10b–5, reflecting the operative language of section 10(b), itself requires that the violation, *i.e.*, the deception, must be "in connection with" the purchase or sale of a security. The language does not, however, require that the defendant be engaged in a security transaction. Thus, companies that release false financial information into a marketplace are liable under Rule 10b–5, even though the company itself does not purchase or sell securities.[221] Correlatively, there is no need to prove in a private suit that the plaintiff is in privity of contract through his purchase or sale with the defendants. Indeed, the in connection with requirement is satisfied even if the target of the fraud is someone other than the purchasing or selling plaintiff.[222] Consequently, untruthful statements about a

---

[215]   421 U.S. at 743.

[216]   *See* Gurley v. Documation, Inc., 674 F.2d 253 (4th Cir. 1982).

[217]   The leading case for this doctrine is Vine v. Beneficial Finance Co., 374 F.2d 627 (2d Cir.), *cert. denied*, 389 U.S. 970 (1967). For post *Blue Chip Stamps* decisions recognizing the doctrine, *see* 7547 Corp. v. Parker & Parsley Dev. Partners L.P., 38 F.3d 211 (5th Cir. 1994) (however, proof that there was a substantial change in the rights, privileges, or preferences of the plaintiff's securities is needed to establish a sale).

[218]   *See* Mosher v. Kane, 784 F.2d 1385 (9th Cir. 1986).

[219]   *See* Mutual Shares Corp. v. Genesco, Inc., 384 F.2d 540 (2d Cir. 1967).

[220]   *Compare* Tully v. Mott Supermarkets, Inc., 540 F.2d 187 (3d Cir. 1976) (upholding injunctive action by a non seller/purchaser) *with* Cowin v. Bresler, 741 F.2d 410 (D.C. Cir. 1984) (strictly applying *Blue Chip Stamps'* reasoning to deny standing to non-trading plaintiff).

[221]   This point was expressly addressed in a landmark insider trading case, *see* Securities and Exchange Commission v. Texas Gulf Sulphur Co., 401 F.2d 833, 860 (2d Cir. 1968) (en banc), *cert. denied*, 394 U.S. 976 (1969) ("We do not believe that Congress intended that the proscriptions of the Act would not be violated unless the makers of a misleading statements also participated in pertinent securities transactions in connection therewith. . . .").

[222]   *See, e.g.,* In re Ames Dept. Stores, Inc. Stock Litig., 991 F.2d 953 (2d Cir. 1993); Heit v. Weitzen, 402 F.2d 909 (2d Cir. 1968).

company's products, certainly in the technology sector where investors can be expected to accord product features on a level akin to earnings per share, can subject such announcements to Rule 10b–5 exposure.[223]

Just what are the permissible bounds of a statement being "in connection with" has been repeatedly muddied by the Supreme Court. In its initial foray into this area, the question was whether a company officer that engineers the board's approval to dispose of bonds it owns violated Rule 10b–5 when the officer's secret intent was to embezzle the proceeds of the resulting sale. One might question on these facts just where the deception was—*e.g.*, the failure to disclose to the board the officer's secret intent—as well as whether the deception required must be one that relates to the inherent value of the security to be sold (as contrasted with the motive for the sale). Instead, Justice Douglas said that the fraud need simply "touch" a securities transaction to satisfy the in connection with requirement.[224] The guidance provided by the Supreme Court has not improved with time. In its decision, *The Wharf (Holdings) Ltd. v. United International Holdings,*[225] the court held the in connection with requirement was met when the defendant did not disclose its intention not to honor an oral option that was granted as part of a transaction. The court reasoned that "even were it the case that the Act covers only misrepresentations likely to affect the value of securities, Wharf's secret reservation was such a misrepresentation" because the defendant's secret intent rendered the option valueless. Thus, the Court gives little insight as to just what determines whether the fraud is "in connection with" the purchase or sale of a security. We might believe from the above quote that *Wharf Ltd.* does wish for the deception to relate to the value of the security transaction to the plaintiff. But in *Bankers Life* there was no misstatement of the value the company would receive for the bonds; the defendant simply failed to disclose his intent to misappropriate the proceeds of that sale. The Court's most recent decision, *SEC v. Zandford,*[226] on this subject returns to the defendant who engineers a security transaction for the purpose of misappropriating the proceeds. What is different from *Bankers Life* in *Zandford* is that the defendant had sole discretion over purchases and sales of the investor's brokerage account. Thus, as a technical matter the investor's judgment was never directly impacted by the defendant's misconduct because the investor had committed that task to the defendant by establishing a discretionary account. The court held that the in connection with requirement was met by allegations that sales were undertaken for the purpose of yielding proceeds that could then be misappropriated. The court did not focus on interdicting the customer's investment judgment. Instead it held there clear was a "scheme to defraud" and that its execution coincided with a securities transaction. Just what constitutes a scheme to defraud would, in light of *Zandford,* appear to include any undisclosed plan to transfer assets from an investor to the defendant. The in connection with requirement is then met if a security transaction is at the heart of that scheme.

---

[223] *See generally* Robert A. Prentice and John H. Langmore, Beware of Vaporware: Product Hype and the Securities Fraud Liability of High Tech Companies, 8 Harv. J. L. & Tech. 1 (1994).

[224] *See* Superintendent of Insurance v. Bankers Life & Casualty Co., 404 U.S. 6, 10 (1971). *See generally* James D. Cox, Fraud Is in the Eye of the Beholder: Rule 10b–5's Application to Corporate Mismanagement, 47 N.Y.U. L. Rev. 674 (1972).

[225] The Wharf (Holdings) Ltd. v. United International Holdings, 532 U.S. 588 (2001).

[226] SEC v. Zandford, 535 U.S. 813 (2002).

[5] Causal Relationship and Damages

Causation is an element of a Rule 10b–5 action. Many courts have divided causation into two subparts: transaction causation and loss causation. Transaction causation requires a showing that but for the violations in question, the transaction would not have occurred (at least in the form that it took).[227] Loss causation requires a showing of a causal nexus between the transaction and the plaintiff's loss.[228]

The Supreme Court in *Dura Pharmaceuticals, Inc. v. Broudo*,[229] made it clear that it is not sufficient to allege that the price was inflated by the misstatement. Instead, a direct causal link must be established between the misstatement and a decline in the price of the stock once the correct information was factored into the price. Moreover, the ability to establish loss causation must be shown at the class certification stage.[230] This is clarified in *Halliburton Co. v. Erica P. John Fund, Inc.*[231] which refused to overrule *Basic, Inc.* and held that the plaintiff is not required to establish that the misrepresentation impacted the security's price. The Court also observed that the defendants, at the class certification stage of the litigation, can seek to overcome *Basic, Inc.'s* presumption through evidence that the misrepresentation did not in fact affect the stock's price. So-called "event studies" are generally used in exploring whether such an impact accompanied the misrepresentation.[232] However, courts have with some recent frequency expressed skepticism over the use of this economic model central to event studies; the model was developed to examine the information content across a portfolio of companies in studying the likely information content in single-firm context.[233]

Inquiry into transaction causation in many instances occurs by inquiring whether the plaintiff relied upon the deception. When this occurs the plaintiff must not only prove that the misstated or omitted fact would have assumed actual significance in the deliberations of the reasonable investors under circumstances similar to those that the

---

[227] Reliance is often equated with "transaction causation." Dura Pharmaceuticals, Inc. v. Broudo, 544 U.S. 336, 341 (2005). Reliance may well affect one's decision to trade or the price at which the plaintiff would have traded had the true facts been known. It can include other steps as well. For example, even if the plaintiff had taken some steps to protect himself in the event of an IPO, had the true facts been disclosed he might well have sought even greater protection. See Castellano v. Young & Rubicam, Inc., 257 F.3d 171 (2d Cir. 2001).

[228] Loss causation is a separate element from transaction causation, and the two cannot be collapsed into each other. AUSA Life Ins. Co. v. Ernst and Young, 206 F.3d 202, 216 (2d Cir. 2000). Loss causation is comparable to the tort law concept of proximate cause. Thus, the damages suffered by the plaintiff must be a foreseeable consequence of any misrepresentation or material omission. Emergent Capital Inv. Management, LLC v. Stonepath Group, Inc., 343 F.3d 189 (2d Cir. 2003). A misstatement is the proximate cause of an investment loss if the risk that caused the loss was within the zone of risks concealed by the misrepresentations. Lattanzio v. Deloitte & Touche LLP, 476 F.3d 147 (2d Cir. 2007). A plaintiff must plead loss causation with sufficient specificity to enable the court to evaluate whether the necessary causal link exists. Teachers' Ret. Sys. of La. v. Hunter, 477 F.3d 162 (4th Cir. 2007).

[229] Dura Pharmaceuticals, Inc. v. Broudo, 544 U.S. 336 (2005).

[230] In re Flag Telecom Holdings, Ltd. Securities Litigation, 574 F.3d 29, 38 (2d Cir. 2009) ("lower courts have an 'obligation'; to resolve factual disputes relevant to [the class certification requirements]"), relying on In re IPO Securities Litigation, 471 F.3d 24 (2d Cir. 2006).

[231] Halliburton Co. v. Erica P. John Fund, Inc., 573 U.S. 258 (2014)(frequently referred to as *Halliburton II*).

[232] See J.B. Heaton & Alon Brav, Event Studies in Securities Litigation: Low Power, Confounding Effects, and Bias, 93 Wash. U.L. Rev. 583 (2015)(close examination of event study methodology that makes case that courts should understand their low statistical predictive power).

[233] See e.g., In re Petrobras Sec. Litig., 862 F.3d 250 (2d Cir. 2017); Waggoner v. Barclays PLC, 875 F.3d 79 (2d Cir. 2017)(when weight of other factors support finding that the security traded in an efficient market there is no need to consider the absence of price impact when issues is whether class enjoys the presumption under *Basic, Inc.*)

plaintiff operated within (this of course is the materiality element), but also that the misstated or omitted fact assumed such significance for the plaintiff that it caused the plaintiff to purchase (or to sell, as the case may be) which the plaintiff would not have done had the defendant not misrepresented the facts.[234] This approach gets tricky, if not ethereal, if the plaintiff is required to prove reliance upon a material fact that was omitted. In such a case, the plaintiff is assisted by the holding of *Affiliated Ute Citizens v. United States*,[235] whose facts are narrower than the language the court used to express its holding; in a non-disclosure case (*i.e.*, pure omission case) reliance can be presumed from a showing that the omitted fact was material.[236] The actual facts of the case suggest the holding might be narrower. The investors were Native Americans who depended upon the defendant bank to sell their securities. All dealings were face-to-face and the bank failed on each trade to disclose that the shares were being resold at a higher price. Thus, the case is not simply an omission case, but one involving a clear fiduciary relationship between the bank and the plaintiffs. This should make it an easier case to conclude reliance *in fact* by the plaintiffs on the bank to deal fairly.

Due to the influence of *Affiliated Ute*, it is common in face-to-face transactions as well as even open market purchases for the plaintiff to enjoy the presumption of his reliance when the defendant has committed only an omission.[237] The presumption, however, can be rebutted. Courts adhering strictly to the unique facts of *Affiliated Ute* where there was a fiduciary relationship between the plaintiff and defendant accord this presumption only when there is a preexisting relationship between the plaintiff and defendant.[238] In cases of misstatements or a combination of misstatements and omissions, proof of reliance by the plaintiff is required.[239]

The major exception to proving the investor's reliance upon the defendant's misrepresentation is the "fraud on the market" theory that was upheld by the Supreme Court in *Basic Inc. v. Levinson*.[240] The theory relieves the plaintiff of proving reliance upon the particular false announcement or representation that is the focus of her claim.

> The fraud on the market theory is based on the hypothesis that, in an open and developed securities market, the price of a company's stock is determined by the available information regarding the company and its business. . . . Misleading statements will therefore defraud purchasers of stock even if the purchasers do not directly rely on the misstatements. . . . The causal connection between the defendant's fraud and the plaintiff's purchase of stock in such a case is no less significant than in a case of direct reliance on misrepresentations.[241]

---

[234] *See* Tricontinental Indus. Ltd. v. PricewaterhouseCoopers, LLP, 475 F.3d 824 (7th Cir. 2007) (plaintiff must allege that it would not have invested in securities if defendant had stated material facts truthfully at time of sale).

[235] Affiliated Ute Citizens v. United States, 406 U.S. 128 (1972).

[236] Affiliated Ute Citizens v. United States, 406 U.S. 128, 153 (1972).

[237] *See, e.g.*, Rowe v. Maremont Corp., 850 F.2d 1226 (7th Cir. 1988).

[238] *See, e.g.*, Cavalier Carpets, Inc. v. Caylor, 746 F.2d 749 (11th Cir. 1984) (court denied the presumption to a plaintiff who carried out his own investigation).

[239] *See, e.g.*, Cox v. Collins, 7 F.3d 394 (4th Cir. 1993).

[240] Basic, Inc. v. Levinson, 485 U.S. 224 (1988).

[241] Peil v. Speiser, 806 F.2d 1154, 1160–61 (3d Cir. 1986), quoted in Basic, Inc. v. Levinson, 485 U.S. at 229.

The theory applies only for securities trading that occurs in a market believed to be efficient.[242] Thus, face-to-face trades, exchanges with the corporation and the like are not transactions whose plaintiffs are the beneficiaries of the fraud on the market theory.[243]

A divided Supreme Court in *Amgen Inc. v. Connecticut Retirement Plans and Trust Funds*,[244] held that class certification does not require the plaintiffs to establish the materiality of the defendant's alleged misrepresentation. The majority reasoned the focus of class certification is whether, among the issues in dispute, the issues that are common to the class predominate over individual issues that may exist. Because "the question of materiality is an objective one that is common to all members of the class" further inquiry into materiality is not required and to do so would "put the cart before the horse."

Just what is an efficient market is rarely litigated, though courts appear to recognize all trading on the New York Stock Exchange as well as larger capitalized companies traded on Nasdaq are covered by the theory.[245] An obvious consequence of the theory is that it facilitates class action certification because when the theory applies there is no inquiry into each class member's reliance. If there were, this would likely render class certification unlikely since common questions of law and fact are not likely to predominate if reliance were required to be established by each class member. This is not to suggest that reliance is not a theoretical impossibility. Even *Basic Inc.* acknowledged that "a plaintiff who believed that Basic's statements were false and that Basic was indeed engaged in merger discussions, and who consequently believed that Basic was artificially underpriced, but sold his shares nevertheless because of an unrelated concern . . . could not be said to have relied on the integrity of the price he knew had been manipulated."[246] We might well question why even this plaintiff should not be permitted to recover. To be sure, the plaintiff hypothesized by the Supreme Court did not rely. But note that because of the defendant's misstatements (denying on three occasions that it was engaged in merger negotiations) defendant did adversely affect the price at which the hypothetical plaintiff sold her shares. Why should the defendant not compensate that plaintiff for the losses causally related to its lies as much as the plaintiff whose decision to sell the shares was based on whim or perhaps the chance throwing of darts? It seems that to require reliance in such cases ignores the role of reliance—to establish a causal nexus between the defendant's violation and the plaintiff's loss. In an efficient market that nexus would appear established by proof that the market price of the shares would have been higher or lower but for the defendant's violation. In an efficient market, investors are to be seen as price takers and, in cases such as *Basic Inc.*, the price so taken is one affected by the defendant's violation.

The issue of reliance can arise by the defendant placing in issue that the plaintiff's reliance upon the defendant's false representation was unreasonable. The essence of this argument is that the plaintiff's recovery should be barred when with modest effort the

---

[242] *See, e.g.*, Regents of Univ. of Cal. v. Credit Suisse First Boston (USA), Inc., 482 F.3d 372 (5th Cir. 2007).

[243] *See, e.g.*, Feinman v. Dean Witter Reynolds, Inc., 84 F.3d 539 (2d Cir. 1996) (broker-customer disputes are not subject to fraud on market theory).

[244] 568 U.S. 455 (2013).

[245] *See, e.g.*, In re Xcelera.com Sec. Litig., 430 F.3d 503 (1st Cir. 2005) (efficient market is one in which market price of stock fully reflects all publicly available information).

[246] 485 U.S. at 249.

plaintiff could have discovered the untruth and thereafter protected himself by either not going forward with the transaction or negotiating a better price. For example, a sophisticated investor was not able to recover from the broker selling it hybrid securities without disclosing the serious risks inherent in the instrument; the court reasoned that given the investor's sophistication a non-reckless investor would have sought advice from knowledgeable advisors.[247] Thus, the sophisticated investor is under some obligation to protect himself from the unscrupulous promoter. However, the courts appear to require some greater departure on the plaintiff's part than the absence of reasonable care, thus placing the plaintiff on a footing equal to the scienter standard by which the fault of defendants is determined.[248]

A special causation issue arises in mergers and recapitalizations that are accompanied by a material misrepresentation and the parties responsible for the deception control sufficient voting power to assure approval of the merger or recapitalization. As will be seen in a later section, the sine qua non of Rule 10b–5 violation is the presence of a material misrepresentation.[249] Without any deception there can be no violation of Rule 10b–5.[250] We might therefore conclude that in such a situation, because the transaction can be effected without the approval of any minority stockholder, there could be no violation of Rule 10b–5. This is true, provided that the state law does not accord the minority an appraisal remedy in the event they should dissent from the transaction.[251] When there is an appraisal remedy, the minority have two alternative investment decisions to consider, each with a different financial outcome. One choice is to accept what is offered in the transaction being supported by the majority. The other choice is to vote against the transaction and pursue their appraisal remedy. This choice is very much an investment decision, being a decision essentially in which forum to dispose of one's shares and at what price. Thus the courts have consistently recognized that the availability of an appraisal remedy resuscitates what would otherwise have been a moribund Rule 10b–5 cause of action.[252]

[6] Primary Participants, Aiders and Abettors, and Control Persons

As discussed above, through the mid-1970s, the Supreme Court acquiesced in the circuit and district courts' expansive view of Rule 10b–5. That trend has not continued. For example, in *Central Bank of Denver v. First Interstate Bank of Denver,* by a five-to-four decision the Court held that there is no implied right of action to redress aiding and abetting a Rule 10b–5 violation.[253] The Court's holding is limited to private rights of

---

[247] *See* Banca Cremi S.A. v. Alex. Brown & Sons, 132 F.3d 1017 (4th Cir. 1997). But when the investors are not as sophisticated, the suit was permitted to proceed even though oral misrepresentations made to the investors were contradicted by warnings in the private placement brochure. *See* Myers v. Finkle, 950 F.2d 165 (4th Cir. 1991).

[248] *See, e.g.,* Mallis v. Bankers Trust Co., 615 F.2d 68 (2d Cir. 1980 Friendly).

[249] *See supra* § 12.12.

[250] *See* Santa Fe Indus., Inc. v. Green, 430 U.S. 462 (1977).

[251] *See* Virginia Bankshares, Inc. v. Sandberg, 501 U.S. 1083 (1991) (though the minority were invited to vote on the cash out merger and their approval was no doubt affected by material misstatements, causation was lacking under the proxy rules because their approval was without meaning since the defendants controlled 85 percent of the voting rights and there was not appraisal remedy provided by state law).

[252] *See, e.g.,* Wilson v. Great Amer. Indus., Inc., 979 F.2d 924 (2d Cir. 1992).

[253] Central Bank of Denver v. First Interstate Bank of Denver, 511 U.S. 164 (1994). *See also, e.g.,* Stoneridge Investment Partners, LLC v. Scientific Atlanta, Inc., 552 U.S. 148 (2008) (defendants were secondary actors and thus could not be held liable as primary violators).

action. After *Central Bank,* there no longer is liability in private suits for aiding and abetting. One must be a primary participant, the scope of which is discussed below, or fall within one of the now narrower instances (*i.e.,* vicarious liability or control person liability, discussed below) for secondary liability. Aiding and abetting may still be charged in SEC injunctive and other enforcement actions as well as in criminal prosecutions.

Central Bank reinforces the narrow approach the Supreme Court has taken in recent years in its interpretation of the scope of the implied causes of action under the federal securities laws. In the course of its opinion, the Court took a literal approach and stressed the importance of looking to the wording of the statute as the primary source of statutory interpretation (including the implication of a private remedy).[254] The most salient part of *Central Bank's* holding is its holding that section 10(b) and Rule 10b–5 proscribe only "the *making*" of a material misstatement (or omission) or "the *commission* of a manipulative act."[255] Thus, to be a primary participant there must be evidence that the defendant *made* a misrepresentation or *committed* a manipulative act. The better view is that principals are bound by the misrepresentations their agents make with apparent authority.[256]

After *Central Bank* two divergent approaches have developed to address whether a defendant can be held to have *made* the misrepresentation that is the gravamen of the case. The most liberal of the two approaches is the substantial factor test which inquires whether the defendant has been a substantial participant in making the false representation. Under this approach, one who drafts, edits, and reviews the document containing the misrepresentation is liable as a primary participant. A far more restrictive approach is the so-called "bright-line" test whereby it is not sufficient for primary participant liability that the defendant have a substantial or even central role in preparing the false statement. Under the bright-line test, no one is a primary participant unless the misrepresentation can be attributed or otherwise identified with having been made by that defendant by the plaintiff. The source of this requirement is the reasoning of *Central Bank* that to permit recovery against one who has merely assisted in making the misrepresentation would allow the plaintiff to circumvent Rule 10b–5's reliance requirement.[257] Thus, for example, in *Wright v. Ernst & Young LLP,*[258] the accounting firm escaped liability for false statements that it had assisted the client in preparing for its press release because the release did not identify the accounting firm as being involved in preparing the release. Carried to its logical extreme, the bright-line test would appear to shield corporate officers from liability for misleading statements they prepare but which are released only under the company's name. Certainly this should not be the case.[259] *Wright* traces the need for the statement to be attributed to the defendant back to *Central Bank's* concern that otherwise reliance would be obviated in Rule 10b–5 cases.

---

[254] *Cf.* Musick, Peeler & Garrett v. Employers Ins. of Wausau, 508 U.S. 286 (1993), holding that there is an implied right to contribution among joint defendants. In the *Central Bank* case, the Court distinguished the *Musick* decision on the basis that the securities laws contain an express statement of controlling personal and joint and several liability, which is in contrast to the absence of a general aiding and abetting provision.

[255] 511 U.S. at 177.

[256] *See* In re Atlantic Financial Management, Inc., 784 F.2d 29 (1st Cir. 1986) (J. Breyer).

[257] 511 U.S. at 180.

[258] Wright v. Ernst & Young LLP, 152 F.3d 169 (2d Cir. 1998).

[259] But such was the result in Copland v. Grumet, 88 F. Supp. 2d 326 (D.N.J. 1999).

In *Stoneridge Investment Partners, LLC v. Scientific-Atlanta, Inc.,*[260] the Supreme Court rejected the theory of "scheme liability" in private securities fraud cases, addressing a conflict among the circuits over whether an injured investor may recover from a party that neither makes a public misstatement nor breaches a duty to disclose but does participate in a "scheme" to violate Rule 10b–5. In this case, investors who alleged losses after purchasing a company's common stock sought to impose liability on the company's customers and suppliers that had agreed to arrangements allowing the company to mislead its auditor and issue a false financial statement affecting the stock price. Traditional reliance was missing, because these third parties had no role in preparing or disseminating the statement that the investors used, and their own deceptive acts were never communicated to the public. Nonetheless, the plaintiffs posited that investors in an efficient market rely not only on the public statements relating to a security but also on the transactions that those statements reflect. The Court, applying the general rule tying reliance to causation, thought that the third parties' acts were too remote to satisfy the reliance requirement. In reaching this conclusion, it expressed reluctance to extend the private cause of action beyond the securities markets into the realm of ordinary business operations governed by state law.

Subsequently, in *Janus Capital Group Inc. v. First Derivative Traders* the Court further narrowed scope of persons who can be held liable under Rule 10b–5.[261] Focusing on the verb "make" in Rule 10b–5(b), the Court ruled that primary liability exists and hence a private right of action may only be brought against someone who *makes* the materially misleading statement in question. The majority of the Court rejected the contention that "make" should be defined as "create," which would allow private plaintiffs to sue a person who provides the false or misleading information that another person puts into a statement.[262] This is a narrow interpretation of Rule 10b–5.

The Court in *Janus* focused on subsection (b) of Rule 10b–5 that expressly refers to someone who *makes* a statement. The impact of the *Janus* decision could be avoided should the SEC decide to reword the language of Rule 10b–5(b) to include someone playing a sufficiently active role in creating the offending statement.

In 2019, the Supreme Court significantly expanded the scope of who might be a primary participant in *Lorenzo v. SEC.*[263] The SEC brought an enforcement action against a broker who circulated among his clients false information prepared by his employer that induced many of the broker's customers to purchase the securities he recommended. He defended that under *Janus* he did not have ultimate responsibility for the false statements since his boss had asked him to circulate the false information. *Lorenzo* holds that the language of both paragraph (a) and (c) of Rule 10b–5 are sufficiently broad to include the dissemination of materially misleading information with the intent to defraud.[264] Thus, even though not within paragraph (b) of Rule 10b–5, a

---

[260] Stoneridge Investment Partners, LLC v. Scientific-Atlanta, Inc., 552 U.S. 148 (2008).

[261] Janus Capital Group, Inc. v. First Derivative Traders, 564 U.S. 135 (2011).

[262] The Court in *Janus* held that notwithstanding the close relationship of a mutual fund and its investment adviser, the adviser will not be held liable as a primary violator for statements made by the fund even where the adviser had a role in drafting the false statements.

[263] Lorenzo v. SEC, 139 S. Ct. 1094 (2019).

[264] Rule 10b–5(a) proscribes those who "employ any device, scheme, or artifice to defraud" and paragraph (c) makes it unlawful "to engage in any act, practice, or course of business which operates or would operate as a fraud or deceit upon any person." 17 C.F.R. § 240.10b–5(c).

person can be a primary violator of paragraph (a) and (c) if false statements are circulated with the intent to induce others to trade in securities.

Though *Lorenzo* was a government enforcement action, the breadth of the opinion does not suggest it should be limited to only SEC suits. It should apply equally in private suits since the Court's rationale is based on the language of section 10(b) and Rule 10b–5(a) and (c). In an analogous situation the Supreme Court rejected the absence of a scienter requirement in SEC enforcement actions because that requirement comes from the terms of section 10(b), not the nature of the action being brought.[265]

Section 20(a) of the Exchange Act[266] imposes secondary liability upon those who are deemed control persons of the primary violator. Most circuits apply a two-prong test to determine whether a person is a control person subject to section 20(a) liability. First, the defendant must have actually exercised general control over the operations or activities of the primary participant. Second, the control person must have had the power or the ability—even if not exercised—to control the specific transaction or activity that gave rise to the violation. Thus, outside directors who serve on the audit committee, and in that capacity approved accounting practices, are control persons with respect to recognizing sales prematurely.[267] However, other outside directors would not be so held, unless involved in the review or release of the misleading information.[268]

Control liability, however, is not absolute. Section 20(a) provides the control person is liable to the same extent as the primary participant, "unless the controlling person acted in good faith and did not directly or indirectly induce the act or acts constituting the violation or cause of action." Note that this arises defensively so that the control person must prove both items. Since most control persons are able to establish that they did not induce the violation, the larger number of litigated cases turn on whether the control person has established her "good faith" defense. Good faith is an elastic expression capable of mandating in some instances only the absence of knowledge. In other contexts good faith implicates the absence of recklessness,[269] and still others good faith calls for the imposition of reasonable procedures to deter and detect misconduct by the controlled party.[270] A minority of the circuits essentially duplicate the good faith inquiry by making it part of the plaintiff's case to establish that a defendant is amenable to being a control person. The adherents of this minority view take the position that Congress intended to impose liability not solely upon a control person, but that the control person must in some meaningful sense have been a culpable participant in the violation either by being an actor in the violation or intended his acquiescence or passivity to further the violation.[271]

---

[265] Aaron v. SEC, 446 U.S. 680 (1980); Ernst & Ernst v. Hochfelder, 425 U.S. 185 (1976).

[266] 15 U.S.C. § 78t(a).

[267] *See* In re Gupta Securities Litig., 1995 WL 338893 (N.D. Cal. 1995); Jacobs v. Coopers & Lybrand LLP, 1999 WL 101772 (S.D.N.Y. 1999).

[268] *See* Bomarko, Inc. v. Hemodynamics, Inc., 848 F.Supp. 1335 (W.D. Mich. 1993) (excusing outside directors from liability but not director who served as firm's general counsel and had reviewed the misleading announcement).

[269] *See, e.g.*, Dellastatious v. Williams, 242 F.3d 191, 194 (4th Cir. 2001) (outside directors satisfied good-faith defense by showing that corporation's system for drafting and reviewing offering documents functioned properly).

[270] Classically this is the case for brokerage firms.

[271] *See* Boguslavsky v. Kaplan, 159 F.3d 715, 720 (2d Cir. 1998); Sharp v. Coopers & Lybrand, 649 F.2d 175, 185 (3d Cir. 1981).

Quite separate from controlling person liability is vicarious liability premised upon the doctrine of respondeat superior. It is quite easy to understand that control person liability is not the exclusive form of vicarious responsibility. Recall that respondeat superior liability is the means for holding the master responsible for torts committed by the servant within the scope of the servant's employment. Under respondeat superior liability it is the employing organization that is liable. Whereas, under control person liability, responsibility can be imposed upon the supervisor of the primary participant, even though the supervisor is not the employing organization. Courts have therefore held that respondeat superior and control person liability coexist, *i.e.*, that control person liability is not the exclusive means to reach the employer.[272] There is some cause for pause, however, that the narrow construction given to the securities laws by the Supreme Court, especially in *Central Bank,* may someday find its impact on the availability of respondeat superior liability. Such a result would indeed twist Congress's intent in providing control person liability. Its intent in crafting into the securities laws control person liability was to expand the scope of liability not to constrict it.

[7] Statutory Restraints on Private Actions via PSLRA and SLUSA

The 103rd Congress bestowed a unique honor on securities fraud actions by enacting the Private Securities Litigation Reform Act of 1995[273] and thereby accorded *securities* class actions their own procedural rules. To date, no other area of private suit has earned its own set of special procedural rules, or more accurately, impediments to the private litigant. At the core of the PSLRA was tweaking the incentives that surround the initiation, prosecution, and settlement of securities class actions. Overall the concern was the relative lack of restraint that Congress believed characterized class action litigation.

An important contribution of the PSLRA to securities class actions is its embrace of the "lead plaintiff," which the Act provides presumptively is the class member with the "largest financial" loss.[274] The lead plaintiff is authorized to make recommendations to the court regarding the selection and dismissal of the suit's counsel. Congress's obvious intent is to harness to the class action's oversight the economic self-interest of such a large claimant. After the PSLRA, being the first lawyer to file a complaint no longer provides a leg up to becoming lead counsel. The evidence to date suggests that securities class actions still are lawyer driven, albeit not of the magnitude as before the PSLRA. A good deal of effort is spent by the lawyers wooing investors with large losses, particularly financial institutions, to petition the court to be a lead plaintiff (all with the understanding that if selected as lead plaintiff the requesting investor would then retain the law firm that recruited the investor).[275] Among the issues posed by the lead plaintiff are whether an aggregation of individual investors who in combination have a larger loss

---

[272] *See, e.g.,* Hollinger v. Titan Capital Corp., 914 F.2d 1564 (9th Cir. 1990).

[273] Pub. L. No. 104–67, 109 Stat. 737 (codified in scattered sections in 15 U.S.C.) [hereinafter PSLRA].

[274] Exchange Act section 21D(a)(3)(B)(iii)(bb), 15 U.S.C. § 78u–4 (2015). For provisions parallel to those described here for Exchange Act based suits that are applicable to suits brought under the Securities Act of 1933, *see* section 27, 15 U.S.C. § 77z–1 (2015).

[275] *See, e.g.,* In re Razorfish, Inc. Sec. Litig., 143 F. Supp. 2d 304 (S.D.N.Y. 2001).

than a single institutional investor is the preferable choice[276] and whether the selection of a lead plaintiff prevents the use of an auction to choose counsel for the class action.[277]

As seen above,[278] the PSLRA introduced something of a "double whammy" by tightening the pleading requirement beyond the standard particularity requirement and barring any discovery until the exhaustion of the defendant's motion to dismiss. The plaintiff "with respect to each act or omission alleged to" be a violation "must plead with particularity facts giving rise to a strong inference that the defendant acted with the required state of mind" to be liable.[279] And, the misrepresentation must be pled with particularity as well as setting forth the facts that support any allegation of misrepresentation that is based upon information or belief.[280] Discovery is not available to assist the plaintiff in satisfying meeting the tightened pleading requirement.[281] The intent of the discovery bar is to revoke the former license the plaintiff's counsel had to conduct a "fishing expedition" into the defendants' files solely by leveling bald accusations of fraud in the complaint.

The PSLRA mandates that the notice of settlement provided class members set forth an estimate of the average recoverable amount per share.[282] A further provision to chasten any bold class action counsel willing to push a questionable case is the PSLRA's mandating that the trial judge at the conclusion of each case make a finding whether the litigants have complied with Rule 11.[283] If so, then appropriate sanctions are to be imposed upon the violating party. Outside of securities litigation, Rule 11 sanctions arise customarily by a motion of one of the parties. The new provision introduced by the PSLRA avoids the possibility of the plaintiff's and defendant's counsel agreeing as part of the settlement that neither will raise Rule 11 sanctions.

Many substantive changes were also introduced by the PSLRA. There is a safe harbor for forward looking statements,[284] a provision for proportionate liability that extends to contribution claims,[285] the elimination of securities claims from being a predicate act that satisfies RICO (unless there has been a prior criminal conviction),[286] and a statute of limitations for contribution claims.[287]

Soon after the PSLRA's passage, there was a noticeable increase in securities fraud filings in state courts. The concern arose that resourceful plaintiff's were, by filing their actions in state courts, circumventing the PSLRA's procedural and substantive provisions. Thus, the second shoe to drop in Congress's focus on securities litigation was the passage in 1998 of Securities Litigation Uniform Standards Act (SLUSA).[288] To

[276] *See* A. Chris Heck, Comment, Conflict and Aggregation: Appointing Institutional Investors as Sole Lead Plaintiffs Under the PSLRA, 66 U. Chi. L. Rev. 1199 (1999).

[277] *See* In re Cendant Corp. Litig., 264 F.3d 201 (3d Cir. 2001).

[278] *See supra* § 12.9[2].

[279] Exchange Act § 21D(b)(2), 15 U.S.C. § 78u–4(b)(2).

[280] Exchange Act § 21D(b)(1), 15 U.S.C. § 78u–4(b)(1) (2015).

[281] Exchange Act § 21D(b)(3), 15 U.S.C. § 78u–4(b)(3) (2015).

[282] Exchange Act § 21D(a)(7)(B), 15 U.S.C. § 78u–4(a)(7)(B) (2015).

[283] Exchange Act § 21D(c)(1), 15 U.S.C. § 78u–4(c)(1) (2015).

[284] Exchange Act § 21E, 15 U.S.C. § 78u–5 (2015). Also this provision exists in the Securities Act § 27A, 15 U.S.C. § 77z–2 (2015).

[285] Exchange Act § 21D(f), 15 U.S.C. § 78u–4(f) (2015).

[286] Racketeer Influence and Corrupt Organizations Act Section 1964(c) (2015), 18 U.S.C. § 1964(c).

[287] Exchange Act § 21D(f)(9) (2015), 15 U.S.C. § 78u–4(f)(9) (2015).

[288] Exchange Act § 28(f), 15 U.S.C. § 78bb(f) (2015).

counter the migration to the state courts, SLUSA preempts state court jurisdictions in *class actions* for certain "covered securities."[289] Class actions are defined as suits seeking damages on behalf of more than 50 persons.[290] Suits arising from misrepresentations made in acquisitions or involving a vote of the stockholders as well as by state pension funds or political subdivisions of the state is among the narrow set cases that are expressly exempted from SLUSA.[291] The most notable of its exclusions is the so-called Delaware carve-out that preserves the state court's jurisdiction to hear certain claims based upon fiduciary principles of the issuer's state of incorporation.[292]

§ 12.10   Rule 10b–5 and Insider Trading

Rule 10b–5 prohibits certain individuals—insiders, misappropriators, and tippees—from engaging in transactions in their company's stock if they do so on the basis of information not available to the investing public. This prohibition has been extended to tipping such information when doing so is a breach of a fiduciary duty.

As seen earlier in this chapter, common law rules pertaining to insider trading did not offer much protection against the trading of shares on the basis of confidential inside information not generally available to the investing public.[293] Section 16(b) of the Exchange Act[294] somewhat fills a gap by providing prohibitions against insider short-swing speculative profits. Recall that section 16(b) applies to a relatively limited number of situations because it requires both a purchase and a sale within six months and applies to equity securities of companies that are subject to the 1934 Act's registration and reporting requirements and reaches only the trading of narrowly defined insiders.[295] Thus, insiders who on the basis of their confidential knowledge trade in securities that are not those of a reporting company, or who have not purchased and sold, or vice versa, within six months, or the person trading is not an officer, director, or an owner of more than 10 percent of a company that is subject to the jurisdictional reach of section 16, can escape the prophylaxis provided by section 16(b).

Origins of "Disclose or Abstain" Rule. The first step toward making Rule 10b–5 the major enforcement weapon for the regulation of insider trading occurred in 1961 in *In re Cady, Roberts & Co.,*[296] an SEC administrative proceeding. The directors of Curtiss-Wright Corporation decided to cut the company's regular dividend, but the decision was not immediately made public. Advance news of the development reached a stockbroker who had been purchasing the stock for his customers; he then liquidated the customers' holdings before the news of the dividend cut depressed the market price. The SEC disciplined the broker for having violated Rule 10b–5.

---

[289] Covered securities are defined in Section 18(b) of the Securities Act, 15 U.S.C. § 77r(b) (2015), and include securities traded on the New York Stock Exchange, American Exchange, and Nasdaq, certain other exchanges that have been designated by the SEC, issued by a company subject to the periodic reporting requirements of the Exchange Act, as well as securities offered pursuant to certain exemptions from the registration requirements of the Securities Act.

[290] Exchange Act § 28(f)(5)(B), 15 U.S.C. § 78bb(f)(5)(B) (2015).

[291] Exchange Act § 28(f)(3), 15 U.S.C. § 78bb(f)(3) (2015).

[292] Exchange Act § 28(f)(3)(A)(i), 15 U.S.C. § 78bb(f)(3)(A)(i) (2015).

[293] *See supra* § 12.7.

[294] 15 U.S.C. § 78p(b). *See supra* § 12.8.

[295] *See infra* § 12.8.

[296] In re Cady, Roberts & Co., 1961 WL 60638, 40 S.E.C. 907 (1961).

Seven years after the *Cady, Roberts* ruling, a highly significant Rule 10b–5 decision was handed down by the United States Court of Appeals for the Second Circuit in *Securities & Exchange Commission v. Texas Gulf Sulphur Company*.[297] In that case, TGS was exploring eastern Canada for possible mining sites. In March 1959, aerial surveys revealed that the Kidd-55 segment had good potential. In late October 1963, ground surveys proved equally optimistic and confirmed the desirability of drilling test holes. Within two weeks, samples from a 655-foot-deep test hole at K-55-1 provided visual evidence of copper and zinc. This was sufficient to convince TGS to acquire the land in question. TGS management decided to keep the test results quiet in order to facilitate an advantageous acquisition of the drill site.

About this time a number of TGS officers began acquiring stock on the open market at less than 18 dollars per share.[298] In early December, laboratory assays of the samples confirmed a high copper, zinc, and silver content. By March 27, 1964, TGS resumed drilling. On April 12, the company issued a pessimistic press release, purportedly to quell rumors, explaining that although the samples were encouraging "[t]he work done to date has not been sufficient to reach definite conclusions and any statement as to size and grade of one would be premature and possibly misleading."[299] At that point, TGS stock was trading at between $30 1/8 and $32. On the very next day, continued drilling revealed that the previous optimism had been justified. Three days later, in an April 16 press release, the company made the facts public. TGS stock climbed to a high of $37 and by May 15 was selling at slightly more than $58; thus making the insiders a substantial profit.

The foregoing facts raised a number of questions, including (1) the accountability of those insiders who profited from their pre-April 16 purchases; (2) the posture of the "tippees," who were not corporate officers but had advance notice of the events surrounding K-55-1; and (3) the corporation's responsibility for the misleading April 12 press release. The court ruled that the corporation violated Rule 10b–5 in negligently issuing the April 12 press release. That part of the holding, which is discussed elsewhere,[300] has been surpassed as by the Supreme Court's ruling that negligence is not sufficient to support a Rule 10b–5 claim.[301]

With regard to the insider trading activity, following the lead of the *Cady, Roberts* ruling, the Second Circuit in *SEC v. Texas Gulf Sulphur* ruled that once there were material facts known only to insiders, they and their tippees were barred by Rule 10b–5 from profiting from such information:

> Thus, anyone in possession of material inside information must either disclose it to the investing public, or, if he is disabled from disclosing it in order to protect a corporate confidence, or he chooses not to do so, must abstain from trading in or recommending the securities concerned while such inside information remains undisclosed.[302]

---

[297] Securities & Exchange Commission v. Texas Gulf Sulphur Company, 401 F.2d 833 (2d Cir. 1968), *cert. denied*, 394 U.S. 976 (1969), s.c., 446 F.2d 1301 (2d Cir. 1971).

[298] This activity continued through April 1964 as the price slowly rose to $30. *See* 401 F.2d at 840, n.2.

[299] 401 F.2d at 845.

[300] *See supra* § 12.9[2].

[301] Ernst & Ernst v. Hochfelder, 425 U.S. 185 (1976).

[302] 401 F.2d at 848.

The court then determined the "materiality" by looking to the dramatic increase in insider stock acquisitions. The court reasoned that this provided strong circumstantial evidence of the time at which the reasonable investor would consider the information a substantial factor in making an investment decision.[303] This resolved the question only with regard to the trading insiders and did not necessarily bear upon the question of materiality insofar as it would affirmatively compel corporate disclosure.[304]

Texas Gulf Sulphur further held that the insiders' good faith was not a defense to an SEC injunctive action, although today it is clear that it must be shown that the defendants acted with scienter.[305] The question of whether a defendant acted with mere negligence or even recklessness rarely arises in insider trading cases since the conduct proscribed can hardly arise by inadvertence. These are not instances, as are many cases involving false statements, where the defendant can lament, "whoops, I have traded on inside information."

In deciding when insiders could trade in the TGS stock, the court reasoned that the disclosure date was not conclusive, because the public needed time to digest and analyze the information once it was released. The court then extended these proscriptions to trading tippees—non-insiders who trade on the basis of advance notice—but it did not address the accountability of the non-trading tippers.

Impact of Chiarella *and Misappropriation Theory.* Insider trading regulation took a momentary setback in *Chiarella v. United States.*[306] The defendant, Vincent Chiarella, a financial printer, worked on a number of tender offers and, using his ingenuity, discovered in advance the identity of the thinly disguised target companies. Armed with knowledge of the impending takeover attempt, the printer purchased stock in target companies with the comforting knowledge that the price would rise with the announcement of the tender offer. The Court overturned his criminal conviction, basing its decision on the absence of a fiduciary relationship between the defendant and any of the companies in which he invested. The Court noted that the purportedly injured sellers had not placed any reliance on the printer's activity and that the impersonal nature of the transactions precluded a 10b–5 violation.

Later the Supreme Court, in dicta, recognized that those not in the permanent employ of the corporation may nevertheless become "temporary insiders" because they have assumed a position of trust and confidence with respect to material information shared with them.

Thus *Chiarella* limits Rule 10b–5's presumption of defendants who traded in the securities of corporations with whom the defendant has a fiduciary relationship. Significantly the court left open the question of what types of fiduciary or other relationships might suffice to establish a duty to disclose or abstain from trading. The potential limiting effect of *Chiarella* was shortlived; drawing on the view expressed by four justices in *Chiarella,* the lower courts have embraced the misappropriation theory as a basis to reach individuals, such as Vincent Chiarella, who breach a fiduciary

---

[303] Materiality is a question of fact depending on all of the surrounding circumstances, yet the courts have been unable to define the concept in a meaningful way.

[304] *See infra* § 12.11.

[305] Aaron v. Securities & Exch. Commn., 446 U.S. 680 (1980) (scienter is required under Rule 10b–5 and section 10b–5 of the 1934 Act but is not an element of a violation of sections 17(a)(2), (3) of the 1933 Act). *See also, e.g.,* Ernst & Ernst v. Hochfelder, 425 U.S. 185 (1976).

[306] Chiarella v. United States, 445 U.S. 222 (1980).

relationship with one entity by using confidential information obtained from that entity to trade in the stock of another corporation.[307]

The misappropriation theory first expands Rule 10b–5 to situations in which a defendant can properly be said to be under a fraud-based duty to disclose or abstain from trading because of a fiduciary relationship not to use confidential information for private gain.

The misappropriation theory reached the Supreme Court for the first time in 1987.[308] The defendant was a financial columnist (writing the influential Wall Street Journal's "Heard on the Street" column) who had tipped his friends in advance as to the contents of upcoming columns that would affect the price of certain stocks. The Second Circuit had held that this information had been misappropriated from the defendant's employer, Dow Jones, and thus, under the disclose-or-abstain rule, the columnist and his friends had violated Rule 10b–5.[309] The Supreme Court granted certiorari and had the opportunity to finally resolve the issue; however, the Rule 10b–5 conviction was affirmed without opinion by an equally divided Supreme Court. Since an affirmance by an equally divided Court does not contain any opinions, there is no indication whether the division was over a wholesale application of the misappropriation theory or on some other grounds.

Though many lower courts embraced the misappropriation theory to expand the reach of insider trading regulation beyond that proscribed in *Chiarella*, two circuits rejected the misappropriation theory.[310] The split between the circuits attracted the interest of the Supreme Court, which, in 1997, once again considered the viability of the misappropriation theory.[311] On this occasion, challenges to this basis of Rule 10b–5 liability were finally put to rest. In *United States v. O'Hagan*, the Court held that a Rule 10b–5 violation can be based on a breach of a duty to the sources of the information even when the violator is not an insider of the company whose securities are being traded. The necessary deception is present by virtue of the defendant failing to disclose her plans to trade in the securities, *i.e.*, "feigning fidelity" to the source of the information.[312] Furthermore, this deception is "in connection with the purchase or sale of any security" even though it cannot be linked to identifiable purchasers or sellers.[313] In other words, the duty underlying the Rule 10b–5 violation need not be owed to a purchaser or seller of securities.

Problems abound in determining what constitutes a fiduciary relationship. Thus, in *United States v. Chestman*,[314] the Second Circuit, sitting en banc, held that the marital relationship was not itself a sufficient basis upon which the misappropriation theory

---

[307] *See* SEC v. Materia, 745 F.2d 197 (2d Cir. 1984) (financial proofreader, facts similar to Chiarella); United States v. Newman, 664 F.2d 12 (2d Cir. 1981), *aff'd on remand*, 722 F.2d 729, *cert. denied*, 464 U.S. 863 (1983) (investment banker misappropriated information about his employer's clients). Lawyers and other law firm employees have similarly been held to have violated Rule 10b–5.

[308] Carpenter v. United States, 484 U.S. 19 (1987).

[309] United States v. Carpenter, 791 F.2d 1024 (2d Cir. 1986).

[310] United States v. O'Hagan, 92 F.3d 612 (8th Cir. 1996), *rev'd*, 521 U.S. 642 (1997); United States v. Bryan, 58 F.3d 933 (4th Cir. 1995).

[311] United States v. O'Hagan, 521 U.S. 642 (1997).

[312] 521 U.S. 642 at 655.

[313] 521 U.S. 642 at 652.

[314] United States v. Chestman, 903 F.2d 75 (2d Cir. 1990), *reh'g en banc*, 947 F.2d 551 (2d Cir. 1991), *cert. denied*, 503 U.S. 1004 (1992).

would operate. In *Chestman,* the defendant learned from his wife, who did not otherwise swear him to preserve the information's confidentiality, certain material non-public information which later was the basis for trading before that information became public.[315] Much needed guidance to the courts is now provided by Rule 10b5–2 which provides a nonexclusive definition of the types of relationships and circumstances that impose a duty of "trust and confidence for the purpose of the misappropriation theory."[316] Rule 10b5–2 provides that trust and confidence can arise by agreement or a history or practice of sharing confidences with reason to believe the confidentiality of the information is to be maintained. Also, information shared among certain family members is similarly deemed confidential, unless the opposite is proven that the person receiving the information did not know and could not reasonably expect that the source of the information expected confidentiality in light of the parties' past practices. Questions have been raised, however, as to whether Rule 10b5–2 goes beyond the scope of the statute in attempting to bring persons under Rule 10b–5's insider trading prohibitions. For example, in one case it was indicated that a mutual expectation of confidentiality is not sufficient to trigger Rule 10b–5's disclose or abstain rule.[317] The SEC takes the position that a contractual duty of confidentiality is sufficient but that view has been challenged.[318]

Tippers and Tippees. In *Dirks v. SEC,*[319] the Supreme Court underscored the importance of a preexisting fiduciary relationship when it held that outsiders may freely trade on an insider's selective disclosure (that is, a "tip") as long as the disclosure was not "improper." Secrist, a former officer of Equity Funding of America, informed Dirks, an investment analyst, that Equity Funding's assets were fraudulently overstated. In the course of aggressively investigating Secrist's tip, Dirks shared Secrist's revelation

---

[315] Chestman learned of the information from Loeb, who learned of the information from his wife, who learned of it from other family members. The majority of the court held that marriage alone did not create a fiduciary relationship. For a different view of the marital relationship, *see* SEC v. Lenfest, 949 F.Supp. 341 (E.D. Pa. 1996) (spouse of director violated confidential relationship by trading on the basis of information obtained from her husband).

Another decision case showing the potential breadth of liability under this view is United States v. Willis, 737 F.Supp. 269 (S.D.N.Y. 1990). A former CEO of Shearson and former president of American Express was considering becoming CEO of BankAmerica. He discussed these plans with his wife, who in turn discussed them with her psychiatrist in the course of her treatment. The psychiatrist traded in the marketplace on the basis of this material nonpublic information and profited as a result. On the basis of the breach of the confidential and hence fiduciary relationship between the psychiatrist and his patient, the court held that the psychiatrist had violated Rule 10b–5.

[316] 17 C.F.R. § 240.10b5–2 (2015).

[317] United States v. Kim, 184 F.Supp.2d 1006 (N.D.Cal.2002) (membership in young executives organization did not create a duty even though there was an expectation of confidentiality since there was not binding obligation to keep information confidential).

[318] The SEC brought charges against Mark Cuban, claiming that he had agreed to keep confidential certain information obtained in connection with a private placement. Among other things, the defense contended that even if such a contractual obligation existed, it is not sufficient to trigger Rule 10b–5's disclose or abstain obligation. *See* SEC's Case Against Cuban Looks Set for Long Fight as Academics Join Fray, 41 Sec. Reg. & L. Rep. (BNA) 295 (Feb. 23, 2009). The district court agreed with the SEC that the duty need not be fiduciary in nature but went on to distinguish between a contractual duty of confidentiality and a contractual non-use agreement. The court dismissed the complaint granting the SEC leave to amend the pleadings to provide a basis for implying a non-use agreement. SEC v. Cuban, 634 F.Supp.2d 713 (N.D. Tex. 2009). Rather than file an amended complaint, the SEC chose to appeal the dismissal and won on appeal. SEC v. Cuban, 620 F.3d 551 (5th Cir. 2010). The Second Circuit has held that a fiduciary duty is not required so long as the information was wrongfully acquired via deception. SEC v. Dorozhko, 574 F.3d 42 (2d Cir. 2009) (defendant hacked computer to obtain non-public information and violated Rule 10b–5 when he traded to his advantage if the information had been obtained via deception).

[319] Dirks v. SEC, 463 U.S. 646 (1983).

with five investment advisers, who caused their advisees to liquidate more than $16 million worth of Equity Funding stock. The Supreme Court held Dirks did not violate Rule 10b–5 because Secrist's disclosure was not improper. The Supreme Court offered an extremely narrow concept of what constitutes an "improper" tip: A disclosure is improper if the insider tips a relative or a friend, or expects to reap a pecuniary gain from the selective disclosure.[320] In reaching this conclusion, the Court demonstrated the pragmatic view that to have held otherwise would have had a chilling effect on the socially desirable activities of security analysts.

The *Dirks'* holding has wider significance than merely to protect analysts: The case restrains the scope of the disclose-or-abstain rule. First, it provides an extremely narrow definition of what constitutes an *improper* tip. Second, even though a tip is improper, only those who are aware the disclosure was improper are subject to Rule 10b–5 liability if they trade or pass the tip on to another. Because of *Dirks,* the bystander who overhears another discussing material nonpublic information may freely trade, provided he is not a friend or relative, or conferred or could confer a pecuniary benefit upon the speaker.[321] But if the parties are not perfect strangers, it is easier to establish the selective disclosure was improper.[322] The tippee liability does not require proof that his tipper knew his tippee would trade; it is enough that the tippee knew that the selective disclosure to him was a breach of the tipper's duty to the employer.[323] When, however, tipping is prosecuted under Rule 14e–3 there is not the same requirement for the selective disclosure to constitute a breach of fiduciary obligation so that the inquiry instead is whether the tippee knew the information was material, non-public, and selectively disclosed after a substantial step had been undertaken toward a tender offer.[324] And, when the act of tipping is within the scope of, for example, the senior officer's employment, the employer can be liable.[325] In most instances, however, tipping and insider trading are outside the scope of one's employment and, hence, does not subject their employer to vicarious liability.[326]

The Supreme Court in *Dirks* explained that in order to create liability the tipper must have received a personal benefit for the tip and that friendship could be sufficient to show a personal benefit.[327] However, in *United States v. Newman,* the Second Circuit held that proof of friendship is not sufficient by itself to show the requisite personal benefit and that the tippee must have been aware of the personal benefit to the tipper.[328] Another decision held that in order to support an inference of a personal benefit, the friendship must be "a meaningful, close, or personal one."[329] The *Newman* decision's

---

[320] 463 U.S. at 663–664.

[321] A paradigm illustration involves a famous football coach who while attending his son's track meet overheard another proud parent discussing an upcoming "deal." *See* SEC v. Switzer, 590 F.Supp. 756 (W.D. Okla. 1984); SEC v. Platt, 565 F.Supp. 1244 (W.D. Okla. 1983).

[322] *See, e.g.,* United States v. Falcone, 257 F.3d 226 (2d Cir. 2001) (conspirators traded on advance knowledge of what companies would be discussed in forthcoming issues of Business Week).

[323] *See* United States v. Libera, 989 F.2d 596 (2d Cir. 1993).

[324] *See* Securities and Exchange Commission v. Mayhew, 121 F.3d 44 (2d Cir. 1997).

[325] *See* SEC v. Geon Industries, Inc., 381 F.Supp. 1063 (S.D.N.Y. 1974), *modified,* 531 F.2d 39 (2d Cir. 1976).

[326] *See, e.g.,* Moss v. Morgan Stanley, Inc., 553 F.Supp. 1347 (S.D.N.Y.), *aff'd,* 719 F.2d 5 (2d Cir. 1983).

[327] Dirks v. SEC, 463 U.S. 646, 664 (1983) ("The elements of fiduciary duty and exploitation of nonpublic information also exist when an insider makes a gift of confidential information to a trading relative or friend").

[328] United States v. Newman, 773 F.3d 438 (2d Cir. 2014).

[329] In re Bolan, Admin. Proc. File No. 3–16178, 2015 WL 5316569 (SEC initial decision Sept. 14 2014).

interpretation of friendship as evidence of a personal benefit represents a narrow reading of the Supreme Court's ruling in *SEC v. Dirks*. In contrast to the Second Circuit in *Newman*, the Ninth Circuit held that a broader view of personal benefit is appropriate.[330] The Supreme Court resolved the conflict between the circuits when it adopted the broader view espoused by the Ninth Circuit. In *Salman v. United States*,[331] Maher repeatedly shared with his brother, Michael, confidential information Maher obtained as an analyst for Citigroup; Michael passed the information on to Salman, Maher's brother in law. By trading on this information, Salman garnered about $1.5 million in profits. The Supreme Court upheld Salman's conviction and effectively overruled *Newman*, reasoning:

> *Dirks* specifies that when a tipper gives inside information to "a trading relative or friend," the jury can infer that the tipper meant to provide the equivalent of a cash gift. In such situations, the tipper benefits personally because giving a gift of trading information is the same thing as trading by the tipper followed by a gift of the proceeds. Here, by disclosing confidential information as a gift to his brother with the expectation that he would trade on it, Maher breached his duty of trust and confidence to Citigroup and its clients-a duty Salman acquired, and breached himself, by trading on the information with full knowledge that it had been improperly disclosed.[332]

In the wake of the Supreme Court's unanimous ruling in *Salman*, tipper-tippee liability is as follows. First, tipping without a personal benefit is not sufficient to hold the tippee liable.[333] A personal benefit does not have to be pecuniary in nature and passing on the information to a friend or relative as a gift clearly is sufficient.[334] When the personal benefit is the result of a gift to a friend, it is not necessary to weigh the closeness of the friendship.[335] Rather, the personal benefit is found in the providing the tip, knowing he or she will trade on it, in lieu of a cash gift to the tippee.[336] Although the Court in *Salman* did not address the issue,[337] there is authority to the effect that in order to hold the tippee liable, the tippee must have known of the personal benefit to the tipper. In addiction, the tipper must have intended that the tippee trade on the information.[338]

---

[330] United States v. Salman, 792 F.3d 1087 (9th Cir. 2015), *affirmed* 137 S. Ct. 420 (2016).

[331] Salman v. United States, 137 S. Ct. 420 (2016).

[332] Salman v. United States, 137 S. Ct. 420, 428 (2016).

[333] Salman v. United States, 137 S. Ct. 420, 427–428 (2016). *See also, e.g.*, United States v. Bray, 853 F.3d 18 (1st Cir. 2017) (upholding conviction).

[334] Salman v. United States, 137 S. Ct. 420, 427–428 (2016). The Court did note, however, that it was not deciding whether a gift to someone who is not a friend or relative would be sufficient.

[335] United States v. Martoma, 869 F.3d 58 (2d Cir. 2017).

[336] *See* United States v. Martoma, 869 F.3d 58 (2d Cir. 2017) ("as the Supreme Court explained in Dirks and reaffirmed again in Salman, the personal benefit one receives from giving a gift of inside information is not the friendship or loyalty or gratitude of the recipient of the gift; it is the imputed pecuniary benefit of having effectively profited from the trade oneself and given the proceeds as a cash gift. *See* Salman, 137 S. Ct. at 427–28; Dirks, 463 U.S. at 664. If under Dirks and Salman it is not correct to characterize the personal benefit at issue in gift-giving as the receipt of friendship, then Newman's discussion of the circumstances in which a jury can infer that a tipper personally benefitted from disclosing inside information as a gift must now be considered inapposite.").

[337] *See Salman*, 137 S.Ct. at 425 ("The Second Circuit also reversed the Newman defendants' convictions because the Government introduced no evidence that the defendants knew the information they traded on came from insiders or that the insiders received a personal benefit in exchange for the tips. 773 F.3d, at 453–454. This case does not implicate those issues.").

[338] *See, e.g.*, United States v. Klein, 913 F.3d 73 (2d Cir. 2019) (upholding conviction notwithstanding defendant's claim that he was bragging and/or joking rather than intend anyone trade on the information).

As noted above, tippee liability does not require proof that his tipper knew his tippee would trade; it is enough that the tippee knew that the selective disclosure to him was a breach of the tipper's duty to the employer.[339] When the act of tipping is within the scope of, for example, the senior officer's employment, the employer can be liable.[340] In most instances, however, tipping and insider trading are outside the scope of one's employment and, hence, does not subject their employer to vicarious liability.[341]

The Court's opinion in *Dirks* stressed the importance of allowing securities analysts to do their job of mining information and helping it flow to investors. However, the license to rely on material nonpublic information that *Dirks* conferred upon analysts has been significantly confined by the SEC's adoption in late 2000 of Regulation FD.[342] In broad overview, Regulation FD (the acronym for "fair disclosure") greatly restricts the freedom public companies formerly enjoyed to make selective disclosures of material non-public information to market professionals or shareholders. The scope of its requirements is examined in a later section of this chapter.[343]

Possession Versus Use. There has been ongoing debate as to whether a case for improper insider trading under Rule 10b–5 can be made by showing that the defendant traded while in *possession* of material non-public information or whether it must be established that he or she in fact *used* the information in making the trades in question.[344] In a 1998 decision, the Eleventh Circuit adopted an "on the basis" rather than "mere possession" test of liability.[345] The court went on to point out, however, that trades while in possession of such information can be used to create a "strong inference" that the defendant in fact used the information.[346] In contrast is the reasoning of Judge Richard Posner that proof that the defendant traded when he had knowledge of insider information should place upon him the burden of establishing that he did not trade on the basis of that information.[347] The SEC has addressed the split in the circuits in its Rule 10b5–1,[348] which essentially equates the meaning of "on the basis" to "in possession."[349] Rule 10b5–1, however, provides a safe harbor for trading when aware of material non-public information if the trade is strictly pursuant to a binding written contract to purchase or sale that was entered into before the defendant became aware of

---

[339] *See* United States v. Libera, 989 F.2d 596 (2d Cir. 1993). For a case deferring to the jury to make factual determinations such as whether the tippee knew the disclosure was improper, *see* Securities and Exchange Commission v. Thrasher, 152 F. Supp. 2d 291 (S.D.N.Y. 2001); U.S. v. Evans, 486 F.3d 315 (7th Cir. 2007) (tippee conviction upheld even though his tipper in another proceeding was not convicted).

[340] *See* SEC v. Geon Industries, Inc., 381 F.Supp. 1063 (S.D.N.Y. 1974), *modified*, 531 F.2d 39 (2d Cir. 1976).

[341] *See, e.g.*, Moss v. Morgan Stanley, Inc., 553 F.Supp. 1347 (S.D.N.Y.), *aff'd*, 719 F.2d 5 (2d Cir. 1983).

[342] Rule 100, 17 C.F.R. § 243.100 (2015).

[343] *See infra* § 12.11.

[344] *See, e.g.*, 2 Allan Bromberg & Louis Lowenfels, Securities Fraud & Commodities Fraud, § 7.4(600), at 7:159, 7:160.14 (1996) (a corporate insider can introduce evidence of nonuse of material non-public information as an affirmative defense); Arnold S. Jacobs, 5A Disclosure and Remedies Under the Securities Laws, § 4.148 (2000) (an insider's decision to buy or sell must be based on his inside information).

[345] SEC v. Adler, 137 F.3d 1325 (11th Cir. 1998).

[346] 137 F.3d at 1337.

[347] *See* Securities and Exchange Commission v. Lipson, 278 F.3d 656, 661 (7th Cir. 2002).

[348] 17 C.F.R. § 240.10b5–1 (2015).

[349] Rule 10b5–1(b) provides that "on the basis" means "if the person making the purchase or sale was aware of the material nonpublic information when the person made the purchase or sale." 17 C.F.R. § 240.10b5–1 (2015).

the inside information.[350] More generally, circumstantial evidence frequently is sufficient to establish that the defendant was in possession of inside information prior to the trade.[351]

Insider trading is also proscribed under Rule 14e–3,[352] being among the many antifraud provisions promulgated by the SEC under the authority conferred on it by the Williams Act amendments to the Exchange Act. The validity of Rule 14e–3 was upheld in *United States v. O'Hagan*.[353] Its proscription of insider trading is triggered when "a substantial step or steps to commence . . . a tender offer" have been taken. This at least occurs when negotiations have commenced between the corporations.[354]

Government Enforcement Actions. Willful violations of the federal securities laws may give rise to a criminal prosecution by the Department of Justice, resulting in fines and/or imprisonment. Furthermore, violations may result in sanctions from the SEC. For example, the Commission may impose administrative sanctions: if the violator is a broker-dealer or other market professional, her license can be suspended or revoked. The SEC is authorized to seek either temporary or permanent injunctive relief in the courts "whenever it shall appear to the Commission that any person is engaged or is about to engage in any acts or practices which constitute or will constitute a violation."[355] More frequently, the SEC seeks some form of monetary recovery in addition to a prospective injunction against future violations.

In the wake of the Supreme Court decisions in *Chiarella*[356] and *Dirks*,[357] Congress enacted even stronger insider trading penalties, available for use by the SEC. The Insider Trading Sanctions Act of 1984 (ITSA) increased civil and criminal penalties for trading while in possession of material nonpublic information: The SEC is authorized to seek disgorgement of profits[358] and a civil penalty of up to three times the profits gained or the loss avoided by the defendant,[359] and the criminal penalty was increased from $10,000 to $100,000. However, while facially applicable to transactions involving misuse of non-public material information, ITSA does not define the scope of permissible conduct. Thus ITSA does not alter the availability of a cause of action, but merely the penalties that may be imposed.

---

[350]   Rule 10b5–1(c), 17 C.F.R. § 240.10b5–1(c) (2015).

[351]   *See, e.g.,* SEC v. Ginsburg, 362 F.3d 1292 (11th Cir. 2004)(evidence of pattern of phone calls by insider who knew of possible mergers and family members trading after the calls permitted an inference that trades were on the basis of information selectively disclosed).

[352]   17 C.F.R. § 240.14e–3 (2015). *See* § 24.5[1] *infra.*

[353]   United States v. O'Hagan, 521 U.S. 642 (1997).

[354]   SEC v. Maio, 51 F.3d 623 (7th Cir. 1995).

[355]   15 U.S.C. § 78t. The SEC's power extends to those who provide substantial assistance to insiders such that they are deemed aiders and abettors of the insider trading offense. *See, e.g.,* SEC v. Naegeli, 1993 WL 15126 (S.D.N.Y. 1993) (attorney aided and abetted client by counselling how to establish a Swiss account through which securities were purchased on the basis of material nonpublic information).

[356]   Chiarella v. United States, 445 U.S. 222 (1980).

[357]   Dirks v. SEC, 463 U.S. 646 (1983).

[358]   On the measurement of the amount of profits to be disgorged, *see* SEC v. MacDonald, 699 F.2d 47 (1st Cir. 1983) (*en banc*) (need disgorge only profits up to the market's reaction to initial disclosure and not the later higher price reached by the security).

[359]   Both disgorgement and treble profits can be recovered as the purpose of ITSA was not to reduce the scope of other relief the SEC may obtain. *See* Securities and Exchange Commission v. Lipson, 278 F.3d 656 (7th Cir. 2002).

ITSA has proven to be an effective enforcement weapon. Following its enactment, the SEC was increasingly vigorous in enforcing insider trading prohibitions and has reached some lucrative settlements. Beyond the increased penalties in ITSA, in October 1990, Congress enacted the Securities Enforcement Remedies and Penny Stock Reform Act, which, among other things, gave the SEC the power in an administrative proceeding to require disgorgement of illegal profits.

The SEC, but not private plaintiffs, can also pursue those who knowingly provide assistance to insiders in carrying out their violation. Thus, the attorney was an aider and abettor to another when he instructed the insider how to open a Swiss bank account through which the unlawful trading was carried out.[360]

Private Rights of Action for Insider Trading. In a face-to-face transaction, an action will lie against someone who sells or purchases while in possession of material inside non-public information.[361] However, in an open-market context, standing to sue is more problematic and, therefore, at one time posed ticklish standing questions.[362] Congress stepped in to change this result. The Insider Trading and Securities Fraud Enforcement Act (ITSFEA) was enacted by Congress in 1988 to supplement any remedy that may exist under Rule 10b–5. The Act provides an express private right of action by contemporaneous traders against persons making improper use of material non-public information.[363] Damages in such an action are limited to the profit (or loss avoided) that is attributable to the defendant's illegal conduct, reduced to the extent that the SEC has secured disgorgement (as opposed to a penalty) under the 1984 ITSA legislation.

§ 12.11   Rule 10b–5 and the Duty to Disclose

Rule 10b–5 plays a major role in ensuring the flow of corporate information to the investing public. The 1934 Exchange Act imposes an affirmative disclosure requirement on corporations that are sufficiently large to fall within the Act's registration and reporting requirements. These provisions require, inter alia, complete financial disclosure, descriptions of the company's operations and future plans, and detailing of management activities, as well as dealing with the more specialized problems of shareholder suffrage, tender offers, and insider trading.[364] Even beyond these express disclosure provisions, the broad prophylactic language of Rule 10b–5 has had a significant impact in the disclosure area.

The duty to not misstate material facts applies regardless of the medium or the intended audience of the misstatement. Thus, a document issued with regard to one type

---

[360] *See* SEC v. Naegeli, 1993 WL 15126 (S.D.N.Y. 1993).

[361] Affiliated Ute Citizens of Utah v. United States, 406 U.S. 128 (1972), *reh'g denied,* 407 U.S. 916 (1972). Causation was not a problem because the purchaser dealt directly with the seller. Further, the Court held that reliance on the nondisclosure could be presumed from the materiality of the information.

[362] Although some courts have imposed liability, most recent decisions have not. The "fraud on the market" theory, however, is far from unanimously accepted in the insider trading context. The Sixth Circuit has held that any duty that is breached is owed to the person from whom the information is appropriated, not to someone in a faceless market. Fridrich v. Bradford, 542 F.2d 307 (6th Cir. 1976), *cert. denied,* 429 U.S. 1053 (1977). Similarly, the Second Circuit has held that a tippee of inside information who is convicted of having violated Rule 10b–5 is not liable to people who are selling their stock at the same time that the defendant is buying on inside information; instead, the person trading on the information must be a corporate official who owes an independent dues to the shareholders who trade on opposite sides of the insiders' transactions, Moss v. Morgan Stanley, 719 F.2d 5 (2d Cir. 1983), *cert. denied,* 465 U.S. 1025 (1984).

[363] 15 U.S.C. § 78t–1 (2015).

[364] *See generally* Homer Kripke, Rule 10b–5 Liability and "Material Facts," 46 N.Y.U. L. Rev. 1061 (1971).

of securities, such as bonds, can have 10b–5 ramifications as to the common stock where the misstatements are material to both.[365] Similarly, statements made in connection with shareholder votes are subject to Rule 10b–5 scrutiny where there is a securities transaction, as is the case, for example, in a merger[366] or in the issuance of additional shares.[367] A purposeful understatement of profits so as not to run afoul of government contracting requirements exposes those releasing the depressed earnings report to liability under Rule 10b–5.[368] Furthermore, a suit exists for investors who purchase the company's shares based on bouncy overstatements regarding the capabilities of the company's new product.[369] The point is that information mediums are seamless so that information intended for one audience can be expected to be accessed by investors whose appetite is insatiable for information bearing on the company's position, performance, and future.

The truly challenging issue under Rule 10b–5 and the securities laws generally arises in providing definitive guidance of when there is a duty to speak. That is, omissions, not misstatements, pose the greatest intellectual challenge under Rule 10b–5. Duty is an element in a Rule 10b–5 action only in the case of the omission of a material fact since a matter in issue is the defendant's obligation to disclose the omitted fact. Note here that the securities laws are quite selective in the instances when there is an express duty to speak. Corporations subject to the registration requirements of section 12 of the Exchange Act[370] must periodically file reports with the SEC.[371] The Exchange Act does not, however, expressly require a corporation to report material information that is not otherwise required by the periodic reporting and shareholder information requirements. The reporting called for by the Exchange Act is periodic, as contrasted with continuous reporting, in part because of the great difficulty in defining when there should be a duty to speak. Hence, there is no affirmative duty to disclose the types of material developments and information mandated by the SEC's periodic disclosure requirements until the corporation's next quarterly or annual report is due. And, those disclosure requirements are relatively focused in terms of the precise types of information that is required to be disclosed. Furthermore, the listing requirements of the major stock exchanges expressly require corporations to make timely disclosure of all information

---

[365] Lanza v. Drexel & Co., 479 F.2d 1277 (2d Cir. 1973).

[366] *E.g.*, Schlick v. Penn-Dixie Cement Corp., 507 F.2d 374 (2d Cir. 1974), *cert. denied*, 421 U.S. 976 (1975).

[367] *E.g.*, Hooper v. Mountain States Sec. Corp., 282 F.2d 195 (5th Cir. 1960), *cert. denied*, 365 U.S. 814 (1961).

[368] *See* Heit v. Weitzen, 402 F.2d 909 (2d Cir. 1968).

[369] *See, e.g.*, Stac Electronics Sec. Litig., 82 F.3d 1480 (9th Cir. 1996).

[370] 15 U.S.C. § 78l (2015).

[371] 15 U.S.C. § 78m. Section 12 requires registration of issuers who have securities traded on a national securities exchange or any class of equity securities with 2,000 shareholders of record but retains the former 500 record holder threshold with respect to investors who are not accredited investors. Sections 12(a), (g)(1)(A), 15 U.S.C.A. § 78l(a), (g)(1)(A) as amended by the Jumpstart Our Business Startups Act (JOBS Act), H.R. Rep. No. 112-3606, § 501 (2012). The record holder calculation excludes shareholders who receive shares as part of an employee compensation plan that is exempt from 1933 Act registration. Section 12(g) was also amended to exclude from the shareholder calculation holders of shares issued pursuant to an exempt crowdfunding offering

In addition, issuers who do not come within the registration requirements but have issued securities pursuant to a 1933 Act registration statement and that have at least 300 holders of those securities are subject to the periodic reporting requirements by virtue of section 15(d) of the Act. 15 U.S.C. § 78o(d) (2015). Section 15(d) issuers have to file the periodic reports but are not subject to proxy regulation (§ 14(a)–(c), 15 U.S.C. § 78n(a)–(c) (2015)); the Williams Act tender offer disclosure requirements (§§ 13(d), (e), and 14(d), (f); 15 U.S.C. §§ 78m(d), (e), 78n(d), (f) (2015)); or the reporting requirements for officers, directors, and 10% beneficial owners (§ 16(a), 15 U.S.C. § 78p(a) (2015)).

that would be material to the reasonable investor, but nevertheless accord the issuer business discretion to withhold information when non-disclosure best serves the corporate interest.[372] Thus, the instances in which Rule 10b–5 imposes a duty to speak are fairly limited.[373] The courts are particularly firm in holding that there is no duty to disclose internal projections or business strategies that may be pursued.[374]

Thus, the starting point in examining the duty to speak is a fairly broad principle that the issuer and others are under no duty to speak absent an independent basis for the duty to disclose.[375] This view is supported by the Supreme Court ruling in insider trading cases that the mere possession of confidential inside information is not sufficient to trigger the duty to disclose or abstain from trading.[376]

The most frequent instances of finding a breach of the duty to disclose material information is where the plaintiff alleges the defendant has committed a half-truth by withholding information that thus rendered what the defendant has disclosed materially misleading.[377] Disclosures made pursuant to the requirements of either the Securities Act of 1933 and the Exchange Act of 1934 not only require that there be disclosed the information set forth specifically in the SEC's disclosure guides, but expressly require that SEC registrant's include in their filings "such further material information . . . as may be necessary to make the required statement, in light of all of the circumstances . . . not misleading."[378] Entangled with the defendant's duty to avoid half-truths is the relative certainty of the information known to the defendant but not disclosed to the plaintiff. This is best illustrated by the issuer of whether the issuer must disclose adverse developments that the business is incurring during the fiscal quarter that it is offering its securities to the public.

Notwithstanding the absence of an affirmative duty to disclose, once a statement has been made, there may be a continuing duty to update and/or correct the information that was previously disseminated. The duty to update refers to the situation in which an earlier statement was true when made, but subsequent facts have rendered the earlier statement materially misleading. In contrast, the duty to correct arises when the earlier statement was false when made, but the party making it did so innocently, *i.e.*, without scienter, but later has knowledge (or is reckless) of the untruthfulness of the earlier statement. Both the duty to update and the duty to correct assume that the earlier-made statement is still influencing investor behavior. If the court is persuaded that the earlier representation is stale, being eclipsed by subsequent information reaching the plaintiff, there is no basis to believe investors are being harmed by the earlier information and, hence, there is no basis for either a duty to update or correct.

---

[372] N.Y.S.E. Company Manual, 3 Fed. Sec. L. Rep. (CCH) ¶ 23,121; American Stock Exchange Company Guide (CCH) ¶ 10,121; Sec. Exch. Act Rel. No. 34–8995 [1970 to 71 Transfer Binder], (CCH) ¶ 77,915 (Oct. 15, 1970).

[373] *See generally* Ian Ayres, Back to Basics: Regulating How Corporations Speak to the Market, 77 Va. L. Rev. 945 (1991).

[374] *See, e.g.*, San Leandro Emergency Medical Group Profit Sharing Plan v. Philip Morris Co., 75 F.3d 801 (2d Cir. 1996).

[375] *See, e.g.*, Murphy v. Sofamor Danek Group, Inc., 123 F.3d 394 (6th Cir. 1997).

[376] Dirks v. SEC, 463 U.S. 646 (1983); Chiarella v. United States, 445 U.S. 222 (1980).

[377] *See, e.g.*, Ansin v. River Oaks Furniture, Inc., 105 F.3d 745 (1st Cir. 1997) (failure to disclose when repurchasing shares from some of its stockholders that it would engage in IPO was material omission).

[378] Securities Act Rule 408, 17 C.F.R. § 230.408 (2015). A similar requirement appears in Exchange Act Rule 12b–20, 17 C.F.R. § 240.12b–20 (2015).

The duty to correct is not absolute because it is triggered only when failure to do so would make the statement made materially misleading.[379] Certainly there is no duty to correct rumors or forecasts that cannot be attributed to the issuer.[380] However, if management confirms the forecast to be made by an analyst or otherwise entangles the issuer with another's statements, there is a duty to correct on the part of the issuer.[381]

Public companies are placed in a difficult position when there are rumors about the company's securities, its fundamental condition, or possible takeover activity.[382] When approached by the press, market researchers, or securities analysts,[383] corporations are faced with a dilemma. They cannot issue a denial if to do so would be materially misleading. Thus, for example, the Supreme Court reaffirmed a materiality standard determined by those facts that a reasonable investor would deem significant in making an investment decision, thus precluding denials of existing merger negotiations.[384]

In such situations, issuers have two alternatives. The issuer can, of course, make full disclosure. Alternatively, the issuer can issue a "no comment" response if the response is given pursuant to an established no-comment policy. There are instances in which the "no comment" response is inappropriate. For example, the SEC has taken the position that if the company or its agents are responsible for leaks of sensitive information or market rumors, there is a duty to correct any misinformation.[385] It follows that public companies should manage their proprietary information, not only for insider trading reasons but also to prevent being forced into premature disclosures by the existence of market rumors due to leaked information. Caution dictates that public companies develop information policies, including the creation of an information ombudsman, as well as limit the issuer's personnel who are authorized to divulge information or respond to outside questions.

As a corollary to the absence of an affirmative duty to disclose, the mere possibility of an event occurring does not trigger a duty to predict or project information that is positive; yet the SEC has long taken the view that material information that is negative must be disclosed. For example, item 303 of Regulation S–K (the SEC's general disclosure guide) requires periodic management discussion and analysis (MD & A) of financial condition operations. As part of this requirement, management is required to disclose and discuss negative trends and uncertainties.[386] The SEC has taken a vigorous enforcement stance on these disclosures.[387] The MD & A disclosures, of course, may also

---

[379] Moss v. Healthcare Compare Corp., 75 F.3d 276 (7th Cir. 1996) (no duty to correct what is merely a tentative estimate); Backman v. Polaroid Corp., 910 F.2d 10 (1st Cir. 1990).

[380] *See, e.g.,* Elkind v. Liggett & Myers, Inc., 635 F.2d 156 (2d Cir. 1980).

[381] *See, e.g.,* In re Cypress Semiconductor Sec. Litig., 891 F.Supp. 1369 (N.D. Cal. 1995), *aff'd sub nom.,* Eisenstadt v. Allen, 113 F.3d 1240 (9th Cir. 1997).

[382] *See* Symposium, Affirmative Disclosure Obligations Under the Securities Laws, 46 Md. L. Rev. 907 (1987); John H. Matheson, Corporate Disclosure Obligations and the Parameters of Rule 10b–5; Basic, Inc. v. Levinson and Beyond, 14 J. Corp. L. 1 (1988).

[383] *See, e.g.,* Helwig v. Vencor, Inc., 210 F.3d 612, 620–621 (6th Cir. 2000) (corporation cannot be held responsible for analysts' statements about its financial health unless corporation takes some affirmative action other than simply providing information to analysts).

[384] Basic, Inc. v. Levinson, 485 U.S. 224 (1988).

[385] *See* In re Carnation Co., 1985 WL 547371 (SEC 1985).

[386] *See* Management Discussion and Analysis of Financial Condition, Sec. Act Rel. No. 33–6835 (SEC May 18, 1989).

[387] *See* In re Caterpillar, Inc., 1992 WL 71907 (SEC 1992) (settlement order involving MD & A analysis and failure to adequately discuss the possible risk of lower earnings in the future). *Compare* Ferber v. Travelers

result in material misstatements or omissions that will form the basis of civil liability in a private action.

It is not clear that in the abstract there are heightened disclosure obligations for face-to-face dealings, at least between strangers. But in the small company seldom are buyer and seller complete strangers. A case in point is *Jordan v. Duff & Phelps, Inc.*,[388] where Jordan, an employee of Duff & Phelps, alleged the chairman of the board was under a duty to disclose a potential merger of the firm that would reward its holders a substantial premium. Jordan, as an employee, had acquired some shares in Duff & Phelp, but was required to sell the shares at their book value to the company when he terminated his employment. Though he gave notice in November of his intent to take a better paying job in Houston, it was agreed he could work through the end of the year so that he could take advantage of the higher end of the year book value of the shares. No hint of a possible merger was made in his conversation with the chairman, Jordan worked until December 31, quit, and was shocked by the announcement January 10 that Duff & Phelps would be acquired. Had he known of the possible merger and remained with Duff & Phelps, he would have received $452,000 for the shares instead of the $23,225 he was paid. A divided court held there was a duty to disclose that the firm was in merger negotiations. Judge Easterbrook found in the relationship between Jordan and Duff & Phelps a fiduciary duty the content of which he divined from what the parties likely would have agreed to when Jordan as an employee had the opportunity to acquire stock in his closely held employer. He did believe that the parties did not contemplate that it was optimal for their relationship that the employee should make decisions regarding the value of the shares in ignorance. Employees trading off the opportunity to work elsewhere would naturally wish to weigh the value of their total gains by remaining with Duff & Phelps. In contrast, Judge Posner in his dissent reasoned that though there may have been a fiduciary relationship there were no disclosure duties that arose naturally from that relationship. He found the detailed provisions of the stock purchase agreement foreclosed any finding of additional obligations owed to Jordan, especially since Jordan as an employee at will could have been summarily fired and thereby have been deprived of sharing in the merger benefits. Other courts have also been willing, once a fiduciary relationship is established, to impose a duty to disclose a possible IPO or merger that would greatly enhance the value of the shares.[389]

The SEC has also imposed pursuant to its Regulation FD[390] a duty on domestic companies that are subject to the Exchange Act's reporting requirements to assure that when it does make certain disclosures that they are not made selectively. In broad overview, Regulation FD greatly restricts the freedom public companies formerly enjoyed to make selective disclosures of material nonpublic information to securities market professionals or its shareholders. Rule 100 of Regulation FD provides that whenever a company or a person acting on its behalf discloses material nonpublic information to securities market professionals or holders of the issuer's securities who the issuer believes may trade on the basis of the information the company must make

---

Corp., 802 F.Supp. 698 (D. Conn. 1992) (finding adequate discussion in MD & A of "known trends" and "uncertainties" relating to problems with issuer's real estate portfolios).

[388] Jordan v. Duff & Phelps, Inc., 815 F.2d 429 (7th Cir. 1987), *cert. denied*, 485 U.S. 901 (1988).

[389] *See, e.g.*, Ansin v. River Oaks Furniture, Inc., 105 F.3d 745 (1st Cir. 1997) (IPO not disclosed); Smith v. Duff & Phelps, Inc., 891 F.2d 1567 (11th Cir. 1990) (must disclose event that will have a material impact on book value of shares at which retiring employee must sell his shares).

[390] 17 C.F.R. §§ 243.100 et seq. (2015).

simultaneous public disclosure of that same information. If such a selective disclosure was "non-intentional," then the issuer should thereafter "promptly"[391] disclose the information publicly. The rule's prohibitions are sufficiently broad to include revelations of non-public information in a luncheon speech or investment forum. Public disclosure can occur by filing the information with the Commission,[392] issuing a press release, or providing public notice and opportunity to the meeting, phone call, or other medium at which the disclosure occurs. What constitutes an appropriate medium for meeting Regulation FD's public disclosure requirement largely depends on whether the information is released through a channel shareholders and the public expect the issuer to use for public announcements.[393]

Rule 100(b) enumerates the types of market professionals swept within its prohibition, including broker-dealers, investment advisers, and investment companies. Significantly, the ban on selective disclosures also extends to any holder of the issuer's security for whom under the circumstances it is reasonably foreseeable that the holder will trade on the basis of the information. A violation of Regulation FD is actionable only by the SEC. The overall effect of Regulation FD has been to force the issuer and its attorneys to consider the type of interaction the issuer's personnel is the have with financial analysts. One step has been more frequent webcasting of meetings with analysts.

§ 12.12 Rule 10b–5 and Control of Corporate Mismanagement

Rule 10b–5's implied private remedy has even played an important role in the regulation of internal corporate affairs,[394] due in large part to the expansive reading that has been given to the rule's "in connection with" requirement. Even in the face of a restrictive Supreme Court decision,[395] the federal mismanagement remedy continues to flourish.[396] However, as will be seen below, a remedy for corporate skullduggery exists under the antifraud provision only if accompanied by deception committed in connection with the purchase or sale of a security.[397]

The plaintiff in *Santa Fe Industries* owned a minority interest in the Kirby Lumber Co., a 95 percent subsidiary of defendant Santa Fe. Utilizing the Delaware "short form"

---

[391] Rule 101(d), 17 C.F.R. § 243.101(d), defines "promptly" to be as soon as "practicable" but not later than 24 hours or the commencement of the next day's trading on the NYSE after a senior official of the issuer learns of the non-intentional disclosure.

[392] The filing is on Form 8-K, *see* Rule 101(e)(2), 17 C.F.R. § 243.101(e)(2) (2015).

[393] *See*, SEC Commission Guidance on the Use of Company Websites, Sec. Exchange Act Rel. No. 58288 (Aug. 7, 2008); SEC Report on Investigation Pursuant to Section 21(a) of the Sec. Exch. Act of 1934: Netflix, Inc. and Reed Hastings, Sec. Exchange Act Rel. No. 69279 (Apr. 2, 2013)(use of personal Facebook page of firm's CEO to announce market-moving information admonished as not consistent with public disclosure).

[394] *See* James D. Cox, Fraud is in the Eyes of the Beholder: Rule 10b–5's Applications to Acts of Corporate Mismanagement, 47 N.Y.U. L. Rev. 674 (1972); Thomas L. Hazen, Treatise on the Law of Securities Regulation §§ 12:89 *et seq.* (7th ed. 2016).

[395] Santa Fe Indus. v. Green, 430 U.S. 462 (1977).

[396] Healey v. Catalyst Recovery of Pa., Inc., 616 F.2d 641 (3d Cir. 1980); Kidwell v. Meikle, 597 F.2d 1273 (9th Cir. 1979); Alabama Farm Bureau Mut. Casualty Ins. Co. v. American Fidelity Life Ins. Co., 606 F.2d 602 (5th Cir. 1979); Wright v. Heizer Corp., 560 F.2d 236 (7th Cir. 1977), *cert. denied*, 434 U.S. 1066 (1978); Goldberg v. Meridor, 567 F.2d 209 (2d Cir. 1977), *cert. denied*, 434 U.S. 1069 (1978).

[397] Similarly, no action lies under the antifraud provision of the proxy rules for mismanagement if the shareholders were not asked to vote via a proxy on the matters giving rise to their loss. *See, e.g.*, General Elec. Co. v. Cathcart, 980 F.2d 927 (3d Cir. 1992).

merger procedure,[398] Santa Fe "cashed out" the plaintiff—that is, forced him to surrender his shares for cash. The plaintiff sued under 10b–5, claiming that the merger was unfair due to the low valuation placed on his shares and, further, lacked any valid business purpose. The Second Circuit upheld the complaint, but the Supreme Court reversed due to the plaintiff's failure to allege an act of deception deriving from a material misstatement or omission.[399] In so holding, the Court was limiting the 10b–5 action to fact settings more closely connected with or similar to the garden variety type fraud in a purchase or sale of a security.

The Supreme Court in the *Santa Fe Industries* decision focused on the statutorily mandated element of deception. It thereby reinforced the basic thrust of the securities laws in requiring disclosure to investors, rather than in protecting shareholders' proprietary interests. The Court noted an emerging split of authority under common law and the various state corporate chartering statutes and expressed its unwillingness to "impose a stricter standard of fiduciary duty than that required by the law of some states."[400] There can be no doubt that the decision operates to narrow the scope of 10b–5, as did the Court's earlier holdings in *Blue Chip Stamps v. Manor Drug Stores*,[401] which requires that the plaintiff be either a seller or purchaser of securities, and in *Ernst & Ernst v. Hochfelder*,[402] which requires an element of scienter before a 10b–5 damage action will lie. On the other hand, these decisions should not be viewed as the death knell for the champions of effective enforcement of the securities laws. In fact, a number of subsequent circuit court rulings have read the *Santa Fe* restriction as being relatively narrow.[403] Moreover, deception can be found in the defendants' failure to disclose their misdeed to all of the directors when the directors approved the transaction.[404]

However, it is clear that, standing alone, a breach of fiduciary duty is not a securities law violation. The utility of Rule 10b–5 as a weapon against corporate mismanagement was further restricted by the Supreme Court. In *Virginia Bankshares, Inc. v. Sandberg*,[405] the Court ruled that a shareholder vote that was not mandated by state law and thus was not an essential cog in the merger machinery could not form the basis of a federal proxy claim. In *Sandberg*, minority shareholders of a corporation involved in a cash-out merger challenged a vote that was allegedly conducted through the use of misleading proxy solicitation materials. The proxies in question did not relate to a vote directly on the merger because management controlled 85 percent of the shares and the minority were not entitled to an appraisal remedy.[406] A failure to secure the shareholder

---

[398] Del. Code Ann. tit. 8, § 253 (2001) permits a simplified merger between a 90% owned subsidiary and its parent corporation, which eliminates the necessity for shareholder approval and does not give statutory appraisal rights to dissenting shareholders of the parent.

[399] 430 U.S. at 470–471.

[400] 430 U.S. at 479 n. 16.

[401] Blue Chip Stamps v. Manor Drug Stores, 421 U.S. 723 (1975).

[402] Ernst & Ernst v. Hochfelder, 425 U.S. 185 (1976).

[403] *See* Virginia Bankshares, Inc. v. Sandberg, 501 U.S. 1083 (1991).

[404] *See* Estate of Soler v. Rodriguez, 63 F.3d 45, 54 (1st Cir. 1995) (two interested directors concealed from other directors that stock was being sold to them at too low a price).

[405] Virginia Bankshares, Inc. v. Sandberg, 501 U.S. 1083 (1991).

[406] In Goldberg v. Meridor, 567 F.2d 209 (2d Cir. 1977), *cert. denied*, 434 U.S. 1069 (1978), the Second Circuit held that a federal Rule 10b–5 claim may be brought if it can be shown that full disclosure might have led to an action under state law against the transaction. Prior to *Sandberg*, four other circuit courts have followed the Second Circuit's ruling that material nondisclosure that denied minority shareholders their opportunity to seek an injunction under state law is sufficient to satisfy the deception requirement of *Santa Fe*. Healey v. Catalyst Recovery of Pennsylvania, 616 F.2d 641 (3d Cir. 1980); Kidwell v. Meikle, 597 F.2d 1273

vote in question would not necessarily have prevented the challenged merger. In a five-to-four decision, the Supreme Court held that there could be no action under the federal proxy rules because the shareholder vote was not an essential link in the transactional chain. Had the plaintiff been afforded an appraisal remedy, they would then have a viable cause of action by alleging that the misrepresentation deprived the minority from voting against the merger so that they would then be able to pursue their appraisal remedy.[407]

(9th Cir. 1979); Alabama Farm Bureau Mut. Casualty Ins. Co. v. American Fidelity Life Ins. Co., 606 F.2d 602 (5th Cir. 1979), *reh'g denied*, 610 F.2d 818 (5th Cir. 1980); Wright v. Heizer Corp., 560 F.2d 236 (7th Cir. 1977), *cert. denied*, 434 U.S. 1066 (1978). *See also* In re PHLCORP Sec. Tender Offer Litig., 700 F.Supp. 1265 (S.D.N.Y. 1988) (failure to disclose appraisal remedy stated a Rule 10b–5 claim).

The Fifth Circuit held that in order for a plaintiff to maintain a Rule 10b–5 action, it is not necessary to prove the success of the state law remedy; rather, all that need be shown is that on full disclosure, the plaintiff in state court would have been able to make out a prima facie case. Alabama Farm Bureau Mutual Casualty Ins. Co. v. American Fidelity Life Ins. Co., 606 F.2d 602 (5th Cir. 1979), *reh'g denied*, 610 F.2d 818 (5th Cir. 1980). *See also* Meyers v. Moody, 475 F.Supp. 232, 244–246 (N.D. Tex. 1979), *judgment aff'd*, 693 F.2d 1196 (5th Cir. 1982), *reh'g denied*, 701 F.2d 164 (4th Cir. 1982). In contrast, the Ninth Circuit has applied an "actual success" test, asking whether the plaintiff would have prevailed in state court. Kidwell v. Meikle, 597 F.2d 1273, 1294 (9th Cir. 1979). *See also* Wright v. Heizer Corp., 560 F.2d 236, 250–251 (7th Cir. 1977), *cert. denied*, 434 U.S. 1066 (1978). *See* Thomas L. Hazen, Breaches of Fiduciary Duty and the Federal Securities Laws, 61 N.C. L. Rev. 527, 531 (1983). All such reasoning is now inconsistent with *Sandberg*. *See infra* § 13.29.

[407] *See, e.g.,* Wilson v. Great Amer. Indus., Inc., 979 F.2d 924 (2d Cir. 1992); Howing Co. v. Nationwide Corp., 972 F.2d 700 (6th Cir. 1992), *cert. denied*, 507 U.S. 1004 (1993).

Chapter 13

RIGHTS AND POWERS OF SHAREHOLDERS: INSPECTION RIGHTS, VOTING, AND PROXIES

Table of Sections

PART A.   SHAREHOLDERS' RIGHTS

§ 13.1 The Nature of the Shareholders' Interest

A share of stock is primarily a profit-sharing contract, a unit of interest in the corporation based on a contribution to the corporate capital. Under their share contract and by virtue of their status as owners of shares, shareholders have three classes of rights against the corporation: (1) rights as to control and management,[1] (2) proprietary rights,[2] and (3) remedial and ancillary rights.[3]

The first class of shareholder rights includes: (a) voting rights for the election—and usually for the removal—of directors, in addition to the incidental right to the holding of annual and special meetings and due notice thereof; (b) voting rights as to the making of amendments to the charter and other fundamental changes in the corporate existence and setup; (c) voting rights as to the making and amending of bylaws, which regulate many matters, including the authority of directors and officers and their compensation; and (d) the right to have the corporation managed honestly and prudently for the benefit and profit of the shareholders within the scope of the authorized business.

---

[1]   There is a lively debate whether the optimal model is one that empowers stockholders or a more director centric approach. *See, e.g.,* Lucian A. Bebchuk, The Case For Increasing Shareholder Power, 118 Harv. L. Rev. 833 (2005); Stephen M. Bainbridge, The Case For Limited Shareholder Voting Rights, 13 U.C.L.A. L. Rev. 601 (2006) (counseling the wisdom of limited shareholder democracy). There also is a growing debate whether shareholders are myopic in their focus on short-term versus long-term results as well as whether there are social costs when manager's favor so-called one time horizon over another. *See* Fried, The Uneasy Case for Favoring Long-Term Shareholders, 124 Yale L.J. 1554 (2015) (demonstrating how through share repurchases managers can, while appearing to favor long-term holders, in fact harm the corporation over time). Much of the debate on short-term versus long-term holder interest is generated by the increased activism by hedge funds where views abound regarding their enduring impacts. *See* Bebchuk, Brav and Jiang, The Long-Term Effects of Hedge Fund Activism, 115 Colum. L. Rev. 1085 (2015) (finding no evidence that short-term gains observed with hedge fund intervention disappear in the long-term).

[2]   *See generally* Julian Velasco, The Fundamental Rights of the Shareholder, 40 U.C. Davis L. Rev. 407 (2006). *For* a discussion of the appropriate mode of governance of the publicly held corporation, *see* Melvin A. Eisenberg, The Structure of the Corporation; A Legal Analysis (1976); §§ 9.1 to 9.4, On the purpose of granting shareholders a vote, *see;* Frank Easterbrook & Daniel Fischel, The Economic Structure Of Law 65–70 (1991) (shareholder voting addresses the problem of incomplete contracting within the corporate context); Robert B. Thompson & Paul H. Edleman, 62 Vand. L. Rev. 129 (2009) (arguing that shareholder voting can correct value-reducing managerial errors, provided there is alignment of the shareholders' voting rights and their underlying financial interest in the firm). Shareholders of the closely held concern may well want a greater voice in the operation of the business, especially in the common situation where the principal shareholders and managers are the same. Thus the close corporation has special needs in forming the corporate structure.

[3]   Share rights, being in essence contract rights, are determined by the terms of the shares as described in the articles of incorporation in conjunction with provisions of the general corporation laws. Stephenson v. Drever, 69 Cal.Rptr.2d 764, 947 P.2d 1301 (Cal. 1997) (minority shareholder's interest was to be repurchased upon termination of employment; shareholder rights were not extinguished upon termination but rather continued until the repurchase was consummated and the former employee was no longer a shareholder of record).

The second class of shareholder rights, designated as proprietary rights, includes: (a) the right to participate ratably in dividend distributions when declared by the management; (b) the right to participate in the distribution of assets in total or partial liquidation; (c) the right to equality and honesty of treatment by the management and by majority shareholders in corporate transactions affecting share interests, such as new issues of shares or amendments of the articles; (d) the right to be registered as a shareholder on the corporate books, subject only to valid and authorized transfers of the shares; and (e) immunity from personal liability for corporate debts, subject to judicial limitations against abuse of this privilege.

Remedial rights of shareholders include: (a) the right to information and inspection of the corporate records; (b) the right to bring representative or derivative suits on corporate causes of action to prevent or remedy mismanagement and unauthorized acts and compel the corporation to enforce its rights; and (c) common law, equitable, and statutory remedies for infringement of individual rights.

PART B.   RIGHT TO INFORMATION

§ 13.2   Basis of Shareholders' Right to Information

A shareholder[4] has a common law right to inspect corporate books and records, in person or by an agent, for a proper purpose in order to protect the shareholder's interest. Most states also provide shareholders a statutory right of inspection, which is generally viewed as supplementing rather than supplanting the common law right.[5] However, some states permit provisions in the corporate charter limiting the right to the statutory right and thus preempting the common law right of inspection.[6]

Many states permit reasonable charter and bylaw provisions regulating inspection.[7] The fact that a transaction was approved by a fully informed shareholder vote does not preclude a shareholder's request for inspection of corporate books relating to the transaction in question.[8]

The shareholder's right to ascertain how the affairs of the business are being conducted by the officers and directors has traditionally been founded on the ownership interest and the necessity of protecting that interest.[9] The common law right of inspection rests on the underlying rights of ownership of the corporate property.[10]

---

[4]   *See, e.g.,* Deephaven Risk Arb Trading Ltd. v. UnitedGlobalCom, Inc., 2005 WL 1713067 (Del.Ch. 2005) (inspecting granted even though shareholder had a net short position).

[5]   *See* Scattered Corp. v. Chicago Stock Exch., Inc., 671 A.2d 874 (Del. Ch. 1994).

[6]   *See, e.g.,* Mannato v. SunTrust Banks, Inc., 708 S.E.2d 611 (Ga. App. 2011) (provision limiting inspection to shareholders with more than 2% stock ownership), applying Ga. Code Ann. § 14–2–1602 (2012) ("the right to inspection enumerated in subsection (c) of this Code section may be limited by a corporation's articles of incorporation or bylaws for shareholders owning 2 percent or less of the shares outstanding.").

[7]   *See, e.g.,* Mannato v. SunTrust Banks, Inc., 308 Ga. App. 691, 708 S.E.2d 611 (2011) (provision limiting inspection to shareholders with more than 2% stock ownership held consistent with Ga. Code Ann. § 14–2–1602, reasoning "the right to inspection enumerated in subsection (c) of this Code section may be limited by a corporation's articles of incorporation or bylaws for shareholders owning 2 percent or less of the shares outstanding").

[8]   Lavin v. West Corporation, 2017 WL 6728702 (Del. Ch. 2017), judgment entered, 2018 WL 565492 (Del. Ch. 2018).

[9]   Otis-Hidden Co. v. Scheirich, 219 S.W. 191 (Ky. 1920).

[10]   State ex rel. Bulkley v. Whited & Wheless, 28 So. 922, 925 (La. 1901) (quasi-ownership).

There has been much litigation over the proper scope of the shareholder's right to inspect corporate books, files, and records. Thus a statute authorizing inspection of "books and records of account" has been held not to authorize inspection of quarterly financial statements,[11] but the statute does reach recordations and contracts of on-going business transactions.[12] A court may limit the scope of a shareholder's inspection to those records that are necessary to protect the shareholder's interest in the corporation.[13]

Courts may, and customarily do, condition inspections on the entry of a reasonable confidentiality order. Records inspected are not presumed confidential and a court should exercise its discretion in deciding whether to impose confidentiality by weighing the shareholder's interest in free communication against the corporation's interest in confidentiality.[14]

§ 13.3   Proper Purposes for Inspection

Shareholders today generally have the right of inspection only for legitimate purposes related to their interest as investors. The common law privilege, however, is not absolute, and the corporation may show in defense that the applicant is acting out of wrongful motives, or that the information sought is not germane or necessary for the stated purpose.[15]

An examination of modern decisions reveals that among the purposes held to justify an inspection demand are to ascertain (1) the financial condition of the company or the propriety of dividends;[16] (2) the value of shares for sale or investment;[17] (3) whether there has been mismanagement;[18] (4) to obtain, in anticipation of a shareholders' meeting, a mailing list of shareholders to solicit proxies or otherwise influence voting;[19] or (5) information in aid of litigation with the corporation or its officers involving corporate transactions.[20] When a shareholder presents suspected wrongdoing or director unfitness

---

[11]   Bitters v. Milcut, Inc., 343 N.W.2d 418 (Wis.App. 1983). 2019 WL 3683525 (Del. 2019).

[12]   *See* Meyer v. Ford Indus., 538 P.2d 353 (Or. 1975) (reaches contracts, records, and correspondence).

[13]   *See, e.g.,* Wells v. League of American Theatres & Producers, Inc., 706 N.Y.S.2d 599, 604 (Sup. Ct. 2000); Troccoli v. L & B Contract Indus., Inc., 687 N.Y.S.2d 400, 401 (App. Div. 1999).

[14]   Tiger v. Boast Apparel, Inc., 2019 WL 3683525 (Del. 2019) (the court must "weigh the stockholder's legitimate interest in free communication against the corporation's legitimate interest in confidentiality").

[15]   Security First Corp. v. United States Die Casting & Dev. Co., 687 A.2d 563 (Del. 1997) (inspection proper to investigate mismanagement during merger negotiations, but denied for records before merger negotiations).

[16]   Gregson v. Packings & Insulations Corp., 708 A.2d 533 (R.I. 1998) (even though financial statements not prepared, access to books granted to determine propriety of bonuses and extraordinary dividend).

[17]   Friedman v. Altoona Pipe & Steel Supply Co., 460 F.2d 1212 (3d Cir. 1972); Pagett v. Westport Precision, Inc., 845 A.2d 455 (Conn. App. Ct. 2004).

[18]   Seinfeld v. Verizon Comm., Inc., 909 A.2d 117 (Del. 2006) (stockholder as a predicate must allege some "credible basis" for inferring possible misconduct); Chitwood v. Vertex Pharm. Inc., 476 Mass. 667, 678, 71 N.E.3d 492, 501 (Mass. 2017)(access granted on showing of particular facts from which it is reasonable to infer wrongdoing or mismanagement). Delaware appears unwilling to grant inspection for the purpose of "second guessing" a decision of the board of directors without alleging that decision constitutes a breach of fiduciary duty or conflicts with the company's articles of incorporation or bylaws. *See* City of Westland Police and Fire Retirement System v. Axcelis Technologies, Inc., 1 A.3d 281 (Del. 2010) (denying request for records related to board's decision not to accept resignation of directors that failed to receive a majority vote pursuant to the company's "plurality plus" provision).

[19]   E.L. Bruce Co. v. State ex rel. Gilbert, 144 A.2d 533 (Del. 1958); Kalanges v. Champlain Valley Exposition, Inc., 632 A.2d 357 (Vt. 1993) (corporation did not meet its burden in proving that request to examine list of stockholders to facilitate attempt to gain control was improper purpose).

[20]   Saito v. McKesson HBOC, Inc., 806 A.2d 113 (Del. 2002) (inspection extended to records before shareholder maintaining derivative suit became a holder).

as a ground for inspection, "a stockholder must establish a credible basis to infer that a director is unsuitable, thereby warranting further investigation."[21] The filing of a shareholder derivative suit does not waive the right to inspect corporate books and records.[22] Many corporations have adopted provisions, usually in their bylaws, that restrict shareholder suits to certain forums. A possible effect of a forum selection clause is limiting the scope of a shareholder's right to inspect corporate records when sought in connection to gathering information relevant to a shareholder's law suit. In *United Technologies Corp. v. Treppel,*[23] the Delaware Supreme Court held trial courts have wide discretion in considering shareholder requests to inspect the books and records of a company so that it would be appropriate to condition access by reference to whether the information to be obtained through the request would be used in litigation inconsistent with a corporation's forum selection class.

A purpose is proper even though it yields no direct benefit to the corporation, but it should not be adverse to the corporation's interest.[24] Among the improper purposes that may justify management denial of a shareholder's claimed right of inspection are: (1) to obtain information as to business secrets or to aid a competitor;[25] (2) to secure business prospects or investment or advertising lists;[26] and (3) to find technical defects in corporation transactions in order to bring strike suits for purposes of blackmail or extortion.[27] In general, a demand is improper if it is motivated merely by idle curiosity or to annoy or harass management.[28]

The decisions place great emphasis on the shareholder's subjective purpose. For example, applying Delaware law, the Supreme Court of Minnesota in *Pillsbury v. Honeywell,*[29] upheld management's refusal to allow an antiwar activist shareholder to have access to the shareholder lists in order to communicate his antiwar beliefs. In so ruling, the court noted: "We do not mean to imply that a shareholder with a bona fide investment interest could not bring this suit if motivated by concern with the long-or short-term economic effects on Honeywell resulting from the production of war munitions."[30] Subsequently the Delaware Chancery Court, in *Conservative Caucus v. Chevron Corp.*[31] distinguished *Pillsbury* as a case where the petitioning shareholder had failed, in making his request for the stockholders' list, to establish any adverse consequences to the corporation from its continuing to manufacture armaments. *Conservative Caucus* granted the shareholder access to the stockholders' list to solicit their support for a proposal to discourage the corporation from continuing to do business in Angola. Delaware courts have indicated that a shareholder's motives in demanding

---

[21]   Central Laborers Pension Fund v. News Corp., 45 A.3d 139 (Del. 2012); Cain v. Merck & Co., 1 A.3d 834 (N.J. Super A.D. 2010).

[22]   King v. VeriFone Holdings, Inc., 12 A.3d 1140 (Del. 2011); Advanced Automation, Inc. v. Fitzgerald, 718 S.E.2d 607 (Ga. App. 2011).

[23]   109 A.3d 553 (Del. 2015).

[24]   COMPAQ Computer Corp. v. Horton, 631 A.2d 1 (Del. 1993) (focusing on whether stated purpose is related to the interests of the shareholder which should not be adverse to interests of the corporation).

[25]   Morton v. Rogers, 514 P.2d 752 (Ariz. Ct. App. 1973).

[26]   E.L. Bruce Co. v. State ex rel. Gilbert, 144 A.2d 533 (Del. 1958).

[27]   Shabshelowitz v. Fall River Gas Co., 588 N.E.2d 630 (Mass. 1992) (improper purpose to seek list to solicit existing shareholders to sell their shares to plaintiff).

[28]   Carpenter v. Texas Air Corp., 1985 WL 11548 (Del. Ch. 1985).

[29]   State ex rel. Pillsbury v. Honeywell, Inc., 191 N.W.2d 406 (Minn. 1971).

[30]   State ex rel. Pillsbury v. Honeywell, Inc., 191 N.W.2d 406, 411 (Minn. 1971).

[31]   Conservative Caucus v. Chevron Corp., 525 A.2d 569 (Del. Ch. 1987).

books and records can be relevant. Thus, for example, where a shareholder's true purpose appeared to be for personal rather than corporate reasons, the inspection request should not be granted.[32]

The majority common law rule does not seem to place the burden on petitioners to show the propriety of examination, nor that the refusal by the officers or directors was wrongful.[33] Similarly, most modern statutes place the burden on the corporation.[34]

§ 13.4 Statutory Regulation of Inspection Rights

In most jurisdictions, the shareholders' right to inspect and examine the books and records of a corporation is not left entirely to the common law but is declared in whole or in part by statutes. Statutory provisions often define the right of inspection only of certain books, such as the stock ledger or list of shareholders. Under this type of statute, the right of inspection of other records, such as books of account, minutes of the meetings of directors and shareholders, and corporate documents, which may be of the greatest importance, are thus left to the common law.[35] Under a statute that provides in general terms that the shareholders of all corporations shall "have the right of access to, inspection and examination of the books, records and papers of the corporation at all reasonable and proper times," it is generally held that inspection will not be allowed for purposes hostile to the interests of the corporation.[36] Ulterior motives may thus be shown by a corporation as a matter of defense. Failure to make a proper demand including proper documentation of share ownership can result in a denial of access to the corporation's books and records.[37]

§ 13.5 Remedies if Inspection Is Denied

If the officers of a corporation wrongfully deny a shareholder the right to inspect its books or papers, the traditional remedy to enforce the shareholder's right was a common law proceeding known as mandamus.[38] Because mandamus was historically used to enforce public rights and duties, the petition was presented in the name of the state on the "relation" or complaint of the party beneficially interested.[39] In a number of states, the real party in interest was named as plaintiff, and the state was not mentioned even as a formal party.[40]

There is a conflict of authority whether a statute appearing to make the right of inspection absolute takes away a court's discretion to refuse the writ of mandamus where inspection is sought for an improper purpose. Most decisions favor the exercise of sound discretion to withhold the writ to protect the just interests of the corporation and the

---

[32] Berkowitz v. Legal Sea Foods, Inc., 1997 WL 153815 (Del. Ch. 1997) (the record indicated that plaintiff's true purpose was not his stated purpose but rather to pursue individual claims against his father and siblings).

[33] NVF Co. v. Sharon Steel Corp., 294 F.Supp. 1091 (W.D. Pa. 1969).

[34] *E.g.,* Del. Code Ann. tit. 8, § 220 (2009).

[35] Tucson Gas & Elec. Co. v. Schantz, 428 P.2d 686 (Ariz. Ct. App. 1967).

[36] State v. Honeywell, Inc., 191 N.W.2d 406 (Minn. 1971). *But see* Lewis v. J & K Plumbing & Heating Co., 418 N.Y.S.2d 244 (App. Div. 1979) (absolute right to inspect balance sheets under N.Y. Bus. Corp. Law § 624(e) (McKinney 1986)).

[37] *See, e.g.,* Central Laborers Pension Fund v. News Corp., 2012 WL 1925724 (Del. 2012).

[38] Stern v. South Chester Tube Co., 390 U.S. 606 (1968) (construing Pennsylvania statute); Miles v. Bank of Heflin, 349 So.2d 1072 (Ala. 1977).

[39] *E.g.,* State ex rel. Foster v. Standard Oil Co. of Kan., 18 A.2d 235, 240 (Del.Super. 1941).

[40] *See, e.g.,* People v. Pacheco, 29 Cal. 210 (1865).

other shareholders against abuse.[41] This discretion is spoken of as inherent in the remedy of mandamus, but it is generally applied in giving equitable relief of a specific nature to avoid injustice and remit the suitor to other forms of relief. There are comparatively few reported cases in which the courts have enforced the right of inspection in equity by injunction. In some jurisdictions, it has been held, however, under statutory provisions or otherwise, especially when ancillary to other equitable relief, that enforcement by an injunction (that is, a mandatory injunction or specific performance) is available.[42]

Modern corporation statutes specifically set forth remedies for enforcing inspection rights. Thus the Delaware statute states that if a corporation does not grant inspection within five business days of a demand, the shareholder may commence an action in the Court of Chancery to enforce the demand.[43] The Model Business Corporation Act as revised in 1984 provides that a court of the county in which the corporation's principal office is located (or, if none in the state, its registered office) may summarily order inspection and copying of the records.[44] Section 16.04(c) of the Model Act provides that the court order of inspection can include an "order the corporation pay the shareholder's expenses incurred to obtain the order."[45]

§ 13.6 Accessing Corporate Reports, Financial Statements, and NOBO List

The notes to the Uniform Business Corporation Act,[46] a predecessor of the Model Act, suggested that each state require detailed annual reports of a corporation's financial condition for the information of shareholders, creditors, and the investing public. This was a response to complaints about the inadequacy of financial statements and reports issued by leading corporations.[47] The great burden and expense to an individual shareholder of exercising the right of inspection of corporate books and records, not to mention bringing suit to enforce that right, make this a poor method of getting needed information. Although the response of state legislatures was not favorable, the federal securities laws filled the need with respect to publicly held corporations.

The Securities Exchange Act of 1934 requires registration and periodic reporting by publicly held companies.[48] Further, the SEC's proxy regulations under that Act require that proxy statements be mailed to shareholders in connection with the solicitation of proxies. These proxy statements must include much financial information as to proposed corporate changes and proceedings. The making of reports and the rendition of financial statements by corporations, however, are generally held not to be substitutes for the

---

[41] In re De Vengoechea, 91 A. 314 (N.J. Sup. Ct. 1914) (mandamus denied due to petitioner's hostile motive).

[42] Otis-Hidden Co. v. Scheirich, 219 S.W. 191 (Ky. 1920).

[43] Del. Code Ann. tit. 8, § 220(c) (2009).

[44] Model Bus. Corp. Act § 16.04(a), (b) (2016).

[45] Model Bus. Corp. Act § 16.04(c) (2016). *See* Grapefields, Inc. v. Kosby, 309 Ga. App. 588, 710 S.E.2d 816 (Ga. Ct. App. 2011) (approving award of over $25,000 to cover shareholder's costs to obtain order compelling inspection.).

[46] The Uniform Act was approved by the American Bar Association at its July 1928 meeting. The annual report requirement is imposed by the Model Act. Model Bus. Corp. Act §§ 16.20 to 16.22 (2008).

[47] William Zebina Ripley, Main Street and Wall Street 209 (1929).

[48] The Public Utility Holding Company Act of 2005, 42 U.S.C. § 16451 (2009).

shareholders' right of inspection and are no excuse for management's refusal to permit a shareholder to examine corporate books and records.[49]

An important constraint on the utility of obtaining a list of the stockholders for a public corporation is that in most instances the list does not identify who votes the shares. The stockholders' list identifies only the names and addresses of the stockholders of record. Most stock in public corporations is held not in the name of the owner of the shares but in the name of the brokerage house where the owner maintains an account. Holding shares in the brokerage house's "street name" greatly facilitates purchases and sales of securities because the owner of the shares does not have to endorse the shares and deliver them to the broker before selling the shares. Indeed, most ownership in public companies is not represented by a certificate but appear only as an electronic entry in the share registry. This is, in part, because holding shares via street names facilitates trading in the shares of public corporations. On purchasing shares investors do not take delivery of any share certificates, but receive only a statement that the shares they have purchased are held in a trust depositary that maintains its own records regarding the identity of the owners of the shares that are on deposit with the trust depositary. The dominant trust depositary in the United States is CEDE & Co.

An examination of the list of stockholders for a public corporation, such as IBM Corporation, will show that a substantial portion of the shares is recorded in the name of CEDE & Co. Separately, CEDE makes available to the corporations whose shares are on deposit with it a list of the brokerage firms holding stock in the CEDE name. This is called the "CEDE breakdown" list. This document, however, does not reveal the names and addresses of customers for whom the broker holds the shares in its street name. The SEC requires brokers to ask each customer who holds stock in a street name if she objects to her name and address being disclosed to the corporation in which she has invested. Those who do not object are then identified to the corporation on the NOBO (non-objecting beneficial owners) list. Thus, it is through the NOBO list that one can determine who the beneficial shareholders are for some of the outstanding shares held in street names (*i.e.*, those in the hands of non-objecting shareholders).

Given the pervasiveness of holding public shares in street names and, hence, the importance of the NOBO list, the question arises whether a shareholder seeking inspection of the list of shareholders is also entitled to the NOBO list. The courts have been unwilling to build upon the principles that underlie the general rights of stockholders to access to company records and their power to communicate with their fellow stockholders by conferring upon the stockholders the power to compel the corporation to acquire a NOBO list. Most courts that have engaged this subject conclude that the requesting shareholder can obtain the NOBO list only if such list is already in the corporation's possession,[50] but the shareholder cannot compel the corporation to obtain or otherwise prepare a NOBO list.[51]

---

[49]   Kerkorian v. Western Air Lines, Inc., 253 A.2d 221, 225 (Del. Ch.), *aff'd*, 254 A.2d 240 (Del. 1969).

[50]   Shamrock Assoc. v. Texas Am. Energy Corp., 517 A.2d 658 (Del. Ch. 1986).

[51]   Luxottica Group S.p.A. v. United States Shoe Corp., 919 F.Supp. 1091 (S.D. Ohio 1995).

§ 13.7 Directors' Right of Inspection

By both case law[52] and statute,[53] the right of a director to inspect corporate books and records is more extensive than that of a shareholder.[54] The director's right has often been said to be absolute and unqualified.[55] It has been held that the right may not be denied on the ground that the director is hostile to the corporation and that his only object is to promote a claim against it; if the hostility goes to the extent of justifying his removal from office, that remedy is to be followed.[56] Even a claim the documents are protected by the attorney-client privilege is not an absolute bar to the director's access.[57]

Inspection should be denied, however, when necessary to prevent abuse by the director or his representative.[58] It has been declared that directors must act in good faith and therefore may not exercise their right of examination for purposes that conflict with their fiduciary obligations.[59] The duties of their positions require directors to keep themselves informed of the business and to be familiar with the affairs of the company.[60] Inspection by a shareholder is primarily for the purpose of protecting her individual interests. Inspection by a director is with a view to enabling him to perform his duties intelligently.

In making an examination of corporate records, a director, like the shareholder, is entitled to expert assistance in order to exercise the privilege effectively and may use attorneys and accountants to help.[61] Wrongful denial of the request allows the director to the sanction provided by law.[62]

PART C. SHAREHOLDERS' MEETINGS AND VOTING

§ 13.8 Shareholders Act at Meetings or by Written Consent

The stockholders' meeting is an important feature of corporate law, but we might well question whether the ritual of a meeting where owners physically come together is a relic of the past. Certainly in the public company we might even question whether the annual meeting has the same importance as it did in the past in terms of providing a medium for management to sense the concerns of the firm's owners. The growing concentration of institutional holders combined with their increasing activism outside

---

[52] *See, e.g.,* Cohen v. Cocoline Prods., Inc., 127 N.E.2d 906 (N.Y. 1955). *See* William C. McLaughlin, Director's Right to Inspect the Corporate Books and Records—Absolute or Otherwise, 22 Bus. Law. 413 (1967).

[53] *E.g.,* Cal. Corp. Code § 1602 (2009).

[54] Kortum v. Webasto Sunroofs, Inc., 769 A.2d 113 (Del. Ch. 2000).

[55] *See, e.g.,* Kortum v. Webasto Sunroofs, Inc., 769 A.2d 113 (Del. Ch. 2000) (prima facie showing of entitlement to documents made by allegation requesting party is a director).

[56] Wilkins v. M. Ascher Silk Corp., 201 N.Y.S. 739 (App. Div. 1923), *aff'd,* 143 N.E. 748 (N.Y. 1924).

[57] *See* Saline v. Superior Court of Orange County, 122 Cal.Rptr.2d 813 (Cal. App. 2002).

[58] *See, e.g.,* Kortum v. Webasto Sunroofs, Inc., 769 A.2d 113 (Del Ch. 2000) (reasonable limits may be imposed if proven director's agent's interests conflict with those of the corporation and the corporation failed to meet its burden of proving that the director or agent has such a conflict; the court was satisfied that the director was not competing with the corporation *when* the request was made).

[59] Chappel v. Applied Control Systems, Inc., 39 Pa. D. & C. 4th 168 (Com. Pl. 1998) (access would be denied if established requesting director was employee of competitor).

[60] *See, e.g.,* Kelley v. Heritage Nat'l Bank, 897 S.W.2d 96 (Mo. Ct. App. 1995) (director's inspection rights based on necessity for knowledge to discharge duties and, therefore, *former* director's access was denied).

[61] *See, e.g.,* Saline v. Superior Court of Orange County, 122 Cal.Rptr.2d 813 (Cal. App. 2002).

[62] *See, e.g.,* McGowan v. Empress Entertainment, Inc., 791 A.2d 1 (Del. Ch. 2000) (equitable to permit recovery of attorneys fees upon showing of bad faith denial of request).

the annual meeting context support the view that the annual meeting is not necessary for such companies to assure interaction between owners and managers. Also, the sheer number of individual investors in many public companies renders the annual meeting setting a weak medium. As the number of owners increases, the collective action problem becomes an ever-increasing obstacle to an effective exercise of their judgment. As seen later in this chapter, the Internet is now being harnessed to corporate governance mechanisms so that the day of increased use of virtual shareholder meetings may well not be far away. Recently, some major corporations have engaged in virtual shareholder meetings.[63] However, there has been pushback by some shareholders and some companies have reverted to face-to-face meetings.[64] In 2019, the American Bar Association approved amendments to the Model Act to permit shareholder meetings solely by remote participation.[65]

As is the case with directors, according to traditional doctrine, a majority of the shareholders have no power to vote or act for the corporation except at a meeting, duly called on proper notice, at which a quorum is present. Absent statutory authorization, written or oral consent to a corporate act by the shareholders or members individually, even though a majority may agree, is not binding on the corporation.[66]

Most modern statutes authorize shareholder action to be taken or approved without a meeting by the written consents of shareholders holding shares with voting power.[67] The Model Business Corporation Act provides for action without a meeting only on unanimous written consent;[68] however, the statutes vary in their requirements from state to state.[69] For example, Delaware permits a majority of the shareholders to act by consent.[70] Failure to adhere to the requirements of the statute for written consents results in the approval never have occurred.[71] A provision common to statutes authorizing action outside a meeting via the consent of less than all the stockholders is

---

[63] *See, e.g.,* Andrea Vittorio, Corporate America's Annual Meeting Tradition Turning Virtual, (Bloomberg Law July 11, 2019). Companies From Fitbit to Ford Meet With Shareholders Virtually, Corporate Law and Accountability Law Report (Bloomberg BNA) (July 10, 2018).

[64] *See, e.g.,* Emily Chasan, Investors Opposing Virtual Shareholder Meetings Notch Wins, https://www.bloomberg.com/news/articles/2018-01-09/investors-opposing-online-only-shareholder-meetings-notch-wins (Jan. 9, 2018).

[65] *See* Corporate Laws Committee, ABA Business Law Section, Changes to the Model Business Corporation Act—Amendments to Chapters 7 and 10 Permitting Shareholders' Meetings Solely by Remote Participation, 74 Bus. Law. 833 (2019).

[66] De La Vergne Refrigerating Mach. Co. v. German Sav. Inst., 175 U.S. 40 (1899).

[67] Cal. Corp. Code § 603(a) (2009); Del. Code Ann. tit. 8, §§ 228, 275(c) (2009); N.Y. Bus. Corp. Law § 615 (McKinney 1986); Tex. Bus. Corp. Act Ann. art. 9.10 (2009).

[68] Model Bus. Corp. Act § 7.04(a)(2016); former Model Bus. Corp. Act § 145 (1969).

[69] Cal. Corp. Code § 603(a) (2009) (authorizes action by consent of as many shareholders as would be needed to pass the action at a meeting unless the articles of incorporation provide otherwise); Del. Code Ann. tit. 8, §§ 228, 275(c) (2001) (same as California except that unanimous consent is necessary for dissolution).

[70] Del. Code Ann. tit. 8, § 228 (2009). *See also* Ark. Code Ann. § 4–27–704 (2009); Fla. Stat. Ann. § 607.0704 (West 2001); Wis. Stat. Ann. § 180.0704 (2009). The right is enforceable by the shareholders. *See, e.g.,* Rich v. Fuqi Int'l Inc., 2012 WL 5392162 (Del.Ch. 2012)(requirement to hold annual meeting is not excused by inability of company to provide audited financial statements per the SEC reporting requirements for public companies); Opportunity Partners LLP v. TransTech Service Partners, Inc., 2009 WL 997334 (Del. Ch. 2009)(blank check company created to facilitate acquisitions must comply with the Delaware statute mandating annual stockholders meeting).

[71] Espinoza v. Zuckerberg, 124 A.3d 47 (Del. Ch. 2015)(affidavit in case challenging transaction that was filed by holder of 61.5 percent of the voting shares ineffective to be ratification of the earlier transaction).

a requirement of prompt notice to all the non-consenting shareholders.[72] Consents are analogous to proxies and are revocable.[73]

§ 13.9 Necessity of Annual Meeting and Convening Special Meetings

Each shareholder has a right to have an annual meeting called and held to elect directors.[74] Modern statutes expressly confer this right.[75] A statutory, charter, or bylaw provision stating that a meeting shall be held every year for the election of directors confers a right on each individual shareholder to have an annual meeting called and held at the time specified or at some later reasonable time.[76] Indeed, statutes commonly provide stockholders with a procedure to compel an annual meeting to be convened when a certain number of months have elapsed since the last annual meeting.[77]

The time and place for a regular annual meeting of the shareholders are usually fixed in the bylaws. In a few jurisdictions, if the charter or bylaws fix the place, the day, and the hour at which regular meetings shall be held, no further notice may be legally necessary.[78] However, under most modern statutes, notice must be given a minimum and a maximum number of days before the meeting to every registered shareholder entitled to vote.[79] The notice must specify the time and place of the meeting, but there is no requirement that it elaborate on the purpose of the meeting unless the articles of incorporation require otherwise.[80]

In the absence of an express provision in the charter or bylaws, special meetings may be called by the board of directors whenever deemed necessary or on demand of the shareholders or a certain percentage of them.[81] Once granted by statute, the shareholders' right to call a special meeting presumably cannot be abridged or altered

---

[72]   *See* Cal. Corp. Code § 603 (2009); Del. Code Ann. tit. 8, § 228 (2009); 805 ILCS § 5/7.10 (2009).

[73]   Calumet Indus. v. MacClure, 464 F.Supp. 19 (N.D. Ill. 1978).

[74]   *See, e.g.,* Saxon Indus. v. NKFW, 488 A.2d 1298 (Del. 1984) (even though corporation was in Chapter 11 bankruptcy, reorganization does not override strong public policy of annual stockholders' meetings).

[75]   Former Model Bus. Corp. Act § 28 (1969) (the right is not absolute in that the shareholder cannot demand that the meeting be held on the bylaw date because the statute gives a 13-month period); Model Bus. Corp. Act § 7.01 (2016) (no express 13-month period). *See also* Cal. Corp. Code § 600(b) (2009); Del. Code Ann. tit. 8, § 211(b) (2009); N.Y. Bus. Corp. Law § 602(b) (2009).

[76]   *See, e.g.,* Morris v. Thomason, 672 So.2d 433 (La. Ct. App. 1996) (directors could not be elected at a special meeting when articles call for their election at annual meeting).

[77]   Some states accord a shareholder the right to compel an annual meeting if no meeting has been held within 18 months. Thus, the annual meeting requirement means a right to have meetings every 18 months rather than every 12 months. Hilton Hotels Corp. v. ITT Corp., 962 F.Supp. 1309 (D. Nev. 1997) (applying Nevada law). Once the statutory grounds for requiring a meeting are established, the right to an order mandating a meeting is "virtually absolute." Speiser v. Baker, 525 A.2d 1001 (Del. Ch. 1987) (plaintiff's complicity in early failures to convene a meetings not enough to bar relief).

[78]   *See* Morrill v. Little Falls Mfg. Co., 55 N.W. 547 (Minn. 1893).

[79]   Model Bus. Corp. Act § 7.05 (2016) (no fewer than ten, nor more than sixty days before the meeting); former Model Bus. Corp. Act § 29 (1969) (same). In counting the number of days, it is proper to exclude either the date of mailing or the date of the meeting, but not both. *See* Hebert v. Stansbury, 248 So.2d 873 (La. Ct. App.), *writ ref'd,* 253 So.2d 61 (La. 1971).

[80]   Model Bus. Corp. Act § 7.05(b) (2016).

[81]   The Model Act provides that special meetings of the shareholders may be called by the board of directors, the holders of not less than one-tenth of all the shares entitled to vote at the meeting, or such other persons as may be authorized in the articles of incorporation or the bylaws. Model Bus. Corp. Act § 7.02 (2016); former Model Bus. Corp. Act § 28 (1969)(same).

unless permitted by statute.[82] Statutes generally confer a right upon 10 percent of the shareholders to convene a special meeting.[83] The Model Act now permits the articles of incorporation to fix a lower percentage as well as a higher percentage, but not to exceed 25 percent.[84] The shareholders' right to call a special meeting provides an important check on the powers of the directors.[85] However, the requested meeting must be for a matter that is a proper subject for stockholder action.[86]

§ 13.10   The Time, Place, and Notice of the Meeting

Charter or bylaw provisions authorizing corporate meetings at a certain time are not intended to prevent meetings at other times on proper notice.[87] The matter of notice is now governed by statute, although statutes permit deviation by the articles of incorporation or bylaws.[88] Corporate statutes frequently require that a general meeting's notice must include notice of any proposal a shareholder intends to submit for a vote; the notice of such proposal should be sufficient to inform shareholders of the proposal's content.[89] For example, the Model Act provides "[u]nless this Act or the articles of incorporation require otherwise, notice of an annual meeting need not include a description of the purpose or purposes for which the meeting is called."[90] Some states deviate from the Model Act. The Sixth Circuit provided a shareholder-friendly interpretation of the Michigan statute that deviated from the Model Act. The Michigan statute called for written notice to set forth the "purposes" of an upcoming annual meeting and include "notice of shareholder proposals."[91] The court held the statute is not satisfied by a general statement that the meeting would deal with any shareholder proposals introduced at the meeting but without describing the subject of proposals the board knew would be introduced at the upcoming meeting. Even though some states do not require notice of the purposes of a forthcoming annual meeting, fiduciary obligations of directors can fill this gap.[92]

In response to pressure from the Uniform Electronic Transmissions Act (UETA) and the federal Electronic Signatures in Global and National Commerce Act (E-Sign), state laws are rapidly embracing wider mediums for notice to be imparted so that increasingly

---

[82]   The Model Act as enacted in most states permits the call of a special meeting by holders of 10% of the votes entitled to be cast. However, beginning in 1995, the Model Act has permitted the articles of incorporation to provide for a lower percentage or a higher percentage up to 25 percent (Model Bus. Corp. Act § 7.02(a)(2)(2016).

[83]   *E.g.,* Model Bus. Corp. Act § 7.02(a)(2) (2016).

[84]   Model Bus. Corp. Act § 7.02(a)(2) (2016).

[85]   *See, e.g.,* Cullen v. Milligan, 575 N.E.2d 123 (Ohio 1991) (proper to call a meeting for shareholders to consider an offer to acquire company's assets as well as to fill vacancies on the board).

[86]   *See, e.g.,* Siegman v. Palomar Medical Technologies, Inc., 1998 WL 51736 (Del.Ch. 1998) (denying request for meeting to approve settlement of litigation on terms proposed by the petitioner).

[87]   In re Hammond, 139 F. 898 (S.D.N.Y. 1905); Scanlan v. Snow, 2 App. D.C. 137 (1894).

[88]   For a case intimating that notice may even arise by custom, *see* State ex rel. East Cleveland Democratic Club, Inc. v. Bibb, 470 N.E.2d 257 (Ohio Ct. App. 1984).

[89]   Gwyn R. Hartman Revocable Living Trust v. S. Mich. Bancorp, Inc., 780 F.3d 724 (6th Cir. 2015)(notice merely stated that a resolution urging the board to amend the bylaws would be introduced at the meeting was not sufficient).

[90]   Model Bus. Corp. Act § 7.05(b)(2016). *See also* Del. Code Ann. tit. 8, § 222(a) (specifying the purpose or purposes of a meeting need be specified for special meetings).

[91]   Gwyn R. Hartman Revocable Living Trust v. S. Mich. Bancorp, Inc., 780 F.3d 724 (6th Cir. 2015)(notice merely stated that a resolution urging the board to amend the bylaws would be introduced at the meeting was not sufficient).

[92]   *See* Stroud v. Grace, 606 A.2d 75, 85–88 (Del. 1992).

reference to the requirement of a writing refers to a message that is in electronic form that can be produced to a tangible written form.[93] Proper notice includes mention of the time and place. As against absent shareholders or members, a meeting is not legal if held before the day or hour specified in the notice of the meeting.[94] And when the hour for a meeting is fixed by the notice, the meeting should be opened at that hour or within a reasonable time thereafter.[95] As against shareholders who are not present and who do not consent, a meeting held at a different place from that specified in the notice of the meeting is a nullity.[96]

Generally, there is no geographical restriction on the location at which a shareholders' meeting may be held, provided proper notice is given. Delaware allows shareholder meetings by means of remote communication if the directors so choose.[97] Meetings outside the state may be binding on the participants even if unauthorized.[98]

Insufficient notice, which deprives any shareholders of the opportunity to attend, argue, and vote on proposed measures renders action taken at a shareholders' meeting voidable at the instance of those who did not participate.[99] If all the shareholders who did not receive notice attend a meeting and participate, this constitutes a waiver of notice, and neither they nor the corporation can question the validity of a corporate act authorized at the meeting.[100] Mere attendance for the purpose of objecting to notice does not constitute waiver of notice.[101] The minutes of a shareholders' meeting should show the proper notice, provide proof of mailing or otherwise that gives notice, or show a waiver of notice either in the minutes themselves or in attached exhibits to which reference is made in the minutes.

Most state statutes authorize shareholders to waive any required notice. Such a waiver must be in writing and can be executed at anytime, and the meeting is not invalid because of the lack of notice if all shareholders entitled to notice but who did not receive it either execute a written waiver or attend and participate in the meeting.[102] To be effective the waiver must be executed by the holder of record, not by the share's beneficial owner.[103]

---

[93] *See, e.g.,* ABA Section of Bus. Law, Committee on Corporate Laws, Changes in the Model Business Corporation Act—Proposed Amendments to Incorporate Electronic Technology Amendments, 64 Bus. Law. 1129 (2009) (defining in section 1.40(6A), (7A) and (28) that a "writing" includes an electronic record which in turn means "information stored in an electronic or other medium and is retrievable in paper form through an automated process used in conventional commercial practice").

[94] People v. Albany & Susquehanna R.R., 55 Barb. 344 (1869), *aff'd,* 12 Sickels 161, 57 N.Y. 161 (1874).

[95] South School Dist. v. Blakeslee, 13 Conn. 227 (1839); State v. Bonnell, 35 Ohio St. 10 (1879).

[96] Miller v. English, 21 N.J.L. 317 (1848); American Primitive Socy. v. Pilling, 24 N.J.L. 653 (1855).

[97] Del. Code Ann. tit. 8, § 211(a) (2009).

[98] Handley v. Stutz, 139 U.S. 417 (1891).

[99] Dolan v. Airpack, Inc., 513 N.E.2d 213 (Mass. App. Ct.), *aff'd,* 513 N.E.2d 217 (Mass. 1987).

[100] Lofland v. Di Sabatino, 1991 WL 138505 (Del. Ch. 1991).

[101] Darvin v. Belmont Indus., Inc., 199 N.W.2d 542 (Mich. Ct. App. 1972); Block v. Magee, 537 N.Y.S.2d 215 (Sup. Ct. App. Div. 1989) (attended meeting, voted no and conspicuous absence from minutes of shareholder's signature).

[102] *See* Cal. Corp. Code § 601 (2009); 805 ILCS § 5/7.20 (2009); N.Y. Bus. Corp. Law § 606 (2009); Model Bus. Corp. Act § 7.06 (2016).

[103] Gim v. Jan Chin, Inc., 362 A.2d 143 (R.I. 1976).

Notice is given to the shareholders of record. Statutes now authorize the board of directors or the bylaws to fix a record date for the purpose of determining who is entitled to notice of and to vote at the meeting.[104]

§ 13.11   Quorum and Voting at Shareholders' Meetings

Nearly all states require the corporation to make available for inspection a list of shareholders entitled to vote.[105] Most states further specify the number of days preceding the meeting that the list must be available for inspection.

At common law, absent a provision to the contrary in statute, charter, or bylaw, a quorum was met by any number of shareholders, provided there were at least two and any required notice of the meeting had been given.[106] However, generally by express provision of the statute, charter, or bylaws, a majority of the shares entitled to vote (or sometimes less if so provided in the charter or bylaws) must be present in person or by proxy to constitute a quorum for the transaction of business; if there are less than the number of shares so present required for a quorum the meeting is not validly convened.[107] The articles of incorporation and corporate statute must be closely examined not only to determine what classes of shares are entitled to vote, but also whether the voting power is equal among all shares of the same class. Considering the contractual nature of the corporation, the articles of incorporation can impose voting restrictions provided they do not conflict with the provisions of the state law. Thus, a provision placing a ceiling on the total number of votes any stockholder could cast, regardless that otherwise her shareholdings would entitle her to a greater vote, was upheld as a permissible variation from the typical one-share one-vote principle.[108] In the typical setting, each share entitled to vote has one voting right. However, many corporations are adopting "tenure voting" whereby holders of shares have greater voting rights the longer they have owned their shares.[109]

The applicable corporate statute, articles of incorporation, and bylaws should be read carefully to determine whether a separate quorum determination is required for each item coming before the stockholders, especially when a corporation has more than one class of stock and the meeting's agenda includes a matter that requires the approval of more than one class of stock. A similar close reading is called for to determine if a greater than majority vote is required. States following the Model Business Corporation

---

[104] *See, e.g.*, Ark. Code Ann. § 4–27–707 (2009); Del. Code Ann. tit. 8, § 213 (2009); N.Y. Bus. Corp. Law § 604 (2009); Model Bus. Corp. Act § 7.07 (2016) (no greater than 70 days before meeting).

[105] *See, e.g.*, Del. Code Ann. tit. 8, § 219 (2009); 805 ILCS § 5/7.30 (2009); N.J. Stat. Ann. § 14A:5–8 (2009); Model Bus. Corp. Act § 7.20 (2016).

[106] Sylvania & G. R.R. v. Hoge, 59 S.E. 806 (Ga. 1907); Morrill v. Little Falls Mfg. Co., 55 N.W. 547, 549 (Minn. 1893) ("[I]t is immaterial whether the number present is only one or more than one").

[107] Former Model Bus. Corp. Act § 32 (1969) ("Unless otherwise provided in the articles of incorporation, a majority of the shares entitled to vote . . . shall constitute a quorum at a meeting of shareholders, but in no event shall a quorum consist of less than one-third . . ."); Model Bus. Corp. Act § 7.25 (2008) (same minimum requirements).

See Committee for New Management of Guaranty Bancshares Corp. v. Dimeling, 772 F.Supp. 230 (E.D. Pa. 1991) (directors were not duly elected at meeting in which quorum improperly determined because treated shares invalidly represented by proxy as not outstanding when calculating the number of shares need for quorum).

[108] *See* Providence & Worcester Co. v. Baker, 378 A.2d 121 (Del. 1977).

[109] *See, e.g.*, Williams v. Geier, 671 A.2d 1368 (Del. 1996).

Act require a separate quorum determination be made for each matter to be acted on at the meeting.[110]

Most courts have held that where a quorum is once present at a shareholders' meeting, the quorum is not broken by the subsequent withdrawal of some of the shareholders, whether present in person or by their proxies.[111] Some courts, however, have held to the contrary, ruling that a withdrawal that leaves the number of shareholders present or represented below the required number destroys the quorum and precludes any further action except a motion to adjourn.[112]

A validly convened meeting can be adjourned to a later date. Many state statutes expressly deal with the question of whether notice of the date and place of the adjourned meeting must be given. Their treatment of this issue varies widely. Some require no notice of the adjourned meeting so long as it is held within a certain number of days;[113] others require notice if a new record date is set.[114] The statutes further condition avoiding the need for any new notice of the adjourned meeting on the new meeting's time and location being announced at the meeting that is being adjourned.[115]

When a quorum is present, the vote of a majority of those present is sufficient to elect directors or to decide any questions, although it need not be a majority of all the shareholders or members, nor a majority of the voting power.[116] By the weight of authority, a plurality of the votes actually cast will be decisive, although some of the shareholders or members who are present may abstain and the majority of the votes cast may not be a majority of the persons present or stock represented.[117] A bylaw or charter provision requiring the affirmative vote of a majority of the shareholders at a corporate meeting means a majority in interest (that is, one vote per share) rather than a majority in number only.[118] These rules are codified in most state corporation statutes, which also generally permit higher voting requirements if specified in the articles.[119] A few statutes still require an extraordinary majority—that is, two-thirds—for approval of charter amendments, mergers, and other organic changes.[120] Also, there may be statutory, charter, or bylaw requirements for class voting by different classes of shares.[121]

---

[110] Model Bus. Corp. Act § 7.25(a) (2016).

[111] Testa v. Jarvis, 1994 WL 30517, 19 Del. J. Corp. L. 1321 (Del. Ch. 1994).

[112] Testa v. Jarvis, 1994 WL 30517 (Del. Ch. 1994) (withdrawal from meeting of one of two 50% holders is tantamount to adjournment).

[113] *See* Me. Rev. Stat. Ann. tit. 13–C, § 705 (2009) (requiring notice if there is a new record date); Cal. Corp. Code § 601 (2009) (45 days).

[114] *See* Del. Code Ann. tit. 8, § 222 (2009); Fla. Stat. Ann. § 607.0705 (2009); Wash. Rev. Code Ann. § 23B.07.050 (2009).

[115] Woodward & Lothrop, Inc. v. Schnabel, 593 F.Supp. 1385 (D.D.C. 1984).

[116] Hill v. Town, 138 N.W. 334 (Mich. 1912).

[117] Inhabitants of First Parish in Sudbury v. Stearns, 38 Mass. (21 Pick.) 148 (1838).

[118] Delaware has upheld an arrangement one vote per 20 shares for all additional shares of a single holder. Providence & Worcester Co. v. Baker, 378 A.2d 121 (Del. 1977).

[119] Model Bus. Corp. Act § 7.25(a) (2016); former Model Bus. Corp. Act § 32 (1969). Extraordinary voting and quorum requirements are frequent control devices in the closely held enterprise.

[120] *E.g.,* Neb. Rev. Stat. Ann. §§ 21–2057, 2072 (2009). *See* Chapter 25.

[121] *See* Elliott Associates, L.P. v. Avatex Corp., 715 A.2d 843 (Del. 1998) (class vote when rights adversely affected by "merger, consolidation or otherwise" arises when firm is acquired).

§ 13.12   Stockholders' Meetings in a Digital Age

The states are slowly, but at a quickening rate, adapting to the digital age by amending various provisions of their corporate statutes to authorize the use of the Internet, Email, etc. in connection with stockholders' meeting. Earlier material reviewed some of these developments as they apply to meetings of the board of directors.[122] The most advanced statute in terms of liberating functions such as notice, voting, and even deliberations from the traditional format for stockholders' meeting is contained in the Delaware statute, which was amended in July 2001 to permit Delaware corporations to take advantage of advances in communications technology.[123] More than half the states now have provisions that authorize the board of directors either to authorize "remote participation" by shareholders[124] or more sweepingly to convene the stockholders' meeting solely "by means of remote communication,", a "remote only" meeting[125] There is a split among the states whether only the directors can authorize remote participation or whether such authorization can be provided generally in the bylaws or the articles of incorporation.[126]

Some major corporations have engaged in virtual shareholder meetings.[127] However, there has been pushback by some shareholders and some companies have reverted to face-to-face meetings.[128]

States impose various conditions for shareholders to enjoy remote participation. Many states follow Delaware's conditions: the corporation shall employ reasonable measures to verify that each person participating remotely is a stockholder or proxyholder; the corporation shall implement reasonable measures to facilitate one participating remotely to read, hear, and vote at the meeting, and the corporation shall have the ability to record the vote or action of the remotely participating party.[129] An equal number of states require only that shareholders be able to hear one another.[130]

---

[122] *See* § 9.9.

[123] Delaware also provides a sweeping definition of what constitutes "electronic transmission." *See* Del. Code Ann. tit. 8, § 232(c) (2001) (defining to cover any form of communication that does not directly involve the physical transmission of paper, so long as a record of the communication is such that it can be retained, retrieved, and reviewed by its recipient and as long as the recipient can reproduce the communication in paper form by automated process).

[124] Several states authorize shareholders to participate in meetings by whatever medium so long as each can hear and communicate with others. *See, e.g.,* Ariz. Rev. Stat. Ann. § 10–708 (2009); Minn. Stat. Ann. § 302A.436(2) (2009) (applies to close corporations); Tex. Bus. Corp. Act Ann. art. 9.10(c) (2009); Gavin A. Beske, Shareholder Meetings Online in Securities In The Electronic Age: A Practical Guide To The Law And Regulation 8–12 (3d ed. John F. Olson & Carmen J. Lawrence, eds. 2002).

[125] Del. Code Ann. tit. 8, § 211(a) (2009).

[126] *See, e.g.,* Ariz. Rev. Stat. Ann. § 10–708 (2009) ("sole" discretion of board), Cal. Corp. Code § 600(a) (2009) ("sole" discretion of board); Colo. Rev. Stat. Ann. § 7–107–108 (2009) (as authorized in articles of incorporation or bylaws) Del. Code Ann. tit. 8, § 211(a)(2) ("sole" discretion of the board), Fla. Stat. Ann. § 607.0701(4) (discretion of the board).

[127] *See, e.g.,* Companies From Fitbit to Ford Meet With Shareholders Virtually, Corporate Law and Accountability Law Report (Bloomberg BNA (July 10, 2018).

[128] *See, e.g.,* Emily Chasan, Investors Opposing Virtual Shareholder Meetings Notch Wins, https://www.bloomberg.com/news/articles/2018-01-09/investors-opposing-online-only-shareholder-meetings-notch-wins (Jan. 9, 2018).

[129] Del. Code Ann. tit. 8, § 211(b) (2009).

[130] *See, e.g.,* 805 ILCS § 5/7.05 (2009); Ind. Code Ann. § 23–1–29–1(d) (2009).

A common corporate provision permits notice of the forthcoming stockholders' meeting to be imparted electronically.[131] However, the statute may condition the effectiveness of such delivery upon the shareholder first consenting to delivery of notice in this form.[132] This would appear to permit email messages to stockholders, but it would be no more appropriate to treat merely placing an announcement on the company's website as notice, as it would have been in a paper-based society to impart notice by a classified advertisement.

A clear majority of the states permit proxies to be executed and transmitted electronically. Though there is broad authorization for the electronic execution and transmission of proxies, this is somewhat qualified by the need for determining the validity of the authorization.[133] There are also provisions for actions without a meeting, a parallel to the written consent procedures discussed earlier, to occur electronically.[134]

In 2001, the SEC approved changes in the NYSE listing requirements that now permit proxy materials to be delivered by electronic means. The SEC rules governing the delivery of proxy materials have gone electronic. Reporting companies now can provide a URL address where holders can access the documents and vote; nonetheless holders still retain the option of a paper copy of the proxy statement to holders who desire such a copy.[135]

§ 13.13 Conduct of Shareholders' Meetings

Section 7.08 of the Model Act envisions a strong, but fair, chair. The official conducting the meeting has a good deal of discretion in controlling the agenda and timing of the meeting. This discretion is necessarily subject to fiduciary obligations to act to further what is believed to be the best interests of the corporation.[136]

The meetings' decorum and over-all order can be assured as well by attention to the rules of parliamentary procedure, although those not versed in the technical niceties of the rules may well prefer the informality of a fair-minded chair.[137]

A leading decision of the New York Court of Appeals[138] illustrates how shareholders, by making their wishes known and commencing removal proceedings against some of the directors, can bring pressure to bear on the directors to change their decisions. The corporation's charter provided for a board of eleven directors. Class A shareholders elected nine of the directors and the common shareholders elected two. The Class A

---

[131] *See, e.g.,* Conn. Gen. Stat. Ann. § 33–603(a) (2009) ("Notice by electronic transmission is written notice"); Fla. Stat. Ann. § 607.0141 (2009) ("notice may be communicated . . . by . . . other electronic means").

[132] *See* Del. Code Ann. tit. 8, § 232 (2009).

[133] *See, e.g.,* Mich. Comp. Laws Ann. § 450.1421 (2009); Nev. Rev. Stat. Ann. § 78.355(2)(b) (2009); N.Y. Bus. Corp. Law § 609 (2009); N.C. Gen. Stat. Ann. § 55–7–22(b) (2009).

[134] *See* Del. Code Ann. tit. 8, § 228(d) (2009) (authorizing electronically executed written consents).

[135] Rule 14a–16, 17 C.F.R. § 240.14a–16, adopted in SEC Securities Exchange Act Rel. No. 34–56135 (July 26, 2007).

[136] *Compare* Merceier v. Inter-Tel (Delaware), Inc., 929 A.2d 786 (Del. Ch. 2007)(upholding board's delay I shareholder on a merger, thereby avoiding certain shareholder rejection) *with* Portnoy v. Cyro-Cell Int'l, Inc., 940 A.2d 43 (Del.Ch. 2008) (filibustering conduct by CEO in delay of meeting to delay vote so as to swing votes in favor of the CEO deemed a breach of fiduciary duty).

[137] *See* A.B.A. Corporate Governance Committee, Handbook for the Conduct of Meetings (2001) (calling for parliamentary procedures to be replaced by a strong concentration of authority in a chair who must operate pursuant a fairness standard).

[138] Auer v. Dressel, 118 N.E.2d 590 (N.Y. 1954), noted in Joe G. Davis, Note, Corporations—Stockholders' Right to Remove Directors, 7 Baylor L. Rev. 313 (1955).

holders instituted a mandamus proceeding to compel the corporation's president to call a meeting of Class A holders, as a bylaw required him to do whenever a specified percentage of the shareholders so requested. Among the purposes advanced in the request were: (1) to vote on a resolution endorsing the administration of a former president, who had been removed by the directors, and to demand that the former president be reinstated; (2) to hear charges against four of the directors, vote on their removal, and select their successors; and (3) to vote on a proposal to amend the charter or bylaws to provide that vacancies on the board arising from the removal of a director or resignation of a director against whom charges were pending would be filled by the class of shareholders that the removed or resigned director had represented. The president opposed calling the meeting on the ground that no proper purpose had been stated. The court, however, held that all of the purposes were proper and affirmed the order compelling the president to call the meeting. While the shareholders could not directly reinstate the former president, the court noted that they were privileged to express themselves and thereby bring shareholder sentiments forcefully to the attention of the directors, who would be standing for election at the next annual shareholders meeting. The court went on to say that shareholders who elect directors have the inherent power to remove them for cause.[139]

In an interesting Delaware case,[140] two factions of shareholders, one led by Tomlinson and the other by Vogel, the corporation's president, were fighting for control of the corporation. As a result of a compromise agreement, each faction designated six directors of the thirteen-person board, and the two factions jointly appointed a thirteenth or neutral director. Friction continued, however, and the neutral director, two Vogel directors, and one Tomlinson director resigned, leaving only five Tomlinson directors and four Vogel directors on the board. At a special directors' meeting, which only the five Tomlinson directors attended, the Tomlinson directors attempted to elect two new directors and thereby gain control of the board. The court, however, invalidated the purported election, holding the meeting invalid for want of a quorum.[141] In the meantime, Vogel, acting in his capacity as president, had called a shareholders meeting for the following purposes: (1) to fill director vacancies; (2) to amend the bylaws to increase the number on the board from 13 to 19 and the quorum from seven to ten; (3) to remove two of the Tomlinson directors; and (4) to fill the newly created positions and the vacancies that would result from the removal of the two Tomlinson directors.

The Chancellor refused to enjoin the meeting, holding that the bylaws gave the president power to call a shareholder meeting even though a majority of the incumbent directors opposed the meeting;[142] that the bylaws so interpreted did not impinge on the statute giving management powers to the board of directors as long as only matters appropriate for shareholder action were considered at the meeting; that the president, without board approval, could propose a bylaw amendment to enlarge the board; that the shareholders have the power to remove directors for cause even though the

---

[139] The fact that the corporation's certificate of incorporation empowered the board to remove a director for cause does not itself deprive the stockholders of their power to remove directors. 118 N.E.2d at 592–593. The court also held that Class A shareholders could amend the bylaws to empower Class A shareholders to elect successors for Class A directors so removed.

[140] Campbell v. Loew's, Inc., 134 A.2d 852 (Del. Ch. 1957).

[141] *See* Tomlinson v. Loew's, Inc., 134 A.2d 518 (Del. Ch.), *aff'd,* 135 A.2d 136 (Del. 1957).

[142] *See also* Republic Corp. v. Carter, 253 N.Y.S.2d 280 (App. Div. 1964), *aff'd,* 204 N.E.2d 206 (N.Y. 1964).

corporation has cumulative voting in director elections; that under the bylaws the shareholders had the power to fill "vacancies" on the board; and that shareholders have the inherent right between their annual meetings to fill newly created directorships.[143]

In many states, the provision of the corporation statute that details the procedure for amending the charter indicates that before shareholders can vote on an amendment, the directors must adopt a resolution setting forth the proposed amendment and directing that it be submitted to a vote at a meeting of the shareholders.[144] No provision is made in these states for a shareholder-initiated amendment of the charter. In a distinct minority of states, the statutory procedure for amending the charter seems to provide leeway for shareholder amendment without director approval,[145] and in a few instances shareholders appear to have successfully utilized a charter amendment to increase the number of directors over the opposition of a majority of the board.[146]

§ 13.14 Shares Entitled to Vote

The general rule is that all legal owners of voting shares in a stock corporation and all members of a non-stock corporation have a right to be present and vote at all corporate meetings.[147]

In the interest of certainty as to voting rights and of the right and duty as to notice of meetings, corporations are universally permitted by statute and charter provisions to look to the corporate records of registered shareholders to determine who is a shareholder entitled to vote, to notice of meetings, to dividends, and to other rights of shareholders.[148] The practice of closing the transfer books for a period of 40 days, more or less, before a meeting is frequently authorized in order to give ample time to make up voting lists of shareholders. In recent years, however, instead of this crude expedient of closing the books against recording transfers, statutes and bylaws have authorized the alternative method of fixing record dates for voting, dividends, and other purposes, so that stock transfers may be continually entered into the books. Those who are registered on the books on the record date remain the shareholders of record for the given purpose, although they may cease to be owners after the record date and before the activity takes place.[149] The Former Model Act, which was typical of modern statutes, permitted the closing of the transfer books at the corporation's discretion for not less than 10 nor more than 50 days or the fixing of the record date by bylaw or directors' resolution to be not

---

[143] The chancellor's opinion covered many other matters, including procedures and rules governing the solicitation of proxies in a contest between factions of shareholders and in a proceeding to remove directors.

[144] *See, e.g.,* Del. Code Ann. tit. 8, § 242(b)(1) (2009) (specifying that every amendment "shall be made and effected" in the manner described); MBCA §§ 10.02, 10.03 (2016); former MBCA § 59 (1969).

[145] *See, e.g.,* Mass. Gen. Laws Ann. ch. 156, § 42 (2009) (amendment may be authorized by a vote of two-thirds of each class of outstanding stock entitled to vote, or by a larger vote as provided in the charter).

[146] *See* Republic Corp. v. Carter, 253 N.Y.S.2d 280 (App. Div. 1964), *aff'd,* 204 N.E.2d 206 (N.Y. 1964).

[147] In re Giant Portland Cement Co., 21 A.2d 697, 701 (Del. Ch. 1941).

[148] Bryan v. Western Pac. Ry., 35 A.2d 909 (Del. Ch. 1944).

[149] *See, e.g.,* Mariner LDC v. Stone Container Corp., 729 A.2d 267, 273 (Del. Ch. 1998) (preferred shares not entitled to vote on acquisition though the articles of incorporation were amended to accord preferred full voting rights prior to merger because the date of record was set before the amendment).

less than 10 nor more than 50 days before the meeting.[150] The Model Act extends the maximum to 70 days.[151]

The right to vote is an incident of stock ownership except insofar as the corporation needs protection by its records against incurring liability to adverse claimants.[152] In some states, the books are prima facie evidence of the right to vote.[153] Other statutes have provided that the transfer of stock is conclusive evidence of the right to vote as to inspectors of the election, but such statutes are not conclusive on the courts as to share ownership, and rival claimants may litigate their rights.[154] The unregistered or equitable owner of shares has the right to compel the holder of the naked legal title to give her a proxy to vote or to vote at her direction.[155]

Most statutes provide that a shareholder who has pledged shares has the right to vote until the shares have been transferred to the name of the pledgee.[156] The person whose name appears on the books of a corporation (or otherwise is designated as the absolute owner of stock) clearly has the right to vote those shares, even though he in fact may hold the shares as trustee. And even when shares are in the name of a person as a "dry" trustee, he or she is entitled to vote them unless the *cestui que* trust objects and takes steps to have them registered in her own name.[157] The Model Act provides that the trustee is entitled to vote as long as the shares are registered in her name.[158] An executor or administrator has the right to vote shares belonging to the estate even though they stand on the books of the corporation in the decedent's name.[159]

If shares are owned by two or more persons jointly, the right to vote is in them jointly, and they must agree in order to vote the shares.[160] This rule of joint action applies to stock held by several executors or trustees unless there is a provision for majority vote on disagreement.[161] Depending on the statutory authority, fractional shares of stock may or may not be used as the basis of voting, cumulatively or otherwise.[162]

§ 13.15   Power to Vote Treasury Shares and Shares Held by a Subsidiary

Shares of its own stock acquired by a corporation are no longer outstanding and are denominated "treasury shares" unless subject to cancellation.[163] Since shares are

---

[150]   Former Model Bus. Corp. Act § 30 (1969). *See* Del. Code Ann. tit. 8, § 213 (2009) (no more than 60 days in advance); 805 ILCS § 5/7.25 (2009) (no more than 60 days in advance); N.Y. Bus. Corp. Law § 604 (2009).

[151]   Model Bus. Corp. Act § 7.07 (2016).

[152]   In re Algonquin Elec. Co., 61 F.2d 779 (2d Cir. 1932).

[153]   Bernheim v. Louisville Property Co., 221 F. 273 (W.D. Ky. 1914) (Kentucky law).

[154]   Lawrence v. I. N. Parlier Estate Co., 100 P.2d 765 (1940).

[155]   Gim v. Jan Chin, Inc., 362 A.2d 143 (R.I. 1976).

[156]   *See* former Model Bus. Corp. Act § 33 (1969). *Cf.* Model Bus. Corp. Act §§ 7.21, 7.24 (2008).

[157]   Sutliff v. Aydelott, 27 N.E.2d 529 (Ill. 1940).

[158]   Model Bus. Corp. Act § 7.24(b)(1) (2016); former Model Bus. Corp. Act § 33 (1969).

[159]   Model Bus. Corp. Act § 7.24(b)(5) (2016).

[160]   Tornga v. Michigan Gas & Elec. Co., 144 N.W22d 640 (Mich. Ct. App. 1966).

[161]   People ex rel. Courtney v. Botts, 34 N.E.2d 403 (Ill. 1941).

[162]   Commonwealth ex rel. Cartwright v. Cartwright, 40 A.2d 30 (Pa. 1944) (decided under Pennsylvania statute: Pa. Stat. Ann. tit. 15, § 1608 (1967)).

[163]   Former Model Bus. Corp. Act § 2(h) (1969). Recent amendments to the Model Act abolish the concept of Treasury shares. *See* §§ 21.9 to 21.11. A corporation's acquisition of its own shares is discussed in Chapter 21.

contracts with the corporation, on surrender to the corporation they can have only a potential or fictitious existence and cannot have voting rights.[164] In virtually all states, shares acquired by the corporation that issued them cannot be voted even when they are held in the name of a trustee[165] or have been pledged by the corporation.[166] It does not violate this principle to permit the parent corporation's directors to constitute a majority of the subsidiary's board, even though this has the indirect effect of allowing individuals who are directors of the subsidiary to decide how to vote the shares issued by the subsidiary.[167] Moreover, the shares held by the issuer as trustee for another can be voted by the issuer in its capacity as trustee.[168]

Shares of a parent company's stock purchased by a wholly-owned subsidiary do not *ipso facto* become treasury shares,[169] but shares of a parent corporation held by its subsidiary should be treated as equivalent to treasury shares at least as far as voting rights are concerned.[170] Otherwise, such shares could be voted by the directors of the parent corporation to continue themselves in office almost as freely as treasury shares could be so voted. The Model Act and most state corporation statutes impose a voting disability on shares a subsidiary holds in its parent.[171]

§ 13.16 Cumulative Voting

Cumulative voting is the privilege of multiplying the number of shares held by the number of directors to be elected and casting the product for a single candidate or distributing the product among two or more candidates.[172] With cumulative voting, shareholders can distribute their votes among some of the vacancies to be filled instead of using "straight voting"—that is, casting votes according to the number of shares held for each vacancy. If five vacancies are to be filled, each share of stock may be voted five times for one individual to fill one position, instead of casting one vote per share for each of the five positions. In other words, a person or persons holding 100 shares may cast 500 votes in favor of one candidate or may distribute the votes in favor of one or more persons for the five vacancies.

---

[164] Atterbury v. Consolidated Coppermines Corp., 20 A.2d 743, 747 (Del. Ch. 1941).

[165] Tapper v. Boston Chamber of Commerce, 126 N.E. 464 (Mass. 1920). Indiana departs from the general rule and allows a corporation to vote its own shares if the corporation is the beneficial owner of the shares. *See* Corre Opportunities Fund, LP v. Emmis Communications Corp., 792 F.3d 737 (7th Cir. 2015) (shares held by corporation in escrow account were "outstanding" and thus under the Indiana statute could be voted by the issuing corporation). In his opinion Judge Easterbrook noted: "in Indiana, apparently alone among the states, a corporation can vote its own shares. Ind. Code § 23–1–22–2(6)." 792 F.3d at 739.

[166] Granite Brick Co. v. Titus, 226 F. 557 (4th Cir. 1915).

[167] State ex rel. Washington Ind., Inc. v. Shacklett, 512 S.W.2d 284 (Tenn. 1974).

[168] *See* Graves v. Security Trust Co., 369 S.W.2d 114 (Ky. 1963).

[169] Golden State Theatre & Realty Corp. v. C.I.R., 125 F.2d 641, 642–643 (9th Cir. 1942). *See* § 21.9.

[170] Speiser v. Baker, 525 A.2d 1001 (Del. Ch. 1987) (subsidiary barred from voting shares of its parent though parent owned less than majority of the subsidiary's shares).

[171] *See* Model Bus. Corp. Act § 7.21(b) (2016); Minn. Stat. Ann. § 302A.447(2) (2008).

[172] An excellent review of the historical decline in state statutes requiring cumulative voting appears in Jeffrey N. Gordon, Institutions as Relational Investors: A New Look at Cumulative Voting, 94 Colum. L. Rev. 124 (1994). Professor Gordon observes that the number of states mandating cumulative voting peaked in 1956 and declined initially because of the belief that they made proxy contests more likely and later, in the 1980s, because of the fear that cumulative voting would facilitate hostile takeovers. *Id.* 147–158. Professor Gordon's overall thesis is that cumulative voting can be an effective means for institutional investors to sustain durable relationships with their portfolio companies. For an excellent discussion of the value and use of cumulative voting today *see* Coyle, Altering Rules, Cumulative Voting, and Venture Capital, 2016 Utah L. Rev. 595 (2016).

The aim of cumulative voting is to allow a minority to secure representation on the board of directors.[173] Without cumulative voting, holders of a bare majority of the shares may elect the full board and thus control the corporation without any representatives of other interests being present at board meetings.

Under cumulative voting, unwary majority shareholders, if they spread their votes over too many offices, may find that a vigilant minority has deprived the majority of control. If there are 1,000 shares outstanding and ten directors to be elected, and one person holds 600 shares, he should be able to elect the majority of the directors. If, however, he casts 600 votes straight for each one of ten candidates, and if the 400 minority shareholders cumulate their 4,000 votes on six candidates, the minority will elect six directors and the majority will elect only four.[174] To be safe under a cumulative system, where there is a substantial block of minority shares, majority shareholders must often abandon the attempt to elect a complete board and must cumulate their votes on such a portion of the members of the board as the number of their shares bears to the total number of shares that will be voted at the election. Thus each group, majority and minority, should ascertain the portion that the number of shares it holds bears to the number of shares it expects to be voted at the election, and then vote its shares cumulatively for that portion of the number of directors to be elected.[175] If after casting his vote a shareholder sees he has made a mistake, he may recall his ballot and change his vote before the presiding officer finally announces the result of the voting.[176]

For cumulative voting to work, all the directors to be elected in a given year must be voted for at one time; each director position cannot be voted on separately.[177] The more directors there are to be elected, the smaller the minority needed to secure a representative. Where the directors are classified, with only one-half or one-third to be elected annually, the benefits to the minority of cumulative voting are greatly diminished.[178] For example, if there are five directors to be chosen and one-fifth of the shares are voted for one nominee, that nominee is practically assured of getting a place on the board, while if only three directors are to be chosen, one-third of the shares would be required for the same assurance.

Constitutional or statutory provisions in some states establish mandatory cumulative voting for all corporations[179]—that is, the privilege of cumulating their votes

---

[173] Maddock v. Vorclone Corp., 147 A. 255 (Del. Ch. 1929).

[174] Dulin v. Pacific Wood & Coal Co., 35 P. 1045 (Cal.), *aff'd per curiam,* 37 P. 207 (Cal. 1894).

[175] The following algebraic formula is sometimes used to determine how many votes of those present is sufficient under cumulative voting to elect a specified number of directors:

$$x = \frac{a \times b}{c+1} + 1$$

with a representing the number of directors it desires to elect, b the number of shares present and voting, c the total number of vacancies to be filled, and x the number of shares necessary to achieve the desired objective. For an example of what can happen when a majority shareholder fails to anticipate the effects of cumulative voting, *see* Stancil v. Bruce Stancil Refrigeration, Inc., 344 S.E.2d 789 (N.C. Ct. App. 1986).

[176] Zierath Combination Drill Co. v. Croake, 131 P. 335 (Cal. Ct. App. 1913).

[177] Wright v. Central Cal. Colony Water Co., 8 P. 70 (Cal. 1885).

[178] Reducing the number of directors to be voted for reduces the chances of minority representation. Accordingly, some corporations, in an attempt to dilute minority representation, have staggered the terms of directors. *See, e.g.,* McDonough v. Copeland Refrigeration Corp., 277 F.Supp. 6 (E.D. Mich. 1967).

[179] Some states have repealed constitutional provisions for mandatory cumulative voting and replaced them with statutes permitting limitation or elimination of cumulative voting. *E.g.,* 805 ILCS § 5/7.40 (2009). *See also* Roanoke Agency, Inc. v. Edgar, 461 N.E.2d 1365 (Ill. 1984).

is granted to the shareholders irrespective of authorization in the charter or bylaws. In most jurisdictions, however, cumulative voting is only permissive and does not exist unless affirmatively authorized by provision in the charter or, sometimes, the bylaws.[180] Today, only six states require mandatory cumulative voting.[181] California also imposes its mandatory cumulative voting requirements on *pseudo foreign corporations* (corporations although incorporated elsewhere that have significant operations or other ties to California).[182] Of the six states mandating cumulative voting, California and Hawaii allow publicly held companies to opt out of cumulative voting.[183]

It has been suggested that the majority shareholders should not have the power to withdraw the privilege of cumulative voting by amendment of the charter or otherwise.[184] If the privilege of cumulative voting is to be granted at all for protection of the minority, it should be made mandatory, not merely permissive at the option of the incorporators or the majority group.

Some states have a constitutional or statutory provision making cumulative voting for directors mandatory and also a statute permitting the staggered election of directors—that is, the classification of directors and the election of each class in a different year—say, for a three-year term. The question of the validity of staggered elections where cumulative voting is mandatory has led to conflicting answers. A Pennsylvania case[185] held that a *constitutional* cumulative voting requirement did not prohibit the classification of directors and the staggering of elections, but in Illinois the staggered election was held to be unconstitutional.[186] Questions may also arise as to the validity of shareholder voting agreements in the face of mandatory cumulative voting.

§ 13.17 Plurality, Majority and Empty Voting; Advance Notice Bylaws

Plurality Voting. The prevailing default rule for the election of directors is that directors are elected under a plurality voting system whereby in director elections the nominees receiving the highest number of affirmative votes are elected, without regard to the number of votes withheld. While this sounds perfectly democratic, plurality voting is not the same as conditioning election on the will of a majority. With plurality voting, if there are five vacancies and five directors nominated, each director will be assured of election, even though none of the directors receive an absolute majority of the votes cast.[187] Thus, under plurality voting, the unopposed nominees who have been chosen by the board are guaranteed a seat as long as they receive at least one vote in their favor, regardless of how many shareholders withhold their votes. When there are fewer vacancies than nominees, the nominees elected are those receiving the most votes to the

---

[180] Maddock v. Vorclone Corp., 147 A. 255 (Del. Ch. 1929).

[181] Arizona, California, Hawaii, Nebraska, South Dakota, and West Virginia. Ariz. Rev. Stat. Ann. § 10–728(b) (2013); Cal. Corp. Code § 708(a); Haw. Rev. Stat. Ann. § 414–149; Neb. Rev. Stat. Ann. § 21–270; S.D. Codified Code § 47–1A–728; W. Va. Code Ann. § 31D–7–728.

[182] Cal. Corp. Code § 2115.

[183] Cal. Corp. Code § 305.5(a); Haw. Rev. Stat. Ann. § 414–149.

[184] *See* Maddock v. Vorclone Corp., 147 A. 255 (Del. Ch. 1929) (unfair exercise of right of amendment by majority but no fraud shown); Harlowe E. Bowes & Ledlie A. DeBow, Cumulative Voting at Elections of Directors of Corporations, 21 Minn. L. Rev. 351, 353 (1937).

[185] Janney v. Philadelphia Transp. Co., 128 A.2d 76 (Pa. 1956).

[186] Wolfson v. Avery, 126 N.E.2d 701 (Ill. 1955).

[187] *See generally*, Claudia H. Allen, *Majority Voting and Shareholder Democracy*, 3 Sec. Litig. Rep. 5 (NO. 6, 2006).

extent there are vacancies. As can be seen, with plurality voting a dominant consideration in the control of the corporation is the process whereby directors are nominated; whoever dominates that process ultimately controls the composition of the board of directors and, quite likely, the corporation itself. Due to shareholder dispersion and the obstacles to collective action, the nomination process historically has been outside the control of the stockholders as a group, except in the closely held corporation. This is because rarely will shareholders be willing to incur a burdensome, expensive, and uncertain process to nominate an alternate slate of directors. Hence, board elections are generally uncontested and the slate of nominees is not customarily formulated in consultation with the public stockholders. And, with the number of nominees being equal to the number of seats up for election, nomination and not voting is where the important event.

Majority Vote Provisions. Activist stockholders in 2004 pushed majority voting via bylaw proposals to replace the minimalist plurality vote requirement with a majority vote requirement.[188] Today, majority voting, in its various forms, is prevalent among the S & P 500 and the trend is trickling down to mid- and small-cap companies.[189]

One form of majority voting is to provide, either by a bylaw or even board-established policy, that a director elected under a plurality standard who does not receive a majority of the votes to tender his resignation to the board, which will then decide whether or not to accept the resignation. A firmer embrace of majority voting are bylaw or charter provisions that change the legal standard for director elections from a plurality to a majority.[190]

One downside to majority voting is that it may result in a failed election, with one or more seats on the board going unfilled, if a candidate does not receive a majority of the votes. That is, when there is a contested election governed by a majority vote provision and the number of nominees exceed the number of board seats pursuant to a majority vote requirement, it is possible that none of the candidates will receive a majority vote. Most majority vote provisions condition the director's election upon receiving a majority of the votes *cast*, rather than a majority of the votes outstanding.[191] So formulated, non-voted shares do not count as part of the denominator in determining whether the director has received a majority vote. An additional protection arises in contested elections; most majority vote provisions contain an exception in contested

---

[188] Claudia H. Allen, *Majority Voting in Director Elections: The New Prevailing Standard,* 22 NO. 9 Corp. Couns. (2008) (In the first year, 12 stockholder proposals were filed asking boards to adopt majority voting for director elections).

[189] For more statistics, *see* ERNST & YOUNG CTR. FOR BD. MATTERS, CORPORATE GOVERNANCE BY THE NUMBERS (2019), https://assets.ey.com/content/dam/ey-sites/ey-com/en_us/topics/cbm/ey-cgbtn-monthly-june-2019.pdf [https://perma.cc/UAT5-HJ84] (statistics current as of June 2019).

[190] *But see* Badlands Trust Co. v. First Financial Fund, Inc., 224 F. Supp.2d 1033 (D. Md. 2002) (requiring seating of two insurgent director nominees who received a majority of the votes cast but not a majority of the vote of the outstanding shares as required by the fund's bylaws; the court held the bylaw invalid with the statute's default rule that a vote of the majority at a meeting is sufficient approval for any matter, unless otherwise provided in the company's articles of incorporation).

[191] Claudia H. Allen, *Majority Voting and Shareholder Democracy,* 3 Sec. Litig. Rep. 5 (NO. 6, 2006). Thus, under the majority cast standard, a candidate is deemed to be elected when the number of "For" votes exceeds the number of "Against" votes as abstaining votes do not count as being "Against." *But see* Badlands Trust Co. v. First Financial Fund, Inc., 224 F. Supp.2d 1033 (D. Md. 2002) (requiring seating of two insurgent director nominees who received a majority of the votes cast but not a majority of the vote of the outstanding shares as required by the fund's bylaws; the court held the bylaw invalid with the statute's default rule that a vote of the majority at a meeting is sufficient approval for any matter, unless otherwise provided in the company's articles of incorporation).

elections, since to do otherwise likely would mean no director is duly elected as none would receive a majority of the votes cast if there were multiple candidates for the same seat. In the event of a failed election, state statutes generally contain holdover provisions which permit incumbent directors to remain in place until a successor can be elected.[192]

Several states have responded to the majority vote movement by adopting legislation that makes it easier to implement majority voting. For example, in 2006 Delaware amended its statute to provide that, "[a] bylaw amendment adopted by stockholders which specifies the votes that shall be necessary for the election of directors shall not be further amended or repealed by the board of directors."[193]

Advance Notice Bylaws. Advance notice bylaws require a shareholder who intends to nominate directors or introduce other business at the shareholder meeting to submit notice in advance.[194] The courts of many jurisdictions enforce reasonable advance notice provisions.[195]

In recent years there has been an increase in proposals by shareholders who have hedged their interest in the company.[196] Investors can effectively buy votes by becoming shareholders on the record date so that they have voting rights, but hedging their position so that they have no corresponding economic interest in the shares. Indeed, derivatives and other capital market developments enable investors to decouple economic ownership from voting rights.[197] Because these shareholders have minimal to sometimes even no economic stake in the firm through share ownership, their interests can be seen as not aligned with those held by fully invested shareholders. Advance notice provisions can address this problem by requiring a shareholder making a proposal to disclose its investment strategy and whether it has entered into any hedging transactions. These provisions provide boards and shareholders with valuable information about whether a stockholder proponent's interest is in line with the interests of other shareholders.

Courts tend to construe narrowly the scope of advance notice bylaws since they do have the effect of constraining the voice of the firm's owners. An interesting illustration of such a narrowed construction is the Delaware Supreme Court's decision in *Hill Int'l,*

---

[192] *See, e.g.,* Model Bus. Corp. Act § 8.05(e) (2016); Del. Code Ann. tit. 8, § 141(b) (2009).

[193] 75 Del. Laws, c. 306, § 5 (2006) (codified at Del. Code Ann. tit. 8, § 216 (2009)).

[194] Md. Code Ann., Corps. & Ass'ns § 2–504(f) (2009).

[195] *See, e.g.,* IBS Fin. Corp. v. Seidman & Assocs., LLC, 136 F.3d 940, 944–45 (3d Cir. 1998); Accipiter Life Sciences Fund, L.P. v. Helfer, 905 A.2d 115, 125 (Del.Ch. 2006). *See,* Lawrence A. Hamermesh, Director Nominations, 39 Del. J. Corp. L. 117 (2014)(advance notice bylaws should be constrained by understanding they exist to promote the orderly electoral process).

[196] Marcel Kahan & Edward B. Rock, *The Hanging Chads of Corporate Voting,* U of Penn, Inst. for Law & Econ. Research Paper No. 07–18, *available at* http://ssrn.com/abstract=1007065.

[197] *See* Henry T. C. Hu & Bernard Black, The New Vote Buying: Empty Voting And Hidden (Morphable) Ownership, 79 So. Cal. L. Rev. 811 (2006).

There is a collateral but related problem of "over voting" where more votes are cast than there are underlying shares. This problem is particularly acute in the context of brokerage firms and institutions "lending" shares to a third person so that person can cover their short sales. A share that is sold short can actually have two beneficial owners: the owner of the shares whose shares are borrowed in order to make delivery to the purchaser of the shares and the purchaser of the shares. The shares that are borrowed for delivery are typically held in street name by the brokerage firm used by the short seller. When the borrowed shares come from a customer rather than from the brokerage firm's own inventory, *i.e.,* they are held in street name, as seen above the NYSE rules require the brokerage firm to vote the shares according to instructions from the customer. Thus, if the customer instructs the broker to vote the shares and the new purchaser of the shares to whom delivery has been made votes the same shares, there is over voting.

Inc. v. Opportunity Partners L.P.[198] Hill's bylaws required notice of any matter to be submitted by a shareholder 60 to 90 days in advance of the date fixed for the meeting. However, the provision provided that if the corporation gives notice less than 70 days before the meeting the shareholder, the shareholder must give notice not later than the tenth day of the corporation's announcement. Hill argued that the 60/90 day time periods were triggered by its announcement that the 2015 meeting would be "on or about June 10, 2015." However, when it later announced the meeting would be June 9, 2015, that announcement was within 70 days of the meeting date. The court held Opportunity's proposed resolutions were timely under the bylaw because the "on or about" was not sufficiently specific to constitute an announcements triggering the commencement of the 60/90 day window. Its proposal however was timely under the ten-day window that applied when the meeting date was announced within 70 days of the stockholders meeting. Of note is that the Supreme Court offered guidance to companies to avoid the advance notice bylaw being ineffective; the court suggested that companies could either peg the notice period to the anniversary date of the corporation's prior meeting or simply announcing the specific date of its annual meeting.

There is a good deal of evidence that the holding period of many institutional investors is measured in weeks, and not months. There also is a widely held view among managers that activist hedge funds are not just opportunists but have short-term horizons. Whether these fears are borne out by the facts for particular firms is of less importance than the reality that such fears are held by company managers. This in turn gives rise to concerns that actual or feared short-term horizons of owners will cause firm managers also to pursue only short-term rather than longterm strategies that would be better for the firm.[199]

Dual Class Voting

Some corporation use dual-class shares whereby the class of common shares issued insiders have super-voting rights whereas shares issued to the public carry one vote per share. It is not unusual for IPO firms to have such a dual class structure. Indeed, when Snap, Inc. (a/k/a Snap Chat) went public only non-voting common shares were available to the public; a handful of its managers held all the voting shares. Earlier, the SEC attempted to prohibit the exchanges from listing dual-class shares, but the court held the SEC lacked authority to enter this area.[200] Although the SEC was unsuccessful in the legal skirmish, it at least won a critical battle. As a result of its continuing pressure, the exchanges adopted voting rights policies that restrict dual-class and tenure voting structures unless they are in place when the company went public, such as what occurred with Snap, Inc.[201] Fear that supervoting shares in the hands of founders and managers insulates the firm from its common shareholders[202] has caused some to champion a

---

[198]   119 A.3d 30 (Del. July 2, 2015).

[199]   *See* Berger, Steven Davidoff Solomon & Aaron J. Benjamin, Tenure Voting and the U.S. Public Company, 72 Bus. Law. 295 (2017); Dallas & Barry, Long-Term Shareholders and Time-Phased Voting, 40 Del. J. Corp. L. 541 (2016) (a 1980 investment in 12 companies that maintained tenure voting through 2013 yielded return six time greater than the S&P 500).

[200]   Business Roundtable v. S.E.C., 905 F.2d 406 (D.C. Cir. 1990).

[201]   *See* NYSE Rule 313.00(A); Nasdaq Rule 5640.

[202]   Super voting shares, particularly those issued initially to the firm's founders, raise concerns whether, at least over time, the arrangement exacerbates agency costs by the twin effects of insider have voting power disproportionate to their equity in the firm and that the super voting power entrenches existing management. *See e.g.*, Ronald Masulis, Cong Wang & Fei Xie, Agency Problems at Dual-Class Companies, 64 J. Fin. 1697 (2009)(finding that the greater that the insider's percentage of total voting power exceeds equity ownership

requirement that these arrangements be "sunsetted" so that they are valid only for a relative short number of years.[203]

The leading case upholding disparate voting rights within the same class of shares and providing the framework for considering supervoting shares, is *Providence & Worcester Co. v. Baker*.[204] Provident & Worcester's certificate provided that each holder of common stock had one vote per share for his first 50 shares, but only one vote per 20 shares for all shares over 50. Thus, as equity ownership increased, voting rights diminished. The court upheld the restrictions under Del. § 212(a), which states that "[u]nless otherwise provided in the certificate of incorporation . . . each stockholder shall be entitled to 1 vote for each share of capital stock held by such stockholder."[205] The court concluded that "if the General Assembly intended to bar the type of restriction on stockholders' voting rights here under review, such prohibition would appear in § 212. . . . Under § 212(a), voting rights of stockholders may be varied from the 'one share-one vote' standard by the certificate of incorporation. . . . "[206]

Tenure or Time-Phased Voting

"Tenure voting" (sometimes referred to as "time-phased voting") refers to charter provisions that provide the number of votes per share increase with the length of time they have been owned. Delaware upheld a plan to establish tenure voting in *Williams v. Geier*[207] whereby the company's shareholders approved a recapitalization in which each share would initially have ten votes; however, upon a change in ownership, a share would revert to having one vote until it was held for three years (shares held in street name were presumed to have short-term owners and relegated to one vote per share).

Frequently, the holding period of many institutional investors is measured in weeks, and not months; this raises concern that institutions seek only short-term gains so that their short-termism inhibits company managers from pursuing long-terms strategies that are better for the firm.[208] Tenure voting can thus be seen as addressing short-termism. On the other hand, super-voting shares, particularly those issued initially to the firm's founders, raise concerns whether, at least over time, the arrangement exacerbates agency costs by the twin effects of insider voting power being disproportionate to their equity in the firm and that the super voting power entrenching existing management has led to calls that the exchanges require listed companies to "sunset" such differential voting right provisions.[209]

---

the greater the evidence of high compensation, value destroying acquisitions, and lower returns on capital investment decisions). Lucian A. Bebchuk & Kobi Kastiel, The Untenable Case for Perpetual Dual-Class Stock, 103 Va. L. Rev. 585, 590 (2017)("as time passes, the potential costs of a dual-class structure tend to increase while the potential benefits tend to erode" so that debate should focus on barring such voting structures or mandating they end after a fixed period of time).

[203] *But see* Jill Fisch & Steven Davidoff Solomon, The Problem of Sunsets, 99 Bos. U. L. Rev. 1071 (2019).

[204] Providence & Worcester Co. v. Baker, 378 A.2d 121 (Del.1977).

[205] *Id.*

[206] *Id. See also* Lacos Land Co. v. Arden Group, Inc., 517 A.2d 271 (Del.Ch.1986).

[207] Williams v. Geier, 671 A.2d 1368 (Del. 1996).

[208] *See* David J. Berger, Steven Davidoff Solomon & Aaron J. Benjamin, Tenure Voting and the U.S. Public Company, 72 Bus. Law. 295 (2017); Lynne L. Dallas & Jordan M. Barry, Long-Term Shareholders and Time-Phased Voting, 40 Del. J. Corp. L. 541 (2016) (a 1980 investment in 12 companies that maintained tenure voting through 2013 yielded a return six time greater than the S&P 500).

[209] *See e.g.,* Ronald Masulis, Cong Wang & Fei Xie, Agency Problems at Dual-Class Companies, 64 J. Fin. 1697 (2009) (finding that the greater that the insider's percentage of total voting power exceeds equity ownership the greater the evidence of high compensation, value-destroying acquisitions, and lower returns on

Very large firms must consider one potential consequence of super-voting shares, possible exclusion from leading stock indices. In 2017 many of the world's largest stock indexes, such as those maintained by S&P (*e.g.*, S&P 500), exclude from their index companies with dual-class shares. This can impact the demand for the shares; for example, about $7 trillion of managed securities are benchmarked to the S&P Index. These changes were introduced in 2017. As a result, certain well-known companies that were already public, such as Alphabet, with dual-class structures were grandfathered into the index.

§ 13.18   Interference with the Stockholders' Franchise

Sometimes, when their control is threatened by an outsider, directors manipulate the timing of a stockholders' meeting to gain a strategic advantage. For example, in a leading Delaware case, *Schnell v. Chris-Craft Industries, Inc.*,[210] the directors, who were engaged in a proxy contest, advanced the date of the stockholders' meeting from the date initially established for the meeting. The directors acted in response to the on-going proxy campaign by an insurgent group and the effect of advancing the date was to reduce considerably the time the insurgents would have to persuade other stockholders to grant their proxies to the insurgents and not management. The court enjoined the convening of the meeting on the ground that the directors acted solely to obstruct the legitimate efforts of dissident shareholders to oust the board.[211] It was not until later, in *Blasius Industries v. Atlas Corp.*,[212] that the approach taken in *Schnell* became fully articulated such that it is now an important principle of corporate law. At a time that Blasius Industries was soliciting written consents to expand Atlas's board and fill the newly created seats with nominees who would support a recapitalization plan, Atlas's board quickly met and added three additional board members. The effect of this was to prevent Blasius's on-going efforts to result in it obtaining a majority of the board seats. Chancellor Allen concluded that the board's actions were taken in good faith and were undertaken in the reasonable belief that the recapitalization plan would not be in the best interests of Atlas or its stockholders. However, he reasoned that good faith alone does not justify the board intentionally interfering with the exercise of the stockholders' franchise. By placing the matter within principal-agent context, where the agent is deemed to act inequitably when taking steps to frustrate the principal's control of the agent, *Blasius* thus imposed upon management the burden of proving a "compelling justification" for acts taken to thwart the exercise of stockholder franchise. *Blasius* is about the validity of directorial power and not an abstract affirmation of shareholder voting rights.

Later Delaware decisions emphasize that in *Schnell* the directors altered the date of a stockholders' meeting that had already been scheduled and that in *Blasius* the procurement of written consents had commenced were pivotal considerations for determining whether directors' actions are judged by the "compelling justification"

---

capital-investment decisions). Lucian A. Bebchuk & Kobi Kastiel, The Untenable Case for Perpetual Dual-Class Stock, 103 Va. L. Rev. 585, 590 (2017)("as time passes, the potential costs of a dual-class structure tend to increase while the potential benefits tend to erode" so that debate should focus on barring such voting structures or mandating that they end after a fixed period of time).

[210]   Schnell v. Chris-Craft Industries, Inc., 285 A.2d 437 (Del. 1971).

[211]   Schnell v. Chris-Craft Industries, Inc., 285 A.2d 437 (Del. 1971).

[212]   Blasius Industries, Inc. v. Atlas Corp., 564 A.2d 651 (Del. Ch. 1988) (Chancellor Wm. Allen).

standard:[213] whether the directors are obstructing the *on-going* exercise of the shareholder franchise.[214] This doctrine is not limited to when there is an on-going contest for control.[215] That is, directors and officers bear a substantial burden of justifying conduct that impedes the *existing* efforts and activities of the shareholders to participate in the corporation's governance.[216] Where the directors' and officers' actions are clearly defensive, but do not interfere with any on-going exercise of the stockholder franchise, their acts are judged by the standard customarily applied to defensive maneuvers.[217] Thus, *Schnell* and *Blasius* do not deprive management of the ability to act strategically, even in the face of on-going efforts to unseat them.[218] The distinction made in the cases serves the justifiable purpose of subjecting to extremely rigorous review those board actions that are taken in order to thwart the efforts of aroused shareholders. We might well question why *Schnell* and *Blasius* should be limited to thwarting the stockholders when engaged in the exercise of their governance rights. Indeed, some flexibility in the doctrine's application appears from time to time. For example, management may well take such steps as calling the meeting where an item known to be controversial will be discussed and purposefully give such short notice as to effectively foreclose any possible opposition from mounting a proxy contest. In this situation, and it would seem others, the fundamental principle should be not whether the opposition is currently taking steps to exercise their shareholder franchise, but whether management has taken steps that prevent such steps from even being commenced. Such an approach does get into difficult factual and problematic factual inquiries. For this reason, having a bright-line test of whether the insurgents are then engaged in steps to oppose management or its position is useful. But it seems that exceptions to this standard can be made where on its face the steps taken by management clearly thwart any possibility of opposition exercising their shareholder franchise.[219]

To trigger *Blasius'* "compelling justification" standard the challenged board action must be taken for the sole or primary purpose of interfering with or impeding exercise

---

[213] *See also, e.g.*, IBS Fin. Corp. v. Seidman & Associates, LLC, 136 F.3d 940 (3d Cir. 1998) (*Blasius* standard is not limited to cases involving a battle for corporate control; directors' reduction of size of board, in advance of annual meeting, was allegedly designed to disenfranchise certain shareholders and thus was not valid without showing a compelling justification).

[214] Stroud v. Grace, 606 A.2d 75 (Del. 1992); Stahl v. Apple Bancorp., 579 A.2d 1115 (Del. Ch. 1990) (*Blasius* inapplicable where meeting date had not previously been set).

[215] *See, e.g.*, IBS Financial Corp. v. Seidman and Assoc., LLC, 136 F.3d 940 (3d Cir. 1998); State of Wisconsin Inv. Bd. v. Peerless Systems Corp., 2000 WL 1805376 (Del. Ch. 2000) (applied when issue was modification to stock option plan and management adjourned meeting so as to secure necessary votes to approve plan).

[216] *See, e.g.*, MM Companies, Inc. v. Liquid Audio, Inc., 813 A.2d 1118 (Del. 2003) (*Blasius* applied to expanding board upon learning that shareholder would nominate two of its own candidates-who were indeed elected—for election as court viewed this as attempt to dilute the influence of the insurgent's nominees if elected); Johnston v. Pedersen, 28 A.3d 1079 (Del. Ch. 2011)(issuance of preferred shares with rights to a class vote on major transaction triggered *Blasius* as issuance occurred after insurgents had obtained written consents for removal of directors); Mercier v. Inter-Tel (Delaware), Inc., 929 A.2d 786 (Del. Ch. 2007)(expressing uncertainty whether *Blasius* is triggered by directors' decision to postpone scheduled shareholder vote where transaction supported by the directors would most certainly be defeated, but finding they did satisfy the compelling justification standard were it to be applied). *See* Jacob A. Kling, Note, Disenfranchising Shareholders: The Future of *Blasius* After *Mercier v. Inter-Tel*, 119 Yale L. J. 2040 (2010).

[217] *See, e.g.*, Aquila, Inc. v. Quanta Services, Inc., 805 A.2d 196 (Del.Ch. 2002).

[218] *See, e.g.*, Glazer v. Zapata Corp., 658 A.2d 176 (Del. 1993) (in face of takeover issuing shares to supporter of management).

[219] *See, e.g.*, Linton v. Everett, 1997 WL 441189 (Del. Ch. 1997) (after failing to convene stockholders' meeting for three years, called meeting with only 30 days' notice which, in granting injunction, court reasoned effectively prevented opposition slate being put forth).

of the shareholder franchise.[220] Cases subsequent to *Blasius* unfortunately have cabined its scope to the voting for directors and matters related to the voting for directors.[221] Thus, the doctrine applies where the board's action impeded the shareholders' ability to elect successor directors.[222] It does not apply where a special committee postpones the vote on a merger in the face of almost certain defeat of that proposal at the upcoming meeting.[223] *Blasius* is not triggered by an impediment that is merely incidental to the objective sought by the board's action.[224] The interference must be on a scale that interferes or impedes the "effective exercise" of the franchise.[225] This is sometimes referred to as precluding the exercise of the shareholder franchise.[226] Causality appears to be an implicit consideration in the courts' application of *Blasius*. For example, the Delaware Supreme Court emphasize that the challenged board action was supported by a group that controlled a majority of the votes.[227] In contrast, *State of Wisconsin Inv. Bd. v. Peerless Systems Corp.*[228] applied *Blasius* where chairman adjourned a meeting at which a controversial proposal was being voted and upon the meeting being reconvened thirty days later the proposal passed by a slim margin. The court emphasized that the vote appeared to be running against the proposal prior to the meeting being adjourned.

Moreover, the shareholders must be in the process of exercising their rights as *Blasius* refers to the *ongoing* exercise of rights. For example, in *Openwave Systems Inc. v. Harbinger Capital Partners Master Fund I, Ltd.*[229] *Blasius* did not apply where board acted to reduce number of board seats after hedge fund filed its Schedule 13G but two months before hedge fund had launched a proxy contest. However the court had observed

---

[220] *See, e.g.,* Williams v. Geier, 671 A.2d 1368, 1376 (Del. 1996). It is not sufficient to show that the interference or impediment *could* be the primary purpose; the mere potential existence of a different purpose is sufficient to remove *Blasius'* application. Kallick v. Sandridge Energy, Inc., 68 A.3d 242, 258 (Del. Ch. 2013)(proxy put provision "*might* have a legitimate purpose of protecting creditors who in fact had insisted" on the provision so the action was deemed within *Blasius*).

[221] *See, e.g.,* Williams v. Geier, 671 A.2d 1368, 1376 (Del. 1996).

[222] MM Companies, Inc. v. Liquid Audio, Inc., 813 A.2d 1118, 1131 (Del. 2003).

[223] Mercier v. Inter-Tel (Delaware), Inc., 929 A.2d 786, 809 (Del. Ch. 2007). *See also* City of Westland Police & Fire Ret. Sys. v. Axcelis Technologies, Inc., 1 A.3d 281,285–89 (Del. 2010) (*Blasius* does not apply to directors' decision not to accept resignation when tendered by director failing to meet "plurality plus" governance standard).

[224] *See, e.g.,* Yucaipa American Alliance Fund II, L.P. v. Riggio, 1 A.3d 310, 330–31 (Del. Ch. 2010) (rights plan that prevented single holder from accumulating more than twenty percent had only an incidental effect on shareholder's right so that *Blasius* did not apply).

[225] Stahl v. Apple Bancorp, 579 A.2d 1115, 1123 (Del. Ch. 1990)(no meeting date had been set so that board's action in setting date beyond traditional date was not deemed to impair or impede the effective exercise of the franchise). More broadly, *Blasius* had not been successfully applied to delays or rescheduling of shareholder meetings. *See* In re MONY Group, Inc. Shareholder Litig., 853 A.2d 661, 676 (Del. Ch. 2004) (setting new meeting and record dates for merger vote that was earlier scheduled did not impede exercise of shareholder rights); H.F. Ahmanson & Co. v. Great Western Financial Corp., 1997 WL 30524 at *16 (Del. Ch. June 3, 1997) (seven-week delay in annual meeting did not frustrate the effective exercise of shareholder franchise). However, where the action prevents voting, the issue transcends cancelling a meeting and *Blasius* is more likely to apply. *See* Perlegos v. Atmel Corp., 2007 WL 475453 (Del. Ch. 2007)(special meeting cancelled thus impeding right of shareholders to vote on replacing directors).

[226] *See* Third Point LLC v. Ruprecht, 2014 WL 1922029 (Del. Ch. Mar. 2, 2014)(10 percent trigger in rights plan did not render successful proxy contest "realistically unattainable").

Hills Stores Co. v. Bozic, 769 A.2d 88, 103 (Del. Ch. 2000); Shamrock Holdings, Inc. v. Polaroid Corp., 559 A.2d 278, 285–86 (Del. Ch. 1989). Thus, action of board proposing an amendment that expanded board's authority was outside *Blasius* when shareholders had full and fair opportunity to vote on the amendment. Stroud v. Grace, 606 A.2d 75, 92 (Del. 1992).

[227] Stroud v. Grace, 606 A.2d 75, 92 (Del. 1992).

[228] 2000 WL 1805376 at * 12–15 (Del.Ch. 2000).

[229] 924 A.2d 228, 242–44 (Del. Ch. 2007).

that *Blasius* would apply if the hedge fund had it instead filed Schedule 13D and thereby indicated an intent to change control.[230]

§ 13.19   Vote-Buying and Coercion

Vote-buying[231] and coercion are two separate but related concepts. Each involves a shareholder voting for or against a matter for reasons other than its intrinsic merits. In vote-buying, a shareholder is enticed with extra benefits that the shareholder would not have received otherwise. Wrongful coercion is where shareholders are threatened through statements that the controlling stockholder, directors, or others will take action that may harm the stockholders' interest.

For the past two decades, vote-buying has been a matter litigated exclusively in Delaware and without success by the party invoking the argument as the foil to prevent the implementation of a transaction requiring stockholder approval. At one time the mere presence of any consideration bestowed for a stockholder's vote was invalid. The rationale for this result was twofold. First, the courts believed that each stockholder owed his fellow stockholders a fiduciary duty when voting to exercise his own independent judgment.[232] This view no longer prevails; only controlling stockholders are held to have a fiduciary duty to other stockholders.[233] Second, during corporate law's formative years analogies to other contexts were made, some analogies, of course, being stronger references than others. Thus, courts reasoned that just as vote-buying by politicians was harmful, so it should be for the purchase of the stockholder's vote.[234]

In 1982, Delaware put an end to vote-buying being per se void. *Schreiber v. Carney,*[235] arose in the context of a corporate restructuring of Texas International Airlines, which required approval of each class of its outstanding securities. One of the three outstanding classes of shares was convertible preferred shares and a majority of those shares were held by Jet Capital, who also held warrants covering 800,000 Texas International common shares. Jet Capital was not favorable to the restructuring because upon its occurrence it would incur a substantial tax liability with respect to the warrants. To secure its approval, Texas International agreed to lend $3.4 million to Jet Capital to enable it to exercise the warrants. In a derivative suit challenging this arrangement on the grounds of unlawful vote-buying, the Delaware Chancery Court voiced a more tolerant approach to vote-buying, reasoning that the despite its unsavory connotation, vote-buying "is simply a voting agreement supported by consideration personal to the stockholder."[236] Instead of being void per se, the court set forth the following two-part approach:

> [V]oting agreements in whatever form . . . should not be considered to be illegal
> *per se* unless the object or purpose is to defraud or in some way disenfranchise
> the other stockholders. That is not to say, however, that vote-buying for some

---

[230]   994 A.2d 228, 244 (Del. Ch. 2007).

[231]   On the subject of vote buying, *see* Douglas R. Cole, E-Proxies for Sale? Corporate Vote-Buying in the Internet Age, 76 Wash. L. Rev. 793 (2001).

[232]   *See, e.g.,* Cone's Ex'rs v. Russell, 21 A. 847, 849 (N.J. Ch. 1891).

[233]   *See, e.g.,* Priddy v. Edelman, 883 F.2d 438, 445 (6th Cir. 1989); Waters v. Double L, Inc., 769 P.2d 582, 583–84 (Idaho 1989).

[234]   For early cases expressing this view, *see* Thomas J. Andre, Jr., A Preliminary Inquiry into the Utility of Vote Buying in the Market for Corporate Control, 63 S. Cal. L. Rev. 533, 541 (1990).

[235]   Schreiber v. Carney, 447 A.2d 17 (Del. Ch. 1982).

[236]   Schreiber v. Carney, 447 A.2d 17, 23 (Del. Ch. 1982).

laudable purpose is automatically free from challenge. Because vote-buying is so easily susceptible of abuse it must be viewed as a voidable transaction subject to a test of intrinsic fairness.[237]

In *Schreiber,* the court found no harm to the other stockholders because the entire purpose of the restructuring was to benefit the other stockholders and the arrangement with Jet Capital was necessary to secure for them the advantages provided by the restructuring. Moreover, the court concluded the loan transaction was intrinsically fair because it was subsequently ratified by the stockholders. After *Schreiber* vote-buying arrangements have with great regularity been upheld.[238]

At one time, many state statutes proscribed vote-buying. Today, remnants of the former hostility to vote-buying can be found among a few corporate statutes that prohibit vote-buying.[239]

Coercion[240] claims have arisen in but a few cases.[241] The leading decision finding coercion is *Lacos Land Co. v. Arden Group, Inc.,*[242] where the CEO threatened to block any future beneficial corporate transactions unless the stockholders approved a corporate restructuring. The restructuring before the stockholders would effectively confer control of the company upon the CEO due to him receiving super voting shares as a result of the restructuring whereas the other stockholders would receive shares with diminished dividend rights and limited transferability. Because of the CEO's threat, the court found the shareholders were being coerced to approve the transactions.[243] It accordingly issued a preliminary injunction against the restructuring. However, in another case involving tenured voting, the court found stockholder approval was not obtained by coercion, despite the proxy statement's disclosure that even absent the sought after two-thirds stockholder approval the arrangement would be carried out with the effect that the shares would be delisted by the NYSE for failure to obtain the two-thirds approval required by the NYSE's listing requirements. The court, somewhat unrealistically, saw this as not a threat, but merely disclosing all the facts necessary for the stockholders to be informed.[244] Thus, what constitutes coercion is not only a factual

---

[237] Schreiber v. Carney, 447 A.2d 17, 25–26 (Del. Ch. 1982).

[238] *See, e.g.,* Portnoy v. Cryo-Cell Intern., Inc., 940 A.2d 43 (Del. Ch. 2008) (adding stockholder to management's slate of nominees in exchange for his support in a proxy fight did not constitute illegal vote buying).

[239] *See* N.Y. Bus. Corp. Law § 609(e) (2009) ("A shareholder shall not sell his vote or issue a proxy to vote to any person for a sum of money or anything of value."); Mont. Code Ann. § 35–1–525(9) (2009).

[240] Delaware provides the following definition of coercion:

Wrongful coercion may exist where the board or some other party takes actions which have the effect of causing the stockholders to vote in favor of the proposed transaction for some reason other than the merits of that transaction. . . . [T]he determination whether a particular stockholder vote has been robbed of its effectiveness by impermissible coercion depends on the facts of the case.

Williams v. Geier, 671 A.2d 1368, 1382–83 (Del. 1996).

[241] Coercion is a major consideration for evaluating defensive tactics and claims that shareholders were coerced arise frequently in the broader context of defensive measures. *See, e.g.,* Omnicare, Inc. v. NCS Healthcare, Inc., 818 A.2d 914 (Del. 2003) (merger became coercive when directors agreed to submit matter to stockholders for approval and the holders of a majority of the shares had contractually bound themselves to vote in favor of the merger); Orman v. Cullman, 2004 WL 2348395 (Del. Ch. 2004). The topic of defensive maneuvers and role coercion assumes in their evaluation is covered in §§ 23.6 & 23.7.

[242] Lacos Land Co. v. Arden Group, Inc., 517 A.2d 271 (Del. Ch. 1986).

[243] Lacos Land Co. v. Arden Group, Inc., 517 A.2d 271, 278–79 (Del. Ch. 1986).

[244] Williams v. Geier, 671 A.2d 1368, 1382–83 (Del. 1996). *See also* Brazen v. Bell Atlantic Corp., 695 A.2d 43 (Del. 1997) (presence of a $550 million penalty payable to its merger partner if the stockholders did not approve the merger not deemed coercive as it represented only 2% of firm's market capitalization).

inquiry, but one for which at least the Delaware Chancery Court appears to have a fairly high level of tolerance of the type of pressure minority stockholders can withstand and still act independently of that pressure.[245] The equitable doctrine against coercion protects preferred as well as common stockholders.[246] It remains to be seen whether other courts will be more willing to find coercion than has Delaware.

PART D.   STATE REGULATION OF THE PROXY MACHINERY

§ 13.20   The Nature of a Proxy

A "proxy" is the authority given by one shareholder to another to vote her shares at a shareholders' meeting.[247] The term is also used to refer to the instrument or paper that is evidence of the authority of the agent, as well as to the agent or proxy holder who is authorized to vote.[248] The proxy holder is an agent whose authority may be general or limited. Being an agent, the proxy holder is thus, in the eye of the law, a fiduciary.[249] As the Delaware court has said: "A person acting as proxy for another is but the latter's agent and owes to the latter the duty of acting in strict accord with those requirements of a fiduciary relationship which inhere in the conception of agency."[250]

It was accordingly held in that case that the proxy holder, as agent, could not bind his principal by an act done with an interest adverse to that of the shareholder, such as the proxy holder's ratification of an issue of stock to himself for an illegal consideration.[251]

At common law, all votes at shareholders' meetings had to be given in person; there was no right to vote by proxy.[252] This is still the rule for directors' meetings.[253] However, as a result of statutory provision, charter, or bylaw provision, the shareholders' privilege of voting by proxy is universal in stock corporations.[254] When the right is given by statute or charter, a shareholder cannot be deprived of it, nor can it be unreasonably restricted by a bylaw.[255]

---

[245] *See* Williams v. Geier, 671 A.2d 1368, 1383–84 (Del. 1996) (announcing that majority stockholder will approve recapitalization so that result is assured is not coercive); Gradient OC Master LTD v. NBC Universal, Inc., 930 A.2d 104 (Del. Ch. 2007) (not coercive to condition exchange of preferred shares on their waiving protective covenants and providing as well that junior preferred shares would be converted to debt if less than ninety percent of the preferred accepted the exchange offer).

[246] Eisenberg v. Chicago Milwaukee Corp., 537 A.2d 1051, 1061 (Del. Ch. 1987).

[247] *See* Reynolds Health Care Services, Inc. v. HMNH, Inc., 217 S.W.3d 797 (Ark. 2005) (distinguishing proxy from voting agreement by the latter commanding how the shares are to be voted whereas the former merely grants the power to vote the shares).

[248] *E.g.*, Eliason v. Englehart, 733 A.2d 944, 946 (Del. 1999).

[249] *See* Preston v. Allison, 650 A.2d 646 (Del. 1994) (trustee of ESOP breached fiduciary obligations to plan participants by voting shares counter to participants' wishes).

[250] Rice & Hutchins, Inc. v. Triplex Shoe Co., 147 A. 317, 322 (Del. Ch. 1929), *aff'd*, 152 A. 342 (Del. 1930).

[251] Rice & Hutchins, Inc. v. Triplex Shoe Co., 147 A. 317 (Del. Ch. 1929), *aff'd*, 152 A. 342 (Del. 1930).

[252] Taylor v. Griswold, 14 N.J.L. 222 (1834); Pohl v. Rhode Island Food Dealers Ass'n, 7 A.2d 267 (R.I. 1939).

[253] *See* §§ 9.7 to 9.10.

[254] *See* Model Bus. Corp. Act § 7.22(a) (2016). Former Model Bus. Corp. Act § 33 (1969).

[255] People's Home Sav. Bank v. Superior Court, 38 P. 452 (Cal. 1894). A bylaw providing that no proxy shall be voted by one not a shareholder is unreasonable and invalid.

A general unrestricted proxy or authorization to attend and vote at an annual meeting, "with all the powers the undersigned would possess if personally present," gives a general discretionary power of attorney to vote for directors and on all ordinary matters that may properly come before a regular meeting, even though specific mention of them is not made in the notice of the meeting.[256] Courts distinguish sharply between what business may be transacted at a regular meeting without notice of specified purposes and what may be transacted at a special meeting. A general proxy is no authority to vote for a fundamental change in the corporate charter or for dissolution or a transfer of all of the property to another corporation, or other unusual transactions, at least where the shareholder has not received proper statutory notice.[257]

A limited proxy may restrict the authority to vote to specified matters only and may direct the manner in which the vote shall be cast.[258] Shares represented by proxy are deemed "present" at a meeting, even though the proxy is granted for the express purpose to "withhold approval" of the slate of directors being put forth by management (when there is no opposing slate of nominees).[259] Failure of proxy holders to produce and file the written evidence of authority will not prevent the votes being counted to make up a quorum to organize a meeting.

There must be satisfactory proof that a proxy has been executed, which minimally requires written evidence of the proxy holder's authority,[260] but courts have recognized proxies executed by a rubber stamp facsimile of the owner's signature[261] as well as by only the owner's initials.[262] When there is a dispute regarding a proxy, in the interest of certainty and expediency courts regularly exclude extrinsic evidence so that only corrections that can be resolved on the face of the proxy will be addressed.[263] Keeping up with technological advances, proxies can be given by electronic transmission and also by telephone so long as certain procedures are followed.[264]

§ 13.21   Revocation, Duration, and Termination of Proxies

A proxy, like an agency in general, is revocable unless "coupled with an interest." Most state statutes provide a proxy's duration cannot extend beyond 11 months, unless the proxy provides a longer period.[265] One who has given a proxy or power of attorney to another to vote her shares may revoke the agency at any time if it is not coupled with an interest, even though it is expressly declared to be irrevocable or a consideration for the appointment is stated.[266] It was formerly against the general policy of the law governing

---

[256] McClean v. Bradley, 282 F. 1011 (N.D. Ohio 1922), *aff'd*, 299 F. 379 (6th Cir. 1924).

[257] Raible v. Puerto Rico Ind. Dev. Co., 392 F.2d 424 (1st Cir. 1968) (reducing par value with the effect of reducing foreclosure costs to pledge).

[258] Bache v. Central Leather Co., 81 A. 571 (N.J. Ch. 1911).

[259] *See* North Fork Bancorp., Inc. v. Toal, 825 A.2d 860 (Del. Ch. 2000).

[260] *See* Dynamics Corp. of Am. v. CTS Corp., 643 F.Supp. 215 (N.D. Ill. 1986) (recognizing strong presumption of proxy validity so that accepted telegraphed proxy even though signature was absent).

[261] Schott v. Climax Molybdenum Co., 154 A.2d 221 (Del. Ch. 1959).

[262] Atterbury v. Consolidated Coppermines Corp., 20 A.2d 743 (Del. Ch. 1941).

[263] *See, e.g.*, Mainiero v. Microbyx Corp., 699 A.2d 320 (Del.Ch. 1996).

[264] Model Bus. Corp. Act § 7.22(b) (2016).

[265] *See, e.g.*, 805 ILCS § 5/7.50 (2009); N.Y. Bus. Corp. Law § 609 (2009); Model Bus. Corp. Act § 7.22(c) (2016).

[266] In re Chilson, 168 A. 82 (Del. Ch. 1933).

corporate control that an irrevocable power of voting, or of directing the vote of stock, should be created even by contract of the shareholder.

Revocation of a proxy need not be made by formal notice in writing to the corporation unless so required by statute. Revocation may be expressed to the proxy holder or to the election judges or may be indicated by a subsequent proxy to another or by sale of the shares.[267] Appearing and asserting the right to vote at a meeting revokes a proxy previously given.[268] Thus a proxy may be revoked orally or by conduct. Just like any other agency, a proxy is terminated by the death of the principal or of the agent or by the loss of capacity by either party, unless this rule is changed by statute.[269]

Even though it is not so stated, a proxy is generally viewed as irrevocable when it is "coupled with an interest" in the shares.[270] What constitutes a sufficient interest in the shares to make a power to vote them irrevocable is an unsettled question.[271] According to the conventional view, the interest must be either (1) a charge, lien, or some property right in the shares themselves; or (2) a security interest given to protect the proxy holder for money advanced or obligations incurred.[272] Under this view, a "recognizable property or financial interest in the stock in respect of which the voting power is to be exercised," which renders the proxy irrevocable, is said to be distinguishable from "an interest in the corporation generally" and from "an interest in the bare voting power or the results to be accomplished by the use of it," neither of which has that effect.[273]

The more recent liberal view holds that the proxy is also irrevocable when the interest protected is in the corporation for which the shares are held as additional security.[274] It seems that modern courts usually find an interest where the proxy is given for the protection of a right of the proxy holder or a third person or to ensure the performance of a duty. Under either view, payment to the shares' owner as compensation for being allowed to vote the owner's shares violates the common law rule against vote-selling such that the arrangement confers no authority on the proxy holder.[275] More recently, the Delaware courts have shifted from viewing vote-buying as *per se* invalid, to being *voidable*, subject to a test for intrinsic fairness.[276] Thus, consideration paid by a corporation that was approved by its outside directors as being in the best interests of the corporation was not invalid.[277] An irrevocable proxy is not terminated by revocation or by death of the creator of the proxy or by his loss of capacity.

---

[267] Concord Fin. Group, Inc. v. Tri-State Motor Transit Co., 567 A.2d 1 (Del. Ch. 1989) (proxies having same date of execution, the proxy with the later postmark was counted).

[268] *See* State ex rel. Breger v. Rusche, 39 N.E.2d 433 (Ind. 1942).

[269] Restatement (Third) of Agency § 3.12 (2006); Restatement (Second) of Agency, §§ 120 to 123 (1988).

[270] Smith v. San Francisco & N.P. R.R., 47 P. 582 (Cal. 1897).

[271] Abercrombie v. Davies, 123 A.2d 893, 906–907 (Del. Ch. 1956), *rev'd on other grounds,* 130 A.2d 338 (Del. 1957).

[272] *See* Calumet Ind., Inc. v. MacClure, 464 F.Supp. 19 (N.D. Ill. 1978).

[273] *See* In re Chilson, 168 A. 82, 86 (Del. Ch. 1933). *Cf.* Smith v. Biggs Boiler Works Co., 82 A.2d 372 (Del. Ch. 1951).

[274] *See* Deibler v. Chas. H. Elliot Co., 81 A.2d 557 (Pa. 1951).

[275] *See* Chew v. Inverness Management Corp., 352 A.2d 426 (Del. Ch. 1976).

[276] *See generally* Robert C. Clark, Vote Buying and Corporate Law, 29 Case W. Res. L. Rev. 776 (1979); *supra* § 13.19.

[277] Schreiber v. Carney, 447 A.2d 17 (Del. Ch. 1982).

A number of states have either tried by statute to avoid the ambiguous term "coupled with an interest" by specifying the circumstances in which a proxy can be made irrevocable. The Model Business Corporation Act more comprehensively defines "coupled with an interest":

> An appointment of a proxy is revocable by the shareholder unless the appointment form conspicuously states that it is irrevocable and the appointment is coupled with an interest. Appointments coupled with an interest include the appointment of:
>
> (1)   a pledgee;
>
> (2)   a person who purchased or agreed to purchase the shares;
>
> (3)   a creditor of the corporation who extended it credit under terms requiring the appointment;
>
> (4)   an employee of the corporation whose employment contract requires the appointment; or
>
> (5)   a party to a voting agreement. . . .[278]

Management customarily solicits proxies seeking authority to vote not only on matters that management knows will arise at the meeting, but also discretionary authority to vote the shares on any other matter that may be proposed at the meeting. In the time between soliciting or even obtaining proxies and the meeting, management may become aware of a matter a stockholder intends to propose for stockholder action at the meeting. Under state law this does not by itself revoke the proxy obtained by management. However, the SEC's position, which applies to companies that are covered by the Securities Exchange Act's proxy rules, is that management cannot exercise its discretionary authority if after obtaining the proxy it learns that a matter will be proposed for stockholder action at the meeting and the proponent intends to solicit proxies in support of that proposal from the holders of at least a majority of the shares.[279]

§ 13.22   The Proxy Voting System

The presence in person or by proxy of holders of a majority of a corporation's shares is generally required to constitute a quorum.[280] It is accordingly of great importance that shareholders unable to attend in person appoint suitable agents to represent them so that elections can be held and other necessary business transacted. As a New Jersey court said of a large steel corporation, "[i]t would be stupid indeed to assume that the 80,000 stockholders may possibly attend the meeting in person."[281] It has similarly been observed: "[I]n the larger corporations the stockholders' meeting is now only a necessary formality; that stockholders' expression can only be had by the statutory device of proxy. As a result, within limitations, realistically the solicitation of proxies is today the stockholders' meeting."[282] In other words, the proxy system is usually a species of

---

[278]   Model Bus. Corp. Act § 7.22(d) (2016).

[279]   *See* Idaho Power Co., SEC No-Action Letter, Fed. Sec. L. Rep. (CCH) ¶ 77,224 (Mar. 13, 1996) (interpreting Rule 14a–4(c)(1)).

[280]   *See* § 13.15.

[281]   Berendt v. Bethlehem Steel Corp., 154 A. 321, 322 (N.J. Ch. 1931).

[282]   Sheldon E. Bernstein & Henry G. Fischer, The Regulation of the Solicitation of Proxies: Some Reflections on Corporate Democracy, 7 U. Chi. L. Rev. 226, 227 (1940).

absentee voting by mail for the slate of directors and the proposals suggested by the management.

Management has a great advantage in the solicitation of proxies because it is lawful for the directors to send out blank proxies printed at the expense of the company and to provide postage paid for by the company, at least if it is not purely a personal contest.[283] The retail investor of a relatively small number of shares has practically no alternative, other than not voting at all, to delegating his vote to a proxy committee of persons whom he does not know, over whom he has no control, and as to whose intended action he is very poorly informed, except as these matters are regulated by the federal rules on proxy solicitation. Institutional investors, who in the last many decades have grown immensely and now own well over half of all publicly traded equities, do not face this constraint; however they do face cost constraints as their overarching goal is garnering returns for their investors or beneficiaries. Thus, institutions frequently do not maintain staffs to closely review the proxies from their portfolio companies. Instead, most subscribe to an independent proxy advisory service and rely on the advisors recommendations.[284]

Although proxy contests are usually limited to closely held businesses, there have been a number of bitterly fought proxy fights in publicly held corporations, in large part due to Securities and Exchange Commission regulation of shareholder suffrage. Notwithstanding the resultant increased emphasis on fairness in shareholder suffrage, the success of groups opposing incumbent management and its policies unless within the context of a takeover attempt has not been great when measured in terms of victories at the ballot box.[285] The primary reasons for the continued success of incumbent management are its control of the proxy machinery and shareholder inertia in voting.

A central concern in proxy voting is that the proxy solicitation materials present a fair and full disclosure of all material information. This concern is addressed by both state[286] and federal law[287] prohibiting material misrepresentations.

The New York Stock Exchange has extensive rules regulating various governance-related activities of listed companies. NYSE Rule 452 restricts in certain areas the discretionary authority of brokers to vote shares they hold in street name. Broadly stated, even though the beneficial owner of the shares has not instructed the broker how to vote the shares, brokers lack discretion to vote the shares on non-routine items. Following a 2012 amendment, the following are matters on which the broker cannot vote:

De-staggering or de-classifying a company's board of directors

Effectuating majority voting in the election of directors

Eliminating supermajority voting requirements

---

[283] Rascovor v. American Linseed Co., 135 F. 341 (2d Cir. 1905) (newspaper advertisement of proposal for exchange of stock).

[284] *See,* Andrew F. Tuch, Why Do Proxy Advisors Wield So Much Influence? Insights from U.S.-U.K. Comparative Analysis, 9 Bos. U. L.Rev. 101 (2019).

[285] *See* Donald E. Schwartz, The Public-Interest Proxy Contest: Reflections on Campaign GM, 69 Mich. L. Rev. 419 (1971).

[286] *See, e.g.,* Arnold v. Society for Sav. Bancorp, 650 A.2d 1270 (Del. 1994); Appel v. Berkman, 180 A.3d 1055 (Del. 2018) (non-disclosures in Schedule 14d-9 disclosures rendered transaction subject to challenge under state law); Morrison v. Berry, 191 A.3d 268 (Del. 2018), as revised, (July 27, 2018) (a company's materially misleading Schedule 14d-9 filing with respect to a tender offer may form the basis of a state law claim that an ensuing shareholder vote was not made upon full disclosure and is therefore invalid).

[287] *See* Securities Exchange Act § 14(a), 15 U.S.C. § 78n(a) and §§ 13.24 *et seq. infra.*

Authorizing the use of written consents by stockholders

Providing rights to call special stockholders' meetings

Overriding certain types of anti-takeover provisions

§ 13.23 Proxy Contest Expenses

In addition to having control of the voting process, management's ability to use company funds during a proxy contest assures its success in most cases.[288] Through its board of directors a corporation may spend reasonable sums in a contested election where the expenditures further the intelligent exercise of judgment by the shareholders.[289] In a contest over policy, as distinguished from purely personal struggles for power, the board may authorize reasonable corporate expenditures to support policies that the directors believe in good faith to be in the corporation's best interest.[290] On the other hand, it has been held that shareholders may vote to reimburse successful insurgents for their expenses.[291] In *CA, Inc. v. AFSCME Employees Pension Plan,*[292] the Delaware Supreme Court held that a proposal to amend the bylaws to provide for reimbursement of an insurgent's proxy campaign expenses, was a proper subject for shareholder action. However, the precise proposal before the court was not a valid because it could cause the directors to provide reimbursement in violation of their fiduciary obligations.[293] It is likely that the proposal would have been appropriate had it included a so-called fiduciary out clause whereby reimbursement would not be required if doing so would have violated the directors' fiduciary obligation. Delaware and the Model Business Corporation Act have since amended its statute to expressly authorize bylaw provisions authorizing procedures to be followed to allow shareholder nominations of directors;[294] and both Delaware and the Model Act expressly authorize bylaws that will provide reimbursement by the corporation of proxy solicitation expenses incurred by a stockholder in connection with the election of directors, subject to such procedures and conditions as the bylaws may prescribe.[295]

At first blush it may seem unjustified to tilt the playing field so heavily in favor of the incumbents by permitting them to use corporate funds and other resources in the proxy contest while requiring the insurgents to finance their own efforts. But consider

---

[288] *See* Mark A. Stach, An Overview of Legal and Tactical Considerations in Proxy Contests: The Primary Means of Effecting Fundamental Corporate Change in the 1990's, 13 Geo. Mason U. L. Rev. 745 (1991).

[289] In practice this enables management to perpetuate itself and control the corporation.

[290] Levin v. Metro-Goldwyn-Mayer, Inc., 264 F.Supp. 797 (S.D.N.Y. 1967); Rosenfield v. Fairchild Eng. & Airplane Corp., 128 N.E.2d 291 (N.Y. 1955).

[291] Steinberg v. Adams, 90 F.Supp. 604 (S.D.N.Y. 1950).

[292] CA, Inc. v. AFSCME Employees Pension Plan, 953 A.2d 227 (Del. 2008).

[293] The court reasoned that the procedural posture of the case required it to consider whether there was any instance in which the proposal in practice would not be proper; such a case would occur if reimbursement was made to an individual who sought a directorship for purely personal reasons.

[294] *See* Del. Code Ann. tit. 8, § 112; MBCA § 2.06(c) (2009). *See generally,* Committee on Corporate Laws, ABA Section of Business Law, Changes in the Model Business Corporation Act-Proposed Shareholder Proxy Access Amendments to Chapters 2 and 10, 64 Bus. Law. 1157 (2009). The official comment provides that section (d) of the provision "allows directors to ensure that such bylaws adequately provide for a reasonable, practicable, and orderly process, but is not intended to allow the board of directors to frustrate the purpose of a shareholder-adopted proxy access or expense reimbursement provision". *Id.* at 1159.

[295] *See* Del. Code Ann. tit. 8, § 113; MBCA § 2.06(c) (2009).

the results if the rules were otherwise.[296] If incumbents had to defend their present control of the board with their own funds, such a defense likely would not be forthcoming. Individuals certainly would be less likely to serve as directors if they thought doing so would require substantial expenditures of their own funds to seek or retain the position. Also, the idea of being easily opposed in an election is not one warmly greeted by those likely to quest a directorship in a public corporation. Certainly any change in the existing rules on reimbursement of proxy context expenses would lead to more proxy contests, as insurgents would not have to worry about the incumbents "playing with other peoples money" as occurs presently. At the same time, there is a serious risk that insurgents who are willing to spend their own funds to gain control of the corporation can be expected to seek some financial benefits from the corporation if they successfully gain control of the board of directors. That is, changes in the existing rules regarding proxy contest expenses may lead to undesirable self-dealing transactions by incumbents and insurgents to recoup the cost of securing their positions. The present rules are far more transparent than what would otherwise occur. Finally, the present rules avoid problematic inquiries regarding when unsuccessful incumbents should be reimbursed.

PART E.   FEDERAL REGULATION OF PROXIES

§ 13.24   Section 14 of the Securities Exchange Act of 1934: An Overview

Nondisclosure of needed information and other abuses foisted on the corporate election system led to federal regulation of proxy solicitation.[297] Section 14(a) of the Securities Exchange Act of 1934[298] declares it unlawful to solicit any proxy or consent or authorization from the holder of any security subject to the act's registration and reporting provisions[299] in violation of such rules as may be prescribed by the Securities and Exchange Commission. Pursuant to this authority, the SEC has promulgated extensive requirements regarding the disclosures that must be made in connection with the solicitation of proxies.[300]

With rare exceptions the only way in which shareholders in a large corporation with shares widely diffused can participate in the election of directors and in voting on fundamental changes in the corporate structure is by the use of proxies. Thus, to participate effectively, shareholders must be informed by the management, or by others soliciting proxies, about the director candidates and measures for which their authorization is solicited. The general purpose of the federal proxy rules is to require that security holders be provided with sufficient information bearing upon and explanation of the matters on which the persons to whom they give proxies are

---

[296] *See* Lucian A. Bebchuck & Marcel M. Kahan, A Framework for Analyzing Legal Policy Towards Proxy Contests, 78 Cal. L. Rev. 1071 (1990).

[297] Thomas Lee Hazen, Treatise on the Law of Securities Regulation ch. 10 (7th ed. 2016).

[298] 15 U.S.C. § 78n(a) (2009).

[299] This includes any security traded on a national securities exchange as well as any company whose total assets exceed $10 and that has a class of equity securities with 2,000 shareholders of record but retains the former 500 record holder threshold with respect to investors who are not accredited investors. Section 12(g)(1)(A), 15 U.S.C. § 78*l*(g)(1)(A) as amended by the Jumpstart Our Business Startups Act (JOBS Act), H.R. 3606, 112 Cong. 2d sess. § 501 (2012). The record holder calculation excludes shareholders who receive shares as part of an employee compensation plan that is exempt from 1933 Act registration. Section 12(g) was also amended to exclude from the shareholder calculation holders of shares issued pursuant to an exempt crowdfunding offering. Rule 3a12–3, 17 C.F.R. § 240.3a12–3, exempts foreign issuers from the proxy rules.

[300] *See, e.g.,* Schedule 14A, 17 C.F.R. § 240.14a–101 (2009).

authorized to cast their votes, so that they may know what they are authorizing. Under the proxy rules, shareholders are also afforded an opportunity to limit the authorization and indicate disapproval as well as approval of management proposals—that is, to specify whether their proxies shall be voted for or against each proposal submitted. Rule 14a–4(c) authorizes the proxy to include discretion to vote on any matter the company's management did not have notice of at least 45 days before the meeting.[301]

Bundling. To avoid the problem of managers coupling unpopular proposals with so-called "sweeteners," the proxy rules now prohibit a group of related proposals to be bundled as a single resolution.[302] This change avoids the problem of stockholders having their natural choice distorted by an artful coupling of value-decreasing proposals with a change that shareholders desire.[303] *Greenlight Capital L.P. v. Apple, Inc.*[304], held that joinder of the following items in a single resolution violated the anti-bundling rule:

> To amend the Apple articles of incorporation to (1) eliminate certain language relating to the terms of office of directors so as to facilitate the adoption of majority voting for the election of directors; (2) eliminate the board of directors authority without shareholder approval to issue preferred stock having superior rights over common; (3) establish a minimum par value for Apple's common shares; and (4) eliminate certain obsolete provisions in Apple's articles related to preferred shares.

The district court observed there is scant authority what constitutes a "separate" item. Nonetheless, citing to the limited insight provided by the 1992 SEC release adopting the anti-bundling provision, the court concluded "the present bundling of items forces shareholders . . . to approve or disapprove a package of items and approve or disapprove matters they would not if presented separately." Moreover, even though the proposals in the whole can be seen as shareholder friendly, the court reasoned that the absence of coercion was not the only objective of the anti-bundling provision. The SEC also sought to allow shareholders to communicate their views to the board which bundling of such disconnected items would frustrate.

Format and Information Requirements. The fundamental requirement of the proxy rules is disclosure of accurate and adequate information by those who solicit a proxy, consent, or authorization. The rules and Schedule 14A must be consulted to determine what information is required for each different item requiring shareholder action, such as election of directors, a plan of remuneration of directors and officers, an amendment of the charter or bylaws, a proposal for merger, consolidation, or sale of assets, or modifications of the corporation's securities.[305] An area of concern is corporate governance in publicly held corporations; the Securities Exchange Commission has responded with detailed disclosure requirements concerning the activities of directors, including the composition and functioning of the various committees of the board as well

---

[301] Rule 14a–4(c), 17 C.F.R. § 240.14a–4(c).

[302] 17 C.F.R. § 240.14a–4 (2009). The standing of shareholders to privately enforce Rule 14a–4's proscription of the impermissible grouping of voting items was recognized in Koppel v. 4987 Corp., 167 F.3d 125 (2d Cir. 1999).

[303] *See* Lucian Bebchuk, Limiting Contractual Freedom in Corporate Law: The Desirable Constraint on Charter Amendments, 102 Harv. L. Rev. 1820, 1836–1830 (1989).

[304] 2013 WL 646547 (S.D.N.Y. 2013).

[305] The Commission specifies in great detail the types of information, both financial and otherwise, that must be disclosed. General Rules & Regulations, Securities Exchange Act of 1934, 17 C.F.R. §§ 240.14a–1 et seq. (2002).

as the directors' individual attendance records.[306] In addition to mandated information, the proxy rules have detailed requirements with respect to how information in the proxy is to be provided. Such format rules not only require the communication be identified boldly as a "proxy" but sets for the size of type to be used as well as providing a means for those voting to abstain or vote against a proposal, *i.e.*, not merely indicate favor.

If fraud or noncompliance with the rules occurs, that constitutes grounds for an injunction against using the proxies and holding the meeting until the proxies have been resolicited.[307] Nothing in section 14 makes action taken at any meeting invalid, even though the action is taken pursuant to proxies obtained in violation of the rules. The only express remedy the Securities and Exchange Commission has for violations of the proxy rules is to seek injunctive relief before the meeting or to give the matter to the Justice Department for criminal proceedings after the meeting.[308] However, as is the case with SEC Rule 10b–5,[309] the most powerful impact of section 14(a) and, in particular, Rule 14a–9, is the antifraud provision, since it provides an implied cause of action available to the corporation or an aggrieved shareholder.[310]

Filing with SEC. The formal proxy solicitation material to be used in a solicitation must be filed with the Commission for inspection at least ten days before the beginning of the solicitation. All other proxy material, such as letters, advertisements, and supplementary material, need not be filed in advance. The material filed is examined by the Commission. On request, informal suggestions may be made by the Commission in advance of the filing date. In many instances, corporations have been required to issue corrected proxies and statements, and meetings have had to be postponed. Full disclosure requirements, of course, have a discouraging effect on the presentation of unfair proposals to the shareholders. The provision of proxy materials to stockholders beginning in 2008 has gone electronic. Reporting companies now can provide a URL address where holders can access the documents and vote; nonetheless holders still retain the option of a paper copy of the proxy statement to holders who desire such a copy.[311]

Under the federal proxy rules, if a security holder wishes to solicit proxies himself, he may require that the management mail to those who are solicited by the management a form of proxy and other material furnished by the applicant/security holder, provided the applicant makes provision for expenses in connection with the mailing. Thus management is required to cooperate in mailing solicitation literature of dissident groups, and shareholders are given a medium of communication with fellow investors. Provision is also made in the proxy rules for a shareholder who desires to present proposals at the annual shareholders' meeting to have her proposal submitted and explained in a management proxy solicitation if she gives timely notice to management of her intention to present the proposal at the meeting.[312]

---

[306] A director's track record, including remuneration and potential conflicts of interest, is relevant to the shareholder's election decision. Berkman v. Rust Craft Greeting Cards, Inc., 454 F.Supp. 787, 789 (S.D.N.Y. 1978).

[307] 15 U.S.C. §§ 78n, 78u (2009).

[308] *See* Thomas L. Hazen, Administrative Enforcement: An Evaluation of the Securities Exchange Commission's Use of Injunctions and Other Enforcement Methods, 31 Hast. L.J. 427 (1979).

[309] 17 C.F.R. § 240.10b–5 (2009). *See* § 12.9.

[310] J. I. Case Co. v. Borak, 377 U.S. 426 (1964). *See infra* § 13.27.

[311] Rule 14a–16, 17 C.F.R. § 240.14a–16 (2009).

[312] 17 C.F.R. § 240.14a–8 (2009).

§ 13.25   Definition of "Solicitation" and "Proxy"

The vast majority of the Securities Exchange Act's disclosure provisions are directed toward requiring full information in the marketplace so that informed and intelligent investment decisions can be made. In contrast, in its concern for shareholder suffrage, section 14(a)'s proxy regulation approaches very closely the fine line separating proxy regulation from the chartering function of the state's general corporation laws.[313] The basic rationale for federal involvement in the internal affairs of large corporations through the Exchange Act's reporting and disclosure requirements is that informing the marketplace of significant corporate developments is necessary to investor confidence and protection. The SEC, although lacking authority to weigh in directly on corporate governance issues,[314] nevertheless does so discretely through its disclosure requirements.

Judicial Interpretation of SEC Definition. To begin with, the Commission has laid down a broad definition of "proxy solicitation."[315] "Solicitation" includes all communications directed to shareholders that are reasonably calculated to affect a voting decision. The regulation has been extended to cover many kinds of communications that are not garden variety vote solicitations. For example, in the course of a merger between two railroads, management's open letter to the Interstate Commerce Commission extolling the virtues of the proposed transaction and urging its administrative approval was held to be subject to the SEC's filing and disclosure requirements, because the shareholder vote had not yet been taken and the letter contained statements that were likely to influence a voting decision.[316]

The courts continue to adhere to the early standard that a communication that itself does not request the giving of any authorization is nevertheless a proxy solicitation when it is "part of a 'continuous plan' intended to end in solicitation and to prepare the way for success."[317] Thus a letter asking several other stockholders to join the request to access the company's list of stockholders was deemed a proxy solicitation because the letter's author intended to use the list in his campaign to solicit proxies. Moreover, a letter to the stockholders that discussed recent activities at the corporation can be deemed a proxy solicitation because the definition includes communications that are designed to discourage stockholders from giving a proxy to someone else.[318]

Sometimes the expansive definition of "proxy solicitation" collides with the First Amendment. In *Long Island Lighting Company v. Barbash*,[319] Long Island Lighting Co. (LILCO) was embroiled in a proxy contest over its mishandling of the design and construction of the Shoreham Nuclear Power Plant. LILCO sued a citizens' group over advertisements it had placed calling for LILCO to be replaced by a Long Island power authority. Even though the ads made no reference to the on-going proxy contest, LILCO argued that the ads were subject to proxy rules. The district court dismissed the suit,

---

[313] *See* Thomas L. Hazen, Corporate Chartering and the Securities Markets: Shareholder Suffrage, Corporate Responsibility and Managerial Accountability, 1978 Wis. L. Rev. 391.

[314] Business Roundtable v. SEC, 905 F.2d 406, 410–12 (D.C. Cir. 1990).

[315] General Rules & Regulations, Securities Exchange Act of 1934, 17 C.F.R. § 240.14a–1 (2009).

[316] *See* Union Pac. R.R. v. Chicago & N.W. Ry., 226 F.Supp. 400 (N.D. Ill. 1964).

[317] Studebaker Corp. v. Gittlin, 360 F.2d 692, 696 (2d Cir. 1966), citing SEC v. Okin, 132 F.2d 784 (2d Cir. 1943).

[318] *See* Sargent v. Genesco, Inc., 492 F.2d 750 (5th Cir. 1974).

[319] Long Island Lighting Co. v. Barbash, 779 F.2d 793 (2d Cir. 1985).

reasoning that otherwise the proxy rules would violate the citizens' group's First Amendment rights.[320] In a divided opinion, the Second Circuit reversed, holding that the proxy rules could apply to communications appearing in the general media and reasoning that it was premature for the court to reach the First Amendment issue. In a strong dissent, Judge Winter argued that the proxy rules should be interpreted to not apply to newspaper advertisements so as to avoid a serious First Amendment issue.[321]

Safe Harbor Provisions. In 1992, the SEC amended the proxy rules to reduce in important ways the earlier restrictions on stockholders to communicate among themselves.[322] New Rule 14a–2(b)(1) broadly (but somewhat ambiguously)[323] exempts from the filing and format requirements communications with stockholders by a person who himself is not seeking proxies and who does not have a "substantial interest" in the subject matter. This exemption is not available to certain classes of individuals, such as officers, directors, director nominees, or one who has in a Williams Act filing disclosed a possible intent to control the issuer. Moreover, a communication by a holder of more than $5 million of the company's stock must file the communication within three days of its use. A further relaxation appears in new Rule 14a–1(l)(2)(iv), which permits holders to announce how they will vote on any matter. A further innovation allows proxy contestants to solicit proxies for less than a full slate of dissident nominees—that is, the dissident can seek proxies for some of its nominees as well as some of the incumbent management's nominees. The function of allowing such "short slates" is to facilitate minority representation on the board.[324]

The scope of Rule 14a–2(b)(1) is not clear; it clearly reaches recommendations that proxy advisors provide their clients. But, as illustrated by *Gas Natural, Inc. v. Osborne*,[325] it is a good deal broader than that. Osborne had been terminated as Gas Natural's CEO and removed from its slate of nominees for the upcoming annual board election. Three weeks before the stockholder meeting, Osborne wrote to the shareholders criticizing Gas Natural's management and "ask[ed] for [the shareholders'] help in running these greedy individuals out of our company." In subsequent communications, he referred to the directors and officers as Nazis, claimed the company was broke, and criticized the decision to rehire its former chief operating officer. Contemporaneous with his initial letter, he requested a list of the stockholders as well as the NOBO list, stating he wished the lists "so I can solicit their support to be reinstated to the Board." He later testified he wanted "to put forward a slate of [directors] who would be supportive of his views." However, he never put forth such a slate and did not, directly or indirectly, seek

---

[320] Long Island Lighting Co. v. Barbash, 625 F.Supp. 221, 222 (S.D.N.Y. 1985).

[321] In SEC v. Wall St. Pub. Inst., 851 F.2d 365 (D.C. Cir. 1988), *cert. denied*, 489 U.S. 1066 (1989), a case under other provisions of the securities laws, the court held that the long-established powers to regulate the securities industry support the reasonableness of the interference with the defendant's speech.

[322] *See* Sec. Exch. Act Rel. No. 34–31326 (Oct. 16, 1992).

[323] In MONY Group, Inc. v. Highfields Capital Management, LP, 368 F.3d 138 (2d Cir. 2004), a shareholder who opposed merger wrote to other shareholders asking them to oppose the merger, including in the communication a duplicate copy of the proxy card earlier circulated by management.

[324] *See* Capital Real Estate Investors Tax Exempt Fund Ltd. Partnership v. Schwartzberg, 917 F.Supp. 1050, 1061 (S.D.N.Y. 1996) (holding that the Rule 14a–1 safe harbor is not available for press releases attacking the integrity of management because the defendant had already taken steps toward challenging management in a proxy campaign. The court also concludes that the disinterested-party safe harbor in Rule 14a–2(b) supported its position, because that provision takes what is presumptively a proxy solicitation and exempts it from many of the proxy rules, but not the antifraud rule of Rule 14a–9, provided the person stays out of the fray).

[325] Gas Natural Inc. v. Osborne, 624 Fed. Appx. 944 (6th Cir. 2015).

the power to act as proxy for another shareholder. The district court granted a permanent injunction against Osborne for not complying with the filing and delivery requirements of the proxy rules. The Sixth Circuit reversed, finding the communication fell within Rule 14a-(2)(b)(1); the panel believed a fair reading of the communications did request "shareholders to withhold or revoke proxies for the" upcoming meeting, Osborne did not request authority to act as a proxy. As such, the communications fell squarely within the scope of the exemption because the exemption excludes communications that do not request the shareholders to execute proxies, do not request authority to act as proxy for any shareholder, and that do not include a proxy form.

Overall, the 1992 proxy rule amendments go a long way toward answering the criticism that the former proxy rules prevented institutions and other sophisticated investors from effectively coordinating their actions to improve the performance and governance of their portfolio companies.[326] Under the new rules, investors can more easily coordinate their actions to maximize their influence at the stockholders' meeting because they are no longer subject to the costly and burdensome prefiling and format requirements. However, their communications continue to be subject to Rule 14a–9's prohibition against misleading communications in connection with a proxy solicitation. However, in late 1999 the SEC did relax the pre-filing obligations of management with respect to announcements related to acquisitions, even though the announcement contained deal related information. Under new Rule 14a–12 the company (or those acting on its behalf) can release announcements related to an acquisition without first filing the information or deliver a proxy statement, provided there is not then a request for a proxy.[327] SEC rules provide that the issuer or a shareholder, as well as a third party acting on behalf of either, can operate an electronic forum that facilitates shareholder interaction[328] and participation in such a forum does not constitute solicitation requiring compliance with the format, pre-filing, etc. requirements for proxies so long as the participant does not solicit personally on behalf of another person.[329]

The filing and disclosure requirements are not applicable solely to incumbent management; under Rule 14a–11, insurgent shareholders are subject to the same rigors.[330] Shareholders who run afoul of the proxy rules may be subjected to the same consequences as management, even including disenfranchisement with regard to the vote in question.[331]

The Securities Exchange Act also provides for SEC regulation of broker-dealer involvement in the proxy process, including the problem of voting or giving proxies for securities held for investors by stock brokerage firms "in street names."[332] Further, the Act requires management disclosure prior to an annual meeting even if management does not solicit proxies.[333]

---

[326] *See* Bernard Black, Shareholder Passivity Reexamined, 89 Mich. L. Rev. 520 (1990).

[327] 17 C.F.R. § 240.14a–12 (2009).

[328] Rule 14a–17, 17 C.F.R. § 240.14a–17.

[329] Rule 14a–2(b)(6), 17 C.F.R. § 240.14a–2(b)(6).

[330] *See* Levin v. Metro-Goldwyn-Mayer, Inc., 264 F.Supp. 797 (S.D.N.Y. 1967). Shareholder proposals are discussed *infra* § 13.26.

[331] *See* Committee for New Management of Butler Aviation v. Widmark, 335 F.Supp. 146 (E.D.N.Y. 1971).

[332] Section 14(b) of the Exchange Act, 15 U.S.C. § 78n(b) (2009). *See, e.g.,* S.E.C., Street Name Study (1976).

[333] 15 U.S.C. § 78n(c) (2009).

§ 13.26   Shareholder Proposals Under the Proxy Rules

Shareholders have made frequent use of Rule 14a–8, which requires management to submit appropriate shareholder proposals to the shareholders for a vote.[334] Among the proposals based on economic or business considerations that shareholders have asked management to submit for consideration at shareholder meetings are the following: (1) to inaugurate a system of cumulative voting for directors; (2) to place a ceiling on the amount of compensation the corporation can pay to any one executive or to the officers as a group or to subject executive compensation to an advisory stockholders vote; (3) to move the location of shareholders' meetings to a place more convenient for shareholders or to provide for the rotation of meeting places; (4) to make available to the shareholders various types of reports, such as a post-meeting report on the annual stockholders' meeting, goals related to company's charitable giving; and (5) requesting management to establish quantitative goals for reducing green house gases.[335]

"Public interest" and "public responsibility" groups have also resorted to Rule 14a–8 to bring social and political issues before the shareholders at annual meetings and thus give those issues publicity.[336] Among commonly recurring proposals of the past have been the following: to terminate a corporation's business activities in South Africa (when apartheid was practiced) or companies activities in the Congo; to prohibit a corporation from participating in the Arab boycott of Israel; to prohibit a corporation from making political contributions here or abroad; to terminate a corporation's manufacture or sale of armaments or other war materials; and to terminate a corporation's sponsorship of television programs featuring violence or sex. Each proxy solicitation season has its "in" topics.

Although shareholders submitting proposals opposed by management infrequently garner a substantial vote at the annual meeting, managements have often modified corporate policies or practices to obtain the withdrawal of a shareholder proposal or simply to remove irritants to good shareholder relations.[337] For example, corporations have now virtually abandoned the practice of holding shareholders' meetings at places inconvenient for large numbers of shareholders, and a growing number of corporations provide shareholders with detailed post-meeting reports on annual meetings. In some instances, however, management will rule a proposal not appropriate for shareholder action or otherwise improper under the proxy rules and thus excludible from the proxy materials. Although the ultimate question of a proposal's propriety for shareholder

---

[334] The pioneer decision demonstrating the usefulness of this rule to a shareholder determined to make changes in certain corporate practices was SEC v. Transamerica Corp., 163 F.2d 511 (3d Cir. 1947), *cert. denied*, 332 U.S. 847 (1948). The proposals before the court in that case had been submitted to Transamerica's management by a dedicated protector of shareholder interests, Lewis Gilbert. He and his brother, John, sponsored numerous proposals for shareholder action.

[335] Interestingly, proposals that attempt to curtail or limit capital expenditures can be omitted on the basis that they concern ordinary business operations. *See, e.g.*, Grimes v. Centerior Energy Corp., 909 F.2d 529 (D.C. Cir. 1990). However, a proposal requiring shareholder approval of all expenditures in excess of $500,000 that are not part of the ordinary business may not be omitted. Storage Technology Corp., SEC No-Action Letter, Fed. Sec. L. Rep. (CCH) ¶ 77,537 (March 18, 1999).

[336] Labor unions have become more active in shareholder issues. *See, e.g.*, Stewart J. Schwab & Randall S. Thomas, Realigning Corporate Governance: Shareholder Activism by Labor Unions, 96 Mich. L. Rev. 1018 (1998).

[337] *See generally* Randall S. Thomas & James F. Cotter, Shareholder Proposals in the New Millennium: Shareholder Support, Board Response and Market Reaction, 13 J. Corp. Fin. 368 (2007).

action is often a matter of state law, it is a violation of Rule 14a–8 not to include a proper proposal in the proxy materials.[338]

Grounds for Omission. While the SEC's rule provides numerous grounds for a proposal's omission, the overriding concern is "[i]f the proposal is not a proper subject for action by shareholders under the laws of the jurisdiction of the company's organization."[339] Because there is very little judicial authority on this topic, the staff of the SEC has over the years been the primary generator of guidance on what is or is not a proper subject for stockholder action. The Delaware legislature in 2008 addressed this awkward situation by authoring the Delaware Supreme Court to receive questions certified to it on the question of the scope of Delaware general corporation law. Thus, in the first use of its expanded jurisdiction, *CA, Inc. v. AFSCME Employees Pension Plan*,[340] the Delaware Supreme Court, responding to a certification filed by the SEC seeking guidance, opined that a proposal to amend the bylaws to provide for reimbursement of an insurgent's proxy campaign expenses, although a proper subject for shareholder action, the precise proposal before the court was not valid because it could cause the directors to provide reimbursement in violation of their fiduciary obligations.[341] It is likely that the proposal would have been appropriate had it included a so-called fiduciary out clause whereby reimbursement would not be required if doing so would have violated the directors' fiduciary obligation.

A Commission enforcement action under the shareholder proposal rules resulted in the Third Circuit[342] compelling management to include in its proxy materials a shareholder proposal (1) to amend the corporate bylaws to provide for independent public auditors, (2) to require notice of all proposed bylaw amendments, and (3) to require that a report of the annual shareholders' meeting be sent to shareholders. In contrast, a federal district court has upheld management's decision to exclude a shareholder's resolution that the company intensify its offshore drilling efforts.[343] The court pointed to the standard statutory mandate that the directors manage the business and affairs of a corporation and then upheld the Commission's finding that the proposal "related to . . . the ordinary business" and "was made 'primarily for the purpose of promoting a general economic or political cause.' "[344] It would appear that any proposal that deals with the *timing* of an act the corporation is already committed to is likely to be deemed as related to "ordinary business."[345]

---

[338] General Rules & Regulations, Securities Exchange Act of 1934, 17 C.F.R. § 240.14a–8(c)(1) (2009).

Under the most recent version of the rule, a shareholder must be the beneficial owner for at least one year of at least 1% or of $2,000 in market value of the securities entitled to vote. General Rules & Regulations, Securities Exchange Act of 1934, 17 C.F.R. § 240.14a–8(b)(1) (2009). The shareholder may submit no more than one proposal with a supporting statement; there is a maximum 500-word limit. *Id.* § 240.14a–8(d). If these requirements are not met, management may exclude the proposal from its proxy statement even if it is a proper subject for shareholder action under state law.

[339] Rule 14a–8(i)(1), 17 C.F.R. § 240.14a–1(i), (j).

[340] CA, Inc. v. AFSCME Employees Pension Plan, 953 A.2d 227 (Del. 2008).

[341] The court reasoned that the procedural posture of the case required it to consider whether there was any instance in which the proposal in practice would not be proper; such a case would occur if reimbursement was made to an individual who sought a directorship for purely personal reasons. *See* § 13.28 (discussing limitations on the corporation's power to reimburse proxy campaign expenses).

[342] SEC v. Transamerica Corp., 163 F.2d 511 (3d Cir. 1947), *cert. denied*, 332 U.S. 847 (1948). *See, e.g.*, Bayless Manning, Book Review, 67 Yale L.J. 1477, 1490 (1958).

[343] Brooks v. Standard Oil Co., 308 F.Supp. 810 (S.D.N.Y. 1969).

[344] Brooks v. Standard Oil Co., 308 F.Supp. 810, 814 (S.D.N.Y. 1969).

[345] *See* Roosevelt v. E.I. Du Pont de Nemours & Co., 958 F.2d 416 (D.C. Cir. 1992).

Uncertain Treatment of Proposals of Broad Social Significance. A leading case on a social and political shareholder proposal is *Medical Committee for Human Rights v. Securities and Exchange Commission.*[346] The proposal was to amend the corporation's charter to forbid it to make napalm without several limitations on its use. The Commission had allowed management to exclude the proposal. The Court of Appeals, D.C. Circuit, remanded the case to the Commission to reconsider the shareholder's claim within the proper limits of the Commission's discretionary powers, as delineated by the court.[347] The company thereafter voluntarily included the proposal in its proxy statement, and the proposal received less than 3 percent of the votes.[348]

From the inception of the shareholder proposal rule, a frequently invoked basis for management to exclude a shareholder proposal is on the grounds, now embodied in subsection (i)(7) of Rule 14a–8, which authorizes exclusion of proposals "relating to the company's ordinary business operations."[349] Just where ordinary business operations cease and fundamental corporate policy issues that affect the character of the enterprise begin is difficult to discern. For example, in one decision, the Court of Appeals for the District of Columbia reasoned that capital expenditures may reach such a level that they no longer merely involve "ordinary business."[350]

Since 1976 the SEC's position has been that a proposal could be excluded whenever it involves business matters "that are mundane in nature and do not involve any substantial policy or other considerations."[351] Under this standard, the SEC consistently held that proposals concerning equal employment opportunities could not be excluded on the basis that they involve ordinary business because they involve important policy questions and were not, under its 1976 interpretative guidelines, merely mundane.[352] In 1992, in the *Cracker Barrel* no-action letter,[353] the SEC retreated from the special treatment accorded proposals involving equal employment opportunities, so that the mere fact that a proposal is tied to a social issue no longer protected it from being omitted if the proposal otherwise focuses on the conduct of ordinary business.[354] Not surprisingly, its retreat stirred a great deal of controversy. Thus, in 1997, the SEC announced it was

---

[346] Medical Committee for Human Rights v. Securities and Exchange Commission, 432 F.2d 659 (D.C. Cir. 1970), *vacated as moot,* 404 U.S. 403 (1972).

[347] Since the proposal, unlike the precatory resolution at issue in Peck v. Greyhound Corp., 97 F.Supp. 679 (S.D.N.Y. 1951), was in the form of a proposed charter amendment, neither management nor the SEC was able to rest its decision on former Rule 14a–8(c)(5)'s ordinary business limitation. The question of propriety was resolved by the SEC against the shareholder under the former subsection (c)(2)'s seemingly subjective purpose test. The court's remand was limited to the Commission's failure to adequately set forth the basis of its decision and thus sheds no light on the proper use of this subsection of the former rule.

[348] Under the current shareholder proposal rule, a proposal is excludable if it has been submitted within the prior five years and received less than 3% of the vote. Rule 14a–8(i)(12), 17 C.F.R. § 240.14a–8(i)(12) (2009).

[349] The current version is found in Rule 14a–8(i)(7), 17 C.F.R. § 240.14a–8(i)(7) (2002).

[350] Grimes v. Centerior Energy Corp., 909 F.2d 529 (D.C. Cir. 1990). And, a proposal that requires all capital expenditures in excess of $300 million can be excluded because it would require submission to the shareholders of routine expenditures incurred after the $300 million level was met. *See* Grimes v. Ohio Edison Co., 992 F.2d 455 (2d Cir. 1993).

[351] Adoption of Amendments Relating to Proposals by Security Holders, Exchange Act Rel. No. 12,999, 41 Fed. Reg. 52,994, 52,998 (Dec. 3, 1976).

[352] For a review of the SEC's course after 1976, *see* Amalgamated Clothing & Textile Workers v. Wal-Mart Stores, Inc., 821 F.Supp. 877 (S.D.N.Y. 1993).

[353] Cracker Barrel Old Country Stores, Inc. No-Action Letter, 1992 SEC No-Act. LEXIS 984 at *43 (Oct. 13, 1992).

[354] Cracker Barrel Old Country Stores, Inc. No-Action Letter, 1992 SEC No-Act. LEXIS 984 at *43 (Oct. 13, 1992). The SEC's power to make this interpretative change was upheld in New York City Employees' Retirement Sys. v. SEC, 45 F.3d 7 (2d Cir. 1995).

considering reverting to its prior practice of reviewing each employment-related proposal to determine if it relates to the ordinary business of the company or to more far-reaching social issues, in which case it would not be excludable from management's proxy statement.[355] In 1998, the Commission officially announced this change in position and the reversal of the position that had been taken in the controversial *Cracker Barrel* no-action letter.[356]

Trinity Wall Street v. Wal-Mart Stores, Inc.[357] is an important decision interpreting the "ordinary business" grounds for a proposal's omission. The proposal called on the board to develop policy and standards to determine whether a retailer should sell a product that "especially endangers public safety," has "the substantial potential to impair the reputation" of the firm, and/or "would reasonably be considered by many offensive to the family and community values integral to the" firm's brand. The narrative portion of the proposal clearly identified a concern that many Wal-Mart stores sold high-capacity guns. The SEC issued a no-action letter supporting the company's decision to omit the proposal on the ground the proposal involved ordinary business matters; ultimately the federal district court ruled the proposal could not be excluded (reasoning the proposal called on the board to oversee and effect company policy as contrasted with directing the board how to manage the firm; alternatively, the district court believed the proposal focused on significant social issues).[358] Under a multi-pronged test, the Third Circuit reversed, holding the proposal was excludable. The court analyzed whether the proposal addressed ordinary business operations by first discerning the proposal's subject matter and second assessing whether that subject matter relates to Wal-Mart's ordinary business. The Third Circuit concluded the subject matter addressed the way the firm decides which products to sell; so viewed, the court easily classified the subject matter as being within the ordinary business rubric. The final area of analysis, per the post-1998/*Cracker Barrell* approach, the Third Circuit evaluated whether the proposal's focus transcended Wal-Mart's day-to-day business operations. Here the proposal failed for too much breadth, as it was not focused on guns or high-capacity magazine guns, but a full array of products that Wal-Mart may choose to sell. The majority believed the proposal instead focused on the retailer-consumer interaction; so viewed, the proposal did not transcend ordinary business. Moreover, the court did not believe the proposal embodied a strong social policy but was rather focused on the heuristics of which products to sell. It was not limited to high velocity pistols and rifles. Seeing the proposal as so focused, the court found support for omission in a long list of SEC no-action letters where the SEC supported exclusion of proposals that addressed products firms sold. Subsequently, the in Staff Legal Bulletin 14H the SEC's Division of Corporation Finance rejected the approach taken in *Trinity Wall St.* and stated it will adhere to its established approach favoring inclusion of proposals that raise significant social issues.

Corporate Governance Proposals. More recently the battleground for shareholder proposals, reflecting the increasing activism of institutional investors, has been proposals focused on changes in corporate governance. SEC no-action letters have rejected company pleas that they be permitted to omit proposals for bylaw changes

---

[355] Amendments to Rules on Shareholder Proposals, Sec. Exch. Act Rel. No. 34–39093, 62 Fed. Reg. 50682–01 (SEC Sept. 26, 1997).

[356] Amendments to Rules on Shareholder Proposals, Sec. Exch. Act Rel. No. 34–40018, 1998 WL 254809 (SEC May 21, 1998).

[357] 792 F.3d 323 (3d Cir. July 6, 2015).

[358] Trinity Wall Street v. Wal-Mart Stores, Inc., 75 F.Supp. 3d 617 (D. Del. 2014).

calling for the redemption of an existing poison pill, stockholder approval of the initiation of a poison pill, separation of the position of board chair and chief executive officers, cumulative voting, and supplanting the plurality vote with a majority vote requirement as a condition for a director's reelection. By far the initiative that has generated the greatest reaction from management and institutional investors has been proposals to amend the company bylaws that would empower stockholders to nominate directors.

Nomination of Director Proposals. The power of shareholders to propose bylaws empowering them to nominate directors has an interesting history. In 2010, the SEC Invoked the authority conferred on it by the historic Dodd-Frank legislation by adopting Rule 14a–11 that provided a mechanism for shareholders of reporting companies who individually collectively owned three percent of the issuer's shares for three years to nominate up to one-fourth of the board. Faulting the SEC for failing to engage in cost-benefit-analysis sufficient to justify the rule, the Court of Appeals for the D.C. Circuit held the rule was adopted arbitrarily and capriciously.[359] With Rule 14a–11 being struck down, activist shareholders have pursued self-help using the SEC's shareholder proposal rule to advance shareholder friendly proxy access resolutions. While these efforts have already met with some modest success, companies have exploited the ground for omitting a proposal when it conflicts with the proposal submitted by management.[360] In a significant no action letter involving Whole Foods, the SEC held that a proposal submitted by shareholders could be omitted because it conflicted with that of management. The SEC staff reached this position even though there were several substantive differences between the shareholder's proposal and that supported by management: management conditioned standing on the individual proponent owning 9 percent of the shares for 5 years, whereas the shareholder initiated proposal allowed a group to meet the ownership requirement, set that ownership requirement at 20 percent, and required ownership for only 3 years. The SEC granted the no-action letter to Whole Foods.[361]

Today, Delaware and the Model Business Corporation Act each expressly authorize bylaw provisions regarding procedures for shareholder nomination of directors as well as reimbursement of the nominee's expenses.[362] The SEC in 2010 amended Rule 14a–8(i)(8) to permit proposals related to the nomination of directors.

§ 13.27 Implied Private Action Under Rule 14a–9

The first time that the Supreme Court gave its imprimatur to an implied cause of action under the securities acts was with regard to Rule 14a–9's antifraud limitations on the use of the proxy machinery.[363] *J.I. Case Company v. Borak*[364] involved a shareholder's claim of misleading statements in management's solicitation of

---

[359] Business Roundtable v. SEC, 647 F.3d 1144 (D.C. Cir. 2011). For a biting critique of the court's reasoning, *see* James D. Cox & Benjamin J.C. Baucom, The Emperor Has No Clothes: Confronting the D.C. Circuit's Usurpation of SEC Rulemaking Authority, 90 Tex. L. Rev. 1811 (2012) (closely analyzing why neither legislative history nor Supreme Court precedents support decision).

[360] Rule 14a–8(i)(9), 17 C.F.R. § 240.14a–8(i)(9) (2010).

[361] Whole Foods Market, Inc., SEC No-Action Letter (available Dec. 1, 2014).

[362] Del. Code Ann. tit. 8, § 112 (2009).

[363] For a close review of these events, *see* Leo Strine, Breaking the Logjam in Washington: Some Constructive Thoughts on a Responsible Path Forward, 63 Bus. Law. 1079 (2008).

[364] J. I. Case Company v. Borak, 377 U.S. 426 (1964).

shareholder support for a proposed merger.[365] The Court relied on the legislative history supporting section 14(a) as requiring basic standards of honesty and the necessity of management's affording at least certain minimum intra-corporate rights to shareholders.[366] While there is a serious question concerning the Supreme Court's continued willingness to imply additional private remedies, under the federal securities laws the Rule 14a–9 implied private cause of action, like the implied cause of action under Rule 10b–5, can no longer be questioned.[367]

It is important to bear in mind that the coverage of the proxy rules is limited. In addition to applying only to solicitation of proxies by Exchange Act reporting issuers,[368] section 14(a) necessarily applies only to issues that are brought before the shareholders for a shareholder vote.

Materiality. The dominant concern in any action under Rule 14a–9 is whether the proxy solicitation contained a *material* omission or misstatement of fact. A fact's materiality is a mixed question of law and fact that arises in pretrial motions as well as at trial. *TSC Industries, Inc. v. Northway, Inc.*[369] is the leading case on the standard to be applied in deciding whether an omission or misstatement is material:

> An omitted fact is material if there is a substantial likelihood that a reasonable shareholder would consider it important in deciding how to vote. This standard is fully consistent with *Mills'* general description of materiality as a requirement that "the defect have a significant propensity to affect the voting process." It does not require proof of a substantial likelihood that disclosure of the omitted fact would have caused the reasonable investor to change his vote. What the standard does contemplate is a showing of a substantial likelihood that, under all the circumstances, the omitted fact would have assumed actual significance in the deliberations of the reasonable shareholder. Put another way, there must be a substantial likelihood that the disclosure of the omitted fact would have been viewed by the reasonable investor as having significantly altered the "total mix" of information made available.[370]

Subsequent Supreme Court decisions have refined without limiting this standard of materiality. Thus, in *Basic, Inc. v. Levinson*,[371] the court held that the standard for determining materiality for soft information, such as financial forecasts, appraisals, and future financial expenditures, that "materiality will depend at any given time upon a balancing of both the indicated probability that the event will occur and the anticipated

---

[365] Mergers and other methods of corporate fusion have provided fertile grounds for proxy-related claims; *e.g.,* TSC Indus. v. Northway, Inc., 426 U.S. 438 (1976); Mills v. Electric Auto-Lite Co., 396 U.S. 375 (1970).

[366] "The section stemmed from the congressional belief that '[f]air corporate suffrage is an important right that should attach to every security bought on a public exchange.'" H.R. Rep. No. 1383, 73rd Cong., 2d Sess. 13, quoted with approval in 377 U.S. at 431.

[367] *See* Thomas L. Hazen, Judicial Federalism: Implied Private Remedies Under Federal Statutes: Neither a Death Knell Nor a Moratorium—Civil Rights, Securities Regulation, and Beyond, 33 Vand. L. Rev. 1333 (1980).

[368] *See* 15 U.S.C. § 781 (2009).

[369] TSC Industries, Inc. v. Northway, Inc., 426 U.S. 438 (1976).

[370] TSC Industries, Inc. v. Northway, Inc., 426 U.S. 438, 449 (1976). The reference is to Mills v. Electric Auto-Lite Co., 396 U.S. 375 (1970), a case not requiring the court to resolve whether an omission was material where the court in dicta stated a fact is material if it "*might* have been considered important" and contradicted itself by stating materiality required "a significant propensity to affect investors."

[371] Basic, Inc. v. Levinson, 485 U.S. 224 (1988).

magnitude of the event in light of the totality of the company activity."[372] Under this sliding scale standard, an event with a low probability of occurrence can nevertheless still be material if its occurrence will have a significant impact on the company's net worth or profits. Thus, in *Basic, Inc.*, false denials that the company was engaged in merger negotiations were material because on the merger the value of the company's shares would increase dramatically.

Contrary to a literal reading of both Rule 14a–9 and *TSC Industries*, the Supreme Court held in *Virginia Bankshares, Inc. v. Sandberg*[373] that opinion statements can be the bases of a materiality claim under Rule 14a–9. In *Virginia Bankshares*, management's proxy statement described the merger's terms as providing the stockholders with a "high" value and elsewhere described the price as "fair." The court held that opinion statements could be materially misleading and just as harmful as misrepresentations of fact. However, *Virginia Bankshares* held that more must be alleged than that the defendant misrepresented their motives, true intentions, or beliefs; otherwise vexatious litigation would arise. The Supreme Court thus conditioned that any suit for materially misleading opinion statements must bear on the substance of the transaction for which approval was sought. This additional requirement was satisfied in *Virginia Bankshares* because the plaintiff alleged the merger's terms were unfair.[374]

It should be apparent that the standard of materiality makes it especially difficult for many matters to be resolved on the basis of pretrial motions. In its breadth the standard is not necessarily pernicious or unwieldy; it simply defies mathematical predictability. Adding to the uncertainty is the statement in *TSC Industries* that the materiality of an item is to be determined by the "total mix" of information made available. This invites consideration of whether an omission, or even a misstatement, is corrected because the correct information is otherwise in the public domain. In particular, the "total mix" criterion invites consideration of the impact of the efficient market hypothesis, which holds that information that is publicly available will be quickly impounded into the pricing of a security. Thus companies whose stock or investors operate in relatively information-rich environments and that are followed by sophisticated traders may well argue that any omission in their proxy statement or otherwise is not a material omission because information available from alternative sources is available and known to investors.

At the same time, there is reason to believe that the context in which the disclosure issue arises is very important in setting forth the parameters of what is the total mix of information. Consider *United Paperworkers International Union v. Specialty Paperboard, Inc.*,[375] where the proponent of a shareholder proposal calling for the company to adhere to certain strict environmental disclosures complained that management's response urging shareholders to vote against the proposal was materially

---

[372] Basic, Inc. v. Levinson, 485 U.S. 224, 238 (1988), quoting with approval SEC v. Texas Gulf Sulphur Co., 401 F.2d 833, 849 (2d Cir. 1968) *(en banc), cert. denied*, 394 U.S. 976 (1969).

[373] Virginia Bankshares, Inc. v. Sandberg, 501 U.S. 1083 (1991).

[374] Indeed, the basis for alleging that the directors misrepresented their opinion statements was that the directors were in possession of at least one report that placed the firm's value at $18 per share higher than the price being paid in the merger and that the offering price would provide no premium for the shares if the assets were determined at their appraised value. *See also* Mendell v. Greenberg, 938 F.2d 1528 (2d Cir. 1990) (undisclosed motive of haste in seeking merger was to produce cash for controlling stockholders' undisclosed motive of need for cash is basis of suit only if also alleged that the merger terms were unfair).

[375] United Paperworkers International Union v. Specialty Paperboard, Inc., 999 F.2d 51 (2d Cir. 1993).

misleading because it failed to disclose that the company had been convicted of numerous environmental violations and generally had a bad environmental record. The company argued that these matters were all disclosed in its annual report and Form 10-K filed with the SEC and as such were all part of the total mix of information before the shareholders. The Second Circuit held these matters should have been disclosed in the proxy statement and that their omission was a material one not corrected by the information being in other reports that were available to the stockholders.

International Paper appears to take the sensible position that when shareholder attention is riveted on a specific document, such as a proxy statement, it is unreasonable to expect stockholders to search through other sources to evaluate the credibility of arguments contained in that document. One can expect, however, that investors considering whether to purchase or sell a company's securities can be more resourceful in considering the merits of that decision, or at least that its publicly available information will be accessed by some market intermediaries whose trading will drive the security's price to a level appropriate in light of such information. Whereas no such arbitrage behavior is possible in the context of proxy voting.

Another troubling question is the social, criminal, and ethical background of directors. On this question, the courts generally have been unwilling to apply the broad tenets of *TSC Industries* to require directors to disclose their prior ethical or legal lapses. For example, several courts have held that the proxy statement in which the directors are seeking reelection does not have to disclose that the directors standing for reelection acquiesced in management's making foreign bribes.[376] Directors also need not disclose that they had willfully acted to thwart the labor laws.[377] One must approach such restrictive opinions with caution, viewing them largely as decisions in which expediency is preferred over the indeterminacy of opening disclosure inquiries to a wide range of social issues.[378] Certainly one can well imagine a wide range of business issues for which advance knowledge of the individual director's social, ethical, or philosophical proclivities would be highly relevant to evaluating that director's ability to serve the stockholders' interests. Though it may keep the size of proxy statements from growing any larger than their present bulk, and this in turn may save a few forests, there is a weak artificiality in holding that proxy statements need not disclose the directors' countenancing the illegal conduct of others or that the directors do not themselves commit the corporation to live within the bounds of the law.

Causation. Questions of causation are especially difficult in the context of misleading proxy solicitations. Therefore, in one case, the failure to disclose details of earlier discussions with a possible merger partner, though concluded by the court to be material, were nonetheless not believed to rise to the level of materiality as to have had a causal impact on the vote of the stockholders.[379] For most issues, the proxy solicitation involves a collective, rather than an individual, decision. Stockholders decide as a group whether to amend the articles, to elect a director, or to merge with another company. Structural decisions, such as the merger or sale of a company, frequently allow dissenters a right to have their shares appraised, so in this regard the decision has both

---

[376] *See, e.g.,* Gaines v. Haughton, 645 F.2d 761 (9th Cir. 1981), *cert. denied,* 454 U.S. 1145 (1982).

[377] *See* Amalgamated Clothing & Textile Workers v. J. P. Stevens & Co., 475 F.Supp. 328 (S.D.N.Y. 1979), *vacated as moot per curiam,* 638 F.2d 7 (2d Cir. 1980).

[378] *See* Gaines v. Haughton, 645 F.2d 761, 778 (9th Cir. 1981), *cert. denied,* 454 U.S. 1145 (1982).

[379] *See* Minzer v. Keegan, 218 F.3d 144 (2d Cir. 2000).

a collective and an individual character. In either case, the causation question is whether the particular omission or misstatement must be shown to have misled the individual stockholder or group of stockholders.

At the same time, it must be recognized that because the decisions are collective decisions and all stockholders are generally bound by the will of a majority, each stockholder's interest is impacted by a misrepresentation that causes her fellow stockholders to approve or forgo a transaction to the extent that transaction impacts the company. Causation is further complicated by the *TSC Industries* standard of materiality, quoted above, which holds that a fact is material without proof "of a substantial likelihood that disclosure of the omitted fact would have caused the reasonable investor to change his vote."[380] Thus a fact is material even though it does not have a dispositive impact on how the individual stockholder votes.

The Supreme Court has treated causation questions in Rule 14a–9 actions somewhat ambiguously. In *Mills v. Electric Auto-Lite Company*,[381] the court stated "a sufficient causal relationship between the violation and the injury . . . [is shown, if] he proves that the proxy solicitation itself, rather than the particular defect in the solicitation materials, was an essential link in the accomplishment of the transaction."[382] *Mills's* loose proscription that the proxy solicitation itself be an essential link takes on some meaning from the facts of that particular case. In *Mills* the Seventh Circuit held that because it was not practicable to ascertain how a defect in the proxy statement influenced each stockholder's voting decision, the court would use the fairness of the transaction as a surrogate for causation. That is, if the transaction was unfair, the court would award relief to the stockholders in the belief that the misleading proxy statement duped them into approving an unfair merger. The Supreme Court rejected this approach, on the sound reasoning that mere evidence of a transaction's fairness does not assure shareholder support. This may strike some as a curious behavioral conclusion, but it rests on the understanding that fairness is a range of values, not a specific point. Thus a merger's terms may be within a range of fairness, but at the low end of the range such that informed stockholders may well vote against the transaction in the belief they should receive a price in the higher range of fairness.

Many have interpreted *Mills* as merely recognizing a rebuttable presumption of reliance by all the stockholders so that the defendant was faced with the nearly impossible burden of proving that the particular defect did not have a causal impact on how the stockholders voted.[383] Overall, the courts responded to *Mills* by according causation a most liberal interpretation, with the effect that a finding of materiality also satisfied causation.[384]

One major requirement of causation is that the alleged omission or misstatement in the proxy statement must pertain to a transaction for which stockholder approval was sought. This is the so-called transaction-causation requirement that is sometimes used

---

[380]　TSC Indus. v. Northway, Inc., 426 U.S. 438, 449 (1976).

[381]　Mills v. Electric Auto-Lite Company, 396 U.S. 375 (1970).

[382]　Mills v. Electric Auto-Lite Company, 396 U.S. 375, 385 (1970).

[383]　*See* Note, Causation and Liability in Private Actions for Proxy Violations, 80 Yale L.J. 107 (1970).

[384]　*See* Mosher v. Kane, 784 F.2d 1385 (9th Cir. 1986) (causation established where defective proxy statement caused bankruptcy court not to approve the transactions such that stockholders never had opportunity to vote).

in the courts' language.[385] To illustrate, consider the court's treatment of numerous cases brought in the 1970s alleging the board of directors failed to disclose in the proxy statement in which they sought election that they had acquiesced in foreign bribery payments carried out by management. With great consistency the courts dismissed Rule 14a–9 actions seeking to hold the directors liable for the bribery payments. The courts ruled that because the bribery payments were not submitted to the stockholders for their approval, transaction causation was lacking—that is, there was no causal relationship between the failure to disclose in the proxy statement the directors' misbehavior and the bribes themselves.[386] There is a more direct link between the nondisclosure of the directors' acquiescence in foreign bribery and their own election. As seen above, the plaintiffs tended to be unsuccessful in those actions because the courts were unwilling to extend the scope of materiality to include the directors' acquiescence in foreign bribery.[387] Generally, therefore, Rule 14a–9 does not provide recovery for damages suffered by the corporation as a consequence of the directors' decisions, even though the directors obtained their election through a misleading proxy statement.[388]

Life has been breathed into the causation area by the Supreme Court's decision in *Virginia Bankshares, Inc. v. Sandberg*.[389] The Court held that causation was not established when the First American Bank of Virginia (Bank) was merged into a wholly owned subsidiary of First American Bankshares, Inc. (FABI), who also owned 85 percent of Bank's shares. The approval of the minority Bank stockholders was solicited by an allegedly misleading proxy statement; state law did not require the approval of the minority stockholders and did not extend an appraisal remedy to dissenters. The plaintiff argued causation was present because, had the proxy statement disclosed the merger's unfairness, it would have been possible for the plaintiff to obtain equitable relief based on a breach of the defendants' state-law-based fiduciary duties.[390] The plaintiff's argument was that certain nondisclosures are material and also establish causation because they are "sue facts," which, if disclosed, would have armed the plaintiff with a state-law-based cause of action to enjoin the transaction.

Justice Souter's opinion in *Virginia Bankshares* rejects the "sue facts" approach to causation. He reasoned that because the plaintiff possessed enough information to allege in his Rule 14a–9 action that the proxy statement failed to disclose the unfairness of the transaction that the plaintiff therefore possessed enough information when he filed his Rule 14a–9 action to have instead sought the relief he alleged was available to him under state fiduciary principles. Justice Souter therefore concluded that the proxy statement did not prevent the plaintiff from seeking such relief as was available under state law. *Virginia Bankshares* thus demonstrates the type of Catch 22 situation that plaintiffs face if they seek to protect themselves under Rule 14a–9 by alleging the nondisclosure prevented the plaintiff from obtaining protection under state law. As discussed earlier in Chapter 12, *Omnicare, Inc. v. Laborers District Council Construction Industry Pension*

---

[385] *See* Rosenbaum v. Klein, 547 F.Supp. 586 (E.D. Pa. 1982).

[386] *See, e.g.,* Abbey v. Control Data Corp., 603 F.2d 724 (8th Cir. 1979); Gaines v. Haughton, 645 F.2d 761 (9th Cir. 1981).

[387] *See, e.g.,* Gaines v. Haughton, 645 F.2d 761 (9th Cir. 1981), cert. denied, 454 U.S. 1145 (1982).

[388] *See, e.g.,* General Elec. Co. v. Cathcart, 980 F.2d 927 (3d Cir. 1992).

[389] Virginia Bankshares, Inc. v. Sandberg, 501 U.S. 1083 (1991).

[390] This approach builds on the reasoning of Judge Friendly in Goldberg v. Meridor, 567 F.2d 209 (2d Cir. 1977), *cert. denied,* 434 U.S. 1069 (1978).

Fund[391] substantially clarifies, if not qualifies, *Virginia Bankshares*. Recall that *Omnicare* examined an opinion statement in terms of whether the person making the statement failed to disclose information necessary to prevent what was stated from being materially misleading.

Certainly the result would have been different in *Virginia Bankshares* if the misleading proxy statement had prevented the minority stockholders from pursuing their appraisal remedy, a course of action that is predicated on stockholders voting against the merger.[392] Also, *Virginia Bankshares* does not appear to affect the causation inquiry where the defendant does not hold enough shares to approve the transactions, as was the case with FABI, which owned 85 percent of Bank's voting shares. Indeed, post-*Virginia Bankshares* decisions continue to hold that the individual Rule 14a–9 plaintiff need not prove either that she relied on the misrepresentation or even exercised her proxy.[393] In sum, *Virginia Bankshares* appears to sharpen somewhat the causation area by holding that potential injunctive relief under state law cannot serve as a bridge between the violation and the harm suffered as a consequence of the transaction. Lower courts have applied *Virginia Bankshares* reasoning to actions under the antifraud provision section 10(b) and under Rule 10b–5.[394]

Remedies. A panoply of remedies is available in Rule 14a–9 actions. The Supreme Court in *Mills* conditioned damages being available to the extent that the transaction's unfairness can be established.[395] On remand, the lower court reviewed the terms of the merger and concluded they were fair, so no damages were awarded.[396] Injunctive relief is especially appropriate where matters have not been pursued so far as to be beyond the prospective relief of a court of equity. Rescission is possible but is inappropriate where the rights of third parties or excessive transaction costs will be incurred.[397]

PART F.　CORPORATE CONTROL DEVICES

§ 13.28　Various Voting Control Devices

The operation of the proxy system has led to almost universal "management control" and a situation in which "ownership of corporate shares without appreciable ownership has become a natural phenomenon of our economic system."[398] Various devices have been used to obtain control of publicly held corporations with their valuable patronage for little or no investment. On the other hand, many of these same devices have proved to

---

[391] ___ U.S. ___, 135 S.Ct. 1318 (2015). *See* James D. Cox, "We're Cool" Statements after *Omnicare*: Securities Fraud Suits for Failures to Comply with the Law, 68 S.M.U. L. Rev. 715 (2015) (reviewing the implications of *Omnicare* with a focus on puffery and forward looking statements).

[392] *Compare* Wilson v. Great Amer. Indus., 979 F.2d 924 (2d Cir. 1992) (antifraud provision applied when misrepresentation alleged to deprive pursuit of appraisal remedy).

[393] *See, e.g.,* Stahl v. Gibraltar Fin. Corp., 967 F.2d 335 (9th Cir. 1992).

[394] *See, e.g.,* Scattergood v. Perelman, 945 F.2d 618 (3d Cir. 1991).

[395] Mills v. Electric Auto-Lite Co., 396 U.S. 375 (1970).

[396] Mills v. Electric Auto-Lite Co., 552 F.2d 1239 (7th Cir. 1977).

[397] For a decision refusing to compel a new proxy solicitation even though the earlier consents were obtained by material misrepresentations, *see* Yamamoto v. Omiya, 564 F.2d 1319 (9th Cir. 1977) (such a cancellation believed to give innocent third party buyer a right to recover damages in an amount greater that the likely loss caused by the omission itself).

[398] Detroit Edison Co. v. SEC, 119 F.2d 730, 739 (6th Cir. 1941).

be useful and legitimate tools in meeting the special needs of close corporations and the desires of the owners of such corporations.[399]

The principal control devices by which groups may seek to gain or retain control of corporations by a combination of voting power or otherwise are as follows: (1) voting agreements entered into by a group of shareholders to assure their voting control; (2) voting trusts; (3) pyramiding, the use of holding companies or a series of holding companies to hold controlling shares of their subsidiaries; (4) classification of common shares into voting and nonvoting, with the voting power vested in a small class of "management stock"; (5) management contracts, often with a parent or affiliated corporation; and (6) classification of directors, with staggered elections of only some of the directors each year. Another device is to provide for per capita rather than per share voting.[400]

Difficult policy questions arise as to how far the law should permit the use of devices that tend to divest the shareholders, who after all are the contributors of capital and the risk-takers, of any chance to share in control. How should these mechanisms by which some seek to obtain the management and patronage of vast aggregations of capital be limited and regulated? How, if at all, should the legal norms vary with the number of shareholders?[401]

§ 13.29 Nonvoting Shares and Voting-Only Shares

Preferred shares are frequently given only contingent rights to vote for directors and on other matters in the event of nonpayment of dividends for a specified period. Under most statutes a corporation may issue nonvoting common stock.[402] The common stock may thus be divided into Class A nonvoting and Class B voting shares. Frequently in such cases the Class A shares will be widely sold to the public and Class B, the voting shares, will be closely held by promoters or managers. It is argued that vesting such control in the active promoters and managers so that no other group can dislodge them is for the benefit of the enterprise. But it may be questioned whether such an arrangement does not deprive investors in the nonvoting shares of potential participation in control, which should be their means of self-defense.[403] At least in close corporations, however, controlling shareholders, while perhaps not fiduciaries to the same extent as directors, are not free to exercise control for their own selfish interests and to oppress or defraud holders of minority or nonvoting shares who have no voice in the selection of management. And notwithstanding their denomination as nonvoting or conditional voting stock, holders of preferred as well as nonvoting common shares are entitled under most modern corporation statutes to vote for organic changes that directly affect their ownership interests.[404]

Control arrangements may also take the form of the corporation issuing shares that have voting rights with few or no accompanying financial interests in the company. For

---

[399] *See* Chapter 14.

[400] Sagusa, Inc. v. Magellan Petroleum Corp., 1993 WL 512487, 19 Del. J. Corp. L. 1304 (Del. Ch. 1993), *aff'd without opinion*, 650 A.2d 1306 (Del. 1994) (upholding per capita voting).

[401] *See* Chapter 14.

[402] *E.g.*, Del. Code Ann. tit. 8, § 151(a) (2009); Model Bus. Corp. Act § 6.01(c)(1) (2008).

[403] William Zebina Ripley, Main Street and Wall Street 86 (1929).

[404] Model Bus. Corp. Act § 10.04(d) (2008).

example, in *Lehrman v. Cohen*,[405] the Lehrman and Cohen families each held a separate class of stock that enabled each family to elect two directors. A third class of stock with no equity in the company but the power to elect the fifth director was issued to the firm's attorney. The arrangement was intended to avoid deadlocks at the board meetings but was challenged when Cohen was replaced as president by the attorney. The validity of the "voting-only" class of shares was challenged. The Delaware Supreme Court held that the arrangement was not a voting trust subject to a ten-year limit because the shares' holder exercised all voting power; the arrangement was not an unlawful delegation of directors' powers; and public policy was not violated by shares having no proprietary interest.

The latter is most important in those states following the Model Business Corporation Act, which defines "shares" as embodying a "proprietary" interest in the firm. At least one other court has upheld the validity of issuing shares that have only voting rights.[406] Overall, the courts are well advised to sustain the validity of shares with unique features where they appear intended to fulfill the special desires of the owners and there is no evidence of fraud or overreaching conduct in their issuance.

§ 13.30 The Voting Trust—Its Use and Abuse

The normal method of delegating voting power is by a proxy, which, as noted earlier,[407] is generally freely revocable unless coupled with an interest. It has been said that the voting trust was developed as a device "to achieve irrevocable proxies."[408]

To meet business needs, adroit lawyers invented the voting trust to give what is in essence a joint irrevocable proxy for a term of years the protective coloring of a trust, thus enabling the trustees to vote as owners rather than as mere agents.[409] In most jurisdictions, the voting trust has met the formal objections to an irrevocable proxy and, subject to certain formalities and limitations on duration, is now validated by statute.[410]

Modern statutes provide broad validation of the voting trust.[411] These statutes typically state that the trust agreement must be in writing and filed with the corporation; they also usually limit the duration of the voting trust, most often to ten years;[412] however, both Delaware and the Model Act no longer limit the duration of a voting trust.[413]

---

[405] Lehrman v. Cohen, 222 A.2d 800 (Del. 1966).

[406] *See* Stroh v. Blackhawk Holding Corp., 272 N.E.2d 1 (Ill. 1971).

[407] *See supra* § 13.20.

[408] Shareholder agreements have been attacked as illegal on the grounds that they represent either an irrevocable proxy or an invalid trust. *See* Abercrombie v. Davies, 130 A.2d 338 (Del. Ch. 1957).

[409] *See generally* Henry W. Ballantine, Voting Trusts, Their Abuses and Regulation, 21 Tex. L. Rev. 139 (1942); Note, 42 N.Y.U. L. Rev. 348 (1967).

[410] *E.g.*, Del. Code Ann. tit. 8, § 218 (2009); N.Y. Bus. Corp. Law § 621 (2009); Model Bus. Corp. Act §§ 7.30, 7.31 (2008).

[411] Model Bus. Corp. Act §§ 7.30, 7.31 (2016).

[412] *See* 1 F. Hodge O'Neal & Robert B. Thompson, O'Neal and Thompson's Close Corporations and LLCs: Law and Practice §§ 4.17 to 4.18, 4.32, 4.36 to 4.37 & 4.41 (rev. 3d ed. 2009); John J. Woloszyn, A Practical Guide to Voting Trusts, 4 U. Balt. L. Rev. 245 (1975).

[413] 8 Del. C. § 218 (2014); Model Bus. Corp. Act § 7.30(c) (2014) ("Limits, if any, on the duration of a voting trust shall be as set forth in the voting trust. A voting trust that became effective when this Act provided a 10-year limit on its duration remains governed by the provisions of this section then in effect, unless the voting trust is amended to provide otherwise by unanimous agreement of the parties to the voting trust").

The voting-trust formalities are considered mandatory,[414] and courts have invalidated voting trusts that exceed the statutory duration[415] as well as for other types of noncompliance with the statute.[416] The modern attitude is to uphold arrangements that do not comply with all the requirements of the state voting-trust statute as long as the arrangement does not otherwise violate public policy.[417] Most statutes today are not intended to invalidate all other voting agreements, and in 1969 the Model Act was amended to reflect this.[418]

§ 13.31   Voting Trusts—Scope of Trustee's Powers

One object of forming a voting trust is to ensure permanency of tenure for the directors and to take from the shareholders the power to change management. Such an arrangement sometimes is a response to some special business need, and good reason can be shown for this drastic change in the rights of the shareholders, who by law and by the corporation's charter have the right to vote on the selection of directors and on fundamental corporate changes.[419] Obviously it is not a legitimate function of a voting trust to capture the voting power of the shareholders for those who propose to use it in their own selfish interest[420] or for purposes hostile to the corporation or its shareholders.[421] A voting trust offers to promoters of a corporation the temptation of seizing and retaining dictatorial control over the investments of others with little or no investment and keeping all the patronage and perquisites of control.[422]

The following are among the purposes usually regarded as legitimate for voting trusts: (1) to aid in reorganization plans and adjustments with creditors in bankruptcy or financial difficulty; (2) to assist financing, to procure loans, and to protect bondholders and preferred shareholders; (3) to accomplish some definite plan or policy for the benefit of the company and to assure stability and continuity of management for this purpose; (4) to prevent rival concerns or competitors from gaining control; (5) to apportion representation and protect minority interests by putting the selection of directors in impartial hands; and (6) as a device in connection with mergers, consolidations, or purchases of a business to assure that the predecessors or constituents, though in the minority, may have representation.[423]

---

[414]   *See, e.g.,* State ex rel. Babione v. Martin, 647 N.E.2d 169 (Ohio Ct. App. 1994), *appeal dismissed,* 646 N.E.2d 178 (Ohio 1995) (agreement did not have formalities necessary for enforceable voting trust nor was it a shareholder pooling agreement).

[415]   Hall v. Staha, 800 S.W.2d 396 (Ark. 1990).

[416]   Hall v. Staha, 800 S.W.2d 396 (Ark. 1990); Abercrombie v. Davies, 130 A.2d 338 (Del. 1957).

[417]   *See* Oceanic Exploration Co. v. Grynberg, 428 A.2d 1 (Del. Super. Ct. 1981) (public policy offended only if noncomplying arrangement was mechanism to secretly acquire control).

[418]   1 Model Bus. Corp. Act Ann. § 34 comment (2d ed. 1971).

[419]   A familiar example is that found within the closely held corporation. *See infra* Chapter 14.

[420]   *See* Sanchez v. Guerrero, 2000 WL 298910 (N.D. Cal.) (reformation of trust appropriate if purpose is no longer to provide stability to company's operations but to perpetuate control of trustee).

[421]   *See* Warehime v. Warehime, 761 A.2d 1138 (Pa. 2000).

[422]   *See* Report of the Securities & Exchange Commission on Investment Trusts and Investment Companies, Part III, ch. V, at 1913 (1940).

[423]   Seward v. American Hardware Co., 171 S.E. 650, 659–660 (Va. 1932).

The trustee of a voting trust is a fiduciary to the beneficiaries of the trust.[424] The voting of the trusts shares to support a transaction in which the trustee has a direct financial interest calls for close scrutiny of the transaction and the trustee's motives.[425]

Warehime v. Warehime[426] presents an interesting illustration of the scope of the voting trustee's powers to vote the trust shares in a manner that advances his interests. John, CEO of HFC, became the sole trustee of two voting trusts established by his father. The shares held by the two trusts represented a majority of the voting power and among their beneficiaries were John and his two siblings. The siblings chafed under John's stewardship of the firm, but bided their time until the trusts' ten-year term expired. In the meantime, John wielded his power to eliminate cumulative voting and installed non-family members on the board. On the eve of the trust's termination, the shares were voted to approve creating a new class of preferred that would be held by the company's 401(k) plan. The shares would enjoy super voting rights in the event (surely to occur) that John and his siblings could not concur on who was to be elected to the board. The plan's trustees were the company's independent directors (the appointees of John) and a majority of them were to decide how the preferred shares were to be voted if they were to be entitled to vote. John's siblings cried foul, alleging quite properly that the arrangement had the effect of extending John's control of the company. The court relied heavily upon the trial court's finding that John acted consistent with his fiduciary duty of good faith as trustee in approving the recapitalization which served the ends of the corporation and its stockholders by providing stable governance and a means to resolve intracorporate disputes. Though not emphasized by the Pennsylvania Supreme Court, a significant consideration in John's strategy was inserting the independent directors into the role of Solomon. The dissenters gave short shrift to this factor and instead saw John's deeds as nothing less than the trustee engaging in self-dealing. Notable in the court's disposition was that it took a broader view of the trustee's obligations; the majority assessed John's actions not solely by their impact on the trust's beneficiaries, but by their impact on the corporation and its shareholders. The majority justified this broader view because of the trust agreement's broad authority that the trustee was to exercise his best judgment and act in good faith.

§ 13.32 The Voting Trust in Operation

The voting trust involves a more complete and formal surrender of the shareholder's legal rights and remedies than any other control device. Voting-trust procedures commonly require that the shares' ownership be transferred to the voting trustee, that there be a formal voting-trust agreement signed by the shareholders creating the trust, and that a copy of that agreement must be filed with the corporation's principal officer.[427] The failure to comply with these provisions at one time led to the arrangement being

---

[424] An interesting question is whether the voting trusts agreement's requirements with respect to how the trust's shares are to be voted are binding on the trustee in his dual capacity as a director of the corporation. *See* Anchel v. Shea, 762 A.2d 346, 357 (Pa. Super. 2000) (director acting consistent with his fiduciary obligations as a director is not restrained by express terms of voting trust agreement that apply to his status as a trustee).

[425] *See, e.g.,* Regnery v. Meyers, 679 N.E.2d 74 (Ill. Ct. App. 1997) (trustee breached obligation by voting trust's shares to approve company's issuance of shares to him at less than their fair market value; also breach by his co-conspirators).

[426] Warehime v. Warehime, 761 A.2d 1138 (Pa. 2000).

[427] Cal. Corp. Code §§ 706, 711 (2009); Del. Code Ann. tit. 8, § 218(a), (b) (2009); N.Y. Bus. Corp. Law § 621 (2009). *See* Model Bus. Corp. Act § 7.30 (2016); former Model Bus. Corp. Act § 34 (1969).

viewed as invalid.[428] More recent decisions have upheld arrangements under state voting-trust statutes when there was less than literal compliance with the statute.[429]

The beneficial owners may cease to be recognized as shareholders of record and may be deprived not only of any right to vote but also of any right of inspection, notice, or information from the corporation or any voice in fundamental changes, such as mergers and consolidations, sales of entire assets, increase and reduction of capital, and bylaw and charter amendments that may adversely affect them. There is ordinarily no justification for such a complete stripping of the shareholders of all the safeguards provided by law for their protection.[430] Persons who have put their shares in a voting trust—that is, the holders of voting-trust certificates—are often spoken of as "equitable owners" of shares of stock. They become in effect equitable tenants in common in the mass of shares transferred to the trustees, with a contract right to receive dividends and retransfer of the shares on termination of the trust. The remedies of the holder of a voting-trust certificate are primarily against the trustees to cancel the trust for fraud, to remove the trustees if guilty of misconduct or for conflicting interests, or to sue for an accounting for secret profits.[431] Voting trustees are subject to the usual fiduciary principles of a trust.[432]

A voting-trust certificate is a profit-sharing security or contract issued by the trustees as a kind of association or holding company, of which the "charter" is the voting agreement. Since voting-trust certificates in effect represent shares in such an association, the transfer thereof can result in a taxable event.[433] Under both state[434] and federal[435] securities legislation, voting-trust certificates are securities and thus are subject to those acts' antifraud and registration provisions.

---

[428] *See* Abercrombie v. Davies, 130 A.2d 338 (Del. 1957). *But see* Del. Code Ann. tit. 8, § 218(c) (2009) (inviting enforcement of voting agreements generally according to their terms).

[429] *See* Reserve Life Ins. Co. v. Provident Life Ins. Co., 499 F.2d 715 (8th Cir. 1974) (omitted address of trustee); Oceanic Exploration Co. v. Grynberg, 428 A.2d 1 (Del. Supr. Ct. 1981) (agreement would be struck down as illegal voting trust only if noncomplying arrangement offended public policy as a mechanism to secretly acquire control).

[430] *Cf.* In re Bacon, 38 N.E.2d 105 (N.Y. 1941), noted in 55 Harv. L. Rev. 868 (1942) (voting trust not specifically including the power to liquidate strictly construed not to include such by implication).

[431] Earle R. Hanson Assocs. v. Farmers' Coop. Creamery Co., 403 F.2d 65 (8th Cir. 1968).

[432] *See* Tankersley v. Albright, 514 F.2d 956 (7th Cir. 1975).

[433] Orpheum Bldg. Co. v. Anglim, 127 F.2d 478, 484 (9th Cir. 1942).

[434] *See, e.g.,* Uniform Securities Act § 202(28) (2002).

[435] 15 U.S.C. §§ 77b(a)(1), 78c(a)(10) (2009).

Chapter 14

CLOSELY HELD ENTITIES

Table of Sections

§ 14.1   Close Corporations and Other Closely Held Entities: Definitions and Distinctive Needs

"Close corporation" (or "closely held corporation") is defined in a number of ways.[1] The term is often used to refer to a corporation with only a few shareholders to distinguish a corporation of that kind from a publicly held company. A popular definition describes a close corporation as one whose shares are not generally traded in the securities markets.[2] "Close corporation" frequently connotes an incorporated business in which the owners consider themselves partners and make decisions and conduct their business affairs as though they were partners.[3] Further, the principal shareholders in a

---

[1]   *See* 1 F. Hodge O'Neal & Robert B. Thompson, O'Neal and Thompson's Close Corporations and LLCs: Law and Practice § 1.2 at 1–4 (rev. 3d ed. 2009).

[2]   Elvin R. Latty, The Close Corporation and the New North Carolina Business Corporation Act, 34 N.C. L. Rev. 432, 439 (1956).

[3]   *See* Ripin v. Atlantic Mercantile Co., 98 N.E. 855, 856 (N.Y. 1912) ("chartered partnerships"); Cuppy v. Ward, 176 N.Y.S. 233, 243 (App. Div.), *aff'd,* 125 N.E. 915 (N.Y. 1919) ("incorporated partnership"). For examples of attribution of partnership characteristics to close corporations, *see* Kann v. Keystone Resources,

close corporation are generally active in management. Summing up the characteristics of a close corporation, a Massachusetts court commented that such a corporation is typified by: "(1) a small number of stockholders; (2) no ready market for the corporate stock; and (3) substantial majority stockholder participation in the management, direction and operations of the corporations."[4]

A family company is generally considered to be a close corporation; in any event a family company has the same needs and problems and should be treated as such in the eyes of the law.[5] A one-person corporation, however, although often thought of and referred to as a close corporation, does not have the same needs and does not present serious management and control problems. This is because the problems generally associated with close corporations involve disputes between shareholders.

A number of states have enacted special legislation to define and govern the close corporation. In Delaware and several other states, for example, this special statutory regulation states that a close corporation's charter must provide that (1) its stock shall be held by not more than a specified number of persons; (2) its stock is subject to transfer restrictions; and (3) it shall not engage in public offerings of its stock.[6] In a few states, the special close corporation statute defines "close corporation" simply as any corporation that elects close corporation status for purposes of the statute.[7] As discussed throughout this chapter, courts recognize the special needs of close corporations even in the absence of statute. This special treatment applies even if a corporation elects not to incorporate under a state's special close corporation statute. However, there is authority in Delaware that corporations desiring to be treated as close corporations must elect to do so under the Delaware Close Corporation Act.[8]

A person taking a minority position in a close corporation may desire and therefore bargain for protection against the power of those holding a majority of a corporation's voting stock to make decisions that will prejudice minority interests. Participants may use some kind of contractual arrangement to set up a control pattern for the corporation that differs from the traditional corporation control structure. The arrangement may take the form of a pre-incorporation agreement among the participants, a shareholders' agreement after the corporation has been organized, a voting trust, special charter and bylaw provisions, irrevocable proxies, or employment contracts between the corporation and the shareholder-employees of the corporation. Most of these arrangements and the laws applicable to them are discussed briefly in the sections that follow.

The issues outlined above and discussed throughout this chapter are not limited to corporate entities. Other forms of doing business such as limited liability companies

---

Inc., 575 F.Supp. 1084 (W.D. Pa. 1983) (not required to observe the strict formalities that are required in large corporations).

    [4]   Donahue v. Rodd Electrotype Co., 328 N.E.2d 505, 511 (Mass. 1975).

    [5]   Family dissention and other aspects of dysfunctional families can lead to legal battles under corporate law. *See, e.g.*, Meiselman v. Meiselman, 307 S.E.2d 551 (N.C. 1983) (controlling shareholder who fired his brother from a family corporation could be liable for interfering with the terminated brother's reasonable expectations); Call v. Call, 2019 Minn. App. Unpub. LEXIS 854 (Minn. Ct. App. 2019) (amid family turmoil, father CEO could not remove his son as president since authority to remove officers is vested in the board). *See also* § 14.10–14.13 *infra* for discussion of disputes in closely held corporations. Legal representation of participants in family corporations can be problematic. *See* Ronald D. Rotunda, Conflicts Problems When Representing Members of Corporate Families, 72 Notre Dame L. Rev. 655 (1997).

    [6]   Del. Code Ann. tit. 8, § 342(a)(1)–(3) (2001) (30 nominal shareholders).

    [7]   *See, e.g.*, Md. Code Ann., Corps. & Ass'ns § 4–101 (Michie 2007).

    [8]   Nixon v. Blackwell, 626 A.2d 1366 (Del. 1993).

(LLCs) and partnerships raise the same issues. The main difference is that corporate law imposes governance structures. In contrast, LLCs and partnerships provide virtually unlimited leeway in drafting agreements and governance structures.[9]

§ 14.2 Close Corporation Statutes—Scheme, Pitfalls, and Objectives

A substantial number of states have enacted special close corporation statutes or have added to their general corporation statute separate supplements or divisions that apply only to close corporations.[10] This special legislation varies from state to state in both format and substance. In most states with special close corporation legislation, a corporation must meet stated requirements to qualify as a close corporation and must elect close corporation status for the special rules to apply.[11]

In some states, the special close corporation statute gives the organizer greater flexibility in molding the corporation's control pattern than the general corporation statute does. For example, in a state in which the general corporation statute contemplates that a corporation will have a board of directors, the close corporation statute may permit the elimination of a corporation's board of directors and the substitution of direct management by the shareholders.[12] Further, special close corporation legislation may provide broader or additional remedies for conflicts among shareholders than is provided by the general corporation statute.

Some close corporation statutes seem to sanction, if not encourage, informal operation of a close corporation and to disregard the usual corporate ritual. Several provide that failure by a close corporation to observe the usual corporate formalities shall not be used by a court as a basis for disregarding the corporation's separate entity and imposing liability on the shareholders for the corporation's obligations.[13] Maryland legislation states that an annual shareholders' meeting need not be held unless requested by a shareholder.[14] The Wisconsin statute provides that provisions required by law to be set forth in a corporation's bylaws can be stated with equal effect in the corporation's articles of incorporation or in a shareholders' agreement.[15]

Corporations electing to be close corporations under the typical close corporation statute must include in their articles a statement that the corporation is a close corporation.[16] If the election is made after shares have been issued, an amendment to the articles of incorporation adding or deleting the provision must obtain the approval of a supermajority of the stockholders.[17] States sometimes require the articles of incorporation to state that the shares of the electing close corporation will be held by no greater number than the number stated in the articles, which can be no greater than a

---

[9]   Limited liability companies and partnerships are discussed in Chapter 1. Issues directly related to LLC dissolution and fiduciary duties are discusses in §§ 14.16, 14.17, *infra*.

[10]   F. Hodge O'Neal & Robert B. Thompson, O'Neal and Thompson's Close Corporations and LLCs: Law and Practice §§ 1.15 to 1.17 (rev. 3d ed. 2009).

[11]   *See, e.g.,* Cal. Corp. Code § 158(a), (b) (West 1990); Del. Code Ann. tit. 8, §§ 343, 344 (2001).

[12]   *See, e.g.,* Del. Code Ann. tit. 8, § 351 (2001).

[13]   *See* Cal. Corp. Code § 300(e) (West 1990); Wis. Stat. Ann. § 180.1835 (West 2002).

[14]   Md. Code Ann., Corps. & Ass'ns § 4–402(a) (Michie 2007).

[15]   Wis. Stat. Ann. § 180.1825 (West 2002).

[16]   *See, e.g.,* Cal. Corp. Code § 158(a) (West 1990); Del. Code Ann. tit. 8, § 343 (2001).

[17]   *See, e.g.,* Cal. Corp. Code § 158(b), (c) (West Supp. 2009) (unanimous vote to add and two-thirds approval to remove); Del. Code Ann. tit. 8, §§ 344 & 346 (2001) (two-thirds vote to elect or terminate election).

number specified in the statute.[18] A transfer of shares that causes the corporation to exceed the limit stated in its articles of incorporation terminates the entity's status as a close corporation. In some states, the corporation is granted a short statutory period of grace in which to take corrective action, such as amending the articles to increase within the statutory limits the number of shareholders specified or reducing the number of shareholders by purchase.[19] California has a unique provision deeming any inter vivos transfer void if it causes the number of shareholders to exceed the specified limit, provided the share certificate contains the statutorily prescribed notice.[20]

The overall objective of electing close corporation status is more than likely to invoke the statutory imprimatur for the close corporation participants to organize the governance of their business and their own participation in a manner different from what customarily follows from being a corporation. The foremost consideration in this regard is the so-called shareholders' agreement that is authorized by most close corporation statutes. Of those states that authorize shareholder agreements, most follow the style first enacted in North Carolina by setting forth various bases on which the agreement cannot be attacked. For example, the Delaware statute provides:

> No written agreement among the stockholders of a close corporation . . . shall be invalid on the ground that it is an attempt by the parties to the agreement or by the stockholders of the corporation to treat the corporation as if it were a partnership or to arrange relations among the stockholders or between the stockholders and the corporation in a manner that would be appropriate only among partners.[21]

On reflection, authorization that takes the form, as does the above Delaware provision, of negating the types of arguments that can be raised against the agreement is a very curious form of legislative authorization. Viewed historically, the statute can be seen as a strong legislative statement rejecting an early line of cases, discussed elsewhere in this chapter, that more often than not invalidated shareholder agreements on the grounds captured today in the statute. But the statute appears to invite the resourceful lawyer to identify a basis not already negated in the statute as the missile to sink the shareholders' agreement. In contrast, the recently enacted Texas close corporation provisions provide a nonexclusive list of many broad topics that may validly be included in a shareholders' agreement.[22]

In sum, close corporation statutes vary widely not simply in the approach each takes toward meeting the unique needs of close corporations but also in the legislature's perception of what areas of the close corporation merit special treatment. This is especially surprising in light of the fact that a perusal of the literature reflects very little disagreement as to how the position of a stockholder in a close corporation differs from that of a stockholder in a public corporation. Though there appears to be no disagreement on this fundamental point, the wide variance among corporate statutes bears testament

---

[18]   *See, e.g.,* Cal. Corp. Code § 158(a) (West Supp. 2009) (35 holders); Del. Code Ann. tit. 8, § 342 (2001) (30 persons).

[19]   *See, e.g.,* Del. Code Ann. tit. 8, § 348 (2001) (30 days).

[20]   *See* Cal. Corp. Code §§ 158(e) (West Supp. 2009), 418(c), (d) (West 1990).

[21]   Del. Code Ann. tit. 8, § 354 (2001). *See also* Cal. Corp. Code § 300(b) (West 1990); N.Y. Bus. Corp. Law § 620(b) (McKinney 2003).

[22]   Tex. Bus. Corp. Act Ann. arts. 12.32 to 12.35 (2003).

to great differences among policy-makers on the appropriate legislative response to meeting the needs of close corporation participants.

§ 14.3　Shareholders' Agreements: Contents

Participants in close corporations frequently enter into agreements among themselves to provide protection to minority shareholders against the principle of majority rule or to tailor the corporate structure to the participants' particular desires and the needs of the enterprise.[23] Minority shareholders often seek agreements that will provide them with representation on the board of directors or will otherwise give them input in the management of the corporation.[24] Although board membership may give the minority access to information on some decisions being made for the corporation, membership alone provides the minority with very little protection against the power vested in the majority by the principle of majority rule. Consequently, the minority may bargain for power to veto some or all corporate decisions or for some other effective participation in corporate affairs.[25] The majority may agree to share their power with the minority in order to encourage potential shareholders to invest in the enterprise, bring into the enterprise valuable patents or know-how, or provide needed executives or scientifically skilled employees as key members of the company.

Shareholders who hold a majority of a corporation's shares sometimes enter into an agreement among themselves with a vastly different objective, usually to guarantee that they will continue to act jointly in making corporate decisions. Shareholders' agreements to which minority shareholders are parties typically cover selection of the members of the board of directors, the naming of corporate officers, employment of shareholders and their salaries, and the amount of time each participant is to devote to the business.[26]

§ 14.4　Forms and Execution of Shareholders' Agreements

A shareholders' agreement may take a number of forms.[27] In a simple shareholders' pooling agreement, the parties agree to vote their shares in the manner set forth in the agreement. The shareholders retain title to their shares and the right to vote them; however, they are contractually bound to vote pursuant to a prearranged plan.[28] A pooling agreement is to be distinguished from a shareholders' management agreement, in which the parties attempt to control corporate decisions that otherwise would be made by the board of directors, such as determining corporate policy, selecting officers, fixing salaries, and declaring dividends.[29]

---

[23]　*See* F. Hodge O'Neal & Robert B. Thompson, O'Neal and Thompson's Close Corporations and LLCs: Law and Practice ch. 5 (rev. 3d ed. 2009).

[24]　*See, e.g.,* Anchel v. Shea, 762 A.2d 346, 359–60 (Pa. Super. 2000) (shareholder agreement calling for each employee to be a director prevented voting trust trustee from removing an employee as a director).

[25]　*See generally* Harvey Gelb, Close Corporation Control and the Voting Agreement, 16 Land & Water L. Rev. 225 (1981).

[26]　*See* Sternheimer v. Sternheimer, 155 S.E.2d 41 (Va. 1967) (failure to include provision dealing with amount of time participants are to work for corporation and extent to which outside part-time activities are allowed can lead to dissension and litigation).

[27]　*See* F. Hodge O'Neal & Robert B. Thompson, O'Neal and Thompson's Close Corporations and LLCs: Law and Practice § 4.3 (rev. 3d ed. 2009).

[28]　5 William M. Fletcher, Fletcher Cyclopedia of the Law of Private Corporations, § 2064 (perm. ed. 2003).

[29]　Annot., Validity and Effect of Agreement Controlling the Vote of Corporate Stock, 45 A.L.R.2d 799 (1956, Later Case Service 1980 & Supp. 1985).

An agreement among shareholders may involve more than a simple contract binding the parties to vote their shares in a specified way. It may, for example, set up irrevocable proxies for the voting of stock or establish a voting trust whereby the stock held in trust is voted by the trustees in the manner determined by the trust instrument.[30] Further, an agreement among shareholders may be embodied in the corporation's charter or bylaws in addition to or instead of being evidenced by a separate document.[31]

More frequently, the objective of a shareholders' agreement is to restrict the freedom of its parties or to arrange their economic rights in a manner different than would follow their proportionate share ownership. For example, in *Wasserman v. Rosengarden*[32] the shareholders' agreement among the minority 20 percent owner and the husband and wife who owned the remaining shares, among other features, assured the minority holder an equal share in profits with the other two holders.[33] The court held that, absent any fraud[34] or apparent injury to public policy, the agreement was valid.

A shareholders' agreement is frequently the document that imposes restrictions on the transfer of shares or even contains covenants not to compete. As would be expected, covenants not to compete are subjected to close scrutiny on policy grounds,[35] and transfer restrictions are subjected to a lower level of review, being upheld in the absence of fraud, duress, or undue influence.[36] A shareholders' agreement can also be the device that accords rights on nonshareholders, such as giving a creditor veto power over board financial decisions.[37]

Many state statutes prescribe specific requirements for shareholders' agreements authorized under their close corporation statutes. For example, California defines "shareholders' agreement" as a written agreement signed by all the shareholders.[38] Several state statutes include authorization for shareholder agreements for those corporations that have duly qualified as close corporations. It is a question of legislative intent whether an agreement that does not comply strictly with such requirements should be held invalid on its face. It would appear wiser to view the statute as merely a safe harbor for such agreements, but not the exclusive means for enforceable agreements to arise.

For example, in a leading case, *Zion v. Kurtz*,[39] the sole stockholders of a Delaware corporation agreed that no business or activities of the corporation would be conducted without the consent of the minority stockholder. The defendant in that action argued, in

---

[30] *See* §§ 13.31 & 13.32.

[31] *See* 1 O'Neal & Thompson, *supra* note 1, ch. 3; *infra* § 14.7. *See also, e.g.*, Hall v. Tennessee Dressed Beef Co., 957 S.W.2d 536 (Tenn. 1997) (bylaw provision treated as contract among shareholders of closely held corporation).

[32] Wasserman v. Rosengarden, 406 N.E.2d 131 (Ill. App. Ct. 1980).

[33] Likewise, a shareholders' agreement can be used to provide a pre-established salary to a party. *See* Roos v. Aloi, 487 N.Y.S.2d 637 (Sup. Ct. 1985).

[34] Fraud would be present if the significance of the agreement on the corporation and relative rights of the shareholders were not fully disclosed. *See* Miller v. Miller, 700 S.W.2d 941 (Tex. Ct. App. 1985).

[35] *Cf.* State v. Nichols, 683 P.2d 565 (Or. Ct. App. 1984) (client's right to choose counsel would be frustrated by transfer restriction on attorney's shares, which provided a lower price in mandatory buyout provision than if attorney had signed covenant not to compete).

[36] *See, e.g.*, Shortridge v. Platis, 458 N.E.2d 301 (Ind. Ct. App. 1984).

[37] *See* Westland Capital Corp. v. Lucht Engg., Inc., 308 N.W.2d 709 (Minn. 1981) (venture capitalists granted power to overrule capital expenditures in excess of $25,000).

[38] Cal. Corp. Code § 186 (West 1990).

[39] Zion v. Kurtz, 405 N.E.2d 681 (N.Y. 1980).

part, that the agreement was invalid because, although several provisions of the Delaware statute authorized the agreement entered into between the parties, that authorization applied only to a corporation that had taken the steps required under Delaware law to formally be a close corporation. The corporation in question had not taken the formalities required to qualify as a close corporation.[40] The New York Court of Appeals held the agreement was valid, reasoning that despite the agreement's noncompliance with the statute's formal requirements, the agreement's substance did not offend Delaware public policy in view of the fact that all the stockholders were signatories to the agreement.

The approach taken in *Zion* is consistent with the cases that have upheld even oral agreements among the shareholders,[41] as well as arrangements that failed to strictly comply with the statutory requirements for that type of provision.[42] Decisions such as *Zion* run the risk of robbing statutory provisions of their significance. One approach may be to view statutory provisions authorizing special arrangements within qualifying close corporations as safe harbors where questions of public policy and affronts to the statutory scheme have been resolved by the legislature; noncomplying agreements would, as in *Zion*, still be scrutinized on these factors and perhaps others.

The Delaware Supreme Court in *Nixon v. Blackwell*[43] expressed less flexibility for its close corporation provisions than the New York court did in *Zion*. The specific issue before the Delaware court was whether non-employee-shareholders could require the corporation to purchase their shares because the shares held by certain employee-shareholders had been purchased. In ruling against the petitioning minority shareholders, the Delaware Supreme Court expressed its unwillingness to create special ad hoc rules for the participants of a small corporation that had not followed the formal procedures to qualify as a close corporation under Subchapter 14 of the Delaware General Corporation Law. Failing to so qualify, the court concluded a corporation is not governed by Delaware's close corporation provisions. Taken literally, it would appear that Delaware would not, as *Zion* concluded, permit the participants in a small corporation to arrange their affairs in a manner that is appropriate only for a "statutory close corporation" if the corporation has not met the technical statutory requirements to be a "close corporation." *Nixon* can be viewed as treating Delaware's close corporation provisions as exclusive safe harbors for agreements that otherwise are impermissible arrangements for corporations. So viewed, only by meeting the statutory requirements to qualify as a close corporation can the corporation's participants invoke the certainty and protection of Delaware's close corporation provisions.

§ 14.5   Validity of Shareholders' Agreements Attacked Because They Limit the Board of Directors' Discretion of Authority

In the past courts looked with much distrust on shareholders' agreements and often condemned not only dishonest schemes but also any agreement that might conceivably

---

[40]   Among the requirements not satisfied was a statement in the articles of incorporation designating the corporation as a close corporation and stating its shares could not be held by a greater number than a stated number of individuals. *See* Del. Code Ann. tit. 8, § 342 (2001).

[41]   *See* Wasserman v. Rosengarden, 406 N.E.2d 131 (Ill. App. Ct. 1980).

[42]   *See, e.g.,* Adler v. Svingos, 436 N.Y.S.2d 719 (App. Div. 1981).

[43]   Nixon v. Blackwell, 626 A.2d 1366 (Del. 1993).

have been injurious to noncontracting shareholders or corporate creditors. Indeed, in some instances courts were overly strict and rejected shareholders' agreements that served a useful purpose and were in the best interest of the corporation and all shareholders and creditors. They applied their concepts of public policy unrealistically, oblivious to the fact that a party to a shareholders' agreement who sets up the illegality of the agreement as a defense often does so simply to escape an honest bargain that has become burdensome.

Most modern statutes provide that shareholders' agreements may stipulate the manner in which the parties will vote their shares,[44] but this does not preclude attacks based on violation of other statutory norms. A common basis for attacking shareholders' control agreements is that they are incompatible with the statutory scheme of corporate management and operation.[45] The statutory section providing that the business of a corporation shall be managed by (or under the supervision of) its board of directors is frequently used to attack the validity of a shareholders' agreement if the agreement purports to control matters within the traditional powers of the directors.[46]

Shareholders' agreements that tend to control directors' actions have often been held invalid even though the agreements were made in good faith and actually were beneficial to the company and its shareholders.[47] Numerous early decisions held that shareholders' agreements, especially agreements by less than all of a corporation's shareholders that restricted the discretion of the directors were invalid as contrary to public policy.[48] The courts reasoned that since the corporation statute provided that the business of a corporation shall be managed by or under the direction of its board of directors,[49] the directors' power of control existed for the benefit of all the shareholders, and they could not bargain away in advance the free exercise of director discretion. Thus shareholders' agreements calling for the election of "sterilized" or dummy directors who would place or maintain designated persons in the corporation's employment were generally held void.[50]

The New York Court of Appeals invalidated a unanimous shareholders' agreement giving broad management powers to designated shareholders because it would "sterilize" the board.[51] The same court refused to enforce a unanimous shareholders' agreement providing that a designated person would serve as president of the company for ten years and not be subject to discharge by the board.[52] The current New York statute is more liberal in sanctioning arrangements that deprive directors of traditional powers, provided those arrangements are placed in the corporation's certificate of

---

[44] *See* Model Bus. Corp. Act §§ 7.30, 7.31 (2016); former Model Bus. Corp. Act § 34 (1969).

[45] *See* Benintendi v. Kenton Hotel, Inc., 60 N.E.2d 829 (N.Y. 1945) (invalidating bylaws).

[46] *See, e.g.,* Conn. Gen. Stat. Ann. § 33–735(b) (2005); Pa. Stat. Ann. tit. 15, § 1721 (Supp. 2009).

[47] *E.g.,* Kennerson v. Burbank Amusement Co., 260 P.2d 823 (Cal. Ct. App. 1953).

[48] West v. Camden, 135 U.S. 507 (1890).

[49] *E.g.,* Model Bus. Corp. Act § 8.01(b) (2016).

[50] *See* Note, The Validity of Stockholders' Voting Agreements in Illinois, U. Chi. L. Rev. 640, 648 (1936).

[51] Long Park, Inc. v. Trenton-New Brunswick Theatres Co., 77 N.E.2d 633 (N.Y. 1948).

[52] Fells v. Katz, 175 N.E. 516 (N.Y. 1931). Some recent decisions purport to follow *Fells v. Katz* but have emphasized that good cause must be shown to discharge an employee covered by agreement. *See* Napoli v. Carrano, 486 N.Y.S.2d 339 (App. Div. 1985); Dubin v. Muchnick, 438 N.Y.S.2d 920 (Sup. Ct. 1981), *modified,* 447 N.Y.S.2d 472 (App. Div. 1982).

incorporation.[53] Further, in a sharply divided four-to-three decision,[54] a New York court, applying Delaware law, upheld an agreement giving a minority shareholder a veto over corporate decisions, even though the agreement was not included in the company's charter or bylaws. The courts' liberal approach toward agreements restricting director discretion can be traced to *Clark v. Dodge*.[55] In exchange for Clark's agreement to disclose a secret formula that would be promoted through their corporation, Dodge agreed to vote as a director to select Clark as the company's general manager and to approve a salary or dividends paid to Clark equal to one-fourth of the company's net income. Several critical points must be observed regarding the facts of *Clark v. Dodge*. First, the agreement restricted the discretion of Dodge as a director on the specific issues of who would be the company's general manager and what compensation the general manager would receive. It was on this point that Dodge later argued that his agreement with Clark was void as against public policy because it removed his discretion as a director to select another as president or to approve a different compensation arrangement for Clark. Second, the action was in equity because Clark wanted specific enforcement of the contract, not damages for its breach. Equity jurisdiction was available because damages could not be determined; Clark's compensation was premised on one-fourth of the net income to be derived by the promotion of his secret process. The profits of such a promotion could only be determined through enforcement of the agreement; hence, damages at law were not adequate. Third, the essence of the agreement was to provide assurance that the secret process could be successfully promoted through the efforts of Clark. This is the reason Clark demanded an agreement that he have unspecified tenure as the company's general manager. Finally, Dodge was obligated to vote for Clark as general manager only so long as he was "efficient and competent."

The New York court in *Clark v. Dodge* departed from precedent and upheld the agreement. The court was influenced not only by the fact that all the stockholders signed the agreement, but also that its limitation on the directors' discretion was limited to specific areas, namely the selection of the general manager and his compensation. Thus, there were many other areas where the directors' discretion was unrestrained by the agreement (*e.g.*, selection of other officers, authority to borrow funds, or approval of corporate expenditures and budgets). In its now classic expression, *Clark* reasoned that rather than an attempt to "sterilize the board of directors" by wholesale removal of its discretion, the agreement before it only "slightly impinged" on the board's discretion. Moreover, the court was impressed that the agreement was among the sole shareholders of the corporation and persuaded that creditors were not harmed by the agreement because there was an *implied* condition of good faith that any payments to Clark would be after making reasonable and adequate provision for creditors. *Clark v. Dodge* thus established a fairly consistent line of case upholding, certainly among the signatories of the agreement, contracts that removed discretion from directors in specific areas, provided enforcement poses no threat to the interest of other stockholders or creditors.[56]

---

[53]   Weber v. Sidney, 244 N.Y.S.2d 228 (App. Div. 1963), *aff'd*, 200 N.E.2d 867 (N.Y. 1964); N.Y. Bus. Corp. Law, § 620(b) (McKinney Supp. 2002).

[54]   Zion v. Kurtz, 405 N.E.2d 681 (N.Y. 1980).

[55]   Clark v. Dodge, 199 N.E. 641 (N.Y. 1936).

[56]   *See, e.g.*, Galler v. Galler, 203 N.E.2d 577 (Ill. 1964) (upholding agreement providing for election of certain persons to specified offices for a period of years).

The recent trend has been toward an increasing statutory and judicial acceptance of shareholders' management agreements.[57] Some courts have upheld shareholders' agreements depriving directors of some managerial powers if they concluded that the agreements took from the directors only relatively unimportant powers and thus impinged only slightly on the statutory norm of director management.

The typical shareholders' management agreement in a close corporation gives minority holders a voice in control and management of the corporation and assures them of employment by the corporation. Such an agreement is now usually held valid, at least if all shareholders are parties and the agreement is not detrimental to prospective shareholders.[58] More recently, courts appear not to emphasize the quantum of discretion removed from the directors by the agreement but instead emphasize the freedom of the stockholders to mold the relationship they prefer through private contractual arrangements, the absence of any harm or fraud on nonsignatories, and the trend toward upholding special arrangements in close corporations.[59] It appears that, whereas courts formerly began their scrutiny with a jealous eye toward the norms and policies believed to be embodied in the local corporate statute, the approach today invariably is contractual.[60] Today, it appears that any limits on the scope or validity of shareholders' agreements are imposed only when there is a clear conflict with the governing corporate statute[61] and, more particularly, if there is any fraud in the agreement's execution or operation.[62]

§ 14.6 Shareholders' Reciprocal Pooling Agreements Controlling Voting for Directors

Agreements to vote for specified persons as directors or to vote as the holders of a majority of the shares in a pool may direct are valid and binding if they do not contemplate limiting the discretion of the directors or the committing of any fraud, oppression, or wrong against other shareholders. The validity of voting agreements therefore depends on their purposes, effects, and tendencies.[63]

Courts consider a variety of factors when determining the validity of a shareholders' agreement.[64] Before such agreements received based approval in most state statutes, a variety of factors were considered in judging their validity: (1) the purpose or object of the agreement, (2) the statutes in force in the particular jurisdiction in which the agreement is made, (3) the conceptions of public policy prevailing in the courts of the jurisdiction regarding the separation of voting power from the beneficial ownership of

---

[57]   *See, e.g.,* Wasserman v. Rosengarden, 406 N.E.2d 131 (Ill. App. Ct. 1980).

[58]   *See* Glazer v. Glazer, 374 F.2d 390 (5th Cir.), *cert. denied,* 389 U.S. 831 (1967), *motion denied,* 274 F.Supp. 471 (E.D. La.), *on remand,* 278 F.Supp. 476 (E.D. La. 1968) (agreement held valid under laws of Tennessee, Ohio, and Florida but invalid under West Virginia law).

[59]   *See, e.g.,* Wasserman v. Rosengarden, 406 N.E.2d 131 (Ill. App. Ct. 1980).

[60]   The strong contractual undercurrent to the courts' approach has caused some commentators to question the desirability of close corporation statutes that may only introduce unneeded technical requirements in the parties' path toward resolving their own relationship through private agreements. *See* Dennis S. Karjala, A Second Look at Special Close Corporation Legislation, 58 Tex. L. Rev. 1207 (1980).

[61]   *See, e.g.,* Gazda v. Kolinski, 458 N.Y.S.2d 387 (App. Div. 1982).

[62]   *See* Miller v. Miller, 700 S.W.2d 941 (Tex. Ct. App. 1985).

[63]   Smith v. San Francisco & N.P. R.R., 47 P. 582 (Cal. 1897).

[64]   The distinction between a mere proxy and a voting agreement is that the latter sets forth the manner in which the shares are to be voted whereas the former simply gives the holder the authority to vote the shares. *See, e.g.,* Reynolds Health Care Services, Inc. v. HMNH, Inc., 217 S.W.3d 797 (Ark. 2005).

shares, (4) the situation of the corporation and the shareholders at the time the agreement was made, (5) whether or not all of the shareholders in the corporation are parties to the agreement, (6) whether the contracting shareholders are also directors or expect to be at the time of the performance of the contract, (7) the length of time during which the agreement will control the shareholders' right to vote their shares, (8) whether the person challenging the validity of the agreement is a party to it or is a creditor or shareholder not party to the agreement, (9) whether the person challenging the agreement is simply trying to "welch" on his undertaking, (10) whether or not there is consideration, other than the mutual promises of the parties to support the undertakings, to vote in accordance with the terms of the agreement, (11) how long the contract has been in operation and the extent to which action has been taken or positions have changed in reliance on it, and (12) the kind of corporation whose stock is subject to the voting arrangement.[65]

Although most modern statutes declare that voting agreements are enforceable according to their terms,[66] this declaration is far from an unlimited validation of all shareholders' agreements. For example, in a famous Delaware case,[67] the two contracting parties, Mrs. Ringling and Mrs. Haley, who between them had sufficient shares to elect five of the seven directors, agreed to act jointly in exercising their voting rights and, in the event of disagreement, to vote in accordance with the decision of an arbitrator. After a disagreement between the two and a decision by the arbitrator as to how the shares of the two were to be voted, Mrs. Haley disregarded the arbitrator's decision and voted her shares contrary to his directions. The Court of Chancery ordered that a new election be held before a master and that effect be given to the agreement. On appeal, however, the Delaware Supreme Court modified the decree by ordering that Mrs. Haley's votes be rejected but that the other votes cast at the shareholders' meeting be counted. The result was that only six directors (instead of seven) were elected, three by Mrs. Ringling and three by Mr. North, the third shareholder. Although this decision of the Delaware Supreme Court frustrated the objective of the agreement, perhaps the decision was justified in a technical sense as a recognition of the rights of Mr. North, who was not a party to the agreement and who had cast his votes properly at a regular shareholders' meeting.

In a subsequent decision,[68] since repudiated by statute, the Delaware court invalidated a pooling agreement on the ground that it was in effect a voting trust that failed to comply with statutory formalities.[69] The court pointed out that the agreement provided for deposit of the parties' stock with irrevocable stock powers conferring on a group of fiduciaries exclusive voting powers over the pooled stock. The court

---

[65] F. Hodge O'Neal & Robert B. Thompson, O'Neal and Thompson's Close Corporations and LLCs: Law and Practice § 5.8 (rev. 3d ed. 2009).

[66] *See* Model Bus. Corp. Act § 7.31 (2016).

[67] Ringling Bros.-Barnum & Bailey Combined Shows, Inc. v. Ringling, 53 A.2d 441 (Del.Supr. 1947), *modifying* 49 A.2d 603 (Del. Ch. 1946).

[68] Abercrombie v. Davies, 130 A.2d 338 (Del. 1957), *remanded*, 131 A.2d 822 (Del. Ch. 1957), noted in 46 Cal. L. Rev. 124 (1958) (criticizes court's holding in *Abercrombie*).

[69] The court pointed to three characteristics of a voting trust: (1) separation of voting rights from other attributes of share ownership; (2) an irrevocable grant of voting rights for a definite period; and (3) the principal object of the arrangement is voting control. The court did not deem it "essential" that there be a transfer of shares on the corporate books, 130 A.2d at 344–346. *See also, e.g.*, State ex rel. Babione v. Martin, 647 N.E.2d 169 (Ohio Ct. App. 1994), *appeal dismissed*, 646 N.E.2d 178 (Ohio 1995) (agreement did not have formalities necessary for enforceable voting trust nor was it a shareholder pooling agreement).

distinguished the *Ringling* agreement, pointing out that it did not create a proxy empowering someone to vote another's shares.[70] In response to this decision, the Delaware legislature enacted a provision stating that the voting trust statute "shall not be deemed to invalidate any voting or other agreement among stockholders or any irrevocable proxy which is not otherwise illegal."[71] Delaware courts today are more supportive of private voting arrangements.[72] In states that do not have this explicit legislative declaration, the Delaware court's reasoning remains a factor to be considered in drafting pooling agreements.[73]

A shareholders' agreement containing a valid irrevocable proxy has the same effect functionally as an ordinary shareholders' pooling agreement that the courts will specifically enforce; it follows that considerations governing the validity of the two should be the same. In either instance, if the agreement has a legitimate business purpose, it should be given effect in accordance with the intentions of the parties.[74]

§ 14.7 Use of Charter or Bylaw Provisions in Lieu of Shareholders' Agreements

Objectives sought in shareholders' agreements can sometimes be achieved by using special charter or bylaw provisions. For example, charter or bylaw clauses imposing an extraordinarily high quorum or voting requirement for shareholder and director action have frequently been employed to allocate control within a close corporation. Such provisions have the effect of giving minority shareholders a veto power over corporate decisions.

In a leading vintage New York case,[75] the court invalidated as contrary to the statutory scheme of corporate governance bylaws requiring: (1) the unanimous vote of the shareholders for shareholder action; (2) the unanimous vote of the shareholders to elect the directors; and (3) the unanimous vote of directors for board of directors action. The court upheld a fourth bylaw requiring the unanimous vote of the shareholders to amend the bylaws. The decision was legislatively repudiated by a statute authorizing the placing of high vote requirements for shareholder or director action in a corporation's charter (but, note, not in its bylaws).[76] Further, almost all states now permit a corporation to insert in its charter a provision setting a high vote for shareholder and director action,[77] and some states permit high vote requirements to be placed in either the charter or the bylaws.[78] In addition, some courts hold that a charter or bylaw provision unanimously adopted by the shareholders may be treated as a contract among

---

[70]   130 A.2d at 346.

[71]   Del. Code Ann. tit. 8, § 218(d) (2001).

[72]   *See e.g.*, Sarissa Capital Domestic Fund, L.P. v. Innoviva, Inc., 2017 WL 6209597 (Del.Ch.2017), judgment entered, 2017 WL 6539590 (Del. Ch. 2017)(ordering specific enforcement of an oral agreement to settle a proxy contest and ordering the company to expand the size of its directors and seat two of the other party's director nominees).

[73]   *See* De Felice v. Garon, 395 So.2d 658 (La. 1980).

[74]   1 F. Hodge O'Neal & Robert B. Thompson, O'Neal and Thompson's Close Corporations and LLCs: Law and Practice § 4.16 at 4–83 (rev. 3d ed. 2009).

[75]   Benintendi v. Kenton Hotel, Inc., 60 N.E.2d 829 (N.Y. 1945).

[76]   *See* Sutton v. Sutton, 637 N.E.2d 260 (1994) (upholding as valid under N.Y. Bus. Corp. Law § 616(b) a unanimous-shareholder-vote requirement for corporate action).

[77]   *See, e.g.*, Cal. Corp. Code §§ 204 (West 1990), 602 (West Supp. 2009); 805 ILCS §§ 5/7.60, 5/8.15 (Smith-Hurd 2004).

[78]   *See, e.g.*, Del. Code Ann. tit. 8, §§ 141(b), 216 (2001); Model Bus. Corp. Act, § 8.24(c) (2016).

the shareholders and thus enforceable as long as there are no new nonapproving shareholders.[79] Even though high vote requirements are clearly permitted, their tendency to lead to deadlock has led some courts to construe them strictly so as to minimize their restrictive effect.[80]

Other special charter and bylaw provisions can be used to depart from the traditional corporate management pattern or to grant protection to minority shareholders. Among special provisions that may be found useful in particular circumstances are the following: clauses requiring cumulative voting for directors; clauses abolishing the board of directors or restricting its powers; clauses authorizing or prohibiting informal operation of the corporation; clauses strengthening shareholders' rights to inspect corporate books and records; clauses controlling dividends and other distributions to shareholders; clauses defining shareholders' preemptive rights; clauses dealing with deadlocks among shareholders and directors; clauses imposing restrictions on the transfer of shares; clauses requiring shareholder approval of officer compensation; clauses giving a shareholder power to dissolve the corporation; clauses prohibiting corporate loans to officers or directors; and clauses providing for arbitration or some other method for resolving disputes among the shareholders.[81]

§ 14.8 Restrictions on the Transferability of Shares; Reasons for Restrictions; Types of Restrictions

In the absence of valid restrictions on their transferability, corporate shares are freely transferable, and the corporation may not refuse to accept a bona fide transferee as a shareholder.[82] In publicly held corporations, free transferability of shares is a valuable attribute in that it encourages contributions to corporate capital by a multitude of investors. In closely held corporations, on the other hand, the participants usually do not want shares to be freely transferable. For similar reasons, LLC members and partners in many partnership ventures may opt to enter in to restrictions of transferability. LLC restrictions on transfer, as is the case with close corporations, are likely to be enforced.[83] Considerable latitude is allowed the participants in imposing share transfer restrictions; restrictions will usually be sustained unless palpably unreasonable under the circumstances.[84] Restrictions may be imposed by the articles of incorporation, the bylaws,[85] or a shareholders' agreement.

Participants in a close corporation may want to restrict the transferability of shares for a number of reasons. Because of the close working relationship that often exists among owners and managers, they may want to retain power to select future associates

---

[79] E. K. Buck Retail Stores v. Harkert, 62 N.W.2d 288 (Neb. 1954).

[80] *See* Blount v. Taft, 246 S.E.2d 763 (N.C. 1978) (finding that bylaws calling for across the board unanimity could be repealed or amended by a simple majority in conformance with the statutory norm).

[81] For a more extensive discussion of special charter and bylaw provisions, *see* 1 F. Hodge O'Neal & Robert B. Thompson, O'Neal and Thompson's Close Corporations and LLCs: Law and Practice §§ 3.15 to 3.61 (rev. 3d ed. 2009).

[82] Mark S. Rhodes, Transfer of Stock § 5.1 (6th ed. 1985).

[83] *See, e.g.,* Eureka VIII LLC v. Niagara Falls Holdings, LLC, 899 A.2d 95 (Del. Ch. 2006) (upholding anti-assignment provision with respect to LLC interest and declaring attempted assignment in violation of the agreement invalid).

[84] Goldberg v. United Parcel Serv., 605 F.Supp. 588 (E.D.N.Y. 1985).

[85] *See* Kansas Heart Hosp., LLC v. Badr, 184 P.3d 866 (Kan. 2008) (bylaw provision empowering board to redeem shares if any holder invested in a competing company was enforceable and not invalid right of redemption of the type that must be included in the articles to be a feature of the shares).

and thus be able to exclude persons who will not be congenial or will not fit into the management team. Further, the participants may desire to restrict the transferability of shares to prevent their purchase by competitors or other persons unfriendly to the corporation.[86] They may also impose transfer restrictions to prevent any one shareholder from gaining absolute control of the corporation by purchasing colleagues' stock. Another reason for restricting the transferability of shares is to preserve the corporation's eligibility to elect the tax status provided by Subchapter S of the Internal Revenue Code[87] or its eligibility to elect to be governed by special close corporation legislation in a number of states requiring close corporations to restrict the transfer of their stock.

There are many different types of share transfer restrictions.[88] The most widely used is the so-called first-option or refusal,[89] which grants the corporation or the other shareholders a right to purchase shares at a set price or at the price offered by a third party, respectively, if a holder decides to sell or otherwise transfer her shares.[90] Other types of transfer restrictions are as follows: (1) absolute prohibitions against transfer; (2) prohibitions against transfer to designated classes of persons, such as competitors;[91] (3) limitation of transfers to stated classes of persons—for example, descendants of the corporation's founders or residents of a designated American state; (4) "consent restraints" that prohibit the disposition of stock without approval of the corporation's directors or shareholders or a stated percentage of one of those groups;[92] and (5) options giving the corporation or the other shareholders the right to purchase the shares of a holder on his death or disability,[93] on the termination of his employment with the corporation,[94] or on the occurrence of some other event.[95] Somewhat related functionally to restrictions on the transfer of stock are buyout agreements, whereby the shareholder agrees to sell stock, and the corporation or the other shareholders agree to buy it, on the occurrence of a stated contingency, such as the shareholder's death or retirement. Such an agreement stipulates a transfer price or sets out a formula for determining price.[96]

---

[86]   This can be a useful device to prevent competitors from acquiring control of a corporation. *See* Joseph E. Seagram & Sons, Inc. v. Conoco, Inc., 519 F.Supp. 506 (D.C. Del. 1981).

[87]   By preventing transfer to a shareholder who does not qualify under Subchapter S or who will refuse to consent to the corporation's election of Subchapter S. *See* I.R.C. §§ 1371 to 1373 (1988).

[88]   *See* 1 F. Hodge O'Neal & Robert B. Thompson, O'Neal and Thompson's Close Corporations and LLCs: Law and Practice § 7.4 (rev. 3d ed. 2009).

[89]   *See, e.g.,* Hall v. Tennessee Dressed Beef Co., 957 S.W.2d 536 (Tenn. 1997) (implying notice requirement from right of first refusal).

[90]   *See, e.g.,* Coury v. Moss, 529 F.3d 579 (5th Cir. 2008) (transfer restriction in articles forms a contract and no right to purchase minority holder's shares until he offers to sell the shares).

[91]   *See, e.g.,* Martin v. Villa Roma, Inc., 182 Cal.Rptr. 382 (Ct. App. 1982) (shares in housing cooperative transferable only to persons meeting requirements).

[92]   *See* Ogden v. Culpepper, 474 So.2d 1346 (La. Ct. App. 1985); Hill v. Warner, Berman & Spitz, 484 A.2d 344 (N.J. Super. Ct. 1984).

[93]   *See* In re Dissolution of Penepent Corp., 96 N.Y.2d 186, 192, 726 N.Y.S.2d 345, 750 N.E.2d 47, 50 (2001) (shareholder agreement giving the corporation the right to purchase a deceased shareholder's shares at a fixed price was not controlling since another shareholder had elected to purchase those shares at fair value in lieu of dissolution prior to shareholder's death).

[94]   *See, e.g.,* Stephenson v. Drever, 947 P.2d 1301 (Cal. 1997) (shares were to be repurchased upon termination of employment; shareholder rights are not extinguished upon termination but rather continue until the repurchase has been consummated and the former employee is no longer a shareholder of record).

[95]   *See* Kansas Heart Hosp. LLC v. Badr, 184 P.3d 866 (Kan. 2008) (bylaw provision empowering board to redeem shares if any holder invested in a competing company was enforceable and not invalid right of redemption of the type that must be included in the articles to be a feature of the shares).

[96]   *See* Horne v. Drachman, 280 S.E.2d 338 (Ga. 1981) (repurchase on termination of employment); Avritt v. O'Daniel, 689 S.W.2d 36 (Ky. Ct. App. 1985) (repurchase on death of shareholder).

Mention should also be made of charter provisions that empower the corporation to redeem ("call") a holder's stock either generally at the corporation's option or on termination of the holder's employment with the corporation.[97] Courts have often been called on to pass on the validity of transfer restrictions against a claim that the restrictions constitute unreasonable restraints on the alienation of property.

§ 14.9 Legal Limits on the Use of Transfer Restrictions

Courts have always looked with disfavor on absolute stock transfer restrictions unlimited in time, regardless of whether they are included in a corporation's articles or bylaws, or in a shareholders' agreement.[98] The courts have, however, generally upheld restraints that they consider reasonable in light of all the circumstances.[99] In passing on the validity of transfer restrictions, the courts have considered a number of factors, including the following: the corporation's size, the extent of the restraint on the holder's power to alienate the shares, the length of time the restriction is to remain in effect, and whether the restriction is conducive to the attainment of corporate objectives and otherwise promotes the corporation's best interests.[100] Generally, courts are more willing to recognize the validity of stock transfer restrictions in close corporations than in publicly held enterprises.[101] However, there are limits on the enforceability of clearly unreasonable restrictions.[102]

The validity of transfer restrictions has frequently been challenged where a great disparity exists between the transfer price provided in the restrictions and the value of the shares. A few courts have held that a restriction, such as a first-option provision, which requires the transfer of shares for considerably less than their value, is an unreasonable restraint on alienation and is thus invalid.[103] Shareholders are not likely to sell their shares if they must first offer them to the corporation or other shareholders at a price that is far below their fair value. Thus a large gap between the option price in a first-option arrangement and the current value of shares may for practical purposes effectively create what is virtually an absolute restraint on alienation.[104] Nevertheless, the great majority of the courts have not invalidated transfer restrictions on the basis that they required the transfer of shares at a price below their value. Even when the value of shares has appeared to be ten, twenty, or even a thousand times greater than

---

[97]   Hamel v. White Wave, Inc., 689 P.2d 709 (Colo. Ct. App. 1984).

[98]   *See* Hill v. Warner, Berman & Spitz, 484 A.2d 344 (N.J. Super. Ct. A.D. 1984).

[99]   *See, e.g.,* Groves v. Prickett, 420 F.2d 1119, 1122 (9th Cir. 1970).

[100]   F. Hodge O'Neal & Robert B. Thompson, O'Neal and Thompson's Close Corporations and LLCs: Law and Practice § 7.7 at 7–34 to 7–35 (rev. 3d ed. 2009).

[101]   *See* B & H Warehouse, Inc. v. Atlas Van Lines, Inc., 490 F.2d 818 (5th Cir. 1974).

[102]   *See, e.g.,* Man O War Restaurants, Inc. v. Martin, 932 S.W.2d 366 (Ky. 1996) (provision in employment contract requiring employee to sell stock back to the corporation for the price originally paid was voided based on the court's strong public policy against forfeiture).

[103]   B & H Warehouse, Inc. v. Atlas Van Lines, Inc., 490 F.2d 818 (5th Cir. 1974) (applying Delaware law, concluded requirement that shares be sold to corporation at set price at one-fifth market price could not be applied to shares not voted in favor of the restriction); Systematics, Inc. v. Mitchell, 491 S.W.2d 40 (1973) (agreement requiring resale to corporation at 20 percent of market value is unfair and fails to comply with statute authorizing restrictions for purchase at "fair" price).

[104]   *Cf.* Man O War Restaurants, Inc. v. Martin, 932 S.W.2d 366 (Ky. 1996) (provision in employment contract requiring employee to sell stock back to the corporation for the price originally paid was voided based on the court's strong public policy against forfeiture).

the transfer price, courts have sustained the restrictions.[105] For example, the Delaware Supreme Court in *Nemec v. Shrader*,[106] held it was not breach of fiduciary duty for corporation to exercise right to purchase retired employees' shares with the consequent effect of shifting millions of dollars of value to the continuing employee-holders who would soon participate in a lucrative buyout of the company whereas dissenters reasoned this violated the implicit term of good faith in the contract.

In many cases, the transfer price was not purposely set low initially; instead it fell below the shares' real value as the company prospered and the value of its shares increased. Even when the transfer price is not fixed in the restriction but is to be determined by formula, the formula price often does not reflect share value accurately for any significant period of time after the restriction is imposed.[107]

In the early cases some courts held that "consent restraints"—that is, restrictions that prohibit transfers unless approved by the directors or other shareholders—were invalid as contrary to public policy and as imposing undue restraints on alienation of property.[108] Many modern courts, however, uphold consent restraints.[109] In a few jurisdictions, however, the validity of consent restraints is still questionable because early decisions have not been overruled.[110]

Since the 1960s most states have enacted legislation governing the validity of stock transfer restrictions. The wording and the substance of the legislation varies from state to state. The Delaware statute provides that stock transfer restrictions or restrictions on the amount of securities that may be owned by any person or group may be imposed either by a corporation's certificate of incorporation, its bylaws, or an agreement among its security holders or among such holders and the corporation, but that a restriction will not be binding with respect to securities issued before adoption of the restriction unless the holders of the securities are parties to an agreement or voted in favor of the restriction.[111]

In addition, the special close corporation section of the Delaware statute, which requires that all of a close corporation's issued stock of all classes be subjected to one or more of the permitted restrictions,[112] provides that if a transfer restriction is held to be unauthorized, "the corporation shall nevertheless have an option, for a period of 30 days after the judgment setting aside the restriction becomes final, to acquire the restricted security at a price which is agreed upon by the parties, or if no agreement is reached as to price, then at the fair value as determined by the Court of Chancery."[113]

---

[105] *See, e.g.,* Helms v. Duckworth, 249 F.2d 482 (D.C. Cir. 1957) (upholding agreement whereby deceased shareholder's estate received only $10 per share for stock worth $80 per share).

[106] 991 A.2d 1120 (Del. 2010).

[107] *See* Note, Stock Transfer Restriction Enforced Despite Nominal Price Term, 16 Stan. L. Rev. 449, 452 (1964).

[108] McNulta v. Corn Belt Bank, 45 N.E. 954, 959 (Ill. 1896) ("[B]y-law is illegal and void . . . because it seeks to keep the future action of the shareholders . . . in subjection to the will of the . . . directors.").

[109] *E.g.,* Schaffer v. Below, 278 F.2d 619 (3d Cir. 1960) (transfer of shares in violation of consent restraint passed equitable title but not legal title to transferee).

[110] *See, e.g.,* Minstar Acquiring Corp. v. AMF, Inc., 621 F.Supp. 1252 (S.D.N.Y. 1985) (plan that provided for nontransferability of rights and adopted in face of hostile tender offer, stricken as unreasonable restraint on alienability).

[111] Del. Code Ann. tit. 8, § 202(b) (2001).

[112] Del. Code Ann. tit. 8, § 342(a)(2) (2001).

[113] Del. Code Ann. tit. 8, § 349 (2001).

Similarly, the Model Business Corporation Act provides that a corporation's articles of incorporation or bylaws or an agreement among shareholders or between shareholders and the corporation may impose restrictions on the transfer of shares but that a restriction does not affect shares issued before the restriction was adopted unless the holders of the shares are parties to the restriction agreement or vote in favor of the restriction.[114] However, the supplement provides a rather extensive list of exceptions to this prohibition.[115]

The Model Business Corporation Act[116] and the general corporation statutes in a number of states require that restrictions be noted conspicuously on the front or back of a share certificate.[117] Unless the restriction is stated, both the Model Business Corporation Act and the Uniform Commercial Code provide that the restriction is not enforceable against a transferee without knowledge.[118]

A further source of caution is the narrow construction courts frequently give to the terms of the transfer restriction. For example, the provision that "no stock in the corporation may be issued, transferred, sold or hypothecated to any person who is not a blood descendant" was held not to reach a testamentary disposition outside the family.[119] Courts frequently appear to manifest bare tolerance of transfer restrictions by strictly construing their scope.[120] The failure of a shareholder to abide by the terms of a valid transfer restriction has been treated as a breach of that shareholder's fiduciary duty.[121]

Similarly, courts sometimes give an expansive meaning to exceptions stated in a transfer restriction.[122] At the same time, courts are not insensitive to the drafters' probable intentions and interpret broad expressions such as "sale" or "transfer" to include transactions not literally within that expression where such a construction carries out the drafters' likely intent.[123]

§ 14.10 Dissension in the Close Corporation

Dissension among the owners of a close corporation has a heavy impact on the enterprise.[124] Because of the participants' intimately close working relationship, in most close corporations, once dissatisfaction or distrust has developed, intracorporate friction is likely to continue to grow. Dissatisfied shareholders of a publicly held corporation have

---

[114] Model Bus. Corp. Act § 6.27(a) (2016).

[115] Model Statutory Close Corp. Supp. §§ 11(b), 12. *See also id.* § 13 (attempted share transfer in breach of prohibition), § 14 (compulsory purchase of shares after death of shareholder).

[116] Model Bus. Corp. Act § 6.27(b) (2016).

[117] *See* Ling & Co. v. Trinity Sav. & Loan Ass'n, 482 S.W.2d 841 (Tex. 1972) (general reference in small type on back of certificate to existence of share restriction in articles not conspicuous but may have placed holder on notice).

[118] Model Bus. Corp. Act § 6.27(b) (2016); U.C.C. § 8–204 (1991).

[119] *See* Valley Nat'l Bank v. Arthur, 490 P.2d 14 (Ariz. Ct. App. 1971).

[120] *See, e.g.,* Louisiana Weekly Publishing v. First Nat'l Bank of Commerce, 483 So.2d 929 (La. 1986) (restrictions on sale and donations causa mortis did not reach inter vivos gift); Durkee v. Durkee-Mower, Inc., 428 N.E.2d 139 (Mass. 1981) (restriction on "sale" does not reach transfer as part of divorce settlement).

[121] *See* Yiannatsis v. Stephanis, 653 A.2d 275 (Del.Supr. 1995).

[122] *See, e.g.,* Sneed v. Silvis Heights Water Corp., 402 N.E.2d 902 (Ill. App. Ct. 1980) (exceptions for transfers by decedent's will or inheritance laws applied to exempt executor's sale of shares to settle the estate because executor's powers arose from state's inheritance laws).

[123] *See* Bruns v. Rennebohm Drug Stores, Inc., 442 N.W.2d 591 (Wis. Ct. App. 1989).

[124] *See generally* F. Hodge O'Neal & Robert B. Thompson, O'Neal and Thompson's Oppression of Minority Shareholders and LLC Members (rev. 2d ed. 2009).

a ready market for their shares, whereas an interest in a closely held corporation does not have a readily available market, at least if the interest is not a controlling one. The marketability of a minority interest in a close corporation is further narrowed if the corporation is racked by dissension. Even if a buyer can be found for a minority interest, the price may be sharply discounted.[125] Furthermore, the existence of transfer restrictions may enable an antagonistic associate to thwart an unhappy shareholder's sale of close corporation shares. Dissension and the inability of unhappy shareholders to get out sometimes results in serious and continuing strife among the shareholders and managers[126] and may result in extensive litigation and serious harm to the corporation and the shareholders.[127]

Deadlocks among the shareholders and in the directorates of closely held corporations may occur because of the way voting shares and positions on the board are distributed. Shares are sometimes divided equally among two or more shareholders or groups of shareholders.[128] And it is not unusual for a close corporation to have an even number of directors; thus a deadlock of directors is likely to occur. Further, in an effort to protect themselves against the power generally vested in shareholders and directors to determine corporate policy by simple majority vote, minority shareholders often bargain for and obtain either a veto over corporate policies and decisions or condition their approval upon a greater than majority vote.[129] Such a veto power increases the risk of corporate paralysis.[130] As one Virginia court eloquently stated, "A recalcitrant . . . shareholder may embalm his corporation and hold it helpless . . . in a state of suspended animation."[131]

Despite the frequency of dissension and deadlock in close corporations, in some states neither legislatures nor courts have provided satisfactory solutions. Therefore, during the organization of a close corporation, counsel must anticipate such problems and may need to provide special contractual arrangements to resolve them. These arrangements usually are set up in the corporation's charter or bylaws or in a shareholders' agreement. They typically take one or more of the following forms: (a) provisions for the buyout of the interests of aggrieved shareholders, (b) the creation of special dissolution rights and procedures, or (c) undertakings to arbitrate disputes. Further possibilities to consider to avoid locking unhappy shareholders into a corporation for an indefinite period of time are: (d) limiting the life of the corporation rather than giving it perpetual existence, (e) setting up a voting trust that gives trustees the power to vote for dissolution, and, where legal, (f) issuing stock that is convertible into notes or debentures.

---

[125] The New Jersey Supreme Court has addressed the issue of whether to apply a marketability discount when a court orders a shareholder to sell his or her stock, concluding that the court must take into account what is fair and equitable. More specifically, a marketability discount cannot be used by the controlling or oppressing shareholders to benefit themselves to the detriment of the minority or oppressed shareholders. Lawson Mardon Wheaton, Inc. v. Smith, 734 A.2d 738, 752 (N.J. 1999).

[126] *See, e.g.*, Hall v. John S. Isaacs & Sons Farms, Inc., 163 A.2d 288 (Del. 1960).

[127] *See, e.g.*, In re Radom & Neidorff, Inc., 119 N.E.2d 563 (N.Y. 1954).

[128] *See, e.g.*, Black v. Graham, 464 S.E.2d 814, 815 (Ga. 1996) (having shown deadlock it was not necessary to further establish any related misconduct).

[129] Roach v. Bynum, 403 So.2d 187, 192 (Ala. 1981).

[130] Veto arrangements are popular. In most jurisdictions, a valid way of setting up effective veto arrangements is available. *See, e.g.*, Zion v. Kurtz, 405 N.E.2d 681 (N.Y. 1980).

[131] Kaplan v. Block, 31 S.E.2d 893, 896–897 (Va. 1944).

§ 14.11   Dissolution for Deadlock

Among the several bases for involuntary dissolution, most corporate statutes include deadlock within the board of directors or among the shareholders. Section 14.30(a)(2) of the Model Business Corporation Act is representative of the position taken by most of the states:

(i)   the directors are deadlocked in the management of the corporate affairs, the shareholders are unable to break the deadlock, and irreparable injury to the corporation is threatened or being suffered, or the business and affairs of the corporation can no longer be conducted to the advantage of the shareholders generally, because of the deadlock; . . .

. . .

(iii) the shareholders are deadlocked in voting power and have failed, for a period that includes at least two consecutive annual meeting dates, to elect successors to directors whose terms have expired. . . .[132]

In fact, the various statutory expressions are but imprecise attempts to capture the true basis on which courts appear to order dissolution under their provisions—namely, that irreconcilable differences exist between the contesting owners. Deadlock is truly a phenomenon of the closely held corporation; it would not long exist within the public corporation. Thus, when equal owners of a corporation are divided over whether the sole corporate asset should be sold or developed, there is little room for compromise. It is ironic that the remedy available in such a case, an order of dissolution, leads to the very result that the shareholder seeking the asset's sale has sought.[133] It is on such facts that some jurisdictions permit shareholders owning 50 percent of the shares to petition for voluntary dissolution.[134] Essentially, what is required is proof that the differences between the shareholders are such that it is no longer reasonable to expect that they will be able to resolve their differences.[135] Acrimony is not required, though it may be present.[136]

Thus statutory requirements such as "irreparable harm" or that the corporation is "unable to conduct business to the shareholders' advantage" are somewhat irrelevant to the courts' inquiry. Courts instead emphasize the deep divisions between the shareholders, the length of those divisions, and the unlikelihood of the division being corrected.[137] Courts do not inquire as to whether a business is going badly or is not expanding. Certainly, the latter inquiry is at best problematic. Just how successful would a business be if cohesion existed among its managers and owners? Thus, one can find more to commend in those statutes that authorize dissolution merely on proof of deadlock, believing this is harm enough.

---

[132] Model Bus. Corp. Act § 14.30(a)(2)(i), (iii) (2016).

[133] See Gillingham v. Swan Falls Land & Cattle Co., 683 P.2d 895 (Idaho Ct. App. 1984).

[134] See In re Security Fin. Co., 317 P.2d 1 (Cal. 1957) (court will grant voluntary dissolution where 50 percent shareholder sought to put end to conflict, but court will exercise its equitable powers if necessary to protect interests of other shareholders).

[135] See Behrens Co. v. B. D. Rawls, 518 So.2d 945 (Fla. Ct. App. 1987) (divisions between shareholders had existed for years).

[136] See In re Hedberg-Freidheim & Co., 47 N.W.2d 424 (Minn. 1951) (director-owner constructed partition around desk to avoid conversation with fellow director-owners).

[137] See Behrens Co. v. B. D. Rawls, 518 So.2d 945 (Fla. Ct. App. 1987).

§ 14.12   Oppression; Protecting Reasonable Expectations

When dissension or deadlock occurs in a corporation, the shareholders can voluntarily dissolve the enterprise, but voluntary dissolution requires the affirmative vote of holders of a majority of the shares in some jurisdictions and a two-thirds vote in others.[138] At one time the courts generally held that unless authority is conferred by statute, courts of equity had no authority over the suit of a minority shareholder to order dissolution of a solvent corporation or to appoint a receiver to distribute its assets and liquidate its affairs.[139] A number of courts, however, recognized that, in the absence of other adequate remedy, there are circumstances under which a court of equity should afford relief to shareholders against fraud and gross mismanagement by appointing a receiver and winding up a solvent corporation.[140] The remedy for deadlock may be used in limited liability companies as well.[141] This is true for oppression by those in control of the LLC.[142]

In many states modern corporation statutes now expressly give the courts power to dissolve a corporation in a suit by a minority shareholder if the directors and majority shareholders are guilty of fraud, illegality, gross mismanagement, or oppression of minority shareholders, or if such dissension exists among the shareholders that the corporate business cannot be carried on or it appears that a winding up of the corporate affairs is necessary to protect the rights of the complaining shareholder.[143] The corporation statutes vary greatly from state to state both on the kinds of situations that trigger a court's power to dissolve and in the percentage of shares a person must hold to be entitled to petition for dissolution.[144] In some states the statutory grounds for involuntary dissolution are rather narrow and specific, such as a deadlock in the board of directors that the shareholders cannot break; in other states the grounds for involuntary dissolution are stated in broad terms, such as for "just or sufficient cause" or "where reasonably necessary for the protection of shareholders."[145]

Public corporations are rarely dissolved involuntarily. The remedy of involuntary dissolution thrives within close corporations, being not merely a mechanism to remedying hopeless deadlocks but also an important avenue for remedying oppressive misconduct by the majority stockholders. Whereas the oppressed minority in a public corporation protect themselves through private actions seeking damages or equitable relief, oppressed shareholders in a close corporation frequently file an action seeking the corporation's dissolution as a means to salvage their investment in the venture. It is therefore safe to say that over the past two decades there has been an extensive and

---

[138] *E.g.,* Model Bus. Corp. Act § 14.02(e) (2016) (majority); Del. Code Ann. tit. 8, § 275(b) (2001) (majority); N.Y. Bus. Corp. Law § 1001 (McKinney 2003) (two-thirds vote).

[139] *See* Grocery Supply, Inc. v. McKinley Park Serv., Inc., 128 F.Supp. 694 (D.C. Alaska Terr. 1955).

[140] *See* Ross v. American Banana Co., 43 So. 817 (Ala. 1907).

[141] *See, e.g.,* Meghan Gruebner, Note, Delaware's Answer to Management Deadlock in the Limited Liability Company: Judicial Dissolution, 32 J. Corp. L. 641 (2007).

[142] *See, e.g.,* Douglas K. Moll, Minority Oppression and the Limited Liability Company: Learning (or Not) From Close Corporation History, 40 Wake Forest L. Rev. 883 (2005).

[143] *See, e.g.,* Cal. Corp. Code § 1800 (West 1990); Del. Code Ann. tit. 8, § 226 (2001).

[144] *See* Sutter v. Sutter Ranching Corp., 14 P.3d 58 (Okla. 2000) (supervote requirement in articles for certain "action by the corporation," including dissolution, did not deprive minority holder of standing to petition for involuntary dissolution which is not action by the corporation).

[145] *See, e.g.,* Gruenberg v. Goldmine Plantation, Inc., 360 So.2d 884 (La. Ct. App. 1978) (minority shareholders can force a corporation into involuntary dissolution when accomplishment of corporate objectives is "impracticable").

significant melding of fiduciary standards to state involuntary dissolution statutes such that it is difficult to isolate the doctrine of fiduciary obligation in close corporations from involuntary dissolution. Much of the focus in this activity has been on the phrase common to dissolution provisions, "oppression". Difficult though it be to so isolate the two areas, the materials in this chapter will nevertheless make an attempt at doing so. The material in the balance of this section focuses almost entirely on how the courts have used the "reasonable expectations" of the shareholders to guide the court in deciding whether grounds for invoking the state's dissolution statute have been established.

In the typical case, the "reasonable expectation" doctrine emerges in a suit by the minority shareholder seeking a close corporation's dissolution under a statute that authorizes involuntary dissolution when those in control of the company have acted in an oppressive manner,[146] or dissolution is necessary to protect the rights or interests of the petitioning stockholder or stockholders generally.[147] Frequently, the specific dissolution provision is limited to close corporations or corporations with a small number of stockholders.[148] In broad overview, the courts that have embraced the talisman of the shareholder's reasonable expectations consider conduct that defeats those expectations as being oppressive or as grounds for concluding dissolution is necessary for the protection of that shareholder. It is worth noting, however, that not all courts have embraced the reasonable expectations analysis.[149]

To be protectable, expectations should be part of an understanding, explicit or implicit, between the participants in the corporation.[150] In a leading case, the North Carolina Supreme Court in *Meiselman v. Meiselman*[151] held that reasonable expectations should be determined on a case-by-case basis, using the full history of the relationship in question—from inception through any later developments.[152] *Meiselman* also required that the expectations must be compared with and known to the other stockholders, so privately held expectations are not reasonable.[153] Furthermore, a

---

[146] Professor Thompson identifies two other constructions for "oppressive": a serious departure from the standard of fair play that shareholders rely on or breach of good faith and fair dealing by the majority stockholder. *See* Robert B. Thompson, The Shareholder Cause of Action for Oppression, 48 Bus. Law. 699, 712 (1993).

[147] The Minnesota statute expressly directs the court to consider the "reasonable expectations" of the shareholders in dissolution petitions. *See* Minn. Stat. Ann. § 302A.751, subd. 3a (West Supp. 1994). *See generally* Joseph E. Olson, A Statutory Elixir for the Oppression Malady, 36 Mercer L. Rev. 627 (1985). McCallum v. Rosen's Diversified, Inc., 153 F.3d 701 (8th Cir. 1998) (CEO/director was divested of his reasonable expectations of an active role in management when those in control fired him so that under the Minnesota statute he is entitled to a buyout of his shares).

[148] *See* N.J. Stat. Ann. § 14A:12–7 (West 2003) (25 or fewer stockholders); N.Y. Bus. Corp. Law § 1104(a) (McKinney 2003) (shares are not publicly traded); Model Statutory Close Corp. Supp. §§ 40, 43 (fewer than 50 stockholders, and articles of incorporation state corporation is a close corporation).

[149] *See* Ritchie v. Rupe, 443 S.W.3d 856 (Tex. 2014) (rejecting reasonable expectations approach under oppression statute).

[150] *See* Longwell v. Custom Benefit Programs Midwest, Inc., 627 N.W.2d 396, 399–400 (S.D. 2001) (reasonable expectations should be analyzed in light of the entire history of the parties' relationship; the court must balance the minority shareholder's reasonable expectations against the corporation's ability to exercise its business judgment); Robert Hillman, The Dissatisfied Participant in the Solvent Business Venture: A Consideration of the Relative Performance of Partnerships and Close Corporations, 67 Minn. L. Rev. 1, 77–81 (1983).

[151] Meiselman v. Meiselman, 307 S.E.2d 551 (N.C. 1983).

[152] Meiselman v. Meiselman, 307 S.E.2d 551, 563 (N.C. 1983). *See also, e.g.,* Royals v. Piedmont Electric Repair Co., 529 S.E.2d 515 (N.C. App. 2000).

[153] 307 S.E.2d at 563.

minority shareholder's reasonable expectations must be balanced against what is reasonably believed to be in the best interests of the corporation.[154]

Meiselman was a dispute between two brothers: One brother held a majority of the stock and was in control of the corporation; the other brother, because he had fallen from grace with the family, had only a minority interest in the company. After the controlling stockholder had removed his brother from his employment position with the company, the removed brother sought the firm's dissolution on the grounds that "liquidation is reasonably necessary for the protection of the rights or interests of the complaining shareholder."[155] The court concluded that dissolution or other equitable relief was appropriate under the "rights or interests" language of the statute when:

> [The plaintiff] ... (1) had one or more substantial reasonable expectations known or assumed by the other participants; (2) the expectation has been frustrated; (3) the frustration was without fault of the plaintiff and was in large part beyond his control; and (4) under all the circumstances of the case plaintiff is entitled to some form of equitable relief.[156]

Meiselman is the most liberal decision yet to define "reasonable expectations." The Meiselman brothers inherited their shares from their father, so their expectations were not those of cofounders of a business enterprise;[157] theirs were expectations formed after the company was in operation. In extending *Meiselman* to its logical conclusion, reasonable expectations are evolutionary, not static. Also, the protectable expectations depend upon the surrounding circumstances. Thus, for example, continued employment by the corporation is not a protectable expectation of all minority shareholders who are also employees.[158] It therefore follows that not every termination of a shareholder's employment will be a breach of fiduciary duty.[159]

Using less sweeping language than that of *Meiselman,* the New York Court of Appeals in *In re Kemp & Beatley,*[160] acting under a statute that authorized dissolution for "illegal, oppressive or fraudulent" conduct, stated that oppression exists "when the majority conduct substantially defeats expectations that, objectively viewed, were both reasonable under the circumstances and were central to the petitioner's decision to join the venture."[161] The court held that an investor in a close corporation may reasonably expect to participate in the active management of the firm as well as to receive a fair return.[162] *Kemp & Beatley* held that dissolution was the only way that the two petitioners, who had been officers and shareholders in the firm for 35 and 42 years, could

---

[154] *See, e.g.,* Willis v. Bydalek, 997 S.W.2d 798 (Tex. App. 1999) (wrongful lockout did not establish oppression).

[155] N.C. Gen. Stat. Ann. § 55–125(a) (1955), since replaced by N.C. Gen. Stat. Ann. § 55–14–30 (2001).

[156] 307 S.E.2d at 564. After remand for reconsideration of the facts in light of the court's reasonable expectation standard, the case was settled.

[157] *See* Gimpel v. Bolstein, 477 N.Y.S.2d 1014 (Sup. Ct. 1984).

[158] *See, e.g.,* Harrison v. Netcentric Corp., 744 N.E.2d 622 (Mass. 2001) (applying Delaware law, upholding termination of minority shareholder as employee).

[159] Harrison v. Netcentric Corp., 744 N.E.2d 622 (Mass. 2001); Crowder Construction Co. v. Kiser, 517 S.E.2d 178 (N.C. App. 1999).

[160] In re Kemp & Beatley, 473 N.E.2d 1173 (N.Y. 1984).

[161] In re Kemp & Beatley, 473 N.E.2d 1173, 1179 (N.Y. 1984).

[162] 473 N.E.2d at 1178. *See also, e.g.,* Muellenberg v. Bikon Corp., 669 A.2d 1382 (N.J. 1996) (minority shareholder had protectable expectation that limited other two shareholders' ability to exercise control to freeze out the minority shareholder; court ordered the unusual remedy of a minority buyout of the majority).

expect a reasonable return on their investment when, after one of them had resigned and the other had been fired, the firm changed its policies so that significant distributions from earnings were no longer based on stock ownership but on the basis of services to the corporation. The New Jersey Supreme Court held that reasonable expectations can be nonmonetary,[163] but required a stronger showing that the expectations include employment of persons other than the petitioning shareholder.[164]

The breadth of the reasonable-expectations standard is that, within the close corporation, participation in management—and certainly the receipt of a salary—are the rewards shareholders customarily seek when investing in a close corporation. This therefore conditions the power of the majority to sever the minority stockholder from the firm's payroll on there being either an adequate return to the owners through dividends or just cause for the employee's termination.[165] Even just cause for terminating an employee-owner may not be sufficient to avoid a court's intervention, as illustrated by *Gimpel v. Bolstein*,[166] where, even though the court refused to protect the salaried position of a co-owner who had engaged in embezzlement, the court nevertheless required the majority to devise some means to provide a financial return commensurate with the petitioning stockholder's investment in the firm. The protection of minority shareholders' interests are not limited to the closely held corporation principles discussed herein. Protectable expectations may exist on the simple basis of an enforceable agreement, even if not in writing.[167]

§ 14.13 Policy Questions Surrounding Dissolution and Alternative Remedies

Today, the remedy most frequently resulting from a court's finding that the state's dissolution statute was satisfied is an order requiring a buyout of the petitioner's shares or some other affirmative relief.[168] There is statutory authority for courts ordering a buyout in many states,[169] but courts have ordered buyouts in the absence of express statutory authorization.[170] The better view is for the courts to consider they have a full panoply of remedies available once the grounds proscribed in the state dissolution statute have been established. The severity of the petitioner's grievance as well as the relative rights of other stockholders and the corporation itself should guide the court in considering what relief is appropriate under the circumstances.[171] It is in this light that

---

[163] *See* Brenner v. Berkowitz, 634 A.2d 1019, 1029 (N.J. 1993) (nexus between alleged misconduct and the interest the plaintiff has in the corporation must be alleged).

[164] Brenner v. Berkowitz, 634 A.2d 1019, 1033–1034 (N.J. 1993).

[165] *See, e.g.,* In re Wiedy's Furniture Clearance Center Co., 487 N.Y.S.2d 901 (App. Div. 1985).

[166] Gimpel v. Bolstein, 477 N.Y.S.2d 1014 (1984).

[167] *See, e.g.,* Penley v. Penley, 332 S.E.2d 51, 64 (N.C. 1985) (protecting interests based on contract principles).

[168] *See* Harry J. Haynsworth, The Effectiveness of Involuntary Dissolution as a Remedy for Close Corporation Dissension, 35 Clev. St. L. Rev. 25, 50 (1986).

[169] *See, e.g.,* 805 ILCS § 5/12.56(b)(11) (Smith-Hurd Supp. 2009); Mich. Comp. Laws Ann. §§ 450.1489, 450.1801 (West Supp. 2009); Minn. Stat. Ann. § 302A.751 (West. 2004); N.J. Stat. Ann. § 14A:12–7 (West 2003). For a state-by-state compilation of the standard for invoking protection and whether there is buyout remedy, *see* John H. Matheson & R. Kevin Maler, A Simple Statutory Solution to Minority Oppression in the Closely Held Business, 91 Minn. L. Rev. 657, 700–709 (2007).

[170] *See, e.g.,* Sauer v. Moffitt, 363 N.W.2d 269 (Iowa Ct. App. 1984).

[171] *See, e.g.,* Sauer v. Moffitt, 363 N.W.2d 269 (Iowa Ct. App. 1984) (partial liquidation and exemplary damages awarded instead of dissolution); In re Trocino, 482 N.Y.S.2d 670 (Sup. Ct. 1984) (dissolution appropriate when all other remedies inadequate).

the Model Statutory Close Corporation Supplement sets forth nine types of relief (in addition to ordering dissolution or a buyout) that the court may order when it finds the bases for dissolution have been established.[172] In addition to court-ordered buyouts, the statutes of some states extend to the corporation or to the nonpetitioning stockholders a mechanism to avoid dissolution by purchasing the petitioning stockholder's shares at their "fair value."[173] The statutes providing this escape from an order of dissolution customarily provide procedures for a neutral party to determine a fair price for the petitioner's shares when the parties cannot reach an agreement.

The commentators are divided on the question of whether a liberal construction of a state dissolution statute is economically efficient. In a classic article, Professors Hetherington and Dooley[174] argue that minority stockholders in close corporations should have a right to require the majority to purchase their shares. They reason that equipping the minority with a "put" for their shares would serve as a low-cost protection against oppression as well as an incentive by the majority to exercise their control so as to maintain the minority's confidence.[175] Professor Hillman voices concern that allowing too easy an exit from the firm not only adds to the enterprise's instability but also is not likely to give sufficient consideration to the costs and burdens this approach visits upon the majority in finding the funds to acquire the minority's shares.[176]

The opposite positions taken by these commentators capture nicely the policy question that courts face in considering their approach to a petition asking the court to provide a means for the minority to exit the corporation with their investment. Consideration of the parties' expectations does not address the concerns that dissolution may be inefficient because of its impact on the resources of the majority and quite likely ultimately the corporation. The reasonable-expectations analysis only provides assurance that dissolution or another remedy is not inconsistent with the parties' probable intentions had they been prescient and contracted *ex ante* a solution for the problem that prompted the minority to seek dissolution. In this way, the reasonable-expectations standard may well be the quintessential illustration of the position taken by many economists that the corporation is but a nexus of contracts, so that the role of a court in response to a dissolution petition is to carry out the probable intent of the

---

[172] Model Statutory Close Corp. Supp. § 41. The types of relief so ordered are:

(1) the performance, prohibition, alteration, or setting aside of any action of the corporation or of its shareholders, directors, or officers of or any other party to the proceedings;

(2) the cancellation or alteration of any provision in the corporation's articles of incorporation or bylaws;

(3) the removal from office of any director or officer;

(4) the appointment of any individual as a director or officer;

(5) an accounting with respect to any matter in dispute;

(6) the appointment of a custodian to manage the business and affairs of the corporation;

(7) the appointment of a provisional director (who has all the rights, powers, and duties of a duly elected director) to serve for the term and under the conditions prescribed by the court;

(8) the payment of dividends;

(9) the award of damages to any aggrieved party.

[173] *See, e.g.,* Cal. Corp. Code § 2000 (West 1990); N.Y. Bus. Corp. Law § 1118 (McKinney 2003).

[174] John A.C. Hethrington & Michael P. Dooley, Illiquidity and Exploitation: A Proposed Statutory Solution to the Remaining Close Corporation Problem, 63 Va. L. Rev. 1 (1977).

[175] In re Dissolution of Penepent Corp., 750 N.E.2d 47, 48 (N.Y. 2001).

[176] *See* Robert Hillman, The Dissatisfied Participant in the Solvent Business Venture: A Consideration of the Relative Performance of Partnerships and Close Corporations, 67 Minn. L. Rev. 1, 77–81 (1983). *See also* Frank Easterbrook & Daniel Fischel, Close Corporations and Agency Costs, 38 Stan. L. Rev. 271, 290 (1986).

parties. This view not only is the embodiment of the reasonable-expectation standard but commends as well the panoply of other possible remedies, discussed above, that courts may substitute in place of ordering the corporation's dissolution or a buyout of the minority.

The current willingness of courts to protect the minority's expectations or to shield a stockholder from unfair treatment in a close corporation is a dramatic change from the position courts took on such matters not that many years ago, when dissolution or ordering a buyout were seen as drastic remedies. For example, in applying a former New York statute that required a showing that dissolution would be beneficial to the shareholders and not injurious to the public,[177] the New York Court of Appeals denied dissolution of a deadlocked corporation that was still operating profitably.[178] In repudiation of this result, New York amended its statute to provide that "dissolution is not to be denied merely because it is found that the corporate business has been or could be conducted at a profit."[179] The amended statute further provides an important consideration in deciding whether to dissolve by providing that in a dissolution proceeding brought by directors or shareholders "the benefit to the shareholders of a dissolution is of paramount importance."[180] The court's consideration of the benefit to the shareholders is included within the reasonable-expectations standard that is now followed in New York such that dissolution is appropriate even for a profitable firm.

Where authorized by statute, a court's appointment of a provisional director is considered less severe than dissolution or receivership and thus has been held to be appropriate where appointment of a receiver or involuntary dissolution would not be.[181] In states not having statutes authorizing judicial appointment of a provisional director, insertion of a provision in the corporation's charter can achieve the functional equivalent of a statutory provisional director. For example, a corporation's charter can be amended to create a separate class of stock with no proprietary rights but with power to elect a director in the event the board becomes deadlocked; that class of shares can then be issued for nominal consideration to an impartial person, enabling that person to elect a deadlock-breaking director.[182] Another device is a charter provision for arbitration in the event of deadlock or dissension; this device can be useful as long as the dispute in question is arbitrable under the applicable state law.[183]

The advantage of arbitration over litigation as a method of dispute settlement in a close corporation is that it is quicker and less expensive.[184] Most objections to arbitration of intracorporate disputes are based on the supposed unfitness of the arbitral process for formulating corporate policy and making managerial decisions. Before deciding to use arbitration in a close corporation, the lawyer should carefully search the statutes and

---

[177] N.Y. Gen. Corp. Law §§ 103, 106, 109 (Thompson's 1939).

[178] In re Radom & Neidorff, Inc., 119 N.E.2d 563 (N.Y. 1954), *motion denied,* 120 N.E.2d 865 (N.Y. 1954), noted 68 Harv. L. Rev. 714 (1955). A corporation's profitability has been given weight by other courts. *See, e.g.,* Baker v. Commercial Body Builders, Inc., 507 P.2d 387 (Or. 1973).

[179] N.Y. Bus. Corp. Law § 1111(b)(3) (McKinney 2003).

[180] N.Y. Bus. Corp. Law § 1111(b)(3) (McKinney 2003). For a discussion of amendments to the New York act that have put it "more in harmony" with the Model Business Corporation Act.

[181] In re Jamison Steel Corp., 322 P.2d 246 (Cal. Ct. App. 1958).

[182] Lehrman v. Cohen, 222 A.2d 800 (Del. 1966) (the Delaware court approved the issuance of such stock).

[183] *See generally* 2 F. Hodge O'Neal & Robert B. Thompson, O'Neal and Thompson's Close Corporations and LLCs: Law and Practice § 9.9 (rev. 3d ed. 2009).

[184] *See* 2 O'Neal & Thompson, *supra* note 140, ch. 9 (pros and cons of arbitration).

judicial decisions of the state of incorporation for corporate norms that would either invalidate arbitration agreements in the particular business situation involved or would otherwise nullify their effectiveness.[185] Further, the lawyer should examine the state arbitration statute and applicable common law principles of the forums in which litigation may arise to determine the proper limits of arbitration.[186]

§ 14.14 Custodians' Resolution of Shareholder Deadlocks and Disputes

The terms "custodian" and "receiver" are frequently used interchangeably. A custodian is appointed when there is a stockholder or director deadlock or other extreme situation for which an extraordinary mechanism is needed to resolve the situation; a receiver is appointed

only when the corporation is insolvent or is being liquidated.[187] The Delaware statute[188] and case law have greatly influenced the efforts of other states[189] that include within their corporate statutes authority for the court to appoint a custodian as a means to resolve internal corporate disputes.

The Delaware statute authorizes the appointment of a custodian[190] in three distinct instances. First, in section 226(a)(1),[191] a custodian may be appointed if at any meeting held for the election of directors a division of the stockholders prevents the election of successors to the current directors whose terms have expired. There is no requirement under the Delaware statute either that the division among the shareholders necessarily must be equal or that they must have failed for more than one successive annual meeting.

The second basis for obtaining a custodian's appointment is provided in section 226(a)(2)[192] and arises when the business is suffering or is threatened with irreparable harm stemming from a division of the directors respecting the management of the corporation's affairs such that a vote required for action by the board of directors cannot be obtained and the stockholders are unable by voting to bring an end to the division among the directors.

---

[185] *See* Ringling v. Ringling Bros.-Barnum & Bailey Combined Shows, 49 A.2d 603, 607 (Del. Ch. 1946), *modified*, 53 A.2d 441 (Del. 1947); Blum Folding Paper Box Co. v. Friedlander, 261 N.E.2d 382 (N.Y. 1970).

[186] *See* Martin Domke, The Law and Practice of Commercial Arbitration (rev. ed. 1984).

[187] *See* Andreae v. Andreae, Fed. Sec. L. Rep. (CCH) ¶ 96,571, 1992 WL 43924 (Del.Ch. 1992) at 92,652 (Del. Ch. 1992).

[188] The current Delaware statute, Del. Code Ann. tit. 8, § 226 (2001), has stood unamended since 1967; before its amendment in 1967 it was extremely difficult in Delaware to address deadlocks effectively because of the great burden of proof placed on the petitioner. The statute was liberalized in 1967 to overcome this problem. *See* Giuricich v. Emtrol Corp., 449 A.2d 232, 238–239 (Del. 1982). *See generally* Ernest Folk, The Delaware Corporation Law: A Commentary and Analysis § 226 & 226.1 (3d ed. 1992).

[189] *See* Kan. Stat. Ann. § 17–6516 (2007) (a comment in an earlier publication of the statute—1988— stated that only slight word changes made in patterning law after Delaware); N.J. Stat. Ann. § 14A:12–7(4) (West 2003) (custodian is alternative to involuntary dissolution, and statute appears to embody principles found in the Delaware statute and case law).

[190] The same bases apply as well to the appointment of a receiver, subject to the qualification, *supra* note 1, that a receiver's charge is to preside over either an insolvent corporation or a solvent corporation's liquidation.

[191] Del. Code Ann. tit. 8, § 226(a)(1) (2001).

[192] Del. Code Ann. tit. 8, § 226(a)(2) (2001). *See, e.g.*, Niehenke v. Right O Way Transp., Inc., 1995 WL 767348 (Del. Ch. 1995) (appointing custodian in the face of deadlock in two-shareholder corporation).

Section 226(a)(3)[193] authorizes a custodian's appointment when the corporation has abandoned its business. In interpreting this provision, the court must walk a line between exercising its role of enforcing the state's statute, intended for the protection of the shareholders' interests, and deferring to the judgment of a board of directors resisting the appointment of a custodian.[194]

It is also within the court's equitable powers to appoint a custodian when those in control of the corporation have engaged in fraud or gross management or have otherwise created a condition of imminent danger of great loss to the corporation that otherwise can be avoided.[195]

The Delaware Supreme Court considered the scope of the custodian's powers in *Shawe v. Elting*.[196] After upholding the Court of Chancery's findings that both the deadlock and irreparable harm requirements of sections 226(a)(1) and (a)(2) were established, the upheld the lower court's order that the custodian be appointed to sell the company. Both the Chancery Court and the Supreme Court believed that further efforts toward mediation would not likely be successful. They each concluded that having the custodian serve as the tiebreaking director or otherwise acting as a mediator would not be overcome the deep impasse separating the parties. Thus, each court held that the sale of the company by the custodian would end the harmful dysfunction the corporation had suffered and could be expected to continue to suffer.

It is also within the court's equitable powers to appoint a custodian when those in control of the corporation have engaged in fraud or gross management or have otherwise created a condition of imminent danger of great loss to the corporation that otherwise can be avoided.[197] New Jersey provides the most sweeping treatment: It allows stockholders of corporations with fewer than 25 holders to petition for the appointment of a custodian or provisional director or for dissolution when directors or those in control of the corporation have acted "fraudulently or illegally" or "mismanaged the corporation" or "acted oppressively."[198] The grounds of illegality and fraud are independent of the oppression ground. Oppression involves conduct *directed* at the minority, whereas conduct that is illegal or fraudulent does not necessarily have to be so directed.[199] The New Jersey statute also authorizes the court to order the majority to sell its shares to the minority shareholders.[200] This remedy, though uncommon, is appropriate where the minority shareholder has been a key factor in the company's success and has the financial capacity to purchase the majority's shares.[201]

---

[193] Del. Code Ann. tit. 8, § 226(a)(3) (2001).

[194] *E.g.*, Francotyp-Postalia AG & Co. v. On Target Technology, Inc., 1998 WL 928382, 24 Del. J. Corp. L. 649 (Del. Ch. 1998) (refusing to appoint custodian).

[195] *See* Hall v. John S. Isaacs & Sons Farms, Inc., 163 A.2d 288 (Del. 1960).

[196] Shawe v. Elting, 157 A.3d 152 (Del. 2017).

[197] *See* Hall v. John S. Isaacs & Sons Farms, Inc., 163 A.2d 288 (Del. 1960); Tansey v. Oil Producing Royalties, Inc., 133 A.2d 141 (Del. 1957) (strong showing of fraud or gross mismanagement is required); Andreae v. Andreae, 1992 WL 43924 (Del. Ch. 1992).

[198] N.J. Stat. Ann. § 14A:12–7(1)(c) (West 2003).

[199] *See* Brenner v. Berkowitz, 634 A.2d 1019, 1028 (N.J. 1993) (failure to file IRS forms W-2 and 1099 deemed marginal violations of law not sufficient to constitute illegality under statute).

[200] N.J. Stat. Ann. 14A:12–7(8) (West 2003). In deciding whether to apply a marketability discount to determine the fair value of shares subject to a judicially ordered buyout, the court must take into account what is fair and equitable. Lawson Mardon Wheaton, Inc. v. Smith, 734 A.2d 738, 748 (N.J. 1999); Balsamides v. Protameen Chems., Inc., 734 A.2d 721, 735 (N.J. 1999).

[201] *See* Muellenberg v. Bikon Corp., 669 A.2d 1382, 1389 (N.J. 1996).

§ 14.15　Fiduciary Duties in the Close Corporation

As the preceding sections of this chapter illustrate, both the legislatures and the courts have recognized the unique needs of the close corporation. In allowing special control devices, such as high vote requirements for shareholder and director action and shareholders' agreements that control action within the traditional province of the board of directors, the law has increasingly recognized the so-called "incorporated partnership." A concurrent development in recent years has been the recognition of partnership-like fiduciary obligations running between the participants in close corporations.[202] The fiduciary duty exists among the close corporation's stockholders, and in appropriate cases continues even though the minority stockholder has been frozen out of his position as an officer of the corporation.[203] The fiduciary duty ordinarily arises in the case of majority shareholders but in fact can apply to any shareholder who has control over corporate actions even if not majority owners.[204] When dealing with other closely held limited liability entities such as the limited liability corporation, it is appropriate for courts to look to the fiduciary duties applicable in closely held corporations and partnerships.[205]

That corporate directors and officers owe a fiduciary duty to their corporation is, of course, well established.[206] Some early decisions[207] and even an occasional recent decision[208] treat this duty as running only to the corporation, not to its shareholders. Most recent decisions and some statutes, however, affirm that this duty is owed to the corporation's shareholders as well as to the corporation itself.[209] Further, most modern courts have accepted the principle that the controlling shareholders as well as the directors and officers owe a fiduciary duty to other shareholders—to public shareholders in a publicly held corporation and to minority shareholders in a close corporation.[210]

A landmark decision recognizing high fiduciary duties among shareholders in a close corporation was *Donahue v. Rodd Electrotype Co.*[211] In that case, a corporation's founder and his sons, to whom he had given some shares, caused the corporation to purchase a portion of the founder's remaining shares without giving the minority shareholder an opportunity to sell her shares to the corporation at the same price per share. The Supreme Judicial Court of Massachusetts analogized the relationship among close corporation owners to that of partners and held that the corporation's purchase

---

[202] *See, e.g.,* Hollis v. Hill, 232 F.3d 460 (5th Cir. 2000) (applying Nevada law; cofounder owed fiduciary duty to other cofounder); Orchard v. Covelli, 590 F.Supp. 1548 (W.D. Pa. 1984) (adherence by majority shareholders to their fiduciary duties is particularly critical in context of closely held corporation).

[203] *See* Rexford Rand Corp. v. Ancel, 58 F.3d 1215, 1221 (7th Cir. 1995) (minority shareholder who two years earlier had been frozen out of the corporation breached duty by acquiring corporation's name after the corporation had been administratively dissolved).

[204] *See, e.g.,* Corwin v. KKR Financial Holdings LLC, 125 A.3d 304 (Del. 2015); Calesa Associates, L.P. v. American Capital, Ltd., 2016 WL 770251 (Del. Ch. 2016).

[205] *See, e.g.,* Purcell v. Southern Hills Investments, LLC, 847 N.E.2d 991 (Ind. App. 2006).

[206] *See* Robert C. Clark, Corporate Law chs. 4–8 (1986), for a discussion of the various ramifications of the fiduciary duty of loyalty that corporate directors and officers owe their corporation.

[207] Carpenter v. Danforth, 52 Barb. 581 (N.Y. Sup. Ct. 1868); Robert S. Stevens, Corporations § 150 (2d ed. 1949).

[208] *See, e.g.,* Lochhead v. Alacano, 662 F.Supp. 230 (D. Utah 1987) (applying Utah law).

[209] *See, e.g.,* Junker v. Crory, 650 F.2d 1349 (5th Cir. 1981).

[210] *See, e.g.,* Mardel Sec., Inc. v. Alexandria Gazette Corp., 320 F.2d 890 (4th Cir. 1963).

[211] Donahue v. Rodd Electrotype Co., 328 N.E.2d 505 (Mass. 1975), noted in 61 Cornell L. Rev. 986 (1976); 89 Harv. L. Rev. 423 (1975).

from the founder had to be rescinded or the minority shareholder had to be given an opportunity to sell her shares to the corporation at the same price per share, since the strict partnership standard of "utmost good faith and loyalty" applies in a close corporation, in contrast to the "less stringent standard of fiduciary duty that applies to larger corporate structures."[212]

In yet another important decision, *Wilkes v. Springside Nursing Home, Inc.*,[213] the Supreme Judicial Court of Massachusetts applied the same strict fiduciary standard in protecting a minority shareholder against arbitrary elimination from the board of directors and discharge from company employment. In that case, the four equal owners of a nursing home had from the inception of the corporation been employed by the home and had participated in management and policy decisions as directors, each receiving the same amount of compensation. After a dispute the other three shareholders, in their capacity as majority members of the board of directors, terminated Wilkes's salary, and at the next annual meeting of shareholders the three failed to reelect Wilkes to the board. The court held that the removal of Wilkes from the board and from employment with the corporation breached fiduciary duties the other shareholders owed Wilkes. Thus, courts have ordered a buyout when that is consistent with the minority's reasonable expectations[214] and denied a buyout when it a buyout was not reasonably expected way to address exclusion from participating in the firm.[215] Where disputes deal with the termination of employment a pivotal consideration generally is whether in fact there exists a business purpose for the termination.[216]

Not all jurisdictions, however, embrace the view that participants in a close corporation are subject to "heightened fiduciary responsibilities" or that those responsibilities are necessarily founded on a liberal construction of their reasonable expectations.[217] The Delaware Supreme Court in *Nixon v. Blackwell*[218] reasoned that it was inappropriate to fashion ad hoc rules according minority shareholders rights not provided them by statute and which were not otherwise contracted for by the shareholders. Subsequently, in *Riblet Products Corp. v. Nagy*[219] the Delaware court

---

[212] 328 N.E.2d at 515.

[213] Wilkes v. Springside Nursing Home, Inc., 353 N.E.2d 657 (Mass. 1976). Compare Blank v. Chelmsford Ob/Gyn, P.C., 649 N.E.2d 1102, 1105 (Mass. 1995) (employee-shareholders may be dismissed as employee where contract permitted such) with King v. Driscoll, 638 N.E.2d 488, 493 (Mass. 1994) (corporation may dismiss employee-shareholder for filing derivative suit, but majority remain liable for breach of their fiduciary duty in engineering dismissal).

[214] Keating v. Keating, 2003 WL 23213143 (Mass. Super. Ct. Oct. 3, 2003).

[215] Brodie v. Jordan, 447 Mass. 866, 857 N.E.2d 1076 (Mass. 2006).

[216] *See e.g.*, McKee v. St. Paul Eye Clinic, P.A., 2015 WL 1757833 (Minn. Ct. App. Apr. 20, 2015); Knights' Piping, Inc. v. Knight, 123 So.3d 451 (Miss. Ct. App. 2012); Daniels v. Thomas, Dean & Hoskins, Inc., 804 P.2d 359, 367 (Mont. 1990). An issue with employee-stockholder squeeze outs is whether the termination is consistent with the complainant's status as an employee at will. Knights' Piping, Inc. v. Knight, 123 So.3d 451, 459 (Miss. Ct. App. 2012)(embracing *Donahue's* high standard but observing the duty does not create "fiduciary-rooted entitlements to their job ... such a result would clearly interfere with the doctrine of employment-at-will"); Metro Comm. Mngt. Serv., Inc. v. Van Istendal, 457 N.J.Super. 66, 197 A.3d 695 (N.J. Super. App. Div. 2018)(acquiring minority position after years of service coupled with employment contract that expressly stated the employment was at will did not provide sufficient facts to support claim of reasonable expectation of continuous employment).

[217] Merner v. Merner, 129 Fed.Appx. 342 (9th Cir. 2005).

[218] Nixon v. Blackwell, 626 A.2d 1366, 1379 (Del. 1993).

[219] 683 A.2d 37 (Del. 1996).

rejected the right of the minority shareholder/employee that had been recognized in Massachusetts in the *Wilkes* decision.[220]

As discussed elsewhere in this treatise, corporate fiduciaries generally carry the burden of proving the fairness of self-dealing transactions.[221] Because of the majority shareholder's superior position, the burden of proving fairness in a close corporation fiduciary case belongs to the majority shareholder.[222]

The essence of most fiduciary duty claims by minority shareholders in closely held corporations is based on the lack of liquidity of their ownership interest. The Delaware Supreme Court has made it clear that absent special considerations or a contractual provision, a minority shareholder has no common law right to have his or her shares repurchased by the corporation.[223]

§ 14.16 Dissolution and Dissention in LLCs

While limited liability company provisions vary widely across the states, the Uniform Limited Liability Company Act of 2006 already is acquiring adopters and its provisions addressing dissolution are representative of the approach taken in the majority of the jurisdictions that have not adopted the ULLCA. Two of its key grounds for dissolution require winding up upon 1) "an event or circumstance that the operating agreement states causes dissolution," 2) "it is not reasonably practicable to carry on the company's activities in conformity with the certificate of organization and the operating agreement," or 3) upon "consent of all the members."[224] Dissolution, winding up and any other "remedy other than dissolution" can occur per a judicial proceeding upon a showing that the managers or members "have acted, are acting, or will act in a manner that is illegal or fraudulent" or "have acted or are acting in a manner that is oppressive or was, is, or will be directly harmful to the applicant."[225] Some states authorize dissolution upon "deadlock," but define this to mean the business "cannot be conducted to the advantage of the members;"[226] this appears to be a condition somewhat more liberal than the ULLCA's "not reasonably practicable to carry on the company's activities in conformity with the certificate of organization and the operating agreement." Deadlock, however, is

---

[220] *See also, e.g.*, Harrison v. NetCentric Corp., 744 N.E.2d 622, 627 (Mass. 2001).

[221] *See* § 10.11 *supra*.

[222] *See, e.g.*, Edelman v. JELBS, 2015-Ohio-5542, 57 N.E.3d 246 (Ohio Ct. App. 10th Dist. Franklin County 2015), appeal not allowed, 145 Ohio St. 3d 1471, 2016-Ohio-3028, 49 N.E.3d 1313 (2016) (in upholding a claim of excessive compensation to the majority, the court noted "when a minority shareholder of a close corporation brings suit against a controlling shareholder for breach of his or her fiduciary duties, a presumption arises that the fiduciary, by virtue of his or her superior position, bears the burden of proof with respect to the fairness of his or her actions. Consistent with this presumption, the fiduciary must demonstrate that his or her actions were fair, reasonable, and based on a full disclosure of relevant information.") (relying on Yackel v. Kay, 95 Ohio App. 3d 472, 642 N.E.2d 1107 (8th Dist. Cuyahoga County 1994)) ("there exists a presumption that the one owing a fiduciary duty by virtue of superior position must go forward with the burden of proof on the fairness of business transactions. The fiduciary must demonstrate that the one to whom the fiduciary duty was owed had full knowledge of and approved the transactions.").

[223] Blaustein v. Lord Baltimore Capital Corp., 84 A.3d 954 (Del. 2014).

[224] ULLCA § 701(a)(1), (2) & (4)(A), (B) (2006).

[225] ULLCA § 701(a)(5) (2006). *See, e.g.*, Decker v. Decker, 298 Wis. 2d 141, 726 N.W.2d 664 (Wis. Ct. App. 2006)(making an offer to purchase the other member's shares with no intention of carrying through on the offer grounds for ordering dissolution).

[226] *See, e.g.*, Ariz. Rev. Stat. Ann. § 29–785(A). *See* Ribadab Properties Corp. v. Eaton, 2006 WL 1734368 (D. Ariz. 2006) (denying dissolution for "deadlock" because failure to agree to a price on which the sole asset of the LLC would be sold to one of the members when parties admitted they were willing to compromise suggest they could reach an agreement without the court ordering dissolution and winding up).

not established by the majority of the members ousting as a manager the founding member.[227]

Delaware has reasoned that its courts being courts of equity have the equitable power to order dissolution for non-statutory bases, such as deadlock.[228] New York has exercised its equitable powers in dissolving an LLC to fashion a buyout remedy.[229] Overall, the judicial approach to ordering dissolution of LLCs is a matter of grave reluctance:

> Given its extreme nature, judicial dissolution is a limited remedy that [courts] grant[ ] sparingly. The court will not dissolve an LLC merely because the LLC has not experienced a smooth glide to profitability or because events have not turned out exactly as the LLC's owners originally envisioned; such events are, of course, common in the risk-laden process of birthing new entities in the hope that they will become mature, profitable ventures. In part because a hair-trigger dissolution [15] standard would ignore this market reality and thwart the expectations of reasonable investors that entities will not be judicially terminated simply because of some market turbulence, dissolution is reserved for situations in which the LLC's management has become so dysfunctional or its business purpose so thwarted that it is no longer practicable to operate the business, such as in the case of a voting deadlock or where the defined purpose of the entity has become impossible to fulfill.[230]

Statutes customarily provide that a petition for judicial dissolution can be filed by a member[231] and some states broaden standing to include managers.[232] In light of the emphasis and deference to private ordering for LLCs, the statutory treatment should be seen as a default rule so that the articles of organization or operating agreement can expand standing to seek judicial dissolution.[233] With member being interpreted strictly, Delaware has held that an assignment of a limited liability company interest does not entitle the assignee full member rights so that assignee lacks standing to petition for dissolution.[234] Delaware has observed it would not be valid for an operating agreement to absolutely preclude dissolution.[235]

The most frequently invoked basis for ground for judicial dissolution is that "not reasonably practicable to carry on the company's activities in conformity with the

---

[227] Kertesz v. Spa Floral, LLC, 994 So.2d 473, 474 (Fla. Dist. Ct.App. 2008).

The operating agreement may provide that when there is deadlock that arbitration is to be used to break the deadlock. This would appear to deflect any petition for dissolution based on deadlock as private ordering has set forth the members' intent how their disagreement should be addressed. *But see*, Ladd v. Ladd Const. LLC., 2008 WL 4416048 (Conn. Super. Ct. 2008) (ordering dissolution even though arbitration called for by operating agreement because the court was persuaded that the designated arbitrator was not impartial).

[228] In re Carlisle, 114 A.3d 592 (Del. Ch. 2015) (ordering dissolution for deadlock at the request of an assignee of a member's interest where standing to seek statutorily authorized dissolution limited to suits by either member or manager).

[229] Mizrahi v. Cohen, 104 A.D.3d 917 (N.Y. App. Div. 2d Dept. 2013).

[230] In re Arrow Investment Advisors, LLC, 2009 Del. Ch. LEXIS 66 (Del. Ch. Apr. 23, 2009).

[231] *See, e.g.*, N.Y. Ltd. Lib. Co. Law § 702; Miss. Code Ann. § 79–29–803(1).

[232] *See, e.g.*, Cal. Corp. Code § 1735(a) (member or manager); Del. Code Ann. tit. 6, § 18–802 (member or manager).

[233] In re Carlisle, 114 A.3d 592 (Del. Ch. 2015)(employee lacks standing to petition for dissolution of Delaware LLC but clearly indicating that statutory provisions on this matter are default rules).

[234] Wiggs v. Summit Midstream Partners, 2013 WL 1286180 (Del. Ch. Mar. 28, 2013).

[235] In re Carlisle, 114 A.3d 592 (Del. Ch. 2015).

certificate of organization and the operating agreement." However, the courts look for clear evidence that the certificate or agreement have been violated.[236] Thus, on the one hand, when there is evidence that two equal owners are at such an impasse, having not communicated for more than a year, dissolution was ordered.[237] On the other hand, on-going disagreements about the conduct of the business and complaints that the party to whom operating agreement delegated management authority acted unilaterally in furtherance of the business was not sufficient basis to order dissolution as the operating agreement empowered such unilateral action.[238] Also, the New York courts have reasoned that this provision is not violated by evidence a member or manager has breached a fiduciary duty owed to the company or members.[239] And, the expulsion of one of the two members does not trigger dissolution under this provision.[240]

It must be borne in mind that dissolution invokes the equitable jurisdiction of the court and that statutes are drafted with the foreknowledge that dissolution is not appropriate for all circumstances notwithstanding the petition clearly satisfying the statutory grounds for judicial dissolution. A classic illustration of this is *Haley v. Talcott*[241] where two equal owners had reached an impasse whether to sell the only asset of the LLC, real estate that was leased to a company controlled by Talcott and a company from which Haley had been summarily terminated by Talcott. The parties had contemplated such an impasse, providing in the operating agreement that a member wishing to continue the LLC could buyout the departing member's interest. However, dissolution was not ordered because the court believed this would be unfair to Haley. The unfairness arose because Talcott and Haley were each personally liable on the mortgage covering the LLC's property. The Vice Chancellor reasoned that forcing Haley to exit either via the buyout or dissolution was inequitable because it left him with no protection against the downside risk of default on the mortgage by the LLC. *Haley* should be contrasted with *Kirksey v. Grohmann*[242] where dissolution was ordered even though the LLC's major operation was profitable; however, the owners were evenly divided over

---

[236] *See* Taki v. Hami, 2001 WL 672399, *6 (Mich. App. 2001) ("not reasonably practicable" means "capable of being done logically and in a reasonable feasible manner"); Spires v. Casterline, 4 Misc. 3d 428, 778 N.Y.S.2d 259 (N.Y. Sup. Ct. 2004) (undertaking a close examination of the operating agreement to conclude that dissolution should be ordered). This does not require proof of wrongful conduct on the part of any party. McConnell v. Hunt Sports Enterprises, 132 Ohio App. 3d 657, 725 N.E.2d 1193 (1999). But wrongdoing and continuing inability to work with one another are persuasive considerations. *See, e.g.*, Saunders v. Firtel, 293 Conn. 515, 978 A.2d 487 (2009).

This standard can be met, however, by a petition joined in by all the members concurring in the statement. *See, e.g.*, Ervin v. Turner, 291 Ga. App. 719, 662 S.E.2d 721 (2008); Tal v. Superior Vending, LLC, 20 Misc. 3d 1103, 867 N.Y.S.2d 21 (Sup. Ct. 2008).

[237] Conners v. Howe Elegant, LLC, 2009 WL 242324 (Conn. Super. Ct. Jan. 8, 2009), modified on reargument, 2009 WL 651735 (Conn. Super. Ct. Feb. 11, 2009).

[238] In the Matter of 1545 Ocean Avenue, LLC., 72 A.D. 3d 121, 893 N.Y.S.2d 590 (N.Y. App. Div. 2010). *But see*, Simmons Family Properties, LLLP v. Shelton, 307 Ga.App. 361, 705 S.E.2d 258 (2010) (failure to call annual meetings since formation of entity 4 years earlier and ignoring request for a meeting seen as not a merely formal deficiency since the operating agreement contemplated shareholders meeting were to be the venue for non-managing members to have their voices heard).

[239] Widewaters Herkimer Co. v. Aiello, 28 A.D. 2d 1107, 817 N.Y.S.2d 790 (N.Y. App. Div. 2006); Artigas v. Renewal Arts Realty Corp., 22 A.D.3d 327, 803 N.Y.S.2d 12 (N.Y. App. Div. 2005). However, the addition of factors of violence and expulsion supported dissolution in *Taki v. Hami*, 2001 WL 672399 (Mich. App. 2001).

[240] The Dunbar Group, LLC, 267 Va. 361, 593 S.E.2d, 219 (Va. 2004) (expulsion of one of the two members did not mean that business set forth in operating agreement could not continue).

[241] 864 A.2d 86 (Del. Ch. 2004).

[242] 2008 S.D. 76, 754 N.W.2d 825 (2008).

the terms for renewing a lease to two of the four members covering some property owned by the entity.

Operating agreements can, and frequently do, provide for the expulsion of a member. Unless the operating agreement provides otherwise, such expulsion is not an event that causes the firm's dissolution.[243]

§ 14.17   Fiduciary Obligations in LLCs

The content of fiduciary obligations in LLC entities continues to evolve. Much like partnerships and the modern trend for close corporations, the courts appear willing to recognize not only do managers owe fiduciary obligations to the LLC and its members but also members stand in a fiduciary relationship to one another.[244] However, the precise content of the fiduciary duty is at this time decidedly ad hoc. There is every reason to expect that the burdens on managers or member-managers in overseeing the management or actually directing the operations of the LLC will be no more demanding than what we have seen applies to corporations generally. Thus, ordinary negligence is unlikely to overcome the presumption of the business judgment rule.[245] On the other hand, gross negligence and self dealing each is likely to invite closer scrutiny of the manager's and member-manager's decision.

The battle ground on the content of fiduciary duties is not likely to be conduct that sounds in care but rather conduct that implicates questions of loyalty. Thus, when a member-manager purchases the interest of another member, he stands in a fiduciary relationship to the non-active member and therefore has a duty of candor to disclose that a third party had offered to purchase the LLC at a substantial premium.[246] *VGS, Inc. v. Castiel*[247] held that member-managers owed a duty of loyalty to their fellow (third) member-manager so that their failure to give notice to the third manager that they would execute written consents for the purpose of increasing their ownership interest and diluting that of the third manager was a breach of fiduciary duty. The decision is particularly significant because neither the statute nor the operating agreement required advance notice of their actions. While the decision might be seen as an unqualified embrace of a duty of loyalty among members, the facts and the Vice-Chancellor's reasoning suggest a more restrained interpretation. The third manager actually controlled a majority of the shares and had the power to appoint a majority of the managers; because the court emphasized this potential for the third manager to protect his interest by changing the composition of the managers, it was a small step to hold that the stealth circumvention was an act in bad faith. In a sense, the approach taken was to imply a missing term, *i.e.*, that any action by a majority of the mangers would be preceded by notice so that the majority member could exercise his right to

---

[243]   Leisher v. Alfred, 2004 WL 693207 (Cal. Ct. App. 2004).

[244]   California expressly provides that the duties a manager owes the LLC and its members are those of a partner in a partnership. Cal. Corp. Code § 17153.

[245]   *See* Uniform Limited Liability Company Act § 409(c) (hereinafter ULLCA), embraces a standard that, even though the duty of a member in a member-managed LLC "is to act with the care that a person in like position would reasonably exercise in similar circumstances" this standard is "subject to the business judgment rule."

[246]   *See* Salm v. Feldstein, 20 A.D. 3d 469, 799 N.Y.S.2d 104 (N.Y.App.Div. 2005). This does not require that the disclosures need be extensive or formal. *See, e.g.*, Metro Communications Corp. BVI v. Advanced Mobilecomm Technologies, Inc., 854 a.2d 121, 158 (Del. Ch. 2004) (effectiveness and economies of LLC would be eroded if "proxy-like" disclosures were mandated in securities transactions between entity and its members).

[247]   2000 WL 1277372 (Del. Ch. 2000).

prevent the action by removing a manager and appointing a person who would carry out his wishes.

One important feature of modern LLC statutes is the statutory authority for the operating agreement to shape in important ways the fiduciary obligations of members and managers.[248] This statutory authority can be very useful in defining business opportunities that a member or manager can acquire without the action being later challenged as a usurpation of a corporate opportunity.[249] Thus, even though some members of an LLC that was organized to obtain a hockey franchise acted individually to obtain a franchise for themselves, this was not actionable because the operating agreement expressly authorized members to engage in a competitive business.[250] However, exculpatory provisions are likely to be interpreted narrowly.[251]

Consistent with the dominating role of the operating agreement, distributions pursuant to dissolution are governed by the operating agreement. When the operating agreement is silent, the courts obtain guidance from the applicable LLC statute and if that is lacking on its inherent equitable powers.[252] Liability of members following dissolution and winding up of the LLC is governed by statute. Member liability for unsatisfied debts of the LLC if members received a liquidating distribution and the LLC failed to fulfill the notice provision common required in winding up businesses.[253]

---

[248] *See, e.g.,* Del. Code Ann. tit. 6, § 18–1101 (providing in paragraph (b) that "[i]t is the policy of this chapter to give the maximum effect to the principle of freedom of contract and to the enforceability of limited liability company agreements"). *But see* Walker v. Resource Dev. Co. Ltd., LLC (DE), 791 A.2d 799, 803 (Del. Ch. 2000) ("legislature never intended this provision to allow the members of an LLC to misappropriate property from another member").

[249] The taking of corporate opportunities is examined in § 11.8, *supra. See* Florida Estate Developers, LLC v. Ben Tobin Companies, Ltd., 964 So.2d 238 (Fla. Dist. Ct. App. 2007) (not self dealing because operating agreement expressly authorizes conveying property to a member); Bernards v. Summit Real Estate Management, Inc., 229 Or. App. 357, 213 P.3d 1 (2009)(to prevail the complaint must set forth allegations of serious wrongdoing as required by the operating agreement).

[250] McConnell v. Hunt Sports Enterprises, 132 Ohio App. 3d 657, 725 N.E.2d 1193 (1999). *See generally,* Moore, Case Note, The Policy of Opting-Out of Fiduciary Duties in a Limited Liability Company: McConnell v. Hunt Sports Enterprises, 725 N.E.2d 1193 (Ohio Ct. App. 1999), 42 S. Tex. L. Rev. 183 (2000).

[251] Solar Cells, Inc. v. True North Partners, LLC, 2002 WL 749163 (Del.Ch. 2002)(interpreting exculpatory provision from "any liability" focused on conflict of interest as not affecting a challenge for injunctive relief) so that a merger with a substantial member was subject to the "entire fairness" standard); Lerner v. Westreich, 12 Misc. 3d 1164, 819 N.Y.S.2d 210 (Sup. 2006) (provision of operating agreement allowing members to compete with LLC did not excuse the member of accounting for any gains derived via self dealing); Kira, Inc. v. All Star Maintenance, 2006 WL 2193006 (W.D. Tex. 2006) (clause in operating agreement excluding liability for corporate opportunities and setting forth a definition of duty of care did not otherwise exculpate "intentional misconduct").

[252] LaFond v. Sweeney, 2015 Colo. 3, 343 P.3d 939 (Colo. 2015) (contingent fees obtained from client after dissolution deemed to below to the firm and must, therefore, be shared with former members).

[253] *See* Croteau v. Nat'l Better Living Assoc., 290 F.R.D. 521 (D. Mont. 2013).

Chapter 15

THE DERIVATIVE SUIT

Table of Sections

§ 15.1 Nature and Basis of Derivative Action

An almost necessary consequence of a wrong to a corporation is some impairment of the value of each shareholder's stock interest. As a general rule, however, shareholders are considered to have no direct individual right of action for corporation wrongs that impair the value of their investment. Injuries to the corporation such as those resulting from negligence, mismanagement, or fraud of its directors or officers normally are not dealt with as wrongs to the whole group of shareholders in their corporate capacity but rather as a violation of the corporation itself, which can be redressed in a suit by or on behalf of the corporation.[1]

The evolution of a proper method of redress by way of a shareholder's suit for corporate wrongs has been a tortuous one, with many troublesome problems. The famous

---

[1] Dodge v. Woolsey, 59 U.S. (18 How.) 331 (1855); Stevens v. Lowder, 643 F.2d 1078 (5th Cir. 1981), *reh'g denied,* 652 F.2d 1001 (1981); Ma'Ayergi and Assoc., LLC v. Pro Search, Inc., 115 Conn. App. 662, 974 A.2d 724 (Conn. Ct. App. 2009) (derivative suit's purpose is to hold corporate insiders to account as well as to assert claims against third parties).

English decision of *Foss v. Harbottle*[2] gave a somewhat grudging recognition to a remedy. A basis of equitable relief was found in the absence of any adequate remedy other than a suit instituted by individual shareholders asking protection of those rights to which the shareholders as a group in their corporate capacity were entitled. But the English court was exceedingly strict in setting forth the conditions precedent to bringing such a suit, in that it required a suing shareholder to make prior demands for action both on the directors and on all the shareholders.

We may question why certain types of misconduct must be redressed only by or through the corporation when the ultimate impact of the misconduct is visited, albeit indirectly, upon the corporation's owners. Would it not make far better sense to allow individual stockholders to seek their own recoveries? Individual suits by shareholders would not result in wasteful multiplicity of suits because the initiating stockholder could use modern class action procedures to sue on behalf of all stockholders.

There are at least three sound reasons that continue to support the continuing distinction between direct and derivative actions. To permit shareholders to sue separately whenever the value of their shares is diminished by a wrong to the corporation would conflict with (1) the separate-corporate-entity concept, (2) the prior rights of creditors, and (3) the duty of management to sue for the protection of all concerned. Further, it would result in confusion in ascertaining the effect of partial recoveries by individuals on the damages recoverable by the corporation for the same wrongful act.[3] A single action by the corporation, or by a shareholder in a derivative suit on its behalf, at least in theory obtains redress for all the shareholders and also protects the priorities of creditors, who may be unable to collect their claims if corporate assets are recovered by the shareholders individually.

The derivative suit plaintiff is self-selected; without election or appointment he presents himself as spokesman for the corporate interest. Because the plaintiff usually has no significant financial interest in the corporation, the possible harmful economic effects of prosecuting the suit cannot be expected to guide his decision to litigate. The derivative suit plaintiff has a fiduciary relationship to the other stockholders of the corporation,[4] yet such a person is not a worthy candidate to decide by himself whether the corporate interest is served by suing on a contract the corporation has entered, a tort allegedly committed to the corporation's property, or any other matter whose initial impact was on the corporation. These are the types of decisions for which the discretionary judgment of the board of directors or its delegates are readily called into play.

As will be seen in succeeding sections, a faint aura of legitimacy accrues to the plaintiff's authority to represent the corporate interest when the demand requirement is excused or otherwise satisfied because the board of directors, due to its own failings or misconduct, is incapacitated from carrying out an independent assessment of the corporate interest served by the suit. To be sure, that aura is not nearly as bright as it would be had the corporation's board of directors, after an assessment from the corporation's perspective of the costs and benefits, crisply resolved to pursue the cause

---

[2]   Foss v. Harbottle, 67 Eng. Rep. 189, 203 (Ch. 1843).

[3]   *See* Brooks v. Land Drilling Co., 564 F.Supp. 1518 (D. Colo. 1983); General Rubber Co. v. Benedict, 109 N.E. 96 (N.Y. 1915).

[4]   *See* Seeburg-Commonwealth Litig. [1974–1975 Transfer Binder], Fed. Sec. L. Rep. (CCH) ¶ 94,969 (S.D.N.Y. 1975).

of action. Nevertheless, within the narrow band of factual settings in which the corporate cause of action is today allowed to proceed at the instance of the derivative suit plaintiff, there is a highly recognizable legitimacy to the right of the plaintiff and her lawyer, under the watchful eye of the derivative suit court, to vindicate the corporation's injury.

Various theories have been suggested to explain the ground on which an individual shareholder may be allowed to sue on a corporate right of action. One theory merely explains the suit as an exceptional procedure to give a remedy for a corporate wrong affecting the shareholders indirectly that would otherwise escape redress due, among other things, to concealment by director—or officer—wrongdoers.[5] It has also been said that "[t]he right of the stockholder to sue exists because of special injury to him for which otherwise he is without redress."[6] The idea that the plaintiff sues because of the special indirect damage to the plaintiff as a shareholder caused by the wrong to the corporation is not an adequate explanation of the basis of the derivative suit. It is more aptly said that "the plaintiff does not sue in his own right, but in that of the corporation."[7] Hence the terms "representative" or "derivative" suit.

A further view, recognized by a number of courts, analyzes the shareholder's suit as in effect a combination of two causes of action—that is, a proceeding having a dual nature. The individual shareholders may be regarded as having a right in equity to compel the assertion of a corporate right of action against the directors or other wrongdoers when the management wrongfully refuses to act. The proceeding may be viewed as a "propulsive" one, to accomplish in one proceeding (1) the enforcement of the obligation owed by the corporation to the plaintiff and to all its shareholders to enforce its claims and (2) the enforcement of the corporation's rights of action against the wrongdoers. The wrongdoers are joined as parties-defendant in order that the corporate duty and right of action may be enforced for the benefit of all in one proceeding.[8] The corporation is the beneficiary of any recovery in the suit.

A shareholder's derivative suit should not be confused with a class suit, in which shareholders having *individual* rights and causes of action against the corporation are represented by a member of the class of shareholders having the rights and causes of action; the transactions and the questions of law and fact involved in the suit are common to all members of the class. In other words, a class action is used for direct shareholder claims against the corporation.

Plaintiffs in a direct suit based on violations of their individual rights—as opposed to a derivative suit—seek redress of an injury peculiar to themselves as shareholders or a class of shareholders, not an injury to the corporation.[9] The suit is brought to enforce a personal cause of action arising from acts independent of wrongful conduct against the corporation; the plaintiff must demonstrate injury in an individual capacity.

A shareholder class action is simply an action on behalf of persons whose individual claims are identical or substantially similar but who are so numerous that their joining in a single action is impractical. This type of action is a practical and inexpensive way

---

[5]   General Elec. Co. v. Bucyrus-Erie Co., 563 F.Supp. 970 (D.N.Y. 1983); In re Longhorn Sec. Litig., 573 F.Supp. 255 (W.D. Okla. 1983); Foss v. Harbottle, 67 Eng. Rep. 189, 203 (Ch. 1843); Burland v. Earle (1902) A.C. 83, 93.

[6]   Home Fire Ins. Co. v. Barber, 93 N.W. 1024, 1029 (Neb. 1903).

[7]   Ross v. Bernhard, 396 U.S. 531, 539 (1970).

[8]   Hawes v. Oakland, 104 U.S. 450, 452 (1882); Liddy v. Urbanek, 707 F.2d 1222 (11th Cir. 1983).

[9]   Green v. Victor Talking Mach. Co., 24 F.2d 378, 381 (2d Cir.), *cert. denied*, 278 U.S. 602 (1928).

for numerous claimants, especially ones with small claims, to obtain relief by pooling their claims into one lawsuit brought by one or a few individuals for and on behalf of the entire group. A direct class action is thus available to corporate shareholders whenever their common injury is not derivative through injury to the corporate entity. As is pointed out in the next section, difficult questions may arise as to the categorization of a particular claim as direct or derivative.

Shareholder derivative suits are the principal remedy by which defrauded minority shareholders may call directors, officers, promoters, and controlling shareholders to account for mismanagement, diversion of assets, and fraudulent manipulation of corporate affairs. In some cases, however, in which a corporate injury results from wrongdoing, an individual right of action may also arise, and a shareholder may be permitted to sue and recover directly and individually for the loss she suffers. For example, a shareholder who is injured by wrongdoing in connection with her initial purchase of stock may have a direct claim against the wrongdoers. Thus, many suits brought under common law rules or the securities acts for fraud in connection with the sale or purchase of securities will be direct, with the class action available where there is an injury common to a number of securities holders or former holders.[10] But, at least conceptually, claims for individual losses and the impairment in the value of shares due to corporate mismanagement are improper allegations in a derivative suit based on a corporate right of action.

§ 15.2 Distinguishing the Shareholder's Individual Suit from the Derivative Suit

As a rule, the shareholder's judicial remedy for mismanagement or other wrongful acts of directors, officers, or third parties is by a derivative or representative suit on behalf of the corporation. This result reflects not only the practical assessment that the misconduct's initial impact is on the corporation itself, with any stockholder harm being consequential to that impact, but also that the duty breached is one owed directly to the corporation such that it is the corporation's right that is violated by the breaching conduct.[11] In some instances, however, a personal right of action is recognized even for corporate wrongs if a separate duty is owing to the individual or a collective proceeding on behalf of the corporation does not give the shareholder redress.[12] In some circumstances, either a derivative suit or a direct action may be brought at the shareholder's election. The characterization of a particular cause of action as derivative or direct (which in appropriate cases may be brought as a class action) brings significant procedural differences, which are explored in succeeding sections. Because of these differences, the initial characterization of a suit can be of critical significance.[13]

The basic distinction between a derivative and a direct action hinges on whether the aggrieved shareholder is claiming an injury to the corporation or the infringement of some right personal to her, although based on her status as a shareholder or otherwise—for example, as an employee. Thus, for example, a suit claiming

---

[10] For general discussions of class actions, *see* John C. Coffee, Jr., Rethinking the Class Action: A Policy Primer on Reform, 62 Ind. L.J. 625 (1987).

[11] *See* Flynn v. Merrick, 881 F.2d 446 (7th Cir. 1989).

[12] *See, e.g.,* Citibank N.A. v. Data Lease Fin. Corp., 828 F.2d 686 (11th Cir. 1987).

[13] *See* Deborah A. DeMott, Shareholder Derivative Actions Law & Practice §§ 2.1 to 2.7 (2019–2020 ed.).

mismanagement by the officers or directors has been described as a "classic derivative suit," as contrasted with an action to compel inspection of the corporate books, which is the plaintiff's individual claim against the corporation as the "real defendant."[14] On the other hand, the directors' gross negligence in approving the selling price of the company gives rise to an individual cause of action.[15] Thus it can be seen that in many instances shareholder suits are not so easily classified as either individual or derivative.

In distinguishing between individual suits and derivative actions, it is helpful to identify some of the underlying policy rationales. Requiring an injury to the corporation to be vindicated either in a suit brought by the corporation itself or in a derivative suit avoids multitudinous litigation that would result from individual shareholder suits.[16] However, the availability of class action treatment would appear a more direct manner to address this concern. A further policy rationale is that, because recoveries in derivative actions generally accrue to the corporation, the derivative suit thus provides a mechanism that assures that the fruits of the derivative suit are channeled so that the relative rights and interests of corporate creditors[17] and *all* shareholders[18] are preserved. This may well argue that the derivative suit mechanism is a necessary prophylaxis for the benefit of creditors.

Perhaps the true rationale for continuing to distinguish the derivative suit from the class action individual-based suit is the availability of a prescreening device on this form of representative suit. That is, as seen earlier, there is a genuine malaise over whether representative suits (that is, class actions and derivative suits) are socially desirable; this concern arises because empirical evidence is consistent with the hypothesis that representative suits are socially destructive because they sometimes (or to their harshest critics, frequently) seek to extort a settlement from the defendants or the corporation. For derivative suits, the corporation has, through the demand requirement,[19] a mechanism that prescreens harmful derivative suits. No such prescreening device is available for class actions. Thus one potential purpose of continuing to distinguish between individual and derivative actions is that the courts can accommodate the corporation's interest in having the corporate voice heard on the desirability of the suit being initiated and prosecuted.

Courts frequently have great difficulty in classifying a plaintiff's claim as individual or derivative. For example, there has been a conflict as to the proper classification of a suit to compel dividends. In a federal case applying Pennsylvania law, the court held such a suit to be direct and individual, reasoning that because "[t]he right to dividends is an incident of [stock] ownership," the shareholder has been injured directly, and recovery "will benefit only the shareholders."[20] In contrast, a New York court held, over

---

[14]   *See* Kramer v. Western Pac. Indus., 546 A.2d 348 (Del. 1988).

[15]   *See, e.g.,* Dowling v. Narragansett Capital Corp., 735 F.Supp. 1105 (D.R.I. 1990) (fraud during sale of company produced not only lower price but lower price for non-defendant stockholders).

[16]   Watson v. Button, 235 F.2d 235, 237 (9th Cir. 1956); Sutter v. General Petroleum Corp., 170 P.2d 898 (Cal. 1946).

[17]   Corporate creditors will be protected because the recovery will go into the corporate treasury, and creditors will have the first claim on the corporation's assets in case of its liquidation or bankruptcy. Watson v. Button, 235 F.2d 235, 237 (9th Cir. 1956).

[18]   Derivative actions protect all shareholders because a recovery by the corporation will raise the value of each share equally. *Id.*

[19]   *See infra* §§ 15.4 and 15.5.

[20]   Knapp v. Bankers Sec. Corp., 230 F.2d 717, 722 (3d Cir. 1956). This is the preferable view.

a strong dissent, that a suit to compel dividends must be brought derivatively because it is grounded on a duty owed by the directors to the corporation, but the New York rule has since been changed by statute.[21] It is possible to justify both views.

On the one hand, an action to compel dividends should be considered an individual action when the complaint is that the majority or management has withheld dividends for the purpose of driving the minority stockholders from the corporation. On the other hand, the suit is properly a derivative action when the complaint is that by failing to declare dividends the corporation risks being subject to punitive excess retained-earnings taxes or that the retained earnings will otherwise be used improvidently.[22] Another sometimes litigated question is the proper classification of a shareholder suit to enforce a shareholder's preemptive rights to a new issuance of shares. Under the better view the action is direct, as it is based on the shareholder's contractual claim against the corporation.[23]

A source of the inconsistency among the courts on their treatment of suits as individual or derivative is a misunderstanding of the effect the court should accord the fact that a class of shareholders has been similarly harmed. Some courts have reasoned that a derivative action is the only basis for a shareholder to complain unless the shareholder has suffered a loss or other injury different from that of the other minority stockholders.[24] This is erroneous. As Justice Traynor so clearly and wisely concluded in *Jones v. H. F. Ahmanson & Company*,[25]

> The individual wrong necessary to support a suit by a shareholder need not be unique to the plaintiff. The same injury may affect a substantial number of shareholders. If the injury is not incidental to an injury to the corporation, an individual cause of action exists.[26]

In *Tooley v. Donaldson, Lufkin & Jenrette, Inc.*[27] where the Delaware Supreme Court, also disapproved both the concept of "special injury" and that a claim is necessarily derivative if the alleged misconduct affects all stockholders equally. The court held that whether a claim is direct or derivative is decided by addressing two considerations: 1) who suffered the alleged harm (the corporation or the suing stockholders individually) and 2) who would receive the benefit of any recovery or other remedy (the corporation or the stockholders individually). Massachusetts reached a startling conclusion regarding this issue where shareholders complained the company's CEO negotiated an unfair merger price so as to garner a $27 million change of control

---

[21] Gordon v. Elliman, 119 N.E.2d 331 (N.Y. 1954). *See* Eisenberg v. Flying Tiger Line, Inc., 451 F.2d 267 (2d Cir. 1971).

[22] *See* Maul v. Kirkman, 637 A.2d 928 (N.J. Super. App. Div. 1994).

[23] Shaw v. Empire Sav. & Loan Ass'n, 9 Cal.Rptr. 204 (Ct. App. 1960).

[24] *See, e.g.,* Grace Brothers Ltd. v. Farley Ind., Inc., 450 S.E.2d 814 (Ga. 1994) (barring direct claim by minority stockholders who complained of unfair treatment in a cash-out merger).

[25] Jones v. H. F. Ahmanson & Company, 460 P.2d 464 (Cal. 1969).

[26] 460 P.2d at 470–471.

[27] Tooley v. Donaldson, Lufkin & Jenrette, Inc., 845 A.2d 1031 (Del. 2004). In reaching its holding, the court expressly disapproved as confusing several earlier Delaware decisions In re Tri-Star Pictures, Inc. Litig., 634 A.2d 319 (Del.Supr. 1993); Lipton v. News Int'l, 514 A.2d 1075 (Del. 1986) and Moran v. Household Int'l, Inc., 490 A.2d 1059 (Del. Ch. 1985) and embraced as illustrative of its present position Parnes v. Bally Entertainment Corp., 722 A.2d 1243 (Del. 1999); Grimes v. Donald, 673 A.2d 1207 (Del. 1996) and Kramer v. Western Pacific Ind., Inc., 546 A.2d 348 (Del. 1988).

benefit. In *Int'l Brotherhood Elec. Workers Loc. No. 129 Benefit Fd. v. Tucci*,[28] the Massachusetts Supreme Court expressly rejected Delaware's approach and held that the suit must be maintained as a derivative suit. The court relied heavily on the state statute, patterned on the Model Business Corporation Act, broadly announcing directors owed a duty to act "in a manner the director reasonably believes to be in the best interest of the corporation."[29] The court believed the statute carried forward its common law rules that in only two instances do directors owe a duty directly to shareholders: 1) in close corporations and 2) for the actions of a controlling stockholder. In contrast, most courts understand the relied upon statutory provision to be aspirational and does not set forth any duty. Moreover, courts in such transactions typically view the directors and officers who negotiate the transaction's terms do so as a representative of both the shareholders and the corporation.

The difference between individual and derivative actions can be illustrated by examples. The following actions have been held to be individual (direct) actions:

(1) A claim founded on a contract between the corporation and the shareholder as an individual[30] or based on the holder's preferred stock rights.[31]

(2) A claim based on false and misleading proxy solicitation.[32]

(3) An action to compel dissolution of the corporation.[33] However, dissolution may also be sought in a derivative suit.[34]

(4) A suit against directors for fraud in the sale or purchase of the individual shareholder's stock.[35]

(5) A claim founded in tort for injury directly upon the shareholder's person or property.[36]

(6) An action against a director for disseminating false reports about the validity or value of shareholder's stock that harms the shareholder in his individual capacity as an investor.[37]

(7) A claim against a voting trustee for a breach of her obligations.[38]

(8) An action to protect the shareholder's relative voting power.[39]

---

[28] Int' Brotherhood Elec. Workers Loc. No. 129 Benefit Fd. v. Tucci, 476 Mass. 553, 70 N.E.3d 918 (2017).

[29] Mass. Gen. Laws ch. 156D, § 8.30(a)(3) (patterned on MBCA § 8.30).

[30] *See, e.g.,* Buschmann v. Professional Men's Ass'n, 405 F.2d 659 (7th Cir. 1969).

[31] Blue Chip Capital Fund II LP v. Tubergen, 906 A.2d 827 (Del. Ch. 2006).

[32] *See* Yamamoto v. Omiya, 564 F.2d 1319 (9th Cir. 1977). However, both cases left open the possibility that a derivative action may also have been appropriate.

[33] Fontheim v. Walker, 141 N.Y.S.2d 62 (Sup. Ct. 1955).

[34] *See, e.g.,* Gottfried v. Gottfried, 50 N.Y.S.2d 951 (Sup. Ct. 1944).

[35] *See, e.g.,* Siegel v. Engelmann, 143 N.Y.S.2d 193 (Sup. Ct. 1955); Von Au v. Magenheimer, 110 N.Y.S. 629 (App. Div. 1908), *aff'd,* 89 N.E. 1114 (N.Y. 1909).

[36] *See, e.g.,* Gieselmann v. Stegeman, 443 S.W.2d 127 (Mo. 1969).

[37] *See, e.g.,* Grogan v. Garner, 806 F.2d 829 (8th Cir. 1986).

[38] *See, e.g.,* Lurie v. Rupe, 201 N.E.2d 158 (Ill. App. Ct. 1964), *cert. denied,* 380 U.S. 964 (1965).

[39] *See, e.g.,* Lochhead v. Alacano, 697 F.Supp. 406 (D. Utah 1988).

(9) A suit to protect a shareholder's inspection rights.[40]

(10) A suit against takeover maneuvers, such as adopting poison pill or issuing stock for the purpose of wrongfully perpetuating or shifting control.[41]

(11) An action to enjoin a threatened *ultra vires* act.[42]

(12) An action to compel payment of a declared dividend.[43]

(13) An action to vindicate a wrong to the individual shareholder, although the same wrongful act may also create a separate corporate cause of action.[44]

(14) A suit against the only other shareholder(s) for injuring the corporation's business where a judgment in a derivative suit would benefit the wrongdoer.[45]

(15) Suit alleging board abdicated its powers to the CEO.[46]

(16) A suit alleging directors breached fiduciary duty when negotiating to sell company.[47]

(17) Suit based on oppressive action designed to force the minority shareholder(s) from the corporation or other coercive action directed at the minority.[48]

The following claims have been held to be derivative:

(1) An action seeking recovery due to managerial misconduct, producing a proportionate decline in the company's shares, such as the waste of corporate assets or usurpation of corporate opportunities.[49]

(2) An action against the purchaser of corporate assets seeking rescission of the sale.[50]

(3) An action under section 10(b) of the Securities Exchange Act of 1934 and SEC Rule 10b–5, where the corporation has purchased or sold securities and the individual shareholder is precluded from relief because he is neither a purchaser nor seller of securities.[51]

---

[40] *See, e.g.,* Gieselmann v. Stegeman, 443 S.W.2d 127 (Mo. 1969).

[41] *See, e.g.,* In re Gaylord Container Corp. Shareholders Litigation, 747 A.2d 71 (Del. Ch. 1999).

[42] *See, e.g.,* Independence Lead Mines Co. v. Kingsbury, 175 F.2d 983 (9th Cir.), *cert. denied,* 338 U.S. 900 (1949).

[43] Independence Lead Mines Co. v. Kingsbury, 175 F.2d 983 (9th Cir.), *cert. denied,* 338 U.S. 900 (1949).

[44] *See, e.g.,* Snyder v. Epstein, 290 F.Supp. 652 (E.D. Wis. 1968).

[45] *See, e.g.,* Fischer v. Fischer, 1999 WL 1032768 (Del. Ch. 1999) (complaint over unfair sale of company's only asset that benefited all stockholders other than the plaintiff).

[46] Grimes v. Donald, 673 A.2d 1207, 1213 (Del. 1996).

[47] Parnes v. Bally Entertainment Corp., 722 A.2d 1243 (Del. 1999) (allegations included charge the directors drove off would-be suitors by demanding side payments to themselves for suitor's offer to be considered).

[48] Strougo v. Bassini, 282 F.3d 162 (2d Cir. 2002).

[49] *See, e.g.,* Phoenix Airline Serv., Inc. v. Metro Airlines, Inc., 403 S.E.2d 832 (Ga.App. 1991).

[50] *See, e.g.,* Bassett v. Battle, 1 N.Y.S.2d 869 (App. Div. 1938).

[51] *See, e.g.,* Ray v. Karris, 780 F.2d 636, 641 (7th Cir. 1985).

(4) An action to recover for injuries to corporate assets caused by fraud or by third parties.[52]

(5) An action to recover damages for an *ultra vires* act.[53]

(6) A suit to compel the directors to dissolve the corporation due to director misconduct.[54]

(7) An action on a contract between the corporation and a third party.[55]

(8) Managerial decisions designed to thwart a takeover and thereby deprive the stockholders of an opportunity to dispose of their shares at a premium.[56]

(9) Breach of fiduciary duty during a merger transaction.[57]

(10) Malpractice or misfeasance by consultants and experts to the corporation.[58]

There are situations in which a claim can be framed either as a derivative or as a direct claim.[59]

In some instances, the nature of the relief claimed has guided the court's determination whether the suit is a derivative suit. For example, in *Cohen v. Mirage Resorts, Inc.*,[60] the plaintiff alleged misconduct leading up to a merger vote was engaged in to assure shareholders would approve a subsequent merger stated a derivative action. The Nevada Supreme Court reasoned that this allegation would render the suit a direct action if relief sought were rescission or a challenge to legitimacy of merger. But this was not set forth in the complaint. The court held that the trial court should have allowed the plaintiff to replead rather than dismiss the suit with prejudice on the grounds a pre-suit demand had not been made.

In voluntary corporate dissolution, where corporate affairs are being wound up or the process of liquidation is completed, the weight of judicial authority allows shareholders to sue the directors individually for wrongs they committed during corporate existence or for abuse of their authority in winding up the corporation.[61] Today, this matter is generally covered by statute. Even in states in which the general corporation statute does not prolong corporate existence after dissolution for winding-up purposes, the winding-up should be treated as continuing the same concern, as is the

---

[52] *See, e.g.*, Green v. Victor Talking Mach. Co., 24 F.2d 378 (2d Cir.) (misappropriation of corporate assets).

[53] *See, e.g.*, Lee Moving & Storage, Inc. v. Bourgeois, 343 So.2d 1192 (La. Ct. App. 1977) (with good faith and due diligence).

[54] *See, e.g.*, Parks v. Multimedia Technologies, Inc., 520 S.E.2d 517, 523 (Ga. Ct. App. 1999).

[55] *See* Boothe v. Baker Indus., 262 F.Supp. 168 (D. Del. 1966) (where right of action existed as to both derivative and nonderivative causes, adjudication of state court nonderivative class action held bar to federal derivative suit).

[56] *See, e.g.*, Nowling v. Aero Serv. Int'l, 752 F.Supp. 1304 (E.D. La. 1990).

[57] *See, e.g.*, In re First Interstate Bancorp Litigation, 729 A.2d 851 (Del. Ch. 1998).

[58] PricewaterhouseCoopers, LLP v. Massey, 860 N.E.2d 1252 (Ind. Ct. App. 2007).

[59] *See* Boothe v. Baker Indus., 262 F.Supp. 168 (D. Del. 1966) (where right of action existed as to both derivative and nonderivative causes, adjudication of state court nonderivative class action held bar to federal derivative suit).

[60] 119 Nev. 1, 62 P.3d 720 (Nev. 2003).

[61] Moore v. Occupational Safety & Health Rev. Comm'n, 591 F.2d 991 (4th Cir. 1979).

case in partnership dissolution. Corporate assets and claims should be administered for the benefit of all concerned, just as they should have been administered before the formal dissolution that terminated the authority of the directors to continue the business.[62]

Several modern cases hold that the individual-derivative distinction assumes relevancy in the close corporation only when there is a justifiable concern that creditors may be harmed if any recovery resulting from the suit does not go to the corporation. Cases have frequently held that in suits between two co-owners of a close corporation that the suit need not be maintained as a derivative suit, even though the suit is premised on conduct that in other contexts would involve only a corporate cause of action.[63] This result appears correct, especially where the record supports the view that creditors are unlikely to be prejudiced should the recovery bypass the corporation. In the tightly held close corporation, where only two or maybe three or four shareholders exist, it is difficult to attribute a *persona* to the corporation when the issue is whose cause of action is being vindicated. Clearly there is no basis to believe there is a true independent voice that can speak through the demand requirement as to the suit's probable impact on the corporation's interests. The American Law Institute encourages such flexibility by recommending that the court exercise such discretion where "it finds that to do so will not (i) unfairly expose the corporation or the defendants to a multiplicity of actions, (ii) materially prejudice the interests of creditors of the corporation, or (iii) interfere with a fair distribution of the recovery among all interested persons."[64]

§ 15.3   Individual Recovery in Derivative Suits

As a general rule, recovery in derivative suits inures to the corporation, with the proceeds becoming a part of the corporate assets.[65] In some situations, however, the shareholder-plaintiff in a derivative suit on a corporate right of action may recover individual damages in lieu of a corporate recovery. For example, where only few stockholders are injured by the breach, there is no fear that creditors may be disadvantaged if recovery does not go to the corporation, and the wrongdoers are still in control of the corporation, recovery may go directly to the shareholder or shareholders who complain.[66] If a corporate recovery will not cure the injury or if granting equitable relief to the corporation by way of rescission would unsettle and disturb significant interests of innocent third parties, the court should be able to give relief according to the needs of the case.

Accordingly, where special circumstances exist,[67] courts have allowed direct pro rata recovery by the shareholders.[68] Courts have decreed individual pro rata recovery in order to facilitate the distribution of corporate funds in a variety of situations: (1) where the corporation is in the process of liquidation, (2) where the wrongdoers retain

---

[62]   George D. Hornstein, Voluntary Dissolution, 51 Yale L.J. 64, 80 (1941). Dissolution and winding up are discussed in Chapter 26.

[63]   *See, e.g.,* Simon v. Mann, 373 F.Supp.2d 1196 (D. Nev. 2005).

[64]   ALI, 2 Principles of Corporate Governance, § 7.01(d) (1992). For a decision adopting the ALI's approach, *see* Barth v. Barth, 659 N.E.2d 559 (Ind. 1995); *contra* Wessin v. Archives Corp., 592 N.W.2d 460 (Minn. 1999).

[65]   *See* Edward J. Grenier, Jr., Pro Rata Recovery by Shareholders on Corporate Causes of Action as a Means of Achieving Corporate Justice, 19 Wash. & Lee L. Rev. 165 (1962).

[66]   *See, e.g.,* Jannes v. Microwave Communications, Inc., 385 F.Supp. 759 (N.D. Ill. 1974).

[67]   *E.g.,* Perlman v. Feldmann, 219 F.2d 173 (2d Cir.), *cert. denied,* 349 U.S. 952 (1955).

[68]   *See* Note, 56 Harv. L. Rev. 1314 (1956).

substantial control of the corporation and corporate recovery would return the funds to their control,[69] (3) where the defendants sell control of the corporation for an unlawful premium and the court seeks to prevent a windfall to purchasers of the wrongdoers' shares,[70] (4) where a majority of the corporation's shares are held by persons who could not bring the derivative suit because of their personal involvement in, or ratification of, the wrongdoing,[71] and (5) where a pro rata recovery fairly resolves the varying equities among differently situated stockholders.[72]

It is difficult to formulate hard and fast rules as to when direct shareholder recovery is appropriate in a derivative suit. Generally, direct recovery is granted where it is the most effective means of dealing with inequities that would otherwise result.[73]

Some of the impetus is removed for individual recoveries in derivative-based suits in the close corporation setting by the increasing willingness of courts to follow the course recommended by the American Law Institute that suits against dominant stockholders in close corporations essentially be treated as individual, not derivative, actions.[74] Such treatment not only lifts the necessity for the minority holder to meet certain substantive requirements to maintain a suit, such as a demand requirement, but also permits recovery for the proportionate harm the dominant stockholder has caused the minority-stockholder-plaintiff.

§ 15.4   Necessity of Demand on the Shareholders

The authority to sue for corporate injuries is vested primarily in corporate management. For a shareholder to show a right to sue on behalf of the corporation, he must allege with some particularity in his complaint that he has exhausted his remedies within the corporation by making a demand on the directors or other officers to sue, or he must allege sufficient reason for not doing so.[75] At one time the requirement that a shareholder exhaust her intracorporate remedies meant that it was insufficient for a shareholder merely to make a demand on the directors that they institute suit; she must also make a similar demand upon the shareholders as a body. It is rare today to find a demand on the shareholders required, in part because most derivative suits allege misconduct that cannot be ratified by a majority vote of the stockholders.[76] However, the derivative suit plaintiff must take care to plead the basis for excusing the demand or otherwise incur the likelihood of dismissal in those jurisdictions that have not abolished this requirement.[77]

An application to the shareholders and the calling of a shareholders' meeting is an exceedingly unreasonable requirement, certainly if the conduct that is the focus of the

---

[69]   *See, e.g.,* Atkinson v. Marquart, 541 P.2d 556 (Ariz. 1975).

[70]   *E.g.,* Perlman v. Feldmann, 219 F.2d 173 (2d Cir.), *cert. denied,* 349 U.S. 952 (1955).

[71]   *E.g.,* Perlman v. Feldmann, 219 F.2d 173 (2d Cir.); *cert. denied,* 349 U.S. 952 (1955), *on remand,* 154 F.Supp. 436 (D. Conn. 1957).

[72]   *See, e.g.,* Rankin v. Frebank Co., 121 Cal.Rptr. 348 (Ct. App. 1975).

[73]   *See, e.g.,* Gabhart v. Gabhart, 370 N.E.2d 345 (Ind. 1977) (allowing individual recovery by former shareholder of merged corporation whose means of redress cut off by merger).

[74]   ALI, 2 Principles of Corporate Governance: Analysis and Recommendations § 7.01(d) (1992).

[75]   *E.g.,* Hawes v. Oakland, 104 U.S. 450, 460–461 (1882); Smith v. Sperling, 354 U.S. 91 (1957); Lewis v. Curtis, 671 F.2d 779 (3d Cir. 1982).

[76]   *See, e.g.,* Gibbs v. Macari, 1997 WL 1261225 (Mass. Super. 1997) (dismissing suit for failure to allege basis to excuse a demand).

[77]   *See, e.g.,* McLeese v. J.C. Nichols Co., 842 S.W.2d 115 (Mo. Ct. App. 1992).

derivative suit can only be ratified by all the stockholders.[78] But the burdens of making such a demand in a public corporation, regardless of the nature of the underlying complaint, are so substantial that it is difficult to understand why the social benefits of making a demand can justify the burdens of this requirement. At best, it erects a needless barrier to legitimate shareholder derivative suits, which are already expensive and burdensome. The requirement is based on a policy of protecting the majority and preventing a large corporation from being unduly vexed by suits brought by shareholders with small holdings whose motives may be hostile to the corporation and who may have made no effort to ascertain the opinion or will of the majority.[79] In general it seems impractical to require, as a condition precedent to bringing a derivative suit, calling a shareholders' meeting or making a demand on many scattered shareholders, in view of the difficulty, expense, delay, and small benefit to be gained thereby.[80] Where an abuse of process is at issue, a refusal by the directors to sue ought to be sufficient to establish a default by the corporation in enforcing its rights, without an additional application to the shareholders. That is, the demand requirement and the special litigation committee are far more effective filters of unwise or harmful derivative suits than we can expect to flow from mandating a demand on the stockholders.[81] Today, the necessity that a demand be made on the shareholders is largely of historical significance.[82] Most modern decisions readily excuse making a demand or the governing statute eliminates the requirement.[83] The American Law Institute's proposals for derivative suits dispense with the requirement of a demand on the shareholders.[84] As a general rule, informed collective shareholder consideration of the proposed litigation is not feasible.

Federal Rule of Civil Procedure 23.1 provides that the plaintiff's complaint must set forth her efforts to obtain action from the stockholders "if necessary." As such, the demand on the stockholders becomes a question in the first instance of substantive state law, save where making a demand would prove inconsistent with federal policy underlying any federal question raised in the derivative suit.[85] As noted above, where state law continues to embody a demand on the shareholders, modern decisions have been most willing to excuse the requirement on one of several possible bases, such as the alleged misconduct being of the type that cannot be approved by a majority vote of the stockholders,[86] or that the defendant holds a majority or controlling block of the voting power,[87] or there is such a large number of stockholders that the plaintiff would incur unreasonable expenses, burdens, and delays in fulfilling the requirement.[88]

---

[78]   This is the central reasoning of the leading modern case. *See* Mayer v. Adams, 141 A.2d 458 (Del. 1958).

[79]   Foss v. Harbottle, 67 Eng. Rep. 189 (Ch. 1843).

[80]   *See* In re Midlantic Corp. Shareholder Litigation, 758 F.Supp. 226 (D.N.J. 1990) (under New Jersey law the demand is excused where it would be expensive and delay would jeopardize the corporation's interests).

[81]   *See infra* §§ 15.4 and 15.5.

[82]   Hawes v. Oakland, 104 U.S. 450 (1882); Fed. R. Civ. P. 23.1.

[83]   *See, e.g.,* Cal. Corp. Code § 800 (West 1990); N.Y. Bus. Corp. Law § 626 (McKinney 1986).

[84]   ALI, 2 Principles of Corporate Governance: Analysis and Recommendations § 7.03(c) (1992).

[85]   *See* Burks v. Lasker, 441 U.S. 471 (1979).

[86]   *See, e.g.,* Mayer v. Adams, 141 A.2d 458 (Del. 1958).

[87]   *See, e.g.,* Gottesman v. General Motors Corp., 268 F.2d 194 (2d Cir. 1959).

[88]   *See, e.g.,* Weiss v. Sunasco, Inc., 316 F.Supp. 1197 (E.D. Pa. 1970).

§ 15.5   The Demand on the Directors Requirement

The derivative suit complaint must plead with particularity the efforts the plaintiff has made to seek the board of directors to prosecute the cause of action the plaintiff seeks to initiate or set forth the reasons for not seeking such action by the board of directors.[89] This is the demand requirement and is the single most challenging hurdle that lies in the path of the derivative suit plaintiff. The requirement of a demand on the directors dates back to the leading Supreme Court case of *Hawes v. Oakland*.[90] It is codified in the Federal Rules of Civil Procedure[91] and is followed in most states.[92]

In general, the directors have discretion to refuse to sue if they decide in good faith not to do so and do not exceed the scope of the business judgment rule. In a leading Supreme Court case,[93] Justice Brandeis declared:

> Whether or not a corporation shall seek to enforce in the courts a cause of action for damages is, like other business questions, ordinarily a matter of internal management and is left to the discretion of the directors, in the absence of instructions by vote of the stockholders. Courts interfere seldom to control such discretion intra vires the corporation, except where the directors are guilty of misconduct equivalent to a breach of trust, or where they stand in a dual relation which prevents an unprejudiced exercise of judgment; and, as a rule, only after application to the stockholders, unless it appears that there was no opportunity for such application, that application would be futile (as where wrongdoers control the corporation), or that the delay involved would defeat recovery.

Even if the directors believe that the corporation has a good cause of action for an injury committed by officers or third parties, that fact does not necessarily make it incumbent on them to bring suit. If in the honest and impartial opinion of the directors the best interests of the company are served by not bringing suit, the directors' decision not to sue is a bar to a shareholder's bringing a derivative suit. In making the decision whether to enforce a corporate cause of action, management generally invokes a cost-benefit analysis. Courts have often said that the question of whether to sue is within the directors' discretion, and that if they act in good faith, their refusal is binding.[94]

Can the law always trust an honest management to decide whether a suit on a clear cause of action is expedient or inexpedient? The distinction cannot be drawn between the directors' neglecting their duty when deciding whether the corporation should bring suit and their committing errors of judgment as to law or policy. Good faith in refusing to sue should not be the only limitation on the discretion of the directors. The proper limit is whether the directors acted not only honestly but within the permissible bounds of intelligent business judgment or discretion. The question whether refusal to sue is wrongful depends on all the circumstances of the case.[95]

---

[89]   *See, e.g.,* Fed. R. Civ. P. 23.1; Cal. Corp. Code § 800 (2009); Del. Ch. Ct. R. 23.1; N.Y. Bus. Corp. Law § 626(c) (2009); Model Bus. Corp. Act § 7.42 (2008).

[90]   Hawes v. Oakland, 104 U.S. 450 (1882).

[91]   Fed. R. Civ. P. 23.1.

[92]   *See, e.g.,* Cal. Corp. Code § 800(b)(2) (2009); Del. Ch. Ct. R. 23.1; N.Y. Bus. Corp. Law § 626(c) (2009).

[93]   United Copper Sec. Co. v. Amalgamated Copper Co., 244 U.S. 261, 264 (1917).

[94]   Burks v. Lasker, 441 U.S. 471 (1979).

[95]   *E.g.,* Abramowitz v. Posner, 672 F.2d 1025 (2d Cir. 1982).

There is good reason to argue that the directors' response to a demand should not carry the same presumptive weight as courts accord directors' judgment in traditional business matters.[96] The considerations that justify the overwhelming deference that courts accord directors' decisions in normal commercial transactions do not justify the same deference when a committee of the directors recommends dismissal of a derivative suit or the board collectively rejects a demand for suit.[97] For example, if a court is asked to upset a directors' decision to acquire Blackacre for allegedly too high a price, the court must weigh that prayer with a healthy respect for the idea that, if it does set aside the directors' judgment, the directors will be liable for the consequential damages of their decision. In contrast, if the court should rule against the directors or a committee of the directors, there is no causal relationship between the directors' decision (that the suit not be pursued) and any harm to the corporation. That is, the directors cannot be held liable for any losses that can be attributed to the court's decision not to dismiss the derivative suit as suggested by the directors. Therefore, the court need not temper its scrutiny of the directors' recommendation in order to spare those directors of personal liability for having reached an improper result. Moreover, the directors' judgment that the suit should be dismissed is not peculiarly within their business expertise. For truly business decisions, courts wisely defer to the managerial, financial, manufacturing, and planning expertise of directors. This indeed is the wisdom of the business judgment rule. But director expertise in evaluating the merits and impact of a suit would appear to be no better, and likely could be a good deal less, than that of a derivative suit court. Courts thus can justifiably be less deferential in the demand-on-director area than they are when asked to review the decisions of directors in other contexts.

The demand requirement gives the board of directors the opportunity to assume control of the decision to litigate.[98] Once a demand is made, the response of the board of directors must be within a reasonable time; if not so forthcoming, the demand required is deemed satisfied.[99] If the directors accede to the shareholder's demands, the corporation supplants the derivative plaintiff for the purpose of enforcing its corporate rights. If the directors refuse to sue despite a proper demand, a few courts have stated that the shareholder is not automatically entitled to pursue the derivative claim.[100] Most courts hold that, if an independent board decides in good faith against the demand (that is, rejects the demand), the directors' refusal to sue falls within the business judgment rule, and the suit must be dismissed.[101] The standard of review of a dismissal recommendation in a demand required case is the same whether the recommendation is proffered by the board or a committee of the board.[102] Only in rare cases will a derivative

---

[96] For an close analysis of the inappropriate use of the heuristics for traditional, non-litigation, oriented business judgment rule approach, *see* Kenneth B. Davis, Jr., The Business Judgment Rule in Wisconsin, 2015 Wis. L. Rev. 475.

[97] *See* Victor Brudney, The Independent Director-Heavenly City or Potempkin Village?, 95 Harv. L. Rev. 597, 630–631 (1982).

[98] *See* Brody v. Chemical Bank, 517 F.2d 932, 934 (2d Cir. 1975).

[99] Lewis v. Sporck, 646 F.Supp. 574 (N.D. Cal. 1986) (three-month delay assured that board had sufficient time); Rubin v. Posner, 701 F.Supp. 1041 (D. Del. 1988) (30 days sufficient where no complex issues posed).

[100] *See* Papilsky v. Berndt, 503 F.2d 554, 556 (2d Cir. 1974), *cert. denied,* 419 U.S. 1048 (1974) (dicta).

[101] *See, e.g.,* Atkins v. Hibernia Corp., 182 F.3d 320, 324 (5th Cir. 1999) (citing Louisiana law, concludes rejection of demand upheld unless plaintiff sustains burden of proving that rejection was not rational, honest and disinterested).

[102] *See* Allied Ready Mix Co., Inc. v. Allen, 994 S.W.2d 4 (Ky. Ct. App. 1998); Harhen v. Brown, 730 N.E.2d 859 (Mass. 2000).

suit be allowed to proceed after the board of directors has rejected the demand.[103] In essence, the inquiry into whether the board lacks the capacity to make the decision not to sue is much like the inquiry into whether the demand should be excused because it would be futile.[104] Because instances are rare when the board of directors approves of the action *and* does not authorize the corporation's counsel to take over the suit, most derivative suits arise where the plaintiff has successfully pleaded facts that excuse any demand on the board of directors.[105] (Common bases for excusing a demand on the board of directors are discussed below.) A plaintiff who has made a demand on the board of directors cannot reverse course and seek to proceed with the suit on the ground that the demand should have been excused.[106]

The demand requirement centralizes in the board of directors a necessary and unique perspective on whether the suit is in the corporation's best interests. Thus the demand requirement protects directors from harassment by litigious shareholders contesting matters clearly within the directors' discretion[107] and helps curtail strike suits by shareholders making reckless charges for personal gain rather than corporate benefit.[108] Shareholders must allege with particularity the efforts made to obtain the action they desire from directors,[109] and the demand must be timely in order to afford the directors a reasonable opportunity to act.[110] Some courts have adopted a permissive view as to the excuse of the demand requirement, viewing the demand requirement as consistent with the flexible standards of modern notice pleading.[111] This in fact is the position taken by the American Law Institute in its proposals for derivative suits in its adoption of the so-called universal demand approach.[112] Others have taken a much stricter view, which characterizes excuse of prior demand as "an exceptional rule of pleading, serving a special purpose. . . ."[113] The wide divergence in the decisions whether to excuse a demand on the board of directors indicates that to a considerable extent the necessity for a demand lies within the sound discretion of the court.[114] The role to accord demand and, more particularly, how easily a demand on the board of directors will be excused, is linked to the degree of deference the legislature or court wishes to accord the board's rejection of any demand made on it. That is, if the board of directors' perspective on the derivative suit's continuation is accorded great deference in all cases, excusing a demand becomes the vehicle for *ex ante* determining the instances in which the board's

---

[103] *See* Ashwander v. Tennessee Valley Auth., 297 U.S. 288 (1936); Stepak v. Addison, 20 F.3d 398 (11th Cir. 1994) (directors in rejecting demand acted with gross negligence when they relied on same law firm that represented defendants in related criminal proceeding).

[104] Grimes v. DSC Communications Corp., 724 A.2d 561 (Del. Ch. 1998) (when demand rejected, plaintiff must bear the burden of proof with particular facts to create a reasonable doubt that the corporation's board wrongfully refused the demand).

[105] *See* Daniel R. Fischel, The Demand and Standing Requirements in Stockholder Derivative Actions, 44 U. Chi. L. Rev. 168 (1976).

[106] *See* Spiegel v. Buntrock, 571 A.2d 767 (Del. 1990) (the making of demand concedes board's independence).

[107] Barr v. Wackman, 329 N.E.2d 180, 186 (N.Y. 1975).

[108] Barr v. Wackman, 329 N.E.2d 180, 186 (N.Y. 1975).

[109] Fed. R. Civ. P. 23.1.

[110] Bartlett v. New York, N.H. & H.R. Co., 109 N.E. 452, 454 (Mass. 1915).

[111] Liboff v. Wolfson, 437 F.2d 121, 122 (5th Cir. 1971).

[112] *See* ALI, 2 Principles of Corporate Governance: Analysis and Recommendations § 7.03 (1992).

[113] In re Kauffman Mut. Fund Actions, 479 F.2d 257, 263 (1st Cir.), *cert. denied*, 414 U.S. 857 (1973).

[114] Kusner v. First Pa. Corp., 395 F.Supp. 276 (E.D. Pa. 1975), *rev'd in part*, 531 F.2d 1234 (3d Cir. 1976).

judgment is not entitled to such deference, perhaps on the ground that the directors are not independent. On the other hand, if the court is prepared to evaluate the board of directors' rejection of a demand made on it, considering such matters as the reasonableness and independence of the directors, there is much less reason for broad grounds for excusing a demand. This essentially is the reasoning of the American Law Institute, which embraces a "universal demand requirement."[115] Although universal demand has been statutorily adopted in many states, courts have been slow to depart from their customary formulations of the demand requirement, or more particularly, when the requirement may be excused on the basis of futility.

In *Kamen v. Kemper Financial Services, Inc.,*[116] the Seventh Circuit held in a derivative action brought under the Investment Company Act of 1940 that a universal demand requirement that abolishes the futility exception should apply to federal question litigation and dismissed the derivative suit for failure to make a demand on the board of directors. The Supreme Court reversed, reasoning that unless a federal statute provides otherwise, federal courts should use state law in determining the necessity of a demand unless to do so would be inconsistent with the policies underlying the federal statute on which the derivative suit is based. The choice of state law was based on the view that "the function of the demand doctrine in delimiting the respective powers of the individual shareholder and of the directors to control corporate litigation clearly is a matter of 'substance' and not 'procedure.' "[117] Thus, to the extent that states differ in their bases for excusing demand, those differences become reflected in federal-question derivative suit litigation unless the specific federal statute should require otherwise. For example, it is inconsistent with federal policies to require a demand in a suit brought on behalf of a mutual fund company where the clear intent of Congress was that such an action is individual, not derivative, although the action would be characterized otherwise under state law.[118] Such an inconsistency is not found with respect to derivative actions brought under the antifraud provisions of the federal securities laws.[119]

Whether a demand is excused for futility is determined at the time the complaint is filed.[120] The courts express in various ways their overall standard for finding futility, but the unique facts of the individual case and the judicial philosophy of the court appear to dominate the outcome more than the general standard that is to guide any finding of futility. When a complaint alleges with particularity that a majority of the board has engaged in fraud, self-dealing, or solely out of self-interest, most courts excuse the demand on the theory that it would be futile, because directors cannot be expected to sue themselves in order to enforce corporate rights.[121]

In the leading New York decision, *Marx v. Akers,*[122] the Court stated that demand should be excused when:

---

[115] ALI, 2 Principles of Corporate Governance: Analysis and Recommendations § 7.03 (1992) (demand is excused "only if the plaintiff makes a specific showing that irreparable injury to the corporation would otherwise result").

[116] Kamen v. Kemper Financial Services, Inc., 500 U.S. 90 (1991).

[117] Kamen v. Kemper Financial Services, Inc., 500 U.S. 90, 96–97 (1991).

[118] *See* Daily Income Fund, Inc. v. Fox, 464 U.S. 523 (1984).

[119] *See, e.g.,* Lewis v. Anderson, 615 F.2d 778, 784 (9th Cir. 1979).

[120] Brody v. Chemical Bank, 482 F.2d 1111 (2d Cir. 1973).

[121] Nussbacher v. Continental Ill. Nat'l Bank & Trust. Co., 518 F.2d 873, 877 (7th Cir. 1975), *cert. denied,* 424 U.S. 928 (1976).

[122] Marx v. Akers, 666 N.E.2d 1034 (N.Y. 1996).

(1) . . . a complaint alleges with particularity that a majority of the board of directors is interested in the challenged transaction. Director interest may either be self-interest in the transaction at issue . . . or a loss of independence because a director . . . is controlled by a self-interested director. (2) . . . a complaint alleges with particularity that the board of directors did not fully inform themselves about the challenged transaction to the extent reasonably appropriate under the circumstances. (3) . . . a complaint alleges with particularity that the challenged transaction was so egregious on its face that it could not have been the product of sound business judgment of the directors.[123]

Though the court in *Marx* concluded that a demand on the board was excused under the first ground with respect to the board establishing its own compensation, the court dismissed the claim because a bare allegation of self-interest failed to establish a cause of action in light of the legislature having expressly authorized boards of directors of New York corporations to fix their own compensation. The court reasoned that the only possible basis for excusing a demand on the facts alleged would be the third ground, namely, that the compensation was excessive on its face.

The leading Delaware case on demand futility is *Aronson v. Lewis*[124] which holds that a demand is excused for futility under one of two alternate standards: (1) whether a reasonable doubt as to the director's disinterest or independence is raised by well-pleaded facts;[125] and, if not, (2) whether the complaint pleads particularized facts sufficient to create a reasonable doubt that the challenged transaction was the product of a valid exercise of business judgment.[126]

Where the defendant is alleged to control a majority of the board, demand is generally excused on grounds of futility only if such control is alleged with sufficient particularity that on the facts so pleaded it is futile to believe a majority of the directors could act independently in the matter.[127] Unsupported allegations that the directors are controlled by the alleged wrongdoers are insufficient to excuse the demand.[128] The most liberal decision to date is *De Haas v. Empire Petroleum Company*,[129] where two of five directors were clearly under the defendant's control and demand was excused on finding that the remaining directors were elected by the defendant notwithstanding that on prior occasions those directors had voted against positions favored by the defendant.

In contrast, the Delaware Supreme Court refused to excuse a demand where the defendant who received an allegedly excessive compensation arrangement and interest-free loans owned 47 percent of the shares and his co-defendants who approved those

---

[123] Marx v. Akers, 666 N.E.2d 1034, 1040–1041 (N.Y. 1996).

[124] Aronson v. Lewis, 473 A.2d 805 (Del. 1984).

[125] *See, e.g.,* Conrad v. Blank, 940 A.2d 28 (Del.Ch. 2007) (demand excused in part on basis that after learning through its own investigation of misconduct, the board took no action).

[126] Aronson v. Lewis, 473 A.2d 805, 814 (Del. 1984).

[127] *E.g.,* Delaware & Hudson Co. v. Albany & S. R.R., 213 U.S. 435 (1909).

[128] *E.g.,* Kaster v. Modification Sys., 731 F.2d 1014 (2d Cir. 1984) (pleading that the alleged wrongdoer owned 71% of the corporation's voting shares did not by itself satisfy futility exception to rule requiring that demand be made on corporation's directors; complaint would have to further indicate that majority shareholder controls vote of board).

[129] De Haas v. Empire Petroleum Company, 286 F.Supp. 809 (D. Colo. 1968), *aff'd,* 435 F.2d 1223 (10th Cir. 1970).

transactions owned an additional 10 percent.[130] The Delaware Supreme Court reasoned that mere proof of majority of the voting powers does not excuse a demand absent further specific allegations that demonstrate "that through personal or other relationships the directors are beholden to the controlling person."[131]

When considering the operation of the demand requirement in cases such as *Marx* and *Aronson* challenging executive compensation, what role does a negative shareholder vote on a say-on-pay resolution have on excusing a demand? Recall from Chapter 11 that public companies must periodically (most are annual) submit senior executive pay to a non-binding shareholder vote approving or disapproving such compensation. Courts have consistently held that demand futility is not established for a suit challenging executive compensation solely on the basis of a negative shareholder advisory vote on executive compensation.[132]

A demand is not required if the directors have made clear that they are opposed to bringing the suit.[133] The most difficult questions for excusing a demand arise when the plaintiff alleges a demand on the board would be futile because the directors have approved the transaction that is the focus of the derivative suit and are thus themselves named as defendants for either having approved the transaction with gross negligence or in bad faith. This is distinguished from the case where the plaintiff pleads that a majority of the directors are financially interested in the transaction that is the subject of the derivative suit. In a case such as financial interest, the demand is easier to excuse than when the basis for arguing futility is based solely on the directors' earlier approval of the suspect transaction or that the demand asks the directors to approve a suit against themselves. In a leading case, the court reasoned that "[i]t does not follow . . . that a director who merely made an erroneous business judgment in connection with what was plainly a corporate act will 'refuse to do [his] duty in behalf of the corporation if [he] were asked to do so.' "[134] The clear majority rule will not excuse a demand on the board of directors on a bare allegation that a majority of the board of directors has acquiesced or approved the transaction that is the subject of the derivative suit. The plaintiff must also plead facts that fairly support the conclusion that, by so approving, the directors engaged in a wasteful or purposeful departure from their fiduciary obligations to the corporation.[135] Being named as defendant in derivative suit involving transactions the director approved as a director, but with no allegations of wrongdoing, does not rob the

---

[130] *See* Aronson v. Lewis, 473 A.2d 805 (Del. 1984).

[131] Aronson v. Lewis, 473 A.2d 805, 815 (Del. 1984). However, the plaintiff subsequently amended the complaint, alleging corporate waste on the part of the approving directors and the court refused the defedants' motion to dismiss. Lewis v. Aronson, 1985 WL 11553 (Del. Ch. 1985).

[132] *See, e.g.,* Weinberg v. Gold, 838 F. Supp.2d 355 (D. Md. 2012)(and merely naming the directors as a defendants does not, in addition to a failed say-on-pay vote, excuse demand); Gordon v. Goodyear, 2012 WL 2885695 (N.D. Ill. 2012). However, sufficiently detailed facts suggesting the award of options were the product of fraud, illegality or were ultra vires has been held to excuse a demand. *See* New England Carpenters Pension Fund v. Haffner, 391 S.W.3d 453 (Mo. Ct. App. 2012)(court's majority emphasized statistical study that there was a one in a million chance the option grant dates were random).

[133] Nussbacher v. Continental Ill. Nat'l Bank & Trust Co., 518 F.2d 873 (7th Cir. 1975), *cert. denied,* 424 U.S. 928 (1976) (directors had previously refused to accept identical suit in another jurisdiction, and chairman of board had stated by affidavit he was opposed to suit).

[134] In re Kauffman Mut. Fund Actions, 479 F.2d 257 (1st Cir. 1973), quoting Bartlett v. New York, N.H. & H. R. Co., 109 N.E. 452, 455 (Mass. 1915).

[135] *See, e.g.,* Werbowsky v. Collomb, 766 A.2d 123 (Md. 2001)(demand not excused solely by allegation the directors participated in or approved the challenged transaction).

director of meeting the independence requirement for a special litigation committee.[136] There is sometimes a tendency to attribute to the foregoing bases for excusing a demand a talisman-like effect so that the presence or absence of some mechanical showing resolves the necessity of the plaintiff making a demand. It would appear far better to consider from the totality of the pleadings whether it is likely that the directors can be expected to render a detached evaluation of the suit; this question, not solely the substantive violations alleged, should be the focus of the inquiry.[137]

The existence of an immunity shield whereby directors are exculpated for breaches of the duty of care complicates the inquiry whether a demand should be excused in cases alleging the directors have breached their duty of oversight. For example, *City of Birmingham Ret. & Relief Sys. v. Good*, addresses whether a board's serial involvement with on-going environmental problems that ultimately caused substantial losses to the corporation supported a claim the directors consciously disregarded their oversight responsibilities so that the derivative suit against them could proceed without making a demand on the board.[138] The majority opinion reasoned that the complaint sought to conflate a "bad outcome" with "bad faith;" the majority did not believe the facts supported the charge the directors on-going efforts to inform themselves regarding problems posed by the utility's coal ash ponds was a conscious disregard of oversight rather than perhaps too deliberate an oversight.[139] The dissent, however, believed sufficient facts were plead to supporting excusing a demand on the board as the facts reflected non-exculpated breaches of the directors fiduciary duty by pursuing business strategy premised in part on flouting environmental laws.[140]

There are now developing several nontraditional bases for excusing a demand. A special excuse can arise in the close corporation where the plaintiff is but one of two directors.[141] Also, if the board of directors responds to the suit by appointing a special litigation committee that has the sole authority to evaluate whether to pursue the litigation, the court can conclude that the board has conceded its disqualification to entertain a demand.[142]

As the foregoing indicates, courts are not willing to lightly excuse the demand requirement. In fact, as noted by a recent federal decision, there has been a trend toward strengthening the demand requirement.[143] Furthermore, there appears to be a strong movement at the state level toward a universal demand requirement; a good many states have modified their statutes to adopt the universal demand requirement put forth in the Model Act.[144] This shift is noted by the Seventh Circuit, which observed that the

---

[136] Sarnacki v. Golden, 778 F.3d 217 (1st Cir. 2015).

[137] *See* Lewis v. Curtis, 671 F.2d 779 (3d Cir.), *cert. denied,* 459 U.S. 880 (1982).

[138] City of Birmingham Ret. & Relief Sys. v. Good, 177 A.3d 47 (Del. 2017). The issue before the court was whether demand was excused on the ground the directors breached their oversight duty. However, the immunity shield protected the directors for mere negligent lapses in oversight. Hence, excusing a demand required particularized allegations that a majority of the directors were at substantial risk of liability.

[139] *Id.* at 55–56.

[140] *Id.* at 68–69.

[141] *See* Bhana v. Patel, 2006 WL 1050519 (S.D. Miss. 2006) (demand futile where two equal owners share control of LLC and suit is against one of them).

[142] *See* Peller v. Southern Co., 911 F.2d 1532 (11th Cir. 1990) (the court intimates different result may occur if corporation filed motion to dismiss for failure to make demand and after filing that motion established special litigation committee).

[143] Boland v. Engle, 113 F.3d 706 (7th Cir. 1997).

[144] A majority of the states now statutorily impose a universal demand requirement.

American Law Institute's Corporate Governance principles have prompted a trend of "both the case law and academic commentary moving strongly in that direction as well."[145]

§ 15.6 Special Litigation Committees[146]

A practice that began in the 1970s has been for the board of directors to delegate the decision of whether to sue on a corporate claim to an independent committee of directors, sometimes with special counsel appointed to assist the committee.[147] Today, it is a common practice for the corporation, either in a demand required or a demand excused case, to establish a committee of independent directors to assess whether continuance of a suit against directors or officers is in the best interests of the corporation.[148] Such committees generally have concluded that continuation of the suit would not promote the best interests of the corporation.[149] Occasionally, a committee will propose a settlement of the action to the derivative suit court.[150] The decision of an independent special litigation committee of a board of directors to refuse a shareholder demand should only be set aside if the committee breached its duty of loyalty or committed gross negligence in reaching its decision.[151] The judicial decisions are in conflict regarding the appropriate standard for reviewing a recommendation of a special litigation committee and a distinct minority of the cases have held such committee action does not merit the attention of the court.

The special litigation committee was created by a melding of the business judgment rule, the demand requirement, and statutory authority for the delegation of board powers. It was intended to provide an efficient means of judging the corporate interest served by a derivative suit when the full board is otherwise disabled by self-interest from gaining the court's attention. The defendant board members' ability to handpick the members of the special litigation committee and defendants' perfect record before these committees, however, have provoked questions about both a committee's ability to render an unbiased assessment of the suit's impact on the corporate interest and the broader issue of whether directors can be impartial in any context when judging their colleagues' actions. The standards for review of the special litigation committee

---

[145] Boland v. Engle, 113 F.3d 706, 712–713 (7th Cir. 1997) (relying on Kamen v. Kemper Financial Services, Inc., 939 F.2d 458, 461–463 (7th Cir. 1991)); Cuker v. Mikalauskas, 692 A.2d 1042 (Pa. 1997), *on remand*, 35 Pa. D. & C.4th 87 (1998).

[146] This section is a current adaptation of James D. Cox & Harry L. Munsinger, Bias in the Boardroom: Psychological Foundations and Legal Implications of Corporate Cohesion, 48 Law & Contemp. Probs. 83, 114–129 (1985).

[147] Lewis v. Anderson, 615 F.2d 778 (9th Cir. 1979), *cert. denied*, 449 U.S. 869 (1980) (under California law, board of directors may delegate to disinterested independent committee business judgment authority to dismiss derivative action against some of directors).

[148] *See, e.g.,* Gaines v. Haughton, 645 F.2d 761 (9th Cir. 1981), *cert. denied*, 454 U.S. 1145 (1982) (committee's determination that not in best interests of corporation to pursue derivative action required dismissal of stockholder's claims).

[149] Myers Minor, The Decisions of the Corporate Special Litigation Committees: An Empirical Investigation, 84 Ind. L. J. 1309 (2009).

[150] *See, e.g.,* Carlton Investments v. TLC Beatrice Int'l Holdings, Inc., 1997 WL 305829 (Del. Ch. 1997) (reviewing the settlement proposed by a special litigation committee pursuant to the two-step review process set forth in *Zapata*, discussed below, and not the "fair and reasonable" standard that is customarily used in reviewing derivative suit settlements).

[151] Espinoza on behalf of JPMorgan Chase & Co. v. Dimon, 124 A.3d 33 (Del. 2015) (answering certified question for the federal Second Circuit Court of Appeals).

recommendations are evolving, and there continues to be a good deal of uncertainty surrounding these standards in many leading cases.

Presuming Impartiality. The most skeptical judicial response to the charge that directors are afflicted by structural bias is *Auerbach v. Bennett,*[152] which holds that it is inappropriate for a court to evaluate a special litigation committee's weighing of the legal, ethical, commercial, public relations, or fiscal grounds that support its recommendation that a derivative suit be dismissed.[153] In this way, *Auerbach* effectively confines judicial review to two narrow areas that have traditionally been open to attack by the plaintiff under the business judgment rule: the directors' independence and good faith.[154] These two areas permit plaintiff challenges to the adequacy and appropriateness of the committee's procedures; the substantive bases for the committee's recommendation, however, are shielded by the business judgment rule and according to *Auerbach* are removed from judicial scrutiny.[155]

Auerbach and its progeny[156] are important, not only for the limitations they impose on judicial review of the committee's recommendation but also because they stand as unwavering testimonials to a wide application of the business judgment rule and to the courts' belief that directors are devoted primarily to the corporate interest. Courts persuaded[157] by *Auerbach*'s articulation of the limited judicial review necessary in special litigation committee cases have in effect announced a substantial presumption that the committee has acted properly, so that its recommendation can be overturned only in extreme situations.[158]

Questioning the Appointive Process. In contrast to *Auerbach, Miller v. Register & Tribune Syndicate, Inc.*[159] expressed the fear that even the most finely tuned adversarial inquiry could not clearly distinguish rationally drawn conclusions from collegial bias. The issue in *Miller* was whether a committee whose members were all nominated to the board after the derivative suit's commencement could cause that suit's dismissal. The Iowa Supreme Court held that it could not.[160] The *Miller* court's approach nevertheless singled out a specific situation in which committee recommendations were disallowed:

---

[152] Auerbach v. Bennett, 393 N.E.2d 994 (N.Y. 1979).

[153] Auerbach v. Bennett, 393 N.E.2d 994, 1002 (N.Y. 1979). *See also,* Desaigoudar v. Meyercord, 133 Cal.Rptr.2d 408, 418–19 (Ct. App. 2003).

[154] Auerbach v. Bennett, 393 N.E.2d 994, 996 (N.Y. 1979).

[155] *See* Auerbach v. Bennett, 393 N.E.2d 994, 996 (N.Y. 1979).

[156] For other jurisdictions following *Auerbach, see, e.g.,* Curtis v. Nevens, 31 P.3d 146 (Colo. 2001).

[157] The popularity of Auerbach may be explained more by historical accident than by courts in sister jurisdictions being persuaded by its logic. A striking statistic is that in the nearly two-year period between *Auerbach* and the Delaware Supreme Court's decision in Zapata Corp. v. Maldonado, 430 A.2d 779 (Del. 1981), which offers an alternative to *Auerbach,* nearly all special litigation committee cases outside New York were brought in the federal courts.

[158] In Hasan v. Clevetrust Realty Investors, 548 F.Supp. 1146, 1149 (N.D. Ohio 1982), the court, similar to *Auerbach,* required actual proof of director bias to establish the lack of the director's good faith. The fact that the committee report was deficient, but not materially so, was thus not sufficient to impeach the committee's impartiality. *Id.* at 1148–1149. The Sixth Circuit Court of Appeals rejected the district court's presumption of the committee members' good faith without rejecting *Auerbach*'s position on court review of the substance of the committee's recommendation. Hasan v. Clevetrust Realty Investors, 729 F.2d 372, 376 (6th Cir. 1984).

[159] Auerbach, Miller v. Register & Tribune Syndicate, Inc., 336 N.W.2d 709 (Iowa 1983).

[160] Miller v. Register and Tribune Syndicate, Inc., 336 N.W.2d 709 (Iowa 1983).

We believe that the potential for structural bias on the part of a litigation committee appointed by directors who are parties to derivative actions is sufficiently great and sufficiently difficult of precise proof in an individual case to require the adoption of a prophylactic rule. We conclude that we should prevent the potential for structural bias in some cases by effectively limiting the powers of such directors in all cases.[161]

Dispatching Skepticism Through Judicial Review. A leading case concerning the review standards for special litigation committee recommendations is *Zapata Corp. v. Maldonado*,[162] which clearly expresses its concern for the directors' potential bias:

[N]otwithstanding our conviction that Delaware law entrusts the corporate power to a properly authorized committee, we must be mindful that directors are passing judgment on fellow directors in the same corporation and fellow directors, in this instance, who designated them to serve both as directors and committee members. The question naturally arises whether a "there but for the grace of God go I" empathy may not play a role. And the further question arises whether inquiry as to independence, good faith and reasonable investigation is sufficient safeguard against abuse, perhaps subconscious abuse.[163]

While recognizing a serious threat of director bias, *Zapata* did not include *Miller*'s sweeping solution. The *Zapata* court reasoned that judicial review of a committee's recommendation should not eviscerate the valuable role the directors' judgments of a suit's worth can play in derivative suit litigation. The court charted what it believed to be a middle course between allowing committee recommendations so much deference that the derivative suit is mortally wounded, on the one hand, and being so skeptical of the committee that the corporation is totally unable to rid itself of a harmful suit, on the other. Into this breach, the Delaware Supreme Court placed a two-step test.

Under *Zapata*'s first step, the court evaluates the committee members' independence, good faith, and bases for their recommendation.[164] *Zapata* reinforced these requirements by demanding a detailed report of the committee's investigation procedures and findings, by placing the burden of establishing these factors on the committee, and by subjecting the committee's reasoning to close scrutiny.[165] This scrutiny represents the court's most sweeping response to the threat of structural bias. In its second step, *Zapata* invited the reviewing court to exercise its independent judgment in determining whether the corporate interest is served by the derivative suit's continuance.[166] This discretion is to be exercised only in limited instances, however.

---

[161] Miller v. Register and Tribune Syndicate, Inc., 336 N.W.2d 709, 718 (Iowa 1983).

[162] Zapata Corp. v. Maldonado, 430 A.2d 779 (Del. 1981).

[163] Zapata Corp. v. Maldonado, 430 A.2d 779, 787 (Del. 1981). Similar concerns were expressed by the New Jersey Supreme Court:

We fully appreciate the distinction between that legal standard [for independence in the review of recommendations of a special litigation committee] and complete impartiality in the everyday sense of the word. Directors understandably are not likely to be enthusiastic about approving the prosecution of a shareholder's suit against members of management with whom the directors maintain an ongoing relationship.

In re PSE & G Shareholder Litig., 801 A.2d 295, 320 (N.J. 2002).

[164] Zapata Corp. v. Maldonado, 430 A.2d 779, 788–789 (Del. 1981).

[165] *See* Zapata Corp. v. Maldonado, 430 A.2d 779, 788–789 (Del. 1981).

[166] Zapata Corp. v. Maldonado, 430 A.2d 779, 789 (Del. 1981). One court has referred to *Zapata*'s second step as invoking an "imprecise smell test." *See* Strougo v. Padegs, 27 F. Supp. 2d 442, 454 (S.D.N.Y. 1998).

The criteria *Zapata* proposed unfortunately are quite vague, so that achieving *Zapata*'s objectives primarily depends on the reviewing court's general concern for structural bias. *Zapata* offers no insight into the meaning of any of the first-level standards. Potentially the standards of independence, good faith, and reasonable bases could be interpreted and applied to generate more penetrating inquiry into the committee's actions than the inquiry likely to result using the standards of *Auerbach*.

The syntax of *Zapata*'s two-step analysis suggests that greater deference be accorded a committee's recommendation in the first step than in the second step. As seen above, the court's independent judgment, exercised at the second step, is reserved for nonfrivolous cases. Frivolity no doubt is in the eye of the beholder. To be sure, it is neither necessary nor appropriate under *Zapata* for a court to exercise its own independent judgment in step two when it concurs in the committee's assessment that the suit lacks merit. Unanswered in *Zapata,* however, is how deeply the court should probe the committee's report at step one, in making its threshold determination of the suit's merits, before it can advance to the second-step analysis. The Delaware Supreme Court's concern that directors retain some power to deflect a wasteful derivative action[167] suggests an approach in which deference is extended to the committee's opinion on the merits, except when a prima facie case can be established solely on the basis of the committee's report showing that the committee's dismissal recommendation is grounded on weak considerations such as the suit's incidental costs exceeding its benefits.[168] *Zapata* may well envision that the committee's view of the suit's merits should enjoy the same level of deference that courts extend to director judgments in other areas in which directors are, under the reasonable basis criterion, free to select from among several reasonably supported alternatives.[169]

The Independence and Good Faith Inquiries. Independence, whether for considering whether a demand should be required or whether a recommendation of a special litigation committee or, for that matter, the board of directors in a demand required case, should cause the suit's dismissal, turns on the ultimate question whether the opining directors have a relationship with the individual defendant or the suit itself that would reasonably be expected to affect the directors' judgment with respect to the litigation.[170] The threshold requirement for the independence of committee members is that they are not themselves defendants in the derivative suit.[171] A committee does not

---

[167] 430 A.2d at 786–787.

[168] *See, e.g.,* Abramowitz v. Posner, 513 F.Supp. 120, 123–124, 131–132 (S.D.N.Y. 1981), *aff'd,* 672 F.2d 1025 (2d Cir. 1982), where the court recognized a probability of securing a favorable judgment but recommended against the suit's continuation in recognition of the defendant's extraordinary services to the corporation, significant remedial action, and concomitant publicity.

[169] *E.g.,* in Elfenbein v. American Fin. Corp., 487 F.Supp. 619 (S.D.N.Y. 1980), the court held that the directors of a parent corporation had a reasonable basis for their exercise of warrants in a subsidiary corporation because they relied on counsel's opinion that the exercise presented no perils under the tax laws, even though two other experts disagreed.

[170] *See* Einhorn v. Culea, 612 N.W.2d 78, 98 (Wis. 2000) (listing the following factors to be considered: whether the director has potential liability in the underlying action including being a defendant therein; director's participation or approval or receipt of benefits from the challenged transaction; director's past or present business dealings with individual defendant; director's family, personal, or social relationships with defendant; director's past or present financial relations with the corporation; number of members of the committee; and roles of corporate counsel and independent counsel).

[171] *See, e.g.,* Gaines v. Haughton, 645 F.2d 761 (9th Cir. 1981), *cert. denied,* 454 U.S. 1145 (1982). *But see* Sarnacki v. Golden, 778 F.3d 217 (1st Cir. 2015)(being named as defendant in derivative suit involving transactions the director approved as a director, but with no allegations of wrongdoing, does not rob the director of meeting the independence requirement for a special litigation committee).

lack independence solely because its members were appointed by the defendants.[172] There is little doubt that the number of committee members is a factor to consider in evaluating its independence from the defendants,[173] specifically that single-person committees raise interesting flags.[174]

Independence has successfully been questioned on a showing that the committee member has a material financial relationship with the corporation.[175] A committee was found to lack independence where just prior to its formation all the directors, including those later appointed to the committee, voted to resist the derivative suit.[176] And, in a case that appears to have all possible indicia of what does not make a committee independent, *Lewis v. Fuqua,*[177] the sole member of the committee

> . . . was a member of the board of directors of Fuqua Industries at the time the challenged actions took place; he is one of the defendants in this suit; he has had numerous political and financial dealings with J. B. Fuqua who is the chief executive officer of Fuqua Industries and who allegedly controls the Board; he is President of Duke University which is a recent recipient of a $10 million pledge from Fuqua Industries and J. B. Fuqua; and J. B. Fuqua has, in the past, made several contributions to Duke University and is a Trustee of the University.

Moreover, the committee's recommendation lacks the force of an independent body where it is purely advisory to the full board of directors most of whose members are defendants in the derivative action.[178]

Close personal friendships naturally raise eyebrows regarding the degree of detachment an individual can be expected to maintain in assessing a suit against his friend. However, in a widely noted case involving a question whether close personal relationships should be the basis for excusing a demand on the board, the Delaware Supreme Court stated:

> Allegations that Stewart [the defendant] and the other directors moved in the same social circles, attended the same weddings, developed business relationships before joining the board, and described each other as "friends," even when coupled with Stewart's 94 percent voting power, are insufficient, without more to rebut the presumption of independence.[179]

The above quote and case holding while initially appearing inconsistent with an earlier decision by Vice-Chancellor Strine in *In re Oracle Derivative Litigation,*[180] on closer examination the contrasting sensitivities to the question of personal relationships

---

[172] *See, e.g.,* Strougo v. Padegs, 27 F. Supp. 2d 442 (S.D.N.Y. 1998).

[173] *See* Houle v. Low, 556 N.E.2d 51, 59 (Mass. 1990).

[174] *See* Hasan v. Clevetrust Realty Investors, 729 F.2d 372 (6th Cir. 1984).

[175] *See* Hasan v. Clevetrust Realty Investors, 729 F.2d 372 (6th Cir. 1984) (single person committee who owned 25% of firm that received substantial fees from corporation managed by derivative suit defendant and also owned 2% of real estate partnership with defendant).

[176] *See* Swenson v. Thibaut, 250 S.E.2d 279 (N.C. Ct. App. 1978).

[177] Lewis v. Fuqua, 502 A.2d 962, 966–967 (Del. Ch. 1985).

[178] In re Par Pharmaceutical, Inc. Derivative Litig., 750 F.Supp. 641 (S.D.N.Y. 1990).

[179] Beam v. Stewart, 845 A.2d 1040, 1050–51 (Del.Supr. 2004).

[180] In re Oracle Derivative Litigation, 824 A.2d 917 (Del. Ch. 2003) (stating the test of independence is "whether a director is *for any substantial reason,* incapable of making a decision with only the best interests of the corporation in mind") (emphasis original).

reflects the differing procedural settings of each decision. *Oracle* arose in a demand excused context where the question before the court was the committee's independence. The *Oracle* court held that the committee had not met its burden to establish that its members were independent when, among other factors, its two members were university professors at a university for which the defendants had been major benefactors to their university and one of the defendants had been the professor to one of the committee members. In its decision in *Beam,* the Delaware Supreme Court emphasized that *Oracle* was a demand excused case so that the burden of proof with respect to independence was with the committee whereas in *Beam* the plaintiff in order to establish the futility of any demand had the burden of proving a majority of the directors were not independent, observing [a]s a practical matter, the procedural distinction relating to the diametrically-opposed burdens and the availability of discovery into independence may be outcome-determinative.[181]

Even though involving a special committee that was established to approve a controlled merger, *Kahn v. M&F Worldwide Corp.*[182] provides a good summary of what is necessary to establish that the committee members are independent. The fact that a director and the controlling shareholder travelled in the same social circles or had past business dealings is not sufficient to rebut the presumption of independence. The court observed that "[b]are allegations that directors are friendly with, travel in the same social circles as, or have past business relationships with the proponent of a transaction or the person they are investigating are not enough to rebut the presumption of independence."[183] What the court believed necessary to show a lack of independence is a showing that the committee member could not "objectively discharge his or her fiduciary duties."[184]

An important consideration, indeed it can be regarded as a separate requirement, for the committee's independence is that the committee be advised by counsel with no historical relationship with the firm.[185] Underlying this requirement is concern that the committee's independent judgment may be compromised whenever the committee's chief legal advisor has a long-standing professional representation of the firm that in no small part depends upon personal relations with the derivative suit defendants. There also is concern that dual representation of the committee and former and on-going representation of the corporation may seriously compromise the confidentiality requirements of the attorney-client relationship.

---

[181] 845 A.2d at 1055.

[182] 88 A.3d 635 (Del. 2014).

[183] 88 A.3d at 649 relying on Beam ex rel. Martha Stewart Living Omnimedia v. Stewart, 845 A.2d 1040, 1051–52 (Del.2004). *See also* 88 A.3d at 648–649. ("To show that a director is not independent, a plaintiff must demonstrate that the director is 'beholden' to the controlling party 'or so under [the controller's] influence that [the director's] discretion would be sterilized.' "), quoting from Rales v. Blasband, 634 A.2d 927, 936 (Del.1993) (citing Aronson v. Lewis, 473 A.2d 805, 815 (Del.1984)).

[184] Kahn v. M&F Worldwide Corp., 88 A.3d 635, 649 (Del. 2014) ("A plaintiff seeking to show that a director was not independent must satisfy a materiality standard. The court must conclude that the director in question had ties to the person whose proposal or actions he or she is evaluating that are sufficiently substantial that he or she could not objectively discharge his or her fiduciary duties."), relying on Cinerama, Inc. v. Technicolor, Inc., 663 A.2d 1156, 1167 (Del.1995) ("[A] shareholder plaintiff [must] show the materiality of a director's self-interest to the . . . director's independence. . . .") (citation omitted); *see* Brehm v. Eisner, 746 A.2d 244, 259 n. 49 (Del.2000) ("The term 'material' is used in this context to mean relevant and of a magnitude to be important to directors in carrying out their fiduciary duty of care in decisionmaking.").

[185] In re Perrigo Co., 128 F.3d 430 (6th Cir. 1997).

Auerbach provides a useful definition of the "good faith" requirement, stating "proof . . . that the investigation has been so restricted in scope, so shallow in execution, or otherwise so *pro forma* or halfhearted as to constitute a pretext or sham . . . would raise questions of good faith. . . ."[186] Thus, a thoughtful, systematic and probing investigation of the facts and report of the findings and conclusions significantly bolster the belief the committee has acted in good faith.[187] Investigations, however, need not be with the formalities of a court proceeding so that stenographic records or testimony under oath are not required to establish the committee's good faith inquiry.[188] The committee's reliance on its independent counsel to perform most of the investigation and the avenues of inquiry that the committee reasonably explained for not exploring is not a basis for finding that its inquiry was so flawed as to constitute a bad faith investigation.[189] A classic illustration of how a committee's report serves to document the absence of good faith is *Hasan v. Clevetrust Realty Investors*,[190] even though the report is 122 pages in length. The derivative suit complaint arose out of greenmail payments made to each of two companies that had acquired a significant percentage of the derivative suit corporation's shares. Reasoning that the committee's failure to interview the personnel of either company was so pertinent to whether the purchase price was fair and was motivated by management's fears for their jobs, the court held that the committee's report was not prepared in good faith. Other cases have also established a lack of good faith based on the superficial quality of the underlying report[191] or that the committee had taken action inconsistent with the report's facts.[192]

"Valuing" the Suit. Significantly, post-*Zapata* decisions fail to recognize the discretionary aspect of *Zapata*'s second step. Courts purporting to follow *Zapata* have instead interpreted the case to require the exercise of independent business judgment in *all* cases.[193] The most insightful application of this interpretation of *Zapata* was by the Second Circuit in *Joy v. North*,[194] which offered the following description of the reviewing court's function:

> [T]he burden is on the moving party, as in motions for summary judgment generally, to demonstrate that the action is more likely than not to be against the interests of the corporation. . . . [T]he function of the court's review is to determine the balance of probabilities as to likely future benefit to the corporation, not to render a decision on the merits, fashion the appropriate legal principles or resolve issues of credibility. Where the legal rule is unclear and the likely evidence in conflict, the court need only weigh the uncertainties,

---

[186]   Auerbach v. Bennett, 419 N.Y.S.2d 920, 929, 393 N.E.2d 994 (N.Y. 1979).

[187]   For excellent descriptions of steps committees have taken, *see* Strougo v. Padegs, 27 F. Supp. 2d 442, 451–53 (S.D.N.Y. 1998).

[188]   *See, e.g.,* Strougo v. Padegs, 27 F. Supp. 2d 442, 452 (S.D.N.Y. 1998).

[189]   *See, e.g.,* Maldonado v. Flynn, 485 F.Supp. 274, 284 (S.D.N.Y. 1980).

[190]   Hasan v. Clevetrust Realty Investors, 729 F.2d 372 (6th Cir. 1984).

[191]   *See, e.g.,* Holmstrom v. Coastal Indus. [1984 Transfer Binder], Fed. Sec. L. Rep. (CCH) 91,486 (N.D. Ohio 1984).

[192]   *See* Watts v. Des Moines Register & Tribune, 525 F.Supp. 1311, 1329–1330 (S.D. Iowa 1981) (special counsel opined that five of the pled causes of action should be pursued).

[193]   *See, e.g.,* Joy v. North, 692 F.2d 880, 888–889 (2d Cir. 1982), *cert. denied,* 460 U.S. 1051 (1983).

[194]   Joy v. North, 692 F.2d 880 (2d Cir. 1982), *cert. denied,* 460 U.S. 1051 (1983).

not resolve them. The court's function is thus not unlike a lawyer's determining what a case is "worth" for purposes of settlement.[195]

The approach advocated in *Joy* is light years beyond the uncritical evaluation embraced in *Auerbach*. Minimally, the *Joy* approach is a more fully textured description of the review process initially proposed in *Zapata*. Moreover, *Joy* is the rare instance in which a court has refused to follow a committee's recommendation to dismiss a derivative action on the substance of the committee's report.[196]

The complaint in *Joy* arose from loans made by Citytrust Bankcorp, Inc. to Katz, a developer in precarious financial condition. The loans ultimately exceeded the lending level to a single borrower imposed by the National Bank Act.[197] Katz's default caused Citytrust to absorb a certain loss of more than $5 million.[198] The special litigation committee was established nearly two years after the derivative suit was commenced. The committee, after nine months, recommended dismissal of the derivative suit against the 23 "outside" defendants, concluding that there was "no reasonable possibility" they would be held liable.[199] As for the remaining seven "inside" defendants, who were senior officers of Citytrust and therefore deeply involved in approving the Katz loans, the committee's recommendation was equivocal. The committee reasoned that there was a possibility that the inside defendants had acted negligently and recommended that settlement negotiations be undertaken with the inside defendants. The committee nevertheless cautioned that its recommendation that settlement negotiations were appropriate did not necessarily imply that the committee believed continued litigation against the inside defendants served the corporate interest.[200]

The *Joy* court's review of the committee's dismissal recommendation nicely frames the dilemma that a special litigation committee poses to a court responding to a recommendation that a derivative suit be dismissed. The court was forced to choose between accepting the committee's evaluation of law and facts, which possibly was contaminated in some indeterminate amount by the directors' bias, or pursuing a final resolution of the legal and factual uncertainties through costly litigation of the claim. The special litigation committee's potential contribution toward shortening the course of wasteful litigation is exemplified by cases such as *Joy,* where the suit's outcome is problematic at the pretrial stage. This situation arises when, on the one hand, the conclusions to be drawn from the facts—such as the defendants' involvement in the alleged wrongdoing or the existence of a business purpose that would exonerate them—remain uncertain even after pretrial investigation or, on the other hand, when the applicable legal duties and defenses are still evolving and are therefore indefinite.[201] When neither the facts nor the law are disputed, however, the special litigation committee adds little to the defendants' arsenal for ridding themselves of a wasteful

---

[195]   Joy v. North, 692 F.2d 880, 892 (2d Cir. 1982), *cert. denied,* 460 U.S. 1051 (1983).

[196]   One other case has rejected the committee's recommendation because of substantive considerations in the committee's report. *See* Holmstrom v. Coastal Indus. [1984 Transfer Binder], Fed. Sec. L. Rep. (CCH) 91,486 (N.D. Ohio 1984).

[197]   12 U.S.C. § 84 (2000).

[198]   692 F.2d at 895.

[199]   Joy v. North, 692 F.2d 880, 884 (2d Cir. 1982), *cert. denied,* 460 U.S. 1051 (1983).

[200]   Joy v. North, 692 F.2d 880, 884 (2d Cir. 1982), *cert. denied,* 460 U.S. 1051 (1983).

[201]   This is an insight overlooked by the Delaware Chancery Court. Chancellor Brown in Kaplan v. Wyatt, 484 A.2d 501 (Del. Ch. 1984), observed that special litigation committees are wasteful because they contribute toward "litigation within litigation." *Id.* at 511.

derivative suit during the pretrial stage. The more conventional pretrial motion for summary judgment (aided by uncontroverted affidavits) or motion to dismiss are available to dispose of a suit.

The American Law Institute and The Model Act. The American Law Institute in its corporate governance project joins the ranks of commentators[202] (and a few courts[203]) who have counseled that the same review standards should apply to demand-required cases as are applied to committee recommendations in demand-excused cases. The ALI carries forward the demand-on-directors requirement[204] and severely limits the bases for excusing these demands.[205] However, later provisions[206] reduce the operational effects of making a demand. The purpose of demand is no longer to provide the target toward which the defendant's colleagues direct their shared beliefs that the suit is not in the corporation's best interest; under the proposal, the response to the suit occurs through a recommendation proffered independently of the demand. The recommendation is made by a committee of directors chosen by the board[207] or, on the corporation's request, by a committee of nondirectors chosen by the court.[208]

The Model Act is even more sweeping under section 7.41 the Model Act requires a demand in all cases, unless serious harm to the corporation would result by any delay due to making such a demand. Section 7.42 provides that the suit can be dismissed if the corporation's request is in good faith and reasonably based. The burden of proof is on those seeking dismissal unless a majority of the board of directors are independent vis-à-vis the suit.

Federalism and the Special Litigation Committee. The Supreme Court in *Burks v. Lasker*[209] held that in federal question litigation, when confronted with a dismissal recommended by a special litigation committee, the federal district court must follow a two-stage analysis. The first inquiry is to determine the extent to which the committee has the power under state law to cause the derivative suit to be dismissed. If the committee has such power under the facts before the court, the court must determine, second, whether dismissal of the suit would be inconsistent with the policy underlying the federal cause of action. Where Congress has addressed the directors' discretionary powers to terminate a derivative suit with such particularity that it would be inconsistent with Congress's obvious intent to permit the directors to deflect the derivative suit, the Court reasoned that dismissal would be inappropriate.[210] The courts

---

[202] *See, e.g.,* James D. Cox, Searching for the Corporation's Voice in Derivative Suit Litigation: A Critique of Zapata and the ALI Project, 1982 Duke L.J. 959, 1009–1010.

[203] *See, e.g.,* Alford v. Shaw, 358 S.E.2d 323 (N.C. 1987). *See generally* James D. Cox, Heroes in the Law: Alford v. Shaw, 66 N.C. L. Rev. 565 (1988).

[204] ALI, 2 Principles of Corporate Governance: Analysis and Recommendations § 7.03(a) (1992). The Pennsylvania Supreme Court has unqualifiedly accepted the proposals of the ALI as the law for Pennsylvania. *See* Cuker v. Mikalauskas, 692 A.2d 1042 (Pa. 1997).

[205] ALI, 2 Principles of Corporate Governance, *supra* note 204, § 7.03(b) ("specific showing that irreparable injury to the corporation would otherwise result").

[206] ALI, 2 Principles of Corporate Governance, *supra* note 204, §§ 7.07 to 7.10.

[207] ALI, 2 Principles of Corporate Governance, *supra* note 204, §§ 7.07, 7.08.

[208] ALI, 2 Principles of Corporate Governance, *supra* note 204, § 7.12.

[209] Burks v. Lasker, 441 U.S. 471, 480 (1979).

[210] 441 U.S. at 484. Two illustrations advanced by the court were the shortswing profits provisions of section 16 of the Securities Exchange Act of 1934, 15 U.S.C. § 78p (2000), and section 36(b) of the Investment Company Act of 1940, 15 U.S.C. § 80a–35(b) (2000). Subsequently, the court held that actions under section 36(b) are not derivative, Daily Income Fund, Inc. v. Fox, 464 U.S. 523 (1984).

have consistently held that *Burks* does not bar a dismissal at the recommendation of a special litigation committee under the antifraud provisions of the federal securities laws.[211]

§ 15.7 Standing to Bring a Derivative Suit

In order to maintain a derivative suit to redress or prevent injuries to the corporation, the plaintiff must be either an owner of shares or have some beneficial interest therein when the suit is brought.[212] Some state statutes apply the contemporaneous ownership to limited liability companies as well as to corporations.[213]

As a general rule, the plaintiff must continue to be a stockholder throughout the life of the suit so that the plaintiff stands to benefit derivatively by the relief given; if the plaintiff ceases to be a shareholder by reason of a transfer of shares, he loses standing to complain.[214] The purpose of the rule is to align the plaintiff's economic interests with the corporate interest to be advanced by the diligent prosecution of the suit.[215] But as is true with any rule whose rigid enforcement can lead to unfair or inequitable results, notable exceptions to this continuous-ownership requirement are recognized in many jurisdictions.[216]

A creditor has no proprietary interest and thus cannot maintain a derivative suit.[217] The authorities are split on whether holders of debentures convertible into stock may bring a derivative suit.[218] The standing of holders of American Depositary Receipts to bring a derivative can be affected by provisions of the deposit agreement.[219] With the exception of the rare corporate statute that provides otherwise, directors and officers who cannot satisfy the share-ownership requirement do not have standing to bring a derivative suit solely because of their capacity as directors or officers.[220] A derivative suit may, however, be brought by a deceased shareholder's administrator or executor having the title to shares in such capacity, by the beneficial owner of shares if a trustee refuses

---

[211] *See, e.g.,* Lewis v. Anderson, 615 F.2d 778 (9th Cir. 1979).

[212] A distinct minority of the states require the derivative suit plaintiff to be an "owner of record." *See* W. Va. Code Ann. § 31–1–103 (2009).

[213] *E.g.,* Del. Code Ann. tit. 6, § 18–1003(2); Tex. Bus. Orgs. Code Ann. § 101.459. *See, e.g.,* In re LoneStar Logo & Signs, LLC, 552 S.W.3d 342 (Tex. App. Austin 2018) (allowing a former LLC member to bring suit would deprive the current members of their rights, the former member is only a bystander in the matter).

[214] *See, e.g.,* Quinn v. Anvil Corp., 620 F.3d 1005 (9th Cir. 2010)(standing lost as a consequence of reverse stock split in a non-public company); Lewis v. Chiles, 719 F.2d 1044 (9th Cir. 1983) (continuing interest protects against plaintiff failing to vigorously prosecute action or accepting an insubstantial settlement because she will not be able to share in any recovery as she no longer is owner of firm).

[215] *See* Schupack v. Covelli, 498 F.Supp. 704 (W.D. Pa. 1980) (only party with present interest in corporation will adequately represent corporation's interests in derivative action).

[216] *Compare* Timko v. Triarsi, 898 So.2d 89 (Fl. Dist. Ct. App. 2005) (standing lost when defendant exercised his right to buyout the plaintiff in a separate proceeding brought by the plaintiff to dissolve the company) *with* Brown v. Brown, 731 A.2d 1212 (N.J. Super. App. Div. 1999) (standing to continue to maintain suit accorded where shares had been transferred to spouse as part of divorce settlement but reserving right to continue the derivative suit).

[217] *See, e.g.,* Darrow v. Southdown, Inc., 574 F.2d 1333 (5th Cir. 1978).

[218] *Compare* Kusner v. First Pa. Corp., 395 F.Supp. 276 (E.D. Pa. 1975), *aff'd in part and rev'd in part on other grounds,* 531 F.2d 1234 (3d Cir. 1976); Simons v. Cogan, 549 A.2d 300 (Del. 1988) (denying standing to convertible debenture holders).

[219] Batchelder v. Kawamoto, 147 F.3d 915 (9th Cir. 1998) (standing denied because deposit agreement provided holders' rights would be determined according to Japanese law, which does not treat holders of ADR's as shareholders).

[220] Schoon v. Smith, 953 A.2d 196 (Del. 2008).

to sue and is made a party defendant,[221] by a pledgee of shares,[222] or by a pledgor of shares, such as a margin customer of a stockbroker holding the stock in the street name for the customer's account.[223]

Under the federal rules[224] and most state statutes,[225] the plaintiff in a shareholder's derivative suit must have been a shareholder of record, a holder of voting trust certificates, or a beneficial owner *at the time of the transaction* that is the subject of the suit. This requirement is also met if the suit's plaintiff acquired her shares by operation of law from one who held the shares at the time of the transaction giving rise to the derivative suit complaint. This requirement is commonly referred to as the "contemporaneous ownership" rule. Where it exists,[226] the contemporaneous ownership rule bars suit by those who acquired their shares or beneficial ownership *after* the misconduct that is the subject of the derivative suit.[227] The rule harmonizes with the basic standing principle that a plaintiff must have sustained a real injury in order to have the right to sue.[228] Most modem courts also agree that a justification for the contemporaneous ownership rule is the prevention of strike suits and speculative litigation.[229] The more dominant rationale for the contemporaneous ownership rule is the prevention of unjust enrichment. As has been seen, any monetary recovery obtained through a derivative suit flows to the corporation, except in those rare cases in which the court orders a pro rata recovery. With the suit's fruits flowing to the corporation, all of its shareholders are the true beneficiaries of the recovery in a derivative suit with each shareholder indirectly reaping a benefit proportionate to his ownership of the firm.[230] In a publicly traded corporation ownership is constantly changing such that there is inherent in any derivative suit a distinct windfall to shareholders who become such after the misconduct that is redressed in the derivative suit. This occurs because shares purchased subsequent to a significant injurious transaction are likely to reflect a decreased market value because of the transaction. A subsequent purchaser normally receives value equal to the purchase price. Therefore, any recovery by the corporation that benefits a subsequent purchaser arguably constitutes unjust enrichment of the purchaser.[231]

This concern, however, does not apply where the value of the stock does not reflect the consequences of the harmful activity until some time after a purchaser has acquired

---

[221] Cal. Corp. Code § 800 (2009); N.Y. Bus. Corp. Law § 626(a) (2009); MBCA § 7.40 (2008); former MBCA § 49 (1980). *See also* Demoulas v. Demoulas Super Markets, Inc., 677 N.E.2d 159, 172 (Mass. 1997) (beneficiary of trust can bring action because trustee may face conflicts in doing so).

[222] Green v. Hedenberg, 42 N.E. 851 (Ill. 1896).

[223] Braasch v. Goldschmidt, 199 A.2d 760 (Del. Ch. 1964).

[224] Fed. R. Civ. P. 23.1.

[225] Del. Code Ann. tit. 8, § 627 (2009); N.Y. Bus. Corp. Law § 626(b) (2009). *See* Deborah A. DeMott, Shareholder Derivative Actions Law & Practice § 4.02 (2019–2020 ed.).

[226] The requirement appears in Fed. R. Civ. P. 23.1 and exists in a majority of the states either by statute, case law, or court rule.

[227] *See, e.g.,* International Broadcasting Corp. v. Turner, 734 F.Supp. 383 (D. Minn. 1990).

[228] This reasoning comes from Home Fire Ins. Co. v. Barber, 93 N.W. 1024, 1029 (Neb. 1903) (one who does not own stock at the time of mismanagement is not injured unless the effects continue and are injurious to him), which is generally credited with giving impetus to the force with which the doctrine is applied today.

[229] Phillips v. Bradford, 62 F.R.D. 681, 685 (S.D.N.Y. 1974).

[230] Bangor Punta Operations v. Bangor & Aroostook R.R., 417 U.S. 703 (1974); Home Fire Ins. Co. v. Barber, 93 N.W. 1024, 1033 (Neb. 1903).

[231] *See* Bangor Punta Operations Co. v. Aroostook R.R., 417 U.S. 703 (1974); National Union Elec. Corp. v. Matsushita Elec. Indus., 498 F.Supp. 991, 1001 (E.D. Pa. 1980).

the shares. Thus on close examination, any strong concern for unjust enrichment most certainly should in most cases doom the derivative suit for publicly traded corporations. Simply put, some level of unjust enrichment is inevitable. One may therefore question just how strong a public policy is served by continuing to embrace the contemporaneous ownership requirement for derivative suit litigation involving public corporations.

Some weakening of the support for the contemporaneous ownership rule appears in statutes that have relaxed the requirement considerably.[232] The proposals of the American Law Institute adopt the novel approach of conditioning a suit on the plaintiff's having become a stockholder "before the material facts relating to the alleged wrong were publicly disclosed or were known by, or specifically communicated to, the holder."[233] In so placing the cut-off for a holder's standing to sue derivatively, the American Law Institute embraces a more realistic test of when the share prices are likely to reflect the impact of the misconduct. Those becoming stockholders after the public becomes aware or the shareholders are aware of the misconduct are more likely to derive a windfall as a consequence of the suit than one who purchased shares subsequent to misconduct that became known only after that purchase.

Problems arise in identifying the time of the wrongful transaction for purposes of the contemporaneous ownership rule. If the alleged wrong is a single act, the critical date is of course easy to identify.[234] When the acts complained of occurred over a period of time, however, many courts have adopted a rule that for a plaintiff to maintain a derivative suit for harmful activity that commenced before her acquisition of shares, the harmful activity must continue to endanger corporate assets thereafter.[235] Whether a court will grant standing to a derivative plaintiff on a "continuing wrong" theory depends on how the court perceives or interprets what constitutes a "transaction."[236] In fact, there appears to be no strong disagreement that the continuing wrong theory is a necessary dimension of the contemporaneous ownership rule, but the courts vary widely in their interpretation of what a continuing wrong is. Thus Delaware has split on whether the wrong is continuing when, on the one hand, the plaintiff purchased before shares were issued but after the resolution authorizing their issuance,[237] and, on the other hand, when the plaintiff purchased after stock option was granted to officers but before the options' exercise,[238] when in each case the complaint was that the shares were being issued for insufficient or no consideration. Statutes in several states embrace the continuing wrong theory by conditioning a suit on the plaintiff having been a stockholder at the time of the transaction "or any part thereof."[239]

---

[232] *See* Cal. Corp. Code § 800(b)(1) (2009) (non-contemporaneous holder may sue when "there is a strong prima facie case in favor of the claim . . . [and] the plaintiff acquired the shares before there was disclosure to the public or to the plaintiff of the wrongdoing" that is the subject of the suit).

[233] ALI, 2 Principles of Corporate Governance (1992).

[234] *See generally* Weinhaus v. Gale, 237 F.2d 197, 199 (7th Cir. 1956).

[235] *See, e.g.,* Bateson v. Magna Oil Corp., 414 F.2d 128, 130 (5th Cir. 1969), *cert. denied,* 397 U.S. 911 (1970).

[236] *See, e.g.,* Goldie v. Yaker, 432 P.2d 841, 843–844 (N.M. 1967).

[237] Desimone v. Barrows, 924 A.2d 908 (Del.Ch. 2007) (a wrong is a continuing one when the alleged wrongful acts is so inexorably intertwined that there is one continuing wrong).

[238] Elster v. American Airlines, Inc., 100 A.2d 219 (Del. Ch. 1953).

[239] *See, e.g.,* Cal. Corp. Code § 800(b)(1) (2009); Wis. Stat. Ann. § 180 (2009).

The plaintiff must be a shareholder at the time of the suit,[240] and most courts take the position that a plaintiff's ownership must have been uninterrupted during the interim period between the complained of transaction and the bringing of the suit[241] and must continue through the life of the suit.[242] This "continuing ownership" requirement poses serious problems when the misconduct that is the focus of the derivative suit occurred in connection with the corporation's acquisition by another entity. For example, assume that the plaintiff was the owner of Beta Company shares just prior to Beta's acquisition by Alpha Company. If Alpha acquired Beta on terms that provide only cash for the Beta stockholders, the plaintiff no longer is a continuing owner of shares. If Alpha exchanged its shares for Beta shares, plaintiff is a shareholder but not a continuing holder of Beta shares.

The courts are badly divided on whether former shareholders of a corporation that does not survive after an acquisition have standing to maintain a derivative suit on behalf of the non-surviving corporation.[243] A cash-out merger that occurs for no apparent purpose other than to deny the plaintiff standing to maintain a derivative suit was held not to cause the suit's dismissal, absent an independent good faith judgment that the suit harmed the corporate interest.[244] A merger that is a "mere reorganization" such as the transfer of the company into its holding company does not destroy the plaintiff's standing.[245] Moreover, the consummated acquisition does not adversely affect the shareholder's individual causes for fraud or unfairness.[246] The American Law Institute proposals provided a reasonable response to cutting the alternative of terminating the derivative suit abruptly on the company's acquisition:

A holder . . . has standing to commence and maintain a derivative suit action if the holder . . . (2) continues to hold the equity security until the time of judgment, unless the failure to do so is the result of corporate action in which the holder did not acquiesce, and either (A) the derivative action was commenced prior to the corporate action terminating the holder's status, or (B) the court finds that such holder is better able to represent the interests of the shareholder than any other holder who has brought suit.[247]

The Delaware Supreme Court in *Lewis v. Anderson*[248] recognized two exceptions: 1) when the merger itself is the subject of the derivative suit claim[249] and 2) when the merger is in reality a reorganization which does not affect the plaintiff's ownership.

---

[240] Schilling v. Belcher, 582 F.2d 995, 999 (5th Cir. 1978).

[241] McNeil v. Southern Golf Invs. of Ga., Inc., 492 S.E.2d 283 (Ga. Ct. App. 1997) (standing lost upon payment of first installment to purchase all of the plaintiff's shares).

[242] *See* Schilling v. Belcher, 582 F.2d 995, 999 (5th Cir. 1978) (standing lost by plaintiff who sold his shares after judgment but before appeal finalized).

[243] Lewis v. Chiles, 719 F.2d 1044 (9th Cir. 1983) (after sale of corporate assets, only acquiring companies and their shareholder could pursue derivative claims).

[244] *See* Merritt v. Colonial Foods, Inc., 505 A.2d 757 (Del. Ch. 1986).

[245] Schreiber v. Carney, 447 A.2d 17, 22 (Del. Ch. 1982).

[246] *See, e.g.,* Cede & Co. v. Technicolor, Inc., 542 A.2d 1182, 1188 (Del. 1988).

[247] ALI, 2 Principles of Corporate Governance: Analysis and Recommendations § 7.02(a)(2) (1992).

[248] 477 A.2d 1040 (Del. 1984). *See also* Arkansas Teacher Ret. Sys. v. Caiafa, 996 A.2d 321 (Del. 2010); Villari v. Mozilo, 208 Cal. App. 4th 1470, 146 Cal. Rptr. 3d 556 (Cal. Ct. App. 2012) (refusing to expand the exceptions beyond those recognized in *Lewis*).

[249] Arkansas Teacher Ret. Sys. v. Countrywide Financial, 75 A.3d 888 (Del. 2013)(fraud exception limited to where "merger itself is the subject of claim of fraud, being perpetrated merely to deprive shareholders of their standing to bring or maintain a derivative action").

The contemporaneous ownership rule appeared before the Supreme Court's decision in *Erie Railroad Company v. Tompkins*.[250] The Federal Rules of Civil Procedure now clearly govern procedural matters in diversity jurisdiction cases, but a number of important substantive issues are governed by state law.[251] For example, whether a suit based on state law is derivative or direct is a state law issue,[252] as is the question of who is a qualified shareholder[253] to bring and maintain a derivative suit. However, it is uncertain whether determining the time of the complained-of transaction for contemporaneous-ownership-rule purposes is a matter of substance or procedure.[254] Thus far, only the Ninth Circuit has definitively ruled on the question, holding that the contemporaneous ownership requirement is procedural, so that it applies in diversity actions.[255] In contrast, the requirement that the derivative suit plaintiff continue to own shares in the corporation is treated as a matter of state substantive law.[256]

§ 15.8   Double Derivative Suits

A parent corporation as a shareholder of a subsidiary can bring a derivative action to redress injury to the subsidiary.[257] In turn, a shareholder of a parent company can maintain a "double derivative" suit to enforce a cause of action in favor of a subsidiary company if the directors of both companies have refused after due request to institute an action in the name of either camp.[258] The parent company has a duty to use its control of the subsidiary to compel the subsidiary to sue to right wrongs done to it, and a shareholder of the parent may in effect compel specific performance of this duty in a double derivative suit.[259] A necessary predicate to a double derivative suit is that the parent has not less than operating control of the subsidiary.[260] It is still an open question whether a shareholder in a corporation that holds less than a controlling interest in a company against which a wrong has been committed is entitled to sue on a double derivative basis,[261] although one court has answered the question affirmatively.[262]

§ 15.9   The Plaintiff as an Adequate Representative

The plaintiff in a derivative suit must fairly and adequately represent similarly situated shareholders.[263] Properly interpreted, this means that the plaintiff must be

---

[250] Erie Railroad Company v. Tompkins, 304 U.S. 64 (1938).

[251] Erie Railroad Company v. Tompkins, 304 U.S. 64 (1938).

[252] *See* Gadd v. Pearson, 351 F.Supp. 895 (M.D. Fla. 1972).

[253] Kauffman v. Dreyfus Fund, Inc., 434 F.2d 727 (3d Cir. 1970), *cert. denied,* 401 U.S. 974 (1971).

[254] *See also* Bangor Punta Operations v. Bangor & Aroostook R.R., 417 U.S. 703 (1974).

[255] Kona Enterprises, Inc. v. Estate of Bishop, 179 F.3d 767 (9th Cir. 1999).

[256] *See* Susman v. Lincoln Am. Corp., 587 F.2d 866, 871 (7th Cir. 1978).

[257] Fed. R. Civ. Proc. 23.1.

[258] An individual shareholder can sue derivatively on a corporation's behalf to enforce its right to enforce the subsidiary's right. *See* Bazata v. National Ins. Co. of Washington, 400 A.2d 313 (D.C. Ct. App. 1979).

[259] *See* Saltzman v. Birrell, 78 F.Supp. 778 (S.D.N.Y. 1955).

[260] *See* Brown v. Tenney, 532 N.E.2d 230 (Ill. 1988).

[261] William H. Painter, Double Derivative Suits and Other Remedies with Regard to Damaged Subsidiaries, 36 Ind. L.J. 143, 152 (1961).

[262] Issner v. Aldrich, 254 F.Supp. 696 (D. Del. 1966).

[263] Fed. R. Civ. P. 23.1.

representative of the shareholders who have been injured.[264] The better view is the defendant has the burden of proving the plaintiff is an inadequate representative.[265]

To meet the fair and adequate representation requirement, a plaintiff must have the same interests as the other shareholders and must be free of interests that conflict with theirs.[266] A plaintiff in a derivative action must also show that he will pursue the claim vigorously and competently.[267] The most frequent basis for finding that a plaintiff is not an adequate representative is when the transparent purpose of the derivative suit is to enable the plaintiff to gain leverage in his personal claims or transactions with the defendants or the corporation.[268] For example, the plaintiff who owned a minuscule 21 common shares but held $21,000 of the corporation's debentures was held to be an inadequate representative for a derivative suit where the court was persuaded the true purpose of the suit was to obtain the full value of his debentures.[269] The right to initiate a derivative suit is not defeated by the fact that the plaintiff-shareholder owns only a few shares of stock in the corporation so that her injury is comparatively trivial and her benefit (through an increase in the value of stock held) from the sought-after recovery will be slight. Theoretically a minority shareholder has the same right as the largest shareholder to insist that the corporation's assets not be wrongfully diverted from the objectives for which it was created.[270] At the same time, the smallness of the plaintiff's holdings may well confirm the court's belief that the plaintiff is seeking to serve a distinct and private agenda through the derivative suit.[271] This concern has prompted some courts to appoint a "lead plaintiff" using the criteria applied in securities law class actions by which the most adequate plaintiff is the shareholder with the largest holdings.[272]

The courts are badly divided as to whether the bidder for control of a corporation is an adequate representative for a suit brought against the incumbent management for misdeeds they allegedly committed in seeking to thwart the bidder's attempt to obtain control.[273] In this area the courts are presented with the tough choice between a bidder

---

[264] *See* Eye Site, Inc. v. Blackburn, 750 S.W.2d 274 (Tex. Ct. App. 1988) (suit barred when all other stockholders are either defendants or have affirmatively stated the plaintiff does not represent their interests).

[265] *See, e.g.,* Smallwood v. Pearl Brewing Co., 489 F.2d 579, 582 (5th Cir.), *cert. denied,* 419 U.S. 873 (1974).

[266] *See, e.g.,* Davis v. Comed, Inc., 619 F.2d 588 (6th Cir. 1980) (providing six factors bearing on adequacy).

[267] In re Southern Peru Copper Corp. Shareholder Derivative Litigation, 52 A.3d 761 (Del. Ch. 2011)(defendant failed to prove plaintiff's inadequacy with facts he inherited shares and had a very limited knowledge of the case and was absent trial); Barrett v. Southern Conn. Gas Co., 172 Conn. 362, 373, 374 A.2d 1051, 1057 (1977).

[268] *See, e.g.,* Blum v. Morgan Guar. Trust Co., 539 F.2d 1388 (5th Cir. 1976) (plaintiff initiated suit after corporation sued him for defaulting on loan).

[269] Owen v. Modern Diversified Indus., 643 F.2d 441 (6th Cir. 1981).

[270] In the close corporation, it quite likely that the derivative suit is the only effective discipline that the small holder has against the much larger owner-defendant. *See* Halsted Video, Inc. v. Guttillo, 115 F.R.D. 177 (N.D. Ill. 1987) (20% owner of close corporation is adequate representative in suit against other owner, who holds 80% interest).

[271] *See* Blum v. Morgan Guar. Trust Co., 539 F.2d 1388 (5th Cir. 1976) (holdings of mere 100 common shares was infinitesimally small to plaintiff's indebtedness to corporation to which he was being sued for being in default).

[272] *See* In re Conseco, Inc. Sec. Litig., 120 F. Supp. 2d 729 (S.D. Ind. 2000) (appointing fund to lead derivative suit).

[273] The following cases have found the bidder is not an adequate representative: Torchmark Corp. v. Bixby, 708 F.Supp. 1070 (W.D. Mo. 1988).

who seeks to serve its private agenda through the successful prosecution of the derivative suit and a plaintiff who can surely be expected to be tenacious in pursuing whatever causes of action the corporation has.

Forum selection bylaws: A number of Delaware corporations have amended their governing documents—bylaws or charter—to provide that in any derivative suit on behalf of the corporation its board of directors can choose whether the suit can proceed only in Delaware or identify another forum in which the suit is then pending. Substantial impetus for such provisions was provided by *Boilermakers Local 154 Retirement Fund v. Chevron Corp.*,[274] where Chancellor Strine upheld a bylaw that was adopted by the board of directors designating Delaware as the forum for resolving disputes involving the internal affairs of a Delaware Corporation. Such a provision is valid even though the state of incorporation is not the forum selected.[275]

The advent of forum-selection clauses comes with several reservations. It remains to be seen whether courts other than Delaware will enforce a forum selection provision if jurisdiction in the forum was properly placed and the burdens on the parties to litigate in Delaware are greater than to continue the suit in the forum. Courts raise concern when the board adopts a forum-selection provision in following the shareholder commencing suit.[276] Moreover, some states have strong public policy against forum selection clauses, at least in corporate contract disputes.[277] Shareholders could also invoke the SEC's shareholder proposal rule to remove such a provision from the company's bylaws.[278] The doctrine of forum non conveniens also is available to the corporation that wishes to oppose the forum selected by the derivative suit plaintiff.[279] At least one federal court outside of Delaware has refused to enforce a forum selection clause in the bylaws in a case where the bylaw was passed after the alleged wrongdoing was claimed to have occurred; the decision was based on federal common law and thus the court did not reach the issue of whether the directors have the power to adopt such a bylaw under Delaware law.[280] Notwithstanding the preceding reservations, forum-selection bylaws are being widely adopted.

Boilermakers premised its reasoning on the shareholders relationship to the corporation being contractual. Taking this same approach, the Delaware Supreme Court subsequently in *ATP Tour, Inc. v. Deutscher Tennis Bund*[281] upheld a board adopted bylaw that abandoned the long-maintained American Rule (whereby litigants bear their own litigation costs) to instead assign the suit's defendant's expenses (which in a

---

[274] 73 A.3d 934 (Del. Ch. 2013).

[275] *See* City of Providence v. First Citizens BancShares, Inc., 99 A.3d 229, 241 (Del. Ch. 2014)(forum selection clause designating North Carolina was valid for Delaware incorporated firm).

[276] The Oregon Circuit Court refused to enforce a forum selection clause adopted by the board in anticipation of the law suit. Roberts v. TriQuint Semiconductor, Inc., No. 1402–02441 (Or. Cir. Ct. Aug. 14, 2014). *Contra* City of Providence v. First Citizens BancShares, Inc., 99 A.3d 229, 241 (Del. Ch. 2014)("That the board adopted . . . [the forum selection bylaw] on an allegedly 'cloudy' day when it entered into the merger agreement . . . is immaterial given the lack of any well-pled allegations . . . demonstrating any impropriety in this timing.").

[277] *See* IDACORP v. American Fiber Systems, Inc., 2012 WL 4139925 (D. Idaho 2012).

[278] Roper Industries, Inc., SEC No-Action Letter, Fed. Sec. L. Rep. (CCH) ¶ 76,937 (Mar. 29, 2012).

[279] *See, e.g.,* In re BP Shareholder Derivative Litigation, 2011 WL 4345209 (S.D. Tex. 2011) (dismissing suit on grounds that defendant corporation and defendant officers allegedly involved in long-term disregard of safety in exploration and production of oil were in England).

[280] Galaviz v. Berg, 763 F. Supp. 3d 1170 (N.D. Cal. 2011).

[281] 91 A.3d 554 (Del. 2014).

derivative suit would include the corporation's costs) to the plaintiff except if the suit proved successful.

In 2015, the Delaware legislature addressed some of the concerns arising from private ordering. Solomon-like, the Delaware legislature split the baby by amending the Delaware General Corporation Law to authorize forum-selection clauses and to prohibit charter or bylaw provisions that would shift to the plaintiff defense costs incurred in connection with shareholder suits that were not successfully concluded.[282] In so acting, the legislature gave managers something they wanted, a way to deal with the scourge of multi-forum litigation[283] while pacifying the local bar that feared lucrative shareholder suits would disappear because of the chilling effect of a loser pay rule for shareholder suits. Delaware's action by no means settles the question of the authority for the board of directors to act unilaterally in adopting a forum selection bylaw. And, since private ordering in the shadow of shareholder suits is not isolated to Delaware corporations,[284] the peace that the plaintiff's bar has now reached via the Delaware legislature may only shift their once Delaware-focused angst to other states. Moreover, the Delaware legislation is narrowly focused; it remains to be seen whether board-adopted bylaws can condition shareholder suits on a range of other actions that impede shareholder suits, such as standing criteria that mandates size and length of the suit's plaintiff's share holdings or even mandating arbitration of such claims. A California court has upheld a forum selection bylaw.[285]

Forum non conveniens: Shareholder suits, whether direct or derivative, enjoy relatively broad choices of venue. However, in derivative suits, and representative suits generally, the plaintiff's interest in a chosen forum can be given less weight because as a practical matter the suit is on behalf of many potential plaintiffs with an equal interest in a particular forum.[286] More limiting than venue is the ability of the plaintiff to serve process on the suit's defendants so that service, not venue, can and often is the constraint that defines the forums available for the suit. Even when venue and service of process can be technically satisfied, the chosen forum may still not be the closest available forum to the center of gravity in terms of the evidence and witnesses. For this reason, federal courts are statutorily empowered to *transfer* a suit to another federal district court when

---

[282] Delaware SB 75, 148th Gen'l Assembly, amending Del. G. Corp. L. §§ 102(f) & 109(b) (prohibiting fee shifting provisions in articles of incorporation or bylaws, respectively) and adding Del. G. Corp. L. § 115 (authorizing forum selection bylaws) was signed by Governor Jack Markell June 24, 2015. The new provision's authorization of forum selection invalidates any provision that would *prohibit* litigation of internal affairs claims in Delaware courts.

[283] *See* Cornerstone Research, Shareholder Litigation Involving Mergers and Acquisitions (March 2013) (finding shareholder suits accompanying 90 percent of merger and acquisition transactions in excess of $100 million). Moreover, about 50% of these deals also resulted in litigation in more than one jurisdiction. *See also* Jill E. Fisch, Sean J. Griffith & Steven Davidoff, Confronting the Peppercorn Settlements in Merger Litigation: An Empirical Analysis and a Proposal for Reform, 93 Tex. L. Rev. 557 (2015)(analysis of merger suits found that supplementary disclosures achieved through settlements produced no effect on shareholder voting). For empirical data to support the position that shareholder deal-focused litigation substitute for the presence of a rival bidder, *see* C.N.V. Krishnan, Ronald W. Masulis, Randall S. Thomas & Robert B. Thompson, 18 J. Corp. Fin. 1248 (2012)(firms subject to such suits complete deals at a lower rate and takeover premia in completed deals is higher for firms subject to shareholder suits).

[284] For a rich account of a challenge in Maryland to a board requiring, among other items, that shareholder disputes be handled through arbitration, *see* Ann Lipton, Manufactured Consent: The Problem of Arbitration Clauses in Corporate Charters and Bylaws, 104 Georgetown L. J. 583 (2016).

[285] Drullias v. 1st Century Bancshares, Inc., 30 Cal. App.5th 696 (6th Dist. 2018).

[286] Koster v. Lumbermens Mutual Casualty Co., 330 U.S. 518, 524 (1947).

maintaining it in the court selected by the plaintiff would seriously inconvenience the parties or the witnesses.[287]

Because of sovereignty concerns, state courts do not enjoy the equivalent power to transfer a shareholder suit to another state court. However, the doctrine of forum non conveniens, a common law doctrine, does allow federal and state courts either to dismiss or stay a proceeding when the court decides the interest of justice would be better served if the suit were maintained in another forum.

Gulf Oil Corp. v. Gilbert,[288] involving a derivative suit, is the leading authority on forum non conveniens within the federal court system. *Gilbert* conditions invoking the doctrine on a consideration of the private and public interests associated with the locus of the suit. Among the private interests are evidentiary sources including witnesses and records as well as the presiding court's power to compel the production of evidence. Public considerations include the difficulty the presiding court may have in applying the applicable legal principles. The U.S. Supreme Court, in a companion decision, *Koster v. Lumbermens Mutual Casualty Co.*,[289] observed that a court could be understandably "reluctant to hear cases involving the administration of the internal affairs of foreign corporations, on the rationale that such administration is better left to the courts of the state where the corporation was incorporated." *Koster* qualifies this observation by noting that because many corporations incorporate in states where they have no significant operations or economic activity, courts should not broadly defer to the corporate domicile—"the ultimate inquiry is where trial will best serve the convenience of the parties," rather than which court has the greater familiarity with the legal principles of the case.[290] *Gilbert* cautions that, unless the balance of such considerations *strongly* favor the defendant, the court should not upset the forum selected by the plaintiff. In light of the fact that that *Gilbert* and *Koster* were decided seven decades ago, there is ample cause to re-evaluate the extent to which the private and public factors they rely on are now eclipsed by important changes in communications, Federal Rules of Civil Procedure, and the Federal Rules of Evidence.[291]

Delaware's approach to forum non conveniens mirrors the federal approach. The Delaware Supreme Court, similar to the federal approach, holds that dismissal on forum non conveniens grounds should rarely occur. Indeed, Delaware has repeatedly held that dismissal, or a stay on the basis of forum non conveniens, cannot be grounded solely on the basis that the legal issue raised in the suit had not been resolved within the state of incorporation.[292] Delaware has invoked the doctrine in an instance where the court believed there would be difficulty compelling the production of evidence and witnesses, who were in Canada and where the case did not raise novel legal issues, but rather typical claims of breach of fiduciary duty that were capable of resolution elsewhere.[293]

---

[287] *See* 28 U.S.C. § 1404.

[288] 330 U.S. 501 (1947).

[289] 330 U.S. 518 (1947).

[290] 330 U.S. at 527.

[291] Martin Davies, Time to Change the Federal Forum Non Conveniens Analysis, 77 *Tulane Law Review*, 309 (2002).

[292] *See, e.g.*, Berger v. Intelident Solutions, Inc., 906 A.2d 134 (Del. 2006); Taylor v. LSI Logic Corp., 715 A.2d 837, 842 (Del. 1998) (dismissed however on grounds that private action being advanced under a Canadian statute that provided exclusive jurisdiction was in Canadian courts).

[293] Hurst v. General Dynamics Corp., 583 A.2d 1334 (Del. Ch. 1990).

On close analysis, it is difficult to conclude that the vast majority of the disputes now heard in Delaware are litigated in the forum that would be considered the center of gravity for the evidence needed to resolve the dispute. Few reported opinions involve companies operating in Delaware; this is consistent with the hallmark of Delaware being the domicile of corporations seeking the multiple benefits of Delaware incorporation, but having their principal place of business elsewhere. Thus, it does not appear persuasive to argue convenience to the parties and efficiency for the court is necessarily served by demanding that the appropriate forum is a state whose only connection with the dispute is purely by virtue of obeisance to the internal affairs doctrine. Moreover, Delaware's assertion that its courts should be the preferred forum so that its judiciary can interpret the law of Delaware stands in contrast to the Delaware Supreme Court's decisions upholding the right of Delaware courts to resolve important unaddressed questions under the corporate statutes of sister states.[294] Delaware's position to argue for applying forum non conveniens in important questions under Delaware law is further undercut by the power of the Delaware Supreme Court to receive certified questions in such situations. Thus, under the traditional formulation of forum non conveniens, Delaware does not appear to have a strong case that it should be deferred to in suits involving Delaware corporations when the center of gravity with respect to witnesses and evidence is outside of Delaware. This hardly suggests there is not a good policy reason for sister courts to defer to Delaware.

§ 15.10   Bona Fide Purchasers of "Tainted" Shares

One of the most significant decisions in the development of the derivative suit is *Home Fire Insurance Company v. Barber*,[295] which, ironically, was not a derivative suit. In *Home Fire Insurance*, Commissioner Roscoe Pound held that a corporation whose sole shareholder acquired his shares from the defendant at an admittedly fair price could not sue that former controlling stockholder for misconduct committed during the years of his control. *Home Fire Insurance* thus established the "vicarious incapacity" principle, under which the corporation is barred from suing for misconduct when its sole or substantial stockholder acquired his shares from those responsible for the misconduct that is the subject of the suit.[296] Such shares are sometimes referred to as "tainted" shares. Courts frequently reach the result by piercing the plaintiff-corporation's veil to identify the real party of interest.[297] But, as seen earlier, veil-piercing is but a mechanism to reach a result believed socially desirable on some other basis; it is rarely a sole justification.

Today the courts emphasize that the objective served by the vicarious-incapacity principle is to avoid the unjust enrichment that otherwise would occur if the holder of tainted shares were allowed to recover from his seller for misconduct that did not cause the current controlling stockholder any economic loss.[298] However, the bar extends to a wider range of issues than preventing the new holder of control from obtaining a windfall. As a general rule, a person who purchases shares in a corporation knowing that

---

[294]   *See, e.g.*, Berger v. Intelident Solutions, Inc., 906 A.2d 134 (Del. 2006); Taylor v. LSI Logic Corp., 715 A.2d 837, 842 (Del. 1998) (dismissed however on grounds that private action being advanced under a Canadian statute that provided exclusive jurisdiction was in Canadian courts).

[295]   Home Fire Insurance Company v. Barber, 93 N.W. 1024 (Neb. 1903).

[296]   *See* Deborah Griffin, Note, Corporate Incapacity to Sue Where Stockholders Would Be Barred from Suing Derivatively-The Vicarious Incapacity Rule: A Public Interest Exception, 54 B.U. L. Rev. 355 (1974).

[297]   *See* Bangor Punta Operations, Inc. v. Bangor & Aroostook R.R., 417 U.S. 703, 716 (1974).

[298]   *See, e.g.*, National Union Elec. Corp. v. Matsushita Elec. Indus. Corp., 498 F.Supp. 991, 999 n.9 (E.D. Pa. 1980); Courtland Manor, Inc. v. Leeds, 347 A.2d 144 (Del. Ch. 1975).

the transferor is estopped by laches, participation, or acquiescence to complain of misapplication of funds or other illegal transactions is in precisely the same position as the transferor and is also estopped.[299] One court has even reasoned that one who purchases control knowing or having reason to know that the seller has mistreated the corporation "is not a *bona fide* purchaser without notice of those facts; therefore the purchaser may not maintain the action."[300] The weight of authority is that a transferee of tainted shares is in the same position as the transferor with respect to suing on transactions that occurred before the transfer, even if the transferee is a purchaser without notice.[301] The high water mark of the vicarious-incapacity principle is *Jannes v. Microwave Communications, Inc.,*[302] where the court partially disallowed a derivative suit because the defendant had acquired 90 percent of the corporation's stock after the alleged wrongs had been committed; thus any recovery on behalf of the corporation would, absent a pro rata recovery, have largely redounded to the benefit of the defendant.

The most significant impact of *Home Fire Insurance* is not its effect on those few cases where the corporation seeks to recover from its former controlling stockholder after a change in ownership. The lasting effects of *Home Fire Insurance* are evident in the wide adoption of the contemporaneous ownership rule, discussed earlier. As seen earlier, concerns about unjust enrichment underlie the continuing force the contemporaneous ownership rule enjoys with the courts and legislatures such that even the few instances of its rigid application being relaxed are guided by a comparative assessment of the unjust enrichment that otherwise will arise.

§ 15.11   Security-for-Expense Statutes

In 1944 the New York legislature, with a view to controlling abuses of derivative suits, took the drastic step of adopting a statute requiring plaintiffs in such suits to give security for the prospective litigation expenses of defendants.[303] Under the current version of the New York statute, a court can require a security deposit unless a plaintiff represents 5 percent of a class of shares or the value of plaintiff's shares exceeds $50,000.[304] The Model Business Corporation Act's security-for-expense provision[305] was deleted from the act in 1982.[306] The current Model Business Corporation Act does not contain a security-for-expense provision but does authorize the court to require the plaintiff to "pay any of the defendant's reasonable expenses . . . if it finds that the proceeding was commenced or maintained without reasonable cause or for an improper purpose."[307]

---

[299] *See* Blum v. Morgan Guar. Trust Co., 539 F.2d 1388 (5th Cir. 1976).

[300] Damerow Ford Co. v. Bradshaw, 876 P.2d 788, 794 (Or. Ct. App. 1994).

[301] *See* Bangor Punta Operations v. Bangor & Aroostook R.R., 417 U.S. 703 (1974); In re REA Express, Inc., 412 F.Supp. 1239 (E.D. Pa. 1976).

[302] Jannes v. Microwave Communications, Inc., 385 F.Supp. 759 (N.D. Ill. 1974).

[303] N.Y. Gen. Corp. Law § 61b, now N.Y. Bus. Corp. Law § 627 (2009).

[304] N.Y. Bus. Corp. Law § 627 (2009).

[305] Former MBCA § 49 (1969) (unless plaintiff's shares represent 5% of the class or have $25,000 in value).

[306] *See* Report of the Committee on Corporate Laws, Proposed Revisions of the Model Business Corporation Act Affecting Actions by Shareholders, 37 Bus. Law. 261, 265–266 (1981).

[307] MBCA Ann. § 7.46(2) (Supp. 1992).

The primary purpose of such a provision is to reduce strike suits.[308] If plaintiff fails to post security as ordered by the court, the result is dismissal of the derivative suit.[309] Courts generally conduct a fairly close review of the pleadings and any supporting affidavits before requiring the plaintiff to post security.[310] As applied to ordinary investors, the security-for-costs requirement is oppressive, and, as a practical matter, it denies the only civil remedy that ordinary shareholders have for breach of fiduciary duties by those entrusted with the management and direction of their corporations. Many writers have vigorously attacked the requirement;[311] others have supported it.[312]

On the whole, security-for-expense statutes have not been a major impediment to the initiation and continuation of derivative suits. Within a decade of its enactment, the New York security-for-expense statute had already proven largely ineffective.[313] Such statutes are rendered impotent by their common exception for suits brought by a plaintiff or plaintiffs who own at least a stated percentage—for example, 5 percent—or stock with a minimum market value. If the original plaintiff does not meet these criteria, he may obtain a stay after a motion for security is made, during which time the plaintiff may procure a list of the stockholders and solicit their participation as plaintiffs in order to satisfy the minimum ownership requirement.[314] Board members, preferring not to have the corporation's dirty linen further aired in such a public manner, frequently prefer not to invoke the statute. Moreover, the plaintiff with a keen eye may skillfully avoid the security-for-expense statute by selecting a forum based on the forum's applicable choice-of-law rules.

For suits in federal court in which jurisdiction is based on diversity of citizenship, the security for expense requirement is considered substantive.[315] However, the federal court abides by the choice-of-law rule of the forum state in deciding whether to apply the security-for-expense statute of the corporation's domicile. Thus, in a leading case the federal court refused to require the plaintiff to post security, although the corporation's domicile would have so required because, under the forum state's choice-of-law rule, the federal court viewed the security-for-expense statute as procedural, not substantive.[316] Similar results should occur if suit is brought in a state other than the state of incorporation and the forum state does not treat security-for-expense statutes as procedural. Suits based on federal issues, such as those brought under the federal

---

[308] Former MBCA § 49 Comment (1969).

[309] *See, e.g.,* Haberman v. Tobin, 626 F.2d 1101 (2d Cir. 1980).

[310] The more extensive review occurs under statutes, such as Cal. Corp. Code § 800(c), which condition ordering of the security on a preliminary showing that there is no reasonable possibility the action will benefit the corporation or that the defendant did not participate in the transaction that is subject of suit.

[311] *See, e.g.,* Henry W. Ballantine, Abuses of Shareholders' Derivative Suits: How Far Is California's New "Security for Expenses" Act Sound Regulation, 37 Cal. L. Rev. 399 (1949).

[312] *See, e.g.,* Ralph M. Carson, Further Phases of Derivative Actions Against Directors, 29 Cornell L.Q. 431, 454–460 (1944).

[313] *See* Note, Security for Expenses Legislation-Summary, Analysis, and Critique, 52 Colum. L. Rev. 267, 281 (1952).

[314] *See, e.g.,* Miller v. Victor, 2015 U.S. Dist. LEXIS 25429 (S.D.N.Y. Mar. 2, 2015) (Under New York statute, it is the holdings at commencement of suit, not before suit was commenced, that must satisfy the 5 percent/$50,000 level for bond to be excused; in dicta the court observed that dilution of the plaintiff's holdings before the suit's commencement do not excuse the need for the statutory amount of holdings to exist when suit is commenced.); Baker v. MacFadden Pub., Inc., 90 N.E.2d 876 (N.Y. 1950).

[315] Cohen v. Beneficial Indus. Loan Corp., 337 U.S. 541 (1949).

[316] *See* Berkwitz v. Humphrey, 130 F.Supp. 142 (N.D. Ohio 1955).

securities acts, do not have to meet the forum state's security-for-expense requirement,[317] although that requirement continues to apply to pendent state claims.[318]

§ 15.12 Limitations, Laches, and Acquiescence as Defenses

The dual aspect of a shareholder's derivative suit—(1) enforcement in equity of a shareholder's right to have the corporation sue on its claims and (2) enforcement in the same proceedings of the basic or underlying corporate right of action against the alleged wrongdoers, which right of action may be legal or equitable—creates questions as to the applicable period of limitations for bringing the suit. The time limit for commencing suit is not necessarily governed by the statute of limitations on equitable proceedings generally, as the shareholder can enforce only such claims as the corporation itself could assert. Accordingly, the general rule has been that the period of limitations is the one that would be applicable to the action if it were brought by the corporation.[319]

In derivative suits courts now generally apply the limitations period applicable to the underlying cause of action.[320] Where the cause of action is for damages in tort or contract, the appropriate legal period of limitations applies.[321] Because the limitations period varies under state statutes depending on the character of the underlying cause of action, courts must classify the action before determining the applicable limitations period. If a state has a statute of limitations expressly applicable to derivative suits, however, the limitations period so provided applies.[322] As many federal laws do not contain an express statute of limitations, the courts at one time in applying those federal laws used an analogous provision under state law, but this practice was overruled recently by the Supreme Court and in 2002 Congress acted to extend the limitations period for securities actions.[323]

The statute of limitations begins to run on the date the cause of action accrues. There invariably is a question whether the running of the statute of limitations should be tolled. Statutes of limitations are statutes of repose intended both to promote judicial economy and to allow individuals to plan for the future free of an indefinite threat of litigation. At the same time, there is obvious unfairness in barring the plaintiff when there is no reasonable basis to believe she could have asserted those rights. Hence, the doctrine of tolling applies. Courts therefore regularly toll the statute for the period during which the defendant has fraudulently concealed her wrongdoing.[324]

In other contexts, courts apply the so-called discovery rule, under which the statute of limitations commences to run when the plaintiff knows or should have reason to know of the wrong.[325] Because the derivative suit redresses a wrong committed against the corporation, and the wrongdoers are usually corporate officers or directors or those in

---

[317] See McClure v. Borne Chem. Co., 292 F.2d 824 (3d Cir. 1961).

[318] See Haberman v. Tobin, 480 F.Supp. 425 (S.D.N.Y. 1979), aff'd, 626 F.2d 1101 (1980).

[319] See Backus-Brooks Co. v. Northern Pac. Ry., 21 F.2d 4 (8th Cir. 1927).

[320] See, e.g., Teren v. Howard, 322 F.2d 949, 954 (9th Cir. 1963).

[321] See, e.g., Hughes v. Reed, 46 F.2d 435 (10th Cir. 1931).

[322] See, e.g., N.Y. Civ. Prac. Law § 213.8 (2009).

[323] Lampf, Pleva, Lipkind, Prupis & Petigrow v. Gilbertson, 501 U.S. 350 (1991).

[324] See, e.g., Rieff v. Evans, 630 N.W.2d 278 (Iowa 2001) (plaintiff has burden of proving either defendant's affirmative concealment or existence of fiduciary relationship to the plaintiff and failure to disclose information underlying the wrongdoing).

[325] See Abbott v. McNeff, 171 F. Supp. 2d 935, 940 (D. Minn. 2001) (numerous bases to conclude that plaintiff was suspicious of the defendant's dealings from the early days of their relationship).

control of the corporation, knowledge is a tricky concept in the context of the derivative suit.[326]

In addition to facing a possible bar to the action under the applicable statute of limitations, since the derivative suit is procedurally equitable the plaintiff is also open to the equitable defense of laches.[327] When successfully invoked by the defendant, laches bars an action because of special facts surrounding the delay in the suit's initiation, even though the delay did not push beyond the limitations period provided at law.

> The equitable defense of laches was based on the theory that upon a person's acquiring knowledge of a wrong affecting his rights, any unreasonable delay in asserting an equitable remedy will bar such form of relief. Further, laches . . . unlike the statute of limitations at law, is not predicated upon the mere passage of time but rather calls for a showing that if the claim sought to be tardily enforced will result in an inequity because of an intervening change in conditions prejudicial to the party raising the defense, then it should be barred.[328]

The three requirements for laches are inexcusable delay, the plaintiff having knowledge of the misconduct, and a bona fide change in position causing prejudice to the party raising the defense.[329] For example, *Houseman v. Sagerman*,[330] even though the applicable limitations period for breach of fiduciary duty was 3 years, laches barred the suit due to a 27-month delay in filing that among other burdens caused defendants to lose the benefits of director and officer liability insurance coverage due to merger. Prompt suit after notice of the misconduct deprives the defense of laches of its most important element, unreasonable delay in prosecuting the action.[331]

The plaintiff's acquiescence can also be the basis of barring her initiation of the suit. Laches and acquiescence are related but distinct concepts:

> Acquiescence is a doctrine springing from the rule that he who seeks equity must do equity. Acquiescence and laches are not correlative terms because they relate to different times within the same spectrum. Laches relates to delay after the act is done, while acquiescence relates to inaction during the time the act is being performed. Laches implies passive assent while acquiescence imports active assent.[332]

Thus a plaintiff is deemed to acquiesce in the misconduct by intentionally failing to complain about a proposed repurchase of shares for an employee stock benefit plan which the plaintiff later challenged as an impermissible defensive maneuver.[333] Acquiescence is far more likely to occur within a small or closely held corporation because it is easier to establish, somewhat objectively, that the plaintiff forbore with full knowledge of the

---

[326] Some courts instead phrase the rule's impact as determining when the cause of action accrues. *See, e.g.,* FDIC v. Manatt, 723 F.Supp. 99, 105 (E.D. Ark. 1989).

[327] *See* Yokochi v. Yoshimoto, 353 P.2d 820 (Hawaiʻi 1960) (burden of proving plaintiff barred by laches is on defendant). For the view that the personal involvement or misbehavior of the plaintiff should not itself be disabling in view that the suit is on behalf of the corporation and not the plaintiff.

[328] Skouras v. Admiralty Enters., 386 A.2d 674 (Del. Ch. 1978).

[329] *See, e.g.,* Herald Co. v. Seawell, 472 F.2d 1081, 1099 (10th Cir. 1972).

[330] 2015 WL 7307323 (Del. Ch. Nov. 19, 2015).

[331] *See* Squaw Mtn. Cattle Co. v. Bowen, 804 P.2d 1292 (Wyo. 1991).

[332] Herald Co. v. Seawell, 472 F.2d 1081, 1099 (10th Cir. 1972).

[333] *See* Herald Co. v. Seawell, 472 F.2d 1081, 1099 (10th Cir. 1972).

underlying facts.[334] But forbearance should not too easily be attributed to the plaintiff; for example, the court wisely concluded that the mere failure to attend the meeting at which the details of the transaction were discussed did not bar the non-attending plaintiff from initiating an action challenging the transaction.[335] Quite apart from the defense of acquiescence is the bar against plaintiffs who purchased their stock with knowledge of earlier or even continuing misconduct from bringing suit for that misconduct.[336] It remains to be seen whether written agreements entered into by shareholders waiving their right to initiate a derivative suit over matters related to the corporation's formation or otherwise will be accorded the same effect as such agreements have had in the partnership or LLC context.[337]

Distinct from the defenses of laches and acquiescence is the defense of in pari delicto which arises most often where an officer or director's misconduct that is the focus of the derivative suit is in fact imputed to the corporation itself so that it is an equal wrongdoer.[338] Even if the misconduct is imputed to the corporation, other considerations that will render the defense of in pari delicto unavailable are:

1. The public cannot be protected because the transaction is complete;

2. No serious moral turpitude is involved; or

3. It would unjustly enrich the defendant at the expense of the plaintiff.

The doctrine of collateral estoppel applies in derivative suit litigation. Therefore, a suit dismissed in Forum A for failure to make a demand cannot be relitigated in Forum B, even if the latter concludes that demand should have been excused in the earlier litigation.[339]

§ 15.13 Derivative Suits and the Right to a Jury Trial and Arbitration

Many courts have held that a jury trial is unavailable in derivative suits.[340] However, in *Ross v. Bernhard*[341] the U.S. Supreme Court ruled that the Seventh Amendment to the Constitution guarantees the right to a jury if the underlying basis of the claim would have been recognized in an action at law. Thus, in *Crane Co. v. American Standard, Inc.*[342] the court held a corporation is not entitled to a jury trial where the

---

[334] *See, e.g.,* Voisine v. Berube, 38 A.3d 310 (ME 2011)(standing denied since plaintiff participated in the transactions that he ultimately complained the other owner had wrongfully engaged); Tagarelli v. McCormick, 614 So.2d 11 (Fl. Ct. App. 1993) (full report received in advance of meeting and plaintiff failed to attend meeting or otherwise object).

[335] *See* Shapiro v. Greenfield, 764 A.2d 270, 284 (Md. Ct. App. 2000).

[336] *See* Blum v. Morgan Guar. Trust Co., 539 F.2d 1388 (5th Cir. 1976).

[337] *See* Elf Atochem North America, Inc. v. Jaffari, 727 A.2d 286 (Del. 1999) (upholding agreement in LLC that waived rights by members to initiate derivative suits for matters related to the operating agreement).

[338] *See* In re American Int'l Group, Inc. Consolidated Derivative Litig., 976 A.2d 872 (Del.Ch. 2009)(dismissing derivative suit to recover damage corporation suffered as a consequence of engaging in bid rigging); In re AMERCO Derivative Litigation, 252 P.3d 681 (Nev. 2011)(wrongful conduct of officers are imputed to the corporation if the officer is the sole actor under the "adverse interest" exception even though officer acted completely and totally adverse to the corporation).

[339] Pyott v. Louisiana Mun. Police Employees' Retirement Sys., 74 A.3d 612 (Del. 2013).

[340] *See, e.g.,* Cohen v. Beneficial Indus. Loan Corp., 337 U.S. 541 (1949).

[341] Ross v. Bernhard, 396 U.S. 531 (1970).

[342] Crane Co. v. American Standard, Inc., 346 F.Supp. 1153 (S.D.N.Y. 1971), *rev'd & remanded,* 510 F.2d 1043 (2d Cir. 1974), *cert. denied,* 421 U.S. 1000 (1975).

plaintiff sought equitable relief and the court, after considering the relative hardships of possible remedies, awarded damages.

§ 15.14   Control, Settlement, and Dismissal of a Derivative Suit

A shareholder's authority to enforce a corporation's cause of action arises from the failure of the official managers to act on its behalf. Assuming the shareholder is a proper representative, the plaintiff does not have absolute control of the litigation but instead has a stewardship function that is exercised under the watchful eye of the derivative suit court to assure that the action's continuation, dismissal, or settlement is in the best interests of the corporation. Thus in a leading case, *Saylor v. Lindsey*,[343] over the objections of the plaintiff, the court approved a settlement supported by his attorney and the defendants. The Federal Rules of Civil Procedure fully reflect the court's role in protecting the corporation's interests with respect to the derivative suit:

> The derivative action may not be maintained if it appears that the plaintiff does not fairly and adequately represent the interests of the shareholders or members similarly situated in enforcing the right of the corporation or association. The action shall not be dismissed or compromised without the approval of the court, and notice of the proposed dismissal or compromise shall be given to shareholders or members in such manner as the court directs.[344]

The question of representation is crucial in safeguarding the interests of all shareholders as well as the corporation.

The final authority to determine whether the action shall be dismissed is the court;[345] a paramount consideration in the court's review is the strength of the plaintiff's case relative to the settlement's terms.[346] Under both statutory and judicially imposed court supervision, the scope of judicial control is not limited to achieving fairness to the particular plaintiff; it extends to the interests of other shareholders, to the corporation as an entity, and to the effect of a settlement on other pending actions. Thus courts frequently consider the continuing costs to the corporation if the suit continues,[347] but a court will have a difficult time accepting a settlement of a viable cause of action when the only tangible benefit to the corporation is avoidance of further costs to the corporation and inconvenience to its employees.[348] The courts, however, rarely provide a close analysis of the costs and benefits of the settlement's terms;[349] they content themselves with broad incantations sounding in fairness to all the interests before them:

> In examining the settlement, the Chancellor need not try the case. Indeed, he is not required to decide any of the issues on the merits. . . . Instead, he . . . exercises a form of business judgment to determine the overall reasonableness of the settlement. . . . [O]ur review is more limited than that of the Court of

---

[343] Saylor v. Lindsey, 456 F.2d 896 (2d Cir. 1972).

[344] Fed. R. Civ. P. 23.1.

[345] Whitten v. Dabney, 154 P. 312, 316 (Cal. 1944).

[346] *See, e.g.,* In re Traffic Executive Ass'n E. R.R., 627 F.2d 631 (2d Cir. 1980).

[347] *See* Shlensky v. Dorsey, 574 F.2d 131, 147 (3d Cir. 1978).

[348] *See* In re Pittsburgh & Lake Erie R.R. Sec. & Antitrust Litig., 543 F.2d 1058 (3d Cir. 1976) (district court's approval of such a settlement reversed).

[349] For a critique of the internal inconsistencies of settlement review criteria and lack of adequate factual basis to undertake a meaningful review, *see* Note, When Should Courts Allow the Settlement of Duty-of-Loyalty Derivative Suits, 109 Harv. L. Rev. 1084 (1996).

Chancery. It is not our function to determine the intrinsic fairness of the settlement or to exercise our own business judgment respecting its merits. We limit ourselves to the question of an abuse of discretion by the trial court in exercising its business judgment.[350]

In discharging their responsibility to review settlements, a court relies on the record and documents—including depositions, interrogatories, and affidavits—already before it as well as any documents filed in support or in opposition to the settlement. A court can convene a hearing on the settlement.

In considering its role in reviewing the proposed settlement the court should take a sobering view of the inherent weaknesses of the suit's participants' incentives to serve the corporation's interests.[351] Simply put, each party lacks a strong economic incentive that can be expected to guide his actions so as to avoid either adopting an overly aggressive litigation strategy or becoming so passive that the resulting settlement is woefully inadequate in light of the suit's intrinsic worth. For example, as seen earlier, the derivative suit plaintiff is not required to have a substantial ownership interest as a condition to bringing suit. Lacking a substantial ownership interest, the plaintiff bears little of the consequences of a suit that produces tangible adverse effects to the corporation. Thus the adverse impact of an ill-advised suit cannot be expected to rein in a maverick plaintiff.

The defendants also enjoy an advantage, however, for they can "play" with other people's money, thanks to the scope of insurance policies and liberal indemnification arrangements, discussed later. Settlement may not totally remove the mud the derivative suit has tossed in the defendants' direction, but it does provide the means for minimizing the defendants' losses, because settlement amounts are carefully tailored to fall within existing insurance and indemnification arrangements.

Thus the carefully drafted settlement arrangement can hold the defendants harmless. While such a settlement earns the gratitude of the defendants for their lawyers, why should derivative suit counsel let the defendants off so easy? The answer lies in the juncture between how the fee for derivative suit counsel is established and the economic principle of diminishing marginal returns. As will be seen later, courts frequently award derivative suit counsel fees based on the time they have invested in the case rather than on a set percentage of the fee recovered. Under this method, the derivative suit counsel, not being neutral to risk, can see that by rejecting a settlement and continuing to pursue the action exposes herself to risk of ultimately recovering nothing or substantially less than the proffered settlement, which risk is not adequately compensated by the marginal expected value of continuing the suit. In sum, the gains of continuing the suit, being on a diminishing basis, do not adequately reward the derivative suit counsel for continuing to aggressively pursue the case.

A further wrinkle to this scenario is that derivative suit counsel obtains a fee award even though no monetary recovery results from the successful prosecution of the suit; therefore defendant's counsel, rather than proposing a cash settlement, most frequently minimizes the drain from the defendants—or the insurance company that stands behind

---

[350] Polk v. Good, 507 A.2d 531, 536 (Del. 1986).

[351] *See* John C. Coffee, Jr., Understanding the Plaintiff's Attorney: The Implications of Economic Theory for Private Enforcement of Law Through Class and Derivative Actions, 86 Colum. L. Rev. 669, 671–677 (1986).

the defendants—by proposing a nonpecuniary recovery.[352] That is, defense counsel, wishing to contain damages, can fulfill this objective by a settlement that ironically places the major financial burden on the corporation itself. This makes possible results such as *In re General Tire & Rubber Company Securities Litigation*[353] where a suit with damages clearly exceeding $100 million was settled on terms that secured for the derivative suit counsel $500,000. The only benefit to the corporation was its undertaking to include two outside directors on its board for two years.[354]

In this area *In re Trulia, Inc. Stockholder Litigation*[355] has had a substantial impact on shareholder litigation. Chancellor Bouchard aimed squarely at the concerns captured in the settlements of shareholder suits where researchers found that in a high percentage of the settlements the only relief was additional disclosures regarding the deal and that these disclosure only settlements did not result in either better terms or have a material effect on voting.[356] *Trulia* therefore held that disclosure only settlements must satisfy a newly established "plainly material" standard whereby:

> [T]he supplemental disclosures address a plainly material misrepresentation or omission, and the subject matter of the proposed release is narrowly circumscribed to encompass nothing more than disclosure claims and fiduciary duty claims concerning the sales process, [provided that] the record shows that such claims have been investigated sufficiently.[357]

Trulia, Inc. is a structured response to disclosure-only settlements that builds on the growing malaise among courts that have increasingly approached the settlements skeptically.

One noticeable impact of *Trulia, Inc.* is the growing prevalence of "mootness fees."[358] This refers to a private agreement between the defendants and plaintiffs for the suit to be withdrawn in exchange for a small payment, but without the defendant obtaining class-wide relief, *i.e.*, the agreement supporting the dismissal is binding only between the defendant and the suit's plaintiff. In this context, the Delaware courts support the withdrawal of the suit on a showing the disclosures were "helpful" or provide "some

---

[352] *See* Roberta Romano, The Shareholder Suit: Litigation Without Foundation?, 7 J. L. Econ. & Organ. 55, 61 (1991) (only 21% of derivative suit settlements produced a cash payment to the corporation or its stockholders).

[353] In re General Tire & Rubber Company Securities Litigation, 726 F.2d 1075, 1088 (6th Cir. 1984).

[354] In re General Tire & Rubber Company Securities Litigation, 726 F.2d 1075, 1079 (6th Cir. 1984).

[355] 129 A.3d 884 (Del. Ch. 2016).

[356] Jill E. Fisch, Sean Griffith and Steven Solomon Davidoff, Confronting the Peppercorn Settlements in Merger Litigation: An Empirical Analysis and a Proposal for Reform, 93 Tex. L. Rev. 557 (2015). *But see* Guiseppe Dari-Matiacci & Erich L. Talley, Being True to Trulia: Do Disclosure-Only Settlements in Merger Objection Lawsuits Harm Shareholders, March 2019 Working Paper, available at https://ssrn.com/abstract = 3347327 (exploring whether there are ex ante benefits to threat of suits that are weakened by removing their likelihood through removing disclosure-only settlements).

[357] In re Trulia, Inc. Stockholder Litigation, 129 A.3d 884, 898 (Del. Ch. 2016). *See also*, In re Walgreen Co. Sh. Litig., 832 F.3d 718 (7th Cir. 2016)(same). *Cf.* Nguyen v. Barrett, 2016 WL 5404095 (Del. Ch. 2016) (plaintiff cannot purposely initiate some disclosure claims prior to the merger's closure and pursue other claims post closure).

[358] *See generally* Matthew D. Cain, Jill E. Fisch, Steven Davidoff Solomon & Randall S. Thomas, Mootness Fees, 72 Vand. L. Rev. 1777 (2019).

benefit.[359] So far, only a single court outside of Delaware has pushed back on mootness fees.[360]

A sobering lesson to be drawn from the explosion of multi-forum litigation is illustrated in *Pyott v. Louisiana Municipal Police Employees' Retirement System*.[361] Derivative suits were filed in the California federal court and Delaware Chancery Court following Allergan's guilty plea accompanied by the payment of a $600 million fine for having actively marketed off-label uses of its blockbuster drug, Botox. Despite proceeding on an expedited calendar in Delaware, the California federal court acted first. In *In re Allergan*, the federal district court dismissed with prejudice the derivative suit on the grounds the derivative suit plaintiff failed to allege sufficient facts to excuse a demand on the board of directors under governing Delaware precedents.[362] Thereupon, the defendants moved to dismiss the Delaware suit, arguing that per collateral estoppel the Delaware suit could not continue, so that dismissal was constitutionally required by the Full Faith and Credit Clause of the Constitution. In an extensive review of the governing law and the factual allegations set forth in the complaint, Vice-Chancellor Laster refused to dismiss the case.[363] The Delaware Supreme Court reversed, holding that California, and not Delaware, law should determine whether privity is lacking due to the derivative suit's dismissal for the failure to excuse demand on the board of directors. It concluded that under California law, privity is satisfied even though the suit is dismissed for failure to excuse a demand.

Professor George Geis invokes *Pyott* to support forum selection bylaws and where the firm does not have such a provision he suggests the outcome be guided by the court's assessment of the adequacy of counsel.[364] This may well reflect the reluctance of some counsel to invest heavily in investigating the facts of the case and devoting time to drafting a complaint, if they are uncertain whether those efforts will be undercut by a swifter proceeding by a rival counsel. If this surmise is correct, it poses a larger concern—that diligence and reflection are ultimately not rewarded but nimbleness and timing are. Ultimately, any difference in zealousness between plaintiff's counsel in the federal court and the Delaware court was addressed with the Ninth Circuit reversing the district court's dismissal, chastising the trial court for repeatedly drawing inferences in the board's favor.[365]

The issue of preclusion played out again in *California State Teachers' Retirement System v. Alvarez*.[366] Following a New York Times story detailing extensive bribery of Mexican officials and suggesting a coverup by senior executives of a Wal-Mart subsidiary, derivative suits were filed against Wal-Mart executives in the Delaware Chancery Court as well as in the federal district court in Arkansas, Wal-Mart's headquarters. Different plaintiffs and law firms were involved in both the suits, but the

---

[359] In re Sauer-Danfoss Sh. Litig., 65 A.3d 1116, 1141 (Del. Ch. 2011).

[360] *See* House v. Akorn, 2019 WL 2576531 (N.D.Ill. 2019)(relying on In re Walgreen Co. Sh. Litig., 832 F.3d 718 (7th Cir. 2016) required showing the disclosures provided by the suit's filing were "plainly material').

[361] 74 A.3d 612 (Del. 2013).

[362] In re Allergan, Inc., 2011 WL 1429626 (C.D. Cal. 2011).

[363] Louisiana Municipal Police Employees' Retirement System v. Pyott, 46 A.3d 313 (Del. Ch. 2012), judgment rev'd, 74 A.3d 612 (Del. 2013).

[364] Geis, Shareholder Derivative Litigation and the Preclusion Problem, 100 Va. L. Rev. 261 (2014) (he also recommends more vigorous application of statutory authority to assign costs for ill-conceived suits).

[365] Rosenbloom v. Pyott, 765 F.3d 1137 (9th Cir. 2014).

[366] California State Teachers' Retirement System v. Alvarez, 179 A3d 824 (Del. 2018).

complaints in both cases relied on facts set forth in the Times story. The Delaware proceeding was stayed after the Chancellor admonished its lawyers to "use the tools at hand"—this expression refers to the plaintiff using her rights as a shareholder under Delaware law to review the company's books and records with the goal of improving upon the bald allegations in the complaint. Otherwise the suit would not likely survive a motion to dismiss. Due to the fierce resistance of Wal-Mart to the inspection request nearly three years passed. During this period, the parallel suit in Arkansas was also stayed.[367] However, the Eighth Circuit Court of Appeals vacated the stay[368] and soon thereafter the Arkansas district court ultimately held that a pre-suit demand on the board of directors was necessary, had not been made, and dismissed the suit with prejudice.[369] Wal-Mart thereupon moved for dismissal of the Delaware proceeding, arguing the Delaware plaintiff was collaterally estopped by the Arkansas holding from relitigating demand futility. *Alvarez*[370] held that because the corporation is the real plaintiff in the derivative suit, privity thereby existed between the litigants in the two forums; the court further reasoned that Due Process is satisfied by the court scrutinizing the adequacy of representation in the Arkansas proceeding. Finding that counsel in that proceeding was adequate, the court held that Delaware plaintiff could not relitigate demand futility that had been resolved earlier by the federal court.

§ 15.15   The Corporation as a Passive Party in Derivative Suits; Defenses

The corporation for whose benefit a derivative suit is brought must be joined as a party defendant.[371] Not only is the corporation an indispensable party, but the suit will be dismissed if the corporation is not served with process as if it were an actual defendant or if it does not voluntarily appear by counsel.[372]

The corporation is commonly referred to as a "nominal" defendant.[373] In general, it is required to adopt a neutral or passive role, with only a limited power to defend itself while the shareholder plaintiff—its volunteer representative—conducts for the corporation's benefit the litigation that its management has failed or refused to bring. The corporation need not file an answer to the complaint or take any steps in the proceedings. It cannot assume the status of a co-plaintiff—the complaining shareholder has the right to control the litigation.[374] If the defendants are corporate directors and officers and control corporate funds, they may well be tempted to exercise their corporate powers to aid their defense. However, apart from reimbursements and advances under indemnification statutes and agreements, it is improper to use corporate funds to give

---

[367] In re Wal Mart Stores, Inc. Shareholders Der. Litig., 2012 U.S. Dist. LEXIS 165632 (Dist. Ark., Nov. 20, 2001)(the defendants moved for a stay so that Delaware could address whether demand could be excused).

[368] Cottrell v. Duke, 737 F.3d 1238 (8th Cir.2013)(holding the a stay was inappropriate because the suit in the federal Arkansas court included federal issues that were not justiciable in the Delaware state court).

[369] In re Wal Mart Stores, Inc. Shareholder Der. Litig., 2015 U.S. Dist. LEXIS 42058 (Dist. Ark., Mar. 31, 2015), aff'd, Cottrell v. Duke, 829 F.3d 983 (8th Cir. 2016).

[370] California State Teachers' Retirement System v. Alvarez, 179 A3d 824 (Del. 2018).

[371] *See* Kilburn v. Young, 536 S.E.2d 769 (Ga. Ct. App. 2000) (granting the plaintiff a reasonable time to join in the suit the absent corporation).

[372] *See, e.g.,* Ross v. Bernhard, 396 U.S. 531 (1970).

[373] *See, e.g.,* Miller v. American Tel. & Tel. Co., 394 F.Supp. 58 (E.D. Pa. 1975), aff'd mem., 530 F.2d 964 (3d Cir. 1976).

[374] Otis & Co. v. Pennsylvania R.R., 57 F.Supp. 680, 682 (E.D. Pa. 1944), aff'd, 155 F.2d 522 (3d Cir. 1946), citing Groel v. United Elec. Co. of N.J., 61 A. 1061, 1064–1065 (N.J. Ch. 1905).

financial aid or to assist in the defense of directors, officers, or other defendants in a derivative suit brought on the corporation's behalf.[375] The plaintiff shareholder is entitled to an opportunity to prosecute the suit without having the resources of the corporation turned against him.

How far the corporation may go in raising defenses to protect its own interests is not entirely settled. The corporation may appear specially to object to service of process or to lack of jurisdiction, and it may resist the appointment of a receiver.[376] Whether the corporate defendant may raise a particular defense depends on the nature of the defense and the interest that the defense is designed to protect.[377] The corporation is allowed to defend when its interests are brought into issue by the suit.[378] Potential defenses can be divided into three groups. First, there are conventional defenses that defeat the corporate right of recovery and are designed to protect the real defendants from liability. The corporation may not assert this type of defense in a derivative suit[379] unless it is a real defendant as to an issue in the litigation.[380] Second are conventional defenses such as laches and ratification. As these defenses are usually designed to protect the alleged wrongdoers, the corporate defendant as a general rule is not allowed to assert these defenses.[381] Third, there are certain defenses that are peculiar to a derivative suit, such as failure to make demand on the board of directors and the necessity for plaintiff to show contemporaneous ownership. These defenses are designed to protect the corporate interest and are therefore ordinarily available to the corporate defendant.

§ 15.16   The Role of Counsel in a Derivative Suit

The individual defendants in derivative litigation frequently seek representation by counsel who also represent the corporation.[382] Questions arise as to the ability of counsel to represent both the corporate and individual defendants. The corporation's true interest in a derivative suit is as a real party plaintiff. Thus where common counsel simultaneously represents in a derivative suit the alleged wrongdoers and the corporation, conflicts of interest may arise.[383] Disqualification of counsel will be ordered where sufficient conflict exists.[384] Courts have held, however, that no conflict exists where the charge is that directors have breached their duty of care in the discharge of their office; the courts reason that this is an attack on the corporation's decisions, and there is no substantial conflict in such a case.[385] Separate attorneys for individual

---

[375] Meyers v. Smith, 251 N.W. 20 (Minn. 1933).

[376] Otis & Co. v. Pennsylvania R.R., 57 F.Supp. 680, 682 (E.D. Pa. 1944), aff'd per curiam, 155 F.2d 522 (3d Cir. 1946).

[377] Foust v. Transamerica Corp., 391 F.Supp. 312 (N.D. Cal. 1975).

[378] See, e.g., Otis & Co. v. Pennsylvania R.R., 57 F.Supp. 680 (E.D. Pa. 1944), aff'd, 155 F.2d 522 (3d Cir. 1946).

[379] See, e.g., Kartub v. Optical Fashions, Inc., 158 F.Supp. 757 (S.D.N.Y. 1958).

[380] See Otis & Co. v. Pennsylvania R.R., 57 F.Supp. 680 (E.D. Pa. 1944), aff'd, 155 F.2d 522 (3d Cir. 1946).

[381] See Barrett v. Southern Conn. Gas Co., 374 A.2d 1051 (Conn. 1977).

[382] See Westinghouse Elec. Corp. v. Kerr-McGee Corp., 580 F.2d 1311 (7th Cir. 1978).

[383] See Murphy v. Washington Am. League Base Ball Club, Inc., 324 F.2d 394 (D.C. Cir. 1963); Cannon v. United States Acoustics, 398 F.Supp. 209 (N.D. Ill. 1975), aff'd in part, 532 F.2d 1118 (7th Cir. 1976).

[384] Messing v. F.D.I., Inc., 439 F.Supp. 776 (D.N.J. 1977).

[385] See, e.g., Bell Atlantic Corp. v. Bolger, 2 F.3d 1304 (3d Cir. 1993); Campellone v. Cragan, 910 So.2d 363 (Fl. Ct. App. 2005) (identifying exceptions as patently frivolous suit, suit alleging mismanagement as distinct from fraud, self dealing, or intentional misconduct, or where degree of corporate participation would be very low).

defendants and the corporations are generally desirable. Also, in the special litigation committee context, the courts customarily assess the committee's "good faith" by considering whether it was represented by counsel who was independent from the officers or directors who are the focus of the derivative suit; hence, counsel that has not historically represented the corporation (and hence developed rapport, and perhaps even economic dependence on the suit's defendants) is called for in such instances.[386]

§ 15.17 The Attorney-Client Privilege in Derivative Suits

Although a corporation, just as any other client, is entitled to the attorney-client privilege,[387] sensitive questions arise if the corporation attempts to assert the privilege in a derivative suit or other action that is initiated by one of its shareholders against the corporation or even its directors or officers.[388] In the leading case of *Garner v. Wolfinbarger*,[389] the court ruled that on a showing of "good cause" that the plaintiff in a derivative suit may discover relevant facts and documents that would otherwise be covered by the privilege.[390] The court commented:

> [I]t must be borne in mind that management does not manage for itself and that the beneficiaries of its actions are the shareholders. . . . Management judgment must stand on its merits, not behind an ironclad veil of secrecy which under the circumstances preserves it from being questioned by those for whom it is, at least in part, exercised.[391]

Among the "indicia" that the court stated bear on whether good cause exists are the following:

> the number of shareholders [requesting the information] and the percentage of stock they represent; the bona fides of the shareholders; the nature of the shareholders' claim and whether it is obviously colorable; the apparent necessity or desirability of the shareholders having the information and the availability of it from other sources; whether, if the shareholders' claim is of wrongful action by the corporation, it is of action criminal, or illegal but not criminal, or of doubtful legality; whether the communication is of advice concerning the litigation itself; the extent to which the communication is identified versus the extent to which the shareholders are blindly fishing; and the risk of revelation of trade secrets or other information in whose confidentiality the corporation has an interest for independent reasons.[392]

---

[386] *See, e.g.,* Einhorn v. Culea, 612 N.W.2d 78 (Wis. 2000).

[387] For a classic description of the attorney-client privilege, *see* United States v. United Shoe Mach. Corp., 89 F.Supp. 357, 358–359 (D. Mass. 1950).

There is, of course, always the predicate question of whether a particular communication is protected as the work-product of an attorney. The courts have many formulations for determining whether a document falls within the privilege. *See* Charles M. Yablon & Steven S. Sparling, United States v. Adlman: Protection for Corporate Work Product, 64 Brooklyn L. Rev. 627, 639–645 (1998).

[388] *See generally* Note, Attorney-Client Privilege for Corporate Clients: The Control Group Test, 84 Harv. L. Rev. 424, 425 (1970).

[389] Garner v. Wolfinbarger, 280 F.Supp. 1018 (N.D. Ala. 1968), *vacated and remanded,* 430 F.2d 1093 (5th Cir. 1970), *cert. denied,* 401 U.S. 974 (1971), *on remand,* 56 F.R.D. 499 (N.D. Ala. 1972).

[390] 430 F.2d at 1103–1104.

[391] 430 F.2d at 1104.

[392] 430 F.2d at 1104. *See also* Wal-Mart Stores, Inc. v. Ind. Elec. Workers Pension Trust Fd., 95 A.3d 1264 (Del. 2014)(responding to a records demand under Del. Gen. Corp. Law § 220, the Supreme Court for the

Garner's "need for information" criterion, where adopted, appears to embody no greater showing than the normal standards for relevance.[393]

The most important limitation on *Garner* is the minority view that *Garner* does not apply when the plaintiff seeks a recovery for themselves rather than on behalf of the corporation.[394] In contrast, the majority view is that the individual nature of the suit is but one of the factors to consider in determining whether good cause has been shown.[395] Some courts have extended *Garner*'s "flexible approach" to permit shareholders in a subsidiary company to discover documents prepared by lawyers for the parent company.[396] Finding *Garner*'s good-cause standard vague and unworkable, some courts have rejected its holding.[397] There is little doubt that as a consequence of *Garner* and its progeny, clients who are aware of *Garner*'s holding are likely to be much less forthcoming in their communications with the corporation's lawyers.[398] And, although *Garner* is invoked in cases involving the derivative suit plaintiff's discovery of documents, evidence, etc. produced by a special litigation committee, the essential guiding principle in addressing such a request is not *Garner* but the bases upon which the plaintiff can challenge the dismissal recommendation of a special litigation committee.[399]

At one time the question of whether the attorney-client privilege attached at all to a communication between a corporation's attorney and an employee or director of the corporation depended on whether the representative communicating with the attorney was within the corporation's "control group"—that is, whether the representative was sufficiently advanced in the corporate hierarchy to have relevant decision-making authority and whether the representative was acting within the scope of his employment.[400] The attorney-client privilege applies to some, but not all, the communications of the general counsel who also has several other corporate roles; the privilege applies to communications that were created solely in the person's capacity as counsel.[401] An alternative to the control group test is the "subject matter" test, which did not confine the attorney-client privilege to such a narrow a set of individuals as occurs under the control group test. Under the subject matter test, communications are within the attorney-client privilege if they are made at the direction of a supervisor and pertain to the subject matter for which the attorney's advice was sought.[402] The control group

---

first time adopted *Garner* doctrine to hold that plaintiff maintaining derivative suit can obtain documents "necessary and essential" to the investigation of wrongdoing).

[393] *See* Herbert E. Milstein, Attorney-Client Privilege and Work Product Doctrine Corporate Applications A–29 (B.N.A. Corporate Practice Series No. 22, 2d ed. 1994).

[394] *See* Weil v. Investment/Indicators, Research & Management, 647 F.2d 18 (9th Cir. 1981) (*Garner* does not apply to individual fraud action against corporation).

[395] *See* Fausek v. White, 965 F.2d 126 (6th Cir. 1992) (after fraudulently freezing minority stockholders out of corporation, controlling stockholder sued for misconduct during his control as well as for losses in connection with freezeout).

[396] *See* Cohen v. Uniroyal, Inc., 80 F.R.D. 480 (E.D. Pa. 1978).

[397] Shirvani v. Capital Inv. Corp., 112 F.R.D. 389 (D. Conn. 1986).

[398] *See* Leo Herzel, The Attorney-Client Privilege: A Pragmatic Approach, 6 Del. J. Corp. L. 443 (1981).

[399] *See* Carlton Investments v. TLC Beatrice Int'l Holdings, Inc., 1997 WL 38130 (Del. Ch. 1997) (deposing the committee's counsel denied).

[400] *See* Diversified Indus. v. Meredith, 572 F.2d 596 (8th Cir. 1978).

[401] *See* Grimes v. LLC International, Inc., 1999 WL 252381 (Del. Ch. 1999).

[402] *See, e.g.,* Harper & Row Publishers, Inc. v. Decker, 423 F.2d 487, 491–492 (7th Cir. 1970), *aff'd per curiam by an equally divided court,* 400 U.S. 348 (1971).

test has since been restricted if not totally rejected with respect to matters before the federal courts by the Supreme Court in *Upjohn Company v. United States.*[403]

In *Upjohn,* the Supreme Court reasoned:

> The control group test adopted by the court below thus frustrates the very purpose of the privilege by discouraging the communication of relevant information by employees of the client to attorneys seeking to render legal advice to the client corporation. . . .

> The narrow scope given the attorney-client privilege by the court below not only makes it difficult for corporate attorneys to formulate sound advice when their client is faced with a specific legal problem but also threatens to limit the valuable efforts of corporate counsel to ensure their client's compliance with the law. . . . The test adopted below is difficult to apply in practice. . . . [I]f the purpose of the attorney-client privilege is to be served, the attorney and client must be able to predict with some degree of certainty whether particular discussions will be protected. An uncertain privilege, or one which purports to be certain but results in widely varying applications by the courts, is little better than no privilege at all.[404]

Thus, after *Upjohn* the position of the communicating employee is not determinative of whether that communication is within the privilege. Questions related to control and the control group, however, should continue to be germane to the issue of whether the communicating employee was "at the direction" of a superior.[405] Thus a district manager's communication to in-house counsel was not within the privilege because there was no evidence that anyone in a supervisory capacity had directed the manager to speak with counsel.[406] Moreover, state courts are not bound by *Upjohn,* which decided the scope of section 501 of the Federal Rules of Evidence, and some states continue to prefer the control person test.[407]

§ 15.18 Award of Attorneys' Fees and Expenses of Suit

As a general proposition, unless there is express statutory authority, courts will not award attorneys' fees to either party to litigation, regardless of the litigation's outcome.[408] A well-recognized exception to this common law rule is the "common fund" or "substantial benefit" doctrine, by which a court may award attorneys' fees where litigation results in a substantial benefit to a number of persons in whose interest the suit was maintained.[409] Under this exception, a liberal allowance for counsel fees and expenses may be made to a successful plaintiff in a derivative action if the corporation and, derivatively, the other shareholders receive benefits from the suit.[410] The rationale

---

[403] Upjohn Co. v. United States, 449 U.S. 383 (1981).

[404] 449 U.S. at 392–393.

[405] *Upjohn* emphasizes at different points that the lower level employees were complying with the directions of their superiors and those superiors were seeking information for the purpose of obtaining legal advice. *See* 449 U.S. at 394.

[406] Independent Petrochem. Corp. v. Aetna Casualty & Sur. Co., 654 F.Supp. 1334 (D.D.C. 1986).

[407] *See* Consolidation Coal Co. v. Bucyrus-Erie Co., 432 N.E.2d 250 (Ill. 1982).

[408] *See, e.g.,* Alyeska Pipeline Serv. Co. v. Wilderness Socy., 421 U.S. 240 (1975); Schlensky v. Dorsey, 574 F.2d 131 (3d Cir. 1978).

[409] *See, e.g.,* Trustees v. Greenough, 105 U.S. 527 (1882); Barton v. Drummond Co., 636 F.2d 978 (5th Cir. 1981).

[410] *See, e.g.,* Mills v. Electric Auto-Lite Co., 396 U.S. 375 (1970).

underlying this doctrine is that the plaintiff's efforts have conferred a benefit on the corporation for which the corporation would otherwise have had to pay, and fairness requires that the plaintiff be reimbursed the necessary expenses of conferring that benefit.[411]

The earliest cases recognizing a right to reimbursement involved litigation that had produced or preserved a "common fund,"[412] but later decisions clearly indicated that a court could order a corporation to reimburse the derivative suit plaintiff's attorneys' fees and expenses of plaintiffs irrespective of whether an actual recovery had been attained in the corporation's favor as long as a "substantial benefit"[413] was conferred as a consequence of the suit.[414] Thus nonpecuniary corporate benefits,[415] such as the cancellation of a disadvantageous contract or transaction, have been held a sufficient basis for allowing counsel fees and expenses.[416]

The plaintiff in a derivative suit has been held entitled to an award of counsel fees where a settlement resulted in replacement of directors and officers.[417] Similarly, an award of counsel fees has been based on protection of the corporate name[418] or the obtaining of a restraining order preventing corporate mismanagement,[419] or the suit caused management to moderate its takeover defenses such that firm ultimately acquired and the stockholders received a handsome premium,[420] or improved disclosure.[421] In a most unusual case, the Delaware Supreme Court held there is no class action or derivative suit prerequisite to an award of attorneys' fees under the common benefit exception.[422] It therefore awarded a fee, even though the *individual* suit arising out of a misleading proxy solicitation was voluntarily dismissed because the corporation had taken action to correct the misrepresentations in its proxy statement. An award of attorneys' fees against a corporation was denied, however, where no corporate fund is established and no assets preserved, and the resulting benefit is to only one class of shareholders as opposed to the corporation;[423] fees were also denied when the purported benefit required the company to include in all vendor contracts an undertaking not to discriminate against vendors on the basis of race when there was no evidence it had so discriminated and the law forbid such discrimination.[424]

---

[411] *See, e.g.,* Bailey v. Meister Brau, Inc., 535 F.2d 982 (7th Cir. 1976).

[412] The common fund approach has been upheld even where the defendant and the plaintiff are the only two shareholders. *See* De Fontaine v. Passalino, 584 N.E.2d 933 (Ill. App. Ct. 1991).

[413] "Substantial benefit" has been defined in a leading case as: "[O]ne that accomplishes a result which corrects or prevents an abuse which would be prejudicial to the rights and interests of the corporation or affect the enjoyment of protection of an essential right to the shareholder's interest." Bosch v. Meeker Co-op. Light & Power Ass'n, 101 N.W.2d 423, 427 (Minn. 1960).

[414] *See, e.g.,* Mills v. Electric Auto-Lite Co., 396 U.S. 375 (1970).

[415] *But see* Rosenbaum v. MacAllister, 64 F.3d 1439 (10th Cir. 1995) (reducing attorneys' fees because, among other considerations, the nonpecuniary benefits were negligible).

[416] *See, e.g.,* Mencher v. Sachs, 164 A.2d 320 (Del. 1960).

[417] Granada Inv., Inc. v. DWG Corp., 961 F.2d 1577 (6th Cir. 1992).

[418] *See, e.g.,* Taussig v. Wellington Fund, Inc., 313 F.2d 472 (3d Cir.), *cert. denied,* 374 U.S. 806 (1963).

[419] *See, e.g.,* Modern Optics, Inc. v. Buck, 336 S.W.2d 857 (Tex. Civ. App. 1960).

[420] Crandon Capital Partners v. Shelk, 157 P.3d 176 (Or. 2007).

[421] Augenbaum v. Forman, 2006 WL 1716916 (Del. Ch. 2006).

[422] *See* Tandycrafts, Inc. v. Initio Partners, 562 A.2d 1162 (Del. 1989).

[423] *See, e.g.,* Missouri Pac. R.R. v. Slayton, 407 F.2d 1078 (8th Cir.), *cert. denied,* 395 U.S. 937 (1969).

[424] Kaplan v. Rand, 192 F.3d 60 (2d Cir. 1999).

§ 15.19 Indemnification and Insurance for Directors and Officers

When an officer or director is named as a defendant in a lawsuit charging misconduct in office, is he entitled to indemnification for expenses if the defense is successful? Further, may he be reimbursed for his costs even in the event that the plaintiff prevails? All states have indemnification statutes.[425] The former Model Business Corporation Act[426] as well as the current Model Business Corporation Act[427] have greatly influenced the overall structure and philosophy of state indemnification statutes. Approximately one-half the state indemnity provisions are substantially similar to the 1969 version of the former Model Business Corporation Act,[428] and all but a handful of the remaining states pattern their indemnification statutes after the current Model Business Corporation Act.[429] The major difference between the two model acts is that the current Model Business Corporation Act makes its provisions the exclusive means for indemnifying directors, empowers the court to approve indemnification in certain instances, precludes indemnification when the defendant receives an improper personal benefit, and requires notice to the shareholders when directors are indemnified.[430] Important variations exist among the states regardless of which particular initiative that state chose as the model for its own indemnification provision.

Both at common law and by statute, the indemnification rules that apply to derivative suits differ from those applicable to suits brought against officers, directors, or corporate agents (outsiders) by third parties.[431] It is well established agency law that, subject to illegality and in the absence of an agreement to the contrary, a principal is bound to indemnify his agent for "expenses of defending actions by third parties brought because of the agent's authorized conduct. . . ."[432]

An important threshold consideration is the breadth of corporate personnel covered by the state's corporate indemnity statute.[433] For example, the Delaware and New York statutes apply to the "director and officers,"[434] whereas a few states extend their statutes to others, such as employees, agents, or other representatives of the corporation.[435]

---

[425] See Model Bus. Corp. Act § 8.50 (2016) (hereinafter MBCA).

[426] See former MBCA § 5 (1969), which was patterned after the Delaware indemnification provisions, see Del. Code Ann. tit. 8, § 145 (2001).

[427] MBCA Ann. §§ 8.50 to 8.58 (2016). The MBCA reflects the changes made in the Model Business Corporation Act in 1980.

[428] MBCA Ann. § 8.50 note on statutory comparison (3d ed. 1994).

[429] MBCA Ann. § 8.50 note on statutory comparison (3d ed. 1994).

[430] See Changes in the Model Business Corporation Act Affecting Indemnification of Corporate Personnel, 34 Bus. Law. 1595 (1979).

[431] For the argument that legislatures, though proscribing suits "by or in the right of the corporation" do not intend to reach direct actions by the corporation against its officers and directors, see Diane H. Mazur, Indemnification of Directors in Actions Brought Directly by the Corporation: Must the Corporation Finance its Opponents Defense?, 19 J. Corp. L. 201, 205–216 (1994).

[432] Restatement (Second) of the Law of Agency § 439(d) (1958).

[433] See generally Who Is an "Executive Officer" of Insured Within Meaning of Liability Insurance Policy, 1 A.L.R. 5th (1992).

[434] Del. Code Ann. tit. 8, § 145(a), (b) (2009); N.Y. Bus. Corp. Law § 722(a), (b) (2009).

[435] See, e.g., Conn. Bus. Corp. Act § 33–777 (2009).

Most statutes provide for indemnification as a matter of right "to the extent" the director or officer is "successful" in his defense and, subject to varying standards and limitations, authorize permissive (that is, discretionary with a body such as the independent directors, independent counsel, or the court) indemnification in other cases. The "to the extent . . . successful" language thus overrules those common law decisions that followed the *New York Dock Company* decision denying the successful director indemnification. In determining whether there has been success, it is important whether the statute envisions a decision on the suit's merits or whether a prejudicial dismissal on procedural grounds entitles the corporate official to indemnification. The statute's inclusion of language such as "on the merits *or otherwise*"[436] obviously invites a broad construction of the meaning of "success." Indemnification as a matter of right may also arise by virtue of supplementary indemnification provisions in the employee's contract with the corporation or by virtue of the bylaws of the corporation that, as discussed below, are authorized in most states.[437]

In a leading case, *Merritt-Chapman & Scott Corp. v. Wolfson*,[438] the Delaware Supreme Court held that the directors were successful within the meaning of the Delaware indemnification statute for their expenses related to the criminal counts, which were dropped as a result of their plea bargaining, entered into after their convictions were reversed on appeal. The defendants pled guilty to a single count that was not dropped as a result of their plea bargain. To avoid requiring partial indemnification of the defendant's expenses under facts such as those of *Merritt-Chapman & Scott*, the current Model Business Corporation Act requires that the defendant have been "wholly successful."[439] A defendant is wholly successful "only if the entire proceeding is disposed of on a basis which involves a finding of nonliability."[440] Courts have also held that a dismissal because of the statute of limitations is deemed a successful defense.[441]

The policy choices within indemnity statutes become more numerous in the case of the unsuccessful corporate officer or director. It is at this point that the greatest variation in approaches and language appears among the state statutes. The former Model Business Corporation Act,[442] following the architecture of the Delaware statute,[443] treats separately indemnification arising from actions by or on behalf of the corporation and all other types of actions. The concern that drives treatment of actions that are by or on behalf of the corporation as separate from others is that of the circularity of otherwise allowing the director or officer to be reimbursed for a recovery that the derivative suit obtained on behalf of the corporation. To allow indemnification for actions by or on behalf of the corporation mocks the therapeutic purposes of the suit because it will be the corporation, not the real defendant, who will be the worse off as a consequence

---

[436] *See, e.g.*, Del. Code Ann. tit. 8, § 145(c) (2009).

[437] VonFeldt v. Stifel Financial Corp., 714 A.2d 79 (Del. 1998) (individual elected to serve on subsidiary corporation's board of directors is covered by provision of parent company's bylaws that extends indemnification as a matter of right to one who perform a function "at the request" of the parent).

[438] Merritt-Chapman & Scott Corp. v. Wolfson, 321 A.2d 138 (Del. Super. 1974).

[439] MBCA § 8.52 (2016).

[440] MBCA Ann. § 8.52 official comment (3d ed. 1994).

[441] *See* Dornan v. Humphrey, 106 N.Y.S.2d 142 (Sup. Ct. 1951), *modified on other grounds*, 112 N.Y.S.2d 585 (App. Div. 1952).

[442] *See* former MBCA § 5(a)(b) (1969).

[443] *See* Del. Code Ann. tit. 8, § 145(a), (b) (2001).

of the suit. The current Model Business Corporation Act takes a different path by barring indemnification in actions by or on behalf of the corporation where the request arises from any proceeding in which the director has received an improper personal benefit or in any proceeding by or on behalf of the corporation in which she has been adjudged liable.[444]

The former Model Business Corporation Act and the Delaware statute distinguish between actions by or on behalf of the corporation and all other actions in that indemnification is allowed for the former only for the defendant's reasonable expenses, but not for any resulting settlement or judgment.[445] Similarly, the current Model Business Corporation Act allows indemnification of the defendant's expenses but not for any amount paid as a fine, judgment, or settlement, provided a court orders such indemnification on a finding that he is "reasonably and fairly entitled to indemnification."[446]

The unsuccessful corporate director or officer is not entitled to indemnification as a matter of right; she must persuade a designated decision-maker to exercise her discretion to indemnify the director or officer. Statutes generally confine the decision-maker to a body of independent directors, independent counsel, or a court.[447] The route the statute lays out for the decision-maker, however, is not a two-way street. There appears in the statute no restraint on the decision-maker refusing to indemnify the unsuccessful director or officer. That is, the petitioner who seeks indemnification for her unsuccessful defense is not entitled to indemnification as a matter of right; the indemnification authorized by the statute for the unsuccessful defendant is permissive.

Moreover, the decision-maker cannot indemnify the unsuccessful defendant unless satisfied that the defendant's conduct meets the standards set forth in the statute. Indemnification provided without meeting the standards is improper, and the amounts can be recovered by the corporation.[448] The most frequent standards to be satisfied are that the defendant acted in good faith and in a manner he reasonably believed to be or not opposed to the best interests of the corporation.[449] The New York Court of Appeals interpreted good faith to require that the officer or director acted for a purpose she reasonably believed to be in the best interests of the corporation.[450] The standard was not met by an officer who engaged in racial discrimination.[451] Good faith can also be interpreted more broadly to be violated by an intentional violation of the law. Thus, in an interesting bribery case, this standard for indemnification was not satisfied, even

---

[444] MBCA § 8.51(d)(2) (2016).

[445] *See* Del. Code Ann. tit. 8, § 145(b) (2001); former MBCA § 5(b) (1969).

[446] MBCA § 8.54(a)(3) (2016). *But see* N.C. Gen. Stat. Ann. § 55–8–57 (2009) (authorizing more expansive indemnification by optional provisions in articles or bylaws or otherwise by agreement).

[447] Del. Code Ann. tit. 8, § 145(d) (2001); MBCA §§ 8.54 & 8.55 (2016); former MBCA § 5(b), (d) (1969).
On the meaning of independent counsel, *see* Schmidt v. Magnetic Head Corp., 468 N.Y.S.2d 649 (App. Div. 1983) (attorney retained by a law firm that customarily performed legal work for corporation deemed independent because of no past relationship with company or its directors).

[448] *See* Behrstock v. Ace Hose & Rubber Co., 496 N.E.2d 1024 (1986).

[449] *See, e.g.,* Cal. Corp. Code § 317(b) (2009); Del. Code Ann. tit. 8, § 145(a), (b) (2001); N.Y. Bus. Corp. Law § 722(a), (c) (2009); MBCA § 8.51(a)(1) (2016); former MBCA § 5(a), (b) (1969).

[450] *See, e.g.,* Biondi v. Beekman Hill House Apartment Corp., 731 N.E.2d 577, 581 (N.Y. 2000) (key to indemnification is director's good faith toward corporation, and mere judgment against director is not dispositive of this issue; in this case, however, director's willful racial discrimination was not in corporation's best interest).

[451] Biondi v. Beekman Hill House Apartment Corp., 731 N.E.2d 577, 581 (N.Y. 2000).

though the bribe was made to advance what the defendant genuinely believed was his employer's interest, because the defendant was believed not to have acted in good faith because he consciously violated the law.[452] And, steps taken by executives to prevent federal regulators from exercising control over the company, even though undertaken for what the executives believed furthered the interests of the company, were nonetheless deemed in bad faith because they sought to undermine the government's regulatory authority.[453] Under statutes that condition reimbursement on whether the executive was "adjudged liable" one court applying this standard upheld indemnification, even though the jury found that the officer had breached his fiduciary duty; since the breach produced no damages the court held that the officer had not been adjudged liable.[454]

When the defendant in an earlier proceeding was found to have breached a fiduciary duty to the corporation and now seeks indemnification, generally the court is the sole decision-maker applying these standards,[455] and the court is under the additional obligation to find that the defendant is "fairly and reasonably entitled to indemnification."[456] Thus, in a decision that makes good sense but no doubt is not politically correct, the court found indemnification of directors was in order where the defendant directors of an all-male club sought indemnification for their continued defense of what they believed the desirable policy for the club.[457] An additional standard is applicable when the defendant seeks indemnification after an unsuccessful defense in a criminal proceeding; the decision-maker must also determine that the defendant "had no reasonable cause to believe his conduct was unlawful."[458]

Most indemnification statutes authorize the corporation to advance expenses to its officers or directors. Advances are especially important when any applicable insurance coverage does not include litigation expenses or, if such coverage exists, the policy has a fairly large deductible before the insurance carrier becomes obligated to assume the defense costs. Even though corporation's power to advance expenses is not unrestrained by the statute, the propriety of making such advances should not depend on the merits of the claim against the officer or director but rather the nature of the underlying claim.[459] For example, the Model Business Corporation Act conditions an advance on "the director delivers to the corporation a signed written undertaking of the director to repay any funds advanced if (i) the director is not entitled to mandatory indemnification . . . and (ii) it is ultimately determined . . . that the director is not entitled to indemnification."[460]

---

[452] *See* Associated Milk Producers, Inc. v. Parr, 528 F.Supp. 7, 8 (E.D. Ark. 1979).

[453] *See* In re Landmark Land Co. of Carolina, Inc., 76 F.3d 553 (4th Cir. 1996); Pilpiak v. Keyes, 729 N.Y.S.2d 99 (App. Div. 2001) (violates public policy to indemnify executive expenses incurred in unsuccessful defense of grand larceny).

[454] *See* Waskel v. Guaranty Nat'l Corp., 23 P.3d 1214 (Colo. App. Ct. 2000).

[455] *See* MBCA §§ 8.51(d)(1), 8.54(a)(2) (2016).

[456] *See, e.g.,* Cal. Corp. Code § 317(c)(1) (2009); Del. Code Ann. tit. 8, § 145(b) (2001); N.Y. Bus. Corp. Law § 722(c) (2009).

[457] *See* Cross v. Midtown Club, Inc., 365 A.2d 1227 (Conn. Super. Ct. 1976).

[458] *See, e.g.,* Cal. Corp. Code § 317(b) (2009) ("had no reasonable cause to believe the conduct of the person was unlawful"); Del. Code Ann. tit. 8, § 145(a) (2001); N.Y. Bus. Corp. Law § 722(a) (2009); MBCA § 8.51(a)(3) (2008); former MBCA § 5(a) (1969).

[459] *See* Ridder v. Cityfed Financial Corp., 47 F.3d 85, 87 (3d Cir. 1995) (interpreting Delaware law).

[460] MBCA § 8.53(a) (2016).

A key policy issue for any legislative body is whether the state indemnity statute should be exclusive. It is over this question that the greatest variation appears among the states. The strong current follows the position of Delaware, whose statute provides:

> The indemnification and advance of expenses provided by, or granted pursuant to, the other subsections of this section shall not be deemed exclusive of any other rights to which those seeking indemnification or advancement of expenses may be entitled under any bylaw, agreement, vote of the stockholders or, disinterested directors or otherwise, both as to action in his official capacity and as to action in another capacity while holding such office.[461]

One court has held that the corporation does not have carte blanche authority in drafting such an extra-statutory indemnification. In *Waltuch v. Conticommodity Services,*[462] the court held that the above quoted provision of the Delaware statute could not authorize indemnification in instances that violate the substantive standards, *e.g.*, "good faith" set forth in the statutory provision circumscribing the corporation's power to indemnify unsuccessful directors and officers. Therefore, the above non-exclusive provision did not permit indemnification of an officer who knowingly violated the law, even though such was called for by his private contract with the corporation. This leaves the above quoted provision authorizing deviations from non-substantive statutory provisions, such as who the decision maker can be and, for example, requiring advances of expenses for which there is no substantive standard.[463]

An analogous concern arises when a broad right to indemnification provided by a contract, bylaw or articles of incorporation in the particular case will conflict with the policy of a state or federal statute if indemnification is made. *Cohen v. Fry*[464] denied indemnification of an executive for liability arising under the clawback provision in the Sarbanes-Oxley act; under the provision executive bonuses can be recovered if the company makes an accounting period covering the period in which the bonus was calculated without the need to establish the executive was responsible for matters leading up to the restatement. The Second Circuit held allowing indemnification of the executive was inconsistent with Congress's intent in providing a broad clawback remedy.

Mandatory indemnification for successful executives provided by statute is not to be reduced by technical requirements found in supplementary bylaw or contractual indemnification arrangements.[465] Some states permit additional indemnification arrangements, provided they are authorized in the articles of incorporation or bylaws.[466] Many other state indemnity statutes expressly state that their provisions are exclusive.[467]

---

[461] Del. Code Ann. tit. 8, § 145(f) (2001).

[462] Waltuch v. Conticommodity Services, 88 F.3d 87 (2d Cir. 1996).

[463] *See* Owens Corning v. National Union Fire Ins. Co., 257 F.3d 484 (6th Cir. 2001) (recognizing authority under above quoted Delaware provision to set forth a presumption of good faith action).

[464] Cohen v. Fry, 622 F.3d 188 (2d Cir. 2010).

[465] *See* Chamison v. HealthTrust, Inc.—The Hospital Co, 735 A.2d 912 (Del. Ch. 1999) (indemnification ordered even though officer had not complied with provision of indemnity contract that required officer to be represented by counsel approved by corporation).

[466] *See, e.g.,* Cal. Corp. Code § 317(g) (2009) (authorized in articles of incorporation); N.Y. Bus. Corp. Law § 721 (2009) (authorized either in articles of incorporation or bylaws).

[467] *See, e.g.,* N.Y. Bus. Corp. Law § 721 (McKinney 1986). *See also* MBCA §§ 8.56(3), 8.58 (2016) (exclusive as to directors but not as to officers).

With the virtual universal acceptance by courts and legislature of at least a limited right to indemnification, the next legal development was liability insurance for corporate officers and directors. The typical directors' and officers' (D & O) policy has two distinct parts.[468] The first part provides coverage to reimburse the corporation for its costs in indemnifying its directors and officers. The second part extends coverage directly to the individual officer or director for which indemnification from the corporation is not available or forthcoming.[469] The latter is sometimes referred to as "Side A" or "last resort" coverage; it comes into effect only when the corporation cannot or will not indemnify the officer or director. Such a denial of indemnification is most frequently the result of a change of control. The standard D & O policy rarely requires the insurer to defend the officer or director[470] and operates on a claims-made basis—that is, the policy covers only those actions brought during the period of the policy.[471] The policy may obligate the insurer to advance sums for the insured's defense.[472] However, if the policyholder gives proper notice to the insurer of a transaction or event that could give rise to a claim at some future date, the claim if made will be covered by the policy even if outside the stated policy period. A 5 percent deductible is not uncommon among policies, and the policies generally exclude from their coverage fines and penalties arising from criminal actions as well as reimbursements for liability arising in civil actions for dishonesty or where the officer or director has personally gained as a consequence of her breach.[473] The standard policy covers non-intentional violations and customarily has many other exclusions, most of which are items likely to be covered by a different type of corporate policy, such as its general liability policy (for the D & O exclusions for libel, slander, environmental liabilities, and other forms of property damage).[474] The key provisions of the policy's coverage are its definition of "wrongful act" and its numerous exclusions. It is standard for the policy to prohibit covered executives from incurring defense costs without the consent of the insurer.

The Model Act empowers a corporation to purchase insurance for any director, officer, employee, or agent for any liability arising out of their corporate capacity "whether or not the corporation would have the power to indemnify or advance expenses

---

[468] Insurance carriers also offer "entity" policies, especially for securities related matters, which provide insurance to the company even though the suit does not name any director or officer. When through the entity coverage the corporation becomes the insured under the D & O coverage, and the corporation enters bankruptcy when claims are to be dispersed from the policy, an issue can arise regarding what portion of the policy belongs to the bankruptcy estate. *See generally* Joseph M. McLaughlin, D & O Insurance Policies in Bankruptcy, 228 N.Y.L.J. 5 (2002).

[469] On the scope of standard D & O policies, *see* J. Olson & J. Hatch, Director and Officer Liability: Indemnification and Insurance § 10.05, at 10–11 (1991).

[470] Courts are fairly consistent in holding that the D & O carrier must pay the attorneys' bill in a timely fashion. *See, e.g.,* Okada v. MGIC Indem. Corp., 823 F.2d 276 (9th Cir. 1986).

[471] *See, e.g.,* Foster v. Summit Medical Systems, Inc., 610 N.W.2d 350 (Minn. Ct. App. 2000) (reasoning that misconduct arose in the preparation of disclosure documents, not the offering of the security itself, court upheld denial of coverage for securities class action claims arising from public offering of securities where policy period commenced on date offering to public commenced).

[472] *See* Commercial Capital Bankcorp., Inc. v. St. Paul Mercury Ins. Co., 419 F.Supp.2d 1173 (C.D. Cal. 2006) (in a duty to defend form of coverage insurer must advance sums necessary for defense even though some of the underlying claims involved intentional misconduct and excluded from coverage; whereas in a D & O policy the allocation agreed upon by insurer and the insured applies).

[473] *See* International Ins. Co. v. Johns, 874 F.2d 1447 (11th Cir. 1989) (settlement returning to corporation amounts received as "golden parachutes" not within exclusion for "personal gains" where court concludes golden parachute arrangement was protected by business judgment rule).

[474] *See, e.g.,* Cincinnati Ins. Co. v. Irwin Co., 2000 WL 1867297 (Ohio Ct. App. 2000) (upholding denial of claim by officers who engaged in inside trading).

to him against the same liability. . . ."[475] Some states, such as New York,[476] place statutory limits on the type of insurance that corporations may provide directors and officers, and, despite the broad language of the Model Act, decisions such as *Waltuch* remind us that liability insurance for gross misconduct may be void as against public policy.[477] This however is largely a theoretical proposition because, as discussed below, insurers exclude from their coverage intentional conduct of the type that poses such public policy considerations.

§ 15.20   Private Ordering and Shareholder Suits

In a highly significant decision, the Delaware Chancery Court held in *Boilermakers Local 154 Ret. Fd. v. Chevron*[478] that the board could, without the concurrence of the shareholders, adopt bylaw provisions that permitted the corporation to choose the forum in which a shareholder-initiated suit would be maintained. Subsequently, in *ATP Tour, Inc. v. Deutscher Tennis Bund*,[479] the Delaware Supreme Court, relying on the reasoning in *Boilermakers*, upheld a board adopted bylaw that abandoned the long-maintained American Rule (whereby litigants bear their own litigation costs) to instead assign the suit's defendant's expenses (which in a derivative suit would include the corporation's costs) to the plaintiff except if the suit proved successful. *Boilermakers* and *ATP Tour, Inc.* each reasoned from the perspective that the shareholders' relationship with the corporation, and in turn their relationship to the board of directors, are contractual so that much of the shareholders' rights can be understood to flow from certain organic documents, and most significantly and pervasively from the company's bylaws. For example, with Delaware corporations the board enjoys the power to amend the bylaws only if granted that authority in the articles of incorporation.[480] With that grant of authority to the board being present in both *Boilermakers* and *ATP Tour, Inc.*, it was a short step for each court to conclude that the board's action was pursuant to the contract shareholders had with their corporation and that the power of the board to amend the bylaws carried with it the power to amend the shareholders' rights.[481] Repeatedly the analysis used by each court referenced the contractual relationship the shareholders had

---

[475] *See* MBCA § 8.57 (2008). *See also* Cal. Corp. Code § 317(i) (2009) (with extensive provisions dealing with propriety of such insurance carrier being affiliated with the corporation); Del. Code Ann. tit. 8, § 145(g) (2001); former MBCA § 5(g) (1969).

[476] *See* N.Y. Bus. Corp. Law § 726(b) (2009).

[477] *See* Vigilant Ins. Co. v. Credit Suisse First Boston Corp., 800 N.Y.S.2d 358 (Supt. Ct. 2003) (denying on public policy grounds claim for sums investment bank was required to disgorge pursuant to an enforcement action by various securities regulators).

[478] 73 A.3d 934 (Del.Ch. 2013). *See generally* Joseph A.Grundfest, The History And Evolution Of Intra-Corporate Forum Selection Clauses: An Empirical Analysis, 37 Del. J. Corp. L. 333 (2012) (tracing development and pattern of early forum selection bylaws).

[479] 91 A.3d 554 (Del. 2014).

[480] Del. Gen. Corp. Law § 109(a). *See also* N.Y.Bus. Corp. Act § 601(a) (charter or bylaws can authorize board to adopt, amend or repeal bylaws). In contrast, most states follow the pattern of the Model Business Corporation Act and grant both the board of directors and the shareholders co-extensive authority to adopt and amend the bylaws, subject to the articles of incorporation restricting the board's authority. MBCA § 10.20(b)(1)(2016). *See also,* Cal. Corp. Code § 211 (shareholders and board empowered to adopt, amend and repeal bylaws).

[481] For an incisive analysis of why consent cannot be found by the shareholders' grant of authority to the board to amend the bylaws, *see* Deborah A. DeMott, Forum-Selection Bylaws Refracted Through an Agency Lens, 57 Ariz. L. Rev. 269 (2015) (a provision in the articles of incorporation authorizing the board to amend the bylaws is too attenuated to constitute consent in part because "nothing in the DGCL or any other Delaware statute explicitly alerts investors to the downstream prospect that limitations may subsequently be imposed" on the shareholders by the board of directors).

through the articles of incorporation and the bylaws with their corporation;[482] hence, the courts believed that contractual relationship was subject to modification through the mechanism provided by the web of the articles of incorporation's authorization for the board to amend the bylaws. With the courts' focus on the contractual basis for their reasoning, the opinions avoid the more ticklish question of whether there are areas of the corporate statute that are beyond the power of the board of directors, acting unilaterally, to change. The corporation-as-contract theory supports other board-adopted bylaw initiatives such as requiring shareholder suits to be subject to binding arbitration.[483]

The preoccupation with the contractual focus demonstrated in *Boilermakers* and *ATP Tour, Inc.* can be attributed to the impact of the contractarian orientation widely espoused among corporate commentators.[484] This perspective is commonly captured in the metaphor that the corporation is but a 'nexus of contracts'. The vision builds on Coase's perspective on why firms exist (the view holds that labor, suppliers, customers, investors, and managers arrange their activities to their optimal benefit), scholars embraced private ordering as the desired norm within corporate law. In a world of private ordering, the state corporate statute is understood to have the limited role of providing default rules in those instances where the parties have not otherwise specified how their affairs or activities are to occur. Corporate participants may well not so specify where contracting around the default rule would be more costly than the perceived ex ante burdens of the default rule. In any case, the default rule is tailored toward what the legislature believes most, but not all, people would have agreed to if contracting were

---

[482] Delaware's invocation of contract principles is illustrated by the following:

[T]he board itself may act unilaterally to adopt bylaws . . . Such a change by the board is not extra-contractual simply because the board acts unilaterally; rather it is the kind of change that the overarching statutory and *contractual* regime the stockholders buy into explicitly allows the board to make on its own. In other words, the . . . stockholders have assented to a contractual framework established by the DGCL and the certificate of incorporation [authorizing the board to adopt bylaws] that explicitly recognizes that stockholders will be bound by bylaws adopted unilaterally by their board." (emphasis added). Boilermakers Local 154 Ret. Fd. v. Chevron 73 A.3d 934, 956 (Del.Ch. 2013).

Because corporate bylaws are "contracts among the corporation's shareholders," a fee shifting provision in a . . . validly enacted bylaw would . . . not be prohibited under Delaware common law." ATP Tour, Inc. v. Deutscher Tennis Bund, 91 A.3d 554, 558 (Del. 2014) (quoting Airgas, Inc. v. Air Products and Chemicals, Inc., 8 A.3d 1182, 1188 (Del. 2010) ("Corporate charters and bylaws are contracts among a corporation's shareholders; therefore, our rules of contract interpretation apply."

Boilermakers also relies on the same broad, undeveloped, state in *Airgas, Inc* as well as a much earlier and less convincing decision, Lawson v. Household Finance Corp., 152 A. 723, 728 (Del. Ch. 1930), upholding the imposition of a right-of-first-refusal transfer restriction set forth in the bylaws where the corporate statute expressly authorized bylaws to restrict shares and the shareholder acquired the shares with full notice of such restriction. Thus, the substantive authority for the bylaw restricting transfer was expressly provided by state statute so that neither *Lawson's* facts nor its reasoning lend themselves to other than a substantive interpretation of a state statute.

[483] On the topic of arbitration bylaws, *see* Claudia H. Allen, Bylaws Mandating Arbitration of Stockholder Disputes, 39 Del. J. Corp. L. 751 (2015).

[484] While the corporation-as-contract banner was carried by many, Frank Easterbrook and Daniel Fischel as well as the celebrated article by Professors Jensen and Meckling provided the intellectual foundation on which others built their multiple contributions. *See* Frank Easterbrook & Daniel Fischel, Voting in Corporate Law, 26 J. L. & Econ. 395 (1983); Frank Easterbrook & Daniel Fischel, Close Corporations and Agency Costs, 38 Stan. L. Rev. 271 (1986); Frank Easterbrook & Daniel Fischel, Corporate Control Transactions, 91 Yale L. J. 698 (1983); and Michael C. Jensen & Wm. H. Meckling, Theory of the Firm: Managerial Behavior, Agency Costs and Ownership Structure, 3 J. Fin. Econ. 305 (1976). For an insightful analysis of the nuance that separates the early scholars whose collective work propelled the contractarian view behind the nexus of contracts metaphor, *see* William Bratton, Nexus of Contracts Corporation: A Critical Appraisal, 74 Cornell L. Rev. 407 (1989).

efficient.[485] Within the nexus of contracts metaphor, forum selection, fee shifting, and even mandated arbitration are just some areas, among many others, that parties can best provide through their negotiations and agreement. Broadly stated, to nexus of contracts adherents, corporate law as provided by the state is merely facilitative of private bargaining; and under this view, corporate law is not public, but private law. In such a realm, the only issue in doubt is what constitutes consent among the affected parties;[486] after all, it is bargaining leading to consent that Coase and contract theory so heavily depend upon as the basis for the efficiency that lies at its end. Even here, the champions of the nexus of contracts approach salve any unease about there being meaningful consent by their obeisance to the efficient pricing of outcomes being reflected in the price of a firm's securities. Thus, owners and others, for example creditors, who believe the 'bargain' may be tilted against them, can overcome any anticipated disadvantage by discounting charges based on the expected costs of any resulting unfairness or harmful contractual provision. Thus, any advantage gained by one party in bargaining can be expected to give rise to counterparty discounting, *e.g.*, paying less for the shares or charging more for the money, goods, or services exchanged.

Consent would appear to be a central concern, if not an overriding requirement, in any contractually-based argument. The *Boilermakers'* orientation finds consent somewhat through the back door. *Boilermakers* and *ATP Tour, Inc.* stand for the broad proposition that boards can act unilaterally to amend the bylaws so as to alter the basic rights of shareholders. Such unilateral action may be argued to entail implicit consent, not by the ongoing reserved powers of the board to amend the bylaws, but rather through the failure of the shareholders to reverse the board's action, by repealing the bylaw earlier adopted by the board. Finding consent, or more likely acquiescence, by the lack of repeal or modification, may not accord sufficient attention to the difficulty of shareholder action. First, there is the ever-present collective action problem of shareholders in public companies. Second, for many public companies shareholder amendments to the bylaws require a greater than majority vote.[487] Furthermore, supervoting shares and multi-classes of shares further weaken the voice of the residual claimants when such distinctions accord a group disproportionate voting rights. Thus, silence on the part of the shareholders may not always be equated to their consent.

Board adopted bylaws that infringe on the shareholders' franchise are vulnerable in the courts. *Blasius Industries, Inc. v. Atlas Corp.*[488] bears significantly on the disconnection between the nexus of contract paradigm and the corporation and shines a light on a core feature of corporate law—the division of authority between the board and

---

[485] Lucian A. Bebchuk, Limiting Contractual Freedom in Corporate Law: The Desirable Constraints on Charter Amendments, 102 Harv. L. Rev. 1820, 1847 (1989) observes that departure from the statutory norm is most likely with respect to rules addressing problems whose 'resolution varies significantly from company to company and when the desirable solution depends on particular features of each company that are better known to the parties than to public officials'.

[486] *See, e.g.,* Deborah A.DeMott, Forum Selection Bylaws Refracted Through the Agency Lens, 57 Ariz. L. Rev. 269 (2015) (authority in charter or statute by which board of directors can be authorized to amend the bylaws is too attenuated for shareholders to envision that such authority would be exercised by the board to limit shareholder rights); Lawrence A. Hamermesh, Consent in Corporate Law, 70 Bus. Law. 161 (2014–15) (arguing that consent is also a necessary component of governance).

[487] One study found that 39.1 percent of Russell 3000 firms mandate a supermajority vote for shareholder initiated bylaw changes Young, Beth. 2009. The Limits of Private Ordering: Restrictions on Shareholders' Ability to Initiate Governance Change and Distortions of the Shareholder Voting Process, Council of Institutional Investors, Working Paper.

[488] 564 A.2d 651 (Del. Ch. 1988).

the shareholders. Upon learning that a substantial blockholder was soliciting shareholders for their consent that would expand the board from 7 to 15 and thereupon appoint 8 nominees to Atlas's board who would support a proposed restructuring of Atlas, the Atlas board moved swiftly to thwart a potential shift in control. The Atlas board filled two of the board seats so that Blasius Industries could not quickly wrest control of Atlas.[489] Chancellor Allen, even though holding that the Atlas board acted in good faith in defending control,[490] nonetheless held the board's actions were beyond the protection of the business judgment rule. He reached this conclusion by observing that the board's actions were not solely steps taken to manage the company but instead were acts that impacted the relationship between principal and agent "with respect to a matter of internal corporate governance."[491] To so act, he believed the board needed to make a stronger case than merely that it acted in good faith when its decision thwarts the shareholders' franchise; he therefore required the board to establish a compelling justification for interdicting the shareholder franchise to elect or nominate directors. Significantly, the justification advanced by the board is not a purpose narrowly focused on whether the *corporate interest* is advanced by management's unilateral interdiction; the compelling justification that is required must be anchored by how, under the circumstances, the board's action furthers the shareholders' franchise. Chancellor Allen reasoned:

> A board's decision to act to prevent the shareholders from creating a majority of new board positions and filling them does not involve the exercise of *the corporation's power* over its property, or with respect to *its* rights or obligations; rather, it involves allocation, between shareholders as a class and the board, of effective power with respect to governance of the corporation. . . . Action designed principally to interfere with the effectiveness of a vote inevitably involves a conflict between the board and a shareholder majority. Judicial review of such action involves a determination of the legal and equitable obligations of an agent towards his principal. This is not, in my opinion, a question that a court may leave to the agent finally to decide so long as he does so honestly and competently; that is, it may not be left to the agent's business judgment.[492]

To be noted as well is that *Blasius'* protection of shareholder franchise arises even though the board is acting in a way that is the exercise of corporate powers; a corporate purpose existed in *Blasius*—to continue the on-going business plan—but a legitimate corporate purpose was not by itself sufficient to justify the board's actions that had the correlative effect of impacting the franchise of shareholders. This observation flows from Chancellor Allen holding the board acted consistent with its obligations for defending the corporation from a threatened change in the board's on-going business policy.

Blasius adheres to the wise advice that "agents whose interests may materially diverge from the interests of their principals should not have the power to unilaterally

---

[489] Because the Atlas Board was classified, with directors serving staggered three-year terms, the consequence of filling two seats was that it would require two annual meetings for Blasius to have any chance to wrest a majority of the board seats.

[490] *Id.* at 658–63.

[491] *Id.* at 659.

[492] *Id.* at 660.

determine or materially vary the rules that govern those divergencies of interests."[493] That is, in the principal-agent realm, the relationship, and the methods for selecting and controlling the agent, are defined by the principal, not by the agent. To this end, and as *Blasius* illustrates, managerial actions that impact the owners' ability to pursue the limited powers owners have to discipline managers—sell, suffrage or sue—are not just of a different order of magnitude; they are within an entirely different sphere of corporate law, that of governance. Because they are not within the board's managerial sphere they are to be judged by a very different standard than applies to questions of management's stewardship of the firm's business.

There is an even stronger and broader message behind *Blasius*: there needs to be recognized among corporate law certain mandatory prophylactic rules whose existence and enforcement is understood as necessary to prevent opportunistic insider behavior And, this bundle of rules is beyond private ordering except pursuant to the most scrupulous attention to consent being granted. As in *Blasius*, escape from such rules' protections or requirements must be jealously protected, perhaps by the "compelling justification" standard invoked by Chancellor Allen.[494] Minimally, there should be a strong presumption that the rules establish a sacred space for shareholders that can rarely be entered by the board.

Sciabacucchi v. Salzberg illustrates one limit on "private ordering" through the bylaws. The case held that an arbitration bylaw can only address matters internal to the corporation and hence could not apply to investor suits under the securities laws.[495] The bylaw adopted by the board reached a wide range of litigation by shareholders, including suits under the federal securities laws which provide for suits in courts. The effect of the opinion is to limit bylaw provisions to matters rooted in the *internal* affairs and operations of the corporation.

---

[493] Lucian A. Bebchuk, The Myth of the Shareholder Franchise, 93 Va. L. Rev. 675, 709–710 (2007) ("[I]t is necessary to constrain board adopted bylaws that opt out of the provided default arrangement to make it more difficult to replace incumbent directors."). Professor Bebchuk suggests a change in such a default rule be conditioned on the bylaw being approved by the shareholders. He offers as support that the Delaware legislature has set the model for this approach by permitting the bylaws adopted after shares have been issued to classify the board only if the bylaw has been approved by the shareholders. *See* Del. Gen. Corp. Law § 141(d). A higher level of approval is also required to provide directors immunity to damages where such a shield must appear in the articles of incorporation, Del. Gen. Corp. Law § 102(b)(7), so that if adopted after shares have been issued requires amendment with the approval of the stockholders.

[494] Unfortunately, the Delaware courts have cabined *Blasius* to the shareholders' right to vote. Moreover, the Delaware Supreme Court has weakened the opinion by laments about its demanding standard. *See* Williams v. Geier, 671 A.2d 1368, 1376 (Del. 1996) ("*Blasius'* burdens of demonstrating 'compelling justification" is quite onerous and . . . therefore [should be] applied rarely"). The Delaware courts appear oblivious to considering whether it is especially appropriate to demand that the board explain conduct thwarting shareholder action when, as in *Blasius*, the circumstances supported the conclusion the board could have sought the approval for its actions from the shareholders.

[495] 2018 WL 6719718 (Del.Ch. Dec. 19, 2018).

Chapter 16

ISSUANCE OF SHARES

Table of Sections

PART A.   SHARE SUBSCRIPTIONS AND UNDERWRITING

§ 16.1 Nature and Form of Subscription Agreements

One may become a shareholder either by (1) subscription contract with the corporation for the issue of new shares; (2) purchase from the corporation of treasury shares—that is, shares already issued and reacquired by the corporation; or (3) transfer from an existing holder of outstanding shares, with the new owner being substituted in the place of the transferor.[1] Share subscribers are persons who have agreed to take and pay for the original unissued shares of a corporation, formed or to be formed.[2] A subscription differs from a contract of sale, a subscription being a contract for the corporation to issue or create new shares, as contrasted with an agreement by a stockholder for the transfer of title to issued shares or shares to be issued.[3]

---

[1]   Corporate capital structure and the various types of ownership interests are discussed in Chapter 18.

[2]   *See, e.g.,* Ashley v. Coleman, 219 So.2d 574 (La. Ct. App. 1969).

[3]   *See* Zukowski v. Dunton, 650 F.2d 30 (4th Cir. 1981).

Unless the corporate statute or charter requires otherwise, a subscription can be oral or written, as long as it is sufficiently definite to satisfy the requirements for a valid contract. This minimally requires evidence of an agreement to purchase a given number of shares in the corporation at a specified price.[4] The states are split as to whether a subscription for stock must be in writing and signed by the subscriber to be enforceable. Approximately one half of the states follow the scheme of the current Model Business Corporation Act or its predecessor by not requiring that the subscription be in writing to be enforceable.[5] Even in jurisdictions that do require a written contract, the subscriber's conduct may estop him from raising the absence of a written agreement as a defense.[6] And in one case, the court interpreted the statute's requirement of a written agreement as affording a defense only to the subscriber; the corporation could have had an unwritten agreement enforced against it by the subscriber.[7] However, courts frequently have held a subscription for stock subject to the statute of frauds, like an agreement for the sale of goods, wares, merchandise, or choses in action.[8]

§ 16.2   Pre-Incorporation Subscriptions—Revocability

The subscriber's power to revoke a stock subscription today is circumscribed by state corporation statutes, which generally render pre-incorporation subscriptions irrevocable for a certain period of time, most frequently six months, unless otherwise agreed or unless all other subscribers agree to the release.[9] In the absence of a statute, courts have sometimes found it difficult to determine the legal principles applicable to pre-incorporation subscriptions.

§ 16.3   Liability on Unpaid Subscriptions to Corporations and Creditors

Under modern statutes, a corporation's board of directors may determine the payment terms of pre-incorporation subscriptions if the subscription agreement does not specify them.[10] A subscriber's default creates a debt due to the corporation, which may be accordingly collected.

Unless liability is imposed by statute, neither subscribers nor shareholders are directly accountable to the corporation's creditors.[11] The subscriber's liability is to the corporation and is pursued by its representatives.[12] In the absence of receivership or bankruptcy proceedings, the usual remedies available to corporate creditors to reach the indebtedness of shareholders for partly paid shares is a creditors' bill in equity or

---

[4]   Klapmeier v. Flagg, 677 F.2d 781 (9th Cir. 1982); AIH Acquisition Corp. LLC v. Alaska Ind. Hardware, Inc., 306 F. Supp.2d 455 (S.D.N.Y. 2004) (specifically enforcing written agreement that contained all essential terms but which had not been signed by the seller where there was clear intent that the agreement was final).

[5]   *See* Bielinski v. Miller, 382 A.2d 357 (NH 1978).

[6]   *See* Duncan v. Brookview House, Inc., 205 S.E.2d 707 (S.C. 1974).

[7]   Putnam v. Williams, 652 F.2d 497 (5th Cir. 1981).

[8]   *See* Cooper v. Vitraco, Inc., 320 F.Supp. 239 (D.V.I. 1970) (decided under U.C.C. § 8–319).

[9]   *See, e.g.,* Ala. Code 1975 § 10–2B–6.20 (Michie 1999); Colo. Rev. Stat. Ann. § 7–106–201 (West 1986 & Supp. 2002); Ga. Code Ann. § 14–2–620 (Michie 1994).

[10]   *See, e.g.,* Ala. Code § 10–2B–6.20 (2009); Ariz. Rev. Stat. Ann. § 10–620 (2009); Wash. Rev. Code Ann. § 23B.06.200 (2009); Va. Code Ann. § 13.1–642 (2009); MBCA § 6.20 (2016); former MBCA § 17 (1969).

[11]   Thomson-Houston Elec. Co. v. Murray, 37 A. 443 (N.J. Sup. Ct. 1897).

[12]   Kerosec v. Yirga, 230 N.E.2d 587 (Ill. App. Ct. 1967).

garnishment, in which creditors must show they have exhausted their remedies at law or are excused from doing so.[13]

§ 16.4   The Underwriting Services of Investment Bankers

It is important for business lawyers to understand the nature of the underwriting arrangements commonly used by issuers and investment bankers in bringing out and distributing issues of corporate securities. However, lawyers should also be aware that securities may be "distributed" to the investing public directly by the management of a going corporation or by the promoters of a new enterprise without the aid of investment bankers or the use of an underwriting agreement. Small concerns often cannot afford underwriting by investment bankers and must rely on corporate officers and agents to sell securities. Large concerns are sometimes able to place large issues of high-grade securities directly with life insurance companies, pension funds, or other institutional investors. In direct private financing, underwriting commissions are saved, as are other expenses such as registration under the securities laws.[14]

The methods for raising corporate capital can be divided into ten basic categories. A corporation—or any other enterprise, for that matter—theoretically at least can raise capital *without an investment banker* by (1) a direct offering of securities to the public or a limited group of people, (2) a direct offering to existing security holders (sometimes called a "rights offering"), (3) a direct private placement, (4) public sealed bidding, or (5) bank loans, mortgage loans, equipment loans, and "lease-backs." The five basic methods *using the services of an investment banker* are (6) a negotiated, underwritten public offering of securities, (7) an underwritten public offering through sealed bids, (8) an underwritten offering to existing security holders, (9) an offering to existing security holders with the investment banker acting as agent, and (10) private placement with the investment banker acting as agent for the issuer. Financial realities and business exigencies frequently limit the actual choices.

"Origination" by underwriters of securities refers to the many steps an investment banker undertakes in preparation for a client company's public offering of securities. These steps include investigating the affairs and needs of would-be issuers, selecting companies that offer good investment opportunities, devising the types and terms of securities to be offered, negotiating with an issuer the spread or discount between the price the underwriters pay the issuer for the securities and the price at which they will be offered to the public or some other arrangement for compensating the underwriters, and arranging for associated underwriters and broker-dealers. "Distribution" involves the managing of selling syndicates, advertising the securities, and presenting them to investors.[15] Largely because of the federal securities laws, there are extraordinarily high due diligence standards for all participants in the distribution process, including underwriters and professionals such as lawyers and accountants.[16]

The relationship between underwriter and issuer generally begins many months before the public offering is commenced. The managing underwriter provides a wide range of services to the issuer preparatory to the offering, including advice on the type

---

[13]   *See* Denniston & Co., Inc. v. Jackson, 468 So.2d 170 (Ala. Civ. App. 1985).

[14]   *See* William M. Prifti, Securities: Public and Private Offerings § 1.10–1.13 (2000).

[15]   At one time, underwriters also had the job of "stabilizing" a soft market, but today such activity is severely restricted by SEC regulation. *See* 17 C.F.R. §§ 240.10b–6, 10b–7 (2002).

[16]   *See* § 11(b)(3), 15 U.S.C. § 77k(b)(3) (2009).

and amount of security to be offered, the offering's timing, and the steps the issuer should take to put its financial and operational status in as favorable a light as possible prior to the offering.

An interesting dimension of underwriting is the matching of underwriter reputation with the relative riskiness of the issuer. The risks of a firm commitment underwriting are that investor demand for the security will be weak so that the underwriter's capital is tied up in the offering. Moreover, its reputation is damaged by having misjudged the marketability of that issuer's securities. It is not surprising, therefore, that lower-risk issuers tend to attract more established, higher-reputation underwriters.

Underwriters' services may be valuable to both issuers and investors. Large investment banking firms have prestige and direct access to the best dealers and customers. Leading underwriters develop a clientele that has faith in the underwriter's investigation, judgment, and responsibility. Thus, by using the services of underwriters, an issuing company may obtain needed funds promptly and save on the terms at which the securities are offered, such as the rate of interest on bonds or debentures or the dividend rate on preferred stock.

Investment bankers frequently establish special relationships with a corporation issuing securities. They may, for example, obtain representation on the corporation's board of directors or acquire control of the corporation by requiring the corporation's shareholders to put their shares into a voting trust with trustees the underwriters select. Underwriters' charges may cover origination costs, compensation for the underwriting risk and syndicate management, and selling compensation. Some underwriters have at times taken advantage of their influence to obtain an undue "spread" between the wholesale price that they pay the issuer and the retail price at which they sell the issue to the public.[17]

Section 11(a)(5) of the federal Securities Act of 1933 imposes responsibility on underwriters for nondisclosure of their arrangements with the issuer and also for misrepresentations in the registration statement or prospectus.[18] The registration statement filed with the Securities and Exchange Commission under the Securities Act must contain information as to the nature of the underwriting arrangements, including a list of all underwriters, as defined in the Act, together with the amount of the issue that each has underwritten. The Securities Act also requires disclosure of underwriting commissions. These disclosure requirements are imposed on participants in the underwriting, including dealers and members of selling syndicates who participate in distributing the securities, unless their compensation is limited to the customary seller's commission. Sections 11 and 12 of the Securities Act thus impose liability on various classes of persons taking part in underwriting and distributing securities in channels of interstate commerce or by the mail.[19] "Underwriter" is a term of art under the Securities Act, and the verbiage of the definition is awkward and vexatious.[20] In substance "underwriter" includes any person who purchases from an issuer, or sells for an issuer,

---

[17] *See* Ferdinand Pecora, Wall Street Under Oath, ch. 10 (1939).

[18] 15 U.S.C. § 77k(a)(5) (2000).

[19] Ernest L. Folk, Civil Liabilities Under the Federal Securities Acts: The *Bar Chris* Case, 55 Va. L. Rev. 1 (1969).

[20] 15 U.S.C. § 77b(a)(11) (2009).

with a view toward the distribution of any security, or anyone who participates directly or indirectly in any such undertaking.[21]

PART B.   THE ISSUANCE OF SHARES

§ 16.5   The Nature of Shares and Share Certificates

A share of stock is a profit-sharing contract, one of a series of units of interest and participation, authorized by the corporate charter, by which capital is obtained in consideration of a proportional right to participate in profits and growth through dividends and other distributions.[22] All subscribers and purchasers of stock make themselves parties to a contract—the corporate charter—which in a broad sense includes not only the articles of incorporation but also the applicable corporation laws as well.[23] The charter contract usually gives the shareholder a vote in the selection of directors, in the adoption of bylaws, and in the making of fundamental changes in the corporate structure. It gives a proportional right to participate in the distribution of assets on dissolution and winding up after payment of debts, as well as certain auxiliary or remedial rights. The share contract is a property right—namely, a fractional interest in the corporate enterprise that includes an indirect interest in its property and earnings, subject to its liabilities.

A certificate for shares certifies that one is a holder or owner of a certain number of shares of stock in the corporation. It is ordinarily documentary evidence of the holder's ownership of shares and a convenient instrument for the transfer of title.[24] The one-time paper crunch on Wall Street has been a major impetus behind the recent move to recognize uncertificated shares.[25] A certificate of stock is in "street name" when it has been issued in the name of an individual or firm and endorsed in blank so that it can be negotiated without further endorsement.[26]

§ 16.6   Issuance, Creation, or Allotment of Shares

Shares of stock are contracts created by mutual assent of the corporation and its shareholders. The shares must first be "authorized" by appropriate provisions in the corporation's charter, which detail the rights attaching to ownership.[27] Once shares are authorized, the power to issue them lies with the board of directors.[28] When shares are sold by the corporation, they are "issued," and those shares are thereafter referred to as "authorized *and* issued." As long as they are not reacquired by the corporation—that is, they remain in the hands of shareholders—they are also "outstanding" (that is,

---

[21]   *See, e.g.,* Harden v. Raffensperger, Hughes & Co., Inc., 65 F.3d 1392 (7th Cir. 1995).

[22]   DRW Builders, Inc. v. Richardson, 679 N.E.2d 902 (Ind. Ct. App. 1997) ("share of stock" defined as instrument conferring proportional part in certain rights in management and profits of a corporation).

[23]   Garey v. St. Joe Mining Co., 91 P. 369, 371 (Utah 1907).

[24]   DRW Builders, Inc. v. Richardson, 679 N.E.2d 902 (Ind. Ct. App. 1997) ("certificate of stock" is merely documentary evidence of title to shares).

[25]   *See* MBCA § 6.26 (2016); former MBCA § 23 (1969). U.C.C. art. 8 (2002 revision).

[26]   *See* R. Baruch and Co. v. Springer, 184 A.2d 206 (D.C. App. Ct. 1962).

[27]   MBCA § 6.01 (2008); former MBCA §§ 15, 54(d) (1969). *But see* James J. Hanks, Jr., Removing the Limits on Authorized Stock, 73 Wash. U. L.Q. 479 (1995) (questioning whether the concept of "authorized" shares should continue to be a component of corporate law).

[28]   *See, e.g.,* Cal. Corp. Code § 406 (2009); Conn. Gen. Stat. Ann. § 33–672 (2009); 805 ILCS § 5/6.05 (2009); MBCA § 6.21 (2016); former MBCA § 18 (1969). Issuance without board approval is void. *See* Foster v. Blackwell, 747 So.2d 1203 (La. Ct. App. 1999).

"authorized, issued, and outstanding"); shares that are "authorized, issued, but *not* outstanding" are shares that were previously issued by the corporation but subsequent to their issuance have been reacquired by the corporation. Such shares are more commonly referred to as "treasury shares" or "treasury stock." Shares issued in excess of the amount authorized, or issued that are not of a type authorized, are void.[29]

The word "issue" is generally employed to indicate the making of a share contract— that is, a transaction by which the directors create new shares and a person becomes the owner of the shares.[30] Share ownership can result either from subscription to an original issue of shares by the corporation or from the transfer of shares from a prior owner and the substitution of the transferee in the place of the prior owner. A corporation usually may resell treasury shares—that is, shares that have already been issued and have been reacquired by the corporation but not retired. Such a resale has the same market impact as the issue or creation of new shares, although the transaction generally gives rise to a different accounting treatment by the corporation.

"Issue" is often associated with the execution and delivery of a share certificate, but the issue of the shares is not dependent on delivery. To become shareholders, in the sense of becoming owners of shares, subscribers need not receive a certificate.[31] However, until the subscriber becomes a holder of record, she ordinarily has no right to vote, to receive notice of shareholders' meetings, and to inspect corporate books; she also has no right against the corporation to participate in dividends.

§ 16.7 Flexibility in Terms of Preferred Shares

As with common stock, the rights, preferences, and restrictions of any class of preferred shares generally are fixed in the charter, *i.e.*, articles of incorporation.[32] The financing of an enterprise may go on year after year, as business expands or the needs for capital arise. New issues of securities may be made from time to time; and, if preferred shares are issued, it may be necessary to meet changing market conditions by variations over time in the dividend rate and other terms of the preferred share contract. Thus the rights, privileges, and restrictions of a series of preferred shares issued at an earlier time quite probably are inappropriate for a contemporary issuance of additional shares. Absent flexible corporate enabling statutes, the serial nature of preferred stock issuances, each with the need for their rights, privileges, and restrictions to meet prevailing market conditions that are different from those of earlier issuances, would necessitate serial amendments to the articles of incorporation to authorize each new series of preferred shares. To avoid the expense and delay of such serial charter amendments, most modern corporation statutes permit a corporation's articles of incorporation to authorize the board of directors to fix the dividend rate, liquidation price, voting rights, and other terms of a class or a series within a class as the board of

---

[29] *See, e.g.*, Blades v. Wisehart, 2010 WL 4638603 (Del. Ch. 2010) (failure to fulfill steps to properly amend articles so as to effect the stock split resulted in shares not being validly issued with consequence their holders were not shareholders); Waggoner v. Laster, 581 A.2d 1127, 1137 (Del. 1990).

[30] Blythe v. Doheny, 73 F.2d 799, 803 (9th Cir. 1934).

[31] Golden v. Oahe Enterprises, Inc., 240 N.W.2d 102 (S.D. 1976) (once corporate stock is paid for, it is issued regardless of whether share certificate is executed and delivered).

[32] *See, e.g.*, Cal. Corp. Code § 202; Fla. Stat. Ann. § 607.0601; 215 ILCS § 5/14.1; Me. Rev. Stat. Ann. tit. 13–A, § 403; MBCA § 6.01 (2016).

directors believes in the best interests of the corporation.[33] These provisions are customarily referred to as "blank stock" authorization. The board of directors' discretion must be exercised within the limits, if any, set forth in the enabling provision of the articles of incorporation, and the articles must set forth the number of shares of the class of shares over which the board of directors has such authority.[34] Such shares are sometimes referred to as "blank stock" preferred shares. Absent such broad authorization, the board of directors lacks authority to so fix the terms of preferred shares.[35]

"Blank stock" preferred assumed a new role beginning with the takeover frenzy of the 1980s as a potentially powerful takeover defensive weapon. Boards of directors seized upon such blank stock authorization as the mechanism to issue "rights" that would confer upon their holders financial or voting rights whose exercise would thwart any hostile takeover of the corporation.[36] The devices, popularly known as "poison pills," are examined extensively later in this treatise.

Most statutes permit enabling charter provisions authorizing the directors to subdivide classes of preferred shares into series.[37]

§ 16.8 Significance of Par Value

"Par value" is a rapidly vanishing feature of corporate law.[38] In broad overview, par value was at one time believed a workable approach toward assuring that the full price was paid for a corporation's shares and that a financial cushion existed for the benefit of creditors against improvident dividend payments and share repurchases. As will be discussed later, the protections that were believed to arise from the shares' par value were largely illusionary because they could be easily circumvented by, among other approaches, the use of shares having a very low par value or even shares without any par value. California began what has become an accelerating trend within corporate statutes to accord no legal significance to a share's par value.[39] Delaware and New York are two important corporate domiciles whose corporate statutes continue to embrace this otherwise outmoded approach toward creditor protection.[40]

What is the significance of the "par value" of shares? "Par value" clearly is not intended to reflect the true value of the shares, as their value will constantly fluctuate. It is not a "value" in any sense. Traditionally, the primary function of par was to fix a minimum subscription or original issue price for the shares.[41] It indicates the amount

---

[33] *E.g.,* Ala. Code 1975 § 10–2B–6.02 (2009); Del. Code Ann. tit. 8, § 151 (2009); Ind. Code Ann. § 23–1–34–6 (2009); Mo. Stat. Ann. § 375.198 (2009); N.Y. Bus. Corp. Law § 502 (2009). *See* MBCA § 6.02 (2016).

[34] Benihana of Tokyo, Inc. v. Benihana, Inc., 906 A.2d 114 (Del. 2006)(broad authority granted to the board in "blank stock" authorization allowed board to issue preferred shares with preemptive rights, even though articles of incorporation had boilerplate statement that there were no preemptive rights).

[35] Waggoner v. Laster, 581 A.2d 1127 (Del. 1990).

[36] *See generally* Thomas R. Wilcox, Delaware's Attempt to Swallow a New Defense: The Poison Pill Preferred Stock, 10 Del. J. Corp. L. 569 (1985).

[37] *See, e.g.,* Ala. Code 1975 § 10–2B–6.02 (2001); Cal. Corp. Code § 202 (West 1990 & Supp. 2002); N.C. Gen. Stat. Ann. § 55–6–01 (2001).

[38] *See* Venture Stores, Inc. v. Ryan, 678 N.E.2d 300, 303 (Ill. Ct. App. 1997) ("Today the concept of par value is an anachronism.").

[39] *See* Cal. Corp. Code § 202(d) (1990) (legislative committee comment).

[40] *See* Del. Code Ann. tit. 8, §§ 102(a)(4), 153 (2009); N.Y. Bus. Corp. Law § 402(a)(4) (2009).

[41] Former MBCA § 18 (1969) ("Shares having a par value may be issued for such consideration expressed in dollars, not less than the par value thereof, as shall be fixed from time to time by the board of

that the original subscribers are supposed to contribute to capital as the basis of the privilege of profit-sharing with limited liability. Par value does not restrict the price of resales of outstanding shares among investors.[42] The aggregate par value of issued shares gives the basis for computing the minimum amount of the corporation's "legal capital." Difficulty can arise when a going concern, after making its original offering of shares, needs to raise more capital by subsequent share issues because the shares cannot be issued for less than par. Unless the corporation has been successful at keeping the market price of the shares above the par value, it cannot market additional shares. To avoid this trap, the practice developed to set an arbitrarily selected low par, for example, $1 per share, with the amount so specified being much below the actual issue price. Though it has been argued that par value can provide a useful method for checking the directors' discretion to issue new shares at a low price and thereby dilute the interest of existing shareholders, clearly the increasing trend today is that par is "outmoded" and "vestigial."[43]

Even in the absence of a statute setting par as the minimum issue price, it has long been the general rule that directors may not fix the issue price at less than par or give a discount from par value.[44] The hardships created by such a rigid approach resulted in the Supreme Court's providing some flexibility in *Handley v. Stutz*,[45] which held that a going concern in need of funds to continue in business may issue additional shares at the best available price free from liability to creditors, even though that price is below the shares' par value. Thus in the absence of a statute, there generally is no shareholders' liability where an operating corporation issues new shares in good faith at the best price that can be obtained, although far less than par, whether in payment of debts or to raise money for the continuance of its business.[46]

§ 16.9 Sale of Treasury Shares at Less than Par

Shares that once were issued as fully paid and have then been reacquired by the corporation and not retired are called "treasury" shares.[47] Such shares are treated as still having the status of "issued" shares for purposes of resale, although they no longer have dividend or voting rights.[48] It has generally been held that the corporation may reissue and sell these treasury shares for less than their par value.[49] Treasury shares are not truly assets to be sold, but merely represent the power to reissue the shares, which is distinguished from the power to create shares by subscription upon original issue.[50] The reason given for this distinction is that the corporation has already received

---

directors."). In 1980 the Model Business Corporation Act was revised to eliminate the concept of par, but many states will probably be slow to adopt this radical change.

[42] *See, e.g.*, Torres v. Speiser, 701 N.Y.S.2d 360 (App. Div. 2000).

[43] California and the 1980 revisions to the Model Business Corporation Act, do away with par value.

[44] *See* CFM of Conn. v. Taufiqul Chowhury, 1993 WL 153152 (Conn. Super. Ct. 1993) (issuance of $40,000 par value shares for only $50 declared void).

[45] Handley v. Stutz, 139 U.S. 417 (1891).

[46] Clark v. Bever, 139 U.S. 96 (1891); Fogg v. Blair, 139 U.S. 118 (1891).

[47] The 1980 revisions to the Model Act abolish treasury shares. Former MBCA § 6 (1980); MBCA § 6.31 (2016).

[48] Former MBCA § 2(h) (1969). *See id.* § 18, which provides that treasury shares may be issued at a price fixed by the board without regard to par.

[49] Borg v. International Silver Co., 11 F.2d 147, 152 (2d Cir. 1925).

[50] *See* Borg v. International Silver Co., 11 F.2d 147 (2d Cir. 1925); Americar, Inc. v. Crowley, 282 So.2d 674 (Fla. Ct. App. 1973) (Carroll, J. dissenting).

a capital contribution for treasury shares and has thereby created for the corporation a stated capital "liability" with respect to the shares so issued, which was not eliminated upon the corporation's reacquisition of the shares. Upon their subsequent reissue, these shares do not increase the corporation's stated capital.[51]

§ 16.10 No-Par Shares; Advantages, Issue Price

New York[52] initiated the movement to authorize the use of shares without par value. No-par shares have since been authorized in nearly every state.[53] The comparative advantages of using no-par and par value shares should be weighed in drafting the stock clauses of a corporation's charter.

The number of no-par shares that may be issued must be specified in the articles of incorporation, or the shares will be void.[54] The great feature of no-par shares is price flexibility in that they require no fixed minimum capital contribution, although the same kind of quality of consideration is required as for par value shares. No-par shares may be issued from time to time at different prices, yet the subscribers and holders of the same class and series of shares will be entitled to participate equally share-for-share in the distribution of dividends and assets. The issue price of no-par shares may ordinarily be fixed by the directors.[55]

§ 16.11 Kinds of Consideration That Validate Payment for Shares

A corporation is not limited to a cash payment for its shares; it may receive payment in property or services if they are of a kind recognized as capable of valuation and are properly valued.[56] Most state statutes set forth the types of consideration the corporation can receive for its shares if the shares are to be "fully paid and nonassessable."[57] The types of consideration commonly authorized are money and real and personal property, including intangible property, as well as services rendered. These traditional forms of eligible types of consideration exclude executory forms of consideration, such as promissory notes or a promise of future services. A minority of the states follow the scheme of the Model Business Corporation Act and allow promissory notes and future services as well as the traditional types of consideration.[58]

---

[51] George S. Hills, Stated Capital and Treasury Shares, 57 J. Acct. 202, 214 (1934).

[52] N.Y. Stock Corp. Law § 12 (1912). *See also* Alfred F. Conard, Cook and the Corporate Shareholder: A Belated Review of William W. Cook's Publication on Corporations, 93 Mich. L. Rev. 1724, n.48 (1995) (commenting that an analysis of the early no-par statutes is provided in Cornelius W. Wickersham, A Treatise on Stock Without Par Value of Ordinary Business Corporations (1927)).

[53] *E.g.*, Del. Code Ann. tit. 8, § 153 (2009).

[54] Triplex Shoe Co. v. Hutchins, 152 A. 342 (Del. 1930). *See also* Staar Surgical Co. v. Waggoner, 588 A.2d 1130 (Del. 1991) ("stock issued without authority of law is void and a nullity"). *See* C. Stephen Bigler & Seth Barrett Tillman, Void or Voidable?—Curing Defects in Stock Issuances Under Delaware Law, 63 Bus. Law. 1109 (2008) (speculating that *Triplex* may have been changed by subsequent enactment in Delaware of UCC provisions that can be interpreted to provide that filing amendment to certificate after shares were issued "cures" the failure of shares to have been duly authorized when initially issued).

[55] *See, e.g.*, Del. Code Ann. tit. 8, § 153(a), (b) (2009).

[56] *E.g.*, West v. Sirian Lamp Co., 44 A.2d 658 (Del. Ch. 1945).

[57] *See, e.g.*, Ariz. Rev. Stat. Ann. § 10–621(B) (2009); Colo. Rev. Stat. § 7–106–202(2) (2009); Del. Code Ann. tit. 8, § 152 (2009); N.Y. Bus. Corp. Law § 504(a) (2009).

[58] Following the modern trend, New York amended its statute in 1998 to authorize future services, N.Y. Bus. Corp. Law § 504(b) (McKinney 2003) (Historical and Statutory Notes); MBCA § 6.21(b) (2016). For a

The difference separating the states adhering to the traditional restrictive forms of valid types of consideration from those following the current Model Business Corporation Act is the choice between embracing prophylactic protections for creditors on the one hand and accommodating commercial practices on the other. The commentary for the current Model Business Corporation Act makes clear that the over-arching view is "that only business judgment should determine what kind of property should be obtained for shares. . . ."[59] Perhaps the biggest question to be raised is whether future service is, from a creditor's perspective, appropriate consideration. For example, if the corporation becomes insolvent before the services are performed, the unperformed obligation hardly enriches the bankrupt company's estate. In most cases, the services to be exchanged for shares have a special value to that corporation, but their value to others is doubtful. Certainly services to be performed is not a type of consideration that can easily be transformed into cash to satisfy creditors (consider here that the creditor's nonpayment arises most likely when the company for which the services were to be performed is insolvent, perhaps ceased its operations, and, moreover, the promised services may have special value for the failed company's operations but are less valuable in another venture). Consider further, just how are the creditors to execute on the promise for future services? In addition, services, particularly those that are promised by the promoters at the corporation's formation, are easily overvalued, and thus a ban may well be justified solely as a necessary prophylaxis for promoter misconduct. Hence, the bar can be seen as a prophylaxis for possible stock watering. Nevertheless, it cannot be overlooked that an important cornerstone to a young company's future is harnessing the creative entrepreneurial talents of key individuals through providing them an ownership interest in the firm proportionate to their prospective contributions. In any case, many creative solutions are available to circumvent the statutory bar to issuing stock for future services.[60] Similarly, there are many means to circumvent the bar to issuing stock for a promissory note,[61] and creditors have the ability to enforce the promissory note, which may well be marketable. The potential for circumvention and the related transaction costs challenges rather than supports the continued vitality of the bar to future services or a promissory note as eligible forms of consideration.

Courts are reasonably liberal in their construction of the statutory prescription of eligible forms of consideration. Thus, for example, shares issued for the goodwill of another corporation have been upheld.[62] For an item to constitute "property" as contemplated by the statute, it must have intrinsic worth and not be illusory, such as having value only upon the occurrence of a substantial condition precedent.[63] Much the same result has been reached by holding that the evidence of the value of such items is insufficient.[64] The overall objective of restricting the issuance of shares to certain types

---

decision holding that the New York amendment does no apply retroactively, *see* Carr v. Marietta Corp., 211 F.3d 724 (2d Cir. 2000).

[59]   MBCA § 6.21, Official Comment (2016).

[60]   *See* David R. Herwitz, Allocation of Stock Between Services and Capital in the Organization of a Close Corporation, 75 Harv. L. Rev. 1098 (1962).

[61]   In Guardian State Bank v. Humpherys, 762 P.2d 1084 (Utah 1988), the court upheld the issuance of shares where the bank loaned cash in exchange for the borrower's promissory note, and the borrower used the loan's proceeds to purchase shares in the bank. An even less questionable circumvention is a loan by one shareholder of the funds used by another to purchase shares.

[62]   Eastern Okla. Television Co. v. Ameco, Inc., 437 F.2d 138 (10th Cir. 1971).

[63]   *See, e.g.,* Scully v. Automobile Fin. Co., 109 A. 49 (Del. 1919).

[64]   *See* Gillett v. Chicago Title & Trust Co., 82 N.E. 891 (Ill. 1907) (rights to unwritten play and prospective patents on scene-shifting devices in payment of $1,999,600 of fully paid stock).

of consideration is to protect creditors by assuring that the corporation receives something having intrinsic worth and also to shield the other stockholders from dilution.[65] The restrictions on the type of consideration shares can be issued for does not apply to treasury shares.[66]

Among the kinds of consideration that have been questioned as valid are promoters' services rendered before incorporation,[67] agreements by promoters, directors, or others to render future services,[68] services in marketing or underwriting securities,[69] services that do not benefit the issuing corporation,[70] future profits,[71] making a loan where shares are issued as a bonus to induce the loan,[72] making a loan in consideration for a pledge of unissued shares as security for the loan,[73] and promissory notes of subscribers.[74] The note of a subscriber has sometimes been viewed as only another promise to pay for the shares; therefore the shares may not be considered as fully paid although the promise itself is binding.[75] More generally, shares issued in exchange for an oral promise to pay that is not enforceable is not an eligible form of consideration.[76] In a leading case,[77] it was held that services to be rendered in the future cannot be a valid consideration for the issue of shares as fully paid and nonassessable under the Delaware constitution calling for "labor done." This does not mean, however, that shares may not be issued in consideration of specified services to be rendered in the future as long as the certificates for the shares are not marked as fully paid but are treated as representing partly paid shares issued on credit.[78]

§ 16.12 Valuation of Consideration for Shares

At one time, a few jurisdictions adhered to what was known as the "strict value rule." According to this rule, payment for shares in property or services was satisfaction as against creditors only to the extent of the true value of the consideration, notwithstanding the good faith of the directors in fixing the value of the property or services.[79] This attempt to allow review of the directors' determination of value has been abandoned in the jurisdictions that had once adhered to it.[80]

---

[65] *See* H. J. Cohn Furn. (No. 2) Co. v. Texas Western Fin. Corp., 544 F.2d 886 (5th Cir. 1977).

[66] *See, e.g.,* Public Inv., Ltd. v. Bandeirante Corp., 740 F.2d 1222 (D.C. Cir. 1984).

[67] Lofland v. Cahall, 118 A. 1 (Del. 1922); Ludlam v. Riverhead Bond & Mortgage Corp., 278 N.Y.S. 487 (App. Div. 1935).

[68] Frasier v. Trans-Western Land Corp., 316 N.W.2d 612 (Neb. 1982).

[69] Ludlam v. Riverhead Bond & Mortgage Corp., 278 N.Y.S. 487 (App. Div. 1935).

[70] Clark v. Cowart, 445 So.2d 884 (Ala. 1984).

[71] *See* Norton v. Digital Applications, Inc., 305 A.2d 656 (Del. Ch. 1973).

[72] Hopper v. Brodie, 106 A. 700 (Md. 1919).

[73] *See* McAndrews v. Idawa Gold Mining Co., 210 N.W. 514 (N.D. 1926), noted in Raymond J. Cook, Comment, Corporations—Pledge by Corporations of Unissued Stock as Security for Debt, 7 B.U. L. Rev. 127 (1927). *But see* Guardian State Bank v. Humpherys, 762 P.2d 1084 (Utah 1988) (bank loaned cash to X who then used the cash to purchase bank's shares deemed to be issuance of shares for cash).

[74] Sohland v. Baker, 141 A. 277, 284 (Del. 1927).

[75] Jacobs v. Frontier Tractor & Equip., Inc., 712 P.2d 493 (Colo. Ct. App. 1985).

[76] MBKS Co. Ltd. v. Reddy, 924 A.2d 965 (Del. Ch. 2007).

[77] Scully v. Automobile Fin. Co., 109 A. 49 (1919).

[78] Norton v. Digital Applications, Inc., 305 A.2d 656 (Del. Ch. 1973).

[79] William E. Dee Co. v. Proviso Coal Co., 125 N.E. 24, 26 (Ill. 1919).

[80] *See* Clinton Mining & Mineral Co. v. Jamison, 256 F. 577 (3d Cir. 1919).

Modern statutes and decisions have established the "good faith rule," under which the judgment of the board of directors, shareholders, or incorporators as to the value of property or services a corporation receives for shares is conclusive unless fraud or intentional over-valuation is shown by the creditor.[81] Statutes frequently express the standard as being "in the absence of fraud" or "absence of *actual* fraud."[82] There are some variations, however, in what amounts to fraud. According to some courts, there must be actual fraud or dishonesty on the part of the directors in order to render the subscriber (or his transferee with notice) liable to creditors for the difference between the actual value paid and the par value or issue price of the shares subscribed.[83] Under this approach, mere proof of excessive valuation does not alone overturn the presumption that normally accompanies decisions of the board of directors.[84] On the other hand, according to other courts and statutes, an actual fraudulent intent is not necessary. "Constructive fraud" is found if the over-valuation is deliberate or intentional, and such intention can be inferred from the surrounding circumstances.[85] Most courts hold that a conscious and intentional over-valuation is fraudulent as a matter of law rather than merely evidence of fraud.[86] Other courts have indicated that a gross over-valuation can amount to "equitable fraud."[87] A conscious or deliberate overvaluation is easier to prove than dishonesty or an intent to deceive creditors. Some courts follow what may be called "a reasonable judgment rule" and regard a determination of value by the directors as fraudulent if the directors fail to make a reasonable investigation to determine the elements of value.[88]

"Fraud" is an elastic concept. Lack of good faith or inequitable conduct on the part of the directors may more readily be found where dilution of the holdings of other shareholders by an unfairly low issue price is involved than where liability to creditors is concerned. The shareholders' interest to be protected against unfair dilution of their shareholdings by discrimination in the issue price of a solvent corporation's shares is stronger than a creditor's claim to enforce a precise capital contribution by shareholders of an insolvent corporation.[89] A leading Delaware case held that even disinterested shareholder approval of the issuance of options to each of the company's directors does not insulate the transaction from closer scrutiny when the magnitude of the option's value to each director is significant.[90]

There is a great need for careful and impartial valuation, especially where there is a potential conflict of interest.[91] Under the older statutes it was proper practice for the

---

[81]　*See, e.g.,* Arkota Ind., Inc. v. Naekel, 623 S.W.2d 194 (Ark. 1981).

[82]　Former MBCA § 119 (1969). *See* Del. Code Ann. tit. 8, § 152 (2009) ("in the absence of actual fraud").

[83]　*See* Diamond State Brewery, Inc. v. De La Rigaudiere, 17 A.2d 313 (Del. Ch. 1941).

[84]　*See* Pipelife Corp. v. Bedford, 145 A.2d 206 (Del. Ch. 1958).

[85]　Bowers v. Rio Grande Inv. Co., 431 P.2d 478, 480 (Colo. 1967) (mere proof of consideration of less than the stipulated par value is not in and of itself proof of such inadequacy in price as to establish constructive fraud or constitute over-reaching).

[86]　Elyton Land Co. v. Birmingham Warehouse & Elevator Co., 9 So. 129, 135 (Ala. 1891).

[87]　*See* § 16.13.

[88]　Pinnacle Consultants, Ltd. v. Leucadia National Corp., 101 F.3d 900, 905 (2d Cir. 1996) (directors' reasonably determined that officers had produced a dramatic turnaround in the company's performance such that being rewarded for their past efforts by issuing warrants was justified).

[89]　Adolf A. Berle, Compensation of Bankers and Promoters Through Stock Profits, 42 Harv. L. Rev. 748, 751, 757 (1929).

[90]　*See* Lewis v. Vogelstein, 699 A.2d 327 (Del. Ch. 1997).

[91]　*See, e.g.,* Doyle v. Union Ins. Co., 277 N.W.2d 36 (Neb. 1979) (fraud occurred by board member submitting his own valuation of property and then supervised the employment of an expert to value the

board of directors, by resolution entered in its minutes, to state its appraisal, after careful investigation, of the fair dollar value of services or property for which shares with or without par value are being used. However, under modern statutes such as the Model Act, there is no need to specify the non-cash consideration or its value since the board's determination of adequacy is presumed to have been made in good faith.[92] An over-valuation without reasonable and impartial investigation into the elements of present value is evidence of lack of good faith. In many situations the board should seek an independent appraisal.

A determination in dollars of the value of the property or consideration received by the corporation is necessary for accounting purposes in stating the cost or value of its assets and in making up balance sheets showing the corporation's financial condition.[93] It is also necessary to designate what part of consideration received for shares is to be attributed to stated capital and what amount, if any, is to be attributed to paid in surplus, particularly in connection with the issue of shares without par value. However, the absence of such a designation should not prevent the shares from being issued, assuming an eligible form of consideration was exchanged for the shares.[94]

As noted above, those states following the Model Business Corporation Act's treatment of the issuance of shares, whereby only the *adequacy* of any consideration is determined by the board of directors,[95] do not require that the directors assign a set value to any non-cash consideration received for the shares when the shares are issued. Under this approach the directors can, if they wish, be more reflective and deliberate and can value the non-cash consideration at some later date. A precise value must at some time be assigned to the non-cash consideration because the corporation's accounting records demand that all assets be recorded in dollars on the company's books at their cost. By requiring the board of directors to pass only on the adequacy of the consideration exchanged for shares before the shares are issued, the Model Business Corporation Act separates the legal consequences of the board's issuance of shares from the accounting questions. Such separation should make successful challenges to the issuance of shares less likely. Moreover, requiring a determination only of adequacy of consideration is consistent with the overall deregulatory and facilitating philosophy of the Model Business Corporation Act.

§ 16.13 Equitable Limitations for Pricing Shares

Directors have a fiduciary duty to fix a reasonable price for issues of shares, both with and without par value. The propriety of the board's issuance of shares is examined in accordance with the business judgment rule, so that a decision arrived at in good faith

---

property; his obvious self-interest was not mediated by the other directors who evidence supported finding were negligent in approving the transaction).

[92] Model Bus. Corp. Act § 6.21 (2016). *See id.* Official Comments.

[93] Garbe v. Excel Mold, Inc., 397 N.E.2d 296 (Ind. Ct. App. 1979); Knickerbocker Importation Co. v. Board of Assessors, 65 A. 913, 915 (N.J. 1907) ("Neither bookkeeping nor mere recitative language in resolutions of a board of directors creating values can be accepted as the equivalent of the proof of bona fide value required by our statute when stock is issued for property purchased.").

[94] *See* Bissias v. Koulovatos, 761 A.2d 47, 49 (Me. 2000) (statute regulating issuance of no-par shares stated the consideration would "be fixed from time to time by the board" interpreted to require only that the "consideration be given for the shares and for such consideration to have a value").

[95] Section 6.21(c) of the Model Business Corporation Act provides simply that before the shares are issued "the board of directors must determine that the consideration received or to be received for shares" is adequate.

by an independent board that has not committed in gross negligence will be upheld.[96] As discussed below, even when the board is not fully independent, directors are given broad leeway in pricing shares.

Timing can be a crucial factor in applying the equitable yardstick of reasonableness. If a newly formed corporation issues no-par or low-par shares to its promoters or others, there is ordinarily no legal restriction on the *amount* of consideration the corporation can receive for the shares, as long as there is some lawful consideration. However, insiders have a heavy burden of establishing the fairness of the transactions when they issue shares to themselves at a significant discount from the price available to outsiders where the issuance of the new shares results in dilution of preexisting ownership interests.[97] If the corporation has been in business for some time and has demonstrated its earning capacity, the price at which additional shares are issued will have a direct effect on the interests of existing shareholders. Too low a price will dilute the interest of the holders of outstanding shares and unfairly impair the values underlying their holdings. Ideally, if new shares are not offered to the existing shareholders, the shares should be issued at a fair price, based on market conditions and the value of the corporation's assets and prospective earnings—subject, however, to a reasonable range of business discretion. As a practical matter, new offerings to the public are frequently priced at a discount as a means of attracting investors and reducing any exposure of underwriters to liability.

When dilution of existing shareholders' interests is at issue, differences in the prices at which shares, either par or no-par, are issued must be justified by showing fairness in light of the circumstances. Shares of the same class may be issued for different amounts of consideration at the same time if the discrimination in price is justified by adequate business reasons and is not a matter of favoritism.[98] Thus, issuing shares at or around the same time at different prices is not by itself invalid and the directors' action will be upheld in the absence of bad faith or wrongdoing.[99] Also, recall that the board's determination of the adequacy of consideration is entitled to deference in the absence of fraud.

Disputes regarding the price at which shares are to be sold rarely arise within companies whose shares are publicly traded. For such firms, the shares' market price provides a powerful benchmark for assessing the board of directors' decision; a rational business purpose is needed to justify offering the shares below their current market value. As stated in a leading vintage Delaware case, *Bodell v. General Gas & Electric Corporation:*[100]

---

[96]   *See, e.g.*, Benihana of Tokyo, Inc. v. Benihana, Inc., 891 A.2d 150 (Del. Ch. 2005) (upholding issuance of $20 million of preferred shares to the firm's holding company that diluted outstanding common shares). Thus, the complete absence of a fair valuation of the consideration exchanged for the shares would be outside the protection of the business judgment rule. *See, e.g.*, Baldwin v. Bader, 585 F.3d 18 (1st Cir. 2009) (upholding the issuance of compensatory shares issued during financial crisis when board made investments in the firm but compensatory shares issued when firm was not experiencing financial distress required some evidence of the value of personal guarantees provided by the share's recipients).

[97]   *See* Schwartz v. Marien, 335 N.E.2d 334 (N.Y. 1975). *See also* Dingle v. Xtenit, Inc., 867 N.Y.S.2d 373 (Sup. Ct. 2008) (no business purpose supported issuance of substantial quantity of shares to majority holder that diluted interests of others).

[98]   Bodell v. General Gas & Elec. Corp., 132 A. 442 (Del. Ch. 1926), *aff'd*, 15 Del.Ch. 420, 140 A. 264 (Del. 1927).

[99]   *See* David R. Herwitz, Business Planning 55–56 (1966).

[100]   Bodell v. General Gas & Electric Corporation, 132 A. 442 (Del. Ch. 1926), *aff'd*, 140 A. 264 (1927).

Notwithstanding ... the absolute terms in which the power of the directors of this corporation to fix the price at which its unissued stock may be sold is expressed, equity will nevertheless by analogy to that reasoning which underlies the doctrine of preemptive right interfere to protect existing stockholders from an unjustified impairment of the values underlying their present holdings.

Bodell related to a question of discrimination regarding the issue price of Class A shares as between two different classes of common shares, Class A and Class B, which were closely related. The Class A shares were in reality a species of participating preferred stock, for they were entitled to a priority over Class B to annual noncumulative dividends of $1.50 per share and to a $25 per-share liquidation preference. After the Class B common had received equal dividends per share, both classes were to share equally in dividends and in distributions of assets subject to the class A's $25 liquidation preference. The directors announced a policy to enhance the attractiveness of Class A shares by giving the privilege of applying yearly dividends thereon toward the purchase of additional Class A shares with a stated purchase price of $25 per share. As a result of this arrangement, the company was able to issue additional Class A shares at $45 and higher. Against a challenge to this arrangement by a holder of Class B shares, the court held that the directors' discretion would not be interfered with except for fraud, such as improper motive, personal gain, arbitrary discrimination, or conscious disregard of the interests of the corporation and the rights of other shareholders. Because the directors articulated a reasonable basis for their decision of making the Class A shares more attractive to investors at a time that the corporation needed to raise cash for expansion, a basis further supported by the high price the Class A shares enjoyed in the market, the court dismissed the action.

The issue in *Bodel* was the relative rights of existing shareholders. On closer analysis, the court may have applied the wrong type of analysis to the dispute in *Bodell*. The arrangement allowed the holder of Class A shares to apply his $1.50 annual dividend toward the purchase of additional Class A shares at a set price of $25. The practical effect of the directors' decisions was to augment the annual dividend with an additional return in the form of a bargain purchase of additional Class A shares. For every sixteen and two-thirds Class A shares owned, a shareholder received a dividend of $25 (16 ⅔ $1.50), plus the gain in the amount that the stated purchase price of additional shares was exceeded by the then fair market value of Class A shares. Thus, if the Class A shares had a fair market value of $45, the holder of Class A shares received a yearly benefit of $45 for every sixteen and two-thirds Class A shares owned, or approximately $2.70 per Class A share. Without doubt, the arrangement was fair and useful to the corporation, because it clearly stimulated investor interest in the Class A shares at a time when the corporation was aggressively issuing Class A shares to outside investors. But the board of directors could have produced the same effect by raising the dividends on the Class A shares from $1.50 to $2.70 per share. But to have done so would have violated the terms of the Class B shares that were to participate fully with the Class A shares after each class of common received its $1.50 per share dividend. Thus the question in *Bodell* was not solely that of whether the directors exercised their discretion fairly and in the best interests of the corporation. The court needed to more fully consider the relative rights of the two classes of common shares in light of a transaction that effectively increased the economic return for one class in the face of contractual arrangements that envisioned that economic returns would be shared equally.

A more frequent basis of complaint in the public corporation is that the board of directors has issued the shares to entrench the incumbent management team. When this is established, appropriate equitable relief is provided, generally to cancel shares that were issued or to enjoin their pending issuance.[101] But the courts will not intrude when a bona fide business purpose supports the shares' issuance, even though a necessary effect of issuing more shares is to entrench management.[102] Moreover, the decision to place a substantial percentage of the stock in "friendly" hands does not itself condemn the shares' issuance where the board of directors after reasonable investigation determines in good faith that such a defensive maneuver is a reasonable response to the threat the hostile bid for control poses to the corporation or its stockholders.[103] The relative freedom of the board of directors to deflect an unwanted suitor is discussed in Chapter 23.

Equitable challenges to the corporation issuing more shares frequently arises in the close corporation, where delicate balances of power and economic participation can be swiftly upset by a board resolution selling shares to one faction of stockholders. The complaint in this setting is invariably that the shares are being sold for less than their fair value or to dilute substantially the plaintiff's ownership interest, or both. As for the concern that the shares have not been fairly priced by the board of directors, the courts emphasize a variety of considerations in determining the fair value of shares in the individual case.[104] For example, a substantial departure from the shares' book value—a highly conservative benchmark, given that book value assumes that the firm's assets have no greater worth than their historical cost less any recorded depreciation or amortization—removes the pricing decision from the business judgment rule.[105] More frequently yet, equitable relief is awarded in the close corporation when the transparent purpose of issuing additional shares is to substantially dilute the plaintiff's voting power.[106] However, a business purpose for issuing the shares and no effort to exclude the plaintiff from purchasing them insulates the shares' issuance from equitable attack.[107]

§ 16.14 The Shareholders' Preemptive Right

The directors' power to issue shares is subject to a common law fiduciary duty not to impair the ratable rights and interests of existing shareholders.[108] The recognition of preemptive rights to an offer of an opportunity to subscribe ratably for new issues arose from an attempt by the courts to create a prophylaxis to unfairness and abusive dilution of existing shares.

Originally, the preemptive right was recognized by the courts as mandatory, but now every state by statute allows the corporate charter to limit or deny the common law

---

[101] *See, e.g.*, Klaus v. Hi-Shear Corp., 528 F.2d 225 (9th Cir. 1975).

[102] *See* Empire of Carolina, Inc. v. Deltona Corp., 514 A.2d 1091, 1097 (Del. 1985) (finding bona fide purpose though did also have effect of entrenching management).

[103] *See* Herald v. Seawell, 472 F.2d 1081 (10th Cir. 1972).

[104] *See* Direct Media/DMI, Inc. v. Rubin, 654 N.Y.S.2d 986 (Sup. 1997).

[105] *See, e.g.*, Hyman v. Velsicol Corp., 97 N.E.2d 122 (Ill.App. 1951).

[106] *See, e.g.*, Gregory v. Correction Connection, Inc., 1991 WL 42992 (E.D. Pa. 1991).

[107] Herbik v. Rand, 732 S.W.2d 232 (Mo. Ct. App. 1987); Crosby v. Beam, 548 N.E.2d 217 (Ohio 1989) (recognizing duty of equal opportunity which can be satisfied by proof of a legitimate business purpose or unequal treatment).

[108] *See* William S. Hochstetler & Mark D. Svejda, Statutory Needs of Close Corporations—An Empirical Study: Special Close Corporation Legislation or Flexible General Corporation Law?, 10 J. Corp. L. 849, 954 (1985) (commenting on inconsistencies in construction of preemptive right provisions).

preemptive right or eliminates the preemptive right unless it is affirmatively granted by corporate charter. By express statutory provision in many states a corporation's article of incorporation may contain provisions limiting or denying preemptive rights.[109] Some such statutes merely refer to the ability to limit or deny the right in a corporation's articles of incorporation, whereas in other states the statute details the scope of the right in the absence of a defining, limiting, or denying provision in the articles.[110] Most frequently, states provide that there are no preemptive rights unless granted in the corporation's articles of incorporation.[111] And even though provided in the articles of incorporation, preemptive rights can be removed through the amendment process.[112] Since preemptive rights are now effectively permissive, drafters of corporate charters should keep in mind the various factors to be weighed as well as the necessity for making clear the extent of any preemptive right.

Preemptive rights aim to safeguard holders against unfairness in the issue of shares, particularly against two possible wrongs: (1) the manipulation of voting control of the corporation by the issuance of shares to one faction of shareholders to the exclusion of other shareholders,[113] and (2) the issue of shares at an inadequate price to favored persons, thereby diluting the proportionate interest of other shareholders to dividends and to corporate assets on dissolution.[114] As the Minnesota high court earlier said, "If a corporation, either through the officers, directors or majority stockholders, may dispose of new stock to whomsoever it will, at whatever price it may fix, then it has the power to diminish the value of each share of old stock, by letting the parties have equal interest in the surplus, and in the goodwill or value of the established business."[115]

The preemptive rights doctrine, however, has never been adequate to cover all situations and, further, has been subject to numerous limitations and exceptions based on practical convenience. Equitable relief remains available to protect against wrongful dilution of financial or voting rights, even though the plaintiff possessed a preemptive right that if exercised would have protected her from the dilution that otherwise occurred.[116] The courts have wisely allowed minority stockholders to choose between invoking self-help through exercising their preemptive right and seeking the protective remedies of a court of equity. The mere availability of a preemptive right should not foreclose other avenues of protection that are available in cases when a preemptive right is not provided. The prophylactic of a preemptive right is available only if the stockholder exercises her right to acquire more of the company's shares. Because the shareholder either may not then have the funds to purchase the shares or could well believe that her monies are better invested elsewhere, the theoretical protection believed to be provided

---

[109] *See* Alaska Stat. § 10.06.210 (2009); Minn. Stat. Ann. § 302A.413 (2009); MBCA Ann. § 10.01 (3d ed. 1995).

[110] *E.g.,* Fla. Stat. Ann. § 607.0202 (2009); N.H. Rev. Stat. Ann. § 293–A:6.30 (2009); N.Y. Bus. Corp. Law § 622 (2009); former MBCA § 26A (1980).

[111] Ariz. Rev. Stat. Ann. § 10–630 (2009); Cal. Corp. Code § 204 (2009); Conn. Gen. Stat. Ann. § 33–683 (2009); Del. Code Ann. tit. 8, § 102(b)(3) (2009) ("no stockholder shall have any preemptive right to subscribe to an additional issue . . . unless, and except to the extent that, such right is expressly granted to him in the certificate of incorporation"); Mich. Comp. Laws Ann. § 450.1343 (2009).

[112] *See* L. L. Minor Co. v. Perkins, 268 S.E.2d 637 (Ga. 1980).

[113] Dickson v. Morrison, 187 F.3d 629 (4th Cir. 1999) (recognizing preemptive right there protected shareholders from management entrenching its control of close corporation).

[114] *See* Katzowitz v. Sidler, 249 N.E.2d 359, 363 (N.Y. 1969).

[115] Jones v. Morrison, 16 N.W. 854, 861 (Minn. 1883).

[116] *See* Schwartz v. Marien, 335 N.E.2d 334 (N.Y. 1975); Katzowitz v. Sidler, 249 N.E.2d 359 (N.Y. 1969).

by a preemptive right can, in many cases, elude the minority stockholder. Hence, a full panoply of remedies of a court of equity should be available, even though the plaintiff is also armed with a preemptive right that theoretically if exercised would avoid the dilution that is at the heart of her prayer for equitable action.

In all jurisdictions, preemptive rights can be denied in a corporation's articles of incorporation; even when not denied, they apply, according to most courts, only to an issue of newly authorized shares and do not extend to a new issue of originally or previously authorized shares, at least not where the issue does not raise funds to expand the business.[117] A few courts, however, have held that preemptive rights extend to original shares that are issued long after the creation of the corporation and a material time after the original offering of shares has come to an end.[118] The latter is the better view because the availability of such an important prophylaxis should not depend on the fortuity of whether less than all the originally authorized shares were issued. This view is even more compelling when the parties have expressly provided for preemptive rights in the articles of incorporation, as they have thereby expressed a desire for affirmative protection against dilution.

The preemptive right is most frequently granted to the holders of common shares.[119] In the absence of a provision in a corporation's articles of incorporation granting holders of a class of stock preemptive rights in issues of another class, it is doubtful to what extent a holder of shares of one class has a preemptive right to an issue of the shares of another class. The cases are in conflict. Should a preemptive right to new issues of common always be given to the holders of preferred shares or only if the preferred shares currently carry voting rights equal to the common shares? Certainly, if preferred is nonvoting and nonparticipating in dividends, there is no basis for dilution of their interest. If preferred shareholders have full voting rights but no participating rights as dividends, or vice versa, the resolution of whether the preferred has a preemptive right is more problematic and should, in the absence of express contractual provisions, turn on the likely intent of the parties.

As the share structure of a corporation becomes more complex, it is very difficult, if not impossible, to grant preemptive rights to a class of preferred shares without some change in the relative rights of other classes.[120] In the absence of a charter provision to the contrary, some jurisdictions limit preemptive rights to holders of shares of the same class as those being issued.[121] Confusion and uncertainty about such matters in a particular jurisdiction may make it desirable to waive or clarify preemptive rights by specific provision in the articles of incorporation.

In a few jurisdictions at least, the preemptive right to subscribe has been extended to convertible securities such as bonds or preferred shares convertible into shares of common stock, thus giving such securities a preemptive right on new issues of the underlying common stock.[122] In light of the sparse supporting authority for this

---

[117] Yasik v. Wachtel, 17 A.2d 309 (Del. Ch. 1941).

[118] Titus v. Paul State Bank, 179 P. 514 (Idaho 1919).

[119] More specifically, the registered owner of the shares is entitled to exercise the preemptive right such that the owner-pledgor of shares may exercise preemptive rights with respect to shares he has pledged to secure a loan. *See* Peri-Gil Corp. v. Sutton, 442 P.2d 35 (Nov. 1968).

[120] *See* Russell v. American Gas & Elec. Co., 136 N.Y.S. 602 (App. Div. 1912).

[121] *E.g.*, MBCA § 6.30(b)(5) (2016).

[122] Wall v. Utah Copper Co., 62 A. 533 (N.J. Ch. 1905).

proposition, however, if such a result is desired, the corporation's articles of incorporation should explicitly so provide.

States adopting the approach taken in the Model Business Corporation Act provide a great deal of certainty to the question of whether the holders of one class of stock have a preemptive right to acquire shares of another class of stock. Under the Model Business Corporation Act, holders of nonvoting shares of one class do not have a preemptive right to acquire shares of another class, regardless of any other preferences those shares may have, unless the articles of incorporation otherwise provide. Moreover, the holders of shares of a class with general voting rights but no preference as to distributions of assets do not have a preemptive right to acquire shares of a class that does have a preference to asset distributions. The twin objectives, therefore, of the Model Business Corporation Act-type of definition of "preemptive rights" are to shield holders from dilution of their voting rights and their economic rights.

The preemptive right ordinarily does not extend to shares issued as consideration for property or services, shares issued to discharge a bona fide debt, or shares issued in a merger.[123] The reasons for these exemptions relate to matters of commercial necessity, practical convenience, and the need for directors to be able to issue shares to accomplish corporate purposes.

Preemptive rights do not ordinarily extend to the reissue or resale of treasury shares.[124] This exception is also based on practical grounds, as treasury shares are usually sold from time to time and not reissued in large amounts. The directors' duty of good faith and fairness, however, applies to a corporation's sale of treasury shares and also to other issues of shares in which no preemptive right is recognized.[125]

Preemptive rights generally do not apply to a corporation's issuance of shares under an employee stock option or employee stock purchase plan. If in a particular state preemptive rights do apply to shares issued under such a plan, or if that matter is in question, waiver of preemptive rights may have to be submitted to the shareholders, or the corporation's articles of incorporation may have to be amended.[126] The value of the employees' right to purchase under such a plan should, of course, have some reasonable relation to the value of the services rendered or to be rendered by the employees.[127]

When a corporation is issuing shares, market conditions may not allow for delay that would result from honoring preemptive rights by offering shares to all the shareholders. In such a situation, the requirement of a preemptive rights offering may harm the shareholders more than it helps them.[128] Thus the conclusion of many courts is that preemptive rights do not apply to shares that are part of those originally authorized. In any event, the existence of a preemptive right can impose a serious timing problem on the corporation's needs to raise capital because any preemptive right

---

[123]   Rogers v. First Nat'l Bank of St. George, 410 F.2d 579 (4th Cir. 1969); Kelly v. Englehart Corp., 2001 WL 855600 (Iowa Ct. App. 2001) (stock for stock no preemptive right unless provided otherwise in articles of incorporation).

[124]   Borg v. International Silver Co., 11 F.2d 147 (2d Cir. 1925).

[125]   Schwab v. Schwab-Wilson Mach. Corp., 55 P.2d 1268 (Cal. Ct. App. 1936).

[126]   *See, e.g.,* Schwartz v. Custom Printing Co., 926 S.W.2d 490 (Mo. Ct. App. 1996) (denying injunction seeking to enforce right of stockholder to obtain proportionate amount of shares to be issued pursuant to a employee bonus plan).

[127]   Dickinson v. Auto Ctr. Mfg. Co., 639 F.2d 250 (5th Cir. 1981).

[128]   Venner v. American Tel. & Tel. Co., 181 N.Y.S. 45, 47 (Sup. Ct. 1920).

postpones sales to outsiders until existing stockholders have been approached. Thus a company that anticipates a future need to raise funds from new investors is well advised to consider removing preemptive rights as a predicate to that offering.

Preemptive rights do not make sense in a public-issue corporation. In fact, their presence can severely hamper future financing. Accordingly, the charters of public companies typically eliminate such rights if the statutes of their domiciles do not do so. If preemptive rights are abrogated or waived, the directors still must not discriminate unfairly in the issue of shares; differences in the issue price of the shares may be made only in the exercise of fair business judgment for the benefit of the corporation.[129] In a close corporation, however, in the interest of preserving the original shareholders' proportionate preemptive rights, they often should not only be retained but also should be extended to cover many of the share-issue transactions that are generally excepted from the rights.[130]

It is thus clear that regardless of preemptive rights, a corporation's directors must observe their fiduciary responsibilities in issuing new shares; otherwise the shares may be subject to cancellation.[131] In the issuance of shares, however, the directors have the latitude, including pricing, given by the business judgment rule.[132] Even though there is some division in the courts as to whether a shareholder suit based on an alleged violation of preemptive rights is direct or derivative,[133] the better view is that the preemptive right, as a right of the individual stockholder, should give rise to a direct cause of action.

Even though a shareholder has a preemptive right to acquire a proportionate amount of a new issue, the board of directors generally fixes a specific date beyond which shareholders can no longer exercise their right to acquire the shares. A shareholder who does not exercise his right within the time so designated is deemed to have waived his right, and the board of directors may offer to anyone else the shares not acquired. When no time is so set, the shareholders' acquiescence by failure to complain is treated as a waiver of her preemptive rights.[134] The better view, however, is that there is no waiver if material facts are misrepresented, the offer's terms are significantly altered, or other unfairness occurs in connection with the stockholder's decision to forgo her preemptive rights.[135]

§ 16.15 The Theory Behind the Legal Capital Concept

The merger of law and accounting is nowhere more evident than in the statutory regulation of the corporation's power to make distributions to its shareholders. The focus of such regulation is threefold: (1) first and foremost, the protection of creditors against unreasonable diminution in the debtor corporation's assets through asset distributions to its shareholders; (2) if there are more than two classes of shares outstanding, the

---

[129] Schwartz v. Marien, 335 N.E.2d 334 (N.Y. 1975).

[130] *See* Fuller v. Krogh, 113 N.W.2d 25, 32 (Wis. 1962).

[131] *See, e.g.,* Mason Shoe Mfg. Co. v. Firstar Bank Eau Claire, N.A., 579 N.W.2d 789 (Wis. Ct. App. 1998).

[132] *See* Schwab v. Schwab-Wilson Mach. Corp., 55 P.2d 1268 (Cal. Ct. App. 1936).

[133] *See* Bellows v. Porter, 201 F.2d 429 (8th Cir. 1953).

[134] *See, e.g.,* Rejsa v. Beeman, 1997 WL 526320 (Minn. Ct. App. 1997).

[135] *See*; Naquin v. Air Engineered Sys. & Serv., Inc., 423 So.2d 713 (La. Ct. App. 1982) (no waiver of preemptive right when defendant has purposely denied plaintiff inspection rights so as to prevent him from being sufficiently informed to exercise his preemptive rights); First Transcable Corp. v. Avalon Pictures, Inc., 585 N.Y.S.2d 195 (App. Div. 1992) (notice defective because lacked complete information necessary to exercise right).

protection of classes having the senior economic rights from erosion of those rights as a result of corporate distributions to the junior shareholders; and (3) the protection of all shareholders from improvident distributions that impair the corporation's power to carry on its business.[136] The bulwark of such protection centers on the concept of "legal capital," the synonyms for which being "stated capital," "capital stock," and "paid-up capital."

Whereas the economist and the accountant both define "capital" as the assets of the business, "capital" in the legal sense is the *amount* the business's proprietors agree to invest in the corporation. Under early corporate statutes, capital was measured by the aggregate par value of the issued shares. Recall that par value is an arbitrary figure, unrelated to a share's intrinsic value, that is fixed in the corporation's charter. The legal significance of par value to a purchaser or subscriber of corporate shares is that it establishes the minimum amount that must be paid for the shares. If less than par value is paid, the corporation and its creditors may recover the deficiency.

§ 16.16   Legal Capital of Par and No-Par Shares

A corporation's legal or stated capital (or, to use an older designation, "capital stock") is established or increased on the issue of shares.[137] Legal capital fixes the margin of net assets or value that must be retained in the business and restricts the distribution of assets to the shareholders. If the shares a corporation issues are par value shares, its legal capital is generally an amount equal to the aggregate par value of the issued shares. When shares without par value were introduced, a different definition of "legal capital" became necessary. Modern corporation acts avoid the use of the old term "capital stock," with its variable meanings, and many statutes substitute the term "stated capital."[138] This latter term is no doubt derived from the practice of specifying what part of the subscription price for low-par or no-par shares is to be attributed to capital and what part to paid-in surplus. Under such a statute, if a corporation's shares are without par value, its stated capital is the aggregate amount of the consideration paid or agreed to be paid that is not allotted to paid-in surplus.[139]

The Concept of Legal Capital. The old terms "capital stock" and "capital" have various meanings and express different concepts in different contexts. As a New York court said in an important dividend case,

> Capital means one thing to an economist, or perhaps more accurately different things to different economists, and it has still different meanings to accountants and to business men. It means different things in different statutes. . . . To determine its meaning in this statute it thus is essential . . . to consider the history of the statute and what our courts have said respecting the statute's predecessors.[140]

---

[136] *See generally* Henry W. Ballantine & George S. Hills, Corporate Capital and Restrictions upon Dividends Under Modern Corporation Laws, 23 Cal. L. Rev. 229 (1935).

[137] *See, e.g.,* Witherbee v. Bowles, 95 N.E. 27 (N.Y. 1911).

[138] *See* Alaska Stat. § 10.06.730 (2009); Del. Code Ann. tit. 8, § 154 (2009); Iowa Code Ann. § 491.110 (2009); Maryland Code Ann. § 2–204 (2009); Minn. Stat. Ann. § 303.02 (2009); former MBCA § 2(j) (1969).

[139] Alaska Stat. § 10.06.730 (2009); *see* Ballantine & Hills, *supra* § 16.15 note 136, at 231–238; Hills, *supra* § 16.9 note 51, at 1360.

[140] Randall v. Bailey, 23 N.Y.S.2d 173, 179 (Sup. Ct. 1940).

Legal capital is an amount that measures the margin of net assets or value that is to be retained in the business as against withdrawals in favor of the shareholders.[141] Legal capital is an amount, a limitation—not the actual corporation assets or property.[142] Corporations under such a regime were permitted to distribute as dividends or as repurchases of their shares the amount by which their assets exceed the sum of the firm's liabilities and legal capital. That is, firms paying dividends or repurchasing their shares are not at liberty to do so to the point that their assets equal their liabilities. Additional sums must be retained in the enterprise—namely, the amount of assets retained within the business following the payment of a dividend or repurchase of shares must not be less than the sum of the firms' liabilities *and* its legal capital. Thus legal capital is the "margin of safety" prescribed by corporate statutes for the benefit of the firm's creditors.[143]

The "trust fund doctrine" that is at the core of the corporate statutes' embrace of the concept of legal capital is primarily a rule against the wrongful withdrawal of assets that should be retained by the corporation for the protection of creditors. There is in fact no true trust fund at all, but only a legal prohibition against withdrawals of corporate assets that reduce the margin of safety for creditors. The margin so identified, however, has no intrinsic relationship to the variables that subject creditors to improper risks or prejudice some of the shareholders themselves.[144] The amount of a corporation's legal capital is an artificial figure, being the product of the number of outstanding shares and their par value or, if any shares are without par value, an amount up to the value of the consideration received for the shares allocated to legal capital by the board of directors. The corporation's legal capital is entered on the liability side of its balance sheet and is deducted from the corporation's net worth (assets minus liabilities) in ascertaining what can be paid to shareholders in dividends or other distributions.

Relation of Issued Shares to Stated Capital. Properly regarded, the relation of stated capital to issued shares is only historical. Under the former version of the Model Act, "stated capital" means (1) the aggregate par value of all issued shares; (2) the amount of consideration fixed for no par stock that is so allocated by the directors; and (3) such amount that the directors have transferred from the surplus accounts "minus all reductions from such sum as have been effected in a manner permitted by law."[145]

Most states do not require that all consideration received for no-par shares be counted in fixing the amount of the legal capital margin. Many states permit the board of directors to allocate to paid-in surplus an unlimited portion of the consideration received on the issue of no-par shares, thus weakening any requirement to establish an adequate stated capital.[146] It has been advocated that there be at least a certain minimum percentage of the consideration—for example, 50 percent—attributed to stated capital.

Although still in force in most jurisdictions, this system has been criticized as archaic.[147] In a forward-looking statute, California was the first state to abandon the

---

[141] Randall v. Bailey, 23 N.Y.S.2d 173, 179 (Sup. Ct. 1940), *aff'd,* 288 N.Y. 280, 43 N.E.2d 43 (1942).

[142] Crocker v. Waltham Watch Co., 53 N.E.2d 230, 237, 238 (Mass. 1944).

[143] Williams v. Western Union Tel. Co., 93 N.Y. 162 (1883).

[144] McDonald v. Williams, 174 U.S. 397 (1899).

[145] Former MBCA § 2(j) (1969).

[146] *E.g.,* former MBCA § 21 (1969); Del. Code Ann. tit. 8, § 154 (2009); N.Y. Bus. Corp. Law § 506 (2009).

[147] *See* George D. Gibson, Surplus, So What?, 17 Bus. Law. 476 (1962).

relationship between par and stated capital.[148] It was followed thereafter by the current Model Business Corporation Act.[149] The current Model Business Corporation Act continues the trend by removing any legal significance to par value and thereby premises the regulation of distributions to stockholders[150] on key financial relationships by requiring that no distribution reduce the firm's assets below its liabilities or render the corporation unable to pay its debts as they mature in the ordinary course of business.[151]

The distinguishing feature of the current Model Business Corporation Act from the impairment-of-capital approach is that the latter required that the assets remaining after the distribution equal not only the firm's liabilities but also its stated capital—that is, the aggregate par value of issued shares. California's modern provision provides somewhat greater protection to creditors than does the present Model Business Corporation Act because it requires that the assets remaining after the distribution equal at least 1 ¼ times the firm's liabilities.[152] The regulation of dividend and share repurchases is discussed in Chapters 20 and 21, where the issues posed by the modern statutes are examined further.

---

[148] Cal. Corp. Code § 500 (2009).

[149] *See* Committee on Corporate Laws, Changes in the Model Business Corporation Act—Amendments to Financial Provisions, 34 Bus. Law. 1567 (1979).

[150] The Model Business Corporation Act subjects both dividends and share repurchases to the same regulatory treatment through its definition of "distribution." *See* MBCA §§ 1.40(6) & 6.40 (2008).

[151] MBCA § 6.40(c)(1), (2) (2016).

[152] Cal. Corp. Code § 500(b)(1) (2009). California is also more conservative than the Model Business Corporation Act by requiring assets be measured pursuant to generally accepted accounting principles, *see id.* at § 114, whereas the Model Act permits assets "on a fair valuation or other method that is reasonable in the circumstances." MBCA § 6.40(d) (2016).

Chapter 17

LIABILITY FOR WATERED, BONUS, AND UNDERPAID SHARES

Table of Sections

§ 17.1   Varieties of Watered Stock

"Watered stock" refers to shares issued as fully paid when in fact the consideration agreed to and accepted by the corporation's directors is something known to be much less than the par value of the shares or lawful subscription price. The term is frequently used to cover bonus shares as well as discount shares and those issued for property or services at an overvaluation.

If shares have been issued by a corporation as paid in full when in fact the subscriber has not paid or agreed to pay the full par value or lawful issue price, in either money, property, or services, the shares are said to be watered to the extent to which they have not been, or are not agreed to be, fully paid.[1] There are various ways in which underpaid or watered shares may come into being. They may be issued gratuitously without any consideration passing to the corporation.[2] They may be issued for cash at a discount below par value,[3] or in exchange for property, labor, or services that are known to be worth less than the par value.[4]

Shares may also be issued as a "bonus" or inducement to the purchaser of bonds or preferred shares. Bonus shares are legitimate when viewed as further consideration for the purchase price that has to be apportioned between them and the other securities.[5] It is often difficult to allocate or apportion the credit where bonus stock has been issued.

---

[1]   *See* E. Merrick Dodd, Jr., Stock Watering (1933).

[2]   *See, e.g.,* Andrews v. Chase, 49 P.2d 938, 941 (1935), *reh'g denied,* 57 P.2d 702 (1936).

[3]   *See, e.g.,* Harman v. Himes, 77 F.2d 375 (D.C. Cir. 1935).

[4]   *E.g.,* Elyton Land Co. v. Birmingham Warehouse & Elevator Co., 9 So. 129 (Ala. 1890).

[5]   In re Associated Oil Co., 289 F. 693 (6th Cir. 1923).

The word "bonus" implies a gift or gratuity and is sometimes used in the sense of shares issued without any consideration.

Another variety of watered stock may be issued in the guise of a stock dividend. In such a case the stock is issued to existing shareholders as shares that represent a transfer of surplus to capital when in fact there is insufficient surplus to justify their issuance.[6]

The sections that follow consider the legal implications of and potential liabilities arising out of watered or over-capitalized shares.

§ 17.2   Evils and Abuses of Stock Watering

Flagrant stock watering was common in the promotion and financing of corporations in the latter part of the nineteenth and the early years of the twentieth centuries.[7] The evils of stock watering consist primarily of injuries to the corporation, innocent shareholders, and creditors perpetrated by promoters and those in control by depriving the corporation of needed capital and of the corporation's opportunity to market its securities to its own advantage, thus hurting its business prospects and financial responsibility. Existing and future shareholders are injured due to dilution of the proportionate interests of those who pay full value for their shares.[8] Present and future creditors are injured when the corporation is deprived of the assets to be contributed by all the shareholders as a substitute for individual liability for corporate debts. Stock watering involves fictitious capitalization and is deceptive both to the corporate management in declaring dividends and to those who deal with the corporation or purchase its securities. Watered stock is invariably accompanied by misleading corporate accounts and financial statements, particularly by an overstatement of the value of assets received for the shares in order to conceal a capital deficit resulting from overvaluation and underpayment of purported capital contributions.[9]

Three developments have significantly reduced the frequency of suits under state corporate statutes for watered stock liability. First, the advent of low-par and no-par stock has to a large extent eliminated watered stock problems in the strict definitional sense. By eliminating par value, the present Model Business Corporations Act also does away with watered stock in its strictest meaning.[10] Finally, the prophylactic effects of state blue sky laws and remedial benefits available under the antifraud provisions, section 10(b) and Rule 10b–5, of the Securities Exchange Act of 1934, have largely supplanted the regulatory impact of state corporate statutes for watered stock, at least with respect to protecting the corporation and later-purchasing shareholders. The discussion that follows closely examines the remedies the corporation and its creditors have for watered stock.

---

[6]   Whitlock v. Alexander, 76 S.E. 538 (N.C. 1912).

[7]   "The great abuses which have been perpetrated, and the deceits which have been practiced upon the public, in the organization of corporations by the issue of stock and bonds, the par value of which has been grossly in excess of the real capital embarked in the business, are too well known to require comment." Altenberg v. Grant, 85 F. 345, 346 (6th Cir. 1898) (construing a strict Kentucky constitutional provision against stock watering).

[8]   Bodell v. General Gas & Elec. Corp., 132 A. 442 (Del. Ch. 1926), aff'd, 140 A. 264 (Del. 1927).

[9]   See Chapter 18.

[10]   However, the same evils can be accomplished by the issuance of shares at a grossly overvalued price.

§ 17.3　Contract and Trust Fund Theories

The liability of shareholders to or for the benefit of creditors on watered or fictitiously paid-up shares has rested on various theories. Some courts look to the artificial "trust fund" theory, while others rely on fraud or holding out. A few jurisdictions base liability to creditors on a common law or statutory obligation to pay for the par value of the shares. The trust fund theory merely describes the rule that the legal obligation to pay par, imposed by common law or by statute, runs to the corporation and may not be released by any agreement with the corporation or by any fictitious or simulated payment, even though accepted by the directors as payment in full. The theory generally is regarded as having originated with Judge Story's 1824 opinion in *Wood v. Dummer*,[11] which was a case not of watered stock liability but of shareholder liability to creditors to restore dividends paid out by an insolvent bank as a distribution of capital.

Under the trust fund theory in its original form, however, the implication of the promise seems to have been based on the policy that the obligation to pay the par value of shares arises from the privilege of exemption from individual liability and that the release from full payment is an evasion of the law as against all creditors.[12] Thus unless the fraud theory is accepted, the creditors' right of action against the holder of watered stock is considered to be an equitable right to reach an asset of the corporation, as in the case of shares issued on credit. The shareholders' liability is thus a legal obligation to the corporation to make a capital contribution required as one of the conditions of doing business with limited liability for the protection of all creditors.[13]

§ 17.4　The Fraud or Holding-Out Theory

The prevailing theory of liability on bonus or watered shares has been founded in tort against the creditors rather than in an obligation to the corporation. The wrong to creditors is fraud and deceit by the directors, participated in by the shareholders, in falsely representing that the par value has been paid or agreed to be paid in full.[14] Under the early form of this theory, subsequent creditors without notice were presumed to have been deceived by this misrepresentation.[15]

The leading case of *Hospes v. Northwestern Manufacturing & Car Company*[16] severely criticized the trust fund theory as a basis of shareholders' liability on watered stock and placed this liability on the ground of fraud, actual or constructive. The "fraud" consists of a supposed representation to creditors as to the amount of capital contributed or subscribed by the shareholders.[17] The creditors are presumed to have extended credit

---

[11]　Wood v. Dummer, 30 Fed. Cas. 435 (C.C.D. Me. 1824) (No. 17944).

[12]　Scovill v. Thayer, 105 U.S. 143, 154 (1882); Sawyer v. Hoag, 84 U.S. (17 Wall.) 610, 620 (1873); Coffin v. Ransdell, 11 N.E. 20 (Ind. 1887); Wetherbee v. Baker, 35 N.J.Eq. 501, 510 (1882).

[13]　It has been said that "where stock of a corporation is issued without being fully paid up, the amount remaining unpaid is, so far as the creditors are concerned, deemed to be money due to the corporation from the stockholders." R.H. Herron Co. v. Shaw, 133 P. 488, 489 (Cal. 1913). *See* Note, 11 Cal. L. Rev. 362 (1923).

[14]　Hirschfeld v. McKinley, 78 F.2d 124 (9th Cir. 1935), *cert. denied*, 297 U.S. 703 (1936).

[15]　*But see* Bing Crosby Minute Maid Corp. v. Eaton, 297 P.2d 5 (Cal. 1956).

[16]　Hospes v. Northwestern Manufacturing & Car Company, 50 N.W. 1117 (Minn. 1892).

[17]　Rhode v. Dock-Hop Co., 194 P. 11, 16 (Cal. 1920).

to the corporation in reliance on the consideration received or to be received for the shares in accordance with legal requirements.[18]

The constructive fraud doctrine, as formulated in the *Hospes* case and followed by many courts, is even less sound and practical as a basis for shareholders' liability than the original trust fund doctrine. The economic reality is that prudent creditors do not look to the capital stock as indicia of creditworthiness.[19] The true victims of the fraud are more likely to be the public subscribers and shareholders with little or no complicity in any misrepresentation to creditors.

In its more recent application, some courts have come to recognize the deficiencies of the fraud or holding-out theory. For example, in *Bing Crosby Minute Maid Corporation v. Eaton*,[20] the California Supreme Court ruled that under the fraud theory the creditor's *actual* reliance on the misstated capital is a "prerequisite to the liability of a holder of the watered stock."[21] This narrower view of shareholder liability comports with current business practice[22] and avoids the hardships of both the trust fund theory and presumption of reliance under a holding-out analysis.[23]

Under the fraud theory, only those creditors who have relied, or who can fairly be presumed possibly to have relied, on the professed amount of capital contributions will be recognized as having a claim against guilty holders of watered stock.[24] In other words, the shareholders' liability is limited to subsequent creditors without notice of the watering. No prior creditors or subsequent creditors with notice can complain. The soundness of the distinction between claims and equities of prior and subsequent creditors is very doubtful where no requirement exists for a creditor to prove reliance. The practical justification, if any, is that of a more or less arbitrary limitation of liability of shareholders, thus avoiding hardship in certain cases.[25]

§ 17.5   The Statutory Obligation Doctrine

Beginning about the middle of the nineteenth century, the evils of stock watering had become so aggravated as to lead many states to adopt constitutional and statutory provisions prohibiting the practice.

The most specific and important type of statute provides that a shareholder shall be liable to creditors, either directly or through the corporation, "to the amount of their

---

[18]   *E.g.,* R.H. Herron Co. v. Shaw, 133 P. 488 (Cal. 1913) (public policy requires that reliance by creditor not be element of watered stock claim).

[19]   As Professor Lattin observed:

A basic fallacy in the fraud theory is that creditors rely upon the stated capital of a corporation in granting credit. Even if they have had access to a recent balance sheet of the company, they are much more interested in the ratio of liquid assets to current liabilities than they are in the fictitious liability item which appears as stated capital or capital stock. Likewise, they are interested in the reputation which the company has acquired through paying its debts promptly.

Norman D. Lattin, Corporations 475 (2d ed. 1971).

[20]   Bing Crosby Minute Maid Corporation v. Eaton, 297 P.2d 5 (Cal. 1956).

[21]   Bing Crosby Minute Maid Corporation v. Eaton, 297 P.2d 5, 9 (Cal. 1956).

[22]   *See* Henry W. Ballantine, Corporations 80 (rev. ed. 1946).

[23]   The *Hospes* rule was subsequently overruled by statute. Minn. Bus. Corp. Act of 1933 § 114 (IV), (V).

[24]   The creditor has the burden of proving that credit was extended after issuance of the watered shares. Once that burden has been met, under one version of the fraud theory the burden then shifts to the shareholder to prove no reliance by the creditor. Randall Printing Co. v. Sanitas Mineral Water Co., 139 N.W. 606 (Minn. 1913).

[25]   2 Garrard Glenn, Fraudulent Conveyances & Preferences §§ 608, 1060–1062 (1940).

stock subscribed and unpaid, and no more" or words to that effect. For example, the pre-1980 Model Business Corporation Act requires that par value stock not be issued for less than par[26] and that no shareholder liability to creditors or the corporation arises "other than the obligation to pay to the corporation the full consideration for which such shares were issued or to be issued."[27]

This construction has been followed by the courts of New Jersey and Delaware, which place shareholders' liability on watered stock on neither the contract theory nor the "trust fund" or "holding out" theory, but on a statutory obligation that the law requires be made good for the benefit of creditors of insolvent companies, without discrimination between prior and subsequent creditors, or between creditors who had notice and those who had no notice.[28] In most other jurisdictions, however, these constitutional and statutory provisions have usually been rendered nugatory, being construed as merely declaratory of the fraud theory developed by the courts and subject to the arbitrary limitations of that theory.[29]

§ 17.6 Liability of Transferees of Watered Stock

Bona fide transferees of watered stock will not be liable unless they may be regarded as having constructive notice of the fictitious payment. When combined with the serious difficulty of proving deliberate or fraudulent overvaluation of shares issued for property or services this rule has made judicial remedies limited if not ineffectual.

According to the better view, the holder of watered or fictitiously paid-up stock cannot escape liability to creditors by transferring the shares to an irresponsible person, an insolvent corporation or person, or to a bona fide purchaser.[30] In some states the transferor remains liable even though the transferee is solvent and took the shares with notice.[31]

§ 17.7 Creditors', Receivers', and Trustees' Remedies

Creditors generally must proceed by a creditors' bill in equity to enforce the liability of shareholders on bonus and watered stock unless there is statutory direct liability.[32] Two exceptions to the general requirement of special statutory authorization for direct liability have emerged: first, when the corporation ceases to do business and is insolvent;[33] and, second, when the officers or directors who are also shareholders act in their corporate capacity to perpetrate the fraud on the creditors.[34]

The more recent exception to the general requirement of special statutory authorization is to allow creditors to sue directly the directors or officers, or shareholders who intentionally perpetrate the fraud of watering the stock even in the absence of

---

[26] *See* former MBCA § 18 (1969).

[27] Former MBCA § 25 (1969). Subsequent versions similarly limit shareholders' liability. MBCA § 6.22 (2016).

[28] Du Pont v. Ball, 106 A. 39 (Del. 1918), *aff'g* John W. Cooney Co. v. Arlington Hotel Co., 101 A. 879 (Del. Ch. 1917).

[29] In re Associated Oil Co., 289 F. 693, 695–696 (6th Cir. 1923) (South Dakota statute).

[30] *See* Palmer v. Scheftel, 186 N.Y.S. 84 (App. Div. 1921), *aff'd*, 142 N.E. 263 (N.Y. 1923) (transferor remains liable because transferee without notice escapes liability).

[31] *See* Graham v. Fleissner's Exr., 153 A. 526, 529 (N.J. 1931).

[32] *E.g.*, Eskimo Pie Corp. v. Whitelawn Dairies, Inc., 266 F.Supp. 79 (S.D.N.Y. 1967).

[33] Providence State Bank v. Bohannon, 426 F.Supp. 886 (E.D. Mo. 1977).

[34] *See* Hoover v. Galbraith, 498 P.2d 981 (Cal. 1972).

statute.[35] For example, a 1967 Massachusetts case[36] recognized direct shareholder liability to creditors where the shareholders/directors transferred no assets in consideration for the corporate stock. All of the shareholders/directors/officers of this closely held corporation had known of the fraud. The court held that, because the corporation was formed for an illegal purpose (to defraud creditors), equity dictated that the creditors be permitted to sue directly as individual creditors.[37]

This ruling of the Massachusetts Supreme Judicial Court seems to be the better policy, particularly when the corporation is closely held. Many courts simply pierce the corporate veil.[38] To require a first suit against the insolvent corporation is time-consuming and unnecessarily increases the creditor's expenses.

Whether the liability on watered stock will be enforced for the benefit of the corporation's creditors by either receivers or trustees in bankruptcy or individual creditors will depend on the law of the state of incorporation.[39] In many states, shareholders' liability on watered, bonus, discount, or subscription shares is recognized as an equitable asset of the corporation held for the benefit of creditors.[40] Conversely, under a fraud rationale, shareholders' liability on watered stock is to the creditors directly and only subsequent creditors may recover because they are presumed to have relied on the misrepresentations.[41] Some courts have ruled that shareholder liability on watered stock is not an asset to the corporation, and its trustee or receiver cannot sue for the benefit of the corporation's creditors.[42]

§ 17.8   Creditors Against Holders of Watered No-Par Stock

A primary advantage to no-par stock is the freedom from any requirement of a fixed minimum capital contribution. Some have questioned whether no-par shares may not pose a serious danger of fraud on existing and possibly on future shareholders as well as on the corporation because there is no statutory restraint on their issuing price.[43] Adequacy of corporate capital is, of course, equally important, whether par value or no-par shares are used. No-par shares involve a relaxation of the requirements as to the establishment of an adequate stated capital and the legal safeguards protecting creditors; a similar effect can be accomplished through the use of low-par shares. As contrasted with that on no-par shares, the liability to creditors of holders of watered par value shares finds its true ground of support either in the contract of the subscriber to pay a definite price in money value for his shares or on a legal or a statutory obligation to pay up to their par value, notwithstanding a corporate release or acceptance of a fictitious equivalent. Par value shares have a minimum issue price in dollars fixed by the charter, which cannot be released as against creditors. With no-par shares this money standard of value may be eliminated, and the price may be fixed in specified property or services or any medium that constitutes valid consideration. If, however, the

---

[35]   Michell Co. v. Fitzgerald, 231 N.E.2d 373 (Mass. 1967).

[36]   Michell v. Fitzgerald, 231 N.E.2d 373 (Mass. 1967).

[37]   Michell v. Fitzgerald, 231 N.E.2d 373, 376 (Mass. 1967).

[38]   *See* § 7.9.

[39]   Harrigan v. Bergdoll, 270 U.S. 560 (1925).

[40]   In re Gribbin Supply Co., 371 F.Supp. 664 (N.D. Tex. 1974).

[41]   Union Guardian Trust Co. v. Barlum, 259 N.W. 297 (Mich. 1935).

[42]   Union Guardian Trust Co. v. Barlum, 259 N.W. 297 (Mich. 1935).

[43]   *See* Carlos L. Israels, Problems of Par and No-Par Shares: A Reappraisal, 47 Colum. L. Rev. 1279, 1289–1300 (1947).

consideration for no-par shares is fixed in money at, say, $20 per share and only $10 is paid in and this is accepted by the corporation as full payment, the subscriber or holder with notice is liable for the balance in event of insolvency, if the balance is needed to pay creditors. A holder with notice of no-par shares will thus be liable for the unpaid balance of the consideration fixed in money if this is paid in property or services at a consciously inflated valuation, as in case of par value shares.

In *G. Loewus & Company v. Highland Queen Packing Company*,[44] the proprietors of a business sold it to the corporation for shares of no-par stock. The agreement stated, "It is understood that the said shares of stock shall be issued at the price of $20 per share and representing a total value of $6000." It was alleged by the receiver that the assets and good will of the business turned over were worth only $1,500. The receiver of the corporation sought an assessment against the subscribers on the ground that the no-par shares were not fully paid and that the prices of the shares had been fixed at $20 per share. The New Jersey court held that the only consideration actually agreed to be given was the transfer of business and that the statement of a price of $20 per share was not intended to fix the consideration to be paid. The duty of the subscribers to pay for the shares was accordingly fully satisfied, and they were not liable for the underpayment. The *Loewus* opinion thus evidences a judicial propensity against recognizing an evasion of the subscriber's obligation to pay for no-par shares.

§ 17.9 Cancellation and Assessment of Diluted or Watered Shares

A few courts hold that shares issued for less than their par value or for an ineligible type of consideration are void, not merely voidable.[45] This result stands on their head the principles on which the violations are based. Why should the holder of watered shares be able to raise her own breach of the state corporate statute so as to avoid liability to creditors of a now insolvent corporation? Or why should a holder who has not given the statutorily prescribed amount or type of consideration but who has enjoyed all the rights of stock ownership, including voting and dividends, not be required to pay fully for those shares when her nonpayment has been discovered? Most courts that have reflected on questions such as these reach the wise conclusion that by treating shares issued for overvalued consideration, as consideration, or an ineligible type of consideration as voidable, the court can thereby more fully address the equities of the individual case.[46]

Thus the equities cry out in favor of allowing creditors to recover for watered shares when the corporation is insolvent; an unfair result would arise if the shares' issuance was treated as a void act.[47] And, as a general rule, in disputes among shareholders, the equities call for treating invalidly issued shares as void.[48] However, where the other stockholders acquiesce in the illegal issuance or otherwise have lulled the shares' holder into believing he enjoyed the full rights of stock ownership, there is a type of waiver of the statutory protections such that it would be inequitable to cancel those shares, even

44 G. Loewus & Company v. Highland Queen Packing Company, 6 A.2d 545 (N.J. Ch. 1939).

45 *See, e.g.,* Foster v. Blackwell, 747 So.2d 1203 (La. Ct. App. 1999).

46 *See, e.g.,* Murray v. Murray Labs., Inc., 270 S.W.2d 927 (Ark. 1954).

47 *See* Belt v. Belt, 679 P.2d 1144, 1148 (Idaho Ct. App. 1984) (as between shareholder who has not paid par value and innocent creditor, shareholder cannot escape liability by arguing shares are invalidly issued).

48 *See* Belt v. Belt, 679 P.2d 1144, 1148 (Idaho Ct. App. 1984).

though they were illegally issued.[49] When the courts hold that the shares issued for less than their par value or for an ineligible type of consideration are void, they are divided as to whether to void all the shares[50] or only those in excess of the amount of shares for which the full par value was received.[51] Similar considerations arise when the complaint is that the issuance of the shares entailed a breach of fiduciary obligation by their recipient.[52] Cancellation may be decreed for only such part of the shares obtained by the promoters as represents an illegal profit, leaving the taker with such number of shares as can be regarded as paid for at a fair price.

---

[49] Frasier v. Trans-Western Land Corp., 316 N.W.2d 612, 616–617 (Neb. 1982).

[50] *See* Frankowski v. Palermo, 363 N.Y.S.2d 159 (App. Div. 1975).

[51] *See* Belt v. Belt, 679 P.2d 1144, 1149 (Idaho Ct. App. 1984).

[52] *See, e.g.*, Bowers v. Rio Grande Inv. Co., 431 P.2d 478 (Colo. 1967); Warren v. Warren, 460 A.2d 526 (Del. 1983).

Chapter 18

CAPITAL STRUCTURE, PREFERENCES, AND CLASSES OF SECURITIES

Table of Sections

§ 18.1 Choices in Debt and Equity Financing

The "capitalization," financial structure, or permanent financing of a corporation is based on the issuance of capital securities. Permanent financing includes not only common stock but also senior securities, which can be (1) an equity interest by way of preferred stock or (2) bonds and debentures, which are the long-term or funded debts. Debt obligations are issued against the corporation's actual or prospective earning power even more than against its assets. The power to issue bonds and other debt obligations is not dependent, as stock issues are, on express authorization by the corporate charter. Debt financing thus provides more flexibility because there generally is no need for prior shareholder approval.

A sound and well-balanced capital structure must be carefully planned. The choice between stocks and bonds of different varieties depends on many considerations, including whether the business has an established earnings record, the ratio of property to its obligations, the rate of return that must be paid, probable marketability and attractiveness to investors, advantages under federal and state tax laws, and the effect on the future credit and ability of the corporation to survive business cycles.[1]

---

[1] For a close treatment of the subject of the considering of the choices available for financing the firm, *see, e.g.,* Georgette Chapman Poindexter, Dequity: The Blurring of Debt and Equity In Securitized Real Estate

The tax laws encourage debt financing by treating interest payments, but not dividends on stock, as deductible from corporate gross income.[2] In order to safeguard against abuse due to thin equity financing, payments on the debt instruments may be treated for tax purposes as disguised dividends.[3] Similarly, too high a debt-to-equity ratio may lead a bankruptcy court to classify debt as stock for the purposes of subordinating claims of shareholder/creditors to those of other creditors.[4]

Attorneys are frequently asked to assist in evaluating the financial soundness of a firm's capital structure. The choice among different kinds of securities should be determined by the organizer and managers, considering the inducements needed to attract different types of investors and the control of management. They must further adequately anticipate the corporation's future financial needs. Questions that inevitably arise include: (1) How can the company raise money at the lowest cost? (2) What are the tax advantages of different forms of securities? (3) How can control be reserved to the organizers without requiring them to invest too large an amount in the corporation? (4) To what extent can the company meet fixed financial charges when its income is fluctuating? (5) How can the company best ensure its credit for future financing to meet expansion and growth?

Preferred shares, which are frequently viewed as a hybrid of debt and equity, may be advisable as an alternative to pure debt because payment of dividends is not a mandatory fixed charge and non-payment will not entail foreclosure or receivership. In addition to the ability to pass on payments without being in default, there is usually no maturity date for retirement of preferred shares, and the redemption provision, if any, is normally an option in favor of the corporation. In the absence of a prohibitory covenant, the corporation has the power to borrow money by issuing notes or bonds that take priority over the preferred shares. Preferred shares may be desirable because they tend to attract a type of investor different from those who invest in pure debt instruments. Special features, such as the right of conversion into a different type of security, further expand the alternative vehicles for raising capital.

The issuance of senior securities such as bonds and preferred shares may be attractive to the issuer for various reasons. First, senior securities create "leverage" for the common shares—that is, a greater chance of possible gain to the common on the total capital investment. Second, senior securities represent money invested for a limited return on the basis of a stable income to the investor; therefore, they have no claim on capital appreciation or increased corporate income. Third, preferred shares facilitate retention of voting control by the initial or current investors, as all senior securities usually have at most only contingent voting rights. This reduces the amount of investment necessary to obtain voting control by way of either initial investment or subsequent acquisition. Fourth, preferred shares and bonds can be used to tap the reservoir of savings of those who seek to avoid the risks of common stocks.

Financing, 2 Berk. Bus. L.J. 233 (2005). *See also* William W. Bratton, Cases and Materials on Corporate Finance (6th ed. 2008).

[2] I.R.C. §§ 163, 301 (2009).

[3] I.R.C. § 385 (2009). *See, e.g.,* Mulcahy, Pauritsch, Salvador & Co. Ltd. v. C.I.R., 680 F.3d 867 (7th Cir. 2012) (payments to shareholders treated as non-deductible dividends and not as salaries).

[4] *See* Costello v. Fazio, 256 F.2d 903 (9th Cir. 1958). The issue here is analogous to the "deep rock" doctrine, which has been used to subordinate shareholder salary claims.

§ 18.2   Bonds and Debt Financing

Bonds or debentures are essentially promissory notes with more elaborate provisions than ordinary commercial loans.[5] They are generally long-term, but in times of fluctuating interest rates shorter-term instruments are not uncommon. Despite its existence as a corporate debt, the longer-term instrument has led to the view of bondholders as "joint heirs in the corporate fortunes—participants in the success or failure who have been given preferential rights in the common hazard."[6]

There are two parts to every bond issue: (1) the trust indenture and (2) the separate bonds. In broad overview, the trust indenture has two distinct parts: The first part sets forth all the obligations and restrictions on the bonds' issuer; the second part not only sets forth the bondholders' rights on default of the conditions set forth in the first part but also, by tracking the standards embodied in the Trust Indenture Act of 1939, sets forth the relationship between the indenture trustee and the bondholders.[7] There are also provisions related to amendment of the indenture as well as protection of any conversion privilege.

The bond is the only writing that the bondholder ordinarily sees. Bonds and debentures may be described as a series of instruments or notes representing units of indebtedness, yet regarded as but parts of one entire debt. The rights of all the bondholders are governed by an underlying trust, deed, mortgage, or indenture between the corporation and a trustee, who is the representative of all the different bondholders. Within this framework the remedies of an individual bondholder are limited.[8] The indenture or mortgage, has grown to be an extraordinarily complicated and elaborate legal instrument.

The Trust Indenture Act of 1939[9] today applies to corporate debt obligations where the aggregate issue price is $10 million or greater.[10] The focus of the Act is on providing "an effective and independent trustee." It addresses this goal by proscribing nine "conflicting interest" relationships.[11] The act also prescribes certain provisions to be contained in the indenture.[12] Additionally, the Act mandates certain minimum capital requirements, calls for high standards of conduct and responsibility on the part of the indenture trustee, preludes seeking preferential treatment for the trustee's claims (as distinct from those of the bondholders the trustee represents) when the obligor is in default, mandates that the issuer provide the trustee with evidence of compliance with the indenture's covenants, and requires the trustee to provide reports and notices to the

---

[5]   William W. Bratton, Corporate Finance Cases and Materials 240–46 (6th ed. 2008).

[6]   Subordination clauses that place the claims of bondholders behind those of subsequent creditors make the bonds more like stock. *See* Robert W. Johnson, Subordinated Debentures: Debt That Serves as Equity, 10 J. Fin. 1 (1955).

[7]   *See* Model Simplified Indenture, 38 Bus. Law. 741 (1983).

[8]   Joseph C. Kennedy & Robert I. Landau, Corporate Trust Administration and Management 238–244 (4th ed. 1992). *See also* Yakov Amihud, Kenneth Garbade, & Marcel Kahan, A New Governance Structure for Corporate Bonds, 51 Stan. L. Rev. 447 (1999) (reviewing weaknesses of present system which addresses poorly the bondholders' collective action problem and sets forth the model of the "supertrustee").

[9]   15 U.S.C. §§ 77aaa et seq. (2009).

[10]   The legislation authorizes the Securities and Exchange Commission to set the dollar level by exercising its rulemaking authority. *See* General Rules and Regulations of the SEC Rule 4a–3, 17 C.F.R. § 240.4a–3 (2009).

[11]   Trust Indenture Act, 15 U.S.C. § 77jjj (2009).

[12]   15 U.S.C. §§ 77jjj to 77rrr (2000).

bondholders. The relationship of the trustee to the bondholders has been subject to various classifications:[13] (1) as fiduciary;[14] (2) as founded in principal-agent law,[15] and (3) based on the contract rights, as defined in the indenture agreement.[16] Of interest is that the Act does not bar the trustee from also being a lender to the obligor of the bonds for which the trustee is the indenture trustee. This reflects the commercial reality that has long existed that most indenture trustees are banks and, as such, are not only in the business of lending funds but use their lending relationships to become the indenture trustee for bonds issued by the bank's clients. A leading case held the indenture trustee breached its fiduciary relationship to the bondholders when it advanced its own interests as a lender to the bond's obligor to the detriment of the bondholders for whom it was the indenture trustee.[17] Neither this fiduciary obligation nor does a fair construction of the Act implicates a broader obligation than undivided loyalty to the bondholders. Thus, in *Elliott Assoc. v. J. Henry Schroder Bank & Trust Co.*, the indenture trustee did not breach its duty to the bondholders by accepting less than the maximum period of notice called for by the indenture before the bonds could be redeemed since the trustee derived no personal gain from its decision.[18]

§ 18.3   Types of Bonds[19]

Open and Closed Mortgage Bonds. A serious error in corporate financing can be the failure to consider future needs for additional capital. The best framed bond mortgages make liberal provision for the increase of indebtedness by future borrowing under the same mortgage, the increase to be made under careful safeguards and restrictions. Such mortgages are known as "open-end" mortgages or bond issues and vary in the degree of openness. A closed bond issue is one in which no more bonds can be issued under a mortgage or deed of trust.

Debentures and Debenture Agreements. There are many varieties of bonds, ranging from those secured by a first mortgage or senior lien on property to those secured by a secondary or junior lien, those secured by a pledge of personal collateral such as stocks or bonds, those secured by the general credit of the corporation and restrictive agreements such as debentures and serial notes, and income bonds, which are sometimes used in reorganizations. Debentures are serial obligations or notes representing indebtedness but not ordinarily secured by any specific mortgage, lien, or pledge of security. They are usually issued under an indenture, in which a trust company agrees to supervise the execution of the covenants of the debtor for the benefit of all the holders. They are usually for a shorter term than mortgage bonds. A prime disadvantage of debenture bonds is that they rest on the credit of the corporation rather than on any specific collateral. The investor must take care to ascertain the protection given by the indenture against excessive dividends and share repurchases as well as against mortgages or future issues of bonds that might be placed ahead of the outstanding

---

[13]   John P. Campbell & Robert Zack, Put a Bullet in the Poor Beast, His Leg Is Broken and His Use Is Past, 32 Bus. Law. 1705, 1723 n.56 (1977).

[14]   York v. Guaranty Trust Co., 143 F.2d 503, 512 (2d Cir. 1944), *rev'd on other grounds*, 326 U.S. 99 (1945).

[15]   *E.g.*, First Trust Co. v. Carlsen, 261 N.W. 333, 337 (Neb. 1935).

[16]   *E.g.*, Hazzard v. Chase Nat'l Bank, 287 N.Y.S. 541 (Sup. Ct. 1936).

[17]   *See* Dabney v. Chase Nat'l Bank, 196 F.2d 668 (2d Cir. 1952).

[18]   Elliott Assocs. v. J. Henry Schroder Bank & Trust Co., 838 F.2d 66 (2d Cir. 1988).

[19]   For a review of the technical features of bonds and their financial significance, *see* Frank J. Fabozzi, Bond Markets, Analysis and Strategies 143–63, 340–45, 389–94 (4th ed. 2000).

debentures or compete for payment from the same general sources of funds. Debentures are frequently protected by "negative pledge" clauses—that is, covenants against new mortgages on the corporate assets or those of subsidiary companies that do not equally secure the debentures.[20]

A further common protective provision is the "successor obligation clause," which requires the bonds to be redeemed when the obligor "sells all or substantially all" of its assets, unless in connection with such disposition the debt is assumed by a responsible party. In *Sharon Steel Corp. v. Chase Manhattan Bank, N.A.,*[21] the debtor attempted to skirt this provision by disposing of its assets in a series of piecemeal sales. If redemption were required, the debtor would be required to pay, in addition to the face amount of the bonds, the redemption premium set forth in the debenture. The court held the sales should be collapsed together so that in combination the clause was triggered, reasoning that the clear intent of the clause was to protect lenders from circumvention of the redemption obligation while permitting borrowers to be acquired by third parties who will assume the obligations to the acquired firm's lenders.[22] *Sharon Steel* is the leading case supporting the importance of according uniform interpretations of standardized—boilerplate—provisions, reasoning that boilerplate such provisions are "not the consequence of the relationship of particular borrowers and lenders and do not depend upon particularized intentions of the parties to an indenture." It therefore held there was no place for parol evidence, or submitting to a jury, for determining the parties' likely intent with respect to the "successor obligation clause," because it was boilerplate.[23]

Redemption Privilege/Obligation. Frequently bonds and preferred stock contain redemption and/or conversion provisions.[24] When a redemption feature is included, the borrower almost invariably reserves the option to call or redeem bonds or debentures on any interest-paying date prior to their maturity after giving appropriate notice to the bondholders. Section 316(b) of the Act provides that the bondholders' "right. . . to receive payment of the principal . . . and interest . . . shall not be impaired or affected without the consent of such holder. . ."[25] This provision does not, however, require bondholder approval of any transaction that impact's their practical ability to be paid as contrasted with altering their legal rights to such payments; hence bondholders did not have a right to approve a transaction that caused the disappearance of a parent's guaranty of its subsidiary's debts.[26]

---

[20] Comment, Protection for Debenture Holders, 46 Yale L.J. 97, 98 (1936); Note, Restrictive Covenants in Debentures: The *Insull* Case, 49 Harv. L. Rev. 620 (1936).

[21] Sharon Steel Corp. v. Chase Manhattan Bank, N.A., 691 F.2d 1039 (2d Cir. 1982).

[22] *But see* Liberty Media Corp. v. Bank of New York Mellon Trust Co. N.A., 2011 WL 1632333 (Del. Ch. 2011) (there be no evidence of a master plan to dispose of all the assets the court held that each of four disposition transactions would be treated separately as each was supported by its own business justification).

[23] *See also* BankAtlantic Bancorp., Inc. Litig., 39 A.3d 824 (Del. Ch. 2012)(successor obligation clause is boilerplate, entitled to uniform interpretation, and purpose of clause is to ensure that borrowers have the flexibility to sell entire business and liquidate, or to liquidate their operating assets and enter a new field free of public debt, so long as the debt is transferred with substantially all of the assets or is otherwise paid).

[24] *See generally* William A. Klein, C. David Anderson, & Kathleen G. McGuinness, The Call Provision of Corporate Bonds: A Standard Form in Need of Change, 18 J. Corp. L. 653 (1993).

[25] 15 U.S.C. § 77ppp(b).

[26] Marblegate Asset Management, LLC v. Education Management Finance Corp., 846 F.3d 1, Fed. Sec. L. Rep. (CCH) P 99606 (2d Cir. 2017).

Without provision for redemption the debtor corporation would have no right to prepay the bonds, which it may wish to do to free itself of high interest payments or restrictions of the mortgage or indenture. A small premium is usually provided in the redemption or prepayment price; although it is not as large a premium as that commonly given for the redemption of preferred stock, it adds to the value and marketability of the bonds.

Conversion Privilege. In order to make a security attractive, corporations often confer upon bond or debenture holders the privilege of exchanging their securities for a predetermined number of shares of stock.[27] This is known as a right or privilege of conversion. The bond indenture will then provide: (1) the kind of security into which the bond may be converted; (2) the ratio of conversion—that is, the number of shares that may be called for in exchange; (3) the period or time limits during which the conversion right extends; and (4) protection against dilution and capital adjustments.[28] In drafting protection of the value a conversion feature, the attorney must take care to identify the types of transactions that can cause dilution[29] as well as whether the objective is to maintain the right to a set proportionate amount of the issuer or, instead, to force the choice between converting or incurring whatever financial consequences flow from the transaction if the bondholder does not convert.[30] It is most common to make both bonds and preferred shares convertible into common shares, although in some instances bonds have been made convertible into preferred shares.[31] Bonds and debentures are frequently issued with a stock purchase warrant giving the option to purchase a certain number of shares at a designated price; this is somewhat similar in its effect to the privilege of conversion.[32] Unlike the conversion privilege, warrants can be marketed separately from the accompanying debenture. In either case, the option or conversion privilege will be adjusted in case of capital changes, split-ups, or dilution of the stock as to which option is to be exercised.[33]

Sinking Funds. Corporations frequently provide a sinking fund for the purchase or retirement of its bonds, thus increasing their security and salability. There are various types of sinking funds.[34] Payments for debenture sinking funds, which may be conditioned on net earnings, typically must be made to a sinking fund agent, who frequently is the trustee under the indenture. Default in sinking fund payments may be grounds for acceleration of the bonds' maturity. Serial bonds are made to mature from time to time, so there is a gradual retirement of part of the bonds without payment of a

---

[27] *See generally* James C. Van Horne & John M. Waschowicz, Jr., Fundamentals of Financial Management 586–97 (10th ed. 1998).

[28] For thoughtful analyses of the standard anti-dilution clause, *see* Broad v. Rockwell Int'l Corp., 642 F.2d 929 (5th Cir. 1981) (*en banc*); Stephen I. Glover, Solving Antidilution Problems, 51 Bus. Law. 1221 (1996); Stanley A. Kaplan, Piercing the Corporate Boilerplate: Anti-Dilution Clauses in Convertible Securities, 33 U. Chi. L. Rev. 1 (1965).

[29] *See, e.g.,* Stephenson v. Plastics Corp. of Am., 150 N.W.2d 668 (1967) (resolving whether a spin off is covered by anti-dilution clause).

[30] This is the issue posed in the classic case. *See* Pittsburgh Terminal Corp. v. Baltimore & Ohio R.R. Co., 680 F.2d 933 (3d Cir.), *cert. denied,* 459 U.S. 1056 (1982).

[31] *See, e.g.,* Augusta Trust Co. v. Augusta, H. & G. R.R., 187 A. 1 (Me. 1936).

[32] *See* Henry B. Reiling, Warrants in Bond-Warrant Units: A Survey and Assessment, 70 Mich. L. Rev. 1411 (1972).

[33] George S. Hills, Convertible Securities—Legal Aspects and Draftsmanship, 19 Col. L. Rev. 1 (1930).

[34] Bringham & Gapenski, Financial Management: Theory and Practice 625–628 (6th ed. 1991).

premium.[35] It is more common, however, to provide for an annual sinking fund to be applied solely to the purchase or to the call and retirement of bonds. Such periodic purchases support the price of outstanding bonds and provide some additional liquidity for their holders. Further, if the bond market is depressed so that the price has fallen below face value, the issuer's ultimate financial burden in retiring the indebtedness is reduced, and, during the time that the bonds continue to be outstanding, the redemption of other bonds supports their value by reducing the company's future financial burdens so there is less risk associated with the payment of their interest and principal. It is common for the indenture to provide that the trustee select by lot the bonds to be retired out of the sinking fund.

Income Bonds. Income bonds, which are not normally issued except during a corporate reorganization, are obligations that call for interest payments only to the extent that income is earned annually or within specified interest periods. Such interest payments ordinarily are not made cumulative. Income bonds remove the menace of fixed charges and depend for their return on the success of the business.[36] In this respect they are very similar to non-cumulative preferred shares. The indenture should define carefully the method for determining the periodic net earnings from which interest is to be paid.

Rights of Bondholders. Some states recognize that under certain circumstances bondholders may become concerned with the management of the corporation and accordingly provide that the bondholders be given inspection rights and voting rights.[37] Ordinarily these rights are contingent and are triggered by default in interest payments or by earnings falling below a certain relation to interest requirements.[38] Conditional voting rights make bonds look more like shares of stock, and it is questionable whether in the absence of a statute such protections can be put into the indenture agreement or articles of incorporation. Voting protection for bondholders, particularly in reorganization, is sometimes provided through a voting trust for common shares.

§ 18.4   Classes of Stock

The ideal financial structure would appear to be the simplest: one class of common shares. In large enterprises, however, especially railroads and public utilities, a reasonable amount of short-term borrowings and of long-term or funded debts is usually included in the capitalization of the firm. Bonded debt has unfortunately often become over-extended, without sufficient basis in existing or foreseeable earnings to give debts a safe margin of protection. This over-extension frequently results in receivership and reorganization. In close corporations, classification of securities is frequently a good device for tailoring control arrangements and participation in profits to the particular desires of the participants.[39]

---

[35]   Floyd Franklin Burtchett & Clifford M. Hicks, Corporation Finance, Policy and Management 186–195 (4th ed. 1964).

[36]   *See* Warner Bros. Pictures, Inc. v. Lawton-Byrne-Bruner Ins. Agency Co., 79 F.2d 804, 816, 818 (8th Cir. 1935).

[37]   *E.g.,* Del. Code Ann. tit. 8, § 221 (2001).

[38]   *See* Tooley v. Robinson Springs Corp., 660 A.2d 293, 295–96 (Vt. 1995) (receipt of late payment does not bar holders from exercising their rights that are provided for default, but will bar them from seeking interest on the late payment).

[39]   *See* James C. Van Horne, Financial Management and Policy 543–46 (11th ed. 1998).

The law does not limit the various classes, varieties, or combinations of preferred shares that may be authorized, as long as the distinction between debt and shares is observed.[40] The organizers and managers of a corporation may wish to subdivide and classify the units of participation in the corporate income, assets, and control. A corporation may thus issue such varieties of preferred shares as the prospects and needs of the enterprise may call for and as the tastes of the investing public may absorb. These classes of shares may differ as to priority of claim on dividends, as to limited or participating dividend rights, as to conversion rights, voting rights, amounts payable on redemption, dissolution, or liquidation, and in protection against dilution and changes of capital structure. A security's precise financial features are driven not only by the prevailing conditions in the market but also by the risk and return objectives of the security's issuer and the various market participants, who can be expected as prospective holders to parcel different components of the security's features among themselves.[41]

Corporations sometimes issue more than one class of "common stock," one being given full voting power and the other either being nonvoting or having only a fractional vote for each share. If the distinction between classes of common stock is not in voting rights but in priority of amount of participation in earnings or assets, the class that has priority is in effect a participating preferred stock as against the other class.[42]

Preferred shares have been called "compromise securities" because they occupy an intermediate position between common shares and debts. It is this intermediate position that causes some to believe they have greater risks than either the common or bondholders.[43] They usually have a specified limited rate of return or dividend and a specified limited redemption and liquidation price. This creates "leverage" because of the greater possible gain to the common shareholders on the total capital invested and the lesser investment necessary to obtain voting control.

§ 18.5   The Preferred Share Contract

Preferred stock is distinctive because of its relationship to common stock. As the highest New York court has declared, "Whatever preferential rights and privileges may thus be granted to a stockholder, the law regards them as contractual. The certificate of stock is the muniment of the shareholder's title, and evidence of his right. It expresses the contract between the corporation and his co-stockholders and himself. . . .' "[44] As such, the traditional rules of construction and interpretation apply to determine the rights of the preferred shareholders as set forth in their contract with the corporation.[45]

---

[40]   *See* Model Bus. Corp. Act § 6.01 Official Comment (2016) (hereinafter MBCA).

[41]   *See generally* Henry Hu, New Financial Products, the Modern Process of Financial Innovation, and the Puzzle of Shareholder Welfare, 69 Texas L. Rev. 1273 (1991). Directors must often resolve conflicts among classes of stock. Value allocation decisions by boards are generally protected by the business judgment rule. The fact that the directors own more of one class than another does not necessarily implicate the directors' good faith or loyalty. Solomon v. Armstrong, 747 A.2d 1098, 1118, 1123 (Del. Ch. 1999), *aff'd*, 746 A.2d 277 (Del. 2000).

[42]   *See, e.g.,* Bodell v. General Gas & Elec. Corp., 140 A. 264 (Del. 1927).

[43]   *See* Lawrence E. Mitchell, The Puzzling Paradox of Preferred Stock (And Why We Should Care About It), 51 Bus. Law. 443, 449–454 (1996).

[44]   Strout v. Cross, Austin & Ireland Lumber Co., 28 N.E.2d 890, 893 (N.Y. 1940), quoting Kent v. Quicksilver Mining Co., 78 N.Y. 159, 180 (1879). Barry J. Benzing, Commentary, Getting What You Bargained For: The Contractual Nature of a Preferred Shareholder's Rights; Korenvaes Investments L.P. v. Marriott Corp., 19 Del. J. Corp. L. 517 (1994).

[45]   *See* Dwoskin v. Rollins, 634 F.2d 285 (5th Cir. 1981); Alta Berkeley VI C.V. v. Omneon, Inc., 41 A.3d 381 (Del. 2012)(using "plain meaning" doctrine to interpret preferred share terms). *See also, e.g.,* Elliott

It is not generally true, however, that the certificate of stock is the authoritative source, evidence, or expression of the preferred share contract.[46] The contract is made with the individual shareholders when they agree to become owners of shares and make themselves parties to the charter contract, not necessarily when a certificate of ownership is issued. In most states all the terms of the preferred share contract must be set forth in the articles of incorporation or charter and cannot be added to or changed by the bylaws, stock certificates, or corporate resolutions.[47] This promotes certainty of information as to the terms of the contract from an authoritative document that is a matter of public record.

§ 18.6   Flexibility Through a "Blank Stock" Authorization

The rigidity that results from having the dividend rate and certain other preferences on classes or series of preferred shares fixed in the charter is relaxed in several states by permission to authorize the board of directors to set the terms of new series of classes of preferred shares or even to create different classes from time to time.[48] A series is a subdivision of a class. These "blank stock" statutes enable the directors to vary the terms as to dividend rates and certain other rights of new series or classes according to what the condition of the financial market and that of the corporation may seem to require for ready sale. Blank stock can thus provide advantages similar to bonds with regard to flexibility of terms.

§ 18.7   Cumulative Dividends

If preferred shares are either expressly or impliedly "cumulative" and dividends are not paid in any year or dividend period, the arrears must be made up in subsequent years, whether earned or not, before any dividends can be declared or paid on common shares.[49] Sometimes dividends on preferred shares are in express terms made to depend on the profits of each particular year, so the holders of the shares will not be entitled to any dividends for a particular year if there are not enough profits in that year to pay them, or they will be entitled only insofar as there were profits. These shares are known as "cumulative if earned," and in the absence of sufficient profits the dividends are non-cumulative and are not made up out of the profits of subsequent years.[50]

Unless a contrary intention appears, dividends on preferred shares have generally been held to be impliedly cumulative.[51] Careful draftsmanship should not leave questions open for judicial interpretation.

Associates, L.P. v. Avatex, 715 A.2d 843 (Del. 1998) (certificate of incorporation gave preferred shareholders a class vote on merger).

[46] The older view was otherwise. *See* Ericksen v. Winnebago Indus., 342 F.Supp. 1190 (D. Minn. 1972) (applying former Iowa statute that did not require redemption to be set forth in the articles of incorporation).

[47] *See, e.g.,* Doppelt v. Perini Corp., 2002 WL 392289 (S.D.N.Y. 2002) (articles and not the offering prospectus governed meaning of dividend preference).

[48] Adolf A. Berle, Corporate Devices for Diluting Stock Participations, 31 Colum. L. Rev. 1239, 1263–1264 (1931).

[49] Bank of Am. Nat'l Trust & Sav. Ass'n v. West End Chem. Co., 100 P.2d 318 (Cal. Ct. App. 1940).

[50] Wabash Ry. v. Barclay, 280 U.S. 197 (1930).

[51] Arizona Power Co. v. Stuart, 212 F.2d 535 (9th Cir. 1954).

§ 18.8   Non-Cumulative Preferred Shares

The great advantage of non-cumulative preferred shares is that they avoid an undue accumulation of dividend arrearages, particularly for years in which dividends are not earned. Non-cumulative shares are frequently employed in reorganizations, when it is necessary to limit dividend rights and the investors must take what the enterprise can carry,[52] but the non-cumulative shares may not be listed on the New York Stock Exchange.[53]

The principal types of non-cumulative preferred share contracts may be divided into three general groups, subject to internal variation: (1) the discretionary dividend type; (2) cumulative if earned, or "mandatory" dividend type; and (3) "dividend credit" type.[54]

Discretionary Dividend Type. An example of a non-cumulative preferred share contract held to be of the discretionary dividend type is found in a leading Supreme Court case holding that even if there are net profits, the preferred stockholder's right to dividends thereon in any year depends on the judgment and discretion of the directors.[55] This right cannot be enlarged beyond the meaning of the contract to give a right to a dividend credit for prior years in which net earnings might have been lawfully distributed.[56] A share contract should not be judicially augmented because the remedies in case of an abuse of discretion in withholding dividends might not be adequate. The dividend right for any particular fiscal year is gone if the directors, without abuse of discretion, withhold a dividend declaration for that year.[57]

The shareholders' protection under such a discretionary non-cumulative contract lies in equitable relief against abuse of discretion rather than in any ability to enforce a series of supposed contract claims.[58] The mere showing that annual profits, accumulated profits, or earned surplus existed from which a dividend might lawfully have been declared is not sufficient to establish a breach of duty on the part of the directors in failing to declare it. No wrong is done unless the withholding of the dividend would be oppressive, fraudulent, or unfairly discriminatory.[59]

Cumulative-if-Earned or "Mandatory Dividend" Type.[60] A non-cumulative preferred share contract may be made a kind of hybrid "cumulative non-cumulative" type

---

[52]   *See* New York, L. E. & W. R.R. v. Nickals, 119 U.S. 296 (1886).

[53]   NYSE Listed Company Manual § A15, ¶ 281.

[54]   *See* W. H. S. Stevens, Rights of Non-Cumulative Preferred Stockholders, 34 Colum. L. Rev. 1439 (1934).

[55]   Wabash Ry. v. Barclay, 280 U.S. 197 (1930).

[56]   The charter and stock certificates provided:

The holders of the Five Per Cent Profit Sharing Preferred Stock A of the Company shall be entitled to receive preferential dividends in each fiscal year up to the amount of five per cent before any dividends shall be paid upon any other stock of the Company, but such preferential dividends shall be noncumulative.

Wabash Ry. Co. v. Barclay, 280 U.S. 197, 202 (1930).

[57]   *Accord,* Guttmann v. Illinois Cent. R.R., 189 F.2d 927 (2d Cir.), *cert. denied,* 342 U.S. 867 (1951).

[58]   *See generally* Adolf A. Berle & Gardiner C. Means, The Modern Corporation and Private Property 172–178, 231–232 (rev. ed. 1967).

[59]   *E.g.,* Levin v. Mississippi River Corp., 59 F.R.D. 353 (S.D.N.Y.), *aff'd,* 486 F.2d 1398 (2d Cir.), *cert. denied,* 414 U.S. 1112 (1973).

[60]   "Mandatory dividend" is a misnomer because, although dividends may accrue if earned, they do not vest and thus become a debt until declared by the board of directors who, except in the most egregious case, have discretion to retain the earnings for the corporation.

by providing in the articles of incorporation that all back dividends, if earned, must be paid ahead of any common stock dividends.[61] A preferred stock provision mandating dividends up to a certain amount so long as there are profits, net earnings, or net income invariably pose important interpretative questions as to the meaning of these expressions. To the extent that terms conditioning the right to dividends have particular significance in the discipline of accounting, as do the terms "profits," "net earnings," and "net income," it is customary to abide by generally accepted accounting principles in applying such terms to a particular situation.[62]

Dividend Credit Rule. The highest court of New Jersey affirmed by an equally divided vote[63] the decision of the Court of Chancery, which had interpreted a non-cumulative provision to be cumulative if earned.[64] A later New Jersey decision explained: "[W]here non-cumulative preferred stock has not been allotted the full dividend to which it is entitled in any one year and the corporation for that year has earned more than the dividend paid to the preferred stockholders, the preferred stock is entitled to have allotted to it such withheld earnings to the extent of its priority before dividends are paid to common stockholders."[65] At one time it appeared that the New Jersey rule was being eroded;[66] however, it has been reaffirmed in subsequent decisions[67] and perhaps even strengthened.[68]

In general, preferences depend not on any statute or rule of law but on the provisions in the preferred share contract. The New Jersey cases are best interpreted as not holding that the bare word "non-cumulative" necessarily means that dividends are cumulative to the extent earned in each fiscal year.[69] Just as cumulative-if-earned dividends can be established in other states by express charter provision, an equally

---

[61]   Wood v. Lary, 47 Hun. 550 (1888), *aff'd*, 124 N.Y. 83, 26 N.E. 338 (1891).

[62]   *See* Kern v. Chicago & E. Ill. R.R., 285 N.E.2d 501 (Ill. App. Ct. 1972).

[63]   Day v. United States Cast Iron Pipe & Foundry Co., 126 A. 302 (N.J. 1924), *aff'g* 123 A. 546 (N.J. Ch.).

[64]   The *Day* court, at 126 A. 304–305, explained its view of the difference between "cumulative" and "non-cumulative" as follows:

> . . . the distinction between the two being that, while dividends (not in liquidation) upon each can, of course, only be paid out of profits or surplus [cite omitted], the dividends upon cumulative preferred stock have at all times and for all years past and present, until paid, priority in payment over any and all unpaid dividends upon common stock, whether the net earnings for any particular past or present year were or were not sufficient to pay the stipulated cumulative dividends upon preferred stock for that year; whereas the like priority of dividends upon noncumulative preferred stock . . . is limited to the unpaid dividends for those years when such net earnings were sufficient (wholly or in corresponding part) to pay such dividends.

[65]   Cintas v. American Car & Foundry Co., 25 A.2d 418, 422 (N.J. Ch. 1942), *aff'd*, 28 A.2d 531 (N.J. 1942).

[66]   12 William M. Fletcher, Fletcher Cyclopedia of the Law of Private Corporations § 5446 (perm. ed. 2004).

[67]   Sanders v. Cuba R.R., 120 A.2d 849 (N.J. 1956).

[68]   *Cf.* Carlos L. Israels, The Corporate Triangle—Some Comparative Aspects of the New Jersey, New York and Delaware Statutes, 23 Rutgers L. Rev. 615, 627 (1969) (recent statutory amendments left rule in intact, thus missing "an opportunity to bring the law and modern corporate finance into a more realistic relationship").

[69]   The dividend-credit rule will imply cumulative-if-earned dividends for non-cumulative preferred shares only where the certificate of incorporation is silent or is so general as to leave adequate room for construction of the contractual arrangements between the parties. Leeds & Lippincott Co. v. Nevius, 144 A.2d 4 (N.J. Super. Ct. 1958), *modified*, 153 A.2d 45 (N.J. 1959).

clear clause in a New Jersey charter can create preferred shares with strictly non-cumulative dividends.[70]

§ 18.9 Participation of Preferred Shares Beyond Their Preference

By express provision, preferred shares may participate in dividend distributions beyond their fixed dividend priority. One or two courts adopted the view that preferred shares are entitled to participate equally with the common shares in any distribution of profits after the common shares have received in the same year a dividend at the same rate as that stipulated as a preference for the preferred, unless the share contract provides to the contrary.[71] A different view, however, is followed in almost all states to the effect that where there is no express stipulation as to participation in the surplus, the preferred is entitled only to its fixed priority or preference.[72] It seems reasonable to infer that in consideration of preferential rights, the preferred shareholders agree to accept priority in dividends at a fixed rate in lieu of further participation with the common. This is the understanding of the investing public, especially in view of the fact that participating preferred stock is an unusual type of security having a special feature that should be specified and defined.

§ 18.10 Preference on Liquidation

When a corporation's assets are distributed among its shareholders as part of dissolution and winding up, the holders of preferred shares have the same, and no greater, right to share proportionately in the net assets as do the holders of common shares unless the holders of preferred shares have a contractual preference.[73] Usually, however, preferred shares contain provisions for not only a dividend preference but also a stated preference in liquidation or winding up. This liquidation preference most often includes a right to receive any arrears of cumulative dividends in priority to any distribution of assets to the common shareholders.[74] It has generally been held that a liquidation preference including accrued dividends is valid, whether or not there are accumulated earnings or surplus available for dividends.[75] The formerly prevalent rule that dividends cannot be paid out of capital is applicable only to a going concern, not on final liquidation and winding up after payment of the corporation's debts.[76] A mere preference as to "payment in full" or as to "assets" in liquidation has been held not to include arrearages of unpaid cumulative dividends.[77]

By the prevailing view, merger or consolidation of a corporation with another is not such a "dissolution" or "liquidation" as to entitle the holder of preferred shares to payment of the liquidation price or preference, unless it is clearly so specified.[78] For

---

[70]   *E.g.*, Leeds & Lippincott Co. v. Nevius, 144 A.2d 4 (N.J. Super. Ct. 1958), *modified*, 153 A.2d 45 (N.J. 1959).

[71]   Niles v. Ludlow Valve Mfg. Co., 202 F. 141 (2d Cir. 1913).

[72]   Englander v. Osborne, 104 A. 614 (Pa. 1918).

[73]   Continental Ins. Co. v. Reading Co., 259 U.S. 156, 181 (1922).

[74]   Buxbaum, *infra* § 21.5 note 53, at 260. *But see* Wouk v. Merin, 128 N.Y.S.2d 727 (App. Div. 1954).

[75]   Fawkes v. Farm Lands Inv. Co., 297 P. 47 (Cal. Ct. App. 1931), noted in Note, Corporations—Dissolution: Dividends in Arrears May Be Paid from Capital, 19 Cal. L. Rev. 450 (1931).

[76]   In re Chandler & Co., 230 N.Y.S.2d 1012 (Sup. Ct. 1962).

[77]   Powell v. Craddock-Terry Co., 7 S.E.2d 143 (Va. 1940).

[78]   *See, e.g.*, Rothschild Int'l Corp. v. Liggett Group, Inc., 474 A.2d 133 (Del. 1984).

example, in *Robinson v. T.I.M.E.-DC, Inc.,*[79] the court held that a spin-off of the company's real estate holdings was not a liquidation because there was no evidence the board intended to wind up the company's affairs.

§ 18.11 Voting Rights of Preferred

In most instances, the participation in corporate governance by preferred stockholders is much the same as for bondholders: they are much like children, to be seen but not heard. Thus the preferred's contract provides for a periodic return through dividends that is either cumulative or non-cumulative, and perhaps a preference on the firm's liquidation. And, like bondholders, rarely do preferred stockholders enjoy voting rights in the election of directors or most other matters requiring a shareholder vote. Under the typical preferred stock arrangement, any voting rights of preferred stockholders arise in those limited situations where the state corporate statute requires the approval of the preferred when an amendment to the articles of incorporation will change or adversely affect the preferred shares. The precise language of the articles of incorporation frequently generally determines whether the preferred get a vote. Thus, in one case the Delaware Supreme Court held the preferred had a right to vote on a recapitalization that was accomplished via a consolidation because the articles provided for a vote when the preferred shares' rights were adversely affected by "amendment" "whether by merger, consolidation or otherwise."[80] However, when the articles more generally provide for a class vote of the preferred by action "to amend" the articles so as to "to alter or change" the rights of the preferred, a merger changing such rights was held not to fall within this provision because the change occurred by virtue of the merger and not by an amendment so that there is no vote by the preferred is required.[81] With their voting rights so narrowly circumscribed, the preferred shareholder generally lacks a means within the traditional corporate governance mechanisms to, for example, assure that their dividends are regularly paid or that the board of directors does not pursue policies that are likely to harm the future returns of the preferred shareholders. To be sure, there is some economic coercion on the directors when the preferred dividends are cumulative because any arrearages delay dividends to the common stockholders who have elected the board of directors. However, the law is replete with cases in which, after many years of failing to pay the preferred their cumulative dividend, the company undergoes a recapitalization that removes the dividend arrearage and allows future participation by the common on a level more favorable than if the preferred dividends had first been satisfied.[82]

A potentially potent force in the hands of the preferred holders is a provision in their contract granting the preferred the right to vote in the election of directors, and perhaps on other matters, if the corporation fails to pay the preferred dividend. Such contingent voting rights, when provided, usually arise only after a certain number of quarterly dividends have not been fully satisfied—for example, four quarters. The listing requirements of the New York Stock Exchange mandate contingent voting rights for

---

[79] Robinson v. T.I.M.E.-DC, Inc., 566 F.Supp. 1077 (N.D. Tex. 1983).

[80] *See* Elliott Assoc. v. Avatex Corp., 715 A.2d 843 (Del. 1998).

[81] *See* Elliott Assoc. v. Avatex Corp., 715 A.2d 843 (Del. 1998).

[82] *See, e.g.,* Goldman v. Postal Tel., Inc., 52 F.Supp. 763 (D. Del. 1943) (common entitled to receive nothing on liquidation, due to arrearages due preferred, received some portion of the reorganized company as an "inducement" for their support).

preferred shares.[83] The drafter should carefully consider whether such contingent voting rights should extend to the power to elect the entire board of directors or a majority of the board, or merely provide minority representation on the board. In *Baron v. Allied Artists Pictures Corporation*,[84] the preferred shareholders obtained control of the board after their contingent voting rights were triggered by successive nonpayments of dividends. The preferred's representatives restored the company to profitability, but because the preferred dividends had not been paid, control over the board had not been restored to the common. The common shareholders sued, arguing unsuccessfully that the mission of the directors elected by the preferred was to extinguish the dividend arrearages so that the control over the board could be returned to the common shareholders. While recognizing that the directors had a fiduciary duty to see that the preferred's dividends were brought up to date, the court nevertheless ruled against the common, holding there was no evidence of bad faith in the current directors' stewardship of the firm.[85]

Some have argued that corporations lack the power to issue shares that have only voting rights. The reasoning behind this argument is that implicit in the meaning and status of "shares" is a proprietary interest. In the only reported decision on this point, the court held that preferred shares are valid even though they carry only voting rights.[86]

§ 18.12 The Redemption Provision: Voluntary or Compulsory for the Corporation

Corporations frequently reserve the option to redeem preferred shares at a certain redemption price in order to facilitate future financing. Where such a right exists, the board of directors must exercise the power to redeem in a manner consistent with the terms set forth in the articles of incorporation.[87] Furthermore, there are limits on mandatory redemption provisions insofar as they may not be honored if there are insufficient funds under the statutory test for share repurchases.[88]

In closely held corporations, redemption provisions, like options to repurchase, may be used to keep control of the corporation's stock among a limited number of shareholders. The corporation's right to redeem is generally discretionary with the corporation's board of directors. Repurchase is subject to the requirement that full disclosure of all material facts be made to the stockholders as well as to the equitable consideration that the repurchase not be coercive. Moreover, any repurchase must not violate the restrictions on share repurchases, discussed in Chapter 21, that are imposed by corporate statute. Thus, when a corporation did not have sufficient funds *i.e.*, surplus, as required by statute for repurchase, it made only a partial redemption; the court held

---

[83]   *See* NYSE Listed Company Manual § 313.00(e)(C) (at least six quarterly dividends, but the power need only extend ability to elected two directors; also recommending same rights for unlisted preferred).

[84]   Baron v. Allied Artists Pictures Corp., 337 A.2d 653 (Del. Ch. 1975).

[85]   There was evidence that payment of the preferred's dividends were delayed due to a deficiency owed the IRS.

[86]   Stroh v. Blackhawk Holding Corp., 272 N.E.2d 1 (Ill. 1971).

[87]   *See generally* White v. Investors Management Corp., 888 F.2d 1036 (4th Cir. 1989).

[88]   *See, e.g.*, SV Inv. Partners, LLC v. ThoughtWorks, Inc., 37 A.3d 205 (Del. 2011) (where corporation did not have sufficient funds legally available under for repurchases under the Delaware statute, only a partial redemption was permitted and the failure to make a complete redemption was not a breach of the terms of the preferred shares in question), *affirming* SV Inv. Partners, LLC v. ThoughtWorks, Inc., 7 A.3d 973 (Del. Ch. 2010), judgment entered, 2011 WL 305074 (Del. Ch. 2011) and judgment aff'd, 37 A.3d 205 (Del. 2011).

this did not constitute a breach of the terms of the preferred shares.[89] In *Eisenberg v. Chicago Milwaukee Corp.,*[90] just after the October 1987[91] stock market collapse (which drove the preferred shares to $41), the board of directors sought to purchase at $55 per share preferred shares whose redemption price was $100. The Delaware Chancery Court enjoined the issuer's tender offer because the directors failed to disclose that they stood to gain by the repurchase as common stockholders because the elimination of the preferred would remove an impediment to their receipt of dividends. Also, the court emphasized that the board's action was coercive because they announced their intention to have the preferred shares delisted from the stock exchange.

Since a corporation's power to redeem shares at a set price is part of the preferred share contract, complaints that a redemption price is unfair vis-à-vis the shares' market value should be unsuccessful. The exercise is subject to the standard requirements of the business judgment rule.[92]

Compulsory redemption provisions and repurchase contracts are sometimes included in preferred share contracts and subscription agreements in order to make shares more attractive to timid investors.[93] Under such contracts the corporation is required to redeem or repurchase its preferred shares at a fixed date or at the option of the owner (essentially granting her a "put" option with respect to the shares), thus giving the shareholders a right to demand a return of their initial investment. Serious harm may result from redemption or repurchase of shares under such contracts. If allowed without restriction, redemptions may injure creditors and other shareholders by depriving the corporation of needed capital.[94]

§ 18.13 The Redemption or Sinking Fund for Retirement of Preferred Shares

A redemption fund, often loosely termed a "sinking fund," may be provided for the purchase or retirement of preferred shares; it is thus similar to a sinking fund used for the gradual or partial retirement of bonds. As with bonds, the sinking fund may consist of a separate account where funds are actually deposited or, as is more commonly the case with preferred shares, it may be unfunded, with balance sheet entries reflecting appropriate restrictions on the surplus accounts. The redemption fund may be accumulated by setting aside specified installments either based on a percentage of the net annual profits, payable out of net assets in excess of capital, based on a periodic small flat percentage of the par value of the preferred shares concerned that are outstanding, or derived from some other source.

---

[89] SV Inv. Partners, LLC v. ThoughtWorks, Inc., 37 A.3d 205 (Del. 2011).

[90] Eisenberg v. Chicago Milwaukee Corp., 537 A.2d 1051 (Del. Ch. 1987).

[91] *See also* Kahn v. United States Sugar Corp., 1985 WL 4449 (Del. Ch. 1985); Cottle v. Standard Brands Paint Co., Fed. Sec. L. Rep. (CCH) ¶ 95,306, 1990 WL 34824 (Del. Ch. 1990).

[92] *See* Hendricks v. Mill Engg. & Supply Co., 413 P.2d 811 (Wash. 1966).

[93] *E.g.,* ThoughtWorks, Inc. v. SV Investment Partners, 902 A.2d 745 (Del. Ch. 2006) (provision allowing board to avoid preferred's put option to the extent funds were necessary for "the" fiscal year's working capital needs did not empower board to accumulate funds over successive years).

[94] In the words of the Supreme Court, "[s]tock which has no retirement provisions is the backbone of a corporate structure." Ecker v. Western Pac. R.R., 318 U.S. 448, 477 (1943).

§ 18.14   Convertible Shares and Warrants

Preferred shares and bonds may be issued with a conversion privilege or with warrants.[95] The conversion privilege confers upon the holder the option of exchanging fixed or limited income securities for shares of common stock at a designated price or prices and within a specified period. A warrant is an option to purchase shares. Corporations issuing convertible shares or bonds or giving stock purchase warrants must be ready to issue the shares and meet the demands of holders who exercise their options at any period within the time frame specified in the contract.[96] The holder of a convertible security does not become the holder of the security acquired through conversion, and that security is not deemed outstanding, until the conversion occurs.[97]

Warrants may be issued accompanying shares of stock or bonds giving the holder the option to subscribe for or to purchase shares of common stock at a stipulated price or prices per share, usually within a limited time.[98] Warrants may be inseparable from the securities with which they are issued. More commonly, however, warrants are separable and are frequently traded on the stock exchanges. Standing alone, a warrant is not an equity interest; the holder's rights are wholly contractual and may expire on dissolution, consolidation, or by lapse of time.[99] Warrants are sometimes issued to shareholders and general creditors in the reorganization of a bankrupt corporation for otherwise unsatisfied claims.[100]

The financial distinction between convertible bonds and warrants is practically nonexistent if one assumes that warrants are issued in connection with their holder's purchase of a senior security, whether that senior security be a bond or preferred stock. The practical distinction between a convertible security and a warrant is that the latter is a separate security, detachable from the senior security that the initial holder was required to purchase in order to obtain the warrants. The warrant also carries with it an exercise price, thus requiring that fresh cash be paid as consideration for the underlying security, whereas the consideration for the underlying security acquired through conversion is the security converted into the underlying security. The value of the warrant and the value of the conversion feature of the senior security are each dependent on the value of the underlying security—that is, the security that can be acquired on exercise of the warrant or conversion of the senior security.

It is commonly stated that warrants and convertible securities are a form of "delayed equity financing." Absent the corporation's right to redeem, the warrant and conversion feature portend the day when their holder will exercise the warrant or convert and thereby acquire the underlying common stock. Obviously, that option is exercised only when the market value of the common shares is materially greater than

---

[95]   *See generally* Richard T. McDermott, Legal Aspects of Corporate Finance §§ 502 to 506 (3d ed. 2000); The Ronald J. Gilson & David M. Schizer, Understanding Venture Capital Structure: A Tax Explanation For Convertible Preferred Stock, 116 Harv.L. Rev. 875 (2003).

[96]   *See generally,* Hildreth v. Castle Dental Centers, Inc., 939 A.2d 1281 (Del. 2007) (failure when convertible preferred shares were authorized to also authorize sufficient common shares to permit full conversion of the preferred shares did not invalidate the authorization or the issuance of the convertible preferred shares).

[97]   *See* Nerken v. Standard Oil Co., 810 F.2d 1230 (D.C. Cir. 1987).

[98]   Adolf A. Berle, Studies in Corporation Finance 131 (1928).

[99]   Helvering v. Southwest Consol. Corp., 315 U.S. 194 (1941). However, they do qualify as "equity securities" under the federal securities laws.

[100]   Ecker v. Western Pac. R.R., 318 U.S. 448, 476 (1943) (dictum).

the exercise price of the warrant or that portion of the bond's value not attributed to its conversion feature (at some point, the principal determinant of a convertible bond's value is the common shares that can be acquired on conversion). The preceding only elaborates on the reasons a warrant or conversion feature, when included in the bundle of rights investors acquire on the issuance of senior securities, is seen as a "sweetener" to the offered financial package. So viewed, one may question whether a warrant or conversion feature truly reduces the cost of raising capital (that is, the benefits referred to in the above excerpt) or merely postpones the full costs of financing until the warrant or the conversion feature is exercised.[101]

§ 18.15 Equitable Protections of Preferred Stockholders

The principle is well established that any protection bondholders and preferred stockholders enjoy arises from the four corners of their contract with the corporation (that is, indenture or terms set forth in the articles of incorporation). There are, however, rare instances when the preferred can invoke the protection of a fiduciary obligation. For example, in *Jackson National Life Ins. Co. v. Kennedy*,[102] the Delaware Chancery court held that preferred stockholders could proceed with claims that the director and controlling shareholder breached a fiduciary duty of candor by failing to disclose certain material facts involved with the forthcoming sale of a significant product line, even though no vote by the stockholders was called for to approve the sale.[103] Furthermore, the court applied a line of Delaware authority holding that directors owe a fiduciary duty to common and preferred stockholders when dividing the consideration received in a merger or other extraordinary transaction.[104] But in most instances, there are no fiduciary obligations that accompany their relationship to the corporation.[105] By far the greatest problems with this classic contract-law approach have arisen when the bond or preferred share enjoys a conversion privilege that places their holder but a step away from full equity ownership. It is with respect to such securities that critics of the classic contract-law treatment of senior securities holders' rights make their strongest case, by emphasizing not only that it is nearly impossible to contract around every possible contingency but that in light of that impossibility there quite likely is purchased within the contract some rough semblance of fair treatment.[106]

---

[101] *See generally* George W. Dent, Jr., The Role of Convertible Securities in Corporate Finance, 21 Iowa J. Corp. L. 241 (1996); William Klein, The Convertible Bond: A Peculiar Package, 123 U. Pa. L. Rev. 547 (1975).

[102] Jackson National Life Ins. Co. v. Kennedy, 741 A.2d 377 (Del. Ch. 1999).

[103] Jackson National Life Ins. Co. v. Kennedy, 741 A.2d 377, 390–91 (Del. Ch. 1999). The case would be even stronger if a shareholder vote were required, *see* Gilmartin v. Adobe Resources Corp., 1992 WL 71510 (Del. Ch. 1992).

[104] Jackson National Life Ins. Co. v. Kennedy, 741 A.2d 377, 390–91 (Del. Ch. 1999). The court relied upon In re FLS Holdings, Inc. Shareholders Litig., 1993 WL 104562 (Del. Ch. 1993), *aff'd*, 628 A.2d 84 (Del. 1993) (unpublished opinion).

[105] *See, e.g.,* Broad v. Rockwell Int'l Corp., 642 F.2d 929, 958–959 (5th Cir.) (*en banc*) (applying New York law), *cert. denied*, 454 U.S. 965 (1981); Metropolitan Life Ins. Co. v. RJR Nabisco, Inc., 716 F.Supp. 1526 (S.D.N.Y. 1989); Metropolitan Sec. v. Occidental Petroleum Corp., 705 F.Supp. 134, 141 (S.D.N.Y. 1989).

[106] The leading critic of rigidly applying classic construction techniques is Professor William W. Bratton. *See* William W. Bratton, Corporate Debt Relationships: Legal Theory in a Time of Restructuring, 1989 Duke L.J. 92; William W. Bratton, The Interpretation of Contracts Governing Corporate Debt Relationships, 5 Cardozo L. Rev. 371 (1984).

Following the developments that have touched modern contract law,[107] gaps in the indenture or preferred stock contract have sometimes been filled, however, by attributing to their contract an implied condition of good faith and fair dealing.[108]

A leading case for invoking an implied condition of good faith and fair dealing is *Van Gemert v. Boeing Company,*[109] involving convertible debentures whose terms required the company to give notice, and provided that such notice could be published in a newspaper, before exercising its option to redeem them. The court concluded that because the debentures did not specify the kind of notice that would be provided, the debenture holders were entitled to expect reasonable notice of the redemption call. The court held that fair and reasonable notice was not provided by the company to redeem its indentures, even though notice was published in the newspapers.[110]

Judicial restraint is very much a two-way street and can also work against the issuer and its fellow stockholders. *Reiss v. Financial Performance Corporation,*[111] concerned whether the exercise price of warrants should be adjusted upward following the corporation undertaking a one-for-five reverse stock split. On three different occasions the firm had issued warrants allowing their holder to acquire common shares at $.10 per share. Only for one of the three earlier transactions was there a provision adjusting the exercise price in the event of an reverse stock split. The corporation asked the court to imply such a provision for the other two warrant transactions so as to avoid their holders reaping an windfall. The Court of Appeals of New York held the parties rights must be determined from their contract and, since the contracts were not ambiguous, it refused to imply a provision as requested by the warrants' issuer.

---

[107] *See generally* Robert S. Summers, The General Duty of Good Faith—Its Recognition and Conceptualization, 67 Cornell L. Rev. 810 (1982).

[108] *See* Rossdeutscher v. Viacom, Inc., 768 A.2d 8 (Del. 2001) (applying New York law to hold there was implied duty of good faith and fair dealing not to manipulate stock price so as to reduce the firm's liability to holders of rights that had variable value depending on how well the post-acquisition price of the firm performed).

[109] Van Gemert v. Boeing Co., 520 F.2d 1373 (2d Cir.), *cert. denied,* 423 U.S. 947 (1975).

[110] *Contra* Lohnes v. Level 3 Communications, Inc., 272 F.3d 49 (1st Cir. 2001) (warrant holders not entitled to personal notice of a forthcoming stock split that would erode the value of outstanding warrants).

[111] Reiss v. Financial Performance Corporation, 764 N.E.2d 958 (N.Y. 2001).

Chapter 19

ACCOUNTING STATEMENTS
AND DIVIDEND LAW

Table of Sections

§ 19.1   The Importance of Accounting to Corporate Law

There is a close interplay between accounting and many corporate transactions. For example, in the preceding chapter it was emphasized that accounting principles play a pivotal role in interpreting bond indentures and the preferred stock's contract when those provisions use expressions that have accounting significance. The connection is equally direct in the case of the states' regulation of corporate distributions, a point examined in the next two chapters. Therefore, because of the frequent interplay between corporate law and accounting, a solid understanding is necessary of the major conventions that underlie accounting principles as well as of the important financial statements produced through the accounting process.[1] This chapter reviews the major conventions on which accounting principles are premised and provides an introduction to the two principal accounting statements: the balance sheet and the income statement.

On certain topics, such as valuation, depreciation, and depletion, the law impliedly adopts what may be termed "good accounting practice" or, as it is commonly and professionally designated, "generally accepted accounting principles" (GAAP).[2] It should be noted, however, that the courts have the final say in interpreting corporation acts and on legal questions, as between conflicting accounting opinions, and tend to follow what will further the legal objective in view.

---

[1]   Proper accounting often depends on legal concepts. *See* Miguel de Capriles, Modern Financial Accounting (Pt. I), 37 N.Y.U. L. Rev. 1001 (1962), (Pt. II) 38 N.Y.U. L. Rev. 1 (1963).

[2]   *See* Ralph J. Baker, Book Review, 21 Tex. L. Rev. 169, 190 (1942):

. . . whether we like it or . . . not the accountants may be making our law. On dividend issues that involve inventory valuations, judges are likely . . . to believe the matter ought to be controlled by good accounting practice. If the case is well tried, with submission of accounting literature as evidence and accounting testimony or depositions [can establish] . . . good accounting practice may be enough even though it falls short of being uniform accounting practice.

There have been recent departures from the traditional legal capital system in California as well as in post-1980 revisions to the Model Business Corporations Act.[3] California expressly references GAAP and thus places the courts in the somewhat unusual position of final arbiter of proper accounting methods.[4]

§ 19.2 Major Conventions of Accounting

Nearly all generally accepted accounting principles are anchored in a set of major tenets, more commonly referred to as "accounting conventions."[5] These conventions are briefly set forth below.

The Separate-Entity Assumption. Just as corporate law distinguishes the corporate entity from its owners, accounting statements reflect the performance and financial position of a distinct entity. Thus the financial statements of a corporation report its assets and income, not those of its stockholders; and this is also true for a partnership and its partners. To be sure, there are principles for presenting the performance and position of companies that are affiliated, known as consolidated financial statements, discussed below, but the overarching principle is that financial reports are developed from the viewpoint of a specific entity.

Cost Convention. The bedrock of accounting principles is that each purchase of assets, services, or expenses, as well as liabilities and owners' equity, is recorded at an item's historical cost (in contrast to the item's fair market value). Thus a building that was acquired ten years earlier is today depreciated on the basis of the cost of acquiring it ten years earlier, even though the building's current fair market value is much above its cost. Similarly, the building is reported on the balance sheet at its historical cost, less depreciation.

To be sure, difficult questions sometimes arise in measuring an item's cost. For example, when stock is issued for Blackacre, there is a need to record a future value for the capital stock account as well as for Blackacre. In this situation the fair market value of Blackacre, assumed to be $500,000, is the cost for Blackacre and is also reported in the capital stock account to reflect what was received for the shares. From that point forward, however, Blackacre continues to be reported at $500,000, its cost, even though the land greatly appreciates in value. But the cost convention is not a two-way street. Should there be a material and permanent decline in an asset's market value, accounting requires the asset's carrying amount be reduced to its new, and lower, value. Thus accounting embodies a highly conservative view of the world in which purchases and assets are recorded at cost and any declines are recognized, but upward appreciation in value is not. Hence the old saying among accountants, "anticipate no gain and recognize all losses."

Constant-Dollar Assumption. Financial reports reflect measurements in a given type of currency, usually that of the company's principal domicile. Whether inflation is

---

[3]   Cal. Gen. Corp. Law § 500 (West 1990).

[4]   This may cause more problems than the dual system of legal and general accounting principles poses because lawyers and judges are often ill equipped to deal with accounting technology. The 1980 revision of MBCA § 45 adopts a reasonableness test as to accounting practices—that is, reasonable under the circumstances. The comments to the Act at 34 Bus. Law. 1867, 1884, state that the statute *does not* constitute a statutory enactment of GAAP. The statute, however, would permit the use of GAAP as a general rule.

[5]   *See generally* Mark E. Haskins, Kenneth R. Ferris, Robert J. Sack, & Brandt R. Allen, Financial Accounting and Reporting ch. 2 (2d ed. 1997).

moderate or high, the true purchasing power of that unit of measurement is reduced over time. Nevertheless, financial reports are prepared on the assumption of a stable monetary unit or, alternatively expressed, that any changes in the monetary unit are not significant. At one time generally accepted accounting practice (GAAP) required public reporting companies to present information in the footnotes of the financial statements reflecting the effects of inflation; however, the recent modest rate of inflation has caused that requirement to be suspended.

Continuity Assumption. Statements are prepared based on the assumption the business will have a continuous existence. This is frequently referred to as the "going-concern assumption." Thus expenditures for such items as future insurance coverage, a new piece of machinery, and inventory are not charged against revenues as an expense if these assets are believed to contribute to the operations in future years. That is, by assuming an indefinite life for the business, the accountant can assign present expenditures to future years on the basis estimates regarding when a purchased item is likely to contribute to operations. If a going concern were not assumed, then all expenditures would be "expensed" in the year the item was purchased.

Discrete Reporting of Time-Periods. Even though a business is assumed to have an indefinite life, accounting reports provide periodic measurements of the firm's performance and financial position. Such periods are called fiscal periods and may be a quarter, a year (calendar year or fiscal year), or sometimes even longer. This requires discrete judgments as to what precise time-period revenues are to be reported and their matching expenses are to be identified. Such decisions are not always clear, and judgment calls invariably arise. Nevertheless, a cornerstone of financial reporting is the need for periodic information regarding the firm's health and operations, even though these reports must be understood not to present a perfectly accurate picture of the firm; perfect accuracy of the firm's overall performance and financial position can be known only when the firm terminates its existence and liquidates. But the users of financial information cannot wait until that day. Hence the assumption that the firm's performance can be divided into defined fiscal periods and reported on.

Realization Principle. A further manifestation of accounting conservatism is the realization principle, which is concerned with the timing of when revenue can be recognized. "Recognized" refers to when the financial statements can report an item's disposition as a sale among its revenues. Simply stated, revenue is not recognized until it is earned. With few exceptions, revenue is not realized until the goods that are sold have been transferred to their purchaser or the services that were acquired have been provided. Thus the primary test of revenue recognition is the completion of the seller's performance; in the case of goods, when title to the goods is transferred.[6]

Matching Principle. If statements were prepared solely on a cash basis, there would be no need for a matching principle. In using a cash basis, expenses are reported as liabilities are incurred or as cash is expended, and sales are recognized when payment in cash occurs. Most business records are not on a cash basis but on an accrual basis, under which the realization principle guides when revenue is reported and the matching principle determines when expenses are recognized. Under the matching principle, accounting decisions essentially entail a two-step process. First, revenues are determined pursuant to the realization principle. Thus goods shipped to customers on

---

[6]　*See generally* Lanny G. Chasteen, Richard E. Flaherty & Melvin C. O'Connor, Intermediate Accounting 329–61 (6th ed. 1998).

account are recorded as sales, even though the customer's cash payment has not yet been received. The important difference, therefore, between the cash and accrual basis of reporting is that the latter allows revenue recognition even though cash has not been received. The second step is *matching* the revenues to be recognized in the fiscal period with all the expenses incurred to produce those revenues. This process requires numerous judgments and estimates as to the connection between realized revenues and their related expenses.

The Consistency Principle. This principle calls for the consistent use of the same method or standard in recording and reporting transactions over successive periods. The consistent use of the same assumptions, approach, and reporting method assures comparability over time. Nevertheless, GAAP does permit assumptions, estimates, and principles to change, provided there is sufficient collateral disclosure.[7]

§ 19.3   The Balance Sheet

The balance sheet sets forth a company's cumulative financial position as of a specific date. Thus the balance sheet reports on the composition of the company's assets, liabilities, and owners' equity at a fixed point in time, whereas the income statement reports the company's operations over a period of time. In separately stating the amount and composition of all the company's assets, and also reporting the totals of its liabilities and owners' equity, the balance sheet follows the established accounting equation where

$$\text{Total Assets} = \text{Total Liabilities} + \text{Total Owners' Equity}$$

As will be seen, the balance sheet is the basic financial report for dividend purposes; most important, it indicates whether, pursuant to an older regulatory pattern, a corporation has sufficient "surplus," or, pursuant to statutes patterned after the current Model Business Corporation Act, its assets are sufficient in light of the firm's liabilities, so that there is a basis for dividends or other distributions to shareholders.

The balance sheet may appear to be inferior to the income statement, the other major financial statement, but when the two are read in tandem, the relationship between them becomes manifest. More specifically, the amount of net income reported on the income statement, together with the amount of dividends, explains the change in net surplus (retained earnings) from the beginning to the end of the accounting period. The balance sheet lists the assets, liabilities, capital, and surplus in two sections or groups: one on the left side—a classified list of the assets with their book values (generally reflecting historical cost less depreciation), the other on the right side—a classified list of the liabilities, capital, and surplus (or shareholders' equity) and their amounts. A vertical arrangement with assets placed at the top may also be used. The capital represented by the different classes of shares and the different kinds of surplus are entered along with the true liabilities on the right side of the balance sheet. The difference between the assets and the liabilities to creditors is sometimes called the net assets or net worth of the enterprise.[8] It is more frequently referred to as the "equity" of the shareholders—their proprietary interest—and indicates the "book value" of the shares.[9] If the value of the assets is less than the sum of the amount of the liabilities

---

     [7]   *See* AICPA APB Opinion No. 20, Accounting Changes (August 1971).

     [8]   For a typical statutory definition of net assets, *see* former MBCA § 2(i) (1969).

     [9]   The objectives of financial reporting, as set forth in Financial Accounting Standards Board (FASB) Concepts Statement No. 1, do not require accounting information to directly measure the value of the business

plus the legal or stated capital, then there is a capital deficit. If the value of the assets, at a proper valuation, is less than the liabilities to creditors properly estimated, then the corporation is insolvent, at least in the bankruptcy sense.[10]

§ 19.4 Classification of Assets on the Balance Sheet

Assets are stated at their acquisition cost, less any changes due to depreciation, depletion, or amortization. Owners' equity reports not only the amount invested in the company but also cumulative increases arising from profitable operations (retained earnings) or decreases due to a net loss from operations. These terms are defined according to generally accepted accounting principles.

In addition to being broadly grouped into assets, liabilities, and stockholders' (owners') equity, the balance sheet's individual items are classified into subcategories according to an underlying characteristic. The most basic subcategories are the following:

Assets	Liabilities	Stockholders' Equity
Current Assets	Current Liabilities	Capital Stock
Fixed Assets	Long-Term Liabilities	Capital in Excess of Par Value
Other Assets	Deferred Credits[11]	Retained Earnings

The above classifications are not exclusive. For example, a parent company's investment in a subsidiary will appear on its unconsolidated balance sheet as "Investments" and appears after Fixed Assets and before Other Assets. Also, over time a highly ambiguous fourth category has developed between Liabilities and Stockholders' Equity, entitled "Deferred Income" or "Deferred Credits." Deferred income refers to advance payments for goods that have not yet been shipped or for services to be provided by the company in the future. In such cases, the *recognition* of revenue is held not yet to have been *realized* because of such non-shipment of goods or non-provision of services. Thus the receipt of revenues in connection with a transaction for which realization has not occurred because of the tenets of the realization convention are reported on the balance sheet as deferred income. Deferred credits most frequently arise because many items or transactions are reported differently in determining taxable income than in determining net income on the company's financial statement. The cumulative differences between the tax expense reported on the company's financial statement and

---

enterprise. That is, balance sheets are not intended to reflect enterprise market value. This value estimation is the role of investment analysis, not accounting. Accounting provides information useful for the analysis.

10 "Insolvency" as defined in the federal Bankruptcy Code is the excess of liabilities over assets valued at fair value. 11 U.S.C. § 101(31) (2000). This is in contrast to defining "insolvency" in terms of the inability to pay debts as they become due.

11 The term "credit" has its own, indeed arbitrary, meaning in accounting. It is not synonymous with a benefit or privilege owned by the company. "Credit" refers merely to an entry that appears on the right-hand side of an account; the left side being the debit side.

the tax liability actually determined on its tax return are reported as deferred tax credits.

Current Assets. Current assets include cash in banks and on hand, accounts receivable, notes receivable, and marketable securities that are readily converted into cash. The current-assets category also includes less liquid assets, such as inventories, finished goods, work in process, raw materials, and factory supplies that may soon be salable. The standard definition of items suitable for inclusion within "current assets" covers items reasonably expected to be converted into cash or consumed within one year or one operating cycle, whichever is longer.[12] The true significance of current assets is their ability to be converted into cash during normal operations. Assets within this category are the first, if not principal, source for satisfying a company's liabilities and other cash needs in the short run. "Working capital" usually refers to the net current assets—that is, the excess of current assets over current liabilities available for use in the business operations.[13] Entries are generally listed at historical cost.

Inventories include goods held for sale, goods in production, or goods that are consumed in the ordinary course of business. Because inventories are constantly being replenished, some assumptions are made regarding the order of their replacement. Common methods used are LIFO (last in, first out) and FIFO (first in, first out). While the latter no doubt reflects the physical flow of most goods, the former more nearly matches cost with actual operations if one sees the act of replenishing inventory as the cost of the goods that gave rise to the need to replenish the inventory.

The basis of valuation for securities and inventories, however, is frequently indicated "at the lower of cost or market" or "cost or market, whichever is lower." Special provision is generally made for slow and doubtful accounts to reflect their actual or discounted worth. The assets are ordinarily listed in the general order in which they may be turned into cash or, as it is often expressed, in the order of their "liquidity."

An entity's financial status for immediate credit purposes is not indicated merely by the proportion that exists between the total assets and the total liabilities but even more so by the current ratio between them. "The current ratio" represents the proportion of the current assets to the current liabilities—that is, between the more immediate liabilities to be met and the various kinds of assets that will be available for meeting them. Even though total assets far exceed the liabilities, forced liquidation may occur if these assets are "frozen,"—that is, are not a kind that may be relied upon to raise needed cash. Working capital and the current ratio thus provide a better indication of a corporation's financial liquidity. It is not, however, *per se* unlawful to declare a dividend when there is a sufficient surplus of assets over liabilities, although there may not be sufficient cash or liquid assets on hand, and borrowing to pay the dividends may be necessary.[14]

Fixed Assets. Fixed assets comprise those that are held indefinitely for the purpose of conducting the business, as contrasted with those that are intended for sale. Assets within this category contribute to future operations through their use or consumption

---

[12]   The operating cycle is the combined time, on average, to acquire, process, and sell inventory, plus the time necessary to realize cash from any sales made on credit.

[13]   That is, if all of the current assets were converted into cash at their book value and all of the current liabilities paid at their book value, working capital would be the amount of cash remaining.

[14]   Steele v. Locke Cotton Mills Co., 58 S.E.2d 620 (N.C. 1950). *See generally* Gabriel A. D. Preinreich, The Nature of Dividends (reprinted ed. 1978).

during a longer time period than one year or operating cycle. They may be tangible or intangible property interests owned by the business and include land, buildings, machinery, and equipment as well as goodwill, patents, trade secrets, and other intangible assets. Overvaluation of tangible or intangible assets has frequently been the cause for skepticism as to whether such assets' fair market value can ever be reliably determined.[15]

The unfortunate term "capital assets" is frequently and incorrectly used as an equivalent to fixed assets. The term is misleading because current assets are just as much capital as are fixed assets and are much more significant to the creditors' security. The astute lawyer should recognize that no particular assets or funds are segregated and earmarked as capital or surplus. That is, the legal capital is an amount of the business, not a res. Impairment of legal capital may result as much from loss of current assets as from loss of fixed assets.[16]

Fixed asset value, as represented on the balance sheet according to GAAP, is not customarily based on a fair market appraisal or realizable value of the asset. Rather, the value is a record of the original cost of the asset, less the estimated depreciation that has accrued to date.[17] In this respect, the balance sheet is largely an historical record, because fixed asset valuations are often greater than any recorded amounts. As a result, the capital and surplus accounts, as far as being dependent on the historical cost of the fixed assets or even on their present appraisal, are usually of little significance as bearing on the ability to pay either debts or dividends. Current assets as opposed to fixed assets are the liquid resources. These assets are customarily (and conservatively) stated on the basis of cost or market, whichever is lower. Generally, the basis of all asset values should be, and is, disclosed more clearly in footnotes to the balance sheet than in its corpus. The Securities and Exchange Commission has formulated extensive policies as to the necessary accounting and valuation bases so as not to make these public disclosures misleading. These standards of reporting are provided by the accounting profession.[18] These recognize that historical cost can no longer be the sole basis of valuation for all purposes.

Deferred Charges and Prepaid Expenses. This special class of debits, seemingly of relatively minor importance, might best not be designated as assets. By definition, a "deferred charge" is an expenditure for a service that will contribute to the generation of revenues in the future. Prepaid expenses, as the name implies, more closely resemble operating expenses but are temporarily designated as assets, until they are consumed by the business. Examples of prepaid expenses are prepaid premiums for insurance covering the protection one or more years in advance, and rent paid in advance. These two examples represent expenses that are not charged against income for the period in which incurred but instead set up as prepayments, to be amortized (or "expensed") as

---

[15] Randall v. Bailey, 23 N.Y.S.2d 173, 177 (Sup. Ct. 1940), *aff'd*, 43 N.E.2d 43 (N.Y. 1942), discussed in § 20.13.

[16] The term "capital losses" is used to distinguish certain unusual losses for accounting purposes from "operating" losses. *See* Stuart Turley, Accounting Standards and the True and Fair View, 5 Company Law 31 (Jan. 1984).

[17] William W. Pyle, Fundamental Accounting Principles 29 (13th ed. 1993) (former authors, William W. Pyle & John Arch White).

[18] The FASB, in its Statement of Financial Accounting Standards No. 33, requires large public enterprises to file supplemental reports with their financial statements to provide, among other information, the increase or decrease in the current costs of inventory and plant and equipment. SEC Accounting Series Release No. 287 adopts the same position. *See* 6 Fed. Sec. L. Rep. (CCH) ¶ 1172, 309.

they are used up. In contrast, deferred charges may be described as long-term prepaid expenses. One example is the unamortized debt on bond discount plus the expense of the bond issue. Likewise, legitimate organizational costs may be regarded as creating intangible assets for a going concern, from which the earning capacity of the business will benefit over long periods. Therefore these too are designated as deferred charges and are also amortized periodically.

§ 19.5   Classification of Liabilities

Liabilities are customarily designated as current or long-term. Current liabilities are those debts and obligations that are reasonably expected to be paid during the upcoming year or operating cycle. Liabilities that do not qualify as current liabilities appear under the heading Long-Term Liabilities and include such items as mortgages payable and bonds payable. Each class of bonds or debentures should be shown on the balance sheet at the face value of the bonds outstanding, with the maturity date and interest rate included. Any discount or premium on the issuance of the bond should also be shown, but in a separate or "contra" account. These contra accounts are customarily amortized using the straight line or the interest rate method, based on the valuation period and the actual and effective interest rates. The two accounts—the face value and the contra entries—are netted to show the amount owing on the account. Furthermore, serial maturities of long-term liabilities should be transferred to the current liability group within the last year before maturity because these amounts then become current.

Current liabilities are usually sub-classified into three or four accounts, such as accounts payable, notes payable, dividends payable, accrued liabilities, and taxes payable. Customarily, debts maturing within a year are current liabilities, although in rare cases, such as when a business's operating cycle is longer than one calendar year, its current liabilities may not mature within that period.

A demand of any sort against a corporation, even though contingent, unliquidated, or disputed, such as a damage claim or a guaranty of another's obligation, is still characterized as a liability. The accountant thus has a difficult task in estimating the nature and amount of contingent liabilities. Once they are recognized, the accountant must choose between determining whether to make the disclosure in the balance sheet itself or in the accompanying footnotes.[19] This choice is necessary because contingent liabilities not sufficiently certain to be estimable are usually reflected in footnotes to the financial statement, rather than specifically in a balance sheet account. Nevertheless, where possible, a reserve against contingencies should be provided if there is a substantial likelihood of such contingent liabilities accruing. Despite their separate treatment, notes to balance sheets, especially qualifications in the accountant's certification to the financial statement with regard to them, must be read with care, as they too can be a basis for the accountant's liability for malpractice or negligence in performing the audit function.[20]

---

[19]   *See generally* William H. McBride, Securities Lawyers' Responsibility and Accountants' Liability: Disclosure of Contingent Liabilities, 53 Tex. L. Rev. 1483 (1975).

[20]   *But cf.* Geoffrey T. Chalmers, Over-Accountable Accountants? Proposal for Clarification of the Legal Responsibilities Stemming from the Audit Function, 16 Wm. & Mary L. Rev. 71 (1974) (accountants' exposure in damages should be limited in some manner that permits them to function without excessive cost to themselves and their clients).

§ 19.6   Stockholders' Equity Accounts

The various classes of shares of stock are all listed in the corporation's balance sheet. The balance sheet displays information as to the number or amount of par value of shares authorized and the number and amount of shares outstanding as well as those shares that have been repurchased and are thus carried on the books as treasury shares.[21] The rights, privileges, and preferences of each class of stock are also presented in summary fashion. In the case of corporations whose shares have a par value, the "capital stock" entry usually sets forth the aggregate par value of the shares authorized and also of those issued and outstanding, each class of shares being shown separately if more than one exists. In the case of no-par shares, the stated capital figure usually represents the aggregate capital contributions of all the issued shares.

Shares of stock outstanding are usually represented at their aggregate par value if they have such, or otherwise at their stated value. Reflecting par value in the capital stock account is more or less mechanical and traditional, for it has little or no reliability as a record of the amount of actual investment of the shareholders in the business. The directors may allocate a larger part of the paid-in capital to stated capital rather than account for it as capital surplus. The customary capital stock entry corresponds more closely to the important concept of stated or legal capital.[22] Therefore once an amount is designated as legal capital, it acts as a limitation to the capital margin. Thus legal capital limits distributions, rather than representing a figure of any independent financial significance.[23] All corporation laws, except California's and those of states adopting the current Model Business Corporation Act,[24] still adhere to the legal-capital basis of accounting and thus requires a working knowledge thereof on the part of corporate counsel.

Legal capital may be best illustrated by way of the following example. Suppose in the early history of a large mining company preferred shares of the aggregate par value of $1 million were sold for cash. Common shares were also issued with an aggregate par value of $1 million for some nominal consideration, such as underwriting or promotion services or speculative mining options. The common shares had no market value at the time of issue. Journal entries were made showing a capital stock item of $2 million, based on the total par value of the issued shares, common and preferred. That amount is the legal capital but not the actual capital invested.[25] The corporation prospers. It later becomes advisable to issue additional shares to raise further capital. A registration statement and a prospectus are required by the federal securities acts, including a balance sheet showing the assets and liabilities of the corporation. Suppose further that a regulatory commission inquiring into the history of the original financing orders a

---

[21]   The stockholder's equity accounts appear under the liabilities of a corporation because both types of accounts are increased by making "credit" entries, as distinguished from assets accounts, which are increased by making "debit" entries. A corporation's "liability" to its shareholders on account of their stock is not a debt; it represents ownership.

[22]   Legal capital is computed as the number of shares outstanding multiplied by their par value, stated value, or issue price (for no-par shares). The amount of legal capital is properly recorded in the capital stock account. Amounts received in excess of legal capital should be recorded in other appropriately designated accounts.

[23]   *See generally* Case v. New York Cent. R.R., 232 N.Y.S.2d 702 (Sup. Ct. 1962), *rev'd*, 243 N.Y.S.2d 620, 19 A.D.2d 383 (App. Div. 1963), *rev'd*, 204 N.E.2d 643 (N.Y. 1965).

[24]   Cal. Gen. Corp. Law §§ 501 et seq. (West 1990).

[25]   *See* Gulf Oil Corp. v. South Carolina Tax Comm'n, 149 S.E.2d 642 (S.C. 1966).

radical "write-down" or restatement at a realistic valuation of the assets originally received in payment for the common shares, involving a reduction in the value of assets of some $1 million. What is the effect of these events on the capital stock liability and on surplus?

Accumulated but undistributed profits are reported in earned surplus/retained earnings. A word about the choice of parlance with this item. "Earned surplus" is the term used in the older varieties of corporate statutes; however, the accounting profession eschews using "surplus" correctly seeing it as an ambiguous expression poorly understood by investors. The accounting profession thus prefers the expression "retained earnings." The amount recorded in earned surplus/retained earnings represents the sum of all profits since the company was formed, less any losses or dividends paid to its shareholders since its formation. Sometimes this account is restricted or appropriated to meet future contingencies or expenditures. The effect of such a restriction (frequently referred to as a "reserve") is to reduce the company's future ability to purchase its shares or declare dividends, since both those acts depend on the amount of *unrestricted* earned surplus or retained earnings.

Losses from operations are recorded as reductions in earned surplus (retained earnings) and, should the losses exceed such accumulated earnings, a deficit will thus appear in earned surplus (retained earnings). In no case will the deficit appear other than in the Stockholders' Equity section of the balance sheet.[26] When earned surplus (retained earnings) has a negative balance, it effectively reduces pro tanto the balance for stockholders' equity.

§ 19.7   The Income or Profit and Loss Statement

The mission of the income statement is to report the net income or loss for a given fiscal period, such as a quarter or year. In broad overview, it reports the revenues realized less the expenses incurred to produce those revenues plus any other gains or losses during that reporting period. Because the accountant assumes the business will have an infinite life, the task of accounting is to provide reliable measurements within discrete fiscal periods of the firm's performance. As a result of dividing reported operations into successive fiscal periods, it becomes necessary to employ a variety of assumptions, estimates, and judgments in the allocation of revenues and expenses among successive fiscal periods. In combination, these decisions introduce a good deal of uncertainty as to the accuracy of what is actually captured on the financial statements.

The income statement usually reflects "earnings from operations" or "profit from operations" in a general format. The income statement may particularize as to the gross sales and net sales or other revenue, as well as "nonrecurring" income, after deducting the cost of sales and operations, administrative and general expenses, maintenance and repairs, and provision for taxes, depreciation, depletion, amortization, and unusual expenses and losses. The income statement is concerned with the earning results and realized gain or loss for an accounting period. Because it best bears on the financial performance of the firm over a recent fiscal period it is viewed by many as the most important financial statement. In the income statement, the cost of goods sold, including selling, administrative, and general expenses, are subtracted from sales, thus bearing a net income (or loss) figure. Depreciation, depletion, and amortization taken during the

---

[26]   *See* First Indus. Loan Co. v. Daugherty, 159 P.2d 921, 930 (Cal. 1945) (Traynor, J. dissenting).

year are also subtracted as normal operating costs or expenses of the business. In a manufacturing operation, such charges become imbedded in the cost of the goods manufactured during the fiscal period. Thus the depreciation of an asset, such as the machinery in the company's plant, is first allocated to the products manufactured during that fiscal period. As recorded, it becomes part of the asset "inventory." It is only when the manufactured product is sold that depreciation is effectively charged against revenues, such charge being imbedded in the cost of goods sold for that fiscal period.

As seen earlier, a major accounting convention is that revenues or income is recognized when earned—whether or not received in cash—and expenses are recognized when incurred—whether or not paid in cash.[27] Most businesses and substantially all corporations use the accrual method of ascertaining income or profit and loss instead of the simpler but less informative cash basis. "Accrual accounting" is a system that matches expenses with revenues but does not require the actual receipt of cash as a precondition for revenue recognition.

Depreciation in the Income Statement. As described above, there can be no profits recognized until all expenses, depletions, and depreciation have been deducted. No one would think of computing the profits of a factory by omitting from the cost of the goods sold the value of the fuel consumed in manufacturing. Likewise, the value of the machinery is consumed in the manufacturing process just as truly as is the fuel. Depreciation reflects this decrease in value due to the "wear and tear" of machinery. Depreciation is an inevitable element of operating cost and must therefore be reckoned in determining profits. The federal income tax laws have done much to improve accounting practice in this respect. Depreciation is thus to be treated as an operating expense, or equivalent entry, that is deductible from current or operating revenue before obtaining the net operating income.

Direct Charges of Certain Losses to Surplus. A serious question is whether unusual losses on items not connected with ordinary operations of the period and extraordinary non-recurring charges are to be included in the annual profit-and-loss statement or whether they should be shown elsewhere. An increase in assets due to the additional investment of funds is not entered in the income account. A question also arises as to whether certain losses that have undoubtedly diminished the net value of the corporation should be reflected in the income statement or instead are to be treated as deductions from earned surplus. At one time, an extraordinary loss, say by earthquake or fire, was sometimes accounted for as a loss of earned or paid-in surplus rather than as a deduction from the profits of the period.[28] The accounting profession has greatly restricted such extraordinary items from bypassing the income statement.[29] Today, extraordinary gains and losses are separately reported in the income statement, not in the statement of earned surplus. The income statement is then reconciled with a surplus statement commonly termed the "statement of retained earnings." This statement shows the opening and closing balance of the earned surplus (retained

---

[27] The major objective of accounting is the determination of periodic net income by matching appropriate costs against revenues. The timely recognition of income and related expenses reflects this objective, which is called the "matching principle."

[28] The effect of an extraordinary item, if material, should be classified separately in the income statement. The Accounting Principles Board, in APB Opinion No. 30 (Oct. 1973), provides, as an authoritative guide, that "extraordinary items" refer to events or transactions that are *both* unusual and infrequent in occurrence. APB Opinion No. 30, AICPA, Professional Standards §§ 2010.16, 2012.10.

[29] *See* APB Opinion No. 30, Reporting Results of Operations (June 1973).

earnings) account and the changes that occurred throughout the fiscal year such as by the payment of dividends or the repurchase of shares. Moreover, the income statement should be reconciled with the balance sheet regarding the increase or decrease of earned surplus shown thereon by reason of unusual sources of gain or loss. An income report for a particular year, like a single balance sheet, should not be relied on to show earning capacity but should be compared with those of preceding years to ascertain the trend of earnings.

Explanatory Comments. Balance sheets and income statements often seem needlessly cryptic and obscure. Supplementary explanatory comments as to the different classes of assets and liabilities, reserves, and surplus are often supplied for the enlightenment of shareholders and investors in connection with the technical financial exhibits. Generally accepted accounting practice mandates the use of footnotes, parenthetical notes, and discussion statements to explain the figures shown on financial statements, especially with regard to foreign investments, contingent liabilities (such as pending lawsuits), bases of valuation, and investments in subsidiary companies.[30] Certain important qualifications, warnings, explanations, or even disclaimers may be called for in the accountant's comments and certificate. This statement, called the auditor's report, consists of a concise report by the auditor or public accountant expressing an opinion on the statement and the representations it contains, and how far the auditor assumes responsibility for its fairness of presentation. Such matters as changes in accounting practice and unusual accounting methods should be disclosed clearly and prominently.

§ 19.8   Consolidated Financial Statements

Where, as often happens, a group of affiliated companies make up one large business enterprise conducted by a parent or holding company, with one or more subsidiaries and affiliates, annual reports generally include consolidated financial statements. The consolidated statements are really an economic concept, valid only as to the creditors and shareholders of the parent corporation. The statements and the financial status of the enterprises, or system as a whole, operate as though they were a single entity.[31] This method does not purport to represent the statements of one particular entity; it is simply a device used for reporting purposes.

A consolidated balance sheet eliminates the parent company's investment in each of its associated companies; the actual assets and liabilities of such companies being substituted therefor. Thus the statement includes assets that legally do not belong to the parent corporation but are instead the property of affiliated corporations. Any minority interest in affiliated companies—that is, the shares held by non-affiliates—must be shown on the right-hand side of the balance sheet, because such outstanding shares, in the public's hands, have an equity interest in the assets of their respective companies. Although the parent company may have an equity interest of only four-fifths of the net assets of its subsidiary companies, the entire complex of assets of all the companies is used in the artificial, consolidated enterprise. As a general rule, consolidated statements will not include a subsidiary unless it is more than 50 percent owned. As noted above, the fact that there is a divided interest in these assets is accounted for by exhibiting on

---

[30]   *See* SEC Regulation S–X, Rule 3–16, 17 C.F.R. § 210.3–16 (2009).

[31]   *See* David R. Herwitz & Mathew J. Barrett, Accounting for Lawyers 115 (1997).

the right-hand side of the balance sheet the portion of the value of the net assets to be allocated to the holdings of the minority or outside shareholders.

Additional modification is necessary in the consolidated balance sheet with regard to intercompany relations where an asset of one of the associated corporations consists of a liability of another member of the group. For financial reporting purposes, the effects of intercorporate transactions must be removed from all consolidated financial statements. Intercompany receivables and payables are also eliminated and should not appear in the consolidated statement. As for liabilities, the consolidated balance sheet shows the combined amounts owing from the parent company and the associated companies to outsiders or public holders. This assures that gain or loss is recognized in consolidated statements only when a member of the consolidated entity has transactions with entities that are not members of the group.

By taking the above-mentioned measures, the consolidated balance sheet thus summarizes the total assets of a group of companies and indicates the parent company's pro rata portion of the cash, inventory, and other assets of the consolidated entities. A consolidated balance sheet thus aims to cut through the artificial legal subdivision of a group of companies and presents the actual assets and liabilities of the entire economic unit. Through this format, consolidated statements provide a comprehensive view of the situation of the combined business as a whole.

Chapter 20

DIVIDEND DISTRIBUTIONS: RIGHTS, RESTRICTIONS, AND LIABILITIES

Table of Sections

PART A.   RIGHTS TO DIVIDENDS

§ 20.1   Declaration and Payment of Dividends

A dividend is properly declared by formal resolution of the board of directors specifying the amount, the time of payment, and the "record date," and fixing the date for ascertaining the shareholders of record. Most dividends are distributed to shareholders in the form of cash. Distributions may also be made in property or in the corporation's own shares. Regardless of the method of declaration or payment, the distribution of dividends among shareholders of the same class must be without discrimination and pro rata unless it is otherwise agreed by all.[1]

---

[1]   Stout v. Oates, 234 S.W.2d 506 (Ark. 1950).

§ 20.2   Directors' Refusal to Declare Dividends

A corporation may have a surplus or accumulated profits legally available for dividends, but the right of the shareholders to the making of any distribution is dependent on the exercise of the directors' good faith discretion with regard to financial advisability at the time.[2] An abuse of this discretion may call for equitable relief.

There are two dangers of abuse of the directors' discretion in declaring or withholding dividends. One is a policy of wastefulness or prodigality—improvident distributions that are injurious to present or future creditors and investors reduce working capital and weaken the corporation as a going concern. The converse abuse is undue accumulation beyond the reasonable needs of the business—the arbitrary refusal to pay shareholders a fair return on their investment when it clearly would be possible and wise to divide accumulated profits. Investors purchasing shares in a business often expect to obtain a return in the form of more or less regular dividends according to the corporation's ability to pay. The management's desire for expansion and more compensation instead of dividends in some cases may defeat the shareholders' just expectations.[3] The law has been concerned primarily with restraining dividend distributions that are dangerous to the rights of corporate creditors.

Directors are the judges of the financial and business situation and what dividends shareholders can have, and when. But as judges they are by no means always fair, unbiased, or impartial. Management and shareholders, particularly in modern large scale corporations, often have conflicting interests. Because the shareholders may own only a few shares, it may be more profitable for the directors, and the officers who influence them, to expand the investment and divert the flow of income to fixed salaries and "incentive" compensation by profit-sharing contracts and bonuses rather than to distribute a large share of the profits to those whom they represent.[4] The directors have wide discretion as to the proper amount of compensation for executive officers, but it may be judicially reviewed. Their discretion does not extend to wasteful diversion of income that fails to leave a fair return to the shareholders.

Many may have the false belief that judicial review of the board's dividend policy is a simple inquiry that calls for little more than reviewing the company's most recent financial statements to ascertain whether operations are sufficient to justify a modest return on the shareholder's investment. This perspective on the question ignores the role that earnings play in the ongoing financial planning of the corporation.

The major source of funds for business expansion is the accumulated but undistributed profits of the business. The board of directors' decision to expand the business opens a host of questions as to how the expansion should be financed—by issuance of equity, by debt, or from undistributed earnings. Even though a school of financial theory counsels that the firm's value is not impacted by whichever of these choices occurs,[5] this "irrelevancy principle" can be seen as placing more emphasis on

---

[2]   An obvious justification is that the corporation does not satisfy the minimum statutory requirements for the payment of dividends. *See, e.g.,* Jones v. Jones, 637 N.Y.S.2d 83 (Sup. Ct. App. Div. 1996).

[3]   Miller v. Magline, Inc., 256 N.W.2d 761 (Mich. Ct. App. 1977).

[4]   E. Merrick Dodd, Jr., Is Effective Enforcement of the Fiduciary Duties of Corporate Managers Practicable?, 2 U. Chi. L. Rev. 194, 197, 205 (1935).

[5]   The seminal work on this topic is Franco Modigliani & Merton Miller, The Cost of Capital, Corporation Finance and the Theory of Investment, 48 Amer. Econ. Rev. 261 (1958).

intangible considerations that are best commended to the board of directors unless an abuse of discretion is otherwise demonstrated. Thus the courts hesitate to substitute their judgment on complicated questions of business policy for that of the elected managers of the business and have limited the scope of judicial review that they are willing to undertake.

It is accordingly a well-settled doctrine that whether or not dividends shall be paid, and the amount of the distribution at any time, is primarily to be determined in the good faith discretion of the directors.[6] Courts examine directors' decisions regarding dividends through the lens of the business judgment rule. In fact the rhetoric of the cases suggests a slightly more deferential standard, stating the court will not intrude upon the decision to not declare dividends absent "fraud or gross abuse of discretion."[7] In sum, dividend declarations are like other matters within the discretion of the board of directors for which director judgments are presumptively valid. The mere fact that a corporation reports a substantial surplus or large profits out of which a dividend might lawfully be declared is not of itself sufficient ground to compel the directors to make a dividend.[8] Directors are given a great deal of discretion to use corporate resources to expand the business, to increase executive compensation by bonuses and profit-sharing contracts, and to establish various reserves if they consider it to be in the interests of the corporation to do so. Thus many reasonable bases have successfully been advanced to justify the directors' decision not to declare dividends: the seasonable nature of the business,[9] new equipment and the possible relocation of a plant,[10] the repurchase of outstanding shares,[11] expansion of business and a contingency for increased competition,[12] and to buffer the corporation against the possible loss of a major account.[13]

However, it is generally supposed that the end and purpose of a business corporation is to do business and earn profits for its shareholders rather than for its management. Ordinarily, it is not the corporate purpose to go on year after year accumulating a surplus indefinitely without prospects of dividends, or to pay out all income in extravagant compensation. Earnings that clearly warrant dividends may not be withheld or diverted fraudulently or for adverse personal motives; in clear and extreme cases of abuse of managerial discretion, a court of equity will give relief.[14]

---

[6]   In re Reading Co., 711 F.2d 509 (3d Cir. 1983); Yates v. Holt-Smith, 2009 WI App. 79, 319 Wis.2d 756, 768 N.W.2d 213 (Wis. Ct. App. 2009)(owners historical sharing in "bonuses" was deemed constructive dividend and refusal to make payment for the apparent purpose of forcing one of the owners to withdraw was a breach of fiduciary duty).

[7]   *See, e.g.,* Baron v. Allied Artists Pictures Corp., 337 A.2d 653, 659 (Del. Ch. 1975).

[8]   In re Estate of Butterfield, 341 N.W.2d 453 (Mich. 1983).

[9]   Iwasaki v. Iwasaki Bros., 649 P.2d 598 (Or. App. 1982).

[10]   In re Reading Co., 711 F.2d 509 (3d Cir. 1983); Zidell v. Zidell, Inc., 560 P.2d 1086 (Or. 1977).

[11]   Kohn v. Birmingham Realty Co., 352 So.2d 834 (Ala. 1977).

[12]   Gay v. Gay's Super Markets, Inc., 343 A.2d 577 (Me. 1975).

[13]   Coduti v. Hellwig, 469 N.E.2d 220 (Ill. 1984).

[14]   Channon v. H. Channon Co., 218 Ill.App. 397 (1920).

Dodge v. Ford Motor Company[15] is the classic case of a court compelling distribution of an excessive accumulated surplus.[16] Two minority shareholders[17] holding one-tenth of the issued shares sued to compel the distribution of an extra dividend of not less than three-fourths of the available surplus. Henry Ford, who controlled the directors, had stated that the greater part of the profits should be put back into expanding the business in order to increase employment and sell more cars at a lower price per car. The court said, "A business corporation is organized and carried on primarily for the profit of the stockholders. . . . The discretion of the directors is to be exercised in the choice of means to attain that end, and does not extend to a change in the end itself, to the reduction of profits, or to the non-distribution of profits among stockholders in order to devote them to other purposes."[18]

In most cases where dividends have been compelled, it has been shown that the directors willfully abused their discretion by withholding distributions because of an adverse interest, a wrongful purpose, or bad faith. In one case, dividends had not been declared in more than 20 years, even though the firm was profitable and its majority stockholder had awarded herself with an excessive salary and had misappropriated the company's assets.[19] More frequently the prevailing minority stockholder is able to link the nonpayment of dividends to a larger scheme to drive the minority out of the corporation.[20]

By far the greatest success plaintiffs have had in challenging the nonpayment of dividends has been within closely held corporations. It would appear that personal hostility is more visible and thus easier to establish in the close corporation. It is also much easier to refute the business justifications advanced for nonpayment in a close corporation. The authority of the directors is usually said to be absolute as long as they act in the exercise of honest judgment. If the refusal to make a distribution of profits is shown to be clearly unjust even though no fraud or intent to harm the shareholders appears, some courts have indicated that relief should be given and that the minority shareholders should not wait indefinitely while profits are needlessly accumulated.[21] Thus, non-payment of dividends in the close corporation invites inquiry whether "oppression" is afoot whereby the directors' decision is assessing in light of the

---

[15] Dodge v. Ford Motor Company, 170 N.W. 668 (Mich. 1919), noted in Note, Dividends—When Equity Will Order Directors to Declare a Dividend, 20 Colum. L. Rev. 93 (1920).

[16] It appeared that on July 31, 1916, the defendant, a close corporation, had a surplus of almost $112,000,000, that it could expect a net annual income of at least $60,000,000 a year, and that it had cash on hand and municipal bonds amounting to virtually $54,000,000.

[17] "After this case, Ford acquired the dissenters' stock. The Dodge brothers used these funds in developing the rival firm that bore their name . . . although the firm later passed under the control of Walter Chrysler." Detlev F. Vagts, Basic Corporation Law 110 (2d ed. 1979).

[18] 170 N.W. at 684. The Michigan Supreme Court affirmed the lower court's decree requiring the distribution of 50% of the accumulated cash surplus as dividends. It reversed the lower court's injunctions, which would have effectively limited Ford's expansion program, however.

[19] *See* Cole Real Estate Corp. v. Peoples Bank & Trust Co., 310 N.E.2d 275 (Ind. Ct. App. 1974).

[20] *See, e.g.,* Yates v. Holt-Smith, 2009 Wis. App. 79, 319 Wis.2d 756, 768 N.W.2d 213 (Ct. App. 2009)(receipt of year-end bonuses based on profits deemed a constructive dividend where evidence supported inference this was done to force another owner from the business); Shostak v. Shostak, 851 A.2d 515 (Me. 2004) (bad faith established by evidence close corporation had historically paid dividends from profits at least to the level of income taxes attributable to each member per IRS Form K-1).

[21] Stevens v. United States Steel Corp., 59 A. 905, 907 (N.J. Ch. 1905).

"reasonable expectations" of the minority.[22] It should be noted that the limitation on the discretion of directors of close corporations may not apply to large corporations with listed stock and a ready market that reflects capital appreciation.[23]

§ 20.3   Rescission or Revocation of Dividend Declarations

A director's resolution declaring a cash dividend probably does not become immediately binding and irrevocable until an announcement to the shareholders or to the public. A leading Massachusetts case held that a directors' vote authorizing a dividend may be revoked if it has not been made public or communicated to the shareholders.[24]

It has been asserted that directors ought to have power, in the exercise of their sound discretion and in the absence of estoppel, to countermand payment of a declared dividend.[25] There are plausible arguments for this view in case of a serious mistake as to business prospects or the destruction of the corporation's plant by fire, earthquake, or other disaster soon after the passage of the resolution. But the arguments against the directors' power to rescind dividends after notice of the declaration seem conclusive. It has thus become established that a cash or property dividend, once announced, cannot be revoked.[26]

§ 20.4   Right to Dividends Declared Prior to Transfer of Shares

In general, any dividend already declared when shares are transferred belongs to the transferor and does not pass by the transfer, and the fact that the dividend is made payable at a future date does not alter the rule. Frequently this problem is solved by the directors' declaration fixing a record date in order to determine who is entitled to the distribution.

The shareholders' right to a corporate distribution becomes fixed by the dividend declaration in the absence of a record date.[27] This general rule, which is codified in many states,[28] is based on the theory that a dividend declaration automatically makes the corporation a debtor to the shareholder.[29] The right or debt thus does not pass on transfer of the shares. Accordingly, when dividends are made payable at a future date, usually for the convenience of the corporation, a transfer between the date of declaration and the date of payment will not affect the transferor's right to the dividends. The dividends will be payable to the owner at the time of declaration rather than at the time of payment.[30]

---

[22]   For a close analysis of the close corporation decisions involving non-payment of dividends, *see* Douglas K. Moll, Shareholder Oppression & Dividend Policy in the Close Corporation, 60 Wash. & Lee L. Rev. 841 (2003).

[23]   In close corporation cases, the courts are more willing to accord less of a presumption of propriety to decisions to withhold dividends than in cases involving public companies. *See, e.g.,* Santarelli v. Katz, 270 F.2d 762, 768 (7th Cir. 1959) ("if a stockholder is being unjustly deprived of dividends that should be his, a court of equity will not permit management to cloak itself in the immunity of the business judgment rule").

[24]   Ford v. Easthampton Rubber-Thread Co., 32 N.E. 1036 (Mass. 1893).

[25]   Robert S. Stevens, Handbook on the Law of Private Corporations 459–461 (2d ed. 1949).

[26]   *See* Comment, Is a Declaration of Subscription "Rights" Revocable? 39 Yale L.J. 1163, 1166, 1173 (1930).

[27]   Ford v. Ford Mfg. Co., 222 Ill.App. 76 (1921).

[28]   *See,* MBCA § 6.40 (2016); former MBCA § 30 (1969).

[29]   Caleb & Co. v. E.I. DuPont de Nemours & Co., 615 F.Supp. 96 (S.D.N.Y. 1985).

[30]   Caleb & Co. v. E.I. DuPont de Nemours & Co., 615 F.Supp. 96 (S.D.N.Y. 1985).

Dividends declared subsequent to the transfer of ownership belong to the transferee.[31] A share of stock has been compared to a fruit tree: the seller may retain any fallen fruit (declared dividends) on sale of the tree but may not shake the tree to recover more fruit after the sale.[32] If the transferor of the stock receives dividends that were declared after the transfer, he is liable to the transferee for them, whether or not the transfer was recorded or registered with the corporation;[33] however, the corporation is not liable to a transferee without notice.[34]

PART B.   RESTRICTIONS ON DIVIDEND DISTRIBUTIONS

§ 20.5   The Purpose of Dividend Restrictions

A difficult and complex branch of corporation law deals with legal capital requirements and the limitations on distributions to shareholders. The rule against capital impairment has long been the fundamental restriction on dividends. Historically, statutes have attempted to provide for the establishment, contribution, and maintenance of some margin of asset values over liabilities for the protection of creditors. But because these statutes did not keep up with changes in generally accepted accounting practices and the insights of modern finance, legal capital has become a dated dividend restriction.[35] One mitigating factor has been the addition of an insolvency test in most statutes.

§ 20.6   The Various Dividend Limitations

Every state statutorily restricts the directors' authority to make dividend distributions based on the corporation's financial condition. These statutes contain one or more of the following restrictions:

(1) A prohibition of dividends when the corporation is insolvent or that would render it insolvent.

(2) The requirement that a general surplus exists from which dividends may be paid and that consists of the value of the net assets or net worth of the corporation over the stated or legal capital margin, determined from the balance sheet and usually excluding any unrealized appreciation of fixed assets.

(3) The requirement that an earned surplus exists, which devises its value from accumulated earnings or profits.[36] All legal-capital statutes permit dividends from capital surplus but the availability of capital surplus has been restricted by several acts to preferred shares.

(4) As an alternative to surplus, the existence of current earnings usually measured for the year in which the dividend is declared or in the preceding

---

[31] *See* Wilcom v. Wilcom, 502 A.2d 1076 (Md. 1986) (purchasers of shares pursuant to stock transfer restriction is equity owner entitled to dividends thereafter, even though transferor refused to transfer title).

[32] De Gendre v. Kent, L.R. 4 Eq. 283 (1865).

[33] Herzfeld & Stern v. Freidus, 330 N.Y.S.2d 479 (Sup. Ct. App. Term 1971).

[34] Richter & Co. v. Light, 116 A. 600 (Conn. 1922).

[35] *See* Thomas C. Ackerman, Jr. & James K. Sterrett, II, California's New Approach to Dividends and Reacquisitions of Shares, 23 UCLA L. Rev. 1052 (1976).

[36] In order to comport with GAAP the California statute speaks in terms of "retained earnings." Cal. Gen. Corp. Law § 500(a) (West 1990).

year will permit "nimble dividends" in a few states, regardless of impairment of capital.

(5) A certain ratio of certain assets to current liabilities, or assets to liabilities, such as 1¼ to 1, may be required to be left after a distribution of dividends in order to avoid impairment of debt-paying ability and working capital position.[37]

(6) An exception to the general dividend restrictions permits a "wasting asset corporation," although not formed for the liquidation of specific property, to distribute the proceeds derived from the consumption of wasting assets without deduction for their depletion or exhaustion.[38] This in effect permits liquidating dividends or a distribution of capital, which may be dangerous to creditors and preferred shareholders.

In addition to the foregoing legal capital restrictions, there is the new balance-sheet approach and "distribution" restrictions adopted in the 1980 amendments to the former Model Business Corporation Act, and these are carried forward in the current Model Business Corporation Act.[39] They prohibit a distribution if, after giving effect to such distribution, the corporation's total assets would be less than its total liabilities plus the maximum amount required for the payment of any liquidation preferences. Nearly one half the states have patterned their statutes after the model acts, and the remaining states continue to adhere to some form of legal capital restriction.

As will be seen in the next chapter, statutory restrictions on the purchase by a corporation of its own shares are often similar to, or at least related to, those on dividend distributions, because both transactions involve the withdrawal of corporate assets in favor of shareholders.[40]

Dividend restrictions also appear in loan agreements as creditors frequently resort to private contracting for protection to supplement the minimum level provided by corporate statutes and fraudulent transfer acts. Where such a provision exists, the limits found in the agreement entered into with a single creditor is much like rain—its benefits fall upon all the corporation's creditors since the debtor's reduced discretion to make distributions to its stockholders has the effect of conserving assets that are available to all of its creditors.[41] Because of the frequency of detailed loan agreements among public companies it is safe to say that the ultimate restriction on distributions to stockholders by public companies is that found in their loan agreements and not corporate statutes or fraudulent transfer provisions.

§ 20.7 The Capital Impairment Limitation

The oldest and still prevalent dividend restriction limits dividends to the extent that there is sufficient surplus, which is defined in the statutes as the amount net assets or

---

[37] This was the alternative approach, as compared with the use of retained earnings in California. Cal. Gen. Corp. Law § 500(b) (West 1990).

[38] *See* § 20.12.

[39] Former MBCA §§ 2(i), 45(b) (1980); MBCA §§ 1.40, 6.40 (2016). The text to the 1980 amendments to the Model Business Corporation Act is reported in 34 Bus. Law. 1867–1889 (1979).

[40] *See, e.g.,* Cal. Gen. Corp. Law § 166 (West 1990). *See generally* Chapter 21.

[41] For an analysis of whether state-imposed dividend restrictions reflect efficient contracting by creditors, *see* John Armour, Share Capital and Creditor Protection: Efficient Rules for a Modern Company Law, 63 Mod. L. Rev. 355 (2000).

net worth is in excess of the legal capital.[42] The laws of Delaware, New York, and a number of other states permit dividends out of surplus of any and all varieties, whether earned or capital surplus.[43] Unlike the pre-1980 Model Business Corporation Act,[44] these states do not draw distinctions between an "earned surplus" and the different kinds of "capital surplus" that may be derived from paid-in surplus or from reduction surplus arising on the reduction of the legal capital. The pre-1980 Model Business Corporation Act distinguishes among different types of surplus, with the result that dividends and share repurchases premised on available earned surplus have much fewer limitations than those premised on other forms of surplus (for example, capital surplus). The pre-1980 Model Business Corporation Act's definitional section divides "surplus" into two components and treats them dissimilarly in important ways. Section 45(a) of the act authorizes dividends in cash or property to the extent of unreserved and unrestricted earned surplus. Because it arises almost invariably from shareholder's investment in the enterprise,[45] capital surplus is burdened with most of the restrictions that surround stated capital. Capital surplus does, however, have some uses accorded earned surplus. For example, even though distributions to the shareholders from capital surplus are allowed, such distributions are conditioned on there being express authorization in the corporation's charter for utilization of capital surplus or approval of a majority of the shares of each outstanding class of stock.[46] Use of capital surplus is prohibited if the corporation's net assets following the distribution are less than the aggregate liquidation preference of a senior class of stock. The prohibition also applies whenever there are any unpaid dividends for any class of stock having a preferential right to dividends. None of these limitations arise when dividends are based on earned surplus. All distributions, whether from earned surplus or capital surplus, must not under the equity test render the corporation insolvent—that is, unable to satisfy its obligations as they mature.

Until the adoption of the current provisions of the Model Business Corporation Act, discussed below, there were few exceptions[47] to the view that unrealized appreciation in value of fixed assets could not be counted in the computation of a surplus as a basis for cash or property dividends.[48] Historically, dividend regulation rested on certain metrics focused on the firm's balance sheet. Since assets under generally accepted accounting principles (GAAP) are recorded at their historical cost, less any depreciation, amortization, or depletion, this approach naturally led to view that unrealized asset appreciation was necessarily foreclosed as a basis of dividends. The presumed intent of the legislature in adopting regulation dependent upon the balance sheet is that the legislature intended the statutory tests to incorporate GAAP for defining the terms used in the statute, that is, terms which historically have significance within the field of accounting should carry forward their meaning from that field. An assumed connection

---

[42]   Del. Code Ann. tit. 8, §§ 170(a), 173, 154 (2001); N.Y. Bus. Corp. Law § 510 (McKinney Supp. 2009).

[43]   Del. Code Ann. tit. 8, §§ 170(a), 173, 154 (2001).

[44]   This was the case prior to the 1980 Model Business Corporation Act amendments. Former MBCA § 45(a) (1969). *See* § 20.14.

[45]   Other sources of capital surplus are transfers from earned surplus to capital surplus on approval of the board of directors, former MBCA § 70 (1969), by a reduction in stated capital, *id.*, or issuances of shares as part of an exchange or conversion of outstanding shares. *Id.* §§ 18, 19.

[46]   Former MBCA § 46 (1969).

[47]   Randall v. Bailey, 43 N.E.2d 43 (N.Y. 1942), *aff'g* 23 N.Y.S.2d 173 (Sup. Ct. 1940). *See* Thomas A. Reynolds, Note, Cash Dividends Payable from Unrealized Appreciation of Fixed Assets—A Reconsideration of *Randall v. Bailey*, 20 U. Pitt. L. Rev. 632 (1959).

[48]   Klang v. Smith's Food & Drug Centers, 702 A.2d 150, 154 (Del. 1997) (directors have the power to use fair value of assets to determine the firm's surplus).

between dividend regulation and GAAP should be powerful because the purposes that underlie GAAP's conservatism and dividend regulation are identical.[49] GAAP's adherence to historical cost and strict rules for the realization of gains and income are based on a number of factors, including: the lack of relevance of market or replacement costs to a fixed asset that is not intended to be sold, the difficulties of valuation, the loss of comparability of financial statements of corporations using different valuation methods, problems of application in depreciation accounting that is intended only to charge asset costs against operations, and the possibilities of employing unrealized appreciation as a purely fictitious basis for dividends.

The leading case for recognizing unrealized gains as a source for dividends is *Randall v. Bailey*,[50] which was decided under an impairment-of-capital statute that permitted dividends as long as "the *value* of its assets remaining after the payment of such dividend, or after such distribution of assets . . . shall be at least equal to the aggregate amount of its debts and liabilities including capital or capital stock as the case may be."[51] When *Randall* was decided not only did practice vary widely among accountants with respect to what was required to recognize income—that is, the realization convention as we understand it today was not then widely practiced[52]—but also courts were far more willing to exercise their judgment as to the meaning of "significant accounting terms."[53] These distinctions, did not, however, enter the Delaware Supreme Court's thinking in *Klang v. Smith's Food and Drug Centers*,[54] when the court permitted unrealized appreciation in assets to meet the state's impairment of capital test:

> The General Assembly enacted the statute to prevent boards from draining corporations of assets to the detriment of creditors and the long-term health of the corporation. That a corporation has not yet realized or reflected on its balance sheet the appreciation of assets is irrelevant to this concern. Regardless of what a balance sheet that has not been updated may show, an actual, though unrealized appreciation reflects real economic value that the corporation may borrow against or that creditors may claim or levy upon. Allowing corporations to revalue assets and liabilities to reflect current realities complies with the statute and serves well the policies behind this statute.[55]

As examined below, the policy referred to by the Delaware Supreme Court may not be well served by permitting unrealized appreciation to be the source of dividend distributions.

Sound policy supports allowing firms to distribute true economic gains to their owners. Such gains are those that are not needed to replace the facilities and resources

---

[49] *See* Current Issues on the Legality of Dividends from a Law and Accounting Perspective, 39 Bus. Law. 289, 292–300 (1983).

[50] Randall v. Bailey, 23 N.Y.S.2d 173 (Sup. Ct. 1940), *aff'd*, 43 N.E.2d 43 (N.Y. 1942).

[51] N.Y. Stock Corp. Law § 58, enacted in 1923 (emphasis added).

[52] *See* James D. Cox, Financial Information, Accounting and the Law 257 (1980). *See also* § 19.2.

[53] *Id.* at 694–695.

[54] Klang v. Smith's Food and Drug Centers, 702 A.2d 150 (Del. 1997).

[55] Klang v. Smith's Food and Drug Centers, 702 A.2d 150, 154 (Del. 1997).

either committed or already consumed within the company's current business.[56] If the land on which the company's plant is built increases in value, that is not a true economic gain that can be distributed to the shareholders—any sale of the land or a parcel of it would possibly necessitate an equal expenditure to replace the land so that operations can continue. Thus pure holding gains are rarely a true advance in a company's fortunes if those gains are associated with an asset without which the business cannot operate. However persuasive such arguments are, they are moot in the face of the clear language of the present Model Business Corporation Act:

> The board of directors may base a determination that a distribution is not prohibited ... either on financial statements prepared on the basis of accounting practices and principles that are reasonable in the circumstances or on a *fair valuation* or other method reasonable in the circumstances.[57]

The official comment to this section expressly states "the statute authorizes departures from historical cost accounting and sanctions the use of appraisal and current value methods to determine the amount available for distributions." There appears little likelihood that the relaxed method of determining distributable dividends under such a provision will occur within a public corporation where dividend practices, particularly for companies in financial distress, have historically been conservative and have been muffled by external lending agreements. But the freedom permitted by the current Model Business Corporation Act is likely to be irresistible within a close corporation, where the rush to grab the assets within a failing company is all too well documented. Certainly one must ponder whether the very meaning of the standards embodied in statutes intended for the protection of creditors should ever be commended to those whose interests are adverse to creditors.

§ 20.8 The Earned Surplus Test

Following the pre-1980 Model Business Corporation Act,[58] many states restricted dividend distributions to earned surplus except in special cases, such as when expressly authorized in the articles of incorporation, when stockholders vote to use capital surplus, when distributions are used to pay cumulative dividends on preferred shares, or when distributions are made from a wasting asset corporation. The role of GAAP in the construction of earned surplus is not clear under the Model Business Corporation Act or, for that matter, under most other statutes.[59] It is generally believed that the earned-surplus test looks to realized gains and accumulated but undistributed profits as the normal basis of dividends on common shares.[60] Similarly, as an alternative test in California, distributions are permitted to the extent of "retained earnings"; thus the current accounting terminology is substituted for the old.[61]

---

[56] This indeed is the notion within the accounting movement calling for current-value accounting. *See* C. Morley Carscallen & Kenneth P. Johnson, Financial Reporting Under Changing Values: An Introduction to Current Value Accounting 16–20 (AMA 1977).

[57] MBCA § 6.40(d) (2016) (emphasis added).

[58] Former MBCA §§ 45, 46 (1969).

[59] The commentators in varying respects argue that the Model Business Corporation Act permits some departure from generally accepted accounting principles. *See* Ray Garrett, Capital and Surplus Under the New Corporation Statutes, 23 Law & Contemp. Probs. 239, 259 (1958) (unrealized gains can be recognized).

[60] Former MBCA § 2(*l*) (1969).

[61] Cal. Gen. Corp. Law § 500(a) (West 1990).

Earned surplus is generally a far more conservative limitation on common share dividends, and on share purchases also, than surplus generally because it links such distributions directly to the financial performance of the company. But even earned surplus may be based in large part on fixed, unmarketable, and frozen assets, such as investments in machinery or real estate. The ability to pay dividends, as distinct from the legal right to pay dividends, depends largely on the liquidity of the financial position—that is, on the so-called current ratio and the sufficiency of working capital to keep the business going.[62] While the existence of the required surplus over capital may satisfy the statutory prohibition, it is the duty of directors to take many other factors into account in the exercise of prudent management.[63]

The earned-surplus restriction is often coupled with prohibitions against capital impairment and payments that would render the corporation insolvent.[64]

§ 20.9 Capital Surplus as a Source of "Distributions" to Shareholders

In many states, including Delaware and New York, capital surplus is available equally with earned surplus for dividends on all kinds of shares.[65] This can create a danger to preferred shareholders and creditors because directors are given the authority by many corporation acts to attribute substantially all of the consideration received on the issue of no-or low-par shares, either common or preferred, to paid-in surplus rather than to capital. A dividend paid out of paid-in surplus would then leave an inadequate capital margin for creditor and preferred shareholder protection. Conceivably, dividends could even be paid to common shareholders out of paid-in surplus received from the issue of the preferred shares and thus divert part of the investment of the senior shares to the holders of the junior shares. Any abuse of this discretion by the directors, however, is properly subject to equitable limitations.[66]

Dividends from paid-in surplus and from capital reduction surplus are a return on capital akin to a partial liquidating distribution, because they represent a distribution of part of the price invested by the original share-subscribers in the business, and, as such, they are not taxable as dividend income, but are treated as a capital return.[67] Most statutes require notice to the shareholders of the extent to which the dividend represents capital surplus.[68] It is surprising that only a few states have required that capital surplus be available for dividends only in the absence of an earned surplus.[69]

---

[62] *See* § 19.4.

[63] *See* David F. Scott, Jr. & C. Wayne Shepherd, Corporate Dividend Policy: Some Legal & Financial Aspects, 123 Am. Bus. L.J. 199 (1975).

[64] Former MBCA § 45 (1969). The insolvency test is also used new or in conjunction with other dividend tests in state statutes. *See* Cal. Gen. Corp. Law § 501 (West 1990).

[65] Del. Code Ann. tit. 8, §§ 154, 170(a) (2001); N.Y. Bus. Corp. Law § 510 (McKinney Supp. 2009); MBCA Ann. 3d § 640 Statutory Comparison ¶ 1(c) (Supp. 1993).

[66] Adolf A. Berle, Investors and the Revised Delaware Corporation Act, 29 Colum. L. Rev. 563, 573–575 (1929).

[67] I.R.C. §§ 316, 301(c)(2) (2009).

[68] A number of state statutes require notice to shareholders of the source of the distribution if not from earned surplus or if from capital surplus. *See, e.g.,* N.Y. Bus. Corp. Law § 501(c) (McKinney 1986).

[69] *See* Ark. Code Ann. § 4–26–619(1)(B) (Michie 2001).

The former Model Business Corporation Act, like other "earned surplus" statutes, permits "distributions from capital surplus" under certain circumstances.[70] In addition to the insolvency limitation, such distributions must be authorized either in the charter or by a majority shareholder vote on a class basis, including nonvoting shares. This authorization is not necessary, however, in the case of distributions in discharge of cumulative dividend rights, provided there is no earned surplus. Distributions out of capital surplus may not be made in a manner prejudicial to preferred shareholders.[71]

Beginning with the 1980 amendments to the Model Business Corporation Act, dividend regulation became even more unconventional. The new approach allows any distribution that meets the solvency test and that does not reduce the corporation's total assets below the sum of maximum liquidation preferences payable and liabilities after giving effect to the distribution.[72] California, in its departure from "legal capital" concepts, provides two alternative tests. It authorizes dividends to the extent there is "retained earnings." Alternatively, California sets forth a test that mirrors that of the Model Act—requires that after giving effect to a distribution, total assets be at least equal the total liabilities[73] The Assets vs Liabilities+Liquidation Preference is carried forward into the present Model Act.

§ 20.10   The Insolvency Limitation

At one time insolvency was the only statutory restriction on dividends in some jurisdictions.[74] Today virtually all statutes have some form of balance-sheet test in addition to an insolvency limitation.[75]

There are two rival definitions of "insolvency":[76] (1) The commercial or equity test of an inability to meet debts and obligations promptly as they fall due;[77] and (2) the bankruptcy or "balance sheet" test, an excess of the amount of liabilities over the total value of the assets.[78] It is not always clear in dividend statutes which of the two possible meanings of "insolvency" should be taken. The rule against impairment of capital should take care of the question of the total assets at least equaling the liabilities,[79] but, if the insolvency limitation is to have any additional force or effect, it should be drawn so as to

---

[70]   Former MBCA § 46 (1969).

[71]   All cumulative arrearages must have been paid, and the distribution cannot reduce the next assets below the aggregate liquidation preference. *Id.* at § 46(e), (d) (1969).

[72]   Former MBCA § 45 (1980); MBCA § 6.40 (2016).

[73]   Cal. Gen. Corp. Law § 500 (West 1990).

[74]   *E.g.*, The Business Corporation Law ch. 434, § 35, 1903 Mass. Acts 418, 435 (1903) (current version of Mass. Gen. Laws Ann. ch. 156D, § 6.40 (West Supp. 2009)); An Act on Corporations, ch. 77, § 21, 1892 Miss. Laws §§ 269, 276 (1892); Act of Dec. 2, 1871, ch. 80, art. III § 28, 1871 Tex. Gen. Laws (2d Sess.) §§ 66, 71 (1871); Act of Feb. 17, 1939, ch. 62, § 28–131, 1939 Wyo. Sess. Laws §§ 66, 71 (1871).

[75]   *E.g.*, former MBCA § 43 (1969).

[76]   *See generally* Stearn, Jr. & Kandestin, Delaware's Solvency Test: What Is It and Does It Make Sense? A Comparison of Solvency Tests Under the Bankruptcy Code and Delaware Law, 36 Del. J. Corp. L. 165 (2011).

[77]   *See* Paratransit Risk Retention Group Ins. Co. v. Kamins, 160 P.3d 307 (Colo. Ct. App. 2007) (equity solvency test contemplates that corporation continues to generate or attempts to generate profits).

[78]   *See* Tumarkin v. Gallay, 127 F.Supp. 94 (S.D.N.Y. 1954).

[79]   Since rules against capital impairment operate on the theory that dividends will be paid out of the excess of net assets over liabilities and stated capital, such a rule requires the total assets to exceed total liabilities. The problem with such determinations is that they are based on the balance sheet values, which do not necessarily correlate with the true market value, particularly in the context of a forced sale. Thus a bankruptcy solvency test may not in fact be incorporated into the capital impairment prohibition and perhaps should be viewed as a distinct limitation, particularly to protect long-term creditors.

cover some objective test of reasonable grounds for believing that the corporation will not be rendered unable to pay its debts and liabilities, both long-and short-term, as they fall due.[80] The plaintiff need only set forth allegations under one of the two statutory solvency tests.[81] Probably the most prevalent interpretation of prohibitions against insolvency in dividend statutes is the equity test.

The equity solvency test should be seen as setting forth a context within which traditional manners of inquiry occur as to whether the directors' decision is protected by the business judgment rule.[82] Within this context, a host of considerations are appropriate:

> [I]n determining whether the equity insolvency test has been met, certain judgments and assumptions as to the future course of the corporation's business are customarily justified, absent clear evidence to the contrary. These include the likelihood that (a) based on existing and contemplated demand for the corporation's products or services, it will be able to generate funds over a period of time sufficient to satisfy its existing and reasonably anticipated obligations as they mature, and (b) indebtedness which matures in the near-term will be refinanced where, on the basis of the corporation's financial condition and future prospects and the general availability of credit to business similarly situated, it is reasonable to assume that such refinancing may be accomplished. To the extent the corporation may be subject to asserted or unasserted contingent liabilities, reasonable judgments as to the likelihood, amount, and the time of any recovery against the corporation, after giving consideration to the extent to which the corporation is insured or otherwise protected against loss, may be utilized.[83]

§ 20.11 Nimble Dividends

Some state statutes allow dividends from the net profits or net earnings of the preceding year or other recent specified period in the absence of any surplus and in spite of a capital deficit.[84] These provisions providing for "nimble dividends"[85] have been criticized by many writers as being unduly lax. The privilege may be justified, however, on the ground that the surplus limitation at times becomes unreasonably strict and arbitrary, as it may permit dividends when they are inexpedient and forbid them when their distribution would be financially sound. The purpose of the law is to establish some minimum test of whether the financial condition of a corporation permits a distribution with a view to the safety of creditors and the investment of the shareholders.

---

[80] *See* 1 Garrard Glenn, Fraudulent Conveyances and Preferences § 32 (rev. ed. 1940) (hereinafter Fraudulent Conveyances); Garrard Glenn, The Law Governing Liquidation §§ 12, 13, 22 (1935).

[81] In re Felt Mfg. Co., Inc., 371 B.R. 589 (Bankr. D.N.H. 2007) (applying New Hampshire Law).

[82] This linkage is expressly made in the present Model Business Corporation Act by premising director liability for unlawful distributions only if the director "did not perform his duties in compliance with section 8.30," which codifies the business judgment rule. MBCA § 8.32(a) (2016).

[83] MBCA § 6.40, Comment 2 (2016).

[84] There is great variety of nimble dividend provisions. *See, e.g.,* Okla. Stat. Ann. tit. 18, § 1049 (West 2010); former MBCA § 34(a) (alternate) (1969). *See* Del. Code Ann. tit. 8, § 170(a) (2001); Kan. Stat. Ann. § 17–6420 (2007). *See* Ark. Code Ann. § 4–26–619(2)(C) (Michie 2001); La. Rev. Stat. Ann. § 12:63(B) (West 1999).

[85] The phrase "nimble dividends" was coined by Professor Baker (*see* Recent Cases, Corporations—Dividends—Virginia Statute Construed to Allow Dividends from Current Profits Despite Capital Deficit, 62 Harv. L. Rev. 130 (1948)), meaning in essence that directors must be nimble in declaring dividends before the earnings are transferred to offset deficits.

§ 20.12 "Wasting Asset" Corporations

A controversial[86] provision in many states permits corporations solely or principally engaged in the exploitation of "wasting assets" to distribute the net proceeds derived from exploitation of their holdings, such as mines, oil wells, patents, and leaseholds, without allowance or deduction for depletion.[87] There may be a vague limitation of making sufficient provision for creditors and the liquidation priorities of preferred shareholders. Such statutes are often accompanied by a requirement of notice that liquidation dividends are being paid without allowance for depletion. The pre-1980 version of the Model Business Corporation Act imposes such limitations in addition to applying them only to corporations engaged principally in the exploration of natural resources.[88] The Act also limits such distributions to depletion reserves and requires authorization in the charter. As a result of the 1980 amendments eliminating legal capital, the wasting asset provision has been deleted.[89] Even in the absence of an express statute, some courts have permitted wasting-asset distributions.[90]

If a corporation is organized to exploit, liquidate, and distribute the proceeds of a particular mineral reserve, estate, or specific lot of assets, the corporation may be described as a "liquidating corporation," which may be excused by statute from making any reserve for depletion or replacement of the assets liquidated. But if the purpose of a corporation that is engaged in the oil or mining or similar business is a continuing one and not the exhaustion and liquidation of a particular property, then, as to keeping its capital intact there is no reason for treating such corporation as different from any other continuing concern, such as a manufacturing corporation.

There is no justification for treating such corporations differently, and such provisions should be repealed. Moreover, there is little evidence that creditors are deserving of less protection for wasting-asset corporations than for other types of corporations. It would therefore appear to be more consistent to settle on a useful prophylactic standard that would work, on average, for all types of corporations.

§ 20.13 The Innovations of the California Statute and the Model Business Corporation Act

Very few parts of the corporate mechanism are more complicated, unworkable, or incomprehensible than the system of legal-capital requirements, with its various attempted restrictions on unsafe distributions of assets to the shareholders.

---

[86] *See* Charles G. Carpenter, A Critical Evaluation of the Wasting Asset Distribution, 25 Bus. Law. 1733 (1970).

[87] *E.g.,* Del. Code Ann. tit. 8, § 170(b) (2001).

[88] Former MBCA § 45(b) (1969).

[89] Former MBCA § 45 (1980); MBCA § 6.40 (2016); 805 ILCS § 5/9.10 (West 2004); Minn. Stat. Ann. § 302A.551 (West 2004); Mont. Code Ann. § 35–1–712 (2009); N.M. Stat. Ann. § 53–11–44 (Michie Supp. 2007); Wash. Rev. Code Ann. § 23B.06.400 (West Supp. 2009).

[90] The California court in an early decision declared that the then California statute, which forbade withdrawal of capital or "capital stock" and confined dividends to "surplus profits arising from the business," did not preclude a mining corporation from distributing the net proceeds of its mining operations without provision for depletion, although the necessary result was that something was subtracted from the value of its mine and from the net worth of its investment. Excelsior Water & Mining Co. v. Pierce, 27 P. 44 (Cal. 1891).

The prevalent limitations as to capital and surplus rest on vague financial standards that are difficult to ascertain and to apply.[91] The margin of safety measured by the legal capital is an arbitrary limit, established on the issue of shares, that has no relation to the kind of business being conducted, the liquidity of assets, the net current asset position, and the ability to meet or refinance obligations as they fall due.[92]

The current version of the Model Business Corporation Act follows California's lead in jettisoning most of the traditional legal-capital concepts. The treasury share enigma is abolished,[93] and both share repurchases and dividends are covered under the concept of "distributions" to shareholders.[94] Also, the equity insolvency test is retained as a basic restriction.[95] The Model Business Corporation Act diverges significantly from the earlier "surplus" approach in rejecting a restriction based on earnings.[96] In lieu of retained earnings or earned surplus, the Model Business Corporation Act and California use a simpler and more flexible balance-sheet test. The new provision prohibits distributions if, after the distribution, a corporation's total assets are less than its total liabilities plus liquidation preferences, if any.[97] The Model Business Corporation Act and California further decline dependency on GAAP by placing the method for valuation of assets and liabilities within the directors' discretion, subject to a standard of reasonableness under the circumstances.[98]

§ 20.14   The Issue of Shares as Stock Dividends and Stock Splits

The term "stock dividend" is an unfortunate misnomer. It is a dividend only in the sense that the corporation has made a pro rata distribution among a class of its stockholders. However, it is unlike the other kinds of dividends discussed in this chapter because the corporation is not distributing any of its assets to its shareholders, and in turn its shareholders receive only additional shares to represent their same proportionate ownership interest. The declaration of dividends in new shares is a kind of psychological, constructive, or symbolic benefit that is sometimes used in order to keep investors satisfied with the retention of profits in the business or for purposes of stock market manipulation by those in control. The customary dividend statutes, discussed in the preceding sections, and the surplus and capital impairment limits do not apply to stock dividends. As explained in a leading case,[99] "a stock dividend does not distribute property, but simply dilutes the shares as they existed before. . . ." It is in no sense a

---

[91]   Homer Kripke, Accountants' Financial Statements and Fact-Finding in the Law of Corporate Regulation, 50 Yale L.J. 1180, 1188, 1190, 1194, 1197 (1941).

[92]   The earning power of a corporation, its ability to pay debts and dividends, may not depend on the amount of its net assets.

[93]   MBCA § 6.40 (and comments) (2016); Cal. Gen. Corp. Law § 510 (West 1990).

[94]   Former MBCA § 1.40(6) (2008); Cal. Gen. Corp. Law § 166 (West 1990).

[95]   Former MBCA § 45(a) (1980); MBCA § 6.40 (2016); Cal. Gen. Corp. Law § 501 (West 1990).

[96]   Both the earned-surplus test (former MBCA § 45 (1969)) and California's retained-earnings test (Cal. Gen. Corp. Law § 500(a) (West 1990)) are based on the concept of paying dividends based on the corporation's earnings or profits rather than on money (capital) paid into the company by the sale of shares.

[97]   Former MBCA § 45(b) (1969); MBCA § 6.40 (2016).

[98]   Former MBCA § 45 (1969). Directors may make asset and liability determinations from financial statements based on accounting practices and principles that are reasonable under the circumstances. See former MBCA § 45, Comment (1969). In many cases the reasonableness standard may require use of GAAP.

[99]   Williams v. Western Union Tel. Co., 57 N.Y.S. 446, 453 (1883).

distribution of surplus. When an amendment to the articles of incorporation is necessary to carry out a stock split or stock dividend, each of the steps must be satisfied.[100]

Neither stock dividends nor stock split-ups themselves increase or decrease the assets or earnings of the corporation. Nevertheless, these two events are treated quite differently by the accounting profession. As will be seen in the next section, surplus equal to the market value of the shares distributed must be capitalized for stock dividends but not for stock split-ups. What distinguishes the two is not the name assigned to the distribution by the board of directors, but whether a material reduction in the shares' market value is likely to accompany the distribution.[101] Investors associate both events with positive news about the corporation, so that rarely is the market value of the corporation's outstanding shares less after the declaration date of either a stock dividend or stock split than before the declaration.[102]

A corporation's distribution of shares held by it in another corporation is properly referred to, not as a stock dividend, but as a property dividend, an actual distribution of corporate assets[103]—and, as such, is subject to the normal restrictions on cash and property dividends. The ordinary stock dividend—that is, the issuance of new shares, is very different in effect from a distribution of other property or of such shares to a different class. A stock dividend does not give the common shareholders any new or different interest in the corporation than they had before; it simply divides the holdings of each shareholder into a larger number of share units, with each stockholder maintaining the same proportionate interest in the corporation.[104]

A share or stock "split-up" is simply a division of outstanding shares by amendment of the articles of incorporation into a greater number of share units, like changing a five dollar bill into five "ones." It is the reverse of a share consolidation or "reverse stock split."[105] A share split-up does not, however, make any representations as to any accumulation of earnings or other surplus or involve any increase of the legal capital[106] as occurs with a stock dividend. In the case of a stock split, the per share par value or stated capital is decreased in the same proportion as the amount of the stock split. Share split-ups may be used for the legitimate purpose of reducing the market value of share units, which may otherwise be too high for general convenience in trading.

Under generally accepted accounting principles, the distinction between a stock dividend and a stock split is whether a material decline in the price of the shares is likely to occur on their distribution. When such a decline is not expected, the distribution is deemed a stock dividend, and surplus must be capitalized, as discussed in the next section, in an amount equal to the aggregate fair market value of the distributed shares. Under accounting standards, a distribution of less than 20 or 25 percent may not produce

---

[100] Blades v. Wisehart, 2010 WL 4638603 (Del. Ch. 2010)(failure to fulfill steps to properly amend articles so as to effect the stock split resulted in shares not being validly issued with consequence their holders were not shareholders).

[101] AICPA, Accounting Research Bulletin No. 43 ch. 7, Stock Dividends and Stock Split-Ups ¶ 11 (1953) (hereinafter AICPA, Bulletin No. 43).

[102] See, e.g., Mark S. Grinblatt, Ronald W. Masulis, & Sheridan Titman, The Valuation of Stock Splits and Stock Dividends, 13 J. Fin. Econ. 461 (1984).

[103] Peabody v. Eisner, 247 U.S. 347 (1918); City Bank Farmers' Trust Co. v. Ernst, 189 N.E. 241 (N.Y. 1934).

[104] Eisner v. Macomber, 252 U.S. 189 (1920).

[105] See Teschner v. Chicago Title & Trust Co., 322 N.E.2d 54 (Ill. 1974).

[106] In re Trust Estate of Pew, 158 A.2d 552 (Pa. 1960).

such an effect.[107] Stock splits are distributions where a material decline in the shares' market value is likely to occur. However, when characterizing a distribution with regard to allocation in trusts between principal and income, some courts have disregarded the dilution effect and instead have looked to the accounting entries made on the corporate balance sheet.

§ 20.15   Capitalization of Surplus for Stock Dividends and Stock Splits

The principal limitation on the issue of the typical stock dividend is a peculiar one—the capitalizing of surplus. Capitalization of surplus refers to the accounting transfer from one of the surplus accounts to the capital stock (stated capital) account. The requirement for such a transfer arises from the commands of the state corporation statute, the listing requirement of the American or New York Stock Exchange, if applicable, and the demands of generally accepted accounting principles. This is more than a mere bookkeeping entry. It decreases surplus and increases the legal-capital margin, which limits dividend distributions. When a share dividend is charged against earned surplus, it has been said that this in effect is the same as a distribution of accumulated profits to the shareholders and a compulsory subscription for shares or reinvestment by them of the amount received in the corporation.[108] The increase of legal capital due to a decrease of surplus restricts the directors' authority to declare dividends payable in cash or property.

By far the least demanding of these is that of the corporation statute that requires that an amount of surplus not less than the aggregate par value of shares distributed as a stock dividend be capitalized.[109] When the shares issued as a dividend are without par value, there is no convenient measure of the amount of surplus to be transferred to capital. Many states leave the amount almost wholly to the directors' discretion.[110]

As seen in the preceding section, there is great concern that investors may misinterpret the true economic effects of a stock dividend. Thus, generally accepted accounting principles require capitalization of surplus equal to the aggregate *fair market value* of the distributed shares in those instances in which a material decline in the per share market value is not believed to accompany the stock dividend's distribution.[111] Since share dividends are usually issued to evidence retention of earnings for reinvestment by the corporation, surplus is transferred and capitalized to give some assurance that such earnings will be retained by the corporation and to prevent misleading investors.[112] It would seem that the padding of the accounts by estimates and conjectures, by reappraising of fixed assets, and by writing up of inventories in order to make a revaluation of surplus for share dividends is undue laxity, which may give a deceptive representation of corporate prosperity to shareholders and to the investing public. GAAP requires transferring earned surplus to the category of permanent capitalization (*i.e.*, "capital stock" and "capital surplus") an amount equal to the fair

---

[107] AICPA, Bulletin No. 43, *supra* note 101.

[108] Trefry v. Putnam, 116 N.E. 904, 911 (Mass. 1917).

[109] Former MBCA § 45(d) (1969).

[110] *E.g.*, Del. Code Ann. tit. 8, § 173 (2001); N.Y. Bus. Corp. Law § 511(a)(2) (McKinney 2003); former MBCA § 45(d)(2) (1969).

[111] AICPA, Bulletin No. 43, *supra* note 101.

[112] *See* AICPA, Bulletin No. 43, *supra* note 101.

market value of the additional shares when a material adjustment in market prices is not likely to follow a stock dividend.[113]

Even though California and the Model Business Corporation Act exclude stock splits and stock dividends from the definition of "distributions," accounting standards still apply, so retained earnings must still be reduced if the states are to comply with generally accepted accounting standards and a material decline in the shares' market value is not likely to accompany the distribution.

PART C. LIABILITIES OF DIRECTORS AND SHAREHOLDERS

§ 20.16 Directors' Liability for Unlawful Dividends

The primary responsibility for protecting capital and keeping dividend distributions within statutory limits rests on the directors by whose authority such distributions are made. Directors' liability is the principal sanction or means of enforcement of dividend restrictions, supplemented by the less effective liability of shareholders and by injunction suits at the instance of shareholders.[114]

Most instances in which directors are held liable for illegal dividends can best be described euphemistically as "bankruptcy planning," through which corporate assets have been purposely deflected by cunning insiders to themselves without satisfying or making provision for outstanding obligations and while the corporation is either insolvent or is winding up its affairs.[115] Absent clear proof that the insiders were aware of their company's financial distress, or otherwise flaunted the statute's restrictions on distributions, director liability is highly unlikely.[116] Simply stated, the cases do not bear out the fear that directors will be hoisted on the petards of arcane principles and technical statutory requirements that so dominate the financial provisions of corporate statutes.[117]

Even in the absence of statutes expressly imposing liability, the directors are liable for participating in violations of the statutory restrictions that are directed to them.[118] All business corporation statutes contain express liability provisions making directors jointly and severally liable to the corporation[119] (or to its shareholders or its creditors)

---

[113] *See* ARB No. 43, *supra* note 101 (suggesting capitalization when the number of shares to be distributed is less than 20–25% of the shares outstanding before the stock dividend is declared).

[114] In most jurisdictions remedies to recover illegal dividends from shareholders are limited to cases of insolvency or knowledge of impropriety.

[115] *See, e.g.,* Retirement Benefit Plan of Graphic Arts Int'l Union Local 20-B v. Standard Bindery Co., 654 F.Supp. 770 (E.D. Mich. 1986).

[116] *See* In re Tufts Elecs., Inc., 746 F.2d 915 (1st Cir. 1984) (no liability for insolvency within one and one-half years of payment to sole shareholder when evidence showed company was solvent immediately after payment made).

[117] *See, e.g.,* Klang v. Smith's Food & Drug Centers, 702 A.2d 150, 156–157 (Del. 1997) (board resolution need not set forth amount of pre-and post-distribution surplus so that understatement of amount of liabilities does not give rise to directors' liability provided sufficient surplus in fact did exist).

[118] A statutory violation is not regarded as being negligence per se or even evidence of negligence, but willful or negligent violation must ordinarily be shown. Directors are not liable for mistakes or errors of judgment if they act in good faith or with due care, as usually shown by considering and checking balance sheets and relying reasonably on reports of subordinates. *See* Blythe v. Enslen, 95 So. 479 (Ala. 1922).

[119] Lerner v. Lerner Corp., 711 A.2d 233, 240–241 (Md. App. 1998) (shareholder lacks standing to complain of illegal dividend, the right of action belongs to the corporation).

for payment of dividends in violation of statutory restrictions.[120] Drafting a satisfactory liability provision requires a delicate balancing between maintaining protection of creditors and avoiding harsh burdens on directors. One of the most interesting questions of construction and legislative policy is whether good faith and due care should be a defense.[121] On the one hand, the legislature may consider that a drastic absolute liability is essential to prevent directors from declaring improper dividends and to give adequate protection to creditors and shareholders. On the other hand, there appears little reason to accord creditors greater protection and directors less protection in the area of illegal dividends than creditors enjoy derivatively in other areas of the directors' discretionary behavior. It would appear that the policy should protect directors whenever they act in good faith and with the reasonable care that the circumstances require. If greater protection is demanded, this should and does occur through the loan agreements that lenders so frequently require for their protection.

Many state statutes have sections on director liability similar to the Model Business Corporation Act. These sections make specific reference to the directors' general standard of care.[122] Accordingly, the business judgment rule is incorporated by reference, as is good faith reliance on counsel, public accountants, and officers or their financial statements and reports.[123] The Model Business Corporation Act reflects the scheme of most state statutes on this subject. Liability is imposed on any director who "votes for or assents to" an unlawful distribution if it is established that he "did not perform his duties in compliance with section 8.30," the provision that codifies the business judgment rule.[124] Any director so held liable has a right of contribution from other directors who similarly breached their statutory duties[125] and from any shareholder for the amount she received knowing the distribution was in violation of the statute or the articles of incorporation.[126]

There is little basis for believing that statutory liability provisions relating to illegal distributions are the exclusive proscriptions for protecting creditors.[127]

§ 20.17 Shareholders' Liability to Return Illegal Dividends

It has already been pointed out that a dividend distribution in violation of statutory restrictions is primarily a wrong done by the directors who declare it. The liability most frequently imposed by specific statutes is placed on the directors who declare the dividend rather than on the shareholders who receive it, although the directors may seek contribution against the shareholders who received the illegal dividend with knowledge.

---

[120] *See* MBCA Ann. § 8.33 (3d ed. 1994).

[121] *See* James E. Tucker, Director and Shareholder Liability for Massachusetts Corporations' Distributions to Shareholders: A Suggestion for Change in Standards of Director Liability, 28 New Eng. L. Rev. 1025 (1994).

[122] *See* MBCA § 8.33 (2008); former MBCA § 48 (1969). *See also, e.g.,* Cal. Gen. Corp. Law § 316 (West 1990); Idaho Code § 30–1–833 (Michie 2005); N.Y. Bus. Corp. Law § 719 (McKinney 2003).

[123] *See* former MBCA § 35, Comment (1969). *See also, e.g.,* Cal. Gen. Corp. Law § 309 (West 1990); Idaho Code § 30–1–833 (Michie 2005); N.Y. Bus. Corp. Law § 717 (McKinney 2003).

[124] MBCA § 8.32(a) (2016).

[125] MBCA § 8.32(b) (2016).

[126] MBCA § 8.32(c) (2016).

[127] A number of cases refute the exclusivity of statutory shareholder liability. *See, e.g.,* In re Kettle Fried Chicken of Am., Inc., 513 F.2d 807 (6th Cir. 1975); Reilly v. Segert, 201 N.E.2d 444 (Ill. 1964). Statutes may also leave open other possibilities of director liability. *See* former MBCA § 48 (1969): "In addition to any other liabilities imposed by law."

The clear trend among statutes is not to impose liability on shareholders unless it can be shown that the dividends were received with knowledge of the company's condition. This is the position taken in the present Model Business Corporation Act, which permits directors to obtain contribution "from each shareholder for the amount the shareholder accepted *knowing* the distribution was made in violation" of the statute.[128] There is no direct shareholder liability to the corporation provided within the Model Business Corporation Act. There is always a question, however, whether a state statute that sets forth rights against shareholders who receive unlawful distributions supplants the common law.[129] Another theory of recovery against shareholders is the creditor's use of an applicable state fraudulent conveyance or fraudulent transfer statute that commonly void transfers without adequate consideration when a transferor is insolvent.[130]

---

[128] MBCA § 8.33(b)(2) (2008) (emphasis added).

[129] *See* Reilly v. Segert, 201 N.E.2d 444 (Ill. 1964) (statute imposing liability on directors for unlawful distributions with a right of contribution from knowing shareholders does not preclude suit by receiver against shareholders).

[130] *See, e.g.*, Federal Nat'l Mortg. Ass'n v. Olympia Mortg. Corp., 792 F. Supp. 2d 645 (E.D. N.Y. 2011).

Chapter 21

REPURCHASES, REDEMPTIONS AND THE REDUCTION OF CAPITAL

Table of Sections

PART A. SHARE PURCHASES AND REDEMPTIONS

§ 21.1 American Rules on Share Repurchases

It is important to understand the financial difference between a corporation's purchase of its own shares and its purchase of shares issued by an independent enterprise. Shares in another entity are assets of possible value to creditors. On a surrender of a corporation's own shares, the purchase price is simply withdrawn from the issuer's business. Nothing of value to creditors takes its place except what is in reality an unissued share, which cannot profitably be reissued when there is a financial reversal. Today all American jurisdictions permit a corporation to purchase its own shares, subject to various limitations such as impairment of capital.

The main objection to share purchases does not spring from *ultra vires* or a lack of relation to the corporate objects and business. Purchases of its shares, like purchases of its bonds, may be regarded as an incident of adjusting its financial structure to the needs of the business.[1] Such powers are customarily conferred expressly by statute or charter

---

[1]   Weiss v. Samsonite Corp., 741 A.2d 366, 371–373 (Del. Ch. 1999) (noting that self-tender offer is conventional method of delivering to shareholders a return on their investment; self-tender offer to acquire 51% of corporation's common stock at a 33% premium was the functional equivalent of an extraordinary dividend).

provisions.[2] It is thus misleading to discuss the regulation of share purchases in terms of the *ultra vires* doctrine.

The underlying reason for limiting share purchases is the same as that of dividends. Safeguards should be imposed against a corporation's depletion of its assets and the impairment of its capital needed for the protection of creditors and other shareholders. This has sometimes been expressed in terms of the trust fund doctrine,[3] which has been used to protect creditors.[4]

Exceptions to a Restrictive Rule. There are certain situations that are considered to give little opportunity for abuse, in which the corporation is generally recognized to have the authority to purchase its own shares even out of capital. Exceptions include: the purchases of preferred shares subject to a redemption provision in the articles of incorporation; purchases to compensate dissenting shareholders under appraisal statutes; employee stock purchase plans that have an option or agreement to repurchase; and purchases pursuant to an authorized statutory method of reduction of legal capital.[5]

The Solvency Limitation. Many statutes retain an insolvency test, however, along with the surplus or capital impairment tests.[6] As will be seen later in this chapter, the timing of these tests assumes special importance when shares are repurchased over a long period, perhaps on an installment basis. The courts are badly divided over whether the surplus and solvency tests are each applied to each installment payment or whether either of these tests should be applied only when the contract of purchase is entered into.

§ 21.2 The Dangers and Abuses of Dealing in the Corporation's Own Shares

The dangers and abuses incident to allowing a corporation, through its management, to make purchases and sales of its own shares are as follows:

(1) Stock repurchases make it possible for favored shareholders to withdraw current assets from the business and impair the capital and the financial responsibility on which creditors have a right to rely.

(2) Repurchases may be used to undermine the equity or margin of safety of preferred shares, to decrease assets, or to decrease surplus and thereby defeat the reasonable expectations of preferred shareholders as to dividend arrearages, future dividends, and liquidation preferences.

(3) Repurchases may be used with similar discriminatory effect against other common shareholders.

---

[2] *See* former Model Bus. Corp. Act § 6 (1969) (Former MBCA); Hayman v. Morris, 36 N.Y.S.2d 756 (Sup. Ct. 1942).

[3] In re Atlantic Printing Co., 60 F.2d 553 (D. Mass. 1932).

[4] In the classic English case, for example, more than one-fifth of the capital of the company had been withdrawn and the company had increased its bank borrowings by a wholesale policy of share-purchasing over a period of years. Trevor v. Whitworth, 12 App. Cas. 409 (1887).

[5] *See* RFE Capital Partners, Ltd. Partnership v. Weskar, Inc., 652 A.2d 1093 (Del. Super. Ct. 1994) (lender's option to "put" warrant to corporation held outside Delaware repurchase statute, which applied only to "capital stock").

[6] *See, e.g.,* former MBCA § 6 (1969); N.Y. Bus. Corp. Law § 513 (McKinney 2003).

(4) Repurchases may be used to juggle the voting control of the corporation and to buy off bona fide opponents of the management. In the context of a takeover attempt, this practice is currently known as "greenmail."

(5) Repurchases may be used for speculation by the corporation or by its management and for manipulation of the market price of the corporation's stock.

In recognition of these and other dangers, state laws not only impose legal restrictions but also regulate the fairness of such transactions.[7] Additional protection is found under federal law, which imposes stringent disclosure requirements as a result of the 1968 Williams Act amendments to the Securities Exchange Act of 1934.[8] In the case of a publicly held corporation, share repurchases can present the opportunity for stock manipulation.[9] In order to avoid manipulation when a corporation purchases its own shares, SEC Rule 10b–18 sets forth a safe harbor for repurchases by publicly held corporations.[10]

§ 21.3 Statutory Restrictions on Repurchases of Shares

Dangers incident to the purchase by corporations of their own shares have led to statutory regulation of the practice. This was not always the case.[11] The repurchase of shares, like the distribution of dividends, is a method of distribution or withdrawal of assets, but the repurchase of shares is subject to even more abuse.[12] What is needed is the imposition of carefully drawn statutory regulations as to the conditions and reasons for which the purchase of shares may be made, the source or basis of permissible withdrawals for payment, the status of the shares after they are reacquired, the effect of later resale, reissue, or retirement of the shares, the accounting practices to be followed on their purchase or reissue, and the liability of directors and shareholders for improper purchases.

Under the pre-1980 Model Business Corporation Act, share repurchases were generally limited to the extent of unrestricted earned surplus or unrestricted capital surplus if specifically authorized by the articles or a majority shareholder vote.[13] The earlier version of the Model Business Corporation Act exempts certain repurchase transactions, such as elimination of fractional shares and retirement of redeemable shares.[14] There is also an insolvency limitation similar to that affecting cash or property dividends.[15] The Act further imposes liability on directors who vote for such illegal share

---

[7]   *But see* Kohn v. Birmingham Realty Co., 352 So.2d 834 (Ala. 1977) (court refused to enjoin meeting at which redemption would be approved where evidence demonstrated corporation had adequate surplus and was solvent, so business purpose for redemption not relevant).

[8]   Pub. L. No. 90–439, 82 Stat. 454 (1968), codified at 15 U.S.C. §§ 78m(d)–(e), 78n(d)–(f) (2009). *See* § 24.1.

[9]   *See, e.g.,* Johnson, Lee & Caneda, A Boom in Stock Purchase Programs: Key Considerations for Management, 22 No. 5 Wall. St. Law. 1 (2018).

[10]   17 C.F.R. § 240.10b–18.

[11]   Loveland & Co. v. Doernbecher Mfg. Co., 39 P.2d 668, 676 (Or. 1934).

[12]   *See* Irving J. Levy, Purchase by a Corporation of Its Own Stock, 15 Minn. L. Rev. 1 (1930).

[13]   Former MBCA § 6 (1969). Most states have adopted similar provisions.

[14]   Former MBCA § 6 (1969). The former Model Business Corporation Act also appears to exempt transactions compromising indebtedness and payment of dissenting shareholders. *Id.* On redemption of redeemable shares, *see* § 18.13.

[15]   Former MBCA § 6 (1969). *See* § 20.16.

purchases.[16] The 1980 amendments to the Model Business Corporation Act's financial provisions, carried forward to the present Model Business Corporation Act, treat share purchases as a form of distribution to shareholders and apply the same limitations to share purchases as to dividends.[17] As seen in the preceding chapter, the new limitations on distributions after the 1980 amendments do away with traditional legal-capital concepts and are much less restrictive than the former earned-surplus test.[18] California's general corporation statute was the first to use this preferable approach of treating share purchases as a distribution.[19] Because the California statute and since 1980 the Model Business Corporation Act provide that repurchased shares are restored to the status of authorized but unissued shares, they have each thereby prevented such shares from being reported as treasury shares.[20]

Some state corporation laws expressly authorize corporations to purchase their own shares "out of surplus."[21] The same limitation may be expressed by a prohibition against purchases that cause an impairment of capital.[22]

These "earned surplus" statutes may allow purchases out of capital surplus when approved in the articles of incorporation or by a majority of the shareholders.[23] Many states allow a corporation to purchase or redeem its redeemable preferred shares out of capital as well as out of surplus—subject, however, to a provision that the capital shall not be impaired as to other preferred shares having priority or equality as to liquidation rights.[24] A general insolvency limitation is often added to these statutes. All such statutes invite inquiry into the extent to which generally accepted accounting principles (GAAP) will guide the statute's application with respect to terms that have accounting significance. As seen earlier, some states expressly incorporate GAAP into their statutes,[25] whereas the present Model Business Corporation Act, following the 1980 amendments to the Model Business Corporation Act, allows "fair valuation or other method that is reasonable in the circumstances,"[26] a result that has occasionally been reached by the courts.[27]

---

[16]   Former MBCA § 48(b) (1969). *See* §§ 21.12, 21.13.

[17]   *See* Model Bus. Corp. Act § 6.40 (2016) (hereinafter MBCA); former MBCA §§ 2(i), 6, 45 (1980).

[18]   The more restrictive earned-surplus test had become a trademark of the Model Business Corporation Act. These amendments present a radical departure to a total-assets-exceed-total-liabilities plus-liquidation-preferences balance-sheet test. The Model Business Corporation Act does retain a basic insolvency test.

[19]   *See* Cal. Corp. Code § 166 (West Supp. 2009); Thomas C. Ackerman, Jr. & James K. Sterrett, III, California's New Approach to Dividends and Reacquisitions of Shares, 23 UCLA L. Rev. 1052 (1976).

[20]   Cal. Corp. Code § 510(a) (West Supp. 2009); former MBCA § 6 (1969).

[21]   La. Rev. Stat. Ann. § 12:55(B) (West 2004); N.Y. Bus. Corp. Law § 513 (McKinney 2003).

[22]   *See* Del. Code Ann. tit. 8, § 160 (2001). *See* American Heritage Inv. Corp. v. Illinois Nat'l Bank, 386 N.E.2d 905 (1979).

[23]   *See* former MBCA § 6 (1969).

[24]   *See* former MBCA § 66 (1969):

No redemption or purchase of redeemable shares shall be made by a corporation when it is insolvent or when such redemption or purchase would render it insolvent, or which would reduce the net assets below the aggregate amount payable to the holders of shares having prior or equal rights to the assets of the corporation upon involuntary dissolution.

The 1980 amendments to the Model Business Corporation Act deleted this section.

[25]   *See* Cal. Corp. Code § 114 (West Supp.1990).

[26]   MBCA § 6.40(d) (2008).

[27]   *See* Klang v. Smith's Food & Drug Centers, 702 A.2d 150, 154 (Del. 1997).

The Delaware Supreme Court in *Klang v. Smith's Food and Drug Centers*[28] provides a sweeping embrace of the authority of the board of directors to resort to unrealized appreciation in assets as a source for the repurchase of shares:

> The General Assembly enacted the statute to prevent boards from draining corporations of assets to the detriment of creditors and the long-term health of the corporation. That a corporation has not yet realized or reflected on its balance sheet the appreciation of assets is irrelevant to this concern. Regardless of what a balance sheet that has not been updated may show, an actual, though unrealized appreciation reflects real economic value that the corporation may borrow against or that creditors may claim or levy upon. Allowing corporations to revalue assets and liabilities to reflect current realities complies with the statute and serves well the policies behind this statute.[29]

This interpretation essentially brings the law of Delaware into line with the discretion the board of directors enjoys under the current Model Business Corporation Act to resort to unrealized gains as a source for distributions to shareholders. One should approach these developments with a healthy appreciation of the risks of allowing such discretion. Corporate law has historically restricted the ability of directors to make distributions to shareholders out of fear that if unrestricted the directors may prefer the interests of shareholders over the pressing rights of creditors. The historical limitations, albeit artificial, nevertheless were guided by metrics that were objective and certainly not within the control of the board of directors. *Klang* and the Model Act weaken such objectivity for the regulation of distributions to shareholders. Also, unrealized gains may well not be true economic profits. True gains are those that are amounts that are not necessary to continue to operate the business at its present state. Thus, the fact that the company's asset in Manhattan has appreciated greatly in value does not mean that the full amount of the appreciation is economic profit. If the parcel's location is central to the company's continued vitality—a vendor of Broadway show tickets—it is not entirely correct to believe the property could be sold, the gains realized, and the historical cost of the property reinvested in New Jersey so that the company can continue its business.

§ 21.4 Executory and Installment Contracts to Repurchase

Particular problems arise with regard to shares' purchase contracts that are executory in nature or where payment by the corporation is delayed by an installment agreement or by the issuance of a debt obligation. There may be important reasons for a corporation to repurchase some of its shares when it has insufficient funds to do so. Repurchase agreements are also common in close corporations,[30] but the commercial purpose for such repurchases may arise when the corporation lacks sufficient cash with which to make the repurchase.[31] A frequent response to these problems is for the corporation to purchase the shares in exchange for an installment note.[32]

---

[28] Klang v. Smith's Food and Drug Centers, 702 A.2d 150 (Del. 1997).

[29] Klang v. Smith's Food and Drug Centers, 702 A.2d 150, 154 (Del. 1997).

[30] *See* 2 F. Hodge O'Neal & Robert B. Thompson, O'Neal and Thompson's Close Corporations and LLCs: Law and Practice §§ 7.10, 7.11 (rev. 3d ed. 2009).

[31] In case of death or disability, the funding problem can be handled with key man insurance.

[32] *See* In re Envirodyne Indus., Inc., 79 F.3d 579 (7th Cir. 1996) (unsecured claims of nontendering cashed-out shareholders of corporation subordinated under Bankruptcy Act § 510(c)).

Making installment payments to former shareholders when the corporation is insolvent is problematic in many states whose statutes or court decisions have not yet defined the moment when the statutory restrictions are to apply to the transaction. The question is whether, when applying the statutory restrictions to an installment repurchase of shares, the transaction should be treated as a single purchase, so that the restrictions are applied at the moment the contract is entered into, or whether the installment repurchase should be treated as a series of successive purchases, so that the statutory restrictions are to be satisfied as to each payment. At a time when states had only a solvency test, the highly influential decision of *Robinson v. Wangemann*[33] held that the state's solvency test should be applied at the moment of payment, not when the parties entered into the installment contract. This so-called insolvency cutoff rule has been widely followed where the question is the timing of a solvency test.[34]

Given the insolvency cutoff rule, with its emphasis on the time of payment and the gradual proliferation of statutory surplus tests for share repurchases, an issue arises as to whether statutory surplus tests should be applied at the time of the purchase or at the time of the actual payments. In *Mountain State Steel Foundries v. Commissioner*,[35] a tax case, the court held that the surplus test must be met only at the time of payment, not when the repurchase agreement was made. This is the so-called surplus cutoff rule. Thus, under the approach taken in *Mountain State*, an installment note for the repurchase of stock was valid even if the corporation did not have sufficient surplus to cover the repurchase at the time the note was given.[36] This surplus cutoff rule, requiring that statutory balance-sheet tests be met at the time of payment, has been accepted in many cases.[37] The cases adopting a surplus cutoff rule, according to one commentator, are the result of an unfortunate failure to "perceive any distinction between the insolvency cutoff rule and a surplus cutoff rule."[38] Even under the stricter surplus cutoff rule, however, where there are no creditors to be protected, a former shareholder may obtain specific enforcement of a note even if it forces the corporation into liquidation.

Not all decisions have followed the surplus cutoff rule. An influential Texas decision relied on a supposed statutory distinction between "payment" and "purchase" in order to enforce a note executed at a time when there was sufficient surplus, although the corporation was insolvent at the time of payment.[39] The bifurcation of the two tests—solvency and surplus—so that the surplus test is applied at the outset and the solvency test is applied to each payment has been followed in the more recent decisions to consider the question.[40] While New Jersey was one of the few states that rejected the insolvency cutoff rule,[41] a subsequent New Jersey decision[42] imposed a surplus cutoff rule. This

---

[33]   Robinson v. Wangemann, 75 F.2d 756 (5th Cir. 1935). Earlier another court addressed this problem with the same effect.

[34]   McConnell v. Estate of Butler, 402 F.2d 362 (9th Cir. 1968).

[35]   Mountain State Steel Foundries, Inc. v. Commissioner, 284 F.2d 737 (4th Cir. 1960).

[36]   *See also* Rainford v. Rytting, 451 P.2d 769 (Utah 1969).

[37]   In re National Tile & Terrazzo Co., 537 F.2d 329 (9th Cir. 1976).

[38]   David R. Herwitz, Installment Repurchase of Stock: Surplus Limitations, 79 Harv. L. Rev. 303, 326 (1965).

[39]   Williams v. Nevelow, 513 S.W.2d 535 (Tex. 1974).

[40]   *See, e.g.,* Walsh v. Paterna, 537 F.2d 329 (9th Cir. 1976).

[41]   Wolff v. Heidritter Lumber Co., 163 A. 140 (N.J. Ch. 1932).

[42]   Kleinberg v. Schwartz, 208 A.2d 803 (N.J. Super. Ct. App. Div.), *aff'd on opinion below,* 214 A.2d 313 (N.J. 1965).

decision was later over-ruled by statute,[43] and that statute has been replaced by a provision patterned after the current Model Business Corporation Act, which applies the statutory tests to each payment only if the corporation did not earlier issue a note or other evidence of indebtedness to acquire shares.[44] Delaware has also statutorily rejected a surplus cutoff rule.[45]

The pre-1980 Model Business Corporation Act, which is similar to the statute that was before the Texas court, speaks in terms of purchases out of surplus and then provides that "no purchase or payment" may be made that would render the corporation insolvent.[46] One commentator has suggested that this language creates a "well-nigh irresistible" inference that the surplus test not be applied at payment.[47] Beginning with the 1980 amendments, the Model Business Corporation Act supplants the surplus test with a requirement that the assets following the distribution not be less than the firm's liabilities and also maintain the solvency test.[48] The statute now applies its own timing standard for the application of both these tests, under which the tests would appear to be applied when the contract to repurchase is entered into, assuming that is the moment when the corporation issues the note embodying its obligation to pay for the shares.[49]

While the surplus cutoff rule certainly protects creditors, it results in the disservice of rendering uncertain the enforceability of bona fide repurchase arrangements should there be insufficient surplus when a later payment is required. To continue to apply both the solvency and the surplus tests to later payments places the withdrawing shareholders in a very difficult position—these shareholders lack the political or equitable powers of stockholders who can protect their future return and also lack the full rights of creditor status. To the extent that the prime concern is the protection of creditors, requiring adequate notice of the corporation's outstanding obligation to make future installment payments would appear to be ample protection. Any creditor unsatisfied with the situation can either demand subordination of the installment obligation or forgo lending money to the corporation.

Some courts have also held that former shareholders may enforce the debt despite insolvency or lack of surplus where there is an underlying lien.[50] One may wonder why the underlying debt that secures a lien should ever achieve greater dignity because of its existence than the debt it secures. Another view holds that a note given as partial consideration to repurchase shares when the corporation was insolvent is illegal, so that the corporation is not obligated to honor the note.[51]

---

[43] N.J. Bus. Corp. Act, ch. 350, § 14A:7–16(6), 1968 N.J. Laws 1011, 1078 (repealed 1988).

[44] N.J. Bus. Corp. Act, ch. 350, § 14A.7–14.1(4) (2003).

[45] Del. Code Ann. tit. 8, § 160(a)(1) (2001).

[46] Former MBCA § 6 (1969).

[47] Herwitz, *supra* note 38, at 323.

[48] Former MBCA § 45 (2008). *See also* MBCA § 6.40 (2016).

[49] Former MBCA § 45 (1980):

In the case of a purchase, redemption or other acquisition of a corporation's shares, the effect of a distribution shall be measured as of the date money or other property is transferred or debt is incurred by the corporation, or as of the date the shareholder ceases to be a shareholder of the corporation with respect to such shares, whichever is earlier. . . .

[50] In re National Tile & Terrazzo Co., 537 F.2d 329 (9th Cir. 1976).

[51] *See* Field v. Haupert, 647 P.2d 952 (Or. Ct. App. 1982).

§ 21.5   Redemption and Purchase of Callable Shares

"Repurchase of shares" is a generic term that includes the narrower concept of redemption pursuant to a contractual right embodied in the share contract and the articles of incorporation. In many cases, it is significant which type of repurchase is involved.

Preferred shares may be made subject not only to redemption that is optional with the corporation but also to compulsory redemption or resale. There are serious objections to compulsory redemption provisions. The normal redemption provision is an option in favor of the corporation to call in and retire preferred shares at a specified redemption price, usually at a premium over the issue price. Any right of redemption, however, must be exercised in strict compliance with the terms of the contract or instrument granting the right.[52] Procedures exercising redemption rights, such as notice to the shareholders and some method of selection by lot, pro rata or otherwise, are usually provided in the charter to prevent discrimination for or against other holders if the entire class of shares is not called.[53] Such provisions have been held by some courts not to preclude a corporation from making independent share repurchases without making a pro rata redemption.[54] Even apart from a pro rata requirement, there are, of course, equitable limitations on both repurchases and redemptions.[55]

The option to redeem is exercised by the board of directors. A resolution adopted in accordance with the charter provisions calling certain shares for redemption creates a contract and, unless expressly conditional, the board's action may not be rescinded or modified.[56]

Traditionally, common shares may not be made redeemable at the option of the corporation.[57] "Stock which has no retirement provisions is the backbone of a corporate structure."[58] The chief function of the provision for redemption in stock or bonds is to facilitate the retirement of senior securities for the benefit of the holders of common shares and to make possible the reduction of capital or refinancing at a lower rate of return on new senior securities by paying off and terminating the old shares that call for a higher dividend. The rule against redeemable common stock must be kept in mind when drafting repurchase agreements.[59] Modern corporation acts make a distinction between the purchase of common shares and the exercise of the right to purchase of callable or redeemable preferred shares. The former is subject to the standard requirement that the purchase can be made to the extent of unrestricted surplus, whereas the acquisition of redeemable shares can rely on the stated capital of the shares

---

[52]   Cotten v. Weatherford Bancshares, Inc., 187 S.W.3d 687 (Tex. Ct. App. 2006).

[53]   Richard M. Buxbaum, Preferred Stock—Law and Draftsmanship, 42 Cal. L. Rev. 243, 265–266 (1954).

[54]   Kansas Heart Hosp., LLC v. Idbeis, 184 P.3d 866 (Kan. 2008) (distinguishing between "redemption" and "purchase" but upholding bylaw that compelled "redemption" of stock held by shareholders who had violated ownership requirements).

[55]   See § 21.6.

[56]   Taylor v. Axton-Fisher Tobacco Co., 173 S.W.2d 377 (Ky. 1943), noted in Recent Decisions, Corporations—Power of Directors to Rescind or Modify Action Calling Stock for Redemption, 42 Mich. L. Rev. 530 (1943).

[57]   Starring v. American Hair & Felt Co., 191 A. 887 (Del. Ch.), aff'd mem., 2 A.2d 249 (Del. 1937).

[58]   Ecker v. Western Pac. R.R., 318 U.S. 448 (1943).

[59]   See In re West Waterway Lumber Co., 367 P.2d 807 (Wash. 1962) (upholding bylaw requiring sale to corporation on leaving the business).

to be redeemed, with any additional amount coming from unrestricted surplus. Thus, the stated capital of redeemable shares is of a somewhat temporary character. If shares are redeemed out of capital, this reduces pro tanto the surplus thereafter available for dividends on the common.

Redemptions are subject of course to the general restriction in favor of the priority of creditors and may not be made when a corporation is insolvent or when the redemption would result in insolvency or inability to meet debts and liabilities as they accrue.[60] Many modern acts also take into account the liquidation preferences of shares to remain outstanding.[61] A charter provision may protect the dividend rights of preferred shareholders—for example, by providing that dividends shall be paid "before any sum shall be paid or set apart for the purchase or redemption of any stock now or hereafter authorized."[62]

§ 21.6 Fiduciary Limitations on Share Repurchases

Share repurchases are subject to abuse to the extent that they provide a facade for an unfair distribution of corporate assets. In a leading Massachusetts case,[63] the majority shareholders caused the directors to repurchase a portion of their holdings at a premium. The court held that the fiduciary duties between shareholders in close corporations demanded equal treatment and a right of the minority to participate on a pro rata basis. Similarly, a Georgia case[64] held that the corporate right to purchase its own shares is not absolute; it is conditioned on good faith. "Good faith is not just a question of what is proper for the corporation. It also requires that the stockholders be treated fairly and that their investments be protected."[65] However, it has been held that the directors may authorize repurchase at a premium in order to protect the corporation against an outside takeover attempt.[66] The Delaware court reached this conclusion by relying on the business judgment rule in the face of a claim that the directors were wasting corporate assets in order to perpetuate their control.[67] This practice, known as "greenmail," is discussed in Chapter 12. Greenmail is a subset of a wide range of concerns that arise when the incumbent management through the board of directors causes the corporation to make a defensive purchase of shares as a step toward thwarting a shift in control.[68] Both privately negotiated repurchases[69] and the redemption of a class of shares held by one stockholder[70] have been upheld when used to remove dissident shareholders.

---

60   Hurley v. Boston R. H. Co., 54 N.E.2d 183 (Mass. 1944).

61   *See* former MBCA § 66 (1969).

62   *See* Peterson v. New England Furn. & Carpet Co., 299 N.W. 208 (Minn. 1941).

63   Donahue v. Rodd Electrotype Co., 328 N.E.2d 505 (Mass. 1975).

64   Comolli v. Comolli, 246 S.E.2d 278 (Ga. 1978).

65   Comolli v. Comolli, 246 S.E.2d 278, 280 (Ga. 1978). The court invalidated a corporate purchase of a deceased brother's shares with borrowed funds in order to perpetuate the control of one of the two surviving brothers, who could not afford to buy the entire holding. The shares had never been offered to the other brother.

66   Cheff v. Mathes, 199 A.2d 548 (Del. 1964).

67   *See* Kors v. Carey, 158 A.2d 136 (Del. Ch. 1960) (upholding corporate repurchase of shares from unsuccessful takeover attempt).

68   *See generally* Robert Gordon & Lewis Kornhauser, Takeover Defense Tactics: A Comment on Two Models, 96 Yale L.J. 295 (1986) (allowing incumbents discretion to acquire issuer's shares greatly skews balance of power in their favor).

69   Martin v. American Potash & Chem. Corp., 92 A.2d 295 (Del. 1952).

70   Hendricks v. Mill Engg. & Supply Co., 413 P.2d 811 (Wash. 1966).

Frequently a corporation will purchase its own shares as a first step in a going-private scheme, a problem that is taken up later.

The right to redeem shares may be balanced with the shareholder's conversion rights. In *Zahn v. Transamerica Corporation*,[71] for example, the Third Circuit invalidated a purported redemption on the grounds that it unfairly denied holders their right to convert and participate with the common shareholders in a distribution of assets. The decision may in fact have been based on inadequate notice and disclosure rather than on any duty of fair dealing.[72] The general question of fairness in corporate reorganizations, recapitalization, mergers, and other transactions is treated in a later section, but these principles nevertheless apply to repurchases and redemptions.

At one time it appeared that SEC Rule 10b–5 had a significant role to play in regulating the fairness of share purchases by a corporation.[73] However, the Supreme Court decision in *Santa Fe Industries, Inc. v. Green*[74] imposed a deception requirement for 10b–5 and held that a showing of unfairness, even tantamount to equitable fraud, did not give rise to a federal remedy. Accordingly, any 10b–5 remedy would be dependent on some sort of nondisclosure or misrepresentation in connection with the share repurchase or redemption.[75]

The Williams Act amendments to the Securities Exchange Act of 1934[76] impose various substantive and disclosure requirements on tender offerors and issuers repurchasing their own shares. The term "tender offer" is not defined in the act. The term includes many share repurchases that are essentially tender offers by the issuer, in light of the expansive interpretations by the SEC and the courts.[77] Although expressly excluded from most of the Williams Act's disclosure, filing, and substantive provisions,[78] the issuer is subject to section 14(e)'s[79] general antifraud provisions,[80] and section 13(e) expressly empowers the SEC to regulate share repurchases by SEC reporting companies.[81] Pursuant to its authority under this provision, the Commission has promulgated a going-private rule[82] as well as a general disclosure requirement for issuer tender offers.[83] An important provision prohibits the issuer from making any purchases of its shares after someone other than the issuer has commenced a tender offer unless certain detailed disclosures are made by the issuer.[84]

---

[71]   Zahn v. Transamerica Corporation, 162 F.2d 36 (3d Cir. 1947).

[72]   *See* Van Gemert v. Boeing Co., 520 F.2d 1373 (2d Cir. 1975).

[73]   Robert J. Malley, Corporate Repurchases of Stock and the S.E.C. Rules: An Overview, 29 Bus. Law 117 (1973).

[74]   Santa Fe Indus., Inc. v. Green, 430 U.S. 462 (1977).

[75]   *See* Thomas L. Hazen, Corporate Mismanagement and the Federal Securities Act's Antifraud Provisions: A Familiar Path With Some New Detours, 20 B.C. L. Rev. 819 (1979).

[76]   Pub. L. No. 90–439, 82 Stat. 454 (1968), codified at 15 U.S.C. §§ 78m(d)–(e), 78n(d)–(f).

[77]   *See* Wellman v. Dickinson, 475 F.Supp. 783 (S.D.N.Y. 1979).

[78]   15 U.S.C. §§ 78m(d)(6)(C), 78n(d)(8)(B) (2009).

[79]   15 U.S.C. § 78n(e) (2009).

[80]   Since subsection 14(d) contains a specific issuer exclusion and 14(e) contains no exclusion, 14(e) logically should extend to all tender offers, even those by an issuer.

[81]   15 U.S.C. § 78m(e) (2009).

[82]   Rule 13e–3, 17 C.F.R. § 240.13e–3 (2009).

[83]   Rule 13e–4, 17 C.F.R. § 240.13e–4 (2009).

[84]   Rule 13e–1, 17 C.F.R. § 240.13e–4 (2009).

PART B.   STATUS OF TREASURY SHARES

§ 21.7   The Peculiar Status of Treasury Shares

Treasury shares carry neither voting rights[85] nor rights to dividends or other distributions.[86] Their existence as "issued shares" is a pure fiction, a figure of speech to explain certain special rules and privileges as to their reissue. A share of stock is simply a unit of interest in the corporate enterprise arising from a contract. When holders of a share surrender their rights to the corporation, it is obvious that the contract is in reality terminated. In cases where the presence, vote, or assent of the majority of the shareholders is required, it must be understood to mean shares that are issued and outstanding and that may be voted.[87] If shares in corporation A are purchased or held by corporation B, which is controlled or dominated by corporation A, the prevailing view is that such shares should not be regarded as treasury shares of the parent. But they should not, and generally may not, carry voting rights because the voting power could be controlled by the management of the parent, and this would be indirect voting by the parent.[88] Treasury stock is in essence authorized stock that may be reissued as fully paid without some of the restrictions on an original issue of shares as to consideration and as to preemptive rights, if any.

Due to the fictional nature of treasury shares, the current Model Business Corporation Act, following the 1980 amendments to the Model Business Corporation Act and the California statute, has abolished the need to recognize treasury stock. Under these provisions[89] all reacquired shares, whether by way of redemption or other purchase, are restored to the status of authorized but unissued unless the articles prohibit their reissue, in which case their repurchase results in an automatic amendment to the articles of incorporation reducing the number of authorized shares.

§ 21.8   The Reissue or Retirement of Treasury Shares

When treasury shares are reissued and sold by the corporation, the shares are issued to the new purchaser, and the corporation is viewed as an intermediate transferee between the former and new shareholders. In reality, the old share contract has been extinguished and the new shares are new units of interest created in their place.

Retirement and Cancellation. Outside of California and states that have patterned their financial provisions after the Model Business Corporation Act, a corporation usually has the option on reacquisition of shares to treat them as treasury

---

[85]   Former MBCA § 33 (1969). An interesting and successful effort to enable the company to gain sufficient voting power so that it could change the onerous terms of the preferred shares was designed to assure that the acquired shares would continue to be "outstanding" was litigated in Corre Opportunities Fund, LP v. Emmis Communications Corp., 792 F.3d 737 (7th Cir. 2015). The company acquired from their holders 60% of its preferred shares in exchange for total return swaps; however, the shares were held in an escrow that would not close for five years during which the company held a proxy to vote the shares. The court upheld the arrangement because a very unusual provision of Indiana law allows the issuing corporation to vote shares it has issued.

[86]   *See, e.g.*, Nev. Rev. Stat. Ann. § 78.283(2) (1994).

[87]   Former MBCA § 33 (1969).

[88]   Italo Petroleum Corp. v. Producers' Oil Corp., 174 A. 276 (Del. Ch. 1934) (99% owned subsidiary); Note, The Voting of Stock Held in Cross Ownership, 76 Harv. L. Rev. 1642 (1963) (hereinafter Note, The Voting of Stock).

[89]   Cal. Corp. Code § 510 (West Supp. 2009).

shares or to retire or cancel them.[90] Treasury shares are carried on the books as authorized and still issued but not outstanding.[91] When retired or cancelled, the shares usually retain the status of authorized but unissued shares.[92] Sometimes the terms "retired" or "cancelled" may be used in the articles of incorporation to mean that once a share is reacquired it may never be reissued. Such a permanent "retirement" results in an automatic reduction in the number of shares authorized by the articles of incorporation. This is common under provisions in the articles in connection with the redemption of preferred shares. To avoid confusion, such provisions in the articles of incorporation should be drafted to expressly prohibit reissue and require reduction of authorized shares where that is desired.[93]

PART C. REMEDIES FOR IMPROPER SHARE PURCHASES

§ 21.9 Recovery by Corporation for Unlawful Share Purchases

There appears little reason in theory to distinguish unlawful share repurchases from unlawful dividends when considering whether innocent shareholders should escape liability. In both cases the danger is the wrongful transfer of assets from the corporation that erodes the creditors' estate. The non-pro-rata nature of a share repurchase raises questions of fairness to nonselling shareholders but does not especially suggest a greater threat to creditors unless the non-pro-rata repurchase is inherently consistent with a richer factual mosaic in which insiders purposely are transferring assets to themselves, such as at the brink of the company's insolvency. And even in this context there appears little gained in the analysis by distinguishing between the treatment of cunning insiders who sell their shares to the corporation and of those who merely pay themselves dividends. Thus, since the 1980 amendments, the former Model Business Corporation Act and the current Model Business Corporation Act impose liability only on guilty shareholders.[94]

Initially, shareholder liability for improper share repurchases was grounded primarily in common law, but today this liability is primarily statutory.[95] Corporation statutes either provide directly for shareholder liability or subject shareholders to the contribution rights of directors.[96] Either form of liability is usually limited to those shareholders acting with knowledge of the impropriety.[97]

---

[90]   Former MBCA §§ 67, 68 (1969). *See also* N.Y. Bus. Corp. Law § 515(b), (e) (McKinney 2003); 15 Pa. Cons. Stat. § 1552 (1995).

[91]   Former MBCA § 2(h) (1969).

[92]   Former MBCA §§ 67, 68 (1969).

[93]   The former Model Bus. Corp. Act § 67 (1969) enables corporations to reduce authorized shares on redemption or repurchase through a provision in the articles. It specifies that reacquired shares have the status of authorized but unissued shares unless an article's provision prohibits reissue.

[94]   MBCA § 8.33 (2016); former MBCA § 48 (1980).

[95]   There continues to be a question as to whether such statutes are exclusive. *See* In re Kettle Fried Chicken of Am., Inc., 513 F.2d 807 (6th Cir. 1975) (court refused to conclude that Delaware general corporation statute § 174's proscription of director liability for unlawful distributions with no reference to shareholder liability exempted shareholders from liability).

[96]   *Cf.* Cal. Corp. Code § 506(a) (West 1990) (shareholder liability to corporation for benefit of creditors) *with* former MBCA § 48(d) (1969) (contribution to directors).

[97]   *See, e.g.,* Palmer v. Justice, 322 F.Supp. 892 (N.D. Tex.), *aff'd per curiam,* 451 F.2d 371 (5th Cir. 1971).

In the case of improper share purchase the directors are liable for causing a corporation to repurchase shares in violation of statutory legal capital requirements.[98] Director liability for improper distributions is usually governed by statutes and is enforced through director liability provisions based on the directors' breach of the duty of care to the corporation.[99] There is some conflict of authority as to whether recovery from directors may be had only for the benefit of existing creditors or also for subsequent creditors. The trend, however, seems to be to allow recovery even to subsequent creditors without notice.[100]

§ 21.10 Right of Recovery by Creditors from Selling Shareholders

The standing of creditors to pursue unlawful share repurchases is no different from their standing to pursue unlawful dividends. When the corporation is insolvent, creditors are usually represented by a receiver or trustee in bankruptcy. However, the individual creditor may bring an action for the improper payments. In this case, rather than suing the shareholder on the creditor's original claim, the creditor usually secures a judgment against the corporation first and then follows the assets of the corporation to the selling shareholders.

---

[98] *See* MBCA § 8.33 (2008); former MBCA § 48(b) (1969).

[99] *See* former MBCA § 48(b) (1969).

[100] For cases stating that recovery may be had for the benefit of subsequent creditors, *see, e.g.*, Coleman v. Tepel, 230 F. 63 (3d Cir. 1916).

§ 21.10 Risk of Recovery by Creditors from Selling Shareholders

Chapter 22

CORPORATE COMBINATIONS

Table of Sections

§ 22.1 Corporate Combinations Overview

The history of American business bears out that corporations transform themselves not solely by growth within but, more important, by acquisition—be they the acquired or the acquirer. This chapter examines the regulatory climate through which corporations acquire other corporations, sell all or substantially all their assets, or acquire the shares of another corporation. In this area the law threads a course between, on the one hand, freeing the entrepreneurial spirit that can mobilize resources to a new and, one hopes, more productive use and, on the other hand, being solicitous of the shareholders' desires not only to participate in that decision but also to protect their interests in the corporation.

The most basic form of acquisition of assets occurs in the simple buy-sell context, where one corporation for a mutually agreed upon price sells assets to another corporation. Not all asset sales merit the attention of state corporate statutes; as will be seen, only sales of all or substantially all the assets outside the ordinary course of business are singled out for special treatment under most corporate statutes. Alternatively, the acquirer and the acquired corporations may choose to merge so that their assets and liabilities are thereafter automatically combined by operation of law. Sometimes the merger of two corporations is structured so that neither corporation survives, but instead, pursuant to their plan of merger, a third corporation is created into which the assets and liabilities of the combining corporations will thereafter exist. This form of acquisition is known as a consolidation. A few state statutes continue to recognize this infrequent form of combination.

Sales of assets, mergers, and consolidations present three different methods of corporate fusion, each with its own financial and legal considerations. A fourth method of corporate combination is a share exchange, whereby all the outstanding shares of an approving class of stock are acquired by another corporation. A variation of this form is the purchase of shares of another corporation (called the "target" corporation). Such purchases can occur either through open market purchases or by a solicitation of the shareholders to sell, generally referred to as a "tender offer." Unlike the other methods of corporate fusion, the tender offer commits to the individual shareholders of the target corporation the decision whether to part with their shares. In contrast, the combination that is consummated by a sale of corporate assets, a merger, or a consolidation is authorized by complex statutory procedures, and generally requires shareholder approval by a set percentage of the class voting by each class of shares affected by the class.[1]

Any method of corporate combination or other fundamental change can work to the substantial prejudice of minority shareholders.[2] Accordingly, both the legislatures and the courts have recognized the need to protect the minority against abuse. The most prevalent mechanism to protect those who oppose the acquisition is the statutory appraisal remedy. This procedure allows dissenting shareholders to receive in cash the fair value of their shares, as determined through an independent appraisal.[3] As will be seen, the so-called dissenters' right is cumbersome and does not always protect the minority's interests. Further, the appraisal remedy does not apply to all types of acquisitions.[4] In recent years there has been a serious conflict as to the availability of a judicial remedy for unfairness when dissenters' rights were available. The trend of

---

[1]   Model Business Corporation Act §§ 71, 72, 72A, 73, 79 (1969) (hereinafter former Model Bus. Corp. Act); Revised Model Business Corporation Act §§ 11.02, 11.03, 11.04, 12.02 (2016) (hereinafter Model Bus. Corp. Act) (the revised Act has deleted the section on consolidation).

[2]   See F. Hodge O'Neal & Robert B. Thompson, O'Neal and Thompson's Oppression of Minority Shareholders and LLC Members ch. 5 (rev. 2d ed. 2009).

[3]   Former Model Bus. Corp. Act §§ 80, 81 (1969); Model Bus. Corp. Act §§ 13.02, 13.03, 13.20 to 13.26 (2016). See §§ 22.23 to 22.27.

[4]   The most striking example is corporate reclassifications, which are covered in only a few jurisdictions, such as N.Y. Bus. Corp. Law § 806(b) (McKinney 2003). See former Model Bus. Corp. Act § 80(a)(4) (1969); Model Bus. Corp. Act §§ 13.02(a)(4) (2016); Chapter 25.

recent decisions is to allow for judicial scrutiny of alleged unfair acquisitions in exceptional cases independent of any statutory remedy.[5]

The federal securities laws have substantial impact on the law relating to corporate combinations. Many methods of corporate combination involve shareholders exchanging their shares either for another class of shares, for shares of another corporation, or for cash. In each case the antifraud provisions of SEC Rule 10b–5 come into play, as is equally true when the corporation rather than the individual shareholder acquires or issues securities.[6] Whenever the issuance of securities is involved, the registration provisions of the Securities Act of 1933 must be considered.[7] Moreover, the federal proxy rules indirectly protect against abuse or ill-planned acquisitions by heightening the disclosure[8] and hence accountability that management is subject to when carrying out acquisitions involving publicly traded corporations subject to section 14(a) of the Securities Exchange Act of 1934.[9] Finally, significant regulatory protection occurs through the 1968 Williams Act amendments to the Securities Exchange Act of 1934 and subsequent state legislation that regulate tender offers and open market purchases of corporate shares.[10]

§ 22.2 Comparison of Methods of Combination or Reorganization

Although the three traditional methods of reorganization—merger, consolidation, and sale-purchase of assets—are distinct, they have a number of similarities. The essential steps to consolidate or merge[11] are as follows:

(1) A consolidation or merger always involves a transfer of the assets and business of one or more corporations to another corporation in exchange for its securities, cash, or other consideration.[12] A merger results in a transfer of the assets to one of the constituent corporations that absorbs the other. With a consolidation a new consolidated corporation is created into which each constituent corporation transfers its assets and liabilities. In each case, the transfer is made by operation of law—that is, by force of the statute operating on the agreement of the constituents to merge or consolidate.[13]

---

[5] Weinberger v. UOP, Inc., 457 A.2d 701 (Del. 1983) (indicating appraisal remedy is exclusive in absence of fraud). *But see* Rabkin v. Philip A. Hunt Chem. Corp., 498 A.2d 1099 (Del.Supr. 1985) (interpreting *Weinberger* as allowing for remedies other than appraisal when specific acts of unfairness are alleged).

[6] 17 C.F.R. § 240.10b–5 (2009).

[7] 15 U.S.C. §§ 77(f), 77(g) (2009).

[8] *Cf.* Skeen v. Jo-Ann Stores, Inc., 750 A.2d 1170 (Del. 2000) (rejecting enhanced disclosure requirement under state corporate law).

[9] *See* § 13.29. *See generally* Edward Ross Aranow & Herbert A. Einhorn, Proxy Contests for Corporate Control (2d ed. 1968).

[10] 15 U.S.C. §§ 78m(d), 78m(e), 78n(d), 78n(f) (2009).

[11] Merger and consolidation are two different forms of combination. In a merger, one corporation merges into another. In contrast, with a consolidation, the two combining companies consolidate into a third.

[12] *See, e.g.,* Shannon v. Samuel Langston Co., 379 F.Supp. 797 (W.D. Mich. 1974); Loving & Assoc., Inc. v. Carothers, 619 N.W.2d 782 (Minn. Ct. App. 2000) (merger does not necessarily terminate a loan guaranty arrangement made with entity that disappeared through merger).

[13] Model Bus. Corp. Act § 11.07 (2016); former Model Bus. Corp. Act § 76 (1969); *infra* § 22.17.

(2) A merger or consolidation entails the assumption of the debts and liabilities of the absorbed company or companies by operation of law.[14]

(3) A necessary effect of a merger or consolidation is the dissolution of the absorbed company or companies.[15] As will be seen, a sale of assets does not constitute a dissolution and does not necessarily call for the liquidation or dissolution of the seller.[16]

(4) A merger or consolidation involves a payment to the shareholders of the absorbed corporation in shares, debt, or cash or securities of the new or surviving corporation. Those who pursue their appraisal remedy can receive cash equal to the appraised value of their shares.

The principal differences between an acquisition by sale of assets and statutory merger or consolidation are:[17]

(1) In case of a sale by one corporation to another, the assets of the selling corporation are transferred by written instruments of conveyance, not by operation of law as occurs in a merger or consolidation.

(2) There are different statutory requirements as to the vote or consent of shareholders. As will be seen, the shareholders of both the successor/ surviving corporation and shareholders of the acquired corporation are generally entitled to vote and, if approved, those who dissent to the merger or consolidation are entitled to their appraisal remedy. In contrast, only the shareholders of the corporation selling its assets are entitled to vote on the transaction[18] because the purchasing corporation acts only through its board of directors.

(3) In a consolidation or merger, the method and basis of exchanging the shares of the constituent corporations for shares, debt, or cash of the successor corporation are set forth in the consolidation or merger agreement. This becomes binding on all parties except dissenting shareholders who elect to invoke their appraisal remedy. Thus, following approval there is a compulsory exchange of new shares for old. In contrast, authority distinct from the stockholders' approval of the sale must be involved to distribute the sales proceeds to the selling corporation's stockholders. Such authority arises after the stockholders have approved the corporation's dissolution. It is also possible, within the limitations of the local state statute, to distribute the sales proceeds through either a dividend or repurchase of shares. That is, neither the dissolution of the selling corporation nor the mechanism for distributing the sales proceeds to the selling corporation's shareholders is embodied in the state statutes

---

[14] *See* Delaware Ins. Guar. Ass'n v. Christiana Care Health Services, Inc., 892 A.2d 1073 (Del. 2006) (duties and liabilities of disappearing corporation are those of the surviving entity).

[15] Knapp v. North Am. Rockwell Corp., 506 F.2d 361, 363 (3d Cir. 1974), *cert. denied,* 421 U.S. 965 (1975).

[16] Cleveland Worsted Mills Co. v. Consolidated Textile Corp., 292 F. 129 (3d Cir. 1923); Goldman v. Postal Tel., Inc., 52 F.Supp. 763, 771 (D. Del. 1943).

[17] *See* George S. Hills, Consolidation of Corporations by Sale of Assets and Distributions of Shares, 19 Cal. L. Rev. 349, 351–352 (1931) (quoting from Henry W. Ballantine, Corporations (1927)).

[18] In Delaware, even the shareholders of the selling corporation do not have statutory dissenters' rights. Del. Code Ann. tit. 8, § 262 (2001).

that authorize corporations to sell all or substantially all their assets. Thus such a distribution pursuant to the plan is a separate transaction following the actual consummation of the sale itself.

(4) Unlike the rules for a merger or consolidation, the general rule for a sale of corporate assets is that the purchasing corporation is not liable for any of the liabilities of the seller.[19] As will be seen, exceptions to this generality abound. A purchaser of corporate assets will be found to have assumed the seller's liabilities in certain circumstances,[20] such as when (a) the purchaser expressly or impliedly has assumed the seller's obligations, (b) the transaction is determined to be a de facto merger, (c) the purchasing corporation is merely a continuation of the selling corporation, or (d) the transaction involved fraud.

(5) A selling corporation is not dissolved by reason of a sale of its entire assets; this requires separate approval by the stockholders and can occur at the same meeting as their approval of the sale of the company's assets. Generally, after such a sale the corporation is liquidated pursuant to a vote approving its voluntary dissolution. A dissolution, however, is not the inevitable consequence of a sale, and the corporation may continue in the same or some new business or in a state of suspended animation.[21]

The ultimate choice of the form a corporate combination is to take is generally a function of legal considerations combined with business and financial realities. One point of primary importance in selecting a method of reorganization is to take advantage of those provisions of the federal tax code that make certain kinds of reorganization exchanges tax-free.[22]

PART A.   SALE OF ASSETS

§ 22.3   Purposes of Sale of Substantially All Assets

The power to sell all of a corporation's assets can be a preliminary step to formal dissolution. Simply put, the authority to sell all its assets outside the regular course of business can be the means for the orderly cessation of business, whether going out of business was caused by financial distress or otherwise.

A purchase and sale of assets may be used not only as a method of expansion or acquisition of a business by another corporation, but also as a method of voluntary reorganization or recapitalization. In such cases a new corporation is organized for the purpose of acquiring the assets and business of the old, and these assets are then transferred to the purchaser in exchange for an issue of its securities to be distributed directly or indirectly to the shareholders of the selling corporation.[23]

---

[19]   *E.g.*, Knapp v. North Am. Rockwell Corp., 506 F.2d 361 (3d Cir. 1974), *cert. denied*, 421 U.S. 965 (1975).

[20]   *See* § 22.8; William L. Cary & Melvin A. Eisenberg, Cases & Materials on Corporations, 1148–1149 (6th unab. ed. 1988).

[21]   Goldman v. Postal Tel., Inc., 52 F.Supp. 763, 771 (1943).

[22]   I.R.C. § 368 (2009). 26 U.S.C. § 368 (2009).

[23]   *E.g.* United Milk Prods. Corp. v. Lovell, 75 F.2d 923 (6th Cir. 1935) (refunding of preferred shares by sale to new corporation formed just for that purpose).

§ 22.4   Statutory Authorization of Sale of Assets

Every jurisdiction now has a statute expressly authorizing a corporation to sell, mortgage, or pledge, and to convey all or substantially all of its property rights with the vote or consent of its board of directors and a specified majority of its shareholders.[24] These statutory provisions have been adopted in order to relax the strict common law rule in many states requiring unanimous consent and thereby to prevent a small minority of shareholders from thwarting the will of the overwhelming majority.[25] These statutory requirements apply even though the corporation is insolvent,[26] which authorization is commercially desirable when the purpose of reorganization is to continue the business in another corporation rather than to liquidate.[27]

Creditors' protection lies in the statutory restrictions on the corporation's distributing the proceeds of the asset sale.[28] Under these statutes, the sale or transfer of all or substantially all of the corporate assets requires authorization by a majority of the board of directors and also the approval of at least a majority of the shareholders entitled to vote. Failure to obtain shareholder approval may subject the seller to liability for conversion.[29] Under most statutes, shareholder authorization can be given only after prior notice of the time, place, and purpose of the meeting at which the vote will be taken and after distribution of a complete and specific statement of the terms and conditions of the proposed sale to be considered.[30] In some jurisdictions, board approval may follow the shareholder action,[31] although generally the plan must first be adopted by the directors.[32] In a few jurisdictions a meeting is not necessary to obtain the shareholders' consent.[33] Under most statutes it is not required that there be final shareholder approval of the complete and final contract of sale;[34] shareholders are considered sufficiently protected if they approve the principal terms of the transaction and the nature and amount of the consideration to be received by the corporation upon the sale. Under the earlier version of the Model Business Corporation Act, even the fixing of consideration can be delegated to the board.[35] When the shareholder vote is subject to the federal proxy rules, there are more stringent requirements of specificity.[36]

---

[24]   Cal. Corp. Code §§ 152, 1001 (West 1990) (simple majority); Del. Code Ann. tit. 8, § 271 (2001) (simple majority; no shareholder vote necessary for mortgage or pledge of assets, *id.* § 272); N.Y. Bus. Corp. Law § 909(a) (McKinney 2003) (two-thirds majority); Model Bus. Corp. Act § 12.02 (2016) (simple majority of the votes entitled to be cast).

[25]   Voeller v. Neilston Warehouse Co., 311 U.S. 531, 535 n.6 (1941).

[26]   *E.g.*, Michigan Wolverine Student Co-op., Inc. v. William Goodyear & Co., 22 N.W.2d 884 (Mich. 1946). *Contra*, Bassett v. City Bank & Trust Co., 165 A. 557 (Conn. 1933).

[27]   *See, e.g.*, Mills v. Tiffany's, Inc., 198 A. 185 (Conn. 1938).

[28]   *See* Chapter 26 as to dissolution and winding up.

[29]   Trifad Entertainment, Inc. v. Anderson, 36 P.3d 363, 369–370 (Mont. 2001).

[30]   *See, e.g.*, statutes cited *supra* note 24.

[31]   *E.g.*, Cal. Corp. Code § 1001(a)(2) (West Supp. 2009).

[32]   3 Model Bus. Corp. Act Ann. § 11.03 (3d ed. 1994).

[33]   *E.g.*, Minn. Stat. Ann. §§ 302A.441, 302A.661 (2004) (requires unanimous consent); Del. Code Ann. tit. 8, § 228 (2001) (generally allowing consent of a majority of shares without a meeting).

[34]   *E.g.*, Cal. Corp. Code § 1001(c) (West Supp. 2009) ("Such sale . . . may be made upon such terms and conditions . . . as the board may deem in the best interests of the corporation").

[35]   Former Model Bus. Corp. Act § 79(c) (1969). The Revised Model Business Corporation Act requires the corporation to notify the shareholders of the consideration to be received. Model Bus. Corp. Act § 12.02(d) (2016).

[36]   SEC Schedule 14A, item 16.

Ordinarily class voting on proposals for the sale of assets is not required. It would seem, however, that a class vote is sound policy whenever the purpose of a sale is to carry out a recapitalization such that as a result of the transaction the relative rights, privileges, and preferences in the share contract will be altered. A class vote of the preferred shares would appear unnecessary when the sale is the prelude to a dissolution and liquidation of the company. In such a case, the entitlements and protection for the preferred shares should be those provided through their contract with the corporation— for example a vote on dissolution or a liquidation privilege.[37] If the purpose of the transaction is to dissolve and liquidate, the same rules as to voting should apply as in cases of dissolution.[38] The holders of common stock may well have the right to decide this question and to pay off the preferred shareholders in winding up if they so desire.

Today's statutes are not specific as to what constitutes "substantially all" of a corporation's assets. The statutory terminology negates the use of a hard and fast rule; one might use an 80 percent rule of thumb borrowed from the tax laws,[39] although courts have gone below this figure. For example, it has been held that stock in another company totaling more than 75 percent of the selling corporation's assets triggered the statutory requirement of shareholder approval prior to its disposition by the corporation.[40] The test has been said to be both quantitative and qualitative and thus depends on the entirety of circumstances surrounding the sale.

The vast majority of the states condition shareholder approval on both the sale being of "all or substantially all the assets" and the sale being "otherwise than in the usual and regular course of business."[41] Delaware is among those states that do not limit the scope of their statutes to sales outside the regular course of business, but in a leading case the Delaware Supreme Court applied such a limitation:

> If the sale is of assets quantitatively vital to the operation of the corporation *and* is out of the ordinary and substantially affects the existence and purpose of the corporation, then it is beyond the power of the Board of Directors.[42]

Thus the inquiry entails a dynamic interaction between a quantitative and qualitative standard. This approach has long been emphasized.[43] The comment to the Model Business Corporation Act explained: The phrase "substantially all" is synonymous with "nearly all" and was added merely to make it clear that the statutory requirements could not be avoided by retention of some minimal or nominal residue of the original

---

[37]   *See* Model Bus. Corp. Act § 10.04 (2016); former Model Bus. Corp. Act § 60 (1969). The Model Business Corporation Act provides for class voting only if the transaction affects special rights of that class, which is generally not the case with a sale of corporate assets not followed by dissolution.

[38]   *See* Chapter 26.

[39]   I.R.C. § 322(b) (2009); 26 U.S.C. § 332(b) (2009); Treas. Reg. § 1.332–2.

[40]   *See* Philadelphia Nat'l Bank v. B. S. F. Co., 199 A.2d 557 (Del. Ch.), *rev'd on other grounds*, 204 A.2d 746 (Del. 1964). *See* Katz v. Bregman, 431 A.2d 1274 (Del. Ch. 1981) (sale of subsidiary that was parent's sole income-producing asset, was 51% of parent's total assets, and provided 45% of parent's net sales held to be sale of substantially all assets).

[41]   *See* Model Bus. Corp. Act § 12.02(a) (2016). The Model Business Corporation Act conditions shareholder approval on a disposition of assets that "would leave the corporation without a significant continuing business activity." A continuing business activity is deemed "significant" if it represents "at least 25 percent of total assets at the end of the most recently completed fiscal year, and 25 percent of either income from continuing operations before taxes or revenues from continuing operations for that fiscal year, in each case of the corporation and its subsidiaries on a consolidated basis."

[42]   Gimbel v. Signal Co., 316 A.2d 599, 606 (Del. Ch.), *aff'd per curiam*, 316 A.2d 619 (Del. 1974).

[43]   *See, e.g.,* Stiles v. Aluminum Prod. Co., 86 N.E.2d 887 (Ill. App. Ct. 1949) (assets sold were twice value of assets retained but were the essential operating assets as those retained were cash equivalents).

assets. A sale of all the corporate assets other than cash or cash equivalents is normally the sale of "all or substantially all" of the corporation's property. A sale of several distinct manufacturing lines while retaining one or more lines is normally not a sale of "all or substantially all" *even though the lines being sold are substantial business.* If the lines retained are viewed only as a temporary operation or as a pretext to avoid the "all or substantially all" requirements, however, the statutory requirements of chapter 12 [of the Model Business Corp. Act] must be complied with.[44]

While the Model Business Corporation Act's comment may appear inconsistent with the statute's language, which has eliminated the "all or substantially all" standard and instead refers to a disposition that would leave the corporation without a "significant continuing business activity,"[45] the comment can best be seen as emphasizing the distinction made earlier between decisions that shift the company assets to new areas,[46] which decisions are committed to the discretion of the board of directors, and decisions that are a prelude to a structural change in the nature of investment, such as sales that are a prelude to liquidation, for which shareholder approval is necessary. Nevertheless, the comment and the statute are far from definitive in their content or scope.

Some courts have held that sales of real estate, even if the company's only asset, is not subject to a statute governing sale of assets.[47] The rationale here is that if the sale of real estate is a purpose for which the company was organized, such a sale is "in the ordinary course of business" and thus within the directors' purview.[48] The sale of property that is the core asset of a real estate investment corporation formed to manage the property's rental is not in the ordinary course of business.[49] There are no exceptions in such statutes for financial exigencies:[50] If the sale of assets is within the ordinary course of business, then no shareholder approval is required.[51]

§ 22.5 Sale of Assets for Securities

At one time there was a conflict as to whether in the absence of a statute a corporation could sell substantially all its assets in exchange for shares or other securities of the purchasing company.[52] Today a corporation may exchange all or part of its assets for securities, but some statutes are silent as to what, other than shares of stock, constitutes legitimate consideration.[53] The statutory authority for these transactions is augmented by tax-free treatment where substantially all of the selling

---

[44] Model Bus. Corp. Act § 12.01 Official Comment (2016) (emphasis added).

[45] Model Bus. Corp. Act § 12.02(a) (2016).

[46] In this regard, the Model Act's Official Comment's use of "former" takes on added significance because it assumes the corporation's continuation.

[47] Roehner v. Gracie Manor, Inc., 160 N.E.2d 519 (N.Y. 1959). *Contra,* Boyer v. Legal Estates, Inc., 255 N.Y.S.2d 955 (Sup. Ct. 1964).

[48] Morris v. Washington Med. Ctr., Inc., 331 A.2d 132 (D.C. Ct. App. 1975).

[49] *See* Boyer v. Legal Estates, Inc., 255 N.Y.S.2d 955 (Sup. Ct. 1964). *See also* Naas v. Lucas, 739 P.2d 1051 (Or. Ct. App. 1987) (transfer of substantially all assets by president to satisfy bona fide debt not within ordinary course of business).

[50] Michigan Wolverines Student Co-op., Inc. v. William Goodyear & Co., 22 N.W.2d 884 (Mich. 1946).

[51] Jeppi v. Brockman Holding Co., 206 P.2d 847 (Cal. 1949) (real estate).

[52] When the circumstances showed such an exigency as to permit a sale of all the corporate property without the aid of a statute, the general rule used to be that the sale could only be for cash unless there was unanimous shareholder consent.

[53] Del. Code Ann. tit. 8, § 271 (2001) ("money or other property, including shares of stock in and/or other securities . . .").

corporation's assets are exchanged solely for all or part of another corporation's voting stock.[54]

§ 22.6 The De Facto Merger Doctrine

In a large majority of jurisdictions, with the important exceptions of Delaware and California, dissenting shareholders are given the right to be paid in cash for the appraised value of their shares in the event of a sale or exchange of all or substantially all of a corporation's assets not in the ordinary course of its business.[55] No showing of fraud, unfairness, or prejudice is required.[56] In Delaware this statutory remedy arises only in connection with statutory mergers and consolidations.[57] In a few states, such as New York and Ohio, as well as the Model Business Corporation Act, the dissenting shareholder is given "a rather full armory of rights which permit appraisal in most cases of fundamental change."[58] Whether or not the scope of appraisal statutes should be so extended is a question of policy depending on the jurisdiction's assessment of how well the appraisal remedy works and whether it does more harm than good.[59]

In a state that does not grant dissenters' rights for sales of assets, there is a serious gap in the shareholder's protection because an effect the same as a merger can be achieved by a sale of assets.[60] For example, assume Corporation A sells its assets to Corporation B and as part of the deal B assumes A's obligations and A dissolves. Thereafter, Corporation A distributes the proceeds of the sale (the B securities) to its shareholders under its plan of dissolution. In reviewing these transactions some courts may determine that there has been a de facto merger, in which dissenters' rights under the merger statute are to be honored.[61] Two significant effects of so treating transactions so the procedural rights that accompany mergers apply are: The shareholders of the "purchasing" corporation will be entitled to vote on the transaction, and an appraisal remedy is available to all shareholders entitled to vote.

A far greater number of jurisdictions, including Delaware,[62] refuse to embrace the de facto merger doctrine. This refusal is based on the doctrine of "independent statutory significance" or equal dignity. This doctrine holds that each authorizing provision of the state's corporation statute is entitled to its own independent significance such that the substantive effects and procedural requirements of one provision are not to be harmonized with another provision under which the same objective could have also been accomplished but pursuant to different procedural requirements. Thus, under the doctrine of independent statutory significance, if the formal requirements of the sale-of-

---

[54] I.R.C. § 368(a)(1)(C) (1988).

[55] *See* former Model Bus. Corp. Act § 80(a)(2) (1969). The Revised Model Business Corporation Act replaced the "all or substantially all" and "usual and regular course of business" language with a standard defined by a disposition of assets that would leave the corporation without a "significant continuing business activity." Model Bus. Corp. Act §§ 12.02(a) (2016). *But see, e.g.,* Del. Code Ann. tit. 8, §§ 253(d), 262 (2001).

[56] Homer v. Crown Cork & Seal Co., 141 A. 425, 434 (Md. 1928).

[57] Del. Code Ann. tit. 8, § 262 (2001).

[58] N.Y. Bus. Corp. Law §§ 806, 910, 1319 (McKinney 1986, Supp. 1994); former Model Bus. Corp. Act § 80 (1969, 1979 rev.); Model Bus. Corp. Act § 13.02 (2016).

[59] Dissenters' rights are taken up in more detail *infra* §§ 22.18 to 22.21.

[60] *See* § 22.4. Even in states granting dissenters' rights they can be eliminated by leaving some assets or by amending the charter to permit such sales in the ordinary course.

[61] *See generally* Ernest Folk, IV, De Facto Mergers in Delaware: *Hariton v. Arco Electronics, Inc.,* 49 Va. L. Rev. 1261 (1963).

[62] *See* Hariton v. Arco Elec., Inc., 188 A.2d 123 (Del.Supr. 1963), *aff'g* 182 A.2d 22 (Del. Ch. 1962).

assets statute are complied with, the transaction will be considered a sale rather than a merger, at least where the contract of sale does not call for dissolution and the selling corporation remains in existence long enough to receive the proceeds of the sale and distribute them to its shareholders.

The leading Delaware decision of *Hariton v. Arco Electronics, Inc.*[63] refused to apply the de facto merger doctrine to a sale of assets even though the sales contract contained an undertaking by the selling corporation to dissolve a new enterprise without the right to appraisal. The Supreme Court of Delaware, although conceding that a sale of assets coupled with a mandatory plan of dissolution and distribution achieves the same result as a merger, held that the transaction was legal. "This is so," said the court, "because the sale-of-assets statute and the merger statute are independent of each other. They are, so to speak, of equal dignity, and the framers of a reorganization may resort to either type of corporate mechanics to achieve the desired end."[64] In other words "the general theory of the Delaware Corporation Law [is] that action taken pursuant to the authority of the various sections of that law constitute acts of independent legal significance and their validity is not dependent on other sections of the Act."[65]

Several decisions in other jurisdictions have applied the de facto merger doctrine.[66] In the leading de facto merger case, *Farris v. Glen Alden Corporation*,[67] Glen Alden and List Industries, a holding company that had purchased large amounts of Glen Alden stock, entered into a "reorganization agreement," subject to shareholder approval in each company. Under the agreement, (1) Glen Alden was to acquire all List Industries assets; (2) Glen Alden was to increase its authorized stock and issue to List several million shares of Glen Alden stock, which in turn were to be distributed to the List shareholders—five shares of Glen Alden in exchange for six shares of List; (3) Glen Alden was to assume List's liabilities, including a $5 million note that List had given to purchase Glen Alden stock some years before, as well as existing stock options, incentive plans, and pension obligations; (4) Glen Alden's name was to be changed to "List Alden Corporation"; (5) the directors of both corporations were to become directors of List Alden, List directors would hold 11 of the 17 directorships on the new board, and the List interests would thus gain control of the new company; and (6) List was to be dissolved.

The Supreme Court of Pennsylvania held the transaction to be a de facto merger, so the plaintiff, a Glen Alden shareholder, was entitled to an appraisal remedy. The court concluded that whenever one corporation combines with another so as to lose its essential nature and alter the fundamental relationships of the shareholders among themselves and their relationships to the corporation, shareholders who do not wish to continue may treat their membership in the original corporation as terminated and may demand payment for the value of their shares. In *Glen Alden* the corporation in which the plaintiff originally held shares, a coal mining company, was to be transformed into a diversified holding company whose interests would range from motion picture theaters to textile companies. This transformation was most striking because the acquired

---

[63] Hariton v. Arco Electronics, Inc., 188 A.2d 123 (Del. 1963), *aff'g* 182 A.2d 22 (Del. Ch. 1962).

[64] 188 A.2d at 125.

[65] Hariton v. Arco Electronics, Inc., 188 A.2d 123, 124 (Del. 1963), *aff'g* 182 A.2d 22 (Del. Ch. 1962), quoting Langfelder v. Universal Labs., 68 F.Supp. 209, 211 n.5 (D. Del. 1946).

[66] Shannon v. Samuel Langston Co., 379 F.Supp. 797 (W.D. Mich. 1974).

[67] Farris v. Glen Alden Corporation, 143 A.2d 25 (Pa. 1958).

company—List, a holding company—was the company that one would have expected to purchase the coal company. The assets of the enterprise in which the plaintiff was to be a shareholder doubled, and its debts increased sevenfold. Control of the new entity would have passed to the directors of List, and the plaintiff would suffer a serious financial loss as the book value of his shares would be reduced substantially.[68]

It has been suggested that the *Glen Alden* case must be taken in the context of its facts as an "upside-down" purchase in which the parties had purposely structured the transaction so that the smaller company acquired the larger.[69] Somewhat more visually, one can view Glen Alden's acquisition of List as a minnow swallowing a whale. The de facto merger doctrine has since been applied where there is no such disparity.[70] Two additional factors may have invited the court's belief that Glen Alden's shareholders needed some extra statutory protection. First, the acquisition was not at arm's length: List had secured through its substantial stock ownership in Glen Alden three nominees to the Glen Alden board of directors. Second, List's substantial ownership of Glen Alden stock was acquired with borrowed funds, so Glen Alden's assets could be used following the combination to satisfy the funds List had borrowed to acquire Glen Alden. When the assets of the acquired company are used by its acquirer to extinguish the debt the acquirer incurred to acquire control, the acquisition is frequently called a bootstrap acquisition. The Glen Alden-List combination was a bootstrap acquisition. The current Pennsylvania statute recognizes the right of appraisal in some situations for the shareholders of the purchasing corporation and thus would appear to preclude the de facto merger doctrine in other situations.[71]

It would be a mistake to believe that the only principle separating the competing approaches illustrated by *Hariton* and *Glen Alden* is a particular jurisdiction's obeisance to the doctrine of independent statutory existence. In a thorough consideration of this area, the late Professor Ernest Folk states that the result achieved in *Hariton* and its progeny rests on two hidden premises.[72] First, the judiciary's view of the vitality and usefulness of the appraisal remedy is argued to have an important bearing on whether a jurisdiction embraces the de facto merger doctrine. If the remedy is seen as socially harmful because it portends a drain of cash from the combining companies, the court is less likely to exercise its equitable powers to accord dissenting shareholders rights that arise in the analogous context of mergers. Similarly, the court may view skeptically the narrow band of transactions for which the legislature has prescribed an appraisal remedy for dissenting shareholders; recent events have shown that shareholders' expectations can be rapidly deflated through transactions and decisions that entail no statutorily prescribed vote or appraisal remedy whatever. In sum, the appraisal remedy can easily be seen as an arbitrary and unwelcome appendage of corporate law such that its expansion through the de facto merger doctrine is equally unwelcome. Second, the decision as to whether to apply the de facto merger doctrine directly confronts one of the

---

[68]   From $38 to $21 per share.

[69]   *See* Ernest Folk, IV, De Facto Mergers in Delaware: *Hariton v. Arco Electronics, Inc.,* 49 Va. L. Rev. 1261, 1267 (1963).

[70]   *E.g.,* Rath v. Rath Packing Co., 136 N.W.2d 410 (Iowa 1965).

[71]   The Pennsylvania statute was amended to provide appraisal rights to the shareholders of the purchasing corporation when such transaction involves an issuance of a majority of the voting shares. 15 Pa. Cons. Stat. § 2544 (1995). *See* Terry v. Penn Central Corp., 668 F.2d 188 (3d Cir. 1981).

[72]   Ernest Folk, IV, De Facto Mergers in Delaware: *Hariton v. Arco Electronics, Inc.,* 49 Va. L. Rev. 1261, 1279–1281 (1963).

most profound questions in corporate law—What is the nature of the shareholder's ownership interest?

> The basic premise implicitly adopted in *Hariton* may perhaps be stated more affirmatively. One does not invest in a unique corporate entity or even a particular business operation, but rather a continuous course of business which changes over a long period of time. Certainly the best investments are growth investments—investments in enterprises which change with time, technology, business opportunities, and altered demand. . . . Viewed this way, the fact that the change—for better or for worse—comes through marriage, whether by merger or assets sale, seems purely incidental. The fact that the corporate entity in which one invested disappears as a result of a merger or of a sale of assets coupled with dissolution is also beside the point. One's investment may gain immortality when it takes a new form, i.e., a share in a successor enterprise.[73]

It may well be that the de facto merger doctrine reaches the socially desirable result but through the wrong means. Almost any combination of two different companies will produce the effects emphasized in *Glen Alden* so that, unless courts are prepared to treat as mergers all combinations structured as a sale of assets, harmful uncertainty will accompany every such transaction. At the same time, the parties have bona fide commercial reasons to structure a transaction as a sale of assets—for example, so that the purchaser can clearly identify the assets and liabilities it wishes to acquire and not acquire. Moreover, the parties may have selected the sale-of-assets procedure to reduce the transaction's cost that would arise if both corporations' shareholders had a right to vote and an appraisal remedy. In this light, the de facto merger doctrine challenges the legislative wisdom of providing for transactions very different procedural rights that can accomplish the same objective. Such a challenge appears to embrace an unduly adventuresome, if not mischievous, role for the courts. At the same time, disquiet arises whenever a statute allows important procedural protections to be bypassed at the option of those who are not intended to be the beneficiaries of such procedural protections. For this reason, some states have essentially codified the de facto merger doctrine by prescribing basic voting and appraisal rights regardless of the form the combination takes.[74]

The de facto merger doctrine is not limited to suits attempting to assert dissenters' rights. It may arise where creditors object to the failure of one corporation to assume liabilities along with the purchase of assets of another. This has been fertile ground for litigation with regard to attempts to avoid products liability damage awards.[75] The cases for successor liability have not been limited to product liability claims.[76] Further, the de facto merger doctrine is not limited to sales of assets: It may arise from other forms of

---

[73]   Ernest Folk, IV, De Facto Mergers in Delaware: *Hariton v. Arco Electronics, Inc.*, 49 Va. L. Rev. 1261, 1280–1281 (1963).

[74]   California was the leader in the movement to codify the de facto merger doctrine. *See* Cal. Corp. Code §§ 168, 1101, 1200 & 1300 (West Supp. 2009). Other states have recognized the doctrine as well. *See* N.J. Stat. Ann. § 14A:10–12 (1998 Supp.).

[75]   *See* § 22.7. *See also* Matheson, Successor Liability, 96 Minn. L. Rev. 371 (2011); Richard L. Cupp, Jr., Redesigning Successor Liability, (1999 Ill. L. Rev. 845).

[76]   *See, e.g.*, Fitzgerald v. Fahnestock & Co., 730 N.Y.S.2d 70 (App. Div. 2001) (suit by former employee of acquired company).

corporate combination, such as a lease of all the productive assets or acquisition of a corporation's control block of stock[77] without merging or liquidating a subsidiary.

§ 22.7 Successor Corporation Liability

As was seen earlier, a distinguishing feature of a business combination carried out as a merger or consolidation is that by operation of law the surviving corporation is subject to all the liabilities of the acquired companies. In contrast, when the combination is structured as an asset or stock purchase-sale, absent special circumstances, the acquiring company is subject only to those liabilities it has agreed to assume. Traditionally, there were just four circumstances in which the selling corporation's creditors could successful proceed against a purchaser who had not so assumed the debt owed to that creditor:

> [T]here are four well recognized exemptions under which the purchasing corporation becomes liable for the debts and liabilities of the selling corporation. (1) Where the purchaser expressly or impliedly agrees to assume such debts; (2) where the transaction amounts to a consolidation or merger of the corporations; (3) where the purchasing corporation is merely a continuation of the selling corporation; and (4) where the transaction is entered into fraudulently in order to escape liability for such debts.[78]

This traditional approach continues to be the great weight of authority, despite the important inroads, discussed below, that modern tort law trends have made on the subject.[79] The most significant testing of the rigidity of these four exceptions has occurred, not surprisingly, in the context of product liability claims brought against corporations that acquired the assets of a company that during its previous life had produced a defective product, which defect did not cause a plaintiff-creditor's injury until after the acquisition.

The first exception referred to above involves little more than a straightforward interpretation of the contract of sale.[80] Buyers wishing to avoid unwanted or contingent liabilities need simply state that the buyer assumes no responsibility for any liabilities of any type or arising from any source, contingent or otherwise, beyond those expressly assumed within the contract.[81]

The de facto merger exception emphasizes the continuity of the acquired company's shareholders in the surviving enterprise. Thus this exception in its most orthodox application arises when stock, rather than cash, is the purchase consideration and the selling corporation dissolves shortly after the acquisition so that the stock is distributed to its shareholders.[82]

---

[77]   *See* Fitzgerald v. Fahnestock & Co., 730 N.Y.S.2d 70 (App. Div. 2001) (acquisition of stock).

[78]   West Tex. Refining & Dev. Co. v. Commissioner, 68 F.2d 77, 81 (10th Cir. 1933).

[79]   *See, e.g.,* Ramlall v. MobilePro Corp., 202 Md. App. 20, 30 A.3d 1003 (Md. Ct. App. 2011).

[80]   *See, e.g.,* Keller v. Clark Equip. Co., 715 F.2d 1280 (8th Cir. 1983), *cert. denied,* 464 U.S. 1044 (1984); Piacente v. J.K. Funding, Inc., 706 N.Y.S.2d 198 (App. Div. 2000).

[81]   Parker v. Western Dakota Insurors, Inc., 605 N.W.2d 181, 184–185 (S.D. 2000) (unambiguous contract with explicit provisions excluding any liability for debts and liabilities not enumerated in agreement weighs against finding of implied assumption).

[82]   *See, e.g.,* R. C. McEntire & Co. v. Eastern Foods, Inc., 702 F.2d 471 (4th Cir. 1983), *cert. denied,* 464 U.S. 849 (1983). *But see* Mudgett v. Paxson Mach. Co., 709 S.W.2d 755 (Tex. Ct. App. 1986) (1979 enactment was intended to remove de facto and continuity of enterprise exceptions).

The third exception arises when the surviving company carries forward a common identity with the selling corporation in terms of its shareholders, management, name, place and nature of business, and employees.[83] It is simply old wine in a new bottle.

The fourth traditional exemption is but a specialized application of the law of fraudulent transfers. Thus, when the successor corporation acquires the predecessor's assets for nominal consideration and continues its operations under the same management, the court can easily conclude the transfer was a fraud on creditors.[84]

The most liberal approach to successor-corporation liability emphasizes the social policy that has driven developments for product liability generally, the question of who is in the best position to absorb the cost of the defect. The so-called product's-line exception has its genesis in *Ray v. Alad Corporation*,[85] where the California Supreme Court held that "a party which acquires a manufacturing business and continues the output of its line of products under the circumstances here presented assumes strict tort liability for defects in units of the same product line previously manufactured and distributed by the entity from which the business was acquired."[86] Two important jurisdictions, New Jersey and Pennsylvania, are among those to quickly adopt the product-line exception.[87] New York is among those states that adhere to the traditional rule[88] but break from its bonds where there is a breach of a duty to warn of a defect, such duty arising from statute, regulation, or negligence.[89]

Another non-traditional approach that is gaining judicial acceptance is the "continuity of enterprise" exception to limited liability, which, like the "mere continuation" exception, focuses on whether the totality of the transaction demonstrates a basic continuity of the predecessor enterprise. However, whereas the "mere continuation" doctrine requires that the two corporations have identical shareholders and directors, the "continuity of enterprise" analysis looks beyond that formal requirement and considers the substance of the underlying transaction—that is, whether the business has been transferred as a going concern. Under this limited exception, the successor corporation may be held liable for the obligations of its predecessor even though the sale of assets is for cash and there is not a complete identity of shareholders.[90]

---

[83]   *See, e.g.*, Cargo Partner AG v. Albatrans, Inc., 352 F.3d 41 (2d Cir. 2003).

[84]   *See, e.g.*, Lumbard v. Maglia, Inc., 621 F.Supp. 1529 (S.D.N.Y. 1985).

[85]   Ray v. Alad Corporation, 560 P.2d 3 (Cal. 1977).

[86]   Ray v. Alad Corporation, 560 P.2d 3, 11 (Cal. 1977).

[87]   *See* Lefever v. K.P. Hovnanian Enters., Inc., 734 A.2d 290, 292 (N.J. 1999) (applying product line exception when successor purchased assets at bankruptcy sale); Ramirez v. Amsted Indus., 431 A.2d 811 (N.J. 1981); Schmidt v. Boardman Co., 958 A.2d 498 (Pa. Super. Ct. 2008) (applying doctrine when it has been established (1)there has been virtual destruction of plaintiff's remedies against original manufacturer, (2) successor possessed ability to assume original manufacturer's risk-spreading role, and (3) the fairness of imposing liability on the successor as a concomitant burden of the goodwill acquired from the original manufacturer); Dawejko v. Jorgensen Steel Co., 434 A.2d 106 (Pa. Super. Ct. 1981) (Pennsylvania considers continuation of product line but one of many factors in the equation).

[88]   *But see* Rothstein v. Tennessee Gas Pipeline Co., 696 N.Y.S.2d 528, 531 (App. Div. 1999) (noting that Appellate Division, Third Department has adopted product line exception; declining to decide issue for Second Department, since successor in this case purchased less than 20% of assets of predecessor, which continued as ongoing, viable business for ten years after transfer).

[89]   *See, e.g.*, Rothstein v. Tennessee Gas Pipeline Co., 696 N.Y.S.2d 528, 531 (App. Div. 1999) (duty to warn may be imposed on successor corporation that maintains sufficient links to purchaser of products manufactured by its predecessor).

[90]   Savage Arms, Inc. v. Western Auto Supply Co., 18 P.3d 49, 55–56 (Alaska 2001) (adopting exception).

Successor liability may also be imposed in the case of an acquisition of a target company's stock. Courts have indicated that successor liability will attach under the de facto merger doctrine when subsequent to the stock acquisition, the target company ceases to have an independent identity and the target's business can only be carried on through the acquiring corporation.[91]

Various federal statutes pose unique obligations for successor corporations. Significant successor liability arises under the "Superfund Law," Comprehensive Environmental Response, Compensation, and Liability Act (CERCLA),[92] which provides that owners as well as operators of property are liable for all costs in cleaning up a site, even though the generator of the waste was a prior owner.[93] Thus, by simply becoming an owner of property on which waste has been disposed of by others, the new owner can become a "responsible party" under CERCLA.[94] And continuity of the work force is an important factor under the labor laws, at least with respect to the successor corporation's obligation to bargain with the union that represented the acquired company's employees.[95]

PART B.　MERGER AND CONSOLIDATION

§ 22.8　Merger and Consolidation Distinguished

A consolidation is the uniting or amalgamation of two or more existing corporations to form a new corporation.[96] The firm resulting from the union is called the "consolidated" corporation. A merger is a union effected by the absorbing of one or more existing corporations by another, which survives and continues the combined business.[97] The disappearing corporation is generally referred to as the "merged" corporation, with the other being the "surviving" corporation. The parties to a combination either by consolidation or merger are called the "constituent" corporations. The chief difference between mergers and consolidations is one of form; the procedure, legal effect, and end-product are the same.[98]

§ 22.9　Attributes and Advantages of Merger and Consolidation

Merger and consolidation are very complex proceedings involving several different transactions affecting many parties, all of which may be accomplished simultaneously

---

[91]　*See* Fitzgerald v. Fahnestock & Co., 730 N.Y.S.2d 70 (App. Div. 2001). The complaint alleged that the defendant acquired all of the target company's stock and the target's business was transferred to the acquiring corporation. The court reversed dismissal of a claim brought against the acquirer based on a judgment that had previously been obtained against the acquired company.

[92]　42 U.S.C. § 9601 (2009).

[93]　CERCLA, 42 U.S.C. § 107 (2000). Carter, Successor Liability Under CERCLA: Its Time to Fully Embrace State Law,156 U. Pa. L. Rev. 767 (2008).

[94]　*See, e.g.,* New York v. Shore Realty Corp., 759 F.2d 1032 (2d Cir. 1985).

[95]　Fall River Dyeing & Finishing Corp. v. NLRB, 482 U.S. 27 (1987) (when majority of successor's employees had been employed by predecessor). More recently, the NLRB took an even broader approach, emphasizing the representations made by the successor of an "intention" to retain the acquired company's workforce. *See* Canteen Company, 317 NLRB No. 153, 317 NLRB 1052 (1995), enfd. 103 F.3d 1355 (7th Cir. 1997).

[96]　*E.g.,* Metropolitan Edison Co. v. Commissioner, 98 F.2d 807, 810 (3d Cir.), *aff'd,* 306 U.S. 522 (1939); former Model Bus. Corp. Act § 72 (1969).

[97]　*E.g.,* Alabama Power Co. v. McNinch, 94 F.2d 601, 610 (D.C. Cir. 1937).

[98]　Delaware retains the distinction between mergers and consolidations. Del. § 264. In contrast, the Model Act has abolished consolidation as a separate form; the transaction can still be accomplished through a share exchange. Model Bus. Corp. Act § 11.03 (2016).

by statute. Legislative authority is essential to authorize a true merger or consolidation.[99] These transactions are fundamental changes of the charter contract and the share contracts and also in the rights of creditors. Each constituent corporation must be authorized under the law of its domicile to enter into a union by merger or consolidation.[100] Each constituent corporation must comply with the procedure set forth by the statute of its state of incorporation.[101] A merger may be preferable to a consolidation in combining corporations because one of the corporations may have nonassignable leases, franchises, or employment contracts that by their terms cannot pass to another entity. Another reason may be that one of the constituent corporations may have qualified to do business as a foreign corporation in a large number of other states and it would be burdensome to qualify a new corporation.[102]

As we have seen, the procedure of selling the entire assets and issuing shares in payment by the purchaser, followed by dissolution and winding up, is often preferable to either merger or consolidation.[103] A sale of assets is particularly helpful when the acquiring corporation is not interested in all of the business of the corporation to be acquired or where it wishes to make a selective assumption of liabilities—subject, of course, to the equitable rights of creditors. Merger or consolidation can be used to acquire some part of the business when preceded or followed by a sale of assets to a third party. Another alternative is to place the unwanted assets in a subsidiary corporation and spin off the shares to the stockholders in the form of a dividend.

The great advantage of a statutory merger or consolidation over combination by sale of assets is that it furnishes a short cut to accomplishing various transactions and may avoid difficulty, delay, and expense such as that attendant on a dissolution, winding up, and the distribution of securities to its shareholders by the selling corporation. By statute, all of the rights and liabilities of the transferor are assimilated into the transferee corporation.

Merger and consolidation are, in essence, the transfer of the property and business of one corporation to another in exchange for securities or cash issued by the purchaser to shareholders of the seller. Merger and consolidation involve the automatic (that is, by operation of law) assumption of all the debts and liabilities of the transferring corporations and a compulsory novation on the part of the creditors.[104] As we have seen, in a combination by sale of assets there may not be a compulsory exchange or distribution of new shares for old or a compulsory substitution of a new debtor as to the debts and liabilities of the seller. In a sale of assets, sufficient funds must be reserved or adequate provision made to take care of the debts and liabilities of the seller; otherwise the transfer would be a fraudulent conveyance, which could be attacked by the creditors. Merger and consolidation are also highly advantageous forms of reorganization because

---

[99] See § 22.10.

[100] See William B. Riker & Son Co. v. United Drug Co., 82 A. 930 (N.J.Err.App. 1912).

[101] E.g., Del. Code Ann. tit. 8, § 252 (2001); N.Y. Bus. Corp. Law § 907 (McKinney 2003); former Model Bus. Corp. Act § 73 (1969); Model Bus. Corp. Act § 11.04 (2016).

[102] See former Model Bus. Corp. Act § 106 (1969).

[103] Norris Darrell, The Use of Reorganization Techniques in Corporate Acquisitions, 70 Harv. L. Rev. 1183 (1957).

[104] Assets are, of course, transferred into the surviving company so that when Alpha acquires Beta there is no transfer of Alpha assets. See e.g., Meso Scale Diagnostics, LLC v. Roche Diagnostices GmbH, 62 A.3d 62 (Del. Ch. 2013)(patents residing in company surviving a reverse merger have not undergone a transfer by operation of law),

they bring the transaction of an exchange of property for shares within the class of tax-free reorganizations under the federal tax laws.[105]

§ 22.10   Statutory Authority for Merger and Consolidation

Mergers and consolidations can be effected only under statutory authority.[106] The power of corporations to merge without unanimous shareholder approval does not exist without statutory authorization, so liability can arise for consequential damages from mergers consummated without complying with the applicable statutory requirements.[107] All jurisdictions have liberal provisions for merger, consolidation, sales of assets, and charter amendments, which on enactment were made applicable to existing corporations as well as to those to be formed.[108] In some jurisdictions constitutional doubts were raised as to the scope of the reserved power to authorize fundamental changes by majority shareholders in preexisting corporations.[109] Although the contrary has long been taken for granted by others, there still may be problems regarding the ability of legislatures to affect the internal rules of existing corporations.[110] The extent to which the authorization of such fundamental changes is dependent on provisions enabling objecting shareholders to demand payment of the fair value of their shares has also been questioned.[111]

§ 22.11   Procedures to Merge or Consolidate

[1] Procedures Generally

The procedure to accomplish a merger is practically the same as that necessary to effect a consolidation. In general the essential steps in each involve: (1) the negotiation and approval of an agreement of merger or consolidation by the boards of directors of the constituent companies and the drafting of a formal agreement to combine in accordance with the applicable statute;[112] (2) the submission of the agreement, either in full or in substance, to the shareholders for their approval by the specified majority vote after lawful notice of a shareholders' meeting; and (3) the execution of the formal agreement by the proper corporate officers, with the formal certificates of due authorization, and the filing of the agreement so duly certified with the secretary of state or other designated official.

As a prelude to exploring their merger, the parties will enter into a range of agreements, including agreeing to maintain the confidentiality of non-public information that may assist the parties in negotiating a business combination. The Delaware

---

[105] *See* Boris I. Bittker & James S. Eustice, Federal Income Taxation of Corporations and Shareholders (6th ed. 1994).

[106] *E.g.,* William B. Riker & Son Co. v. United Drug Co., 82 A. 930 (N.J.Err.App. 1912); Colgate v. United States Leather Co., 72 A. 126 (N.J.Err.App. 1909).

[107] Nelson v. All Am. Life & Fin. Corp., 889 F.2d 141 (8th Cir. 1989).

[108] This was highly desirable, if not necessary, for the sake of uniformity and the facilitation of business. *See, e.g.,* Brundage v. New Jersey Zinc Co., 226 A.2d 585 (N.J. 1967).

[109] E. Merrick Dodd, Jr., Dissenting Stockholders and Amendments to Corporate Charters, 75 U. Pa. L. Rev. 585, 723, 735–737 (1927).

[110] *See* Nelson Ferebee Taylor, Evolution of Corporate Combination Law: Policy Issues and Constitutional Questions, 76 N.C. L. Rev. 687 (1998).

[111] *See* Nice Ball Bearing Co. v. Mortgage Bldg. & Loan Ass'n, 166 A. 239 (Pa. 1933).

[112] There is no duty under state law to disclose such negotiations. *See, e.g.,* Eldridge v. Tymshare, Inc., 230 Cal.Rptr. 815 (Ct. App. 1986).

Supreme Court upheld a 4-month injunction against Martin-Marietta's use of confidential information obtained pursuant to the confidentiality agreement to structure its hostile tender offer for Vulcan.[113]

Once a merger agreement is in place, it will create contractual obligations between the parties to the agreement. Merger agreements typically contain a "material adverse change" or "material adverse effect" provision allowing the contract to be avoided when material changes or effects are discovered after the merger agreement is made.[114] The provision's purpose is to protect the buyer from unanticipated changes in the seller's business between the signing of the agreement and the closing. A noteworthy decision is *IBP Inc. v. Tyson Foods Inc.*[115] where the court held that a 64 percent drop in sales and a $60 million accounting restatement were not sufficient to trigger the material adverse change provision as an escape from the merger agreement. This and other decisions reveal that a generalized material adverse change provision will not always provide meaningful protection with respect to changed conditions. If the parties foresee specific contingencies, they would be well advised to enumerate them in the merger agreement as examples of what constitutes a material adverse change.

[2] Voting Requirements

Most states now provide for majority approval by the shares entitled to vote,[116] although some adhere to the older practice of a two-thirds requirement.[117] Recent amendments to the Model Act if adopted by state legislatures would dilute the shareholders' power in reducing the required vote from a majority of those entitled to vote, to a plurality of those actually voting.[118]

In view of the fact that the interests of different classes of shares, particularly preferred and common, frequently conflict in a merger or a consolidation (they do as in the case of amendments to the articles of incorporation), a class vote is frequently accorded to each class of stock affected in a proscribed manner by the merger or consolidation. Jurisdictions following the scheme of the Model Business Corporation Act define how the stock is "affected" broadly to include not only by any changes in the existing rights, privileges, and preferences of an outstanding class of stock but also by any dilution in their economic or voting rights through the issuance of additional shares of that class or of a class that will compete for assets with an outstanding class.[119] In

---

[113] Martin Marietta Materials, Inc. v. Vulcan Materials Co., 56 A.3d 1072 (Del.Ch. 2012), *aff'd*, 2012 Del. LEXIS 342 (Del. 2012).

[114] *E.g.*, Pine State Creamery Co. v. Land-O-Sun Dairies, Inc., 201 F.3d 437 (4th Cir. 1999); Great Lakes Chemical Corporation v. Pharmacia Corp., 788 A.2d 544 (Del. Ch. 2001); Raskin v. Birmingham Steel Corp., 1990 WL 193326 (Del. Ch. 1990).

[115] IBP, Inc. v. Tyson Foods, Inc., 789 A.2d 14 (Del. Ch. 2001), *aff'd sub nom.*, Tyson Foods, Inc. v. Aetos Corp., 818 A.2d 145 (Del. 2003).

[116] *E.g.*, Del. Code Ann. tit. 8, § 251(c) (2001); former Model Bus. Corp. Act § 73 (1969); Model Bus. Corp. Act § 11.03 (2008).

[117] Mass. Gen. Laws Ann. ch. 156D, § 11.04(5) (LexisNexis. Supp. 2009) (articles may authorize a lower vote); N.Y. Bus. Corp. Law § 903(a)(2) (McKinney 2003) (two-thirds of all shares; if class vote required, majority of all shares of each class).

The New York statute was amended in 1998 to require only a majority of those shares entitled to vote. The amendment applies prospectively only to corporations incorporated after February 22, 1998. N.Y. Bus. Corp. Law § 903 (2001).

[118] *See* Committee on Corporate Laws, Changes in the Model Business Corporation Act Pertaining to Appraisal Rights and to Fundamental Changes—final Adoption, 55 Bus. Law. 405 (1999).

[119] *See* Model Bus. Corp. Act §§ 11.02(a) (2016).

contrast, a class vote is not provided in many states, such as Delaware, so that they grant inadequate protection to the holders of preferred shares.[120]

The modern trend among corporate statutes is to include a "small acquisition" exception to the right of shareholders to vote on mergers or consolidations. This exception removes mergers and consolidations from the necessity of any vote of the stockholders of the *surviving* corporation, provided the articles of incorporation are not amended to change their rights, privileges, or preferences, the number of shares each owns is not affected by the merger or consolidation, and the number of voting shares outstanding after the combination is not increased by more than 20 percent from the number of outstanding voting shares before the acquisition.[121] This exemption reflects the drafters' wisdom that some acquisitions are of such small impact to the corporation in terms of their dilutive effects that they should fall exclusively within the discretion of the board of directors to carry out. In a sense, in terms of the shareholders' involvement the transaction is treated no differently than if the board of directors had first sold common shares (not to exceed 20 percent of those already outstanding) for cash and used the cash to acquire another corporation.

[3] The Agreement of Merger or Consolidation

The foundation of the merger or consolidation is an agreement negotiated and approved by the directors of each constituent corporation and approved by the requisite number of the outstanding shares. This agreement yields the "plan of merger" that is approved by the shareholders. In the case of consolidation, the agreement to consolidate or the articles of consolidation contemplates the articles of incorporation of the newly formed corporation. It should set forth matters required by statute to be stated in articles of incorporation. In the case of a merger, the agreement should state any matters as to which the articles of incorporation of the surviving corporation are to be amended. However, in a merger, separate procedures are required to carry out that amendment. In each case, the agreement should set forth the terms and conditions of the union and the mode of carrying it into effect, as well as the basis of converting the shares of the constituent corporations into shares of the consolidated or surviving corporation. Under the Delaware statute, once the agreement has been approved by the directors and officers, it is to be executed and filed publicly.[122] The Model Business Corporation Act requires the filing of "articles of merger or share exchange" with the secretary of state, which must include the articles of incorporation or any amendments thereto.[123] This document sets forth specific information regarding the shareholders' approval of the combination. The merger becomes effective on the effective date specified in the filed articles of merger or exchange.[124] In some states, the plan of merger itself is filed.[125] In

---

[120] *See* SEC Report on Reorganization Committees Part VII 329, 376, 388, 397, 411, 530–536 (1938); Comment, 45 Yale L.J. 105, 113–114 (1935).

[121] *See, e.g.,* Model Bus. Corp. Act §§ 6.21(f), 11.04(g) (2016).

[122] Del. Code Ann. tit. 8, § 251(c) (2001).

[123] Model Bus. Corp. Act § 11.06 (2016); former Model Bus. Corp. Act § 74 (1969).

[124] Model Bus. Corp. Act § 11.06(d) (2016).

[125] Cal. Corp. Code § 1103 (West Supp. 2009); Del. Code Ann. tit. 8, § 251(c) (2001); Kan. Stat. Ann. § 17–6704(d) (2001).

some states a "certificate of merger" is filed with the proper state and/or county officials.[126]

[4] Distributions to Shareholders

Statutes commonly provide that the plan of merger submitted to the shareholders for approval must set forth the manner and basis for converting shares of each constituent corporation into shares of the surviving corporation's shares, the shares of a third corporation, or cash or other property.[127]

§ 22.12 "Short-Form" Mergers

Most states now provide for a simplified procedure in mergers of certain subsidiaries into the parent corporation or vice versa, or into another subsidiary.[128] Since the procedure is less complex than the normal statutory merger, such transactions are referred to as "short-form" mergers. Under these short-form merger statutes, no vote is required by the shareholders of either the surviving parent or the absorbed subsidiary, and the approval of the board of directors of the subsidiary is not required.[129] However, if the parent corporation is merged into the subsidiary, a vote of the parent shareholders will be required.[130] A significant result of the short-form procedure is the denial of dissenters' rights to the shareholders of the surviving parent, although such rights are given to the shareholders of the merged subsidiary.[131] Though the subsidiary's shareholders do not have an opportunity to dissent in a short-form merger, their avenue for appraisal is to give notice of their intent to seek appraisal after receiving notice of the parent's board's approval of the acquisition. In Delaware, California, and those states that have adopted the Model Business Corporation Act, the short-form merger is available for subsidiaries where 90 percent of the outstanding shares of each class are owned by the parent.[132] Some states impose a greater ownership requirement, although most have now adopted the 90 percent rule.[133]

The short-form merger can be the final step in a freeze-out or a going-private transaction, and the procedure has been condemned by some as not sufficiently protecting minority shareholders.[134] Another view is that the short-form merger statute avoids the hollow ritual of a 90-percent-plus owner convening a meeting to approve its decision to acquire the subsidiary; although the minority shareholders are disenfranchised, they still have their right to exit through the appraisal remedy.[135] And

---

[126] *E.g.*, Mass. Gen. Laws Ann. ch. 156D, § 11.06(d) (LexisNexis Supp. 2009); N.C. Gen. Stat. Ann. § 55–11–05 (Supp. 2001); 15 Pa. Stat. §§ 1926, 1927 (1995).

[127] *See* Auserehl v. Jamaica Builders Supply Corp., 404 N.Y.S.2d 421 (App. Div. 1978) (no violation for failure to refer to manner in which ten shares in acquiring corporation are to be converted into same number of shares in surviving corporation).

[128] *See* former Model Bus. Corp. Act § 75 (1969); Model Bus. Corp. Act § 11.05 (2016); Comment, The Short Merger Statute, 32 U. Chi. L. Rev. 596 (1965).

[129] Cal. Corp. Code § 1110 (West Supp. 2009); Del. Code Ann. tit. 8, § 253 (2001).

[130] *See* Model Bus. Corp. Act § 11.05 (2016). *But see* Del. Code Ann. tit. 8, § 253(a) (2001).

[131] Del. Code Ann. tit. 8, § 253(d) (2001); former Model Bus. Corp. Act § 80(c) (1969); Model Bus. Corp. Act § 13.02(a)(1) (2016).

[132] Cal. Corp. Code § 1110(b) (West Supp. 2009); Del. Code Ann. tit. 8, § 253 (2001); Model Bus. Corp. Act § 11.05 (2016); former Model Bus. Corp. Act § 75 (1969).

[133] N.Y. Bus. Corp. Law § 905 (McKinney 2003), (formerly 95%, now 90%); Wis. Stat. Ann. § 180.1104 (West Supp. 2009) (formerly 100%, now 90%).

[134] *See, infra* § 23.3.

[135] *See* Teschner v. Chicago Title & Trust Co., 322 N.E.2d 54 (Ill. 1974).

any business purpose required for ridding the organization of its minority shareholders is easily established.[136] The subsidiary's minority shareholders need not be given an opportunity to receive any interest in the surviving corporation.[137] Instead, they may be forced to accept cash payment as determined by the buy-out terms of a merger plan or, if they dissent, as determined by the statutory appraisal process.

§ 22.13 Triangular Mergers and Share Exchanges

[1] Triangular and Reverse Triangular Mergers

Generally speaking, there have been three traditional forms of corporate combinations: (1) merger or consolidation, (2) purchase or sale of assets, and (3) acquisition of the stock of another corporation, any of which may be entered into on a nontaxable basis. An ingenious variation that may also take advantage of the federal tax laws is the three-party or triangular merger. There are three principal reasons for utilizing the triangular merger: (1) to avoid the automatic assumption of liabilities,[138] which can be particularly desirable when acquiring a high-risk enterprise;[139] (2) to avoid a vote by the acquiring parent corporation's shareholders and their attendant appraisal rights; and (3) to continue the existence of the acquired corporation as a subsidiary of the parent acquiring corporation.[140] The triangular merger also avoids several disadvantages of a purchase of assets[141] and a straight stock acquisition of another company.[142]

Straight Triangular Merger

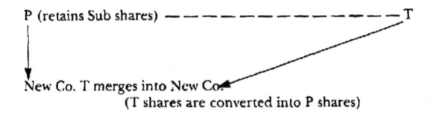

P (retains Sub shares) — — — — — — — — — — — T

New Co. T merges into New Co.
(T shares are converted into P shares)

---

[136] *See* Cross v. Communication Channels, Inc., 456 N.Y.S.2d 971 (Sup. Ct. 1982) (avoids annual meetings, eliminates conflicts of interest involving inter-company transactions, and establishes a uniform set of goals).

[137] Stauffer v. Standard Brands, Inc., 187 A.2d 78 (Del.Supr. 1962).

[138] *See* In re Beck Indus., 479 F.2d 410 (2d Cir. 1973).

[139] Charles Michael Ginnings & Raymond M. Jones, Triangular Mergers in Texas, 12 Houston L. Rev. 307 (1975).

[140] Among the possible advantages of a continued existence are the opportunity to maintain ongoing agreements with prior creditors and the ability to retain existing labor contracts.

[141] Such advantages include (1) greater flexibility in the consideration to be paid without jeopardizing tax-free status because a qualifying purchase of assets must be solely for voting stock, I.R.C. § 368(a)(1)(C) (2009); (2) avoidance of transfer-of-title problems; (3) there is no need to liquidate as a second step and the acquired corporation may remain in existence if desired; (4) the avoidance of a shareholder vote in those states requiring such for a purchase of assets.

[142] (1) There is greater freedom in the consideration for tax-free acquisitions; (2) the acquiring company is assured of complete control; (3) there is no need to worry about the various tender offer provisions of state and federal securities laws. However, with a triangular merger the shareholders of the acquired company will be given dissenters' rights, but this is equally true of clean-up mergers that frequently follow tender offers.

In the straight triangular merger, the acquiring corporation forms a subsidiary[143] for the purpose of merging with the target. A merger then occurs between the subsidiary and the target. Although standard merger law generally requires a vote of each merging corporation's shareholders, this is not a problem in the triangular merger because the subsidiary's shares are held exclusively by its parent (Acquiring Corporation), whose board of directors votes those shares. When Target merges into Subsidiary, Target's shareholders receive the stock of Acquiring Corporation. This can be accomplished by having capitalized Subsidiary with the parent's stock in exchange for the Subsidiary's shares. Alternatively, the stock can be issued directly by Acquiring Corporation to Target's shareholders. One possible pitfall is that the transactions must be structured to avoid the claim that the parent's shares have been issued for invalid consideration. Statutes in most states now authorize the use of shares of another corporation as consideration for mergers. Since the parent is not a party to the merger no parent shareholder vote is required, assuming that there had already been authorized in the charter sufficient shares to be issued pursuant to the merger plan, because directors have the power to issue previously authorized shares. As a bona fide parent-subsidiary structure, the subsidiary, not the parent, assumes the liabilities of the merged target company.

After the transaction described in the preceding paragraph, Acquiring Corporation owns 100 percent of Subsidiary, and Subsidiary has all the assets and liabilities of Target. If the parent corporation does not wish to continue Subsidiary's existence, it can use the short-form merger provision to merge Subsidiary into itself. In so structuring the transaction, the parent corporation's shareholders never have an opportunity to vote on its acquisition of Target. Thus the triangular merger is a straightforward mechanism to avoid the acquiring corporation's shareholders having a direct vote, and, for that matter, an appraisal remedy, in an acquisition of another company.

Reverse Triangular Merger

A variation on the above procedure is the reverse triangular merger. In the reverse transaction, Subsidiary is merged with Target, so Target survives and becomes a subsidiary of the original parent. The advantage to the reverse method is that it allows the acquired company to continue to exist, unlike in a traditional two-party merger or consolidation. The continued existence of the target avoids the necessity of negotiating new labor contracts and making formal transfers of the target's property.[144] Additionally, the target's continued existence may be required by the terms of outstanding bonds or

---

[143] The subsidiary may also be referred to as a "phantom corporation," which has led to the alternative appellation "phantom merger." *See, e.g.,* Marcou v. Federal Trust Co., 268 A.2d 629 (Me. 1970).

[144] *Cf.* PPG Indus. v. Guardian Indus. Corp., 597 F.2d 1090 (6th Cir.), *cert. denied,* 444 U.S. 930 (1979) (surviving company could not avoid patent infringement under license granted to acquired company that permitted "transfers" only by consent).

other types of agreements it has with creditors. The triangular and reverse triangular methods of combination are not limited to mergers; they can also be used for a purchase-of-assets acquisition.

[2] Statutory Share Exchange

It sometimes is desirable to structure an acquisition so that the acquired company continues as a separate, albeit wholly-owned, subsidiary of the acquiring company or a holding company, rather than ceasing to exist. Ideally suited for this objective is the "share exchange," a procedure now authorized in numerous states that have patterned their own enactments after the Model Business Corporation Act.[145] Following board of director and shareholder approval by each corporation, the shares of the acquired corporation are exchanged for cash or stock of the acquiring corporation or a third corporation. The agreement between the corporations can provide that only designated classes of stock of the acquired company will be exchanged, so that following a share exchange some classes of the acquired corporation are unaffected. In any case, following the share exchange, all the shares of one or more classes of stock are acquired by the acquiring corporation, and the existence of the acquired corporation continues.

§ 22.14 Rights of Creditors of Constituent Companies

Absent contractual provisions to the contrary, the creditors of a corporation cannot prevent its consolidation or merger with another corporation even if the new debtor corporation is not as satisfactory to them as the old.[146] Accordingly, it is not uncommon to find express restrictions, such as consent requirements, in credit agreements as well as in debt indentures and preferred-share contracts.[147] In general, the only recourse of the creditors of the constituent corporations is to sue the united corporation directly or to pursue the assets of the constituents into the hands of the new corporation under a theory of fraudulent conveyance.[148]

§ 22.15 Leveraged Buyouts as Fraudulent Conveyances

Fraudulent conveyance provisions trace their roots to the sixteenth century. Their proscriptions remain nearly as simple today as they were then, whether they appear in the state's version of the Uniform Fraudulent Conveyance Act,[149] the Uniform Fraudulent Transfer Act,[150] or the Bankruptcy Act's own version of this avoidance provision.[151] It is in their simplicity that these provisions raise highly troubling questions in the complex leveraged buyout (LBO) transaction.[152]

---

[145] *See* Model Bus. Corp. Act § 11.03 (2016).

[146] Western Air Lines, Inc. v. Allegheny Airlines, Inc., 313 A.2d 145, 153 (Del. Ch. 1973).

[147] Similarly, noncompliance with statutory requirements for shareholder approval of a sale of assets outside the ordinary course of business is not a defect creditors can raise. *See* Phillips Petroleum Co. v. Rock Creek Mining Co., 449 F.2d 664 (9th Cir. 1971); McDermott v. Bear Film Co., 33 Cal.Rptr. 486 (Ct. App. 1963).

[148] *See, e.g.,* Cameron v. United Traction Co., 73 N.Y.S. 981 (App. Div. 1902); Del. Code Ann. tit. 8, § 259(a) (2001); N.Y. Bus. Corp. Law § 906(b)(3) (McKinney 2003); former Model Bus. Corp. Act § 76(e) (1969); Model Bus. Corp. Act § 11.07(a)(4) (2016).

[149] 7A U.L.A. 427 (1985).

[150] 7A U.L.A. 639 (1985).

[151] 11 U.S.C. § 548 (2000).

[152] For the view that public policy should exclude LBOs from fraudulent conveyance laws, *see* Douglas G. Baird & Thomas H. Jackson, Fraudulent Conveyance Law and Its Proper Domain, 38 Vand. L. Rev. 829 (1985).

Leveraged buyouts can take many forms. A most common form involves creating a thinly capitalized corporation to purchase the corporation that is to be acquired. The funds for the purchase are borrowed by the newly formed corporation, usually through bridge loans from a syndicate of financial institutions. The loan's proceeds are used to purchase the shares of the acquired corporation. Upon the merger of the acquired corporation and the newly formed corporation, the acquired corporation's assets can be used to satisfy the loan. Thereafter the two corporations are combined, permanent financing is arranged, and the earnings and assets of the acquired corporation are used to meet these financial obligations. It is when all the various steps are collapsed together that the issue of the acquisition constituting a fraudulent conveyance arises.[153] In considering a collapse of the various steps of the LBO, courts frequently emphasize the interdependence of the various steps.[154]

§ 22.16 Accounting for Corporate Combinations

For the longest time, there were two alternative methods of accounting for corporate mergers and other forms of combination: the purchase method and the "pooling-of-interest" approach.[155] As discussed more fully below, the purchase method requires a revaluation of the acquired company's assets based on the purchase price in connection with the merger. In contrast, the pooling method simply consolidated the existing balance sheets of the constituent companies.

In 1999, the Federal Accounting Standards Board voted unanimously to abandon the use of the pooling method of accounting for corporate mergers.[156] FASB chairman Jenkins explained that "the purchase method of accounting gives investors a better idea of the initial cost of a transaction and the investment's performance over time than does the pooling-of-interest method."[157] There then ensued many months of intense lobbying to deflect the FASB from its position or to prevent an absolute bar to this popular method for accounting for company acquisitions. All such efforts were to no avail as the FASB ultimately adopted FASB Statement 141 that bars the pooling method of accounting for acquisitions completed after June 30, 2001.[158]

Statement of Financial Accounting Standard No. 141 was revised in 2007, tightening several aspects, most notably emphasizing the central role of identifying the "identifiable assets" acquired in a business combination, embracing methods for their fair valuation, and imposing a requirement to "re-measure" any assets given as consideration by the acquirer in the business combination including any contingent consideration as of the acquisition date. While the acquirer may—under the 2007 revision—adjust the amounts recorded by using new information acquired up to one year after the acquisition date, this adjustment is limited to reflect new information only to the extent it bears on facts and circumstances that existed as of the acquisition date.

---

[153] *See* Raymond J. Blackwood, Applying Fraudulent Conveyance Law to Leveraged Buyouts, 42 Duke L.J. 340 (1992).

[154] *See* Moody v. Security Pac. Bus. Credit, Inc., 127 B.R. 958 (W.D. Pa. 1991).

[155] *See generally* William W. Bratton Corporate Finance: Cases and Materials Appendix A–10–A–36 (6th ed. 2008).

[156] *See* FASB to Bar Pooling Method for Mergers; Trade Groups Unhappy, 31 Sec. Reg. & L. Rep. (BNA) 543 (April 23, 1999).

[157] FASB to Bar Pooling Method for Mergers; Trade Groups Unhappy, 31 Sec. Reg. & L. Rep. (BNA) 543 (April 23, 1999).

[158] Pooling-of-interest accounting, however, can still be used for combinations of companies that are under the common control.

Thus, post acquisition events cannot be the basis to adjust figures. The most controversial portion of the 2007 revision of SFAS No. 141 is its requirement, contrary to the treatment in the preparation of the company's tax return, that acquisition-related costs (*e.g.*, advisory, accounting, valuation, legal) shall be accounted for as expenses in the period in which the costs are incurred and the related services are received. There is an exception to this expensing requirement for costs incurred in connection with the issuance of securities.

Commencing with fiscal years that begin after December 15, 2001, FASB Statement No. 142 requires that goodwill and other tangible assets that appear on the balance sheet must be evaluated annually pursuant to see if their carrying value is impaired. The impairment assessment for goodwill is a two-step process. First, the fair value of the reporting unit for which the goodwill is associated must be determined. This figure is compared to the carrying amount (including goodwill) for that reporting unit on the parent's books. If the overall value of the reporting unit equals or exceeds the carrying amount, there is no impairment. However, if the carrying amount exceeds the fair value so determined, the second step must be taken. This requires that the "implied fair value" of the goodwill must be ascertained and compared with its carrying amount. The implied fair value of goodwill is determined by allocating the aggregate fair value of the reporting unit among its assets with the residual of any unallocated amount being attributed to its goodwill. The amount, if any, that the implied fair value of goodwill that is so determined is less than its carrying amount is the amount of impairment that must then be expenses on the company's financial statements.

In broad overview, under the "purchase method" the acquired companies' assets are listed at their fair market value as determined by the consideration paid by the acquiring company. Because the purchase price will reflect the going-concern value rather than the liquidation or replacement value of the assets, under the purchase method it is necessary to list goodwill as an asset of the surviving corporation. Overvaluation of goodwill can give rise to fraud claims against directors.[159] Under generally accepted accounting practices (GAAP) goodwill must be amortized so that it is charged to earnings on a periodic basis.[160] Under the pooling-of-interests method of accounting, the assets of the constituent companies are pooled and are listed at their pre-combination book values; the constituents' retained earnings are similarly combined.

PART C.   REMEDIES OF DISSENTING SHAREHOLDERS

§ 22.17 Alternative Remedies of Dissenting Shareholders

Shareholders in constituent corporations are put to a statutory election in merger and consolidation proceedings, and sometimes asset sales and recapitalizations, to take the securities specified in the agreement or withdraw from the enterprise and obtain payment in money for the appraised value of their shares by following the strict statutory appraisal procedure.[161] Dissenters cannot simply retain the old securities and assert any rights under them; if they fail to demand appraisal they are bound by the lawful action

---

[159] *See, e.g.*, Williams v. Bartell, 225 N.Y.S.2d 351 (App. Div. 1962) (Bergan, J. dissenting) (amount of goodwill lowered as a result of SEC letter of consent).

[160] *See* APB Opinion No. 17 (1970).

[161] Porges v. Vadsco Sales Corp., 32 A.2d 148, 1150 (Del. Ch. 1943).

of the majority, just as if they had consented to the action taken.[162] In recent years, however, the exclusivity of statutory dissenters' rights has been subject to some isolated erosion, but generally the appraisal remedy displaces other state law remedies, discussed next, except in the case of fraud or illegality.[163] Denial or loss of statutory dissenters' rights is considered to be an injury to the shareholders' property (*i.e.*, their stock) for statute of limitations purposes.[164]

[1] Injunction

Prior to the consummation of a merger, consolidation, or sale of assets, a dissenting shareholder may sue to enjoin its completion either on the ground of lack of authority or compliance with a statute or on the ground of fraud or abuse of power.[165] Similarly, an injunction will lie to prevent violations of the securities laws' disclosure provisions.[166] Dissenting shareholders may lose their right to equitable relief by injunction by laches— that is, by failing to bring suit with the utmost promptitude before the rights of third persons have intervened.[167] Another limitation on injunctive relief is the maxim that equity is not available if an adequate remedy at law exists.[168]

[2] Rescission

Suits are sometimes brought for rescission of a completed merger or consolidation or sale of assets. Theoretically such a transaction may be voidable on the ground that it is unauthorized or procured by fraud or abuse of power. But as a practical matter the only relief granted in such suits is an award of pecuniary compensation or a cash settlement to redress the injury to the dissenting shareholder for loss of his investment. This is on the ground that the task of readjusting the rights and interests of the constituent corporations, the creditors, and perhaps the thousands of shareholders and investors concerned is so insurmountable as to make any attempt to do so, upon a rescission, utterly fantastic.[169] As an early Alabama court reasoned, "It would be a painful travesty upon justice if a court of equity, in order to conserve the rights of a few stockholders in one of the parent companies, should destroy the property rights of innocent stockholders in the new company."[170] A suit for rescission, therefore, is usually in practical effect treated as simply a suit for the value of the shareholder's interest as fixed by a judicial, non-statutory appraisal.[171]

---

[162] National Supply Co. v. Leland Stanford Jr. Univ., 134 F.2d 689 (9th Cir. 1943), *cert. denied*, 320 U.S. 773 (1943).

[163] Umstead v. Durham Hosiery Mills, Inc., 578 F.Supp. 342 (M.D.N.C. 1984).

[164] Willard v. Moneta Bldg. Supply, Inc., 551 S.E.2d 596, 599–600 (Va. 2001).

[165] *E.g.*, Under some recent cases the proposed combination may be enjoined on the basis of gross unfairness. *E.g.*, Bryan v. Brock & Blevins Co., Inc., 490 F.2d 563 (5th Cir. 1974); Young v. Valhi, Inc., 382 A.2d 1372 (Del. Ch. 1978).

[166] Bryan v. Brock & Blevins Co., 343 F.Supp. 1062 (N.D. Ga. 1972), *aff'd on other grounds*, 490 F.2d 563 (5th Cir.), *cert. denied*, 419 U.S. 844 (1974).

[167] Federal United Corp. v. Havender, 11 A.2d 331 (Del. 1940).

[168] Dan B. Dobbs, Law of Remedies § 2.5 (2d ed. 1993).

[169] McMillan v. Intercargo Corp., 768 A.2d 492, 500 (Del. Ch. 2000) (completed merger cannot be unwound once "the metaphorical merger eggs have been scrambled").

[170] Alabama Fidelity Mortgage & Bond Co. v. Dubberly, 73 So. 911, 915 (Ala. 1916).

[171] *See, e.g.*, Harman v. Masoneilan Int'l, Inc., 418 A.2d 1004 (Del. Ch. 1980).

[3] Individual Shareholder Action for Damages

Where, in voting to dissolve, merge, consolidate, or sell substantially all corporate assets, the majority have exceeded their lawful powers, have failed to comply with statutory conditions, or have been guilty of abuse of powers, objecting shareholders frequently were allowed to sue and recover for the value of their holdings on the theory that their equitable interest in the corporation had been misappropriated, "converted" or destroyed by the wrongful or inequitable action of the corporation.[172] Because the purchase, merger, or transfer under such circumstances is illegal or wrongful, the purchaser or successor may be held personally accountable to the dissenting shareholder for the value of the shares or of his proportional interest either on the ground of participation therein or on the ground that the successor is subject to the liabilities of the predecessor.[173] An individual shareholder's direct right of action to recover for the destruction of the value of his shares, often explained on the artificial theory of conversion, is an exception to the general rule that a shareholder cannot recover damages payable to himself personally for what is primarily a wrong done against the corporation in the absence of some wrong peculiar to him.[174]

[4] Direct Actions Under the Securities Laws

Under SEC Rule 10b–5 defrauded purchasers or sellers may sue for damages resulting from misrepresentation or nondisclosure that resulted in their being deceived.[175] Similarly, a business combination consummated through a misleading proxy statement gives rise to individual recoveries under Rule 14a–9 of the Exchange Act, and various express liabilities exist for the purchaser of new securities that may be issued pursuant to the place of merger, consolidation, or sale of assets.[176]

[5] Statutory Dissenters' Rights

The foregoing remedies for dissenting shareholders are available through the courts. These remedies are supplemented and in many cases replaced by the statutory appraisal remedy. As discussed in the sections that follow, statutory appraisal rights have been adopted in every state although they vary in scope, application, and the extent to which they are the exclusive remedy available to dissenting shareholders.

[6] Quasi-Appraisal

The quasi-appraisal proceeding is correctly seen not as a cause of action but rather as a measure of damages for a breach of fiduciary duty. The resulting damage award arises in the successful prosecution of breach of fiduciary duty in a transaction that appraisal existed, but due to the breach, for example a failure of disclosure, the

---

[172] Parnes v. Bally Entertainment Corp., 722 A.2d 1243, 1245 (Del. 1999) (permitting direct suit by shareholder challenging merger).

[173] American Seating Co. v. Bullard, 290 F. 896, 900 (6th Cir. 1923).

[174] 13 Comment, 23 Cal. L. Rev. 174, 178–179 (1935).

[175] 17 C.F.R. § 240.10b–5 (2002). *See* §§ 12.9 to 12.12.

[176] Securities Act 1933, §§ 11, 12(a)(1), 12(a)(2), 15 U.S.C. §§ 77k, 781(a)(1), 781(a)(2) (2000).

shareholder did not follow the steps necessary to obtain statutory appraisal.[177] The remedy is however equitable and thus subject to equitable defenses such as laches.[178]

§ 22.18 The Statutory Appraisal Remedy

Every state has adopted "appraisal" statutes, which give dissenting shareholders a right to demand payment of the fair value of their shares.[179] The statutes vary broadly in their coverage. The right is given in case of certain fundamental changes, such as merger or consolidation, and often in case of sale of the entire assets, and sometimes in case of amendments that change the rights of a certain class of outstanding shares and some other changes.[180] There is a widely adopted but debatable exception for a corporation whose shares are publicly traded.[181]

The expansion of commerce in the nineteenth century created a need for bigger and more complex corporations. The rule of unanimity impeded corporate growth because any shareholder could prevent a corporate combination if he did not agree. Because of the importance of contract and property rights, courts held grave doubts regarding the constitutionality of permitting corporate actions over the protest of any single shareholder. It is from these concerns that the appraisal remedy was born.[182]

In 1858, Pennsylvania authorized the merger of two railroads, which a dissenting shareholder sought to enjoin. In the ensuing case, *Lauman v. Lebanon Valley Railroad*,[183] the court, fearing that the merger would be unconstitutional if the shareholder was forced to accept shares in another corporation, held that the Pennsylvania legislature must have meant to provide dissenters with an appraisal remedy. The court enjoined the merger but only until security was given for the appraised value of the plaintiff's shares. There appears to be no basis for the court inferring the legislature intended to provide such relief to dissenters. The Pennsylvania legislature took the court's hint and passed the first appraisal statute (limited albeit to railroads), and the corporate landscape has never been the same since.

The justification for the appraisal remedy has other foundations today. The principle is well ingrained that the majority may combine their corporation with another and alter existing rights among shareholders without fear of serious constitutional challenge. At the same time, it is rarely the remedy of other than the "wine and cheese" crowd, for seldom is appraisal sought by investors whose holdings are less than $100,000,

---

[177] *See*, In re Orchard Enters., Inc. Shareholder Litig., 88 A.3d 1, 43–50 (Del.Ch. 2014).

[178] *See e.g.*, Houseman v. Sagerman, 2015 WL 7307323 (Del. Ch. Nov. 19, 2015)(suit barred due to 27-month delay in filing action which delay rendered defendants unable to resort to D&O coverage to defend).

[179] *See generally* Peter V. Letsou, The Role of Appraisal in; Bayless Manning, The Shareholder's Appraisal Remedy: An Essay for Frank Coker, 72 Yale L.J. 223 (1962).

See also Proposed Changes in the Model Business Corporation Act—Appraisal Rights, 54 Bus. Law. 209 (1998).

[180] Peters Corp. v. New Mexico Banquest Investors Corp., 188 P.3d 1185 (N.M. 2008) (appraisal protects minority who object to fundamental corporate change which was found in case flowing from the company's redemption of the substantial holdings of one of its stockholders).

[181] *See, e.g.*, Del. Code Ann. tit. 8, § 262(b)(1) (2001). *See* Note, A Reconsideration of the Stock Market Exception to the Dissenting Shareholder's Right of Appraisal, 74 Mich. L. Rev. 1023 (1976).

[182] *See generally* Elliott Weiss, The Law of Take Out Mergers: A Historical Perspective, 56 N.Y.U. L. Rev. 624, 624–630 (1981).

[183] Lauman v. Lebanon Valley Railroad, 30 Pa. 42 (1858).

and few appraisal proceedings in fact occur.[184] The more visible benefit of appraisal is that it does provide a safety valve through which dissenters' unhappiness can be ventilated without interrupting the acquisition. A more ethereal, but no less important, rationale is that the existence of an appraisal remedy complements other monitoring mechanisms for self-dealing or ineptitude on the part of the board of directors.[185] Certainly the directors will be less sanguine about a proposal they submit to the shareholders for approval if they believe there is an efficient mechanism for shareholders to realize an alternatively determined value for their shares than that being recommended by the board of directors.[186] So viewed, an important consideration is whether the procedures for exercising the appraisal remedy as well as the substantive guidelines for determining fair value are indeed efficient and have the right social balance.[187]

It is important to consider the policy and purpose of the statutory remedy. As seen above, the impetus for creating the appraisal remedy was to remove possible doubt about the constitutionality of statutes authorizing fundamental changes as to existing corporations and the contract rights of shareholders.[188] In part, the purpose of these provisions has been to give dissenters a simple and direct remedy not only where there is a harmful change in the share contract but also where they simply do not desire to accept shares in a different corporation or shares different from those they purchased. As Professor Lattin put it, the purpose has been "[t]o placate the dissenting minority and, at the same time, to facilitate the carrying out of changes of a desirable and extreme sort."[189]

While in theory the ostensible purpose of the statutory appraisal remedy is to protect the minority and afford them a way out in case of fundamental changes, in reality it appears that the purpose is even more to aid and protect the majority. The proceeding by dissenting shareholders for the appraisal of their shares does not delay or prevent the completion of the consolidation, merger, sale of assets for securities, or recapitalization by amendment; the change takes place subject to a collateral proceeding to value the shares of the dissenting shareholders. However, appraisal proceedings do burden the

---

[184] *See* Joel Seligman, Reappraising the Appraisal Remedy, 52 Geo. Wash. L. Rev. 829, 829 n.3, 830 n.5 (1984). *See also,* Jiang, Li, Mei & Thomas, Reforming the Delaware Appraisal Statute to Address Appraisal Arbitrage: Will It Be Successful, 59 J.L.& Econ. 697 (2016)(appraisal arose in about 14 percent of transactions involving Delaware corporations during 2000–2014 and nearly one-third of the claimants holdings were below $1 million); Korsmo & Myers, The Structure of Stockholder Litigation: When do the Merits Matter?, 75 Ohio St. L. J. 829, 878–882 (2014)(finding appraisal garnered a 19.5 percent return over the merger consideration).

[185] *See generally* Hideki Kanda & Saul Levmore, The Appraisal Remedy and the Goals of Corporate Law, 32 UCLA L. Rev. 429 (1985).

[186] *But see* Paul G. Mahoney & Mark Weinstein, The Appraisal Remedy and Merger Premiums, Am. L. & Econ. Rev. 239, 272 (1999) (in examination of 1,350 mergers involving public companies found that the existence or non-existence of appraisal remedy had no statistically significant impact on shareholder returns even in acquisitions involving self-interested managers; thus, they conclude, "The potential for self-dealing . . . is not a sufficient condition for appraisal to be valuable to public shareholders.").

[187] Thus, among the objectives of the recently completed American Law Institute project was to reduce the procedural entanglements of seeking appraisal, allowing common counsel to be used in those proceedings, and providing a means for earlier payment of dissenters while not disturbing the strong presumption of propriety in non-self-dealing situations. *See* ALI Principles of Corporate Governance: Analysis and Recommendations §§ 7.21 to 7.25 (1994).

[188] *See* Lauman v. Lebanon Valley R.R., 30 Pa. 42 (1858).

[189] Norman D. Lattin, Remedies of Dissenting Stockholders Under Appraisal Statutes, 45 Harv. L. Rev. 233, 237 (1931).

constituent corporations, who may be more inclined to offer a generous exchange in an effort to avoid exercise of the appraisal remedy.

Those who have drafted and sponsored many of these statutes have been careful to avoid possible undue interference and obstruction by minority shareholders acting in bad faith and thus have made as little concession to the dissenters as possible.[190] Those who wish to avail themselves of the statutory remedy must act with exceeding quickness in order to meet the stringent conditions precedent. Simply stated, most appraisal statutes contain multiple steps, each with a specific and short time period within which dissenters must comply to preserve and perfect their right of appraisal.[191] For example, under the Model Business Corporation Act, if a shareholder vote is required for the fundamental change, the shareholders must give written notice of their intent to dissent prior to the vote and then must refrain from voting in favor of the plan.[192] After the vote the dissenting shareholders will be informed of the procedures to be followed and must again make a written demand for payment of the fair value of their shares. The statutes vary greatly on the technical procedures to be followed. Under the Delaware Act, after the vote the corporation must within 10 days give notice of the right to dissent, and thereafter the shareholders have 20 days within which they must make a written demand.[193] Under the Model Business Corporation Act there is no time limit on the corporation's post-approval notice. The shareholders must be given at least 30 days.[194]

Failure to conform to the multiple statutory requirements to obtain appraisal leads to the remedy being lost.[195] On the other hand, there appears no reason why a stockholder who has made a timely request for appraisal can reverse course and opt to receive what was offered in the merger, if the change is communicated within the period in which notice of intent to pursue appraisal was to occur.[196]

In 2016 Delaware amended its appraisal statute so that the Chancery Court can dismiss a petition if the total amount of shares represented do not exceed one percent of the outstanding class or the value of the consideration provided in the transaction for those shares is less than $1 million.[197]

In most states, shares are not qualified for appraisal if they have voted in favor of the transaction.[198] Because most statutes do not require, as was once the case, that the

---

[190] For cases strictly applying the procedural requirements dissenters must pursue, *see* Meadows v. Bicrodyne Corp., 573 F.Supp. 1030 (N.D. Cal. 1983) (notice of short-form merger directed to record address, although incorrect, was proper notice, so shareholder could not resurrect right to dissent for lack of proper notice).

[191] Companies may be held to have waived technical failures of dissenting stockholders by continuing to deal with the dissenter. *See, e.g.,* VSI Enterprises, Inc. v. Edwards, 518 S.E.2d 765 (Ga. App. Ct. 1999).

[192] Model Bus. Corp. Act § 13.21 (1984); former Model Bus. Corp. Act § 81(c) (1969). An excellent review of the Revised Model Business Corporation Act appears in Harry F. Johnson & Paul Bartlett, Jr., Is a Fistful of Dollars the Answer? A Critical Look at Dissenters' Rights Under the Revised Model Business Corporation Act, 12 J.L. & Com. 211 (1993).

[193] Del. Code Ann. tit. 8, § 262(d)(2) (2001).

[194] Model Bus. Corp. Act § 13.21(a) (2016); former Model Bus. Corp. Act §§ 81(b), 81(c) (1969).

[195] Tiscornia v. Natural Resources USA Corp., 2012 WL 5874448 (D. Utah 2012)(stockholder failed to submit alternative value for shares within statutory 30 days of company's payment and, hence, waived right of appraisal).

[196] *See* Roam-Tel Partners v. AT&T Mobility Wireless Operations Holdings, Inc., 2010 Del. Ch. LEXIS 247 (Del. Ch. 2010).

[197] Del. Code Ann. tit. 8 § 262(g), as amended in 2016.

[198] Del. Code Ann. tit. 8, § 262(b) (2001). *See* In re Appraisal of Ancestry.com, Inc., 2015 Del. Ch. LEXIS 2 (Del. Ch. Jan. 5, 2015) (appraisal can be pursued without petitioner showing the shares were not voted in

shareholder actually vote against the combination, it is a misnomer to any longer refer to the appraisal remedy as the "dissenter's" remedy. In recent years there has been a substantial increase in Delaware appraisal actions as hedge funds capitalize on liberal provisions regarding standing to seek appraisal[199] and the relatively high rate of interest paid on appraised amounts. Such suits are generally referred to as "appraisal arbitrage" as appraisal is pursued with respect to shares purchased after the record date by a holder who never voted for the transaction but is pursuing appraisal on the affected shares.[200]

Recent cases that have made appraisal arbitrage less attractive were triggered by two 2017 Delaware Supreme Court decisions. In *DFC Global Corporation v. Muirfield Value Partners, L.P.*,[201] the Delaware Supreme Court declined to establish a presumption in favor of the negotiated deal price in an appraisal hearing. Nonetheless, Chief Justice Strine stated that the deal price should have received more weight because "economic principles suggest that the best evidence of fair value [is] the deal price, [if] it result[s] from an open process, informed by robust public information, and easy access to deeper, non-public information, in which many parties . . .had a chance to bid."[202] In *Dell, Inc. v. Magnetar Global Event Driven Master Fund Ltd*, the Delaware Supreme Court reaffirmed its decision not to establish a presumption in favor of the negotiated deal price in an appraisal hearing.[203]

Even though not establishing a presumption in favor the deal price the approach now taken by Delaware allows the companies to supports anchoring the appraised value in the deal price through facts supporting their argument that the transaction was the product of a process designed to secure a fair price. Factors such as the presence of competing bidders, the length of time accompanying the negotiations, the publicity surrounding the negotiations, the restrictions of any deal protection provisions, and the like are all relevant in determining whether the directors acted to pursue the best price.[204]

---

favor of the merger by the shares' previous holder); In re Appraisal of Transkaryotic Therapies, Inc., 2007 Del. Ch. LEXIS 57 (May 2, 2007)(so long as record holder can show that the number of shares it did not vote in favor of the merger is at least as many as those for which it sought appraisal the petitioner has met the requirement that the shares for which appraisal is sought were not voted in favor of the merger).

[199] In re Appraisal of Transkaryotic Therapies, Inc., 2007 Del. Ch. LEXIS 57 (May 2, 2007) (so long as record holder can show that the number of shares it did not vote in favor of the merger is at least as many as those for which it sought appraisal the petitioner has met the requirement that the shares for which appraisal is sought were not voted in favor of the merger).

[200] Minor Myers & Charles R. Korsmo, Appraisal Arbitrage And The Future Of Public Company M&A, 92 Wash. U. L. Rev. 1551 (2015) (empirical analysis of rise in appraisal actions and are targeted at transactions where merger price are vulnerable to review); George S. Geis, An Appraisal Puzzle, 105 Nw. U. L. Rev. 1635 (2011)(close analysis of the legal regime that enables appraisal arbitrage).

[201] DFC Global Corporation v. Muirfield Value Partners, L.P., 172 A.3d 346 (Del. 2017). *See* Dell, Inc. v. Magnetar Global Event Driven Master Fund Ltd., 177 A.3d 1, 21 (Del. 2017) (rejecting a presumption to favor the deal price).

[202] DFC Global Corporation v. Muirfield Value Partners, L.P., 172 A.3d 346, 349 (Del. 2017). *See* Dell, Inc. v. Magnetar Global Event Driven Master Fund Ltd., 177 A.3d 1, 21 (Del. 2017) (rejecting a presumption to favor the deal price).

[203] Dell, Inc. v. Magnetar Global Event Driven Master Fund Ltd, 177 A.3d 1, 21 (Del. 2017) (rejecting a presumption to favor the deal price).

[204] *See*, Lawrence A. Hamermesh & Michael L. Wachter, Finding the Right Balance in Appraisal Litigation: Deal Price, Deal Process, and Synergies, 73 Bus. Law. 961 (2018)(reasoning that the template for this inquiry is the "enhanced scrutiny" standard established in *Revlon, Inc. v. MacAndrews & Forbes Holdings, Inc.*, 506 A.2d 173 (Del. 1986)).

Lower appraisal values, however, remain likely under the Delaware Supreme Court's approach of not according the deal price a presumption of fair value. Chancery Court decisions illustrate this effect. For example, in *In re AOL Inc.*, Vice Chancellor Glasscock used his own discounted cash flow in attempt to correct for widely varying appraisal values as a result of three potential cash flow projections.[205]

A question similar to the role of deal price arises with respect to market price for the security being appraised. Just how much of a thumb on the appraised value scale should market price assume? In *Verition Partners Master Fund Ltd. v. Aruba Networks, Inc.*,[206] Vice Chancellor Laster expanded on the position taken in AOL. In his opinion, Vice Chancellor Laster used the unaffected market price to establish the fair market value because "the unaffected market price provides a direct indication of the value of the subject company based on its operative reality independent of the merger."[207] Vice Chancellor Laster indicated that the 2017 Delaware Supreme Court decisions represented a fundamental shift in appraisal methodology.[208] However, the Delaware Supreme Court reversed and rejected the Chancery Court's presumption in favor of the deal price.[209] The opinion noted:

> When a public company with a deep trading market is sold at a substantial premium to the pre-announcement price, after a process in which interested buyers all had a fair and viable opportunity to bid, the deal price is a strong indicator of fair value, as a matter of economic reality and theory.[210]

Statutes differ as to the status of dissenting shareholders after demand for payment. Under other statutes, the rights cease only after payment of the appraised price.[211]

Under the Model Business Corporation Act, a shareholder who has perfected his rights to appraisal loses all rights as a shareholder, unless he withdraws from the appraisal process.[212] The shareholder is thereafter entitled to be paid the amount the corporation believes is the fair value of his shares.[213] And the shareholder can continue to press his claim in a formal appraisal proceeding for any additional amounts above paid by the corporation that the shareholder argues is necessary to raise the total payment to the shares' fair value.[214] Both the shareholder and the corporation have obligations with respect to initiating formal appraisal proceedings under the Model Business Corporation Act. The shareholder must, among other requirements, demand

---

[205] In re AOL Inc., 2018 WL 1037450, *11 (Del. Ch. 2018) (finding the Management Projections were the best cash flow estimates because they were made in the regular course of business). *See also, e.g.*, In re of SWS Group, Inc., 2017 WL 2334852 (Del. Ch. 2017), summarily affirmed Merlin Partners, LP v. SWS Group, Inc, 181 A.3d 153 (Table) (Del. Feb. 23, 2018) (rejecting appraisal arbitrageur's proposed valuation).

[206] Verition Partners Master Fund Ltd. v. Aruba Networks, Inc., 2018 WL 2315943, *1 (Del. Ch. 2018), judgment entered, 2018 WL 3379909 (Del. Ch. 2018), *reversed* 2019 WL 1614026 (Del. 2019).

[207] *Id.*

[208] *Id.*

[209] Verition Partners Master Fund, Ltd. v. Aruba Networks, Inc., 210 A.3d 128 (Del. 2019).

[210] *Id.* The court concluded that the proper valuation was $19.10 a share; this amount was determined by working from the deal price of $24.67 per share and deducting the value of anticipated synergies that the companies priced into the merger.

[211] *See* Johnson v. C. Brigham Co., 136 A. 456 (Me. 1927) (under prior Maine statute requiring specific negative vote).

[212] Model Bus. Corp. Act § 13.23 (2016).

[213] Model Bus. Corp. Act § 13.24 (2016).

[214] Model Bus. Corp. Act § 13.26(a) (2016).

payment of his estimate of the shares' fair value within 30 days,[215] and the corporation must within 60 days of that demand initiate the proceeding or be obligated to pay the shareholder the full amount sought.[216]

In an appraisal proceeding, evidence of value must be taken and a record must be kept.[217] An appraiser's report must usually be filed with the clerk of court, and the parties may take exception to the report.[218] After a hearing as to the exceptions, argument on the report, and the consideration of evidence, the court will confirm, modify, or reject the report.[219]

The expenses of an appraisal proceeding are a factor of serious importance, as they involve appraisers' fees, attorneys' fees, and fees for expert accountants and witnesses before the appraisers. This may be an undue burden on the dissenter, but it may also allow a shareholder acting in bad faith to cause the corporations to spend substantial sums.[220] Only a few statutes make adequate provision for attorneys' fees and other expenses of the petitioner.[221]

§ 22.19   Scope of Statutory Appraisal Rights[222]

Though it is well recognized that dissenters' rights only arise in those transactions specifically proscribed in the statute,[223] courts sometimes invoke the remedy by analogy to the type of transactions covered by the statute. Thus, in *Moreley Brothers v. Clark*,[224] the court held a shareholder was entitled to appraisal when the corporation's issuance of new shares reduced the present stockholder's interest from 100 percent to 19.9 percent.[225] Correlatively, a transaction that formally is of the type specified in the state's appraisal statute substantively may not involve the type of change that appraisal was intended to apply. For example, a merger carried out to reincorporate under the laws of another state was held not to be within the type of merger transaction proscribed in the state appraisal statute.[226] Such a judicial gloss, though perhaps reaching the "right" result, creates a good deal of uncertainty when planning unorthodox transactions. A wise approach would be to apply appraisal statutes literally when considering the scope of this legislatively created remedy.

---

[215] Model Bus. Corp. Act § 13.26 (2016).

[216] Model Bus. Corp. Act § 13.30(a) (2016).

[217] Model Bus. Corp. Act § 13.30 (2016); former Model Bus. Corp. Act § 81(h) (1969).

[218] *See* Note, Rights of Dissenting Stockholders Pending Statutory Appraisal Proceedings, 21 Va. L. Rev. 825 (1935).

[219] *See* Francis I. duPont & Co. v. Universal City Studios, Inc., 312 A.2d 344 (Del. Ch. 1973), *aff'd*, 334 A.2d 216 (Del. 1975).

[220] *See* Dimmock v. Reichhold Chem., Inc., 360 N.E.2d 1079 (N.Y. 1977) (ten-year proceeding produced an increase in value of $13,000 after expenses of $50,000).

[221] *See, e.g.*, Hernando Bank v. Huff, 609 F.Supp. 1124 (N.D. Miss. 1985), *aff'd*, 796 F.2d 803 (5th Cir. 1986) (expense assigned to corporation because appraisal yielded significant increase in amount to be paid by corporation).

[222] Model Bus. Corp. Act § 13.02(a) (2016); former Model Bus. Corp. Act § 80(b)(2) (1969).

[223] *See* Valando v. Data Boutique, Ltd., 323 N.Y.S.2d 608 (Sup. Ct. 1971).

[224] Morley Brothers v. Clark, 361 N.W.2d 763 (Mich. Ct. App. 1984).

[225] *See also* Orchard v. Covelli, 590 F.Supp. 1548 (W.D. Pa. 1984) (statute not exclusive and will protect minority in close corporation from oppression).

[226] China Prod. of N. Am., Inc. v. Manewal, 850 P.2d 565 (Wash. Ct. App. 1993).

Serious gaps exist in the statutory protection for minority shareholders against fundamental corporate actions that may be prejudicial to their interests.[227] In some states, including Delaware, appraisal rights do not attach to sales of assets or charter amendments; thus this remedy is limited to mergers or consolidations.[228] In most states a corporation's sale of all or substantially all of its assets "not made in the usual and regular course of its business" triggers statutory dissenters' rights.[229] However, even with a sale of assets, dissenters' rights possibly can be avoided if some substantial asset—for example, a tract of real property—is left in the selling corporation.[230] Most statutes do not give dissenters' rights to shareholders of the purchaser of assets, and, subject to the infrequently applied de facto merger doctrine,[231] a transaction can thus be structured to avoid the statutory remedy.[232]

Appraisal rights extend to charter amendments under the Model Business Corporation Act.[233] There are no states in which dissolution per se triggers dissenters' rights,[234] although in some states a sale of all or substantially all assets in a dissolution proceeding will invoke the statutory right.[235] Under the Model Business Corporation Act, appraisal rights also apply to a planned exchange of shares to which the corporation is a party if the shareholder is entitled to vote on the exchange.[236]

Many states that have control-share anti-takeover provisions in their corporate statutes provide a remedy similar to the more traditional appraisal remedy. These provisions require a person making a "control share" acquisition to purchase the shares of any requesting shareholder. A "control-share acquisition" is variously defined but generally refers to one whose ownership interest reaches 20–25 percent and whose purchase has not been approved by the incumbent board of directors.[237]

The Corporate Governance Project of the American Law Institute contains sweeping recommendations as to the instances to which an appraisal remedy should be applied.[238] While the Corporate Governance Project covers mergers, consolidations, exchanges of shares, sales of assets, and amendments to the articles, a broad policy of the provision is

---

[227] F. Hodge O'Neal & Robert B. Thompson, O'Neal and Thompson's Oppression of Minority Shareholders and LLC Members §§ 5.28 to 5.29 (1985).

[228] Del. Code Ann. tit. 8, § 262 (2001); Kan. Stat. Ann. § 17–6712 (2007). A number of states deny dissenters' rights to shareholders in a surviving parent corporation that used a short form procedure to merge with a subsidiary. See § 22.14.

[229] *E.g.*, 805 ILCS § 5/11.60 (1994).

[230] There is surprisingly little authority on what constitutes "substantially all." *See* F. Hodge O'Neal & Robert B. Thompson, O'Neal and Thompson's Oppression of Minority Shareholders and LLC Members § 5.19 (rev. 2d ed. 2009).

[231] *See, e.g.*, Pratt v. Ballman-Cummings Furn. Co., 495 S.W.2d 509 (Ark. 1973), *appeal after remand*, 549 S.W.2d 270 (Ark. 1977) (partnership formed by two corporations held to be a de facto merger entitling minority shareholders to appraisal rights).

[232] For another avoidance device, *see* the discussion of triangular mergers *supra*.

[233] *E.g.*, N.Y. Bus. Corp. Law § 806(b)(6) (McKinney 2003); former Model Bus. Corp. Act § 80(a)(4) (1969); Model Bus. Corp. Act § 13.02(a)(4), (5) (2016). *See* § 25.5.

[234] There is disagreement as to whether such protection is necessary. *Compare* Melvin A. Eisenberg, The Legal Roles of Shareholders and Management in Modern Corporate Decisionmaking, 57 Cal. L. Rev. 1, 81 (1969), *with* Manning, *supra* note 179, at 250.

[235] Flarsheim v. Twenty Five Thirty Two Broadway Corp., 432 S.W.2d 245 (Mo. 1968).

[236] Model Bus. Corp. Act § 13.02(a)(2) (2016); former Model Bus. Corp. Act § 80(a)(3) (1969).

[237] *See, e.g.*, Me. Rev. Stat. Ann. tit. 13–A, § 1110 (more than 25% of the shares); 15 Pa. Cons. Stat. Ann. §§ 2541 to 2548 (1995) (20% of the shares); Mich. Comp. Laws Ann. § 450.1719 (West 20052) (acquiring person acquires more than majority of all voting power).

[238] *See* ALI Principles of Corporate Governance: Analysis and Recommendations § 7.21 (1994).

not to necessarily condition the remedy's existence on the particular transaction requiring the particular shareholder's approval. This is something of a double-edged principle. Appraisal is not required, even though shareholders are required to approve the transaction, if a body of shareholders will not own less than 60 percent of the combined enterprise[239] and accords shareholders an appraisal remedy in a combination accomplished without their approval if they emerge from the transaction owning less than the 60 percent figure.[240] Because the scope of the appraisal remedy is predominantly a matter of state statutory law, the operative effect of this portion of the American Law Institute's treatment of the appraisal remedy is largely to influence the drafters of corporate statutes. However, where ambiguity exists under local statutes, the American Law Institute's treatment could be highly influential.

The Model Business Corporation Act[241] and some states now deny appraisal rights to holders of shares registered on a national securities exchange.[242] In Delaware, for example, where appraisal rights attach only to merger and consolidation, the statute now excludes transactions where shares of any class or series are either listed on a national exchange or held by more than 2,000 stockholders.[243]

In addition to the substantive limitations on the scope of the appraisal remedy, the risk of considerable expense as well as the procedural difficulties in pursuing the remedy further decrease its effectiveness in protecting minority shareholders. Even if a dissenting shareholder proceeds promptly and in compliance with all procedural requirements, the price to be received for his shares is unpredictable, whether or not the shares are publicly traded.

Further, federal tax laws discourage shareholders from exercising their right to have the dissenter's shares purchased. If the dissenter's rights are invoked, the shareholders receive cash for their shares, and there is a tax on whatever capital gain is realized.[244] If by going along with a merger or other fundamental change the shareholders receive stock or securities, they may be able to avoid recognition of gain on the exchange.[245]

An important question regarding the scope of the appraisal remedy is whether its existence or rights set forth in the statute can be the subject of private ordering. The justification for a provision waiving the appraisal remedy is they remove the uncertainty otherwise created by the remedy so that firms on average will experience higher premia when acquired. For many years, Delaware has recognized that through provisions in the articles of incorporation or even private agreement preferred shareholders can waive their statutory right of appraisal.[246] More recently, the Delaware Court of Chancery upheld an agreement in the subscription agreement by common shareholders to waive

---

[239] ALI Principles of Corporate Governance: Analysis and Recommendations § 7.21(a) (1994).

[240] *See* ALI Principles of Corporate Governance: Analysis and Recommendations § 7.21 (1994). *See, e.g.,* Morley Bros. v. Clark, 361 N.W.2d 763 (Mich. Ct. App. 1984).

[241] Model Bus. Corp. Act § 13.02(b) (2008).

[242] Note, A Reconsideration of the Stock Market Exception to the Dissenting Shareholder's Right of Appraisal, 74 Mich. L. Rev. 1023 (1976).

[243] Del. Code Ann. tit. 8, § 262(b) (2001).

[244] I.R.C. § 1002 (repealed 1976); I.R.C. § 1001 (2009).

[245] I.R.C. § 354(a)(1) (2009). *See also* I.R.C. § 356 (2009).

[246] *See,* In re Appraisal of Fold Holdings, Inc. Preferred Stock, 698 A.2d 973, 976–77 (Del. Ch. 1997).

the statutory right of appraisal.[247] Such private ordering is more easily justified when it arises in the one-off negotiations between sophisticated parties. It remains to be seen, however, whether enforceable private ordering focused on the appraisal remedy can occur through bylaws adopted by the board or a majority of the shareholders after shares have been issued. In this context, there is a weaker argument of meaningful consent by a holder who did not earlier support the bylaw provision.[248]

§ 22.20 Valuation of Shares in Appraisal Proceedings

The most difficult task in obtaining relief under appraisal statutes is establishing the fair value of the dissenting shares. The statutes use a variety of terms to describe what the dissenting share is worth. These include "value," "fair value,"[249] "fair cash value," or "fair market value." These different expressions in effect mean the same thing.[250] The use of the word "fair" indicates that market quotations for a particular day or even the average over a period of time is not conclusive as to the valuation of the shares.[251] Legislatures and the courts have not been able to establish any definite measure or standard of value. The Model Business Corporation Act simply provides that fair value should be determined "using customary and current valuation concepts and techniques generally employed for similar businesses in the context of the transaction requiring appraisal."[252] Although varying terms are used, the vague general standard leaves it up to the appraisers to fix a fair price as between the parties. The appraiser is expected to consider all the elements and factors, both positive and negative, that would be considered by practical and experienced business people in estimating the value of the shares as an investment. The process must take into account not only the liquidating value of the corporation's net assets but also the future prospects and earning power of the corporation as a continuing enterprise.[253] The appraisal, whether by an appraiser or the court, must be reasonable and fair.[254]

More important than the adjectives used to express the value that dissenters are to receive are the assumptions regarding the context in which such value is to be realized. One can assume the value of the firm based on its piecemeal liquidation, assuming that

---

[247] Manti Holdings, LLC. v. Authentix Acquisition Co., 2018 WL 4698255 (Del Ch. Oct. 1, 2018).

[248] *See* § 15.20 *supra.*

[249] "Fair value" as used in corporate statutes is accorded a variable meaning. For example, Delaware provides that the corporation must pay "fair value" for fractions of shares that arise as a consequence of a reverse stock split. Del. Code Ann. tit. 8, § 155 and also provides in its appraisal statute that dissenters are entitled to receive "fair value" for their shares. Del. Code Ann. tit. 8, § 262. In a reverse stock split decision, the Delaware Supreme Court justified its use of market price (averaged over a ten-day period and in an efficient market) as the exclusive as the sole measure of fair value per section 155 of fractional shares arising in reverse stock split while taking into account a wider range of considerations in determining fair value under the general appraisal statute.

[250] *But see* Swope v. Siegel-Robert, Inc., 243 F.3d 486, 492 (8th Cir. 2001) (applying Missouri law; "fair value" in minority stock appraisal cases is not the equivalent of "fair market value" since dissenting shareholders do not have access to willing and ready buyers on an open market, but instead are unwilling sellers with no bargaining power).

[251] *See, e.g.,* Bell v. Kirby Lumber Corp., 395 A.2d 730 (Del. Ch. 1978), *aff'd in part and rev'd in part,* 413 A.2d 137 (Del. 1980).

[252] Model Bus. Corp. Act § 13.01(4)(ii) (2008).

[253] *See also* Cede & Co. v. Technicolor, Inc., 875 A.2d 602 (Del.Supr. 2005) (upholding use of forecasts of capital expenditures and depreciation as well as revenue predictions).

[254] *See* Gonsalves v. Straight Arrow Publishers, 701 A.2d 357, 361 (Del.Supr. 1997) (reversible error for court to choose one party's expert over the other party's expert who espouses one method—capitalization of average earnings for past five years—over another expert's approach who utilizes capitalization of most recent year's earnings without considering some combination of the approaches used by each expert).

the firm is to go out of business and that there will be no purchaser of its assets as an operating economic unit. This assumption in most cases will produce the most conservative valuation of the firm because it does not permit consideration of the synergies the assets produce through their interaction as a going concern. This assumption is frequently referred to as the net asset value of the firm. If one values the corporation assuming it is a going concern, three different scenarios are possible: (1) the firm is auctioned off to the highest bidder; (2) the sale is at arm's length but without encouraging competing bids; or (3) the role of a third-party buyer is not considered[255] and the business is valued in light of its present income and risks. By far the most liberal valuation occurs under the assumption there is an auction; the more conservative ignores the impact of a third-party buyer on the intrinsic value of the firm.[256] By making the amount obtained through an arm's-length acquisition presumptive of fair value unless the dissenter proves otherwise by clear and convincing evidence, the American Law Institute discreetly reinforces the presumption of propriety that normally accompanies director actions not involving self-dealing. On the other hand, this presumption does not arise in self-dealing acquisitions, so these types of transactions can be put to something akin to a market test by measuring fair value in an auction setting.[257]

In arm's-length transactions, the American Law Institute recommends that the bargain struck is presumptively the shares' fair value, unless the dissenter proves otherwise by clear and convincing evidence.[258] And when the transaction is self-interested, the American Law Institute recommends those in control "match the highest realistic price that any other willing, able, and fully informed buyer would have paid. . . ."[259]

In determining the adequacy of particular appraisal prices, many courts, being influenced by the reasoning of earlier Delaware decisions, have used a weighted average of four values: (1) asset value, (2) market value, (3) earnings value, and (4) dividend value, with the relative weight to be decided according to all of the surrounding circumstances.[260] Where there is no ascertainable market value, the courts generally look to the other three factors.[261] The four factor analysis is generally known as the "Delaware block" method, which is a misnomer today because the Delaware Supreme Court has now discarded its strict adherence to a weighted-average approach and has instituted a method of valuation based on all relevant factors.[262] In other words, Delaware will now accept as evidence "proof of value by any techniques or methods which

---

[255] M.P.M. Enterprises, Inc. v. Gilbert, 731 A.2d 790 (Del. 1999).

[256] *See generally* Lucian Bebchuk & Marcel Kahan, Fairness Opinions: How Fair Are They and What Can Be Done About It?, 1989 Duke L.J. 27, 31–33.

[257] *See* ALI, Principles of Corporate Governance 319–324 (1994).

[258] ALI, Principles of Corporate Governance § 7.22(b).

[259] ALI, Principles of Corporate Governance at 316.

[260] *See, e.g.*, Bell v. Kirby Lumber Corp., 395 A.2d 730 (Del. Ch. 1978), *aff'd in part and rev'd in part,* 413 A.2d 137 (Del. 1980); Gibbons v. Schenley Indus., 339 A.2d 460 (Del. Ch. 1975); In re Delaware Racing Ass'n, 213 A.2d 203 (Del.Supr. 1965).

[261] *E.g.*, Foglesong v. Thurston Nat'l Life Ins. Co., 555 P.2d 606 (Okla. 1976).

[262] Weinberger v. UOP, Inc., 457 A.2d 701 (Del. 1983).

are generally considered acceptable in the financial community and otherwise admissible in court."[263]

The determination of value is a factual one[264] and is thus done on a case-by-case basis. Certain principles, however, have been said to govern every valuation: (1) net asset value should not be heavily weighted, unless valuation is being made for liquidation, because the value of corporate assets bears little relation to the value of the stock;[265] (2) extraordinary gains, such as gains from a sale of fixed assets or "gains" achieved by changes in inventory accounting should not be considered, because these gains will not be repeated in the future, and therefore they are not indicative of future earnings potential;[266] (3) market value can be ignored or discounted[267] when shares are so thinly traded as to question the reliability of their market value;[268](4) the discounted cash flow analysis is nearly always a consideration in appraisal proceedings; the approach while well-established is nonetheless sensitive to the unique facts before the court.[269] In addition to these considerations, of interest is the Delaware Supreme Court holding that according deference to the price set in the merger negotiations, even if at arms' length, would "inappropriately shift the responsibility to determine fair value from the court to the private parties."[270] In valuing shares of a closely held corporation, reference to comparable public corporations is sometimes appropriate when the comparative group has similar earnings and other financial relationships.[271]

With its decision in *Weinberger v. UOP, Inc.*,[272] Delaware broke free of the rigid adherence to the formulas of the Delaware block method[273] by holding that all relevant factors should be considered when appraising shares.[274] The underlying assumption in an appraisal valuation is that the dissenting shareholders would be willing to maintain their investment position had the merger not occurred. Consequently, the corporation must be valued as an operating entity.[275] This invites the use of modern financial valuation models used in business and finance to be used in appraisal proceedings. For example, a fairly widely used financial technique for valuing businesses is the

---

[263] Weinberger v. UOP, Inc., 457 A.2d 701, 713 (Del. 1983). Another case has also taken an unstructured approach to valuation.

[264] Piemonte v. New Boston Garden Corp., 387 N.E.2d 1145 (Mass. 1979).

[265] *See* Hernando Bank v. Huff, 796 F.2d 803 (5th Cir. 1986).

[266] In re Valuation of Common Stock of Libby, McNeill & Libby, 406 A.2d 54 (Me. 1979).

[267] Munshower v. Kolbenheyer, 732 So.2d 385 (Fla. App. 1999) (applying a 20% nonmarketability discount to shares in a closely held corporation).

[268] *See* Swope v. Siegel-Robert, Inc., 243 F.3d 486, 493 (8th Cir. 2001) (applying Missouri law; since fair market value is irrelevant in determining fair market value, market forces do not affect ultimate assessment of fair value in appraisal proceeding).

[269] For a thoughtful illustration of estimating future free cash flow, the appropriate growth rate in determining the firm's terminal value, and the discount rate used, *see* Global GT LP v. Golden Telecom, Inc., 993 A.2d 497 (Del. Ch. 2010); Maric Capital Master Fund, Ltd. v. Plato Learning, Inc., 11 A.3d 1175 (Del.Ch. 2010).

[270] Golden Telecom, Inc. v. Global GT, LP, 11 A.3d 214, 218 (2010).

[271] *See* In re Radiology Assoc., Inc., 611 A.2d 485 (Del. Ch. 1991).

[272] Weinberger v. UOP, Inc., 457 A.2d 701, 713 (Del. 1983).

[273] The rigidity of this method is best illustrated by *Universal City Studios v. Francis I. duPont & Co.*, 334 A.2d 216 (Del.Supr. 1975), wherein the court mandated use of the five-year earnings average, though the trend line in earnings was steeply rising, countering this ultimate conservatism by imprecisely using lower discount rate with which to capitalize earnings.

[274] Universal City Studios v. Francis I. duPont & Co., 334 A.2d 216 (Del.Supr. 1975).

[275] Paskill Corp. v. Alcoma Corp., 747 A.2d 549, 553 (Del. 2000); M.G. Bancorporation, Inc. v. Le Beau, 737 A.2d 513, 525 (Del. 1999).

"discounted cash flow technique," which was sometimes emasculated within the "earnings value" component of the Delaware block method. The discounted-cash technique, a variation on the method's application, is now well accepted in Delaware.[276]

The new Delaware appraisal method imposes some limits on what may be considered in arriving at a fair value. For example, the Delaware Supreme Court held that it was proper not to give any weight to "real world" offers for the target company shares.[277] The court pointed out that since the Delaware statute, as is the case with the Model Act, expressly provides that fair value shall be determined "exclusive of any element of value arising from the accomplishment or expectation of the merger."[278] According to the court, this means that synergies arising from an actual or expected transaction cannot be considered in determining fair value. The court explained that an arm's-length third-party offer is more likely to represent the synergistic value of the proposed acquisition rather than the fair value of the target company.[279]

The overall objective of the appraisal process is to determine the dissenter's proportionate value *of the firm,*[280] which is not the same as stating the value of her shares in the firm. In determining the value of the shares, the latter emphasis would consider such intangibles as whether the shares represent majority or minority interests in the firm. If minority shares, they are not nearly as valuable as majority shares because they lack the power to direct the company's operations. This is the so-called minority discount that some courts subtract from the dissenter's shares in determining their value. Some courts have employed a minority discount in valuing shares.[281] However, the great majority of the more recent decisions have emphasized that the appraisal statutes call for a value of the shareholder's proportionate interest in the firm, not simply their shares, so that it is inappropriate to deduct a minority discount.[282] The 1999 amendments to the Model Business Corporation Act follows the majority trend by taking the position that fair value is to be determined on a proportionate basis without considering a minority discount.[283]

A number of courts have disapproved the application of a marketability discount, which adjusts for a lack of liquidity when there is a limited supply of buyers for the stock.[284] A marketability discount reflects the reality that shares that are not marketable

---

[276] *See* Cede & Co. v. Technicolor, Inc., 1990 WL 161084 (Del. Ch. 1990).

[277] M.P.M. Enterprises, Inc. v. Gilbert, 731 A.2d 790 (Del. 1999). Although the trial court admitted evidence of the offer, it decided not to give it any weight in the valuation process.

[278] M.P.M. Enterprises, Inc. v. Gilbert, 731 A.2d 790, 795 (Del. 1999); Del. Code Ann. tit. 8, § 262(h) (2001).

[279] 731 A.2d at 797:

A merger price resulting from arms-length negotiations where there are no claims of collusion is a very strong indication of fair value. But in an appraisal action, that merger price must be accompanied by evidence tending to show that it represents the going concern value of the company rather than just the value of the company to one specific buyer.

[280] *See, e.g.,* Advanced Communication Design, Inc. v. Follett, 615 N.W.2d 285, 290 (Minn. 2000) ("fair value" means pro rata value of corporation's value as a going concern).

[281] Offenbecher v. Baron Services, Inc., 2001 WL 527522 (Ala. Civ. App. 2001) (upholding lower court's application of 50% minority discount).

[282] *Compare* Shawnee Telecom Resources, Inc. v. Brown, 354 S.W.2d 542 (Ky. 2011)(applying a minority discount) *with* Swope v. Siegel-Robert, Inc., 243 F.3d 486, 495–496 (8th Cir. 2001) (applying Missouri law; minority status of stock is irrelevant in appraisal proceeding).

[283] Model Business Corporation Act § 13.01 (2016).

[284] *Compare* Shawnee Telecom Resources, Inc. v. Brown, 354 S.W. 2d 542 (Ky. 2011)(applying a marketability discount) *with* Swope v. Siegel-Robert, Inc., 243 F.3d 486, 493 (8th Cir. 2001) (applying Missouri

likely carry a lower value to their holder and any prospective purchaser.[285] Again, the 1999 amendments to the Model Act provide that in determining "fair value" the appraisal proceeding should not take into consideration a marketability discount.[286]

Under many state statutes, the dissenting shareholder is not to be allowed a value enhanced by the prospective benefits of the merger, consolidation, or sale in which he refuses to participate.[287] Courts more recently have permitted post-transaction benefits to be included in determining the fair value of dissenter's shares.[288] It has been suggested, however, that fairness demands that the minority shareholders be compensated for their share of the synergism produced by the merger.[289] The synergistic formula was accepted by the Seventh Circuit in the context of determining fairness under the federal proxy rules and in upholding the terms of the merger.[290] However, it has been criticized by a number of commentators.[291] In 1999, the Delaware Supreme Court ruled that the appraisal statute prohibits considerations of synergies which would be created by the proposed business combination.[292]

§ 22.21 Exclusivity of Statutory Appraisal Rights

There has been a good deal of debate as to whether statutory provisions that permit dissenting shareholders to demand payment for their shares may or should be exclusive of other legal and equitable remedies by which minority shareholders seek to enjoin or attack changes such as merger or consolidation.[293] In some states the appraisal statutes are silent as to what effect the statutory right of appraisal has on the availability of other remedies.[294] In a few states, the statute expressly provides that appraisal is the exclusive remedy,[295] but this flat restriction is usually tempered by either other statutory language or judicial interpretation.[296]

In 1983, the Delaware Supreme Court indicated that in the absence of fraud or illegality, the appraisal remedy will be exclusive.[297] Failing to provide details related to

---

law; marketability discount is incompatible with purpose of appraisal, that is, to enable dissenting shareholders to recapture their complete investment when they are unwillingly subjected to substantial corporate changes).

[285] Lawson Mardon Wheaton, Inc. v. Smith, 716 A.2d 550, 562 (N.J. Super. App. Div. 1998) (unlike minority discount on the basis that marketability discount reflects illiquidity and should be applied to all shares of stock, not just those of the dissenters).

[286] Model Business Corporation Act § 13.01 (2016).

[287] Perlman v. Permonite Mfg. Co., 568 F.Supp. 222 (N.D. Ind. 1983) (Indiana law).

[288] *See* M.P.M. Enterprises, Inc. v. Gilbert, 731 A.2d 790 (Del. 1999).

[289] *See, e.g.,* Cawley v. SCM Corp., 530 N.E.2d 1264 (N.Y. 1988) (nonspeculative benefits arising from the acquisition may be considered).

[290] Mills v. Electric Auto-Lite Co., 552 F.2d 1239 (7th Cir.), *cert. denied,* 434 U.S. 922 (1977).

[291] Victor Brudney & Marvin A. Chirelstein, Fair Shares in Corporate Mergers and Takeovers, 88 Harv. L. Rev. 297, 308–309 (1974).

[292] M.P.M. Enterprises, Inc. v. Gilbert, 731 A.2d 790 (Del. 1999).

[293] *See generally* Steven D. Gardner, A Step Forward: Exclusivity of the Statutory Appraisal Remedy for Minority Shareholders Dissenting from Going-Private Merger Transactions, 53 Ohio St. L. Rev. 239 (1992).

[294] *E.g.,* Del. Code Ann. tit. 8, § 262 (2001). Broadcasting Co. v. Mahurin, 365 S.W.2d 265, 270 (Ark. 1963). Joseph v. Wallace-Murray Corp., 238 N.E.2d 360 (Mass. 1968).

[295] *E.g.,* Conn. Gen. Stat. Ann. § 33–373(f) (West 1987). *See* In re Jones & Laughlin Steel Corp., 398 A.2d 186 (Pa. Super. Ct. 1979), *aff'd,* 412 A.2d 1099 (Pa. 1980).

[296] *See* Miller v. Steinbach, 268 F.Supp. 255, 270 (S.D.N.Y. 1967) (former Pennsylvania statute's exclusivity limited to "good faith" and transactions that are not "sham or subterfuge").

[297] Weinberger v. UOP, Inc., 457 A.2d 701 (Del. 1983).

the exercise of the appraisal remedy, such as when and where to submit the dissenter's shares, as required by the statute, is enforceable outside the appraisal procedure, although the relief is likely constrained to the harm proximately caused by any delay, etc. in pursuing appraisal.[298] Material nondisclosures in connection with the transaction will preclude the exclusivity of the statutory appraisal remedy.[299] The Delaware Supreme Court has not elaborated on what types of unlawful conduct other than fraud will avoid the exclusivity of the statutory appraisal remedy. The court has merely stated that direct judicial review of a transaction may be found when the plaintiff establishes fraud or other misconduct.[300]

The meaning of "fraud," "illegality," and other such types of misconduct that prevent the appraisal statute from being the shareholder's exclusive recourse is fairly much decided on a case-by-case basis. The courts are fairly consistent in refusing to allow an exception to the appraisal statute when the sole complaint is that the merger does not offer a fair price for the dissenter's shares.[301] A bare allegation that the merger freezes the minority out of the corporation is generally not successful in overcoming the exclusivity of the appraisal remedy.[302] In some jurisdictions, the appraisal remedy is exclusive, even though the plaintiff charges that the majority was engaged in self-dealing and thereby sought to acquire the company at an unfair price.[303] The better view is to at least permit equitable relief in such a situation.[304] Appraisal does not foreclose complaints that the merger never secured the necessary approvals,[305] other procedural improprieties,[306] the corporation's failure to initiate dissenters' rights proceedings,[307] or for misconduct before the merger.[308] Finally, in *Cede & Co. v. Technicolor, Inc.*[309] the Delaware Supreme Court held that a shareholder who had begun an appraisal proceeding and thereafter, before that proceeding's conclusion, learned of fraud in the merger, could join in one proceeding the fraud and the appraisal actions so that if fraud were indeed proven appraisal would be moot; otherwise, appraisal could be pursued.

Many courts have invoked this rule despite the availability of appraisal where the parties controlling the transaction have misled the complaining shareholder or appraiser

---

[298] *See, e.g.,* Galligan v. Galligan, 741 N.E.2d 1217 (Ind. 2001).

[299] *E.g.,* Nagy v. Bistricer, 770 A.2d 43 (Del. Ch. 2000).

[300] Rabkin v. Philip A. Hunt Chemical Corp., 498 A.2d 1099, 1105 (1985) ("While a plaintiff's mere allegation of 'unfair dealing', without more, cannot survive a motion to dismiss, averments containing 'specific acts of fraud, misrepresentation, or other items of misconduct' must be carefully examined"; quoting from *Weinberger*).

[301] *See, e.g.,* Mitchell Partners, L.P. v. Irex Corp., 53 A.3d 39 (Pa. 2012).

[302] *See* Kademian v. Ladish Co., 792 F.2d 614, 630 (7th Cir. 1986).

[303] Walter J. Schloss Associates v. Arkwin Indus., 460 N.E.2d 1090, 1108 (N.Y. 1984).

[304] *See* Walter J. Schloss Associates v. Arkwin Indus., 460 N.E.2d 1090 (N.Y. 1984) (appraisal exclusive if shareholder seeks damages but not for equitable protection against freeze-out).

[305] *See* Shidler v. All Am. Life & Fin. Corp., 775 F.2d 917 (8th Cir. 1985).

[306] Rabkin v. Philip A. Hunt Chem. Corp., 498 A.2d 1099 (Del.Supr. 1985) (second step of acquisition purposely delayed to avoid paying higher consideration promised in first stage if merger completed within one year).

[307] Galligan v. Galligan, 741 N.E.2d 1217, 1225–1226 (Ind. 2001) (shareholders may proceed with separate claim against persons responsible for breach of fiduciary duty to initiate dissenters' rights proceedings).

[308] *See* Kademian v. Ladish Co., 792 F.2d 614 (7th Cir. 1986).

[309] *See* Cede & Co. v. Technicolor, Inc., 542 A.2d 1182 (Del. 1988).

by fraudulent misrepresentations[310] concerning the value of the shares,[311] or have not complied with the procedural requirements for a merger or other fundamental corporate change.[312] One question that arises under the statutes making appraisal the exclusive remedy unless the conduct is "unlawful or fraudulent,"[313] and in decisions by courts phrasing the rule in terms of "fraud or illegality"[314] is whether a breach of fiduciary duty will be sufficient to overcome appraisal's exclusivity. Some courts have held that it is.[315] Other courts have held that a claim based only on a breach of fiduciary duty (without claims of self-dealing, waste, or fraud) will not avoid the appraisal remedy's exclusivity.[316] However, the better view is that pre-transaction breaches of fiduciary duty can be considered in determining the fair value of the dissenting stockholder's shares.[317]

Whatever the local position is as to the exclusivity of the appraisal remedy, the existence of an appraisal remedy does not bar any available action under the federal securities laws for deception. Thus inadequate disclosures during proxy solicitation have often resulted in challenges to the legitimacy of mergers and other corporate combinations.[318] For example, undervaluation of a constituent company's assets,[319] failure to disclose the control of one constituent company by the other,[320] and the inflated value of the shares to be received[321] have all given rise to such suits. Courts also give relief to complaining shareholders where the parties controlling the transaction have deceived the shareholders as to the substantive fairness of a plan of merger or consolidation and thus have induced them not to invoke the right of appraisal.[322]

---

[310] Victor Broadcasting Co. v. Mahurin, 365 S.W.2d 265, 270 (Ark. 1963).

[311] Cole v. Wells, 113 N.E. 189 (Mass. 1916).

[312] *E.g.,* Starrett Corp. v. Fifth Ave. & Twenty-ninth St. Corp., 1 F.Supp. 868 (S.D.N.Y. 1932).

[313] *See* N.Y. Bus. Corp. Law § 623(k) (McKinney 1986); former Model Bus. Corp. Act § 13.02(d) (1969, as amended); Model Bus. Corp. Act § 13.02(d) (1984).

[314] *E.g.,* Weinberger v. UOP, Inc., 457 A.2d 701 (Del. 1983).

[315] *E.g.,* Galligan v. Galligan, 741 N.E.2d 1217 (Ind. 2001) (appraisal right did not preclude separate suit for breach of duties on part of management to adhere to notice requirements of appraisal statute); Gardner v. Major Automotive Companies, Inc., 2012 WL 3614353 (E.D. N.Y.2012) (same applying Nevada law).

[316] *See, e.g.,* Moon v. Moon Enterprises, Inc., 65 Ark.App. 246, 986 S.W.2d 134 (1999) (shareholder's failure to make written demand for payment under appraisal statute waived claim and precluded claim for breach of fiduciary duty in connection with challenged sale).

[317] *See, e.g.,* Sound Infiniti, Inc. v. Snyder, 186 P.3d 1107 (Wash. Ct. App.), *pet. rev. granted,* 203 P.3d 379 (Wash. 2009).

[318] *See* Robert M. Goolrick, Some Disclosure Problems in Acquisition Proxy Statements and Prospectuses, 28 Bus. Law. 111 (1972).

[319] Gerstle v. Gamble-Skogmo, Inc., 478 F.2d 1281 (2d Cir. 1973).

[320] TSC Indus. v. Northway, Inc., 426 U.S. 438 (1976).

[321] Schlick v. Penn-Dixie Cement Corp., 507 F.2d 374 (2d Cir. 1974).

[322] *See* Wilson v. Great Amer. Indus., 979 F.2d 924 (2d Cir. 1992).

Chapter 23

EQUITABLE LIMITS ON ACQUISITIONS AND DEFENSIVE MANEUVERS

Table of Sections

§ 23.1 Fiduciary Obligations in Acquisition Transactions

The classic paradigm for an acquisition is two or more corporations combining in an arm's-length transaction.[1] Shareholder approval follows the negotiation and approval of the plan of merger by the board of directors of the constituent corporations. When shareholder approval is required—that is, it is not avoided through the "small acquisition" exception discussed earlier—the desirability of the transaction is judged by the collective judgment of the shareholders and their board of directors. A major consideration is the full and fair disclosure of all material facts of the acquisition. When the parties are dealing at arm's length, there is little justification for judicial scrutiny, any more than for the business decisions of the board of directors or officers generally. This is not to suggest that mistakes, errors in judgment, or bad results do not flow from acquisitions; they most certainly do. The law's caution here mirrors the concerns examined in Chapter 10 that capitalism works best when it is Adam Smith's invisible hand, not causes of action, that guide the deployment of resources. That is, the preeminent force in placing resources to their highest use is not judicial intervention but the judgment of the firm's managers and its shareholders. Although courts will review the fairness of arm's-length acquisitions, the shareholder-plaintiff bears the substantial burden of proving "such gross disparity as will raise an inference of improper motives or

---

[1]   *See* Jeffrey J. Schick, Comment, Toward Transaction-Specific Standards of Directorial Fiduciary Duty in the Tracking-Stock Context, 75 Wash. L. Rev. 1365 (2000).

reckless indifference to or intentional disregard of stockholders' interests."[2] Under such a standard, the plaintiff is rarely successful.[3]

But not all acquisitions fit within the orthodox mold of corporations dealing at arm's length. There has long been a history of judicial review of combinations between affiliated corporations, most particularly when the subsidiary is acquired by its parent. In the 1980s two additional acquisition forms became more prevalent—the merger freeze-out and the management buyout. In the freeze-out a majority stockholder initiates a transaction that eliminates the minority's continuing equity participation, generally by the terms of the merger forcing the minority to receive cash for their shares. The frequency of merger freeze-outs is enhanced by modern statutes, which today not only condition an acquisition's approval on a majority vote but also authorize the plan of merger to provide that cash or any other property can be exchanged for shares. Thus modern statutes authorize transactions that eliminate the minority, which classically, at least, were authorized only by short-form merger statutes.

The merger freeze-out poses a question that classic self-dealing acquisitions do not pose. While both freeze-outs and self-dealing acquisitions invoke concerns that the terms offered the minority are the product of self-interested negotiations, the merger freeze-out raises the additional concern as to whether, and in what contexts, the majority is able to exercise its power to terminate the minority's continuing participation in the firm. The management buyout (MBO) also eliminates the shareholders from the corporation. The transaction is part of a larger objective: to take the company private and for its present management to have a larger stake in its future operations and success. The MBO varies from other types of self-interested acquisitions because in the MBO those initiating the transaction and emerging as part of the control group previously did not have a controlling shareholder interest in the corporation. They nevertheless are not dealing with the corporation or its shareholders at arm's length unless, as discussed later, active steps are taken to interject an independent negotiator into the transaction.

The fount of the majority's fiduciary obligations in acquisitions is *Sterling v. Mayflower Hotel Corporation,*[4] where the court imposed an "entire fairness" standard on the majority:

> Hilton as a majority stockholder of Mayflower and the Hilton directors as its nominees occupy, in relation to the minority, a fiduciary position in dealing with Mayflower's property. Since they stand on both sides of the transaction, they bear the burden of establishing its entire fairness, and it must pass the test of careful scrutiny by the courts.[5]

---

[2]   Baron v. Pressed Metals of Am., Inc., 123 A.2d 848 (Del. 1956); Wittman v. Crooke, 707 A.2d 422 (Md. Ct. App. 1998) (the merger enjoys protection of business judgment rule even though directors recommending the merger would assume positions with the acquiring company since all the material facts were disclosed before the shareholders approved the merger).

[3]   One instance of such success is Gimbel v. Signal Co., 316 A.2d 599 (Del. Ch.), *aff'd per curiam,* 316 A.2d 619 (Del. 1974), where a preliminary injunction was issued, subject to the posting of a sizable bond (which was never provided), for the sale of a subsidiary allegedly at below its fair market value.

[4]   Sterling v. Mayflower Hotel Corporation, 93 A.2d 107 (Del. 1952).

[5]   Sterling v. Mayflower Hotel Corporation, 93 A.2d 107, 109–110 (Del. 1952). *See also* McMullin v. Beran, 765 A.2d 910 (Del. 2000) (directors who approved unfair merger at the insistence of the controlling stockholder and did not adequately inform themselves will be deemed to have breached their fiduciary duty).

Sterling then embraced the give-get formula for measuring fairness, reasoning that "the test of fairness which we think [is] the correct one [is] that upon a merger the minority stockholder shall receive the substantial equivalent in value of what he had before."[6] The Delaware Supreme Court, and other courts,[7] now recognize that the minority should also participate proportionally in any nonspeculative gains generated by the acquisition.[8]

The procedural context in which the transaction is formulated, proposed, and approved has assumed increasing importance. For example, the Delaware Supreme Court has distinguished between "fair dealing" and "fair price" such that it more readily concludes the appraisal remedy is exclusive as to the latter but not necessarily as to the former.[9] "Fair dealing" is defined to include questions regarding the acquisition's timing, how it was initiated, structured, and negotiated, and the approvals of the directors and stockholders obtained.[10] In essence, fair dealing examines whether the transaction is the product of overreaching misbehavior by which those in a fiduciary relationship to the target corporation use their power to deprive the target corporation of fair and independent representation in the acquisition.[11] For example, *Weinberger v. UOP, Inc.*[12] held the parent corporation violated the requirement of fair dealing because two of its officers also sat on the subsidiary's board of directors and, even though they prepared a report of the subsidiary's value using the subsidiary's information, they did not share that report with their fellow subsidiary directors. Had they done so, their fellow directors would have learned that a 14 percent increase in the purchase price would have had minimal effect on the expected return the parent expected to garner from the acquisition.

These problems are circumvented by interjecting an independent negotiating committee between the parent and the target corporation.[13] A further means to clothe the controlled corporation with an independent voice is by conditioning the transaction's consummation on the approval of a majority of the disinterested shares.[14] In *Weinberger* this avenue was unsuccessful, however, because the proxy statement failed to disclose all the material facts. It withheld, for example, the contents of the earlier described report.[15] However, the burden of proving the acquisition's entire fairness does not shift if the procedures followed are not truly independent. For example in *Kahn v. Tremont Corp.*,[16] the Delaware Supreme Court held that the creation of a special negotiating

---

[6]　Sterling v. Mayflower Hotel Corporation, 93 A.2d 107, 114 (Del. 1952).

[7]　*See, e.g.,* Mills v. Electric Auto-Lite Co., 552 F.2d 1239 (7th Cir.), *cert. denied,* 434 U.S. 922 (1977).

[8]　*See* Weinberger v. UOP, Inc., 457 A.2d 701 (Del. 1983).

[9]　*See* Rabkin v. Philip A. Hunt Chem. Corp., 498 A.2d 1099 (Del. 1985).

In Cede & Co. v. Technicolor, Inc., 542 A.2d 1182 (Del. 1988), the court explained the exclusivity of the appraisal remedy in terms that appear to again distinguish between fair dealing and fair price. The court emphasized the Delaware appraisal remedy relief against the corporation; that relief is the value of the dissenter's shares. By contrast, fraud is a more expansive remedy, being available against parties other than the corporation and providing relief that is more encompassing than the intrinsic value of the shares. The court thus permitted both types of action to be maintained in the same suit, recognizing that appraisal may not provide complete relief for unfair dealing or fraud.

[10]　*See* Weinberger v. UOP, Inc., 457 A.2d 701, 711 (Del. 1983).

[11]　*See* Parnes v. Bally Entertainment Corp., 722 A.2d 1243 (Del. 1999) (allegations that chairman and controlling stockholder favored his interests over interests of other shareholders tainted entire process such that if established fair dealing part of "entire fairness" standard would not have been satisfied).

[12]　Weinberger v. UOP, Inc., 457 A.2d 701 (Del. 1983).

[13]　*See* Rosenblatt v. Getty Oil Co., 493 A.2d 929, 937–939 (Del. 1985).

[14]　Kahn v. M&F Worldwide Corp., 88 A.3d 635 (Del. 2014).

[15]　457 A.2d at 712.

[16]　Kahn v. Tremont Corp., 694 A.2d 422 (Del. 1997).

committee to approve the sale of the company to its controlling stockholder did not change the burden of proving entire fairness where the most active member of the committee enjoyed long-standing commercial ties to the controlling stockholder and the other two committee members were not active in the committee's deliberations. Furthermore, the committee's advisors were not seen as being independent since they were indirectly tainted because they were selected on the recommendation of the committee's chair who the court concluded was not himself independent.

Most recently in *Kahn v. M&F Worldwide Corp.*,[17] the Delaware Supreme Court held that a business judgment review rather than the entire fairness test should apply to a controlling shareholder merger if certain conditions are satisfied.[18] Specifically, the court, in a unanimous decision, explained that the more exacting entire fairness analysis would not apply if "(i) the controller conditions the procession of the transaction on the approval of both a Special Committee and a majority of the minority stockholders; (ii) the Special Committee is independent; (iii) the Special Committee is empowered to freely select its own advisors and to say no definitively; (iv) the Special Committee meets its duty of care in negotiating a fair price; (v) the vote of the minority is informed; and (vi) there is no coercion of the minority."[19] In the course of its opinion, the court explained that the presumption of independence may be rebutted only by a showing that a committee member was "beholden" to the controlling shareholder. The fact that a director and the controlling shareholder travelled in the same social circles or had past business dealings is not sufficient to rebut the presumption of independence.[20] The ties to the controlling shareholder must be sufficient to show that the committee member could not "objectively discharge his or her fiduciary duties."[21] Somewhat at odds with the opinion is its footnote suggesting that a complaint alleging serious price inadequacy would survive a motion to dismiss;[22] the Delaware Supreme Court has since clarified that in such transactions a care violation arises "only by showing that the Special Committee acted with gross negligence, not by questioning the sufficiency of the price."[23] The New York Court of Appeals has adopted the Delaware rule.[24]

§ 23.2 Equitable Limitations on the Power of Sale or Merger

A controlling shareholder or parent corporation that dominates and controls another corporation is not as a matter of law precluded from purchasing the entire property and assets of the controlled corporation, either when the assets of a going concern are sold or when the corporation is being wound up. However, such a purchase by a controlling person or the company's managers implicates the same concerns

---

[17] 88 A.3d 635 (Del. 2014).

[18] In *Flood v. Synutra Int'l, Inc.*, 195 A.3d 754, 761–64 (Del. 2018), the court held the six-part process could apply even if the interested party's initial proposal did not include both independent director and shareholder approval so long as those components had been embraced and were in place before negotiations commenced. A vigorous dissent in the case reasoned that *Kahn* requires the initial proposal to embrace the six procedural steps. *Flood v. Synutra Int'l, Inc.*, 195 A.3d 754, 775–777 (Del. 2018).

[19] 88 A.3d at 645.

[20] 88 A.3d at 649.

[21] *Id.* Flood v. Synutra International, Inc., 195 A.2d 754 (De. 2018) (upholding transaction approved by a special committee of independent directors and a vote by a majority of disinterested shareholders).

[22] Kahn v. M & F Worldwide Corp., 88 A.3d 635, 649 n.14 (Del. 2014).

[23] Flood v. Synutra Int'l, Inc., 195 A.3d 754, 768 (Del. 2018),

[24] In re Kenneth Cole Productions, Inc., 27 N.Y.3d 268, 32 N.Y.S.3d 551, 52 N.E.3d 214 (2016). *See also, e.g.*, In re Baltic Trading Stockholders Litigation, 160 A.D.3d 599, 76 N.Y.S.3d 117 (1st Dep't 2018); In re Martha Stewart Living Omnimedia, Inc. Stockholder Litigation, 2017 WL 3568089, *23 (Del. Ch. 2017).

examined in Chapter 10 regarding self-dealing such that close or rigorous judicial scrutiny occurs.[25]

The template most commonly followed for addressing the minority holder's complaint that the merger of the firm with its controlling stockholder (or an entity under the controlling stockholder's influence) is *Weinberger v. UOP, Inc.*[26] The *Weinberger* court held that when the appraisal remedy is not exclusive,[27] the reviewing court should "carefully scrutinize the board's actions to ascertain whether the board instituted measures to ensure a fair process, and whether the board achieved a fair price for the disinterested stockholder minority."[28] This formula is more frequently stated as the "entire fairness" inquiry with fairness thus having two distinct components: fair dealings and fair price. The court undertakes a unified assessment that involves balancing the process followed and the price received by the minority.[29] Just as we saw earlier in Chapter 10, when there is a self-dealing acquisition, it is inappropriate to apply the presumption of propriety that accompanies the business judgment rule. When there is a self-dealing acquisition the controller party has the burden of proving entire fairness.[30]

In assessing the fairness of the process, the court will consider:

> [T]he board's composition and independence, the timing, structure and negotiation of the transaction; how the board and shareholder approval were obtained; and the extent to which the board and the shareholders were accurately informed about the transaction.[31]

Important considerations in such a fairness inquiry are the presence of an independent committee to represent the interest of the minority holders in negotiating the transaction, the approval of a majority of the minority shares after full disclosure of all material facts, and the use of independent advisors for the outside directors considering the transaction.[32] Thus, fair dealing was not satisfied when the financial consultant to the independent directors had close ties to the law firm that customarily represented the controlling stockholder.[33] Fair dealing does not require, however, that the shareholders be provided with financial data needed to make an independent judgment.[34] The ratifying vote of a fully informed majority of the minority shifts the burden of proving fairness; such ratification has limited benefits to the defendant because the transaction

---

[25]   In re Morton's Restaurant Group, Inc. Shareholders Litig., 74 A.3d 656 (Del. Ch. 2013) (entire fairness standard not triggered with merger with owner of 27.5 percent of company's shares who placed two of its employees on the board).

[26]   Weinberger v. UOP, Inc., 457 A.2d 701 (Del. 1983). *See also* Berger v. Intelident Solutions, Inc., 911 A.2d 1164 (Del. Ch. 2006).

[27]   On the exclusivity of the appraisal remedy, *see* § 22.21.

[28]   Lerner v. Lerner Corp., 750 A.2d 709, 711 (Md. Ct. App. 2000).

[29]   *See* Cinerama, Inc. v. Technicolor, Inc., 663 A.2d 1156, 1179 (Del. 1995).

[30]   For evidence that burden-shifting impacts the frequency of litigation in acquisitions, *see* Robert B. Thompson & Randall S. Thomas, The New Look of Shareholder Litigation: Acquisition-Oriented Class Actions, 57 Vand. L. Rev. 133 (2004).

[31]   Ryan v. Tad's Enterprises, Inc., 709 A.2d 682, 690 (Del. Ch. 1996).

[32]   *See* Kahn v. Lynch Communication Systems, Inc., 638 A.2d 1110, 1119 (Del. 1994) (special committee or minority plebiscite only shifts the burden on issue of entire fairness, but for a committee to do so "the majority shareholder must not dictate the terms of the transaction" and "the special committee must have real bargaining power that it can exercise with the majority shareholder on an arms length basis" that is "the power to say no").

[33]   *See* Ryan v. Tad's Enterprises, Inc., 709 A.2d 682, 693 (Del. Ch. 1996).

[34]   *See, e.g.,* McMullin v. Beran, 765 A.2d 910 (Del. 2000).

still is subject to scrutiny under the entire fairness standard, albeit the burden shifts to the plaintiff to prove the transaction was not entirely fair.[35] There is no effective ratification if the vote is the product of coercion.[36] Fair price has been defined as meaning the amount a reasonable seller "would regard in the range of fair value."[37] *Weinberger's* entire fairness inquiry applies, however, only when a parent corporation or individual controlling shareholder stands on both sides of the challenged transaction.[38]

Though Delaware has pioneered in making law for the protection of minority shareholders frozen out via a merger, its approach is qualified. In *Glassman v. Unocal Exploration Corporation*,[39] the court held that the parent company that exercises its right under the short-form merger provision[40] to rid itself of the minority shareholders in the subsidiary does not have to establish the entire fairness for its actions. In such a case, the exclusive remedy to the minority, absent fraud or illegality, is the appraisal remedy.[41] The court reasoned that the legislative intent in providing a short-form merger procedure would be frustrated if the parent corporation were subject to the entire fairness review standard. Also, because the decision to accept a tender offer is an individual one, the entire fairness standard does not apply to a controlling stockholder's tender offer for the minority shares.[42]

Building on the reasoning of *Glassman*,[43] a series of Delaware Chancery Court decisions have substantially qualified the application of *Weinberger's* "entire fairness" test in freezeouts involving a tender offer followed by a short-form merger. This new approach is succinctly stated in *In re Pure Resources Shareholders' Litigation*[44] holding that the entire fairness test is met when 1) the tender offer is free of any material misrepresentation, 2) the tender offer must be subject to a non-waivable majority of the minority provision whereby the ultimate freezeout will not occur unless shares held by at least a majority of the minority are tendered, 3) the controlling stockholder promises to promptly consummate a short-form merger at the price as that offered in the tender offer, and 4) there is no coercion such as retributive threats in connection with the tender offer.[45] A preliminary injunction was, however, granted in *Pure Resources* because the

---

[35]   *See* Kahn v. Lynch Communication Systems, Inc., 638 A.2d 1110 (Del. 1994).

[36]   *See* Weiss v. Samsonite Corp., 741 A.2d 366 (Del. Ch. 1999).

[37]   Weiss v. Samsonite Corp., 741 A.2d 366 (Del. Ch. 1999).

[38]   Emerald Partners v. Berlin, 787 A.2d 85, 90 (Del. 2001).

[39]   Glassman v. Unocal Exploration Corporation, 777 A.2d 242 (Del. 2001).

[40]   Short-form mergers are discussed in § 22.14.

[41]   Glassman v. Unocal Exploration Corporation, 777 A.2d 242 (Del. 2001).

[42]   *See* In re Siliconix, Inc. Shareholder Litigation, 2001 WL 716787 (Del. Ch. 2001).

[43]   *See also* Solomon v. Pathe Comm. Corp., 672 A.2d 35 (Del. 1996).

[44]   In re Pure Resources Shareholders' Litigation, 808 A.2d 421, 441 (Del. Ch. 2002).

[45]   *See* Next Level Comm., Inc. v. Motorola, Inc., 834 A.2d 828 (Del. Ch. 2003) (no coercion when there was disclosure of target company's financial difficulties, failure to give assurances controlling stockholder would relax loan conditions that would enable target company to obtain external financing, and disclosure of risk of delisting on Nasdaq where Nasdaq had issued such warnings).

Until resolved by the Delaware Supreme Court, there appears to be a division within the Chancery Court decisions on the appropriate review standard. Thus, *In re Cox Comm., Inc. Shareholder Litig.*, 879 A.2d 604 (Del.Ch. 2005), conditions a freezeout on the recommendation of an independent committee or independent minority plebiscite. Whereas In re Pure Resources, Inc. Shareholder Litig., 808 A.2d 421 (Del. Ch. 2002), conditions the freezeout on a minority plebiscite and a promise to undertake a cleanup merger at the same price. Finally, *In re Siliconix, Inc. Shareholder Litig.*, focuses solely on whether the offer is coercive. This division prompted the Vice-Chancellor Laster to certify the question to the Supreme Court, In re CNX Gas Corp. Shareholders Litig., 4 A.2d 397 (Del. Ch. 2010), which was not reviewed by the reviewed. In re CNX Gas Corp. Shareholder Litig., 4 A.2d 397 (Del. 2010).

material information had not been disclosed, the other conditions were deemed satisfied even though a special committee created by the majority to consider the offer lacked the authority to negotiate a better price and was rebuffed in its efforts to adopt a shareholder rights plan to block the tender offer.[46]

In 2013, Delaware amended its statute to enable the boards of two independent companies to combine without a formal vote of the acquired firm's shareholders. The procedure is generally referred to as a "streamlined back-end merger" for which the predicate is the acquiring firm obtaining via a friendly tender offer enough target shares to assure approval of the merger. The procedure is set forth in section 251(h) of the Delaware General Corporation Law which provides:

1. The merger agreement expressly provides it is governed by section 251(h);

2. The acquiring consummates a tender offer for "any and all" of the outstanding stock of the firm to be acquired which stock is of the class entitled to vote on the merger;

3. The acquiring corporation owns at least the required amount of stock necessary to approve the merger;

4. No party to the merger is an "interested stockholders" of the acquired firm;

5. The corporation consummating the offer merge with or into the acquired firm; and

6. The outstanding shares of the acquired firm that are not cancelled by the merger are converted through the merger into, or into the right to receive, the same amount of cash, property, rights or securities paid for the shares in the tender offer.[47]

§ 23.3 Merger Freeze Outs of Minority Shareholders

Abuses that may accompany a controlled merger or other conflict-of-interest transaction are magnified when the minority shareholder is cashed out and thus is not able to share in the profits of the surviving corporation. These cash-outs, also known as "squeeze-outs" or "freeze-outs," which are not new, have been accomplished in a variety of ways.[48] The short-form merger is the simplest of the various statutory liberalizations and has led to an increase in the use of merger, consolidation, or sale of assets as a freeze-out technique. This is a rapidly developing area in which there has been a great deal of judicial and scholarly energy directed toward the proper treatment of freeze-out transactions.[49] The cases recognizing a freeze-out remedy have focused on two factors: (1) the purpose of the transaction and (2) fairness to the minority shareholders. While some courts require a showing of no valid purpose as a threshold to scrutiny of the

---

[46] 808 A.2d at 430.

[47] Del. Gen. Corp. Law § 251(h). A similar provisions was adopted in Maryland in 2014. Md. Gen. Corp. L. § 3–106.1.

[48] For comprehensive treatment, *see* F. Hodge O'Neal & Robert B. Thompson, O'Neal & Thompson's Oppression of Minority Shareholders and LLC Members, ch. 5 (2009).

[49] *E.g.*, Michael J. McGuinness & Timo Rehbock, Going-Private Transactions: A Practitioner's Guide, 30 Del. J. Corp. L. 437 (2005) (closely examining two distinct but commonly used going private approaches); Faith Stevelman, Going Private at the Intersection of the Market and the Law, 62 Bus. Law. 775 (2007) (characterizing Delaware's opinions as being in disarray and proposing a sweeping entire fairness review in all freeze outs).

transaction's fairness,[50] older Delaware cases, at least in their language, put the burden of proving both on the defendants.[51] While briefly imposing a business purpose requirement for a freeze out,[52] the Delaware Supreme Court subsequently abandoned the business purpose requirement.[53] In the close corporation setting, merger freezeouts are frequently examined in the context of whether the minority holder's reasonable expectations have been defeated.[54]

The utility of the business purpose test appears to be its invitation to the court to review somewhat more widely the overall terms, objectives, and motivations surrounding the acquisition. There is little evidence that the business purpose test otherwise provides strong and predictable protection to the minority or ensures the majority against the unnecessary scrutiny of a fair transaction. It is important in this regard to stress that the emphasis of the business purpose test is on the purpose for the acquisition itself;[55] the business purpose test applied by the courts does not inquire as to why the acquisition's terms provide cash, rather than a continuing equity participation, to the acquired corporation.

The range of legitimate commercial purposes for an acquisition is so extensive that the business purpose test effectively proscribes only the most egregious types of misconduct.[56] On the other hand, if courts wish to recognize the right of shareholders to continue their participation in an enterprise, they would focus on the reasons for cashing the minority shareholders out of the corporation. Such a narrowed focus on the justification for eliminating the minority would likely reduce the frequency of merger freeze-outs. In one famous case, a freeze-out was justified by the objective of removing from the corporation an obstreperous minority shareholder who was blocking the majority's acceptance of a beneficial offer from a third party.[57] By either not requiring a business purpose or focusing their inquiry on the more general purpose for the acquisition, the courts strongly embrace the concept of majoritarism within the American corporation, whereby the minority's interest can be terminated, albeit at a fair price, by the will of the majority. Any preoccupation with the fairness of the price offered the minority must confront the question of whether the appraisal remedy should be the minority's exclusive right to complain.[58]

An important consideration in evaluating the exclusivity of the appraisal remedy in the context of a self-interested acquisition is the procedural setting in which the relief is sought. Courts should be more willing to avoid the exclusivity of the appraisal remedy when the object of the action is a temporary or preliminary injunction. In this context, courts grant their relief when there is reason to believe purposeful manipulation of

---

[50]   *E.g.*, M&W, Inc. v. Pacific Guardian Life Ins. Co., Ltd., 966 P.2d 1098 (Hawai'i Ct. 1998); Gabhart v. Gabhart, 370 N.E.2d 345 (Ind. 1977).

[51]   Roland Int'l Corp. v. Najjar, 407 A.2d 1032 (Del. 1979).

[52]   Singer v. Magnavox Co., 380 A.2d 969 (Del. 1977).

[53]   Weinberger v. UOP, Inc., 457 A.2d 701 (Del. 1983).

[54]   *See, e.g.*, U.S. Bank N.A. v. Cold Spring Granite Co., 802 N.W.2d 363 (Minn. 2011).

[55]   *See, e.g.*, Romero v. United States Unwired, Inc., 2006 WL 2366342 (E.D. La. 2006) (some independent rationale for a merger must be provided), *rev'd in part on other grounds.*

[56]   *See generally* William Carney, Fundamental Corporate Changes, Minority Shareholders, and Business Purposes, 1980 A.B.F. Res. J. 69 (1980).

[57]   *See* Matteson v. Ziebarth, 242 P.2d 1025 (Wash. 1952).

[58]   Where the stockholders are not accorded an appraisal remedy, one court concluded they were entitled to equitable protection to assure they received fair value for their shares. *See* Stoneman v. United Nebraska Bank, 254 Neb. 477, 577 N.W.2d 271 (1998).

disclosure practices or operations has been carried out to artificially depress the price of the company's shares,[59] the transaction is purposely timed to deprive the minority of a higher price they would have received if the transaction's timing had been more neutrally determined,[60] or there appears to have been no independent determination by the board of directors of the fairness of the price offered to minority.[61] A Delaware Supreme Court decision provides discipline to the controlling shareholders in a merger freeze-out; the court held that shareholders who are frozen out in the second stage of a two-step acquisition are entitled in the appraisal process to a proportionate share of the gains arising from a business plan that was agreed to be followed after eliminating the minority in the second step of the acquisition.[62]

A management buyout (MBO) customarily takes the form of a purchase of the target corporation by a newly formed corporation largely with funds borrowed from financial institutions and the old management and their new partners holding a significant, if not exclusive, portion of the new company's equity. From a theoretical point, the MBO deals directly with the classic agency problem that arises from the separation of ownership and management. Managers become the sole or dominant owners after the MBO, so the firm's destiny is their own. Because they, not dispersed shareholders, reap the full benefits of the venture's upside potential, managers have powerful incentives to assure the venture's success.[63] On the other side of the social equation, questions abound when the managers are purchasing the corporation in such a setting.[64] First, there is the concern over the superior information advantage the managers have over the shareholders. Second, the stockholders' approval may not fully reflect their true sense of the fairness of the transaction when other offers or options have been constrained by the very managers proposing to purchase the firm. Third, there must be concern whether the price and terms of payment are the product of negotiations in the strictest sense of the meaning. Certainly, negotiations are difficult to imagine if the directors who recommend the proposal to the stockholders are also the purchasers.

Because the management buyout is the purest form of self-interested acquisition, it is subject to the closest scrutiny for fairness of the price, but more significantly for the process for approving the acquisition. There is no breach of fiduciary duty merely because the target corporation's assets and earnings will be used to purchase the firm's outstanding shares or because the managers gain from the transaction, absent proof they have reaped a unique advantage from their fiduciary position.[65] At the same time, what objective evidence exists that assures that the managers are offering a fair price? A convenient answer to this concern arises when there are competing offers. In this context

---

[59]   *See* Berkowitz v. Power/Mate Corp., 342 A.2d 566 (N.J. Super. Ch. 1975).

[60]   *See* Rabkin v. Philip A. Hunt Chem. Corp., 498 A.2d 1099 (Del. 1985).

[61]   *See* Kahn v. Lynch Communication Sys., Inc., 638 A.2d 1110 (Del. 1994).

[62]   *See* Cede & Co. v. Technicolor, Inc., 684 A.2d 289 (Del. 1996). For a review of the implications of *Technicolor, see* Jesse A. Finkelstein & Russell C. Silberglied, *Technicolor IV:* Appraisal Valuation in a Two-Step Merger, 52 Bus. Law. 801 (1997).

[63]   *See* Michael Jensen, Agency Costs of Free Cash Flow, Corporate Finance and Takeovers, 76 Amer. Econ. Rev. (Papers and Proceedings) 323 (1986); Robert Kaplan, The Effect of Leveraged Buyouts on Operations and Value, 24 J. Fin. Econ. 217 (1989).

[64]   *See generally* Richard Booth, Management Buyouts, Shareholder Welfare and the Limits of Fiduciary Duty, 60 N.Y.U. L. Rev. 630 (1985); Deborah A. DeMott, Puzzles and Parables: Defining Good Faith in the MBO Context, 23 Wake Forest L. Rev. 15 (1990); Thomas L. Hazen, Management Buyouts and Corporate Governance Paradigms, 25 Wake Forest L. Rev. 1 (1990).

[65]   *See* Field v. Allyn, 457 A.2d 1089 (Del. Ch. 1983).

the focus is to assure a free dynamic auction of control. Thus, in a leading MBO case, *Mills Acquisition Company v. Macmillan, Inc.*,[66] the Delaware Supreme Court struck down a lockup option granted to the MBO's financial partner because the corporation's directors, most of whom were participants in the MBO, were viewed as having skewed the results of the bidding competition through the lockup and several other actions they took. Other indicia of objective fairness are resorting to investment bankers' opinion letters[67] and constituting a group of independent directors to serve as a negotiating committee with the MBO group. If a duly constituted independent body of directors is not given the task of negotiating the acquisition with either the managers or the controlling stockholder, the burden of proving entire fairness of the acquisition falls on the interested party.[68]

Notwithstanding its subsequent rejection in Delaware, the business purpose test continues to be an issue in many other jurisdictions.[69] Further, the business purpose test is not limited to mergers; it has also been applied, for example, where the directors issued additional shares to themselves to perpetuate their control.[70]

§ 23.4 Going-Private Transactions Under the Securities Laws

A very popular subspecies of the freeze-out merger is the going-private transaction.[71] This has been described as any organic corporate change, such as merger, reverse stock split, repurchase of shares, or recapitalization, that results in a publicly traded company being delisted or closely enough held so as no longer to be subject to the 1934 Exchange Act's reporting requirements.[72] There are various possible motives behind going private—for example, a company may decide that the burdens of SEC reporting are too expensive or it may be the final step in a takeover by another company.[73] All of the fairness considerations applicable to any freeze-out transactions necessarily apply with equal force to this special subspecies. In addition, there has been both SEC involvement and state law concern based on the fact that going-private transactions lessen the standards of corporate conduct.

Beyond the state law fiduciary standards for directors and controlling shareholders,[74] relief may be found under SEC Rule 10b–5,[75] the federal proxy rules if a shareholder vote is involved, and section 14(e) of the 1934 Exchange Act, which deals

---

[66] Mills Acquisition Company v. Macmillan, Inc., 559 A.2d 1261 (Del. 1989).

[67] *See* Lucian Bebchuk & Marcel Kahan, Fairness Opinions: How Fair Are They and What Can Be Done About It?, 1989 Duke L.J. 27.

[68] *See* Rosenblatt v. Getty Oil Co., 493 A.2d 929 (Del. 1985).

[69] *E.g.,* Bryan v. Brock & Blevins Co., Inc., 490 F.2d 563 (5th Cir. 1974) (Georgia law); Gabhart v. Gabhart, 370 N.E.2d 345 (Ind. 1977).

[70] Lichtenberger v. Long Island Mach. Sales Corp., 420 N.Y.S.2d 507 (App. Div. 1979).

[71] *See* Lynch v. Vickers Energy Corp., 383 A.2d 278 (Del. 1977).

[72] SEC Rule 13e–3, 17 C.F.R. § 240.13e–3 (2009).

[73] *See generally* Victor Brudney, A Note on Going Private—Juggling Shareholder Protection with Corporate Flexibility: Will the States Drop the Ball?, 1978 Wis. L. Rev. 797 (1978).

[74] Bird v. Wirtz, 266 N.W.2d 166 (Minn. 1978); Berkowitz v. Power/Mate Corp., 342 A.2d 566 (N.J. Super. Ch. Ct. 1975).

[75] 17 C.F.R. § 240.10b–5 (2009).

with tender offers.[76] Issuer tender offers are specifically regulated under Rule 13e–4 of the Exchange Act.[77]

The SEC in Rule 13e–3 has promulgated extensive disclosure requirements and a special antifraud rule for going-private transactions.[78] In broad overview, Rule 13e–3 imposes special disclosure obligations on non-arm's-length mergers, recapitalizations, tender offers, and the like by the issuer or its affiliate that either (1) will cause delisting by a securities exchange or NASDAQ of *any* class of the issuer's securities or (2) will reduce the number of its record stockholders below 300 so that it will be exempt from the registration and reporting requirements of the Securities Exchange Act.[79] Several exceptions to the going-private rule are provided, the most significant being (1) the second step of a pre-announced two-step acquisition, provided the consideration is at least equal to that offered in the earlier tender offer, the second step occurs within one year of the earlier tender offer, and the earlier tender offer fully disclosed the intention to undertake a second-step acquisition;[80] (2) the transaction provides that all the issuer's security holders receive only an equity security that has substantially the same rights as the equity security given up and is registered under the Securities Exchange Act;[81] and (3) issuer redemptions, calls, and other acquisitions pursuant to the rights established in the instruments (articles of incorporation) creating that class of security.[82] The term "affiliate" enjoys a fairly broad construction under the rule so that the issuer's combination with another company indirectly controlling the issuer can trigger the disclosures required by Rule 13e–3.[83]

If an exemption is not available, the issuer or its affiliate involved in a transaction subject to Rule 13e–3 must provide to each affected security holder of record the extensive disclosures required by the rule. This must be provided to the holders not later than 20 days prior to the purchase of the shares or the date when their consent or vote on such transaction will be sought.[84] The disclosure required by Rule 13e–3 is extensive. For example, Item 8(a) of Schedule 13E-3 requires the directors to express their opinion of the transaction's fairness to the frozen-out stockholders.[85] Further, Item 8(b) of Schedule 13E-3 requires a reasonably detailed discussion of the "material factors upon which the belief stated in Item 8(a) is based."[86] In applying these disclosure requirements, the SEC demands more than mere itemization of the factors relied on; it requires their discussion.[87] Thus a general statement that the board of directors considered $29.50-per-share fair in light of the company's book value of $3.77-per-share was held incomplete absent any discussion "of the reasons and extent to which book

---

[76]   15 U.S.C. § 78n(e) (2009).

[77]   17 C.F.R. § 240.13e–4 (2009).

[78]   17 C.F.R. § 240.13e–3 (2009).

[79]   Rule 13e–3(a)(3), 17 C.F.R. § 240.13e–3(a)(3) (2009).

[80]   Rule 13e–3(g)(1), 17 C.F.R. § 240.13e–3(g)(1) (2009).

[81]   Rule 13e–3(g)(2), 17 C.F.R. § 240.13e–3(g)(2) (2009).

[82]   Rule 13e–3(g)(4), 17 C.F.R. § 240.13e–3(g)(4) (2009).

[83]   *See, e.g.,* Brewer v. Lincoln Int'l Corp., 148 F. Supp. 2d 792 (W.D. Ky. 2000) (agreement by acquiring company with person controlling 90% of the voting power that the latter would vote in favor of a step necessary for the acquisition to occur in exchange for ultimately receiving 50% of the acquiring company could make the acquiring company an affiliate).

[84]   Rule 13e–3(f), 17 C.F.R. § 240.13e–3(f) (2009).

[85]   *See* 17 C.F.R. § 240.13e–100 (Item 8(a)) (2009).

[86]   *See* 17 C.F.R. § 240.13e–100 (Item 8(b)) (2009).

[87]   *See* 17 C.F.R. § 240.13e–100 (Item 8(b)) (2009).

value is or is not an accurate reflection of the Company's value and therefore was accepted or rejected as a criterion for judging the fairness of the transaction."[88] The full force of Rule 13e–3's disclosure demands appears in the Supreme Court's holding that opinion statements, such as those elicited by the going-private rule, can in appropriate circumstances be material misrepresentations that give rise to private recoveries.[89] Violations of Rule 13e–3's disclosure demands subject the violator not only to the full panoply of the SEC's enforcement remedies, but also to the private actions that are available under the rule for affected shareholders.[90]

§ 23.5 Defensive Tactics[91]—Shark Repellant Provisions

In recent years tender offers[92] have become a popular alternative means of corporate acquisition. Tender offers are often not as time-consuming as proxy battles and, because they do not involve action by the target company, no dissenters' rights are involved. There are many different tender offer techniques, which are often the first part of a multistep acquisition,[93] freeze-out, or going-private transaction. Tender offers may be consummated with the support of the target's management,[94] or can evolve into contested battles for corporate control.[95] Once a tender offer has been made, the target company's management must respond.[96] If management decides to go along amicably with the takeover, it will be bound to adhere to the fiduciary standards that apply to any controlled takeover.[97]

The defense against a takeover attempt is generally covered by the business judgment rule, which allows management the use of reasonable corporate funds to defend its policies.[98] The business judgment rule does not apply, however, to decisions by directors who have a self-interest in the transaction. Often a charge is made that a takeover defense is motivated by the directors' desire to entrench themselves in office. Accordingly, the courts have to decide in which instances the directors will be insulated by the business judgment rule and in which instances their self-interest will limit their discretion to act.

Defensive tactics vary widely but can be placed in two categories: responsive or preventive. Some of the most popular responsive defensive tactics include arrangements

---

[88] Meyers Parking Sys., Inc., Exchange Act Release No. 26,069 [1988–1989 Transfer Binder] Fed. Sec. L. Rep. (CCH) ¶ 84,333 (1988).

[89] *See* Virginia Bankshares, Inc. v. Sandberg, 501 U.S. 1083 (1991).

[90] *See* Howing Co. v. Nationwide Corp., 826 F.2d 1470 (6th Cir. 1987), *cert. denied*, 486 U.S. 1059 (1988).

[91] For a recent overview of tender offers and defensive tactics, *see* Ronald W. Masulis, Cong Wang & Fei Xie, Corporate Governance and Acquirer Returns, 52 J. Fin. 1851 (2007) (data supporting conclusion that firms protected by antitakeover provisions are less subject to the disciplinary power of the market for corporate control).

[92] Although there is no statutory definition of "tender offer," both the courts and the SEC have taken an expansive approach to include certain privately negotiated control transfers and some open market purchases. *See, e.g.,* Wellman v. Dickinson, 475 F.Supp. 783 (S.D.N.Y. 1979) (privately negotiated "lock-up" of control).

[93] *See, e.g.,* Radol v. Thomas, 534 F.Supp. 1302 (S.D. Ohio 1982).

[94] *See, e.g.,* Smallwood v. Pearl Brewing Co., 489 F.2d 579 (5th Cir.), *cert. denied*, 419 U.S. 873 (1974).

[95] *See, e.g.,* Piper v. Chris-Craft Indus., Inc., 430 U.S. 1 (1977).

[96] *See* Elliott Weiss, Tender Offers and Management Responsibility, 23 N.Y.L. Sch. L. Rev. 445 (1978).

[97] *See* Marc I. Steinberg, Fiduciary Duties and Disclosure Obligations in Proxy and Tender Contests for Corporate Control, 30 Emory L.J. 169 (1981).

[98] Kaplan v. Goldsamt, 380 A.2d 556 (Del. Ch. 1977).

and mergers with "white knights,"[99] the issuance of additional shares to dilute the tender offeror's holdings,[100] or the self-tender for shares from either the raider[101] or the other shareholders.[102] There is, of course, always a characterization issue whether a step taken by the board of directors or the company officers is a defensive maneuver.[103]

There are, of course, many other varieties and combinations of defensive tactics available to the target's management. A common feature of defensive maneuvers such as these is that they can be, and are, taken solely on the authority of the board of directors, without prior authorization or approval by the corporation's shareholders. The most frequently invoked measures are discussed in the next two sections.

A quite different type of defensive measure is the preventive measure, frequently called a "shark repellant" or "porcupine" provision. These measures place in the corporation's articles of incorporation or bylaws a provision or provisions designed not only to protect the corporation's shareholders from certain harmful effects that may accompany a shift in control but also to discourage attempts to make a hostile bid for control.

Three types of shark repellant or porcupine provisions have been identified.[104] The first type of amendment impedes the transfer of corporate control. This includes a staggering of directors' terms of office, which necessarily increases the time it will take to effect a turnover in management, the use of a classified board,[105] a provision that the removal of directors requires cause, the reservation to the board of the right to fill vacancies or add directors, the limitation of the use of consent and special meetings, and the setting of the date for shareholder meetings.[106] Management may further attempt to lock in these provisions by requiring a supermajority to further amend the charter or bylaws.[107]

The second type of amendment creates barriers to the second step in two-tiered transactions by requiring a supermajority for the authorization of a merger following a

---

[99] *See, e.g.*, Piper v. Chris-Craft Indus., 430 U.S. 1 (1977).

[100] A valid business purpose is required for the dilution. It is not allowable if merely a defensive tactic. *See* Norlin Corp. v. Rooney, Pace, Inc., 744 F.2d 255 (2d Cir. 1984).

[101] This is popularly known as submitting to "greenmail." *See* Cheff v. Mathes, 199 A.2d 548 (Del. 1964).

[102] The leading case upholding the self-tender for shares excluding the shares owned by the raider is Unocal Corp. v. Mesa Petroleum Co., 493 A.2d 946 (Del. 1985) (corporate self-tender for shares excluding the shareholder making the hostile tender offer is allowable if there is any rational business purpose for doing so).

[103] *See, e.g.*, Williams v. Geier, 671 A.2d 1368 (Del. 1996) (recapitalization that was supported by owners of more than 50% of the voting shares that had the effect of entrenching their control was not defensive maneuver).

[104] Lewis S. Black, Jr. & Craig B. Smith, Antitakeover Charter Provisions: Defending Self-Help for Takeover Targets, 36 Wash. & Lee L. Rev. 699, 715–716 (1979).

[105] *See generally* Lucian Arye Bebchuk, John C. Coates IV & Guhan Subramanian, The Powerful Antitakeover Force of Staggered Boards: Theory, Evidence, and Policy, 54 Stan. L. Rev. 887 (2002) (staggered boards during 1996–2000 study period increased likelihood of company remaining independent from 34% to 61% and reduced odds of first bidder being successful from 34% to 14%); Robert Daines, Do Classified Boards Affect Firm Value? Takeover Defenses After the Poison Pill, J. Fin. & Quant. Analysis (2002).

[106] *See* Mentor Graphics Corp. v. Quickturn Design Systems, Inc., 728 A.2d 25, 40–41 (Del. Ch. 1998) (upholding bylaw amendment providing that special meeting could not be convened in less than 90–100 days).

[107] *See* Chesapeake Corp. v. Shore, 771 A.2d 293, 343 (Del. Ch. 2000) (bylaw amendment required a 90% shareholder turnout for approval deemed to be preclusive, and if not preclusive, was unreasonable to the threat posed).

tender offer.[108] The percentage required is usually chosen as the average number of shareholders who regularly attend the meetings, so that near unanimity at the meetings is required. Often management collectively controls enough stock to block the required supermajority.

The third type, the fair price amendment, is different from the first two in that, while it may deter a corporate raider, it operates mainly to benefit the shareholders rather than to preserve the management. A fair price amendment may be passed to waive the supermajority requirement for approval of a merger if the second-step buyout price is above a specified amount. Another amendment of this type grants shareholders the right to have their shares redeemed at a certain price after a partial tender offer. This right of redemption is derived from the English Companies Act[109] and was apparently first used in the United States in 1978.[110] It deters tender offers because it removes control from them over how many shares they must purchase and it gives the target shareholders an incentive not to tender their shares at the initial offering.[111]

Much controversy remains over whether the use of various defensive tactics is legal, is within the power of the management at all, or is a breach of management's fiduciary obligations,[112] and whether such use has a positive or negative impact on economic and public policy.[113] Provisions are customarily examined under both the *Unocal* standard, discussed below, and the *Blasius* standard, discussed earlier.

§ 23.6   Defensive Maneuvers and the Business Judgment Rule

There is now abundant evidence that defensive measures on average reduce shareholder welfare.[114] Until the mid-1980s, under the business judgment rule the prevailing approach upheld the directors' defensive maneuvers, unless the plaintiff established that the primary motive behind management's defense was their own personal interest in retaining their jobs with the corporation.[115] Under this approach, defensive maneuvers of all types and magnitude were upheld on a showing that the bidder would likely operate the target company in a manner that diverged from the course followed or recommended by the incumbent management.[116] Because a bidder can always be expected to change at least some of the target company's operations if it successfully acquires control of the

---

[108] Young v. Valhi, Inc., 382 A.2d 1372 (Del. Ch. 1978) (charter provision required approval of 80% of the issued and outstanding common shares in order to accomplish a merger with any offeror holding at least 5% of the corporation's stock).

[109] 11 & 12 Geo. 6, ch. 38, § 209(2) (1948).

[110] Proxy of Rubbermaid, Inc., (Mar. 24, 1978), *reprinted in* Martin Lipton & Erica H. Steinberger, 2 Corporate Takeovers and Freeze-Outs 400–447.

[111] Id. at 414–417.

[112] *See, e.g.,* Asarco, Inc. v. Court, 611 F.Supp. 468 (D.N.J. 1985) (blank-check preferred stock defense is *ultra vires* and void. Unlawful discrimination between shareholders of the same class).

[113] John C. Coffee, Jr., Regulating the Market for Corporate Control: A Critical Assessment of the Tender Offer's Role in Corporate Governance, 84 Colum. L. Rev. 1145 (1984).

[114] For a close review of the empirical studies of the negative impact defensive measures have on share values and the overall wealth of shareholders and with the view that in assessing the data researchers must give close attention to how the defenses interact, *see* Lynn A. Stout, Do Antitakeover Defenses Decrease Shareholder Wealth? The Ex Post/Ex Ante Valuation Problem, 55 Stan. L. Rev. 845 (2002); John C. Coates IV, Takeover Defenses in the Shadow of the Pill: A Critique of the Scientific Evidence, 79 Tex. L. Rev. 271 (2000).

[115] *See, e.g.,* Johnson v. Trueblood, 629 F.2d 287, 292–293 (3d Cir. 1980) (what is needed is "a showing from which a factfinder might infer that impermissible motives predominated in the making of the decision in question").

[116] *See, e.g.,* Panter v. Marshall Field & Co., 646 F.2d 271 (7th Cir.), *cert. denied,* 454 U.S. 1092 (1981); Cheff v. Mathes, 199 A.2d 548 (Del. 1964).

target, an approach that emphasizes solely the directors' motives for defending control strikes down defensive measures only when managers act in haste without developing an adequate record for their actions.[117] One can therefore conclude that a standard that arises only if the directors' primary motive is to save their jobs is an ineffective standard for protecting the interest of shareholders in receiving a valuable offer for their shares.

The most commonly used template for assessing defending control is *Unocal v. Mesa Petroleum Company*,[118] where the Delaware Supreme Court steered a course between the above two contending positions. In *Unocal* the court upheld Unocal's board of directors' decision to self-tender for its own shares in order to thwart a takeover attempt by Mesa Petroleum. Mesa had commenced a front-end loaded two-tiered tender offer for 37 percent of Unocal's outstanding stock—that is, those accepting its offer would receive $54 in cash, and any shares not purchased were to be acquired in the second-stage cash-out merger for a bundle of securities purporting to be worth $54. Unocal's board, with the aid of their investment advisors, believed not only that $54 was an inadequate price, but also that action was necessary to protect the shareholders from a coercive offer. They therefore approved purchasing at $72 per share any Unocal shares not acquired by Mesa if Mesa acquired 50 million Unocal shares through its own tender offer.

After a review of earlier Delaware precedents, *Unocal* embraced a two-step process for judging defensive maneuvers. Under the first step, incumbents have the burden of proving they acted in good faith after reasonable investigation.[119] *Unocal* calls for the burden of proof to be placed on the target board of directors because of the "omnipresent specter that a board may be acting primarily in its own interests, rather than those of the corporation and its shareholders."[120] This level of the *Unocal* process invokes the same areas of concern historically examined under the business judgment rule, except for the location of the burden of proof. Important in resolving this inquiry in favor of the Unocal board was their use of outside investment advisors, the fact that a majority of its directors were outside directors, and the deliberateness of the board's consideration of the issues posed by the Mesa bid.[121]

The second step of the *Unocal* test demands that the defensive measure "must be reasonable in relation to the threat posed."[122] This standard, interpreted literally, suggests courts are required to balance the particular defensive maneuver against the harm threatened by a particular bid. Such an approach necessarily invites more scrutiny of the directors' decisions than normally occurs when the court has already satisfied itself that the directors have acted in good faith after reasonable investigation. However, this step has been largely eroded in later decisions, discussed below.

At the opposite end of this interpretation of *Unocal* is the belief that the two steps in fact collapse into one, such that a board satisfying its burden of proving it acted in good faith after reasonable investigation can "just say no." In one of the most significant corporate decisions of the twentieth century, *Paramount Communications, Inc. v. Time,*

---

[117] *See* Bennett v. Propp, 187 A.2d 405 (Del. 1962) (hasty purchases of shares when no outward threat to acquire control outside protection of business judgment rule).

[118] Unocal v. Mesa Petroleum Company, 493 A.2d 946, 954 (Del. 1985).

[119] Unocal v. Mesa Petroleum Company, 493 A.2d 946, 954 (Del. 1985).

[120] Unocal v. Mesa Petroleum Company, 493 A.2d 946, 954 (Del. 1985).

[121] *See* 493 A.2d at 952–956.

[122] Unocal v. Mesa Petroleum Company, 493 A.2d 946, 954 (Del. 1985).

Inc.,[123] the Delaware Supreme Court interpreted *Unocal's* reasonable relationship standard as being much closer to the "just say no" approach than to one inviting acute assessments of the proportionality between the defensive maneuver and the perceived threat.

The seeds of *Paramount Communications* were planted in the quest by Time's board of directors for a strategic merger partner that, after several years of searching, had focused on Warner Communications. Time proposed a combination of the two firms in which Warner would be acquired by Time in a stock-for-stock transaction that would have required a vote of the Time shareholders. Though Warner was structured as the seller, it was by far the larger entity; after the acquisition 62 percent of the combined companies would be held by the former Warner shareholders. Management succession was worked out so that the vitally important "Time culture" would be preserved. Just shortly after the boards' approvals, Paramount Communications announced an all-cash $175 per-share bid for Time. Because the amount that Paramount bid (which later was raised to $200 per share) was greatly in excess of the amount at which the market was valuing Time shares in light of its proposed acquisition of Warner, it was clear that Time shareholders would never approve its acquisition of Warner. Thus, after discussing alternative defenses to Paramount's bid, Time's board ultimately decided to alter the original agreement to provide that Time would pay cash to acquire Warner so that a vote of the Time shareholders would not be required. This change would require Time to borrow $7–10 billion to carry out the all-cash acquisition.

The Delaware Supreme Court deemed the alteration of the acquisition's consideration from stock to cash as a defensive maneuver that should be examined under *Unocal.*[124] In a major victory for target company directors, *Paramount* holds that the nature of the threat for which defensive measures can be crafted transcends questions of fair price or a coercive offer. For example, in *Paramount* the bid posed a threat to Time's preexisting long-range strategic plans as well as running the risk of confusing the shareholders' approval of a stock-for-stock transaction had that plan been submitted to the Time shareholders for their approval.

Thus *Paramount* reaffirms the board of directors as a presumptively infallible decision-maker regarding the long-term benefits of an incumbent board's strategic plan. The proxy machinery remains available to discipline through nonelection those directors whose policies the shareholders believe do not maximize shareholder wealth. *Paramount* does not appear cleanly to authorize a "just say no" approach because the court reasoned that the reasonable-relationship standard is not violated merely because it made a bidder's acquisition more difficult—Paramount could still acquire Time but, following Time's acquisition of Warner, Paramount's acquisition would necessarily be much larger, but not impossible.[125] In this manner, it is possible to interpret *Paramount* as reasoning that the reasonable-relationship standard would be violated if the defensive maneuver would *preclude* any acquisition whatever of the target company or its successor. Thus a fair reading of *Paramount* is that it alters *Unocal* substantially by inquiring not as to whether on a careful weighing of the facts the defensive maneuver is disproportionate to the threat posed by the bidder or its offer, but whether the effect of the defensive

---

[123] Paramount Communications, Inc. v. Time, Inc., 571 A.2d 1140 (Del. 1989).

[124] Paramount Communications, Inc. v. Time, Inc., 571 A.2d 1140, 1150 (Del. 1989).

[125] Paramount Communications, Inc. v. Time, Inc., 571 A.2d 1140, 1153 (Del. 1989).

maneuver is to preclude any takeover of the target at all.[126] This is a dramatic change in the court's role as initially set forth in *Unocal* and, as such, *Paramount* is correctly viewed as a watershed case.

Even after *Paramount,* the *Unocal* test remains fairly open-ended[127] such that results are determined on a case-by-case basis with little guidance evolving from such factually diverse inquiries. One likely consideration is whether the hostile bid is believed to be coercive. If not, courts appear less willing to uphold defensive steps.[128]

The *Unocal* enhanced duty standard does not apply in every instance that a corporation decides to reject an acquisition proposal.[129] Thus, for example, a board that has no significant financial self-interest, can reject a takeover offer and still have the benefit of the business judgment rule.[130]

The Delaware court has since made it clear that even under the enhanced review standard of *Unocal*, a corporation's board has a wide range of discretion in reacting to hostile takeover attempts. Indeed, there is cause to doubt that little additional scrutiny is introduced through the second step of *Unocal*.[131] As seen in the above discussion of *Paramount,* a showing of preclusion has replaced the earlier proportionality test first embraced in *Unocal*. Moreover, in considering whether a board has acted improperly in refusing to redeem the corporation's poison pill so that a formal takeover of the firm can be considered by the stockholders, the Delaware courts have assumed that the theoretical possibility of a proxy contest renders the pill non-preclusive.[132] Also, under *Unocal's* first step, though the burden of proof is on the target management a good deal of deference still is accorded its decision. Thus, in *Unitrin, Inc. v. American General Corp.,*[133] the court explained that, unless the defensive measures are "draconian" or outside a "range of reasonableness," the board's response should be upheld. A defensive measure is draconian when it is either coercive or preclusive.[134] As explained by the court

---

[126] Hints of proportionality rather than the more demanding preclusive standard appears from time to time. *See* Chesapeake Corp. v. Shore, 771 A.2d 293, 342–43 (Del. Ch. 2000).

[127] *See generally* Ronald Gilson & Ranier Kraakman, Delaware's Intermediate Standard for Defensive Tactics: Is There Substance to Proportionality Review?, 44 Bus. Law. 247 (1989) (examining post-*Unocal* decisions with suggestions for achieving greater certainty by considering type of threat raised as justification for defensive maneuver).

[128] Two pre-*Paramount* decisions struck down defensive maneuvers where the hostile bid was not coercive because cash was offered for all the target shares. AC Acquisitions Corp. v. Anderson, Clayton & Co., 519 A.2d 103 (Del. Ch. 1986); Robert M. Bass Group, Inc. v. Evans, 552 A.2d 1227 (Del. Ch. 1988).

[129] Gantler v. Stephens, 965 A.2d 695, 705 (Del. 2009) (claims of disloyalty unconnected with a defensive action to a hostile takeover are not subject to *Unocal's* heightened scrutiny).

[130] Kahn v. MSB Bancorp, Inc., 1998 WL 409355 (Del. Ch. 1998), *aff's* 734 A.2d 158 (Del. 1999) (customary directors' fees did not in itself create a conflict of interest situation; furthermore, directors' stock ownership meant that the directors' rejection of the offer denied them the takeover premium that was offered).

[131] *See generally* Mark J. Lowenstein, *Unocal* Revisited: No Tiger in the Tank, 27 J. Corp. L. 1 (2001). For an empirical review of how defensive maneuvers have fared in Delaware, especially in the Delaware Supreme Court, since *Unocal* was decided, *see* Robert B. Thompson and D. Gordon Smith, Toward a New Theory of the Shareholder Role: "Sacred Space" in Corporate Takeovers, 80 Tex. L. Rev. 261, 284–286 (2001) (pronouncing the death of *Unocal*).

[132] *See* Ronald J. Gilson, Unocal Fifteen Years Later (And What We Can Do About It), 26 Del. J. Corp. L. 491, 500 (2001).

[133] Unitrin, Inc. v. American General Corp., 651 A.2d 1361 (Del. 1995).

[134] "This court's choice of the term 'draconian' in *Unocal* was a recognition that the law affords boards of directors substantial latitude in defending the perimeter of the corporate bastion against perceived threats. . . . [D]epending upon the circumstances, the board may respond to a reasonably perceived threat by adopting individually or sometimes in combination: advance notice bylaws, supermajority voting provisions, shareholder rights plans, repurchase programs, etc." *Id.* at 1388 n.38.

in *Unitrin*, "[w]hen a corporation is not for sale, the board of directors is the defender of the metaphorical medieval corporate bastion and the protector of the corporation's shareholders."[135] A court should not substitute its judgment for that of the board of directors.[136] The *Unitrin* court refused to compel the target company to redeem its poison pill absent proof that a proxy fight to unseat the target management "would be either mathematically impossible or realistically unattainable."[137] Delaware courts place an especially high burden of proving fairness when the primary purpose of the board's defensive action is to interfere with the shareholders' voting franchise. In such a case, the defendants must present a "compelling justification" for the action.[138] As observed by the Delaware Supreme Court, this heightened standard of review "is quite onerous, and is therefore applied rarely."[139]

Coercion has emerged in Delaware as a prevalent litmus for assessing the validity of corporate action. Coercion is, under the *Unocal-Unitrin* analysis, a basis for invalidating a defensive maneuver. Coercion is actionable when a shareholder is forced into a "choice between a new position and a compromised position for reasons other than those related to the economic merits of the decision."[140]

A central consideration in the *Unocal* analysis is the perceived "threat" posed by the unwanted suitor. In *Unocal* the threat was clearly present, because not only was the bidder a well-known greenmailer, but also its bid was coercive in that it was a front-end loaded two-tier offer that would leave any late-tendering or non-tendering shareholder with junk bonds. Post-*Unocal* decisions have greatly expanded the range of considerations that constitute a threat, applying the broad litmus of *Unitrin* whereby considerations short of a coercive bid are permissible threats if they fall within the "range of reasonableness" standard.

> The *ratio decidendi* for the "range of reasonableness" standard is a need of the board of directors for latitude in discharging its fiduciary duties to the corporation and its shareholders when defending against perceived threats. The concomitant requirement is for judicial restraint. Consequently, if the board of directors' defensive response is not draconian (preclusive or coercive) and is within a "range of reasonableness" a court must not substitute its judgment for the board's.[141]

The highly deferential view reflects not just the unwillingness of courts to enter the role of business decision makers, but also their likely awareness that they would not be very good at such inquiries if they chose to be more active.[142] When a corporation is not for sale,[143] the board of directors thus is given considerable discretion in repelling hostile

---

[135] Unitrin, Inc. v. American General Corp., 651 A.2d 1361, 1388 (Del. 1995).

[136] The court in *Unitrin* overturned the Chancery Court's temporary restraining order and remanded for determination of whether the poison pill and repurchase program were within the range of reasonable defensive measures available to the board.

[137] Unitrin, Inc. v. American General Corp., 651 A.2d 1361, 1381 (Del. 1995).

[138] Blasius Indus. v. Atlas Corp., 564 A.2d 651 (Del. Ch. 1988).

[139] Williams v. Geier, 671 A.2d 1368, 1376 (Del. 1996).

[140] In re General Motors Class H Shareholders Litig., 734 A.2d 611, 621 (Del. Ch. 1999).

[141] Unitrin v. American General Corp., 651 A.2d 1361, 1388 (Del. 1995).

[142] *See generally* Ronal J. Gilson & Reinier Kraakman, Delaware's Intermediate Standard for Defensive Tactics: Is There Substance to Proportionality Review?, 44 Bus. Law. 247, 270–271 (1989).

[143] When a corporation's board of directors has placed the company up for sale, then the *Unocal* test does not apply and the board's duty is to maximize shareholder value.

assaults. Thus, as in *Time,* when a proposed acquisition does not coincide with the target company's established long-term business plan, it may reject the offer to merge.[144]

Preclusion and coercion are not, of course, the sole focus of *Unocal.* Actions by a self-interested board or acts without a reasoned, informed deliberation while vulnerable under the standard applications of the business judgment rule are more so under *Unocal* in view of the burden of proof on such matters being on the board of directors. Thus, in *Chesapeake Corp. v. Shore,*[145] even though the board had established slight price inadequacy, its approval of a supermajority bylaw was invalidated because the directors were self-interested and acted in a "grossly insufficient" manner in approving the bylaw change.

There is some basis to conclude that courts outside of Delaware that invoke the *Unocal* standard accord directors less deference under the first step of *Unocal.*[146] Also, *Unocal* is not the only approach to assessing defensive maneuvers. Other judicial review standards for defensive maneuvers exist, but none is as widely adopted as *Unocal.* Some courts continue to emphasize the standards of good faith (that is, proper motive) and reasonable investigation, but clearly give the directors' defensive actions closer scrutiny than other challenges to their stewardship of the corporation's affairs.[147] Some courts require a compelling or independent business justification for the act that thwarts the bidder's attempt to gain control.[148] In an insightful study, Professor Michal Baruza finds that the most significant factor influencing whether non-Delaware courts follow *Unocal's* heightened review standard is the relative strength of state anti-takeover statutes of the corporation's domicile.[149] For example, the Maryland court reasoned that with the legislature enacting strong anti-takeover provisions for domestic companies it would be inconsistent to follow *Unocal*[150] Thus, in this area, probable legislative intent not only matters, but matters a lot. The alternative to *Unocal's* heightened scrutiny is the

---

[144] Kahn v. MSB Bancorp, Inc., 1998 WL 409355 (Del. Ch. 1998), *aff'd,* 734 A.2d 158 (Del. 1999) (bank holding company that was in the process of acquiring another bank was justified in rejecting unsolicited merger proposal from another bank holding company).

[145] Chesapeake Corp. v. Shore, 771 A.2d 293 (Del. Ch. 2000).

[146] *See, e.g.,* Flake v. Hoskins, 55 F. Supp. 2d 1196, 1217 (D. Kan. 1999).

[147] *See* Dynamics Corp. of Am. v. WHX Corp., 967 F.Supp. 59 (D. Conn. 1997) (applying New York business judgment rule to conclude decision not to redeem pill was reasonable in light of superior terms of merger supported by management).

[148] *See* Klaus v. Hi-Shear Corp., 528 F.2d 225 (9th Cir. 1975) (compelling business reason for transferring shares to ESOP).

[149] Michal Barzuza, The State of Antitakeover Law, 95 Va. L. Rev. 1973 (2009). *But see* Hanson Trust PLC v. ML SCM Acquisition, Inc., 781 F.2d 264, 273 (2d Cir. 1986) (rejecting *Unocal* for a New York corporation before that state had enacted any anti-takeover provision). After enacting an "other constituency" statute a court invoked that statute's enactment to justify continuing not to apply *Unocal.* Dynamics Corp. of Am. v. WHX Corp., 967 F. Supp. 59, 64–65 (D. Conn. 1997).

[150] Hudson v. Prime Retail, Inc., 2004 WL 1982383 (Md. Cir. Ct. Apr. 1, 2004). Before the legislature had adopted the anti-takeover provision codifying the business judgment rule a federal court had assessed the defensive maneuvers under *Unocal. See* NCR Corp. v. American Telephone & Telegraph Co., 761 F. Supp. 475 (S.D. Ohio 1991).

For states without an anti-takeover statute that have adopted the approach in *Unocal, see* Flake v. Hoskins, 55 F. Supp. 1196, 1212 (D. Kan. 1999) and weak statutes do not preclude *Unocal. See* Amanda Acquisition Corp. v. Universal Foods Corp., 798 F. Supp. 984 (E.D. Wis. 1989) (concluding statutes appeared consistent with Delaware's approach to defensive maneuvers).

standard application of the business judgment rule where the director's actions are presumed a valid exercise of authority.[151]

The American Law Institute's approach allows directors to take any step that "has the foreseeable effect of blocking an unsolicited tender offer" and then proceeds to provide that in considering whether the board's response is reasonable the "board may take into account all factors relevant to the best interests of the corporation and the shareholders," including "whether the offer, if successful, would threaten the corporation's essential economic prospects."[152] By placing the burden of proof on the person challenging the defensive maneuver, the American Law Institute embraces a less intrusive approach than occurs in Delaware and in most other states.[153] A further qualification and defensive maneuver arises when the directors must facilitate an auction for control.

Although we might well conclude that there has been a weakening of the law's moderating influence on management's tendency to deflect socially beneficial shifts in control (most notably before the Delaware Supreme Court), a more holistic view suggests that any weakness in the law may be counterbalanced by other developments. The wide practice of boards of directors being independent of the officers they monitor, the rise in stock and other incentive plans, and an increasingly more competitive product markets are each developments that are counter to the management entrenchment thesis. Such developments may account for why the level of takeover activity, while first declining in the years immediately following corporate law developments that tended to entrench managers, has returned to historically high levels.[154]

§ 23.7 Judicial Treatment of Specific Types of Defensive Maneuvers

Nowhere is the lawyer's creativity better documented than in the seemingly endless varieties of defensive maneuvers that have developed and continue to evolve. Moreover, the flexibility—or perhaps the indeterminacy—of the prevailing review standards (as seen in *Unocal*, discussed in the preceding section) becomes quite evident in examining how the very different features that distinguish defensive maneuvers from one another are treated under *Unocal*.

Poison Pills. The most common type of defensive measure is a shareholder rights plan, more commonly known as a "poison pill." The device begins with a corporation's distribution, generally in the form of dividend, of "rights" pro rata among its stockholders. A right entitles its holder to purchase stock or other security upon a certain triggering event. The precise triggering (or activating) event depends on the type of pill. As will be seen, in the "flip-over" variety of pill, the triggering event is a second-step transaction, such as a merger or asset purchase by the bidder of the target corporation.

---

[151] Torchmark Corp. v. Bixby, 798 F. Supp. 1010 (W.D. Mo. 1988)(absent evidence of fraud or self-dealing the board's actions entitled to deference).

[152] ALI, Principles of Corporate Governance: Analysis and Recommendations § 6.02(a)(b) (1994). An important qualification is that non-shareholder interests may be considered "if to do so would not significantly disfavor the long-term interests of shareholders." *Id.* at § 6.02(b)(2).

[153] ALI, Principles of Corporate Governance: Analysis and Recommendations § 6.02(c). An insightful critique of the undue conservatism of the ALI's approach appears in Elliott J. Weiss, Whose Rules Should Govern Takeovers: Delaware's, the ALI's, or Martin Lipton's?, 33 Ariz. L. Rev. 761 (1991).

[154] *See* Marcel Kahan & Edward B. Rock, How I learned to Stop Worrying and Love the Pill: Adaptive Responses to Takeover Law, 69 U. Chi. L. Rev. 871, 881–884 (2002).

In the "flip-in" variety of pill, the triggering event is usually a first-step transaction, such as the bidder launching a tender offer for, or completing the purchase of, a certain percentage of the corporation's stock—for example, 20 percent of its outstanding stock. The precise right that a holder has upon the triggering event's occurrence depends on the type of poison pill.[155] Many pills contain a "post-trigger safety valve" that allows the target board to redeem the pill after an acquirer has triggered it, provided the board determines the acquisition does not harm the corporation.[156]

A flip-over poison pill allows the target company's shareholders to acquire the bidder's stock at a substantial discount, usually at half price (for example, the purchase of $200 worth of the bidder's common shares by paying only $100) if the two corporations merge. The flip-over pill becomes operative, therefore, when the bidder, after acquiring a substantial ownership interest in the target, merges the target into itself or another entity that it controls. The overall effect of the target shareholders' exercising their flip-over rights is to dilute substantially the value of the bidder's common shares. It is because of this possibility that the flip-over provision acts as a disincentive to unwanted suitors. Its primary benefit to the target shareholders is to protect them against an unfair, coercive second-step merger that forces them to give up their target shares for securities or cash of the bidder.

Another variety of poison pill is the "back-end" plan, under which the target corporation's board of directors designates a price deemed fair for the target shares. Thereafter, the target shareholders have a right to require the target corporation to acquire their shares at that price, provided the bidder has not already acquired the shares at that price. As with the flip-over pill, the primary objective of a back-end pill is to protect stockholders from a coercive second-step merger.

The flip-over pill is not operative, however, if the bidder does not merge with the target. Thus a flip-over provision can be avoided if the bidder operates the target as a controlled subsidiary. Even this arrangement does little to salve the unease that the target management may have for the unwanted bidder. Target management is not without mechanisms to discourage a nonmerging bidder—it may resort to a "flip-in" poison pill. A flip-in rights plan allows the holders to acquire stock or other securities of the target company at prices substantially below their market value. The triggering event for the flip-in pill is generally the bidder announcing a tender offer for a certain percentage of the target's shares and/or its purchase of a stated percentage of the target's shares. Because the amount specified is generally in the 20 to 30 percent range, the flip-in pill can be triggered even though control may not in fact be threatened.[157]

Consequently, if the rights are triggered and thereafter exercised by their holders, the cost of the acquisition to the bidder increases substantially as the value of its holdings is diluted by the ability of other holders to purchase additional shares of the target below their fair market value. The potency of poison pills in dampening the

---

[155] For an unfortunate unintended result involving a flip-in provision, *see* Emeritus Corp. v. ARV Assisted Living, Inc., Case No. 793420 (Super Ct. Orange Cty. 1999) (issuing shares to friendly investment group inadvertently triggered rights plan that hostile bidder could take advantage of).

[156] *See* Versata Enterprises, Inc. v. Selectica, Inc., 5 A.3d 586 (Del. 2010).

[157] *See* Dynamics Corp. of Am. v. CTS Corp., 794 F.2d 250 (7th Cir. 1986), *rev'd on other grounds,* 481 U.S. 69 (1987) (invalidating flip-in pill where trigger was activated by bidder's purchase of 15% of the target shares, even though that bidder did not intend to seek control of bidder).

appetite of would-be suitors of target corporations has been documented by several studies that reflect that negative stock effects accompany the adoption of poison pills.[158]

Poison pills have spawned a good deal of litigation regarding their validity under state statutes and the directors' fiduciary obligations with respect to a poison pill defense.[159] A common and necessary feature of any rights plan is that the bidder receives no rights and cannot acquire any rights from another. That is, the dilutive effects vis-à-vis the bidder could easily be overcome by the bidder's purchase of the rights from their holders, if those rights could be so acquired. Thus rights plans commonly provide that the rights are not issued to the bidder and are not transferable. Only a few courts have invalidated rights plans because of their discriminatory treatment within the same class of shares.[160] Rights plans that do not include the bidder can have unanticipated and unwanted effects even if the rights are nontransferrable.[161]

The leading case applying *Unocal* to uphold the adoption of a poison pill plan is *Moran v. Household International, Inc.,*[162] where the Delaware Supreme Court reasoned that a flip-over provision was analogous to the antidilution provisions that customarily exist to protect holders of senior securities in mergers. With this predicate, the court then reasoned that a poison pill was a reasonable and proportional response to a threat of a harmful second-step coercive merger at a price unfair to the target shareholders. *Moran* emphasized that the rights were redeemable prior to their activation by the triggering event.

As *Moran* emphasized, the rights' redemption feature is a key element to their legal validity as a takeover defense and is central to understanding why poison pills are created in the first place.

Two pre-*Paramount Communications* decisions held that the target directors cannot refuse to redeem the pill in the face of an offer that is neither coercive nor unfair on its face.[163] An important feature of both these decisions was the non-coercive nature of the bidder's offer. On the other hand, there are a larger number of decisions that evidence the patience and deference courts accord the target board of directors' decision not to redeem the pill, at least to the extent of allowing the target board to devise or execute a plan for a greater return for the target shareholders.[164] *Paramount Communications'* deference to the target management being able to adhere to its preexisting strategic plan is consistent with the view that great deference is to be accorded decisions not to redeem a pill. Thus the traditional route of a proxy contest

---

[158] *See* Dosoung Choi, Sreenivas Kamma & Joseph Weintrop, The Delaware Courts, Poison Pills, and Shareholder Wealth, 5 J. L., Econ. & Org., 375 (1989); Gregg A. Jarrell, James A. Brickley, & Jeffrey N. Netter, Market for Corporate Control: Empirical Evidence Since 1980, 2 J. Econ. Persp. 49 (1988).

[159] *See* Gearhart Indus. v. Smith Int'l, Inc., 741 F.2d 707 (5th Cir. 1984) ("springing" feature of warrant was not manipulative under section 14(e)).

[160] *See* Avon Prod., Inc. v. Chartwell Assoc. L.P., 907 F.2d 322 (2d Cir. 1990).

[161] *See, e.g.,* Emeritus Corp. v. ARV Assisted Living, Inc., Case No. 793420 (Super Ct. Orange Cty. 1999) (defensive tactic that involved issuing shares to friendly investment group inadvertently triggered rights plan that hostile bidder could take advantage of).

[162] Moran v. Household International, Inc., 500 A.2d 1346 (Del. 1985).

[163] Grand Metro. Public Ltd. v. Pillsbury Co., 558 A.2d 1049 (Del. Ch. 1988) (restructuring response proposed by target management not clearly better than that of bidders because it would require long-term holdings to recoup predicted greater rewards than immediate cash all shares bid).

[164] *See, e.g.,* Dynamics Corp. of America v. WHX Corp., 967 F.Supp. 59 (D. Conn. 1997) (concluding the plaintiff-bidder continued to have the inferior offer so that pill need not be redeemed to preserve merger with another company offer greater premium).

would be necessary to dislodge the recalcitrant board as a prelude to acquiring a controlling interest in a target firm.[165]

eBay Domestic Holdings Inc. v. Newmark,[166] is one of the very few recent decisions to invalidate the adoption of a poison pill. Moreover, the case arose in a closely held, not a publicly held corporation.[167] Two owners of more than 70 percent of craigslist Inc.'s stock approved the issuance of a pill designed to prevent eBay from either acquiring more craigslist shares or selling the shares it owned. The Delaware Chancery Court, applying *Unocal's* two-prong test struck down the pill. The court reasoned that the board's action failed to meet *Unocal's* first step by not advancing a proper *corporate* purpose and as to the second prong it was not reasonably related to the goal of preserving the company's culture.

The most draconian form of the poison pill is the so-called "dead hand" poison pill, so named because its distinguishing feature is its continuing director provision which permits the rights to be redeemed only by the directors who were in office when the rights plan was put into place.[168] Thus, under a dead hand poison pill a new board of directors, whose members support the firm's acquisition, cannot redeem the rights that stand as an obstacle to the firm being acquired. On its face, such a continuing director provision conflicts directly with the well-established principle that contractual provisions that restrain the discretion of the board of directors are void as against public policy. Emphasizing the strong public policy in the boards' power to manage the affairs of the corporation, the New York Supreme Court invalidated the dead hand poison pill of Irving Bank Co.[169] The Delaware Supreme Court invalidated what it described as a "no hand" or "delayed redemption provision" of a rights plan.[170] The delayed redemption provision provided that, if the shareholders replace a majority of the directors, the newly elected board could not redeem the rights for six months if the purpose or effect of the redemption were to facilitate a transaction with an "interested person." The court explained that such a provision by limiting the new directors' ability to redeem a poison pill could prevent them from authorizing a transaction that their fiduciary duty would otherwise require.[171] The Delaware Chancery Court struck down a "dead hand" poison

---

[165] *See* Lyman Johnson & David Millon, The Case Beyond *Time,* 45 Bus. Law. 2105 (1990) (arguing that *Paramount* endorses the "just say no" defense).

[166] eBay Domestic Holdings, Inc. v. Newmark, 2009 WL 3806162 (Del. Ch. 2009).

[167] *See* Kurz v. Holbrook, 989 A.2d 140, 183 (Del. Ch. 2010)("fiduciary duties [such as those in *Unocal*] apply regardless of whether the corporation is registered and publicly traded, dark and delisted, or closely held").

[168] *See generally* Lese, Preventing Control From the Grave: A Proposal for Judicial Treatment of Dead Hand Provisions in Poison Pills, 96 Colum. L. Rev. 2175 (1996).

[169] *See* Bank of New York Co. v. Irving Bank Corp., 528 N.Y.S.2d 482 (Sup. Ct. 1988).

[170] Quickturn Design Systems, Inc. v. Shapiro, 721 A.2d 1281 (Del. 1998).

[171] As the court explained:

One of the most basic tenets of Delaware corporate law is that the board of directors has the ultimate responsibility for managing the business and affairs of a corporation. Section 141(a) [of the Delaware statute] requires that any limitation on the board's authority be set out in the certificate of incorporation. The Quickturn certificate of incorporation contains no provision purporting to limit the authority of the board in any way. The Delayed Redemption Provision, however, would prevent a newly elected board of directors from completely discharging its fundamental management duties to the corporation and its stockholders for six months. While the Delayed Redemption Provision limits the board of directors' authority in only one respect, the suspension of the Rights Plan, it nonetheless restricts the board's power in an area of fundamental importance to the shareholders—negotiating a possible sale of the corporation. Therefore, we hold that the Delayed Redemption Provision is invalid under section 141(a), which confers upon any pill,[172] since it would conflict with the Delaware statute imposing fiduciary duties on the new directors,[173] because it violates the rule that the "shareholder vote has primacy in our system,"[174] and also because the dead hand poison pill is disproportionate and thus violates the Delaware Supreme Court's rulings in its *Unocal* and *Unitrin* decisions.[175] In contrast, a federal district court upheld a poison pill,[176] stressing the unrestrained language of the state corporation statute that authorizes poison pills for Georgia corporations. There is ample reason to believe that the federal district court misinterpreted the Georgia legislature's intent in amending the state's business corporation act to more clearly empower the board of directors to issue poison pills.[177] More importantly, there are serious policy reasons that counsel against subjecting the corporation to the effects of continuing director provisions; a dead hand on the tiller is not much comfort to the vessel's passengers.[178] Nevertheless, in another federal district court decision, decided under Pennsylvania law, the court refused to give a declaratory judgment invalidating a dead hand poison pill with a delayed redemption provision.[179] The court there also noted that the dead hand features were not indefinite and handcuffed the new board for a specified period of time.[180]

The presence of a poison pill and a classified board whereby directors serve staggered three-year terms greatly enhances the potency of the poison pill. A strategy to takeover a firm with a poison pill is to do so in two steps: step one is launching a proxy campaign to gain control of the board and step two is for the newly elected directors to redeem the pill. The presence of a classified board means that a party wishing to overcome a pill by first gaining control of the board will have to be very patient as it will require two annual meetings for a new majority to be elected to the board. Most bidders are not patient. Recall that all pills contain a provision allowing the board to redeem the pill before the trigger is engaged and the pill's catastrophic effects occur. Despite the additional and substantial protection that a classified board adds to the pill, the addition of a classified board to the pill does not, however, appear to make the pill more vulnerable under *Unocal-Unitrin*. *Air Products and Chemicals, Inc. v. Airgas, Inc.* upheld a poison pill that was coupled with a staggered board. The Chancellor reasoned, in part, that Delaware continues to uphold reasonably based board decisions not to redeem the pill. Very persuasive to the Chancellor that the board had so acted in refusing to redeem the pill in view of the fact that the bidder had been successful in having its nominees elected

---

newly elected board of directors the full power to manage and direct the business and affairs of a Delaware corporation.

721 A.2d at 1291–1292. *Accord,* Carmody v. Toll Brothers, Inc., 723 A.2d 1180 (Del. Ch. 1998).

[172] Carmody v. Toll Brothers, Inc., 723 A.2d 1180 (Del. Ch. 1998).

[173] Carmody v. Toll Brothers, Inc., 723 A.2d 1180 (Del. Ch. 1998).

[174] Carmody v. Toll Brothers, Inc., 723 A.2d 1180, 1195 (Del. Ch. 1998).

[175] Carmody v. Toll Brothers, Inc., 723 A.2d 1180, 1194–1195 (Del. Ch. 1998).

[176] *See* Invacare Corp. v. Healthdyne Technologies, Inc., 968 F.Supp. 1578 (N.D. Ga. 1997).

[177] *See generally* Lucas O. Harsh, Note, Dead Hand Poison Pills: Will Georgia Corporations Continue to Issue a Lethal Dose, 16 Ga. St. U. L. Rev. 665 (2000).

[178] For a review of the many arguments against continuing director provisions, *see* Lese, Preventing Control from the Grave: A Proposal for Judicial Treatment of Dead Hand Provisions in Poison Pills, 96 Colum. L. Rev. 2175 (1996).

[179] AMP, Inc. v. Allied Signal, Inc., 1998 WL 778348 *8 (E.D. Pa. 1998) (unpublished case).

[180] AMP, Inc. v. Allied Signal, Inc., 1998 WL 778348 *8 (E.D. Pa. 1998) ("Being finite in time, the duration must be viewed in light of the ordinary business judgment rule that is allowed directors, as well as the presumptions of good faith for disinterested majorities established in section 1715(d) in matters dealing with potential or proposed acquisition of control of the corporation.").

so that they became one-third of the board only to see its newly anointed nominees join the other directors in concluding the bidder's offer was inadequate.[181]

Poison pill rights plans have brought into question the relative power of shareholders and directors. Who has the final word in the adoption of poison pills—the shareholders or directors? The pill comes into existence by the fiat of the board of directors exercising its authority under the "blank stock" provision of the articles of incorporation. Having the general authority to issue shares with such "rights, privileges and preferences" as the board believes is appropriate, no further approval from the stockholders is necessary for the rights to be issued.[182] In *International Brother-hood of Teamsters General Fund v. Fleming Companies,*[183] the Oklahoma Supreme Court upheld a shareholder adopted bylaw that restricted the board of directors' ability to adopt a rights plan. Among other things, the court noted that unlike some other states, Oklahoma does not have a statute specifically authorizing such rights plans, although it does have a statute authorizing stock options and rights generally. The absence of a statute specifically authorizing poison pill rights plans is a basis for distinguishing *Fleming* in those states having specific statutory authorization. According to the Oklahoma court in *Fleming,* the Delaware and Oklahoma statutes are similar. In a related development, the SEC indicated that in the absence of clear Delaware law on point, it was unable to conclude that the mandatory bylaw amendment was not a proper shareholder matter.[184]

Issuer Repurchases and Restructurings. One response that target management can make to a hostile bid believed to offer an inadequate amount for the target corporation's shares is to develop a plan that offers a greater amount. The simplest approach is for the target corporation to initiate its own tender offer for a certain percentage of its shares. This is unlikely to thwart the unwanted bid, however, as target shareholders would still be able to tender to the bidder the shares that were not acquired by the target in its self-tender offer. Thus all that a simply designed self-tender offer accomplishes is to reduce ultimately the number of shares the bidder must purchase to obtain control (that is, after the target corporation's self-tender, there are fewer outstanding shares, so control requires an absolute smaller number of shares to be held). To scuttle an unwanted offer a self-tender offer must be structured so as to coerce the shareholders to choose the issuer's offer over that of the outside bidder.[185] Such an effect has been held to violate *Unocal* because of its coercive nature and because it likely will not be judged to be reasonably related to the threat posed when the bidder's offer was for all the outstanding shares.[186] Recall that the defensive maneuver upheld in *Unocal* was a self-tender offer that excluded the shares of the hostile bidder; that offer was

---

[181] 16 A.3d 48 (Del.Ch. 2011) (the court also embraced a "realistically attainable" standard for assessing the legality of a provision conditioning removal of the entire board upon a two-thirds vote of the outstanding shares concluding this was met by evidence that if the shareholders received a "sufficiently appealing" offer that their approval would be forthcoming).

[182] *See* Leonard Loventhal Account v. Hilton Hotels Corp., 780 A.2d 245 (Del. 2001) (power recognized by *Moran* would be meaningless if rights plan required stockholder approval).

[183] International Brotherhood of Teamsters General Fund v. Fleming Companies, 975 P.2d 907 (Okla. 1999).

[184] General DataComm Industries, Inc. SEC No-Act LEXIS 1037 (SEC No-Action Letter Dec. 9, 1998). This was a reversal of the Commission's previous position.

[185] For a close analysis that defensive repurchases, like third party tender offers, pressure firm shareholders and accordingly each should be similarly regulated, *see* Michael Bradley & Michael Rozenzweig, Defensive Stock Repurchases, 99 Harv. L. Rev. 1377 (1986).

[186] *See* AC Acquisitions Corp. v. Anderson, Clayton & Co., 519 A.2d 103 (Del. Ch. 1986).

upheld, however, because the bidder's offer posed the threat of a second-step unfair cash-out merger of the target shares not acquired in its first-step tender offer. A repurchase is also effective if it causes the insiders' percentage ownership to increase such that they can veto any actions of the unwanted suitor.[187] When the outside bid is for *all* the target shares, the target shareholders have the freedom to compare that offer with what is offered by the target management. Thus there appears no practical justification to protect the corporation or the shareholders from the coercive features of target management's response.[188]

A means for the target to offer greater value than is being offered in the hostile tender offer is to undertake a restructuring of the corporation. Restructuring includes a variety of ways by which a corporation can generate cash to distribute pro rata among its stockholders by selling major divisions and by borrowing significant amounts of money with the effect of increasing the financial leverage within its capital structure. After these steps are taken, the existing shareholders are offered a package of securities (equity and debt) and cash that in combination have a value greater than that offered by the hostile bid. Many successful restructurings are indistinguishable in their effects from a leverage buyout, as the target corporation borrows to the full extent of is debt capacity, raising concerns for future financial distress that may require additional asset disposals to reduce the crushing burden of its newly incurred debt. Courts have been reluctant to enjoin restructurings, viewing them as alternative means to maximize the value of the firm for the benefit of its shareholders.[189]

Greenmail. Another form a defensive repurchase can take is "greenmail," whereby the target board of directors approves the corporation acquiring the target shares held by a raider at a premium above-market price so as to fend off a takeover.[190] For such a purchase to be protected by the business judgment rule, the record must reveal a good faith reasonable belief of the target board of directors that the corporate interest is served by the repurchase. In a few instances, the courts have ruled favorably on pretrial motions brought by plaintiffs challenging a greenmail transaction. A leading case is *Heckman v. Ahmanson*,[191] where the court preliminarily enjoined a greenmail payment by Walt Disney Productions Inc. that offered approximately a $60 million profit to the Steinberg Group. There was insufficient evidence that a corporate purpose was served by the repurchase, so the inference arose that the repurchase was guided only by the naked desire of the incumbents to retain their positions of control.[192]

In response to concern over greenmail, the Tax Reform Act of 1986 included provisions that disallow any deduction "for any amount paid or incurred by a corporation in connection with the redemption of its stock,"[193] and in 1987 Congress imposed a 50

---

[187] *See* American Gen. Corp. v. Unitrin, Inc., 1994 WL 698483 (Del. Ch. 1994).

[188] This point was recognized in Shamrock Holdings, Inc. v. Polaroid Corp., 559 A.2d 278 (Del. Ch. 1989), but management's coercive self-tender offer was not enjoined because the court was persuaded that shareholders would have difficulty comparing the two choices before them because of the indefiniteness of determining the future value of a significant patent infringement action the issuer had against another major corporation.

[189] *See* British Printing & Communication Corp. v. Harcourt Brace Jovanovich, Inc., 664 F.Supp. 1519 (S.D.N.Y. 1987).

[190] *See* David Manry & D. Strangeland, Greenmail: A Brief History, 6 Stan. J. L. & Bus. 217 (2001).

[191] Heckmann v. Ahmanson, 214 Cal.Rptr. 177 (Ct. App. 1985).

[192] For similar reasoning, *see* Lou v. Belzberg, 728 F.Supp. 1010 (S.D.N.Y. 1990).

[193] 26 U.S.C. § 162 (2000).

percent excise tax on the gain or other income arising from a payment that is not made on the same terms to all shareholders.[194] The tax laws, therefore, provide a substantial disincentive for greenmail transactions.

Share Issuances and ESOPs. The most direct assault on a hostile bid is by the target board of directors issuing a substantial block of voting shares to a holder who can be depended on to support the incumbent management team.[195] In such a situation, the target board of directors has a heavy burden of proof either that its primary motive in approving the issuance of shares was not related to control of the corporation[196] or that the hostile bid posed a threat to the corporation or its shareholders. The most common form this defensive maneuver takes is the target corporation issuing shares to an employee stock ownership plan (ESOP). ESOPs are tax-favored devices[197] designed to provide retirement benefits for a corporation's employees through the collective stock ownership of their employer.

Challenges to ESOPs on the grounds that they are an invalid defensive maneuver have largely depended on whether the reviewing court is persuaded that the primary motive for transferring shares to the ESOP was to entrench management. Absent evidence that the corporate interest is in improving employee morale and productivity, an ESOP adopted in the heat of a takeover will most likely be enjoined.[198] To date, the most sympathetic reaction to an ESOP created in the heat of a takeover battle was that taken by the Delaware Chancery Court in *Shamrock Holdings Inc. v. Polaroid Corporation,*[199] where the court, applying the review standard of intrinsic fairness,[200] was persuaded that the ESOP was designed to improve employee productivity, that no substantial out-of-pocket costs were incurred by the corporation because funding came largely from the employees, and any immediate dilutive effects on share values would be recouped over time through expected gains in productivity.[201] Transfers of additional shares after a takeover bid to an ESOP created before that bid requires close consideration of whether the subsequent transfer of shares to the ESOP was part of the on-going strategy to improve employee productivity.[202] In contrast, an ESOP hastily initiated after the commencement of a hostile bid and approved without adequate

---

[194] 26 U.S.C. § 5881 (2000).

[195] *See, e.g.,* Unilever Acquisition Corp. v. Richardson-Vicks, Inc., 618 F.Supp. 407 (S.D.N.Y. 1985) (issuing preliminary injunction against dividend in preferred stock that would dilute the offeror's control).

[196] *See, e.g.,* Klaus v. Hi-Shear Corp., 528 F.2d 225 (9th Cir. 1975) (injunction granted where target board failed to establish a compelling business justification for share issuance); Condec Corp. v. Lunkenheimer Co., 230 A.2d 769 (Del. Ch. 1967) (injunction granted where primary purpose was to preserve control).

[197] An employer can establish an ESOP in many ways, but the maximum tax advantages arise if the funds for the shares contributed to the ESOP are borrowed. The lender or employer can exclude from gross income 50% of the interest received from a loan to the employer or ESOP when the loan proceeds are used to acquire employer securities. In any case, employers are allowed to deduct the dividends paid on the ESOP shares when those dividends are distributed by the ESOP or the employer to the plan's participants. Finally, when an ESOP is created by the termination of a qualified plan, any excess assets that existed in the qualified plan that are transferred to the ESOP are exempt from the 10% excise tax that otherwise applies. *See generally* CCH Guide to Employee Benefits ¶¶ 271–277 (1986).

[198] *See, e.g.,* Norlin Corp. v. Rooney, Pace, Inc., 744 F.2d 255 (2d Cir. 1984) (requires proof of a basis independent from threat posed by bidder for creation of ESOP).

[199] Shamrock Holdings, Inc. v. Polaroid Corp., 559 A.2d 257 (Del. Ch. 1989).

[200] Because the directors did not themselves purport to judge their actions as defensive maneuvers such that their decision embraced the considerations demanded by *Unocal,* the court treated this as a standard conflict-of-interest case, whereby the directors have the burden of proving intrinsic fairness. *Id.* at 271.

[201] Shamrock Holdings, Inc. v. Polaroid Corp., 559 A.2d 257, 272–273 (Del. Ch. 1989).

[202] *See* Danaher Corp. v. Chicago Pneumatic Tool Co., 633 F.Supp. 1066, 1071–1073 (S.D.N.Y. 1986).

information as to the ESOP's benefits to the company is outside the protection of the business judgment rule.[203]

Lock-Up Options and Other Deal Protection Arrangements.[204] When confronted by two or more opposing bids for control, target management sometimes enters into an arrangement with one of the bidders that has the effect of conferring on that bidder a significant strategic advantage in the contest for control vis-à-vis the other bidders. These arrangements can take several forms, such as an option by the preferred bidder to acquire significant target assets at a favorable price (called a "lock-up option"), an agreement not to seek other bidders (called a "no-shop clause"), the payment of a significant fee if that bidder's offer does not result in the bidder obtaining control (called a "termination fee," "hello fee" or "goodbye fee"),[205] or agreeing to share certain proprietary/inside information only with that bidder.[206] Because of their dampening effect on continued bidding for control, these arrangements are correctly characterized as defensive maneuvers and will be examined under *Unocal*. They also are more frequently examined under the special requirements of *Revlon*, discussed in the next section.

Termination fees can be examined either under contract law, where the question is whether it is an enforceable provision for liquidated damages or under corporate law.[207] Some courts instead view termination fees as an alternative form of performance.[208] Under the former the first question is whether damages would be uncertain if the deal were not consummated. If so uncertain, the final test of the provisions validity is whether the amount so stated is reasonable.[209] From a corporate perspective the questions are examined under *Revlon* and/or *Unocal* being persuaded by such considerations as the provision being necessary to obtain the bid.[210] Fees of one to five percent of the transaction's value are believed reasonable.[211]

Another common provision requires a board to submit the merger proposal to its shareholders (generally referred to as a "force the vote" provision) or bars the target management from actively pursuing other bidders (referred to as a "no-talk/shop" provision). Each type of agreement inherently restricts the freedom of a board of

---

[203] *Compare* NCR Corp. v. American Tel. and Tel. Co., 761 F.Supp. 475 (S.D. Ohio 1991) *with* Katz v. Chevron Corp., 27 Cal.Rptr.2d 681 (Ct. App. 1994) (upholding creation of credit facility that acquired company's shares).

[204] *See generally* Sean J. Griffith, Deal Protection Provisions In The Last Period of Play, 71 Ford. L. Rev. 1899 (2003); R. Franklin Balotti & A. Gilchrist Sparks, III, Deal Protection Measures and the Merger Recommendation, 96 Nw. U. L. Rev. 467 (2002); Leo E. Strine, Jr., Categorical Confusion: Deal Protection Measures in Stock-for-Stock Merger Agreements, 56 Bus. Law. 919 (2001).

[205] *See, e.g.,* In re Lear Corp. Shareholder Litig., 967 A.2d 640 (Del. Ch. 2008) (not outside business judgment rule to approve $25 million termination fee in exchange for suitor increasing bid $1.25 per share when shareholder disapproval looked likely and there were no other suitors).

[206] There is extensive literature on lock-ups. *See* John C. Coates IV & Guhan Subramanian, A Buy-Side Model of Lockups: Theory and Evidence, Marcel Kahan & Michael Klausner, Lockups and the Market for Corporate Control, 48 Stan. L. Rev. 1539 (1996) (arguing lock-ups are socially harmful because they reduce the first bidder's gains and place too much discretion with managers). For a more favorable view of lock-ups.

[207] Beebe v. Pacific Realty Trust, 578 F.Supp. 1128, 1150 (D. Or. 1984).

[208] St. Jude Medical, Inc. v. Medtronic, Inc., 536 N.W.2d 24, 28–29 (Minn. Ct. App. 1995).

[209] *See* Brazen v. Bell Atlantic Corp., 695 A.2d 43, 48 (Del. 1997) (relying upon Lee Builders v. Wells, 103 A.2d 918 (Del.Ch. 1954)).

[210] *See* J.P. Stevens & Co., Shareholders Litigation, 542 A.2d 770 (Del. Ch. 1988); Shaper v. Bryan, 371 Ill. App.3d 1079, 1082, 864 N.E.2d 876, 880–981 (1st Dist. 2007).

[211] *See* Dennis J. Block & Jonathan M. Hoff, Protective Provisions, Fiduciary Outs in Merger Agreements, 224 N.Y.L.J. 5 (Aug. 24, 2000).

directors and meets the historical reluctance of courts to uphold agreements that interfere with the directors' discretion. That is, the board of director's fiduciary obligation is paramount to any contractual obligation.[212] At the same time, the contractual requirements cannot simply be ignored under the guise that the directors are fiduciary.[213] Hence, there is an interesting dynamic that arises whereby the validity of the contractual restrictions is assessed in terms of whether ex ante entering into the contractual restrictions was pursuant to the directors' fiduciary responsibilities. For example, the Colorado Supreme Court held that the target board was not prevented by its contractual obligation to use its "best lawful efforts" to obtain stockholder approval from withdrawing the board's recommendation that the company be sold after a sudden rise in commodity prices greatly increased the value of the firm.[214] In this context, a blanket no shop and no talk provision which both bars seeking bidders or even talking to unsolicited suitors would be of doubtful validity.[215] In the leading case, *Paramount Communications, Inc. v. QVC Network, Inc.,*[216] the Delaware Supreme Court held that merger agreement terms that mandated directors act in a certain fashion or that the directors forbear were invalid. Thus, the Delaware Supreme Court held that a no-shop provision was unenforceable because it unduly restricted the board in fulfilling its fiduciary duties in responding to changing circumstances that typically occur in takeover contests.[217] However, the case is distinctive because the merger posed a change of control such that the company had entered the *Revlon* moment, discussed below, and was not seen as the product of the board acting in a deliberate and open-minded manner. In *Ace Ltd. v. Capital Re Corp.,*[218] the Delaware Chancery court avoided invalidating such an agreement because the provision permitted the target board to escape the clause if there was an unsolicited superior bid and it was advised by counsel that not to consider the competing bid would constitute a breach of their fiduciary duties. The latter clause in *Capital Re* is known as a "fiduciary out" provision. A board that does not have such a contractual right to exit may nevertheless provide cover for itself if it develops second thoughts about the merger.

In 2003, in *Omnicare, Inc. v. NCS Healthcare, Inc.,*[219] the Delaware Supreme Court in a 3 to 2 opinion, struck down a deal protection provision because it failed to include a "fiduciary out" provision. The case involved a merger agreement between NCS Healthcare, Inc. (NCS) and Genesis Health Ventures, Inc. (Genesis) which required the NCS board to submit the plan of merger to the stockholders for approval, even if the NCS board decided to no longer recommend the merger. Collateral to the merger agreement were separate agreements by two NCS stockholders who held a majority of the voting power to vote their shares in favor of the NCS-Genesis merger. The agreement also contained a $6 million termination fee. All was peaceful until Omnicare offered to acquire NCS for a sum substantially above that being offered by Genesis. Evaluating the deal protection provisions under *Unocal,* the slim majority concluded that while the

---

212   *See* Paramount Communications v. QVC Network, Inc., 637 A.2d 34 (Del. 1994).

213   *See* Corwin v. deTrey, 16 Del. J. Corp. L. 267 (Del. Ch. 1989).

214   *See* Great Western Producers Co-Operative v. Great Western United Corp., 613 P.2d 873 (Colo. 1980).

215   *See* Jewel Companies v. Pay Less Drug Stores Northwest, Inc., 741 F.2d 1555 (9th Cir. 1984) (striking down such an agreement).

216   Paramount Communications, Inc. v. QVC Network, Inc., 637 A.2d 34, 38–41 (Del. 1994).

217   Paramount Communications, Inc. v. QVC Network, Inc., 637 A.2d 34, 50–51 (1994).

218   Ace Ltd. v. Capital Re Corp., 747 A.2d 95 (Del. Ch. 1999).

219   Omnicare, Inc. v. NCS Healthcare, Inc., 818 A.2d 914 (Del. 2003).

directors met their burden under *Uncocal's* first prong that they acted in good faith (*i.e.*, if they did not agree to submit the plan to the shareholders they would have risked losing the Genesis offer), the deal protection measures failed under *Unocal's* second prong because they were coercive. The majority reasoned that although the minority holders were not forced to vote in favor of the merger, they were required to accept it because when coupled with the voting agreement with the majority holders the minority holders were effectively presented with a *fait accompli*.[220] Moreover, the court found this deal protection provision was outside *Unitrin's* range of reasonableness as absent a fiduciary out provision the measure made "mathematically impossible" for any other proposal to succeed.[221] It may well be that an important unarticulated consideration in the majority's opinion is that the two stockholders whose agreement to support the NCS-Genesis merger, while owning a majority of the voting shares, in fact held a distinct minority of the equity of the NCS.

There are at least three distinctive bright-line rules that flow from a broad reading of *Omnicare*.[222] First, the *Unocal* standard applies to all transactions regardless of whether there will be a change in control. Second, absent a "fiduciary out" clause, a "force the vote" provision, such as that in *Ominicare*, linked with affirmative voting agreements that effectively lock up the transaction will be invalid. Indeed, *Omnicare* raises doubts whether directors can, absent statutory authority, irrevocably commit to submit a matter to the stockholders for approval. And, third, the directors have a fiduciary obligation to the minority when the majority holders work together as a cohesive group to approve a transaction. Subsequent lower court decisions in Delaware have turned heavily on their facts, and some have even characterized *Omnicare* as "aberrational,"[223] and overall the opinions have emphasized the validity of deal protection provisions is to be determined from a close analysis of the surrounding circumstances with an eye toward whether the directors' actions were intended to secure the highest price and not driven by selfish motives.[224] Several decisions outside of Delaware manifest a more deferential view toward the target board's use of deal protection measures, examining the board's actions under the standard business judgment rule.[225]

Following *Omnicare*, the Delaware legislature enacted a limited "force the vote" provision:

> A Corporation may agree to submit a matter to a vote of its stockholders whether or not the board of directors determines at any time subsequent to approving such matter that such matter is no longer advisable and recommends that the shareholders reject or vote against the matter.[226]

---

[220] 818 A.2d at 936.

[221] 818 A.2d at 936.

[222] *See generally* Justin W. Oravetz, Is A Merger Agreement Ever Certain? The Impact Of The Omnicare Decision On Deal Protection Devices, 29 Del. J. Corp. L. 805 (2004).

[223] In re Toys "R" Us, Inc. Shareholder Litig., 877 A.2d 975, 1016 n. 68 (Del.Ch. 2005).

[224] In re Lear Corp. Shareholder Litig., 926 A.2d 94 (Del. Ch. 2007) (upholding no-shop provision in presigning period but providing a 45 day "go-shop" period post signing).

[225] *See, e.g.,* In re Guidant Corp. Shareholders Derivative Litig., 2006 WL 290524 (S.D. Ind. 2006) (upholding no shop provision, termination fee, and adoption of poison pill).

[226] Del. Code Ann. tit. 8, § 146.

Several other states have also followed Delaware and provide express statutory authority for directors to agree to submit an acquisition proposal to their shareholders.[227] However, none the enacting states remove the power for the directors to either make no recommendation or to recommend that the stockholders reject the proposal.

Many state provisions permit the board to submit mergers to their shareholders without a board recommendation.[228] Thus, the board, having this statutory option, could withhold its recommendations, make full disclosure of all the facts, and allow the shareholders then to decide whether to approve the acquisition. The crucial variables in determining the validity of such agreements are whether the agreement has the effect of terminating the "bidding process," whether the agreement was important in obtaining a bid from the present suitor or significantly improving its prior bid, and whether the target company has entered the *Revlon* moment, discussed below, because there is a prospective change of control. Standstill agreements entered into by parties exploring their possible combination also raise questions regarding the extent that the directors' discretion can be restrained.[229]

A unique defensive tactic used in recent years is the acquisition of another business by the target company, creating a potential antitrust threat to impending tender offers.[230] A somewhat related strategy of imposing a regulatory obstacle in the suitor's path is to purchase assets of a type such that any change in their ownership requires prior governmental clearance. For example, the purchase of a radio station or some other heavily regulated business can tie up the takeover attempt in any administrative proceedings that may be needed to approve a change of ownership in the regulated business. Another type of asset acquisition that becomes a defensive maneuver is the "Pac-Man" defense, where the target company makes a tender offer for control of the original tender offeror.[231]

§ 23.8   The Directors' Role as Auctioneers—the *"Revlon* Moment"

A significant qualification of *Unocal* was announced by the Delaware Supreme Court in *Revlon Inc. v. MacAndrews & Forbes Holdings, Inc.*,[232] which arose from the competing efforts of Pantry Pride, Inc. and Forstmann Little & Company to acquire control of Revlon, Inc. Pantry Pride had begun its hostile bid at $47.50 per share and successively raised its bid as Revlon embraced a series of defensive maneuvers and soon authorized its investment banker to negotiate with other parties who might have been interested in acquiring Revlon. An interested bidder was found in Forstmann Little & Company, Revlon's white knight, but by then Pantry Pride had increased its offer to $50, then $53, and still higher, to $56.25 per share. After Pantry Pride's offer had reached $53 per share, Revlon's board considered a leverage buyout headed by Forstmann Little & Company that, among other features, would require the sale of two important Revlon

---

[227] *See* Md. Code Ann. § 3–105(d) (Michie 2007); Minn. Stat. Ann. § 302A.613 (Supp. 2008) (Repealing earlier provision and authorizing submission to shareholders even if board changes opinion of proposed offer); Okla. Stat. Ann. tit. 18, ch. 22, § 1027(I) (Supp. 2006).

[228] *See, e.g.,* Del. Code Ann. tit. 8, § 251(c) (2001); MBCA § 11.04(b) (1999). *See* William T. Allen, Understanding Fiduciary Outs: The What and the Why of an Anomalous Concept, 55 Bus. Law. 658 (2000).

[229] *See* Crane Co. v. Coltec Ind., Inc., 171 F.3d 733 (2d Cir. 1999) (interpreting notice requirement of a standstill agreement).

[230] *See* Consolidated Gold Fields PLC v. Minorco, S.A., 871 F.2d 252 (2d Cir. 1989) (affirming the issuance of a preliminary injunction against tender offer on antitrust grounds).

[231] *See* Martin Marietta Corp. v. Bendix Corp., 549 F.Supp. 623 (D. Md. 1982).

[232] Revlon, Inc. v. MacAndrews & Forbes Holdings, Inc., 506 A.2d 173 (Del. 1986).

divisions for approximately $1.2 billion. To assure that Forstmann Little would be the victor, Revlon's board granted it the option to acquire two other product lines for $100–175 million below their fair market value if another bidder acquired 40 percent of the outstanding Revlon shares. It was this feature that the Delaware Supreme Court, pursuant to the language of the court, set out below, held was inconsistent with the duties of directors under the facts to become "auctioneers." Citing *Unocal*, the court upheld the directors' various defensive actions taken in response to Pantry Pride's initial bid of $47.50 because the court was persuaded that the board had "acted in good faith, and on an informed basis, with reasonable grounds to believe that there existed a harmful threat to the corporate enterprise."[233]

> However, when Pantry Pride increased its offer to $50 per share, and then to $53, it became apparent to all that the break-up of the company was inevitable. The Revlon board's authorization permitting management to negotiate a merger or buyout with a third party was a recognition that the company was for sale. The duty of the board had thus changed from the preservation of Revlon as a corporate entity to the maximization of the company's value at a sale for the stockholders' benefit. This significantly altered the board's responsibilities under the *Unocal* standards. It no longer faced threats to corporate policy and effectiveness, or to the stockholders' interest, from a grossly inadequate bid. The whole question of defensive measures became moot. The directors' role changed from defenders of the corporate bastion to auctioneers charged with getting the best price for the stockholders at a sale of the company.[234]

Revlon should be seen as a qualification of *Unocal* rather than an alternative. It does not prohibit defensive maneuvers but requires that their reasonableness be measured not in terms of the threat to control but by the objective of obtaining the best offer for the target shareholders. Thus *Revlon* does not prohibit lock-up options when the directors have entered the "*Revlon* moment." The court stated "A lock-up is not per se illegal under Delaware law. . . . Such options can entice other bidders to enter a contest for control of the corporation, creating an auction for the company and maximizing shareholder profit."[235] Because the lock-up granted Forstmann Little did not result in a substantial improvement in its bid and did not attract a new bidder to the contest, the court viewed its only impact as bringing the intense bidding contest to a close for an insubstantial benefit to the target shareholders.[236]

Revlon can be seen as a natural extension of *Unocal* in the sense that both cases set standards for the target board of directors to act in their shareholders' best interest. This view is supported by the body of commentators who believe that the legitimacy of defensive maneuvers is facilitating an auction.[237]

---

[233] Revlon, Inc. v. MacAndrews & Forbes Holdings, Inc., 506 A.2d 173, 181 (Del. 1986).

[234] Revlon, Inc. v. MacAndrews & Forbes Holdings, Inc., 506 A.2d 173, 182 (Del. 1986).

[235] Revlon, Inc. v. MacAndrews & Forbes Holdings, Inc., 506 A.2d 173, 183 (Del. 1986).

[236] Not insignificantly, the court also observed that the Revlon directors were benefited personally by favoring Forstmann Little who promised to support the value of earlier issued bonds whose holders were suing the Revlon directors for their failure to support, as they had represented they would, the bond covenants that were designed to prevent an LBO's occurrence that would increase the risk of those bonds.

[237] *See, e.g.*, Ronald J. Gilson, A Structural Approach to Corporations: The Case Against Defensive Tactics in Tender Offers, 33 Stan. L. Rev. 819, 868–875 (1981).

The mere commencement of a hostile bid does not trigger *Revlon* duties on the part of the target directors, even though that offer puts the target company into play.[238] In the period immediately following, *Revlon*, Delaware Supreme Court decisions vaguely identified three alternative bases for applying *Revlon*'s auctioneering standard:[239]

(1) When the target initiates an active bidding process seeking to sell itself or effect a restructuring that will lead to the break-up of the company.[240]

(2) When the target abandons its long-term strategy and seeks an alternative plan that entails the break-up of the company.[241]

(3) Where the effect of the plan supported by the target board of directors is to bring about a change in control of the corporation.[242]

However, *Revlon*'s reach today is in the "change of control" situation. Thus, in *Lyondell Chemical Co. v. Ryan*,[243] the Delaware Supreme Court clearly stated that a company's directors did not become subject to *Revlon* duties by the company being "in play," but instead *Revlon* applies when the company "embarks on a transaction-on its own initiative or in response to an unsolicited offer-that will result in a change of control."[244]

In Delaware cases, the ultimate test for *Revlon*'s application is whether the structure of the transaction "embarked on"[245] by the board of directors entails a change of control. In broad overview, for analysis purposes transactions can fall into three types: all-cash, all-stock, and a blend of cash-and-stock. It is clear that an all-cash structure triggers *Revlon*; disputes in all-cash transactions focus not on whether *Revlon* applies but at what point did the board's actions moved them from the *Unocal* mode to the more focused *Revlon* mode.[246] *Revlon* is inapplicable to an all-stock structure when ownership

---

[238] *See* Paramount Communications, Inc. v. Time, Inc., 571 A.2d 1140, 1151 (Del. 1989).

[239] *See* Odyssey Partners, L.P. v. Fleming Companies, Inc., 735 A.2d 386 (Del. Ch. 1999).

[240] Flake v. Hoskins, 55 F. Supp. 2d 1196, 1215 (D. Kan. 1999) (applying Missouri law which stated to parallel Delaware to conclude that seeking a white knight does not constitute shopping the firm such as to trigger *Revlon*).

[241] 571 A.2d at 1151.

[242] Paramount Communications, Inc. v. QVC Network, Inc., 637 A.2d 34 (Del. 1994). The following accurately captures the meaning of "change of control" as it has evolved in the case law:

[A] board sells "control" and thus triggers *Revlon* duties . . . when it agrees to exchange a controlling stake in the company, either for cash or non-voting securities, or for voting shares in an acquirer with a controlling shareholder but not when it exchanges 100% of its voting shares for voting shares in a widely held acquirer, most commonly through a stock-for-stock merger. . . .

The exchange of all of the target's voting shares for voting shares of another widely held company is *not* a sale of control, and thus does not trigger *Revlon*, on the logic that control of the target company was before, and control of the combined company remains afterward, in a "fluid aggregation of unaffiliated stockholders."

Bernard Black & Reinier Kraakman, Delaware's Takeover Law: The Uncertain Search For Hidden Value, 96 Nw. U. L. Rev. 521, 534–35 (2002).

[243] Lyondell Chemical Co. v. Ryan, 970 A.2d 235 (Del. 2009).

[244] Lyondell Chem. Co. v. Ryan, 970 A.2d 235 (Del. 2009).

[245] Lyondell Chem. Co. v. Ryan, 970 A.2d 235 (Del. 2009) (board is not placed in *Revlon* merely by being on notice of an expressed interest of a potential buyer); In re Micromet, 2012 Del. Ch. LEXIS 41 (Del. Ch. Feb.29, 2012) (board subject to *Revlon* the moment it starts to seriously contemplate sale or begins negotiations of a sale).

[246] *See* Lyondell Chem. Co. v. Ryan, 970 A.2d 235 (Del. 2009); Koehler v. NetSpend Holdings, Inc., 2013 WL 2181518 (Del. Ch. 2013); In re Delphi Fin. Group, 2012 WL 729232 (Del. Ch. 2012); In re Micromet, 2012 Del. Ch. LEXIS 41 (Del. Ch. Feb.29, 2012). *Cf.* Air Prods & Chem., Inc. v. Airgas, Inc., 16 A.3d 48 (Del. Ch. 2011) (explaining why *Revlon* did not apply).

shifts from a large unaffiliated group of public holders to an even larger group of unaffiliated owners.[247] However, as held in *Paramount v. QVC, Inc.*,[248] if the all-stock transaction results in an entity with a controlling stockholder or stockholder group, so that the target stockholders are relegated to minority status, *Revlon* applies. There is some uncertainty with respect to the blend of cash-and-stock. In an earlier decision, the Delaware Supreme Court held that a merger involving 33 percent cash and the remainder stock did not trigger *Revlon*.[249] However, a 50/50 division between cash and stock prompted the Delaware court to assume *Revlon's* application.[250]

The case law outside of Delaware is not refined on when *Revlon* applies even in jurisdictions that purport to follow Delaware. What case law exists does not provide insight to the possible scope of *Revlon* or non-Delaware qualifications to *Revlon*. Among the few decisions that exist there is support for *Revlon's* application to all-cash mergers initiated by the board[251] and when issuance of shares places control in the hands of an individual or organized group.[252]

The efficacy of imposing heightened duties for change of control instances is that shareholders are entitled to participate in the control premium when as a result of a board-approved transaction there will emerge in that company a controlling stockholder when previously the company had no controlling stockholder.

. . . *Revlon* imposes the following obligation:

[T]he directors must focus on one primary objective—to secure the transaction offering the best value reasonably available for the stockholders—and they must exercise their fiduciary duties to further that end. . . . In determining whether the directors have met this responsibility, the Court applies a threshold examination under the enhanced scrutiny test [called for by *Revlon*] which consists of:

(a) a judicial determination regarding the adequacy of the decisionmaking process employed by the directors, including the information on which the directors based their decision; and (b) a judicial examination of the reasonableness of the directors' action in light of the circumstances then existing. The directors have the burden of proving that they were adequately informed and acted reasonably. . . .

However, . . . the Court's responsibility is not to second-guess the decisionmaking process of the directors. . . . Accordingly, a court applying

---

[247] In re KKR Financial Holdings LLC Shareholder Litig., 101 A.3d 980 (Del. Ch. 2014).

[248] 637 A.2d 34, 42–43 (Del. 1994). *See also* C & J Energy Services, Inc. v. City of Miami Gen'l Employees' & Sanitation Employees' Ret. Turst, 107 A.3d 1049 (Del. 2014) (as result of acquisition, a third party would own 53 percent of the combined firm so *Revlon* applied).

[249] In re Santa Fe Pacific Corp., 669 A.2d 59 (Del. 1995). *See also,* In re Synthes Shareholder Litig., 50 A.3d 1022 (Del. Ch. 2012) (blend of 35 percent cash and 65 percent stock does not trigger *Revlon*).

[250] In re Smurfit-Stone Container, 2011 Del. Ch. LEXIS 79 (Del. Ch. 2011). *See also* In re Dollar Thrifty, 14 A.3d 573 (Del. Ch. 2010)(assuming *Revlon* applied to a transaction involving 80 percent cash).

[251] Shenker v. Laureate Education, Inc., 411 Md. 317 (Md. 2009).

[252] Collins v. Warrell, 2011 N.J. Super. LEXIS 2087; Matter of Bear Stearns Litig., 870 N.Y.S.2d 709 (N.Y. Sup. Ct. 2008).

enhanced judicial scrutiny should be deciding whether the directors made a reasonable decision, not a perfect decision. . . .[253]

There are at least two features of *Revlon*'s intensified review:

(a)   a judicial determination regarding the adequacy of the decision making process employed by the directors, including the information on which the directors based their decision; and

(b)   a judicial examination of the reasonableness of the directors' action in light of the circumstances then existing. The directors have the burden of proving that they were adequately informed and acted reasonably.[254]

Unlike the bare rationality standard customarily applied under the business judgment rule, *Revlon* examines the directors' actions under a reasonableness standard.[255] Nonetheless, the heightened *Revlon* review is not a license for the judiciary to second guess debatable reasonable choices that directors have made in good faith. Nor does the standard mandate that the board conduct either an auction or targeted market canvass for a better offer.[256]

Revlon demands that the board's actions in favoring or disfavoring a particular bidder must have a reasonable relation to the advantage sought to be obtained.[257] The target board can enter into arrangements with one bidder that "tilt the playing field," provided doing so is in the shareholders' interest.[258] Thus, an asset lock-up such as that struck down in *Revlon* is valid when undertaken to draw a new bidder into the contest or to entice a present bidder to change materially its prior bid.[259] The auctioneering duty requires a quest of the best offer that, because of timing and valuation considerations, is not synonymous with the highest price.[260] At the same time, there is no duty to seek additional bidders when a company is confronted by a hostile bid.[261] Traditional business judgment rule considerations regarding the director's independence and reasonable investigation continue to assume even greater significance when the target board has entered the *Revlon* moment.[262] Since such judgments are made under the unique circumstances of the case, an important variable in assessing the board's performance is whether rigid deal protective provisions were concurred to which prevented the possibility of other bidders stepping forward. For example, *In re Pennaco Energy, Inc.*

---

[253]   Matador Capital Mgmt. Corp. v. BRC Holdings, 729 A.2d 280, 290–91 (Del. Ch. 1998) *quoting in part* Paramount Comm., Inc. v. QVC Network, Inc., 637 A.2d 34, 45 (Del. 1994).

[254]   In re Toys "R" Us, Inc. Shareholder Litig., 877 A.2d 975, 1000 (Del. Ch. 2005) (citing Paramount Comm., Inc. v. QVC Network, Inc., 637 A.2d 34 (Del. 1994)).

[255]   In re Netsmart Technologies, Inc. Shareholders Litig., 924 A.2d 171 (Del. Ch. 2007).

[256]   In re Toys "R" Us, Inc. Shareholder Litig., 877 A.2d 975, 1000 (Del. Ch. 2005) (citing Barkan v. Amsted Industries, 567 A.2d 1279, 1286 (Del. 1989)).

[257]   *See, e.g.,* Black & Decker Corp. v. American Standard, Inc., 682 F.Supp. 772, 786 (D. Del. 1988) (triggering of contractual rights in pension plan and officer's if third party acquired control deemed unfair treatment of third party versus the favored MBO participants).

[258]   *See* West Point-Pepperell, Inc. v. J. P. Stevens Co., 542 A.2d 770 (Del. Ch. 1988).

[259]   *See, e.g.,* Cottle v. Storer Communication, Inc., 849 F.2d 570 (11th Cir. 1988).

[260]   Citron v. Fairchild Camera & Instrument Corp., 569 A.2d 53 (Del. 1989) (upholding board's preference of $66 cash offer for all shares over $70 cash offer for 42% of the company with the remaining shares to be later acquired in a share-for-share exchange).

[261]   *See* Barkan v. Amsted Indus., 567 A.2d 1279 (Del. 1989).

[262]   *See, e.g.,* Hanson Trust PLC v. ML SCM Acquisition, Inc., 781 F.2d 264 (2d Cir. 1986).

Shareholders Litigation,[263] while noting that the directors did not demonstrate a textbook illustration of thoughtful methodical procedures to determine the fair value of the firm, they did not foreclose a post-effective market check by agreeing to a termination fee equal to three percent of the value of the acquisition. Hence, the board's flexibility to address any later emerging bid and the fact that no later third-party bid occurred supported the directors' actions.[264]

The more limited discretion that directors have under *Revlon* compared with *Unocal* is illustrated by the very different treatment granted management's defensive maneuvers in two recent decisions, *Paramount Communications, Inc. v. QVC Network, Inc.*[265] and *Paramount Communications, Inc. v. Time, Inc.*[266] As seen earlier, the Delaware Supreme Court in *Time, Inc.* upheld management's defensive maneuver under *Unocal* and refused to apply *Revlon* when Time's management, in response to a bid from Paramount Communications, altered the form of its combination with Warner Communications from the issuance of Time stock to the payment of cash for Warner shares. In contrast, *Revlon* was applied in *QVC Network, Inc.* when Paramount's own merger with Viacom, Inc. was threatened by a higher offer from QVC so that it entered into a no-shop agreement as well as an agreement granting Viacom a large termination fee and an option to purchase a significant number of Paramount shares at a substantial discount, all triggered if QVC acquired control of Paramount. In both cases the defensive maneuver did not make a hostile acquisition of the target corporation impossible; the particular defensive maneuvers merely made such an acquisition more expensive. However, by assessing the defensive maneuvers in *QVC Network, Inc.* under *Revlon*, the Delaware Supreme Court was able to conclude that the directors had prematurely terminated bidding, so their actions were inconsistent with their roles in obtaining the best offer for their shareholders. In contrast, the court reasoned in *Time, Inc.* that changing the acquisition from a stock-based to cash-based acquisition so as to avoid a stockholders' vote would avoid the threat that the higher bid made by Paramount for Time, Inc. posed to the Time shareholders who may not have fully comprehended the full value of the long-range strategy reflected in management's support of the Time-Warner combination. The only apparent variable that separates these two significant decisions is the court's application of *Revlon* in *QVC Network, Inc.*

A point worthy of emphasis in the contrasting results reached in *Time, Inc.* and *QVC Network, Inc.* is the basis for applying *Revlon* in one but not the other. In both cases the target shareholders would emerge from the management-supported combination owning a distinct minority of the combined company. However, the court concluded in *Time, Inc.* that such a change of control does not trigger *Revlon*, even though the former Warner Communication shareholders would own 62 percent of the combined company (hence, the former Time shareholders would own only 38 percent), because control would be held by a fluid aggregation of unaffiliated stockholders both before and after the

---

[263] In re Pennaco Energy, Inc. Shareholders Litig., 787 A.2d 691, 705–07 (Del. Ch. 2001).

[264] In re Pennaco Energy, Inc. Shareholders Litigation, 787 A.2d 691, 707 (Del. Ch. 2001). *See also* Samjens Partners I v. Burlington Industries, Inc., 663 F.Supp. 614 (S.D.N.Y. 1987) (holding 2% termination fee, negotiating lower "hello fee" and alterations obtained in no shop clause suggests no undue preferential treatment).

[265] Paramount Communications, Inc. v. QVC Network, Inc., 637 A.2d 34 (Del. 1994). *See generally* Lawrence C. Cunningham & Charles M. Yablon, Delaware Fiduciary Duty Law After *QVC* and *Technicolor:* A Unified Standard (and the End of *Revlon* Duties?), 49 Bus. Law. 1593 (1994).

[266] Paramount Communications, Inc. v. Time, Inc., 571 A.2d 1140 (Del. 1989).

acquisition.[267] In contrast, the transaction in *QVC Network, Inc.* resulted in control of the target corporation being held by a corporation controlled by a single individual.[268] The court clearly rejected the argument that some evidence of a break-up of the target firm was also necessary for *Revlon* to apply. A clear illustration of where there would be no change of control such that *Revlon* must be met is where the sale of the company is at the suggestion of that company's majority holder; in such an instance, the courts reason it is unrealistic to believe that a meaningful auction would occur.[269] Hence, the focus is whether the directors acted reasonably and in good faith in securing a fair price for the company.

The crucial factor under *QVC* is thus whether there would be a transfer of control as a result of the challenged transfer.[270] Should such a control transfer be involved the result presumably would be the consumption of a control premium that would otherwise be potentially available to the complaining shareholders. In other words, had control of Paramount been transferred to Viacom which was controlled by a single shareholder, the former Paramount shareholders would no longer be able to enjoy any indicia of control of their corporation notwithstanding their ownership of Viacom shares. As explained by the Delaware Supreme Court, there are thus three instances in which the courts will require target managers not to seek the best value for their shareholders: (1) When a corporation has initiated active bidding to put itself up for sale or seeks to effect a reorganization that would result in a breakup of the corporation; (2) when the target company abandons a long-term strategy and seeks a suitor in order to fend off a takeover attempt; or (3) when approval of the transaction results in a sale or change in control.[271]

Ryan v. Lyondell,[272] considered whether the target directors breached their duty of good faith by developing a wait and see approach for two months following the suitor's 13D filing. The Delaware Supreme Court held that *Revlon* duties did not commence until the directors began to negotiate with the firm's suitor; it therefore reversed the Chancery Court's holding that *Revlon* duties were triggered by the bidder filing Schedule 13D announcing it held 8.3 percent of the Lyondell shares and had an interest in acquiring Lyondell. The court, therefore, rejected the Chancery Court's position that the duties commenced upon the suitor's Schedule 13D filing that place the firm "in play." The Chancery Court reasoned that the directors acted improperly once they did commence negotiations, believing that they failed to conduct an auction or undertake a market check of the firm's value (they also agreed to a $385 termination penalty and no-shop clause). While recognizing the facts likely would invite continued discovery if the suit were premised on a breach of the directors' duty of care, the Supreme Court reasoned that because Lyondell's charter provided directors an immunity shield for care violations

---

[267] Paramount Communications, Inc. v. QVC Network, Inc., 637 A.2d 34, 47 (Del. 1994).

[268] Paramount Communications, Inc. v. QVC Network, Inc., 637 A.2d 34, 48 (Del. 1994).

[269] *See, e.g.*, McMullin v. Beran, 765 A.2d 910 (Del. Supr. 2000) ("When the entire sale to a third-party is proposed, negotiated and timed by a majority shareholder . . . the board cannot realistically seek any alternative because the majority shareholder has the right to vote its shares in favor of the third-party transaction it proposed for the board's consideration.").

[270] *See, e.g.*, Krim v. ProNet, Inc., 744 A.2d 523, 527–528 (Del. Ch. 1999) (since public shareholders retained control after merger, directors did not breach their duty of care by failing to hold auction).

[271] Arnold v. Society for Savings Bancorp, Inc., 650 A.2d 1270 (Del. 1994) (since neither of the three cited situations existed, the court upheld a merger that followed the rejection of an earlier proposal to buy pieces of the target company).

[272] 970 A.2d 235, 242 (Del. 2009).

that any breach of *Revlon* duties would require proof of a "conscious disregard for those duties."

Directors' decisions must be reasonable, not perfect. . . . The trial court denied summary judgment because Lyondell directors "unexplained inaction" prevented the court from determining that they had acted in good faith. But, if the directors failed to do all that they should have under the circumstances, they breached their duty of care. Only if they knowingly and completely failed to undertake their responsibilities would they breach their duty of loyalty. The trial court approached the record from the wrong perspective. Instead of questioning whether disinterested, independent directors did everything that they (arguably) should have done to obtain the best sale price, the inquiry should have been whether those directors utterly failed to attempt the best sale price.

Viewing the record in this manner leads to only one possible conclusion. The Lyondell directors met several times to consider Basell's premium offer. They were generally aware of the value of their company and they knew the chemical company market. The directors solicited and followed the advice of their financial and legal advisors. They attempted to negotiate a higher offer even though all the evidence indicates that Basell had offered a "blowout" price. Finally, they approved the merger agreement, because "it was simply too good not to pass along [the stockholders] for their consideration. We assume, as we must on summary judgment, that the Lyondell directors did absolutely nothing to prepare for Basell's offer, and that they did not even consider conducting a market check before agreeing to the merger. Even so, this record clearly establishes that the Lyondell directors did not breach their duty of loyalty by failing to act in good faith. . . .[273]

In *C & J Energy Services, Inc. v. City of Miami Gen'l Employees' & Sanitation Employees' Ret. Trust*,[274] the Delaware Supreme Court reaffirmed that a passive market check can satisfy *Revlon*. The court reached this result despite deficiencies in the process of selling control, such as conflicts with the primary financial advisor, limited direct board oversight or involvement in the sale, and aggressive compensation and severance packages. The plan of merger provided a broad fiduciary-out clause and a breakup fee of 2.27 percent that the court considered reasonable. Chief Justice Strine emphasized that *Revlon* and similar decisions arose where the target board was resisting bids of higher bidders whereas there were no competing bidders in *C&J Energy Services* and the shareholders had the uncoerced vote to approve or disapprove the acquisition that was being supported by a private equity fund that owned ten percent of the target's stock. The court, therefore, concluded the petitioner had failed to establish "a reasonable probability of success on the merits" so as to obtain a preliminary injunction.

Of even greater significance is *Corwin v. KKR Fin. Holdings LLC*[275] holding that in an arms-length transaction a fully informed non-coerced vote of approval by the stockholders displaces *Revlon*:

---

[273] 970 A.2d at 243–244.

[274] 107 A.3d 1049 (Del. 2014).

[275] Corwin v. KKR Financial Holdings LLC, 125 A.3d 304 (Del. 2015).

When the real parties in interest—the disinterested equity owners—can easily protect themselves at the ballot box by simply voting no, the utility of a litigation-intrusive standard of review promises more costs to stockholders in the form of litigation rents and inhibitions on risk-taking than it promises in terms of benefits to them. The reason for that is tied to the core rationale of the business judgment rule, which is that judges are poorly positioned to evaluate the wisdom of business decisions and there is little utility to having them second-guess the determination of impartial decision-makers with more information (in the case of directors) or an actual economic stake in the outcome (in the case of informed, disinterested stockholders). In circumstances, therefore, where the stockholders have had the voluntary choice to accept or reject a transaction, the business judgment rule standard of review is the presumptively correct one and best facilitates wealth creation through the corporate form.[276]

Corwin's significance occurs on two important fronts. First, and most obviously, it allows stockholder approval to supplant *Revlon*, provided the transaction is not one that otherwise triggers an entire fairness inquiry because it is with a related party. Second, and of great significance to corporate law, *Corwin* holds that the shareholder vote compelled by statute for the transaction to be duly undertaken can also serve as a vote ratifying any lapse under *Revlon* or for that matter any other fiduciary principle. The burden does not shift if material facts are withheld from the approving shareholders.[277] The burden of establishing non-disclosure is on the complaining stockholder.[278]

Whether the directors have fulfilled their *Revlon* duties can be affected by a conflict of interest on the part of an investment bank advising the target company. For example, *In re El Paso Corporation Shareholders Litig.*[279] involved the target, El Paso, considering whether to be acquired by Kinder Morgan, Inc. or whether to remain independent but spin-off its exploration and production (E&P business) to its shareholders. Morgan Stanley advised El Paso on the merger with Kinder Morgan instead of its long-time investment bank, Goldman Sachs, due to Goldman Sachs having a substantial financial investment in Kinder Morgan. Nonetheless, Goldman Sachs remained very much in the

---

[276]   125 A.3d at 313.

[277]   In re Saba Software, Inc. Stockholder Litigation, 2017 WL 1201108 (Del. Ch. 2017), as revised, (Apr. 11, 2017) (merger alleged undertaken quickly to avoid company being deregistered for failure to comply with SEC filing requirements so there was some element of compulsion but court emphasized management's failure to fully disclose shareholders' options if deregistration did occur). The shareholder approval can include the vote of its controlling stockholder in an otherwise arms-length acquisition since presumably the large holder's interests are aligned with that of other stockholders. *See* In re Merge Healthcare Inc., 2017 WL 395981 (Del. Ch. 2017).

[278]   In re Solera Holdings, Inc. Stockholder Litigation, 2017 WL 57839 (Del. Ch. 2017). *See also* Appel v. Berkman, 180 A.3d 1055 (Del. 2018) (disclosures were not as full as they might have been and rendered the vote subject to challenge under Corwin v. KKR Financial Holdings LLC, 125 A.3d 304 (Del. 2015)); In re Straight Path Communications Inc. Consolidated Stockholder Litigation, 2018 WL 3120804 (Del. Ch. 2018) (sufficient allegations that transaction was unfair under entire fairness test); Sciabacucchi v. Liberty Broadband Corporation, 2017 WL 2352152 (Del. Ch. 2017) (the requirements of *Corwin* were not satisfied because the stockholder vote on the transaction at issue was "structurally coercive."); In re Massey Energy Company Derivative and Class Action Litigation, 160 A.3d 484 (Del. Ch. 2017) (the *Corwin* defense was inapplicable to fiduciary claims for pre-merger conduct that was not specifically ratified by a stockholder vote in connection with a merger); Dieckman v. Regency GP LP, 155 A.3d 358 (Del. 2017) (sufficient allegations that general partner misled shareholders in their vote approving the challenged transaction); In re Saba Software, Inc. Stockholder Litigation, 2017 WL 1201108 (Del. Ch. 2017), as revised, (Apr. 11, 2017) (shareholder vote without full disclosure rendered transaction subject to challenge).

[279]   41 A.3d 432 (Del. Ch. 2012).

picture, advising El Paso on the merits of the spin off as well as the terms of the advisory fee for Morgan Stanley. Goldman counseled El Paso to structure Morgan Stanley's compensation so that it would receive a large fee *only* if its acquisition by Kinder Morgan Inc. was completed. Further intrigues flowed when El Paso's CEO learned that Kinder Morgan would likely sell the E&P business following the merger; the CEO, without disclosing any of this to El Paso board, approached some fellow El Paso managers with a proposal that they form a group to purchase the E&P business should the Kinder Morgan merger occur. Chancellor Strine held there was a reasonable probability of success on the merits that *Revlon* duties were not met. Somewhat more extreme, because it involved an investment bank's conflict of interest that was not known to the target, is *In re Del Monte Foods Company Shareholder Litig.*[280] Barclays actively concealed from Del Monte's board its role in putting Del Monte in play. Indeed, Barclays had even brought the two potential buyers together. And, through most of the process of advising Del Monte, Barclays did not disclose that it would earn a fee by providing financing to the buyers. After assisting Del Monte in its negotiations including the terms of a no-shop deal protection provision, Barclays ultimately asked for permission for the substantial fees it would receive for financing to the buyers. In response to this request, Del Monte's board did not, among other approaches, ask whether the buyers could obtain financing without Barclay and the late revelation did not prompt the board to probe further into Barclay's relationship with the buyers. While recognizing that the immunity shield likely protected the Del Monte directors from personal liability, the court believed the Del Monte board nonetheless failed to exercise appropriate oversight of the negotiations, particularly in light of their heightened *Revlon* duties. It therefore delayed voting on the merger should be postponed for 20 days to permit the possibility of a competing topping bid.

Quite independent of *Revlon* is the more general question of whether directors can, consistent with their fiduciary duties, enter into an enforceable agreement with a bidder not to actively pursue or support competing offers. An early federal decision held that directors can at least bind themselves not to *accept* a competing merger offer until the shareholders have voted on an initial agreement.[281] The Nebraska Supreme Court held that directors were bound by the fiduciary duties to the shareholders to submit with a favorable recommendation a subsequent higher bid, even though they had agreed with an earlier bidder to support that offer.[282] Importantly, the Delaware Supreme Court has held that contractual provisions that bar the board of directors from actively pursuing another bidder must complement the directors' fiduciary obligations. Thus directors who have entered the *Revlon* moment cannot enter into a no-shop agreement if it is inconsistent with their likelihood of securing a better offer through the pursuit of other bidders and bids.[283]

Outside of Delaware, *Revlon* has had a checkered fate. Persuaded by the experience of the Delaware courts, *Revlon* is frequently adopted as the applicable standard.[284] On the other hand, many courts believe the standard business judgment rule, including its

---

[280] 25 A.3d 813 (Del. Ch. 2011).

[281] *See* Jewel Co. v. Pay Less Drug Stores Nw., 741 F.2d 1555 (9th Cir. 1984).

[282] *See* ConAgra, Inc. v. Cargill, Inc., 382 N.W.2d 576 (Neb. 1986).

[283] *See* Paramount Communications, Inc. v. QVC Network, Inc., 637 A.2d 34 (Del. 1994).

[284] *See, e.g.,* Priddy v. Edelman, 883 F.2d 438, 444 (6th Cir. 1989) (believing Michigan would follow *Revlon*, but nevertheless examined the case under the more restrained business judgment rule).

presumption the directors have acted properly, is the appropriate approach.[285] There also is the view that directors are not under a duty to initiate an auction when control is to be transferred;[286] such a view rejects the fundamental tenet of *Revlon*.

In broad overview, the vigor with which a state's own antitakeover statutes protect domestic corporations is highly correlated with whether the court follows *Revlon*.[287] States with no or weak antitakeover statues tend to apply a heightened level of inquiry, similar to that in *Revlon*, in sale of control transactions.[288] In contrast, when the state legislative scheme reflects moderate-to-strong antitakeover measures, *Revlon* is typically supplanted by the presumptions accompanying the business judgment rule. Illustrative of a strong embrace of the business judgment rule is Indiana's other constituency statute that expressly provides that Delaware's approach to mediating disputes involving a change of control was "inconsistent with the proper application of the business judgment rule."[289] Following the statute's enactment, Indiana courts have consistently invoked the business judgment rule in challenges arising in change of control transactions.[290] Similar holdings appear in other states with strong statutory antitakeover provisions.[291]

---

[285] *See*, Shenker v. Laureate Education, Inc., 411 Md.317, 341, 983 A.2d 408, 422 (2009) (in Maryland *Revlon*-like considerations within the business judgment rule and a provision in Maryland statute stating there is no higher duty in change of control transactions relates to review of defensive measures and not other actions of the board).

[286] Lewis v. Celina Fin. Corp., 655 N.E.2d 1333 (Ohio. Ct. App. 1995).

[287] *See* Michal Barzuza, The State of Antitakeover Law, 95 Va. L. Rev. 1973, 2013 (2009).

[288] *See* O'Neill v. Church's Fried Chicken, Inc., 910 F.2d 263 (5th Cir. 1990) (decided before Texas, the state of incorporation, had adopted its other constituency statute); Flake v. Hoskins, 55 F. Supp.2d 1196 (D. Kan. 1999) (interpreting Missouri's weak other constituency statute as not precluding *Revlon*, but then concluding none of the instances in which the doctrine applies were present in the case).

Maryland appears to be in limbo since Shenker v. Laureate Education, Inc., 411 Md. 317 (Md. App. 2009), held that the state's other constituency statute did not reject a heightened obligation on the part of the directors when selling control). Subsequent Maryland cases have nonetheless invoked by business judgment rule by distinguishing *Shenker. See, e.g.,* Timm v. Impac Mortg. Holdings, Inc., 2013 Md. Cir. Ct. LEXIS 1 (Md. Cir. Ct. 2013).

[289] Burns Ind. Code Ann. § 23–1–35–1(f).

[290] *See, e.g.,* G & N Aircraft, Inc. v. Boehm, 743 N.E.2d 227, 238 (Ind. 2001). *See also* Shepard v. Meridian Ins. Group, 137 F. Supp. 2d 1096 (S.D. Ind. 2001) (relying on state antitakeover statute's strong embrace of the business judgment rule to dismiss challenge to sell company to a buyer preferred by the board).

[291] *See, e.g.,* Dixon v. ATI Ladish LLC, 667 F.3d 891 (7th Cir. 2012) (applying business judgment rule in reliance on Wisconsin's statute); Dynamics Corp. of America v. WHX Corp., 967 F. Supp. 59 (D. Conn. 1997) (interpreting New York legislative scheme as inviting a variation of the business judgment rule).

Chapter 24

FEDERAL AND STATE TAKEOVER LAWS

Table of Sections

---

§ 24.1 Federal Regulation of Takeovers

The vociferousness of contested takeover battles as well as the potential for abuse with negotiated or controlled offers has led to the federal regulation of tender offers, most notably through the 1968 Williams Act amendments to the Exchange Act.[1] The Williams Act provisions impose disclosure requirements on various persons in connection with tender offers and stock acquisitions. The required disclosures include identification of the entity launching the takeover attempt and a description of the purpose of the proposed action and related future plans. Disclosure is required of any person who acquires more than five percent of the outstanding shares of any class of equity security subject to the Act's reporting requirements.[2] This provision serves to prevent secret creeping acquisitions—that is, acquisitions in which the target company learns of the takeover attempt too late to take any action. At the same time, an overall effect of the Williams Act disclosure requirements as well as its many substantive rules regulating the conduct of tender offers is to increase the cost of a takeover, to increase the premiums that are paid to target shareholders, and to raise the uncertainty as to whether a bid for control will be successful.[3]

Under section 14(d), similar disclosure is required for "a tender offer for or request or invitation for tenders of" any equity security subject to the reporting requirements of the Exchange Act.[4] Disclosure and SEC filings must also be made by anyone resisting,

---

[1]   Pub. L. No. 90–439, § 2, 82 Stat. 454 (1968) (codified at 15 U.S.C. §§ 78m(b)–(c), 78n(d)–(f) (1997 & Supp. 2009)). In the case of an exchange offer, as opposed to a cash tender offer, the new securities will be subject to the 1933 Act's registration requirements. 15 U.S.C. §§ 77f, 77g (1997 & Supp. 2009).

[2]   15 U.S.C. § 78m(d) (2015). *See id.* § 78m(e) (1997 & Supp. 2009), which prohibits misstatements, omissions, and fraud in connection with such SEC filings.

[3]   *See* Gregg A. Jarrell & Michael Bradley, The Economic Effects of Federal and State Regulation of Cash Tender Offers, 23 J.L. & Econ. 371 (1980).

[4]   15 U.S.C. § 78n(d) (2015). *See also id.* § 78n(f) (2015), which requires disclosure of any agreement concerning management turnover.

opposing, or supporting any tender offer.[5] Section 14(e) of the Exchange Act is not limited to reporting companies; in effect it applies Rule 10b–5 standards to all conduct and statements in connection with a tender offer.[6]

Other rules and regulations that affect tender offers include SEC Rule 14e–5, which prohibits tender offerors from buying shares through means other than the tender offer itself,[7] and Rule 14e–4, which prohibits short tendering and hedged tendering during a tender offer.[8] Rules 14e–1[9] and 14e–2[10] govern the behavior of the tender offeror and the target management, respectively. Rule 14(e)–3 is a general prohibition of insider trading during a tender offer.[11]

While section 14(e) provides an express remedy only for the SEC or criminal enforcement,[12] the bulk of 14(e) litigation has arisen from implied private causes of action.[13] Section 14(e) is the preferred provision to proceed under, as it depends on the plaintiff's status as a target of some deceptive act in connection with a tender offer rather than on the narrower purchaser/seller requirement of Rule 10b–5.[14] There remains some question as to the requirement of scienter.[15] It seems clear, however, that section 14(e) does require detrimental reliance in order to establish a private remedy.[16]

In proceeding under 14(e), the plaintiff may be the tender offeror (but not a defeated tender offeror seeking damages),[17] the target management,[18] or shareholders of the target company.[19] There is no set definition of "manipulation," and there has been much controversy as to what is required for a 14(e) action. The Supreme Court recently examined this question in *Schreiber v. Burlington Northern, Inc.*, discussed below, and held that in order to state a cause of action there must be some element of non-disclosure, misrepresentation, or deception.[20] Accordingly, fully disclosed conduct that may be manipulative will not support an implied cause of action.

---

[5]   15 U.S.C. § 78n(d) (2015).

[6]   15 U.S.C. § 78n(e) (2015).

[7]   17 C.F.R. § 240.14e–5 (2015) which replaced Rule 10b–13, 17 C.F.R. § 240.10b–13 (2002).

[8]   17 C.F.R. § 240.14e–4 (2015). These practices consist of tendering securities not owned or tendering securities subject to a put or call option.

[9]   17 C.F.R. § 240.14e–1 (2015).

[10]   17 C.F.R. § 240.14e–2 (2015).

[11]   17 C.F.R. § 240.14e–3 (2015). The Supreme Court upheld the rule as a valid exercise of the SEC's rule-making power. United States v. O'Hagan, 521 U.S. 642 (2015).

[12]   Section 14(e) declares certain conduct unlawful but does not make any mention of a private remedy.

[13]   It is clear that a defeated tender offeror cannot maintain an action for damages under section 14(e). Piper v. Chris-Craft Indus., Inc., 430 U.S. 1 (1977). *See also* Sedighim v. Donaldson, Lufkin & Jenrette, Inc., 167 F. Supp. 2d 639, 650 (S.D.N.Y. 2001). However, most federal courts recognize an implied cause of action for target shareholders under section 14(e) only to prevent or offset damages incurred in the decision to tender shares during a tender offer.

[14]   15 U.S.C. § 78n(e) (2015); 17 C.F.R. § 240.10b–5 (2015).

[15]   *See infra* § 24.5; Schreiber v. Burlington N., Inc., 472 U.S. 1 (1985); Mobil Corp. v. Marathon Oil Co., 669 F.2d 366 (6th Cir. 1981), *cert. denied*, 455 U.S. 982 (1982).

[16]   *See* Panter v. Marshall Field & Co., 646 F.2d 271 (7th Cir.), *cert. denied*, 454 U.S. 1092 (1981).

[17]   Piper v. Chris-Craft Indus., Inc., 430 U.S. 1 (1977).

[18]   Rondeau v. Mosinee Paper Corp., 422 U.S. 49 (1975).

[19]   In re Digital Island Sec. Litig., 357 F.3d 322, 325 (3d Cir. 2004); Panter v. Marshall Field & Co., 646 F.2d 271, 287 (7th Cir.), *cert. denied*, 454 U.S. 1092 (1981).

[20]   Schreiber v. Burlington Northern, Inc., 472 U.S. 1 (1985).

Materially misleading tender offer filings violate the Williams Act.[21] In addition to any federal remedies that may exist, state law claims may also be available. For example, shareholders may challenge a shareholder vote that was influenced by a materially misleading Williams Act filing.[22]

§ 24.2   Filing Requirements of Section 13(d)

Any person other than the issuer who acquires, directly or indirectly, beneficial ownership[23] of more than 5 percent of a class of equity security registered pursuant to section 12 of the 1934 Act[24] must file appropriate disclosures with the SEC within ten days after reaching the five percent threshold, pursuant to section 13(d)(1).[25] In 2010, the SEC was given the authority to shorten the ten day filing window. Somewhat similar disclosures are required of an issuer's purchases of its own shares (or through its affiliate) by virtue of section 13(e).[26]

Any person acquiring five percent of a class of equity securities must, within ten days after reaching the five percent threshold, file with the Commission six copies of a statement reflecting the information required by section 13(d)(1).[27] Thus, under section 13(d)(1) the purchaser has a ten-day window between the crossing of the five percent threshold and the disclosure date. This gives the hostile bidder some important running space to gain momentum towards acquiring control of the target company. There is no express limitation on the amount of securities that may be purchased prior to filing the required Schedule 13D. An SEC advisory group recommended amending the rules to require filing in advance of the five percent purchase,[28] but no such change has taken place.

The appropriate filing under section 13(d)(1) is embodied in Schedule 13D.[29] Holders of less than 20 percent of the class of securities who certify that they do not have an intent to exercise control of the issuer (referred to as a "passive investor"), may use Schedule 13G in place of Schedule 13D.[30] Certain "qualified institutional investors" also

---

[21] *See, e.g.,* Securities Exchange Act § 14(e), 15 U.S.C. § 78n(e).

[22] *See* Appel v. Berkman, 180 A.3d 1055 (Del. 2018) (non-disclosures in Schedule 14d-9 disclosures rendered transaction subject to challenge under state law); Morrison v. Berry, 191 A.3d 268 (Del. 2018), as revised, (July 27, 2018) (a company's materially misleading Schedule 14d-9 filing may form the basis of a state law claim that an ensuing shareholder vote was not made upon full disclosure and is therefore invalid).

[23] Many questions arise as to who is a beneficial owner for the purposes of the Williams Act. For example, a nominee with voting power who may vote only at the instruction of third parties is not the beneficial owner of the shares in question and thus is not subject to the section 13(d) filing requirements. Calvary Holdings, Inc. v. Chandler, 948 F.2d 59 (1st Cir. 1991).

[24] Until 2012, section 12(g)(1), as modified by Rule 12g–1 required registration of any class of equity security with more than 500 shareholders where the issuer had more than $10 million in assets. 15 U.S.C. § 78l(g)(1) (2015); 17 C.F.R. § 240.12g–1. As amended section 12(g) requires registration of companies having $10 million in assets and 2,000 or more shareholders of record but retains the former 500 record holder threshold with respect to investors who are not accredited investors. Section 12(g)(1)(A), 15 U.S.C. § 78l(g)(1)(A) as amended by the Jumpstart Our Business Startups Act (JOBS Act), H.R. Rep. No. 112–3606, § 501 (2012). The record holder calculation excludes shareholders who receive shares as part of an employee compensation plan that is exempt from 1933 Act registration. Section 12(g) was also amended to exclude from the shareholder calculation holders of shares issued pursuant to an exempt crowdfunding offering.

[25] 15 U.S.C. § 78m(d)(1) (2015). Section 12, 15 U.S.C. § 78l (2015).

[26] 15 U.S.C. § 78m(e) (1997 & Supp. 2009); 17 C.F.R. § 240.13e–3 (2015).

[27] 15 U.S.C. § 78m(d)(1) (2015).

[28] *See* 15 Sec. Reg. & L. Rep. (BNA) 156 (June 17, 1983).

[29] 17 C.F.R. § 240.13d–1 (2015).

[30] 17 C.F.R. § 240.13d–1(c) (2015). *See also* Edelson v. Ch'ien, 405 F.3d 620, 623 (7th Cir. 2005).

may report their holdings on Schedule 13G regardless of whether their holdings are 20 percent or greater of a class of the issuer's securities, provided the institutional investor does not intend to control the issuer.[31] Passive investors must amend the Schedule 13G within forty-five days after the end of the calendar year to report any change in information on their previous report.[32] Moreover, amendments to the Schedule 13G must occur "promptly" when the passive investor's holdings exceed ten percent of the class of securities and thereafter a prompt amendment is required to report an increase or decrease by more than five percent when the passive investor's holdings are greater than ten percent but less than twenty percent.[33] Finally, upon acquiring twenty percent or more, or, as pointed out below, upon a change of intent to control the issuer, the former passive investor is no longer considered passive and, therefore, must report the acquisition on Schedule 13D within 10 days and is subject to a "cooling off" period. During the cooling off period the investor is prohibited from voting any securities of the issuer until ten days after filing of a Schedule 13D.[34] A similar cooling off period applies when the passive investor or qualified institutional investor has a change of intent regarding controlling the issuer.[35]

As discussed below, the failure to make a timely Schedule 13D filing may result in an injunction against future purchases, at least until the violation is cured.[36] The SEC has also obtained disgorgement of profits made on shares acquired during the period between when a filing should have been made and when the defendant filed its Williams Act disclosures.[37]

The long-form Schedule 13D requires the following disclosures.[38] Item One must contain a description of the security purchased and its issuer. Item Two elicits information regarding the beneficial owner, including the principal business of the person making the filing and whether the filer has been convicted within the past five years of criminal violations or has been the subject of a civil order arising out of a violation of the securities laws. Item Three requires detailed disclosures of the source and amount of funds or other considerations being used to acquire the securities.[39] Item Four requires a description of the purpose(s) of the transaction, including any plans the purchaser may have that likely will result in a reorganization or a business combination such as mergers, consolidations, sales or acquisition of substantial assets, tender offers, changes in dividend policies and the like.[40] The level of detail is generally less when the shares are acquired only for investment.[41] Item Five requires the person filing the Schedule 13D to provide detailed information regarding the number of the target

---

[31]   17 C.F.R. § 240.13d–1(b) (2015). Qualified institutional investors are defined as registered broker dealers, banks, insurance companies, registered investment companies, registered investment advisers, employee benefit plans, parent holding companies, control persons, and savings associations. *Id.*

[32]   17 C.F.R. § 240.13d–2(b) (2015).

[33]   17 C.F.R. § 240.13d–2(d) (2015). Qualified institutional investors must file within 10 days after the close of the month in which such change in ownership occurred. 17 C.F.R. § 240.13d–2(c) (2008).

[34]   17 C.F.R. § 240.13d–1(e)(2)(i) & (f)(2)(i) (2015).

[35]   17 C.F.R. § 240.13d–1(e)(2)(i) (2015).

[36]   *See, e.g.,* SEC v. First City Fin. Corp., 890 F.2d 1215 (D.C. Cir. 1989) (enjoining future violations).

[37]   *E.g.,* SEC v. First City Fin. Corp., 890 F.2d 1215 (D.C. Cir. 1989).

[38]   *See* 17 C.F.R. § 240.13d–101 (2015).

[39]   *See, e.g.,* SEC v. Levy, 706 F.Supp. 61 (D.D.C. 1989).

[40]   *See, e.g.,* In re Phillips Petroleum Sec. Litig., 738 F.Supp. 825 (D. Del. 1990).

[41]   In some such cases there may be an exemption from section 13(d)'s filing requirements. *See* 15 U.S.C. §§ 78m(d)(6), 78m(f) (2015).

company's securities owned by the filer and its affiliates. Item Six elicits descriptions of all contracts, arrangements, understandings, or relationships between the persons filing the Schedule 13D and any person with respect to the target company's securities.[42]

In addition to the initial filings, the person acquiring the five percent threshold must make amendments reflecting any significant changes in the information contained in Schedule 13D or 13G.[43] In determining whether a change in circumstances necessitates an amendment, the general doctrine of materiality is applicable.[44] Under SEC Rule 13d–2(a)[45] a one percent or larger change in beneficial ownership is presumptively a material change.

The greatest interpretative problems in completing Schedule 13D arise with respect to Item 4, which requires a description of the control aspirations of the purchasers. For example, a purchaser's intent to acquire a twenty percent equity interest, thereby obtaining some representation on the target company's board, was held to create an obligation to disclose a plan to acquire control.[46] In considering such questions, the courts have applied Rule 12b–2(f)'s definition of "control"[47] to determine when a purchaser's objective is to affect control. In view of the overall objective of the Williams Act amendments, which is to provide an early warning of a potential change in control, it is not surprising that disclosure of a control purpose is required even when the purchaser does not yet have a formalized concrete plan for exercising that control.[48]

By virtue of section 13(d)(3),[49] when two or more people combine their efforts, such as by forming a partnership, limited partnership, syndicate, or other group for the purpose of acquiring, holding, or disposing of a target company's securities, that group is deemed to be a "person" for the purposes of section 13(d).[50] Accordingly, a Schedule 13D must be filed when members of a group aggregately acquire five percent of a class of equity securities subject to the Exchange Act's reporting requirements. The Second Circuit has held that the determinative factor is whether a group has been established that holds the securities pursuant to an express or implied agreement, thus presenting the *potential* for a shift in control; no agreement to buy further securities is necessary.[51] Furthermore, it is not necessary that the agreement be in writing.[52] The Second Circuit has also held that the members' agreement to acquire control may be established by

---

[42]　　*See* CSX Corp. v. Children's Inv. Fund Mgmt. (UK) LLP, 562 F. Supp. 2d 511, 556 (S.D.N.Y. 2008), *aff'd in part, vacated in part, remanded*, 654 F.3d 276 (2d Cir. 2011) (failure to disclose actual swap agreements did not amount to a material nondisclosure).

[43]　　15 U.S.C. § 78m(d)(2) (2015); 17 C.F.R. § 240.13d–2 (2015). Once a Schedule 13D has been filed, a sale of the stock so acquired must be disclosed promptly. In re Cooper Labs., Inc., 1985 WL 548418 (S.E.C. Release 1985).

[44]　　*See* 17 C.F.R. § 240.12b–2 (2015).

[45]　　17 C.F.R. § 240.13d–2(a) (2015).

[46]　　Dan River, Inc. v. Unitex Ltd., 624 F.2d 1216 (4th Cir. 1980), *cert. denied*, 449 U.S. 1101 (1981); Chromalloy Am. Corp. v. Sun Chem. Corp., 611 F.2d 240 (8th Cir. 1979).

[47]　　17 C.F.R. § 240.12b–2 (2015).

[48]　　Chevron Corp. v. Pennzoil Co., 974 F.2d 1156 (9th Cir. 1992) (triable issue of fact as to whether Schedule 13D was materially misleading in failing to adequately disclose intent to obtain board position and exert degree of management influence over target company).

[49]　　15 U.S.C. § 78m(d)(3) (2015).

[50]　　For a similar provision with regard to tender offers, *see* section 14(d)(2), 15 U.S.C. § 78n(d)(2) (2015).

[51]　　GAF Corp. v. Milstein, 453 F.2d 709 (2d Cir. 1971), *cert. denied*, 406 U.S. 910 (1972).

[52]　　CSX Corp. v. Children's Inv. Fund Mgmt. (UK) LLP, 562 F. Supp. 2d 511, 553 (S.D.N.Y. 2008); SEC v. Drexel Burnham Lambert, Inc., 837 F.Supp. 587 (S.D.N.Y. 1993), *aff'd in part, vacated in part, remanded*, 654 F.3d 276 (2d Cir. 2011).

purchase of enough securities to reach the five percent threshold.[53] On the other hand, discussions by various persons of the possibility of entering into an agreement do not alone establish the formation of a group.[54] The Seventh Circuit requires a greater showing of concerted activity to establish the formation of a group than does the Second Circuit. The Seventh Circuit requires the group to have an agreement not only to exert control, but also to have an agreement to acquire additional shares for the purpose of exerting control.[55] A group may be deemed to exist when parties agree to act in concert to purchase additional shares, regardless of the absence of a common plan with respect to the target corporation beyond the acquisition of additional shares.[56] Quite separate from section 13(d)(1) is the question of whether failure to disclose the existence of a group in Schedule 13D constitutes a material misstatement or omission. Generalizations in this area are difficult since the determination of a group often depends on the facts of the case.

§ 24.3   Definition of "Tender Offer"

Whereas section 13(d)(1)'s filing requirements are aimed at creeping acquisitions and open-market or privately negotiated large block purchases,[57] section 14(d)(1)'s filing and disclosure provisions are called into play when there is a "tender offer." Although "tender offer" is not defined in the act, it is important in that it determines the applicability of section 14(d)(1)'s[58] filing requirements, section 14(e)'s[59] general antifraud proscriptions, and section 14(f)'s[60] disclosure requirements relating to new directors.

On more than one occasion Congress has considered and rejected[61] an objective definition of "tender offer," such as the one embodied in the proposed Federal Securities Code.[62] In contrast, most state tender-offer statutes contain objective definitions.[63] The SEC has declined to use its broad rule-making power to promulgate objective standards[64] to determine the existence of tender offers.[65] This position was "premised upon the dynamic nature of [the] transactions [involved] and the need for the Williams Act to be interpreted flexibly."[66] Needless to say, the SEC's preference for flexibility comes at the

---

[53]   Corenco Corp. v. Schiavone & Sons, Inc., 488 F.2d 207 (2d Cir. 1973).

[54]   Lane Bryant, Inc. v. Hatleigh Corp., 517 F.Supp. 1196 (S.D.N.Y. 1981).

[55]   Bath Indus., Inc. v. Blot, 427 F.2d 97 (7th Cir. 1970) (enjoining group acquiring nearly 50% control from ousting incumbent management). *See also* Edelson v. Ch'ien, 405 F.3d 620, 630 (7th Cir. 2005).

[56]   Mid-Continent Bancshares, Inc. v. O'Brien, 1981 WL 1404 (E.D. Mo. 1981).

[57]   15 U.S.C. § 78m(d) (2015). *See* § 24.2 *supra.*

[58]   15 U.S.C. § 78n(d) (2015). *See* § 24.4 *infra.*

[59]   15 U.S.C. § 78n(e) (2015). *See* § 24.5 *infra.*

[60]   15 U.S.C. § 78n(f) (2015). *See* § 24.6 *infra.*

[61]   *See, e.g.,* Full Disclosure of Corporate Equity Ownership and in Corporate Takeover Bids, Hearings on S.510 Before the Subcomm. on Securities of the Senate Comm. on Banking and Currency, 90th Cong., 1st Sess. 131 (1967).

[62]   The proposed code would have required an offer or solicitation directed toward more than 35 persons. *See* A.L.I. Fed. Sec. Code § 292 (1979); *id.* § 299.9(a) (Tent. Draft No. 1, 1972). The comments explain that although the present law has a "public connotation" of "tender offer," it is too vague and open-ended.

[63]   *See generally* Report, State Takeover Statutes and the Williams Act, 32 Bus. Law. 187 (1976). The applicable state legislation is considered in § 24.8 *infra.*

[64]   *See, e.g.,* Sec. Act Rel. No. 33–5731 [1976–1977 Transfer Binder], Fed. Sec. L. Rep. (CCH) ¶ 80,659 (SEC Aug. 2, 1976).

[65]   The SEC quickly withdrew its 1979 proposed definition of "tender offer"; *see* Proposed Rule 14d1(b)(1) (1979).

[66]   *See* Sec. Exch. Act Rel. No. 34–16385 (Nov. 29, 1979).

cost of sleeplessness for corporate planners, who quite naturally quest certainty for their client's acquisitions. The Commission's long-standing position is that the definition of "tender offer" "is not limited to the classical 'tender offer' where the person desiring to acquire shares makes a public invitation or a written offer to the shareholders to tender their shares. Nor is there a requirement that the shares be tendered through a depositary. The change in control may be effected by direct purchase from shareholders without a public or a written invitation for tenders having been made."[67] The essence of the SEC's position is that "tender offer" covers more than traditional takeover attempts involving public solicitation and may, under appropriate circumstances, include privately negotiated and open-market purchases.

In a widely cited decision, *Wellman v. Dickinson*,[68] the court adopted an eight-factor test to determine whether a tender offer exists. The eight factors can be summarized as follows:

(1)   active and widespread solicitation of public shareholders;

(2)   solicitation for a substantial percentage of the issuer's stock;

(3)   whether the offer to purchase is made at a premium over prevailing market price;

(4)   whether the terms of the offer are firm rather than negotiable;

(5)   whether the offer is contingent on the tender of a fixed minimum number of shares;

(6)   whether the offer is open only for a limited period of time;

(7)   whether the offerees are subject to pressure to sell their stock; and

(8)   the existence of public announcements of a purchasing program that precede or accompany a rapid accumulation of stock.[69]

These factors are simply broad guidelines.

Arguably, a series of control-related open-market purchases would fall within the "tender offer" definition as well. The cases, however, have taken a contrary view. Thus, a plan of successive open-market purchases was held not to be a tender offer where the aggregate number of shares so purchased fell short of the five percent threshold.[70] Even where the five percent threshold was exceeded, an attempt to exercise voting control after a series of open-market purchases was held insufficient to make the acquisition a tender offer.[71] Similarly, the purchase of twenty-five percent of a company's stock in a two-day period was held not to be a tender offer where only one of the *Wellman*'s eight factors was present.[72] The most compelling case to date for characterizing a series of

---

[67]   Cattlemen's Inv. Co. [1971–1972 Transfer Binder], Fed. Sec. L. Rep. (CCH) ¶ 78,775 at 81,627 (SEC Staff Reply, April 24, 1972).

[68]   Wellman v. Dickinson, 475 F.Supp. 783, 823–824 (S.D.N.Y. 1979), *aff'd on other grounds*, 682 F.2d 355 (2d Cir. 1982), *cert. denied*, 460 U.S. 1069 (1983). *See also* SEC v. Carter Hawley Hale Stores, Inc., 760 F.2d 945 (9th Cir. 1985).

[69]   The eight-factor test, which is not contained in any formal SEC rule, has evolved over a period of time.

[70]   Gulf & W. Indus., Inc. v. Great Atl. & Pac. Tea Co., 356 F.Supp. 1066 (S.D.N.Y. 1973), *aff'd*, 476 F.2d 687 (2d Cir. 1973).

[71]   Water & Wall Assocs., Inc. v. American Consumer Indus., Inc., 1973 WL 383 (D.N.J. 1973).

[72]   Brascan, Ltd. v. Edper Equities, Ltd., 477 F.Supp. 773 (S.D.N.Y. 1979).

open-market purchases as a tender offer is *Hanson Trust PLC v. SCM Corporation*,[73] where twenty-five percent of the target company's outstanding stock was acquired quickly through negotiated and market purchases after canceling its earlier publicly announced tender offer.[74] Such purchases are commonly referred to as "street sweeps." The court in *Hanson Trust* reasoned that the price of the purchases was at the market price and that the privately negotiated purchases were accomplished without any pressure or secrecy.[75] A different result might have followed had the withdrawal of the tender offer been part of a plan designed to evade the protections of the Williams Act.[76]

A number of decisions have discussed whether privately negotiated transfers of a controlling block of shares can constitute a tender offer. The cases conflict, but most hold that privately negotiated transactions are susceptible to being categorized as tender offers even though most privately negotiated purchases will not fall within the definition of "tender offer." Any privately negotiated purchase that interferes with a shareholder's "unhurried investment decision" and "fair treatment of . . . investors"[77] defeats the protections of the Williams Act and most likely is a tender offer.[78]

§ 24.4 The Williams Act Requirements for Tender Offers

As discussed more fully below, section 14(d) and applicable SEC rules require filing with the SEC certain mandated disclosures at a tender offer's commencement.[79] In addition, there are certain substantive requirements in Regulations 14D and 14E for tender offers subject to section 14(d)(1).

[1] Filing Requirements

Section 14(d)(1) of the Exchange Act[80] requires that all "tender offer material" for equity securities subject to the registration requirements of section 12 be filed with the Commission and be accompanied by the appropriate disclosures.[81] Section 14(d)(1) requires disclosures of the type specified in Schedule 13D,[82] in addition to such other information as the SEC may require.[83] As is the case with a Schedule 13D filing for acquisition of five percent or more of a class of a target company's stock,[84] section 14(d)(1)

---

[73] Hanson Trust PLC v. SCM Corp., 774 F.2d 47 (2d Cir. 1985).

[74] These purchases were made within hours of the withdrawal of the tender offer.

[75] Hanson Trust PLC v. SCM Corp., 774 F.2d 47 (2d Cir. 1985).

[76] *Cf.* Field v. Trump, 850 F.2d 938 (2d Cir. 1988), *cert. denied*, 489 U.S. 1012 (1989), wherein the court found that a privately negotiated purchase sandwiched between the withdrawal of one tender offer and the initiation of a second, both at a lower price, was part of a single tender offer.

[77] Cattlemen's Inv. Co. v. Fears, 343 F.Supp. 1248, 1251 (W.D. Okla. 1972) (finding a tender offer to have occurred). *See also, e.g.,* Telenor East Invest AS v. Altimo Holdings & Invs. Ltd., 567 F. Supp. 2d 432, 443 (S.D.N.Y. 2008) (noting the difference between those in need of protection of the Act and those who do not; specifically, "privately negotiated transactions with sophisticated investors do not constitute tender offers").

[78] Wellman v. Dickinson, 475 F.Supp. 783 (S.D.N.Y. 1979), *aff'd on other grounds*, 682 F.2d 355 (2d Cir. 1982), *cert. denied*, 460 U.S. 1069 (1983).

[79] Filing requirements are not limited to the tender offeror but apply to anyone who is recommending in favor of or against a tender offer covered by the Act. *See* Schedule 14D-9.

[80] 15 U.S.C. § 78n(d)(1) (2015).

[81] 15 U.S.C. § 78n(d)(1) (2015).

[82] 15 U.S.C. § 78m(d) (2015).

[83] *See* SEC Schedule TO and Rule 14d–1, 17 C.F.R. § 240.14d–100 (2015). Schedule TO was formerly Schedule 14D-1.

[84] 15 U.S.C. § 78n(d) (2015). *Cf.* 15 U.S.C. § 78m(d) (2015), which is discussed *supra* § 24.2.

filings must be updated to reflect material changes and developments.[85] Section 14(d)(1) does not apply to an issuer's acquisition of its own shares; those transactions are governed by section 13(e), not section 14(d)(1). However, the SEC's regulations for issuer tender offers are comparable to those in Regulation 14D's rules for third-party offers.[86]

Regulation 14D sets forth the Commission's filing and disclosure requirements under section 14(d)(1). Rule 14d–1[87] provides the basic definitions for covered tender offers and incorporates by reference all general definitions applicable under other provisions of the Exchange Act. Rule 14d–3 requires filing Schedule TO with both the SEC and the target company as well as with the exchange on which the target shares are listed and, if not listed, with the National Association of Securities Dealers (NASD). In addition to the long-form filing embodied in Schedule TO,[88] the tender offeror must file ten copies of all additional tender-offer materials with the Commission no later than the date on which it is first published or disseminated.[89] All documents used in the tender offer and the solicitation must thus be on file with the Commission prior to their use.[90] When the bidder's consideration includes non-exempt securities, the offer must be disseminated to the target shareholders through a prospectus, in compliance with the federal Securities Act of 1933. In all other cases (that is, cash or exempt securities) the bidder has three alternative methods to disseminate its bid: the long-form publication, summary publication, or, using a list of stockholders, through a communication directly to the target shareholders.[91]

[2] Commencement of the Tender Offer

Rule 14d–2[92] provides that a tender offer begins at 12:01 a.m. on the day it is first sent to securities holders or published.[93]

[3] Schedule TO

All bidders must file Schedule TO. "Bidder" is defined as any person who makes a tender offer or on whose behalf a tender offer is made, however, an issuer seeking to acquire its own securities is not within the definition.[94] Schedule TO requires certain basic information regarding the bidder and the bid. For example, Schedule TO requires disclosure of the name of the bidder, the name of the target company, and the title of the class of securities being sought. It also requires that all "persons" reporting under the Schedule provide their names and addresses as well as disclose whether or not they belong to a "group" within the meaning of section 14(d)(2).[95] But the disclosures demanded of the bidder are more extensive than mere background information. There must be disclosure of the source of funds to be used in connection with the tender offer

---

[85]   15 U.S.C. § 78n(d) (2015).

[86]   15 U.S.C. § 78m(e) (1997 & Supp. 2009). In 1986, the SEC amended Rules 13–4 and 14e–1 so as to subject issuer self-tenders to the same time periods and substantive regulation as third-party offers covered by section 14(d) and Regulation 14D.

[87]   17 C.F.R. § 240.14d–1 (2015).

[88]   17 C.F.R. § 240.14d–100 (2015).

[89]   17 C.F.R. § 240.14d–3(b) (2015).

[90]   17 C.F.R. § 240.14d–3 (2015).

[91]   *See* Rule 14d–4, 17 C.F.R. § 240.14d–4 (2015).

[92]   17 C.F.R. § 240.14d–2 (2015).

[93]   Rule 14d–2(a), 17 C.F.R. § 240.14d–2(a) (2015).

[94]   17 C.F.R. § 240.14d–1(g)(2) (2015).

[95]   17 C.F.R. § 240.14d–100 (2015).

and the identity and background of the person filing the document, including the disclosure of any criminal convictions or civil orders arising out of a securities violation within the past five years of the person presenting the tender offer. The tender-offer document must also disclose all contracts, transactions, or negotiations in the preceding three fiscal years between the bidder and the target company, its directors or its officers, the purpose of the tender offer, and the bidder's plans and proposals for the future with regard to the target company. The Schedule TO must divulge the bidder's current interest and holdings of securities of the target company as well as any contracts, arrangements, understandings, or relationships between the bidder and the target company. Present or proposed contracts, arrangements, understandings, or relationships between the bidder, its officers, directors, controlling persons, or subsidiaries and the target company or any of its officers, directors, controlling persons, or subsidiaries that are material to a stockholder's decision must likewise be disclosed. Schedule TO must identify all persons retained, employed, or compensated in connection with the tender offer. The bidder must also disclose extensive information regarding its financial position if the bidder's financial position is material to an investor's decision regarding whether or not to tender shares in the target company.

Certain prospective information must be disclosed—such as any steps towards compliance, with necessary administrative approval for the offer, the possible impact of the antitrust laws, or the margin requirements,[96] as well as a summary of pending material legal proceedings.[97] When there have been material misstatements in a Schedule TO filing, they can be cured by subsequent correction, provided that adequate prominence is given to the curative changes.[98]

[4] The Bidders' Access to the Target Company's Shareholders

Rule 14d–5 spells out the target company's obligation to respond to requests for a shareholder list in connection with tender offers.[99] Briefly, if the bidder or other person presents the request according to the rule's requirements, the target company's management must comply, but the reasonable cost of compliance can be charged to the bidder. Faced with such a request, the target company has two options. First, within three business days it may deliver the stockholder lists to the bidder making the request.[100] Or secondly, it can mail the bidder's materials, within three business days of receipt, to the target company's holders.[101] The SEC dictates the proper form for the bidder's written request.[102] Also, a bidder's request for such lists subjects the bidder to

---

[96] *See, e.g.,* Irving Bank Corp. v. Bank of N.Y. Co., 692 F.Supp. 163 (S.D.N.Y. 1988).

[97] *Cf.* Fry v. Trump, 681 F.Supp. 252 (D.N.J. 1988) (upholding section 14(a) claim based on failure to disclose 10 of 18 pending legal proceedings).

Additionally, the filed copies of Schedule TO must contain the following exhibits: copies of all tender offer material published, sent, or given to security holders by or on behalf of the bidders in connection with the tender offer; any loan or agreement used to finance the tender offer or otherwise disclosed in Schedule TO; any documents setting forth the terms of any contracts, arrangements, understandings, or relationships referred to in Schedule TO; any written legal opinions referring to relevant pending legal proceedings; and the prospectus for any securities to be issued in an exchange offer.

[98] *See, e.g.,* American Insured Mortgage Investors v. CRI, Inc., 1990 WL 192561 (S.D. N.Y. 1990) (material changes had to be highlighted through the use of boldface and italic typeface).

[99] 17 C.F.R. § 240.14d–5 (2015).

[100] 17 C.F.R. § 240.14d–5(c) (2015).

[101] 17 C.F.R. § 240.14d–5(b) (2015). The bidder is to be informed of the progress of any such mailing undertaken by the target company.

[102] 17 C.F.R. § 240.14d–5(e) (2015).

certain requirements, including the return of any lists furnished by the target company.[103]

[5] Withdrawal and Duration of Tender Offer

Rule 14d–7[104] provides that withdrawal rights may be exercised throughout the period that the tender offer remains open, which must be for at least twenty business days.[105] Any increase or decrease in the consideration offered under the tender offer requires that the tender offer's duration be extended for an additional ten business days from the date of change in consideration.[106] The rule also prescribes how the notice of withdrawal is to be given. The overall effect of the SEC's regulations respecting the duration of tender offers and providing withdrawal rights through the life of the tender offer is not only to remove pressure from the target shareholders to rush their acceptance of the bidder's offer but also to create a climate within which competing bids may arise.

[6] Proration and "Best Price" Rules

Rule 14d–8[107] requires pro rata acceptance of shares tendered where the tender offer by its terms does not obligate the tender offeror to accept *all* shares tendered. This takes pressure off the target company's shareholders, who would otherwise have to make a quick decision were acceptance to be on a first-come basis. Proration occurs at the tender offer's close. Thus, target shareholders can delay their acceptance of a bid until near its closing without fear they will be treated differently if the bidder's offer is oversubscribed. A tender offeror may not extend the proration period after expiration of the offer where the effect would be to alter the pro rata acceptance of the shares tendered.[108]

Section 14(d)(7) of the Securities Exchange Act[109] provides that whenever a bidder varies the terms of a tender offer or request before the expiration thereof by increasing the consideration offered to the holders of the securities sought, the bidder must pay to all persons tendering securities pursuant to their requests that same price, whether or not the securities were tendered prior to the variation of the tender offer's terms. This can be especially important if a series of transactions are integrated and held to be parts of a single tender offer.[110] This best price requirement is applicable to both issuer self-tenders and tender offers by third-party bidders.[111] The SEC "best price" requirement applies only to shares purchased during a single tender offer. As such, unlike state "fair

---

[103] 17 C.F.R. § 240.14d–5(f) (2015).

[104] 17 C.F.R. § 240.14d–7 (2015).

[105] 17 C.F.R. § 240.14e–1 (2015).

[106] 17 C.F.R. §§ 240.13e–4(f)(1)(ii), 240.14e–1(b) (2015).

[107] 17 C.F.R. § 240.14d–8 (2008).

[108] Pryor v. United States Steel Corp., 794 F.2d 52 (2d Cir. 1986); Pryor v. USX Corp., 1991 WL 346368 (S.D.N.Y. 1991) (tender offeror could not accept shares tendered after the deadline when this would affect proration rights of shares previously tendered; tender offeror was liable to shareholders who had wrongfully been denied their tender offer premium), s.c., 806 F.Supp. 460 (S.D.N.Y. 1992) (denying summary judgment because terms of offer were susceptible to differing interpretations as to whether late-tender shares would fall within the proration period).

[109] 15 U.S.C. § 78n(d)(7) (2015).

[110] *See, e.g.,* Gerber v. Computer Assocs. Int'l, 303 F.3d 126, 136 (2d Cir. 2002) (finding the payment to be made during and not after the tender offer since "giving effect to every purported withdrawal that allows a discriminatory premium to be paid to large shareholders would completely undermine the 'best-price rule'" (citing Field v. Trump, 850 F.2d 938, 944 (2d Cir. 1988))).

[111] 17 C.F.R. §§ 240.13e–4(f)(8)(ii), 240.14d–10(a)(2) (2015).

price" statutes,[112] the SEC does not regulate two-tiered offers consummated in two distinct steps. The SEC best-price requirements do not prohibit different types of consideration, and the different consideration need not be substantially equivalent in value as long as the tender offer permits the security holders to elect among the types of consideration offered.[113]

Bidders sometimes become ensnared by Rule 14d–10 due to there being no definition of tender offer. In a leading case, *Field v. Trump*,[114] Trump announced a $22 bid for Pay'n Save, only to cancel the bid five days later to "facilitate negotiations" with two Pay'n Save directors who opposed the offer. That same night Trump struck a deal of $23.50/per share, plus $900,000 for "fees and expenses" (roughly equal to $1.50 on a per share basis) with the two recalcitrant directors. The next day Trump announced a $23.50 bid. The Second Circuit concluded that an offer announced on September 7, withdrawn on September 12, and reannouncing a bid on September 13 constituted the same tender offer and supported a claim under Rule 14d–10. Other courts have preferred a bright-line approach focused on the formal announcement and discontinuance of the bid.[115] Also, to provide some clarity with respect to severance pay, covenants not to compete and the like, Rule 14d–10(d)(2) now provides a safe harbor for severance and other compensation arrangements if they are approved by a body of independent directors of the target or bidder when the compensation is not based on a per share calculation.[116]

When different types of consideration are offered, the tender offeror may limit the availability and offer it to tendering shareholders on a pro rata basis.[117] As is the case with the "all holders" requirements, discussed below, the Commission has given itself the power to grant exemptions from the operation of the best-price requirement.[118] As with the rules respecting the duration of tender offers and the withdrawal rights of tendering shareholders, the liberal proration rules and best-price rules shield the target shareholders from being pressured to tender their shares. In combination these rules contribute to an auction environment by making competing bids possible by assuring that the target shareholders are free within relative broad time periods to place their shares with the highest bidder. While this may well reduce the incentive for bidders to initiate a takeover, it is equally likely that the bidder that offers the highest price, on average, is the company that can put the target corporation's assets to their highest use. To the extent that this leads to a better allocation of resources, the concomitant greater costs imposed by the Williams Act are not all that bad.

---

[112] *E.g.*, Md. Code Ann., Corps. & Ass'ns §§ 3–602, 3–603 (LexisNexis 2007). *See* § 24.8 *infra*.

[113] 17 C.F.R. §§ 240.13e–4(f)(9), 240.14d–10(c) (2015).

[114] Field v. Trump, 850 F.2d 938, 100 A.L.R. Fed. 421 (2d Cir. 1988). *See also*, Epstein v. MCA, Inc., 50 F.3d 644, 655, 31 Fed. R. Serv. 3d 611 (9th Cir. 1995), judgment rev'd on other grounds, 516 U.S. 367 (1996) (considering whether the various steps were an integral part of the tender offer).

[115] *See* In re Digital Island Securities Litigation, 357 F.3d 322, 334 (3d Cir. 2004); Lerro v. Quaker Oats Co., 84 F.3d 239, 244–45, 34 Fed. R. Serv. 3d 974 (7th Cir. 1996) (compensation promised to target management for future consulting and non-competition agreements the day before announcing a bid not part of the tender oer). Contra Gerber v. Computer Associates Intern., Inc., 303 F.3d 126, 59 Fed. R. Evid. Serv. 1321 (2d Cir. 2002) ($5 million payment to target CEO for ve-year covenant was within the tender oer period).

[116] 17 C.F.R. § 240.14d–10(d)(2) (2015).

[117] 17 C.F.R. §§ 240.13e–4(f)(9), 240.14d–10(c) (2015).

[118] 17 C.F.R. §§ 240.13e–4(g)(7), 240.14d–10(e) (2015).

[7] The "All Holders" Requirement

In 1985, the Delaware Supreme Court upheld a company's defensive self-tender offer that excluded a hostile tender offeror from the self-tender offer.[119] Since that decision, the SEC has adopted an "all holders" rule, so that such an exclusion is now prohibited. Even though there is no explicit statutory requirement that a tender offer be made to all shareholders, the SEC takes the position that the "all holders" requirement is "necessary and appropriate" to implement the Williams Act.[120]

There is an exception in the "all holders" requirement for tender offers that exclude one or more shareholders in compliance with a constitutionally valid state statute.[121] In addition to reserving general exemptive power under the "all holders" rules,[122] the SEC has promulgated a specific but limited exemption for odd-lot tender offers by issuers. An "odd-lot offer" is one that is limited to security holders owning less than a specified number of shares under one hundred.[123]

[8] Exemptions from Regulation 14D; Mini Tender Offers

Section 14(d)(8) of the Act[124] exempts certain tender offers or requests for tenders from the scope of section 14(d)'s requirements. When the acquisition of the securities sought together with all other acquisitions by the same person of securities of the same class within the preceding twelve months does not exceed two percent of the outstanding securities of the class, section 14(d) does not apply.[125] Similarly, section 14(d) does not apply where the tender offeror is the issuer of the security.[126] The Securities Exchange Act also gives the SEC exemptive power by rule, regulation, or order from transactions "not entered into for the purpose of, and not having the effect of, changing or influencing the control of the issuer or otherwise as not comprehended within the purposes of this subsection."[127]

Although not couched in terms of an exemption, section 14(d) provides that its provisions do not apply to tender offers when after completion of the offer, the bidder would hold less than five percent of a class of the target company's equity securities.[128] Tender offers falling below this threshold became known as mini tender offers. In the 1990s various fraudulent practice developed in connection with these largely unregulated mini tender offers, including offering to buy back stock at a price lower than the current market price.[129] In order to prevent the abuses of mini tender offers, the SEC

---

[119] Unocal Corp. v. Mesa Petroleum Co., 493 A.2d 946 (Del. 1985).

[120] *See* Sec. Exch. Act Rel. No. 34–23421 [1986–1987 Transfer Binder], Fed. Sec. L. Rep. (CCH) ¶ 84,016 (SEC July 11, 1986).

[121] 17 C.F.R. §§ 240.13e–4(f)(9)(ii), 240.14d–10(b)(2) (2015).

[122] 17 C.F.R. §§ 240.13e–4(f)(7), 240.14d–10(e) (2015).

[123] 17 C.F.R. § 240.13e–4(h)(5) (2015).

[124] 15 U.S.C. § 78n(d)(8) (2015).

[125] 15 U.S.C. § 78n(d)(8)(A) (2015).

[126] 15 U.S.C. § 78n(d)(8)(B) (2015).

[127] 15 U.S.C. § 78n(d)(8)(C) (2015).

[128] 15 U.S.C. § 78n(d) (2015).

[129] By labeling the offer a "tender offer," unwary investors were duped into tendering their shares and receiving less than they would have had they sold the shares on the market.

issued guidelines that essentially require full disclosure with respect to mini tender offers.[130]

§ 24.5　The Antifraud Provision—Section 14(e)

Section 14(e) of the Exchange Act[131] prohibits material misstatements, omissions, and fraudulent practices in connection with tender offers. The jurisdictional reach of this antifraud provision is broader than other provisions of the Williams Act because it applies to *any* tender offer in interstate commerce, regardless of whether the target company is subject to the Exchange Act's reporting requirements.[132] Whether a fact is material depends on whether a reasonable investor would consider it significant in making an investment decision.[133] Materiality is based on a highly factual inquiry and thus is difficult to predict. For example, it is not necessary to disclose preliminary merger discussions that may lead to a tender offer.[134] At the same time, a denial of such negotiations, even though they are at a very early stage, is not advisable in light of the Supreme Court's holding that whether a denial of preliminary merger negotiations is material is a question of fact.[135]

As in other areas of the securities laws, courts approach materiality determinations cautiously so as to preserve a healthy balance between the need of investors for information and the fact that too-demanding disclosure requirements ultimately will work against the interests of the corporation's shareholders.[136] Accordingly, subjective motivation behind fully disclosed transactions need not be spelled out as long as all material facts underlying the transaction are disclosed.[137]

Scienter, meaning a misrepresentation committed with either knowledge of its falsity or with reckless disregard for the truth, is required for section 14(e) actions.[138] And if damages are sought, detrimental reliance by the plaintiff must also be alleged.[139] The plaintiff can, as in Rule 10b–5 actions, invoke the fraud-on-the-market approach to satisfying reliance, provided the affected security traded in an efficient market.[140] However, in a section 14(e) action, the plaintiff need not be a purchaser or seller, as under Rule 10b–5, provided "he has been injured by fraudulent activities of others perpetrated in connection with a tender offer."[141]

---

[130] *See* Commission Guidance on Mini-Tender Offers and Limited Partnership Tender Offers, Release No. 34–43069, 2000 WL 1190808 (SEC July 24, 2000).

[131] 15 U.S.C. § 78n(e) (2015).

[132] In contrast, the other provisions of the Williams Act are limited to securities of issuers subject to section 12's registration requirements. 15 U.S.C. § 78l (1997 & Supp. 2009).

[133] TSC Indus. v. Northway, Inc., 426 U.S. 438 (1976).

[134] Staffin v. Greenberg, 672 F.2d 1196 (3d Cir. 1982).

[135] Basic, Inc. v. Levinson, 485 U.S. 224 (1988).

[136] Macfadden Holdings, Inc. v. JB Acquisition Corp., 802 F.2d 62, 71 (2d Cir. 1986), *relying on* Data Probe Acquisition Corp. v. Datatab, Inc., 722 F.2d 1, 5 (2d Cir. 1983), *cert. denied*, 465 U.S. 1052 (1984).

[137] Diamond v. Arend, 649 F.Supp. 408, 415–416 (S.D.N.Y. 1986).

[138] *See, e.g.*, Chris-Craft Industries, Inc. v. Piper Aircraft Corp., 480 F.2d 341, 362, 25 A.L.R. Fed. 534 (2d Cir. 1973); Bloor v. Carro, Spanbock, Londin, Rodman & Fass, 754 F.2d 57, 61 (2d Cir. 1985).

[139] *See, e.g.*, Salsitz v. Peltz, 227 F. Supp. 2d 222, 225 (S.D. N.Y. 2002).

[140] *See* Semerenko v. Cendant Corp., 223 F.3d 165, 178 (3d Cir. 2000).

[141] Smallwood v. Pearl Brewing Co., 489 F.2d 579, 596 (5th Cir. 1974).

The Supreme Court has held that there is no private remedy under section 14(e) *for damages* in the hands of a competing tender offeror.[142] Lower courts have consistently recognized private actions for the target company or its shareholders for damages or such equitable relief as is appropriate under the circumstances.[143] The courts have also recognized the right of the bidder as well as a competing bidder to obtain injunctive relief.[144]

In an important decision, *Schreiber v. Burlington Northern, Inc.*,[145] the Supreme Court limited the thrust of section 14(e). Burlington Northern had made a hostile tender offer to purchase 25.1 million shares of El Paso Gas from the public at $24 per share. After negotiations with El Paso management, the original offer was withdrawn, El Paso management was given "golden parachute" severance payments, and a new tender offer was made for 21 million shares from the public and 4.1 million shares from El Paso at $24 per share. It was claimed that a combination of El Paso management's golden parachutes and a decision to reduce the size of the offer to the public in order to infuse more cash into El Paso (presumably to pay for the golden parachutes) artificially affected the price of the El Paso stock and thus constituted manipulation. The source of the plaintiff's actual complaint was that because fewer shares would be purchased pursuant to the revised bid, as contrasted with the initial bid, the plaintiff would, under the proration rule, have fewer of her shares purchased. Rather than directly face the issue of defining "manipulative conduct," the Court held that " 'manipulative' as used in § 14(e) requires misrepresentation or nondisclosure."[146] The Court thus found section 14(e) was not violated because no omission or misstatement was alleged to have occurred in connection with the cancellation of the first tender offer.

A significant impact of *Schreiber* is it stopped a potential intrusion of federal law into the regulation of defensive maneuvers, an area historically regulated by state fiduciary duty law. Before *Schreiber* was decided, some lower courts held section 14(e) was violated by defensive measures when the tactic prevented further bidding so that the defensive measure could be seen as "locking" the target shares into a price established by the defensive maneuver.[147] These controversially expansive holdings had the potential of opening new frontiers for the federal regulation of tender offers, although it represented a minority view.[148] The *Schreiber* decision made it clear that defensive tactics cannot violate section 14(e), even if manipulative, unless accompanied by a material misstatement or omission.

Unless the Court retrenches from its sweeping conclusion in *Schreiber,* it would appear that any rules promulgated under section 14(e) are at risk to the extent that they go beyond disclosure. This could result in a significant cutback on Regulation 14E and also would be a most questionable narrowing of the scope of the section. The statute

---

[142] Piper v. Chris-Craft Indus., Inc., 430 U.S. 1 (1977).

[143] *See, e.g.,* Seaboard World Airlines, Inc. v. Tiger Int'l, 600 F.2d 355 (2d Cir. 1979) (recognizing the 14(e) remedy but finding no substantive violation).

[144] *See, e.g.,* Humana, Inc. v. American Medicorp., Inc., 445 F.Supp. 613 (S.D.N.Y. 1977). *Cf.* Rondeau v. Mosinee Paper Corp., 422 U.S. 49 (1975).

[145] Schreiber v. Burlington Northern, Inc., 472 U.S. 1 (1985). *See, e.g.,* Norman S. Poser, Stock Market Manipulation and Corporate Control Transactions, 40 U. Miami L. Rev. 671 (1986).

[146] 472 U.S. at 12.

[147] Mobil Corp. v. Marathon Oil Co., 669 F.2d 366 (6th Cir. 1981).

[148] *See, e.g.,* Radol v. Thomas, 772 F.2d 244 (6th Cir. 1985), *cert. denied,* 477 U.S. 903 (1986).

expressly talks in terms of "manipulative" in addition to "fraudulent and deceptive conduct," and the Supreme Court cannot properly excise that term from the statute.

The SEC has promulgated a series of rules under section 14(e), which appear as Rule 14E. Collectively they regulate certain conduct within tender offers regardless of whether the target corporation is subject to the reporting provisions of the Securities Exchange Act. Rule 14e–1[149] requires that any person making a tender offer must hold the offer open for at least twenty business days from the date on which it is first published. The *Schreiber* decision, discussed above, requires deception as an element of any section 14(e) violation. To the extent that the reasoning carries over to the SEC rule-making power, that decision casts a cloud over the validity of Rule 14e–1 because the rule regulates the duration of the offer and thus goes beyond mandating full disclosure.[150] It can, of course, be argued that the SEC's power to mandate a period during which the tender offer must remain open is justified because it gives investors and the market the time necessary to digest the information mandated by the Williams Act's affirmative disclosure requirements.[151]

Rule 14e–1(b) further provides that the tender offeror may not increase or decrease the terms of the offer, the type of consideration, or the dealer's soliciting fee unless the tender offer remains open for at least ten business days from the publication of the notice of such change in the terms of the offer.[152] It also declares it to be an unlawful practice for a tender offeror to fail to pay the consideration offered or to return the securities tendered promptly after either the withdrawal or termination of the tender offer.[153] Rule 14e–1(d)[154] makes it unlawful to extend the length of the tender offer without issuing a notice of such extension by press release or other public announcement, and the notice must give sufficient detail of the time period of the tender offer and its extension.

Whenever a tender offer is made for a target company's shares, the target company has ten business days from the first date on which the tender offer is published to respond.[155] Rule 14e–2[156] requires that the target company's management make one of the following responses within the ten-day period: (1) a recommendation of acceptance or rejection of the tender offer; (2) an expression of no opinion with a decision to remain neutral toward the offer; or (3) a statement that it is not able to take a position with respect to bidder's offer. The Rule 14e–2 statement must also include all reasons for the position taken, or the stance of neutrality, as well as any explanation of the inability to take a position. In setting forth its reasons, the target company's management is, of

---

[149] 17 C.F.R. § 240.14e–1(a) (2015).

[150] *But see* Polaroid Corp. v. Disney, 862 F.2d 987 (3d Cir. 1988), which upheld the SEC's "all-holders rule" (Rule 14d–10, 17 C.F.R. § 240.14d–10 (2015)), reasoning that requiring the offer be made to all shareholders furthers the disclosure goals of the Williams Act.

[151] *Cf.* Polaroid Corp. v. Disney, 862 F.2d 987 (3d Cir. 1988).

[152] 17 C.F.R. § 240.14e–1(b) (2015). *See also* 17 C.F.R. § 240.13e–4(f)(1)(ii) (2015) (imposing same requirement for tender offers by issuers).

[153] 17 C.F.R. § 240.14e–1(c) (2015).

[154] 17 C.F.R. § 240.14e–1(d) (2015).

[155] 17 C.F.R. § 240.14e–2 (2015).

[156] 17 C.F.R. § 240.14e–2 (2015).

course, subject to all of the rules concerning materiality[157] as well as to potential civil and criminal liabilities for material misstatements.

Rule 14e–3[158] prohibits insider trading during a tender offer. The Rule 14e–3 prohibitions expressly apply not only to insiders of the target company but also to others possessing nonpublic information about an upcoming tender offer. In 1997, the Supreme Court upheld the validity of Rule 14e–3 but left undecided the question of whether the SEC's rule-making authority is broader under section 14(e) than it is under section 10(b).[159]

An important anti-manipulation rule is Rule 14e–5 which prohibits a tender offeror from purchasing the target securities other than through the tender offer once the offer has commenced and until it is completed.[160] It has been held that violations of Rule 10b–13 (Rule 14e–5's predecessor) supported a private damage action,[161] but not all courts seem to agree.[162]

Rule 14e–4 prohibits short tendering[163]—the practice of tendering or guaranteeing securities not owned by the person making the tender or guarantee.[164]

§ 24.6 Director Turnover and Williams Act Section 14(f)

As is the case with any transfer of corporate control, tender offers will frequently result in a shift in corporate management.[165] Accordingly, it is not uncommon to find tender offers containing agreements relating to management turnover and the election of new directors. These control transfers can raise problems under state law relating to invalid control premiums and other breaches of fiduciary duty.[166] The Williams Act adds certain disclosure obligations when the bidder has arranged for at least a majority of the directorships to change. Under section 14(f) of the Exchange Act,[167] when in connection with a tender offer for equity securities subject to the Act's reporting requirements of section 14(d)(1) or a purchase of shares subject to section 13(d)(1) agreements arise concerning the designation of new directors who will be at least a majority of the target's board of directors and such change will occur otherwise than through a formal vote at a meeting of securities holders, extensive disclosure is required. Essentially, the information that must be disclosed is of a scale equal to that required in connection with

---

[157] *See, e.g.,* Schwarzschild v. Tse, 1992 WL 448796 (N.D. Cal. 1992) (allegation that directors did not adequately disclose assumptions underlying fairness examination were unsupported by evidence). *See* § 24.1 *supra.*

[158] 17 C.F.R. § 240.14e–3 (2015).

[159] United States v. O'Hagan, 521 U.S. 642 (2015).

[160] 17 C.F.R. § 240.14e–5 (2015).

[161] City Nat'l Bank v. American Commw. Fin. Corp., 801 F.2d 714 (4th Cir. 1986), *cert. denied,* 479 U.S. 1091 (1987).

[162] Beaumont v. American Can Co., 797 F.2d 79 (2d Cir. 1986).

[163] 17 C.F.R. § 240.14e–4 (2015).

[164] *See* Merrill Lynch, Pierce, Fenner & Smith, Inc. v. Bobker, 636 F.Supp. 444 (S.D.N.Y. 1986), *rev'd,* 808 F.2d 930 (2d Cir. 1986) (denying proration to shareholder who sold short while tendering).

[165] *See* Thomas L. Hazen, Transfers of Corporate Control and Duties of Controlling Shareholders— Common Law, Tender Offers, Investment Companies and a Proposal for Reform, 125 U. Pa. L. Rev. 1023 (1977).

[166] This subject is discussed in Chapter 12 *supra.*

[167] 15 U.S.C. § 78n(f) (2015).

a stockholders' meeting at which directors will be elected.[168] Contemplated management turnover, including any arrangement regarding the make-up of the majority of directors, also must be disclosed.[169] Thus, for example, where a stock purchase agreement permits the purchaser to designate a majority of the issuer's directors, section 14(f)'s disclosure obligation is triggered.[170] When the agreed upon shift in control occurs, a second filing obligation arises.[171]

§ 24.7   Remedies for Violations of Sections 13(d), 13(e), and 14(d)

Most of the litigation concerning the question of the existence of implied private rights of action under the Williams Act has arisen in the context of section 14(e)'s general antifraud proscriptions.[172] The courts recognize the existence of at least a limited implied remedy under section 14(e).[173] Since sections 13(d), 13(e), and 14(d) all apply to issuers subject to the Securities Exchange Act's registration and reporting requirements[174] and involve mandatory filings with the Commission, there are a number of other remedies for material misstatements or omissions in these filings.

In *Rondeau v. Mosinee Paper Corporation,*[175] the defendant delayed filing his Schedule 13D more than four months after he acquired more than 5 percent of Mosinee Paper Corporation's stock. The Supreme Court reversed the Seventh Circuit's grant of an injunction, holding that such relief requires proof that the target company's shareholders have been irreparably harmed by the violation. The meaning of "irreparable harm" is an interesting question under the Williams Act, whose provisions ostensibly are designed to provide shareholders and investors sufficient information to enable them to make intelligent decisions when faced with a tender offer, while, at the same time making sure not to tip the balance in favor of incumbent management in the battle for control.[176] Moreover, fashioning any retrospective, corrective equitable relief must be timed so as not to occur too late or it is like trying to unscramble scrambled eggs.[177] At the same time, premature interference has the natural effect of altering the economic bargaining positions of the contestants, and these effects may well be irreversible.

Because time is of the essence in takeover battles, frequently the relief sought in an action under 13(d)(1), 13(e), or 14(d)(1) is for preliminary injunctive relief. Plaintiffs in such actions bear an especially high burden in light of the dual requirement that they prove both a substantial likelihood of success on the merits and irreparable injury if the preliminary injunction is not issued. Failure to meet either of these requirements will

---

[168] Rule 14f–1 provides for specific disclosures in the event there is going to be a change in the majority of directors other than at a shareholder meeting, in a transaction subject to either section 13(d) or section 14(d). 17 C.F.R. § 240.14f–1 (2015).

[169] 15 U.S.C. § 78n(f) (2015). *See* 17 C.F.R. § 240.14f–1 (2008).

[170] Drobbin v. Nicolet Instrument Corp., 631 F.Supp. 860 (S.D.N.Y. 1986).

[171] *Id.*

[172] 15 U.S.C. § 78n(e) (2015). *See* § 24.5 *supra.*

[173] *See* § 24.5 *supra.*

[174] 15 U.S.C. §§ 781 (1997 & Supp. 2009), 78n(a) (2015).

[175] Rondeau v. Mosinee Paper Corporation, 422 U.S. 49 (1975).

[176] *See* S. Rep. No. 550, 90th Cong., 1st Sess. 2 to 3 (1967); H.R. Rep. No. 1711, 90th Cong., 2d Sess. 4 (1968).

[177] Electronic Specialty Co. v. International Controls Corp., 409 F.2d 937, 947 (2d Cir. 1969).

result in a denial of preliminary relief.[178] However, serious violations will warrant preliminary relief, because waiting until a full trial on the merits usually means that the challenged transaction will take place years before the case is resolved. As one court has put it, "[e]ffectively the only relief available to an issuer, under the prevailing view, is an order requiring the 5 percent owner to file a corrected 13D and perhaps enjoining further acquisitions pending the corrections."[179]

With regard to section 13(e) in general, it has been held a private remedy exists because the issuer's security holders constitute a class for whose special benefit the legislation was enacted.[180] The Sixth Circuit has recognized a private remedy for violation of section 13(e)'s going-private provisions that allegedly resulted in the loss of the plaintiff's state law appraisal remedy due to material misstatements or omissions.[181]

In addition to any federal remedies that may exist for Williams Act violations, state law claims may also be available. For example, shareholders may challenge a shareholder vote that was influenced by a materially misleading Williams Act filing.[182]

§ 24.8   State Regulation of Tender Offers

Approximately two-thirds of the states have statutes that regulate tender offers. In less than twenty years, the states went through three generations of takeover statutes.[183] Prior to the adoption of the Williams Act in 1968, there was virtually no specialized regulation of tender offers at either the federal or state level. In most instances, the transparent intent behind state tender offer acts is to protect incumbent management and to preserve the payrolls of local companies that are potential takeover candidates. The statutes' effectiveness arise because they impose additional and substantial impediments to a takeover thus inhibiting or at least slowing any transaction.

Whereas the Williams Act can be seen as maintaining a level playing field between the bidder and the target corporation's shareholders, most state anti-takeover acts make no pretense of such even-handedness. Hence, they are collectively condemned under the rubric "anti-takeover statutes." The discussion that follows is designed to present an overview of similarities within the three distinct types of state anti-takeover statutes. One must be mindful, however, that while general observations about broad categories of anti-takeover statutes are possible, important, albeit sometimes subtle, distinctions exist among the states in their implementation of such a common approach. In the words

---

[178] *See* Gelco Corp. v. Coniston Partners, 811 F.2d 414 (8th Cir. 1987).

[179] Hubco, Inc. v. Rappaport, 628 F.Supp. 345, 354 (D.N.J. 1985).

[180] Howing Co. v. Nationwide Corp., 826 F.2d 1470 (6th Cir. 1987), *cert. denied,* 486 U.S. 1059 (1988) (implied private damage action).

[181] Howing Co. v. Nationwide Corp., 972 F.2d 700 (6th Cir. 1992), *cert. denied,* 507 U.S. 1004 (1993) (decided under section 13(e)'s going-private rules). *See also* Brewer v. Lincoln Int'l Corp., 148 F. Supp. 2d 792, 807 (W.D. Ky. 2000).

[182] *See* Appel v. Berkman, 180 A.3d 1055 (Del. 2018) (non-disclosures in Schedule 14d-9 disclosures rendered transaction subject to challenge under state law); Morrison v. Berry, 191 A.3d 268 (Del. 2018), as revised, (July 27, 2018) (a company's materially misleading Schedule 14d-9 filing may form the basis of a state law claim that an ensuing shareholder vote was not made upon full disclosure and is therefore invalid).

[183] *See* Thomas Lee Hazen, State Anti-Takeover Legislation: The Second and Third Generations, 23 Wake Forest L. Rev. 77 (1988).

of one commentator, "State takeover acts are similar to snowflakes—if you think you have found identical ones, you are probably not looking closely enough."[184]

The various state statutes employ a wide range of jurisdictional provisions. The vast majority of the state acts base jurisdiction on the target company's incorporation within the state, or on the location within the state of the target company's principal place of business and/or substantial target company assets.[185] Another important variation among the states is how they define "tender offer." The state statutes generally include precise but diverse statutory definitions, including the number of solicited target company shareholders required before the act applies.[186]

State anti-takeover laws have evolved through successive generations. Today, only the second and third generation statutes have survived constitutional challenges.

First Generation Anti-Takeover Statutes. Following the pattern of the state blue sky laws, many of the first generation anti-takeover statutes went beyond the disclosure philosophy of the Williams Act by giving the state administrator the power to review the merits of the tender offer's terms and the adequacy of the bidder's disclosures.[187] The administrator was frequently empowered to hold hearings, which could be initiated by either the administrator,[188] by the target company,[189] or by a certain percentage of the target company's shareholders.[190] Moreover, first generation statutes frequently imposed a waiting period of ten, twenty,[191] or thirty days[192] between the filing of the tender offer and the date on which it was to become effective. After the SEC in 1979 adopted Rule 14d–2(b),[193] which establishes that a tender offer commences on publication of its terms, and because many substantive Williams Act regulations are then triggered by such commencement,[194] a conflict between state and federal law arose such that the SEC believed all such waiting periods were preempted.[195]

In *Edgar v. MITE Corporation*,[196] the Supreme Court declared the Illinois anti-takeover statute unconstitutional. The Illinois statute imposed a waiting period and provided for a hearing on the tender offer's terms. The court's majority believed the

---

[184] Symposium, State Regulation of Tender Offers, 7 J. Corp. Law 603 (1982) (footnote omitted).

[185] *See, e.g.,* Conn. Gen. Stat. Ann. § 36b–41(1) (West 2004 & Supp. 2009); Ohio Rev. Code Ann. § 1707.041(A)(1) (West) (2004, Supp.2009) (amended 1990).

[186] *See, e.g.,* N.H. Rev. Stat. Ann. § 421–A:2(VI)(a) (LexisNexis 2009) (" 'Takeover bid' does not include: (3) Any . . . offer to acquire an equity security, or the acquisition of such equity security pursuant to such offer . . . from not more than 25 persons . . .").

[187] *E.g.,* La. Rev. Stat. Ann. § 51:1501(E) (West 1987) (repealed); 70 Pa. Cons. Stat. § 74(d) (Supp. 1993) (repealed).

[188] *E.g.,* Mo. Stat. Ann. § 409.521 (West 2001).

[189] *E.g.,* 70 Pa. Cons. Stat. § 74(d) (Supp. 1993) (repealed).

[190] *E.g.,* Conn. Gen. Stat. Ann. § 36b–44(a) (West 2004) (owners of "aggregate ten percent of the outstanding equity securities of the class involved in the tender offer" may petition the commissioner to schedule a hearing).

[191] *E.g.,* Del. Code Ann. tit. 8, § 203(a)(1) (1983) (repealed); 70 Pa. Cons. Stat. § 74(a) (Supp. 1993) (repealed).

[192] *E.g.,* N.C. Gen. Stat. Ann. § 78B–4(a) (1985) (repealed).

[193] 17 C.F.R. § 240.14d–2(b) (2015).

[194] *See* §§ 24.3, 24.4 *supra.*

[195] *See* Sec. Act Rel. No. 33–6158 (SEC Nov. 29, 1979).

[196] Edgar v. MITE Corporation, 457 U.S. 624 (1982).

Illinois law violated the Commerce Clause because of the burdens it placed on interstate commerce in light of the state's interest in regulation:[197]

> While protecting local investors is plainly a legitimate state objective, the State has no legitimate interest in protecting nonresident shareholders. Insofar as the Illinois law burdens out-of-state transactions, there is nothing to be weighed in the balance to sustain the law.[198]

A plurality of the justices found the Illinois law also violated the Supremacy Clause in conflicting with the desire for even-handedness embodied in the Williams Act. *Edgar v. MITE Corporation* was the death knell for first generation statutes.

Second Generation Anti-Takeover Statutes. Relying on some helpful language in *Edgar v. MITE Corporation*,[199] a number of states enacted second generation takeover statutes, which were designed to overcome the constitutional infirmities of the Illinois statute that was struck down in *MITE*. The basic thrust of many of these second generation statutes is to regulate tender offers through state law rules relating to corporate governance rather than through state securities laws and administrative regulations. That is, adhering to the traditional choice-of-law rule that questions regarding the internal affairs of a corporation are to be resolved according to the state of the company's incorporation, the second generation anti-takeover statutes introduce many corporate law requirements that operate to the serious disadvantage of the bidder for control. Ohio was the first state to adopt second generation legislation.[200] Many other states have since enacted second generation statutes.

A few second generation statutes are disclosure-oriented and are easily analogous to the states' historical administration of their blue sky laws.[201]

The most common and effective form of second generation anti-takeover statute is the "control share acquisition" statute. For example, the Ohio statute, which governs all forms of takeovers and is not limited to tender offers, applies to Ohio corporations having fifty or more shareholders and a principal place of business, principal offices, or substantial assets within the state.[202] The Ohio act then classifies takeover transactions by the percentage of shares owned by the acquiring person, with each control zone triggering the act's substantive requirements.[203] Acquiring persons must deliver to the target company a disclosure statement describing the proposed acquisition. The target company's board then has ten days to call a special shareholders' meeting, which must take place within fifty days. At that meeting the transaction requires approval of a majority of the disinterested shares not owned or controlled by the acquiring person or any affiliate.

---

[197] The Illinois statute required the bidder to notify the secretary of state 20 business days before commencing its tender offer, and the secretary of state was empowered to convene a hearing in which case the tender offer could not proceed until the hearing's completion.

[198] 457 U.S. at 644.

[199] Edgar v. MITE Corporation, 457 U.S. 624 (1982).

[200] Ohio Rev. Code Ann. § 1701.832 (2004) (amended 1993).

[201] *See* Cardiff Acquisitions, Inc. v. Hatch, 751 F.2d 906 (8th Cir. 1984), *appeal after remand,* 751 F.2d 917 (8th Cir. 1984).

[202] Ohio Rev. Code Ann. § 1701.831 (LexisNexis 2004 & Supp. 2009).

[203] For example, the Pennsylvania statute sets three control thresholds: 20%, 33⅓, and 50%. 15 Pa. Cons. Stat. Ann. § 2562 (West 1995 & Supp. 2009).

An alternative to the "control share acquisition" type of statute is the "fair price" statute. For example, Maryland takes a more structural approach in regulating share acquisitions. The Maryland statute requires any takeover be approved by at least eighty percent of the shareholders and two-thirds of the disinterested shareholders unless all shareholders receive the best price paid by the acquiring person within a five-year period.[204] The best-price approach, patterned after fair price charter amendments adopted by many corporations, is designed to fend off two-tiered offers. The Maryland Act excludes "friendly" offers from its coverage. A number of states have adopted fair-price statutes, some of which vary the terms of the Maryland act. Another means by which fair price is determined is by the statute providing target shareholders an appraisal remedy in control acquisition transactions.[205]

Another form of statute within the second generation is the "constituency" or "stakeholder" statute,[206] which permits management to consider interests other than those of the shareholders in making decisions.[207] These statutes generally make it clear that although management may consider other interests, it does not have to. Still another approach taken in some of the second generation statutes is to give dissenters' rights to a wide variety of control transactions.

The Supreme Court in *CTS Corporation v. Dynamics Corporation of America*[208] upheld the constitutionality of Indiana's control share statute. Under the Indiana statute, voting rights are denied to shares held by anyone whose ownership exceeded twenty percent of the outstanding voting shares unless the "independent" target shareholders at a meeting to occur within fifty days of the threshold being crossed vote to grant voting rights to those shares. The bidder in *CTS Corporation* reasoned that the Indiana statute delayed the consummation of tender offers by fifty days, the length of time it needed to assure itself that it had indeed acquired voting control. Such delay, it was argued, conflicted with the Williams Act, which contemplates that tender offers need be of no greater duration than twenty business days. In an opinion whose language appears more often to support the bidder's than the target's position,[209] the Supreme Court swept the bidder's concerns aside. It first reasoned that the bidder was not disadvantaged because it could make its offer to purchase the shares conditional on later shareholder approval. Next, the Court advised that even if disadvantaged by a fifty-day delay, this delay was not unreasonable. Clearly a factor in the Court's reasoning is the spectre of having to cast aside the rich history of the "internal affairs" doctrine, which so clearly supports the state of a corporation's incorporation regulating its substantive affairs.[210]

---

[204] Md. Code Ann., Corps. & Ass'ns §§ 3–602, 3–603 (LexisNexis 2007).

[205] *E.g.,* 15 Pa. Cons. Stat. Ann. §§ 2545 to 2547 (West 1995).

[206] Ind. Code Ann. § 23–1–35–1(d) (LexisNexis 1999 & Supp. 2007).

[207] *See* Cal. Corp. Code § 309 (West 1990 & Supp. 2002); Ind. Code Ann. § 23–1–35–1 (LexisNexis 1999 & Supp. 2007).

[208] CTS Corporation v. Dynamics Corporation of America, 481 U.S. 69 (1987).

[209] *See generally* Donald C. Langevoort, The Supreme Court and the Politics of Corporate Takeovers: A Comment on *CTS Corp. v. Dynamics Corp. of America,* 101 Harv. L. Rev. 96 (1987).

[210] The Indiana statute applied to target corporations that (1) were incorporated in Indiana and (2) had their principal place of business or substantial assets within Indiana and a certain number of shareholders in Indiana. The latter two-point bases were not emphasized by the court, and logic would suggest that being incorporated within the state justifies applying its anti-takeover provisions.

Third Generation Anti-Takeover Statutes. Finding few limits in *CTS Corporation v. Dynamics Corporation of America*,[211] states have spawned a third generation of anti-takeover provisions even more draconian than their predecessors. A version of the third generation takeover statutes is modeled on the New York "freeze" statute,[212] also known as a business-combination statute. The idea behind such statutes is to delay any transaction that would complete the second step of a two-step acquisition where the first step was not agreed to by target company's management. Thus, for example, the New York statute prohibits a merger or other business acquisition within five years of the control acquisition date unless the transaction was approved by the target company's directors *prior* to the control acquisition date. Other states followed New York's lead, including Delaware, which adopted a three-year-freeze statute.[213] The Delaware statute withstood early challenges to its constitutionality,[214] and the constitutionality of the Wisconsin freeze statute was upheld by the Seventh Circuit.[215] Statutes are still likely to fall victim to the Commerce Clause when they treat foreign bidders more harshly than local bidders.[216]

The varieties of third generation statutes continued to proliferate. In the spring of 1990, Pennsylvania adopted the most ambitious anti-takeover statute to date. In addition to adopting a control share statute, the Pennsylvania legislature enacted a provision requiring any person owning more than twenty percent of a company's voting shares to disgorge any profit realized within an eighteen month period.[217] The impact of this provision is to discourage suitors by locking them in as shareholders in the event that their takeover attempt is unsuccessful. Pennsylvania has taken yet another approach by expressly sanctioning use of poison pills as a defensive measure.[218] Also in 1990, Massachusetts enacted a statute that mandates dividing the directors into groups and staggering the election of directors.[219] A corporation's board by a majority vote may choose to opt out of the law, should the directors decide to have all directors elected annually. Shareholders can opt out of staggered elections only on a two-thirds vote.

---

[211] CTS Corporation v. Dynamics Corporation of America, 481 U.S. 69 (1987).

[212] N.Y. Bus. Corp. Law § 912 (McKinney 2003).

[213] Del. Code Ann. tit. 8, § 203 (2001 & Supp. 2008).

[214] *See* BNS, Inc. v. Koppers Co., 683 F.Supp. 458 (D. Del. 1988).

[215] Amanda Acquisition Corp. v. Universal Foods Corp., 877 F.2d 496 (7th Cir. 1989), *cert. denied*, 493 U.S. 955 (1989).

[216] Campeau Corp. v. Federated Dept. Stores, 679 F.Supp. 735 (S.D. Ohio 1988).

[217] 15 Pa. Cons. Stat. Ann. §§ 2571 to 2576 (West 1995).

[218] *See* Pennsylvania Enacts Law Against Hostile Takeovers, 20 Sec. Reg. & L. Rep. (BNA) 502 (April 1, 1988).

[219] Mass. Gen. Laws Ann. ch. 149, § 184 (LexisNexis 2008).

Chapter 25

AMENDMENTS TO THE CORPORATE CHARTER

Table of Sections

§ 25.1 Power to Authorize Fundamental Changes

Corporation statutes vest the management of corporate business in the board of directors. The board's authority extends to the making of contracts of any kind, incurring indebtedness, and authorizing any other act, unless otherwise limited by the articles of incorporation or by a provision in the state corporation statute.[1] Any statutory limitation on the board of directors' authority to carry out corporate business arises when the transaction is of a type for which the statute requires shareholder approval to be obtained. Shareholder approval is so required in those instances where the transaction poses a fundamental change in the corporation or the stockholders' economic or voting rights.[2] Fundamental corporate transactions are those characterized by their extraordinary nature as well as by the unusual changes they bring either to the corporate business or to the rights of its shareholders. It is because of their effects on the business and the shareholders that the authority to undertake such transactions is not commended solely to the discretion of the board of directors, but must be authorized by some specified vote or written consent of the shareholders. The shareholders' competence to assess the merits of the proposed fundamental change is found in their self-interest and in the fact that the skills called into practice are analogous to those exercised in investing generally. That is, the type of structural decision for which stockholder approval is required under most corporate statutes bears directly on the risks and returns associated with an ownership interest in the firm.

While we may doubt that stockholders will diligently review and reflect on the significance of the transaction for which their approval is sought before they vote, there is no reason to believe fundamental transactions involve skills that are alien to the stockholder investor such that their involvement is harmful. Thus the concurrent approval of the shareholders is required to authorize a new class of stock or to increase

---

[1]   *See* Cal. Corp. Code § 300 (West 1990 & West Supp. 2009); N.C. Gen. Stat. Ann. § 55–2–02 (2002); MBCA §§ 8.01(b) (2016).

[2]   Under this traditional pattern of corporate governance, no direct power can be exercised by the shareholders unless by unanimous consent. *See* Manson v. Curtis, 119 N.E. 559 (N.Y. 1918).

the authorized number of shares of an existing class of stock;[3] to reduce the legal capital;[4] to convey, transfer, or lease all or substantially all the property of the corporation;[5] to amend the articles of incorporation;[6] to authorize a merger or consolidation with another corporation;[7] to dissolve the corporation voluntarily;[8] or to renew or extend the period of corporation's existence.[9] This chapter examines the power of the corporation as well as the procedures to amend the articles of incorporation.

To understand the formal procedures that accompany the process of amending the articles of incorporation invites a reconsideration of the earlier discussion that a corporation is but a "nexus of contracts." This metaphor describes the unique contractual relationship that exists among the shareholders, the corporation, and the state of incorporation. At the heart of this contract are the corporation's articles of incorporation as well as the statute under which it is incorporated. By conceptualizing the shareholders' relationship with their corporation as contractual, with the terms of that contract set forth in both its articles of incorporation and the local corporate statute, a certain rigidity in that relationship appears. Thus, absent some authority in either the articles of incorporation or the laws of the governing state, an amendment of the articles of incorporation would appear to require the consent of all shareholders. This statement merely reflects the basic principle of contract law that the terms of any contract cannot be changed except by mutual consent.[10] Surely, in a long-term business relationship and within a dynamic commercial setting, corporate activity and shareholder interests cannot long survive if change in the rights of owners requires the approval of each affected owner. At the same time, one must have a healthy regard for the vulnerability of minority stockholders if their rights can be changed at the will of the majority. Hence, as statutes and doctrine have over the years become increasingly more permissive of amendments that alter the rights of shareholders on the approval of a majority of the shares, a question of growing importance is what equitable limitations or other protections should exist to shield the minority stockholders from unfair or coercive amendments of their rights, privileges, or preferences?

§ 25.2 Constitutional Limitations—the *Dartmouth College* Case

The Constitution declares that "[n]o State shall . . . pass any . . . Law impairing the Obligation of Contracts. . . ."[11] When the legislature of a state grants a charter to a private corporation, whether it be of a business or a charitable nature, the charter embodies a contract between the state and the corporation and later its shareholders.

---

[3]   *See* Chicago City Ry. v. Allerton, 85 U.S. (18 Wall.) 233 (1874); Hill v. Small, 183 S.E.2d 752 (Ga. 1971) (stock issued by directors in violation of charter is void; stockholders did not authorize the stock issued). But *cf.* 805 ILCS § 5/10.15 (Smith-Hurd 1993) (directors may amend to split shares); MBCA § 10.05(4) (1999).

[4]   *E.g.,* W. Va. Code Ann. § 31–1–115 (Michie 2001, repealed); former MBCA § 69 (1969) (the current MBCA does not carry forward the approach in the former MBCA).

[5]   *E.g.,* Ky. Rev. Stat. Ann. § 271B.12–020 (Banks-Baldwin 1989); Tex. Corps. & Ass'ns Code Act Ann. § 5.10 (Vernon 2003 & West Supp. 2008).

[6]   *E.g.,* Cal. Corp. Code § 900 (West 1990); Del. Code Ann. tit. 8, § 242 (2001 & Michie Supp. 2008); former MBCA § 58 (1969).

[7]   *E.g.,* Ky. Rev. Stat. Ann. § 271B.11–030 (Banks-Baldwin 1989); N.C. Gen. Stat. Ann. § 55–11–03 (2000 & West Supp. 2008).

[8]   *E.g.,* Cal. Corp. Code § 1900 (West 1990).

[9]   *E.g.,* Cal. Corp. Code § 909 (West 1990).

[10]   *E.g.,* Allen v. Royale "16", Inc., 449 So.2d 1365 (La. Ct. App. 1984) (any change in corporate charter must conform to corporation law).

[11]   U.S. Const. art. I, § 10, cl. 1.

The leading case on the power of the state to authorize changes in the shareholders' contract with the corporation was decided by the United States Supreme Court in 1819 and is known as the *Dartmouth College* case.[12] Dartmouth College, a charitable corporation, had been created by a charter granted in 1769 by the governor of the colony acting in the name of King George III. The charter provided that the purpose of the institution was the instruction of Indian, English, and other youths. Management and control of the institution were entrusted to a self-perpetuating board of 12 trustees and their successors. In 1816, the New Hampshire legislature passed three special acts amending this charter. The newly enacted legislation changed the name of the corporation to Trustees of Dartmouth University; it rearranged the control and administration of its affairs by increasing the number of trustees to 21 and created a board, to be appointed by the governor, of 25 overseers with power superior to the trustees.

The corporation brought an action attacking the charter amendments as void under the constitutional prohibition against impairment of the obligation of contracts. The state court upheld the legislation on the ground that the corporation was a public institution subject to the control of the legislature. The state court reasoned that the charter was not a contract within the meaning of the Constitution. The case was argued before the Supreme Court of the United States by Daniel Webster for the plaintiffs in error and William Wirt for the defendant in error. The Supreme Court reversed. The Court held that the corporation was a private entity founded and endowed by private means, that corporate charter was a contract within the meaning of the Constitution, and that the acts of the New Hampshire legislature impaired the contract and were void.

The *Dartmouth College* case clearly recognizes that the articles of incorporation and the corporation laws existing at the time of incorporation can therefore be regarded as a contract among the stockholders. Indeed, the reasoning of *Dartmouth College* captures nicely the threefold contract that embodies the rights the shareholders hold in the corporation. The links in contract are: (1) between the state and the corporation, (2) between the corporation and the shareholders or members, and (3) among the shareholders themselves.[13]

§ 25.3 The Reservation of Power to Amend the Corporate Statute

In the *Dartmouth College* case, discussed in the previous section, Mr. Justice Story suggested that in granting a charter the state might reserve the power to amend or repeal the grant and thereby avoid the vested-rights problem. Since that decision, such statutory reservation has become universal.[14] Some states have a constitutional provision reserving such power,[15] but a statute or constitutional provision reserving the power to amend or repeal cannot amend or repeal the charter of a corporation that was created before the reservation[16] unless the corporation expressly or impliedly submits to

---

[12] Trustees of Dartmouth College v. Woodward, 17 U.S. (4 Wheat) 518 (1819).

[13] *See* Staar Surgical Co. v. Waggoner, 588 A.2d 1130, 1136 (Del. Ch. 1991) ("[A] corporate charter is both a contract between the State and the corporation, and the corporation and its shareholders. . . . The charter is also a contract among the shareholders themselves.").

[14] *E.g.,* Cal. Corp. Code § 900(a) (West 1990); Del. Code Ann. tit. 8, § 394 (2001 & Michie Supp. 2008).

[15] *E.g.,* N.Y. Const. art. 10, § 1.

[16] Dodge v. Woolsey, 59 U.S. (18 How.) 331 (1855).

it.[17] In states where existing corporations are subject to the reserved power to amend, a new statute or even a comprehensive new corporation code may apply to all corporations then existing as well as to those formed thereafter.[18]

The legislature's reserved power enters into and forms part of the charter contract of corporations created after its enactment. The reservation permits rearranging relative rights by amendment of the contract between the corporation and its shareholders or members[19] as well as changing the contract between the corporation and the state. The reserved power thus extends beyond mandatory changes made by amendment of the corporation laws. It also covers changes authorized by a specified majority of the shareholders, even if a particular class of shares suffers materially.[20]

The power reserved to the legislature to alter or amend the laws governing existing corporations is not unlimited.[21] Under the due process and contract clauses of state and federal constitutions, the power does not extend to contracts and property *acquired* under the charter; it extends only to rights that are governed by the charter. For example, the reserve clause may validly be relied on to authorize the elimination of dividends that are in arrears but not to authorize cancellation of dividends that have been declared but not paid. The reservation does not authorize legislation depriving a corporation, its shareholders or its creditors of property rights without due process of law.[22]

§ 25.4 The Amendment Process

In most instances the amendment of the articles of incorporation requires the approval of both the board of directors and the shareholders entitled to vote. Many states follow the lead of the former Model Business Corporation Act and the current Model Business Corporation Act to permit certain types of amendments solely on the authority of the board of directors.[23] In most cases, such authorization is confined to certain "housekeeping" changes, such as deleting the names or addresses of the initial directors, substituting the full expression "corporation" or "incorporated" for the abbreviated version, or vice versa, or to deleting the name or address of the initial registered agent. Some substantive changes are also authorized to be made solely on the authority of the board of directors, such as the power to extend the duration of the corporation if the corporation was formed at a time when a limited duration was required by law,[24] to change the par value of a class or series of shares,[25] or to create a series of shares within an authorized class.[26] In Illinois, a majority vote of the board of directors can authorize a stock split, provided that no class or series of shares is adversely affected.[27]

---

[17]   *See* Golconda Mining Corp. v. Hecla Mining Co., 494 P.2d 1365 (1972).

[18]   Bennett v. Lonoke Bancshares, Inc., 356 Ark. 371, 155 S.W.3d 15 (2004) ("reservation of powers" clause becomes part of every corporate charter by operation of law, and all shareholders implicitly consent to state's authority to amend, alter, or repeal any corporation statute).

[19]   Adair v. Orrell's Mut. Burial Ass'n, 201 S.E.2d 905 (1974).

[20]   Looker v. Maynard, 179 U.S. 46 (1900); Goldman v. Postal Tel., Inc., 52 F.Supp. 763 (D. Del. 1943).

[21]   *See* Phillips Petroleum Co. v. Jenkins, 297 U.S. 629 (1936).

[22]   Superior Water, Light & Power Co. v. City of Superior, 263 U.S. 125, 137 (1923).

[23]   *See, e.g.,* MBCA §§ 10.02, 10.03 & 10.05 (2016).

[24]   *See* MBCA § 10.05(a) (1999).

[25]   *See* Fla. Stat. Ann. § 607.1002 (West 2007).

[26]   *See* Wis. Stat. Ann. § 180.1002 (West 2002).

[27]   805 ILCS § 5/10.15(d) (2004 & West Supp. 2008).

Subject to appropriate approval by the board of directors and the shareholders entitled to vote, all states expressly authorize amendments to the articles of incorporation if the provisions of the amendment could lawfully be contained in the original articles at the time the amendment is made.[28] However, the extent of the authority to amend the articles of incorporation depends on the wording of the governing provision in the corporation statutes. The most common state statutory approach is to provide a laundry list of amendments that are permissible;[29] other states provide a broad grant of power to amend the articles of incorporation.[30] Regardless of which statutory approach is taken, the power of amendment in most states generally requires approval by a vote of at least a majority of the shares eligible to vote;[31] a handful of states still require a two-thirds vote of the shareholders.[32]

The Model Business Corporation Act has a somewhat more intricate approach to determining the approval required to amend the articles of incorporation. In states adopting the Model Act's approach, the articles of incorporation are amended pursuant to a bare majority of the votes cast affirmatively or negatively at a stockholders' meeting at which a quorum is present; if the amendment is of the type that gives rise to a class vote the required approval (*i.e.*, a majority of the votes cast provided a quorum of that group of shares is satisfied) of such class of shares must also be obtained.[33] The articles of incorporation may specify a greater quorum or voting requirement for resolutions to amend the articles of incorporation.

State statutes commonly require in specific types of amendments to the articles of incorporation that a class or series of shares is entitled to vote and the approval of a requisite percentage of the shares of that class or series must approve.[34] Such class voting is an important right to a class or series of shares. A class vote affords the possibility for a class affected by the amendment to veto the amendment. This power provides them with important bargaining power in assuring that any amendments of their rights, privileges, and preferences are not simply in the best interest of the corporation but are also in the economic interest of that class of shareholders. Some states have phrased their statutory provisions to grant a class vote only where the amendment would "adversely affect"[35] a class or series of shares,[36] and then proceed to enumerate a list of amendments that are deemed to adversely affect the rights of

---

[28]   *See, e.g.,* Del. Code Ann. tit. 8, § 242(a) (2001 & Michie Supp. 2008).

[29]   *See, e.g.,* Del. Code Ann. tit. 8, § 242(a) (2001 & Michie Supp. 2008).

[30]   *See, e.g.,* Cal. Corp. Code § 900(a) (West 1990).

[31]   *See* Del. Code Ann. tit. 8, § 242(b)(1) (2001 & Michie Supp. 2008).

[32]   *See, e.g.,* 805 ILCS § 5/10.20(c) (West 2004 & West Supp. 2008).

[33]   The actual means for accomplishing this result is a bit complex. MBCA § 10.03(e) (2016) sets forth the requirement for shareholder approval and refers the reader to MBCA § 10.04 (2016) to determine whether a class vote is required. The actual approval required, absent a charter provision calling for a greater requirement is the general shareholder voting requirements of MBCA §§ 7.25 & 7.26 (2016). *See* MBCA § 10.03 Official Comment (2016).

[34]   The Model Business Corporation Act introduces new terminology by using "voting groups" in place of a class or series. *See* MBCA § 10.04 (2016).

[35]   For a case considering whether a class is "adversely affected," *see* Dalton v. American Inv. Co., 490 A.2d 574 (Del. Ch. 1985) (not adversely affected by amendment switching from redemption by lot to redeeming via market and negotiated purchases 5% each year for 20 years).

[36]   *See, e.g.,* Mass. Gen. Laws Ann. ch. 156B, § 71 (2005 & LexisNexis Supp. 2009); N.Y. Bus. Corp. Law § 804(b) (McKinney 2003 & West Supp. 2009).

holders.[37] Delaware is distinctive in the brevity with which its statute proscribes amendments triggering a class vote.[38]

An appraisal remedy, also known as dissenters' rights, is a method an unhappy shareholder may use to mitigate any unfairness that arises in a fundamental change within the corporation. The appraisal remedy provides shareholders with a right, subject to certain procedural preconditions, to dissent from certain types of changes and to obtain payment in cash for the fair value of their shares.

The Model Business Corporation Act grants appraisal rights when an amendment to the articles of incorporation, with respect to a class or series of shares, reduces the number of shares of a class or series owned by a shareholder to a fraction of a share if the corporation has the obligation or right to repurchase the fractional share.[39] As the Official Comment explains:

> The reasons for granting appraisal rights in this situation are similar to those granting such rights in cases of cash-out mergers, as both transactions could compel affected shareholders to accept cash for their investment in an amount established by the corporation. Appraisal is afforded only for those shareholders of a class or series whose interest is so affected.[40]

In addition, the Act grants appraisal rights in the event of any other amendment to the articles of incorporation to the extent provided by the articles, bylaws, or board resolution.[41] Some states also provide an appraisal remedy for amendments that materially alter the rights, preferences or privileges enjoyed by the shares' holder.[42]

Failure to comply with the temporally significant steps to effect an amendment results in the amendment not being effective so that, for example, if the amendment sought to create newly authorized shares the shares would not be deemed validly authorized.[43]

§ 25.5   Equitable Limitations on Changes in Outstanding Shares

The problem of fairness in recapitalization has frequently been litigated in connection with charter amendments and other transactions undertaken to eliminate dividend arrearages on preferred shares.[44] The purpose for eliminating the preferred's accumulated dividends is not hard to understand. A board of directors that believes the

---

[37]   *See* Mass. Gen. Laws Ann. ch. 156B, § 77(a)–(e) (2005 & LexisNexis Supp. 2009).

[38]   Delaware provides a class vote only for amendments that (1) increase or decrease the aggregate number of authorized shares of the class, (2) increase or decrease the par value of the shares of the class, or (3) alter or change the powers, preferences, or special rights of the shares of the class. *See* Del. Code Ann. tit. 8, § 242(b)(2) (2001 & Michie Supp. 2008).

[39]   MBCA § 13.02(a)(4) (2016).

[40]   MBCA § 13.02 Official Comment (2016).

[41]   MBCA § 13.02(a)(5) (2016).

[42]   Celauro v. 4C Foods Corp., 38 Misc. 3d 636, 956 N.Y.S.2d 821 (Sup. 2012) (listing decisions in New York finding that an amendment altered rights of outstanding shares in such a way as to trigger appraisal under the New York statute).

[43]   *See* Blades v. Wisehart, 2010 WL 4638603 (Del.Ch. 2010) (failure to satisfy steps to amend the articles so as to effect the stock split resulted in shares believed to have been approved not being validly issued so that their holders were not stockholders).

[44]   *See, e.g.,* State v. Bechtel, 31 N.W.2d 853 (Iowa 1948). *See generally* Ben Walther, The Peril And Promise Of Preferred Stock, 39 Del. J. Corp. L. 161 (2014)(examining the erosion over time of protections courts once extended preferred shareholders).

corporation, after years of desuetude, has "turned the corner" toward continuing profitability may question whether honoring the preferred arrearages is necessarily the right choice. Recall that the board of directors is elected by the common shareholders and that the directors may themselves be the owners of common shares. Until the arrearages are paid or eliminated, dividends cannot be paid to the common stockholders. Hence their natural tendency is to reduce or eliminate the right to arrearages of dividends and any other features of the preferred share contract they believe is burdensome to the corporation. Additionally, substantial preferred arrearages cast a dark cloud over the ability of the corporation to attract new investors in its common stock because of the corporation's need to satisfy all accumulated dividends on the preferred before declaring dividends on its common shares. And new investors may be needed in this case because the new financial vigor of the corporation may be sustainable only with an expansion of its resources.

The courts are deeply divided on the approach to be taken when considering whether a recapitalization should be enjoined on the basis of unfairness. Recall that the preferred are viewed in the same light as bondholders when they stand before the court; they are not residual claimants to the firm. The firm's obligations to them are provided by the terms of their contract, and, hence, the courts do not view either the preferred stockholders or bondholders as standing in a fiduciary relationship to the firm or its managers. The least protective of the approaches requires evidence of fraud or bad faith before a court will enjoin a recapitalization.[45] More frequently the courts apply a fairness standard in assessing a recapitalization.[46] Few instances exist in which courts have used their equitable powers to protect the preferred shares' claim that the amendment of their rights was unfair or even fraudulent.

It is now generally understood that, in addition to securing the requisite shareholder approval after full disclosure of the material facts to the recapitalization, fairness demands only some reasonable compensation for the changes or sacrifices that an amendment visits upon the affected class. Thus the elimination of accrued dividends has been held fair because the preferred increased their equity interest in the corporation[47] or voting control shifted to the preferred.[48] In making these determinations, one should initially be guided by the objective standard that, after the recapitalization, the preferreds' share of the firm's future value approximates their claim before the acquisition. This approach may be seen as placing too much weight on the economic feature of the shares and not giving sufficient attention to their other features, such as voting rights. Some courts therefore have applied rough estimates of fairness based on considering the shares' voting rights, liquidation rights, or future claims on dividends or earnings.[49] The far wiser approach is to view the economic rights of the parties on the assumption the firm will continue as an operating entity and to consider their positions primarily in financial terms. This assumption appears imminently

---

[45] *See* Aldridge v. Franco Wyoming Oil Co., 14 A.2d 380 (Del. 1940); McNulty v. W. & J. Sloane, 54 N.Y.S.2d 253 (Sup. Ct. 1945).

[46] *See* New Faunce v. Boost Co., 83 A.2d 649 (N.J. Super. Ch. Ct. 1951); State v. Bechtel, 31 N.W.2d 853 (Iowa 1948).

[47] *See* Hottenstein v. York Ice Mach. Corp., 136 F.2d 944 (3d Cir. 1943); McQuillen v. National Cash Register Co., 27 F.Supp. 639 (D. Md. 1939).

[48] *See* Porges v. Vadsco Sales Corp., 32 A.2d 148 (Del. Ch. 1943).

[49] *See* Page v. Whittenton Mfg. Co., 97 N.E. 1006 (Mass. 1912) (liquidation value); Page v. American & British Mfg. Co., 113 N.Y.S. 734 (App. Div. 1908).

reasonable because the very purpose of the recapitalization in most instances is to permit the firm to continue its operations, and the issues before everyone are predominantly how to share the future free cash flow of the business.

Thus proportionality should be informed in the first instance by the stockholders' relative shares in the firm's value before its recapitalization. This is at best a highly impressionistic beginning point, not only because valuing the firm and each class of stock's share of the firm is a highly subjective inquiry, but also because questions such as how voting rights are to be shared in a recapitalized firm do not lend themselves to quantification. Moreover, there should be some substantial room for bargaining differences between the two classes of stock so as to capture a host of intangible considerations that are not easily included in financial models. As such, equitable protections may be limited to those rare instances where the recapitalization plan appears as a transparent effort to reduce the influence or financial interest of the minority by a discrete block of shareholders who hold a majority of the shares.[50]

§ 25.6 The Debate over Power to "Opt Out" of State Laws

The modern trend continues to provide greater and greater freedom for corporations to amend their articles of incorporation. This trend moves hand-in-hand with the increasing tenor of corporate statutes to be enabling rather than regulatory. It remains to be seen whether this trend will continue, as some have argued it should, to permit corporations to amend their articles so as to "opt out" of certain types of regulatory provisions that normally apply. Several influential scholars have argued quite persuasively that corporations should be allowed to decide selectively what corporate regulatory provisions they wish not to have apply to that corporation.[51] Such an opt-out arrangement is a natural extension of the nexus-of-contracts view of corporations: if one accepts that a corporation is but the intersection of differing contractual relations, it is equally logical to accord the contracting parties freedom to arrange their rights and protections in a manner they believe appropriate, with little paternalism from the state. Not surprisingly, those who reject the nexus-of-contracts view strongly oppose the opt-out arrangement.[52] Any such opt-out arrangement appears to place a good deal of faith in the belief that the shareholders are fully informed as to the consequences of the choices placed before them and that they will respond effectively. In a large public corporation not only is the proxy mechanism poorly devised for such thoughtful participation but also the full ramifications of the proposal will be extremely hard to assess.[53] Nevertheless, the American Law Institute proposes an approach akin to an opt-out choice by providing protection of directors and officers in limited circumstances against charges of self-dealing, of usurpation of corporate opportunity, or of competing

---

[50] See, e.g., Starr v. Engineering Contracting Co., 31 N.W.2d 213 (Neb. 1948).

[51] See, e.g., Frank Easterbrook & Daniel Fischel, The Corporate Contract in the Economic Structure of Corporate Law (1991); Richard Posner, Economic Analysis of the Law 393–397 (4th ed. 1992); Ralph Winter, State Law, Shareholder Protection, and the Theory of the Corporation, 6 J. Legal Stud. 251 (1977). For a thoughtful reply to Judge Easterbrook and Professor Fischel, see William W. Bratton, The Economic Structure of the Post-Contractual Corporation, 87 Nw. U. L. Rev. 180 (1992).

[52] See, e.g., Victor Brudney, Corporate Governance, Agency Costs, and the Rhetoric of Contract, 85 Colum. L. Rev. 1403 (1985); Robert Clark, Agency Costs Versus Fiduciary Duties in Principals and Agents: The Structure of Business 55 (J. Pratt & R. Zeckhauser eds. 1985); John Coffee, No Exit? Opting Out, the Contractual Theory of the Corporation, and the Special Case of Remedies, 53 Brook. L. Rev. 919 (1988); Thomas L. Hazen, The Corporate Persona, Contract (and Market) Failure and Moral Values, 69 N.C. L. Rev. 273 (1991).

[53] See generally Lucian Bebchuck, Limiting Contractual Freedom in Corporate Law: The Desirable Constraints on Charter Amendments, 102 Harv. L. Rev. 1820 (1989).

with their corporation, when they have acted in accordance with valid standards of conduct embraced by the corporation in its bylaws or articles of incorporation.[54]

Perhaps the most visible and widely used opt-out provision is the director immunity shield whereby most state statutes authorize the articles of incorporation to include a provision that protects directors from liability for damages for grossly negligent acts.[55] The Model Business Corporation Act sets forth a variety of opt-out provisions, including an appraisal remedy for preferred shares when their rights are affected by amendment.[56]

---

[54]   In ALI 1 Principles of Corporate Governance: Analysis and Recommendations § 5.09 (1994), the ALI protects directors and officers who rely on a standard of the corporation for transactions involving dealings with their corporation, acquiring property for their personal benefit, and competing with their corporation. "Standard of the corporation" is defined as a rule of governance that appears either in the bylaws or the articles of incorporation whose validity is to be judged "by its consistency with corporate statutes, the principles of corporate law, and applicable rules of general law." *Id.* § 1.36 Comment. When a corporation has taken advantage of a liability opt-out provision, the exculpatory defense is an affirmative defense that must be made by the defendants. Emerald Partners v. Berlin, 726 A.2d 1215, 1223–1224 (Del. 1999).

[55]   Immunity shield provisions are discussed in § 10.7.

[56]   MBCA § 13.02(c) (1984).

Chapter 26

VOLUNTARY DISSOLUTION, ADMINISTRATIVE DISSOLUTION, AND WINDING UP

Table of Sections

§ 26.1 Voluntary Dissolution Versus Informal Liquidation

Voluntary dissolution of a corporation involves two legal steps: (1) the dissolution itself, which involves the termination of the corporate existence, at least as far as the right to continue doing ordinary business is concerned, and (2) the winding up of affairs, payment of debts, and distribution of assets among the shareholders. Winding up may precede or follow the dissolution, depending on the jurisdiction's statutory procedures. For convenience in winding up, the corporate existence is usually continued either indefinitely or for some period limited by law in order to dispose of the corporation's assets and pay creditors.[1] This enables the directors to function as a board with title in the corporation rather than as trustees of the liquidation process. During the course of winding up, a corporation's assets will be collected and realized, the claims of creditors will be settled, and the remaining assets will be distributed to the shareholders.

The pre-1984 Model Business Corporation Act provides a two-step process to dissolve. First, a statement of intent to dissolve that has been approved by the shareholders is filed with the Secretary of State. Additionally, notice of the intent to dissolve must be given to known creditors during this step. Second, when the winding up process is completed, the articles of dissolution must be filed. The Secretary of State then issues a certificate of dissolution and the corporation is dissolved.[2] The current Model Business Corporation Act and a clear majority of the states have simplified the process by requiring only that the articles of dissolution to be filed, with the dissolution becoming effective as of the date of the filing.[3]

---

[1]   *See, e.g.,* Cal. Corp. Code § 2010 (West Supp. 2009); Del. Code Ann. tit. 8, § 278 (2001); 805 ILCS § 5/12.75, 12.80 (West 2004); N.Y. Bus. Corp. Law §§ 1005, 1006 (McKinney 2003); MBCA § 14.05 (1984).

[2]   Former MBCA §§ 83, 84–87 (1969).

[3]   MBCA §§ 14.03(b) & 14.06 (2016).

A corporation's legal existence terminates only when it is dissolved by legal authority, expires by limitation of its term of existence, or is dissolved by forfeiture.[4] Although it is not a formal dissolution, an informal liquidation may occur by sale of all the corporate assets, the abandonment of corporate activities, and the distribution of the corporation's property among the creditors and shareholders. This is sometimes referred to as a practical or de facto dissolution. However, a liquidation of assets does not terminate the corporate existence as a matter of law.

There may be reasons for retaining a corporation as a shell, such as for reactivation at a later date or for use in a corporate merger or consolidation. Directors and shareholders should follow the proceedings prescribed by law for voluntary dissolution and the winding up process; otherwise, the directors and shareholders risk liability due to unauthorized return of capital to the shareholders.[5] That is, absent dissolution, distributions to shareholders are lawful only to the extent that they do not exceed the regulatory limits for dividends or share repurchases.

§ 26.2 Statutory Authority for Voluntary Dissolution

Every state provides for the voluntary dissolution of a corporation when authorized by a vote of the shareholders. The vote is generally initialized with an adoption of a resolution and a submission of a proposal of dissolution by the directors.[6] Most states require that the resolution to dissolve include a recommendation by the directors to approve the dissolution before the shareholders may vote. Jurisdictions based on the current Model Business Corporation Act require a recommendation, but provide for an exception when there is a conflict of interest.[7] Only a small number of states do not mandate any type of director approval prior to a shareholder vote to dissolve.[8] In all jurisdictions, however, notice of the dissolution vote must be given to the shareholders prior to the meeting at which the vote is to take place.[9]

The number of shareholder votes required for approval of the dissolution varies widely among the states, with most requiring a majority of the shares entitled to vote.[10]

Most states authorize dissolution based solely on the approval of the incorporators or the initial board of directors. Each jurisdiction that authorizes this method of dissolution when either one or both of the following two factors are present: 1) the corporation has not issued shares; or 2) the corporation has not commenced business activities. In jurisdictions based on the pre-1984 Model Business Corporation Act both factors must be present,[11] while jurisdictions based on the current Model Business Corporation Act require the presence of either one of the two factors.[12] The remaining

---

[4]   *See* In re Clark's Will, 178 N.E. 766 (N.Y. 1931).

[5]   *See* Central Nat'l Bank v. Connecticut Mut. Life Ins. Co., 104 U.S. 54 (1881).

[6]   All states authorize the directors of a corporation to submit a proposal of dissolution to the stockholders. *See, e.g.,* Del. Code Ann. tit. 8, § 275(a) (2001).

[7]   MBCA § 14.06 (2016).

[8]   *See, e.g.,* Cal. Corp. Code § 1900(a) (West 1990); 805 ILCS § 5/12.15(a)(2) (West 2004) (allowing for a proposal of dissolution to be submitted to the shareholders upon written request by one-fifth of shareholders entitled to vote on dissolution).

[9]   *See, e.g.,* Del. Code Ann. tit. 8, § 275(a) (2001).

[10]   *See* Ariz. Rev. Stat. Ann. § 10–1402 (2004) (requiring a majority of shares entitled to vote unless articles of incorporation specify a greater percentage).

[11]   Former MBCA § 82 (1969).

[12]   MBCA § 14.01 (2016).

jurisdictions that authorize this method of dissolution either require only that the corporation not have issued shares,[13] or require only that business activities have not commenced.[14]

Following the completion of a statutorily approved method of voluntary dissolution, a certificate of dissolution is filed by the corporation and the dissolution becomes effective.[15]

In most states only the voting shares have a voice as to dissolution under many corporation acts.[16] Filing of a certificate of dissolution and, in some states, the publication of notice are required steps. After the statement of intent to dissolve has been duly adopted and filed, notice thereof is generally required to be sent to all known creditors. When a corporation conducts business in several states, it must dissolve according to the law of the state that granted its charter.

§ 26.3   Equitable Limitations on Voluntary Dissolution

In the case of a voluntary dissolution, as in the case of mergers, consolidations, and other fundamental changes to a corporation, management and majority shareholders are given wide latitude. Nevertheless, as Justice Traynor observed in *In re Security Finance Company,*[17] a leading case, "[t]here is nothing sacred in the life of a corporation that transcends the interests of its shareholders, but because dissolution falls with such finality on those interests, above all corporate powers it is subject to equitable limitations."[18]

The most common method of voluntary dissolution begins with a proposal to dissolve by the board of directors, and becomes effective by a majority vote of the shareholders.[19] Many states provide appraisal rights for dissenting shareholders, ensuring that they receive fair value for their shares, but only when the dissolution is accompanied by a sale of substantially all the corporation's assets.[20]

Voluntary dissolution, even when authorized by statute, is contingent upon the majority acting without fraud, bad faith, or oppression of the minority.[21] Thus, in *In re Security Finance Company,* although the holder of fifty percent of the shares was within his statutory right to initiate voluntary dissolution, the court recognized that he, as a major stockholder, had a duty to act in good faith.[22] The court found this standard was more than satisfied under the facts because the evidence did not show that the dissolution was a means to freeze out the other shareholders or that the price to be

---

[13]   *E.g.,* Cal. Corp. Code § 1900.5 (West Supp. 2009).

[14]   *E.g.,* Kan. Stat. Ann. § 17–6803 (2007); 15 Pa. Cons. Stat. Ann. § 1971 (West 1995).

[15]   The current MBCA as well as a majority of states require only that the articles of dissolution be filed for the dissolution to become effective. However, states based on pre-1984 versions of the MBCA require a two step process to dissolve, with the articles of dissolution becoming effective only after the winding up period.

[16]   *See, e.g.,* Cal. Corp. Code § 1900(a) (West 1990) (50% of shares entitled to vote); Del. Code Ann. tit. 8, § 275 (2001) (majority of all shares entitled to vote thereon).

[17]   In re Security Fin. Co., 317 P.2d 1 (Cal. 1957).

[18]   *Id.* at 5.

[19]   *See supra* § 26.2.

[20]   *See* MBCA § 13.02(a)(3) (2016).

[21]   *See* In re Security Finance Co., 317 P.2d 1 (Cal. 1957).

[22]   *Id.* at 5.

received through liquidation was unfair.[23] In contrast, dissolution cannot be used to exclude the minority shareholders from participating in the business that will be continued by the majority.[24]

Dissolution is one of several mechanisms to accomplish a minority freeze-out.[25] Though dissolution may be used to transfer an existing corporation to a new corporation controlled by the majority shareholders, as is the case of merger freeze-outs, the majority does not have carte blanche power to expel the minority through voluntary dissolution. If the minority shareholders are excluded or deprived of the fair value of their investment in the course of reorganizing a corporation under the control of the majority, the minority may obtain equitable relief in the form of an injunction against being unfairly frozen out of the corporation.[26] The minority shareholders, however, do not have an unqualified right to continue their participation in the corporation.

Courts are reluctant to nullify the corporation's dissolution or rescind other major changes once they have already been carried out. Nonetheless, occasionally rescission, or reinstating the corporation, is the most appropriate remedy. Generally, however, the most convenient remedy is payment of damages or compensation for the misappropriation of the interest of the shareholders. The court may award damages to the frozen-out minority based on their interest in the company before its dissolution.[27]

§ 26.4 Dissolution by Expiration of Stated Duration and Administrative Dissolution

A corporation may be dissolved upon expiration of a certain period of time or the occurrence of a specified event, if provided in its corporate charter.[28] The corporation's right to exist as a *de jure* corporation ceases after that time[29] unless it is extended or renewed by vote of the shareholders or amendment of the articles of incorporation under legislative authority.[30] According to some authorities, there may be an existence by estoppel or a *de facto* corporation as a result of the continuation of corporate activities after the expiration of the charter.[31] By express statutory provision, the existence of a corporation, even when created for a limited time, is usually prolonged for the limited purposes of winding up business affairs, paying debts, distributing assets, and pursuing and defending claims stemming from activities occurring prior to dissolution.[32]

A corporation may be dissolved administratively for failure to fulfill state requirements, such as nonpayment of state taxes and fees, failure to appoint or give timely notice of a change in its registered agent, failure to file the mandated annual

---

[23] The assets of the corporation were to be sold to a third party and majority stockholder had received six offers for the company's assets. *Id.* at 3.

[24] *See* Callier v. Callier, 378 N.E.2d 405 (Ill. App. 1978) (holding that dissolution was improper when a fifty percent shareholder used it to siphon off going-concern value of existing corporation in order to form a new corporation under his control).

[25] *See* F. Hodge O'Neal and Robert B. Thompson, O'Neal's Oppression of Minority Shareholders § 7.04 (2d ed. 1985).

[26] *See, e.g.,* Lebold v. Inland Steel Co., 125 F.2d 369 (7th Cir. 1941).

[27] *See* Grato v. Grato, 639 A.2d 390 (N.J. Super. App. Div. 1994).

[28] *See, e.g.,* Cal. Corp. Code § 200(c) (West 1990); Del. Code Ann. tit. 8, § 122(1) (2001).

[29] *See, e.g.,* Woodroffe v. Woodroffe (In re Estate of Woodroffe), 742 N.W.2d 94 (Iowa 2007).

[30] *See, e.g.,* Cal. Corp. Code § 909 (West 1990); Del. Code Ann. tit. 8, § 242 (2001).

[31] *See supra* Chapter 6.

[32] *See, e.g.,* Cal. Corp. Code § 2010 (West Supp. 2009); Del. Code Ann. tit. 8, § 278 (2001).

report with the secretary of state, or expiration of the period of duration stated in the articles of incorporation.[33]

Usually when a corporation is dissolved for failure to comply with corporate filing and fee requirements, its corporate powers are suspended but not forfeited. Almost all states have statutes allowing corporations to apply for reinstatement upon compliance with the state requirement that gave rise to the dissolution.[34] The majority of these states' statutes provide that reinstatement relates back to the effective date of the dissolution; therefore, the corporation is free to resume business as if it was never dissolved. Courts interpret these statutory provisions as validating corporate transactions that occurred during the period in which the corporation was dissolved.[35] The relation back provision also retroactively restores a corporation's power to sue, which provides legislative incentive to pay taxes and fees and file annual reports in a timely manner.

§ 26.5   Grounds for Judicial Dissolution

Judicial dissolution is a remedy that may be sought in an action by individual shareholders, the state, or, in some instances, creditors of the corporation. Although the power to dissolve a corporation is conferred upon the court by statute, dissolution proceedings are fundamentally equitable in nature. Dissolution is generally regarded as an extreme remedy and courts have been reluctant to grant it except as a last resort.

Action by Shareholders. The subject of voluntary dissolution in response to a petition by shareholders is examined in Chapter 14. Most statutes provide for judicial dissolution in a suit by minority shareholders in some or all of the following four situations:[36] (1) when the directors are deadlocked, the shareholders cannot break the deadlock, and irreparable injury to the corporation is suffered or threatened; (2) when the directors, controlling managers, or majority shareholders are acting in an illegal, oppressive, or fraudulent manner; (3) when the shareholders are deadlocked and cannot elect directors; and (4) when corporate assets have been misapplied or wasted. The emphasis of such actions is the protection of the interests of the shareholders. The two categories of judicial dissolution discussed below—dissolution by action of the state and dissolution by action of creditors—arise out of concern for the non-stockholder interests if the corporation's existence is not terminated.

Action by the State. Historically, the common law quo warranto action was the only action available to the state to cause the forfeiture of a corporation's existence or to prevent the corporation from continuing its harmful activities.[37] Today nearly all jurisdictions have enacted statutes that permit judicial dissolution in an action brought by the state upon a showing of an established ground for dissolution.[38] Often, certain state officials or a state's attorney generally may initiate judicial dissolution in limited circumstances.[39] Permissible grounds include (1) where "the corporation obtained its

---

[33]   *See, e.g.,* MBCA § 14.20 (2016).

[34]   *See, e.g.,* Del. Code Ann. tit. 8, § 312 (Supp. 2008).

[35]   *See, e.g.,* eServices, LLC v. Energy Purchasing, Inc., 2012 WL 404957 (E.D. Ky. 2012).

[36]   *See, e.g.,* MBCA § 14.30(a)(2).

[37]   *See* People ex rel. Carey v. Lincoln Towing Serv., Inc., 369 N.E.2d 94 (Ill. App. Ct. 1977).

[38]   *See, e.g.,* Del. Code Ann. tit. 8, § 284 (2001); MBCA § 14.30(a)(1).

[39]   *See, e.g.,* MBCA § 14.30(a)(1) (2016); Cal. Corp. Code § 1801(a) (West 2009); Del. Code Ann. tit. 8, § 284(a) (West 2009).

articles of incorporation through fraud"; or (2) where the corporation has continued to exceed or abuse the authority conferred upon it by law. Some states provide additional grounds for dissolution, such as nonuse of corporate powers.[40]

Thus, Most states have adopted mechanisms by which the state can administratively dissolve corporations for the failure to meet corporate filing and fee requirements.[41] The procedure generally commences with the secretary of state giving notice to the corporation of the particular defect that, if not corrected within a stated length of time—generally 60 days—will cause the corporation's administrative dissolution. Most state statutes provide that, even though a corporation has been administratively dissolved, its existence can be reinstated by curing the defect that gave rise to its dissolution, such as payment of past and current fees that are due the state.[42] The effect of administrative dissolution in most states is to suspend the corporation's powers, not terminate its existence outright. Such suspension bars any action on the corporation's behalf except as necessary to wind up its affairs.[43]

Petition by Creditors

In most states, judicial dissolution proceedings may be initiated by a creditor upon certain conditions.[44] Under statutes modeled after the Model Business Corporation Act, for example, an action may be commenced by a creditor against an insolvent corporation when the creditor has obtained a judgment which is left unsatisfied after an attempt to execute it, or when the corporation has admitted, in writing, that the creditor's claim is due.[45] A small number of states do not provide for judicial dissolution in a suit by creditors. Some of these states, such as Delaware, permit creditors to petition for appointment of a receiver when a corporation is dissolved.[46]

Provisions authorizing dissolution initiated by creditors should not to be confused with involuntary proceedings under the federal bankruptcy act, which may be brought by three or more creditors and may culminate in liquidation or reorganization.[47] Bankruptcy proceedings are a matter of federal law and do not result in dissolution because only the state has the authority to dissolve a corporation.

§ 26.6 Winding up and Statutory Continuation of Existence After Dissolution

All states now have statutes that provide for the continued existence of a dissolved corporation for winding up purposes.[48] Although the detail in which winding up procedures are described in these statutes varies widely from state to state, all states

---

[40] *See, e.g.,* Cal. Corp. Code § 1801(a)(4) (West 1990) (providing for dissolution by state for failure to pay taxes for five years); Del. Code Ann. tit. 8, § 284(a) (2001) (providing for dissolution by state for nonuse of corporate powers).

[41] *See, e.g.,* Del. Code Ann. tit. 8, § 510 (2001).

[42] *See, e.g.,* Iowa Code Ann. § 490.1422 (West 1999) (within two years); R.I. Gen. Laws § 7–1.1–88.1 (1999) (within five years); N.Y. Tax Laws § 203–a(7) (McKinney Supp. 2002) (within 90 days).

[43] *See* Graham, Inc. v. Mountain States Tel. & Tel. Co., 680 P.2d 1334 (Colo. Ct. App. 1984).

[44] *See, e.g.,* MBCA § 14.30(a)(3)(2016).

[45] *Id.*

[46] *See, e.g.,* Del. Code Ann. tit. 8, § 279 (2001); Kan. Stat. Ann. § 17–6808 (2007); Okla. Stat. Ann. tit. 18, § 1100 (West 1999).

[47] 11 U.S.C. § 303 (2000). Where there are fewer than 12 creditors, any one of them may institute involuntary bankruptcy proceedings. *Id.* § 303(b)(2).

[48] *See, e.g.,* Del. Code Ann. tit. 8, § 278 (2001).

require that a corporation cease all business activities upon dissolution, except those germane to winding up the affairs of the corporation. The current M.B.C.A. and statutes patterned after it go as far as to provide a list of various steps to be taken during the winding up period. These steps include: (1) collecting the corporation's assets; (2) disposing of properties that will not be distributed in kind to the shareholders; (3) discharging or making provision for the liabilities of the corporation; (4) distributing the remaining property among shareholders; and (5) doing every other act necessary to wind up and liquidate the corporation's business and affairs.[49] A recent amendment to the current M.B.C.A. gives further structure to the winding up process by imposing on the directors of a dissolved corporation the duties of making provision for liabilities and distributing the remaining assets to the shareholders.[50]

Personal liability may be imposed on those who exceed the scope of winding up activities permitted by statute, and continue business as a going concern.[51] This liability may be explicitly stated in statutes that govern administrative dissolution,[52] or derived from statutes that prohibit persons from acting on behalf of a nonexistent corporation.[53] However, liability for continuing to operate a dissolved corporation is generally contingent on personal knowledge that the corporation has been dissolved.

Today, dissolution does not alter the general governance of the corporation. The current M.B.C.A. and statutes patterned after it explicitly reverse common law notions by specifying that dissolution does *not*: (1) transfer title to the corporation's property; (2) prevent transfer of its shares or securities; (3) subject directors and officers to different standards of conduct; (4) change quorum or voting requirements for the board or shareholders; (5) prevent commencement of a proceeding by or against the corporation; (6) abate or suspend a proceeding pending by or against the corporation on the effective date of dissolution; or (7) terminate the authority of the registered agent of the corporation.[54]

---

[49] MBCA § 14.05 (1984).

[50] MBCA § 14.09 (1984) (added by 2000 amendment). Several states have adopted this provision.

[51] *See, e.g.,* Messing v. Paul, 147 Fed. Appx. 437 (6th Cir. 2005).

[52] This is the case in a very small number of states.

[53] *See* Ariz. Rev. Stat. Ann. § 10–204 (2004).

[54] MBCA § 14.05(b) (1984).

Table of Cases

Table of Statutes

Table of Regulations

Table of Rules

Index

References are to Sections